WORLD POLICE ENCYCLOPEDIA

BOARD OF EDITORS & ASSOCIATE EDITORS

Samuel Bwana
Senior Research and Information Manager
Kenya Anti-Corruption Commission
Kenya National Police
Nairobi, Kenya

Mark Ming-Chwang Chen
Professor
Department of Border Police
Central Police University
Kwei-Shan, Taiwan

Lucia Dammert
Researcher
Editor
Police Practice and Research: An International Journal
Latin American Faculty of Social Science (FLACSO)
Santiago, Chile

Mintie Das
WPE Project Assistant to the Editor-in-Chief
International Police Executive Symposium (IPES)
South Burlington, Vermont, USA

Ramesh Deosaran
Professor of Criminology
and Social Psychology, and Director
Centre for Criminology and Criminal Justice
Faculty of Social Sciences
The University of the West Indies
St. Augustine, Trinidad and Tobago

Robert F. J. Harnischmacher
Editor-in-Chief Polizeiforum
Lecturer, Department of Criminology
Criminal Politics and Police Sciences
Faculty of Law
Ruhr-University
Bochum, Germany

Peter Hobbing
Associate Fellow
Centre for European Policy Studies (CEPS)
Brussels, Belgium

Peter Johnstone
Associate Dean
College of Human Ecology
East Carolina University
Greenville, North Carolina, USA

Želimir Kešetović
Associate Professor of Crisis Management
Faculty of Civil Defense
University of Belgrade, Serbia

Marke Leong
University of New England
Armidale, NSW, Australia

Colleen Lewis
Associate Professor of Criminal Justice and Criminology
Faculty of Arts, and Co-Director of the Parliamentary Studies Unit
Monash University
Melbourne, Australia

Paulo R. Lino
Guest Lecturer
Lutheran University of Brazil
Consultant to the Organization of American States
Director
International Police Executive Symposium (IPES)
Rio Grande, Brazil

Agbonkhese Shaka Moses
Department of Sociology
Ambrose Alli University
Ekpoma, Nigeria
Editor
Police Practice and Research: An International Journal
Ekpoma, Nigeria

William Mubanga
Former Lieutenant
Zambia Police Department
Lusaka, Zambia

Tonita Murray
Former Head of Canadian Police College
Police and Gender Advisor
Afghan Ministry of the Interior
Kabul, Afghanistan

John P. Mutonyi
Police Superintendent, Kenya
Department of Criminology
University of Leicester
Leicester, United Kingdom

Mike Rowe
Lecturer in Policing and Public Order Studies
Department of Criminology
University of Leicester
Leicester, United Kingdom

John Scott
Lecturer
School of Social Science
University of New England
Armidale, NSW, Australia

Jakkrit Singhsilarak
Police Colonel
Thai National Police
Bangkok, Thailand

Mark Ungar
Associate Professor
Brooklyn College
City University of New York
New York, New York, USA

Ernesto Lopez Portillo Vargas
President
Institute for Security and Democracy
Mexico City, Mexico

Arvind Verma
Associate Director of India Studies
Department of Criminal Justice
Indiana University
Bloomington, Indiana, USA

WORLD POLICE ENCYCLOPEDIA

Volume 1
A-K
INDEX

Dilip K. Das

EDITOR

Michael J. Palmiotto

Managing Editor

Routledge
Taylor & Francis Group
New York   London

Published in 2006 by
Routledge
Taylor & Francis Group
270 Madison Avenue
New York, NY 10016

Published in Great Britain by
Routledge
Taylor & Francis Group
2 Park Square
Milton Park, Abingdon
Oxon OX14 4RN

Printed in the United States of America on acid-free paper
10 9 8 7 6 5 4 3 2 1

International Standard Book Number-10: 0-415-94250-0 (Hardcover)
International Standard Book Number-13: 978-0-415-94250-8 (Hardcover)
Library of Congress Card Number 2005044342

Library of Congress Cataloging-in-Publication Data

World police encyclopedia / Dilip K. Das, editor in chief, Michael J. Palmiotto, managing editor.
   p. cm.
  Includes bibliographical references and index.
  ISBN 0-415-94250-0 (set : alk. paper) -- ISBN 0-415-94251-9 (v. 1 : alk. paper) -- ISBN 0-415-94252-7 (v. 2. : alk. paper)
  1. Police--Encyclopedias. 2. Criminal justice, Administration of--Encyclopedias. 1. Das, Dilip K., 1941- II. Palmiotto, Michael.

HV7901.W64 2005
363.2'03--dc22   2005044342

Taylor & Francis Group is the Academic Division of T&F Informa plc.

Visit the Taylor & Francis Web site at
http://www.taylorandfrancis.com

and the Routledge Web site at
http://www.routledge-ny.com

TABLE OF CONTENTS

INTRODUCTION

Policing is both a local and global activity, a practice within nations and a responsibility shared between them. It is thus the aim of the *World Police Encyclopedia* to present in one publication a comprehensive survey of policing around the world, providing the reader with rounded descriptions and keen analyses of national policing systems while placing each national system within an international policing perspective.

The *Encyclopedia* recognizes that every nation has a police system and no two police systems are the same. Every country polices its own territory with distinct methods and judicial procedures, with varying penalties and prison standards, and within unique cultural and historical contexts that apply specific pressures and pose specific challenges. Thus, the encyclopedia contains articles on each of the member nations of the United Nations as well as the non-member nation of Taiwan, covering the globe in two comprehensive volumes.

To enable the work to function systematically as a cross-cultural, global reference work, each article is also executed with a uniform design. Where possible, articles share the same structure and contain the same kinds of information, enabling readers to compare historical contexts; policing institutions; cultural, ethnic, and religious forces; and other demographic variables that contribute to the formation, shape, and dynamic of policing systems. Readers can research how various nations educate and train police, how they finance and administer police systems, what political oversight they exercise, and how they legitimize or ban practices such as the death penalty, life imprisonment, or public surveillance.

Critical to any reference work, especially one that seeks to offer a great diversity of information within a comparable format, a thorough analytical index is included. The index guides the reader to topics of interest wherever discussed within the work. It also encourages exploration of the contents so readers may discover new information and easily see connections that they otherwise may have overlooked.

A reference work of this kind also recognizes the changes in policing systems around the world and the growing need to understand them because local practices are taking on more and more global significance. With the accelerated expansion of communications, trade, and transnational political organizations, issues such as judicial, penal, and policing protocols, while locally administered, are increasingly subject to international review, praise, and critique. This encyclopedia will contribute to the reader's ability to evaluate these practices, where they have arisen, and the direction they are evolving.

With the globalization of organized criminal activities, the drug trade, illicit arms deals, prostitution, and terrorism, the need for countries to cooperate and coordinate their policing efforts has increased dramatically into the twenty-first century—a theme throughout the book. Indeed, international criminal activities have made international policing efforts a priority. Imperative and expensive, these efforts have entered the business of our daily lives as never before. However, the context and history of such efforts also demand our understanding. Hopefully, this encyclopedia will aid readers to an informed and balanced understanding of accomplishments and challenges involved in any policing effort.

Organization of the Book

There are 193 entries in *World Police Encyclopedia*. Given the range and scope of these entries, the following tools have been employed to ensure easy navigation of the volume and access to essential information:

- An alphabetical list of all entries;
- A comprehensive index; and
- A template format, applied to each entry.

Every entry in *World Police Encyclopedia* includes the following sub-headings, summarizing as much relevant information as is available for the particular nation in question:

Background Material
Each entry begins with a brief overview of that nation's history and current statistical information,

including population, ethnic composition of the population, and GDP per capita.

Contextual Features

In this section, the political structure of the government of the nation in question is discussed. Other information relevant to an understanding of the police of any given nation is also included in this section, including information on crime, the criminal justice system, and penal codes and prisons.

The primary section of each entry is titled **Police Profile**. This section is broken down further, under the following subheadings:

Background covers the history and development of the police system.

Demographics provides statistical information on the police force, including total number of members and the gender and ethnic composition of the police force.

Organizational Description describes who controls the police, ranks and hierarchy structure, special response units, and support services (as applicable).

Functions provides an overview of police powers in regard to various police functions, discussing administrative duties as well as criminal justice matters.

Training covers the requirements for joining the police force, including any special schooling.

Police Public Projects may cover crime prevention, traffic control, or school-based police outreach programs, if any such programs exist in the nation in question.

Police Use of Firearms describes laws and regulations relating to police firearm use and ownership.

Complaints and Discipline provides an overview of police accountability regarding citizen complaints, as well as police respect for human rights.

Terrorism describes any terrorist organizations that are active in the nation in question and police efforts to combat terrorism.

International Cooperation enumerates international assistance being provided to the police of the nation in question, exchange of officers among nations, if any, and any international policing efforts to which the police have contributed.

When applicable, entries also include a section on **Police Education, Research, and Publications**. This section provides an overview of:

· Institutions of higher education for the police;
· Leading researchers, authors, reporters, and columnists, with affiliations;
· The extent and sources of funding for police research, and areas of recent research;
· Leading police journals, magazines, and newsletters;
· Major police publications (books or reports);
· Police-related websites.

Each entry concludes with a **Bibliography** of relevant cited sources, as well as suggestions for further reading.

A Note on Coverage

Every attempt has been made to provide comprehensive coverage of policing practices in every nation. However, a number of factors have prevented equal coverage of all countries. Accessibility to reliable information varies widely from country to country, for a variety of reasons. Some nations do not make public statistical or demographic information regarding their national security forces. In the case of numerous countries, primarily several located in Africa, data relating to the police and policing activities is simply not consistently recorded. The editors of the *World Police Encyclopedia* have relied on 125 contributors and 25 associate editors, the vast majority of whom are either criminal justice scholars or working professionals in each of the countries or geographical regions addressed, to make every reasonable attempt to procure as much reliable and detailed information as possible. It is unfortunately the case that, in general, far more statistical data and information is available for Western nations, as opposed to less developed and developing nations. It is the editors' hope that any perceived lack of data in the *Encyclopedia* will inspire further archival work and research among scholars and police professionals to ensure access to police-related information for every interested party in every nation.

LIST OF CONTRIBUTORS

Felipe Abbott. University of Chile, Santiago, Chile.

Pavel Abraham. Professor, President, Romanian Antidrug Agency, Bucharest, Romania.

Marcelo F. Aebi. University of Lausanne, Lausanne, Switzerland; Autonomous University of Barcelona, Barcelona, Spain.

Biko Agozino. Assistant Professor, Department of Social and Behavioural Sciences, Cheyney University of Pennsylvania, Cheyney, Pennsylvania, USA.

Maria Pia Scarfo Allocca. Specialist in Central America, New York, New York, USA.

Oyesoji Aremu. Department of Guidance and Counselling, University of Ibadan, Ibadan, Nigeria.

Ahmet Hamdi Aydin. Lecturer, Kahramanmaras S. University, Kahramanmaras, Turkey.

David Baker. Head of Criminal Justice and Criminology, Monash University, Melbourne, Australia.

Oleg Balan. Director of Public Administration Department, Academy of Public Administration, Chisinau, Moldova.

Adrian Beck. Senior Lecturer, Scarman Centre, University of Leicester, Leicester, United Kingdom.

G.Q. Billings. Central Missouri State University, Missouri State Highway Patrol, Warrensburg, Missouri, USA.

Christopher Birkbeck. Professor of Criminology, University of Los Andes, Merida, Venezuela.

Ivor Blake. Divisional Commander, Royal Saint Christopher & Nevis Police Force, Basseterre, Nevis.

József Boda. Director of Ministry of Interior International Training Centre, Budapest, Hungary.

Margaret Brignell. Team Leader, Collections Management, Canadian Police College Library, Ottawa, Canada.

Christopher Brooks. School of World Studies and African American Studies, Virginia Commonwealth University, Richmond, Virginia, USA.

Antanas Bukauskas. Lecturer, Department of Public Administration, Mykolas Romeris University, Lithuania.

Michele Caianiello. Professor, International Criminal Justice, University of Bologna and University of Camerino, Italy.

Irena Cajner-Mraovic. Assistant Professor and Head of the Department of Criminology, Police College, Zagreb, Croatia.

Henry F. Carey. Assistant Professor, Department of Political Science, Georgia State University, Atlanta, Georgia, USA.

Cathy Casey. Program Leader, Crime and Justice, Auckland University of Technology, Auckland, New Zealand.

Jacqueline Azzopardi Cauchi. Professor, Department of Sociology, University of Malta, Malta.

Adam Chapman. Postdoctoral Fellow, Centre for Cross Cultural Research, Australian National University, Canberra, Australia.

Wisootrujira Chatsiri. Border Patrol, Royal Thai Police, Bangkok, Thailand.

Mark Ming-Chwang Chen. Professor, Department of Border Police, Central Police University, Kwei-Shan, Taiwan.

Pavel Cincar. Police Presidium of the Czech Republic, Deputy Head, International Police Co-Operation Division, Prague, The Czech Republic.

Gonzalo Jar Couselo. Brigadier General of Guardia Civil, Madrid, Spain.

Marcos Josegrei da Silva. Professor, Criminal Law, Law School, Tuiuti University, Parana, Brazil.

Mintie Das. WPE Project Assistant to the President, International Police Executive Symposium (IPES), South Burlington, Vermont, USA.

Carmen Rosa de León-Escribano. Author and Researcher, Guatemala City, Guatemala.

Monica den Boer. Dean of Studies, Police Academy of The Netherlands and Police Academy Professor, Free University Amsterdam, Amsterdam, The Netherlands.

Osman Dolu. Kent State University, Kent, Ohio, USA.

Bruno Domingo. Center for Police Study and Research, (CERP), Toulouse, France.

Fiona Donson. NGO Worker, Phnom Penh, Cambodia.

Vejnović Duško. Director of the Center for Geostrategic Studies, University of Banja Luka, Banja Luka, Bosnia and Herzegovina.

Maximilian Edelbacher. Senior Advisor, Federal Police, Vienna, Austria.

Andreas Egeryd. Senior Administrative Officer, Division for Police Issues, Stockholm, Sweden.

Jean-Etienne Elion. Colonel, Department of Police and Security, Brazzaville, Republic of Congo.

Theodora Ene. School of Sociology and Social Work, University of Bucharest, Bucharest, Romania.

Eduardo E. Estevez. Coordinator, Public Security, Ministry of Interior, Buenos Aires, Argentina.

Charles Fields. Professor of Criminal Justice, College of Justice and Safety, Eastern Kentucky University, Richmond, Kentucky, USA.

Daniel Fontanaud. National Expert to the European Commission, Paris, France.

Javier Galarza. Police Captain, Ecuador National Police, Quito, Ecuador.

Victor Manuel Garcia. Visiting Police Executive, Central Police University, Kwei-Shan, Taiwan.

Farid Gardashbayov. Public Finance Monitoring Center, Baku, Azerbaijan.

Gilbert Geis. Professor (Emeritus), Department of Criminology, Law, and Society, University of California-Irvine, Irvine, California, USA.

Roland Genson. Councellor for Justice and Home Affairs, Permanent Representation of the Grand-Duchy of Luxembourg to the European Union, Brussels, Belgium.

Ruth Geva. Chief Superintendent, Israel Police (retired), Consultant, Community Safety and Crime Prevention, Jerusalem, Israel.

Rune Glomseth. Assistant Professor, National Police Academy, Oslo, Norway.

Georgi Glonti. Institute of State and Law, Tbilisi, Georgia.

Paulo Gomes. Portuguese Ministry of the Interior, Lisbon, Portugal.

Recep Gultekin. Head of Foreign Relations Department, Turkish National Police, Ankara, Turkey.

Ismail Dincer Gunes. Department of Sociology, University of North Texas, Denton, Texas, USA.

Nelson Armando Vaquerano Gutiérrez. Professor, Human Rights and International Law, University of El Salvador, Salvador, El Salvador.

Robert F.J. Harnischmacher. Editor-in-Chief, *Police Forum*, Lecturer, Department of Criminology, Criminal Politics and Police Sciences, Faculty of Law, Ruhr-University, Bochum, Germany.

Michele Harrigan. Ph.D. Candidate, Transnational Police Co-operation, Institute of Social Psychology, Department of Sociology, London School of Economics & Political Science, London, United Kingdom.

Anthony Harriott. Senior Lecturer, Department of Government, University of the West Indies (Mona Campus), Mona, Jamaica.

William Harry. Commissioner of Police, Royal St. Vincent and the Grenadines Police Force, Kingstown, St. Vincent.

Abdul Qadir Haye. Inspector General of Police (retired), Rawalpindi, Pakistan.

Haruhiko Higuchi. Police Policy Research Center, National Police Agency, Tokyo, Japan.

Brunon Hoyst. Faculty of Law and Administration, University of Łódź, Lódź, Poland.

Paul Ibbetson. Ph.D. Candidate, Wichita State University, Wichita, Kansas, USA.

Analida Ivankovich. Police Researcher, John Jay College of Criminal Justice, Managing Editor, *Police Practice and Research: An International Journal*, New York, New York, USA.

Andrew Jackson. Assistant Director, European Asylum Policy Unit, Asylum and Appeals Policy Directorate, Brussels, Belgium.

Yateendra Singh Jafa. Member of Indian Police Service (retired), and Fellow, Jawaharlal Nehru University, New Delhi, India.

Mark Jones. Professor, East Carolina University, Greenville, North Carolina, USA.

Arunas Juska. Assistant Professor, East Carolina University, Greenville, North Carolina, USA.

Andreas Kapardis. Author and Researcher, University of Cyprus, Nicosia, Cyprus.

Zoran Keković. Assistant Professor, Faculty of Civil Defense, Police College, Serbia and Montenegro, Belgrade, Serbia.

Karin Keller. Canton Police Executive, Zurich, Switzerland.

Želimir Kešetović. Associate Professor, Crisis Management, Faculty of Civil Defence, University of Belgrade, Belgrade, Serbia.

Ranjan Koirala. Senior Superintendent, Armed Police Headquarters, Kathmandu, Nepal.

Betsy Wright Kreisel. Associate Professor, Criminal Justice Department, Central Missouri State University, Warrensburg, Missouri, USA.

Peter Kruize. Faculty of Law, University of Copenhagen, Copenhagen, Denmark.

Hamid R. Kusha. Associate Professor, Criminal Justice, Department of Social Sciences, Texas A&M International University, Laredo, Texas, USA.

Ahti Laitinen. Professor, Criminology and Sociology of Law, University of Turku, Turku, Finland.

Velibor Lalić. Associate Researcher, Center for Geostrategic Studies, University of Banja Luka, Bosnia and Herzegovina.

Uwe Langenbahn. Deputy Chief, National Police of Liechtenstein, Verwaltungsgebaude, Liechtenstein.

Musa Bockarie Lappia. Sierra Leone Police Headquarters, Loidu, Sierra Leone.

Marke Leong. University of New England, Armidale, NSW, Australia.

Colleen Lewis. Associate Professor of Criminal Justice and Criminology, Faculty of Arts, and Co-director of the Parliamentary Studies Unit, Monash University, Melbourne, Australia.

Meruert Makhmutova. Director, Public Policy Research Center, Almaty, Kazakhstan.

Mary Fran Malone. Lecturer, Department of Political Science, University of New Hampshire, Durham, New Hampshire, USA.

Francesco Marelli. Consultant, United Nations Interregional Crime and Justice Research Institute (UNICRI), Turin, Italy.

Joan R. Mars. Assistant Professor, Department of Sociology, Anthropology & Criminal Justice, University of Michigan-Flint, Flint, Michigan, USA.

Noel McGuirk. University of Ulster, Ulster, Northern Ireland.

Kenethia L. McIntosh. Department of Criminal Justice, University of Maryland-Eastern Shore, Eastern Shore, Maryland, USA.

Erica McKim. Policy Analyst, National Security Policy and Planning Section, Criminal Intelligence Directorate, Royal Canadian Mounted Police, Nepean, Ontario, Canada.

Cindy McNair. Department of Criminal Justice, Indiana University, Bloomington, Indiana, USA.

Jean-Louis Messing. Commissioner of Police, Yacuande, Cameroon.

J. Mitchell Miller. Director of Graduate Studies in Drug and Addictions and Associate Professor, Department of Criminology & Criminal Justice, University of South Carolina, Columbia, South Carolina, USA.

Ruth Montgomery. Editor, Canadian Association of Chiefs of Police (CACP) Publications, Ontario, Canada.

Agbonkhese Shaka Moses. Department of Sociology, Ambrose Alli University, Ede State, Nigeria.

Thomas Mosley. Department of Criminal Justice, University of Maryland-Eastern Shore, Eastern Shore, Maryland, USA.

Aogán Mulcahy. Department of Sociology, University College Dublin, Dublin, Ireland.

Tonita Murray. Police and Gender Advisor, Afghan Ministry of the Interior, Kabul, Afghanistan.

Yem Xuan Nguyen. Deputy Director of Standing Office on Drug Control, Da Nang, Vietnam.

Gilbert Norden. Institute of Sociology, University of Vienna, Vienna, Austria.

Evaristus Obinyan. Fort Valley State University, Fort Valley, Georgia, USA.

Jonathan C. Odo. Department of Criminal Justice, University of Maryland-Eastern Shore, Eastern Shore, Maryland, USA.

Ihekwoaba D. Onwudiwe. Associate Professor, Department of Criminal Justice, University of Maryland-Eastern Shore, Eastern Shore, Maryland, USA.

Michael O'Shea. Asia Centre, University of New England, Armidale, Australia.

Milan Pagon. Dean, College of Police and Security Studies, Ljubljana, Slovenia.

Michael J. Palmiotto. Professor of Criminal Justice, Wichita State University, Wichita, Kansas, USA.

Nancy Park. Library Manager, Canadian Police College, Ottawa, Canada.

Vassiliki Petoussi. Lecturer, Sociology of Law and Deviance, Department of Sociology, University of Crete, Crete, Greece.

João José Ramalhete Marques Pires. Cabinet of External Affairs and Cooperation, National Directorate of Public Security Police, Lisbon, Portugal.

Nii-K Plange. Professor, Sociology, School of Social and Economic Development, The University of the South Pacific, Suva, Fiji.

A. R. Ramsaran. Law Department, Faculty of Law and Management, University of Mauritius, Reduit, Mauritius.

Husnija Redžepagiæ. Principal, High School of Internal Affairs, Serbia and Montenegro, Belgrade, Serbia.

Michael Reid. Press Office, Belize Police Department, Belize City, Belize.

Aigi Resetnikova. Researcher, Institute of Law, University of Tartu, Tartu, Estonia.

Fiorella Espinosa Ribeiro. National Police of Uruguay, Montevideo, Uruguay.

Annette Robertson. Scarman Centre, University of Leicester, Leicester, United Kingdom.

Walter Rombaut. Police Advisor, Belgian Federal Police, Brussels, Belgium.

Mike Rowe. Lecturer, Department of Criminology, University of Leicester, Leicester, United Kingdom.

Daniel Linares Ruestra. Financial Investigation Unit, National Police, Lima, Peru.

Mohammad Salahuddin. Department of Criminal Justice. Indiana University, Bloomington, Indiana, USA.

Juan Carlos Valenzuela Sanchez. Visiting Police Executive, Central Police University, Kwei-Shan, Taiwan.

Kim Yong Sang. International Program Coordinator, National 119 Rescue Services, Seoul, Korea.

Martijn Schilstra. Policy Advisor, Amsterdam City Hall, Department of Public Order and Safety, Amsterdam, The Netherlands.

Eric Schultz. Senior Assessment Coordinator, Criminal Justice Training Assessment, Excelsior College, Albany, New York, USA.

John Scott. School of Social Sciences, University of New England, Armidale, Australia.

Sankar Sen. Indian Police Service (retired) and Senior Fellow, Institute of Social Sciences, New Delhi, India.

Amanda Marie Sharp. Department of Criminal Justice, East Carolina University, Greenville, North Carolina, USA.

Hasan Shkembi. Police Academy, Tirana, Albania.

Martin Sitalsing. Deputy Chief Constable, Regional Police Force, Friesland, Amsterdam, The Netherlands.

Nils-Henrik Sjölinder. Administrator, Ministry of Justice, Division for Police Issues, Public Order and Safety, Stockholm, Sweden.

Nelly Sonderling. Communication Research, South African Police, Pretoria, South Africa.

Trpe Stojanovski. Senior Executive, Ministry of the Interior, Republic of Macedonia, Skopje, Macedonia.

Kathleen Sweet. CEO and President, Risk Management Security Group, Assistant Professor, Purdue University, West Lafayette, Indiana, USA.

Ian Taylor. School of International Relations, University of St. Andrews, St. Andrews, Scotland.

Samih Teymur. Department of Information Sciences, University of North Texas, Denton, Texas, USA.

Mark Ungar. Associate Professor, Brooklyn College, City University of New York, New York, USA.

Endang Usman. Corruption Crime Department, Jakarta Metropolitan Police, Jakarta, Indonesia.

L.N. Uusiku. Office of the Inspector-General, Namibian Police, Windhoek, Namibia.

Ernesto Lopez Portillo Vargas. President, Institute for Security and Democracy, Mexico City, Mexico.

Nicole Vartanian. Senior Research Associate, Institute of Education Sciences, Washington, DC, USA.

Bryan Vila. National Institute of Justice, U.S. Department of Justice, Washington, DC, USA.

S. George Vincentnathan. Professor and Chair, Department of Criminal Justice, University of Texas-Pan American, Edinburg, Texas, USA.

Anwar Yehya. Director of Training, Internal Security Forces, Beirut, Lebanon.

Lola Gulomova Zarifovna. The Paul H. Nitze School of Advanced International Studies (SAIS), Johns Hopkins University, Baltimore, Maryland, USA.

Sitora Gulomova Zarifovna. Female Lawyers League, and Tax & Law Institute, Dushanbe, Tajikistan.

LIST OF ENTRIES A-Z

Kazakhstan
Kenya
Kiribati
Korea, North
Korea, South
Kuwait
Kyrgyzstan
Laos
Latvia
Lebanon
Lesotho
Liberia
Libya
Liechtenstein
Lithuania
Luxembourg
Macedonia
Madagascar
Malawi
Malaysia
Maldives
Mali
Malta
Marshall Islands
Mauritania
Mauritius
Mexico
Micronesia
Moldova
Monaco
Mongolia
Montenegro
Morocco
Mozambique
Myanmar
Namibia
Nauru
Nepal
Netherlands, The
New Zealand
Nicaragua
Niger
Nigeria
Norway
Oman
Pakistan
Palau
Panama
Papua New Guinea
Paraguay
Peru
Philippines
Poland
Portugal

Qatar
Romania
Russia
Rwanda
St. Kitts and Nevis
Saint Lucia
Saint Vincent and the Grenadines
Samoa
San Marino
São Tomé and Príncipe
Saudi Arabia
Senegal
Serbia
Seychelles
Sierra Leone
Singapore
Slovakia
Slovenia
Solomon Islands
Somalia
South Africa
Spain
Sri Lanka
Sudan
Suriname
Swaziland
Sweden
Switzerland
Syria
Taiwan, Republic of China (ROC)
Tajikistan
Tanzania
Thailand
Togo
Tonga
Trinidad and Tobago
Tunisia
Turkey
Turkmenistan
Tuvalu
Uganda
Ukraine
United Arab Emirates
United Kingdom
United States
Uruguay
Uzbekistan
Vanuatu
Venezuela
Vietnam
Yemen
Zambia
Zimbabwe

AFGHANISTAN

Background Material

The Islamic Republic of Afghanistan is a land-locked country situated in south-central Asia. Its neighbours are Turkmenistan, Uzbekistan, Tajikistan and China to the north, Pakistan to the east and southeast, and Iran to the southwest and west. The country is slightly smaller than the state of Texas, and is semiarid and mountainous. It has thirty-two provinces, and the capital is Kabul.

Agriculture and pastoralism constitute 80% of the economy. Natural resources include natural gas, coal, copper, and precious and semiprecious stones. Fresh water is limited, and the country suffers from deforestation, desertification, soil degradation, and air and water pollution. There is some small-scale manufacturing, particularly of textiles and handwoven carpets, but exports did not exceed $98 million in 2002. Much of the infrastructure is either destroyed or broken down as a result of war. There are only 2,793 kilometres of paved road, the electricity supply is unreliable, and there is a shortage of housing and medical care. The country is the most heavily mined in the world, and many Afghan men and boys have lost their lives or limbs from stepping on land mines.

The estimated population of Afghanistan in 2004 was slightly more than 28 million. Living standards are among the lowest in the world. Twenty-three percent of the population lives below the poverty line. Life expectancy at birth is 42.46 years. The fertility rate is 6.78 children per woman, and infant mortality is 1.65 per ten live births. Many children die before their fifth birthday.

Afghanistan is ethnically diverse. Pashtuns form 42% of the population, Tajiks 27%, Hazara and Uzbeks 9% each, and other groups a smaller percentage. Half the population speaks an Afghan version of Farsi, 35% speak Pashtu, and other minority languages are also spoken. About 36% of the population is literate.

The location of Afghanistan has influenced its long and turbulent history. It has been successively invaded from the west by Alexander the Great, from the northeast by Genghis Khan and Tamerlane, from India by the British, and by Russia from the north. Invasions of Muslim Arabs starting in about 650 AD introduced Islam into Afghanistan.

Events in the last quarter of the twentieth century devastated the country. In 1973, the king was deposed, and a government with Marxist leanings came to power. Its weaknesses led to a

Russian invasion in late 1979. After meeting fierce opposition from Afghan religious fighters, or *mujahidin*, the Russians withdrew in 1989. Civil war followed, in which various tribal factions and warlords united to oust the Marxist government before starting to fight among themselves. In 1996, the Taliban faction emerged as the dominant group in most of the country, with the exception of the north, which was held by the Northern Alliance.

The Taliban government imposed an extreme religious regime on the country. Television, films, and music were banned. Men were required to follow strict religious practices, while the Taliban took particularly repressive measures against women. Women were not allowed to work, go to school, seek medical attention from male doctors, or be alone on the streets. They were compelled to wear the *birqa*, a garment that covered them completely except for a netting grill over the eyes. The behavior of both sexes was monitored by the Department for the Promotion of Virtue and the Prevention of Vice, or the "Vice and Virtue Police." The punishments these police ordered included whippings, amputations, imprisonment, and execution.

The Taliban also gave Osama bin-Laden and the international terrorist organization, al-Qaeda, a base from which to operate. After the al-Qaeda attacks of September 11, 2001, in New York and in Washington, D.C., the United States mounted a successful military action against the Taliban with the help of allied forces and the Northern Alliance. This brought an end to the twenty-three years of war that began with the Russian invasion and during which no civilian police force existed.

During the war, many Afghans fled to Pakistan or to Iran. There were 3 million refugees in Pakistan, and 1.5 million in Iran. While many returned after the war, Afghanistan nevertheless lost a significant proportion of its intellectual capital needed to rebuild the country.

With international support, Afghan leaders met in Bonn, Germany, in late 2001 to form an interim government for the reconstruction of Afghanistan. This meeting was followed in June 2002 in Afghanistan by a *loya jirga*, or grand council, which created the Transitional Islamic State of Afghanistan (TISA) and elected Hamid Karzai as president by secret ballot. In January 2004, the TISA held another *loya jirga* to adopt a new constitution for the country. In October 2004, in a free and general election, Hamid Karzai was again elected president.

Since the fall of the Taliban, Afghanistan has been the recipient of several billion dollars of international aid from more than sixty donor countries. Aid ranges from military and civil security to education, health, agriculture, job and housing improvements, and infrastructure rebuilding. In 2003, the GDP rose 29% as a result of such aid and the end of a four-year drought.

Afghanistan faces enormous challenges. One of the most important is the need for security to support social stability, a healthy economy, and a democratic society that respects human rights. The warlords and their private armies undermine the authority of the central government and often engage in armed skirmishes among themselves. There are also sporadic terrorist outbursts and attacks on foreign aid workers, particularly in provinces close to the border with Pakistan and the Tribal areas, where remnants of al-Qaeda are reputed to have their mountainous bases.

There is a U.S. military force in Afghanistan, and NATO oversees an international security assistance force (ISAF) composed of soldiers from various nations, which is based mainly in Kabul. Outside Kabul there is little security, and even in the city there are no guarantees. Other measures to improve security include disarmament and demobilization of the *mujahidin* and private armies and their reintegration into civil society. Such efforts have fallen short because, among other things, there are few jobs, and the soldiers are usually illiterate and have no experience outside of fighting. Another measure for reconstructing Afghanistan and improving security is the creation of provincial reconstruction teams, led by individual countries, to rebuild and establish security in Afghaanistan province by province.

Contextual Features

The transitional Afghan government is headed by an elected president, who is both the chief of state and head of government. The transitional government includes representatives from various ethnic groups and factions in the country, including such major political groupings as the Northern Alliance and the former Taliban. The ministers responsible for running government departments are appointed by the president.

A new constitution was proclaimed in January 2004. It includes many elements similar to those of the constitution introduced by King Mohammed Zahir in 1964, which was described as one of the finest in the Muslim world at the time. It guarantees universal suffrage, a wide range of human rights for all Afghans, and entrenches the Independent Human Rights Commission to which citizens can complain in cases of violation of their fundamental rights.

The constitution further provides for the election of a president and a national assembly consisting of 220 to 250 members, including at least one woman from each province. The president appoints ministers with the approval of the national assembly. The national assembly consists of the Wolesi Jirga, or House of the People, and the Meshrano Jirga, or House of Elders. The former is elected, while two thirds of the latter are composed of representatives from provincial and district councils and a third is chosen by the president consisting of experts and experienced individuals. Women make up 50% of the latter. The constitution also provides for a judiciary and a nine-member supreme court appointed by the president and approved by the Wolesi Jirga for a nonrenewable term of ten years. There is also a Loya Jirga, which is a supreme council consisting of members of the national assembly and chairpersons of the provincial and district councils. This body is convened when needed to decide issues related to independence, national sovereignty, territorial integrity, constitutional amendment, or prosecution of the president.

The constitution declares Afghanistan to be an Islamic republic and acknowledges Islamic or Shari'a law as the law of Afghanistan. The Hanafi branch of Islamic law is practiced in Afghanistan. This emphasizes precise conduct in observing religious duties, allows the use of legalistic methods to avoid certain prohibitions of the Koran, and permits women to be *qadi*, or religious judges, in certain circumstances.

In addition to Islamic law, statute and customary laws exist. Islamic law is the preserve of religious scholars, or *mullahs*, while statute law is the province of the secular government. While not entirely clear-cut, Islamic law applies to personal and interpersonal matters such as religious observance, the family, contracts, torts, and crimes against the person. Statute law applies to the administration of the state and its institutions, the constitution, international matters, and to crimes against the public interest such as forgery, smuggling, embezzlement, and bribery.

Customary law is local law, which varies from region to region, and the preserve of tribal elders who deliberate in tribal councils, or *jirgas*. A *jirga* decides on matters by consensus, and its decisions are binding on the parties in dispute. Customary law has an important place in the Afghan legal system, and property, family, and other matters are decided by customary law.

One of the major codes in customary law is the Pashtunwali, which is practiced by the Pashtun, the majority tribe in Afghanistan. It is based on notions of chivalry, hospitality, and gender boundaries, which, taken together, form the tribal code of honor. Men and women have their own separate spheres of authority and influence under the Pashtunwali and work and socialize almost exclusively within their own gender group. Women are usually the family leaders; they manage family resources and choose wives for their sons, while men have a more public role.

The constitution provides for an independent judiciary consisting of a supreme court composed of nine members appointed by the president for ten years, high courts, and appeal courts. The attorney general's office, which is a part of the executive branch but independent of its deliberations, is responsible for the investigation and prosecution of crime and for discovery via the police, as in the European legal model.

A dual legal system means there is a dual judiciary and dual court system. Judges who apply Islamic law and those who apply statute law are separately trained and have a separate court system. Islamic judges are trained in religious schools or *madrassas*, or in the Islamic law faculty at Kabul University, and secular judges are trained in the Faculty of Law and Political Science at Kabul University. Neither has much understanding of the other's system of law, despite earlier efforts to unite both court systems under the Court of Cassation and to cross-train.

In addition to the higher courts, each of the thirty-two provinces has a provincial court with original jurisdiction over matters such as smuggling, press offenses, and charges against public officials. They also have appellate jurisdiction over the decisions made by primary courts. Judges of primary courts recognize the authority of customary law and can either refer matters to tribal elders or incorporate the decisions of tribal elders into the decisions of the primary court.

Despite the appearance of well-developed legal, judicial, and court systems, the opposite in fact prevails. The transitional government is unable to assert its legitimate authority much beyond Kabul, and there are still serious abuses of human rights. Statutory law exists largely on paper and Islamic and customary law prevail. After twenty-three years of war, most written statutes have disappeared or been destroyed by the Taliban, so judges and the legal community have little access to a written body of law. Moreover, the various ideologies that have held sway since the 1960s, each translating chosen priorities into law, means that there are several strata of statutory laws prevailing.

The courts are in disarray and those hearing secular cases seem to have largely disappeared. The court system is underfunded and understaffed, and seems to be operating in a consistent manner only in Mazar-e-Sharif and Kabul.

Italy is the lead donor nation for reconstruction of the legal system and has begun the process with the help of the International Development Law Organization and the Afghan Judicial Reform Commission. They are assembling complete sets of laws, rebuilding and equipping courthouses, and training judges and other judicial system officers. Austria is funding reform of the juvenile justice system. It is establishing a youth court in Kabul and building a residential correctional facility for juveniles.

Prisons and correctional facilities are also malfunctioning. There are 354 government correctional systems. Most are very small and are in such poor condition that they are unable to hold people satisfactorily. Nineteen provincial prisons have been destroyed, and the remaining fourteen require varying degrees of rebuilding. Prison conditions do not meet international standards. Sanitation, food, and overcrowding are serious concerns. Men, women, children, and criminal and political prisoners occupy the same establishments, although they are segregated where possible. While the Ministry of Justice is nominally responsible for the correctional system, according to Amnesty International, correctional facilities are controlled by various armed groups, and there are frequent human rights violations. Correctional facilities are understaffed, and existing staff are untrained and not paid regularly. There are few programs for the education or rehabilitation of prisoners.

Rebuilding of prisons and reform of the correctional system have not been energetically pursued by the international community. There are plans to remedy this situation. The Kabul correctional facility has been rebuilt, and there are plans to build provincial detention centers and establish a training center for correctional staff, and then to construct eight regional correctional complexes. There are also plans for the development of programs and activities to aid rehabilitation of prisoners.

There are few official statistics on crime in Afghanistan, so most of the information is anecdotal. Moreover, it is difficult to distinguish between crimes committed for a political, factional, or private purpose. Carrying arms is a way of life in Afghanistan, and violence is therefore prevalent. Family violence and violence against women are reported to be high. There have been cases of arson and bombings of girls' schools to express disapproval of female education, sexual assault is reported to be common, and, within the family, women may suffer beatings, burnings, and even death at the hands of their husbands or mothers-in-law. The fear of violence is said to prevent many women from participating in public life. This is particularly so in the conservative west of the country around Herat.

With the return of the refugees after the war, there were reports of rising crime, especially in Kabul, where the normal population of roughly 250,000 swelled to 2 million and more. For ten months in 2001, there were a reported 48 murders, 80 thefts, 12 kidnappings, and 54 drug-related crimes. Although it is likely that many crimes were not reported, the figures appear almost negligible compared to cities with similar populations in the West. Islamic values help to the keep crime rate low.

The increase in opium cultivation and trafficking since the fall of the Taliban contributes to international organized crime. Afghanistan is the world's largest producer, supplying opium for most of the heroin used in Europe. In 2002, despite eradication programs, 30,750 hectares of poppies were cultivated, capable of yielding 1,278 metric tons of opium. Processing of opium has also begun. All of these activities exacerbate security problems, help fund terrorist activities, and threaten the stability of neighboring countries. It is also reported that growing numbers Afghans are using opium themselves.

Police Profile

Background

The Afghan National Police (ANP) is a centralized, militaristic state organization under the direction of the Minister of Interior Affairs. It is modeled on the European police system. The present ANP owes its origins to Mohammed Zahir Shah who built up a professional, national police force in the 1960s and 1970s with German help. In 1989, the Federal Republic of Germany built a police academy in Kabul. Three years later when Kabul was overrun by the *mujahidin*, the academy closed. During the period of conflict from the late 1970s to 2002, there was no effective civilian police. Generally, the military, intelligence agencies, Vice and Virtue Police, warlords, or other armed groups usurped the police function and emphasized their own political and security goals. After the fall of the Taliban in December 2001, the urgent need to reestablish security and civil society made police reform a priority. Germany agreed to lead international efforts to help the Afghan government reconstruct its national police force.

Demographics

ANP numbers have been variously reported at anything from 50,000 to 170,000. This means that the ANP has a police-to-population ratio ranging from 1:164 to 1:560. The aim is ultimately to set the number of members of the ANP at 50,000, which would bring it into line with international standards. This is expected to take a number of years to accomplish.

The reasons for uncertain knowledge on the size of the ANP is the lack of substantive records and what a German study calls the "nominal affiliation" of "back-door policemen," *mujahidin*, and conscripts swelling police numbers. Conscription has ceased, but before 2002, young men were given a choice of conscription into the army or the police for two years. Conscripts, which make up the majority of police personnel, are largely illiterate and have little police training. They are provided with a uniform, food, accommodation, and health services. They live at their posts and take turns to stand watches throughout the day and night. They live in an all-male society, with little opportunity for family and social interaction outside the police post.

There are two higher levels of police officers, equivalent in military terms to noncommissioned and commissioned officers. They are educated, but their training dates back to the 1970s and 1980s. Starting in 2002, they began receiving some limited in-service training. Many of these officers are approaching the end of their careers but, owing to the war, there is no educated generation behind them to take over. There is, therefore, a sense of urgency to train as many new recruits at these levels as possible.

The number of police women in the ANP in 2003 was about sixty, of which all but a handful were in Kabul. Recruitment and training of women is a priority; however, it is difficult to attract women because of family disapproval, the low status and pay of police officers, and religious limitations. Women take the same training as male police officers. To attract more women and to redress the effects of the repression of women during the Taliban years, the police academy admits illiterate women to a special program where they gain literacy skills in conjunction with police training.

Since each province has its own ethnic character, police reflect the ethnicity of the provincial population from which they were recruited. While in theory there is equal opportunity for all ethnic groups in the ANP, whether by design or accident, some ethnic groups may receive more advantages than others. For example, Amnesty International reports that 90% of some classes at the police academy have been composed of northern Tajik participants. Because provincial police organizations reflect the local ethnic composition, they tend to assert provincial autonomy from central control and, in some cases, demonstrate more allegiance to local tribal leaders and warlords than to the central government.

Organizational Description

The police operating budget for the Ministry of Interior in fiscal year 2004–2005 was 3.24 billion afghanis or roughly US$75.7 million. In addition, donor countries make funds available for specific reconstruction and reform projects. Nevertheless, financing is inadequate; police salaries are low; working conditions poor; accommodation, food, and medical care inadequate; uniform and equipment lacking; and police can go for several months without being paid. Most engage in secondary employment to augment police pay.

Under the transitional government, the terms and conditions of employment of ANP members is governed by the 1973 Law of Employment, Promotion and Retirement of Police and Gendarmes. The law regulates the employment, education, and rights and privileges of police and gendarmes. It creates three categories of employees: police and gendarmes, military conscripts, and civilian specialist officers such as mechanics, veterinarians, and topographers.

There are four levels of police and gendarmes in the rank system and a number of ranks within each level. The first or highest level includes ranks equivalent to brigadier general or assistant deputy commissioner and above. The second level contains ranks equivalent to major to colonel, or chief inspector to chief superintendent. The third level includes ranks equivalent to company sergeant major to captain, or police staff sergeant to inspector. The fourth level includes ranks equivalent to constable to sergeant.

The Ministry of the Interior has a strong role in influencing police practices. While there is provision for a chief commander of police and gendarmes, in practice there appear to be a number of high-ranking commanders, often representing various factions whose fortunes ebb and flow according to the political climate of the moment.

Each of the thirty-two provinces has a police commander who heads the provincial organization. They too are often pulled into the political orbit. Some owe more allegiance to local warlords than to the central government, and their police leadership abilities are mixed. Some have had professional police training; some are former military officers with no police experience; and some are illiterate with no police training, who were appointed for their exploits during the war. Those appointed by the transitional government since 2002 are competent reformers, but they have frequent difficulties because the allegiance of officers under their command may be subject to other more powerful local influences.

Each province is divided into a number of districts and further divided into a number of localities with police stations. There are specialist units at the district and provincial levels for investigation, traffic, and other police functions.

Functions

The role and functions of police and gendarmes are defined in the Law of Police and Gendarmes (1973), which contains provisions for the organization, duties, and authorities of police and gendarmes. The role of the police is to ensure security, order, and well-being of the public; crime prevention; safeguarding people's rights and freedoms, protection of the public interest; application of the courts' verdicts; and law enforcement. They are empowered to warn, stop, summons, impose fines up to 500 afghanis for minor offenses, arrest, and search and seize. Other statutes influencing the functions of the police include the Penal Code (1976) and Criminal Procedure Law (1965).

Gendarmes are responsible for border patrols, entry and departure of people at the borders, customs inspections, and national security at the borders. While having the power to investigate smuggling, passport, and border violations, they refer criminal matters to the police. The border police force is broken down, and urgent efforts are underway to create a new one, which will also be responsible for the interdiction of illicit drugs. The work of conscripts is mainly to serve as stationary guards at checkpoints or to perform a range of menial tasks including cleaning and making tea.

While the laws that govern the police incorporate some recognition of human rights, set out the limits to police powers, and are in effect until an elected government replaces them, Amnesty International argues that they fall short of meeting international policing standards. Given literacy standards and the chaotic state of both the law and policing, it cannot be assumed that the police are even aware of legal provisions.

There are little or no written policies, procedures, or standing orders, since most were destroyed under the Taliban. Few records are kept, particularly at the police station level where perhaps only the commander can read or write. Nevertheless, there is a strong oral tradition in Afghanistan, so police have well-developed memories for remembering procedures, names, or instructions, and, at the local level, may be very knowledgeable about their communities.

Training

The basic requirements for entering the police school are Afghan citizenship, age between seventeen and twenty-two years, good physical and mental health, height of at least 1.70 meters, no criminal record, and a minimum nine years of schooling. After the successful completion of one year of police training, a recruit can be appointed as a constable.

The higher the level in the police hierarchy, the longer the training. Noncommissioned officers train for a year at the police academy. Commissioned officers receive three years of academic training interspersed with a year of practical training between the second and third and another at the end of the third year, forming in total a training program of five years. A U.S. screening and training program was introduced in 2003 to ensure that former conscripts retained in the ANP are suitable for police work and receive eight weeks of basic police training.

The commandant of the Police Academy in Kabul is an officer of the ANP, and some police officers are involved in the training; however, training in police procedures such as traffic control, patrol, crowd control, emergency response, protective duties, investigative techniques, forensic science, management, and human rights is provided by police trainers from donor countries. The Ministry of the Interior prefers that training takes place in Afghanistan and that local conditions are taken into consideration, but occasionally Afghan police officers have the opportunity to train abroad at the police schools of other countries.

Given the almost complete loss of civilian police expertise during the war, reform efforts are concentrated on restoring police professionalism and dealing with the immediate problems of security, traffic chaos, narcotics trafficking, and rebuilding the border police. Police training reflects this preoccupation. Instilling an understanding and knowledge of human rights is also a central feature. Training in management is also given some attention to support police capacity-building efforts.

Eight regional police training centers have been set up with foreign aid. In addition, senior operational officers who were trained before the war provide some practical training at the provincial, district, and local levels.

Police Use of Firearms

The Law of Police and Gendarmes sets out the conditions in which firearms and explosives can be used by the police. It stipulates that the level of force used should be minimized. While use of firearms and explosives against a crowd is permissible in certain situations, the use of either against children is not permitted. Police must also give due warning before using firearms or explosives.

The Afghan police do not normally carry sidearms but issue weaponry when required. In theory, records of issued firearms and ammunition are kept; in practice, recordkeeping is faulty. Firearms are not serviced regularly, and therefore are not in good condition. There appears to be no regular firearms training, and frequently there is no money for ammunition.

Complaints and Discipline

It is reported that the Afghan police frequently offend against human rights and engage in corrupt practices. There is no internal code of discipline published throughout the ANP and no external police oversight or complaint mechanisms. The ANP has created a human rights unit, which maintains links with the Afghan Independent Human Rights Commission, but the Commission has no legally mandated control over the police. In general, there is no redress for citizens against wrongful treatment. The Ministry of the Interior and the ANP are working to improve discipline and eliminate human rights abuses by developing internal policies and procedures and by training.

Terrorism

Terrorist activities are prevalent in Afghanistan. Remnants of the Taliban and al-Qaeda sympathizers attack foreign aid workers and Afghans who work for them with bombs, mines, rockets, and firearms. Others have fire-bombed girls' schools and other targets that challenge tribal traditions.

Other outbreaks are the result of factional fighting. In general, the police are not responsible for repressing terrorism. This is undertaken by the U.S. and NATO-led international armed forces. On occasion, however, the central government has sent a contingent of police to restore order when there has been conflict between local factions. While the police contribute to intelligence gathering and investigation of terrorism, the National Army has the lead responsibility.

International Cooperation

Afghanistan is the recipient of significant aid for reconstruction of the ANP and for traffic and crime control. Germany leads the reconstruction effort, while a number of donor countries concentrate on specific aspects of reform. The German police are responsible for five areas of concentration: (1) reestablishing the police academy and providing recruit training; (2) restructuring the police organization; (3) supplying equipment; (4) providing advice on reconstruction; and (5) coordinating other international police reconstruction efforts.

Major international efforts include rebuilding the border police, the training and development of counternarcotics units, and traffic enforcement training. Another initiative that involves policing is the creation of provincial reconstruction teams. A donor country takes responsibility for the complete rebuilding of the infrastructure of a province from water and roads to health and education. Security is a fundamental part of these efforts. Programs for disarmament, demobilization, and reintegration of private armies also contribute to security and policing reform.

While some countries are not involved directly in police reform, they help finance it. The international community created the Law and Order Trust Fund for Afghanistan. The fund is used principally for paying police salaries but may also be used for the acquisition of nonlethal equipment, rehabilitation of police facilities, capacity building, and institutional development.

Police Education, Research, and Publications

The Afghan police are a subject of study by Western journalists and international organizations, but war and the flight of millions to Pakistan, Iran, and elsewhere just about extinguished intellectual life of Afghanistan, and continuing hardship is an obstacle to its renaissance. Consequently, research and publication of news or studies of the police are virtually nonexistent, and even the Police

Academy concentrates on practical training rather than police theory and research. While there is no police website, the government maintains one (*www.afghanistangov.org*), where the new constitution and information on Afghan reconstruction aid, including aid to the police, are published.

TONITA MURRAY

Bibliography

Afghan Ministry of Interior. National Police, Law Enforcement & Stabilization Public Investment Programme: Submission for the SY 1383–1385 National Development Budget. Kabul: Ministry of Interior, 2003.

Amnesty International. *Afghanistan: Police Reconstruction Essential for the Protection of Human Rights*, 2003. Available at: www.web.amnesty.org/library/index/engasa110032003. Accessed November 20, 2004.

Amnesty International. *Afghanistan: Open Letter to Participants in the International Conference on Reconstruction Assistance of [sic]Afghanistan*, 2004. Available at: www.web.amnesty.org/library/eng-afg/index/110062004. Accessed November 20, 2004.

CANADEM. *Mission to Support Police Reform in Afghanistan*. Ottawa: Canadian International Development Agency, 2003.

Etling, Bruce. *Legal Authorities in the Afghan Legal System (1964–1979)*, 2003. Available at: www.law.harvard.edu/programs/ilsp/etling.pdf. Accessed November 20, 2004.

Ewans, Martin. *Afghanistan: A Short History of Its People and Politics*. New York: HarperCollins Publishers, 2002.

Ghani, Ashraf. *A Report on the Accomplishments of the Government of Afghanistan, September 2002–2003*. Kabul: Ministry of Finance, 2003.

Kakar, Palwar. *Tribal Law of Pashtunwali and Women's Legislative Authority*, 2003. Available at: www.law.harvard.edu/programs/ilsp/kakar.pdf. Accessed November 20, 2004.

Lau, Martin. *Islamic Law and the Afghan Legal System*, 2003. Available at: http://bglatzer.de/arg/arp/lau.pdf. Accessed November 20, 2004.

ALBANIA

Background Material

The Republic of Albania is located in the southwestern part of the Balkan Peninsula along the Adriatic and Ionic Seas. Since antiquity, major centers such as Buthroti (Butrinti), Dyrrahu (Durresi), Apollonia, Lisi (Lezha), Scodra (Shkodra), Antipatrea (Berati), Bylisi (Hekli), and Amantia (Plloca) have flourished in the area. Prior to the Greeks, the most ancient inhabitants of the Balkan Peninsula were the Pellazge, whose language was different from Greek. In 2001, the Albanian population totaled about 3.087 million, with an average population density of 107 inhabitants per square kilometer. The capital is Tirana, a city of 700,000 inhabitants. The average age of the population is about 29 years old. Less than half the population, about 42%, lives in towns and cities; the other 58% live in villages. The population is homogeneous; 98% is of Albanian origin, whereas 2% is composed of other minorities. The official language is Albanian.

The three major religions in Albania are Catholicism, Christian (Greek) Orthodox, and Islam, which coexist well with each other. The republic of Albania is a secular country that respects and encourages the rights of all religions. Annual per capita income of the population in 2002 (based on GDP) was $1,471. Agriculture dominates the Albanian economy and is the main component of overall production in the country. Industry consists of small- and medium-sized companies in light industry and food-processing businesses. Several branches of the economy, including transportation, business, and tourism, have made significant progress. Albania also has important mineral resources. Since 1990, Albania has been involved in the movement toward democratization.

Contextual Features

Albania is a parliamentary republic based on a free, general, and periodic system of elections. The head of state is the president of the country, who is elected by the People's Assembly. The governing system in Albania is based on checks and balances among the legislative, executive, and judicial powers.

The People's Assembly is composed of 140 deputies chosen through general parliamentary elections every four years. All citizens eligible to vote can also be candidates as deputies. The Assembly performs a double function in the administration of internal and external policies and the legislative role as the only legislative body.

The executive power has two levels: central and local level. The central executive power is exercised through the government composed of the premier and the ministers, who together comprise the Council of Ministers. The prime minister represents the Council of Ministers and ensures the implementation of legislation and the program of the government approved by the parliament and political decisions approved by the Council of Ministers. The communes, town halls, and circuits of respective territorial units exercise executive power at the level of local government. The representative units of the local government are the councils, elected every three years through general direct elections. The executive of the town hall is the chairman, who is elected directly by the people. The circuit is composed of a number of local governing bodies with traditional, economic, and social links. It is there that regional policies are designed and implemented and where they are harmonized with state policies. Its representative body is the Council of the Circuit.

The Judiciary System and Legislation

The judicial police investigate penal proceedings when the attorney has delegated such powers. The principle of presumed innocence functions in the penal process. According to Article 31 of the constitution, everyone enjoys the right to self-defense or legal defense (a lawyer) to appeal against a court decision to a higher court. Based on these principles, the Albanian justice system is considered to be adversarial. In order to ensure a fair system of defense for the legal freedoms and rights of the individual, there is the law on civil service and the ombudsman as a constitutional institution, which is independent and nonpartisan.

The main types of crimes are crimes against persons (assault, homicide), illegal trafficking (of human beings, arms, and drugs), corruption, organized crime, armed robbery, traffic accidents, and financial crimes and evasion. A breakdown of the 1,589 cases recorded in 2002 follows: homicide, 179; sex crimes, 76; armed robbery, 214; economic and financial crimes, 753; drug crimes, 250; illegal trafficking, 544; and crimes against property, 1,322.

Judicial power is based in the High Court, as well as the First Scale Court, which are established by law. Lawyers are independent and submit to the constitution and legislation. The High Court issues decisions implemented by the state bodies in the name of the republic. In the Republic of Albania, the Constitutional Court functions to guarantee respect for the constitution and to give final interpretations. Decisions taken by the Constitutional Court are obligatory and terminal. This Court has only the right to abolish the acts that it examines, and it proceeds only by the request of institutions or subjects established in the constitution.

The organization and functioning of the detention system, execution of judicial decisions, and the imprisonment and treatment of detainees, arrested, or persons convicted of crimes is performed by the General Directorate of Prisons, directly subordinate to the Ministry of Justice.

Police Profile

Background

According to historical sources, the beginnings of the Albanian Police date back to the second half of the eighteenth and first half of the nineteenth century. The establishment of the Albanian Police as an official institution corresponds to the time when Albania was proclaimed independent, and the first Albanian state was established in 1912. About one month later, with a special decision of the Council of Ministers, the Public Order Forces (Police and Gendarmerie) were formed on January 13, 1913. According to the first organization of the police, the Police Directorate functioned at the local level with the office of police commissariats in prefectures and subprefectures. The gendarmerie was organized with the High Committee at the center and battalions, companies, and gendarmerie posts at peripheral levels. Of great support to the formation of the public order forces was the Dutch Mission (1913–1914). After 1914, the profile of the Public Order Forces was affected by historical change. During World War I, the Albanian police forces followed the model of the invaders' military forces in Albania (Austria-Hungary, France, Italy). Between 1920 and 1924, police structures and the legal framework underwent a change. The regulation of police duties was designed in 1921. The period between 1925 and 1938 is characterized by the progressive development of the police and gendarmerie.

Elements of Western police structures are reflected in the police and gendarmerie legislation.

During World War II, the structures were mainly assimilated and later modeled according to the interests of the invading countries. During the two invasions, Albanian forces were integrated with the invaders' military structures and were named the Police Armed Corps. In 1943, in the liberated zones, partisan structures operated for the maintenance of order and public serenity as the Circuit Command and Country Commandant voluntary guards. In November 1944, these forces were reorganized under the People's Defense Forces.

After World War II, the organization and structure of the police followed the eastern model. On May 14, 1945, military restructuring resulted in the creation of the People's Police, a part of the Ministry of Interior. From 1945 to 1990, aside from changes in organizational form and structure, the main function of the People's Police was the prevention and detection of offenses. Although the Albanian Police had a separate school for personnel development and qualification, the education institution was strongly dominated by ideological and political indoctrination. In April 1991, the Public Order Police was created, and a new organization was under way. This was done at two levels. A new legal framework was provided, and this was accompanied by depoliticizing reforms.

From 1992 to 1996, the Albanian police undertook a process of reform, which at the beginning had a significant impact. Later it was accompanied by frequent changes of personnel structure and lack of professional criteria that did not secure understanding and furtherance of goals. A decision by the Council of Ministers in June 1999 launched the reform of the State Police that began with Law No. 8553, dated November 25, 1999. The basic document was the Strategy of Reform in the State Police, which implemented a new legal infrastructure and structural organization of State Police according to the standards of Western countries.

Organizational Description

According to the new organization and Law No. 8553, the State Police are not part of the armed forces; they have civil status under the Minister of Public Order. The mission of the police is to protect order and public security and to guarantee law enforcement. The State Police have a unique organization that covers all national territory, according to administrative divisions of the country, and it is depoliticized. The total number of State Police workers is 12,454, of whom 65 are women, and the average age of police personnel is 36.7 years. The ratio of police worker to citizen is 1:246. Of the total number, 84.5% are in active (operating) services, and the others serve in auxiliary services. The numbers of police workers in various units follow:

- Criminal Investigation Department (CID), 1,404
- Public Order, 5,205
- Border Police, 1,716
- Traffic Police, 769
- Forensics, 118
- Rapid Intervention Forces, 996
- First response officers, 337

The Minister of Public Order, at the top of the hierarchy, has the responsibility of guiding and controlling all police activity and exercising civil control within the government program. The general director of the police is the highest administrative and technical leader within the police and reports to the Minister of Public Order. The general director takes measures to implement the normal police activities; he is chosen from the high-ranking leaders of the police on the basis of skills and successful professional experience. He is proposed by the minister and appointed by the Council of Ministers. The general deputy director is the right arm of the general director of police and performs the tasks delegated to him. The procedure for appointing the deputy director is the same as for the director.

The new structural organization of the State Police has both central and local organizational levels. The central level is composed of the General Directorate of Police, responsible for the direction, job coordination, and control of all structures of police services, including the Order Police, Criminal Police, Border Police, Traffic Police, and Rapid Intervention and Special Forces, as well as auxiliary structures of personnel, logistics, finance, and administration. The Rapid Intervention and Special Forces are in a state of alert and are to be used to restore order, to work in difficult operations in the fight against crime or terrorism, and to aid in accidents and natural disasters.

At the local level, the highest administrative body is the Directory of the Police Circuit, which falls under the General Directorate of Police and is responsible for the direction, coordination, and control of police activity within respective territorial jurisdictions. Within their structures are the commissariats of police districts (forty-two) and police stations (five). The regional offices concerned with terrorism, illegal trafficking, organized crime, and economic and financial crime are simultaneously part of the directorates and also depend on the Central Directory of Criminal Police in the ministry. In general, police organization at the local (circuits) level corresponds to the main structures of central services in the ministry.

Since 1999, the State Police has had a system of police rankings. According to functions and tasks performed by the police, workers are divided into four roles and division of ranks:

1. Basic role: agent, first agent, assistant, first assistant, and chief assistant (9,488 police workers)
2. Medium role/middle police managers: vice inspector, inspector, and chief inspector (2,166)
3. High role/command personnel: vice commissar, commissar, chief commissar (398)
4. Major role/senior command personnel: leader, first leader (9).

The criteria for promotion are education, training, and professional qualifications. The law clearly defines the standards to achieve promotion to higher rank, and movement in rank and career are based on the roles and functions that the police workers perform. The General Director orders promotion of police at the basic role, with the proposal of the respective commission on promotions. For the medium and high role, promotion requires an order of the Minister based on the proposal of the respective commission on promotions and the job positions available. For the major role, promotion is made by a decree of the president of the prepublic, with the proposal issued by the minister and approved by the prime minister.

Functions

The institutional duties of police are to:

- Secure order and public safety
- Guarantee the exercise of individual freedoms and rights
- Take measures to prevent and detect crime
- Control the state border of the country
- Supervise the road traffic
- Protect the highest state authorities
- Safeguard the institutions and the most important public properties
- Guarantee the implementation of laws and sublegal acts
- Help in cases of misfortunes and accidents

In the basic role (agent, chief assistant), police workers perform functions or executive tasks with limited initiative, as well as commanding and leading functions (of assistants) of a team or group in accordance with the requests of the law and their qualifications. Other functions may be patrol police, traffic, security police, and assistant inspector in public order, crime agent, operator, patrol responsible, and team commander. Middle police managers (vice inspector, chief inspector) perform specific tasks such as pursuing and investigating, giving instruction in professional training activities for agents and assistants, and leading and arranging for operational units. The specific functions are criminal police inspector, chief of the office, chief of the council, chief constable, lectures in police college, and so on. Selection criteria include three years of police higher education, professional qualifications, experience, good job evaluations, and competition. Command personnel (vice commissars and chief commissars) perform the leading functions of police organizations and sectors. They serve as chief of the office, chief of department, academy instructor, chief of the commissariat, vice director, police director in the ministry or in a circuit, and leader of auxiliary structures. Senior command personnel (leader or first leader) are responsible for management of all police structures. They are selected among chief commissars, and their movement from one rank to the other is done without a schedule.

To exercise its powers, the police have responsibility for order, public security, and judicial police. To perform their duties in accordance with legislation, the police have been given the following rights:

Arrest. This right derives from the Law on the State Police, the Law on the Judicial Police, and the Code of Penal Procedure, and it is exercised by police workers who perform agent duties or officers of the judicial police. Arrest is made in cases of flagrant acts or when an order is being executed after being issued by competent bodies such as prosecutors or courts. All international standards of freedom and human rights are respected.

Detention. The police have the right to take the lawbreaker, even forcefully, to the police offices or authorities that have issued the warrant. The detention cases are determined by the constitution and in the law on police.

Use of firearms. Firearms are used as the last resort and only when there is no other means to respond to an eminent danger of high risk to life. Use of force is the intervention of the police to prevent violence from the lawbreaker, and it is used when the violator resists the police, tries to escape arrest or detention, during serious public disorders, and so on. Entering buildings, even forcefully, is allowed in dwellings or other environments when there is information that a crime is being committed, to escape from an eminent danger, and to offer help in cases of accidents and natural disasters. Police officers may be called to verify the circumstances of penal acts and the execution of decisions on administrative infringements. Provisional blocking of parts of roads and surrounding areas is allowed in cases of accidents. Police have the right to control the crime scene, the gathering of evidence (crime items and forensic investigation), and the proceedings in the criminal event. They may have physical control of persons, their clothes, and their cars without a warrant in cases such as the prevention of eminent danger, for public security, and for prevention of a criminal act.

Another police power is to check individuals for identity cards in cases when they are present at a crime scene, when an order by the court has to be executed, when there is a law on infringement or disturbance of public serenity, and at border checkpoints. Police also have the right to proceed in cases of administrative infringements of law (fines, temporary sequester, blocking of activities, administrative proceedings, and so on). It should be noted that minors under the age of fourteen may not be taken to police premises in the absence of parents.

Terrorism

The investigation and prevention of terrorism are handled by the State Police and State Information Service Police in a special structure within the General Directorate of Police, called the Sector for the Fight Against Terrorism and Anticonstitutional Crimes. At the local level, the regional offices of the war against terror and anticonstitutional crime fall directly on the respective sector in the Ministry of Public Order. As of 2002, there was no known terrorist organization operating in Albania, and there have been only sporadic acts of arson performed by individuals against public and private property such as shops and dwellings. On October 15, 2001, the Albanian assembly approved a resolution that Albania is part of the broad international alliance in the war against terrorism. Albania has approved and adheres to a number of covenants and agreements on international terrorism. As a consequence of the cooperation of Albanian intelligence officials with North

Atlantic Treaty Organization (NATO) institutions and those in neighboring countries, Islamic terrorist elements sheltered in Albania during and after the turmoil of spring 1997 were identified, expelled, or extradited.

Since 1992, there has been great interest by international organizations and Albanian and foreign nongovernmental organizations (NGOs) to initiate projects on police within the framework of human rights. The Council of Europe, the Red Cross, and others have developed one-week projects for police training in human rights. The Albanian Human Rights Centre and the Ministry of Public Order have a long history of cooperation in the field of police education through training courses, legal counseling, and professional development by both Albanian and foreign experts. Beginning in January 2000, a three-year project was implemented to train Albanian Police on human rights. This project was developed in cooperation with the Danish Human Rights Centre, financed by Danish Assistance to Albanian Police (DANIDA), and has been extended to twelve prefectures of the country; and training consists of two days of seminars directed by police experts in the Police Academy and by legal experts in the justice field. This training is also given to the students of the police academy.

Police Use of Firearms

The use of firearms by the police is determined in law No. 2990, dated December 24, 1998, and authorized in the following situations:

1. For the protection of the police officer's life or the life of a citizen when attacked with firearms or threat to life, and when the attack cannot be prevented by other means
2. For the daily performance of duties according to the laws and when the attack cannot be prevented by other means
3. When objects are guarded by armed policemen
4. When a crime has been committed (destruction or damage to property, robbery, bank theft, high-value object theft, rape by a group of people)
5. When a person has committed a serious crime and is attempting to escape a police pursuit
6. When the arrested or sentenced person attempts to escape from imprisonment centers or detention rooms or attempts to violently free other arrested or punished persons
7. When a group of people attempts to pass through a checkpoint or use firearms near a police checkpoint

Firearms are not used against vulnerable groups or people in public gatherings, and they are not used when an illegal order has been given. The law on the right to carry firearms identifies persons who are allowed to keep firearms. The two main categories are high-ranking authorities of the state and other persons such as civilian guards for the security of objects or banks, and police workers (tax police, municipals, and so on). Firearms are a state monopoly in Albania.

Complaints and Discipline

The police worker has the right to complain about arbitrary actions against him to his superior or to a higher authority of the disciplinary commission (the highest disciplinary committee), to an ombudsman, or to the Court. Disciplinary measures, according to the regulation, include warning, warning with rejection, five-day loss of pay, delay of promotion up to one year, decrease in rank, job suspension up to three months, and dismissal from police. These measures are taken by superiors directly or by the superior in a scaled way.

Importance is paid to the treatment of complaints addressed to police by the public. During 2002, 157 complaints were received from the public, of which 70 cases were for maltreatment, and 87 cases were for infringement of law during search and seizure.

There have been numerous critiques by the media, international organizations, and NGOs of human rights abuses by police. A significant report was the annual report on practices on human rights issued by the democracy bureau of the U.S. State Department in March 2002. These critiques target arbitrary arrests and abuses with suspects, detainees, and prisoners, as well as cases of mistreatment of minors, journalists, local representatives, and so on. There have also been cases of use of deadly force. NGOs, the Albanian Helsinki Committee, and the Albanian Center for Human Rights have launched investigations of illegal arrests and rights violations of detained persons. There have also been allegations of torture of crime victims.

International Cooperation

Because of the internationalization of certain types of crime, war against illegal trafficking, organized crime, and terrorism, international cooperation is both a strategic priority and a necessity. The main directions of cooperation are:

- Agreements and bilateral protocols of cooperation in the fight against illegal trafficking, organized crime, and terrorism, with more than fourteen countries including Italy, Greece, Turkey, Macedonia, Montenegro, Egypt, China, Russia, and Slovenia
- Unilateral agreements of cooperation on war against crime, especially its organized forms in the framework of the European Union (EU) on the Black Sea
- Transborder crime in Southeastern Cooperation Initiative (SECI) framework
- Fight against illegal trafficking (Albania, Greece, Italy, and Germany)
- Programs of material and technical assistance for the Albanian Police from the European Union (ECPA mission) and the United States (ICITAP)
- Education, training, and scholarships for police personnel abroad

Police Education, Research, and Publications

The only postsecondary educational institution responsible for the preparation and qualification of police workers is the Police Academy in Tirana. The mission of the Police Academy is to form, prepare, and qualify specialists for all roles in the State Police, to be skillful and committed to protect order and public security, as well as to develop scientific research in the field of policing. The Police Academy is composed of the three-year academy that responds to the need for formation and qualification of medium- and high-ranking police workers (inspectors, commissars) and the Police Institute that forms and qualifies police workers for basic roles (agents, assistants). The research and scientific activity at the Academy is directed by the Scientific Council of the Academy and focuses on research, study, and scientific treatment of policing issues. In addition to the pedagogical process, the teaching staff, respective sectors, and students engage in scientific research activity to ensure increased research capacity of the teaching staff, access to scientific information in lectures, and development of applied studies in the field of policing. An office for studies and research in the field of policing has been established that will cooperate with other similar institutions within and outside the country. It will publish materials for the needs of the Academy and police in general and will also be responsible for qualification of the upper ranks. Since 2000, this office has published the magazine *Crime, Order and Policing*. This scientific magazine covers issues of crime, order, public security, and democratic policing. It offers positive experiences, recommendations, and concrete solutions to police problems. The main publication on the police is the monthly magazine *Police Today*. Financing for these publications and other materials is included in the police budget and that of the Police Academy. The following are leading researchers and authors in the area of police and policing in Albania:

Bajram Yzeiri, director, Police Academy
Hasan Shkembi, chief, section of studies and research center, Police Academy
Ilir Mandro, deputy director, Police Academy
Luan Veliqoti, adviser, public order minister
Pandeli Taci, director, studies center, and qualifications, Police Academy
Piro Lazi, chief, professional department, Police Academy
Jani Papandile, external lecturer, Police Academy.

Examples of recent research on police and policing are listed below.

Law and the police, police management, by Dr. Bajram Yzeiri
Criminology, identification of firearms, crime scene investigation in homicide via firearms cases, Ilir Mandro
History of police, Albanian police legislation (historical review), Hasan Shkembi
Forensic photography, Luan Veliqoti
Criminology and penology, Jani Papandili and Ilir Mandro
Police frustration in focus, Piro Lazi

Explanatory vocabulary of CID terms, Pandeli Taci.

HASAN SHKEMBI

Bibliography

Albania, Republic of. Constitution of the Albanian Republic. Albanian Parliament. Tirana, 1998.
———. Penal Code of the Republic of Albania. Albanian Parliament. Tirana, 1995.
———. Penal Procedure Code of the Republic of Albania. Albanian Parliament. Tirana, 1995.
———. On the State Police. Law No. 8553. Albanian Parliament. Tirana, 25 November 1999.
———. On Ranks in the State Police. Law No. 8463. Albanian Parliament. Tirana, 20 July 2000.
———. On the Organization and Function of the Judiciary Police. Law No. 8677. Albanian Parliament. Tirana, 2 November 2000.
———. Disciplinary Regulation of the State Police. Decision of the Council of Ministers. Tirana, 2000.
———. Organization and Function of the Police Academy. Decision of the Council of Ministers, No. 281. Tirana, 2 June 2000.
———. Police Personnel Regulation of the State Police, No. 280. Tirana, 2 June 2000.
———. Regulation of the Police Academy. Ministry of Public Order. Tirana, 2001.
———. Statute of the Police Academy. Tirana, 2001.
———. Strategy of Reform in the State Police. Ministry of Public Order. Tirana, 1999.
Crime, Order and Policing. Police Academy. No. 1, 2002, Tirana.
Qiriazi, Perikli. *Albanian Geography*. Tirana, 1998.
Shkembi, Hasan. *History of the Police*. Tirana: Police Academy, 1996.
Taci, Pandeli and Shkembi, Hasan. Personnel Prognosis of the State Police: Review. Ministry of Public Order. Tirana, 2000.
Thengjilli, Petrika. *History of the Albanian People*. Tirana, 2000.

ALGERIA

Background Material

Algeria is bordered by Mauritania, Morocco, and Western Sahara, the Mediterranean Sea, Tunisia and Libya, and Niger and Mali. Algeria differs from its close neighbors in that it is state dominated by the military. The great majority of the population consists of Sunni Muslims of Arab Berber descent. Arabic and Tamazight (a Berber dialect) are the official languages, even though French is widely spoken. The area is in turmoil, and police or gendarmes may well be part of the problem. Algeria is a nation at war with itself. As the news has reported for more than a decade, Algeria has been embroiled in one of the bitterest civil wars in modern history.

The police have played a significant role in the nationalist movement that began to develop after World War I. The war for independence against European colonialism began three decades later in 1954. Independence was achieved in 1962, and the country became a nonaligned state but championed the movements against white minority rule throughout Africa. However, after Islamic fundamentalists, the Front Islamique du salut (FIS), won 42% of the vote in first-round elections in 1991, the army cancelled the elections and forced the president to resign. The fundamentalist party was banned, and its leaders were arrested. A state of emergency was declared, which remains in force today, and an armed insurrection has continued into the present. In 1994, General Liamine Zeroual became president, but resigned in 1999. In new elections, Abdelaziz Bouteflika, the military oligarchy candidate was sworn in as president. The government has been plagued by accusations of discrimination against Berbers and widespread corruption. Algeria assumed a two-year seat on the UN Security Council in January 2004. For more than a decade, one of the world's most brutal wars has been played out in Algeria. The alleged combatants are "Islamists" and "security forces." Over 200,000 people have perished in the struggle. It is also a civil war that has divided the army and the people, although the actual fighting has largely been between the paramilitary forces and a small, violent faction of Islamic extremists. Unfortunately, the security forces or police have been involved in bloody massacres and numerous documented human rights violations, along with the terrorists.

The policies of Algeria's ruling military junta, or "le pouvoir," have helped cause and perpetuate its civil war. The corruption and incompetence of its senior generals has squandered much of the nation's wealth, and its repression has pushed legitimate political opposition to engage in extreme violence. The end result suggests the conclusion that Algeria's army has done more to destroy the nation than protect it.

Contextual Features

Ordinary criminal cases are heard in the regular civil court system by judges appointed by the Ministry of Justice through an independent board. Criminal cases are heard in forty-eight provincial courts, which have jurisdiction over more serious crimes as well as appellate jurisdiction over lower courts in local tribunals (*tribunaux*), which have original jurisdiction for less serious offenses. According to the U.S. State Department's *Country Reports on Human Rights Practices* for 1992, the judiciary is generally independent of executive or military control, except in cases involving security or public order.

In December 1992, special antiterrorist courts with civilian judges were established to try crimes specifically relating to terrorism. According to the State Department, these courts are believed to have been formed so that the government might have greater influence over the outcome of security-related criminal cases. A State Security Court, which had previously tried cases involving endangerment of national security, had been abolished in 1989 as part of a political reform program. Muslim Sharia law predominated in local courts, but there were no Islamic courts as such. Military courts dealt with offenses by military personnel and all types of espionage cases. During the 1991 state of emergency, about 700 persons were tried in military courts whose jurisdictions had been widened to include acts endangering national security. The trials of seven opposition leaders in 1992 were among those heard by military courts. Some of the rights normally accorded in civil courts were ignored or circumscribed in the military courts.

Outwardly, defendants in civil courts usually have full access to counsel who are supposed to be able to function freely without governmental interference. The Algerian Bar Association provides pro bono legal services to defendants unable to pay for their own lawyer. In connection with criminal investigations, detention for questioning normally cannot exceed forty-eight hours, but an antiterrorist law issued in 1992 permits prearraignment detentions of up to twelve days.

Similar to Western protocols, detainees must be informed immediately of the nature of charges against them. Once charged, a person can be held under pretrial detention indefinitely while the case is being investigated. No bail system exists, but provisional liberty may be granted if the detainee can demonstrate availability at all stages of the inquiry. Lawyers are entitled to have access to their clients at all times under visual supervision of a guard. Defendants have the right to confront witnesses and present evidence. Trials are public, and defendants have the right of appeal.

Prior to the civil unrest of 1991 and 1992, the government had introduced political reforms that liberalized the justice system with respect to actions deemed to threaten internal security. Previously, citizens could be arrested for expressing views critical of or different from those of the government, for disturbing public order, for associating with illegal organizations, or, in extreme cases, for threatening state security. The constitution of 1989 provides the right to form political parties and civic associations and to strike and strengthens the right of freedom of expression and opinion. Nevertheless, under legislation introduced in 1990, persons convicted of publishing information endangering state security or national unity can be sentenced for a term of up to ten years. Criticizing Islam or another revealed religion can bring a penalty of up to three years' imprisonment or worse.

According to Amnesty International, more than 100 persons were under sentence of death at the close of 1992. At least twenty-six Islamists were sentenced to death after the banning of their party (the FIS) in 1992, but no executions were actually carried out in 1992. More than 100 civilians and supporters of Islamic opposition groups were killed by security forces during 1992, and more than 1,000 people were in detention at the end of 1992, according to government sources.

Under the 1991 state of emergency and the 1992 martial law decrees that gave military and security authorities wide latitude to enforce public order, large numbers of Islamists were detained. The government acknowledged that it detained 9,000 persons at eight desert camps without formal charges in 1992. By the end of the year, 1,000 were still held in four remaining camps, despite government plans to close them down. Opposition leaders claimed that the number of those rounded up by the government had actually reached 30,000.

The constitution originally stated that detention in criminal cases should not exceed forty-eight hours before the suspect is charged or released (the *garde a vue* law). According to the Code of Algeria, Country Information Criminal Procedure this may be extended to four days. Also, under the Anti-Terrorist law of 1992, persons who are suspected of subversive or terrorist activities can have their detention extended to a maximum of twelve days. The individuals should be informed of the charges against them. However, changes to the Criminal Procedure Code in June 2001 significantly extended the legally permitted period of pretrial detention. Previously, anyone accused of a crime, whatever its nature, could be held for no longer than sixteen months while their case was being investigated by the examining magistrate. Now, those accused of crimes punishable by sentences of at least twenty years' imprisonment can be held for twenty months while their case is investigated by the examining magistrate; those accused of "crimes considered to be terrorist or subversive acts" for thirty-six months; and

those accused of a "transnational crime" for up to sixty months.

Algeria adopted a penal code in 1966, retaining the death penalty. Algerian criminal law includes the death penalty for crimes against state security, crimes against life, and economic sabotage. Military criminal law also has the death penalty. The 1992 counterterrorism law has also made it possible to impose the death sentence for subversive or terrorist activities for which the Algeria criminal code previously only had the maximum of life imprisonment. Since the end of 1993, the execution of the death penalty has been suspended.

The legal system is based on socialist, French, and Islamic law. Judicial review of legislative acts is conducted by an ad hoc Constitutional Council composed of various public officials, including several Supreme Court justices. Algeria has not accepted International Court of Justice jurisdiction. Postindependence governments were quick to take steps to eliminate the French colonial judicial legacy. In 1965, the entire system was reformed by a decree that instituted a new judicial organization. This decree was followed a year later by the promulgation of new legal codes—penal code, code of penal procedure, and code of civil procedure. A provincial court in each province and nearly 200 widely distributed tribunals were eventually created. The Algerian authorities announced legislative changes in June 2001 as an important step in bringing domestic law into line with international standards, pointing to textual changes to strengthen the presumption of innocence; increase the control of law enforcement agents by the judiciary; bolster the rights of detainees held in the custody of the security forces; limit the recourse to pretrial detention; and establish the right of an individual wrongfully held in pretrial detention to compensation.

The judiciary now consists of three levels. At the first level is the tribunal, to which civil and commercial litigation is submitted and which takes action in penal cases of the first instance. At the second level is the provincial court, which consists of a three-judge panel that hears all cases and functions as a court of appeal for the tribunals and for the administrative jurisdictions of the first instance. At the third and highest level is the Supreme Court, which is the final court of appeal and of appeals against the decisions of the lower courts. In 1975, the Court of State Security, composed of magistrates and high-ranking army officers, was created to handle cases involving state security. The constitution of 1996 instituted two new high courts to complement the Supreme

Court. The Council of State acts as an administrative equivalent to the Supreme Court, hearing cases not ordinarily reviewed by that body; and the Tribunal of Conflicts was instituted to regulate any jurisdictional disputes that might arise between the other two high courts.

Police Profile

Organizational Description

The security apparatus consists of the army (ground, naval, and air defense forces); national gendarmerie; national police; communal guards; and local self-defense forces. All of these elements have been involved in counterinsurgency and counterterrorism operations. The Ministry of National Defense and Ministry of Interior are tasked with overseeing the maintenance of law and order. While the government has generally maintained minimum control of the security forces, there have been repeated instances in which elements of the security forces allegedly acted independently of government authority. These acts resulted in the human rights violations already mentioned. Allegations of such abuses have continued to decline since 2001 but have persisted.

The government's security apparatus is composed of the armed forces (army 107,000 including 75,000 conscripts, air force 10,000, and navy 7,000) and paramilitary forces of 181,200, including an estimated 100,000 self-defense militia and communal guards, as well the gendarmerie of approximately 60,000 (U.S. State Department Briefing Notes, August 2000). The gendarmerie has been blamed for using excessive force in dealing with unrest in the Berber area of Kabylie, where an insurrection began in spring 2001. Responsibility for maintaining law and order is shared by the Gendarmerie Nationale and the Surête Nationale. Unusually and similar to a military force, members wishing to be discharged must have their resignation approved by a special police commission. Leaving the force without authorization can incur punishments ranging from a fine to imprisonment, much like the concept of absence without leave in Western militaries.

The Gendarmerie Nationale serves as the main rural police force. It is responsible for maintaining peace in villages, towns, and rural areas and providing security surveillance over local inhabitants, as well as representing government authority in remote areas. The force is organized into battalions, whose companies and platoons are dispersed to individual communities and outposts. It is a heavily armed force and works under the Algerian Ministry of Defense. In a much publicized effort to combat terrorism in rural areas, it is supposed to work in close cooperation with the army. In conjunction, the Corps de Garde Communale (local police) provide standard policing on a local level and when requested also support the security forces in the fight against terrorism.

The Gendarmerie Nationale was commanded in 1993 by Major General Abbas Ghezaiel, who reported directly to the minister of national defense. In 1993, specific gendarmerie personnel constituted a total force of approximately 35,000. Although generally regarded as a resourceful and competent force, the gendarmerie has been severely tested in dealing with constant civil disorder. It frequently has lacked adequate manpower, and its units have been inadequately trained and equipped for riot control. The gendarmerie, however, have demonstrated, at least according to the government, the ability to root out terrorist groups operating from mountain hideouts.

As stated, the gendarmerie is organized into battalions, whose component companies and platoons are dispersed to individual communities and desert outposts. Its regional headquarters are in the same cities as the six military regional headquarters; it has subdivisions in the forty-eight *wilayat* (provinces). A highly mobile force, the gendarmerie possesses a modern communications system connecting its various units. They are also in direct contact with the army. Gendarmerie equipment includes light armored weapons and transport and patrol vehicles. The force in 1993 had forty-four Panhard armored personnel carriers, fifty Fahd armored personnel carriers, and twenty-eight Mi-2 light helicopters. In addition to using training provided by the French since independence, the gendarmerie operates its own schools for introductory and advanced studies. The gendarmerie's main training center is at Side Bel Abbes, the former headquarters of France's Foreign Legion. The academy for officers is at Isser, about 150 kilometers east of Algiers.

The Sûreté Nationale is the primary policing authority in Algeria's principal cities and other urban areas. Subordinated administratively to the Ministry of Interior, the Sûreté is charged with maintaining law and order, protecting life and property, investigating crimes, and apprehending offenders. In addition, it performs other routine police functions, including traffic control. Under the direction of its inspector general, the Sûreté consists of a force of approximately 16,000, and is believed to be organized along the lines of its French counterpart, with operational and investigative branches and supporting services. The judiciary police branch is responsible for criminal investigations, working in close coordination with the Office of the Public Prosecutor in the Ministry of Justice. Police elements assigned to the capitals of the *wilayat* are under the nominal control of the individual governors. A special riot police force is equipped with modern riot-control gear. Although the police were able to cope with urban disturbances and violence during the early and mid-1980s, the military has frequently been called in to control larger outbreaks of violence.

Elements of the Sûreté also play a role in countering threats to the government arising from political subversion. The Sûreté assigns police contingents to work with customs inspectors at legal points of entry to control illegal activities. The force has concentrated on apprehending illegal immigrants and drug traffickers.

Military Security is the principal and most effective intelligence service in the country. Its former chief, General Mohamed Médiène, was believed to number among its more influential officers. After President Boumediene took power in 1965, he relied on Military Security to strengthen his control during the difficult process of consolidating "external" and "internal" personnel, some of whom were of questionable loyalty. Military Security became the dominant security service in the 1970s, responsible to the head of state for monitoring and maintaining files on all potential sources of opposition to the national leadership.

Although theoretically bound by the same legal restrictions as the Sûreté and gendarmerie, Military Security is less circumscribed in its operations. Frequent allegations of incommunicado detention of suspects have been linked mainly to Military Security. An important role in the area of national security was later assumed by the General Delegation for Documentation and Security (Delégation Générale de Documentation et Sûreté, DGDS) as the principal civilian apparatus for conducting foreign intelligence and countering internal subversion. The security services are engaged in attempting to infiltrate Islamist groups and to employ paid informers for monitoring opposition movements. They are not held to the same constitutional standards as normally recognized in the West, especially as they relate to phone surveillance and search and seizure limitations. During and after the riots of October 1988, widely published accounts told of torture and other human rights abuses of detainees. Both Military Security and the DGDS were implicated in the brutal treatment of detainees to obtain confessions or extract information on clandestine political activists. Government officials have acknowledged individual cases of improper behavior but have failed to adequately investigate them or punish the offending officers. Promises of internal self-policing and investigation of abuse, although repeatedly promised, have failed to materialize.

In September 1990, the dissolution of the DGDS was announced after criticism of its repressive role in the 1988 riots. The dissolution coincided with other government verbal reforms to remove barriers to individual liberties. Informed sources believed, however, that this action did not represent an end to domestic intelligence operations but rather a transfer of DGDS functions to other security bodies. Surveying the overall intelligence picture, the French periodical *Jeune Afrique* concluded that Military Security, with its abundant documentation on the leadership and organization of the violent Islamist groups, remained the senior intelligence body concerned with internal security. Other intelligence groups include the Coordinating Directorate of Territorial Security, Antiterrorist Detachment, and a working group of the High Council of State charged with political and security matters. The precise functions and jurisdictions of these bodies remain a mystery to outsiders.

In addition to the Corps de Garde Communal, various local defense militias exist. In January 1997, the Algerian Prime Minister signed an executive decree that made the existence of militias official and set out their parameters. Thus, groups acting outside the normal framework of law enforcement have been entrusted to carry out law enforcement functions. The decree states that members of these "groups of legitimate violence" can use force and firearms in cases of aggression or attempted aggression or in case of a "duty to assist persons in danger." Their conduct has been documented in numerous human rights violations publications, especially those of Amnesty International. In November 1994, the African Commission on Human Rights even adopted a resolution on Algeria that included its concern over extrajudicial executions, torture, and arbitrary detention. The resolution called on the international community to recognize the situation in Algeria, but was later not renewed.

KATHLEEN SWEET

Bibliography

Algeria. 1963. Constitution. Available at: http://www.marx ists.org/history/algeria/1963/09/constitution.htm.

asylumlaw.org. 2002. Country Information Algeria. April. Available at: www.asylumlaw.org/docs/algeria/IND0402_algeria_ca.pdf.

Cordesman, Anthony H. 2001. *Tragedy of Arms: Military and Security Developments in the Maghreb.* Westport, Conn.: Greenwood Publishing Group. Available at: http://site.ebrary.com/lib/ncent/Doc? id=10002045&ppg=120.

Human Rights Watch. 2001. *Human Rights Developments. Algeria. World Report 2001.* Available at: www.hrw.org/wr2k1mideast/algeria.html.

U.S. Embassy, Algeria. 2005. Home page. Available at: http://algiers.usembassy.gov/.

U.S. Library of Congress. 2004. Country Studies. Availble at: http://lcweb2.loc.gov/frd/cs/dztoc.html.

United Nations. 1995. Conclusions and Recommendations of the Committee on Economic, Social and Cultural Rights, Algeria. U.N. Doc. E/C.12/1995/17. University of Minnesota. Available at: www.umn.edu/humanrts/esc/ALGERIA.htm.

U.S. State Department. 2004. Algeria. Background Note. Available at: www.state.gov/r/pa/ei/bgn/8005.htm.

U.S. State Department. 2004. Algeria. Country Reports on Human Rights Practices. Bureau of Democracy, Human Rights, and Labor, February. Available at: www.state.gov/g/drl/rls/hrrpt/2003/27924.htm.

ANDORRA

Background Material

Andorra consists of a range of mountains and valleys wedged between France and Spain, with a total area of 467.76 square kilometers. The first mention of the name "Andorra" goes back to the year 843. In the thirteenth century, a period of struggle between the bishops of Urgell and the counts of Foix for the sovereignty of Andorra was settled with the signing of two conventions. These "Paréages" (1278 and 1288) established co-sovereignty between the two powers. Through dynastic marriages, the rights held traditionally by the counts of Foix were conferred to the Kings of France.

During the nineteenth and twentieth centuries, Andorra consolidated its political institutions, increasing its legitimacy and profile on the international scene. In 1993, the Andorran people approved, by referendum, the Constitution of the Principality, and the country became a member of the United Nations. Also in 1993, a treaty of friendship and cooperation was signed between Andorra and France and Spain (by which the co-princes (see below) formally recognized the sovereignty of Andorra).

The population of Andorra is 66,000 (36% Andorran, 40% Spanish, 10% Portuguese, 7% French). Its capital is Andorra-la-Vella. The official language is Catalan, but Spanish and French are widely used. The major religion is Catholicism. Andorra enjoyed a position of economic self-sufficiency, based around agricultural production and mining, for a significant period of time. Since the 1930s, it has developed its economy on tourism, trade, and banking activities (GNP: US$15,250 per capita in 2000).

Contextual Features

Andorra is a parliamentary co-principality and a sovereign state governed by the rule of democratic law. Its constitution proclaims the principles of freedom, equality, justice, tolerance, defense of human rights, and dignity of the individual. Andorran political institutions are organized on a pyramidal basis. At the base, individuals are grouped into quarters; quarters are gathered into seven parishes, and each has a representative body (*comu*). Comus have the legal authority and represent the autonomy of Andorran local communities. The parliamentary assembly, "General Council of the Valleys," ensures representation of the citizens and parishes. It exerts legislative power, approves the state budget, and directs and controls the government's political action. The government, composed of the head of the government (*cap de govern*) and ministers, directs the national and international policy, proposes draft laws to parliament, and exerts the state authority. Since 1993, it has been autonomous (before 1993, the executive power was exerted directly by the co-princes via their local representatives, the *viguiers*). The co-princes are the bishop of Urgell

(Spain) and the President of the French Republic. They have identical capacities and assume, jointly and in an undivided way, the function of head of state.

Despite its bonds with France and Spain, Andorra is not a member of the European Union (EU); and there are still frontier checks at the Andorran borders. Nevertheless, a trade agreement (including a partial customs union) between the EU and Andorra was signed in 1990. Andorra has been a member of the Council of Europe since 1994.

The constitution guarantees the principles of law, public legal standards, non-retroactivity of laws establishing a more severe sanction, legal safety, accountability of public authorities, and prohibition of arbitrary action. In the same way, Andorra integrates into its legal system the relevant principles of international law. Andorra has a penal code (November 7, 1990) and a code of penal procedure (October 12, 1998) supplemented by a series of legal texts on the organization of criminal justice (dated March 9, 1993, and including the law on public ministry of December 12, 1996, among others). Criminal trials and sentencing are public, and oral procedures are preferred.

Crime is primarily related to tourist activity (shoplifting, credit card theft, drugs). The smuggling of high-duty goods such as alcohol, cigarettes, and food is also a problem for Andorra, which is often referred to as a commercial and tax paradise. The Andorran state is also vigilant in regard to money laundering. The rate of homicides is low (from zero to three murders each year since 1996).

The constitution of 1993 guarantees the right of justice formerly held by the co-princes and exerted by their representatives (*viguiers*). Justice is held by the Andorran people; judges are independent and nominated in public competition.

The first instance court, called the Batllia, considers penal contraventions and minor offenses. The first are judged by a single judge, the others by a panel. The Batllia also acts as an examining judicial body. The Court of Corts judges the most serious offenses in first instance and hears appeals of the decisions by the Batllia. The Superior Court of Justice judges major offenses in appeal. The public prosecutor's office (Ministeri Fiscal) was created in 1975 to represent society as a whole in court, exert public action in penal matters, and ensure the respect of fundamental rights and civil liberties. The Superior Council of Justice, by appointing judges and exerting disciplinary power over them, ensures the independence and correct operation of justice.

The penal code establishes the penalties, distinguishing between "principal penalties" (such as imprisonment, admonition, and fine) and "additional penalties" (for example, fine, prohibition of stay, expulsion of foreigners, and confiscation). The death penalty was abolished in 1993, with the last execution occurring in 1943. Andorra has two prisons, one for long-term imprisonment, and the other for provisional detention. The administrative and legal authorities frequently have recourse to the expulsion of foreign delinquents.

Prison conditions generally meet international standards. Men and women are held separately, as are juveniles from adults. Pretrial detainees are also held separate from convicted criminals. The government permits visits by independent human rights observers.

Police Profile

Background

For centuries the valleys of Andorra did not have a police force. A popular militia called the Sometent was officially created in the fifteenth century by the *viguiers* and was in charge of defense against external attacks. In 1931, the construction of a road and a hydroelectric power station gave rise to a police force (one armed person in charge and six agents) assigned to maintain law and order, assist judges, and stop delinquents. This police force, under the orders of the *viguiers* and judges until 1993, is now subject to orders of the head of government but also to judges and the public prosecutor's office in regard to legal questions. The towns, exercising some authority in police matters, employ police officers to enforce law and order within their territory and to control traffic and parking.

Organizational Description

The Andorran national police force ensures the citizens' safety through its preventive and deterrent capabilities. The force numbers 207 people, including 161 police officers (13 women). The largest number belongs to the uniformed police force (132) with 29 non-uniformed members assigned to criminal matters). The rest are technical and administrative staff. The national police force is governed by the decree of July 3, 1989. The services, organized in three large sectors, are headed by a director.

1. The Public Safety sector consists of four units. The public safety unit carries out patrols by car and by foot on public highways to assist citizens and prevent the commission of offenses. For this purpose, it provides listening offices to citizens in all parishes. It also includes the explosives section (detection and destruction of explosive devices) and the canine section (specializing in avalanches, narcotics, and explosives, among others). The public service unit coordinates the operational activity of police services and answers phone calls by citizens for information and complaints. The border unit is in charge of immigration, as well as surveillance of the Andorran borders. The traffic unit ensures traffic control, including procedures after road accidents. This unit provides escorts for the Andorran authorities and personalities visiting the country and accompanies all special transports. It provides assistance to drivers whose cars break down or who encounter weather-related problems; Andorran roads are frequently snow-covered in winter.

2. The Criminal Investigation Department consists of the investigation unit in charge of criminal matters (with several specialized sections for minors, narcotics, economic and financial delinquency, information on sects, and terrorism). A general invesiagtion unit and the Andorran National Central Office for Interpol are also attached to this sector.

3. The Police Support sector includes the department of analysis and data processing, which ensures the filing of administrative and legal police documents and centralizes information for criminal analysis. It also hosts a department of prevention and social orientation that carries out investigations in social matters such as drug addiction, alcoholism, family conflicts, juvenile delinquency, and abuse of children and women. It also includes the department of management and maintenance (buildings, cars, and other police equipment), the department of human resources (initial and continuous staff training), and the legal department (providing advice on legal questions).

The police hierarchy is structured on the ranks of commissioners, officers, sergeants, and agents.

Police officers are recruited by open competition. Requirements for candidates are Andorran nationality, good moral standards, ability to speak and write Catalan correctly, ability to speak French and Spanish, and familiarity with the basic legal provisions on the Andorran police services. They must hold a minimum school level (second-degree diploma of the Andorran education system or equivalent for trainee agents; two years of university for officers; four years of university law studies for commissioners) and be suited physically and mentally.

Hierarchy

Ranks	Number
Commissioner 1st class	1
Commissioner 2nd class	4
Officer 1st class	2
Officer 2nd class	2
Sergeant major	4
Sergeant 1st class	1
Sergeant 2nd class	18
Police agent	129
Trainee police agent	18

Functions

The Andorran police force cooperates with the administrative authorities, for example, regarding the implementation of immigration and road traffic regulations. It also ensures the monitoring of the numerous sporting and cultural events. It mainly acts in a preventive way, but also has powers to investigate, apprehend, and seize persons, among others. For example, police legally may detain persons for 48 hours without accusing them of a crime. Warrants are required for arrest. The government declined to amend the law to provide individuals under arrest with immediate access to an attorney despite a request by the Council of Europe's Committee for the Prevention of Torture in 2000. Legislation provides, however, for legal assistance beginning 25 hours after the time of arrest.

Training

Police staff can reach the rank of sergeant by means of internal competition. For the higher ranks, internal promotion occurs according to merit. It is, however, relatively difficult to advance to the highest ranks of the hierarchy because of the limited number of opportunities available in this small police force.

Initial training lasts six to seven months with theoretical courses and practical training. For officers, initial training lasts one year at the school of the Guardia Civil in Spain; commissioners receive two years of training at the higher police school in Lyon, France. Police officers are instructed in human rights during initial training.

Use of Firearms

Police officers on duty must carry their service weapon. Use of these weapons is limited by the law to specific cases: self-defense or of others, escape of prisoners, driver refusal to stop at traffic control, fugitives trying to elude apprehension, and defense of persons or buildings against attacks. Nevertheless, police officers must make the least possible use of their weapons and fire to wound and not to kill. In cases of hostage taking, and even in situations of self-defense, the police must be expressly authorized to fire.

Complaints and Discipline

Andorran law provides that police officers must not engage in other professions, that they are bound by professional secrecy, and that they must respect the principles of human rights in their work (such as courtesy, prohibition against inflicting inhuman or degrading treatment). Disciplinary measures are in place for infractions, from minor (including tardiness, inaccuracy with respect to the public, and failure to observe uniform dress code details, among others), to significant (for instance, failure to observe chain of command, political propaganda, racial or religious discrimination), to major ones (such as, unauthorized absence from duty, insubordination, and professional misconduct). Andorran legislation specifies a range of disciplinary sanctions, including oral or written warnings and suspension of bonus payments up to discharge.

Terrorism

As of early 2005, Andorra was not threatened by terrorist activities. Nevertheless, the police force supervises the movement of people at the borders within the framework of cooperation with the French and Spanish police forces.

International Cooperation

In 1987, the Andorran police became a member of Interpol. The central national Interpol bureau is closely associated to the activities of the operational services (direct hierarchical and functional links, in particular with the investigation unit in charge of combating organized crime). The Andorran police maintain relations with French and Spanish police services in the context of a regional and operational network and by adopting protocols of cooperation that include mutual assistance in investigation, exchange of information and best practices, exchange of civil servants, and joint training activities.

Andorra has signed several instruments of the Council of Europe relating to police and justice matters, including, among others, the Convention for the Prevention of Torture; Convention on the Transfer of Convicted Criminals; Convention Concerning Money Laundering, the Discovery, Seizure and Confiscation of Products of Crime; European Convention on Extradition; European Convention on the Prevention of Terrorism; and Penal Convention on Corruption. In addition, Andorra has signed several United Nations agreements, such as the Convention Against the Illegal Traffic in Drugs and Narcotic Substances; Convention on the Suppression of Financing for Terrorism; Convention Against Transnational Organized Crime; Convention Against Torture and Other Cruel, Inhuman or Degrading Penalties.

Police Education, Research, and Publications

Laws are published in the *Andorran Official Journal*. It is possible to find certain elements of Andorran law on the website of the Law Library of Congress. As of 2004, there were no publications dedicated to Andorra's police force. The only data available are delivered by international organizations such as Interpol. It is also possible to find short descriptions on Internet sites of the Principality of Andorra.

BRUNO DOMINGO

Bibliography

Alis Salguero, Ivan. *La police dans un micro-état européen: l'exemple de la principauté d'Andorre* (The police in a European micro-state: the example of Andorra). Toulouse: Centre d'Etudes et de Recherches sur la Police, Institut d'Etudes Politiques, 2000.

Council of Europe. *Report to the Andorran Government on the Visit to Andorra carried out by the European Committee for the Prevention of Torture and Inhuman or Degrading Treatment or Punishment (CPT) from 27 to 29 May 1998*. Strasbourg: Council of Europe, 2000.

Degage, Alain, and Antoni Duro i Arajol. *L'Andorre*. Paris: Presses Universitaires de France, 1998.

Interpol. International Statistics Series, Andorra. Available at: www.interpol.int.

ANGOLA

Background Material

The Republic of Angola is located on the western coast of southern Africa. It has an area of 1,246,700 square kilometers and a population of 10,978,552 (2004 estimate). The capital is Luanda, while other major cities are Benguela, Cabinda, Huambo, Lobito, Lubango, and Namibe.

A majority of the population is Bantu. The official language of Angola is Portuguese. Other languages spoken include Umbundu, Kimbundu, Kikongo, and Tchokwe. Just over half (51%) of the population identifies as Catholic, while 17% profess Protestantism, 30% adhere to traditional/animist beliefs, and 2% practice other religions.

Angola's main exports are petroleum, diamonds/minerals, wood, fish, coffee, cotton, and sisal. The GDP per capita (purchasing power parity) is US$1,900 (2003 estimate).

Angola was a Portuguese colony following the arrival of the Portuguese in 1482. The first city, Luanda, was established in 1605.

Angola achieved independence on November 11, 1975, after fourteen years of armed struggle. The first government was composed of members of the Popular Movement for the Liberation of Angola (MPLA), which was first established in 1956. Angola has begun to enjoy the fruits of peace since the end of a twenty-seven-year civil war in 2002. Fighting between the MPLA and the National Union for the Total Independence of Angola (UNITA) followed independence from Portugal. Peace seemed imminent in 1992 when Angola held national elections, but UNITA renewed fighting after losing to the MPLA at the polls. Up to 1.5 million lives may have been lost, and 4 million people displaced, in the quarter-century of fighting. The death of Jonas Savimbi, the leader of UNITA, ended that group's insurgency and strengthened the MPLA's hold on power.

Angola's economy has been in disarray because of the prolonged period of nearly continuous warfare. Although an apparently durable peace was established in 2002, consequences of the conflict continue, including widespread landmines. Subsistence agriculture provides the main livelihood for 85% of the population. Oil production and ancillary activities are vital to the economy, contributing about 45% to GDP and more than half of exports. Much of the country's food is still imported. To fully take advantage of its rich natural resources—gold, diamonds, extensive forests, Atlantic fisheries, and large oil deposits—Angola will need to continue reforming government policies and to reduce corruption. While Angola made progress in bringing inflation down from 325% in 2000 to about 106% in 2002, the government has failed to make sufficient progress on reforms recommended by the International Monetary Fund, such as increasing foreign exchange reserves and promoting greater transparency in government spending. Increased oil production supported a 7% GDP growth rate in 2003.

Contextual Features

The government of Angola is a multiparty democracy with a semipresidential system composed of the following state organs: president of the republic, national assembly, government, and tribunals. Angola is administratively organized into 18 provinces with 163 municipalities.

Adopted in November 1975, Angola's first and only constitution dedicated the new republic to eliminating the vestiges of Portuguese colonialism. The constitution provides numerous guarantees of individual freedom and prohibits discrimination based on color, race, ethnic identity, sex, place of birth, religion, level of education, and economic or social status. The constitution also ensures freedom of expression and assembly.

Constitutional revisions in 1976 and 1980 more clearly established the national goal of a revolutionary socialist, one-party state. As revised, the constitution vests sovereignty in the Angolan people, guaranteed through representation of the party, and promises to implement "people's power." It also emphasizes the preeminence of the party as policy-making body and makes the government subordinate to it. Government officials are responsible for implementing party policy. Economic development is founded on socialist models of cooperative ownership.

Other constitutional guarantees include health care, access to education, and state assistance during childhood, motherhood, disability, and old age. In return for these sweeping guarantees, each individual is responsible for participating in the nation's defense, voting in official elections, serving in public office if appointed or elected, working (which is considered both a right and a duty), and generally aiding in the socialist transformation.

Despite its strong socialist tone, the constitution guarantees the protection of private property and private business activity within limits set by the state. National economic goals are to develop agriculture and industry, establish just social relations in all sectors of production, foster the growth of the public sector and cooperatives, and implement a system of graduated direct taxation. Social goals include combating illiteracy, promoting the development of education and a national culture, and enforcing strict separation of church and state, with official respect for all religions.

The constitution also outlines Angola's defense policy. It explicitly prohibits foreign military bases on Angolan soil or affiliation with any foreign military organization. It institutionalizes the People's Armed Forces for the Liberation of Angola (Forças Armadas Populares de Libertação de Angola, FAPLA) as the nation's army and assigns it responsibility for defense and national reconstruction. Military conscription applies to both men and women over the age of eighteen.

At independence, the Ministry of Justice administered the civilian legal and penal systems, although its jurisdictional boundaries with the Ministry of State Security, Ministry of Interior, Ministry of Defense, and regional military councils were unclear. The civilian court system, known as the People's Revolutionary Tribunal (Tribunal Popular Révolucionario), was established in 1976 to deal with capital offenses against national security. These courts had jurisdiction over crimes against the security of the state, mercenary activities, war crimes, and so-called crimes against humanity, and they could unilaterally assume jurisdiction over any criminal case that had a significant impact on national security. Such tribunals, composed of three to five judges, were established in each provincial capital, but administered by a national directorate in Luanda.

In 1983, military tribunals were set up in each military region and empowered to try crimes against the security of the state, including alleged offenses committed on behalf of UNITA such as terrorism, espionage, treason, sabotage, destabili-zation, and armed rebellion; "economic crimes" such as speculation, hoarding, and currency violations; disobedience of directives from the regional military council; and other acts that might "damage or endanger the interests of collective defense and security." The independence of the judicial structure and process was severely circumscribed by political control of the court system and the fact that the judges of the military tribunals were military officers whose appointment, reassignment, and removal were controlled by the minister of defense. Military courts frequently handed down death sentences, which were usually carried out by firing squad. Although persons sentenced to death by military courts were legally entitled to automatic appeal to the Armed Forces Military Tribunal, the highest military court, such appeals were not known to have been lodged.

Article 23 of the constitution provides that citizens shall not be arrested and tried except in accordance with the terms of law and states the right of accused persons to legal defense. However, the extent to which these provisions were observed was uncertain. Amnesty International reported the detention without charge or trial of dozens of political prisoners and trials by military tribunals of hundreds who were not given adequate opportunity to prepare their defense or appeal sentences.

Angolan law provided that persons suspected of having committed serious crimes against the security of the state could be detained without charge by the Ministry of State Security for up to three months, and that this period could be extended an additional three months. Unlike common criminals, such detainees did not have to be brought before a judge within forty-eight hours of arrest and could not challenge the basis of detention. Political prisoners had to be informed of the accusations against them after six months in detention and then had to be referred to a public prosecutor or released. If charges were pressed, there was no stated time period within which a trial had to be held, and delays of several years were common.

There is little reliable and accurate information available on the prison system in Angola. Prisons are apparently very basic, and authorities apparently have wide discretion in dealing with prisoners. Detention facilities are overcrowded, diets are substandard, and sanitation and medical facilities are minimal. Intimidation, prolonged interrogations, torture, and maltreatment, especially of political prisoners, are common. Visits by families, friends, and others appear to be restricted arbitrarily. Prisoners are sometimes held incommunicado or moved from one prison to another without notification of family members.

The Ministry of the Interior and the Ministry of State Security reportedly administer penal institutions, but their respective jurisdictions are unknown. The main prisons are located in Luanda, where a maximum security institution was opened in early 1981, and in several provincial and local jurisdictions. The principal detention centers for political prisoners are the Estrada de Catete prison in the capital and the Bentiaba detention camp in Namibe Province. The government-run detention center at Tari in Cuanza Sul Province has been identified as one of the main rural detention centers. Tari was a former sisal plantation turned into a forced-labor farm, where prisoners lived in barracks or in their own huts while doing forced labor. In 1983 it was reported that Tari's prisoners included those already sentenced, awaiting trial, or detained without trial as security risks.

It is difficult to generalize about the incidence of crime in Angola. It is likely that Angolan society exhibits criminal patterns similar to those of societies in other developing countries experiencing uncontrolled rural-to-urban migration, rapid social change, unemployment and underemployment, the spread of urban slums, and the lack or breakdown of urban and social services. It is also likely that such patterns are more pronounced because of three decades of endemic conflict and massive dislocation. Historic and comparative patterns suggest that crimes against property increase with urban growth and that juveniles account for most of the increase.

Available evidence suggests that the crime rate in Angola is rising. Smuggling, particularly of diamonds and timber, is frequently reported as a major criminal offense, occasionally involving senior government officials. Dealing in illegal currency is supposedly another common crime. Persons acting as police or state security agents sometimes abuse their powers by illegally entering homes and stealing property. Intermittent police crackdowns on black market activities have only short-term effects. Endemic production and distribution problems and shortages give rise to embezzlement, pilfering, and other forms of criminal misappropriation. The extent of this problem was indicated by an official estimate in 1988 that 40% of imported goods did not reach their intended consumers because of the highly organized parallel market system. The government later approved new measures to combat economic crime on a national scale.

Police Profile

Organizational Description

In order to fully comply with its responsibilities, the National Police consists of the following levels of command: General Command, Provincial Command, and Municipal Command.

The National Police is divided into the following areas and departments: Public Order, Criminal Investigation, Traffic and Transport, Investigation and Inspection of Economic Activities, Taxation and Frontier Supervision, and Rapid Intervention.

Functions

The National Police is a militarized force whose basic duties include the following generic duties:

1. Defense of democratic legality.
2. Preservation of public order and calm.
3. Respect for the regular exercise of the fundamental rights and liberties of citizens.
4. Defense and protection of state, collective, and private property.
5. Prevention of delinquency and reduction of criminality.
6. Collaboration in the implementation of national defense policies, in terms established by the law.

Its exclusive duties follow:

1. Ensure the registry, organize the records, and oversee the marketing, use, and transport of arms.
2. Ensure that preventive measures of manufacture and marketing of munitions and explosive substances and their equipment are followed.
3. Guarantee the personal security of members of government agencies and of other national and foreign entities, and of other citizens when subject to situations of significant threat.
4. Exercise the policing, supervision, and control of national borders.

Finally, the special duty of the National Police is to guarantee the security of strategic economic objectives.

Complaints, Discipline, and Human Rights

Angola is a signatory to several international human rights conventions, including the Convention on the Political Rights of Women of 1953, Convention on the Elimination of All Forms of Discrimination Against Women, Geneva Conventions of 1949 Relative to the Treatment of Prisoners of War and the Protection of Civilian Persons in Time of War, and Convention and Protocol Relating to the Status of Refugees of 1967.

However, the human rights organization, Freedom House, consistently gives Angola the lowest ratings on its scale of political rights and civil liberties, and *The Economist World Human Rights Guide* assigned Angola an overall rating of "poor." Amnesty International and the U.S. Department of State have also issued reports highly critical of human rights practices in Angola.

The lack or disregard of international human rights standards in Angola is evident in several respects. Arbitrary arrest and imprisonment without due process are among the most common abuses. Although Angolan law limits the amount of time one can be detained without charge, there does not appear to be a specific period within which a suspect must be tried, and as many as several hundred political prisoners may have been detained for years without trial. The regional military councils have broad authority to impose restrictions on the movement of people and mate-

riel, requisition supplies and labor without compensation, and try crimes against state security.

Amnesty International also reported numerous instances of torture during the late 1970s and early 1980s. Ministry of State Security officials were reported to have permitted or sanctioned the torture of criminals and political prisoners by such methods as beating, whipping, and electric shock. Political detainees arrested for offenses such as criticizing government policies were deprived of food and water for several days and subjected to frequent and severe beatings during interrogation and confinement. Although allegations of torture and mistreatment remained common in the mid-1980s, such practices did not appear to have been systematic.

JEAN-ETIENNE ELION

Bibliography

U.S. Library of Congress. A Country Study: Angola. The Library of Congress, 1989. Available at: http://lcweb2.loc.gov/frd/cs/aotoc.html.

ANTIGUA AND BARBUDA

Background Material

The islands of Antigua and Barbuda are located in the middle of the Leeward Islands in the Eastern Caribbean, roughly seventeen degrees north of the equator. Antigua is composed 280 square kilometres and Barbuda, 161 square kilometres. In comparison, the combined area of the two islands is 2.5 times the size of Washington, D.C.

Christopher Columbus explored the island of Antigua in 1493. The name Antigua follows from the Church of Santa Maria de la Antigua in Seville, Spain. Britain colonized Antigua around 1632 and Barbuda around 1678. The country joined the West Indies Federation in 1958. When the West Indies Federation disintegrated, the country became one of the West Indies Associated States. It then started handling its own internal affairs. The country became fully independent in November 1, 1981. The capital is Saint John's (Antigua).

The population totals 68,320 (2004 estimate). Most are descendants of slaves who used to work in the sugar plantations. There are also some Europeans, mostly British, with a few Portuguese, along with Lebanese and Syrians. The Anglican form of Christianity is the most widely followed religion, although other Protestant denominations and Roman Catholicism are also represented. The official language is English, although local dialects are also spoken.

Tourism continues to dominate the economy, accounting for more than half of the GDP. Reduced tourist arrivals since 2000 have slowed the economy. The dual-island nation's agricultural production is focused on the domestic market and constrained by a limited water supply and a labour shortage arising from the lure of higher wages in the tourism and construction industries. Manufacturing consists of enclave-type assembly for export with major products being bedding, handicrafts, and electronic components.

Contextual Features

The government of Antigua and Barbuda is a constitutional monarchy with a United Kingdom—style parliament. The executive branch is headed by a governor general, although the chief of state is the British monarch. The head of government is the prime minister. The cabinet consists of the Council of Ministers; ministers are appointed by the governor general on the advice of the prime minister.

The highest body of the judicial branch is the Eastern Caribbean Supreme Court, based in Saint Lucia. One judge of the Supreme Court is a resident of the islands and presides over the Court of Summary Jurisdiction. The Supreme Court Chief Justice is elected by unanimous vote by the prime ministers of the member-states. At present, the Eastern Caribbean Supreme Court justice presiding over the Court of Summary Jurisdiction is a resident of Antigua and Barbuda.

Antigua and Barbuda's judiciary is structured around the High Court, the Court of Appeals, and the Magistrates Court. Of a total of eleven judges, three sit in the High Court, four in the Appeals Court, and four in the Magistrates Court. Some High Court judges act as resident judges. The judicial branch in Antigua and Barbuda does not have budgetary autonomy; resources derive from the executive branch.

The legal system of Antigua and Barbuda is based on English common law. The judicial system is part of the Eastern Caribbean legal system, and reflects historical ties to the United Kingdom. The constitution designates the Privy Council in London as the final court of appeal, which is always employed in the case of death sentences. There are no military or political courts.

Antigua's legal system is strongly influenced by and based on the British system. Criminal and civil disputes are resolved through oral public debate between parties. Civil cases are presented to the High Court. In both cases, the right of appeal is allowed to the Court of Appeal with a final right of appeal to England's Privy Council. Both civil and criminal procedures are oral and adversarial. Civil cases can last four or five years (in the High Court), while criminal cases do not generally last more than one year.

Criminal defendants have the right to a judicial determination of the legality of their detention. The police must bring detainees before a court within forty-eight hours of arrest or detention. The law prohibits forced exile, and the government does not use it in practice. The constitution provides for an independent judiciary, and the government generally respects this provision in practice.

The constitution provides that criminal defendants should receive a fair, open, and public trial. In capital cases only, the government provides legal assistance at public expense to persons without the means to retain a private attorney. Courts can reach verdicts quickly, with some cases coming to conclusion in a matter of days. Antigua and Barbuda does not currently have an institutionalized legal aid system, although an effort is being made to implement one.

The most pressing crime problem in Antigua and Barbuda is gang activity. There are six gangs in Antigua and Barbuda made up of young persons, ranging in age from fourteen to thirty-five, although the majority are between fourteen and twenty-five. Gang members number about 200 persons. At least two of these gangs were formed and are led by persons who lived in the United States, one of whom was deported to Antigua after committing criminal offences. These gangs are involved in robberies, drug trafficking, and assaults on persons. At least one of them has also been involved in causing disturbances in schools. Three members of one gang were charged with murdering a police inspector who was in a shop they were robbing.

Antigua and Barbuda serves as a transhipment point used by drug traffickers, with cocaine being the primary drug that is transhipped through the islands. Traffickers use boats, air drops, ships, and commercial containerized shipping to move illicit drugs to the islands for transhipment to the United States via Puerto Rico and to Europe. Traffickers also use couriers to smuggle small amounts of cocaine and heroin through Antigua and Barbuda. The drugs are concealed either on the couriers, in their luggage, or carried internally. Antigua and Barbuda is also a significant country for international money laundering. Antigua and Barbuda's offshore banking sector was established in the mid-1980s and grew rapidly. This growth, along with limited regulatory capabilities, has made Antigua and Barbuda one of the more vulnerable financial centres in the Caribbean to money laundering. In addition, internet gambling in Antigua and Barbuda is used, to a smaller extent, for money laundering. According to the U.S. State Department, by the end of December 2000, the government of Antigua and Barbuda (GOAB) reportedly had licensed more than eighty internet gaming websites and about twenty-six offshore banks.

Other crimes include but are not limited to vandalism, street crime, burglaries, and break-ins.

The Ministry of Legal Affairs is responsible for the prison system in Antigua and Barbuda, which is administered by Her Majesty's Prison. Visits are permitted by independent human rights groups.

The prisons are generally overcrowded, and facilities are antiquated. Prison conditions are poor and primitive. There have been reports of abuse.

Police Profile

Demographics

The police is a constabulary of 687 police officers, and the Antigua and Barbuda Defence Force, The Royal Antigua and Barbuda Police Force allow women to enroll. Statistics on the number of men and women presently working are not available.

Organizational Structure

The police department serving the islands of Antigua and Barbuda is the Royal Antigua and Barbuda Police Force. The Royal Police Force of Antigua and Barbuda was created in February 1967, following the dissolution of the then-Leeward Islands Police Militia, the defence units on the islands before many of them gained political independence from Britain. Both of these forces report to the deputy prime minister, but they are independent of one another. However, in certain special circumstances, the Royal Police Force works in conjunction with the Defence Force. The Coast Guard is subordinate to the Police Department.

The Antigua and Barbuda Police Force presently consists of the main headquarters of twelve police stations located around the two islands. There is no special telephone number to call for emergencies. For any matter concerning the police department, residents call the main switchboard numbers offered in the local telephone directory. Six different telephone numbers are offered for the police headquarters. There is a special crime hotline number available to the public.

The Antigua and Barbuda Police Force has two criminal investigation units. The Criminal Investigation Department/Narcotics is solely responsible for the investigation of money laundering and drug trafficking offences and is provided with additional assistance from the Antigua and Barbuda Coast Guard and the Defence Force. The Minor Offences Department investigates crimes not addressed by the Criminal Investigation Department/Narcotics.

The police have introduced a domestic violence unit. This unit has been established due to the visit of a domestic violence team sponsored by the Florida Association of Voluntary Action in the Caribbean area. This unit will train the police department on how to deal with domestic violence issues.

Functions

Duties include patrol, traffic control, crowd control, arrests, and recordkeeping of arrests. The police generally respect human rights; basic police-reporting statistics, however, are confidential.

Although the director of public prosecution is charged with investigating criminal cases, this process can also be initiated by the police, who may even act as prosecutors.

In addition to the aforementioned duties, the police force act as the governor general's honour guard.

Training

The police forces are trained, organized, and supervised according to British law enforcement practices. All this training is conducted in the Police Training School presently situated in Antigua. Actual training procedures are not available to the public.

ANALIDA IVANKOVIC

ARGENTINA

Background Material

Argentina is located in the southeast part of South America, bordering the South Atlantic Ocean and the countries of Uruguay and Brazil to the east, Paraguay to the northeast, Bolivia to the north, and Chile to the west. The Argentine Republic is the second largest country of the region.

Argentina was a Spanish colony until the May Revolution (May 25, 1810) and the Independence

Declaration (July 9, 1816). Military leader José de San Martín, a national hero, played a decisive role in the independence wars against Spanish rule. Nation-formation during the nineteenth century evolved under political conflict and civil armed struggles. Throughout the twentieth century, major players were the military and two political parties, the Radicals (Unión Cívica Radical, UCR) and Peronists (Partido Justicialista, PJ). From the 1930s to 1983, Argentina suffered military interventions in politics. From the 1960s, during periods of dictatorship as in most Latin American countries, the prevailing security concept emphasized the prevention and combat of threats from internal enemies that included counterinsurgency warfare, militarization of law enforcement targeted against society, a distorted military role turning inward to oversee national boundaries—all major elements of the so-called national security doctrine, which was a kind of ideological setting to justify military regimes.

The year 1983 brought the return to democracy, but a consensus arose about the need to redefine the role of the military. To address the military problem, measures were taken in the following areas:

Judicial: Military junta members and guerrilla leaders were arrested, put on trial, and sentenced on human rights violations that occurred during the "Dirty War" (1976–1983).

Political: Civilian control over the armed forces was restored. The National Commission of the Disappeared was established by then-President Raúl Alfonsín (UCR), chaired by writer Ernesto Sábato; the Commission issued a final report, titled *Never More*, which verified 9,000 disappearances.

Legislative: The 1988 National Defense Law distinguished defense (external security) from law enforcement and public security (internal security) and prohibited military intelligence from conducting activities related to domestic political matters. The 1992 Internal Security Law established civil management functions and bodies to control police forces, and the controversial Full-Stop and Due Obedience laws that limited indictments of military personnel.

President Carlos Menem (PJ) later granted presidential pardons to all those convicted or under trial (October 1989 and December 1990, respectively). Offenses related to missing children during the Dirty War (kidnappings) remained under judicial investigation.

After decades of economic decline and hyperinflation, during the 1990s President Menem launched a modernization program based on macroeconomic stabilization, privatization, trade and financial liberalization, and state reform. Under the 1991 convertibility law, parity (US $1 = 1 peso) allowed price stability. However, unemployment, income distribution, and poverty rates became worse under conditions of eroded competitiveness, heavy reliance on capital inflows, and exposure to external shocks. By late 1998, the economy went into recession. Under the presidency of Fernando De la Rúa (Alianza, a center-left coalition of UCR and Frepaso), Argentina's sustained economic decline forced an austerity program, triggering political, economic, and social crisis. After months of protests by *piqueteros*—groups of unemployed people who demonstrated in the streets—in the third week of December 2001, looting broke out in suburban areas and in Buenos Aires and other cities, resulting in civilian deaths (twenty-three) during a stage of siege. De la Rúa resigned, and the National Congress appointed Senator Eduardo Duhalde (PJ) as president. He devalued the peso and confronted the economic crisis, and social protest diminished during 2002.

Contextual Features

Under the constitution approved in 1853 and modified in 1994, Argentina adopted a representative, republican, and federal form of government with three independent powers: executive, legislative, and judicial. Suffrage is universal and mandatory from age eighteen. Executive power is vested in a president and vice president, who are directly elected by popular vote. They hold office for a four-year term and are eligible to run for a second consecutive term. Legislative power is vested in the National Congress, which has two chambers. The Senate (seventy-two seats) is composed of three senators per province and three senators for the Autonomous City of Buenos Aires (Buenos Aires City), elected by popular vote to six-year terms. The Chamber of Deputies (257 seats) includes representatives directly elected by the people in proportion to each district population, for four-year terms with half standing for reelection every two years. Judicial power is exercised by the Supreme Court of Justice, to which the president appoints the nine members with Senate consent, and by other lower federal courts —appellate, district, and territorial.

Each of the twenty-three provinces and Buenos Aires City has a constitution in compliance with the National Constitution and a provincial government with three independent powers (executive, legislative, and judicial). Provincial court systems are similarly organized, comprising provincial supreme, appellate, and lower courts. There is a single penal code; each province has a code of penal procedure approved by its legislature, and there is a National Code of Penal Procedure for the federal jurisdiction.

The corrections system is decentralized, including both federal and provincial penitentiaries that are currently overcrowded (in 2000, the adult incarcerated population totaled 39,917). The mission of the Federal Penitentiary Service (SPF) is the custody, guarding, and treatment of persons deprived of liberty. Subordinate to the Minister of Justice for Security and Human Rights, through the Undersecretary for Criminal Policy and Penitentiary Affairs, the penitentiary service is headed by the National Director, assisted by General Directorates for Penitentiary Corps, Correctional Regimes, and Administration. It includes thirty centers throughout the country, the nation's Penitentiary School, Penitentiary Studies Postsecondary Academy, and Noncommissioned Officers (NCO) School.

Reflecting its Roman and Spanish traditions, the Argentine justice system is a mixture of accusatory and inquisitorial systems. The criminal process consists of two principal stages. First is the preliminary instruction, or investigatory stage, carried out by instructional judges or by prosecutors and characterized by secrecy. Second, the trial is, in principle, a public, oral, and adversarial proceeding in order to issue the sentence—finding of guilt or innocence and a sanction—which is given by the court, usually a panel of three judges. There is no jury, and there is no death penalty in Argentina.

In the wake of reforms of the criminal justice system and penal procedures, at the provincial level there is a trend toward the accusatory system, the establishment of courts for minors, and the acknowledgment of victim's rights. Probation and mediation are in developmental stages.

Based on the 1994 constitutional reform, international declarations and conventions have constitutional rank, complementing the rights and guarantees recognized therein. The reform also established two independent bodies: (1) the Ombudsman, within the legislative sphere, for defense and protection of human rights and other rights; and (2) the Public Ministry, the Nation's General Attorney and General Defender, with functional autonomy and financial autarky to promote the performance of the judiciary in defense of legality and general interests of society. Since 1994, official statistics have shown a significant increase in overall crime rates, including homicide. Based on data available from public health reports, a World Bank economist affirmed that comparable historical statistics of homicide rates show that Argentina has been and to a large extent still is a relatively peaceful society. Homicide rates from 1979 to 1993 were clearly below those of Brazil, Mexico, and the United States (Lederman 1999: 1). The homicide rate for the last decade of the twentieth century averaged 7.86 per 100,000, and the total crime rate averaged 2.15 (Sistema Nacional de Información Criminal 2001).

For 2001, the homicide rate (number of homicides per 100,000 population) was 8.23. Among the most significant types of offenses in 2001 were crimes against property (66% of total recorded crimes), with theft at 49% and theft without violence at 40%. Violent crime, or offenses against persons, followed with 18% of total recorded crimes.

Victimization survey data show that 39.6% of the inhabitants of Buenos Aires City were victims of some type of offense in 2001. The reporting rate for residents of the city victimized at least once in the same period and reporting the incident to the police dropped 7.9% from 1997 (31%) to 2001 (23.1%). Writing in 1999, the cited economist observed that the

> recent crime wave is being driven by a combination of factors including the deteriorating growth rate and the worsening in the distribution of income.... [T]here is strong evidence that Argentina suffers from low quality public institutions, which not only impair its economic development, but also tend to contribute to the upward trend in crime rates by making citizens less willing to report crimes and reducing the probability of convicting criminals.

(Lederman 1999: 5)

Police Profile

Background

Postcolonial police duties developed in the early 1800s. In 1821, the post of police chief for Buenos Aires Province was established, providing the basis of the first state police, and was headquartered at Buenos Aires City. In December 1880, the Police of the Capital City and the Policías de la Provincia de Buenos Aires (PPBA) were established as separate bodies. In January 1945, the Policía Federal Argentina (PFA) replaced the Police of the Capital City, extending federal jurisdiction and responsibilities to the national territories, which eventually became provinces.

The Prefectura Naval Argentina (PNA), or Argentine Coast Guard, dates back to the early 1800s. In 1819, the Captaincy of Ports of Río de la Plata United Provinces was established. The PNA was consolidated in 1896, and this was made law decades later in 1969.

The first bills for the creation of a gendarmerie were drafted in the first decade of the twentieth century, during the tenures of Presidents Roque Sáenz Peña and Hipólito Yrigoyen. In July 1938, the Gendarmería Nacional (GN), or National Gendarmerie, was created by law, replacing the Army Regiment border surveillance activities. Since 1947, the Argentine Police Agreement for technical cooperation between provincial police forces—PFA, GN, and PNA—and the National Aeronautical Police (Air Force, Ministry of Defense) has been in effect. In 1970, specific missions, functions, and jurisdictions for the federal forces were established by law. In 1994, after decades under military or defense jurisdiction, the GN and PNA were subordinate to the Interior Ministry. In July 2002, internal security functions and responsibilities of the Interior Ministry were transferred to the newly created Ministry of Justice, Security and Human Rights (MJSyDDHH); PFA is subordinate to the president through the MJSyDDHH, and the GN and PNA are subordinate to the MJSyDDHH.

Policing in Argentina is the responsibility of federal and provincial governments. The Internal Security System provides a policy framework for the twenty-six armed and uniformed police bodies. By the late 1990s, increase in violent crime, insecurity, and public concern about policing prompted police reorganizations and reforms with disparate outcomes. At the national or federal level, the three police bodies are grouped under the category of security forces, that is, intermediate forces and not armed forces, that fulfill missions and functions within both the internal security and the defense spheres. At the provincial level, each government organizes and governs its police force. The jurisdiction of the federal police and security forces is limited to defined federal crimes and territories, and the provincial police forces are limited to nonfederal crimes within their boundaries. Federal forces are integrated in the internal security system established by the Internal Security Law of 1992. The political head of the system is the minister of justice,

security, and human rights, assisted by the Internal Security Secretariat. The national police effort is the coordinated action of the PFA, GN, PNA, and the twenty-three provincial police forces for the purpose of maintaining internal security as defined by law.

There are two main types of police functions:

- Security Police: activities related to public order and safety, crime prevention and control, criminal intelligence, traffic control, and several administrative policing activities.
- Judicial Police: policing activities performed under judicial supervision and related to criminal investigations. With the exceptions of Córdoba, Buenos Aires, and Mendoza Provinces, which established separate bodies, every police force exercises both functions.

Sharp increases in urban crime along with complaints of use of excessive force and abuses associated with police led to general concern about policing. In the late 1990s, police reform initiatives were undertaken in Buenos Aires Province (with a population of 13,818,677, of which Greater Buenos Aires accounts for 8,684,953), and in Mendoza Province (population 1,576,585). Beginning in December 1997, the plan for Buenos Aires police reform and a systemic approach to public security was drafted by León Arslanián and Alberto Binder. The appointment of a civilian as chief of police with intervention powers over the former Policía Bonaerense, which was renamed Policías de la Provincia de Buenos Aires, was followed by a significant purge of police personnel. The force was split into separate bodies to achieve decentralization and specialization: Security Police, organized in each of the eighteen judicial departments; Investigations Police; Transit Police; and a service for the custody and transfer of detainees. The Ministry of Justice and Security was established to enhance civilian control. Other measures established by law included rules of conduct for police personnel, guidelines for detentions, prohibitions regarding citizens' privacy, control of corruption and abuses office, education guidelines, and community participation mechanisms.

Since 1999, the Mendoza Province police reform has followed a similar pattern. Another official initiative, the 2001 transfer of PFA urban structures and functions from the national level to Buenos Aires City government jurisdiction, fell short of expectations. Córdoba, Chubut, Neuquén, Río Negro, Santa Fe, and Buenos Aires City underwent a "wave" of community policing or community participation.

Organizational Description

The PFA is a civil armed institution and the major police force. According to Organic Decree-Law of 1958 and related legislation, the PFA performs security and judicial policing in Buenos Aires City (population 2,768,770) and in the country's federal jurisdiction acts as fiscal (revenue) police and state security police and is responsible for the protection of top officials and government buildings and for issuing passports and identity cards.

The PFA organization includes the chief of police office; vice chief of police office; 12 superintendents (interior; metropolitan security; investigations; dangerous drugs; scientific police; internal affairs; institutional counseling; personnel and education; administration; welfare; federal firemen; communications); several general directorates; and lower level units (departments, divisions, sections, police stations, delegations, and special bodies). Throughout Argentina, the PFA has 751 components; fifty-three police stations are located in Buenos Aires City alone.

Rank structure includes nine officer levels (subaltern officers; chief officers, including subcommissioner and commissioner; senior officers including commissioner inspector, major commissioner, general commissioner); and seven NCO levels. From a high of 41,334 personnel in 1983, the PFA totaled 30,573 personnel in 1998, and women represent about 11% of the force.

As a security force of military nature, the GN performs duties within territorial borders, has federal security and judicial policing functions, and protects assigned strategic targets. The law regulates its organization, missions, and functions. Concerning internal security, the GN prevents and counteracts drug trafficking, terrorism, organized crime, and related crimes; breach of the peace, at the request of a competent authority when the situation exceeds the control of the police forces; crimes against the constitutional order; offenses against environment and health preservation; and international and interjurisdictional traffic and road technical security infringements. The GN also undertakes criminal investigations in areas that are under integration or regional cooperation agreements.

The basic organization of the GN consists of the national director; deputy national director; national directorate general and special staffs; and the regional headquarters with mobile detachments and other specialized and support elements. GN border security areas are international border crossings and tunnels, international linking routes, parks and environmental reserves, lakes situated on international borders, and other places as assigned by the executive or upon federal justice request.

As the country's maritime authority, the PNA is both a security force and specialized police force established by law. It is responsible for performing police functions in jurisdictional waters and ports in the fields of safety of navigation, safety and public order enforcement, federal judicial police, navigational issues police, drug interdiction, and reestablishment of security at the request of a competent authority. The PNA also provides services as environmental preservation police and maritime and river fishing police.

The PNA organization includes the Commandant's Office and support offices (General Secretariat, Intelligence Service, Naval Technical and Legal Advisory Service, and High Rank Officer Council, and consultative councils); Vice Commandant's Office; Safety of Navigation Police Directorate; Safety and Judicial Police Directorate; Environment Protection Directorate; personnel, material, training, and administration directorates; and the Operations Directorate. The three federal forces act as immigration and customs auxiliary police.

The police reform in Buenos Aires Province in 2001 introduced new organizations and a new policing model. With approximately 45,000 personnel, PPBA is the largest in the country.

Federal police forces total 66,547 members (PFA, 33,378; GN, 18,259; PNA, 14,910). With the addition of the provincial police forces of 139,459 personnel, the estimated total is 206,006. The ratio of police to population is one for every 175 inhabitants, or 5.7 per 1,000 population.

Training

Federal educational systems provide basic training, specialized training, and professional improvement for their personnel. Minimum recruitment standards for officer candidates are secondary school studies; Argentine citizenship; single marital status, without children; no criminal record; age seventeen to twenty-five (PFA), age seventeen to twenty-two (PNA); and age seventeen to twenty-three (GN). Selection includes psychological, medical, physical, and intellectual examinations. PFA has a one-year study plan that requires a university degree; the three-year plan requires only secondary school education. The PNA requires candidates to have completed three years of secondary school studies to apply for NCO rank. Since 1996, within the career path for promotion to officer rank of PFA subcommissioner, a tertiary or university degree is required; to reach NCO rank of first sergeant, secondary school studies are required.

New PFA basic policies and doctrine were published in 1999. As new policing objectives, community problems including victim support, domestic violence, offenses against minors, and ecology issues were proposed. Subsequent priorities have included expanding personnel; specialization through continuing education methodologies; implementing structural changes such as re-creation of Mounted, Transit, Infantry Guard bodies, police station schedules, and reorganization of divisions; and implementing a technology investment plan for communications and personnel protection equipment.

Police Use of Firearms

The use of firearms is covered by a 1975 decree that confers conditions on legitimate users and enables federal and provincial police to bear firearms. In 1999, the PFA issued an internal regulation limiting compulsory bearing of firearms only to ordinary or additional policing services.

Complaints and Discipline

According to Article 35 of the Internal Security Law, police and security forces must strictly observe the American Human Rights Convention. The UN Code of Conduct for Law Enforcement Officials has been adopted, and human rights courses and topics have been introduced in federal forces training programs. Police disciplinary matters are governed internally by a system of sanctions, applicable to an officer who violates the police code of conduct and enforced hierarchically through the chain of command. There are no police unions.

Oversight systems continue to be developed. Under reform legislation in Buenos Aires Province, the Corruption Control and Functional Abuses Office—Internal Affairs Auditor and Ethics Tribunal—was established at Ministry level to resolve police corruption and serious misbehavior cases. Since 1999, the Mendoza Ministry of Justice and Security has had a civilian general inspector of security office and a disciplinary board; the former is in charge of overseeing the legality of police activities, and the latter, a mixed body of civilians and police officers, enforces the disciplinary code. In other jurisdictions, citizens have the option of judicial complaint. In January 2000, due to public concerns, the internal affairs area was upgraded to superintendency level under the direct authority of a PFA chief.

A 2001 report issued by an Investigative Commission on Forged Police Procedures, established in June 2000 under the General Attorney's Office, discovered fifty-five cases forged by PFA members that had contributed to flagrant human rights violations. Another controversial issue has been police authority to detain individuals for identity or police records verification,

Based on data available from newspapers, the Legal and Social Studies Center (CELS), a human rights organization, has compiled cases of civilians and police killed in direct confrontations for the period 1993 to 2001. During that time, an average of four civilians died in Buenos Aires City or in Greater Buenos Aires for every PFA or PPBA member killed. For 2001, the highest figures for the period, 261 civilians died in confrontations, and police deaths reached 78. More than 25% of those civilians were eighteen years old or younger, while 22% were nineteen to twenty-one years old (CELS 2002: 1–14).

Terrorism

Counterterrorism is an intergovernmental and interagency task that requires coordination among law enforcement, intelligence, and other government agencies that may contribute to preventing terrorist acts. In the 1990s, Argentina suffered two serious terrorist bombings; the first was on March 17, 1992, at the Israeli Embassy, and the second was on July 18, 1994, at a Jewish community center building—Asociación Mutual Israelita Argentina (AMIA).

In 1997, the PFA's Department of Antiterrorist Investigations Unit (DUIA) was created for the main purpose of assisting in the judicial investigations of terrorist bombings. In February 2001, the General Directorate for International Terrorism and Complex Offences was established under the direct authority of the PFA Chief. This structure included Interpol; DUIA; Complex Offenses Directorate; Discriminatory Behavior Investigations Division; Special Federal Operations Group Division, an elite response team for crisis situations; and the Triple Border Section, based in Puerto Iguazú (Misiones Province) and responsible for obtaining and processing information from the border region among Argentina, Brazil, and Paraguay.

To deal with international terrorism threats since 1993, the GN progressively developed its intelligence structures both at the coordination and operational levels in Buenos Aires City headquarters and Puerto Iguazú. Responsibility lies with the Intelligence Directorate and the Special Counter-Terrorism Intelligence Unit. Other GN components include the Special Forces Section, Special

Bomb Disposal Group, Scientific Police Department, and Special Unit for Judicial Investigations and Procedures.

The PNA's intelligence units throughout its territorial jurisdiction operate under functional control of the PNA Intelligence Service and the Antiterrorist Division and also play a role in counterterrorism. Although the National Aeronautical Police organization is not part of the Internal Security System, it does contribute to counterterrorism by keeping airport security measures fully operational. A special investigations unit was established by decrees in 2000 and 2001 to assist in judicial investigation and to provide operational support and coordination. The unit consists of members of the following: PFA's Department of Antiterrorist Investigations Unit (DUIA); the Intelligence Secretariat's Department on International Terrorism and Transnational Crimes; PNA's Antiterrorist Division; GN's Division for Coordinating Antiterrorist Activities; the Federal Penitentiary Service's Intelligence Department; and the Anti-corruption Office, MJSyDDHH.

International Cooperation

In May 1996, the Triple Border Tripartite Command was established. Composed of permanent members of the police and security forces of Argentina, Brazil, and Paraguay, its primary purpose is to strengthen border cooperation in domestic security through exchange of information and joint and combined actions in order to combat international terrorism, drug trafficking, money laundering, smuggling of weapons, munitions, and explosives, and other offences related to transnational organized crime. Following the September 11, 2001, terrorist attacks in the United States, steps were taken to revitalize subregional counterterrorism tasks, improving cooperation and coordination of activities. At the subsequent meeting of interior ministers of the Common Market of the Southern Cone, Bolivia, and Chile, the Specialized Working Group on Terrorism was created.

The PFA Interpol Department performs duties of the National Central Office under the mandate given by the International Criminal Police Organization. PFA took part in several international peacekeeping missions, including action in Slovenia in 1996 and in Eastern Slovenia, and by contributing advisors in El Salvador in 1998. The GN also takes part in peacekeeping missions, humanitarian assistance, and police monitoring, including UN missions in Guatemala (since 1995); Bosnia-Herzegovina and Croatia (1996); Angola (1991–

1995); Haiti (several multinational actions since 1994); UN Protection Force, former Yugoslavia (1992–1995); UN Transitional Administration for Eastern Slovenia, Baranja, and West Sirimum, UN Civilian Police (1996–1997) and UN Police Support Group (since 1998); White Helmets in Luanda, Lebanon-Beirut, and Rwanda-Kigali (since 19 96); UNTAET, Timor Oriental-Indonesia (1999); and NATO Multinational Specialized Unit, Bosnia-Herzegovina.

Police Education, Research, and Publications

Federal Forces Education

Federal Police College (Escuela Federal de Policía "Coronel Ramón L. Falcón")
Federal Academy for NCOs and Agents (Escuela Federal de Suboficiales y Agentes "Comisario General D. Alberto Villar")
Federal Postsecondary Academy (Academia Federal Superior "Gral.Br. Cesario A. Cardoso")
University Institute of PFA (Instituto Universitario de la PFA)
Officers Training Academy (Escuela de Oficiales "Gral.D. Martín Miguel de Guemes")
NCO Training Academy (Escuela de Suboficiales "Cbo. Raúl Remeberto Cuello")
Staff College (Escuela Superior "Gral.Br.D. Manual María Calderón")
Professional Training Center (Centro de Formación y Capacitación para GNA)
Training Center for Foreign Missions (Centro de Capacitación para Misiones al Exterior)
Officer College (Escuela de Oficiales "General Matías de Yrigoyen")
NCO School (Escuela de Suboficiales "Coronel Martín Jacobo Thompson")
Staff College (Escuela Superior PNA).

Education in PPBA

Police College (Escuela de Policía "Juan Vucetich").
Police Staff College (Escuela Superior de Policía "Crio. Mayor Emilio García").
Secondary School for police agents (Escuela de Educación Media N° 24).

Other Relevant Initiatives

Mendoza Province: Fundación Instituto Universitario de Seguridad Pública; offers graduate and postgraduate level careers and courses.

Río Negro Province: Carrera de Tecnicatura en Administración y Gestión de la Seguridad (technician in security administration and management), Centro Universitario Regional Zona Atlántica, Universidad Nacional del Comahue, Viedma.

Leading Researchers/Authors/Reporters/Experts

University Researchers

Gregorio Kaminsky, Ph.D., institutional analyst; researcher at Universidad Nacional de Lanús, Buenos Aires Province.

Máximo Sozzo, lawyer; professor and researcher at Universidad Nacional del Litoral (UNL), Rosario, Santa Fe Province; specialist in criminology; editor of: *Seguridad Urbana: Nuevos Problemas, Nuevas Perspectivas* (*Urban Security: New Problems, New Perspectives*) (Santa Fe: UNL, 1999).

Authors with Police Background

Adrián Pelacchi, retired general commissioner; former PFA chief; former secretary of internal security.

Eduardo Pérez Rejón, retired senior PPBA officer; lawyer; author of *Seguridad Pública: Profesionalismo Policial—Vigilancia Comunitaria* (*Public Security: Police Professionalism—Community Policing*) (Buenos Aires: Primo Editora, 1999); *Patrulla Policial* (*Police Patrol*) (Buenos Aires: Primo Editora, 1997).

Journalists as Authors

Martin Edwin Andersen, former *Washington Post* and *Newsweek* correspondent in Argentina and adviser to U.S. Senate and Justice Department; researcher at Freedom House, based in New York.

Ricardo Ragendorfer, journalist; author of *La Secta del Gatillo—Historia Sucia de la Policía Bonaerense* (*The Trigger Sect—Dirty History of the Bonaerense Police*) (Buenos Aires: Editorial Planeta, 2002).

Experts in Police and Security Policy

Eugenio Burzaco, political scientist; member of Grupo Sophia.

Marcelo Saín, political scientist; professor at the Universidad Nacional de Quilmes, Buenos Aires Province; former undersecretary for planning, Buenos Aires Province Ministry of Security.

Research on Police Policy and Practice

Research project, "Crime Prevention Policies, Urban Security and Police Institution in Santa Fe Province," Universidad Nacional del Litoral, project no. 168, 2000–2003, director Julio de Olazábal, co-director Máximo Sozzo. Related article: Sozzo M., et.al. "¿Más Allá de la Disciplina Policial? Transformaciones de los Mecanismos de Control Interno de la Actividad Policial en la Provincia de Santa Fe" ("Beyond Police Discipline? Transformation of Internal Oversight Mechanisms of Police Activities in Santa Fe Province"), *Delito y Sociedad. Revista de Ciencias Sociales*, no. 14 (2000): 123–160.

Research project "Violence, Citizen Security and Public Policies: Police Institutional Culture and Building of Identities Through the Educational Devices," code 04-06788-B-category II.11 Violence and Urban Security; approved in 1999; funded by the Science and Technology Research Fund (FONCYT), National Agency for Science and Technology Promotion, director, Gregorio Kaminsky, Universidad Nacional de Lanús.

Project "Citizen Security and Control of Fulfillment of the Law on the Part of Public Security Institutions," Centro de Estudios Legales y Sociales, funded by The Tinker Foundation and the Foreign and Commonwealth Office, for a two-year period.

Magazines and Journals

Published by PFA

Mundo Policial. Comisario (R) Plácido Donato—Catamarca 1272, Ciudad de Buenos Aires (1246); tel. (5411)4962-3713.

Policía y Criminalística. Comisario General (R) Roberto Rosset, Lavalle 2629 Piso 1°, Ciudad de Buenos Aires (1052); tel. (5411)4963-6095; e-mail: polycrimi@policiafederal.gov.ar.

Related to PNA

Revista Guardacostas; *Cuaderno de Bitácora.* Publisher: Editorial Guardacostas—Tacuarí 471, 6° A, Ciudad de Buenos Aires (1071); tel. (5411)4331-6092; website: *www. editguardacostaspna.org.ar/frames.htm.*

In Field of Criminology

Delito y Sociedad—Revista de Ciencias Sociales. Juan Pegoraro —Av. Congreso 2491, Ciudad de Buenos Aires (1428); e-mail: pegoraro@mail.retina.ar; subscriptions: centro_publicaciones@unl.edu.ar.

Selected Publications Since 2001

Andersen, Martin. *La Policía: Pasado, Presente y Propuestas para el Futuro* (*The Police: Past, Present and Proposals for the Future*). Buenos Aires: Editorial Sudamericana, 2002.

Gayol, Sandra, and Kessler, Gabriel, Eds. *Violencias, Delitos y Justicias en la Argentina* (*Violences, Crimes and Justices in Argentina*). Buenos Aires: Editorial Manantial, 2002.

Saín, Marcelo. *Seguridad, Democracia y Reforma del Sistema Policial en la Argentina.* (*Security, Democracy and Reform of Argentina's Police System*). Buenos Aires: Fondo de Cultura Económica, 2002.

Yrimia, Héctor. *Proyecto DACSSI para Situaciones de Crisis con Toma de Rehenes* (*DACSSI Project for Hostage-Taking Crisis Situations*). Buenos Aires: Gráfica Sur Editora, 2001.

Stanley, Ruth. "How Deviant Is Deviance? 'Cop Culture,' Mainstream Culture, and Abuse of Police Power in Buenos Aires." Paper presented at conference of the Research Group on Armed Forces and Society of the International Political Science Association, 27–30 June 2002, Bucharest, Romania. Available at: *www.msubillings.edu/dzirker/ Romania/Stanley02d.htm* (17 January 2003).

EDUARDO E. ESTÉVEZ

Bibliography

Annicchiarico, Ciro. *Seguridad (In)Seguridad: Problemática Bonaerense (Security (In)Security:The Buenos Aires Problematic)*. Buenos Aires: Némesis, 2002.

Argentine Government. Report of the Argentine Republic on its implementation of Security Council resolution 1373 (2001). Document S/2001/1340. Security Council, United Nations, 31 December 2001. Available at: www. un.org/Doss/sc/committees/1373/1340e.pdf (21 December 2002).

———. Supplementary Report of the Argentine Republic on the Implementation of Security Council Resolution 1373 (2001). Document S/2002/1023. Security Council, United Nations, 13 September 2002. Available at: http:// ods-dds-ny.un.org/doc/UNDOC/GEN/N02/495/88/PDF/ N0259488.pdf (6 January 2003).

Argentina, Poder Ejecutivo Nacional. "Jurisdicción 40– Ministerio de Justicia, Seguridad y Derechos Humanos" (Jurisdiction 40–Ministry of Justice Security and Human Rights"). Proyecto de Ley de Presupuesto Año 2003, Argentina, 2002. www.mecon.gov.ar/onp/ html/proy2003/jurent/pdf/P03J40.pdf (3 December 2002).

Burzaco, Eugenio, with Carlos Etcheverrigaray, Diego Gorgal, and María Eugenia Vidal. *Rehenes de la Violencia (Hostages of Violence)*. Buenos Aires: Editorial Atlántida, 2001.

Centro de Estudios Legales y Sociales (CELS). *Violencia en las Prácticas Policiales (Violence in Police Practice)*. Chapter 4 of the Informe sobre la Situación de los Derechos Humanos en Argentina 2002 (Report on Human Rights Situation in Argentina 2002). Buenos Aires: CELS. Available at: www.cels/org.ar/Site_cels/ publicaciones/informes_pdf/2002_Capitulo4.pdf (6 January 2003).

Corrales, Juan Carlos. "Seguridad Interior y Defensa Nacional—1° Parte 1930–1973 (Internal Security and National Defense—1st Part 1930–1973)." In *Revista de Gendarmería Nacional (GN)*, Cuaderno no. 5, 1–151. Buenos Aires, July 1993.

Dirección Nacional de Política Criminal, Departamento de Investigación. "Estudio de Victimización Ciudad Autónoma de Buenos Aires 2001" ("Victimization Study of the Autonomous City of Buenos Aires"). Ministerio de Justicia, Seguridad y Derechos Humanos. Buenos Aires, September 2002. Available at: www.jus.gov,ar/polcrim/victimiz/vic2001/Ciudad BsAs/VictiCBA2001.htm (5 January 2003).

Jankowski, H.R. "Programas de Proximidad—Policía del Neuquén" ("Proximity Programs—Police of Neuquén Province"). Paper presented at the II Congreso Internacional "La Policía del Futuro: Calidad y Policía Comunitaria," organized by the Government of the Province of Neuquén and the Barcelona University, Spain, October 30–November 2, 2001, San Martín de los Andes, Province of Neuquén, Argentina.

Lederman, Daniel. "Crime in Argentina: A Preliminary Assessment." Washington, D.C.: World Bank, December 7, 1999. Available at: http://wbln0018.worldbank.org/LAC/lacinfo client.nsf/d29684951174975c85256735007fef12/ 2a64c740 3be80d218525688100639cd2/$FILE/Crime%20in%20Ar gentina.pdf (27 December 2002).

Maier, Julio. "Breve Historia Institucional de la Policía Argentina" ("Brief Institutional History of the Argentine Police"). In *Justicia en la Calle: Ensayos sobre la Policía en América Latina (Justice in the Streets: Essays on the*

Police in Latin America), edited by Peter Waldmann, 127–140. Medellín: Biblioteca Jurídica Diké, 1996.

National Directorate of Criminal Policy, Research Department. "Victimization Studies, City of Buenos Aires 1997–2001." Buenos Aires: Ministry of Justice, Safety and Human Rights of Argentina, October 2002. Available at: www.jus.gov.ar/polcrim/victimiz/vic2001/Ciu dadBsAs/Evolucion1997-2001/Evolution%20study%20 City%20of%20Buenos%20Aires%201997-2001.PDF (5 January 2003).

Palmieri, Gustavo, Rodrigo Borda, and Cecilia Ales. "Justice Facing Police Violence." (*Derechos Humanos en Argentina Informe 2002*, part II, chapter IV [Buenos Aires: Center for Legal and Social Studies, June 2002].) Available at: http://www.cels.org.ar/english/4_documents/docu ments_pdf/police_violence.pdf (24 January 2002).

Pelacchi, Adrián. *Tratado Sobre Seguridad Pública* (*Discussion on Public Security*), Vol. 318. Buenos Aires: Editorial Policial, 2000.

Policía Federal Argentina (PFA). *Ideas Centrales del Tercer Milenio: Al Servicio de la Comunidad* (*Central Ideas of the Third Millenium: Serving the Community*), Vol. 317. Buenos Aires: Editorial Policial, 1999.

Prefectura Naval Argentina (PNA). *Reseña Histórica de la Prefectura Naval Argentina* (*Historical Account of the Argentine Coast Guard*). Colección Historia Institucional,

Serie Ensayos, No. 07. Buenos Aires: PNA, Secretaría General, Departamento Asuntos Históricos, 1994.

Rodríguez, Adolfo E. and Eugenio J. Sappietro. *Historia de la Policía Federal Argentina: A las Puertas del Tercer Milenio* (*History of Argentine Federal Police: At the Gates of the Third Millenium*). Buenos Aires: Editorial Policial, 1999.

Sistema Nacional de Información Criminal (SNIC). "Informe Anual de Estadísticas Policiales Año 2001" ("Annual Police Statistics Report 2001"). Buenos Aires: Dirección Nacional de Política Criminal, Ministerio de Justicia y Derechos Humanos. Available at: http://sntweb.jus.gov. ar/polcrim/bajadaDeArchivos/SNIC%202001.pdf (14 January 2003).

"Tema Central: Crisis y Alternativas en el Sistema de Seguridad Pública en la Argentina" (Central Theme: Crisis and Alternatives in the Argentine Public Security System." *Colección: Revista de la Escuela de Ciencia Política de la Universidad Católica Argentina*, no. 10 (2000): 13–182. Available at: www.uca.edu.ar/facultades/derecho/ coleccion/n10/n10.htm (29 January 2003).

Wood, J. and E. Font. "Building Peace and Reforming Policing in Argentina: Opportunities and Challenges for Shantytowns." Paper presented at conference "In Search of Security: An International Conference on Policing & Security," Montréal, Québec, February 2003.

ARMENIA

Background Material

The Republic of Armenia borders Turkey to the west, Georgia to the north, Azerbaijan to the east, and Iran to the south. While the historic Armenian kingdom once extended into northeast Turkey and northwest Iran—from the Caspian to the Mediterranean Seas—present-day Armenia represents the smallest of the former Soviet Socialist republics, at only 29,800 sq km (11,490 square miles) in size. The United Nations estimated the 2003 population at 3.1 million, with 2001 government figures showing 67% urban dwellers and 33% rural dwellers. Armenia's inhabitants are largely monolithic: The country is predominantly filled with ethnic Armenians (98%), and the primary language is Armenian, with Russian largely spoken as a second language. Armenia was the first nation to adopt Christianity as its state religion, and the Armenian Apostolic Church serves over 90% of the population.

An ancient nation on the frontier of Europe and the Near East, Armenia was the first republic to regain its independence following the dissolution of the Soviet Union in 1991. Thereafter, the country experienced a severe economic decline in the 1990s as a result of the economic transition of the Soviet breakup; a devastating earthquake in 1988, which took the lives of an estimated 45,000 people and left another 500,000 homeless; a war with neighboring Azerbaijan over the historically Armenian enclave of Nagorno-Karabakh, and for which a tenuous ceasefire exists; and a crippling blockade imposed by Azerbaijan and Turkey (in coalition with ally Azerbaijan and related to Turkey's ongoing denial of its execution of the 1915 Armenian Genocide). In spite of posting a double-digit growth rate in both 2002 and 2003, at least 40% of Armenians live below the poverty line, and some indicators of structural poverty are already identifiable. Armenia's per capita national income is estimated at about $790.

As a result of the effects of these domestic challenges, the International Organization for Migration has estimated that 800,000 to 1,000,000 people have migrated from Armenia since 1991, although the process has slowed due to a period of economic recovery, with some émigrés returning. In 2004, the United Nations ranked Armenia among countries with medium human development based on life expectancy, education, and income. Armenia (eighty-second) ranks behind most European nations, but ahead of neighbors Turkey (eighty-eighth), Azerbaijan (ninety-first), Georgia (ninety-eighth), and Iran (101).

Contextual Features

The Republic of Armenia was established in 1991, after the country declared its independence from the Soviet Union. Prior to that, the short-lived but historic First Armenian Republic had been established in 1918 but was subsumed under the rubric of the Soviet Union on November 29, 1920.

The Armenian constitution delineates authority among three principal branches of government. The executive branch consists of the nation's president—who serves a five-year term—prime minister, and council of ministers. The legislative branch is composed of the National Assembly, which reflects the multiparty system served by 131 members of parliament. Ombudsman legislation was adopted in 2003, and the Ombudsman Office began work in early 2004. The universal right to vote in Armenia is granted at the age of eighteen.

Finally, the judicial branch oversees the country's court system, including the Constitutional Court. Beyond these divisions can be found administrative subdivisions in the form of ten *marzes* (provinces), in addition to the city of Yerevan, which has the status of a province.

Armenia's legal and judicial system operates under a system of civil law and is guided by the Third Republic of Armenia's Constitution, which was approved in 1995 by a referendum, although three draft initiatives for constitutional changes—similar in content, but originating from coalitions on both sides of the opposition and the government—are being considered. Within this constitutional framework, the country's courts of jurisdiction are delineated in the following categories:

- The Constitutional Court, which is made up of nine members, considers cases related to the constitutionality of laws, the National Assembly, government resolutions, orders and decrees of the president, and international treaties.
- Seventeen judges preside over the Courts of First Instance in each of Armenia's ten provinces as well as seven centers in Yerevan. These courts have jurisdiction over civil, criminal, military, and administrative cases; detentions; search warrants; and privacy of communication.
- Fifteen judges comprise the Economic Court, which rules on cases that are business oriented.
- The system provides for two Courts of Review, one of which presides over civil appeals, and the other which has jurisdiction over criminal and military appeals.
- The highest court of appeals is the Court of Cassation.

As a requirement for the nation's ascension into the Council of Europe, Armenia transferred the jurisdiction of the penitentiary system from the Ministry of the Interior to the Ministry of Justice in October 2001, under the auspices of the Law on the Status of the Penitentiary Service. Another significant related piece of legislation is the Law on Treatment of Arrestees and Detainees, passed in February 2002, which "defines the general principles, conditions and procedures for keeping of arrestees or detainees under arrest or detention in accordance with procedures set out in the Criminal Procedural Code of the Republic of Armenia, as well as the rights of arrestees and detainees, guarantees for ensuring their rights, their responsibilities, and procedures for releasing these persons from arrest or detention." The Law on Penitentiary Service followed in 2003, further outlining regulations and procedures associated with the detention of convicted prisoners. Official figures for 2003 indicate that there were approximately 4,500 prisoners being held in Armenian prisons.

Police Profile

It was during the creation of the first Republic of Armenia (1918–1920) that the Armenian police force was established under the Ministry of the Interior. The first law on the police was passed on April 21, 1920, which enumerated the broad authority that the police exercised in the country as a central unit of the Interior Ministry, with responsibilities reaching beyond the overall maintenance of law and order. In fact, the Ministry had been given additional oversight for the spheres of communications, railroads, and public schools in the young republic.

After the dissolution of the first Republic of Armenia, the police continued to exist throughout the period of Soviet rule (1920–1991), although the unit went through numerous titular and administrative incarnations. During this period, the Ministry of the Interior became the People's Commissariat of Internal Affairs, which sought to identify opponents of the socialist revolution. For its part, the police were charged with carrying out the policy of mass executions and oppression favored by the Stalinist regime and took no mercy on its own ranks: from 1920 to 1940, ten of thirteen directors of the police were executed. A decade later, the units responsible for police and special services were separated into the Ministry of Internal Affairs and the Committee on State Security (known as the KGB), respectively.

With the emergence of the modern Republic of Armenia and the disbanding of the Soviet Union, the domestic police force took on new roles. One of these included patrolling the border regions during the war against Azerbaijan in the 1990s; as the violence escalated, hundreds of police officers lost their lives as volunteers in defense units. At the same time, other officers had to contend with the increasing presence of organized crime within the country. By 1992, the president of Armenia had established the Interior Troops unit as an auxiliary arm of the Ministry of the Interior and transformed the School of Police into the Police Academy. The current Republic of Armenia Police (hereafter referred to as RA Police) falls under the umbrella of the Ministry of Internal Affairs and takes its authority from Armenia's constitution. The National Assembly signed the Law of the Republic of Armenia on Police on April 16, 2001. The law was revised to incorporate prerequisites for accession into the Council of Europe, and the ensuing Law on Police Service was passed on June 30, 2002, authorizing the Internal Affairs Ministry to regulate the activities of the RA Police. Article 2 of the law outlines the main objectives of the police, which are protection of the life, health, honor, rights, freedoms, and legal interests of individuals against criminal and other illegal assaults/actions; protection of the interests of society and the state; restraint, prevention, and precaution on crimes and administrative offences; discovery and disclosure of crimes; ensuring of the public order and public safety; and protection of all types of ownership.

The administrative structure of the police is situated in a central headquarters, which is led by the chief of police, one first deputy, and several deputies (who are assigned areas of responsibility by the chief)—all of whom are appointees of the president. The chief oversees the efforts of eleven departments (one each for the ten *marzes* and one for Yerevan), fifty-two precincts, and several specialized directorates and divisions. The commander of the Interior Troops is also appointed by the president and holds the title of ex-officio deputy chief of the police. Major units that fall under the RA Police's jurisdiction include Organized Crime Enforcement, Drug Enforcement, Economic Crime, Criminal Investigations, Public Safety, Public Relations and Press, Road Inspection, Transportation, Passport and Visa Directorate, and Criminal Forensics. The police's Penitentiary Division was reorganized under the Justice Ministry, and the Fire Department was transferred to the Emergency Management Department. In order to serve in the RA Police, individuals must graduate from the five-year training program at the Police Academy. The police ranks are soldier, police soldier, junior officer personnel, police middle/secondary officer personnel, senior officer personnel, and supreme officer personnel. Individuals are not allowed to maintain membership in any political organizations while employed with the RA Police. The weapons issued to officers are primarily Soviet-made firearms and ammunition, which include Makarov and TT handguns, and AKS, AKM, and AK-74 automatic rifles. The Law of the Republic of Armenia on Arms outlines three categories of firearms: civilian, service, and combat. Registration, licensing, and training requirements for civilians are outlined in the legislation. Petty crimes such as pickpocketing and mugging, predominantly at night, represent the majority of street crimes. This is notable in the context of the economic challenges facing Armenia, including 43% of the population living below the poverty line and an estimated 25% level of unemployment. Even in light of these figures, the country continues to boast a low rate of violent crime. According to the 2004 *Statistical Yearbook of Armenia*, of the 11,073 crimes recorded in 2003, thefts represented the largest percentage of offences at roughly 26% of the total. Following thefts were road accidents (5%), "hooliganism" (3%), and drug-related crimes (3%). Premeditated and attempted homicide represented only 1% of the total, and rape and attempted rape were reported even less frequently. In demographic terms, the 2003 crime figures were overwhelmingly committed by males (94%); the largest percentage of offenders were between the ages of eighteen and twenty-four (27%) or thirty to forty-nine (44%);

and, the largest proportion of those committing the crimes were neither employed nor attending school (56%).

In an attempt to address the issue of youth-related crime and juvenile delinquency, the Police Bureau of Juveniles has taken on new projects to broaden its outreach efforts to young people across Armenia. One example is the Armenian Legal Socialization Project, implemented by the nonprofit organization Project Harmony (which is headquartered in the United States with an Armenian branch) in twenty-two schools across Armenia. The project's objectives include assigning police officers to make regular visits to schools in order to help spread awareness about laws and the legal system among Armenia's youth, as well as helping to forge more positive attitudes toward law enforcement officers. In addition, the Bureau of Juveniles works with the Children's Admission and Orientation Center of Armenia, which serves youths from unstable homes and provides them with support while they are experiencing periods of transition. These efforts are a part of a broader movement to develop a juvenile and family court system, which has been lacking in the country and leaves children vulnerable in the absence of proper protection under the law.

Regarding human rights, Article 3 of the Law of the Republic of Armenia on Police emphasizes the priority role it plays: "Police activity shall be based on the principles of preservation of legality respect for human rights and freedoms." The Police Academy curriculum includes the study of the European Convention on Human Rights and Freedoms, and Armenian law regarding the protection of human rights is included in the curricula of the Police Academy, Training Center, and ongoing official training of police personnel.

However, the RA Police came under broad international and domestic criticism for activities that took place in March and April 2004, surrounding protests and rallies staged by opposition parties against the incumbent government that had retained power after contentious elections the previous spring. Several watchdog groups, such as Human Rights Watch, documented a range of abusive activities conducted by the RA Police during the two-month period, ranging from failing to approve applications for holding the rallies, to restricting travel into Yerevan so that protesters would not have access to the rallies, to exercising excessive force, arrests, and aggression against protesters, activists, and journalists.

Corruption is another issue that has taken center stage in Armenia, with the government instituting the Anti-corruption Strategy and Implementation Action Plan. The plan designates the RA Police as one of the primary agencies to carry out the criminal prosecution of corruption-related activities, yet recognizes that structural and institutional reforms will need to take place internally before the RA Police can be fully vested in this process. It goes further to recommend an increase in the salaries and social security of law enforcement personnel, which are repeatedly cited as primary factors in the vulnerability to corruption within the RA Police ranks.

There are no international terrorist organizations or activities in Armenia on record. The government has taken steps to join international efforts to impede the spread of terrorism and participates in the International Convention for the Suppression of the Financing of Terrorism and all of the Council of Europe's antiterrorism conventions. Armenia also adopted UN Security Council Resolution 1373, which freezes the bank accounts and assets of terrorists and their supporters.

Police Education, Research, and Publications

Since 1992, when the Republic of Armenia joined Interpol, the RA Police has cooperated with a number of foreign governments in issues and training related to criminal justice. In particular, the RA Police works with counterparts in the Interior Ministries of other newly independent states (NISs), both in terms of crime prevention and training of personnel. In addition, cooperation with the Interior Ministry of France has taken the form of exchange visits and training. Further, Armenian police officers participated in training sponsored by the Egyptian Police Academy, as well as in India.

Domestically, the police also cooperate with accredited international organizations that work within Armenia via their embassies and representative offices in the country. The Yerevan office of the Organization for Security and Cooperation in Europe (OSCE), for example, has committed $2 million to partner with the RA Police on matters related to community policing and emergency response and has worked with the Armenian Police Training Center to strengthen courses for police recruits and officers undergoing refresher training. In addition, the OSCE has offered guidance on Western-style methods for restructuring police services and resources, using modern law enforcement tools and techniques and training officers on human rights and freedoms.

The U.S. Embassy provides a range of assistance to the RA Police on matters that include general law enforcement, rule of law, counternarcotics, and money laundering via the Bureau for International Narcotics and Law Enforcement Affairs (INL). For example, the INL has donated a computer lab to the Police Training Center for use by students and officers studying there. Also under the auspices of the INL, senior police officers from Glendale, California, conducted training for RA Police officers, touching on issues that included crime scene preservation and management, evidence identification and collection, latent fingerprint collection, crime scene photography, and homicide and other death investigations. Further, Armenian officials have begun working with law enforcement agencies in Glendale in an effort to counteract organized crime rings, particularly with regard to money laundering, smuggling, and immigration fraud.

The primary means for disseminating public information on behalf of the police are in the form of a weekly newspaper and television show, both named "02."

NICOLE E. VARTANIAN

Bibliography

American Bar Association and Central and East European Law Initiative. 2002. *Judicial Reform Index for Armenia.* Washington, D.C.: American Bar Association. Available at: www.abanet.org/ceeli/publications/jri/jri_armenia.pdf.
Armenia, Republic of. 2004. *Anti-Corruption Strategy and Implementation Action Plan.* Available at: www.gov.am/enversion/programms_9/korup_prog.htm#5.
Bournoutian, George. 2002. *A Concise History of the Armenian People: From Ancient Times to the Present.* Costa Mesa, Calif.: Mazda Publishers.
Embassy of the Republic of Armenia. Home page. Available at: *www.armeniaemb.org.*
Human Rights Watch. 2004. *Cycle of Repression: Human Rights Violations in Armenia.* Available at: http://hrw.org/backgrounder/eca/armenia/0504/armenia-election.pdf.
Interpol. European police and judicial systems, Armenia. Available at: www.interpol.com/public/region/Europe/pjsystems/Armenia.asp#23.
Legislation Online. Prison Service, Armenia. Available at: www.legislationline.org/index.php?country=4&org=&eu=0%topic=12.
National Statistical Service of the Republic of Armenia. *Statistical Yearbook of Armenia,* 2004. Available at: www.armstat.am/StatData.

AUSTRALIA

Background Material

The first inhabitants of the Australian continent were the Aborigines, whose ancestors travelled across the seas at least 60,000 years ago. The first Europeans settlers in the late eighteenth century encountered a harsh and challenging land. The majority of early settlers were convicts transported from England. Gradually, white settlement spread outward from Sydney into the rugged hinterland. The gold rushes of the 1850s created wealth for individual immigrants, especially in the colony of Victoria. By the 1880s, Australia had become a prosperous land with thriving cities. Industrial development was accompanied by the rise of a strong labour movement, but this was crushed by the depression and great strikes of the early 1890s. Six colonies formed the federation of Australia in 1901, based on a determination to maintain British ways and exclude non-Europeans. Australia lost 60,000 men in World War I. The rapid Japanese advance in the Pacific in World War II threatened Australian national security for the first time. Australian foreign policy allegiance and protection shifted from Great Britain to the United States. A vigorous postwar immigration policy favouring Europeans was adopted to populate the country. The 1960s witnessed bitter social upheaval and division with opposition to the Vietnam War and conscription. The economic boom of the eighties was followed by recession in the nineties. The Bali bombing (12 October 2002) shattered Australian illusions that they were immune from terrorism.

Australia is a sparsely populated country with more than 12,000 miles of coastline on the rim of

Southeast Asia. Water scarcity in such an arid country is becoming a basic concern. Official unemployment is over 6% and is significantly higher among younger people. Treatment of aboriginal communities by authorities and police has been an ongoing problem. The depletion of the ozone layer, especially along coastal regions such as the Great Barrier Reef, is a major environmental problem. Since September 11, 2001 (S11) and the bombings in Bali (October 2002) and at the Marriott Hotel (Djatjarta, August 2003), national security has become a pressing and immediate concern.

On August 7, 2001, there were 18,972,350 people (9,362,021 males and 9,610,329 females) counted in Australia. This represents a modest increase of 1,079,927 people (6.0%) since the 1996 census, and an increase of 2,122,016 people (12.6%) since the 1991 census. The population estimate for July 2003 was 19,731,981. Life expectancy for men is 77 years, and for women, 83 years.

Australia is a multicultural country with approximately one quarter of its population born outside Australia. English was stated as the only language spoken at home by 15,013,965 people (80.0%) in the 2001 census. The three most common languages spoken at home other than English in the 2001 census were Chinese, 401,357 (2.1%); Italian, 353,605 (1.9%); and Greek, 263,717 (1.4%).

Australia is nominally a Christian country with approximately 5 million professing to be Catholic, 3.9 million Anglican, and 1.25 million Uniting Church. A total of 2.9 million claim no religious affiliation.

The median weekly individual income for people aged 15 years and over in 2001 was $300 to $399 ($400 to $499 for men and $200 to $299 for women). The state or territory in Australia with the highest median individual income in the 2001 census was the Australian Capital Territory ($500 to $599), followed by the Northern Territory ($400 to $499). All states had a median individual income in the 2001 census of $300 to $399.

Traditional activities of agriculture and manufacturing were mainstays of the Australian economy throughout much of the twentieth century. Australia has a prosperous, Western, capitalist economy. The main economic sectors are services, agriculture, and industry. The labour force by sector is composed of services (73%), industry (22%), and agriculture (5%) (1997 estimates). The main industries are mining, industrial and transportation equipment, food processing, chemicals, and steel. Major agricultural pursuits are wheat, barley, sugar cane, fruits, cattle, sheep, and poultry. A severe drought has afflicted much of Australia in recent years.

Contextual Features

Australia's system of law includes legislation passed by the federal parliament, state parliaments, and the legislative assemblies of the Northern Territory and Australian Capital Territory (statute law). It is also composed of delegated or subordinate legislation made under federal, state, and territory acts. Australian common law (judicial decisions), which developed from English common law, also applies, as does common or statute laws of England that have not been repealed.

State and territory parliaments make laws on matters of relevance to their jurisdiction. However, in certain circumstances as defined in the Australian Constitution, commonwealth law may override state law when it is not consistent with it. Criminal justice issues are overwhelmingly a matter for state and territory parliaments and governments.

Australia has a hybrid political system. It combined elements of the British system of responsible government with the U.S. federalist system and adapted both to shape its own federalist structure. It consists of a central parliament, the federal parliament, also referred to as the commonwealth parliament, six state parliaments (New South Wales, Victoria, Queensland, South Australia, Western Australia, and Tasmania), and two territory parliaments (Northern Territory and Australian Capital Territory).

In Australia's parliamentary democracy, parliamentarians are elected through free, open, and regular elections. It has a written constitution that distributes power between the federal government (the commonwealth) and state and territory governments. In all Australian parliaments, questions can be asked "without notice," and the proceedings of parliament are publicly recorded in Hansard.

The commonwealth and the states and territories follow the principles of responsible government. Each of the state parliaments, with the exception of Queensland, has two houses—a legislative assembly and a legislative council (bicameral parliaments). The Queensland Parliament voted to abolish its legislative council in 1922, and since then has only had a legislative assembly (unicameral parliament). The party that wins the majority of votes in the legislative assembly forms the government, and according to convention the leader of the winning party becomes premier and in the case of the territories the chief minister.

The federal parliament consists of the Queen, who is represented in Australia by the governor-general; the Senate (also referred to as the States' House); and the House of Representatives. Each state elects the same number of representatives (senators) to the Senate. In the House of Representatives, the number of members from each state depends on the size of a state's population. By convention, the leader of the party commanding a majority in the House of Representatives becomes the prime minister of Australia.

The Australian Constitution divides the powers of government among the legislature, executive, and judiciary. In Australia, the executive (cabinet) forms part of the legislature (parliament), so theoretically Australia does not have a "pure" separation of powers. State parliaments are bound by the Australian Constitution as well as their own state constitutions. While the Australian Constitution does not include a bill of rights, it does offer some limited protection against legislative or executive action infringing on people's rights. For example, Section 51 states that acquisition of property must be "on just terms"; Section 80 protects the right to trial by jury in relation to some criminal offences; and Section 116 protects the right to practice any religion.

The independence of the judiciary and its separation from the legislative and executive arms of government are sacrosanct in Australia. It is taken for granted that territory, state, and federal judges will interpret and apply the law independently of any government. Federal judges' security of tenure is guaranteed by the constitution, and in the states and territories, legislation ensures security of tenure for judges.

The Australian Constitution provides for the judicial power of the commonwealth to be vested in the High Court of Australia. It also requires that the High Court consist of a chief justice and not less than two other justices. Today's High Court has six other justices.

The High Court has an original and appellate jurisdiction and is the final court of appeal in relation to all matters, whether they are decided in federal, state, or territory jurisdictions. The High Court's original jurisdiction extends to criminal matters in relation to indictable offences under commonwealth law; however, this jurisdiction is rarely exercised.

Each state has its own independent system of courts made up of a supreme court, intermediate court (known as the district or county court), and local courts of summary jurisdiction, commonly referred to as the magistrates court. State and territory courts have original jurisdiction over all matters pertaining to state or territory laws, and in respect to matters that come under federal laws, where the commonwealth parliament has conferred jurisdiction. Each of the states and territories has a court of criminal appeal that is constituted by at least three judges of the supreme court. Most criminal matters, even if they arise under commonwealth law, are dealt with by state or territory courts.

The supreme courts are the highest state and territory courts and deal with the most important civil litigation and the most serious criminal cases. They also exercise appellate jurisdiction from the lower state courts. A full court of a supreme court can hear appeals from a decision of the supreme court when constituted by a single judge.

The intermediate courts, which are presided over by a single judge, decide the great majority of serious criminal offences. They also deal with civil matters up to certain monetary limits. The names given to these courts vary. For example, in Victoria, they are known as county courts, and in New South Wales as district courts.

The courts of summary jurisdiction are presided over by a magistrate and deal with most of the ordinary (summary) offences, such as traffic infringements, minor assaults, and street offences. Magistrates also conduct committal proceedings in relation to the more serious offences to determine if there is a prima facie case to be determined by a judge and jury, either in an intermediate court or a supreme court.

At the federal level, there is also the Family Court of Australia and the Industrial Relations Court of Australia. Some states also have specialist courts; for example, New South Wales has established a compensation court and a drug court, and Victoria has created a children's court and a drug court. Each jurisdiction has a coroner's office.

In Australia, the most common crimes recorded by Australian police during 2002 were theft (679,460), unlawful entry with intent (394,374), and assault (159,548). In the last quarter of the year, 50,541 people were in community-based correction programs (Australian Bureau of Statistics, available at: *www.abs.gov.au*).

As of June 30, 2002, there were 22,492 prisoners in Australia; 93% were male (21,008), and 7% female (1484). New South Wales, the most populated state, had the largest prisoner population (8,759), with Queensland the third most populated state having the next largest number of prisoners

(4,721). The highest imprisonment rate of 466 prisoners per 100,000 adults was recorded in the Northern Territory. This is three times the national rate. The median age of prisoners is 31 years for males and 30 years for females, and the majority (56%) are young adult males aged between 20 and 34 years.

The federal government does not operate a prison system. People convicted of federal crimes serve their sentence in a state or territory prison. Each state and territory has its own prison system, and male and female prisoners are housed in separate prisons. Juveniles (offenders under eighteen years of age) who are sentenced to detention are housed in juvenile correctional centres. In some states, prisons are operated by private providers.

New South Wales has 26 correctional centres (25 public and 1 private), and Victoria has 13 (12 public and 1 private). The state of Queensland has 10 public and 2 private institutions, and Western Australia 14 public and 1 private. South Australia has 10 correctional institutions, 9 public and 1 private, and Tasmania has 4, all of which are public institutions. The Northern Territory and the Australian Capital Territory each have two public correctional institutions (information available at: *www.aic.gov. au/publications/tandi/ti84.pdf; www.dcs.nsw.gov.au/ correctional;* and *www.aic.gov.au/research/correc tions/facilities/nt.html*).

Police Profile

Background

In the nineteenth century, the six Australian colonies all established independent police forces organised and supported by centralized bureaucracies. Tasmania was the last colony to unify its police system in 1898. With the advent of the Federation of Australia in 1901, each of the six states maintained its policing autonomy under a centralized, disciplined, all-male bureaucratic system.

During the twentieth century, there were a variety of attempts to establish commonwealth policing (first embodiment in 1917). The early attempts to establish and define the role of a federal police agency were subjected to "apathy, suspicion, ridicule and derision by state organisations" (Bryett et al. 1994: 86). Some stability resulted in 1979 with the formation of the Australian Federal Police (AFP), which was an amalgam of the Australian Bureau of Narcotics, Commonwealth Police, and Australian Capital Territory police. The AFP's mandate is to enforce commonwealth law and provide the community policing of the Australian Capital Territory by a

semiautonomous branch of the AFP. The Northern Territory runs its own police force. These eight centralized public police departments (six state, AFP, NTP) are large-scale organisations: the New South Wales (NSW) Police Service numbers more than 14,000 sworn members, and the Victoria Police has more than 10,000 members. Apart from the AFP and the Northern Territory, state governments finance policing across Australia. State-run bureaucracies providing policing services across a large geographic area can create inflexibility. Approximately 47,000 sworn police serve a population of 19 million Australians. There is no unitary police administration in Australia (unlike the strongly centralized, unitary New Zealand police system).

These eight police agencies in Australia acknowledge a legacy to the model of Sir Robert Peel's London Metropolitan Police. Just as Peel's 1829 creation needed some form of administration to impose control and social order over its 900 selected police, so the colonial police forces in Australia needed similar administrative control mechanisms and replicated the English policing institutions. Although in theory policing was meant to be civil in nature, both in organisation and operation it often was militaristic (Haldane 1995; McCulloch 2001). Police departments adopted many procedures and symbols of the military: uniform, ranks, batons, drill, ceremonies, and procedures.

The NSW Police is Australia's oldest and largest police organisation, and one of the world's largest with more than 17,000 employees, including 14,000 sworn police members. As of 30 June 2002, there were 45,395 sworn police officers in Australia; this constitutes a rate of about one police officer per 430 people. One-fifth of the sworn members were female. Few women occupy senior executive and other highly paid roles in Australian policing. In total, police services in Australia employed 57,830 people in mid-2002.

Organizational Description

In Australia, major policing decisions and policies have traditionally been enacted by a few men at the top (police command) in organizations featuring centralized, graded authority. Ranks include constable, senior constable, sergeant, senior sergeant, inspector, chief inspector, superintendent, chief superintendent, assistant commissioner, and commissioner. Rules and protocols abound in the formal organisations. Entry requirements and intensive training are necessary before one enters the ranks of constable with its corresponding duties. In all police services in Australia, promotion is on merit, not length of service.

The AFP in the 1990s dramatically restructured according to the model of an FBI law enforcement body. A series of radical changes were made to the fragmented and inefficient bureaucratic organisation including fixed term appointments, performance-based contracts, promotion by merit, accelerated advancement, lateral entry, and a unified police and civilian workforce. In 1996, the rank structure was abolished, as the AFP management instigated one level for all operatives, that of investigative federal agent. The flattened rank structure has set the AFP apart from the six state police bureaucracies with the traditionally ranked military structure (for example, constable, senior constable, sergeant, senior sergeant, inspector, superintendent, chief superintendent, assistant commissioner, and commissioner) to a team-based, professionally oriented organisation. The contemporary organisation is fundamentally an investigative police service, and since S11 and the Bali bombings (October 12, 2002), it has emerged together with the Australian Security Intelligence Organisation as the leading Australian organisations in the "war against terrorism." Subsequently, the AFP, with its offshore interventions, has received increased powers and funding and much greater federal government support and media prominence.

All the state police agencies have some form of special response units. Victoria boasts an elite special operations group and a specific crowd control force response unit. McCulloch (2001) argues that there has been a blurring of distinctions between police and military training and activities in Australia.

Functions

Each police agency is responsible for protecting life and property, maintaining peace and order, enforcing the law, controlling crime, regulating normal everyday life, and co-ordinating emergency responses. However, each state agency, as the controlling functionary, maintains its authority as the legitimate coercive agency of that particular state and remains the visible symbol of state authority. The AFP is a unique police organisation in that it performs the three fold law enforcement functions of the local policing of the Australian Capital Territory (suburban Canberra), and national and international policing.

Some states dropped the word "force" from the title as being too aggressive and substituted the more approachable "service" (such as Queensland Police Service, New South Wales Police Service). Philosophical change has witnessed Australian policing adopting community policing and problem-oriented policing models rather than the traditional militaristic policing model. Programs such as Blue Light discos, Crime-Stoppers, and Neighbourhood Watch are features of the police department and community nexus. All state police agencies have established various liaison units to develop cooperation with outside bodies (for example, elderly, Koorie, Asian, ethnic, gay, and industrial disputation). Some specific Victoria Police community projects include Community Safety Week, Confident Living for Older Victorians, Women's Safety Strategy, Youth Leadership Program, Schools Involvement Program, and an outdoor adventure program.

With Australia's recent priorities of combating people smuggling, transnational crime, and terrorism in the Southeast Asian region, the AFP's intelligence-gathering role is intrinsic to the enforcement of the federal government's interventionist role in the region.

Police in Australia have adopted modern business plans and practices, corporate images, performance management programs, and client-oriented philosophy. Tertiary education, additional training, and promotion on merit have revolutionised career paths. Approximately 15% of police in Australia are female (this figure was little over 1% in 1970), and females comprise about 30% of recruits in training. In 2001, the Victoria Police appointed the first female in Australia to head a police organisation. There has been a rapid increase in non-sworn staff performing traditional police duties, while privatisation of certain traditional police functions remains controversial.

State police, under statutory authority, have the power to detain individuals and deprive them of their liberty in certain circumstances. Police can search a person, make arrests, question, and demand name and address, as well as ultimately use coercive powers if reasonable in the circumstances. Police in all states are allowed to carry a firearm; it is mandatory on operational duty. All police possess discretionary powers that involve personally based decision making. Such discretion is most commonly exercised at the street level by lower-ranked police, often working autonomously without direct supervision (Edwards 1999: 12–14).

Section 37 (2) of the Australian Federal Police Act 1979 empowers the Minister for Justice and Customs to direct the general policy pursued by the AFP in performing its functions. In April 2002, state and territory leaders agreed to permit the AFP to investigate state offences if they were incidental to "multijurisdictional crime." The commonwealth has assumed the preeminence in the war against terrorism, people smuggling, and organised crime. A revamped AFP has been given the power to take over state investigations if declared "transnational crimes" such as national bikie groups, international drug syndicates, and money laundering. The June 2002 federal legislation enacted terrorism as a crime and subsequently provided the AFP with a mandate against extremists and subversives.

Police Public Projects

Please refer to the police-community projects outlined in the Functions section.

Police Use of Firearms

Australian Police Forces are armed.

Complaints and Discipline

The Australian Federal Police and each state and territory police service has its own internal investigation section that investigates complaints against police. However, since 1985 all Australian police services have been subjected to varying forms of civilian oversight of complaints against police processes.

The Australian Federal Police has an internal professional standards unit that is responsible for investigating and managing complaints against police. Since 1981 the Commonwealth Ombudsman has had the power to monitor and review the internal investigation process, and in some instances to conduct its own investigation. Complaints can be made in writing, by telephone, or orally to the AFP or to the ombudsman's office. In June 2004, the federal government announced that it intends to establish the Inspector General of Australian Law Enforcement that would be given the powers of a standing royal commission to oversee federal policing.

In New South Wales, the Commonwealth Ombudsman gained jurisdiction over police complaints in 1979. It monitors and reviews the majority of police complaints, and in some limited instances investigates in its own right. In 1996, as a result of a recommendation from the Royal Commission into the New South Wales Police Service (Wood Inquiry), an additional police oversight body, the Police Integrity Commission, was established. It is responsible for the prevention, detection, or investigation of serious police misconduct and for managing or overseeing other agencies in the detection and investigation of serious and other police misconduct (Police Integrity Commission, available at: *www.pic.nsw.gov.au/About Us.asp*).

Complaints against the police in the Northern Territory are investigated by the internal Professional Responsibility Division of the police force and are monitored and reviewed by the Office of the Ombudsman. In some circumstances, the Ombudsman's office can also conduct its own investigation.

One of the major recommendations of Queensland's 1987–1989 Commission of Inquiry into Possible Illegal Activities and Associated Police Misconduct (the Fitzgerald Inquiry) was the creation of an independent body to monitor, review, and investigate complaints against police: the Criminal Justice Commission (CJC). For several years after its establishment, the CJC through its Official Misconduct division also assisted the police to investigate organised and major crime. In 1997, the Queensland Crime Commission (QCC) was established and took over this function. In January 2002, the Criminal Justice Commission and the Crime Commission were merged to form the Crime and Misconduct Commission (CMC) (see home page, available at: *www.cmc.qld.gov.au/police-workingtogether.html*). In September 2002, a new process of police discipline and complaint investigation was introduced whereby the quasi-independent Ethical Standards Command, within the Queensland Police Service, works with the Crime and Misconduct Commission to investigate allegations of police misconduct. The CMC maintains an overview responsibility, but can also investigate in its own right if it decides to do so.

The Crime and Misconduct Division also works proactively with the Queensland Police Service (QPS) by assisting it to establish improved policing strategies and strategies by which the Service can monitor its own performance. Through its public research papers and reports, the CMC also helps to inform the Queensland public about policing issues and the progress of the Fitzgerald-inspired reform process (documents available at: *www.cmc.qld.gov.au/OVERSEEINGQPS.html*).

Since 1985, South Australia has had a dedicated Police Complaints Authority. It receives complaints against police, keeps a register of them, and notifies the police of the complaint. It then monitors and reviews investigations conducted by the South Australia Police Internal Investigation Unit and determines if any further action is required.

In some circumstances, it conducts its own independent investigation (see *www.austlii.edu.au/au/ special/rsjproject/rsjlibrary/rciadic/national/vol4/ 41.html*).

The Tasmanian Ombudsman's office has had the power to review police complaints investigated by the Tasmania Police since 1978.

Following calls for a royal commission into the Victoria Police in 1996, the Victoria Police established the Ethical Standards Department. Its primary role is to investigate complaints against police and to prevent, detect, and investigate corruption, crime, malpractice, and breaches of discipline within the Victoria Police. It is a large department with approximately 200 personnel, and consists of five divisions: the Corruption Investigation Division (prevents, detects, and investigates corruption and serious criminality); the Complaint Investigation Division (manages and investigates specific operational incidents including use of firearms, pursuits, deaths in custody, and other incidents involving police that are likely to be of public concern); the Investigation Support Division (provides operational support to investigations through telecommunications interception, surveillance, integrity testing, and covert investigation coordination; and the Strategic Initiatives Division (a largely proactive role helping Victoria Police and other government departments to develop and promote policies aimed at raising standards of integrity and professionalism. The Services Division is the first point of contact for people making complaints.

Other internal units are the Discipline Advisory Unit, which is responsible for the administration of the Victoria Police disciplinary system, and the Internal Sources Unit, which provides case management support for internal sources (see *www. police.vic.gov.au/showcontentpage.cfm?contentpage id=2320*).

In terms of independent oversight, up until early 2004 the Deputy Ombudsman (Police Complaints) largely performed a monitor and review role with respect to police complaints. Following a series of allegations involving police corruption and links to organised crime, the position of Deputy Ombudsman (Police Complaints) was abolished and replaced by the position of Police Ombudsman. This change was also accompanied by an increase in coercive powers for the Police Ombudsman and a $10 million increase in resources. This office was located in the Ombudsman's Office and the two functions, Ombudsman and Police Ombudsman, were performed by the same person. A few months after the creation of the Police Ombudsman, the position was replaced by Director, Police Integrity within the Office of Police Integrity, both of which reside in the Ombudsman's Office. Again, the Ombudsman and Director, Police Integrity, are the same person.

As a result of recommendations by the recent Royal Commission into the West Australia Police (Kennedy Inquiry), a new oversight body, the Corruption and Crime Commission (CCC), was established in 2003. It replaces the Anti-corruption Commission, which had responsibility for investigating serious police misconduct, and the West Australian Ombudsman's role, which was primarily to monitor and review complaints investigated by the police internal affairs unit and occasionally to conduct its own investigation of such matters.

The West Australia Police Commissioner will retain responsibility for the handling and investigation of complaints about police misconduct, but the CCC will oversee the police investigations. In doing so, it will have the powers of a royal commission and be able to conduct public hearings and compel witnesses to testify. It will also be able to conduct integrity tests in relation to police (*Sydney Morning Herald*, 26 February 2003).

Penalties associated with misconduct in all Australian States and Territory police forces and at the federal level can range from admonishment, a fine, to a reduction in rank all the way through to dismissal. The majority of complaints received in respect to all Australian police forces and services are minor in nature and are often resolved informally. Civilian oversight bodies can recommend a particular sanction; however, the final decision as to which penalty is imposed rests with the commissioner of police.

Terrorism

In Australia, confrontation and conflict between civil police forces and terrorists have been rare because the instances of terrorist actions have been rare themselves. Prior to the 1978 Hilton bombing, Australia had little direct experience of international terrorism. No confirmed terrorist organisations, prior to S11, have targeted Australia or have confirmed operations in Australia. The perceived danger is the activities of Jemaal Islamiyah and its Southeast Asian cells, with alleged training bases linked to al-Qaeda.

Both state and federal police have been granted increased resources and legal powers to act as intelligence and information-gathering agencies as well as perform security and paramilitary operations. In order to enhance federal and state counterterrorism cooperation, joint counterterrorism investigation teams have been established. These teams combine the community and local contacts of state and territory police with the AFP's international access. The teams are under the centralised command of the AFP in order to collate the voluminous intelligence about significant arrests and suspicious criminal transactions. Each team is linked to the AFP's Transnational Crime Co-ordination Centre, a twenty-four-hour operation aimed at disseminating terrorist information.

Full cooperation among policing agencies is not automatic, especially since state policing jurisdictions precede the AFP's formation by a century or more. Local police and emergency services personnel are the immediate response groups after a terrorist attack. Local police are the ones normally contacted about suspicious behaviour; effective communication and coordination between police and security agencies are essential. Approximately 50,000 police around Australia present a massive intelligence-gathering capability.

All state police services have counterterrorist units. The NSW Police Service under Commissioner Peter Ryan led Australian counterterrorism precautions for the 2000 Sydney Olympics. Backed by each state's antiterrorism capacity, the AFP is playing the pivotal role in overt and covert intelligence and security operations. Traditionally, the AFP has been a law enforcement organisation that investigates crimes for prosecution; the contemporary AFP is increasingly gathering intelligence in a global and undefined war. The AFP is at the forefront of the fight against terrorism due to its national jurisdiction, joint state/commonwealth task force arrangements, national interface with the Australian intelligence community and Australian Defence Force, long-established overseas liaison network, and experience in transnational crime investigation. The AFP's new proactive and preemptive role takes the fight into the international arena in order to combat terrorism; not just to monitor it, but to provide early interdiction against it. The Bali bombing investigation and victim identification process comprised the largest operation in the AFP's history. The effective working relationship between the AFP and the Indonesian POLRI stemmed from the understanding that only co-police could develop.

The advent of "failed states" arouses fears of easy facilitation of terrorist bases and finances, weapon smuggling, drug dealing, money laundering and people smuggling. The 2003 Australian-led contingent to the Solomon Islands constitutes 155 AFP agents and 90 Australian Protective Services members protected by 1,500 Australian Defence Force personnel. It is anticipated that most of the military will leave by the end of 2003, but the police are expected to remain for some time, probably several years. The operation is directed at ridding the islands of gang warfare, disarming the militias, and restoring the infrastructure of law and order. A total of 300 police, both federal and state, have been signalled for duties in Papua-New Guinea.

International Cooperation

The AFP's cooperation with regional forces into counterterrorist operations is viewed as a natural corollary of cooperative work already undertaken in the region regarding drugs and people smuggling. The AFP had previously taken the fight against transnational crime offshore; today, that includes the AFP working offshore in policing partnerships to prevent threats to the Australian community.

There has been a dramatic increase in the number of police training activities, joint operations, and regional visits conducted by the AFP and state police in Asia and the Pacific. Extensive training programs dealing with intelligence, investigations, and forensics for regional law enforcement officers are being conducted. Having originated from Australian leadership of the South Pacific Forum, a new $A15-million, Australian-financed training venture is proposed at Suva (Fiji) for police officers of the South Pacific region, and this potentially could form the basis of a regional police force.

In 2003, more than 100 AFP agents were working full-time on counterterrorism, together with analysts and intelligence experts. The AFP has a well-integrated network of liaison agents operating overseas who gather intelligence and share information with other policing agencies. Fifty-eight such agents operate in thirty strategic locations, including fourteen posts within Asia. Officers based in London, Washington, D.C., and Kuala Lumpur are dedicated to counterterrorism intelligence. Shared operations and intelligence have assisted investigations of drug trafficking, money laundering, sex tourism, fraud, people smuggling, arms sales, and terrorist activities. The AFP has sponsored seminars in Singapore, Bangkok, Hong Kong, and elsewhere on issues of importance. The AFP provides community policing services to Australia's non-self-governing external territories—

Norfolk Island, Cocos (Keeling) Islands, and Christmas Island.

The AFP has implemented counterterrorism agreements signed with Singapore, Malaysia, Thailand, and the Philippines, as well as Indonesia. Not all countries have embraced Australian policing overtures: Singapore and Malaysia remain hesitant. The escape of a leading Jemaah Islamiyah operative from Manila's main prison in 2003 highlighted the tenuous control of criminal justice agencies even over captured alleged terrorists.

The AFP's Law Enforcement Cooperation Program (LECP) is based on the AFP's international liaison officer network and plays a significant role in fostering cooperation. AFP officers in the network are dedicated to creating links between countries by facilitating the exchange of information and enhancing communication and understanding. This is done in a variety of ways, including international conferences and seminars, promoting the LECP, and developing bonds with the law enforcement officers of their host country.

While the LECP initially focused on countries in the Asia Pacific region, an injection of an additional $8.082 million over a four-year period is enabling the program to expand globally.

Australia has a long tradition of providing police for peacekeeping duties mainly in respect to service with the United Nations. Since 1979, the AFP has been building strong relationships with external organisations involved with peace operations, including the UN, The Royal Canadian Mounted Police, Singapore Police Force, and other law enforcement agencies.

Australian police have served in many UN peacekeeper operations, including Cambodia, Cyprus, East Timor, Mozambique, and Somalia. They have also served in non-UN peacekeeping operations in Bougainville (UN sanctioned, led by Australia and New Zealand); Haiti (UN sanctioned, led by United States); and Solomon Islands (led by Australia and New Zealand). AFP police officers are currently deployed to peace operations in Cyprus, East Timor, and the Solomon Islands.

Australia established the Human Rights and Equal Opportunity Commission in 1986. It aims to promote greater understanding and protection of human rights in Australia and to address the human rights concerns of the Australian people at an individual and group level. The Commission focuses on issues such as race, sex, and disability discrimination, as well as the rights of Indigenous Australians (Human Rights and Equal Opportu-

nity Commission, available at: *www.hreoc.gov.au/info_sheet.htm*).

The number of Aboriginal people in Australian prisons is thought by many to be a human rights issue. They are heavily overrepresented in Australian prisons, and this has remained the case despite the findings of the final report of the Royal Commission into Aboriginal Deaths in Custody in 1991 (Aboriginal Deaths in Custody, available at: *www.hreoc.gov.au/social_justice/statistics/*).

Australia is a signatory to several UN Declarations that address human rights issues.

Police Education, Research, and Publications

The Australian Institute of Criminology is the national focus for the study of criminal justice in Australia and for the dissemination of criminal justice information. Recent publications have included intelligence-led policing, a safe and secure environment for older Australians, and researching heroin supply. The Australian Institute of Police Management at Manly, NSW, conducts courses and seminars for senior police officers from Australian police jurisdictions and Asia Pacific countries. A number of universities have units developed to police or criminal justice research. Some of the leading institutions in this field are Monash University, Charles Sturt University, University of New South Wales, Griffith University, and University of Melbourne.

Some of the main researchers on policing in Australia and their recent publications include:

Bryett, K., A. Harrison, and J. Shaw. *The Role and Functions of Police in Australia*, Vol. 2. Sydney: Butterworths, 1994.

Chan, J. *Changing Police Culture: Policing in a Multicultural Society*. Sydney: Cambridge University Press.

Chappell, D., and P. Wilson, eds. *Australian Policing: Contemporary Issues*, 2d ed. Sydney: Butterworths, 1996.

Dixon, D. *Law in Policing: Legal Regulation and Police Practices*. Oxford: Clarendon Press, 1997.

Edwards, C. *Changing Police Theories for 21st Century Societies*. Sydney: Federation Press, 1999.

Enders, M., and B. Dupont, eds. *Policing the Lucky Country*. Sydney: Hawkins Press, 2001.

Finnane, M. *Police and Government: Histories of Policing in Australia*. Oxford: Oxford University Press, 1994.

Graycar, A., and P. Grabosky, eds. *The Cambridge Handbook of Australian Criminology*. Cambridge: Cambridge University Press, 2002.

Lewis, C. *Complaints Against Police: The Politics of Reform*. Sydney: Hawkins Press, 1999.

McCulloch, J. *Blue Army: Paramilitary Policing in Australia*. Carlton: Melbourne University Press, 2001.

Prenzler, T., and J. Ransley, eds. *Police Reform: Building Integrity*. Sydney: Hawkins Press, 2002.

There has been limited research of the individual police agencies in Australia, but the three most significant institutional histories are:

Clyne, R. *Colonial Blue: A History of the South Australian Police Force 1836–1916*. Adelaide: Wakefield Press, 1987.

Haldane, R. *The People's Force: A History of the Victoria Police*. Carlton: Melbourne University Press, 1995.

Johnston, R.W. *The Long Blue Line: A History of the Queensland Police Force*. Brisbane: Boolarong Press, 1992.

The Criminology Research Council funds criminology research by providing research grants to researchers in universities, government departments, and similar institutions within Australia. Policing is one designated research area that is policy oriented, and research outcomes should have practical application. The Australasian Centre for Policing Research in South Australia conducts practical research aimed at policy and strategic development in policing. Researchers can apply to the nationally competitive Australia Research Council for grants to conduct research on criminal justice issues, including police.

Refereed articles on policing appear in *Current Issues in Criminal Justice*, the journal of the Australian and New Zealand Society of Criminology. The Australian Institute of Criminology publishes an occasional paper series under the title *Trends and Issues*.

The AFP produces a quarterly magazine *Platypus*, which discusses aspects of the AFP's policing task (available at: *www.afp.gov.au/page.asp?ref=/Publications/Platypus/Home.xml*).

The AFP's Annual Report discusses recent performance, and the AFP produces a range of other research projects, bulletins, reports, and corporate publications. Most are available online on the AFP's publications page (available at: *www.afp.gov.au/page.asp?ref=Publications/Home.xml*).

Internal state police publications and magazines include *Police Life* (Victoria), *Vedette* (Queensland), *Newsbeat* (Western Australia), and *The Drum* (Northern Territory).

Listed below are police-related websites:

www.afp.gov.au
www.police.vic.gov.au
www.nt.gov/pfes/.au
www.police.qld.gov.au
www.sapolice.sa.gov.au
www.police.wa.gov.au
www.police.tas.gov.au
www.police.nsw.gov.au
www.aic.gov.au

DAVID BAKER AND COLLEEN LEWIS

Bibliography

Bryett, K., A. Harrison, and J. Shaw. *The Role and Functions of Police in Australia*. Vol. 2. Sydney: Butterworths, 1994.

Chan, J. *Changing Police Culture: Policing in a Multicultural Society*. Cambridge and Sydney: Cambridge University Press, 1997.

Chappell, D., and Wilson, P., eds. *Australian Policing: Contemporary Issues*. 2nd ed. Sydney: Butterworths, 1996.

Clyne, R. *Colonial Blue: A History of the South Australian Police Force 1836–1916*. Adelaide: Wakefield Press, 1987.

Dixon, D. *Law in Policing: Legal Regulation and Police Practices*. Oxford: Clarendon Press, 1997.

Edwards, C. *Changing Police Theories for 21st Century Societies*. Sydney: Federation Press, 1999.

Enders, M., and B. Dupont, eds. *Policing the Lucky Country*. Sydney: Hawkins Press, 2001.

Finnane, M. *Police and Government: Histories of Policing in Australia*. Oxford: Oxford University Press, 1994.

Graycar, A., and P. Grabosky, eds. *The Cambridge Handbook of Australian Criminology*. Cambridge: Cambridge University Press, 2002.

Haldane, R. *The People's Force: A History of the Victoria Police*. Carlton: Melbourne University Press, 1995.

Johnston, R. W. *The Long Blue Line: A History of the Queensland Police Force*. Brisbane: Boolarong Press, 1992.

Lewis, C. *Complaints Against Police: The Politics of Reform*. Sydney: Hawkins Press, 1999.

McCulloch, J. *Blue Army: Paramilitary Policing in Australia*. Carlton: Melbourne University Press, 2001.

Prenzler, T., and J. Ransley, eds. *Police Reform: Building Integrity*. Sydney: Hawkins Press, 2002.

AUSTRIA

Background Material

Since its first naming of "Ostarrichi" in 996, Austria has experienced several basic changes in its territorial and legal identity. Under the Babenbergs (976–1246), it became a duchy in 1156. As the "House of Austria," the Habsburg dynasty (1282–1918) grew to a dominant power in European history, acquiring kingdoms, duchies, and counties through the centuries. The Austro-Hungarian Empire was divided after the end of World War I in 1918. Among the "succession states" was the First Republic of Austria, which became part of the German Third Reich in 1938. The Second Republic began at the end of World War II in 1945, at first under the control of the Allies. Austria became an independent neutral state in 1955 and joined the European Union (EU) in 1995.

The politico-cultural heritage of the Austro-Hungarian Empire is a significant historical asset of present-day Austria, which, with its 83,859 square kilometers is a relatively small country. It is an Alpine country located along the Danube, Europe's second longest river. Austria is bordered on the west by Switzerland and the Principality of Liechtenstein, on the northwest by Germany, on the north by the Czech Republic, on the northeast by Slovakia, on the east by Hungary, on the south by Slovenia, and on the southwest by Italy. Austria consists of nine federal provinces: Vorarlberg, Tyrol, Carinthia, Salzburg, Upper Austria, Styria, Lower Austria, Burgenland, and Vienna, which is also the capital city.

According to the national census of 2001, Austria has a population of 8.03 million. Based on the area of the country as a whole, the average population density is ninety-six people per square kilometer, rather low for Europe. This figure is misleading, however, because only 39% of the land is suitable for habitation. If calculated based on habitable area only, population density is as high as 240 people per square kilometer, equal to that of Germany. About one-fifth of the Austrian population lives in Vienna, the only Austrian city with a population of over 1 million. Other major cities are the provincial capitals of Graz, Linz, Salzburg, and Innsbruck, which have fewer than 250,000 inhabitants each. Almost half of Austria's resident population lives in small communities of up to 5,000 inhabitants. No other Western European country has as many people residing in the countryside and small towns as Austria.

Of the total population living legally in Austria, 8.9% are foreigners, and an additional 3.6% are foreign-born persons who have been naturalized. There are also an estimated 150,000 foreigners living in Austria illegally. In Vienna, the proportion of legal foreigners among the Viennese population is 16%. The largest foreign groups are the (multiethnic) Yugoslavs and the Turks. While many of them are part of an "ethnic underclass," a sizeable proportion of Vienna's foreign community (about 15%) can be characterized as an international "overclass" that includes members and families of UN organizations (for instance, Crime Prevention Department), UN Industrial Development Organization (UNIDO), International Atomic Energy Agency (IAEA), Organization of Petroleum Exporting Countries (OPEC), and Organization for Security and Co-operation in Europe (OSCE). As for the colloquial language, 95.5% of Austrian citizens speak German exclusively; 4.1% speak German and an additional language; and 0.4% speak another language than German in everyday life. Other languages include Slovene (used by 2.4% of the citizens in the province of Carinthia), and Croatian and Hungarian (used by 6.5% and 1.8% of the citizens in the province of Burgenland, respectively). All figures are based on the 2001 census.

The population of Austria as a whole is largely Roman Catholic (73.6%), although only 49.2% of the Viennese are Catholic. The Protestant population is 4.7%, most of whom are Lutheran, but there are twenty-four communes that are over 50% Protestant. Among the resident population, 4.2% are Muslim, and 3.4% belong to other religions. Of the remainder, 12% are not members of a religious community, and 2% provided no information in the 2001 census.

In 2000, Austria's gross national income per capita was US$25,220, which places it fourteenth in the world and third in the EU (World Development Indicators 2002). Unemployment is relatively low compared with most other EU countries. This is due in part to the still large share of all employment in the public sector.

Austria takes first place among all Organization for Economic Co-operation and Development (OECD) countries in terms of employment related to tourism and gross national product (GNP) share of tourism. Austria also has a relatively large agricultural sector with its large number of "mountain farms." More than 10% of all Austrian farms are "organic farms," a higher share than in any other EU country. The predominant feature of Austria's industrial sector is the high proportion of small- and medium-sized enterprises. The major branches of Austrian industry are basic and heavy industries (due to the country's natural resources), consumer goods (foods, textiles, clothing), chemicals, transport and vehicles, and electrical and metal industries.

Austria was a forerunner in the field of environmental protection. It upholds very stringent regulations in the field of waste disposal, chemicals, and air pollution from furnaces. A 1978 plebiscite prevented the opening of an atomic power station at Zwentendorf (Lower Austria) and resulted in the enactment of the Atomic Power Ban law. Austria relies on hydroelectric power from the Danube River and the Alps.

Contextual Features

Austria is a democratic republic whose head of state is the federal president, elected by popular vote for a term of six years. The president has mainly ceremonial functions but also appoints the members of the federal government. The head of the government is the federal chancellor. The legislative body is the parliament, which consists of two houses: the National Council of 183 representatives, elected every four years; and the Federal Council of 64 members representing the federal provinces. Each province is administered by its own government, which is headed by a governor elected by the provincial parliament. Delegates to these parliaments, or diets, are elected according to the same principles as those to the National Council. The provinces are responsible for such matters as regional and local planning, social infrastructure, hospitals, and elementary schools.

Austria is a party democracy governed by political parties and political interest groups with a powerful federation of trade unions that serve as invisible partners of the government. In addition to trade unions, Austria also has a system of self-governing trade and sectoral organizations (that is, Chambers of Labor, Commerce and Industry, and Agriculture), and professional chambers, with compulsory membership. These chambers perform a variety of "delegated" state functions, and serve, therefore, something of a semiofficial role within and outside the governmental administration. The chambers and unions are closely linked to one or the other of Austria's two large political parties, the moderately left Social Democratic Party and the more conservative People's Party. Representatives of the major chambers, unions, industrial management, and government form the so-called "Parity Commission on Wages and Prices" that was created in 1957. This commission works mainly behind closed doors and tries to mediate and reach consensus in such essential questions as redistribution of wealth and wage and price policies. The commission is the most important institution of the Austrian "social partnership" system, which has contributed greatly to Austria's social peace for more than four decades. Until recently, for example, there were practically no strikes. Since the beginning of the twenty-first century, however, Austria faces a serious challenge to its highly developed welfare state due to demands of an aging population and the "downsizing" of the labor market.

The first comprehensive criminal code in Austria, enacted in 1768, contained illustrated directions for the application of "painful interrogation," or torture, if the judge entertained suspicions regarding a defendant. The Josephine Code of 1787 was generally more humanitarian. Capital punishment was prohibited, but reinstituted in 1795. It was again prohibited between 1919 and 1934, and finally abolished in 1950. Imprisonment and fines remained the main punishments. In 1974, a great reform of penal legislation emphasized the avoidance of jail sentences whenever possible because of the potentially antisocial effects of even short prison terms. Vagrancy, begging, and prostitution were specifically decriminalized. The penal code was changed from an offense-related law (according to which a criminal is charged for the crime committed regardless of personal factors, background, or state of mind) to an offender-oriented law (which means that such factors are taken into account in sentencing).

Criminal offenses are categorized either as crimes—cases in which the possible sentence is from three years to life imprisonment—or misdemeanors for all other cases. Misdemeanor cases, for which the jail sentence cannot exceed one year, are heard by a single judge in District Courts. Cases in which the possible sentence is no more than five years of imprisonment are heard in Regional Courts before a single judge. If the possible sentence is from five years to life, cases are heard in Regional Courts before Magistrates Courts (Schoeffengerichte), or in the case of certain severe crimes, before Assize Courts (Geschworenengerichte). Assize Courts (juries) consist of three professional judges and eight lay assessors, and Magistrates Courts have two professional judges and two lay assessors. In the latter, the lay assessors decide together with the professional judges whether someone is guilty and how the person should be sentenced. In Assize Courts, only the lay assessors make such decisions.

There are 150 District Courts (each covering an area extending over one or more communes) and 18 Regional Courts (each covering several District Courts). The four Courts of Appeal are situated in Vienna (covering the city, Lower Austria, and Burgenland), Graz (covering Styria and Carinthia), Linz (covering Upper Austria and Salzburg Province), and Innsbruck (covering Vorarlberg and the Tyrol). The final court of appeal is the Supreme Court. All courts function only at the federal level. All courts operate in conformity with the law. Professional judges (approximately 1,675) are independent in the exercise of their offices and may neither be dismissed nor transferred.

Prosecutions are brought by the staff of the Public Prosecutor's Office, which is completely independent of the courts themselves. The individual members of the Public Prosecutor's Office attached to the lower courts (District and Regional Courts) report to senior Public Prosecutors (the members of the Public Prosecutor's Office attached to the Courts of Appeal). They in turn, together with the Attorney General at the Supreme Court, report to the federal Ministry of Justice. Altogether there are about 200 public prosecutors in Austria.

The penal system in Austria includes seven penitentiaries for men, one for juveniles, one for women, three special institutions, and sixteen jails at the seats of Regional Courts. In 2002, the average prison population was 7,800. Of this number 26% were prisoners on trial. Of the total inmate population, 35% were foreigners, 5% were women, 2% were juveniles (ages fourteen to eighteen years), and 6% were young adults (ages nineteen to twenty-one years). The rate of incarceration was 97 per 100,000 population, about the same as in most Western European countries, but higher than in Scandinavia. More unfavorable than in Scandinavia is also the justice officer to prisoner ratio of 1 to 2.5 in Austria. Regulations stipulate that all able-bodied prisoners will be put to useful work. If proceeds from an individual's work exceed the costs to the state of his maintenance, the prisoner is paid a wage. Part can be used for pocket money;

the remainder is paid to the offender after release. Where facilities are inadequate or the situation justifies work or education beyond what is available on the prison grounds, those not considered dangerous or likely to attempt escape can work or attend classes in the nearby area.

Probation service is provided by an association called "Neustart." Staff members of this association also implement so-called extrajudicial arrangements, which are granted under certain circumstances by law. In this system, some first offenders are no longer sentenced but given a chance to make good. In 2002, such extrajudicial arrangements were made in the cases of 8,710 offenders.

In 2002, the criminal rate in Austria amounted to 6,793 criminal offenses per 100,000 inhabitants. In other words, law enforcement authorities recorded a total of 591,584 criminal offenses liable for prosecution: 121,320 were defined as crimes, an increase of 17% over 2001; 470,264 were misdemeanors, an increase of 12%. A comparison of offense rates over a longer period of time is problematic because count sheets were used for data collection until February 2000, and data are now collected electronically. Criminal offense figures increased moderately in the 1960s and early 1970s, and then increased greatly until the mid-1990s. From the 1950s to the 1990s, there was an average yearly increase of 70 registered criminal offenses per 100,000 inhabitants.

In terms of the types of offenses, by far the largest category, 72% of all recorded criminal offenses in 2002, were offenses against another's property (all categories of theft, burglary, robbery, fraud, damage to property); 14% were offenses against life and limb (homicide, bodily injury). Whereas for crimes such as homicide the clearance rate is traditionally high, the anonymous crimes such as theft and burglary have a low clearance rate. The clearance rate for all criminal offenses in 2002 was 40.8%, the lowest in decades.

Nevertheless, Austria is still among the safest countries in the world. For example, in car theft statistics it continues to rank in the lower third among the EU member-states. With 0.9 recorded homicides per 100,000 people in 2003, Vienna is one of the safest capitals in the world. The drug problem, along with drug-related crime, has in no way reached the same proportions as in some Western European cities and the United States. In 2003, the police removed addictive drugs valued at 8.2 million euros from the illegal market. Organized drug traffic in Austria is dominated mainly by foreign criminal groups that use Austria as a transit country to reach other European points. Foreign criminal groups such as the Russian and

Italian mafia use Austria primarily as a "recreation zone" (holding meetings, conferences, strategic planning) and as an investment country (running enterprises, buying real estate, and sometimes money laundering). In addition, traveling criminal groups from Eastern Europe, largely involved in robberies, burglaries, and thefts, are active in Austria. Austria's borders have been turned into the "edge of affluence" by the opening of former Iron Curtain countries to the West. Since the early 1990s, the importation of criminal activity and illegal immigration have become the main foci of internal security. In 2001, the number of detained persons who had entered Austria illegally represented a twenty-fold increase over 1993. In 2002, 24.4% of all criminal suspects investigated by the police did not have Austrian citizenship.

Police Profile

Background

Militias were the chief law enforcement bodies in the Middle Ages, along with police forces maintained by local rulers and the cities. In the sixteenth century, the City Guard was deployed at the town gates of Vienna. By the end of the Thirty Years War (1618–1648), the city had established the Public Order Watch, which was responsible for the maintenance of order and security, especially in those parts of the city where the City Guard did not go. Serious friction between the two bodies was the consequence. In the era of "benevolent despotism" in the eighteenth century, a "police welfare state" with a central police bureau and commissariats was established. In this era, "administration" mainly meant police administration. It was understood as the execution of laws for the maintenance and promotion of the general welfare, and police power was practically unrestricted. In the late eighteenth and early nineteenth centuries, the concept of an "absolutist welfare police" was replaced by the concept of "security police," in which the protection against and suppression of any danger to law, order, and public security was the single most important task of the police. However, this concept was perverted by the Metternich regime of neoabsolutism, with its strong police reign. Consequently, in the 1848 Revolution, the major criticism of the absolute state was concentrated on the police force that was seen as maintaining a solidified political system. In the aftermath of the Revolution and with the rise of political liberalism, important legal steps were taken to limit police power with laws regarding the protection of personal freedom (1862) and protection of

domestic rights (1862), and the basic state law regarding the general rights of citizens (1867). The structures of the security-executive forces that have proved to be remarkably stable were created at that time. The Gendarmerie, or rural police (also referred to as Security Guards of the Country), was founded on the French model in 1849 after the disorder and looting that had accompanied the uprising of 1848. First organized as part of the military, the Gendarmerie was then wholly severed from it. The Police, found in the cities, are successors of the Imperial and Royal Viennese Security Guards, established in 1869 on a Paris and London model meant to replace military police in the city. The Criminal Police go back to the 1870 institution of Imperial and Royal Police Agents in Vienna. Finally, in 1870, police matters were definitively conferred on the Ministry of the Interior, which had been established in 1848, transformed into the Supreme Police Authority in 1852, and into a police ministry in 1859 (and abolished in 1867). This security-executive forces structure was taken over virtually unchanged by the First Republic after the empire had collapsed in 1918. It represented the one and only authority to provide order in the postwar era, and it contributed greatly to the transition from the old state authority to the new one.

The organization of the security-executive forces of the Second Republic adopted the system in place between the wars, thus adopting the organization under the earlier monarchy as well. Consequently, some features of police bureaucracy can be traced back to the time before democratization.

Organizational Description

Police power in Austria is exclusively assigned to the federal government, as far as legislation and execution is concerned. The federal minister of the interior is responsible for the security-executive forces. Next in the hierarchy is the head of the Directorate-General for Public Security, a division of the Ministry of the Interior; it consists of the Central Command of the Gendarmerie, the Federal Security Guard, the Federal Criminal Investigation Department, the Federal Department for the Protection of the Constitution and Fight against Terrorism, and the Administrative Police. In each federal province, the Director of Public Security is the highest authority in security matters. He is appointed by the Federal Minister of the Interior but must be acceptable to the Chief of the Provincial Government. Lowest instance are the District Administration Authorities (Bezirkshauptmannschaften) or Federal Police Authorities (Federal Police Directorates). The latter are found in Vienna and thirteen of the larger cities: Schwechat, St. Poelten, Wiener Neustadt (all Lower Austria), Linz, Steyr, Wels (all Upper Austria), Salzburg (provincial capital), Innsbruck (Tyrol), Eisenstadt (Burgenland), Graz, Leoben (both Styria), and Klagenfurt, Villach (both Carinthia). The police in each city are headed by a chief; the president of the Viennese police is also director of public security because Vienna is both the capital city and a federal province. Forty-five Austrian communes have their own local police forces separate from the Federal Police or the Gendarmerie. The greatest of these is the Urban Security Guard in Baden (Lower Austria).

The Federal Police are organized in corps, which are assigned to one of the fourteen Federal Police Directorates. In Vienna, for example, the Federal Police Directorate is divided into:

1. Presidia Division (bureau for organization, control, and internal revision; bureau for questions of law and data protection; bureau for budget, logistics and infrastructure; staff department; bureau for information and public relations).
2. Provincial Department for the Protection of the Constitution and Fight against Terrorism
3. Criminal Department Vienna (Criminal Investigators' Inspectorate, Criminal Direction 1, severe and white-collar crimes; Criminal Direction 2 with five commissariats; Criminal Direction 3, criminal investigation, records, and Criminal Advisory Service).
4. Administrative Police Department (aliens' police, administrative bureau, bureau for club, association, and assembly matters and press law affairs, bureau for penal records, police department at the Public Prosecutor's Office, Vienna).
5. Security and Traffic Police Department (traffic office, police prison, the fourteen police commissariats).
6. Inspectorate-General for the Security Guard.

The gendarmes operate in rural areas and in towns without a contingent of Federal Police or local police, acting locally on behalf of the District Administration Authorities. Thus, the Gendarmerie, which unlike the Federal Police Directorates has no authoritative power, is responsible for the security of about two thirds of the Austrian population. It is organized into eight provincial command units, which form part of the Provincial Public Security Directorates. The provincial headquarters have spe-cial departments for various functions: staff department, criminal department, technology department, organization department, economic department, and traffic department. Below the provincial headquarters are eighty-six district Gendarmerie headquarters, corresponding to the District Administration Authorities, and then the Gendarmerie posts (825). A post can have up to thirty gendarmes; most have about ten. Border posts are served by Border Gendarmes and Alpine posts by Gendarmerie Alpinists and guides.

The Gendarmerie and Federal Police Directorates had their own mobile commando units (emergency units) until 2002, when a unified commando group named "Eko Cobra" was formed. The unit consists of 336 officers and is stationed in Wiener Neustadt, Graz, Linz, and Innsbruck, with branch offices in Krumpendorf (Carinthia), Feldkirch-Gisingen (Vorarlberg), and Salzburg City.

Staffing levels in 2002 follow:

Gendarmerie: 13,472 officers; 5% women
Federal Security Guard: 9,670 officers; 11% women
Criminal Investigation unit: 2,324 plain-clothes officers; 6% women
General administration of Federal Police: 2,818 officers; 75% women

There is one Federal Police officer for every 233 residents in the cities that it patrols, and one gendarme for every 386 inhabitants in the areas under Gendarmerie supervision. Overall the police to civilian ratio in Austria is 1:315, which compares favorably with similar countries. Austria is a well-policed country, and private security services are of minor importance. The private security guard to civilian ratio is 1:1,231, although there has been partial privatization of some public security services.

Police reform and reorganization to unify the Federal Police and Gendarmerie is planned for the first decade of the twenty-first century. There are concerns that these changes will result in further centralization of the Austrian police force.

Functions

The Austrian police force is divided into Security Police and Administrative Police. The Administrative Police are responsible for the protection of specific matters of administrative law and for ensuring compliance with legal regulations pertaining to specific areas of administrative authority. Violations of these regulations result in the imposition of administrative fines by the police authority that has jurisdiction over the activity or subject matter in question, such as buildings, industry and trade, foodstuffs, traffic, aliens, firearms and explosives, clubs, associations and assemblies, and newspapers and related matters. The Security Police deal with administrative aspects of criminal justice, which are defined in the Code of Criminal Procedure, and are also responsible for the security of the state and for the maintenance of public peace and order. They also have the general duty of providing assistance. Related to these tasks and duties are responsibilities for warding off dangers, crime prevention, and "special" protection as stated in the Security Police Act 1991:

1. "Special protection" includes protection of helpless people, of national government institutions, of foreign state representatives, and of public places.
2. Prevention of probable and dangerous assaults against life, health, freedom, morals, property, or environment. This refers to cases for which there is clear reason to believe that a criminal offense is about to take place.
3. Prevention of further dangerous assaults after a hazardous attack has already occurred. The operation of the security-executive forces is focused on "re-securing measures" after an executed attack.
4. Protection against an impending dangerous attack that threatens life, health, freedom, and property. If it is possible, Security Police authorities must inform the relevant population about the threat.

When fulfilling their tasks, the Security Police can only interfere with the rights of persons if such a measure is provided for in the law, if no other means are suitable to fulfill the task, and if the relationship between cause and expected success is maintained. In other words, "Sparrows must not be shot at with cannon balls, and tanks must not be attacked with catapults."

Training

The requirements for joining the Police or Gendarmerie include: Austrian citizenship; no criminal record; no administrative record (drunken driving, and so on); nine years of education (minimum education that is compulsory for every Austrian); age eighteen to thirty years, men only after military service; minimum height (men 168 centimeters, women 163 centimeters); "normal" weight (body length minus 100 ± 15%); good health (by passing a five-hour medical examination); and passing the entrance examination (written test in spelling and grammar, and intelligence and personality tests lasting four to five hours). For those who pass the entrance examination, basic training is provided at the education centers of the security-executive forces (there is one center for each of the nine federal provinces). Training consists of theoretical education (the main part), practical training on the job, and analysis and discussion of the practical experiences in preparation for the final test. Subjects taught include the following: law, psychology, criminology, ethics, tactics, first aid, self-defense, shooting, electronic data processing, rhetoric, English, and sports. Trainees study or work from Monday to Friday, forty hours per week for twenty-one months. The trained officer finishes as an inspector and starts to work as a security guardian in one of the police districts or as a gendarme, at the level of employment group E 2b (which comprises also the revier inspectors to which all officers are promoted later on automatically).

After some years of work, the officer may continue training after first passing an examination. The entrance examination for security guard officers who want to become criminal investigators (employment group E 2a) includes work on a trial basis for one week, selection by an assessment center, and a final written and oral test. This course and all other courses for becoming noncommissioned officers (NCOs) (employment group E 2a) take nine to twelve months. The NCO ranks are group inspector, district inspector, department inspector, control inspector, and chief inspector.

The training of commissioned officers (employment group E 1) is open only to officers of the employment group E 2a who meet the educational and/or working requirements. Training lasts for twenty-four months and is carried out at the Academy for Security Affairs in Traiskirchen (Lower Austria). Gendarmerie post commanders with university entrance qualification (Matura) may attend the course after at least one year of work as a commander; those without university entrance qualifications may attend after at least three years of work as a commander. The corresponding requirements for security guard officers and criminal investigators are similar. The extensive entrance examination takes several days and includes writing an essay, dictation, interview, sports, and so on. Trainees have classes in jurisprudence, management, social sciences, empirical social research, and foreign languages. Successful completion of the course depends on writing a kind of diploma work and passing the final examination, after which Academy graduates are promoted to lieutenant. The further ranks of commissioned officers are first lieutenant, captain, major, lieutenant-colonel, colonel, brigadier, and general.

A plan to transform the Academy for Security Affairs into a specialized college and to grant a degree upon successful completion of six semesters of study to become an E 1 officer has not been implemented. It is thought that qualified commissioned officers would have better opportunities for promotion to top positions in the police. At present, such positions are often occupied by police jurists, lawyer-officers who normally do not have the training of a police officer, but do have additional training from their university studies in jurisprudence. Their employment is a special feature of the Austrian police system. The ranks of the police jurists are commissary, first commissary, councilor, first councilor, privy councilor, vice-president, and president of police. An important criterion for promotions into high ranks is politics.

Police Public Projects

The Criminal Advisory Service (Kriminalpolizeilicher Beratungsdienst, now Kriminalpolizeiliche Beratung), founded in 1974 in Vienna, gives advice to the population free of charge at 107 information centers throughout Austria. Consultations are held not only in the centers, but also in homes. In 2001, officers provided 63,848 personal consultations. Officers give lectures to target groups, sometimes in connection with special projects. Examples include "Totally Okay" (production of a CD containing songs against violence and drug addiction, together with school classes in St. Johann/Salzburg in 1999); "Self-reliance" (production of a film on shop-lifting together with school classes in Hallein/Salzburg in 1999); "Skater Cops" (special traffic education program introduced in Carinthia in 1999); "Inspector Lux" (crime prevention show and distribution of a corresponding booklet at primary schools in Salzburg and Burgenland in 2001–2002); "Out—the Outsiders" (antiviolence film shown at schools in the whole of Austria in 2001–2003); "Kindergendarmerie" (Gendarmerie identity cards for children who can answer certain safety-related questions, in Vorarlberg in 2003). Self-defense courses have been offered in Burgenland, for example, since 1998. In the cities, Traffic Kindergartens are provided to give traffic training.

In addition, various community policing projects have been carried out. Contact officers were introduced in Vienna in 1977 and were followed by youth contact officers (Vienna, 1984); contact officers for the foreign population (Vienna, 1996); contact officers for soccer fan groups (since 1999 in towns with first-league soccer clubs in order to prevent hooliganism); contact gendarmes (villages without Gendarmerie posts, since 2002); "Meet your Cops" (introduced in several districts of Vienna in 1994); Mobile Police Stations (introduced in several districts of Vienna in 1995); mobile consultation rooms (introduced in 2001 in Burgenland); security panels, security places, security partnerships, security committees, and security advisory boards, in which officers, politicians, citizens, and perhaps firemen, taxi drivers, representatives of rescue parties, associations, and housing construction cooperatives can cooperate with each other (introduced first in Schwechat in 1991, then in other towns and districts); and "Police and Africans" (introduced in Vienna, 2000). In the "Rayon" (French) officers project in Vienna, in addition to the contact officers, each of the officers tries to make contact with the people of one of the 1,721 rayons, or local areas, into which Vienna is subdivided by the police. Another project is "Youth Meets Security Executive," joint computer workshops for officers and pupils at schools in Lower Austria and Styria.

Police Use of Firearms

Federal Police and Gendarmerie contingents are armed with pistols, and these can be supplemented with automatic rifles, carbines, and machine pistols. The officers are allowed to use the firearms as justifiable self-defense and as a last resort to stop crime or prevent dangerous criminals from escaping. Before the weapons are used, warnings must be given. The warnings are "stop, police here!" and firing into the air. When shooting at the offender, the officer is to avoid killing if possible.

Selling and owning firearms is restricted in Austria. Hunters and sportsmen are specially treated. There are two categories and documents for the possession of weapons. Weapons can only be carried if a person can prove he or she has a dangerous job and is a responsible person; 1.2% of Austrians have this document. The second possibility is to own a weapon kept at home; 2.6% of the Austrians use this option. In both cases, owners are checked by the police.

Complaints and Discipline

Although there are constitutional guarantees and police officers are trained to respect human rights (for example, forty hours in basic training), there are complaints about police violence and human rights violations against the security-executive forces in Austria. There have been graphic media reports about "police attacks," and the human rights organization Amnesty International criticized the security-executive forces in certain cases. All charges were investigated by the Office of Internal Affairs at the Federal Ministry of the Interior and by public prosecutors and judges. Most charges proved to be unfounded. Nevertheless, as a consequence of the charges, the Human Rights Advisory Board (HRAB) was established. It monitors the activities of the security-executive forces. Members of this board are experts in the fields of medicine, psychology, sociology, social welfare work, and jurisprudence, who are appointed by the Federal Minister of the Interior for a period of three years. They are fully independent when implementing their tasks and act on an honorary basis. In 2002, the six expert committees of the board made 396 inspection visits to police stations and observed 34 police interventions, resulting in 101 recommendations to the Federal Minister of the Interior. The board publishes one annual report on its activities. The recommendations are included in the annual Security Report by the Federal Government to the National Council.

Terrorism

In 2002, 326 rightwing extremist–motivated acts took place. Most of them were violations of the law banning Nazi activities. In the field of leftwing extremism, fifty-nine offenses were recorded. Extremism is pursued by the Department for the Protection of the Constitution and Fight Against Terrorism (former State Police). The activities of this department, which include counterintelligence, are under the control of a special permanent subcommittee of the National Council.

International Cooperation

Austria's participation in the early development of international police cooperation is documented by an event in 1923 when Interpol was established in Vienna, with the valuable cooperation of then-chief of police of Vienna, J. Schober. Interpol was headquartered in the Austrian capital until 1938. Later, Austria continued to play an active role as exemplified by its participation in UN, OSCE, Western European Union (WEU), and EU security operations. In recent decades, more than 1,000 members of the Gendarmerie and Federal Police have participated in such operations in foreign countries, ensuring human rights, supervising free and fair elections, and participating in the training of police forces. Another example is the setting up of the Middle European Police Academy (MEPA), which was an Austrian initiative.

As a member of the EU, Austria is also involved in Europol, the Association of European Police Colleges (AEPC), and the Collège Europèen de Police (CEPOL), and it is the headquarters of the Ad-hoc Center for Border Guard Training (ACT). Austria and five other Alpine countries form the "Alpine partnership" for police cooperation. Another police cooperation group is the "Salzburg Group," formed with Poland, Slovakia, Slovenia, Hungary, and the Czech Republic. Furthermore, special cooperation in border management should be mentioned, including joint border patrols with Swiss police officers; bilateral contact bureaus at the borders with Hungary and Slovakia, respectively; and trilateral contact bureau at the border crossing point Thörl-Maglern (Carinthia) with Italian and Slovenian police. In March 2003, Austrian police officers assisted Liechtenstein police on the occasion of an international soccer game.

Police Education, Research, and Publications

At the yet-to-be-established specialized college for the training of commissioned police officers, research capabilities may be established.

Leading researchers include Arno Pilgram, Heinz Steinert, Wolfgang Stangl, Walter Hammerschick, Gerhard Hanak, and Inge Karazman-Morawetz, all of whom are affiliated with the Institute for the Sociology of Law and Criminology.

The most important funding agency is the Federal Ministry of the Interior. A few projects are funded under the European Commission.

Areas of recent research include:

Tasks of the security-executive forces: Hauer, A. 2000. *Ruhe, Ordnung, Sicherheit. Eine Studie zu den Aufgaben der Polizei in Oesterreich* (*Peace, Order, Security. A Study on the Tasks of the Police in Austria*). Vienna: Springer.
Training of the police: Stangl, W. and Hanak, G. 1999. "Theorie und Praxis in der Offiziersausbildung" (Theory and Practice in the Commissioned Officer's Education). Research report. Vienna: Institute for the Sociology of Law and Criminology. Institute of Conflict Research. Forthcoming.

"Wissenschaftliche Betreuung bei der Entwicklung eines Kernlehrplanes für die Grenzpolizei im europäischen Raum" (Scientific Care for the Development of a Basic Curriculum for the Border Police in Europe). Research report. Vienna: Institute of Conflict Research.

Crime prevention activities of the police: Karazman-Morawetz, I. 2002. "Die suchtpraeventive Arbeit des Kriminalpolizeilichen Beratungsdienstes (BGD) und Effekte seiner Interventionen (beratende und begleitende Taetigkeit) an Schulen" (Addiction Prevention Activities of the Criminal Advisory Service and Effects of its Interventions in Schools). Research Report. Vienna: Institute for the Sociology of Law and Criminology. Stangl, W., Hanak, G., and Karazman-Morawetz, I. Forthcoming. "Crime-Related Fears within the Context of New Anxieties and Community-Based Crime Prevention (INSEC)." EU-Project. Local Report. Vienna: Institute for the Sociology of Law and Criminology.

Conflicts between police and citizens: Fehervary, J., and Stangl, W., eds. 1999. "Gewalt und Frieden. Verstaendigungen über die Sicherheitsexekutive" (Violence and Peace. Understanding the Security-Executive). Vol. 1. Vienna: Academy for Security Affairs of the Federal Ministry of the Interior.

Police and human rights: Fehervary, J. and Stangl, W., eds. 2000. "Menschenrecht und Staatsgewalt. Analysen, Berichte, Diskussionen" (Human Rights and Supreme Power. Analyses, Reports, Discussions). Vol. 2. Vienna: Academy for Security Affairs of the Federal Ministry of the Interior.

Police and foreigners: Haller, B. 2001. "Wie ist die Haltung der Exekutive zu Fremden in Oesterreich und wie geht sie mit ihnen um" (What Is the Attitude of the Security-Executive Forces in Austria Towards Foreigners and How Are They Dealing with Them?). Research Report. Vienna: Institute of Conflict Research.

Leading police journals include *Gendarmerie, Das Sicherheitsmagazin. Die Nr. 1 in Oesterreich, der kriminalbeamte, kriminalpolizei, Kriminalsoziologische Bibliografie, Oeffentliche Sicherheit. Das Magazin des Innenministeriums,* and *Sicherheit & Recht.*

Major recent police publications include:

Stangl, W. and Hanak, G., eds. 2003. *Innere Sicherheiten (Internal Security).* Yearbook of Sociology of Law and Criminology 2002. Baden-Baden: Nomos Verlagsgesellschaft.

Fehervary, J. and Stangl, W., eds. 2001. "Polizei zwischen Europa und den Regionen. Analysen disparater Entwicklungen" (Police between Europe and the Regions. Analyses of Disparate Developments). Vol. 3. Vienna: Academy for Security Affairs of the Federal Ministry of the Interior.

Police-relatedweb sites include:

www.bmi.gv.at
www.gendarmerie.gv.at
www.polizei.gv.at
www.diebundespolizei.at
www.polizeijuristen.at
www.kripo-online.at
www.polizeigewerkschaft-fsg.at

MAXIMILIAN EDELBACHER AND GILBERT NORDEN

Bibliography

Edelbacher, M., ed. 1998. *Organisierte Kriminalitaet in Europa. Die Bekaempfung der Korruption und der organisierten Kriminalitaet (Organized Crime in Europe: Fighting Corruption and Organized Crime).* Vienna: Linde.

Edelbacher, M. 2001. "Austrian International Police Co-operation." In *International Police Co-operation: A World Perspective,* edited by Koenig, D.J. and Das, D. K., 121–128. Lanham, Md.: Lexington Books.

Edelbacher, M. 2003. "Crime Prevention: A Community Policing Approach." In *International Perspectives on Community Policing and Crime Prevention,* edited by Lab, S.P. and Das, D.K., 14–27. Upper Saddle River, N.J.: Prentice Hall.

Edelbacher, M. 2003. "Organized Crime: A Perspective from Austria." In *Organized Crime: World Perspectives,* edited by Albanese, J.S. and Das, D.K., 188–211. Upper Saddle River, N.J.: Prentice Hall.

Edelbacher, M. and Fenz, C. 2002. "Juvenile Justice System: An Austrian Perspective".

Edelbacher, M. and Kutnak Ivkovic, S. 2004. "Ethics and the Police: Studying Police Integrity in Austria." In *The Contours of Police Integrity,* edited by Klockars, C.B., Kutnjak Ivkovic, S., and Haberfeld, M.R., 19–39. Thousand Oaks, Calif., London, New Dehli: Sage Publications.

Edelbacher, M. and Norden, G. 2000. "Challenges of Policing Democracies: The Case of Austria." In *Challenges of Policing Democracies: A World Perspective,* edited by Das, D. K. and Marenin, O., 215–241. Amsterdam: Gordon and Breach Publishers.

Hinterstoisser, H. and Jung, P. 2000. *Geschichte der Gendarmerie in Oesterreich-Ungarn (History of the Gendarmerie in Austria-Hungary).* Vienna: Stoehr.

Hoermann, F. and Hesztera, G., eds. 1999. *Zwischen Gefahr und Berufung. Gendarmerie in Oesterreich (Between Danger and Vocation: The Gendarmerie in Austria).* Vienna: Museum Association Werfen, Federal Ministry of the Interior, Central Command of the Gendarmerie.

Hufnagl, W. 1999. *Spezialeinheiten der oesterreichischen Polizei und Gendarmerie (Special Units of the Austrian Police and Gendarmerie)*. Stuttgart: Motorbuch Verlag.

Lichtenberger, E. 2000. *Austria: Society and Regions*. Vienna: Austrian Academy of Science Press.

Schnabl, F. and Seyrl, H. 2002. *Notruf 133. 133 Jahre Wiener Polize (Emergency Call 133. 133 Years of Vienna Police)*. Vienna: Echo Verlag.

Winterdyk, J.A., ed., 1997. *Juvenile Justice Systems: International Perspectives*. Toronto: Canadian Scholar's Press.

AZERBAIJAN

Background Material

The Republic of Azerbaijan is located in the Caucasus, bordering on Armenia, Georgia, and Turkey on the west, Iran on the south, the Russian Federation on the north, and the Caspian Sea on the east. Its size is 86,600 square kilometres (about 20% under occupation by Armenia), about the size of the U.S. state of Maine. The capital of the country, Baku, is the country's largest city, with 1,807,000 people (as of 2001). The second most populated city is Ganja, with 301,000 people, and the third is Sumgait, with 287,000 people. Geographically, Azerbaijan has both extensive mountain ranges and flatlands, and just under 20% of the land is arable.

The total population is 8.213 million, with an annual growth rate of 0.44%. Ethnic makeup is 90% Azeri, 2.6% Lezgi, 2.5% Russian. Armenians make up another 2%, almost all of them in the separatist Nagorno-Karabakh region. The remainder of the population consists primarily of Avars, Ukrainians, Tatars, Jews, Talysh, Turks, Georgians, Kurds, and Udins. Of the population, 27.7% are under 14 years of age, 64.7% are between 15 and 64, and 7.6% are over 65. A little over half of the population resides in urban areas.

Azerbaijan is in conflict with Armenia over the Azeri republic of Nagorno-Karabakh, under Armenian military control since 1988. This occupation has resulted in the mass movement of about 1 million Azeri refugees and internally displaced persons (IDPs) into Azerbaijan, accounting for about a seventh of the country's population. Islam is the religion of 93.4% of the population, with Russian Orthodox (2.5%), and Armenian Orthodox (2.3%) minorities. The official language is Azeri, but most people also speak Russian. Education is compulsory for children between the ages of six and seventeen, with a literacy rate of 97%. The 2003 mortality rate was 9.68 for every 1,000 people.

In addition to its well-known oil and gas reserves, Azerbaijan it is a producer of cotton, tobacco, fruits, and vegetables. However, the increase of oil as a share of exports—from 65% in 1998 to over 90% in 2001—is causing the oil sector to suppress other sectors of the economy. Azerbaijan's parliament has adopted economic liberalization reforms through privatisation, monetary regulation, a balanced budget, and removal of prices and production controls. GDP for 2002 was $28.61 billion, and GDP per capita, $3,700. In 2002, oil brought in $2 billion of export revenue, and the other major industries earned $1.8 billion. The external debt is $1.4 billion (2002). About 41% of the 3.7-million workforce is in agriculture and forestry, with 52% in services and 7% in heavy industries.

Contextual Features

The Republic of Azerbaijan is a secular democracy, which adopted a new constitution in November 1995. The government is based on the separation of powers among its legislative, executive, and judicial branches. The executive is headed by the president, who serves a five-year term and can be elected only twice. The president is head of state and supreme commander-in-chief, appoints the prime minister, and forms the government. The president also appoints the heads of executive power in the Republic's towns and sixty-five administrative *rayons* (districts), with parliament approving most of his appointments.

The legislature is the unicameral, 125-member Parliament of the Republic of Azerbaijan, the *Milli Majlis* (National Meeting). One hundred seats are elected from single-mandate districts, and twenty-five are allocated from political party lists of the country's thirty registered political parties. Parliamentarians serve five-year terms. The most recent parliamentary elections were won by the ruling Yeni (New) Azerbaijan Party (YAP).

The Constitutional Court is Azerbaijan's highest judicial body, and the Constitution of the Republic of Azerbaijan is the supreme law. The general public prosecutor operates as the level of the Supreme Court of Azerbaijan, the city public prosecutor in the Court of Appeals, and the Court of Appeals is the court of first instance (city/districts courts). The Nakhcivan Autonomous Republic has its own separate parliament, budget, and Supreme Court. Azerbaijan has an independent judiciary, which is structured by the 1994 Judicial Organization Law. As in the other former Soviet republics, it is headed by the Supreme Court, whose twelve members serve five-year terms and are appointed by the Chamber of Deputies after initial selection by the Judicial Council. The high court has four chambers, with three justices in each. Two of the chambers review civil cases, one handles criminal cases, and the fourth adjudicates on administrative, social, and mining cases. In addition to hearing appeals from lower courts, the Supreme Court has original jurisdiction on matters such as charges against top officials or disputes over state contracts. Like the U.S. Supreme Court, Azerbaijan's Supreme Court has the authority of judicial review.

Also at the top of the judiciary is a Constitutional Court, established in 1998, which handles habeas corpus petitions, conflicts between government branches, and the constitutionality of legislation, presidential decrees, and international treaties. Superior courts, at the next level of the judicial hierarchy, hear appeals from trial judges, who have original jurisdiction over civil, family, commercial, and labor cases, as well as those involving minors, criminal violations, and misdemeanors. In the judicial process, finally, the institutionally independent attorney general's office prosecutes crimes, and the public defender's office provides support for defendants.

Legal proceedings are carried out by local courts. There is also a court on grave crimes, which handles most criminal cases. The Penal Code of Azerbaijan includes a wide range of crimes, but among the most clearly defined are thefts and frauds (1,943 and 1,114, respectively, in 2002) (Interpol, International Crime Statistics), crimes of violence (1,028), and bribery (915). An ineffective judiciary, however, leads to many unpunished abuses of labor laws on working conditions, wages, and union rights. More strictly enforced are antitrafficking provisions, supported by a special drug police and courts, as well as several separate prisons for many

traffickers. About 20% of all prisoners are held for narcotics crimes.

The regular prison system, run by the Ministry of Government and administered mainly by the police, holds 15,520 prisoners and is characterized by harsh conditions and overcrowding (Interpol, International Crime Statistics). About 70% of these inmates have not been charged or sentenced, according to the Ministry of Internal Affairs, and inmates are not separated by crime, age, and other factors. Youths detained falsely or on minor charges, for instance, are routinely placed with violent criminals. But reforms in the late 1990s brought some improvements. A 1996 law allows the release of prisoners if no charges are brought for eighteen months, for example, and the Justice Minister introduced new bail laws, hired more public defenders, and released thousands of debtors from prison.

A total of 2,131 crimes were registered in January and February 2004, which is 16.2% more than the previous year. Of these, 10.5% were serious crimes, such as murder, rape, and grave injury, and 51.7% were less serious, such as robbery. As a result of operational search measures, 63.5% of all registered crimes are resolved, and guilty parties are taken to the courts. In January and February 2004, from the revealed 1,888 facts of law infringements, 1,595 persons were submitted to criminal proceedings. Of these, 84.1% were able-bodied persons of working age, but not working and not in school; 8.8% had been arrested before. The most widespread offences are larceny, traffic violations, hooliganism, and swindling. According to the latest data, there are 26 crimes per 100,000 persons in the Republic.

Police Profile

The structure of the police in Azerbaijan has never changed, even as political and economic conditions change dramatically. In addition, the police support the government in power.

Background

Before the Soviet Union was formed, Azerbaijan was not an independent country, and thus did not have an independent police force. When Soviet power was established in Azerbaijan on April 28, 1920, so was the Russian militia. Then Azerbaijan was a part of Russia, which has a police system called the Jandarmeria, which held the functions of the modern police. The jandarms were elite militas. When Azerbaijan first announced its independence on May 28, 1918, the police system was formed with the support of the Turkish police. Turkey sponsored numerous training programs in Azerbaijan. They had a well-educated military and strong police structure.

The first police forces in Azerbaijan were poorly trained and abusive during first era of independence, from 1898 to 1920, and then during Soviet rule. When the Soviet Union's disintegration led to Azerbaijan's independence on October 18, 1991, the new country created its first organized state police force, first changing the name of the militia to the "police." The police organizational structure reflected that of a highly centralized government. Measures to professionalize and modernize the police were not taken, and the State Police organ was not officially established until the Police Law of 1995, which formalized the system that was in effect throughout the first half of the twentieth century.

In addition, OPON (Detachment of Police of Special Purpose—a highly trained unit of about 500 officers, much like the U.S. Federal Bureau of Investigation) played a significant role in the country's political and public life, with large military bases and powerful officials unaccountable for their actions. The chief was Rovshan Javadov, who was deputy minister of internal affairs. Although it was the military's strongest force, OPON opposed government orders in the war for Karabakh with Armenia. There was mutiny in Baku in 1993, when a revolutionary group tried to return Ayaz Mutallibov, Azerbaijan's first president, to power. Rovshan Javadov was killed when the OPON mutinied in Baku in the same year. Subsequently, the OPON command was dismissed, and the agency dismantled. Internal security forces were then created within the Ministry of Internal Affairs instead of the Ministry of Defense. These forces also have units to suppress unrest during meetings, processions, and other activities. One outbreak of such unrest occurred after the presidential elections of October 16, 2003, instigated by the opposition party Musavat to protest election results. Even before the election results were announced, there was unrest in which, informal sources estimated, 400,000 people participated. Unrest also broke out after the disintegration of the Soviet Union, but was resolved by newly elected president Heydar Aliyev.

Demographics

According to Interpol, the police and prosecutors have powers of identity checking, arrest, questioning, and searches of persons and premises. Police can detain persons on the orders of judges, whose powers are limited to identity check, arrest, and custody. By law, neither the police nor the military has the right to strike.

According to the Ministry of Internal Affairs, last year there were 15,520 registered crimes, 22% less than in 1995. In this period, the number of crimes dropped from 264 to 193 per 100,000 people. Of all reported crimes, 42.7% were committed in Baku, 4.7% in Sumgait, and 2.6% in Ganja. Of all registered crimes, 1,486 of them (9.6%) resulted in death. There were 1,767 crimes committed by groups, 1,534 by persons who previously committed crimes; 420 by minors or with their participation; and 525 by inebriated persons. In 2002, minors committed or participated directly in 420 (3%) crimes out of all registered crimes. A total of 432 persons was subject to criminal responsibility, of whom 7.2% were girls. In 2002, inspectors dealing with crimes by minors registered 726 children with criminal tendencies.

In 2002, 2,190 crimes were registered, 14% of which were related to drugs. In comparison with 2001, the number of crimes committed by drug abusers increased from 18% to 21%. A total of 1,955 persons committing crimes under the influence of drugs and other strong substances were captured. Of those crimes, 28% were committed by persons under 30 years of age, 94% by men, and 93% by persons who were not employed or in school. At the beginning of 2003, 15,698 persons using drugs for nonmedical purposes were subject to dispensary and preventive registration.

In 2003, Azerbaijan's 52 prisons held 17,795 people—down from 23,504 in 2000. Of that population, 10.3% were pretrial detainees/remand prisoners. About 1.7% were female, 1.4% foreigners, and 0.5% juveniles and minors. The prison system's official capacity is 24,670, and so the occupancy rate was 72.1%.

Organizational Description

The main law enforcement body is the Ministry of Internal Affairs, which encompasses a supervision division, protection unit of state bodies and authorities, the state traffic police, internal armies, and a police body for special purposes. Headed by Ramil Usubov since 1994, the ministry is very powerful and closely connected to the president.

Azerbaijan has a military composed of 72,000 soldiers (Human Rights Watch, Human Development Report 2002), and a military expenditure of $121 million in 1999 or 2.6% of GDP (CIA World Factbook 2001). According to the Stockholm International Peace Research Institute, the UN Arms Register, and the Human Development Report, Azerbaijan had no arms imports before September 11, 2001, mainly because of U.S. sanctions imposed in 1993. Azerbaijan did not receive any U.S. weapons between 1990 and 2001, except for $38,000 in direct commercial sales deliveries (DCS) in 1996 (although $541,000 had been licensed in 1996). In 1997, Azerbaijan was granted $6,000 worth of DCS, but no weapons were part of this licensing. In 2001, however, the country received $513,227 in military training, according to the Foreign Military Training Report. Since September 11, in fact, Azerbaijan has benefited from the removal of U.S. sanctions. In the 2001 emergency supplemental bill passed after September 11, Azerbaijan received $3 million in nonproliferation, antiterrorism, de-mining, and related programs (NADR) funding and was allocated an additional $3.23 million in NADR funding for FY2003. The NADR funding is part of a $45.5 million fund for "specialized training and equipment to prevent and respond to terrorist incidents." The funding also includes the $42.2 million allocated for military training and equipment for border security forces in Central Asia. Azerbaijan was allotted $4 million in (FMF) in FY2002, $3 million in FMF in FY2003, and promised $2.5 million in FMF for FY2004. Moreover, Azerbaijan was allocated $750,000 for (IMET) in FY2003 and $900,000 for IMET in FY2004. Azerbaijan was also appropriated $46 million as part of the (FSA) in FY2003 and $41.5 million in FSA funding for FY2004.

Training

Police training is underdeveloped in Azerbaijan. There are several police schools, but the Police Academy is the only high-level police academy. The Ministry of Internal Affairs also holds training for police officers, and there are "internal troops" controlled by the Ministry of Internal Affairs and used mainly in defense of the government in conditions such as demonstrations and uprisings.

Complaints and Discipline

Azerbaijan's police are generally corrupt, often stopping people in the streets to take bribes. This is particularly true of the Road Police (Dovlat Yol Polisi), to which the population often pays hefty bribes of up to three times the monthly minimum wage of 60,000 manats ($12). Much of this corruption stems from a lack of resources, which even often forces many officers to buy their own uniforms. This unprofessional working climate and structure at times pushes individual officials into criminal activities, ranging from robbery to murder. The government is trying to address this problem, and in 2002 reduced personnel and increased wages of the Dovlat Yol Polisi.

Many state-appointed lawyers do not adequately defend detainees, while others report that they are not given access to their clients. Even when lawyers do obtain access, Azerbaijani law does not offer medical examinations to prove the physical abuse that is often used to obtain forced confessions from their clients. Contrary to international standards, detainees do not have the right to be treated or visited by their own doctors. The prosecutor has a duty to examine all complaints of mistreatment, but rarely does so in practice.

Terrorism

Regarding terrorism, Azerbaijan is not considered to be facing a serious terrorist threat or as a source of international terrorism. Most of the terrorism that does exist is carried out by groups in Nagorno-Karabakh, territory currently occupied by Armenia. Crimes against foreigners are rising, but are mainly limited to petty theft. One of the main criminal policies of the country is the fight against drug operations, robbery, and rapidly growing threats of murder against people if they go to the police. Because of possible drug operations in occupied Nagorno-Karabakh, Azerbaijan is sometimes considered a drug-transit country.

Police Education, Research, and Publications

One of the active organizations in this field is Prison Watch of the Azerbaijan Association. Leading authors on policing include Kamil Salimov, Hasan Bagirov, A.M. Aliyev, Elchin Hasanov, and A.N. Gajizade.

FARID GARDASHBAYOV

B

THE BAHAMAS

Background Material

British settlement of the islands of The Bahamas began in 1647. The islands became a British colony in 1783. The Bahamas attained independence in 1973. Since then, the nation has prospered through tourism and international banking and investment management. Because of its geography, the country is a major transshipment point for illegal drugs, particularly shipments to the United States, and its territory is used for smuggling illegal migrants into the US.

The Bahamas are located in the Caribbean. They are a chain of islands in the North Atlantic Ocean, southeast of Florida, northeast of Cuba. It has a total area of 13,940 sq km and a population of 299,697 (2004). The ethnic composition of the population is as follows: black, 85%; white, 12%; and Asian and Hispanic, 3%. The religious composition of the population is as follows: Baptist, 32%; Anglican, 20%; Roman Catholic, 19%; Methodist, 6%; Church of God, 6%; other Protestant, 12%; none or unknown, 3%; other, 2%.

English is the official language, although Creole is spoken among Haitian immigrants.

The capital is Nassau.

The Bahamas are a stable, developing nation with an economy heavily dependent on tourism and offshore banking. Tourism alone accounts for more than 60% of GDP and directly or indirectly employs half of the archipelago's labor force. Steady growth in tourism receipts and a boom in construction of new hotels, resorts, and residences has led to solid GDP growth. The GDP per capita is $16,700 (2003 est.).

Contextual Features

The Bahamas are a constitutional parliamentary democracy. The legal system is based on the British model, with executive, legislative (Parliament), and judiciary branches. The country is divided administratively into 21 districts. The chief of state is the British monarch, who is represented in the Bahamas by a governor general. The head of government is the prime minister. The cabinet is appointed by the governor general on the prime minister's recommendation. The governor general is appointed by the monarch.

The bicameral Parliament consists of the Senate (a 16-member body appointed by the governor general upon the advice of the prime minister and the opposition leader for five-year terms) and the House of Assembly (40 seats; members are elected by direct popular vote to serve five-year terms).

The highest court is the Privy Council. It is the final Court of Appeal. Other courts are The Bahamas Court of Appeal, the Supreme Court, and the Stipendiary and Circuit Magistrates Courts.

Police Profile

Background

The Royal Bahamas Police Force is based on the traditional British constable system. When Queen Elizabeth II and Prince Philip visited The Bahamas in February 1966, the prefix "Royal" was conferred on the force. On March 7, 1967, the Police Reserve was established, with a strength of 200.

Demographics

The Royal Bahamas Police Force is a small paramilitary force. It has approximately 2,200 personnel as well as approximately 200 members of the Reserve.

Organizational Description

The Royal Bahamas Police Force is organized into three districts: New Providence, Grand Bahama, and the Family Islands. Each district has several divisions and subdivisions. These divisions and subdivisions are overseen by Gazetted Officers—that is, officers with a rank of Assistant Superintendent or higher.

The Royal Bahamas Police Force also oversees the fire department.

Functions

The Royal Bahamas Police Force performs all duties related to the maintenance of law and order throughout the Bahamas Islands.

Training

The Bahamas Police Academy is located in Oakes Field, Nassau, New Providence. The Academy provides training for all potential regular police, fire police, police reservists, and members of the police band. In addition, continuing education programs are available for members of the police force and members of other governmental security departments.

Police Use of Firearms

In the Bahamas, the police are armed. They carry modern small arms.

Bibliography

"Bahamas, The." *CIA World Factbook*. www.cia.gov/cia/publications/factbook/geos/bf.html.
Latin American Military - Bahamas - Royal Bahamas Police Force (RBPF). www.LAMilitary.com.
"Mutual Legal Assistance in Criminal Matters and Extradition." Organization of American States. www.oas.org/juridico/MLA/en/bhs/.
"Royal Bahamas Police Force." www.rbpf.org/.

BAHRAIN

Background Material

Bahrain is an independent and fully sovereign Arab Islamic State located on the eastern shore of the Middle East Gulf States (Persian Gulf). This sheikdom of approximately 600,000 (1997 estimate) is about 231 square miles located on two main islands (Bahrain or Aval and Al Muharraq) connected by a causeway. The capital and primary port, Al Manamah, is on Bahrain/Aval. Under British control from 1880 until 1971, the country's current system of government dates back to 1973 when Muslim fundamentalists developed a constitution that, by Middle East standards, promotes a democratic society. The government of Bahrain is a hierarchical monarchy with a ruling family (Khalifa) that is upheld and guided by Islamic religious principles. Although the constitution of Bahrain and governmental operations claim to be rooted in a democratic process wherein all powers lie with the people, Islamic tradition and the ruling family almost entirely define social order and justice. Nearly 70%

of the population of Bahrain is Muslim, making for a highly homogenous society wherein Arabic is the official language.

Contextual Features

Islam, the official religion of the State, is the primary source of Bahrainian law; in fact, the second article of the constitution states that Islamic Shari'a (Islamic Law) is to be a main source of legislation (Shura Council, 2004). There is no meaningful distinction between religion and state. Another significant influence on the Bahrainian legal system is British law, most notably through the Penal Code of 1860, the Criminal Procedure Code of 1861, and the Contract Act of 1872. By the mid 1970s, a Bahrainian legislative committee had developed its own independent legal system based on a combination of Egyptian, British, and Shari'a principles. Today, the 1976 Penal Code of Bahrain serves as the law, supplemented periodically by Amiri decrees from the supreme ruler (Amir)—interventions that have the full force of law and are made on behalf of the citizens.

Judicial procedure in Bahrain, as in other Islamic and civil law countries, does not recognize the right to jury trial. Additionally, there is no assurance of appellate review of convictions and only minimal rights to appeal length of sentences. Although the accused are represented at trial by defense counsel, there is typically no representation at critical stages of the interrogation process. Many defendants, especially the indigent, see their defense attorney for the first time only minutes before their trial. Many defenses are limited to apologies for offenses and using the court's time.

Bahrain does enjoy, however, relatively low overall crime rates and especially low rates of violent crime, perhaps reflecting the combined deterrent effects of religion and state reinforced by high conviction rates. In 1986, less than 5% of over 5,000 felonies were in the category of theft. Common crimes include forgery, fraud, bribery, simple assaults, and narcotics and alcohol violations.

Whereas comparative criminologists have observed the social processes and covariates effecting low rates of crime in Bahrain, there is a great dearth of research on law enforcement in the country. At the 10th International Police Executive Symposium (IPES), which was held in Bahrain, the IPES President Professor Dilip Das praised the professionalism of the Bahrain police and was joined by National Assembly members in the suggestion that Bahrain serve as a model for democratic policing in the region, generally, and in post-Saddam Hussein Iraq, specifically.

Police Profile

Demographics

There are approximately 2,000 officers, mostly assigned to traffic management, property crime investigation, and security duties, in the national police (All References 2003). Women are a small minority group in the police force and generally work in one of the following divisions: criminal investigations, inquiries, or airport security (All References 1993). Women will soon be able to work in the traffic division, an area where they previously have not been allowed (Saffarini 2004).

Organizational Description

Law enforcement in Bahrain is a national militaristic police force operating out of eight main patrol stations (Adhari, Adliya, Al Mudaifa, Ali Bin Ebrahim, Central Market, Hussain Yateem, Lulu, and Sanabis). The Ministry of the Interior serves as an umbrella agency over virtually all police services (Shura Council 2004).

Recently, Bahrain has decided to assemble a community police force that will consist of 500 citizens, only 25% of whom are female (Economic Development Board 2004). In addition to the 500-person community police force, the Kingdom of Bahrain is also proposing to recruit 100 men and women from each of the five governorates to increase the current police force size (Economic Development Board 2004). Also of note is the recent charge to "fight crime" with more training and increased patrol units working the streets (EDB 2004).

Functions

Inasmuch as the military and law enforcement are one and the same, Bahrainian police also investigate and facilitate court martials. The National Guard, a semiautonomous institution, guards the border and oil fields and acts as a reserve unit for regular military operations and metropolitan police needs alike. Kuwait state security, Security and Intelligence Service (SIS), investigates security-related offenses and terrorist threats, particularly those suspected of collaboration with Iraq as Bahrain is an ally of the United States and Great Britain, both of which use the country as a base of Middle East operations. (Bahrain is a primary coalition naval base and the point of origin for coalition air operations against Iraq.)

The newly instituted community police force will be challenged to "maintain peace and security" without the right to carry a gun while sworn officers can carry guns to help govern public gatherings.

Training

Officer candidates attend a three-year program at a national police academy, and National Guard officer candidates attend the Kuwaiti Military College (Federal Research Division of the Library of Congress, 2003).

Complaints and Discipline

Claims of democratic transformation have been checked by various human rights watch groups, who observe that Bahrain's system of justice is often arbitrary and sexist. Accusations have focused on quick resort to martial law, the extraction of confessions by torture, and the noticeable absence of defense attorneys in cases with maximum sentences of less than three years. The "inclusion" of women into traffic divisions of the police force, while touted by police administrators as a positive step for the society and a giant leap for the country's

advancement, actually limits female officers to conducting driving license tests. Women accused of crime are almost entirely at the mercy of the system, and the incommunicado detention of their children is, allegedly, an oft-used interrogation tactic.

J. MITCHELL MILLER

Bibliography

All References. (1993). "Police and the Criminal Justice System." 2 Sept. 2004. www.reference.allrefer.com.
Amnesty International. (2004). "Women and Children Subject to Increasing Abuse in Bahrain." 27 Nov. 2004.
Capital Governate. (2002). "Police Stations." 24 Nov 2004. www.capitol.gov.bh/.
Economic Development Board. (2004). "Defense and Security News." 19 Oct. 2004. http://biz.bahrainedb.com/.
Federal Research Division of the Library of Congress. (2003). "Country Studies." 22 Nov. 2004. http://countrystudies.us/.
Helal, Adel, and Charisse Coston. (1991). "Low Crime Rates in Bahrain: Islamic Social Control-Testing the Theory of Synnomie." *International Journal of Comparative and Applied Criminal Justice* 15 (1): 125–144.
Saffarini, Reema. (2004). "Bahraini Women Likely to Join Traffic Police Soon." 27 Nov. 2004. www.gulfnews.com/.
Shura Council. (2004). "Glances from the Council's History." 12 Nov 2004. www.shura.gov.bh/en/.

BANGLADESH

Background Material

Bangladesh was a part of British India, and then of Pakistan, from 1947 through 1971. Beginning in the middle of the eighteenth century, the British ruled the Indian subcontinent for about two hundred years. After nine months of bloody war against Pakistan, Bangladesh emerged as an independent nation in December 1971. It is situated in the southern part of Asia and is nearly surrounded by Indian territory, except for a small strip in the southeast bordered by Myanmar (previously Burma). The total land area is 144,000 sq km, and its population is 126 million. The main religion in Bangladesh is Islam, and Bengali is the

primary language. Muslims account for nearly 83 percent of the total population, Hindus 16 percent, and less than 1 percent is Buddhist. Most of these groups retain the ethnic features inherited from their ancestors, who came from Burma, Thailand, Assam, and elsewhere in the Southeast (Afsaruddin, 1990). Since its separation from Pakistan in 1971, Bangladesh has had a troubled history of political instability with periods of military rule, but effective democracy was restored in 1991.

Bangladesh inherited a colonial economic system without substantial industrialization. The British policies prevented urban and industrial development in Bangladesh, resulting in a purely agricultural economy dominated by rice and jute. The economy remains mainly agrarian, relying on the export of ready-made garments, jute, tea products, shrimp, and unskilled workers. Presently, one fourth of the country's GDP comes from agriculture. The annual growth rate remained stagnant during the decade, and GDP growth rate varied between 4% and 5%. State ownership and private ownership exist side by side; however, the dominance of the private sector has gradually increased in recent years. The adult literacy rate is 62% (BBS 2001), and the per-capita income is about US$380 (World Development Report 2003).

Contextual Features

The country has a written constitution that was adopted in 1972. The entire country is broadly divided into six territorial divisions. Divisions are divided into small administrative districts. Districts are further divided into *Thanas*, rural-based administrative units. The legislative branch of the government is a unicameral Parliament, composed of 300 members who are directly elected from territorial constituencies (Heitzmen and Worden 1989). Additionally, 30 female members are chosen by the Parliament.

The administration of criminal justice in Bangladesh is highly centralized. The Ministry of Home Affairs administers police and correctional functions, while the Ministry of justice controls prosecutorial functions. The basic principles underlying the criminal justice system are derived from the constitution. The constitution guarantees fundamental rights to citizens. But in practice, constitutional guarantees are found to be inadequate protection of the rights of the accused. For example, unlike the U.S. practice, the defense attorney's presence is not permitted during police interrogation.

Evidence suggests that Bangladesh in general utilizes widespread pretrial detention. Detainees may be held without trial for extended periods, and the rights of the accused are limited both in theory and practice (Malik 1993). Additionally, periodic enactment of various laws by the government has increased the punitiveness of the criminal justice system.

Police reports indicate that violent crime such as murder has increased significantly in recent years. Between 2001 and 2003, a total of 10,331 murders occurred in Bangladesh. The most common crimes were armed robbery, mugging, extortion, kidnapping, and rape (Khan 2004).

The legal institutions of Bangladesh have their foundations in the English colonial era. The criminal law and procedure continue to reflect both their customary law and the elements of common law. The colonial procedural and substantive laws, particularly criminal laws as designed by the British colonial power more than 150 years ago to rule and subjugate the alien people of the Indian subcontinent, are still in operation. Bangladesh inherited the "Penal Code," first promulgated in 1850 as the Indian Penal Code; the "Code of Criminal Procedure," of 1898; the Police Act of 1861; and the Prison Act of 1894 from the British (Heitzman and Worden 1989). Additionally, special laws such as Special Powers Act of 1974, Anti Terrorism Act 1992, Public Safety Act 2000, and Speedy Trial Act 2002 were promulgated since the independence of Bangladesh in 1971.

Bangladesh adopted elements of the Common Law and new procedures based on customary law to create a system that meets the society's needs. "Personal Laws" such as the laws of inheritance, marriage, and divorce are mainly based on Islamic laws for the Muslims.

The judicial system is composed of the Supreme Court, the Court of Sessions, the Metropolitan Magistrate's courts, and the Magistrates' court of grades I through III (courts of first instance). There is no separate system of juvenile courts in Bangladesh. The trial system is non-adversarial in nature, and plea-bargaining does not exist in the court system. All the courts administer justice according to the same law. Jury trials do not exist in Bangladesh.

The Supreme Court of Bangladesh is the highest court and has two divisions: One High Court Division (a superior court of records) and one Appellate Division. The Supreme Court has responsibility for affairs of state such as the interpretation and enforcement of the constitution and alleged violations of the fundamental rights of the individual. The High Court has supervisory powers over the lower adjudicatory bodies in the hierarchy of court structure. The Appellate Division reviews judgments of the lower courts and the High Court.

An interesting feature of the court system is the role of police officers in adjudication process. The police perform the prosecutorial functions in the court of first instance (Magistrates' court), although they have no professional knowledge or legal training. Most importantly, the court system has no administrative control over police prosecutors (Huque 1980). On the other hand, in the Session Courts, the government appoints prosecutors on a contractual basis to perform the job of public prosecutors.

However, in the metropolitan cities of the country, "Metropolitan Magistrate Courts" have been set up where magistrates are exclusively engaged in the trial of cases. Statistics show that 80 percent of the criminal cases of the country are being adjudicated by them. Unlike U.S. practice, the defense attorney's presence is not permitted during police interrogation.

The prison system of Bangladesh had its inception in the legislation of the Prison Act of 1894, which was basically derived from the England Prison Act of 1877. The jail is the only correctional institution in Bangladesh and assumes the combined functions those jails and prisons serve in the United States. Most of the jails were built during the British regime, and many of the jails do not have sufficient numbers of personnel to maintain adequate supervision.

The correctional system is administratively centralized. Although 54 years ago Bangladesh cast off British rule, Bangladeshi jails are still administered under the century-old colonial Prison Act.

There are 80 jails, which vary greatly in size, as well as many other characteristics. They are divided into three categories: central, district, and *thana* jail. A separate department of the Government (Ministry of Social Welfare) handles the limited use of probation. Most importantly, a probation sentence is not combined with a period of imprisonment. Most of the modern alternatives to imprisonment are not being practiced in Bangladesh.

Police Profile

Background

The Bangladeshi police follow the 200-year-old British police system, with some minor modifications. During British rule, the police were a repressive institution, and their main purpose was to serve the interest of the ruling class. In other words, the basic structure of the police remained unchanged. Historically, the police have been extremely partisan toward those in power by serving the ruling party and its leader by enforcing laws against opposing groups. It is found that the ruling elites not only interfere with police functions but also victimize officers in many ways, such as affecting transfers and promotions of those who fail to oblige them.

Organizational Structure

The police in Bangladesh are centralized as a national force. Police functions are controlled by the Ministry of Home affairs, while the operational responsibilities are vested in Police Headquarters. The Inspector General is the chief executive of the police department. Police administration is carried out under the century-old Colonial Police Act of 1861. The Home Ministry has the power to issue administrative regulations on personnel and police operations.

There are three main branches in the police department: the Traffic, Special, and Detective branches. In addition to that, there is a Central Investigation Department (CID), which deals with the high profile and serious cases. In 2003, a new unit of the police called the "Rapid Action Battalion" was introduced. They are responsible for investigating and detecting serious crime. Unlike in many countries, police departments in Bangladesh do not have separate vice units to fight prostitution, gambling, and narcotics.

The Bangladeshi police are composed of 64 administrative districts unevenly divided into five police ranges (regional headquarters) headed by DIG. Policing activities are carried out from a central office (*Thana*) in both urban and rural areas. There are presently 539 police stations in Bangladesh. The officer in charge, properly known as the O.C. of a police station, is responsible for maintaining law and order and for prevention and detection of crimes in his jurisdiction. The metropolitan police, a separate wing within the police department, is responsible for policing the major cities of the country. There are five regional headquarters headed by Deputy Inspector General. Evidence suggests that police departments utilize their resources mainly in their crime control missions.

There is a single criminal code and standardized criminal justice procedures for the entire country. As of 2003, the police department in Bangladesh had an estimated 109,000 personnel. Women composed less than 1% of the total police force. Muslims account for more than 90%. Police officers are categorized as gazette and non-gazette, roughly analogous to commissioned and non-commissioned officers in the military services. The Inspector General is the chief executive of the police department. The remaining top four managerial positions are Additional Inspector General, Deputy Inspector General (DIG), Additional DIG, and Superintend of Police (SP). The non-gazette category consists of Inspector, Sub-Inspector (SI) and Assistant Sub-Inspector (ASI). In reality, Superintend (SP) of a district and Officer-in-Charge (OC) of a *thana* are the two most powerful officers in the police administration. In each metropolitan police station, there are one Inspector (Officer-in-Charge), eight Sub-Inspectors, four Assistant Sub-Inspectors, and 20 constables.

Recruitment in police service is being done at three levels: Constable, Sub-Inspector, and Assistant Superintend of Police (ASP). The Superintendent of Police recruits constables in their respective jurisdictions. Sub–inspectors are recruited through a competitive examination conducted by police headquarters. Assistant Superintends are members of the civil service, recruited through a competitive examination by the public service commission.

Training

The cadet Sub-Inspector and the Assistant Superintendent of the police (ASP) are required to complete one year of foundational training at the police Academy, which consists of physical conditioning, operation of light and heavy arms, criminal law and procedures, and driving. After successful completion of the academy training, Sub-Inspectors are required to undergo two years of in-service training in various police units. On the other hand, new constables are required to complete six months of training at the police training schools. Presently, there are four such schools in the country. There is a detective training school in Dhaka for the members of the detective branch. There is also a traffic training school that offers courses on traffic management (Chowdhury 1996).

In 2000, the government established a Police Staff College in Dhaka. The college is designed for the training of senior-level police officers. Since its inception, the college has offered a number of short courses (ranging from 6–12 weeks) on human rights. The main components of the program include controlling human rights violations and increasing awareness among the police officers. The senior-level police executives, retired IG's, judge, justice, university teachers, and lawyers, are engaged in conducting the training. The Police Staff College has received financial assistance from the United Nations Development Programme (UNDP) and other international agencies.

In the past, senior-level officers received foreign training in Japan or the United Kingdom on a regular basis. But in recent years, the opportunity for higher training is virtually absent, primarily due to resource constraints. As compared to non-gazetted officials, the gazette officers are well trained and well paid. The lower echelons of the police, known as constables, who constitute more than 70% of the police force, are poorly trained with low levels of education. Interviews suggest that the curricula for training, especially for the constables, are not adequate. As a result, constables generally have a weak grasp of procedural laws and the proper use of force in dealing with criminals. After completing four years, the SI's can take a departmental promotion test in order to qualify for the next promotion (Inspector).

After completing one year of foundation training at the police academy, trainee Assistant Superintendents undergo a six-month-long in-service training. They are then required to pass a law test conducted by the Public Service Commission (PSA). Assistant Superintendents further receive four months of basic training for administration at the Public Administration Training Centre (PATC). Promotion basically depends on individual performance, as evaluated by superior officers. Although there is a provision that 33% of the total posts of Assistant Superintendents will be filled through departmental promotion, in reality very few Inspectors are being promoted to Assistant Superintendents (Personal Interview, Sept. 30, 2003).

Evidence suggests that professionalism in police work has yet to fully develop in Bangladesh. The use of traditional methods, inadequate training, an absence of modern communication technologies, corruption, and improper use of political influence in police work have hindered the professionalism. According to the Police Commission Report of 1988, only 38% of the total force were actually involved in functions like crime prevention, detection and investigation of crimes, prosecution of criminals, and law and order maintenance. The rest of the officers are involved in non-crime-related functions such as protection of the VVIPs, VIPs, and other dignitaries, escort, and other functions.

Police in Bangladesh suffer from a distorted self-image. A recent survey by the author found that more than 80% of the respondents have no confidence in the police (Kashem 2003). The use of excessive force, rape and killing of those in police custody, and other questionable practices raised serious questions about the legitimacy of the police in recent years. Police are not provided the necessary budget and equipment to fight crime and disorder. Also, the lack of modern communication systems (e.g., petrol car, two-way radio) makes it very hard and often impossible to respond to crimes and disorders. There is a centralized 999 telephone system to request police service. However, it is reported that people hardly use this service. The use of computers for record keeping is virtually absent. As a result, police departments are unable to maintain computerized files on criminal history information, warrants, and arrests. According to police officers, introduction of computers in police work will greatly improve their crime control functions. Police investigative functions such as fingerprint processing, laboratory testing of substances, or ballistics testing is very limited. This is mainly because the laboratories are not well equipped to conduct these tests.

Data on the number of officers indicate that officers assigned to police stations are overworked. Street level officers (constables) and Sergeants work at least 12–15 hours daily and are not entitled to weekly holidays. It was found that Sub-Inspectors and Assistant Sub-Inspectors posted at a police station are overburdened with clerical work. Police officers, especially the constables, are not well equipped. They use heavy weight rifles that are 100 years old. Carrying of such heavy arms in fact restricts their mobility. Sub-Inspector and above ranking officers are authorized to carry various types of revolvers. Police officers are authorized to use one or more types of nonlethal weapons such as chemical agents (e.g., pepper spray, tear gas) in maintaining public order. Among these, the police in Bangladesh most commonly use tear gas. All police departments maintain written policy directives on the use of deadly force. Surprisingly, street level officers (constables) have very limited power. For example, a traffic police posted at a busy intersection of a city cannot write a ticket for violation of traffic rules.

The rate of police corruption in Bangladesh is very high. The present form of corruption is highly organized (Kashem 2003). Unlike many countries, there is no Civilian Complaint Review Board for dealing with complaints against the police. That is, a separate unit within the police department called "Police Security Cell" handles the complaints. In other words, investigations of police misconduct are solely internal. A press report revealed that more than 20,000 complaints against the police were pending. Lawsuits alleging the use of excessive force, brutality, and assault can be filed in state courts. However, the court systems of Bangladesh rarely take any actions against the police.

Police Public Projects

In the absence of community policing, there are no major police public projects in Bangladesh.

International Cooperation

The Bangladeshi police force has been honored for its contribution to the maintenance of international peace. It has participated in peacekeeping and democracy building activities under UN supervision in various parts of the world, including Namibia, Cambodia, Mozambique, Rwanda, Yugoslavia and Haiti. In 1976, Bangladesh became a member of Interpol.

Police Education, Research, and Publications

Besides the police academy and training schools for the police officers and constables, courses on policing are not offered at any level of undergraduate or graduate programs in Bangladesh. Besides some journalistic articles on police corruption and brutality, empirical research on policing is virtually absent in Bangladesh. Presently, police departments publish a monthly magazine in Bengali entitled *Detective* that basically covers departmental news. Recently, the Department of Sociology at the University of Chittagong has introduced a graduate course on policing. Professor Mohammed Bin Kashem teaches this course. In addition, Professor Kashem has started a research center at the University of Chittagong called the Center for Crime Prevention. The main purpose of the center is to conduct research on police methods of crime prevention and police crime control effectiveness. However, obtaining funds for police research seems to be difficult. Government sources, for example the Home Ministry, do not sponsor any kind of police research. Responses from the international donor agencies located in Bangladesh are not encouraging. Recently, the Moulana Bhashani University of Science and Technology established a new department entitled Criminology and Police Science. The program is the first of its kind in Bangladesh.

The following are the leading crime reporters working at the national daily newspapers of Bangladesh: Sakir Ahmed, *The Daily Ittefaque*, Dhaka; Towhidul Islam, *The Daily Inqilab*, Dhaka,;and Sankar Dey, *The Daily Janakantha*, Dhaka.

The following are the notable researchers: Mohammed Nurul Alam, Former Additional IG, and Commandant, Police Staff College, Dhaka; and Motiar Rahman, Additional DIG, Police Headquarter, Dhaka.

MOHAMMED BIN KASHEM

Bibliography

Afsaruddin, M. *Society and Culture in Bangladesh*. Dhaka: Book House, 1990.

Bangladesh Bureau of Statistics (BBS). *Statistical Yearbook of Bangladesh*. Dhaka, Bangladesh: Ministry of Planning.

Chowdhury, Ahmed Amin. *Bangladesh Police: Uttaridikhar O Babostapona*. Dhaka: S. S. Pringers, 1996.

Heitzman, J., and Worden, R. L., eds. *Area Handbook Series: Bangladesh a Country Study*. Washington, D.C.: Federal Research Division, 1989.

Kashem, Mohammed Bin. "Preventive Crime: Police and Crime Control in Bangladesh." [Paper presented at the Annual Meeting of the Asian Association of Police Studies, July 2002, Hong Kong.]

Kashem, Mohammed Bin. "The Social Organization of Police Corruption: The Case of Bangladesh." *Police Corruption: An International Comparative Perspective.* Ed. Dilip K. Das and Rick Sarre. PA: Lexington Books, 2003.

Khan, Pervez. "Crime Increased, Brutality in Murder: A New Trend." *Prothom Alo*, 6. No. 56, January 2004: 1, 2.

Malik, S. "The Preventive Detention Laws of Bangladesh." *Preventive Detention and Security Law*. Ed. A. Harding and J. Hatchard. Dordrecht, Netherlands: Martinus Nijhoff Publishers, 1993. 41–57.

World Development Report, 2004. World Bank, Washington, D.C.

BARBADOS

Background Material

The island of Barbados was settled by the British in 1627. The island was uninhabited before that date. Social and political reforms were adopted throughout the 1940s and 1950s. Independence was achieved in 1966.

Barbados is located in the Caribbean. It is an island in the north Atlantic Ocean, northeast of Venezuela. It has a population of 278,289 (2004 est.). The population is 90% black, 4% white, and 6% Asian and mixed. The following religions are practiced, with percentages denoting the portion of the population adhering to that religion: Protestant 67% (Anglican 40%, Pentecostal 8%, Methodist 7%, other 12%); Roman Catholic 4%; none 17%; other 12%. English is spoken in Barbados.

Historically, the Barbadian economy has been dependent on sugar cane cultivation and related activities, but production in recent years has diversified into light industry and tourism.

The GDP is $15,700 (2003 est.).

Contextual Features

Barbados is a parliamentary democracy. It operates as an independent sovereign state within the Commonwealth. It is divided administratively into eleven parishes.

The legal system is based on English common law. There is no judicial review of legislative acts.

The chief of state is the reigning monarch of the UK and the Commonwealth. The monarch is represented in Barbados by the Governor General, who is appointed by the monarch. The head of the government is the Prime Minister. Following legislative elections, the leader of the majority party or the leader of the majority coalition is usually appointed prime minister by the governor general; the prime minister recommends the deputy prime minister.

The bicameral Parliament consists of the Senate (21-member body appointed by the governor general) and the House of Assembly (30 seats; members are elected by direct popular vote to serve five-year terms).

The Supreme Court of Judicature is the highest body of the judiciary. Judges are appointed by the Service Commissions for the Judicial and Legal Services.

Crime in Barbados is characterized by petty theft and street crime. Incidents of violent crime, including rape, occur.

Police Profile

Demographics

The Royal Barbados Police Force is composed of 200 special constables and 1,250 police officers.

Organizational Description and Functions

The Royal Barbados Police Force has a unit that focuses on enforcing drug laws and slowing drug trafficking. This is necessary because the Caribbean region is a major transit point for drugs coming from South America to Europe and to the United States. This force makes use of British-trained drug-sniffing dogs, which are used at the airport to find individuals attempting to smuggle illegal narcotic substances into Barbados. The Barbados police work with the United States Coast Guard to combat drug trafficking.

The Barbados Defence Force is responsible for national security. It is an all-volunteer force with headquarters in St. Anne's Fort. The Force is entrusted with maintaining order during emergencies. The Force is also called in to help when prisoners escape from prison.

The Royal Barbados Police Force Band is regionally and internationally known. It plays regularly at government and cultural functions.

Bibliography

"Barbados." *CIA World Factbook*. www.cia.gov/cia/publi cations/factbook/geos/bb.html.

"Barbados: Consular Information Sheet." US Department of State. http://travel.state.gov/travel/cis_pa_tw/cis/cis_1022.html.

"Royal Barbados Police Force." http://barbados.allinfo about.com/police.html.

BELARUS

Background Material

The Republic of Belarus (formerly the Byelorussian Soviet Socialist Republic) is a founding member of the Commonwealth of Independent States (CIS). The country is located in the central part of Eastern Europe and shares common borders with Poland, Lithuania, Latvia, Russia, and Ukraine. The territory of the Republic is 207,000 sq km.

In the thirteenth century, after the fall of the Kievan Rus to the Mongols, Belarus was incorporated into the Lithuanian-Polish Commonwealth (LPC). In 1795, the LPC was partitioned, and its eastern territories, including Belarus, were annexed by the Tsarist Russia.

By the late nineteenth century, Belarus experienced an emergence of nationalism. In 1918 following the collapse of the Russian Empire, a short-lived People's Republic of Byelorussia was created, only to be crushed by Bolshevik revolutionaries. On January 1, 1919, the Byelorussian Soviet Republic was formed, and it came under the total political and economic control of the central au.thorities in Moscow.

During the Soviet period, Belarus became one of the most assimilated of the Russia Soviet republics. Pro-independence sentiments in Belarus during Gorbachev's reforms of the late 1980s were much weaker than in the neighboring Baltic republics and Ukraine. On August 25, 1991, the country declared independence, mostly in response to the crisis of the central authority in Moscow.

The population of Belarus is 10.3 million (2004 est.); 81.2% are Belarusian; 11.4% Russians, Poles, and Ukrainians; 7.4% others. Major religions are Eastern Orthodox (80%), Catholics (14%), and Protestants (2%) (1997 est.). Seventy percent of the population lives in cities. The capital, Minsk, has a population of 1.6 million. The state languages are Belarusian and Russian.

Although Belarus inherited from the Soviet era a relatively well-developed (but militarized) industrial infrastructure and highly educated work force, economic transition was difficult and slow. Reforms have especially slowed down since 1994 when authoritarian president Alyaksandr Lukashenka assumed control of the country. By 1996, because of repeated human rights violations and non-democratic practices in the electoral process, the country found itself in political isolation. Most of the Belarusian economy remains under direct control of the government. In response to growing political isolation, Belarus pursued a course toward European Union style unification with the Russian Federation. This unification process is currently stalled because of disagreements with Russia over constitutional and other types of issues.

In 2003, Belarus reported economic growth of 6.1%. About one third of the national product is created by industry (machinery and transport equipment, chemicals, foodstuffs, metals, and textiles).

The Belarusian GDP in 2003 was $17.5 billion; per capita GDP $1,765. However, the country's long-term economic prospects are hampered by serious structural problems (dependence on Russian subsidies, majority of enterprises operating at a loss, high inflation, arbitrary and corrupt legal system, price controls).

Contextual Features

Belarus is a presidential republic. Administratively, the country is divided into six *voblastsi* (provinces), and one municipality (*horad*); they in turn are divided into *rayony* (districts) and cities that are, in turn, composed of towns, villages, and settlements. Executive power is exercised by the President of the Republic of Belarus (elected directly by the people of the Republic for a five-year term), who is the head of state. The Prime Minister heads the government, which consists of the Council of Ministers (the cabinet). The Prime Minister in Belarus is appointed by the President, with the consent of the House of Representatives. The government is accountable to the President of the Republic and the Parliament of the Republic of Belarus. The legislative branch consists of a bicameral legislature, with the lower house of 110 members and an upper house of 60 members. The judicial branch consists of the Supreme and Constitutional Courts. The 1996 referenda (declared illegitimate by the European Union observers) provided the Presidential office extraordinary powers, including the right to appoint and dismiss certain judges, legislators and local office holders, and lifetime immunity from prosecution.

The judicial system of the Republic of Belarus is based upon the principles of territorial delineation and specialization. Judicial power is vested in the court system headed by the Constitutional Court.

Besides the Constitutional Court, two more types of courts exist. General jurisdiction courts are subdivided into three tiers: Supreme Court of the Republic of Belarus; regional, district (city) courts; and military courts. They rule in both civil and criminal matters, with the exception of areas covered by the other judicial branches. There are also economic courts, consisting of the Supreme Economic Court of the Republic of Belarus, economic courts of Districts and Cities, and the City of Minsk Specialized Economic Court.

The Supreme Court of the Republic of Belarus is the superior body in the hierarchy of the general jurisdiction courts. Located in Minsk, it has the following structure: the Plenum of the Supreme Court; the Presidium of the Supreme Court; and four Judicial Chambers: Military, Civil Cases, Criminal Cases, and Patents.

The Plenum of the Supreme Court provides guidelines to courts on proper application of the law, and it supervises activities of the judicial chambers. The main function of the judicial chambers is to review cases filed for cassation as well as consider cases in which the newly discovered evidence was presented. The regional courts serve as courts of second or higher instance for district (city) courts. The ratio of professional judges is estimated to be 10.03 per 100,000 inhabitants (in 2000).

The dissolution of the Soviet Union in 1991 led to a drastic decline of the standard of living, a general breakdown of law and order, and a dramatic increase in crime in Belarus. By 1993, the murder rate increased by almost 50%; larceny/theft by almost 60%. In the first post-independence decade, the crime rate grew on average by 6% annually and by 2001 reached a rate of 1,127 per 10,000. The rate of homicide and attempted homicide increased to 11.9; thefts to 608.3, and drug offenses to 38.1 per 10,000. In addition, there was a significant rise in organized crime as the country became a route for transporting illegal drugs and trafficking of women to the European Union countries. Crime rates in Belarus continue to rise, although at a slower rate, mainly due to an increase in robbery, burglary, fraud, and thefts.

The Committee of Observance of Punishment of the Ministry of Interior is in charge of the correctional system, which includes penitentiary facilities and alternative forms of punishment such as restitution, probation, parole, and suspended sentences. Belarus signed a number of international treaties, such as the European Convention of Human Rights and the European Prison Rules, which safeguard the rights of prisoners in the country.

Imprisonment and fines are the most commonly used forms of penalties in Belarus. The imprisonment rate is 595.50 (2000). Prison conditions in the country remain poor. The incarcerated population exceeds official prison capacity by 21%; there are shortages of food and medicine, and an increase in tuberculosis, syphilis, and HIV/AIDS infections. The death penalty has not been abolished in Belarus. In 2002, seventy-seven persons were executed in Belarus.

Police Profile

Background

The internal security of the Republic of Belarus is provided by a group of forces and services that include the Committee for State Security, the Ministry of Interior (MI), the Presidential Guard, the Emergency Ministry, the State Customs Committee, and the State Committee of Border-Security Forces.

Since the late 18th century, when Belarus was incorporated into the Russian Empire, the development of the Belarusian law enforcement system had been wedded to the Russian and Soviet models. The situation did not change substantially in the post-independence period. Structurally and functionally, the Belarusian police system remains very close to the law enforcement model of the Russian Federation.

The Ministry of Interior of Russia was created in 1802 by the decree of the Emperor Alexander I, and it marked the beginning of a professional police force in Russia, as well as in Belarus.

After the Revolution of 1917, the imperial police in Belarus was abolished and replaced by a people's militia directly administered from Moscow. In its early period, the Belarusian militia was divided into two forces: territorial and transport police. The first centralized police unit—the criminal investigative branch—was established in 1918 to combat a dramatic rise in crime in the post-revolution period. Later, the departmental guard, traffic police, the fire service, and the internal passport services were also established.

In Soviet times, the police functioned first and foremost to maintain and preserve the political and economic system of the communist state. Following Belarusian independence in 1991, the law "On police" was adopted to replace the Soviet era legislature.

Organizational Description and Functions

The quasi-militarized and centralized structure of Belarusian police reflects the legacy of both the Tsarist and Soviet periods. The administrative and command center of the police force is in Minsk.

Police personnel are divided into a hierarchy of ranks. The highest officers (Superior management) have a rank of major general and above; senior officers (Complex Units Commanders) have ranks of major through colonel; middle officers (Smaller Units Commanders) have ranks of junior lieutenant to captain; the lowest officers (supervising) are sergeants and petty officers; and below this are the soldiers (operational execution).

The Ministry of Interior consists of the following services:

- Organized Crime and Corruption Committee;
- The Criminal Police, made up of: Criminal Investigative Department, the Anti-Drug and Anti-Social Crimes Department, Department of Economic Crimes, Department of High-Tech Crimes, the National Crime Laboratory, the National Interpol Bureau, the Research and Information Department; and a Special Counterterrorist Squad;
- Public Safety and Special Police services, consisting of the Department of Public Order and Preventive Measures, the State Automobile Inspectorate, the Internal Passport Department, the Department of Migration, the Correctional Institutions Committee, the State and Private Property Protection Department;
- The Investigating Committee of the Ministry of Interior; and
- The Troops of the Ministry Interior.

The Ministry of Interior sets and implements national policing policy, monitors law enforcement in the country, compiles statistics, and trains police officers and personnel.

The Belarusian police function under supervision of two institutions: the MI and the local governmental bodies.

Crime investigations in Belarus are headed by the State Prosecutor's Office, which oversees the investigative branches of the police and the State Security Committee.

The mission of the internal troops of the MI is:

- to facilitate local police efforts in maintaining public order and safety;
- to enforce the state emergency regulations;
- to guard correctional facilities and other objects (i.e., cargoes, infrastructure);
- to assist in the search for missing persons or escaped prisoners.

The Deputy of the Minister of Interior is the commander of 16 MI troop regiments stationed throughout the country. Rank-and-file soldiers of the troops are composed of conscripts, while all commissioned officers are career employees of the MI.

Training

Police in Belarus are recruited from citizens no older than 35 years of age. Soldiers must have a general secondary education; candidates for middle and senior officer positions must have a specialized college or university degree. Each candidate must undergo a medical examination and background check for criminal records and disability.

Police staff are trained primarily (although not exclusively) by educational institutions administered by the MI. Police training is conducted on three levels. The basic police training for soldiers is provided in specialized short-term courses where basic policing techniques and the general principles of the law enforcement are taught.

The second tier of police training is carried out on the university level, while the highest level of training is equivalent to postgraduate education. Police colleges provide associate law degrees, whereas the MI Academy provides associate law degrees as well as postgraduate degrees. Among the most important national police educational institutions are police colleges in Baranavichy and Mahilyov, the special MI police training center in Minsk, and the MI Academy in Minsk. Graduates of police colleges and the MI Academy receive the rank of lieutenant.

After a number of years in service, all police officers and staff are required to undergo a subsequent training. Promotion in the police force depends not only on the number of years served, but also on the officer's service evaluation, which is measured according to a professional qualification index, shooting skills, and physical condition.

Police Use of Firearms

All officers carrying firearms must undergo annual firearms training to keep their shooting skills up to the required level. The law prohibits off-duty police officers from carrying a gun. The exceptions are detectives and members of special force units.

The Legislature's definition of conditions under which a police officer can use a firearm are not entirely unambiguous. Arms may be used for self-defense or to defend citizens against the deadly assault, for hostages' release, for suppression of acts threatening public safety, against armed attacks or assault on a police station or on any other guarded object, and for apprehending a person offering armed resistance. Police personnel can also use a firearm to issue a warning and to call out for help, to neutralize dangerous animals, and to stop vehicles if a driver doesn't react to a legitimate demand to stop driving. Before discharging a gun, a police officer is required to issue a warning cry. An internal investigation may be launched if police officers use firearms inappropriately.

Police Public Projects

Policing of the local community is carried out in a combination of overt and covert methods. The majority of patrols are carried out in patrol cars equipped with mobile radio communication systems.

For policing purposes, the territory of the country is divided into precincts. Every precinct has one or more precinct officer (*uchastkovyi*), who usually resides in that precinct and personally knows the majority of the community members. The precinct officer keeps a public office where members of a community can present their claims and complaints. On average, Belarusian police investigate five million administrative violations annually. As the scope of organized crime in the country has grown, undercover investigative techniques have also been increasingly applied. However, current Belarusian legislation on undercover policing is

inadequate to ensure the protection of individual privacy. The MI is currently engaged in developing and implementing community policing approaches. Police officers are also participating in social programs and partnerships involving various populations at risk.

Complaints and Discipline

According to numerous reports of international human rights organizations, Belarusian security forces frequently commit serious human rights abuses: peaceful demonstrators are routinely detained and occasionally beaten; in police interrogations beatings and psychological pressure is often used. Politically motivated intimidation and arrests continue, although the majority of arrestees are released in a relatively short period of time. Despite legal protections, investigators routinely fail to inform detainees of their rights and conduct preliminary interrogations without providing the opportunity to seek legal counsel.

Terrorism

Domestic and international terrorism is virtually nonexistent in Belarus. Between 1996 and 2004, the State Prosecutor Office investigated four cases classified as local terrorist acts. In October of 2004, the Belarusian parliament ratified two treaties: On Joint Counterterrorist Activities on the Territory of CIS, and the International Convention for the Suppression of the Financing of Terrorism, which was adopted by the General Assembly of the United Nations on December 9, 1999. The Committee of the State Security is in charge of anti-terrorism activities in Belarus.

International Cooperation

Belarus is a member of two CIS-based organizations: the Bureau on Coordination of Struggle Against Organized Crime, and the Counterterrorist Center. The MI has also established the National Interpol Bureau in Minsk.

Police Education, Research, and Publications

One of the most serious drawbacks of police education and training in Belarus is the lack of training in crowd management and human rights enforcement. Nevertheless, in recent years a growing amount of literature on various aspects of policing has been produced. Academic studies (although of uneven quality) are regularly published in such journals as *Voprosy kriminologii, kriminalistiki i sudebnoj ekspertizy* (questions of criminology and judicial examination), *Justicija Belarusi* (Belarusian Law), and the bi-weekly newspaper of the MI *Na strazhe* (*The Guardian*).

Most of the academic research is carried out in the educational institutions of the Ministry of Interior and the Ministry of Justice. Among the most significant recent publications in the field are studies by V.F. Yermolovich, I.A. Kibak, O.L. Bazhanov and others.

SERGEY YEVDOKIMOV AND ARUNAS JUSKA

Bibliography

Amnesty International. 2003. *Amnesty International Annual report 2003*. http://web.amnesty.org/report2004/blr-summary-eng.

Bazhanov, O.L. *Prestupnost' v Belarusi 1992–1999*. Minsk: Izdatel'stvo Ministerstva Justicii Respubliki Belarus, 2002.

Chigrinov P.G. *Ocherki Istorii Belarusi*. Minsk: Izdatel'stvo Vyshaja Shkola, 2000.

Garnett, Sherman W., and Robert Legvold. *Belarus at the Crossroads*. Washington D.C.: Carnegie Endowment for International Peace, 1999.

Human Rights Watch. 2003. *Human Rights Overview 2003. Belarus*. http://hrw.org.

Institute of Problems Criminology and Judicial Examination of the Ministry of Justice. http://ncpi.gov.by/minjust/nii/index.htm.

Kibak, I. A. *Professional'no-psihologicheskaja Podgotovka Kursantov Akademii MVD Respubliki Belarus Kak Faktor Aktivacii Stanovlenija Specialista*. Minsk: Izdatel'stvo Akademiji Ministerstva Vnutrennich Del, 1999.

Kuznetsov I.M., and V. A. Shelkoplias. *Istoria Gosudarstva i Prava Belarusi*. Minsk: Izdatel'stvo Vyshaja Shkola, 1999.

Marples, David R. *Belarus: A Denationalized Nation*. I.s.: Hardwood Academic Press, 1999.

The Ministry Interior. http://www.mvd-belarus.nsys.by/; http://www.amia.unibel.by.

The Ministry of Justice. http://ncpi.gov.by/minjust/.

The Ministry of Statistic and Analysis of the Republic of Belarus. 2004. *The Republic of Belarus in Figures, 1990–2003*. http://president.gov.by/Minstat/en/main.html.

The National Centre of Legal Information of the Republic of Belarus. http://ncpi.gov.by/eng/index.htm.

Shelley, Louise. *Policing Soviet Society: The Evolution of State Control*. New York: Routledge, 1996.

U.S. Department of State. 2003. *Belarus: Country Report on Human Rights Practices 2003*. http://www.state.gov/g/drl/rls/hrrpt/2003/27827.htm.

United Nations. 2001. *Seventh United Nations Survey of Crime Trends and Operations of Criminal Justice Systems, covering the period 1998–2000*. http://www.unodc.org/pdf/crime/seventh_survey/7sc.pdf.

Vishnevskij A.F. *Organizacija i Dejatel'nost' Milicii Belarusi 1917–1940: Istoriko-pravovye Aspekty*. Minsk: Izdatel'stvo Tesey, 2000.

World Fact Book. *Belarus*. http://www.odci.gov/cia/publications/factbook/geos/.

Yermolovich V.F.. *Kriminalisticheskaya Characteristika Prestyplenya*. Minsk: Izdatel'stvo Amalfea, 2001.

Yermolovich V.F. *Sposoby i Mechanism Prestuplenya*. Minsk: Izdatel'stvo Amalfea, 2000.

BELGIUM

Background Material

Visited throughout the centuries by the armies of most European countries, Belgium became independent from The Netherlands in 1830 and was occupied by Germany during World Wars I and II. It has prospered in the past half century as a modern, technologically advanced European state and member of NATO and the EU. Tensions between the Dutch-speaking Flemings of the north and the French-speaking Walloons of the south have led in recent years to constitutional amendments granting these regions formal recognition and autonomy.

With a total population of 10,258,762 (2001), Belgium has the following age pyramid and gender distribution:

0–14 years: 17.48% (male: 916,957; female: 876,029)

15–64 years: 65.57% (male: 3,390,145; female: 3,336,908)

65 years and over: 16.95% (male: 709,212; female: 1,029,511)

The ethnic population breakdown is as follows: Fleming 58%, Walloon 31%, other 11% [mostly from Turkish (3.5%) and Moroccan (6%) origin]; 0.5% are Europeans.

The population speaks the following languages: Dutch (58%), French (41%), and German (1%).

Belgium is 75% Roman Catholic and 25% Protestant.

Belgium's modern, private-enterprise economy has capitalized on its central geographic location, highly developed transport network, and diversified industrial and commercial base. Industry is concentrated mainly in the populous Flemish area in the north, although the government is encouraging investment in the southern region of Walloon. With few natural resources, Belgium must import substantial quantities of raw materials and export a large volume of manufactured goods, making its economy unusually dependent on the state of world markets.

Approximately three quarters of its trade is with other EU countries. Belgium's public debt is expected to fall below 100% of GDP in 2002, and the government has succeeded in balancing the budget. Belgium became a charter member of the European Monetary Union (EMU) in January, 1999. Belgium's currency is the EURO. Economic growth in 2000 was broad based, putting the government in a good position to pursue its energy market liberalization policies and planned tax cuts.

Some economical indicators (2000 est.) were:

GDP purchasing power parity—241.2 billion Euro

GDP—real growth rate: 4.1%

GDP—per capita: purchasing power parity— 23,500 Euro.

Contextual Features

Belgium is a federal parliamentary democracy under a constitutional monarch. It is composed of 10 provinces: Antwerpen, Brabant Wallon, Brussel (Bruxelles), Hainaut, Liege, Limburg, Luxembourg, Namur, Oost-Vlaanderen, Vlaams-Brabant, West-Vlaanderen. In addition, there is the Brussels Capitol Region, which is not included within the 10 provinces. At the local level, Belgium consists of a total of 589 municipalities.

The chief of state is King Albert II (since August 9, 1993); the Heir Apparent is Prince Philippe, son of the monarch. The head of the government is Prime Minister Guy Verhofstadt (since July 13, 1999). A Council of Ministers is appointed by the monarch and approved by Parliament. The monarchy is hereditary, and the prime minister is appointed by the monarch and then approved by Parliament.

The bicameral Parliament consists of a Senate and a Chamber of Deputies. The Senate, or Senaat in Dutch, Senat in French has 71 seats (40 members

are directly elected by popular vote; 31 are indirectly elected). Members serve four-year terms. The Chamber of Deputies, or Kamer van Volksvertegenwoordigers in Dutch, Chambre des Representants in French, has 150 seats (members are directly elected by popular vote on the basis of proportional representation to serve four-year terms).

As a result of the 1993 constitutional revision that furthered devolution into a federal state, there are now three levels of government (federal, regional, and linguistic community) with a complex division of responsibilities. This reality leaves six governments, each with its own legislative assembly.

Belgium has a continental European legal system, overseen by the Supreme Court of Justice or Hof van Cassatie (in Dutch) or Cour de Cassation (in French). Judges are appointed for life by the monarch. The complete Belgian criminal justice system is composed of five Courts of Appeal, 26 District Criminal Courts, a Federal Public Prosecution Office, and 26 Public District Prosecution Offices.

The Belgian criminal law system has various types of penalties, including service to the community, financial fines, confiscation, imprisonment, with or without penal service. There are several types of prisons in the territory, including specific institutions for minors, females, and males. The most frequently committed crimes in Belgium are theft, theft with aggravated circumstances, violence against individuals, fraud, and drug-related crimes.

Police Profile

Background

In the past, Belgian policing activity was primarily carried out by the Gendarmerie (17,000 officers) founded in 1796 but demilitarized in 1992; the Criminal Police attached to the Public Prosecutors called Judicial Police (3,500 officers), founded in 1919; and the 583 Municipal police forces (18,459 officers). The Belgian police system was overhauled by the 1998 police reform law, which created an integrated police, structured at two levels instead of three.

Organizational Description

Police anti-crime–related activity is performed in Belgium under the supervision and control of the federal or the local Public Prosecution Office, or under the supervision of an Examining Magistrate, who is attached to the Districts Courts. A biannual National Security Plan and the Local

Security Plans provide the necessary guidelines for policing in Belgium.

The Federal police and the 196 local police forces work under the scrutiny of a General Inspection (IAG). They are also overseen by an external body of the Belgian Parliament, the "P Committee." Both the IAG and the P Committee are responsible for all kinds of complaints and discipline-related matters.

Aimed to combat serious criminal activities (e.g., organized crime, terrorism, drug trafficking, serious crimes) at the national level and to support the local police forces, the Federal Police is divided in two levels:

- A central level or Headquarters, composed of five major General Directorates (DG's) coordinated by a General Commissioner (CG). The General Directorates (DG's) deal with the following matters:

  o Administrative police-related matters; border control; air, rail, and sea transports; maintenance of law and order; general police reserve and highway patrol (DGA).
  o Criminal investigations, forensics, coordination and support of the Criminal Field Offices (DGJ).
  o Operational support to police actions, Special Units, National Criminal Data bases, air support, international police cooperation, support to the local police forces (DGS).
  o Staff and human resources management and training (DGP).
  o Finance and logistics (DGM).

- A field level composed of 26 Criminal Field Offices (SJA's), each headed by a Criminal Director (DirJu), and 26 (criminal) Coordination and Support Departments (SCA's) headed by a Criminal Coordinator (DirCo). Coordination between SJA's and SCA's activities is performed at the district level.

The 196 Local Police forces are autonomous and headed by a Head of Zone under the supervision of local mayors and municipal counselors elected by popular vote. The Heads are appointed (as are all police managers) for a mandate of five years with possible extension for a further five-year term.

The typical missions of the local police forces include the following:

- Local policing in general (e.g., road patrol, maintenance of law & order)
- Local criminal investigation
- Support to the Federal Police

The various ranks of the local police forces are identical to those of the Federal Police.

Functions

Police officers can interrogate offenders, witnesses, or victims. They can seize objects if these have been used to commit offences or if these objects are the result of offences.

Police officers are entitled to arrest offenders disturbing public order and safety (so-called administrative arrest). Offenders may be detained for a maximum of 12 hours, after which they have to be released.

Police are also entitled to arrest suspects of criminal offences, who may be detained for a maximum of 24 hours. The arrest must then be confirmed by a King's Prosecutor at a District Court. If the arrest is not confirmed, the suspect has to be released.

Training

Various police colleges ensure the selection and uniform training of the Belgian Police Officers (Federal Police and Local police forces) under the supervision of the General Directorate for the Human Resources (DGP).

The federal police colleges are:

- The College of the Federal Police—DPEF (basic and continued training) with bases located in Antwerp, Brussels, Gent, Jumet, and Vottem.
- The National College of Investigation— DPER (criminal and forensic investigative techniques).
- The College for Officers—DPEO (senior police management).

Selection and basic training are also provided by ten local police schools that are located in the following cities: Antwerp, Arlon, Asse, Brugge, Brussels— Capital, Gent, Genk, Jurbise, Liege, and Namur.

Police Public Projects

The police, often in cooperation with the government, have developed several public awareness programs on the national as well as the local level. These programs focus on such areas as traffic safety, protection of children, protection against theft, prevention of shoplifting, robbery, and (lately) car and home jacking.

Police Use of Firearms

According to Belgian legislation, police officers are armed. The standard service weapon is a handgun. The use of firearms is limited to self-defense or to the protection of other individuals.

Terrorism

The fight against terrorism is basically coordinated by the Interforces Anti-terrorism Group (G.I. A), a department which gathers human resources from the Intelligence Special Services and from the Federal Police. This standing department assesses any potential terrorist threat and makes recommendations to the Executive Branch of the government.

From a criminal investigation perspective, the Federal Police and, more specifically, its General Directorate for Criminal Affairs (DGJ) is tasked to fight against terrorism.

The last time Belgium experienced terrorist attacks was in the early 1980s, when the Cellules Communistes Combattantes (C.C.C.) were active in the country. Recently, it has been established that various terrorist groups originating from abroad mainly use Belgium as a logistic backyard. Dealing with forged traveling documents, weapons, and supplying strategic or tactical intelligence, terrorists maintain close contacts at the international level with their operational groups. This fact has been once again confirmed after the terrorist attacks against the United States on September 11, 2001.

International Cooperation

Belgium has always been at the forefront of international police cooperation. It is part of the EU-Schengen mechanism, a founding member of INTERPOL since 1923, a member of EUROPOL, and also has been very active in the framework of signing international, multilateral, and bilateral police cooperation agreements.

One of the missions of the Federal Police is to direct the management of the international police cooperation. This responsibility is therefore taken on by specific departments, according to the operational or strategic nature of the issues that have to be dealt with.

Department of the International Police Cooperation Policy (CG/CGI)

The General Department under the hierarchical control of the General Commissioner of the Federal Police (CG) develops and manages the international cooperation policy with the foreign services and organizations directly and indirectly involved in police matters.

To this end, CGI keeps up, develops, and organises all the necessary international contacts with those services and organisations. CGI manages the representation of the Belgian police services abroad, including Belgian liaison officers holding a post abroad.

The CGI General Department is made up of policemen and civilians, including lawyers (whose contribution is especially significant), and they represent the Belgian Federal Police in nonoperational working sessions organized on the strategic level by the different international authorities concerned about law enforcement issues.

During those meetings, the CGI officials take part in various forums at the European level, where different policy and implementation issues are discussed. They seek to fight all forms of criminality, to coordinate security policies, to address problems related to illegal immigration, to improve maintenance of law and order during big political demonstrations or sports events, and to propose the necessary measures to keep public peace and security.

CGI is the principal negotiator for the Belgian government, working with the representatives of the Ministries of the Interior, Justice, and Foreign affairs when bilateral or multilateral agreements on police cooperation are negotiated.

Belgium has signed agreements on police cooperation with Bulgaria, Estonia, Hungary, Latvia, Lithuania, Morocco, Poland, Romania, Russia, Slovakia, Slovenia, Czech Republic, Germany, France, Luxembourg, The Netherlands and The United Kingdom.

Department of Operational Police Cooperation (DGS/DSO)

This Department (DSO), the activities of which are similar to those of Interpol's NCB's, develops and manages, under the hierarchical control of the General Director of Operational Support of the Federal Police (DGS), all the operational aspects of international police cooperation, notably:

- Keeping up direct international and operational contacts with the foreign police services, with the European police service (Europol), and with Interpol;
- Acting as a central operational point of contact within the scope of cooperation multilateral relationships or of international organizations in charge of police cooperation;
- Executing the operational management of and the international circulation of descriptions, notably by the structures and the systems that have been multilaterally implemented to this end;

81

- Acting as an operational point of contact for foreign liaison officers holding a post in Belgium;
- Acting as an operational point of contact, in order to provide a logistic and administrative support to the Belgian liaison officers holding a post abroad; and
- Providing follow-up and support to operational points of contact.

Police Education, Research, and Publications

The structure of the Belgian police services has changed due to several reforms, which led to the formation of a brand new police service. In 2001, the three regular police corps in Belgium, namely the Municipal Police, the Gendarmerie, and the Judicial Police, gave way to a new integrated police, structured on two levels (a federal level and a local level).

The main feature of this new police organization is the creation of a single status for the policemen on both federal and local levels. This principle of equivalence applies to all levels: administrative, financial, union, disciplinary, rank, safeguarding of legal rights, etc. and, consequently, to training as well, which is an essential sphere of activity for the creation of a new police culture.

Mainly based on the "community policing" concept, the training of the Belgian police staff remains an important factor for the creation and implementation of a police policy respectful of the values of democratic society, the rule of law, and the dignity of citizens.

By focusing police work on the citizen, the police officers are expected to serve the population and meet its needs and expectations. This philosophical and strategic approach also aims at close cooperation between police services and the population in order to solve crimes, to reduce insecurity, and to prevent problems inherent to life in society and to local delinquency.

This concept, which is broader than a simple strategy, aims at another vision of police in society as well as a total change of police culture and structure, to which the educational process undergone by police staff has to correspond.

Simultaneously, the efforts made by the staff during the training must be highlighted as much as possible. Therefore, the police training has to enable any police officer to develop positively in his career as well as to master special knowledge and skills.

In concrete terms, the wide range of training options offered to the police staff enables the latter to have access to all levels and functions of the police structure.

In the same way, the training is also harmonized with a common basic education, in order to implement the important principle of mobility of staff within the Belgian police services, without making any distinction concerning the (local or federal) level of the service to which the police officer belongs or is appointed.

The primary objective of Belgian police training is to allow staff to acquire, even to increase, the skills which enable them to entirely fulfill their tasks and take on their responsibilities within the police organization.

All training measures concern the following four main themes:

- Knowledge and comprehension of the legal provisions and regulations;
- Use of specific police techniques;
- Implementation of tactical principles and methods;
- Learning of relevant elements in the field of human behavior and relationships.

The training measures are organized in modules and generally alternate theoretical and practical school activities with training courses.

Finally, the training measures are based on qualification profiles; that is, on the sum of knowledge, aptitudes, attitudes, and potentials needed by the police officers in order to fulfill the tasks and take on the responsibilities connected with the post they are holding or applying for.

Professional training of Belgian police is divided into four main categories: basic training, functional training, advancement training, and continuing training.

Basic Training

Recruitment procedure: Before starting his basic training, the applicant is recruited according to specific admission criteria, provided that he has certain qualifications. He is then recruited through a procedure composed of four different tests:

- A test measuring necessary cognitive skills;
- A personality test based on recruitment techniques adapted to the function;
- A medical and physical aptitude test in connection with the post applied for;
- A selection test taken before a selection committee and resulting in a final global evaluation.

Structure of basic training: Basic training is to be followed by the four categories of operational staff: auxiliary, basic, middle-rank, and superior-rank officers.

Each basic training aims at endowing the candidate with professional skills. His future profile will enable him to competently hold a post within the police organization; to detect, analyze and understand changing and complex situations; to find appropriate solutions to the problems arising; and to implement those solutions in accordance with the laws.

This training is characterized by its orientation towards the roots of the police job, and it stimulates life skills, police ethics, and deontology, the development of learning strategies, and the suitability between profile and system of evaluation.

Functional Training

Any police officer already holding a basic post may accede to functions that often require a high level of knowledge and know-how, as well as extensive aptitude and understanding of social behavior. The candidate must then correspond to a specific profile and meet certain conditions, notably the obligation to follow and succeed in a *functional training*, which will then result in the granting of a certificate.

Advancement Training

This is a form of professional training aimed at acquiring new aptitudes and knowledge or at deepening skills in some aspects of the police function. This training is organized for some members of the staff, who may get advancement if they succeed at it.

Continuing Training

Whatever his/her rank or (basic or special) function may be, any police officer has to continue training during his/her career. Those measures allow him/her to maintain, update, and increase skills and knowledge as well as to learn some new ones, in order to do a high-quality job and, if the case arises, to reach a higher salary scale.

Examples of areas of continuing training include violence and hazardous situations management, stress control, conflict solving, aid to victims, intervention techniques, and transport of funds.

Besides these different training measures meant for the members of the operational staff, some continuing and functional training measures specifically oriented towards the civilian personnel of police (administrative and logistic staff, or "CaLog") have to be organized as well, such as strategic analysis and integration into the police sphere.

The Training Department was created within the framework of the reform of the Belgian police services and its effects on the police structure. This body is directly dependent on the General Department of Human Resources of the Federal Police and is in charge of initiating, developing, coordinating, assessing, and coordinating all training on the national level and for all Belgian policemen.

As a real information and coordination platform, its activities notably focus on the analysis of the training needs, as well as on the creation of a global training plan for the integrated police. As a think tank, it might give some advice relating to training to the services concerned.

It regularly creates and develops specific educational tools, on request or on its own initiative. It also has a support and information relay function towards the responsible Belgian authorities.

In practice, it also attends to the good implementation of the different training programs, notably by means of management contracts signed with the police schools and through the documents submitted to them for approval. In the same way, it monitors the compliance of the implementation of the legal provisions, as well as the quality of the training. It guarantees the equity of financing between the various police schools.

The role of the Training Department extends to the European level, considering its full representativeness in the field of police training. Consequently, the Training Department is also entrusted with the task of representing the Belgian interests, resources, and needs on the European and international level, as far as police cooperation regarding training is concerned. As such, it is considered to be the most appropriate authority for the coordination and chairmanship of the Belgian representatives within the board of the European Police College. Finally, it manages cross-border cooperation projects regarding police training, notably with France.

In order to reach its objectives, the Training Department works in close cooperation with various partners, principally the police schools. These are the essential elements of professional training. All the basic, functional, advancement, and continuing training cycles are indeed organized and taught in those schools for all the members of the integrated police (federal or local) or to the operational or administrative and logistic staff.

Among those schools, a distinction has to be made between the schools *recognized* or *instituted* by the Ministers of the Interior and Justice.

The Minister of the Interior has recognized, in the ten provinces of Belgium (except Walloon Brabant), a training institution for police staff. These institutions have their own status (either non-profit-making associations or provincial or interregional institutions). There are a total of ten; the one in the Brussels region is bilingual.

The schools work by virtue of approval given by the Minister of the Interior to the appropriate authority for each kind of training. A management contract is concluded every year between the school management and the Minister of the Interior through the Training Department.

Even if the schools do not directly belong to the police structure, as they have their own authority, they nevertheless play an essential part in police training.

As far as the instituted schools are concerned, they directly belong to the federal police structure. The general Department of Human Resources acts as the competent authority. The Minister of the Interior has instituted two schools: a Federal School and a *National School for Officers*.

Briefly, the first one is in charge of the organization of functional and continuing training and of the backing of recognized schools (especially the management of students and the provision of trainers). The second one deals with the organization of basic and advancement training for police officers, and some functional and continuing training.

The Minister of Justice also has instituted a national research school in charge of organizing the judicial functional training of the basic, middle, and officer members of the staff. This school also organizes the continuing training of the federal and local judicial investigation units.

WALTHER ROMBAUT

Bibliography

WEBSITES OF BELGIAN POLICE

- Federal police: www.fedpol.be
- Training Department: www.police.ac.be
- Police in general: www.police.be
- Local police forces: www.info-zone.be
- Recruitment: www.jobpol.be; www.poldoc.be

Contact address: Federal Police General Department of Human Resources Training Department Avenue de la Force Aérienne 101040 Etterbeek, Belgium Telephone: + 32 2 342 69 05 Fax: + 32 2 642 69 36. E-mail: dpf@police.ac.be.

Beaupère Christian, and Christophe Schiffers. *Buurtpolitie, definitie en organisatiemodel* (Neighbourhood police, definition and organization model). Brussels, Permanent Secretariat for the Prevention Policy, 2000.

Bourdoux Giles, and Christian De Valkeneer. *De politiehervorming, kommentaren op de wet van 7 december 1998* (Police Reform, comment on the Law of December 7th 1998)Brussels: Larcier, 2001.

Bourdoux, Giles L., Eddy De Raedt, Dirk Lybaert, and Marc De Mesmaeker. *Wet op het politieambt* (Law on the police function). Brussels: Politeia, 1999.

Bourdoux Giles, Eddy De Raedt, Marc De Mesmaeker, and Alain Liners. *Wet op het politieambt, handleiding.* (Law on the Police uinction: manual of the police function). Brussels: Politeia, 2001.

Fijnaut, Cyrille, Brice de Ruyver, and Franky Goossens. *Reorganisatie van de politie* (Reorganization of the police). Leuven: University Press, 1999.

Fijnaut, Cyrille., Franky Goossens, F. Hutsebaut, and D. Van Daele. *De Belgische politie* (Belgian Police). Leuven: Kluwer Jurisprudence Belgium, 1999.

Meijlaers Stefan, Marian Verbeek, Jozef Wiertz, Raf Truyens, and MarcGeerits. *Het politiecollege en de Politieraad, een nieuwe rol voor burgemeesters en mandatarissen* (Police Colleges and Police Council: the new role of the mayor and the mandataries in the local police). Brussels: Politeia, 2001.

Tange, Carrol. *Community policing*. Brussels: Sociopolitical Research and Information Centre, 2000.

Vandenhoute, Thierry. *De politiehervorming in België* (Police reform in Belgium). Brussels: Bruylant, 2000.

Van Outrive, Lode. *De Politiehervorming* (Police reform). Brussels: Sociopolitical Research and Information Centre, 1997.

BELIZE

Background Material

At last head count (2000), the population census for the small Central American nation of Belize stood at just under 250,000. Formerly British Honduras, and the last-released of Britain's many former colonies, Belize was once home to a thriving and advanced Mayan civilization that spanned a period from 1200 BC to 900 AD. Today, Belize's population is heterogeneous with mixes of African and Asian extractions, Maya Indian, Hispanics, Garinagu, and Caucasians all thrown together by an interesting chain of events.

Situated on the east coast of the Central American mainland, Belize faces the Caribbean Sea and is bounded on the north by the Mexican State of Quintana Roo and on the west and south by the Republic of Guatemala. The country measures approximately 8,867 square miles with a maximum length from north to south of 174 miles. The official language of the country is English, but Spanish is also widely spoken. Garifuna, Mayan, and Chinese are also spoken by respective races. The country is mostly prime rainforest and pristine marine reserves with a landscape dotted with decayed reminders of its rich Mayan heritage. Ruins like Lemonai, Xunantunich, Caracol, and Altun Ha offer a breathtaking window into this past. Offshore, the three largest atolls in the western hemisphere and the second largest barrier reef in the world give way to a coral wonderland that diving pundits the world over have proclaimed to be among the most beautiful anywhere. Considered to be relatively underpopulated, Belize boasts more wildlife per square foot than any other county, and it offers as colorful and diverse an array of fauna, bird, and marine life as can be found anywhere on the planet.

Belize is divided into six districts and a new capital, Belmopan, which was constructed in 1972 to provide high sanctuary from the hurricanes that threaten each year between June and November. Twice Belize was almost completely destroyed by hurricanes, once in 1931 and again in 1961.

Somewhere near the middle of the nineteenth century, Mestizo refugees from the Caste Wars in Yucatan settled the northern districts of Corozal and Orange Walk. In the South, sparse remains of the once teeming Mayan civilization, primarily the Ketchi and Mopan, resettled the southernmost district of Toledo. The Garinagu, descendants of a once-proud warrior nation vanquished by the British and banished to exile in Honduras around the end of the nineteenth century, settled the other southern district of Stann Creek. Today, the Mayans are still struggling for acceptance and recognition, but the Garinagu have become a major presence in Belize. They have contributed much in the way of education and the arts, particularly music. Unfortunately, so too have they contributed to the dereliction of law and order, and while they comprise a mere 6% of the entire population, they account for 15% of the prison population.

While undoubtedly Central American by geography, Belize has a distinct West Indian flavor and historical content to its culture. By this distinction, Belize sits in a strategic position to serve as bridge between these two relatively close but distinctly different subregions of the western hemisphere.

Like Guyana to the south, with whom it shares more than a few similarities, Belize has also been touted as a potential breadbasket for the vastly overpopulated and mostly tourism-oriented islands to its seaboard side. One has to wonder, however, if this potential will ever be realized, as an aggressive international campaign of its own has sent tourist arrivals skyrocketing. Consequently, Belizeans these days seem increasingly more inclined to the quick, easy dough available from tourism than to the slow kneading of dough to fill anyone's breadbasket, even its own.

As recently as 1960, Belize was relatively unknown to the outside world, struggling to feed itself on a few citrus, banana, and sugar cane crops while leaning heavily upon the United Kingdom for subsistence. However, the latter half of the last century saw a significant swell in Belize's population and at the same time, a major shift in the ethnic and cultural makeup.

Sometime after 1961, the year of Hattie, a hurricane which left 2,000 dead and thousands homeless, a mass exodus occurred whereby many Belizeans immigrated to the United States. The mass migration to the north created a "brain drain," while also leaving a vacuum in the citrus and banana industries. In an attempt to compensate, Belize turned to refugees from war-torn neighboring republics like Guatemala, Honduras, and El Salvador. Those who migrated were mostly the young, energetic, skilled, and educated, leaving behind the very young and the very old. When those migrating to the United States did bring their children with them, those children often went neglected by parents working long hours. A few managed to take advantage of educational opportunities and blended well into the American landscape, but a large number became casualties of America's metropolitan ghettos. Many of these migrant children dropped out of school and turned to drugs and crime.

Some parents eventually sent their children back home with the hope that an environmental change could provide a remedy. What this did instead was to contribute significantly to the already deteriorating conditions in Belize. Many of these problem children became imbedded into the mainstream of the American underworld and are now being deported back to Belize in large numbers (approximately 150 per annum), many after having done time in America's prisons. By the mid 1980s, street gangs had been introduced to the streets of Belize, and with all factors considered, the task of policing this young nation has become quite daunting indeed.

Contextual Features

Belize obtained its independence in 1981 but remains within the British Commonwealth and still recognizes the Queen of England as the head of state. Belize has a constitution with a preamble that outlines the basic principles and beliefs upon which the nation is founded. Foremost is the belief that the nation is "founded on principles which acknowledge the supremacy of God." A Governor General, according to the constitution, is "appointed by Her Majesty and shall hold office at her Majesty's pleasure and who shall be her Majesty's representative in Belize." The Governor General's role is mostly ceremonial, but there are some important constitutional functions performed by the holder of that office. The appointment is made on the nomination of the government of the day, and to date, there have been two separate governor-generals under two separate governments. While Belize's political arena has seen a fair share of independent candidates and much rhetoric about third-party formation, politics in Belize is still basically a two-party system: People's United Party (PUP) and the United Democratic Party (UDP). Since Independence, each party had consecutive terms in office until 2003 when the People's Unity Party won a second landslide term.

Like most of Britain's former colonies, Belize adapted the British Westminster Parliamentary model of government with responsibilities for governance divided between branches of the Executive, Legislative, and Judiciary. The principal executive instrument of policy for the direction and control of government is the Cabinet of Ministers, with the Prime Minister at the helm.

The legislature, as defined by the constitution, is a bicameral legislature composed of an elected House of Representatives and an appointed Senate. The House of Representatives is composed of twenty-nine seats and the Senate of thirteen. Members of the House of Representatives are elected via general elections that are held every five years. The Governor General appoints members of the Senate upon advice from the ruling party, the opposition, and the private sector.

The judges, the Director of Public Prosecutions, and the Governor General, acting in accordance with the advice of the Advisory Council, make up the judicial system. Within the structure of the Judiciary, there are four levels of courts, namely: Magistrate's Court, Supreme Court, Court of Appeal, and the Privy Council. The Privy Council serves as the final court of appeals for Belize, but a move is afoot to replace the Privy Council with a Caribbean Court of Justice (CCJ). The popular perception in Belize and throughout the Caribbean is that the Privy Council is too far removed from native cultures and therefore cannot effectively implement sentences, in particular with regards to the death penalty. This has led many skeptics to refer to the CCJ as the Hanging Court since it is widely believed that one of the first decrees of the CCJ will be to reinstate the death penalty in member countries.

In 1989, Belize established a Family Court to deal with an increasing number of domestic disputes and other family matters. There is also a Municipal Court, which handles traffic offenses and other matters pertaining to local government.

The first prison was built in Belize in the early 1900s and was designed to house a maximum of 300 prisoners. This proved to be adequate for most of the twentieth century, but following the aforementioned events and somewhere around the late 1970s, the prison population began to expand rapidly, and by early 1990, the population had swollen to over 800. Due to this expansion in prison population and to concerns for security, the government decided to build a new prison and move it to a remote area some 16 miles out of Belize City. In 1993, prisoners were relocated to the new prison, and in 2002, management for the prison was transferred to a non-profit organization composed primarily of concerned Rotarians known as the Kolbe Foundation. The current population of the prison system stands at just over a thousand inmates, including 23 females and 70 youths under the age of 18.

Police Profile

Background

The first system of organized policing was introduced to the then-colony of British Honduras back in 1886. The British Honduras Constabulary Force was formed with members mainly recruited from the island of Barbados. In 1888, many of the Bajans returned to their native island, and the colony turned to Jamaica for new recruits. By the year 1893, most of the Jamaicans who had arrived in the colony, upon the completion of their five-year contracts, returned to their native island.

In 1902, the constabulary force was abolished, and the police adopted the title of British Honduras Police Force. On January 6, 1964, by an important constitutional change, internal self-government was granted to British Honduras, and responsibility for everything except Internal Security, Defense, and discipline was passed to an elected Minister of Government. The Governor retained responsibility for security and related matters. In 1969, the first Belizean Commissioner was appointed, and in that same year, a Police Special Force was organized with its members trained in not only general policing but also military duties. This new elite force was tasked with internal security, riot duties, and search-and-rescue missions. In 1978, the Belize Defense Force was established, and some members of this special force transferred to the military while some remained with the police as members of a smaller tactical support unit. This unit was tasked with the responsibility of providing a quick response in the event of serious crime or disorder, and for the first time, the police began to openly carry firearms.

In 1985, the government decided that the functions of this Special Branch of the Force should be taken over by a new independent body, namely the Security Intelligence Service. This arrangement lasted until 1990, when a new Government disbanded the Security Intelligence Service. The functions of Special Branch were re-instated and subsequently modified, in view of the collapse of communism and in consideration of the increasing threat to society from the use and trafficking in controlled drugs and the rise in criminality.

Meanwhile, The police force gradually handed over to new departments most of the work of Immigration, Customs, and Vehicle Licensing, as these functions were considered separate from the duties of the police. In the ensuing year, the Belize Police Force grew in strength and developed into an efficient, civil police organization based on the British system of policing to meet the needs of the country as it developed into a nation state.

Organizational Description

The Belize Police Department is administered from Police Headquarters, Belmopan City, where the Commissioner of Police, along with his senior executive/desk officers, is based. The administration is divided into the following functional departments, some of which are further divided into branches and sections:

- Office of the Commissioner
- Management Services
- Operations

The following branches/sections fall under the desk of Management Services:

- Deputy Management Services

- Administration
- Personnel, Welfare, and Sports
- Internal Affairs and Discipline
- Planning, Performance Review, and Inspection
- National Prosecution
- Director Training
- Police Training Academy
- Financial Controller

The following branches/sections fall under the desk of Operations:

- National Crimes Investigation Branch/Deputy Operations
- Special Branch, including the Criminal Intelligence Unit
- Anti-Drugs Unit
- Joint Intelligence Coordinating Center
- Community Policing
- National Traffic
- Dragon Unit
- Maritime Unit
- Uniform Operations
- Tourism Police Unit
- All Police Districts and Sub-stations

The Commissioner of Police is responsible for the overall command and control of the Belize Police Department, with accountability to the Minister of Home Affairs. A Staff Officer is assigned to the office of the Commissioner of Police to assist in the daily supervision. This office is held by a Superintendent of Police.

Management Services is responsible for the effective and efficient administration of the Belize Police Department on a daily basis, the provision of a high standard of police service to the public, and career development and welfare of all subordinates. This office is held by an Assistant Commissioner of Police.

The Deputy Management Services office assists the Commander Management Services in discharging the functions of his office in an effective and efficient manner. This office is held by a Senior Superintendent of Police.

The Administration office is responsible for the development and maintenance of systems through which all general administration matters of the Department are efficiently implemented, managed, and maintained. This office is held by a Superintendent of Police.

The Personnel, Welfare, and Sports office is responsible for all personnel matters, including service records, promotions, transfers, annual leave, welfare, and all sporting activities of the department. This office is held by a Superintendent of Police.

Internal Affairs and Discipline is responsible for the thorough and requisite investigations of all matters of internal discipline. This office is held by an Assistant Superintendent of Police.

Planning, Performance Review, and Inspection is responsible for the inspection of Police Formations, systems, and the research and preparation of papers for the development of the Department. This office is held by a Superintendent of Police.

National Prosecution maintains the efficient working of the branch in all matters concerned with the actual prosecution of cases before the Magistrate Courts as well as the preparation and presentation of evidence in regard to the conduct of Preliminary Inquiries. This office is held by an Assistant Superintendent of Police.

Director Training plans, implements, monitors, and reviews all training of the department, including the management of the Police Training Academy. This office is held by a Superintendent of Police.

The Police Training Academy is responsible for recruitment and training of new recruits, the planning and conducting of in-service and refresher training for the department. This office is held by an Assistant Superintendent of Police.

The Financial Controller is responsible for the preparation of the budget, the professional control of expenditure of public finances, and personnel management within the department. This office is held by a civilian equivalent to an Assistant Commissioner of Police rank.

The Operations office is responsible for the planning, coordinating, and conducting of Police-led operations countrywide and the maintenance of close liaison with other government agencies. This office is held by an Assistant Commissioner of Police.

The National Crimes Investigation Branch is responsible for overseeing the investigation of all crimes in Belize. This office is held by a Senior Superintendent of Police who is also the Deputy to the Commander Operations Branch.

The Special Branch is responsible for the efficient and effective development of systems through which the internal and external security of the country is kept at the highest possible level. This office is held by a Superintendent of Police.

The Anti-Drugs Unit enforces the drugs law and conducts the operations aimed at those persons involved in the illicit drug trade. This office is held by an Assistant Superintendent of Police.

The Joint Intelligence Coordinating Center oversees the collection, collation, analysis, and dissemination of intelligence relating to drugs and other criminal activities. This office is held by an Assistant Superintendent of Police.

Community Policing is responsible for coordinating the implementation and continued development of the Department's Community Policing Program. This office is held by a Superintendent of Police.

National Traffic is responsible for the development and maintenance of systems to be used for traffic enforcement countrywide. This office is held by an Assistant Superintendent of Police.

The Dragon Unit is responsible for joint BDF/Police border patrols; narcotics, firearm, and human smuggling interdiction; and the conduct of anti-crime operations countrywide. This office is held by an Assistant Superintendent of Police.

The Maritime Unit is responsible for policing the entire coastal waters and inland waterways of the country in addition to the cays, etc. This office is held by a Sergeant of Police.

The Uniform Operations office is responsible for the high visibility of uniform officers on the streets countrywide patrolling in a proactive manner. This office is held by a Superintendent designated as Officer Commanding Patrol Branch.

The Tourism Police Unit is responsible for providing security to tourists, providing patrols within tourist areas and destinations, and the enforcing the Belize Tourist Board Legislation. This office is held by an Assistant Superintendent of Police.

Police Districts and Sub-Stations are responsible for all operational and administrative aspects of policing, including the delivery of quality service to the public within their jurisdiction.

Belize is divided into six Police Formations, each Formation being under the command of a Formation Commander. The Police Formations are:

- Eastern Division—commanded by an Assistant Commissioner of Police
- Corozal—commanded by a Superintendent of Police
- Orange Walk—commanded by a Superintendent of Police
- Cayo—commanded by a Superintendent of Police
- Stann Creek—commanded by a Superintendent of Police
- Toledo—commanded by a Superintendent of Police

Each formation is autonomous, with the Commanding Officer being directly responsible to the Commissioner of Police for the efficient and effective policing of his or her formation.

In all the divisions, the main Police Station is located in the District head town. Responsible to these main stations are a number of subsidiary Police Stations located in some of the main villages, the majority of which are one-man village stations, manned either by a Police Corporal or a Constable.

In 2003, the Belize Police Department acquired a new vehicular fleet composed of fifty Ford Focus Cars and fifty Ford Ranger (Diesel) pickup trucks. All existing vehicles were subsequently auctioned off, with the proceeds used to defray the cost of the new vehicles. All Police Formations and Branches were issued new vehicles. The department received a donation of seven motorcycles in the past year bringing the number of motorcycles owned by the department to fifty-five.

Functions

The Belize Police Department is the only police organization in Belize. It is charged with the preservation of law and order, the prevention and detection of crime, and the apprehension and prosecution of offenders. The department is also responsible for the licensing of firearms and, as a result of its statutory obligations, is involved in criminal law as well as administrative functions.

The Belize Police Department is a member of the International Police Community (INTERPOL), and members of the Department are trained and equipped to perform the duties entrusted to it by society. Responsibilities include: to prevent and detect crime, to protect life and property, to preserve peace and maintain law and order, and to perform all duties in accordance with the Constitution of Belize and with justice and integrity.

The Police Department is within the portfolio of responsibilities of the Minister for Home Affairs, who is responsible to Parliament for the Police Department and all its activities. The Chief Executive Officer of the Ministry of Home Affairs and the Security Services Commission share administrative control. Operational command of the Department is vested in the Commissioner of Police.

Training

The educational standard required for entering the Belize Police Department is a minimum of a high school diploma; however, exceptions are made where persons possessing only a primary school certificate are accepted. Applicants must be Belizean, physically fit, of good character, and have a minimum height of 5 feet 4 inches. The age limit for enlistment is 18 to 35 years. In 2003, the department, in order to attract applicants possessing certain qualifications, introduced an Accelerated Promotion Policy, where persons possessing a Master's Degree in areas deficient within the organization are recruited as Recruit Constables, and

they undergo the initial five months training. Upon successful completion of initial training, they are commissioned to the rank of Acting Inspector of Police. Thereafter, the officers undergo a two-year, on-the-job training at various branches and formations. At the conclusion of the two years, based on aptitude and recommendation from their superior, the officesr will be promoted to the rank of Inspector of Police.

Police Public Projects

The following community service programs were established by the Belize Police Department:

In 2000, The Belize Police Department launched a comprehensive five-year strategic plan aimed at improving efficiency and garnering support and cooperation from the community at large. In an effort to reduce crime, maintain order, and improve road safety, the department placed emphasis on the following strategic priorities:

- Increase effectiveness of preventative patrols;
- Improve road safety;
- Target drug traffickers and reduce availability of hard drugs;
- Increase professionalism and quality service in order to foster better cooperation;
- Improve investigative procedures to increase detection and conviction of offenders.

In July of 1994, a youth cadet service was established whereby the department recruited boys and girls between the ages of 8 to 14. Youth Cadets meet twice weekly and have annual camps where cadets from around the country gather at a designated location for social and sporting activities.

In 1991, a first offenders program was started as a pilot project with the full support of the Chief Justice, Director of Public Prosecutions, Chief Magistrate, Chief Education Officer, Human Development Department, and School Principals. The program proved successful and was extended nationwide. The program is aimed at rehabilitating youths under the age of eighteen who are arrested and found to be first offenders. First Offenders are dealt with by the schools in the case of students and by a Social Worker in the case of a non-student.

The press officer/public relations officer keeps the public informed of Police activity via a daily press release, as well as being available for comment in the event of newsworthy occurrences. The Public Relations Office also hosts a weekly radio talk show titled "Linkup" in order to keep the public informed and offer a venue for suggestions and critiques.

Neighborhood Watches are currently being established in many areas countrywide, and the response from the public has been encouraging. In November of 2002, a Neighborhood Watch Coordinator was hired to help establish and sustain watches in all areas.

As a part of the emphasis on Community Policing, the department has established specific zones throughout the country and has assigned Zone Beat Liaison Officers in all zones. A dedicated officer is selected and assigned to respective zones with responsibility for interfacing with residents, businesses, and schools on a daily basis. Zone beat officers assist with concerns and provide feedback as necessary.

Following internal analysis by the department that indicated areas of high prevalence of crime, Special Police Areas were established throughout the nation. Appropriate signs reflecting these areas were posted, and the department maintains special attention to these areas, including 24-hour patrol, regular stop and search operations, and house searches.

Following the acquisition of a hundred new vehicles in 2003, Police commenced regular patrols of all highways. Permanent checkpoints have also been established on both major highways and are manned on a 24-hour basis.

Gun Amnesty/Cash for Information Program

A National Crimes Control Council (NCCC) was initially established in September of 1991 and held consultations with the Judiciary, Business Community, Prisons Department, Police Department, Bar Association, Religious Leaders, and Social Services Organization. The NCCC was tasked with monitoring the crime situation in Belize and with developing and implementing crime prevention programs and strategies. The NCCC remained dormant from 1992, however, and was not revived until June of 2003. The NCCC currently holds meetings on the third Wednesday of every month, and a press release is sent out at the end of each meeting.

In July 2003, the NCCC commissioned a subcommittee to develop a program aimed at removing illegal guns from the street. The program was implemented in two stages, the first being a month amnesty period that ran from August 6 through September 6, 2003. All persons in possession of illegal firearms were given the opportunity to turn them in with no legal action being taken. A total of 13 weapons were turned in during this phase of the program. Following the completion of the Amnesty Period, the second phase of the

program came into effect. The Cash for Information Program saw the establishment of a hotline (922) whereby citizens were encouraged to "call in" and get a reward for information leading to removal of illegal firearms from the streets. Trained operators manned the phones, and citizens were assured tha all information was treated with the strictest of confidence. A system was devised whereby callers were given a code with which they could collect a cash reward if the information proved fruitful. Monies for the program came from the government, with all funds matched by the private sector. To date the program has been hailed as a success, removing an average of one gun per day from the streets of Belize. This program is schedule to run indefinitely with funds being replenished by special fund-raising projects and by a percentage of the fines levied on those found in possession of illegal weapons.

In an attempt to curtail continued criminal activity by persons deported from the United States or other countries (in particular those who were deported after serving prison sentences), the Belize Police Department has in place a sign-in program. All deportees must sign in once per week, effective immediately upon arrival. Deportees are required by law to actively seek gainful employment and are not allowed to associate with known gang members or frequent places where such persons hang out.

In 2002, the Belize Police Department recognized that the increasing number of persons employed by private security firms and those working as independent security guards, if properly screened and trained, could serve as a valuable resource in the everyday fight against crime. The criteria for employment in that field was evaluated and modified, and a Guardnet System was implemented which gave security firms and private business places direct access to a radio network, which was placed in the control room of the Police Department and which is manned on a continuous basis. The Belize Chamber of Commerce donated some $10,000 worth of communication equipment that was distributed in all six districts. As more firms and businesses come on board, the program promises to be hugely successful.

A major concern of the Belize Police Department is the alarming number of traffic accidents that occur, in particular on the highways. Following the acquisition of new vehicles in 2003, the traffic arm of the department began regular patrols of the country's highways. In 2002, a total of 77 persons lost their lives due to traffic accidents. This showed an increase of six deaths or

	Authorized Establishment 2002–2003	Actual Strength 2001	Actual Strength 2002
Commissioner	1	1	1
Assistant Commissioner	2	2	1
Senior Superintendent	3	3	4
Superintendent	13	12	13
Assistant Superintendent	15	7	12
Inspector	33 + 1	18	26
Assistant Inspector	-	29	7
Officer Cadet	-	-	-
Sergeant	82	58	78
Corporal	139	132	135
Constables	700 + 4	594	621
Total	988 + 5*	856	898
		Tourism Officers 45	37
		Auxiliary Police 42	36
		Special Constables	58

*Authorized supervisory ranks assigned to offices/posts outside the Department.

8.5% over the previous year. The department has embarked on aggressive educational programs geared in particular toward drunk driving. Members of the department pay regular visits to schools and have joined forces with other agencies to battle the problem.

Police Use of Firearms

While the Belize Police Department is authorized by law to carry arms, the Department has chosen to remain primarily an unarmed organization. All officers are normally issued a regulation baton. The members of the specialized branches, however (e.g.,Crimes Investigation Branch, Special Branch, Dragon Unit, and Anti Drug Unit), are normally issued weapons while in the execution of their duties. The Belize Police Department possesses an assortment of weapons (e.g., .38 Smith and Wesson revolvers, 9 mm pistols, M-16 Rifles, SLR, single action shotguns, pump action shotguns, and rifles). The .38 Smith and Wesson revolver and the 9 mm pistols are the weapons more frequently used. All

officers received firearm and weapon handling training while undergoing basic training. Additionally, a number of officers have received refresher training. All members also receive instructions on laws governing the use of firearms, including Justifiable Force and Harm. In 2001, the Belize Police Department also promulgated a "White Card" which was issued to all its members and forms a standard part of their accoutrements. The "white card" is a guideline governing the use of firearms by Police Officers.

The authorized establishment as approved by Government for the Belize Police Department is 988 + 5 all ranks. The actual strength of the department at the end of 2002 was 898 officers all ranks. This figure comprised 797 male officers and 101 female officers. Below is the breakdown by rank at the end of 2002.

Like all mission statements, the Police Department's mission statement expresses its philosophy, values, beliefs, and assumptions underlying the Police Department's culture. It provides a sense of purposefulness and direction for its officers, and it

National Composition of the Department

The National Composition of the Department as at December 31, 2002 Was as Follows:

	Compol	Asst. Compol	Sr. Supt.	Supt.	Asst. Supt	Insp.	Asst. Insp.	Sgt.	Cpl.	Const.	Total
Belizean	1	1	4	13	12	26	7	78	135	621	898

ORGANIZATION OF THE BELIZE POLICE DEPARTMENT

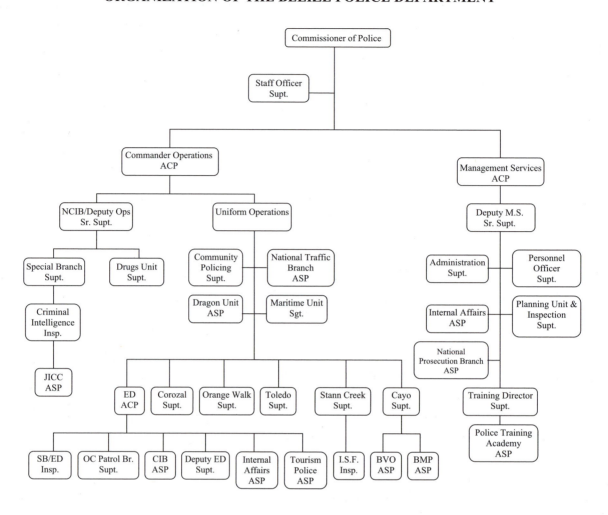

helps unify the department with the community. An environmental scan or SWOT analysis shown above would enable the department to maximize its strength, minimize its weaknesses, take advantage of its opportunities, and counteract its threats so as to further enhance its growth and success. As depicted above, the SWOT analysis highlights the greatest strides taken by the Belize Department and challenges encountered over the last five years.

G. MICHAEL REID

Bibliography

Annual Achievement Report, 2002.
Belize Police Force Standing Orders.
Belize Policing Plan, 2000–2005.
Chief Justice's Report on Judiciary, 2001.
Kolbe Foundation Report on Prison, 2002–2004.
Political Reform Commission's Report, January 2000.
Many thanks to Superintendent Allen Whylie and Mr. Marvin Skeen from the Kolbe Foundationwhose valuable contributions made this document possible.

Major Crimes and Statistics

	2001	2002	2003
Murder	64	87	57
Rape	56	54	42
Robbery	546	571	631
Burglary	1,942	1,956	1,320
Theft	1,855	1,886	1,357

BENIN

Background Material

The Republic of Benin is located in Western Africa. It has an area of 112,620 sq km. The population is 7,041,490 (estimated 2003). Porto-Novo is the official capital; Cotonou is the seat of government. The nation enjoys a multi-party democratic rule, with a unicameral national assembly. French is the official language, while Fon and Yoruba are the common vernaculars. In terms of religion, the population breaks down as indigenous beliefs, 50%; Christian, 30%; and Muslim, 20%.

Benin adopted its constitution in 1990. The legal system is one of French civil law and customary law. The main crimes are child trafficking, domestic violence, vigilantism, and drug trans-shipment. There is a National Police force and a National Gendarmerie. Ministries responsible for policing are the Ministry of Defense (Gendarmerie), Ministry of Interior, Security and Decentralization (National Police), and Ministry of Justice (Judicial police). Benin participates in the following international organizations: United Nations, Economic Community of West African States (ECOWAS), African Union, World Health Organization, International Monetary Fund, Interpol, and United Nations.

The Republic of Benin is a constitutional democracy situated in West Africa. It is flanked by Togo to the west, Nigeria to the east, Burkina Faso and Niger to the north, and the Bight of Benin to the south. Known as Dahomey until 1975, Benin was previously part of French West Africa. Europeans first arrived in the area in the eighteenth century and established trading stations around the coastal areas. The Portuguese, French, and Dutch traded weapons for slaves. In 1900, the province came completely under French rule. In 1958, it became an autonomous republic within the French community and gained full independence in 1960.

Initially, there were persistent insecurity and sporadic unrest, owing to chronic rivalries between the north and south and five military coups d'état. In 1972, the Deputy Chief of Staff of the Armed Forces, Major Mathieu Kérékou, overthrew the existing government and replaced it with one built on Marxist-Leninist principles. The state took control of most areas of the economy and the legal and educational systems. Kérékou maintained power until the early 1990s. Influenced by France and other democratic countries, he then introduced a democratic constitution and held presidential and legislative elections. Prime Minister Nicephore Soglo won the presidential election, and his political associates claimed victory in the National Assembly. In elections held in 1996 and 2001, Kérékou was returned to power.

The majority of the seven million inhabitants of Benin live in the southern section of the country, near the major port city of Cotonou, the capital city of Porto-Novo, and the Royal City of Abomey. The population is ethnolinguistically diverse. The majority of citizens belong to four ethnic groups: Adja, Bariba, Fon, and Yoruba. While French remains the official language, more than half of the inhabitants speak Fon. Other key languages include Yoruba, Mina, Bariba, and Dendi. About 50% of the Beninese population is animist, with the remainder divided almost evenly between Christians (in the South) and Muslims (in the North).

The Benin economy is grounded primarily in agriculture. Cotton accounts for about 40% of its GDP, and for about 80% of national export earnings. It also produces cocoa, palm products, textiles, various oil seeds, pineapples, cassava, rice, beans and fish, both for local consumption and exportation to Europe. Benin started producing offshore oil in October, 1982.

Since its transition to democratic governance, the World Bank and the International Monetary Fund (IMF) have supported a debt-reduction package for Benin. In 2004, the average per capita annual income was below $400. New privatization policies of the government are expected to help stimulate economic growth. Benin is a member of the Economic Community of West African States (ECOWAS) and is reportedly dependent on Ghana for its electricity.

Benin maintains favorable foreign relations with France and the United States. It played mediating roles in crises in Liberia, Guinea-Bissau, and Togo and contributed personnel to the United Nations contingent in Haiti and, in 2003, to an ECOWAS stabilizing mission to Ivory Coast. Its relations with Nigeria are also stable. Despite being poor, its civilian rule and participation in peacekeeping missions command international respect for Benin.

Through the U.S. Agency for International Development (USAID), the United States supports programs in Benin for primary education, family health and planning, women's and children's health, and combating diseases such as AIDS. It also supports the development of a civil society, participation in national decision-making, transparency and accountability in government, decentralization of private and local initiatives, and the enhancement of the electoral system.

Contextual Features

Benin is a model democratic society in Africa. Its government functions under a multiparty democratic rule. The President, elected by popular vote for a five-year term, is the chief of state and head of government and exercises executive power. Subject to parliamentary approval, the President appoints a cabinet known as the Council of Ministers. The National Assembly is a unicameral legislature of 83 deputies, elected by universal suffrage and whose members serve four-year terms. There are four women in the Cabinet and six in the National Assembly, one of whom is the leader of the largest opposition party.

A new constitution was approved in a national referendum in 1990. It prohibits arbitrary arrests and detention; forced exile of citizens; and arbitrary interference with privacy, family, home, or correspondence. It supports freedom of religion, speech, and the press; academic freedom; and the right of peaceful assembly and association. Although there are sporadic reports of police abuses, the police have generally respected these rights.

The constitution provides for a constitutional court, a supreme court, and a high court of justice. These courts were established to counterbalance executive authority. The Supreme Court is the court of last resort in all administrative and judicial matters. The Constitutional Court is charged with deciding the constitutionality of laws, disputes between the President and the National Assembly, and disputes regarding presidential and legislative elections. The President of the Constitutional Court is a woman.

The constitution provides for the right to a fair and public trial. A defendant enjoys the presumption of innocence and has the right to be present at trial and to be represented by an attorney. The legal system is based on French civil law and on customary law. While the judiciary is constitutionally independent, it is reported to be inefficient, poorly trained, and susceptible to corruption, mainly because of low pay.

There are some reported inconsistencies in human rights. Child labor is a problem; employment opportunities for persons with disabilities are limited, and there are reports of occasional police beatings for those who criticize the police or government. Detention for questioning often exceeds the stipulated 48 hours. There is also societal discrimination against women, particularly in rural areas, where they perform most of the labor on subsistence farms. Educational opportunities for girls are lower than for boys, and female literacy rates (18%) are lower than male rates (50%). Female genital mutilation is also widely practiced, despite its illegality.

There are roughly 6,000 detainees in Benin prisons. Conditions are harsh. It is reported that overcrowding, lack of proper sanitation, and limited medical amenities threaten inmates' well-being. Diets are inadequate, and prisoners regularly suffer from malnutrition. The government is attempting to improve these conditions. It reported to the United Nations Committee on Torture that in 2002 it planned to spend 300 francs a day on each prisoner and that all had been vaccinated against meningitis, typhoid fever, and tetanus.

The eight civil prisons in Benin are under the jurisdiction of the Justice Ministry. Female and male inmates are separated, but youths are sometimes lodged with adult prisoners and pretrial detainees with convicted offenders; however, care is taken to separate them from chronic offenders and those on death row. Except for the facility in Natitingou in Atacora Province, every prison in the country is filled to three times capacity. A new 1,000-person prison being built in Akpro-Misserete is delayed because of funding problems.

Trafficking in children is a problem in Benin, particularly in rural areas. They are kidnapped or given by their parents in return for promises of education or other incentives. The children are taken to Nigeria, Gabon, Ghana, Togo, or Ivory Coast, where they become agricultural, domestic, or construction laborers. They may be abused sexually or otherwise, or forced into prostitution. There is also child traffic into Benin from neighboring countries. A 1999 study in Benin concluded that 49,000 rural children, or 8% of rural children aged between 6 and 16 years, work abroad, and that the number was probably nearer 80,000 if those who had left for other reasons were included. Boys constituted 61% of the number, and girls 39%. Between January 1 and September 1, 2003, the police intercepted 136 trafficked children in the country.

Other crimes include domestic violence, in particular wife beating and infanticide. Benin is also a transshipment country for illegal drugs passing from Nigeria to Europe and the United States. A particularly difficult problem is vigilantism or mob justice. Reported episodes include the burning alive of 25 thieves and an attack on civilians by 40 paratroopers carrying sharp weapons in retaliation for an injury sustained by a colleague in a bar fight.

Police Profile

Background

Policing in Benin is based on the French model. The National Gendarmerie is part of the military and comes under the Minister of Defense. It polices rural areas. The National Police comes within the jurisdiction of the Minister of Interior, Security, and Decentralization, while the judicial police in both organizations are responsible to the Minister of Justice. The National Police and the National Gendarmerie are responsible for such functions as maintenance of order, control and prevention of crime, and traffic regulation. In fulfilling these responsibilities, they are described as the "administrative police." The Gendarmerie is reported to include approximately 2,000 officers, and the National Police about 1,000. Given the population, these numbers appear low. In 1997, as part of a security and crime fighting initiative, the government planned to increase the security forces by 200 constables (guardians of the peace), 200 gendarmes, and 200 military personnel, each year for five years.

The investigation of crime is the responsibility of the judicial police. They belong to one or other of the two police forces, but have specific training and the responsibility to discover crimes, gather evidence, and seek out offenders. Some members of the two police organizations have the status of both administrative and judicial police. In their investigative capacity, the judicial police work under the supervision of the judiciary. While they may opportunely collect evidence to establish that a crime has been committed, they must present the evidence to the court and, once legal proceedings commence, they are subject to the direction of the examining magistrate (*juge d'instuction*) and the prosecutor.

Organizational Description

The National Police is organized into four corps: sergeants and constables (brigadiers and guardians of the peace); peace officers, police inspectors, and police commissioners. Within each corp, there are a number of levels. For example, there are probationary constables, second- and first-class constables, corporals, sergeants and staff-sergeants in the sergeants and constables corps. There are three levels of peace officer, five levels of inspector, and six levels of commissioner. The latter corps consists of probationary commissioner, second- and first-class commissioner, principal commissioner, divisional commissioner, and controller general of police. Passage from one corps to another is possible if a candidate passes a professional examination, takes the necessary educational upgrading, and is promoted.

Training

Recruits are selected by competition for direct entry into one of the four corps. They must be of Beninese nationality, have satisfied the law with respect to military service, not be deemed ineligible by certain terms of the penal law, and have passed a background investigation. They then enter a police school to receive the training appropriate to their corps. After successful completion, they become probationers.

The National Gendarmerie School is situated in Porto-Novo. The school trains gendarmes and non-commissioned officers for certificates in use of firearms, professional aptitudes, and brigade commander. Non-commissioned ranks of the judicial police are also trained in investigation and criminal identification. They receive their training from academics and lawyers. The National Police School is at Cotonou, where it is likely it has a similar training program.

Remuneration is based on an index figure which differs from corps to corps and rank to rank. They also receive special allowances for special duties and qualifications. They receive 30 days vacation a year, free lodging or a lodging allowance, free health care for themselves and their families, and a pension at the end of their service.

In principle, promotion within a corps is automatic when someone advances to greater responsibility. Each year a promotion table of names is prepared in order of merit. Where there is equal merit, seniority in a rank, in a corps, in the National Police or, if necessary, seniority in age is taken into account. The table is published on December 15 to take effect on the following January 1.

Police Public Projects

There are some special units of the police. One is for the protection of minors. These have been increased in size in recent years to deal with the problem of trafficking in children. Their activities include criminal prosecution, protection of the victims of trafficking, and prevention.

While the police generally refrain from torture and human rights violations, they are not well regarded by the public. A 1998 study found that 92% of the respondents did not have confidence in the police, and 94% believed the justice system to be slow, corrupt, and to have one law for the rich and another for the poor. There are claims that owing to inadequate training and faulty equipment used to screen passengers and cargos, the police at the borders are inadequately prepared to identify false documents or to interview suspected criminals, terrorists, and others.

Police Education, Research, and Publications

The University of Benin, located in Cotonou, was founded in 1970. It provides most of the professional training in Benin. The French government provides aid to subsidize university education. Apart from the police schools of the Gendarmerie and the National Police, the Ministry of Interior has announced on its website plans to build a school for advanced studies in policing. In addition, the International Criminal Investigative Training Assistance Program (ICITAP) has instituted a management development program for gendarmerie and national police officers responsible for security at major seaports in Benin. In 2003, ICITAP presented six iterations of its two-day first police responder course, which focused on the fundamentals of crime scene management. It is also involved in providing training to the Beninese police in the handling of travel documents and fraud investigations.

IHEKWOABA D. ONWUDIWE

Bibliography

Banks, S. Arthur, and Thomas C. Muller. *Political Handbook of the World: Governments and Intergovernmental Organizations.* New York: CSA Publications, 1998.

Bénin, Government of. *Loi 93-010 du 4 août 1993 portant statut spécial des personnels de la police nationale.* Agence intergouvernemental de la francophonie, Droit francophone, http://portail.droit.francophonie.org/doc/html/bj/loi/fr/1993/1993dfbjlg8.html, November 20, 2004.

Carter, Gwendolen, M. *Five African States: Responses to Diversit.* New York: Cornell University Press, 1963.

Decaldo, Samuel. Historical Dictionary of Benin. Metuchen, New Jersey and London: The Scarecrow Press, Inc., 1987.

The Europa World Year Book. London: Europa Publications Limited, 1999.

Institut international de droit d'expression et s'inspiration françaises. *La direction de la police judiciare et son contrôle par les autorités judiciaires au Bénin.* Juriscope – 1999, http://juriscope.org/publications/etudes/police.htm, November 20, 2004.

International Criminal Investigative Training Assistance Program (ICITAP). "Project Overviews: Benin," www.usdoj.gov/criminal/icitap/upcoming.html, 29 June, 2004.

Kurian, George Thomas. *World Encyclopedia of Police Forces and Penal Systems.* New York: Facts on File, 1989.

Legun, Colin. *Africa: Contemporary Record.* New York and London: African Publishing Company 1992–1994.

Mars-Proietti, Laura. *Nations of the World: A Political, Economic and Business Handbook.* Millerton, New York: Grey House Publishing, 2004.

Onwudiwe, Ihekwoaba D. *The Globalization of Terrorism.* Aldershot: Ashgate Publishers, 2001.

Ramsay, Jeffress. *Global Studies: Africa.* An Annual Edition's Publications. Connecticut: The Dushkin Publishing Group, 1993.

The World Fact Book. "Benin: Country Facts Sheet. " 2003. http://strategies.gc.ca/epic/internet/inimr-ri.nsf/en/gr-05028e.html, 21 June, 2004.

U.S. Department of State. "Benin: Country Reports on Human Rights Practices" 2003, www.state.gov/g/drl/rls/hrrpt/2003/27712pf.htm (29 June, 2004).

BHUTAN

Background Material

The Kingdom of Bhutan is a land-locked country in the Himalayan mountain range. Wedged between India and China, it has a common 605-km border with India and a 470-km frontier with China. It borders Tibet to the north, the Indian States of Assam and West Bengal to the south and east, and the Indian State of Sikkim to the west. It has an area of 46,580 sq. km, about the size of Switzerland. The northern area is in the sparsely populated Greater Himalayas, which reach heights of over 7,300 meters (23,950 ft.). The southern areas are composed of the fertile valleys of the Lesser Himalayas fed by the Wang, Sunkosh, Trongsa, and Manas Rivers.

The population of Bhutan is 2,185,569, although some estimates put it as low as 810,000 (CIA 2005). The first recorded settlers arrived in Bhutan 1,400 years ago. Three main ethnic groups, the Sharchops, Ngalops, and the Lhotshampas (of Nepalese origin), make up Bhutan's population. The Sharchops reside predominantly in eastern Bhutan. Their origin can be traced to the tribes of northern Burma and northeast India. The Ngalops migrated from the Tibetan plains, and they brought Buddhism to the kingdom. Most of the Lhotshampas migrated to the southern plains in search of agricultural land and work.

Bhutan is the only country in the world to retain the Tantric form of Mahayana Buddhism (Drukpa Kagyu) as its official religion. The Buddhist faith permeates all strands of secular life, bringing with it a reverence for the land and its well-being. Bhutan's official language is Dzongkha. English is the medium of instruction in schools, and the national language, Dzongkha, is taught as a second language. A number of different dialects are spoken in Bhutan due to the geographic isolation of many of its highland villages.

The economy is based on agriculture and forestry, which provide the main livelihood for 90% of the population. The central uplands and the Himalayan foothills support the majority of the population. Agriculture consists largely of subsistence farming and animal husbandry (CIA 2005). Farming is the most common occupation, and working family farms is the predominant way of life. People in higher altitudes undertake cattle and yak breeding, and their herds graze in high pastures. Cardamom, citrus fruit, and spices are the major agricultural exports. Cement and electricity are also exported. Bhutan has strong trade and monetary links with India, which finance nearly three fifths of the country's budget expenditure. Hydroelectric power and tourism are its key resources. The gross national product per capita is estimated to be $700.

Bhutan has never had a rigid class system. Social and educational opportunities are not affected by rank or by birth. Bhutanese women enjoy equal rights with men. Polygamy is allowed, provided the first wife consents to it. Divorce is common. The law requires that the marriages must be registered. It also favors women in matters of alimony. The inheritance law provides for equal inheritance among all sons and daughters, though traditional inheritance practices vary among the ethnic groups. Customs in a particular ethnic group may permit heirs to forego their legal rights, while favoring the girls in other groups, which seems to explain why a large number of shops and other businesses are run by women (US Department of State 2005). There are no laws providing for the right to privacy, but the Bhutan culture deeply respects personal privacy.

Contextual Features

Drukpa Shabdrung Ngawang Namgyal, a Tibetan lama of the Drukpa Kagyu school of Tantric Mahayana Buddhism, who arrived in Bhutan in 1616, introduced the present dual system of religious and secular government in the country. He unified the country and established himself as the country's supreme leader and vested civil power in a high office known as the Druk Desi. Religious affairs were entrusted to another leader, the Je Khenpo (Chief Abbot of Bhutan). Following Shabdrung's demise, civil wars intermittently broke out for two centuries, and the regional Penlops (governors) became increasingly more powerful. This ended when, under the British influence, an assembly of representatives of the monastic community, civil servants, and the people elected the Penlop of Trongsa, Ugyen Wangchuck, as the First King of Bhutan in 1907. Bhutan became a protectorate of the British Empire. It gained independence simultaneously with India in 1947. The hereditary monarchy survives.

The King governs with the assistance of a National Assembly and Council of Ministers. There is no written constitution. In December 2001, the King appointed a committee to draft the country's first constitution. The National Assembly has 150 *chimis* (members). One hundred *chimis* are elected indirectly by the heads of households for a three-year term. They do not belong to any political party, as political parties have no legal status in Bhutan and only function in exile. Ten members are nominated by the Buddhist clergy, 34 by the King from among the bureaucracy and the government to represent him, and six are Royal Advisory Counselors. All major ethnic groups are represented in the National Assembly. Fourteen ethnic Nepalis are also members. Women are underrepresented in the National Assembly: it has fifteen women members. The constituency of a member of the National Assembly consists of a number of villages, and each village nominates one candidate. Since there is no electoral system, the villages nominate a member by consensus. The National Assembly has no independent authority, and the sovereign power is vested in the King. The citizens have no right to change their government. The Assembly does not have an Opposition Party.

The administrative organization is based on Shabdrung Namgyal's administrative system of the seventeenth century. Bhutan is divided into 20 *Dzongkhags* (districts), each with its own *Dzongda* (district chief). The *Dzongda* is appointed by the Royal Civil Service Commission and is directly responsible to the Ministry of Home Affairs. He is in charge of administration, implementation of government policies and development projects, and maintenance of law and order. A *Drungpa* (Subdistrict Officer) assists him in the administrative matters, and the Superintendent of Police assists in maintaining law and order. In 1988, four *Dzongde* (zones) were set up as administrative units between the district level and the central government. A group of four districts make up one zone, which is headed by the *Dzongde Chichab* (Zonal Administrator) with authority over the district chiefs in the area.

In recent years, efforts have been made to enhance administrative decentralization. All districts are divided into administrative units (*Gewog*, blocks). Each block consists of a cluster of villages. Government orders at the block level are transmitted through an elected representative, the *Gup* (village headman). There is a *Dzongkhag Yargey Tshogdu* (District Development Committee) in each district, whose declared objective is to increase community participation in social and economic development activities. These committees consist of representatives of the local administration, farmers, and businessmen. More recently, *Gewog Yargey Tshogchungs* (Block Development Committees) have been created, which are the lowest people's bodies and practically have no authority.

No statistics on crime have been reported by Bhutan to the United Nations (Winslow, 2004). Petty crime, such as pick pocketing and purse snatching, is occasionally reported. White-collar and violent crime is increasing; four such cases were reported in April 2003. It appears that the main causes of rise in crime are the influx of foreign laborers, widening economic disparities, and greater contact with foreign cultures (Winslow, 2004). Juvenile crime is also rising. The highest rate of juvenile crime was recorded in 2003, with 63 youths convicted across the country. There was no evidence that the incidence of rape or spousal abuse is extensive. For example, there were 10 cases of rape in 1999 nationwide.

The legal traditions of Bhutan are based on the religious laws of Buddhism. Its civil and criminal codes are rooted in the Tsa Yig, a code established in 1616 by Shabdrung, the Monk-ruler. This code was revised in 1957, but it retained the substance of the seventeenth-century code. There is no comprehensive legal regime pertaining to civil and criminal cases. Most laws are yet to be codified. An Office of Legal Affairs (OLA) was established in 2000 to conduct state prosecutions, draft and review legislation, and render legal counsel. The OLA is composed of a Legal Services Division, with domestic, international and human rights sections; and a Prosecution Division with a criminal section and a civil section. Programs to develop written laws are progressing, and new civil and criminal procedures and criminal codes are being drafted (UNCHR 1995).

Family problems, such as marriage, divorce, and adoption, are usually resolved on the basis of the Buddhist or Hindu religious laws: the Buddhist tradition for the majority of the people, and the Hindu custom for the ethnic Nepalis in southern Bhutan. The country is modernizing its family law. The general law of 1957 guarantees women equality before the law, the Inheritance Act of 1980 equal rights to women in inheritance of land and property, and the Marriage Act of 1980 equality in marriage and family life. The 1996 Amendment to the Marriage Act of 1980 has raised the legal marriage age for men and women from 16 to 18. The 1996 Rape Act seeks to protect women against sexual abuse by imposing stringent financial penalties and prison sentences on the offenders. The Rape Act of 1996 clearly defines a criminal sexual assault and specifies penalties. The rape of minors brings imprisonment ranging from five to 17 years. In extreme cases, a rapist may get life imprisonment. On March 24, 2004, Bhutan abolished the death penalty.

Bhutan has not accepted the jurisdiction of the International Court of Justice. However, in 1988 it ratified a SAARC convention on terrorism, which provides for the extradition of terrorists.

The judicial system has a three-tiered hierarchy, consisting of the village, district, and national levels. The village headman (*Gup*) constitutes the basic court at the lowest level. He adjudicates alone, on the basis of equity, in minor civil disputes and administrative matters. There are two subdistrict courts in a district, which function as the courts of first instance. Each of 20 districts has a district court, where appeals are lodged against the decisions of the *Gup* and the subdistrict courts. A judge (*Thrimpon*) aided by a junior assistant (*Rabjam*) heads the district court. The Chief Justice of the High Court appoints the district judges. A district court has jurisdiction over the territory of his district. It has original jurisdiction in criminal and civil matters and is also competent to review administrative decisions of a *Gup*, a *Dzongda*, or a *DYT* committee. The district court has a lone district Judge. However, Thimpu district has two judges: one for the civil, and the other for the criminal, matters. Bhutan does not have the intermediary appellate court system. The next higher court after the district court is the High Court in Thimphu.

The High Court has original jurisdiction in matters relating to the state security and international treaties. The proceedings are brought before the High Court by the Public Prosecutor's Office, which works under the supervision of the Ministry of Home Affairs. The United Nations Centre of Human Rights (UNCHR) mission in June-July 1995 found that the High Court judges did not have formal legal education and were selected from among the members of the civil services. However, the government intended to employ for judicial functions some people who had received legal education abroad and were mostly working as assistants/trainees at the High Court.

For offences against the State, the State-appointed prosecutors file charges and prosecute cases. In other cases, the concerned organizations and departments of the government file charges and conduct the prosecution. An accused should receive written charges in the language he understands and get time to prepare his defense. In case a defendant cannot write his defense, the court assigns judicial officers to assist. However, ethnic Nepali refugees allege that this practice is not always followed. The legal system of Bhutan does not provide for lawyers, and there is no private legal practice in the country. A legal education program is gradually developing a body of trained legal experts.

The trials should be conducted in open and public hearings, but there are allegations from ethnic Nepali refugees that in practice this is not always so. The accused in criminal cases can appoint a *jambi* (legal representative) who must be a Bhutanese citizen. Traditionally *Jambis* are villagers who have some legal knowledge and are experienced in arguments and negotiations. According to a report on Bhutan of the UN Working Group on arbitrary detention, the people do not widely use this facility, as they are not aware of its existence. It recommended development of this system so as to help the litigants and defendants. The government accordingly established a national training course for the *jambis*. Until the end of 1996, the High Court had run two such courses. The *jabmis* are given three-month training and a license to practice. A special focus is on the legal procedures relating to the land and property disputes. Political dissidents are of the view that the

jabmis hardly understand the legal intricacies, as they do not have a formal legal education. Now some persons who have retired from the judicial service have started the private practice of assisting people in filing petitions and applications to the courts. The justice administration system of Bhutan is yet to be modernized.

Prison conditions are reported to be adequate, although austere.

The government of Bhutan has prepared a draft Administration of the Juvenile Justice Act in order to coordinate national law and policy with the provisions of the Convention on the Rights of the Child, which Bhutan has ratified. The proposed Act seeks to provide for the establishment of institutions required for the care, protection, treatment, development, and rehabilitation of delinquent juveniles. The Juvenile Justice Act will extend to the entire country. It contains guidelines for the conduct of the police, courts, and the correctional centers in respect of the juvenile offenders and criminals (United Nations, 1999). A juvenile rehabilitation center functions at Tsimasham, Chukha District. In view of the increase in juvenile crime, a workshop presided over by the Chief Justice of Bhutan was held in September 2004 to familiarize officers of the police and other law-enforcement agencies with the international standards and instruments of juvenile justice administration.

Police Profile

Background and Demographics

The Royal Bhutan Police (RBP) was established on September 1, 1965 with 500 personnel reassigned from the army. More personnel were subsequently inducted directly. The RBP currently employs 3,417 personnel (117 officers, 952 noncommissioned officers and 2,348 constables).

Organizational Description

The organization, structure, duties, and powers of the RBP are defined in the Royal Bhutan Police Act, 1980. The RBP is under the direct control and supervision of the Chief of the Royal Bhutan Police. He works under the control of the Ministry of Home Affairs. A Deputy Chief of Police assists him. The Chief of the Royal Bhutan Police exercises full power of administration over the force. He has vast disciplinary powers, including the power to remove or demote any police personnel and sentencing them to imprisonment. He makes rules and orders relating to the organization, classification, and distribution of the Police Force, the particular duties to be performed by them, inspections, and the collection and dissemination of intelligence.

The RBP headquarters at Thimpu has three functional branches. The General Division looks after the general welfare of the police and prison administration. The Crime Division deals with crime detection, investigation of special report cases, maintenance of crime records, traffic control, and police research work. The Administrative Division deals with training, VIP security, motor transport, communication systems, arms and ammunition, publication, and sports activities. The heads of all Branches at the headquarters are under the direct command of the Chief of Police.

The field structure consists of the Range Officers, and under their command are the district Police Officers. There are three Ranges in Bhutan. Range I has its headquarters at Phuntsholing, Range II at Gaylegphug, and Range III at Samdrupjongkhar. Each range has three Police Districts. Phuntsholing, Thimpu, and Wangdue Phodrang are the districts in Range I. Gaylegphug, Chirang, and Thonsa fall in Range II; and Samdrupjongkhar, Tashigang, and Mongar in Range III. Each Police District has a number of Police Stations and Outposts. The Check-posts and Outposts are deemed to be police stations. The head of a Police Station is designated as Officer-in-Charge (OC). In his absence, the next in command functions as OC. The police hierarchy has a tall structure, with thirteen ranks. The lowest rank is Constable (*Gagpa*), and the highest is the Chief of Police. These ranks are mentioned in Section 5 of Part Two of the Act, along with the equivalent ranks of the army.

Under Section 11, Part One of the Police Act, the Chief of Police may deputize a representative of the Police for a village or a group of villages where a police station cannot be established or whenever it is deemed necessary to police such a village or villages. Under Section 12, a police representative deputized under Section 11 shall be entitled to all facilities and benefits of the regular police. He shall perform duties assigned to him by the Chief of Police and shall be liable for punishment under Section 5 of the Act for negligence of duty. Section 12 also provides that where a Police representative has not been appointed under Section 11, the *Chipons* of their respective villages shall report matters of importance to the nearest Police Station.

Functions

According to Section 14, Part One of the Police Act, 1980, it shall be the duty of every Police official to promptly execute all lawful orders issued in writing by a competent authority, collect and communicate intelligence affecting the public peace, prevent the commission of crime, detect crime and bring the offenders to justice, and apprehend all persons for whose apprehension sufficient grounds exist. The Police also manage traffic on the streets and roads. Section 17 enjoins upon the Police the duty of maintaining order in public places, including public roads, airfields, and bus stops. Section 19 indicates that the Police responsibilities extend to enhancing public hygiene and decency. For instance, they can without a warrant take persons into custody who slaughter cattle, throw dirt, treat animals cruelly, consume alcohol, indecently expose their bodies, or ease themselves in public places. Section 39 authorizes the Police (and therefore casts upon it the duty) to enforce measures for cleanliness and prevention of disease at public fairs and gatherings. Section 40 makes the Police responsible for damage control during outbreak of fire. Besides performing these standard police duties, the RBP functions as border guards and firefighters and provides first aid (Rigden and Tsering 2001). It is also responsible for maintaining internal security, a task in which the Royal Bhutan Army, Royal Bhutan Guards, and a national militia assist it. Section 43 lays down that the Police shall act in accordance with the provisions of the Prisoners Act for the administration of prisons and prisoners.

The Police Act and the Prison Act provide the legal framework for police activities in Bhutan. The police powers enumerated in Part One of the Police Act are:

- Section 8. Conduct of Police on Duty—No Police official shall interfere or accost any person without reasonable grounds to believe that he has broken the law or is about to break the law unless such individual is moving around at odd hours or travelling on the highway after the specified restricted hours. Section 14, however, says that it shall be the duty of every Police personnel "to prevent the commission of crime, to detect and to bring offenders to justice and to apprehend all persons for whose apprehension sufficient ground exists...."

- Section 13. No Arrest or Search without Warrant—The Police shall not arrest, seize or search a person or a place without a warrant from a court of law.

- Section 14. Duties of Police—It shall be lawful for every Police Officer without a warrant to enter and inspect any bar, gambling house or other resorts of bad characters.

- Section 19, part one. It shall be lawful for any Police Officer to take into custody, without a warrant, any person who in his view, slaughters any cattle or cleans a carcass or cruelly rides, drives or trains an animal; who wantonly or cruelly bats or tortures any animal; who obstructs a passage by leaving his cattle or cart in a public place so as to cause inconvenience or danger to others or who parks for unduly long time his animal or cart for loading/unloading passengers or articles; who exposes any goods for sale on public roads or thoroughfares; throws dirt or litter in a street; who is found drunk or riotous on the road or is incapable of taking care of himself; who indecently exposes his body or eases himself in public place; or exposes the public to a contagious disease; neglects to fence any dangerous well, tank or any other structure.

- Section 27. Power of Arrest—Any Police personnel may arrest any person without a warrant who:

  (i) abuses or physically assaults another person;
  (ii) moves suspiciously about at odd hours and cannot give a satisfactory account of himself;
  (iii) conceals his identity with a view to commit a crime;
  (iv) attempts to dishonor a female;
  (v) is suspected to be dealing in illegal business;
  (vi) possesses illegal arms/ammunition, etc.;
  (vii) uses false weights and measures;
  (viii) peddles harmful drugs;
  (ix) damages public property;
  (x) is a wanted criminal or a deserter from the uniformed services;
  (xi) does fishing and hunting on legally prohibited days and months;
  (xii) receives stolen property;
  (xiii) obstructs a police officer in the execution of lawful duties.

- Section 28. Use of Handcuffs—A person below 13 years shall not be handcuffed.

- Section 29. Power of Search and Arrest—Any Police Officer may search any place or any person if he has sufficient reason or grounds to believe that such a search is necessary to prevent any crime. The search shall, however, be conducted in the presence of two respectable and disinterested witnesses and the search report shall be signed by the searching officer, the accused, and the witnesses.

- Section 30. Arrest without Warrant and Report thereof—Any Police Officer may arrest a person for any offence, which does not require a warrant from a court of law. The arrested person, however, shall be produced before a court of law within 24 hours, exclusive of the time taken for the journey from the place of arrest. If the arrested person cannot be produced within 24 hours, then a report shall be sent to the court within 24 hours to that effect and action shall be taken according to the direction of the court.

- Section 31. Power of Seizure—Any Police Officer who is investigating a case or performing a lawful duty within Bhutan shall seize anything, which is prohibited under the law, and forward a report to the nearest court of law. It shall be lawful for every Police Officer to demand the production of any documents that may be necessary for him to satisfy himself regarding the bona fides of a person.

Training

All police personnel undergo training conducted at the training centers, under the guidance and control of the Chief of police. The training courses run by the training centers are:

- Basic training course for constables—nine months. Their basic training consists of drill with or without arms, weapons training, tae kwon do, law, investigation techniques, checkpost duties, public relations and escorting visitors.
- Basic training course for Officers—six months.
- Refresher course—six weeks.
- Condensed course of six weeks in respect of scientific investigation, police accounts, police administration, handling of dogs, photography. The Chief of Police may prescribe other condensed courses, with emphasis on games, physical training, and weaponry.

Indian police advisers and instructors helped in raising the Bhutan Police, and they have been training its personnel. From 1975 onwards, Bhutanese police instructors, trained in India for one year, began training recruits at the Zilnon Namgyeling Police Training Center. After 1981, a second training center was set up at Jigmiling, Geylegphug District. Both training institutions are under the direct control of the Chief of Bhutan Police. A Principal who is a police officer heads a training center. Trained Assistants, who supervise and control indoor and outdoor training, work under his command.

Advanced training for selected police officers in criminology, traffic control, and use of police dogs has taken place in India and other countries. Bhutan police officers are trained at India's National Police Academy and training institutions located in various States, such as the police training colleges of Delhi and Punjab Police. Some officers have also attended the Police Executive Development Course in Singapore (Srivastava, 2002). Following specialized training in India, a Bhutan woman police officer established in 1988 a fingerprint bureau at Thimpu (Bhutanese Information Resource, 1991). After their basic training at Trashigatsel, Chukha, the Officer Cadets who were recruited in May 2004 would be sent for advanced training to police academies in India. Outstanding trainees among them will receive training in Australia in subjects like scientific interrogation and forensics (*Kuensel* 2004).

Complaints and Discipline

Under the Police Act, the Police may not arrest a person without a warrant and must produce a person within 24 hours of his arrest. "Legal protections are incomplete, however, due to the lack of a fully elaborated criminal procedure code and deficiencies in police training and practice. Arbitrary arrest and detention remain a problem, but are not routinely used as a form of harassment" (US Department of State 1996). Some members of the Police are reported to have committed human rights abuses against ethnic Nepalese. The government denied these reports, and also claimed that it had investigated and punished three government officials. But the details of these cases were not made public (US Department of State 2001). A subsequent report indicates improvement in the situation. It stated that the law prohibits arbitrary arrest and detention, and the government generally observed these prohibitions (US Department of State 2005).

Reports indicate that the government's human rights record is unsatisfactory, but it is trying to improve it. Ethnic Nepalis who settled in large numbers in southern Bhutan at the turn of the century had equal rights with the natives. However, on account of large-scale illegal immigration of Nepalis, the government enacted the Citizenship Act in 1985. It requires that a child could be a citizen of Bhutan only if both of his parents were citizens. Thousands of Nepalis were expelled during 1989–1992. According to the UN High Commissioner for Refugees (UNHCR), over 100,000 ethnic Nepalis from the country have been living in seven camps in southeastern Nepal since the early nineties (US Department of State 2005).

Many ethnic Nepalis are reported to have been detained in the early 1990s on suspicion of supporting a dissident movement, and it is alleged that suspected dissidents were tortured during confinement, primarily as a tactic for reducing the presence of ethnic Nepalis in southern Bhutan. According to human rights groups, the police regularly conduct house searches for suspected political dissidents without legal justification. The government restricts the rights of Bhutan citizens. There are limitations on the right to a fair trial, assembly, privacy, and workers' rights. There are, however, no reports of political or other extra-judicial killings or politically motivated disappearances (US Department of State 2005).

Though there are reports of human rights abuses by the police and security forces, the government of Bhutan is responding to global concern on these issues. Representatives of the ICRC periodically visit prisons in Bhutan, and the government has allowed them access to the detention centers, including those in southern Bhutan inhabited by the ethnic Nepali minority, which has shown dissident tendencies. The UN High Commissioner for Refugees and the chairman and member of the United Nations Human Rights Commission Working Group on arbitrary detention visited Bhutan in 1994 (US Department of State, 1996). Upon request from the government, the Center for Human Rights sent a mission in 1995 to assess the human rights needs of the country and identify the priorities for cooperation with the government, including technical assistance activities to be implemented. The report of the mission contained various recommendations for improving the administration of justice, reporting on human rights violations and discharging international obligations. The one-year project was aimed at strengthening the institutional capacity of Bhutan to deal with human rights issues and its understanding of international human rights, norms, and mechanisms (United Nation 1996).

Terrorism

The main threat to peace in Bhutan comes from the activities of Indian insurgent groups who have established their hideouts and training bases in southern Bhutan. It was reported in 2002 that three main Indian militant groups had their bases in Bhutan: the United Liberation Front of Assam (ULFA), the National Democratic Front of Bodoland (NDFB), and the Bodoland Tiger Force (BLTF) (Kumar 2002). It was estimated that about 400 ULFA activists and 1000 BODO militants had camped in southern Bhutan. Militants are reported to be involved in killings, extortion, and kidnappings. The BLTF kidnapped a Bhutanese immigration officer as a warning to the Bhutan government that it would suffer if it stopped sheltering the militants (*Kathmandu Post* 2001). Under pressure from India, the Bhutan government issued an ultimatum to the militants to leave by December 2001 and launched a military operation in December 2003 in which many terrorists and their camps were destroyed. Insurgents are suspected to be attempting retaliatory attacks against Bhutan. For instance, there was a bomb blast in Gelephu town on September 5, 2004, which killed two persons and injured 27. According to the police, it could be the handiwork of the NDFB (*Kuensel* 2004). The government is taking legal and police/military action to contain the terrorist threat. On September 4, 2004, the courts sentenced 111 persons to prison terms ranging from four years to life imprisonment for aiding and abetting the activities of the ULFA, NDFB, and other militants who had camped illegally in Bhutan. The culprits included civil servants, businessmen, and laborers (*Kuensel* 2004).

YATEENDRA SINGH JAFA

Bibliography

Amnesty International (2003). "Combating Torture: a manual for action." *Bhutan: Gaining access for ICRC visits.* www.amnesty.org.
Amnesty International (2004). http://aiaispacific.amnesty.org/apro/aproweb.nsf/pages/highlights_sa.
ASIP (Asia Social Issue Program) (2003). *Bhutan's Transition to Constitutional Monarchy:Challenges for Change.* www.asiasource.org/asip/bhutan.cfm.
Bhootan.org (2002). *Bringing Bhutan Closer to the World.* www.bhootan.org/index.php?module=Static_Docs& func=view&f=usdept/state_de.
Bhootan.org (2002). Bringing Bhutan Closer to the World. www.bhootan.org/index.php?module=Static_Docs& func=view&f=usdept/state_de.
BHUTAN. Bureau of Democracy, Human Rights and Labor-2004. www.state.gov/g/drl/rls/hrrpt/2004/41739.htm.
Bhutan at a Glance. (2000). A Country Profile. www.geo cities.com/bhutaneserefugees/at_aglance.html.
Bhutan at a Glance. (2000). *A Country Profile.* www.geo cities.com/bhutaneserefugees/ataglance.html.
Bhutan Broadcasting Service (2004). "Police familiarized with Juvenile Justice System." (26 September). www.bbs.com.bt/ARCHIVES%202003/Archives-%20September.htm.
Bhutan Information Resource. (1991). http://reference.all refer.com/country-guide-study/bhutan/bhutan86.html.
Bhutannewsonline (2004) *Political System of Bhutan.* www.bhutannewsonline.com/political_system.html.
CIA (10 February 2005). *The World Factbook-Bhutan.* http://cia.gov/cia/publications/factbook/geos/bt.html.
Kathmandu Post (31 January, 2001). "Bhutan Under Threat from Northeast Militants."
Kaye, Ronald (1989). "Criminal Justice in Bhutan." Published in *Alumni for Life.* University of California, Los Angeles. UCLA School of Law. Fall/Winter 2000/2001 Issue.
Kuensel Online (11 December 2004). "Juvenile Crime highest in Thimpu." http://kuenselonline.com/article.php?sid=4799.
Kumar, Surendra (2002). *Flushing out Indian Insurgents from Bhutan: The Stumbling Blocks.* Institute of Peace and Conflict Studies, Article No. 737. 26April 2002.
Rigden, Tenzing, and Tashi Tsering (2001). *Strategis Affairs-Analysis.* The ULFA Problem from a Bhutan Point of View. No.0016/Issue:March 1, 2001.p.6. www.stratmag.com/issueMar-1/page06.htm.
Srivastava, Divya (2002). *Institute of Peace and Conflict.* Databases. Bhutan. www.ipcs.org/newDatabaseIndex2.jsp?database=1002&country2=Bhutan.
United Nations Centre for Human Rights (1995). *Bhutan. Mission Report.* p.12.
United Nations (26 January 1996). "Economic and Social Council. Bhutan." www.unhchr.ch/Huridoca.nsf/0/3745369261c58623802566b40064618a.
US Department of State (28 February 2005). *Country Reports on Human Rights Practices, 2004.*
US Department of State (2004). Bureau of Consular Affairs, Washington D.C. *Consular Information Sheet.* http://travel.state.gov/travel/cis_pa_tw/cis/cis_1068.html.
US Department of State (23 February 2001). *Country Reports on Human Rights Practices, 2000: Bhutan.* www.terrorismcentral.com/Library/Government/US/StateDepartment/DemocracyHumanRights/2000.
Winslow, Robert (2004). San Diego State University. *A Comparative Criminology of the World.* www.rohan.sdsu.edu/faculty/rwinslow/asia_pacific/bhutan.html.

BOLIVIA

Background Material

Bolivia is a land-locked country in the heart of South America, bordering on Brazil in the east, Peru and Chile in the west, and Argentina and Paraguay on the south. Its size of 425,000 square miles (1.1 sq km) is the size of Texas and California combined. Geographically, the country has two distinct areas. The western half of the country is a high plateau (*altiplano*), among the highest parts of the Andean mountain chain, with a semiarid and cold climate. The eastern half is made up of temperate and semitropical valleys, as well as tropical lowlands, with a mostly humid climate. The country has two capital cities: the administrative capital and largest city, La Paz, has 793,290 people; and the constitutional capital, Sucre, has a population of 215,770. The second largest city in population is Santa Cruz, with 1,135,530 people; the third is the eastern lowland city of Cochabamba, with 517,020 people; and the fourth is El Alto, which surrounds La Paz, with 649,960 people.

The total population is 8.27 million, with an annual population growth rate of 2.74%. Between 56% and 70% of Bolivians belong to the country's three dozen indigenous groups, the largest of which are the Quechua (2.5 million people), the Aymara (2 million), the Chiquitano (180,000), and the Guarani (125,000). The remaining 30% to 42% of people are of European and mixed descent. There is a small amount of German, former Yugoslav, Asian, Middle Eastern, and other minorities, many of whom have lived in Bolivia for several generations. The vast majority of people are Roman Catholic, though much of Roman Catholicism has been combined with indigenous religious norms and practices. There is also a significant and growing Protestant minority. The official language is Spanish, but most people's primary languages are Quechua, Aymara, and Guarani. Education is compulsory for children between the ages of seven and 14, with a literacy rate of 85.5%. The 2000 infant mortality rate was 62 for every 1,000 births.

Economically, Bolivia is one of the poorest and least-developed countries in the western hemisphere, with a GDP of $8.4 billion, an annual growth rate of 1.2%, and a per capita income of just $1,012. Almost two thirds of the population lives in poverty. Of the total work force of 2.9 million people, about 1.26 million work in non-agricultural employment, with 70% in services and government, and 30% in industry and commerce. Most of the economy is based on agriculture and extraction of natural resources, mainly hydrocarbons (natural gas, petroleum) and mining (zinc, tungsten, antimony, silver, lead, gold, and iron). Only 27% of the land is arable, and agriculture composes 15% of GDP. The major agricultural products are soybeans, cotton, potatoes, corn, sugarcane, rice, wheat, coffee, beef, barley, and quinine. Industries include manufacturing, commerce, textiles, food processing, chemicals, plastics, mineral smelting, and petroleum refining.

Total exports amount to $1.35 billion, and the major ones are natural gas, tin, zinc, coffee, silver, tungsten, wood, gold, jewelry, soybean, and byproducts. Imports amount to $1.7 billion, with principal imports including machinery and transportation equipment, consumer products, and construction and mining equipment. Bolivia's biggest trading partners are Brazil, the United States, Colombia, Argentina, Peru, Chile, and the United Kingdom.

The Bolivian *altiplano* was settled for several centuries prior to Spanish conquest in the 1500s. The Tiahuanaco Empire began in the seventh century and extended all the way to the Peruvian coast. After its collapse, the area was ruled by 12 Aymara nations and the Quechua-speaking Inca Empire. Under Spanish rule, the area of Bolivia was known as Upper Peru, and the population was used as forced labor in the mines. The world's biggest silver mine was discovered in Potosí in 1545, making it the colonies' biggest city, but the mines were exhausted by the end of the 1700s. The independence movement got under way with revolts in 1809, but Bolivia was one of the last countries to be liberated, declaring independence on August 6, 1825. Revolutionary leader Antonio José de Sucre became the first president, and he presided over an economy shattered by a lack of mining wealth. After nitrates were discovered along Bolivia's coast in the 1870s, English-financed Chilean interests aggressively moved in, spurring a Chilean military invasion after Bolivia signed a treaty with Peru and then increased tax rates. In the ensuing War of the Pacific of 1879–1884, Chile soundly defeated Bolivia and Peru, annexing all territory up to the Peruvian border and thus robbing Bolivia of its coast. In the Chaco war with Paraguay of 1933–1935, Bolivia then lost a significant amount of its territory to Paraguay.

For most of its history, Bolivia's governments were based on narrow elite interests and the armed forces. Most of those governments were short-lived, with 78 different rulers since independence. The rocky road to democracy began with a revolution by tin-miners in 1952, which led to a regime that nationalized the largest mines, began a comprehensive land reform program, adopted universal suffrage, and promoted indigenous rights. The current constitution was enacted in 1967 and revised in 1994. A series of short-lived governments ruled until Hugo Banzer Suarez seized power in a 1971 coup and established a repressive regime. U.S. pressure led to elections in 1978, which resulted in a series of unstable governments and a fragmentation of the main parties into 70 smaller parties. A particularly brutal, drug-trafficking military dictatorship from 1980 to 1982 further weakened civil society and the rule of law. Siles Zuaro was elected in 1982, but resigned three years later after the economy collapsed into hyperinflation. Paz Estenssoro of the Nationalist Revolutionary Movement (MNR) was elected in 1985 and introduced a policy of economic liberalization. The 1989 elections brought Paz Zamora of the *Movimiento de la Izquierda Revolucionaria* (MIR: Movement of the Revolutionary Left) to office, followed by the MNR's Gonzalo Sánchez de Lozada in 1993. Building on resentment of Lozada's economic liberalization, former dictator Hugo Banzer was elected in 1998 and began an intensive militarization eradication of coca with heavy U.S. support. When illness forced Banzer to resign in August 2001, he was succeeded by his Vice President, Jose Quiroga. In the May 2002 Presidential election, Sánchez de Lozada barely won with 22.5% of the vote over 21% for Evo Morales, the leader of the coca growers, known as *Cocaleros*.

Contextual Features

Politically, Bolivia is divided into nine departments. But as a constitutionally "unitary" republic, nearly all power rests with the federal government, which makes most department appointments and determines resource allocation. The federal government consists of executive, legislative, and judicial branches. The executive branch is headed by a president, elected for a nonrenewable four-year term, and a cabinet. The legislative branch is a bicameral Congress, with a 27-member Senate of three senators from each department, and a 130-member Chamber of Deputies that includes proportional representation of minorities. Bills introduced in Congress require an absolute majority for approval into law. Among the most important laws enacted by Congress have been those in the area of labor, including provisions to guarantee the constitutional rights to employment and a fair wage. More recently, Congress enacted a new Criminal Procedure Code, described in detail below.

The judicial branch, structured by the 1993 Judicial Organization Law, has five levels of jurisdiction. It is headed by the Supreme Court, whose 12 members serve ten-year terms and are appointed by the Chamber of Deputies after initial selection of candidates by the Judicial

Council. The high court has four chambers, with three justices in each. Two of the chambers review civil cases; one handles criminal cases; and the fourth adjudicates on administrative, social, and mining cases. In addition to hearing appeals from lower courts, the Supreme Court has original jurisdiction on matters such as charges against top officials or disputes over state contracts. Also at the top of the judiciary is a Constitutional Court, established in 1998, which handles *habeas corpus* petitions, conflicts between government branches, and the constitutionality of legislation, presidential decree, and international treaties. Superior Courts, at the next level of the judicial hierarchy, hear appeals from trial judges, who have original jurisdiction over civil, family, commercial, and labor cases, as well as those involving minors, criminal violations, and misdemeanors. In the judicial process, finally, the institutionally independent Attorney General's Office prosecutes crimes, and the Public Defender's office provides support for defendants.

Bolivia also has an expanding range of additional judicial safeguards. Indigenous law and legal structures, attacked and altered since the beginning of Spanish rule, have been resuscitated with constitutional recognition of indigenous juridical standards and mechanisms of dispute resolution. Above all, the country's reformed constitution declares for the first time that Bolivia is a multi-ethnic state. Indigenous rights are also fortified by the 1994 Law of Popular Participation, which expands the jurisdiction and responsibilities of municipal governments, and the Forestry Law and Agrarian Reform Law of 1996, which gives indigenous people more control over their land. More generally, Law 1770 of 1997 also provides for arbitration of disputes, based on an agreement between the disputing parties and a time limit of six months. Two of the most important additions to the legal structure, the ombudsman (The *Defensoría del Pueblo*) and the Judicial Council, are discussed below.

The Penal Code of Bolivia includes a wide range of crimes, but among the most clearly defined are labor and drug-trafficking violations. Bolivia has a wide range of labor regulations on working conditions, wages, and union rights. Economic uncertainty and lack of effective judiciary, however, have led to many unpunished labor abuses. More strictly enforced are anti-trafficking provisions, supported by a special drug police and courts, as well as several separate prisons for many traffickers. About 55% of all prisoners, in fact, are held for narcotics crimes.

The regular prison system, run by the Ministry of Government and administered mainly by the police, is characterized by harsh conditions and overcrowding. Reforms in the late 1990s brought some improvements. A 1996 law allows the release of prisoners if no charges are brought for 18 months, for example; and the Justice Minister introduced new bail laws, hired more public defenders, and released thousands of debtors from prison. Despite subsequent population reductions, though, prisons remain overcrowded: Although its physical capacity is just under 5,000 prisoners, the correctional system holds over 8,000. At least 60% of these inmates have not been charged or sentenced, according to the Ministry of Justice and Human Rights; and inmates are not separated by crime, age, and other factors. Youths detained falsely or on minor charges, for instance, are routinely placed with violent criminals. Inmates with money can "buy" visiting privileges, day-pass eligibility, place or length of confinement, as well as cells, which cost between $20 and $5,000, paid to prior occupants or to prisoners who control cell blocks. In La Paz's San Pedro Prison, one of the country's largest, the majority who cannot buy their cells are crammed into tiny airless cells, of about three by four by six feet, with no ventilation, lighting, or beds, and even then crowding forces many inmates to sleep sitting up. Others are forced to sleep on stairs and in hallways (as determined by author interviews in San Pedro prison, July 19, 2000). Even the FELCN's small high-security La Paz facility of the special drug police force squeezes an average of four inmates into dark cells of about six by ten feet (as determined by author interviews in La Paz FELCN prison, July 20, 2000). Cells in police stations throughout the country also lack minimum standards, without adequate illumination or basic sanitation. According to the Ministry of Government's Director General of the Penal System, in addition, nearly 700 children under age six live with a parent in prison, and many of those children are forced to ferry weapons and drugs in and out of the facility. Prison food is inadequate and unhealthy; medical clinics lack basic medicines and even beds; and functioning rehabilitation programs are rare. Over the past several years, finally, three prisoners have been burned in their cells, and others have died from apparent neglect by prison authorities. There was a November 1998 agreement between the *Defensoría del Pueblo* and the Ministry of Government to close down or repair prisons with subhuman conditions, but the government lacks funding to fully implement these and other changes.

Police Profile

Background

Throughout Bolivia's history, the police have been at the center of the country's political and economic turmoil. Amid social unrest, economic crisis, and frequent changes in government, the police have been essential in maintaining public order and carrying out state policy—even since the return of democracy in 1982.

The first police forces in Bolivian territory were poorly-trained and abusive militias during Spanish rule. A year after becoming independent in 1825, the new republic established both a constitution and its first organized state police force. The police's structure reflected that of a highly centralized government, which directly ruled the country's nine departments, based on colonial territorial divisions. But measures to professionalize and modernize the police were not taken, and the National Police (*Policía Nacional*) was not officially established until the Police Law of 1886, which formalized the system that remained in effect throughout the first half of the twentieth century. After Bolivia's defeat to Chile in the 1879–1883 War of the Pacific, the country split into two parties, the Conservatives and Liberals. In 1898, the two sides clashed in a civil war which the Liberals, representing the middle classes and centered in La Paz, eventually won. The Liberal Party, which ruled from 1899 to 1920, then re-wrote the constitution, creating a balance of power between the three branches of government, and took steps to make the police more efficient and to better incorporate it into the state.

The aftermath of the 1933–1935 Chaco War led to more changes. A huge number of returning soldiers transferred into the police force, leading to a highly militarized, pyramid-based hierarchal police structure characterized by extreme discipline. It was this change that many officers regard as the origin of the police's authoritarian practices and attitudes. In 1937, the police became institutionalized with the creation of the National Corps of Carabineers (*Cuerpo Nacional de Carabineros*) and its professional training school, the Police School (*Escuela de Policía*), later renamed the National Police Academy (*Academia Nacional de Policías*). The *Carabineros* were a post-war merger of the Military Police, the Gendarmerie (*Cuerpo de Gendarmería*), the paramilitary Security Police (*Policía de Seguridad*), and the army's Carabineer Regiment (*Regimiento de Carabineros*). The Organic Law of Police and Carabineers of 1950 further revised the police system.

The Chaco War also precipitated important shifts in society, the most important of which was an alliance of the middle and rural working classes that led to the 1941 formation of the *Movimiento Nacionalista Revolucionario* (MNR). After a period of economic decline, the MNR led a successful revolution against the US-backed oligarchy. In power, the party nationalized the tin mines, initiated land reform, granted universal suffrage, and financed broad new social development programs. Until the 1952 Revolution, the police corps was subordinate to the Ministry of National Defense and the army, which assumed most police functions and treated the corps as a reserve to be called on only during emergencies. As a result of its active support of the 1952 Revolution, however, the national police was modernized, took over much of the power of a drastically-reduced military, and was transferred to the jurisdiction of the Ministry of Interior. Though the Interior Ministry was limited to administrative supervision, the police resented being commanded by an army officer and having lower status and pay than the military.

The police continued to be favored over the armed forces in the provision of resources until the 1964 military coup led by Vice President Rene Barrientos Ortuno, who continued most MNR policies. Barrientos' death in 1969 generated a period of populism in which the left grew in power. But after taking over in a 1971 coup, Banzer repressed labor and leftist leaders in an authoritarian regime known as the *Banzerato*. Heavy use of police power continued through the military regimes that ruled the country until 1982.

Demographics

The majority of the National Police's approximately 20,000 personnel are classified as uniformed personnel, and the rest are technical, auxiliary, or identification personnel, and civilian police investigators involved in crime detection, forensic science, administration, and logistics. The police hierarchy is headed by the body of superior officials, with ranks identical to those of the military, from general to sub-lieutenant. Below superior officials are subordinate officers, and the remaining 85% of the force are officers without rank. Each of the four general classifications—*jefes* (field officers), *oficiales* (company officers), *clases* (NCOs), and privates (tropas)—has graded ranks within each class. Uniformed personnel are promoted on the basis of examinations given when they attain the required time in the grade, which is either four or five years.

Classification of civilians was based on a nonmilitary two-category system composed of superiors (*funcionarios superiores*) and subalterns (*funcionarios subalternos*).

Organizational Description

Along with democracy, the 1982 transition brought clearer organization and rules to the police, mainly through the 1985 *Ley Orgánica de la Policía Nacional*. Part of the Executive Branch's Interior Ministry, the police are divided into a General Command, a High Disciplinary Tribunal (*Tribunal Disciplinario Superior*), and ten national offices, including Personnel, Intelligence, Planning and Operations, Auxiliary Technical Services, Instruction and Training, Identification, and Control of Dangerous Substances. Daily policing is the responsibility of "operative" forces in each of the country's nine departments. Each of these forces include a Transit unit, responsible for road safety and quality; the Order and Security unit, in charge of regular patrols and property protection; and a "Special Security" battalion to ensure public order during social conflict.

Most departmental police are also roughly divided between urban and rural forces. The urban force, divided into patrol and criminal investigation sections, operates police stations and local jails. Much of the rural force, including Customs Police to combat smuggling and illegal border crossing, are assigned to border posts and ports of entry. Overall, most police personnel work in the three departments with the three largest cities: about 23% in La Paz Department, about 16% in Santa Cruz Department, and about 14% in Cochabamba Department. The La Paz Departmental Police also has an Explosives Brigade (*Brigada de Explosivos*) and a Feminine Police Brigade (*Brigada Policial Femenina*). All municipalities are entitled to raise local police forces to enforce local ordinances. But only the city of La Paz has established such a force, the La Paz Municipal Police (*Policía Municipal de La Paz*). Other police forces included antiriot, anti-narcotics, and antiterrorist units. The Special Security Group (GES: *Grupo Especial de Seguridad*) is in charge of reestablishing public order and responding to attacks against property. Antiterrorism courses to GES members, which began in 1987, led to creation of an antiterrorist command, the Multipurpose Intervention Brigade (BIP: *Brigada de Intervención Polivalente*) to handle "uncommon violence," such as kidnapping, hostage-taking, and subversion. In the 1990s, the Zamora government gave primary antiterrorist responsibility to the Special Elite Antiterrorist Force (FEAE: *Fuerza Especial Antiterrorista de Elite*).

There are also smaller decentralized police forces, including an ecological agency. One of the more recent and important police agencies is the Judicial Police (*Policía Técnica Judicial*), which depends in part on the Judiciary, under regulations separate from those of other police units. Composed of professional investigators, detectives, forensic experts, and other professionals, the PTJ is responsible for the detention and processing of suspects, investigation and verification of crimes, and investigative procedures such as evidence collection.

Most influential regarding police structure and functioning since the 1980s, though, has been the creation of several coca eradication police forces, with about 6,000 members. The central narcotics force is the Special Antinarcotics Force (FELCN: *Fuerza Especial de Lucha Contra el Narcotráfico*) created in 1987, which has been the principal actor in the drug efforts in the Beni, Chapare, and Yungas regions. In 1989, FELCN also got its own intelligence service to collect evidence on drug-trafficking suspects. FELCN also runs a subordinate force, the Rural Area Police Patrol Unit (UMOPAR: *Unidad Móvil de Patrullaje Rural*) popularly known as The Leopards (*Los Leopardos*), which was formed in 1983 under a United States-funded program, in accordance with four narcotics treaties. Run by the Government Minister through the Social Defense Secretariat (*Secretaría de Defensa Social*), UMOPAR is focused exclusively on drug trafficking and related concerns. Is has nearly 1,500 officers, many of whom are used to infiltrate drug trafficking networks. Its funds come mainly from the United States and are not specified in any government document or budget. UMOPAR has three operation centers—in Cochabamba, Chimoré, and Yapacaní—but its main center is in Chapare, the main coca-growing region.

Functions

Despite relative political and economic stability, increases in crime and anti-government protest—along with the huge anti-coca operations—have resuscitated the police's militarized approach. But its internal weaknesses remain, including administrative limitations, widespread corruption, continuing rights abuses, and difficulty in implementing criminal regulations. The police have three broad areas of activity: preventative control over crime, investigative procedures of crimes that do occur,

and administrative control over correctional facilities such as prisons. While this combination of powers makes the police integral, current pressures have cast doubt over all of them. But the police not only fall short of completing its tasks, but often obstruct them as well.

This gap between the police's goals and daily practice is most evident in its failure to halt rising crime. Bolivia is still one of the safest countries in the region, but reported crime quadrupled between 1993 and 1999, to more than 200,000 cases in 1998 alone. Like many others, the police blame poverty, unemployment, mass migration to the cities, and, according to some officers, entry of Peruvians with criminal records. But the police complain of woefully inadequate government support. Despite external funding and new equipment through projects such as the $26 million Citizens' Security and Protection Plan in 1999, the police's overall budget is shrinking. In 1999, it was reduced by 25% and in 2000 by slightly more.

Police facilities reveal the effects of such cuts. Even at PTJ headquarters in La Paz, equipment is lacking; the physical plant is deteriorating, and officials are cramped into small rooms where up to four different cases are handled simultaneously. Higher officials are frustrated by the government's slow and convoluted responses to crime, such as long delays in passing the Security and Protection Plan. Being on the front lines against crime, police also believe that they should be part of policy formation, and they pointedly complain that they are not included in the development of even basic laws.

Training

Recruitment and training have gradually improved, but they remain largely inadequate. Officers and higher civilian employees are drawn mainly from the small urban middle class and the army. But poor pay, conditions, and prestige at the lower levels attract few people outside of the poor and poorly-educated sectors of the population. Education varies according to specialization, and most enlisted personnel receive most of their training during the first months on the job. The Higher Police School (ESP: *Escuela Superior de Policías*) was created in 1969 to train officers in the ranks of lieutenant colonel and above to manage command departments, operational units, and training institutes. The Young Men's Basic Police School (EBPV: *Escuela Básica Policial de Varones*) provides a one-year training course at the operational level for subalterns. Officers without rank are given a three-year education at the *Escuela Nacional de Policías*, but the entrance requirement of a secondary school degree remains out of reach of most Bolivians. The National Police Academy offers a four-year course for officers, covering criminal law, penal and civil investigation, criminology, ballistics, laboratory science, narcotics, traffic, and human and public relations. The academy has also offered a course based on the counterinsurgency course of the United States Army Special Warfare School, as well as a program in which selected personnel are sent to training courses overseas and then teach unit-level courses back in Bolivia. In the past, admission to the academy depended on political reliability and loyalty to the government. By the early 1980s, applicants had to undergo medical, physical, and mental examinations, as well as general knowledge tests. Cadets accepted to the academy are not subject to the age limitations for military service and are exempted from military obligations. The normal student body ranges from 480 to 500 cadets, who, upon graduation, receive a bachelor of humanities and commission as second lieutenant. Officers are commissioned by graduation from the National Police Academy, by transfer from the army, by direct political appointment for demonstrated ability, or by outright patronage. Most civilians were political appointees and had some relevant experience.

Complaints and Discipline

Annual salary for the police chief is about US$20,000, a detective around US$3,200, and a street officer under US$1,300. Amid constantly rising costs of living, such low pay has led to frequent and very violent police strikes, walkouts, and takeovers of government buildings. It also forces many officers to moonlight for private security firms and makes all of them susceptible to corruption. Officers at the lower ranks routinely extort money from small businesses, entertainment halls, brothels, gang members, detainees, and informal economy workers, such as those who sell goods on the street. Traffic police openly take bribes from drivers breaking (or not breaking) traffic laws. Higher ranking officers, meanwhile, extract money for speeding up or slowing down court cases, covering up crimes, issuing licenses, and ignoring illicit activity by powerful people. Top judicial police officials have been accused of the torture of detainees. Senior policemen organized a string of burglaries in 1999, and the police chief allegedly misused a pension fund. Police are also involved in kidnapping, robbery, organized crime rings, the "disappearance" of cars, and cover-ups of crime. Contraband and drug trafficking are the most

lucrative forms of corruption. Most inquiries into such abuses lack teeth: A police officer conducting an internal corruption inquiry was reportedly beaten unconscious by two other policemen in a police cell. After criminal gangs were found to include police, bombs exploded outside police headquarters in the city of Santa Cruz. Under pressure, though, more police are being held accountable. Since 1997, four police chiefs have been fired under allegations of corruption and involvement in crime, but 25 of the police's 77 senior commanders face investigations still not concluded.

Corruption and poor crime fighting have led to widespread public distrust of the police. Polls show that a majority of Bolivians rank the police as first or second among the most corrupt and least trustworthy institutions in the country and regard investments in the police as having little impact. Such distrust aggravates the police's own hostility toward an ungrateful population, increasing support for an "iron fist" approach to control social problems and, by the police's own admission, an attitude of "brutality, authoritarianism, and violence" toward citizens (Colonel Jaime Gutiérrez Terrazas, Director Nacional de DDHH de la Policía Nacional, in an interview with the author, July 13, 2000). Part of the problem lies with education and the law. Not a single one of the *Ley Orgánica's* 138 articles discusses human rights at length—not even Chapter Nine, which covers police education. Training is instead highly technical, centered on the use of arms and control of social groups.

However, even built-in checks may be inadequate. Most of the written laws are clear and adequate, admit many police officials, but the problem is the poor and inconsistent application of them. Most police officers do not adequately follow the *Ley Orgánica*, and even the police chief doubts that they are trained sufficiently to implement the new penal code procedures of gathering evidence, interviewing suspects, and protect crime scenes.

As in the past, human rights abuses flourish amid this lack of education and accountability. The most common targets of abuse are people on the street, particularly vulnerable minorities such as youth, rural *campesinos*, and community or rights activists. Excessively unwarranted use of force, humiliating treatment of women, and mistreatment of detainees are all common. Members of the Permanent Assembly of Human Rights (APDH) have been arrested and tortured by police officials. Constitutional rights are eroded, not just by police practices, but by certain laws. Even after some of its more controversial provisions were eliminated, for example, anti-trafficking Law 1008 of 1988 violates basic rights, such as by prohibiting pretrial release, and it fosters discrimination against indigenous people. Rights officials in coca regions try to counter these trends, but in doing so must tread carefully between local communities and law enforcement agencies, both of whom are suspicious of them. In addition, military officials controlling coca-producing zones have been accused of beatings, violating the inviolability of the home, illegal confiscation, violent raids, extra-judicial shooting, and collusion with cocaine traffickers. But nearly all military officials who have been charged with abuses have been acquitted.

A big source of police corruption, inefficiency, and abuse is the national criminal justice system. Even under democracy, criminal justice officials lose documents, manipulate investigations, fabricate evidence, mistreat detainees, and bend to pressure from political officials. Such biased and slow criminal investigation encourages the police to skirt due process procedures, while poor judicial oversight fuels abuses among officers, and a lack of popular trust in justice dampens moral among the police force.

Police Public Projects

In the mid-1990s, though, an activist Ministry of Justice and Human Rights (particularly under René Blattmann, who was Minister between 1994 and 1996) initiated an overhaul of the system. The biggest reform was the 1999 formulation of a new Criminal Procedure Code, which took effect in June 2001. It replaces written trials with oral trials, hands over criminal investigations from police and judges to newly appointed public prosecutors (fiscales) with independent powers of investigation, and, for the first time, requires police to give evidence in court. Though the code reduces the police's judicial power, it also supports policing work by drawing clearer boundaries and responsibilities.

Along with the new penal code came a new legal conciliation center, improvements in the administration of the public ministry and judiciary, new commercial and intellectual property codes, and a constitutional tribunal to review all laws. In 1998, Bolivia also established a Judicial Council (Consejo Judicial), whose five members are authorized to propose candidates for most courts, formulate and administer the judicial budget, and investigate and discipline all judicial personnel. It has already filled a record number of court openings and made great headway against inefficiency and corruption.

The council has also broken the Presidency's long-standing control over the courts. Recent appointees to the 12-member Supreme Court, for example, were selected more for their professional competence than for their political connections.

But the reform that affects the police most is the establishment of a national ombudsman, the *Defensoría del Pueblo* (People's Defender), which was created as part of the 1992 constitutional reforms and began operating in 1998 with appointment of the first *Defensor*, who heads the agency. The *Defensoría* is empowered to investigate the practices of all state agencies, including the courts, public administration, prisons, private utilities, and police. Poor conditions in police cells, for example, were exposed by the *Defensoría*. To address such problems, it can formulate policy recommendations and utilize legal recourses such as *habeas corpus*. Advocating on behalf of societal groups, the agency enjoys a high level of public support. Its multilingual radio broadcasts and regional information gathering, for instance, have exposed patterns of discrimination and regional imbalances in resource distribution.

But the *Defensoría*—as well as the other promising new agencies—is being undermined by ongoing politicization and inefficiency. In particular, the *Defensoría* is constrained by obstruction and stonewalling by the executive and the inefficiency of the courts, which are slow to take up the problems exposed by the agency. The current *Defensor*, Ana María Romero de Campero, complains that she is constantly submitting legal recourses to stop unconstitutional state actions, such as unannounced roadblocks, intrusions on citizen privacy, and the use of clandestine agents (author interview, July 12, 2000). Like the *Defensoría*, the judicial council has been hampered by political, legal, and bureaucratic obstacles. Its overhaul of court management and accounting triggered attacks by the agencies previously in charge of budgets, as well as by the Senate, which accused the council of corruption and excessive spending.

The council's investigation of corruption brought down even greater political wrath. In its first 15 months, the council sanctioned nearly a hundred judicial personnel for crimes such as bribery. But before long the backlashes began. One started with the dismissal and trial on drug collaboration charges of a court officer, who appealed to the Constitutional Court on the grounds that the dismissal violated his due process rights. After the court ruled in the officer's favor and reinstated him in his post, Congress eliminated the council's power to dismiss judges and limited punishment to suspension to a range of three months to three years—effectively eliminating the council's ability to prosecute serious crimes (according to Luis Carlos Paravicini, Judicial Council member, in an author interview, July 14, 2000).

Politicization also affects other criminal justice agencies. Explaining his government's failure to pass a law regulating the MP, for example, Bolivia's Fiscal General said that the constitution is being interpreted in a way that "makes Congress appear as the MP's boss" and allows for constant interference in the MP's work by outside officials (Oscar Crespo Soliz, Fiscal General de la República de Bolivia, in an author interview, July 24, 2000). The MP's yearly reports to Congress, in fact, complain that external interference, unclear guidelines, and weak functional autonomy prevent it from carrying out its constitutional obligations (Ministerio Público de la Nación, Fiscalía General de la República de Bolivia, 1996). In the coca regions, as discussed below, political pressure is also placed on local fiscals responsible for investigating police and military involvement in drug trafficking.

Disarray within the courts also undermines criminal justice. Judicial personnel regularly strike to protest low salaries, broken promises of raises, and the huge salary differences between higher and lower ranking judicial officials. Like Colombia and Peru, Bolivia has "faceless" or other special courts for drug-trafficking and terrorism, many created by Law 1008. Public defense also is weak, and there are far to few public defenders to serve the many defendants unable to afford an attorney, despite efforts like the 1995 "Public Defense Program" to strengthen or create public defense offices in under-serviced regions.

Along with politicization and uncertainty in the legal system, social unrest also complicates contemporary policing. Throughout history, one of the police's biggest responsibilities has been to contain social unrest and opposition to state policy. Above all, the country's rural and mainly indigenous laborers, *campesinos*, have not hesitated to take up action. Unable to attain meaningful remedies or control over their lands, for example, *campesinos* have organized strong unions and movements, especially after the 1952 revolution and the 1953 Agricultural Reform Law. Unpopular mass eradication of coca plants, clumsily applied crop substitution policies, and fatigue with neoliberalism have only re-enforced these state–society tensions since the 1980s. Most of the Aymara, Quechua, and Guaraní peoples, who comprise the majority of Bolivia's population, still regard state policy and law as encroachment on their autonomy.

Programs such as the Popular Judicial Consultancies, started in 1978 by the Center of Juridical Studies and Social Investigation (CEJIS), attempt to bring social grievances into the legal system. Using their increased political power, though, many indigenous peoples have preferred to use their own legal norms. Along with Colombia, Ecuador, and Peru, in the 1990s Bolivia enacted constitutional provisions recognizing the legal traditions of indigenous peoples and allowing them to administer justice in their regions. Employing legal traditions that prioritize participation, respect, and social harmony over written laws, many communities have created forums to judge disputes and dispense sanctions. Encouraging this trend, in the mid-1990s the Justice Ministry launched its "Traditional Justice Project," which includes development of local Peace Justice network (the *Justicia de Paz*) to carry out traditional conflict resolution through pilot forums and judges in at least 40% of the country's municipalities.

The use of community justice can all be seen in the sprawling urban areas of El Alto, surrounding the city of La Paz, where poor rural indigenous people have immigrated in massive numbers and set up justice forums ranging from structured disciplinary tribunals to neighborhood councils (*juntas de vecinos*). These forums enjoy strong popular support because they are elected, utilize indigenous customs well suited to community problems, and are fast. Of the 152 cases taken to a *junta* of the typical El Alto neighborhood of Villa Bolívar "D," for example, 51% were resolved in a week or less and 15% in less than three weeks. Though the cases taken to the forums reflect the community's biggest strains—such as physical altercations, robbery, and domestic violence—over 92% of council sanctions are obeyed. Despite such success, those sanctions vary widely and are inconsistently applied, and often lead to abuses of power, such as illegal seizure of private property. But one proposed solution, to combine forums with local courts and police, would only heighten underlying conflicts. Most justice forums report serious crimes such as rape and murder to the PTJ, which in turn recognizes forum procedures to resolve them. But attempts to carry out punishments that violate national law—such as the death penalty—have made the police and courts increasingly reluctant to respect the forums. For these and other reasons, the Traditional Justice Project got stalled by criticism in Congress. Because the disputes dominating community forums are rooted in broad societal hardships, long-term resolution also requires effective policies against crime, poverty, and other sources of violence. Without them, residents are more likely to turn to options such as vigilantism. In some El Alto neighborhoods, in fact, even many residents on justice councils use whistles to alert each other of "criminals," whom they then beat up or kill. Some community forums also clash with the police, especially when local leaders elected to the forums are engaged in organized crime such as drug trafficking.

International Cooperation

The United States plays a heavy role in Bolivian policing, triggering strong resentments and raising questions of national policing sovereignty. In the early 1990s, the International Criminal Investigative Training Assistance Program (ICITAP) of the U.S. Department of Justice provided Bolivia's National Police with criminal investigative capabilities and forensics technical assistance, complementing other U.S. programs in prosecutorial assistance. Between 1993 and 1998, ICITAP helped to improve the PTJ's investigative capabilities, training programs, educational standards, technology base, and case management systems—culminating in the 1998 implementation of the National Criminal Information System (SNIC). ICITAP stepped up assistance in 1999 to help the police implement the new Criminal Procedure Code, developing a National Training Plan to integrate the changes into the policies and procedures of the police and other criminal justice agencies. Training courses have been given to over 1,400 investigators, prosecutors, public defenders, judges, and other personnel throughout Bolivia. A curriculum for the Criminal Investigative School has been completed and training materials consistent with the new CPC developed. With ICITAP assistance, a Police Education Commission (PEC) has been constituted to revise the entire police education system, including addressing the issue of transferring management of the Criminal Investigative School to the National Police Academy. Hardware and software for nationwide interconnection of the SNIC have been installed in PTJ and prosecutor offices in the major cities. Training to support the system has been given to technicians in those cities, and a SNIC training computer has been established at the Police Academy for ongoing investigator training. ICITAP also assisted in the development of the new Police Organizational Law, which will streamline police hierarchy and coordinate promotion procedures. To combat corruption, finally, the police Disciplinary Code is being modified, and a Directorate of Professional Responsibility (DGPR) is being established.

But it is the U.S.-backed militarization of Bolivia's police which has been a main source of power and controversy. The police's favored position returned after the fall of the 1980–1982 dictatorship, and has since grown with their involvement in the war against drug trafficking and illegal coca cultivation. Article 5 of the *Ley Orgánica* places the police under army command during international armed conflict—a controversial measure partly blamed for the abuses that have accompanied the coca eradication. Although the police have 70% more personnel than the armed forces, the police budget is only about 60% the size of the military budget. Compared with the military, where over 25% of personnel are officers, in the police no more than 15% are officers. But police force has been at the center of the eradication, propelled by its military hierarchy, weapons and technology far more sophisticated than those of a police force limited to routine policing, and with wide autonomy from the state agencies responsible for overseeing it.

Most explosive has been the U.S.-financed eradication of coca, long an integral part of Bolivian culture and medicine. When the economic liberalization that began in 1985 accelerated migration to the cities, coca was one of the few relatively secure sources of income in regions like Chapare. When the modern eradication campaign began in the late 1980s, the Bolivian government restrained it out of fear of backlashes. Efforts were stepped up in the mid-1990s, when Bolivia received more money for the war on drugs than any other Andean government. Resulting in the loss of about $500 million each year to Bolivia's economy (Farthing and Kohl 2001), eradication led to widespread social protest and a six-month government state of siege in 1995 that included a curfew, banned meetings, and mass detentions, and ended only with voluntary eradication by *cocaleros*. When Banzer assumed office in 1997, he stepped up eradication with *Plan Dignidad*, which successfully eliminated all illegal coca in Chapare. But the plan provided very few of the promised economic alternatives for *Cocaleros*, and in 1999 was criticized by the Defense Ministry's own Defense Policy Analysis Unit (UDAPDE) for underestimating the violence and social costs involved. The main eradication force is the U.S.-funded Joint Task Force (JTF), a combined police and military agency whose 1998 establishment has generated ongoing popular protest and violence. The JTF has fired upon unarmed protestors, and *Cocalero* self-defense committees have killed some security officers. Working alongside the JTF is the Expeditionary Task Force (ETF), created in January 2001 with 500 members. Though headed by military commanders, the ETF is not part of the police or military and receives most of its funds from the United States. The ETF has been responsible for human rights abuses and several killings, and the *Defensor* regards it as illegal, since the military cannot increase its personnel without Congressional approval. But even after criticism from the U.S. Congress, the United Nations, and international rights organizations, the ETF expanded to 1,500 members in January, 2002.

Tensions were eased by negotiations sponsored by the Church, the *Defensoría*, and the Permanent Human Rights Assembly. But they rose again after the November 2001 enactment of Supreme Decree 26415, which prohibits the drying, transport, and sale of coca leaf grown in the Chapare in previously legal markets. The *Defensor* regards the Decree as unconstitutional, since a supreme decree, which does not require congressional approval, cannot override Law 1008, the penal code, or the constitution. After violent clashes in the coca market in January 2002, in which four security officers were killed, the GES raided the *cocaleros'* federation building, beating and detaining scores of activists. Later on in 2002, Supreme Decree 26415 was allowed to expire. But even though 57 *cocalero* deaths by security forces have been documented since 1987, only three of these cases made it to court—and none were concluded. The Chapare District Attorney rarely completes the investigation report, without which a judge cannot open the case. Although the *fiscal's* office is autonomous, as discussed above, it comes under enormous pressure by the government. Despite the constitutional provision that civilian courts handle all human rights cases, in addition, many of them have been sent to the military courts.

As with increasing strains from crime, poverty, and economic uncertainty, coca eradication is challenging the Bolivian police's integrity and efficiency. But there is hope that new laws and institutions, as well as democracy itself, will help hold the police accountable as well as support the work they do on behalf of all Bolivians.

MARK UNGAR

Bibliography

Comisión de Derechos Humanos de la H. Cámara de Diputados. *Denuncia de torturas a ciudadanos de alzamiento armado.* La Paz: CEDOIN, 1995.

Farthing, Linda, and Ben Kohl. "The Price of Success: Bolivia's War Against Drugs and the Poor." *NACLA Report on the Americas*, July-August 2001.

González Mendivil, Franklin. *Docrtrina Policial.* La Paz: Policía Nacional/Comando General, 1988.

Ministerio de Justicia y Derechos Humanos, República de Bolivia y Centro de Asesoramiento Social y Desarrollo Legal. *Justicia Comunitaria, Vol.4: Las Zonas Urbano Marginales de la Paz y Cochabamba.* La Paz: Ministerio de Juticia y Derechos Humanos, 1998.

Ministerio Público de la Nación, Fiscalía General de la República de Bolivia. *Informe del Fiscal General de la República: Gestiones 1994–1995.* Sucre, Bolivia: Editorial Judicial, 1996.

World Bank (International Bank of Reconstruction and Development). *Staff Appraisal Report: Bolivia Judicial Reform Project*, World Bank: 1995.

BOSNIA AND HERZEGOVINA

Background Material

Officially named the Republic of Bosnia and Herzegovina (also Bosnia-Hercegovina), the country is bordered on the north, west, and south by Croatia, on the east and southeast by the republics of Serbia and Montenegro, and on the southwest by the Adriatic Sea along a narrow extension of the country. Roughly triangular in shape, it occupies an area of 19,741 square miles (51,129 square kilometers). The larger region of Bosnia occupies the northern and central parts of the republic, and Herzegovina occupies the south and southwest. The capital is Sarajevo.

Bosnia and Herzegovina's declaration of sovereignty in October 1991 was followed by a declaration of independence from the former Yugoslavia on March 3, 1992 after a referendum boycotted by ethnic Serbs. In March 1994, Bosniaks and Croats reduced the number of warring factions from three to two by signing an agreement creating a joint Bosniak/Croat Federation of Bosnia and Herzegovina. On November 21, 1995, in Dayton, Ohio, the warring parties signed a peace agreement that brought to a halt the three years of interethnic civil strife (the final agreement was signed in Paris on December 14, 1995). The Dayton Agreement retained Bosnia and Herzegovina's international boundaries and created a joint multiethnic and democratic government. This national government was charged with conducting foreign, economic, and fiscal policy. Also recognized was a second tier of government consisting of two entities roughly equal in size: the Bosniak/Croat Federation of Bosnia and Herzegovina and the Bosnian Serb-led Republika Srpska (RS). The Federation and RS governments were charged with overseeing internal functions.

In 1995–1996, a NATO-led international peacekeeping force (IFOR) of 60,000 troops served in Bosnia to implement and monitor the military aspects of the agreement. IFOR was succeeded by a smaller, NATO-led Stabilization Force (SFOR), whose mission is to deter renewed hostilities. In 2004, an EU-led force took over for NATO.

Within Bosnia and Herzegovina's recognized borders, the country is divided into a joint Bosniak/Croat Federation (about 51% of the territory) and the Bosnian Serb-led Republika Srpska or RS (about 49% of the territory); the region called Herzegovina is contiguous to Croatia and the Federal Republic of Yugoslavia (Montenegro) and traditionally has been settled by an ethnic Croat majority in the west and an ethnic Serb majority in the east.

The country is 40% Muslim, 31% Orthodox, 15% Roman Catholic, 4% Protestant, and 10% adhere to other religious beliefs.

The Croatian, Serbian, and Bosnian languages are spoken.

In the period immediately following the 1991 war in Croatia, Bosnia and Herzegovina's official economy collapsed. Huge increases in the price of oil, falling imports and exports, hyperinflation, shortages of food and medicine, insolvent banks, and unpaid pensions all resulted in a swelling black market, or informal economy. In addition, war after independence caused widespread destruction, so that any eventual peace would have to be followed by a complete rebuilding of the economy.

The bitter interethnic warfare in Bosnia caused production to plummet by 80% from 1990 to 1995, unemployment to soar, and human misery to multiply. With an uneasy peace in place, output recovered in 1996–1999 at high percentage rates from a low base; but output growth slowed in 2000 and 2001. GDP remains far below the 1990 level. Economic data are of limited use because, although both entities issue figures, national-level statistics are limited. Moreover, official data do not capture the large share of activity that occurs on the black market. The *marka*—the national currency introduced in 1998—is now pegged to the euro, and the Central Bank of Bosnia and Herzegovina has dramatically increased its reserve holdings. Implementation of privatization, however, has been slow, and local entities only reluctantly support national-level institutions. Banking reform accelerated in 2001 as all the communist-era payment bureaus were shut down. The country receives substantial amounts of reconstruction assistance and humanitarian aid from the international community but will have to prepare for an era of declining assistance.

Contextual Features

An agreement negotiated in Dayton, Ohio in November 1995 established Bosnia and Herzegovina as a state composed of two largely autonomous entities, the Serb Republic and the Federation of Bosnia and Herzegovina. The latter is a decentralized federation of Croats and Bosniacs and established one internationally supervised district—Brcko district (Brcko Distrikt). Each entity has its own legislature and president. The central institutions of Bosnia and Herzegovina include a directly elected tripartite presidency with one Bosniac, one Serb, and one Croat member. The presidency appoints a multiethnic Council of Ministers with one Bosniac and one Serb cochairman, on a two-year rotating basis, and one Croat vice-chairman. The parliament is bicameral. Members are directly elected to the 42-seat lower house (House of Representatives), in which 28 seats are reserved for the federation and 14 for the Serb Republic. Members of the upper house (the House of Peoples, with five members from each ethnic group) are chosen by the entity parliaments.

Bosnia and Herzegovina has a civil law sysem, also called Romano-Germanic law, the law of continental Europe, based on an admixture of Roman, Germanic, ecclesiastical, feudal, commercial, and customary law, while its criminal law system could be called mixed or quasi-adversarial.

The criminal justice system is composed of the courts, the Prosecutors, the prisons and correctional institutions, and the Police.

The Bosnia and Herzegovina Constitutional Court consists of nine members: four members are selected by the Bosniak/Croat Federation's House of Representatives, two members by the Republika Srpska's National Assembly, and three non-Bosnian members by the president of the European Court of Human Rights. A new state court, mandated in November 2000, has jurisdiction over cases related to state-level law and appellate jurisdiction over cases initiated in the entities; the entities each have a Supreme Court; each entity also has a number of lower courts; there are 10 cantonal courts in the Federation, plus a number of municipal courts; the Republika Srpska has five district courts, plus a number of municipal courts.

Reliable statistics for crime offences and crime trends are not available for the entire nation of Bosnia and Herzegovina. Bosnia and Herzegovina has been affected by a high rate of corruption and organized crime in the post-war period.

Penal institutions in Bosnia and Herzegovina are under the jurisdiction of the Ministry of Justices. There are 11 penal institutions in total in Bosnia and Herzegovina and three separate departments of these institutions.

In the territory of the Federation of Bosnia and Herzegovina, there are five penal institutions and three departments (penal institutions in Zenica, Tuzla, Bosnia and Herzegovinaac, Mostar, Sarajevo, department of Tuzla penal institution in Orasje, department of Tomislavgrad penal institution in Busovaca, and department of Sarajevo penal institution in Ustikolina). All the penal institutions in the Federation of Bosnia and Herzegovina are semi-open, except the one in Zenica, which is closed.

In the territory of the Republika Srpska, there are six penal institutions (in Banja Luka, District Penal institution in Bijeljina, District penal institution in Doboj, penal institution in Foca/Srbinje, penal institution—"Kula"—Srpsko Sarajevo, and District penal institution in Trebinje). All penal institutions in the territory of Republika Srpska are semi-open, except the one in Foca/Srbinje, which is closed.

The entity laws, as well as the Rule Books in existence in penal institutions, are in compliance with the European Rules for Penal institutions.

Police Profile

Background

At the end of the war, lingering hostilities were one of the priorities of the International Community. Reconstruction of the police forces took place as part of the general overall reconstruction efforts. The task of police development was assigned to the International Police Forces (IPTF).

Recognizing the importance of establishing professional democratic police forces that respect international standards, human rights, and fundamental freedoms, UN Security Council Resolution 1035 (December 21, 1995) articulated the mandate for the International Police Task Force (IPTF). As with IFOR, however, the real basis for the IPTF originates in the Dayton Peace Agreemen (DPA).

Annex 11 clearly states that responsibility for maintaining a "safe and secure environment for all persons" rests with the signatories themselves. However, to assist in discharging their public security obligations, the Parties requested that the IPTF perform the following functions:

Monitor and inspect judicial and law enforcement activities, including conducting joint patrols with local police forces;
Advise and train law enforcement personnel;
Analyze the public security threat and offer advice to government authorities on how to organize their police forces most effectively; and
Facilitate law enforcement improvement and respond to requests of the parties, to the extent possible.

In response to the DPA, IPTF developed a three-point plan, which concentrated on:

Restructuring a post-communist and post-paramilitary police force;
Reforming the police through training, selection, certification, and de-certification procedures;
Democratizing the police forces by establishing a de-politicized, impartial, accountable, multi-ethnic police force, that abides by the principles of community policing.

The Petersberg Declaration of April 1996 obligated the Federation to reduce its police personnel to 11,500 from the estimated 32,750 (29,750 in Bosniak areas/3,000 in Bosnian–Croat areas) police officers active in December 1995. Although this left a ratio of police officers to citizens nearly double the European standard, it nevertheless reduced their forces by almost two thirds. RS police remained unwilling to submit to the IPTF restructuring formula until late 1997, rejecting the IPTF limit of 6,000 policemen, and insisting on a force equal in strength to the Federation's.

The IPTF was an essential participant in persuading the Federation and the RS to restructure their forces. In April 1996, the IPTF Deputy Commissioner proposed the creation of a Commission on Restructuring in each entity for exchanging information about the restructuring process and gaining cooperation from the relevant authorities.

The agreement between the European Union and Bosnia and Herzegovina on the activities of the European Union Police Mission (EUPM) in Bosnia and Herzegovina was signed on October 4, 2002. The EUPM action is based on an agreement with the Bosnia and Herzegovina authorities, by which the local authorities have committed themselves to cooperating fully in pursuit of the EUPM objectives.

The European Union Police Mission will be the first civilan crisis management operation under the European Security and Defence Policy (ESDP). It will add an important component to other European programs, such as institution building and reconstruction, working towards achievement of the Union's overall policy in the region. The aspirations of Bosnia and Herzegovina to be integrated into the EU should be accompanied by a strong commitment of the Bosnia and Herzegovina authorities to support the accomplishment of the EUPM objectives.

The Mission will be conducted following the principle of intensive presence and co-location of international police and civilian experts alongside mid and senior level Bosnia and Herzegovina police officials in police institutions and Ministries, at State, Entity, Canton/PSC, and Brcko District level. The headquarters in Sarajevo will control and administer the mission.

The EU Police Mission will be an integral part and a key element of the OHR Rule of Law Pillar. It will be the lead agency in Bosnia and Herzegovina in all matters concerning law enforcement issues. The EUPM will be able to remove from office non-compliant officers, whose performance and behaviour do not fit the agreed standards, through a recommendation by the EUPM Head of Mission (HoM). The Police Commissioner to the High Representative in Bosnia and Herzegovina. EUPM, within the context of its mandate, will be responsible for assisting the development of Bosnia and Herzegovina police capacities in all aspects of law enforcement. The EUPM will monitor, mentor, and inspect Bosnia and Herzegovina police efforts to ensure that Bosnia and Herzegovina will be capable of investigating and countering the full range of criminal activities, including organised crime and terrorism with a State-level capability forming an effective part of the administration of justice. The establishment of EUPM has been widely welcomed by the international community. On February 28, 2002, the Steering Board of the Peace Implementation Council (PIC) accepted the offer made by the European Union to establish the EU Police Mission from January 1, 2003. The UN Security Council Resolution 1396 welcomed the PIC decision on March 5, 2002. On December 16, in a Presidential Statement, UN Security Council support for EUPM was reiterated.

At the moment, the EUPM is in the final stages of setting up the mission. The HQ is 70% staffed; virtually all the co-location teams have been fully deployed.

The Mission will be fully operational on January 1, 2003.

Organizational Description

On November 15, 1999, the three members of the Bosnia and Herzegovina Joint Presidency accepted the invitation of the United Nations Security Council to appear before it on the eve of the fourth anniversary of the Dayton Peace Accords. The Presidency agreed that the future of Bosnia and Herzegovina is as a part of Europe. They further agreed that this will require full integration into European institutions, and the creation of the type of strong, functioning common institutions found in other democratic, European countries.

The three Presidents agreed, among other issues, to the establishment of a State Border Service on the basis of certain principles and within the framework of the High Representative's efforts. This commitment by the Presidency to other agreed principles was released in a document called "The New York Declaration." Bosnia and Herzegovina's State Border Service (SBS) was officially inaugurated at Sarajevo airport on June 6, 2000 by the Special Representative of the Secretary-General, Jacques Paul Klein.

The State Border Service is a multi-ethnic institution, based on professional competence. Once the Border Service is complete, some 3,000 officers will control 1,660 kilometers of borders. As Mr. Klein said, the establishment of the Border Service is a crucial step in the fight against trafficking in women and cross-border trade in illegal goods. Without an effective border service, Bosnia and Herzegovina would also continue to be a major transit point for illegal immigration to Europe.

There are about 1,666 kilometers of border in Bosnia and Herzegovina, of which approximately 40% is "blue border," the trade name for the border when formed by a river or the sea. In Bosnia and Herzegovina, the rivers Una, Sava, and Drina make up the blue borders.

It is estimated that about 3,000 personnel would be required for an effective State Border Service. Additionally, a Training Centre staff, an Air-wing and a Boat or Marine Squadron will also be necessary for the service.

On June 20, 2002, the State Information and Protection Agency (SIPA) was established. It carries out a variety of different tasks related to crime prevention, protection of VIPs, as well as diplomatic and consulate offices and State buildings. The Agency is situated in Sarajevo. The Agency has 574 employees consisting of 60 administrative staff members; the rest of the employees are operational staff.

SIPA is organized in three departments, as follows:

1. Department for criminal information. This department is responsible for collecting and dispensing information being of great importance for legal enforcement of international and criminal laws in Bosnia and Herzegovina, including information related to drug production and trade, international and domestic terrorism, illegal trade of nuclear materials, illegal trade of biological-chemical weapons, internationally organized crime, and criminal acts liable to punishment according to international, war, and humanitarian law.

2. Department for protection of very important persons (VIP). This department safeguards the members of the President's administration, the Chairman of the Ministerial Council of Bosnia and Herzegovina, the Chairman of the House of Representatives of the Bosnia and Herzegovina Parliament Assembly, judges of the Constitutional Court of Bosnia and Herzegovina, the President of the Bosnia and Herzegovina Court, the Bosnia and Herzegovina Prosecutor, foreign officials visiting Bosnia and Herzegovina, and other individuals as ordered by the President.

3. Department for protection of diplomatic-consulate and state buildings. This department carries out physical security of property for the diplomatic-consulate mission and the buildings of Bosnia and Herzegovina.

The structure of the federation police forces consists of the federal Ministry of Interior and cantonal ministries of the interior. Each canton has its own Ministry of the Interior, due to the fact that the Bosnian and Herzegovinian Federation is composed of 10 cantons. The cantons are responsible for a range of tasks and duties. The Law on Internal Affairs for Bosnia and Herzegovina Federation determines internal affairs beyond the scope of the Bosnia and Herzegovina Federation authority, as well as other tasks related to cantonal internal matters. Internal affairs under the authority of Federation are as follows:

- Prevention and illumination of crimes and terrorist acts, illegal drugs trade, organized crime in intercantonal area, tracking and arresting perpetrators of committed crimes, and bringing them before competent bodies;
- Federation citizens' businesses;
- Protection of certain persons and buildings in Federation;
- Protection of human rights and civil freedoms in the area of internal affairs.

The Federal Ministry is in charge of law enforcement, and it advises the Federation Government and suggests appropriate measures to be taken in each case. The police force of Brcko District was established in 2000 on the initiative of the international community. The police force's main tasks are the protection of personal safety, law enforcement, the maintenance of public peace and order, the protection of property, the prevention of crime, the protection of certain persons and buildings, control over buying, possessing and carrying weapons and ammunition, traffic safety and road control, and control over transport, usage and storage of dangerous materials.

Functions

Police undertake measures and activities relative to:

- establishing the identity of individuals;
- giving warnings;
- summoning individuals in order to give information and warning;
- referring persons to the Investigative judge in cases anticipated by law;
- detaining persons;
- deprivation of freedom;
- use of other people's vehicle and communication means;
- restriction of movement in certain areas;
- entering people's homes and other premises;
- searching of the home and other rooms, vehicles, individuals and space;
- use of the means of force (use of physical force, use of special vehicles, trained dogs, rubber batons, horses, chemical means, placing obstacles, use of firearms);
- temporary seizure of items, documents, and files.

Training

There are two police academies (in Republika Srpska and in the Bosnia and Herzegovina Federation) for schooling of the future members of the police force. The Ministry of Interior announced an open competition for admission to the police academy. One training session in the police academy lasts twelve months, consisting of six months of theoretical teaching and six months of practical, on-site training in police stations.

Upon successful completion of the course, the candidate has fulfilled the conditions necessary to become a member of the police force.

Police Public Projects

The UN's IPTF mission had a mandate to conduct major multi-media publicity campaigns to alert the public to the resources available to victims of domestic violence, to expand awareness of the State Border Service, and to increase awareness of police responsibilities through the "Your Police Serving You" campaign.

Police Use of Firearms

Authorized police individuals during the performance of their tasks related to their work can use the firearms in the following situations: to protect others' lives, to protect their own life, to divert an attack on the person or building they are guarding, or to prevent the flight of persons who have committed a crime.

If there is a well-grounded condition for the use of firearms, a police officer must introduce himself or herself officially and give a clear warning that he or she is going to use firearms. The police officer is to give enough time for his warning to be enforced, unless there is a risk that his and other people's lives can receive serious threats and require an urgent action for protection of life. When firearms are used, a detailed explanation is required. The police officer must submit a report to his or her shift leader before the end of his or her shift, if he or she has used a firearm during that shift. A copy of each report is forwarded to the Department of Internal Control within 24 hours.

The acquisition, transport, and repair of firearms are carried out under the supervision of the Ministry of Interior. Firearms can be purchased only when approved by the Ministry of Interior, based on a legal act valid for six months from the issuing date. Ammunition can be supplied upon approval from the same body and only for the type of ammunition for which the weapon permit has already been issued.

Human Rights

During its mandate, the United Nations mission in Bosnia and Herzegovina carried out human rights and human dignity training for all members of the police forces.

From December 1995 to December 2002, the UN's IPTF during its mandate investigated or assisted with local investigations of over 13,000 cases of alleged human rights abuses by law enforcement personnel, of which 11,000 cases have been resolved.

Terrorism

According to the US Department of State, Bosnia and Herzegovina is one of only two countries in southeast Europe with known exsisting al-Qaeda networks (the other being Albania).

In the immediate aftermath of September 11, 2001, the Bosnian and Herzegovinian Ministers Council established a Coordinating Body for the monitoring of terrorism on the state level.

In early 2002, the US Federal Bureau of Investigation asked Bosnia and Herzegovina to immediately block bank accounts linked to the addresses Mula Mustafa Beseglije 72 and Young Muslims Road 30. The American investigators found strong evidence of connections between these addresses and al-Qaeda.

The American government has a black list of organizations that give financial support to terrorists. The organization named "Bosnian Ideal Future" came under suspicion and was added to this list. Its director, Munib Zahiragic, under the pressure of the American administration, was arrested.

International Cooperation

The United Nations brokered the Regional Cooperative Law Enforcement Arrangement (Croatia, Bosnia and Herzegovina, FRY-Serbia/Montenegro—and, as of 2002, Hungary) that established a Committee of Ministers and a Regional Task Force to combat on a regional basis organized crime, illegal migration, and, post-September 11 2001, international terrorism. The "Common Purpose" operation was established to combat organized crime and to monitor known/suspected terrorist groups. A national bureau of Interpol has been established in Sarajevo.

Police Education, Research, and Publications

The UN has administered compulsory basic training courses in Human Dignity, Transitional Training, Community Policing, and Traffic Awareness for every currently serving police officer and a Management course for Supervisors. Other specialized training courses included drug control, organized crime, crowd control, firearms, computers, and senior management. The UN trained more than 1,163 cadets, including 409 females, at the two police academies in Sarajevo and Banja

Luka, which the UN mission in Bosnia and Herzegovina helped establish. Also established, in close cooperation with SFOR, was a joint training program for specialized local police units in crowd control and major incident management. The service now has its own professional training center in Suhodol, near Sarajevo, which has conducted 42 specialization courses with 534 participants. Another 529 officers have undergone transition training. In April 2002, 50 cadets commenced training at Suhodol.

The US Justice Department's International Criminal Investigative Training and Assistance Program (ICITAP) was largely responsible for drawing up and distributing guidelines and standards for democratic policing. The doctrine of democratic policing includes: orientation to democratic principles, adherence to a code of conduct worthy of the public trust, protection of life, public service, a central focus on crimes against people and property, respect for human dignity, and non-discrimination.

Police Education and Publications

There are two institutions in Bosnia and Herzegovina for police higher education: The Faculty of Criminology Science in Sarajevo, and the Faculty for Internal Affairs in Banja Luka.

The leading police journals are *Securitas*, the journal of the Federal Ministry of Internal Affairs of the Federation of Bosnia and Herzegovina, and the journal *Dendology*, which is based in the Republic of Srpska.

Very little police-oriented research is currently being conducted and made readily available in Bosnia and Herzegovina.

Police-Related Websites

www.eupm.org
www.unmBosnia and Herzegovina.org
www.vladars.net
www.fmup.ba

VEJNOVIC DUSKO AND LALIĆ VELIBOR

Bibliography

"Agreement on International Police Task Force," Annex 11. *The Dayton Peace Accords General Framework Agreement for Peace in Bosnia and Herzegovina*. Paris, 14 December 1995.

Call, Charles T. "Institutional Learning Within ICITAP," in Robert Oakley, Michael Dziedzic and Elliot Goldberg (eds.), *Policing the New World Disorder: Peace Operations and Public Security*, Institute for National Strategic Studies, Washington: National Defence University Press, 1998.

Dziedzic, Michael, and Andrew Bair, op cit. p.285.

———. Human Rights Watch. "Politics and the Policing Agenda of the United Nations International Police Task Force." *Human Rights Watch Report*, June 1998.

———. Charles T. Call, op cit.

———. "Bosnia and Herzegovina Anti-Corruption Police Trained," *Oslobodjenje* (Sarajevo daily newspaper).

International Crisis Group. *Is Dayton Failing? Bosnia Four Years After The Peace Agreement*, op cit. p.47.

International Crisis Group. *Is Dayton Failing? Bosnia Four Years After The Peace Agreement*. ICG Balkans Report No 80, Sarajevo, 28 October 1999. 44.

———. Interview, Michael O'Rielly, op cit.

NATO, IFOR AFSOUTH Transcript, Sarajevo Coalition Press Information Centre, 30 May 1996.

"Total Of 15 RS Officers Trained In Great Britain." Onasa News Agency. 11 April 2000.

Training identified in Michael Dziedzic and Andrew Bair, *Bosnia and the* International Police Task Force, and in the International Crisis Group, *Is Dayton Failing? Bosnia Four Years After The Peace Agreement*, op cit.

Wilkinson, Tracy, and Dean Murphy. "Bosnia Foes Pull Back." *Los Angeles Times*, Home Edition. 20 January 1996:1.

———. International Crisis Group, "IPTF Report", op cit.

BOTSWANA

Background Material

Botswana is a republic in southern Africa with a total area of 581,730 square kilometres. The capital is Gaborone. Between the 1880s and its independence in 1966, Botswana was a neglected British protectorate known as Bechuanaland. For its first five years of political independence, with Seretse Khama as its first president (1966–1980), Botswana remained financially dependent on Britain to cover the full cost of administration and development. The planning and execution of economic development only took off in the early 1970s with the discovery of diamonds. Since independence, Botswana has been an extremely rare bird in Africa, namely a state that has been peaceful and prosperous. It has had one of the fastest growing economies in the world and is a fully functioning liberal democratic state, currently under the presidency of Festus Mogae (head of state since Sir Ketumile Masire retired as president in 1998).

Challenges facing the country centre primarily around intense inequality and the threat posed by AIDS. Less than 25% of Botswana's work force is formally employed. Indeed, Botswana has 47% of the population living below the poverty datum line and a GINI coefficient of 0.54. Countries whose GINI coefficients are 0.5 and above are considered to have high levels of income inequality. Few households produce enough crops to even cover their own subsistence, and four out of five rural households survive on the income of a family member in town or overseas. With regard to HIV/AIDS, Botswana has the world's highest adult prevalence (35.8%). At the purely economic level, both the production and the consumption levels of Botswana's economy are continually touched, having ramifications for future foreign direct investment and undermining confidence in making long-term investments in the country. One need only realise the extent of the pandemic in Botswana: if the US had a similar proportion of infections, there would be 50 million infected people. In Botswana, as many babies are infected in four days as are infected in one year in the United States.

Data from the 2001 population census suggest a population of 1.7 million people. As part of its self-proclaimed status as a "non-racial" republic, censuses in Botswana do not ask questions related to race or ethnicity, nor tribal status. Indeed, no attempt to count population by ethnic origin has been made since the only full ethnic national census in 1936, and the last racial national census in 1964. Any discussion of the population breakdown is thus conjecture. However, it is probable that probably less than half the population is "ethnic Tswana." The official language of Botswana is English, used for all government correspondence and as the medium of instruction from post-elementary primary education upwards. The national language, however, is Setswana, which is used in spoken communications to the public, and is also used (alongside English) in Parliament. Setswana is spoken or understood by most adult citizens, while English enjoys a very wide understanding, even with those with a basic education. Among home languages, Yeyi is the main language of the north-west, Kalanga of the north-east, Tswapong

of the far east, and Setswana of central and south-eastern Botswana. There are, however, about 34 languages in use in the country. The main religions in Botswana are indigenous African religions (65%) and Christianity (34%). There is a small number of Muslims, primarily immigrants from the Indian subcontinent.

Per capita income is around US$3,056 (compared to US$12 at independence), and this income is stable at 4.3% annual growth. Over the past three decades, Botswana's real per capita income grew by more than 7% per year, comparable to rates of growth achieved by the Asian Tigers. Agriculture provides a basic livelihood for more than 80% of the population but supplies only about 50% of Botswana's food needs and only 4% of its GDP. Diamond mining and tourism are highly important to the economy, and mining in particular has generated the growth rates enjoyed by Botswana in the last three decades. Indeed, since the early 1980s, the country has been the world's largest producer of gem diamonds. Three large diamond mines have opened since independence. The government has consistently maintained budget surpluses and has substantial foreign exchange reserves totalling about $7 billion.

Contextual Features

Botswana has a dual legal system, in which Roman Dutch law operates side by side with traditional customary law. The local systems of "tribal" law and custom operate in the rural districts, which rule everyday disputes and property relations but are subordinate to statutory law. The civil legal code of Botswana dates back to 1890, when the laws of the Cape Colony were adopted by the colonial state. The Cape code is Romano-Dutch, as modified by English common law. The civil code has itself been modified by cases and precedents since 1890, as well as by legislation.

Tswana customary law, as represented by the laws and precedents of the eight recognised "tribes," is also recognised in matters of property, inheritance, and personal dispute arbitration in rural areas. Most citizens encounter the legal system through the customary courts (dikgotla), under the authority of a traditional leader. These courts handle minor offences involving land, marital, and property disputes. In customary courts, the defendant does not have legal counsel, and there are no precise rules of evidence. Tribal judges, appointed by the tribal leader or elected by the community, determine sentences, which may be appealed through the civil court system.

The quality of decisions reached in the traditional courts varies considerably. In communities where chiefs and their decisions are respected, plaintiffs tend to take their cases to the customary court; otherwise, persons seek justice in the civil courts. The structure and role of courts in Botswana are composed of the Court of Appeal, the High Court, and the Magistrates' Courts. The Court of Appeal is a superior court of record, with jurisdiction in respect of criminal and civil cases emanating from the High Court. The Court of Appeal is broad-based, with judges drawn from the commonwealth countries (e.g. Ghana, Nigeria, South Africa, and the United Kingdom). Subordinate Courts are magistrates' courts, which vary in their grades and powers. There are five grades of magistrate: Chief Magistrate, Principal Magistrate, Senior Magistrate, Magistrate Grade I, and Magistrate II. All these courts have jurisdiction to try all offences except capital offences like murder and treason. Supervision of these courts is through appeals to the High Court and the making of monthly returns in criminal cases. The courts are empowered to pass sentences of corporal punishment.

If need be, cases can be heard at the High Court. The High Court is headed by the Chief Justice, appointed by the President. Some of the members of this court are Puisne Judges. These Judges are appointed by the President, in accordance with the advice of the Judicial Service Commission. The Court sits in Lobatse and Francistown. This court supervises proceedings of the magistrate court and is held in public and in English.

All appeals from final judgments of subordinate courts and from the customary court of appeal lie with the High Court. This also includes appeals from court martials and industrial courts. The High Court has unlimited jurisdiction, both in criminal and civil cases, and is also a superior court of record. It also has the power to decide any questions regarding the interpretation of the constitution. Capital punishment still exists, but the High Court has the discretion to pass, or not to pass, the death sentence, depending on the circumstances of the case. The President has the prerogative of mercy.

The Department of Prisons has its headquarters in Gaborone, although the system is somewhat decentralised, with two Divisional Offices—the dividing line being the Tropic of Capricorn. There are 21 prisons in Botswana, with a capacity of 3,198. However, over-crowding is a serious problem, with the current prison population standing at more than double the capacity. The government has started constructing two new prisons to bring capacity to over 4,000.

Rehabilitation programmes for prisoners were intensified in the early 1980s. The programmes include a variety of training projects, such as arable and dairy farming, poultry, bee-keeping, tailoring, welding, pottery and carpentry, to name but some. There are also education programmes. Recently, a parliamentary bill was passed that allows the Prison Commissioner authority to release terminally ill prisoners and prisoners in the last 12 months of their sentences. The Prisons Act provides for a governmental visiting committee for each prison, the members of which are appointed by the Minister of Labour and Home Affairs. Members of these committees serve one-year terms and visit their prison four times within their first term and issue a report both to the Commissioner of Prisons and the Ministry of Labour and Home Affairs. The Prisons Act grants relatives, lawyers, magistrates, and church organisations the right to visit prisoners for "rehabilitative purposes."

The main crimes in Botswana are as follows:

Offence	1999	2000
Murder and attempted murder	219	222
Rape and attempted rape	1,345	1,383
Store breaking and theft	3,482	4,158
Defilement of girls under 16	143	184
Road traffic offences	87,433	93,809
Common nuisance	2,247	2,360
Motor vehicle theft	3,462	4,223
Affiliation Procedure Act	1,394	1,950
Immigration Act	4,169	4,545
Housebreaking and theft	4,623	5,328
Burglary and theft	3,259	3,835

Of those people summoned and convicted for crimes committed, 15,181 were adult males, 3,099 adult females, 400 juvenile males, and 44 were juvenile females. During the last year, two males and one female were sentenced to death.

Police Profile

Background

Before 1884, law was enforced on a traditional, "tribal" basis. However, with the advent of settler expansionism northwards from the Cape Colony, the Bechuanaland Field Force (BFF) was established as an *ad hoc* company of men to protect the White settlers on their way to the north. On May 21, 1884, the territory of Bechuanaland was declared a British Protectorate. As a result, in 1885 The Bechuanaland Border Police (BBP) was formed, absorbing the BFF, as well as a small force known as the Bechuanaland Mounted Police. Made up of one hundred Whites, the BBP was established with its headquarters in Making (in South Africa) and with outposts at Fort Gaberone's (now Gaborone) and Fort Elebe in the north. The first commander of the BBP was Colonel Carrington. Prime duties included protecting the local population from cattle rustling by renegade Boers. The BBP, known as the Blue Blooded Police due to the high ratio of British aristocrats in its ranks, was a mounted infantry unit and was used to guard the rearguard bases in the gradual occupation of what is now western Zimbabwe. Indeed, elements of the police from Bechuanaland played a role in the opening up of Rhodesia to European settlement in the First Matabele War.

The eastern part of the Protectorate was transferred to the British South Africa Company in 1895, and most of the men of the BBP were transferred to the British South Africa Company Police. The BBP itself was disbanded. The name of the force changed to the British South Africa Police (BSAP) in 1898, policing Southern Rhodesia and eastern Bechuanaland, with the police in Bechuanaland being designated Division Number One. Interestingly, most of Bechuanaland's junior administrative officers were not entirely subject to the authority of the British Resident Commissioner, as they were officers in the BSAP. Even the capital of the territory was not inside the Protectorate but in Making in South Africa, as it was the temporary local police headquarters in expectation of the transfer of the Protectorate's administration to Salisbury in Southern Rhodesia.

The Bechuanaland Protectorate Police (BPP) was itself formed in 1902 by amalgamating the Bechuanaland section of the BSAP (Division One) with the Native Police. This new force remained officered by whites who had been in the BSAP. The force remained quasi-military in nature and played an important role in defending the British territory from Boer incursions during the Anglo-Boer War (1899–1902). It should be noted that a substantial number of the men involved in the ill-fated Jameson Raid of 1895, which helped stimulate the Boer War, were former BBP officers and troopers, and the raid itself was launched from Bechuanaland.

In 1923, two branches of the BPP were established: one for Africans, and one for Europeans. Military ranks were reserved for the Whites. African policemen (recruited mostly from Basutoland—now Lesotho) did not have the power of arrest, and a

tribal police known as *barongwa ba kgosi* ("messengers of the chief") were left to patrol tribal reserves. The BPP itself by this time was mostly involved in border patrols and guarding traders and government officials. An African Police Reserve was formed to patrol disease cordon fences within the country.

The BPP was reorganised in 1934 by Colonel Godley, who advocated a smaller force to act as a stopgap until help arrived from the police in Rhodesia. This reorganisation saw the number of police posts throughout the country rise from the six that existed in 1923 to 23. "Godley" reforms also led to the creation of the Police Mobile Unit in 1936, which was used to quell civil disturbances and might be seen as a precursor to today's Special Support Group. The BPP's officer ranks remained staffed by Whites (mostly British or Rhodesian), and local Africans could only be constables or troopers. This was to change after the Second World War, when Deputy Commandant Masterman pushed through a programme to replace subordinate white personnel with local African staff. This meant that in 1948, the rank of European Trooper was abolished. The command of the African Branch of the BPP was also changed to permit Africans to obtain high command. Motor vehicles were introduced to supplement the traditional camel patrols (an interesting form of transport still used by the police in some remote desert outposts in Botswana), and military ranks were finally discarded in favour of standard police ranking. Promotion became open to all, although the officers remained largely white. Indeed, it was not until 1971 that a local African became Commissioner of the now newly named Botswana Police after independence as the Republic of Botswana in 1966. The headquarters of the police was moved from Making to Gaborone in 1965 in preparation for independence, which saw the newly named Botswana Police constituted with a strength of six hundred men. Today, the Botswana Police has nearly six thousand personnel (see below) and is headed by the Commissioner of Police, who comes under the supervision of the Office of the President.

A development of note after independence was the formation of the Botswana Defence Force in 1977. Until then, Botswana had no army and relied on the Botswana Police for both internal and external security. However, in the late 1970s Botswana was attacked on a number of occasions by Rhodesian forces, intent on nullifying the presence of Zimbabwean guerrillas and supporters on their western border. As a result of such provocation, the Botswana Defence Force (BDF) was created in 1977, recruiting its members initially from the Botswana Police. The

BDF's first commander was Major-General Mompati Merafe. The BDF often works alongside the police, particularly in investigating poaching.

Demographics

No figures exist for the ethnic breakdown of the Botswana Police, nor do the police provide figures based on gender. However, as noted below, more females are currently joining the service than are men. The Botswana Police operates with three divisions, 14 districts, and 74 police stations. In addition to these divisions, the service also operates a number of specialised branches, namely: Security Intelligence, Criminal Investigation Department (CID), Special Support Group, Departmental Management Services, the Police Training College, Transport and Telecommunications Branch, Traffic Division, and the Performance Improvement Co-ordination Unit.

Organizational Description

As of December 2000, the Botswana Police had a strength of 5,903 personnel, making it actually under-strength according to the official establishment figures:

In 2000, 391 civilians worked for the Botswana Police. These were personnel performing the following duties: cooks, kitchen hands, office cleaners, groundsmen, herdsmen, pumpers, and a camel trainer.

Functions

The Criminal Investigation Department (CID) has a number of specialised units within its structure. The Criminal Record Bureau provides support to other units in the Police and other government departments with fingerprint classifications and identifications. Fingerprinting is done for the purpose of criminal identification, immigration enquiries, security employment purposes, and scenes of crime. The Diamond and Narcotic Squad within the CID investigates cases related to precious and semi-precious stones, drugs, and ivory smuggling. It also facilitates the movement of diamonds from the mines to the central selling point. In the last year, the Squad dealt with 359 cases of cannabis possession, totalling 844 kilograms. Of those caught, the vast majority were local citizens, while Zimbabweans, South Africans and Zambians made up the bulk of the rest. There was only one case of cocaine smuggling, a packet of 508 grams posted to a local citizen from Germany and intercepted by the Police.

The Serious Crime Squad is charged with the investigation of motor thefts, fraud, crime intelligence, bank surveillance and clearance of motor vehicles for import/export purposes. The Motor Vehicle Theft Section dealt with 498 stolen vehicles in 2000. The vast majority of these cars were stolen in South Africa and in transit, usually to Zambia and other countries further afield. The Crime Intelligence Section has not yet been fully established and is thus not operational at present. However, trials have been conducted which have contributed to the breaking up of vehicle theft syndicates. Similarly, the Bank Surveillance Section is in its embryonic stage.

Botswana has recently been experiencing a rise in fraud cases, and the Fraud Section deals with these. Most fraud relates to misuse of credit cards as well as computer fraud and the use of the internet for criminal activities. False passports and identification documents have also been uncovered, usually to facilitate illegal immigration from other African countries. Having said that, the promulgation of Corruption and Economic Crime Act in 1994, which created new offences of corruption, including being in control of disproportionate assets or maintaining an unexplained high standard of living, has lifted the burden of investigating corruption from the police. To deal with these offences, a new body, the Directorate on Corruption and Economic Crime (DCEC), was created and given special powers of investigation, arrest, search and seizure. The DCEC has its headquarters in Gaborone and an office in Francistown, and it is staffed by over 100 officers. Now, only low-level cases of corruption are investigated by the police, the bulk being referred to the DCEC.

Rank	Establishment	Strength	Vacancies
Commissioner	1	1	
Deputy Commissioner	2	2	
Senior Asst Commissioner	9	7	2
Assistant Commissioner	9	9	
Senior Superintendent	60	54	6
Superintendent	157	138	19
Assistant Superintendent	269	226	43
Inspector	434	412	22
Sub Inspector	566	569	3
Sergeant	1,052	1,019	33
Constable	3,754	3,447	307
TOTAL	6,294	5,903	391

Training

Recruitment into the Police requires a secondary school certificate, citizenship of Botswana, and one must be between 18 and 30 years of age. In the last year for which data exist, 404 recruit constables and 21 cadet officers were trained. Of these, 213 were female recruit constables, and eight were female cadets. The government has built a police instruction college in Otse, south-west of Gaborone, to improve the training and instruction of new recruits, as well as providing further education for existing officers.

Police Use of Firearms

The Central Arms Registry maintains records of registered firearms and administers the Arms and Ammunitions Act. In 2000, there were 30,622 registered firearms in the country. The vast majority were owned by farmers for the control of vermin and for slaughtering purposes. The use of armed weapons for criminal purposes in Botswana is uncommon, and there is no "gun culture" in the country—unlike in South Africa. The police remain unarmed except for special units, although the Police Act allows for the Botswana Police to use guns for military purposes if required to do so.

The Special Support Group (SSG) is the unit within the Botswana Police that is armed at times. It was founded in 1978 and provides support to other police units, usually operating mobile patrols and road blocks as well as providing presidential escorts and the escorting of precious minerals (mostly diamonds) from the mines to the central selling point. It is the SSG that carries out border patrols. The SSG is a paramilitary unit and has a strength of approximately 200 men. They have received training from various nations, primarily South Africa. It is also the SSG that represses internal disturbances (such as student demonstrations if they get out of hand), and the unit has been criticised for its over-enthusiasm in quelling disturbances. The unit is not shy to use force and has been involved in some controversial incidents where people have been shot. Recently, the SSG was criticised by the Zimbabwean media for roughing up Zimbabwean migrants in Botswana.

Human Rights

The government of Botswana generally respects the human rights of its citizens, although the treatment of the country's indigenous inhabitants, the Basarwa ("bushmen") is a matter of concern. There have been allegations that the police sometimes beat or otherwise mistreat criminal suspects in order to obtain evidence or coerce confessions. The authorities have taken action in some cases against officials responsible for such abuses. The Constitution prohibits arbitrary arrest and detention, and the Government generally respects these prohibitions.

Suspects must be informed by the police of their legal rights upon arrest, including the right to remain silent, to be allowed to contact a person of their choice, and generally to be charged before a magistrate within 48 hours. A magistrate may order a suspect held for 14 days through a writ of detention, which may be renewed 14 days. Most citizens charged with non-capital offences are released on their own recognisance; some are released with minimal bail. Detention without bail is highly unusual, except in murder cases, where it is mandated. Detainees have the right to hire legal counsel of their choice, but in practice most are unable to do this. However, poor police training and poor communications in rural villages make it difficult for detainees to obtain legal assistance, and authorities do not always follow judicial safeguards. The Government does not provide counsel for the indigent, except in capital cases. The BCHR provides free legal services, but its capacity is limited. Another NGO, the University of Botswana Legal Assistance Centre, provides free legal services in civil, but not criminal, matters. Constitutional protections are not applied to illegal immigrants, although the constitutionality of denying them due process has not been tested in court.

International Cooperation

Botswana is a member of the Association of Chiefs of Police (IACP) and is a member of Interpol. The Botswana Police enjoy particularly close bilateral links with the police in South Africa, Zambia and Zimbabwe. Meetings with these forces are usually held under the auspices of regional Defence and Security Joint Commissions. The force is an active member of the Southern African Regional Police Chiefs Cooperation Organisation. Until this year, the Botswana Police employed an expatriate Police Advisor, seconded from the United Kingdom.

The Botswana Police regularly run joint operations with other forces. Of note recently was a joint operation with South Africa, which recovered thirty stolen cars, arrested 90 illegal immigrants, and impounded 21 taxes; a joint operation with Zimbabwe, which impounded 65 suspect vehicles; and an operation with Namibia, which uncovered 633 traffic offences, 109 illegal immigrants, and impounded 33 vehicles. The Botswana Police also are involved in ongoing cooperation concerning diamond smuggling.

Police Education, Research, and Publications

The Botswana Police educates its staff both internally (the college at Otse), at local institutions, and overseas. Internally, the various departments and wings within the force operate their own training courses. For instance, the CID ran courses on Crime Intelligence, Crime Investigation, Vehicle Investigation, etc. These courses run from between four and 16 weeks. Similarly, the Traffic and Driving Wing operates courses on Defensive Driving, Traffic Safety Management, Motor Cycling, etc. The main local institution used for training selected officers is the University of Botswana. Diplomas, honours degrees as well as masters degrees were being offered to individual officers in subjects as diverse as Research and Evaluation, Statistics, Electrical Engineering, and Law. The Botswana Accountancy College hosts a number of policemen taking courses in accountancy, while the Institute of Development Management, based in Gaborone, probably trains the most officers in total, with courses on Human Resources Management, HIV/AIDS Counselling, and Effective Written Communication. A few officers have been sent overseas for further training, mostly to do masters degrees in Criminology, although the United Kingdom runs an International Commanders Programme, which last year hosted 12 high-ranking officers from Botswana. Sweden also runs a Traffic Safety management programme, which taught 20 Botswana Police members.

The Botswana Police publishes a journal entitled *Botswana Police Magazine*. The editor is Superintendent Christopher Mbulawa, and the editorial offices are at: Botswana Police Public Relations Unit, Private Bag 0012, Gaborone, Botswana. The major police publication in Botswana is the *Botswana Annual Report of the Commissioner of the Botswana Police*, published once a year in English.

IAN TAYLOR

Bibliography

Botswana Police. *Annual Report of the Commissioner of the Botswana Police for the Year 2000*. Gaborone: Government Printer, 2001.

Dingake, Oagile. *Key Aspects of the Constitutional Law of Botswana*. Gaborone: Pula Press, 2000.

Masterman, J. *A Historical Sketch of the Bechuanaland Protectorate Police*. Mafeking: Government Printers, 1946.

Mpho, Maine. "The Role and Development of the Bechuanaland Protectorate Police Force, 1898-1966." BA dissertation, University of Botswana, 1989.

Obeng, Kenneth. *Botswana: Institutions of Democracy and Government*. Gaborone: Associated Printers, 2001.

Republic of Botswana. *Police Act*. Gaborone: Government Printers, 1979.

Republic of Botswana. *Corruption and Economic Crime Act, 1994*. Gaborone: Government Printers, 1994.

Republic of Botswana. *Botswana National Atlas*. Department of Surveys and Mapping, 2000.

Tlou, Thomas, and Alec Campbell. *History of Botswana*. Gaborone: Macmillan, 1997.

BRAZIL

Background Material

Brazil was discovered in 1500 and remained a colony of Portugal until its declaration of independence on September 7, 1822. It is situated in South America and has an area of 8,514,215.3 sq km, the largest country in the region, and 15,735 km of borders with Argentina, Uruguay, Paraguay, Bolivia, Peru, Colombia and Venezuela.

According to the last general census in 2000, the population is 169,799,160 people, of which 49.22% are men, and 50.78% are women; 81.25% live in urban areas, and 18.75% in rural areas. It is the most populated and the largest country in South America.

Brazil's only language is Portuguese, which, in spite of slight differences in regional accents, is understood in all parts of the country. Brazil is divided into five regions: south, southeast, center-west, northeast, and north. Some are very distinct from one another in terms of ethnic, cultural, topographical, and economic aspects. Politically, the country encompasses 26 states and the Federal District, which is where the Federal Administration sits, with a status of both State and Municipality. As part of these 27 federative units, there are 5,541 municipalities, of which 449 are in the Northern region, 1,792 in the Northeast region, 1,688 in the Southeast region, 1,189 in the South Region, and 463 in the Center-West Region.

According to the Federal Constitution passed on October 5, 1988, each state shall have its own State Constitution and Governor, with an autonomy which, due to its status as a Federation, is relative, since they are limited to issues allowed by the Federal Constitution, which prohibits the States from having their own criminal and criminal procedural laws, except in first jurisdiction, after specifically authorized by the National Congress.

Brazil is a country formed by several races. No records exist of any open racial conflicts. Federal laws prohibit racial and religious discrimination of any kind, setting tough prison sentences for their violators. Nevertheless, discrimination against blacks and Indians does exist, especially in middle-class circles, which have triggered protests from anti-discrimination, non-governmental organizations. Among the 169,799,160 residents of Brazil, 91,298,042 declared to be White; 10,554,336 considered themselves black; 761,583 yellow; 65,318,092 mixed-races, and 734,127 proclaim to be Indian; another 1,206,675 did not answer the question made by the government in 2000.

In 2000, research was also conducted on the religion proclaimed by each respondent, and the conclusion was that 124,980,132 of the people were Catholics; 26,184,941 Evangelical; 2,262,401 Spiritualists; 525,013 claimed Afro-Brazilian religions; and 3,044,013 believe in other religions, among which are 1,104,886 Jehovah's Witnesses, 214,873 Buddhists, 86,825 Jews, and 27,239 Muslims. 12,492,403 declared not to have any religion.

Contextual Features

In 2002, the per capita income in Brazil was US $7,360.00. The United Nations Human Development Index (HDI) (2002) puts Brazil in 73rd place, among the 173 countries that were studied. Brazil has an economically active population of 78 million. The main economic activities are: wood and mineral exploration (in the North Region), agroindustry and tourism (in the Northeast Region), prospecting and livestock (in the Center-West Region), industry and services (in the Southeast Region), agribusiness and industry (in the South Region).

Brazil adopted the Civil Law legal system, based on the Portuguese legal experience, which was itself inspired by the Italian, French and German systems. Great importance is given to written laws, although the Brazilian legal system adopts as criteria for legal decisions precedents originating from the country's higher courts.

Brazil adopted a federal constitution in 1988, which provides the legal principles that guide the nation, among which are the separation of the branches of government—the Executive Branch (headed by the President of the Republic); the Federal, State and City Legislative Branch; the Judicial Branch; and the Department of Justice, which formally is an integral part of the Executive Branch, but not headed by the President, having full independence and autonomy. These three branches (plus the Department of Justice) are, as provided for in the Brazilian Constitution, "independent and harmonious among them."

The death penalty and life imprisonment sentences are barred by the Brazilian Constitution, and no judge may sentence someone to this type of punishment, except in cases when war has been declared.

Brazil has also a Penal Code and a Code of Criminal Procedure, both launched in 1940 and still in effect, having passed through numerous legal amendments so they could adjust to modern times. The country also has Special Criminal Laws that specify procedures for certain criminal acts. The laws are continually adapted to reflect current needs. For instance, in 2002 Law 10.409 altered the laws on drug trafficking crimes and possession for self use, implementing new procedures to reduce the action of traffickers. In 2003, Law 10.695 changed the penalties for copyright infringement, including the downloading of music from the internet and its subsequent illegal selling.

The Judicial Branch is made up of the Federal Supreme Court, with 11 Justices, the highest judicial organization; right below, the Superior Court of Justice; the Superior Labor Court (to hear labor cases); the Superior Military Court (for military cases); and the Electoral Superior Court (which functions only during election periods). They all sit in Brasilia, the Federal District.

This entry focuses on the State and Federal courts, which have sole jurisdiction over criminal matters.

State Courts exist in every state. They are made up of first jurisdiction judges and at least one Appeals Court, with the creation of a greater number being allowed should the workload justify. They decide more common cases, which involve private individuals and all types of crimes, except those that the Federal Constitution has determined to be handled by federal courts.

Federal courts are divided into five administrative regions. First jurisdiction federal judges sit only in the most populated and economically important cities in each state. For appeals, there are five Federal Courts, which have jurisdiction to decide appeals filed against decisions made by first jurisdiction judges under his/her competence. They judge all cases of federal interest and crimes provided for in the Federal Constitution as being of its attribution, such as: international drug trafficking, crimes included in international treaties ratified by Brazil, crimes against federal agents in the line of work, those of international interest, crimes on board aircrafts and vessels, money counterfeiting, federal tax evasion, crimes against the financial system, and money laundering, among others.

Small claims courts also exist in the federal sphere as well as in states, to which cases of a less significant economic value and lesser crimes are submitted, with penalties that include sentences of a maximum of two years of incarceration. Trials are speedier and settlements can be reached among the parties.

In Brazil, first instance judges are selected by a screening process. No elections exist for judges in the country. As a rule, the minimum age of 24 years of age is required and two years of professional experience as a practicing attorney. This results in Brazilian judges being very young in general. To have an idea, according to the Federal Judiciary Administration, the average age for a federal judge is 34 years. Selection tests are very tough, and candidates abound. When enrolling for the exams, the candidate chooses an area of law in which he intends to focus—whether a state, federal, military or labor judge.

Appeals judges are selected by promoting first jurisdiction judges, and a number of the seats in theses courts are reserved for long practicing lawyers with notable legal knowledge, and for public prosecutors under the same conditions, who will become second jurisdiction judges directly. A similar process takes place to fill seats in the Superior Courts.

In Brazil, magistrates have important guarantees, such as life-term appointment after two years of work (they cannot be dismissed until they retire, except when serious acts are committed and a judicial decision can prove the accusations).

The average income of a Brazilian judge is currently US$65,000,00 annually. There are around 14 thousand judges in Brazil, among all categories, which represents one state judge for every 26,854 inhabitants and one federal judge for every 147,826 inhabitants.

Members of the Department of Justice have similar guarantees and wages. The form of recruiting is also the same. As with judges, public prosecutors are divided into state, federal, labor and military and practice only in the area of their choosing. They formulate indictments and follow up on police investigation.

The punishments for crimes committed in Brazil vary from a simple fine or obligation to perform public service in social work entities to 30 years of incarceration. The longest punishment provided for in the Brazilian penal system is for the crime of kidnapping followed by death and varies between 24 and 30 years in prison. The punishment for drug trafficking varies from three to 25 years in prison, without the right to any benefit, since it is considered a heinous crime as provided for by Law 8.072 of 1990, together with kidnapping, first-degree murder, torture, genocide, rape, counterfeiting prescription medication and terrorism. The minimum age limit to be tried for a crime is 18 years of age. Under this age limit, the criminal is sent to a reformatory by a legal order for the maximum term of three years.

The Brazilian prison system holds currently about 285 thousand inmates. In the last few years, a substantial increase in the prison population has taken place in the country as a consequence mainly of the increase in the number of convictions by judges and intensified law enforcement work. As an illustration, in 1995 the country had 95 thousand people in prison. In the state of Sao Paulo alone 1,500 new convictions are added every month. In 2003, the state will spend in excess of US$71,000,000,00 to maintain the prisons in the country. Brazil has 46,514 guards to handle inmates in the prisons. In general, prisons are state run; however, in some states, such as Parana, some were recently built and transferred to the private sector, which manages them and is paid a monthly remuneration which varies State by the State (on average US$400.00 per inmate). For this reason, a significant shortage exists which, in many cases, causes the system to house a greater number of prisoners than the recommended numbers in each prison, falling below the internationally required standards and reducing inmates' rights.

The following data are made available by the National Prison Department:

No federal prisons exist in Brazil, although their implementation has been considered. Thus, those convicted by the Federal Courts are sent to state-run prisons. The federal administration implemented a program to build maximum-security federal prisons in some states. Those convicted by Federal

Courts (as well as tougher criminals such as more complex and violent crime organization leaders

Prisional Establishments Statistics:

Quantity:

Total number of establishments	1,431

Inmates per 100,000 inhabitants:

Population	Total
Brazil's population	169,799,170
Prison population	284,989
Brazil's population	169,799,170
Inmates p/100,000 inhab.	168

Shortage of cell vacancies:

Data Brazil	Total
Vacancies available	180,726
Prison population	284,989
Deficit (Brazil)	104,263

Prison population statistics:

Prisoners by sex	Total
Men	272,462
Women	12,527
Brazil's population	169,799,170
Total prisoners	284,989

that have become commonplace in the last few years) will be sent to these facilities.

The largest crime incidences in Brazil are reported in a study conducted in 2000 by the National Secretary for Public Safety.

For each group of 100,000 inhabitants

1. Theft (excluding vehicle theft): Average/ Brazil: 774.19 (per 100,000 vehicles)
2. Vehicle Theft: Average/Brazil: 713.54 (per 100,000 vehicles)
3. Aggravated Vehicle Theft: Average/Brazil: 576.58 (per 100,000 vehicles)
4. Assault: Average/Brazil: 500.88
5. Theft (excluding vehicle theft and theft resulting in death of victim): Average/Brazil: 299.50
6. First Degree Murder: Average/Brazil: 23.52 (from these, 61.2% were committed with the use of a firearm)
7. Sexual Assault: Average/Brazil: 7.13
8. Theft with Death of Victim: Average/Brazil: 0.94
9. Ransom Kidnapping: Average/Brazil: 0.14

It is clear that crime is related to property, which is explained by the huge economic gaps that exist in Brazil between rich and poor, which leads to a high level of larceny and theft. Due to high crime rates, according to the Center for Crime Studies at the Federal University of Minas Gerais (2002), 84.3% of Brazilians do not feel safe when going out in large cities, and 77.7% adopt some type of measure to avoid being the victim of violence when leaving home. It is estimated that the annual economic losses resulting from the commission of crimes, direct or indirect—such as the decrease in the number of tourists, foreign investment and consumption, and workdays lost—run around 10% of the country's GDP.

Police Profile

Background and Demographics

Historically, the Brazilian police have been linked to the armed forces and to the ideological tendencies of the administration in power. According to information available in *Alerta Geral – violência, criminalidade e segurança pública no Brasil* (*General Alert—Violence, Crime and Public Safety in Brazil*, 2003), from the transition from a monarchy to a republic in 1889, the history of law enforcement is divided into several periods, reflecting the position adopted by police officers in fighting criminals in different times in history. Until 1893, the police were used as a military force, primarily to assist army brigades. From 1894 to 1930, the police were used in regional political struggles to fight local revolutionary movements. From 1930 to 1945, the police were used as an instrument to repress political opposition. From 1946 to 1964, the state police were strengthened, with intensified investment in arms to preserve each state's interests. The police were used primarily as an instrument of political repression from 1964 to 1985. Since 1985, the police have been primarily focused on combating the overall increase in crime.

Organizational Description and Functions

According to the Federal Constitution of 1988, law enforcement in the streets is performed countrywide by the so-called "military police," a state-run force whose structure varies from state to state. Brazil has 358,166 military police officers (211.3 for every 100,000 inhabitants), who are paid wages that can vary from US$2,950.00 to US$5,350.00 annually, depending on the state. These are the salaries for those named "soldiers," which is the initial position in their career, and increases are given as the police officer goes up in rank. Entrance is made by a public selection process in which it is required that the candidate complete at least middle school and pass a series of exams. A clear criminal record is also required. Training after selection lasts from 10 to 12 months, depending of the State. State troopers, responsible for patrolling state highways, are part of the Military Police.

The country also has a number of "civil" police forces, which are also state entities and perform their duties in police precincts. They are responsible for investigating and turning cases over to state prosecutors for indictments to be presented to state judges. Their members, according to the data available through the National Secretary for Public Safety, are 102,554; that is, 60.5 for every group of 100,000 inhabitants countrywide, and the initial pay, form of entrance, and training are similar to those of military police.

The Federal Police are charged with dealing with federal cases, investigating all crimes in which federal interest is involved and, subsequently, referring the case to federal prosecutors. According to 2003 numbers provided by the Federal Police itself, there are 7,403 federal police officers in action throughout Brazil, and annual salaries vary from US$19,310.20 (beginning officers) to US$43,376.73 (police chiefs). These officers have to have a college degree and, after passing intellectual and psychological exams, are submitted to a training program, which varies from four to eight months at the National Police Academy in Brasilia, Federal District, provided they do not have a police record.

Brazil also has a federal Highway Police Department, responsible for patrolling the country's federal highways, repressing crime, and guiding traffic in these locations. Currently, 7,300 police troopers are in action, with an annual beginning pay of US $17,017 for all troopers. The selection process follows the same standards as for the other police carriers. It is required that future officers have completed middle school at a minimum.

Brazil does not have a municipal police force. There is, however, the so-called Municipal Guards, whose duties are to provide security in schools, public buildings and parks, and to direct traffic. There are 60,000 municipal guards in the country, and their wages are around US$3,100.00 annually.

The organization of police forces varies from state to state. Military police forces adopt a structure similar to that maintained by the army, having ranks such as soldiers, lieutenants, sergeants, captains, majors and colonels. For the last four ranks,

a four-year program at the Police Academy is required. Salaries are substantially higher than those of lower-rank officers and, in the majority of the states, salaries of the last two ranks are close to that of state prosecutors. They command the police organization, planning actions and determining how they are executed by police officers on the beat. The duty of the police force is basically to maintain order in society and to take preventive action. It is the police force in uniform. When a crime takes place, and after the suspect has been detained, he/she is taken to a civil or federal police station, depending on whether the crime is of state or federal interest. Subsequently, they go back to the streets.

Civil police forces in each state are made up of investigators and police chiefs, who act as supervisors.

The federal police have a similar structure. Federal police officers are generally recognized for their efficiency and capability in quickly resolving cases that are referred to them. Therefore, they are often called upon to investigate complex cases, even at the state level, by specific order of the Minister of Justice.

These two police forces are called judiciary police forces, since they work closely with public prosecutors in order to find evidence against suspects and later present them to judges. The existing procedure for this is called a "police inquiry." Police officers must conduct investigations as specifically dictated by law. At the conclusion of an investigation, summarizing documents are sent to the Ministry Justice. There is a series of formalities that must always be followed by police officers during the course of an investigation and, without them, the investigation is not accepted by a judge.

Highway patrol forces perform their duties on the highways, and, when a crime comes to their attention on these roads, they detain the suspects and send them to a federal or civil (state) police station, depending on whether it is federal or state jurisdiction respectively.

Training

Training of law enforcement officers is provided by police academies. Curriculum has always varied according to the historical climate in the country. Thus, in authoritarian periods it was centered on political and military issues, focusing on guerrilla groups and opposition to the regime in power at the time. Currently, and since Brazil abandoned a totalitarian military regime in 1985, it has been investing in improving the teaching of law enforcement techniques, of cordiality and support to citizens, who are seen as a police officers' partners and not as potential enemies to national security, as was previously the case. In addition, notions of human rights are also being introduced in police academy curricula throughout the country in order to drastically reduce police violence which, unfortunately, still exists in certain places, certainly fruit of a misguided culture ever present since the middle of the twentieth century that good police officers show force and raise fear in their fellow citizens by their potential for violence.

Internal and external mechanisms exist to control Brazilian police forces, and to prevent and punish abuses eventually committed by law enforcement in the exercise of their duties. The internal mechanisms are the Internal Affairs Divisions, which are an integral part of the force itself. These internal entities conduct the investigation of reports of corruption, assault and battery, tortures, and other reported improper behavior, by victims as well as citizens, in many instances by anonymous telephone calls. In this respect, the federal administration implemented the "dial-torture" program, consisting of a free call line for abuses committed by any police officer anywhere where they are reported in the country. Externally, since the federal Constitution was implemented in 1988, public prosecutors have been placed in charge of controlling police work, overseeing actions of police forces and preventing abuses in law enforcement. Undoubtedly, it is a device that needs to be perfected so that it can solidify as quickly as possible due to its relevance.

Police Use of Firearms

The weapons most commonly used by the police forces are the 38-caliber revolver, the 9 mm machine gun, the 40-caliber pistol, the 30-caliber riffle, and the 7.62-caliber shotgun. However, this varies from state to state and also depends upon the police force in question, since elite groups, for example, may use more sophisticated weapons for special actions.

Terrorism and International Cooperation

There is no evidence of the formation of any known terrorist cells in Brazil. However, the activities of some domestic crime organizations such as the "Red Command," the "Third Command," and the "First Command of the Capital," pose challenges to the Brazilian police community. These organizations engage in drugs and arms trafficking, extortion, money laundering, and theft.

International police cooperation has been increasingly strengthened through the promotion of workshops bringing together police organizations from other countries and sending Brazilian law enforcement officers to conduct improvement courses in other countries. Cooperation is more evolved in relation to the other countries of South America, the United States, Germany, and Australia.

In terms of improvement, it is important to note that valuing police work in Brazil is very recent and started to improve after the implementation of the Federal Constitution of 1988, where a program of increase in police pay was started, especially the Federal Police and high rank positions within state police, reequipping and professional training. However, the country is resentful of years of lack of investment in improving police work and, without a doubt, it will still take decades so that new investigation methods, based on the respect for human rights and investment in technology and intelligence, be actually understood as being crucial for police officers and for society itself so that one can confront criminals effectively. In 2000, the Minister of Justice implemented the National Secretary for Public Safety, who coordinates all actions in Brazil related to public security involving state as well as federal law enforcement agencies, in addition to heads of the correctional system with the aim of integrating all law enforcement agencies in the country, and thus, to modernize them and fight crime more efficiently. For this purpose, the Secretary had available in 2003 a budget of US$ 131,000,000, complementing budgets of each one of the States. A detailed National Public Security Plan was also prepared, and in 2003 the Unified Public Security System began to be implemented by means of which police action in Brazil will be unified, lessening regional differences. Formally, all States in Union have joined this system, and the implementation phase is underway. After its conclusion, the country intends to have a police that is better equipped and trained, using standard procedures in all states.

Police Education, Research, and Publication

Publications involving law enforcement issues in Brazil originate in Police Academy classrooms and workshops promoted by police forces. Such publications are generally produced by official law enforcement agencies, with some university research centers dedicated to the issue and private organizations having a significant role as well.

The following are notable law enforcement research, teaching, and statistics organizations:

Center for Crime Studies and Public Safety, Federal University of Minas Gerais *www.est. ufmg.br*

Brazilian Institute for Crime Sciences *www. ibccrim.org.br*

Laboratory for Studies on Violence *www.cfh. ufsc.br/~raiva/raiva.html*

Boletim Conjuntura Criminal *www. conjunturacriminal.com.br*

São Paulo Foundation Against Violence *www. spcv.org.br/info/brasil.htm*

Center for Studies on Violence at the University of Sao Paulo *www.nev.prp.usp.br*

Department of Political Science at the University of Sao Paulo *www.fflch.usp.br/dcp*

The following is a list of police departments and other law enforcement agencies:

Ministry of Justice of Brazil – National Secretary for Public Safety *www.mj.gov.br/senasp*

Civil and Military Police in Brazil *www.mj.gov. br/senasp/senasp/inst_sspestados.htm*

Federal Police Department *www.dpf.gov.br*

Federal Highway Patrol Department *www.dprf. gov.br*

MARCOS JOSEGREI DA SILVA

Bibliography

Amorim, Milra de Lucena Machado, Lucinda Siqueira Chaves Freire, e Yana Palankof, eds. *A atuação da Justiça Federal na esfera criminal.* Conselho da Justiça Federal, Centro de Estudos Judiciários, Secretaria de Pesquisa e Documentação. Brasília: CJF, 2000.

Athias, Gabriela. "Planalto quer fortalecer guarda municipal." *Jornal Folha de São Paulo*, de 9 de novembro de 2003. C1.

Barros, Ricardo Paes de, Ricardo Henriques, e Rosane Mendonça. *A Estabilidade Inaceitável: Desigualdade e Pobreza no Brasil.* São Paulo: IPEA, 2001.

BRASIL. "Instituto Brasileiro de Geografia e Estatística." www.ibge.gov.br (9 Nov., 2003).

———. "Secretaria Nacional de Segurança Pública." www.mj.gov.br/senasp (9 Nov., 2003).

———. "Secretaria Nacional de Segurança Pública." Criminalidade no Brasil: diagnósticos e custos. [Paper presented at the Câmara dos Deputados Federais. 2003, Brasília, available www.camara.gov.br/internet/Eventos/Sem_Conf_Realizados/2003/pdf/Custos/Criminalidade_MinisterioJustica.pdf].

Gomes, Paulo Tarso de Oliveira. "Crime Organizado e Lavagem de Dinheiro." [Paper presented at the Escola da Magistratura Federal do Paraná. March 2003, Curitiba.].

Mendroni, Marcelo Batlouni. *Crime Organizado: Aspectos Gerais e Mecanismos Legais.* São Paulo: Editora Juarez de Oliveira, 2002.

———. *Curso de Investigação Criminal.* São Paulo: Editora Juarez de Oliveira, 2002.

Neto, Theodomiro Dias. *Policiamento Comunitário e Controle sobre a Polícia.* São Paulo: IBCCRIM, 2000.

Oliveira, Flávia, e Luciana Rodrigues. "Educação segura o Brasil." *Jornal O Globo*, de 8 de julho de 2003, Caderno de Economia.

Oliveira, Roberto da Silva. *Competência Criminal da Justiça Federal.* São Paulo: Editora Revista dos Tribunais, 2002.

Sadek, Maria Tereza. *O Ministério Público e a Justiça no Brasil.* São Paulo: Editora Saraiva, 1997.

———. *O sistema de Justiça.* São Paulo: IDESP, 1999.

———. *Delegados de Polícia.* São Paulo: IDESP, 2003.

Soares, Plácido. *Alerta Geral: Violência, Criminalidade e Segurança Pública no Brasil.* Curitiba: Livraria do Chain Editora, 2003.

BRUNEI DARUSSALAM

Background Material

Nageri Brunei Darussalam (Brunei), founded in 1363, is a small country in Southeast Asia, bordered by the South China Sea and the Malaysian State of Sarawak. Brunei is broken into four districts: Brunei-muara, Tutong, Belait, and Temburong. Now an independent country, Brunei was a British protectorate from 1888–1984. Brunei is a constitutional sultanate, ruled by a Sultan, who serves as the Prime Minister, Defense Minister, Finance Minister, and head of the religion of Brunei, as well as the ruler of the country. The same family has ruled Brunei since the fourteenth century.

Brunei has a total area of 5,770 sq km (land: 5,270 sq km, water: 500 sq km). The capital is Bandar Seri Begawan. The population is 365,251, comprised of Malay (67%), Chinese (15%), Indigenous (6%), and other ethnic groups (12%). The languages spoken are Malay (official), English, and

Chinese. Religions represented are Muslim (official, 67%), Buddhist (13%), Christian (10%), and Indigenous beliefs/other (10%). The per capita income is US$18,600, and major economic industries include crude oil, natural gas, and refined products.

Contextual Features

Brunei's government is an independent sultanate, based on a written Constitution. His Majesty The Sultan is the sole authoritarian figure in Brunei and also assumes the position of Prime Minister. His Majesty oversees four councils: (1) The Council of Cabinet Ministers, (2) The Council of Succession, (3) The Privy Council, and (4) The Religious Council. Each Council is responsible for specific tasks; His Majesty must approve all actions.

The Council of Cabinet Ministers is by far the largest and includes twelve different departments, each specializing in a specific area. The twelve offices are (1) The Prime Minister's office, (2) Ministry of Defense, (3) Ministry of Finance, (4) Ministry of Foreign Affairs, (5) Ministry of Home Affairs, (6) Ministry of Education, (7) Ministry of Industries and Primary Resources, (8) Ministry of Religious Affairs, (9) Ministry of Development, (10) Ministry of Culture, Youth and Sports, (11) Ministry of Health, and (12) Ministry of Communication.

The Council of Succession determines matters concerning succession to the throne. The council uses the constitution as well as the Regency Proclamation of 1959 to support their decisions. The Privy Council's main objective is to advise His Majesty in multiple areas, specifically concerning constitutional matters and issuance of pardons. The Religious Council advises the Sultan (who also serves as head of the faith) in areas concerning the Islamic religion.

Violent criminal activity in Brunei is rare, although the amount of burglary/theft is rising. Individuals in violation of Brunei law may be subject to expulsion from the country, arrest, and/or imprisonment. There are very high penalties for illegal drug offenses. Brunei has a mandatory death penalty for possession of certain amounts of narcotics. Drug trafficking and importation of illegal drugs both carry a mandatory death sentence. Caning is used as punishment in nearly 80% of criminal convictions. Prostitution is illegal in Brunei, and women who move to Brunei for the purpose of prostitution are quickly deported.

There are two court systems in Brunei: a national system dealing with laws in the Constitution (consisting of three individual courts), and a system that is applied to Islamic law. The National system includes The Subordinate Court, the Intermediate Court, and the Supreme Court. The Subordinate Court is where most cases appear. The Intermediate Court (established in 1991) deals with more serious criminal and civil matters, but does not handle capital offenses. The Supreme Court, the highest court in Brunei, is composed of The High Court and the Court of Appeals. The Supreme Court not only handles appeals, but also tries cases which carry a capital sentences. The second court system, Syariah Courts, co-exists with the Supreme Court. This court is reserved strictly for matters dealing with Islamic law.

Since 1988, caning has been a mandatory punishment for 42 different criminal offenses. Caning occurs in the presence of a doctor, who can stop the punishment at any time, for medical reasons. Many criminals prefer caning to long terms of incarceration.

Prison sentences in Brunei are extremely long. Some minor drug possession charges are known to carry a minimum sentence of 21 years. There are no reported cases of police misconduct concerning prisoners. The prisons meet minimum international standards, and a new prison was finished in 1998, due to the increasing number of prisoners in Brunei. Overcrowding of prisons in not a problem in Brunei. Prisoners are entitled to visits from their family, and the families are allowed to bring food into the prison for the inmates.

Police Profile

Background

The Royal Brunei Police Force (RBPF) was established in 1921. In 1923, the duties of the RBPF were expanded to include fire services, prisons, immigration, issuance of licenses, vehicle registration, and alien registration. By 1951, the RBPF set up a training camp in Seria. In 1959, the Brunei Constitution required the Sultan (who serves as the Inspector General of Police) to have a Commissioner of Police for the Force. In 1967, a second training center was established in Jalan Aman, Berakas. In 1974, the Women Contingent was created. In 1984, the RBPF joined INTERPOL and ASEANAPOL.

Demographics

The Royal Brunei Police Force employs 3,297 individuals. Of these, 204 are civilian employees who work as gardeners, cleaners, technicians, and clerical staff. The remaining 3,093 are police personnel. Of the

3,093 officers, only 428 are female. All employees are required to be citizens of Brunei, and all applicants for the force are required to hold at least the Brunei Junior Certificate of Education (BJCE).

Organizational Description

At the head of the Royal Brunei Police Force is His Majesty the Sultan, who serves as the Inspector General of Police. Directly beneath him is the Commissioner of Police. Under the Commissioner is the Deputy Commissioner of Police. These individuals oversee five departments as well as the seven individual police districts.

The five departments of the RBPF include (1) Department of Administration and Finance, (2) Department of Operations, (3) Department of Criminal Investigation and Intelligence, (4) Department of Logistics, and (5) Department of Traffic Investigation and Control. Each department is responsible for different tasks to ensure the procedures of the Royal Brunei Police Force are properly carried out.

The Department of Administration and Finance handles personnel administration and the force's budget. The Department of Operation oversees the daily routines of the RBPF and coordinates all operations. The Department of Criminal Investigation and Intelligence advises and transmits information concerning criminal activities to the highest-ranking officials. The Department of Logistic undertakes the department's logistical requirements as well as provides technical support. The Department of Traffic Investigation and Control is responsible for investigating all cases concerning automobile accidents.

There are seven police districts within Brunei. The majority of officers enter the Royal Brunei Police force as a Rank and File Officer (also known as a Constable), who patrols the districts. For promotion to Inspectorate, His Majesty the Sultan must approve the promotion. The Commissioner of Police may make recommendations for promotion to Inspectorate of individuals within the force, or from direct entry (hired immediately as Inspectorate without prior experience in the RBPF). To be promoted to Assistant Superintendent of Police, all recommendations must come from the Commissioner and must be approved by the Sultan.

In 1993, the Royal Brunei Police Force added a Special Investigations Unit, headed by a superintendent. This unit handles cases concerning murder, suspicious death, armed robbery, and arson. Officers from this unit attended a Forensic Science Course taught by the FBI in Malaysia.

In 1997, a Woman and Child Abuse Unit was established to combat the rising abuse problems. A female assistant superintendent heads this unit. The Woman and Child Abuse Unit is also responsible for handling rape cases. Officers from this unit attended a Rape Investigation Course in Singapore in an effort to improve their personnel skills. This unit also plays a role in the prevention of prostitution in Brunei.

Functions

The objectives of the Royal Brunei Police Force include minimizing the number of law violations, and maximizing the detection and conviction of individuals in violation of Brunei law. The force is also prepared to restore public order, should disruptive incidents occur. They also run educational programs for the public, dealing with traffic rules and regulations. The force is also responsible for maintaining the resolutions adopted by the ASEANAPOL and INTERPOL conferences.

The force is responsible for all criminal investigation matters. This includes preparing an annual plan for crime prevention. The RBPF does not only deal with criminal matters; they also have administrative responsibilities. The force is responsible for preparation of their annual budget as well as reviewing policies and introducing amendments to the Police Regulations.

Training

The requirements for joining the police force vary slightly for males and females. The chart below breaks down the differences. The most important requirement is that all candidates must be mentally and physically able to perform as an officer in the RBPF.

Police Public Projects

The Police Force stresses the importance of involving the community to combat crime. They encourage individuals who witness criminal activities to report the transgressions. The force also holds traffic rules and regulations classes to educate the public about traffic safety. The Woman and Child Abuse unit, added in 1997, was specially designed to combat the unethical treatment of women and children in Brunei.

REQUIREMENT	MALE	FEMALE
Nationality	Brunei citizen	Brunei citizen
Age	18–28	18–25
Education	Brunei Junior Certification Of Education (BJCE)	Brunei Junior Certification Of Education (BJCE)
Height	Minimum 5 ft 3 in	Minimum 5 ft.
Weight	49.8 kg (110 lbs.)	47.6 kg (105 lbs.)
Marital Status	Single or Married	Single

Police Use of Firearms

It is written into law that the RBPF may use force, including lethal weapons, in circumstances in which the officer feels there is no other way to stop an individual who has committed a criminal act. The officer may also use firearms to overcome resistance presented by an individual, to prevent escape, or to disburse an unlawful group.

Complaints and Discipline

Although freedom of speech is guaranteed in the Brunei Constitution, it is the custom that individuals do not openly speak out against the government. Due to this, complaints against the RBPF are rare. The prisons in Brunei meet international standards and thus are approved of by International Human Rights Groups.

Terrorism

There are no known terrorist organizations functioning in Brunei, and no terrorist acts have been committed in Brunei. Brunei has signed a treaty with Malaysia, Singapore, and Indonesia to combat the possibility of terrorist cells crossing the countries' borders.

There is some concern that the terrorism group Jemaah Islamiyah (JI) may have the capabilities to carry out terrorist acts in Southeast Asian nations, including Brunei. JI is known to have connections with al-Qaeda and may have active cells in parts of Southeast Asia. There have been no warnings of attacks, but the government is monitoring the situation to be prepared in the event of a terrorist attack.

International Cooperation

Although there is not an exchange of officers between Brunei and any other country, Brunei maintains good relations with other countries. Brunei is a member of INTERPOL (International Criminal Police Organization) and ASEANAPOL (Association of South-East Asian Nations Police).

Brunei is home to 23 international embassies and has 30 embassies abroad.

Police Education, Research, and Publications

All applicants of the Royal Brunei Police Force must possess a Junior Certificate of Education. Higher Education degrees are either obtained at the University of Brunei or abroad.

Most of the research conducted by the police force occurs inside the organization. Research is funded from inside the country. Special groups are assembled to conduct the research. These groups include the Criminal Intelligence and Research Unit, Gambling Suppression and Anti-Vice Unit, and the Major Crime Unit.

The Government Gazette is published, printed, and sold by the government of Brunei. The information included is by discretion of the Sultan and may include notice of amendments to any act, new governmental appointments, and new statutes. The Government Gazette can be purchased for an annual fee or in single issues. The Government Gazette can be obtained from:

The Director of Printing
Government Printing Department
Bandar Seri Begawan BB3510 Brunei
  Darussalam

Extensive information concerning Brunei and the Royal Brunei Police Force can be found at *www.police.gov.bn*.

AMANDA MARIE SHARP

Bibliography

CIA World Factbook. *Brunei*. Retrieved December 7, 2004, from www.cia.gov.cia/publications.factbook/geos/bx/html.

Government of Brunei Darussalam official website. *Brunei Darussalam*. Retrieved December 7, 2004, from www.brunei.gov.bn/index.htm.

Government of Brunei Darussalam official website. *Royal Brunei Police Force*. Retrieved January 5, 2005, from www.police.gov.bn/.

Map Zones. *Brunei Darussalam*. Retrieved December 8, 2004, from http://kids.mapzones.com/world/brunei.

U.S. Department of State (2005). *Consular Information Sheet: Brunei*. Retrieved January 4, 2005, from http://travel.state.gov/travel/cis_pa_tw/cis/cis_1073.html.

U.S. Department of State (2001). *Country Reports on Human Rights Practices: Brunei*. Retrieved December 7, 2004, from www.state.gov/g/drl/rls/hrrpt/2000/eap/index.cfm?docid=675.

World Statesman. *Brunei Darussalam*. Retrieved December 8, 2004, from www.worldstatesmen.org/Brunei.html.

BULGARIA

Background Material

Bulgaria became a People's Republic in 1946. Communist domination ended in 1990, when Bulgaria held its first multiparty election since World War II and began moving toward democracy and a market economy. The country joined NATO in 2004.

Bulgaria is located in the south-east portion of Europe. It has boundaries with Serbia and the Former Yugoslav Republic of Macedonia to the west, Greece and Turkey to the south, and Romania to the north.

Bulgaria consists of a total area of 110,912 sq km, with a population of 7,517,973 (July, 2004 est.). The ethnic composition of the population is Bulgarian (83.9%), Turk (9.4%), Roma (4.7%), and other (2%) (including Macedonian, Armenian, Tatar, and Circassian). The religious composition of the population is Bulgarian Orthodox (82.6%), Muslim (12.2%), Roman Catholic (1.7%), Jewish (0.1%), Protestant, Gregorian-Armenian, and other (3.4%).

Bulgarian is the official language, although many ethnic groups also speak their own languages.

The capital of Bulgaria is Sofia.

The GDP per capita is US$7,600 (2003 est.).

Contextual Features

According to the Constitution which came into force on 13th July 1991, Bulgaria is a democratic republic with a clear separation of powers between the legislature, the executive, and the judiciary.

The legislative branch of the government is represented by a single-chamber national assembly, made up of 240 members. The National Assembly elects the Council of Ministers. The President and Vice-President are both elected by direct universal suffrage for five-year terms. The President nominates the Prime Minister. He is normally the leader of the party with the largest representation in the National Assembly.

Bulgaria is divided into nine regions and 273 municipalities. Each region is headed by a governor and each municipality by a mayor who is elected by the municipal council.

The personnel, organisational, and financial management of the judicial system are performed by the Supreme Judicial Council. This council consists of 25 members: 11 are elected by the Parliament; 11 magistrates are elected in a two-stage election procedure, with the chairmen of the supreme courts and the Chief Prosecutor as *ex officio* members. The Supreme Judicial Council manages the judicial system, but it has no authority to rule on the justice of particular cases.

Bulgaria has the following types of courts: regional courts, district courts, courts of appeal, Supreme Court of Appeal, and a Supreme Administrative Court.

The office of the prosecutor is structured to correspond with the structure of the courts, and it is composed of the following: chief prosecutor, chief prosecutor's office of appeal, chief administrative prosecutor's office, appellate prosecutors' offices, martial appellate prosecutors' offices, district prosecutors' offices, and regional prosecutors' offices.

More than 700,000 crimes were reported in Bulgaria between 1970 and 1990. The People's Militia reported an annual rate of 570 crimes per 100,000 people in 1989. Beginning in 1990, the incidence of crime increased sharply, however. Compared with the 15,000 crimes committed during 1989, the People's Militia received reports of more than 4,600 crimes in Sofia alone during the first six months of 1990. Approximately 70% of these crimes were committed by repeat offenders, and a very high percentage were petty crimes against property. By 1989, however, homicides had increased by 30%, burglaries by nearly 40%, and rapes by 45%. Organized crime was increasingly evident; more than ten criminal organizations reportedly operated in Sofia. They were involved in black-market activities and were reputed to have connections to organized crime in other countries.

Smuggling of drugs, arms, and other contraband was a persistent problem during and after the Zhivkov regime. The press noted cooperation between customs authorities and the United Nations (UN) Commission for Narcotics Control in efforts to curtail international drug trafficking. The UN supported these efforts by funding construction of modern border checkpoints in Bulgaria. The International Criminal Police Organization (Interpol) also certified that Bulgaria had a good record in international law enforcement. In Bulgaria the Directorate of Customs and Customs Control of the Ministry of Finance was responsible for preventing drug trafficking; however, the People's Militia and Border Troops also were active in the counter-narcotics effort.

Under the penal code inherited from the Zhivkov era, crimes against the socialist economy or socialist property generally were punished more severely than crimes against persons. Major economic crimes, misappropriation, and serious malfeasance were punished rigorously. Six-year prison terms were levied for crimes such as conducting private economic activity while representing a state enterprise and receiving economic benefits for work or services not rendered. Illegally crossing national borders was punishable by a fine of 3,000 *leva* and a five-year prison term, with heavier penalties for recidivists.

In the reform period, an increasing number of minor offenses were changed to receive administrative punishments such as fines up to 300 *leva*. These administrative proceedings represented rather arbitrary justice because the accused did not have the right to trial or legal counsel. The administrative proceedings were an expedient designed to alleviate a tremendous backlog of minor cases. Beginning in 1990, the dismantling of the state enterprise system called for shifting the emphasis of the criminal code from protection of state property to protection of the individual. This shift was attempted in the new constitution ratified by the National Assembly in July 1991.

Until 1990, the Ministry of Internal Affairs operated the penal system through its Central Prison Institutions Department and its Prison Service. The latter organization trained and administered prison guards. In 1990, the system included 13 prisons and 26 minimum-security facilities housing 6,600 prisoners. Major prisons were located in Bobov Dol, Pazardzhik, Plovdiv, Sofia, Stara Zagora, Varna, and Vratsa. In 1990, authorities reported that the total prison population had declined by 10,000 as a result of amnesties granted to political prisoners during the previous three years. The remaining prison population included a high percentage of repeat offenders and prisoners convicted of serious crimes. The institution at Pazardzhik reported more than 560 inmates, including more than 50 imprisoned for murder, 60 for rape, 140 for other crimes against persons, and the balance for crimes against property. Offenders guilty of less serious crimes served time in minimum-security facilities, including open and semiopen labor camps. Prison strikes and demonstrations began with the Zhivkov ouster, continuing and escalating through the first half of 1990. Sparked by the release of large numbers of political prisoners, massive strikes elsewhere, and the suddenly volatile sociopolitical climate, the strikes became violent, and several inmates reportedly immolated themselves to protest prison conditions. Red Berets were called upon to reinforce Prison Service guards. By 1991, Bulgaria had already implemented one stage of prison reform to improve its international human rights image: prisons were put under the Ministry of Justice instead of the Ministry of Internal Security.

Police Profile

The Ministry of Internal Affairs controlled the People's Militia (police) and the special militarized Internal Security Troops known as Red Berets. In response to public demands for reform, a new Independent Trade Union Organization of Militia Employees set forth reforms to improve the organization's public relations, which remained very poor in 1990. Declaring that membership in a party was incompatible with nonpartisan law enforcement, the union called for the depoliticization and professionalization of the militia. The force also sought to change its name from "militia" to "police." The Commission on National Security of the National Assembly supported this proposal, and the Ministry of Internal Affairs itself drafted a new law on the People's Militia for consideration by the National Assembly.

The People's Militia controlled several subordinate organizations, including the Territorial Militia, Road Militia, Commercial Militia, Central Investigations Department, Training Department, and Administration Department. The Territorial Militia provided law enforcement at the local level. Directorates for the Territorial Militia in each province of the country reported to the People's Militia at the national level. The Road Militia acted as a traffic enforcement authority similar to a highway patrol or state police force. The Commercial Militia investigated economic crimes, fraud, and thefts. The Training Department supervised the training of personnel for the People's Militia. It operated a special secondary school to train sergeants and a national academy to train officers. Candidates studied law codes, criminology, criminal procedure, and foreign languages.

The Internal Security Troops, familiarly known as the Red Berets, were also part of the Ministry for Internal Security. They were a militarized, light infantry force responsible for preventing riots and other civil disturbances. Their 15,000 personnel were organized into 15 regiments.

The Bulgarian police today continue to come under the authority of the Ministry of Internal Affairs, assisted by a General Secretary to whom three Secretaries report. Each Secretary directs a number of police services. The Interpol NCB in Sofia reports directly to the General Secretary.

The main police law enforcement services are the Central Service for Combating Organized Crime, the National Police Service, and the National Investigation Service (this service has now been placed under the authority of the Ministry of Justice).

The main functions of the Central Service for Combating Organized Crime (CSCOC) are to collect and process criminal intelligence about national and international criminal cases which apparently involve structured criminal groups. In this respect, it also acts as a coordinating body for the other police services in the country. Its principal areas of activity cover international drug trafficking, international terrorism, internal terrorism, blackmail and kidnappings, trafficking in weapons, strategic raw materials and human beings, trafficking in goods of cultural and historical value, financial and currency crimes, and illegal entertainment.

The National Police Service is responsible for combating general crime (crimes against persons, property, and public order) throughout Bulgaria. It is staffed by both uniformed and plain clothes personnel. The National Police Service is also divided into criminal and financial sections. It provides logistic support (surveillance, checks, arrests etc.) for the CSCOC and the National Investigation Service.

The National Investigation Service is responsible for preparing all documents relating to prosecution proceedings in connection with cases under investigation (reports, statements, etc.). Its officers report to the prosecutor or to the examining magistrate.

Police investigations can be carried out in response to requests from foreign judicial authorities, subject to the agreement of the Chief Prosecutor. Requests for such investigations should normally be made by letters via diplomatic channels. However, in urgent cases Interpol channels can be used to forward the letters, and enquiries can begin as soon as the Chief Prosecutor has given his approval. Foreign police officers may be present during such investigations but may not take any active part in them.

Bibliography

"Bulgaria." *CIA World Factbook*. www.cia.gov/cia/publications/factbook/.

"Bulgaria." *Library of Congress Country Studies*. http://lcweb2.loc.gov/frd/cs/bgtoc.html.

"Bulgaria." *Interpol website*: www.interpol.int/Public/Region/Europe/pjsystems/Bulgaria.asp.

BURKINA FASO

Background Material

The Democratic Republic of Burkina Faso is located in Western Africa. It has a population of 13,500,000 (2004 est.). While French is the official language, there are several national languages, including Moré, Dioula, Fulfudé, and others. Forty percent of the population practices animist religion, while Islam (40%) and Christianity (20%) are also followed.

This Republican democracy features a National Assembly elected by universal suffrage. The Constitution was accepted in 1991. The legal system is based on French civil law and customary law. In 2001, the nation suffered 53,418 criminal offenses.

Police organizations are: the National Police, National Gendarmerie, and municipal police. Ministries responsible for policing are: the Ministry of Defense (Gendarmerie), Ministry of Security

(National Police), and Ministry of Territorial Administration (municipal police). Burkina Faso is a member of the following international organizations: the Economic Community of West African States (ECOWAS), All-African Chiefs of Police, Interpol, and the United Nations.

Formerly known as Upper Volta, the Democratic Republic of Burkina Faso is a land-locked country located in West Africa south of the Sahara. It covers an area of 105,900 square miles. Mali is located to its north and west; Ivory Coast, Ghana and Togo to its south; and Benin and Niger to the east. Ouagadougou is the capital city.

Burkina Faso is a poor country. The basis of its economy is subsistence agriculture and pastoralism. Water is scare, and only 14% of the land is cultivated. Life expectancy is 44.2 years, and 45% of the population lives below the poverty line. The literacy rate is 24%, and health problems include meningitis, hepatitis, malaria, and HIV/AIDS.

Originally inhabited by the Bobo, Lobi, and Gurunsi people, the area was invaded in the eleventh century by several indigenous kingdoms, the most powerful being the Mossi. France conquered the territory in the late nineteenth century, made Upper Volta a colony in 1919, and administered the area indirectly through Mossi authorities. A peaceful struggle for independence continued throughout the 1950s.

Independence was attained on August 5, 1960, and a new constitution was adopted. President Thomas Sankara renamed the country Burkina Faso, which means "land of men of dignity." He was assassinated in a coup that brought Captain Blaise Compaoré to power in 1987. Campaoré introduced a new constitution in 1991 that separated the ruling party from the state, legislative, and judicial branches, established a multiparty system, and guaranteed freedom of the press and opinion. Campaoré was re-elected in both 1991 and 1998.

The GDP is US$2.3 billion (2001).

Contextual Features

Burkina Faso is politically stable, owing to the absence of ethnic polarization and limited political violence. Under the 1991 Constitution, executive power is vested in the president and his ministers, and is counterbalanced by a legislative National Assembly of 111 members and an independent judiciary.

The president, who must be a civilian and at least 35 years of age, is elected for a term of five years with a two-term limit. Delegates to the National Assembly are elected for a five-year term, and there is universal suffrage. Women compose eight per-

cent of the Assembly. The president appoints a prime minister, subject to parliamentary approval. A council of ministers is appointed by the president on the recommendation of the prime minister.

The Constitution provides for public freedoms, the equality of all citizens before the law, and other political and social rights. The *Family and Citizens Code*, known as a "code for women," came into effect in 1990. It promotes the principles of the equality of the couple in a marriage, the abolition of forced marriages, and institutes the principle of monogamy.

Burkina Faso has a strong and dynamic civil society, consisting of non-governmental organizations, advocacy groups, trade unions, the media, village groups, traditional chieftains, and religious groups. The Burkinabé Movement for Human Rights and the Rights of Peoples observes elections in other African countries. The *African Charter on Human and Peoples' Rights*, which was adopted by the Organization of African Unity in 1981, was ratified by Burkina Faso. The Ombudsman of Faso was established in 1994 to settle disputes between the administration and citizens.

The system of law is based on French civil law. Traditional or customary law is still in effect and used to solve many disputes. The police, gendarmerie, religious authorities, or neighborhood representatives are often consulted informally to resolve conflicts. There are reports that the justice system is distanced from the citizen. Administration of justice is hampered by an insufficient number of courts and judges, limited documentation, lack of professional training, and poor pay and working conditions. Detention for questioning often lasts three to six months beyond the legal 72 hours, and detainees are kept in poor conditions. Thereare significant politicization of the magistracy, interference by the executive, and lack of confidence by persons subject to trial. Court fees are prohibitive, and legal aid is rarely applied. Nevertheless, progressive laws are being enacted, such as the 1997 law prohibiting female genital mutilation.

The 1991 Constitution provides for the independence of the judiciary, which is accountable to the Higher Council, chaired by the President. Judges are appointed by the executive arm of the government. Under a 1993 law, the Ministry of Justice manages the judicial system.

The responsibility for justice is assigned to the Supreme Court, courts of appeal, and the courts of first instance (high courts, magistrates' courts, departmental courts, and labor courts). There are also courts of special jurisdiction, such as the High

Court of Justice (created to deal with political offences committed by senior political figures), and military tribunals.

The Supreme Court regulates the judicial activity of all courts. It has both financial and administrative authority. A law passed in 2000 split the Supreme Court into four separate divisions: the Constitutional Chamber, the Administrative Chamber, the Judicial Chamber, and the Audit Chamber.

The Constitutional Chamber rules on the constitutionality of legislation, implementation of constitutional provisions, and electoral matters. The Administrative Chamber has jurisdiction over the legality of administrative activities and the accountability of the administration to the public. It hears electoral appeals pertaining to provincial and municipal elections. The Audit Chamber has jurisdiction over public and de facto accountants.

The Court of Appeal hears questions of fact or law previously submitted to the high courts. It has a separate criminal division to deal with crimes where there is the possibility of appeal.

Courts of first instance hear civil and commercial cases involving sums of no more than 100,000 CFA, and criminal infractions such as crop or property damaged by wandering cattle. The Magistrates' Courts are responsible for hearing civil and commercial cases with a value between 100,000 CFA and one million CFA. They also serve as police courts and have appellate jurisdiction for decisions of the departmental courts. Collegiate high courts are located in each province, and they are responsible for civil and commercial cases involving amounts of more than one million CFA, and criminal offences. They also hear appeals from decisions made by the magistrates' courts. The labor courts handle social conflicts arising from labor contracts.

The National Police report the following crime statistics.

The correctional institutions include detention centers, prisons, juvenile reform schools, and agricultural penitentiaries. There are reports that prisoners are subjected to overcrowding, unsanitary conditions, and inadequate food, which has driven authorities to find other locations such as stores and offices to use as detention centers.

Police Profile

Background and Organizational Description

The police system of Burkina Faso is French in organizational structure, equipment, and nomencla-

Offence	1999	2000	2001
Counterfeit currency	33	28	38
Arms dealing	7	24	43
Drug trafficking	26	51	63
Forgery	41	23	38
Misappropriation of public funds	2	15	8
Criminal conspiracy	12	19	9
Assassination	12	16	19
Murder	32	44	34
Poisoning	10	19	10
Infanticide	4	13	4
Parricide	1	6	2
Manslaughter	220	141	188
Assault & Battery	3,151	4,014	31,143
Kidnapping of a minor	229	258	259
Armed robbery	650	1,004	1,038
Rape	59	103	90
Theft	9,543	12,558	13,957
Fraud	1,062	976	1,261
Possession of stolen goods	451	696	772
Breach of trust	3,031	8,342	4,179
Arson	68	132	233

ture. Public security includes a gendarmerie of approximately 4,200 personnel under the jurisdiction of Ministry of Defense but in operational matters responding to the agency requiring its services; the national police controlled by the Ministry of Security; and the municipal police, controlled by the Ministry of Territorial Administration. The Presidential Guard is an autonomous security force, although it is technically subject to the jurisdiction of the armed forces and part of the army. There is also a reserve militia of 45,000 men and women aged between 20 and 35, who are trained for military and civil duties and serve part-time for two years.

The national police are headed by the Director of Security Services with a rank of at least Chief Commissioner. The General Directorate of the National Police manages both internal and external matters of the organization. It has three main branches of Judicial Police, General Information, and Public Security.

The gendarmerie is organized militarily. Most police services are delivered at the brigade level. It is chiefly concerned with controlling crime in the rural areas, most of which occurs mainly in the form of illegal immigration and contraband trade across the frontiers, fraud in the mining enterprises, and black marketeering.

The municipal police come under the authority of a mayor and operate within a community under a municipal police commandant. Their functions are to assist mayors in applying police regulations,

Prison Statistics

Number of establishments (2002)	11
Total 2002 prison population (National Police Administration)	2,800
Rate of prisoners per 100,000 of population (pop. base 12.2 million)	23
Pre-trial detainees or remand prisoners in prison population (2001)	58.3%
Percentage of women in prison population (2001)	1.0%
Percentage of juveniles, minors, young prisoners (2001)	2.4%
Official capacity of prison system (2002)	1,650
Occupancy level as percentage of the official capacity (2002)	169.70%

Source: International Centre for Prison Studies, King's College, London, England

supporting other municipal services, and providing ceremonial services when needed.

In addition to these organizational divisions, there is a legal division between the functions of administrative and judicial police, although the distinction is not always apparent, since police personnel can act in both functions. Administrative police are generally responsible for order maintenance, security, public peace, and public health. Its role is said to be preventive. The role of the judicial police is described as repressive; that is, it is responsible for criminal investigation. These two functions are exercised in both the national police and the gendarmerie, although the two are governed by different legal instruments. In the judicial role, police are officers of the court in company with examining magistrates and prosecutors. The judicial police tend to be short-staffed, under-resourced, ill-equipped and trained, and are not well-regarded by the population.

Although reforms have been made, there are reports of interference in the independence of the justice system and agreement that conditions have worsened.

Training

France plays a large part in police training in Burkina Faso. Basic training is provided to officers in public security and order; traffic stops and traffic accident investigations; fraud; airport and border policing; police laws; and investigation techniques. In 2004, human rights and investigative training was given to the judicial police to help improve the quality of investigation. Advanced training is also offered in France at the schools of the French National Police.

France has also funded projects relating to public security and civil order in Burkina Faso. In 1998, such projects included the funding of a police unit to manage problems in maintaining public order in the urban area and the acquisition of new vehicles for the gendarmerie in the departments. France also provided four million francs for the renovation of the National Police School in Ouagadougou, its transformation into an academy for basic and continuous training for all police, the

provision of teaching and training equipment, office supplies, and the development of a policy of continuous training. In 2001, Turkey and Burkina Faso signed an agreement for training of the gendarmerie.

Complaints and Discipline

The Burkinabé Movement for Human Rights (MBDHP) and Amnesty International report that security forces were responsible for extrajudicial killings and human rights abuses of detainees of criminal suspects during a campaign against crime in 1997 and 1998. The Minister of Security denied these allegations but admitted that security forces had killed some people in battles with armed bands. President Campaoré declared March 30, 2001 a National Day of Pardon and apologized for past government crimes, paving the way for financial compensation for victims of political crime. Amnesty International reports that extrajudicial executions by the police continued in 2002.

The Zongo affair illustrates the fragility of the justice system in Burkina Faso. Norbert Zongo was a journalist who died with his brother and two other men in a suspicious car fire in 1998. He had been investigating the alleged killing of the driver of the President's brother by members of the Presidential Guard. The Independent Investigatory Commission created to investigate the affair found that Mr. Zongo was killed for political reasons. A judge was appointed to try the six members of the Presidential Guard but no progress in the trial was made.

Terrorism

Jane's Terrorism Intelligence Centre reports there are no active insurgent groups in Burkina Faso, although representatives of foreign rebel groups are believed to have visited Burkina Faso to trade in weaponry and diamonds. The UN reports that with the assistance of Burkina Faso,

Liberia is actively breaking Security Council embargoes on weapons imports into its own territory and into Sierra Leone. The Burkina Faso government has been attempting to disassociate itself from these groups. In 2002, a European investigation into al-Qaeda financing found evidence that the Liberia and Burkina Faso governments hosted senior terrorist operatives who oversaw a diamond-buying operation of $20 million.

International Cooperation

Burkina Faso is a member country of the Economic Community of West African States (ECOWAS), a political and economic community. To combat international crime, the police forces of the member countries have cooperated in creating extradition treaties and reciprocal warrants for the arrest of fugitives, with the exception of political criminals. Since 1990, ECOWAS has deployed ECOMOG, a regional peacekeeping military force, to supervise and enforce a ceasefire in the Liberian civil war and in Sierra Leone. In 1991, ECOWAS leaders agreed to sign a security protocol administered through four regional bureaus, one in Ouagadougou.

Burkina Faso is a member of Interpol, and officials participate in the biennial All-African Chiefs of Police Conference. In addition, Burkina Faso has contributed police officers to the UN mission in the Democratic Republic of the Congo and to the 2004 UN Stabilization Mission in Haiti. One of the participants in Haiti was a female police commissioner from Burkina Faso.

NANCY PARK

Bibliography

A la découverte du Burkina Faso (Discovering Burkina Faso— Government of Burkina Faso web site). www.prima ture.gov.bf.

Amnesty International. *Annual Report 1999: Burkina Faso.* www.amnesty.org/ailib/aireport/ar99/afr60.htm.

Bayart, Jean-Francois, Stephen Ellis, and Beatrice Hibou. *The Criminalization of the State in Africa.* Bloomington and Indianapolis: Indiana University Press and The International African Institute in association with James Currey, Oxford, 1999.

Central Intelligence Agency. The World Factbook 2002. "Burkina Faso." 2004. www.odci.gov/cia/publications/factbook/geos/uv.html.

Economist Intelligence Unit. *Country Profile 2002—Burkina Faso.* www.eiu.com.

Embassy of France in Burkina Faso. *Service de Coopération Technique Internationale de Police (SCTIP).* www.france-burkina.bf/SCTIP/Sctip.htm.

Englebert, Pierre. *Burkina Faso: Unsteady Statehood in West Africa.* Boulder, CO: Westview Press, 1999.

Hagberg, Sten. "Enough is Enough: an enthnography of the struggle against impunity in Burkina Faso." Journal of Modern African Studies 40, no. 2 (2002): 217–245.

Institut international de droit d'expression et d'inspiration françaises. *La direction de la police judiciare et son contrôle par les autorités judiciaires au Burkina Faso.* Juriscope—1999. (November 11, 2004). http://juriscope.org/publications/etudes/police.htm.

International Commission of Jurists. "Burkina Faso-Attacks on Justice 2000." www.icj.org/news.

Kacowicz, Arie M. "Negative International Peace and Domestic Wars: The West African Case, 1957–1996" [Paper presented at the International Studies Association Convention, March 18–22, 1997, Toronto, Canada.].

U.S. Department of State, Bureau of Democracy, Human Rights and Labor. *Burkina Faso—Country Reports on Human Rights Practice—2001.* 4 Mar 2002. www.state.gov/g/drl/rls/hrrpt/2001/af/8271.htm.

Yonaba, Salif. *Indépendance de la justice et droits de l'homme: le cas du Burkina Faso.* Geneva: Centre for the Independence of Judges and Lawyers, 1997.

BURUNDI

Background Material

Burundi has never had a genuinely national police force.

In the sixteenth century, Burundi was a kingdom characterized by a hierarchical political authority and tributary economic exchange. A king (*mwani*) headed a princely aristocracy (*gwana*,) which owned most of the land and required a tribute, or tax, from local farmers and herders. In the mid-eighteenth century, this Tutsi royalty consolidated authority over land, production, and distribution with the development of the *ubugabire*—a patron-client relationship in which the populace received royal protection in exchange for tribute and land tenure.

Although European explorers and missionaries made brief visits to the area as early as 1856, it was not until 1899 that Burundi came under German East African administration. In 1916, Belgian troops occupied the area. In 1923, the League of Nations mandated to Belgium the territory of Ruanda-Urundi, encompassing modern-day Rwanda and Burundi. The Belgians administered the territory through indirect rule, building on the Tutsi-dominated aristocratic hierarchy. Following World War II, Ruanda-Urundi became a United Nations Trust Territory under Belgian administrative authority. After 1948, Belgium permitted the emergence of competing political parties. Two political parties emerged: the Union for National Progress (UPRONA), a multi-ethnic party led by Tutsi Prince Louis Rwagasore; and the Christian Democratic Party (PDC), supported by Belgium. In 1961, Prince Rwagasore was assassinated following an UPRONA victory in legislative elections.

Full independence was achieved on July 1, 1962. In the context of weak democratic institutions at independence, Tutsi King Mwambutsa IV established a constitutional monarchy composed of equal numbers of Hutus and Tutsis. The 1965 assassination of the Hutu prime minister set in motion a series of destabilizing Hutu revolts and subsequent governmental repression. In 1966, King Mwambutsa was deposed by his son, Prince Ntare IV, who himself was deposed by his prime minister Capt. Michel Micombero in the same year. Micombero abolished the monarchy and declared a republic, although a *de facto* military regime emerged. In 1972, an aborted Hutu rebellion triggered the flight of hundreds of thousands of Burundians. Civil unrest continued throughout the late 1960s and early 1970s.

In 1976, Col. Jean-Baptiste Bagaza took power in a bloodless coup. Although Bagaza led a Tutsi-dominated military regime, he encouraged land reform, electoral reform, and national reconciliation. In 1981, a new constitution was promulgated. In 1984, Bagaza was elected head of state, as the sole candidate. After his election, Bagaza's human rights record deteriorated, as he suppressed religious activities and detained political opposition members.

In 1987, Maj. Pierre Buyoya overthrew Colonel Bagaza. He dissolved opposition parties, suspended the 1981 constitution, and instituted his ruling Military Committee for National Salvation (CSMN). During 1988, increasing tensions between the ruling Tutsis and the majority Hutus resulted in violent confrontations between the army, the Hutu opposition, and Tutsi hardliners. During this period, an estimated 150,000 people were killed, with tens of thousands of refugees flowing to neighboring countries. Buyoya formed a commission to investigate the causes of the 1988 unrest and to develop a charter for democratic reform.

In 1991, Buyoya approved a constitution that provided for a president, nonethnic government, and a parliament. Burundi's first Hutu president, Melchior Ndadaye, of the Hutu-dominated FRODEBU Party, was elected in 1993. He was assassinated by factions of the Tutsi-dominated armed forces in October 1993. The country then plunged into civil war, which killed tens of thousands of people and displaced hundreds of thousands by the time the FRODEBU government regained control and elected Cyprien Ntaryamira president in January, 1994. Nonetheless, the security situation continued to deteriorate. In April 1994, President Ntayamira and Rwandan President Juvenal Habyarimana died in a plane crash. This act marked the beginning of the Rwandan genocide, while in Burundi, the death of Ntaryamira exacerbated the violence and unrest. Sylvestre Ntibantunganya was installed to a four-year presidency on April 8, but the security situation further declined. The influx of hundreds of thousands of Rwandan refugees and the activities of armed Hutu and Tutsi groups further destabilized the regime.

At 206.1 persons per sq. km., Burundi has the second-largest population density in Sub-Saharan Africa (the total population is 6,231,22). Most people live on farms near areas of fertile volcanic soil. The population is made up of three major ethnic groups—Bahutu (Hutu), Batutsi or Watusi (Tutsi), and Batwa (Twa). Kirundi is the common language. The primary religion is Christianity (Roman Catholics and Protestant), although indigenous beliefs and Islam are represented. Intermarriage takes place frequently between the Hutus and Tutsis. The terms "pastoralist" and "agriculturist," often used as ethnic designations for Watutsi and Bahutu, respectively, are only occupational titles which vary among individuals and groups. Although Hutus encompass the majority of the population, historically Tutsis have been politically and economically dominant.

The mainstay of the Burundian economy is agriculture, accounting for 58% of GDP in 1997. Agriculture supports more than 90% of the labor force, the majority of whom are subsistence farmers. Although Burundi is potentially self-sufficient in food production, the ongoing civil war, overpopulation, and soil erosion have contributed to the contraction of the subsistence economy by 25% in recent years. Large numbers of internally displaced persons have been unable to produce their own food and are largely dependent on international humanitarian assistance. Burundi is a net food importer, with food accounting for 17% of imports in 1997.

The main cash crop is coffee, which accounted for 78.5% of exports in 1997. This dependence on coffee has increased Burundi's vulnerability to seasonal yields and international coffee prices. Coffee is the largest state-owned enterprise. In recent years, the government has tried to attract private investment to this sector, with some success. Efforts to privatize other publicly held enterprises have stalled. Other principal exports include tea and raw cotton.

Little industry exists, except the processing of agricultural exports. Although potential wealth in petroleum, nickel, copper, and other natural resources is being explored, the uncertain security situation has prevented meaningful investor interest. Industrial development also is hampered by Burundi's distance from the sea and high transport costs. Lake Tanganyika remains an important trading point. The trade embargo, lifted in 1999, negatively impacted trade and industry.

Burundi is heavily dependent on bilateral and multilateral aid, with external debt totaling $1.247 billion in 1997. A series of largely unsuccessful five-year plans initiated in July 1986 in partnership with the World Bank and the International Monetary Fund attempted to reform the foreign exchange system, liberalize imports, reduce restrictions on international transactions, diversify exports, and reform the coffee industry. IMF structural adjustment programs in Burundi were suspended following the outbreak of the crisis in 1993. The World Bank has identified key areas for potential growth, including the productivity of traditional crops and the introduction of new exports, light manufactures, industrial mining, and services. Other serious problems include the state's role in the economy, the question of governmental transparency, and debt reduction.

Contextual Features

In November 1995, the presidents of Burundi, Rwanda, Uganda, and Zaire announced a regional initiative for a negotiated peace in Burundi facilitated by former Tanzanian President Julius Nyerere. In July 1996, former Burundian President Buyoya returned to power in a bloodless coup. He declared himself president of a transitional republic, even as he suspended the National Assembly, banned opposition groups, and imposed a nationwide curfew. Widespread condemnation of the coup ensued, and regional countries imposed economic sanctions pending a return to a constitutional government. Buyoya agreed in 1996 to liberalize political parties. Nonetheless, fighting between the army and Hutu militias continued. In June 1998, Buyoya promulgated a transitional constitution and announced a partnership between the government and the opposition-led National Assembly. After Facilitator Julius Nyerere's death in October 1999, the regional leaders appointed Nelson Mandela as Facilitator of the Arusha peace process. Under Mandela, the peace process has revived, and important progress has taken place.

To protest the 1996 coup by President Buyoya, neighboring countries imposed an economic embargo on Burundi. Although the embargo was never officially ratified by the United Nations Security Council, most countries refrained from official trade with Burundi. Following the 1996 coup, the United States suspended all but humanitarian aid to Burundi. The regional embargo was lifted on January 23, 1999, based on progress by the government in advancing national reconciliation through the Burundi peace process.

The government is a Republic, with power vested strongly in the executive branch (the president). It is a transitional government, and a *de facto* military regime. There is a 121-member National Assembly (81 elected, 40 appointed), a Supreme Court, and subsidiary courts.

A draft constitution was promulgated on March 13, 1992 and suspended following the July, 1996 coup. A Transitional Constitutional Act, promulgated on June 6, 1998, legitimizes the authority of the president and establishes the political platform for the transitional regime.

Police Profile

Background

On January 3, 2005, Burundi's president Domitien Ndayizeye announced that he had signed two laws setting up a new army and police force, which will include the central African country's former rebels. The creation of new security forces is part of a political and military process under way to implement agreements on peace and a new administration to end a decade-long civil war which claimed more than 300,000 lives.

The former army, dominated by the Tutsi minority which traditionally ran the small country, had

43,000 troops, and the number of ex-rebels drawn from the Hutu majority population is estimated at 27,000. Some 20,000 men on either side are to be demobilized over a four-year period, which began late in 2004. The new army is to include 30,000 men, with a police force of 20,000.

The new army and police will consist evenly of Hutus and Tutsis, officials have agreed. At present, Hutus comprise 85% of the population but between only 35% to 40% of the armed forces, according to military sources. Burundi has never had a genuinely national police force in the past. In the past year, most members of six of seven rebel groups have been gathered at 12 sites across the country. Each movement has been responsible for its own members, and the FDD runs six of the sites.

In line with a ceasefire accord signed by the government and the FDD in November 1993, all troops will be called back to barracks apart from those guarding the borders. A single rebel group, the National Liberation Forces (FNL), has refused to sign the peace accords and is still fighting in Bujumbura Rural, the province around the capital, but peace has been restored in all the other 16 provinces in the country. FDD members joined the transitional government in November 2003.

Complaints and Discipline

In the event of a violation of human rights or infringement of a right, the injured citizen is entitled to appeal to the courts and tribunals for restoration of his rights. Similarly, when a citizen is prosecuted, he is guaranteed the right to a defence and to a fair trial.

The responsible authorities include the following: the Prosecuting Counsels of the Prosecutor's Office, the officers of various police forces, the judicial police of the prosecutor's offices, the ordinary courts and tribunals, the Supreme Court, the special courts, and the military courts (courts martial, military appeal courts). These courts are bound, in conformity with the regulations, to protect certain rights, and these include human rights.

AGBONKHESE SHAKA MOSES

Bibliography

"Burundi President Creates New National Defense Force to Include Former Rebels." *VOA News.* 03-January-2005 2201.

Peace Agreements Digital Collection: Burundi Arusha Peace and Reconciliation Agreement for Burundi Protocol III.

United States Institute of Peace Library: Peace Agreements Digital Collection: Burundi.

United States Institute of Peace Library Peace Agreements Digital Collection: Arusha Peace and Reconciliation Agreement for Burundi.

United States Institute of Peace Library Peace Agreements Digital Collection: Protocol III Peace and Security for All.

United States Institute of Peace Library Peace Agreements Digital Collection: Chapter II the Defence and Security Forces

C

CAMBODIA

Background Material

Cambodia is approximately 181,000 square kilometers in size, although its borders with both Thailand and Vietnam are the subjects of long-running disputes. The country's recent history has been dominated by civil war and political conflict that have left the country struggling to develop. Indeed, Cambodia is currently ranked 130th out of 175 on the UN Human Development Index. However, Angkor Wat—the symbol of the nation—testifies to a time when the Khmer empire dominated Southeast Asia. The golden age of that civilization was during the Angkor period (889–1434), a time in which the empire dominated the areas now covered by Thailand, Cambodia, Vietnam, and part of Laos.

As France came to dominate the region in the nineteenth century, Cambodia became a French protectorate. The French control lasted until independence was granted in 1953, negotiated by then King Norodom Sihanouk, who abdicated to become the country's Royal Chief of State. However, with independence came destabilization both inside and outside the country's borders as the situation in Vietnam spilled over and started to impact on its neighbors.

In 1970, the government of Norodom Sihanouk was toppled in a coup, after which the country descended into civil war with fighting between the new rightwing government headed by General Lon Nol and communist forces led by Pol Pot. Many people fled the country, including members of the legal and criminal justice system.

The victory by the communist Khmer Rouge forces in 1975 heralded a new and horrific era for the country. The capital city of Phnom Penh was captured, and all cities and towns were ordered to be evacuated. Millions of Cambodians died, either executed by the authorities or from starvation and overwork on the collective farms established by the Khmer Rouge as it attempted to establish Maoist, peasant-based agrarian cooperatives.

The Khmer Rouge government lasted until 1978 when the Vietnamese invaded and installed a new government, the People's Republic of Kampuchea, controlled by the Vietnamese. Although the Vietnamese invasion ended the brutality of the Khmer Rouge, it did not restore peace to the country. Two decades of fighting followed between the Vietnamese-controlled authorities and opposition parties including Khmer Rouge soldiers.

In 1991, the four main parties involved in the conflict signed the Paris Peace Accord, an international peace agreement. The parties came together to form a temporary government until UN-sponsored democratic elections in 1993. Although flawed and subject to complex domestic political maneuvering, the transition to democratic government has generally been regarded as bringing a greater degree of stability to the country. Yet the country still bears deep scars from the traumas that the years of civil war and communist control inflicted on it.

The problems facing the country as it tries to rebuild itself are reflected to a large extent in the situation of the police and criminal justice system. These problems, including poor education, rampant corruption, and general insecurity, are considered here.

The country's population numbers 13,363,421. As a result of recent history, the age profile of the population is extremely young with the median age being 19.5 years.

The Cambodian population is 90% ethnically Khmer. Significant ethnic minorities include ethnic Vietnamese (5%), ethnic Chinese (1%), and a minority Cham (Muslim) population. There are also several "hill tribes" in the northeast of the country.

The official language of Cambodia is Khmer, although English and French are widely spoken. The official religion is Theravada Buddhism and is practiced by approximately 95% of the population. Other notable religions include Islam, animism, and Christianity.

According to the World Bank, the gross national income per capita for Cambodia in 2003 was US$310. The percentage of the population living on less than $2 a day, and therefore considered poor, is 78%.

Subsistence agriculture is the main economic activity for Cambodians. However, the major export products of Cambodia are garments, rice, rubber, wood and wood products, corn, and rubies. Garment manufacturing is by far the largest export product at the present time. In 2002, the textiles sector accounted for 76% of the country's total exports.

Contextual Features

The current political system in Cambodia was established following the Paris Peace Accord of 1991. The peace treaty paved the way for democratic elections organized by the United Nations Transitional Administration of Cambodia. The first elections under this system in 1993 produced a coalition government between the Cambodian Peoples Party and the royalist FUNCINPEC party.

A new constitution was also adopted in 1993 and brought about the reestablishment of the monarchy under King Norodom Sihanouk. The constitution allows the King to play a key ceremonial role, representing the best interests of the state and its people.

The political system is based upon a multiparty democratic system of government. Since 1993, two National Assembly elections were held in 1998 and 2003, while the first local commune elections took place in 2002. The 2003 national election led to an eleven-month political deadlock during which there was no official government. ADHOC, a local human rights nongovernmental organization (NGO), noted in its 2004 Human Rights Situation Report that

> It has become almost customary that a political crisis occurs ... [after] every election. This situation mirrors the vulnerability of Cambodia's democratic institutions and the immaturity of its politicians, who have dealt with the political crisis by modifying the Constitution in the wake of every election irrespective of the impacts on the spirit of the supreme law of the country.

(ADHOC 2005: 1)

The deadlock was finally resolved in June 2004 when the CPP and FUNCINPEC agreed to form an expanded coalition government with a 332-seat cabinet, one of the world's largest.

The legislative branch of the Cambodian government is made up of the National Assembly, which is elected, and the Senate, which is currently appointed. The National Assembly is the primary law-making body, while the Senate acts to review those laws before they can be adopted.

The executive branch is known as the Royal Government of Cambodia (RGC), and is made up of the Council of Ministers led by the Prime Minister assisted by seven Deputy Prime Ministers, and a number of State Ministers and State Secretaries. The Council of Ministers is the dominant body within the executive branch, carrying out the functions of the state.

As with most criminal justice systems, Cambodia's is deeply affected by both its political and legal history. In order to understand the current criminal justice system, it is therefore necessary to have at least an overview of major developments that have contributed to the shaping of that system. The following discussion provides a brief discussion of these developments.

French colonial rule provided Cambodia with a strong legal system that was modeled on the French legal system. This system was operating in the urban centers at the time of Cambodian independence from France in 1953. The formal system was mixed with customary law, which operated to a large degree in rural areas. The customary laws were developed over centuries by Cambodians at the local level based largely on the traditional values and norms operating at the village level. In practice, the system involved the village chief playing a central role in the reconciliation of disputes.

Following independence the legal system was sustained until the outbreak of civil war and the subsequent rise of the Khmer Rouge. Between 1975 and 1979, the Khmer Rouge Regime of Democratic Kampuchea (DK) implemented policies that led to destruction of the legal system and its institutions. The removal of those who might be considered to be opponents of the regime included lawyers and judges. Although the 1976 constitution of the DK included references to tribunals and judges, the regime never implemented any form of legal system. By the time the Khmer Rouge were defeated, it is said that "only ten law graduates, including five judges, were known to remain in the country" (Coghill 2000: 52).

The new government established in 1979 by the Vietnamese was essentially a communist system of government. The justice system was therefore in effect an arm of the executive, and was overwhelmingly political in nature. It operated under the close supervision of the Ministry of Justice, even to the extent that the Ministry reviewed all judgments handed down by the courts of first instance for factual and legal accuracy, and reviewed sentencing to ensure that the system was fair.

The current criminal justice system has its basis in the 1993 constitution, which produced a fundamental change within both the legal and political system. With a liberal democratic system came a judicial system based on independence from political institutions, and the previous socialist systems were abolished.

However, the change has not been entirely effective in practice, and the current system continues to show clear influences of all the major political and legal changes that have affected its recent history. Customary law continues to operate in rural areas with informal legal solutions often dominating over formal court-based systems.

Many senior officials within the criminal justice system were trained and worked under the socialist system of the 1980s. As a result, their understanding and implementation of the system remains heavily influenced by this experience. Change, even when set down in the constitution, has not been swift or easy for these officials.

Cambodia inherited a civil law system from the French colonial powers. Such a system is traditionally based on a statutory code setting out the laws that govern the functions of all parts of society.

The courts play the role of interpreting and applying the law in each case. Judgments are normally not provided in written form, and judicial decisions do not develop a system of precedent. In Cambodia, the courts follow this approach.

However, Cambodia does not yet have a clear and effective statutory code; instead the laws are drawn from diverse sources; in many cases they are incomplete and do not reflect or adequately respond to the most serious problems affecting the country. Thus, in the context of criminal law, we find the sources of the law arising from the constitution, international law, UNTAC transitional law, laws from previous regimes such as those still in force from the socialist period, and more recent laws passed by the National Assembly. The result is a rather confused picture with conflicting laws being followed by different courts. At present, work is being undertaken on a number of new laws including a draft penal code.

Cambodian law is therefore in desperate need of revision. However, law reform suffers from problems of delay, which has been compounded by the eleven-month political stalemate after the 2003 election. Ongoing difficulties in reforming the law on a major scale have led to the passing of piecemeal legislation, which in turn has produced conflicts and confusion.

According to the Ministry of Interior, the number of crimes committed in 2003 was 5,691, down from 5,848 in 2000. In 2004, the Ministry also reported that 1,259 robbery cases, 498 murder cases, 25 kidnapping cases, 360 rape cases, and 17 human trafficking cases were reported. However, the gathering and storing of crime statistics by the authorities are unreliable. As a result, any analysis offered is based to a large extent on the priorities set by the criminal justice authorities and human rights and legal aid NGOs working in Cambodia.

Briefly, criminal offenses causing serious concern within Cambodia include violent crime, especially sexual violence and violent assaults and murders. Other major crime problems reflect the pressures that a developing country can experience, such as human trafficking, drug trafficking and use, land grabbing, and more recently, terrorism.

Courts of first instance can be found in the provincial, municipal, and military courts. There are nineteen provincial courts and two municipal courts hearing all nonmilitary cases arising within their geographical area. There is no separation in the courts between the criminal and civil benches.

Within the court system, there are both investigating and trial judges. The investigating judge investigates criminal cases when requested to do so by the prosecutor. S/he informs the accused about their rights, makes decisions on pre-trial detention, and can order an acquittal if s/he finds that there is insufficient evidence against the suspect. The investigating judge is not meant to act as a trial judge, although in practice this does happen because of the lack of qualified judges in the country.

The Appeal Court is located in Phnom Penh and hears cases from all first instance courts. Appeal Court trials are heard by three judges, called the "Trial Council," and attended by a prosecutor. There are seven Appeal Court judges in total.

The Supreme Court is located in Phnom Penh, and is the highest court in Cambodia. It contains a civil chamber made up of four judges, and a penal chamber made up of five judges. The president of the court is required to be present at all hearings.

The Supreme Court is the highest court and hears three different types of cases. First, it will hear cases raising questions of law from appeals to the Appeal Court. Second, the Supreme Court will take appeals from the Appeal Court where that court has failed to follow the judgment of the Supreme Court. Finally, the Supreme Court will hear a "Complaint to Review" by a convicted person. In this type of case a person who has already been convicted of an offense asks the court to consider new evidence that may establish his or her innocence.

The Supreme Court has no power to review legislation, executive regulations, or to develop its own case law. The court does not hand down written judgments or even offer justifications for their decisions, with the result that there is no development of a system of precedent.

Finally, the constitution provides for the creation of the Supreme Council of Magistracy, which is designed to play the role of advising the King on matters of appointment, transfer, discipline, and promotion of judges and prosecutors. However, it has thus far failed to fully implement its full constitutional role due to a number of problems, including a lack of independence from the executive, the busy timetables of its members and the interference in matters under its mandate by the executive.

The management of prisons in Cambodia comes under the remit of the Ministry of Interior. In practice, the running of prisons operates on what appears to be military style procedures and working practices. All decisions are made by the Ministry of Interior, the Directorate General of the National Police, and the relevant Provincial/Municipal Police Commission.

Cambodia's prisons are in a poor state, characterized by overcrowding, underfunding, and poor infrastructure. Allegations of torture and excessive detention are common, as are demands for bribes by underpaid prison guards.

Police Profile

In recent years, it has consistently been stated that police practice is still deeply influenced by the communist regime that ruled the country between 1979 and 1992. As has already been stated, the criminal justice system under the communist regimes was to all intents and purposes a political structure. The primary focus of the system was to ensure the security of the state rather than of the individuals living within the state. Examining the police in Cambodia, an Asian Human Rights Commission report noted that the primary role of the police during this period was in fact to undertake surveillance on the population.

The structure of the police during this time was also highly political with various political cadres controlling their own police forces. Concerns have continued that political control, extrajudicial killings, and impunity generally operate in Cambodia. These linkages may not be so transparent now, but fears persist that recruitment is based on political affiliation and party membership.

Organizational Structure

At the present time, numerous police agencies operate under the overall control and supervision of the Ministry of Interior, including Security, Tourism, Traffic, Economy, Immigration, Judiciary, Firefighters, Antinarcotics, Antiterrorism, Anti-Human Trafficking, Border Patrol, and Bodyguard. The overall police force is estimated to be approximately 64,000.

The operation and structures of the police have continued to reflect their historical political and military functions, with military titles being the norm. Appointments and promotions tend not to reflect an officer's ability, but rather tenure and political affliation.

Training

The Cambodian police have received a significant amount and variety of human rights and professional training offered by both local NGOs and international organizations. Cooperation with other countries to improve crime prevention and investigation includes training from Australian and Canadian police forces, among others. Funding comes from a variety of sources, including the British Embassy and the U.S. State Department. Training has particularly been focused in high-profile sensitive crime areas such as drug trafficking, child sex abuse, and human rights.

This training is aimed not only at reforming and improving the Cambodian police and their practice; it is also aimed at reducing crime and improving prevention, detection, and prosecution. However, the problems of the criminal justice system not only relate to the police, and in fact in some sectors, including, for example, the antinarcotics unit, police practice has shown some signs of improvement. However, without similar improvements in the overall system, it will remain deeply corrupt and ineffective. The good work in improving policing will also be undone if police officers see other criminal justice officials taking bribes and undermining their work by letting known offenders walk away unpunished.

Police Use of Firearms

In relation to weapons, the police are not allowed to sell, hire, exchange, borrow, or lend their weapons or ammunition. Police regulations state that the police should not use their weapons to threaten and intimidate people. The police should not shoot unless there are orders to do so, or unless it is necessary in self-defense or to save life or public or private property.

Complaints and Discipline

The current role of the police within Cambodia is now governed by the Criminal Law and Procedure Act, which was passed in 1992 during the UNTAC era, and the Law of Criminal Procedure Act passed in 1993. These laws were meant to bring them into line with the appropriate role of the police in a liberal democracy providing a clearer understanding of the role of the police, especially in relation to criminal investigation and prosecution.

However, problems from the previous regime continue to undermine such efforts. In particular, it would appear that in practice the primary role of the police in relation to the investigation of crime is to achieve a confession from a suspect. As a result, the use of violence and torture in interrogations is reported to be common.

Indeed, in June 2004 the deputy director general of the national police publicly justified the use of torture by his officers to obtain information from suspects. It was only after strong local and international criticism from human rights organizations that he withdrew his statement. However, the impression remains that the police regard such behavior as entirely acceptable in order to achieve successful criminal convictions.

Police involvement in criminality compounds the view that a culture of impunity operates within the police forces in Cambodia. An example of such criminality can be found in relation to the drug trade. Allegations that the police are involved in drug-related corruption are common and have given rise to concern, as the level of drug use and drug trafficking has risen in Cambodia, which stands at a key geographical location in the region's drug trade.

A less dramatic but more common problem is that of corruption. Corruption by poorly paid officials among Cambodia's public authorities is an annoying but everyday fact of life in the country. However, despite it being a clear breach of the police rules of discipline, such corruption is widespread and can take the form of unofficial fines for traffic offenses and charges for services provided, as well as illegally negotiated compensation agreements between victims and offenders through which the police get a proportion of the financial settlement. This practice has resulted in serious offenses such as rape going unpunished by the formal criminal justice system.

Declaration (Prakas) 006 on the Discipline of the National Police Forces was created in 1995 by Ministry of Interior, responsible for the overall running of the police. The Prakas sets out the guidelines for the conduct of the police and the internal regulation of police behavior. It makes clear that the police are required to be politically neutral, and that their role is to serve the people rather than serve any political masters. To this end, it also makes clear that the police are not above the law, and must apply all laws strictly in accordance with justice and fairness.

Under the Prakas, the police can be disciplined in a number of ways:

- If a police officer is found to have received a bribe of less than 5,000 Riel, then they will be subject to the minimum penalty of a warning or reprimand.
- A police officer may be demoted or dismissed from service if s/he shoots a weapon without order or legitimate reason, receives bribes of over 5,000 Riel, uses her/his position to threaten others for private gain, falsifies documents, uses state assets for private advantage, imposes improper fines, fabricates evidence, commits an act of torture, or spends the state's budget improperly.
- A police officer will be prosecuted if s/he conspires or commits the following: provides a weapon or ammunition to someone that is illegal and/or results in danger to life, and tortures

or beats an accused during interrogation causing death.

However, as the discussion above has indicated, there appears to be little practical enforcement of these rules of discipline.

Terrorism

In recent years, Cambodia has moved to establish a specialized antiterrorism unit to deal with what is considered to be the increasing threat of terrorism both internally and regionally. In fact, it has been claimed that for a while Cambodia became a safe haven for Islamic terrorists who were using Islamic schools as a front for their activities. These claims led to arrests and prosecution of a number of Muslim men who had been teaching in such a school.

As a result, at the end of 2004 a court in Phnom Penh sentenced the infamous Indonesian Islamist known as Himbali, along with three others, to life imprisonment. Himbali was convicted in absentia of plotting with the two Thais and one Cambodian to bomb the British and American embassies in Phnom Penh. While the embassies welcomed the convictions, many human rights organizations voiced their concerns about a trial where virtually no evidence had been presented.

As well as claims that Islamic terrorists are operating in Cambodia, domestic terrorist activity has been found in the form of the Cambodian Freedom Fighters (CFF). The U.S.-based CFF, established in 1998, has as its clearly stated aim the overthrow of the Cambodian government. In 2002, nineteen people were convicted of terrorism and/or membership in "an armed group." The offenses relate to an attack in Cambodia in 2000. They were sentenced to imprisonment of between five years and life.

FIONA DONSON

Bibliography

Cambodian Human Rights and Development Association (ADHOC). *Human Rights Situation Report 2004*. Phnom Penh: ADHOC, 2005.

Cambodian League for the Promotion and Defense of Human Rights (LICADHO). *Report: Prison Conditions 2002–2003*. Phnom Penh: LICADHO, 2004.

Cambodian League for the Promotion and Defense of Human Rights (LICADHO). *Report: Rape and Indecent Assault Cases and the Cambodian Justice System*. Phnom Penh: LICADHO, 2004.

Coghill, S. *Resource Guide to the Criminal Law of Cambodia*. Phnom Penh: International Human Rights Law Group and Cambodia Defenders Project, 2000.

Fernando, B. *Problems Facing the Cambodian Legal System*. Hong Kong: Asian Human Rights Commission, 1998.

Human Rights Watch. "Essential Background: Overview of Human Rights Issues in Cambodia." World Report 2005, Index. New York: Human Rights Watch.

World Bank, Asian Development Bank, and Japan Bank for International Cooperation. *Connecting East Asia: A New Framework for Infrastructure*. Washington, DC: World Bank, 2005.

Yigen, K. *The Police in Cambodia*. Copenhagen: Danish Centre for Human Rights, 2001.

CAMEROON

Background Material

Cameroon is situated in central Africa, slightly above the Equator. With a land base of 475,442 square kilometres, the country is rich in biodiversity and culture. Cameroon's population is estimated at 16 million, and the country shares a long border of nearly 1,000 kilometres with the Federal Republic of Nigeria in the west, Chad in the north, the Central Africa Republic in the east, and Equatorial Guinea, Gabon, and Congo Brazzaville in the south.

Cameroon's history has always been associated with France and Great Britain, but this country was really colonized by Germany, which, in 1884 under the supervision of Gustav von Nachtigal, succeeded in signing with the chiefs of Douala—situated at the estuary of the Wouri River facing the Pacific Ocean—the Protectorate treaties.

After the German defeats in 1917 and 1945, Cameroon was placed under the Mandate of the League of Nations and under the trusteeship of the United Nations and administered by the victors, France taking the eastern part and Great Britain the western part of the country.

This dual administration is partly responsible for the numerous problems of integration that the country is facing today. In fact, in the exercise of their trusteeship powers, each country tried to inculcate in its "zone" the influence of its administration so much so that it was difficult to merge the two systems of administration at independence, and such a hypothetical integration could only give rise to claims from minority groups.

The eastern part of the country declared independence on 1 January 1960 in a climate rife with uprising and repressions orchestrated by national liberation movements and by local political authorities backed by the French administration.

As for the western part of the country, it obtained independence on 1 October 1961. The unification of the two Cameroons was achieved under President Ahmadou Ahidjo, and the country was renamed the United Republic of Cameroon. This was a step toward the merging of customs, habits, and feelings—in short a step toward the building of a true nation. This laudable ambition, however, has been difficult to achieve, as some citizens cultivated hatred and a will of domination, while others simply had the feeling that they were oppressed in the new state in which 237 ethnic groups cohabit with many languages and dialects.

French and English were adopted as the two official languages of Cameroon. At the religious level, it should be noted that the secularity of the state of Cameroon was affirmed. However, it can be noted that one-quarter of the population is animist. Muslims represent 22% of the population, and are mostly found in the northern part of the country. Catholics represent 33% and Protestants 17%, and are mostly based in the southern region of the country.

Contextual Features

At the political level, Cameroon is a republic endowed with solid and reliable democratic institutions, and functions on a semipresidential system.

With a powerful president elected by direct and secret universal suffrage for a seven-year term of office renewable once, the new institutions have been rejuvenated by the adoption of the Constitution of 18 January 1996, which put an end to the anachronisms of the previous constitution adopted in 1972, and ushered in a real democratisation process by recognising the separation of powers, the primacy of man, decentralisation as a source of administrative efficiency, and the relative control of the executive, among other things.

After a period of calm following independence, the fall of the Berlin Wall, aid attached with strings imposed by international financial institutions (International Monetary Fund and World Bank), and the Cold War exacerbated the divergences that were shelved by the authoritarian practices of the one-party system.

The privileged ties that exist between France and its former colonies, including Cameroon, and Francophone and France-Africa summits pushed the country into embracing democracy on the one hand, and the turmoil of demonstrations, repression, and recuperation, on the other.

Nevertheless, what happened in Cameroon during the political turmoil of 1991 outweighed the negative outcomes of many years of colonialism and its aftermath. Considerable losses in property and human lives occurred, to the extent of jeopardizing the very existence of the State. One year after the liberalisation of political activities, there were 117 political parties. Apart from the party in power, the CPDM, and the UPC (party that opted for armed struggle to obtain independence since 1956), NUDP, and SDF (1), the other political parties represented only a particular tribe, clan, and most often, a family.

The last presidential election on 11 October 2004, in which H.E. Paul Biya emerged as the winner gave a true picture of the political game made up of alliances, treachery, and political mendacity. The party in power, the CPDM, led by Biya is the master of the political game. Sure of its establishment throughout the national territory, this party has never hesitated to form alliances with other parties. This has given birth to what political pundits call the "presidential majority." This has resulted in widespread electoral successes.

Opposition parties on the contrary have never found a common platform with a view to proposing a plausible alternative that complies with the law. Their demagogic gesticulations made through alliances formed behind the backs of their respective parties, their reputation as turncoat politicians, their tendency to shy away from discussing issues affecting the daily lives of Cameroonians make these parties political outcastes whose activities are only felt when elections are at hand, especially as financial manna is always available from the state or they lodge a complaint nationally and worldwide to denounce "massive irregularities," or claim a stolen victory, or threaten to resort to violence to quench their thirst for power.

The Supreme Court, Courts of Appeal, and other courts of justice generally exercise the judicial power, which is independent of the executive and the legislative powers (see Article 37, paragraph 2) of the constitution.

Presently, Cameroon is practising two legal systems. In the French-speaking region, the French "Code d'Instruction Criminaelle" as well as the Civil Code are applicable, while the Common Law is applicable in the English-speaking region.

At the penal level, there is a Penal Code in force throughout the national territory, except in the English-speaking region where the "bail system" remains applicable for the majority of offences recorded by the courts. Criminal Investigation Department officers are called on to back up their proceedings during court hearings in the English-speaking region.

Clarification of both judicial systems has shown the limits of mental and institutional harmonization in the country forty years after independence and thirty years after unification.

A bill on penal procedure is under study, and it is hoped that all Cameroonians will be subject to the same rule, and consequently, to the same sanctions without any feeling of nostalgia. Once the sentence has been announced and even before it is announced, one should make sure that the defendant is ready to pay his debt toward society.

Prisons that were built about forty years ago have neither been renovated nor adapted to modern standards in order to cope with the growing number of delinquents in the cities to effectively serve as reformatory institutions. The most glaring example is offered by the two main cities, Yaounde and Douala.

Yaounde, the political capital city of Cameroon has a population of about 2.2 million. The Kodengui Central Prison had an initial intake of 1,200 inmates, but as of 30 June 2004, it housed more than 4,000 inmates. In spite of the efforts made by judicial authorities (easing of procedures, rapid enrolment of cases, and so on), and administrative authorities (building a central prison), the problem of overcrowding continues.

The situation is more critical in the city of Douala, the economic capital, with a population of about 2.7 million. The Central Prison of New Bell, initially conceived to house 1,500 inmates, had almost 5,000 inmates as of 30 June 2004.

In the absence of prisons for minors and maximum-security prisons, there is also the problem of the dilapidation of existing ones.

Criminality in Cameroon takes root in the surrounding poverty. The causes of poverty are many; only those happenings that are politically and economically motivated are mentioned here. Since 1988, Cameroon has been going through an unprecedented economic and financial crisis, which was exacerbated by the structural adjustment programme introduced by the World Bank and the International Monetary Fund (IMF). The following causes can be cited:

- Devaluation in January 1994 of the CFA Franc by 50%

- Liquidation of some state corporations and the subsequent loss of jobs
- Rural exodus
- Unemployment of youths
- Proliferation of firearms
- Massive escape of prisoners from prisons
- Poor state of roads
- Absence of streetlights

Violent crime consists of all attempts on the physical integrity of citizens, and this takes the form of attacks during the day or during the night, in public or private places, with or without firearms or knives, resulting in the loss of life or injury, and/or of valuable objects and cash. Homicide, assault and battery, aggravated theft, rapes, and other violent crimes are rampant in big cities, while highway robbery is usually found in rural areas. The cities of Yaounde and Douala registered the highest rate of crime in 2003.

Whitecollar crime is most often practised by intelligent, astute persons, and sometimes by "respectable" persons. Whitecollar criminality is usually known as "feymania," a group-organized moral and financial swindle; people who wish to get rich quick easily fall prey to this group. It manifests itself through the following:

- Corruption
- Breach of trust
- All kinds of swindles
- Forgery
- Counterfeiting
- Embezzlement of public funds

A wide range of modern crime networks have found a fertile ground in our Cameroon, namely:

- Importation and consumption of hard drugs
- Women and child trafficking for hard labour or prostitution
- Trafficking in human organs
- Cybercrimes

A recent report on households reveals that more than 60% of cases of armed robbery in Yaounde and Douala are perpetrated by youths between 18 and 25 years.

Police Profile

Background

The history of the Cameroon Police Force is similar to that of the entire country. After the German defeat in World War I, Cameroonians developed an interest in the management of public affairs. The expansion of some cities brought about security problems, which the French gendarmes alone could not cope with. As from 1925, the French administration, which was the trusteeship authority at the time, opened the first police stations in Douala and Yaounde via the Order of 7 November 1925. These police stations had the special duties of ensuring public order, applying laws and regulations, and combating delinquency. In the English-speaking zone, these missions were entrusted to the Nigerian Police Force.

After the World War II, and most especially in the wake of the famous Brazzaville Conference, which recognised the rights of "peoples to self-determination," events took a decidedly different turn with the formation of national liberation movements.

The trusteeship authority was now confronted with clamours for independence. This situation was worsened by the inappropriate assessment of facts by the then High Commissioner of the French Republic. He had to fall back on the local police force in order to mercilessly quell these manifestations and establish a regime of terror in areas controlled by these movements. It is within this context of unrest that independence was obtained in 1960.

The new independent regime made use of the same authoritarian and autocratic methods to assert its authority. The police force was never militarised; as the secular arm of the state, it lent total support to the new institutions. The police force was now looked on as a force of repression rather than a security force. It was instead seen as a hated and suspicious instrument, rather than as an instrument that guarantees security, peace, and public tranquillity.

The sight of a policeman brought about feelings of suspicion. This perception lasted until 1991 when the special laws dating from 1964 were abolished and replaced by laws instituting democracy, multiparty politics, and the primacy of the individual in society.

Since the police force is a reflection of a given society, the Cameroonian Police Force underwent profound changes both in the general organization and in the carrying out of its sovereign missions at the service of institutions, and protection of persons and their properties. As a full public service, the police force unavoidably moved from the republican concept to the concept of the citizen.

Demographics

Presently, the National Security force numbers about 17,000 elements of all grades in the ratio of one policeman to 1,000 inhabitants. At first sight, the situation seems to be unrealistic, but given that three quarters of this manpower are based in big cities, one has every reason to be reassured because 12,000 are gendarmes and the other quarter are in charge of security in the suburbs and other remote areas. The government intends to increase personnel to 34,000 by 2008.

Organizational Description

The Cameroon Police Force is a large administration having its own means to accomplish its missions. Decree No. 2002/003 of 4 January 2002 to organize the General Delegation for National Security is the reference instrument for reforming and restructuring the police corps.

A glance at this important instrument leads to the discovery that the substance remains unchanged in spite of the new trend to adapt existing structures to the evolution of Cameroonian society and demands of globalisation. The original "national security" appellation of the Cameroonian Police Force makes it a command and administration corps placed under the authority of the President of the Republic who is the Supreme Commander.

The following synoptic diagram outlines the structure of national security.

In a bid to build a modern country, the best method of recruitment into the police force remains a competitive entrance examination and merit based on the following criteria:

- Superintendents of police are recruited from among Cameroonians who are holders of the bachelor's degree or the medical doctor degree.
- Assistant superintendents of police are recruited from among Cameroonians who are holders of the GCE advanced level or an equivalent certificate.
- Police inspectors are recruited from among holders of the GCE ordinary level, and police constables from among holders of the primary school certificate.

Considering the delicate missions assigned the police forces, in addition to the required certificates, other conditions are also needed, namely age, good moral character, good health, and Cameroonian citizenship. This excludes any discrimination linked to the candidate's gender, ethnic group, or religion.

Functions

The police force's fundamental mission consists of ensuring the respect and protection of institutions, public liberties, persons, and properties. In addition, it ensures the respect and implementation of laws and regulations, performs administrative and judicial police duties, and is a regular force called upon to ensure the national defence.

While falling under the direct authority of the President of the Republic, the police force carries out missions entrusted by government authorities within the framework of their respective competencies in compliance with the instructions of the Head of State.

Training

The training of policemen is ensured at local and higher levels by the National Police College of Yaounde. Before 1990, this institution was in charge of training superintendents and assistant superintendents of police. The training lasted for two years for Cadet Superintendents of Police who were holders of the bachelor's degree and four years for holders of the GCE advanced level. After the reform, the four-year training cycle was suppressed, and Cadet Superintendents of Police and Assistant Cadet Superintendents of Police now undergo a two-year training programme, while those on professional internship and special courses do one year.

The institution still trains nationals from Benin, Chad, Central African Republic, and Equatorial Guinea on a regular basis.

At the lower level, the Mutengene Police Training Centre takes care of the initial and further training of police inspectors and constables. It also serves as a Training Centre for specialized techniques of maintaining public order and of military tactics.

Police Public Projects

Cameroonians are eager to know what their police force does. For that reason, the public is informed about what is being done in other countries, especially as concerns highway robbery and criminality.

Through its radio programme, "At the Service of One and All," broadcast on the national radio station (CRTV) every Saturday afternoon, practical pieces of advice are given to citizens on certain aspects of social life, on the conduct to adopt in a given situation and the police unit to contact, as well as useful phone numbers.

Complaints and Discipline

Since everyone does not always accept police actions, there are ways and means of guaranteeing the rights of citizens without ruling out the need to maintain public order and peace. These consist of internal control mechanisms, which are purely police mechanisms, and external control mechanisms.

The Decree to organize the General Delegation for National Security provides for mechanisms of control of police action at all command levels.

Control at the high level is exercised by the Delegate General for National Security Inspectors General, Directors within the framework of their specific functions, and the Special Division for Control of Services. At the regional level, control is exercised by the Provincial Delegate for National Security or his assistant, and other regional officials.

The official in charge of the activity makes a rectification of the acts committed by the policeman by giving him the right guidelines, or he simply takes note of his inefficiency, which is likely to discredit the entire police corps. He may be compelled to open a disciplinary file for the accused, and depending on the nature of the facts, the sanctions that will be meted out will range from an additional spell of duty to dismissal.

In 1991, Cameroonian lawmakers set up a National Commission of Human Rights and freedoms. This important institution is, among other things, in charge of keeping an eye on the conditions of detention of individuals in prisons, police cells, and gendarmerie cells. To that effect, it has free access to cells at any time and can, if it deems it necessary, listen to detainees and forward complaints to government authorities. Considering its composition—magistrates and personalities of the civil society—and seriousness, the establishment of this Commission enables each official to take adequate measures so that nothing problematic will be seen that may be attributable to him. Magistrates have free access to police stations and other units so as to keep an eye on detentions. They release detainees and give guidelines on how to speed up investigations.

Terrorism

Although Cameroon may not yet be harbouring terrorist networks of worldwide reputation, security services should remain vigilant. Given the extreme mobility of persons thanks to modern transportation and computers, no country in the world can boast of being beyond the reach of terrorist attacks. Given the fact that Cameroon hosts several diplomatic missions, and the interests of some countries involved are found in the intense fight against terrorism, or those indirectly supporting liberation movements in the Near and Middle East, one understands why Cameroon should not lag behind in the fight against this phenomenon.

Besides the judicious exploitation of information and intelligence reports on terrorist activities, Cameroon has resolutely pledged to participate in every initiative taken by the United Nations in order to arrive at an appropriate regulation.

International Cooperation

Cameroon, fully aware that no sustainable development can take place if peace is not guaranteed, has decided to abide by the objectives of the international community. Since 1992, a first contingent of seventy policemen was sent to Cambodia. After one year of service, the same experience was repeated in 2000 and 2002 in Kosovo. In 2004, contingents were sent to Côte d'Ivoire, Haiti, and the Democratic Republic of Congo, and observers were sent to Burundi.

Presently, about 300 Cameroonian policemen are participating alongside other policemen in the world in peacekeeping operations, and by so doing are acquiring the experience needed in this domain never before exploited by us. In a bid to improve on the output of its manpower, the National Security force regularly sends police officers abroad, especially to France, Great Britain, United States, Belgium, and Switzerland, for practical internships on human rights, and the fight against highway robbery, drugs, and other illegal transnational activities. Police officers are also sent to Egypt and South Africa for these courses. It should also be noted with satisfaction that the French government contributes to the training of the Cameroon Police Force through its police international cooperation service, by providing great assistance in the form of teaching staff, teaching material, and counselling, and by so doing facilitates effective training on the spot of police officers at a preferential cost.

Police Education, Research, and Publications

As regards publications, the Cameroon Police Force has the following:

Quarterly police information magazine entitled *Servir*

Monthly magazine entitled *Thermopolice*, which gives an account of the actions undertaken by the police supervisor and the achievements of regional services

Two news bulletins: *Le Moule des Cadres*, published by the National Police College Yaounde, and *Le Reflet*, published by the Mutengene Police Training Centre.

JEAN LOUIS MESSING

Bibliography

Levine, V. T. *Le Cameroun*. Paris: Nouveaux Horizons, 1970.

Mbome, F. "L' Etat et les Eglises au Cameroun." thesis, Paris, 1979.

Messing, J. L. "La Problematique du maintien de 1° ordre dans les Etats d'Afrique noire francophone, le cas du Cameroun (1960–1992)." these de 3e cycle en droit public, Yaounde, 1995.

Mveng, E. *Histoire du Cameroun*. Paris: Presence Africaine, 1963.

Ngongo, L. P. *Histoire des Institutions et des faits Sociaux*. Paris: Berger-Levrault, 1987.

Pondi, P. *La Police au Cameroun*. Yaounde: Cle, 1988.

CANADA

Background Material

Canada lies to the north of the United States. Geographically, it is the second largest country in the world, covering 9,984,670 square kilometers. It stretches from the Atlantic Ocean in the east to the Pacific Ocean in the west, and from the U.S. border north to the Arctic Ocean. While only 5% of its land is arable, it has rich agricultural regions, ample fresh water, and large tracts of forest.

In 2001, the Canadian population was close to 31.5 million. Natural population increase has slowed, so immigration is an important contribution to population growth. More than 18% of the population was born outside of the country.

Canada is a multicultural society, and largely tolerant of racial and cultural differences. Until the late 1950s, most Canadian immigrants were drawn from the British Isles, Europe, and the United States. By contrast, of those who immigrated during the 1990s,

58% were from Asia and the Middle East, 20% from Europe, 11% from the Caribbean and Central and South America, and 8% from Africa. Other than Aboriginal people, 4 million people identify themselves as non-Caucasian in race or nonwhite in color. The three largest visible minority groups are Chinese, South Asian, and blacks.

There are three Aboriginal groups in Canada: North American Indian or First Nations peoples, Inuit (Eskimo), and Métis, who are people of mixed Indian and French or Scottish ancestry. In general, the Inuit inhabit northern Canada, particularly the Inuit-governed territory of Nunavut in the eastern Arctic. The Métis are concentrated in the western provinces, while the First Nations, who comprise many different family and linguistic groups, are dispersed throughout the country. While the non-Aboriginal birth rate is declining, that of Aboriginal peoples is rising. One third of the Aboriginal population in 2001 was under 14 years of age.

English and French are the two official languages of Canada. In addition, many immigrants retain their mother tongues. The Inuit speak Inuktituk, and people of the First Nations speak a variety of distinct languages. The number of native language speakers is dwindling, and many languages have disappeared.

Roughly 77% of the population is Christian, of which more than half is Roman Catholic. Muslims constitute 2% of the population; Jews, Buddhists, Hindus, and Sikhs represent about 1% each; and 16.5% of the population has no religious affiliation. Canada is usually at the top or near the top of the United Nations quality of life index. Life expectancy at birth is 79.96 years, and the infant mortality rate is 4.82 per 1,000 live births. Health and other social benefits are provided by government, including maternity leave, and some preschool support. In 2000, average annual earnings of employed people over 15 years of age were $31,757. More than 30% of employed people earned over $60,000 annually, although 41% earned less than $20,000 a year. Earnings were strongly linked to educational level and age. Over 60% of people in the top income level have a university degree, while over 60% in the lower income level have only high school education or less. Women earn 64 cents for every dollar earned by men. Immigrants earn substantially less.

Education from kindergarten to high school graduation is provided free of charge to children. In 2001, 20% of the population had university qualifications. Another 21% had a college diploma, and 12% a trade certificate. The percentage of male and female university graduates was roughly equal. Over 1 million of the working-age population had doctorates, masters, or other qualifications above the bachelor's degree level, and six out of ten immigrants of working age had trade, college, or university credentials.

Canada is a highly technical and industrialized society. In 2004, the estimated GDP per capita was almost $30,000. It has rich natural resources and is a major producer of lumber, pulp and paper, wheat, fish, oil, natural gas, nickel, uranium, copper, iron ore, zinc, and other minerals. It both exports these as raw materials, and uses them for its own manufacturing industries. It also exports motor vehicles, rail cars, and machinery. Canada is also involved in technology production, particularly telecommunications. Computer and internet use is among the highest in the world. Canada also participates in aerospace development. Membership in the North American Free Trade Area (NAFTA) with Mexico and the United States has stimulated the Canadian economy, and 85% of its exports go to the United States.

Contextual Features

Canada is a confederation of ten provinces and three territories, and a parliamentary democracy. While it has retained British political features from its earlier status as a British dominion, the Canadian political system is influenced by proximity to the republican United States and adherence to international agreements. The confederation was created in 1867 among the provinces of Nova Scotia, New Brunswick, Canada East (now Quebec), and Canada West (now Ontario). Over time, Manitoba, Prince Edward Island, British Columbia, Saskatchewan, Alberta, and Newfoundland joined the confederation. The Yukon, Northwest, and Nunuvut territories are situated in the north and have insufficient population to acquire provincial status.

The Canadian head of state is Queen Elizabeth II of the United Kingdom. Her Canadian representative is the Governor General, appointed by the Queen on the advice of the Canadian government.

In 1982, Canada repatriated its constitution in the form of the British North America Act of 1867, from the United Kingdom, and proclaimed it as the Constitution Act. It governs the division of powers and responsibilities between the federal government and the provinces. In general, the Act makes the federal government responsible for "peace, order and good government," and the provinces for "property and civil rights." The federal law also has precedence over provincial law, and the federal government can disallow provincial statutes. In practice, there are some areas of shared jurisdiction, or where the federal government has some influence in provincial matters, such as health, by virtue of federal spending power.

The Charter of Rights and Freedoms is part of the constitution. It guarantees equality before the law, and protection against discrimination based on race, national or ethnic origin, color, religion, sex, age, or mental or physical disability. It also guarantees language rights for Francophones and Anglophones; freedom of conscience, religion, thought, belief, opinion, and expression; peaceful assembly and association; the right to vote; the right to enter, remain, and leave Canada; the right to life, liberty, and security of the person; to be secure against unreasonable search and seizure; not to be arbitrarily detained or imprisoned and, on arrest, to be informed promptly of the reasons why; to retain and instruct counsel and to have the right of habeas corpus; to be tried by a jury within a reasonable time; not to witness against oneself; to be presumed innocent until proven guilty; not to be denied reasonable bail without cause; not to be tried twice for the same offense; and not to be subjected to any cruel or unusual treatment. A "notwithstanding" clause allows a constitutional provision to be set aside in special circumstances, but it has never been invoked.

The federal parliament is responsible for legislating criminal law, which is mainly contained in the Criminal Code, and for passing and enforcing laws on a wide variety of matters from trade and commerce to foreign affairs, health protection, transport, resource protection, defense, security, and other matters. The provinces are responsible for education, health programs, highways and traffic regulation, forests, municipalities, property rights including companies and securities matters, and the administration of justice, which includes the police, civil and criminal courts, and corrections. This means that criminal law is the same throughout Canada, but there are some differences in justice practices because of provincial control of police, courts, and corrections.

The legal system is based on English common law except in Quebec, which as a former French colony retains French law for civil matters. Jurisdiction for the courts and the judicial system is divided between the federal and provincial governments. Provincial authority for the administration of justice means that each province has the responsibility to constitute, organize, and maintain a system of courts. The judges of the lower or provincial courts are appointed by the provinces. The judges of the superior trial and appeal courts in a province are appointed and paid by the federal government. Sometimes, in the interests of social policy or efficiency, provinces operate special-purpose courts such a small claims, family, and traffic courts.

The federal courts system consists of the Federal Court for hearing matters against the federal government, the Federal Appeal Court, the Tax Court, and the Supreme Court of Canada. The jurisdiction of the Supreme Court of Canada includes both the common law and the civil law of Quebec. It hears appeals from the court of last resort, usually the provincial or territorial appeal courts and the Federal Appeal Court. The Supreme Court of Canada also gives opinions on matters referred by the provincial and federal governments. In 2000–2001, the total cost of the Canadian courts system was C$1.039 billion; prosecutions cost C$335 million and legal aid programs C$512 million.

Responsibility for corrections is divided between the federal and provincial governments. Offenders given a sentence of two years or more serve them in the federal correctional system, and those with sentences of less than two years serve them in a provincial facility. Correctional facilities are classified as maximum, medium, and minimum security, and operate commensurate security regimes. Inmates are assigned to a security level dependent on their behavior rather than their crime. Separate facilities exist for women. Because there are so few women in federal correctional facilities, it is difficult to ensure that they are provided with the same rehabilitative opportunities as men. Another problem is the overrepresentation of Aboriginals in the correctional population. The provincial and federal governments cooperate in various arrangements to ameliorate conditions for inmates. Many offenders also serve their sentences in community correctional settings. Under the Youth Criminal Justice Act, most young people in conflict with the law are treated by means other than the formal criminal justice system. They may go through a process of restorative justice and make some form of restitution.

The provinces also operate remand centers for those awaiting or undergoing hearings. In most cases, arrested and accused persons are released on bail rather than held in custody. Provincial parole boards make decisions on the release of provincial offenders, and the National Parole Board does the same for federal inmates. Usually a convicted person is eligible for parole after serving one third of a sentence, or after seven years, whichever is the least. Unless held by special order, inmates having served two-thirds of a sentence are released under mandatory supervision in the community. Persons found guilty of a serious personal injury offense and demonstrating a persistent pattern of aggressive behavior, can be designated dangerous offenders and ordered to be held indefinitely. In 2002, there were 32,512 correctional inmates, and 124,196 people under community supervision in Canada. The total cost of correctional services was close to $2.5 billion.

In 2003, the crime rate per 100,000 population was 8,132, excluding traffic violations, and drug and other federal statute offenses. The homicide rate was 1.7, the attempted murder rate 2.2, and drug offenses were 271.8 per 100,000 population. The rate of theft under $5,000 was 2,220.4, and over $5,000, 63.6 per 100,000 population. Apart from small fluctuations, crime has been declining since the early 1990s, and has tended to stabilize.

While "street" crime is well contained, organized crime and high-technology crime pose a considerable threat. In company with other members of the G7, Canada pays particular attention to the control of international organized crime. It also has an obligation to participate in international efforts against terrorism. Canada has special mechanisms, and works with the United States on such measures as the Integrated Border Enforcement Teams (IBETS) to prevent international terrorist activity in the two countries.

Firearm ownership and use are regulated in Canada. Licenses are required to own firearms and, with few exceptions, firearms must be registered, and owners must take gun-safety training. Some exceptions apply to Aboriginals who hunt for subsistence.

Police Profile

Background

Each of the ten provinces makes laws for the direction of its police. The laws prescribe standards for such matters as governance, recruitment, training, uniform, or use of firearms. They also require municipalities attaining a certain population size, usually 5,000 inhabitants, to provide and pay for their own policing. Thus, municipalities are responsible for urban policing, while provinces provide policing outside of municipalities.

In total, there are about 300 police organizations in Canada. The figure fluctuates because provincial governments are amalgamating many small municipal police services into larger more efficient organizations. These amalgamated police services operate regionally, and so introduce another level of government into what is already a complex system. In practice, however, the system works smoothly because mechanisms exist to promote cooperation and standardization. Some of these mechanisms include regular meetings of federal, provincial, and territor-

ial officials responsible for justice and policing to discuss joint policies and actions, and the existence of professional associations, such as the Canadian Association of Chiefs of Police, Canadian Association of Police Boards, and Canadian Professional Police Association, a national umbrella organization for police unions.

Demographics

There are close to 60,000 police officers in Canada, of which 27%, or 15,634, are sworn Royal Canadian Mounted Police (RCMP) officers. The police-to-population ratio varies from province to province and municipality to municipality, but in 2004, it was 188 for every 100,000 of the Canadian population. This is about 20% lower than the United States and Australia, and about 25% lower than England and Wales.

In addition to sworn police officers, there are over 22,000 nonsworn employees working in police organizations, or one for every 2.7 police officers. Nonpolice employees perform clerical, dispatch, forensic science, intelligence analysis, identification, specialized investigation, victim assistance, training, administration, management, and executive functions. Many major police services have at least one civilian on their executive team and a number of civilian managers.

There are almost 10,000 female police officers, or over 16.5% of the police population. The number of women and visible minorities in policing is growing as a result of employment equity programs. Women meet the same physical and intellectual standards as male police officers, carry out the same duties, and receive the same rate of pay. Women have been in policing since the late nineteenth century, but have been accepted on an equal footing with men only since the early 1970s. Since then, women have reached executive and other senior ranks and served as chiefs of major police organizations.

In 2004, 7.6% of RCMP sworn members were Aboriginal, 6% visible minorities, and 3% persons with disabilities. Because racial/ethnic data are normally only voluntarily reported, however, the total racial and cultural representation in Canadian policing is unknown. Nevertheless, government policies have spurred police forces to strive for multicultural representation among their employees. Modifications to uniforms and internal rules are sometimes made to make this possible. For example, some police services have modified their rules to allow Sikh police officers to wear turbans, and First Nations police officers to wear their hair in braids. Few aboriginal or visible minority police officers have yet achieved promotion above the junior management level, probably because minority recruiting and integration into mainstream policing are relatively recent.

Police agencies range in size from less than ten to 22,000 in the RCMP. The Toronto Police Service has roughly 7,000 members. Many Canadian police services have less than 100 officers. A police organization usually requires 100 police officers to provide a full range of services. Consequently, many of the smaller Canadian police services rely on larger police organizations for specialist services such as homicide investigation. The inability of small police forces to provide a full range of services is one of the reasons why many are being amalgamated.

Organizational Description

The RCMP is a federal police force governed by the Royal Canadian Mounted Police Act. Under its terms, the RCMP is accountable to the Minister of Public Safety and Emergency Preparedness, who is the cabinet minister responsible to the federal parliament for the RCMP, the Canadian Security Intelligence Service, Canadian Correctional Services, and National Parole Board. The RCMP is responsible for enforcement of federal statutes, national security investigations, security of federal institutions, important persons and foreign missions, and relations with foreign police services. In this role, it carries out such activities as organized crime, narcotics, cybercrime and commercial crime investigations, intelligence gathering, and protective policing, and places liaison officers in Canadian embassies and high-level commissions around the world.

In addition to its federal role the RCMP also provides policing services under paid contract to eight of the ten provinces. The two exceptions are Ontario and Quebec, which have their own provincial police. The RCMP is also responsible for policing in the three territories. The RCMP is thus dispersed throughout Canada from large, urban population centers to isolated Arctic communities of Aboriginal people.

In the provinces where it forms the provincial police service, municipalities may choose to use the RCMP rather than maintain their own police forces. Two hundred municipalities across Canada are therefore policed by the RCMP. In its contract role, the RCMP performs a full range of policing duties from enforcement of the Criminal Code and provincial statutes, to answering calls for service and emergency response. The provincial police of Ontario and Quebec also undertake contract policing in their provinces on the request of a municipality.

Through the RCMP, the federal government also provides a number of national operational support services to Canadian police forces. These are called the National Police Services. They comprise forensic laboratories which, among other things, perform DNA profiling and maintain a national DNA data bank; a national police information system accessible from police patrol cars, which contains data on criminal records, outstanding warrants, motor vehicle ownership, and other matters; an automated fingerprint identification system; a national criminal intelligence system; national registries for missing children, sex offenders, and bomb data; and the Canadian Police College, which provides advanced and specialized training to Canadian and foreign police officers. These services promote standardization of policing across the country and overcome the fragmentation occasioned by multijurisdictional policing.

In addition to police services, there are a number of federal and provincial regulatory or law enforcement agencies. They enforce the regulatory and penal aspects of administrative statutes for such matters as customs and excise, immigration, health and food safety, consumer protection, resource protection, or trade and commerce.

Private security companies and agents are said to outnumber police officers in Canada. They carry out a number of functions ranging from static guard duty to private investigations. Sometimes their activities resemble those of the police, such as when they perform security functions for private residential enclaves, public housing projects, or large indoor shopping malls. In general, however, they lack formal powers and are regulated by the provinces.

Aboriginal reserves with their own governing bodies can choose their own mode of policing. They may contract with another police service to provide services, or they may establish their own police service. The federal government contributes 58% of the cost, and the province in which the reserve is situated pays 48%. The arrangements are governed by tripartite agreements signed by the federal, provincial, and band governments, which stipulate the standard of policing to be provided on the reserve.

With the exception of RCMP members, police officers are unionized. The unions tend to be conservative; support tougher law, sentencing, and punishment; and nurture a strong police subculture. Their policies and activities have done much to improve working conditions and material advantages of police officers.

Functions

Police possess the powers to enter premises, stop, detain, search, seize, arrest, and use force. The force used must be the least possible and a last resort. Use of interpersonal skills is the preferred means of controlling situations. The rule of law and the Charter of Rights and Freedoms prescribe the circumstances in which powers may be exercised. In some circumstances, police must first obtain a warrant to exercise their powers. Police are also able to exercise discretion; that is, to deal with situations differentially, depending on circumstances. For example, they can decide not to take action against young persons in conflict with the law, to issue warnings, to use restorative justice mechanisms, or to process them through the criminal justice system.

Police officers carry semiautomatic side arms, but there are policies and procedures governing when they can be drawn. A police shooting causing death usually attracts considerable media attention, and is invariably investigated. Police officers who have used deadly force inappropriately may be charged criminally. Police also use weapons of less-than-lethal force, such as the taser gun, which administers an electrical shock, bean bag guns, and pepper spray. Tear gas may be used in extreme cases.

The police role includes maintenance of order, enforcement of laws, criminal investigation, crime prevention, and emergency and general services to the public. Community policing, including response to call, vehicle and foot patrols, school liaison programs, and other activities are usually carried out by general duty officers. Specialist functions such as criminal investigation, traffic law enforcement and collision investigation, crime scene investigation and identification, youth crime, family violence, explosives dismantling, or intelligence and criminal profiling are usually carried out by trained specialist police officers in specialized units. Public confidence in the police is regularly measured in public opinion polls and usually reaches more than 80%.

Training

Canadian policing is a bottom entry profession. Everyone enters as a junior constable and progresses through the ranks by promotion. While there is considerable rank variation among Canadian police services, in municipal police services there are generally three nonmanagement ranks of constable, senior constable, and sergeant; two management ranks of inspector and superintendent; and executive ranks of deputy chief and chief. Some police

services have ranks roughly equivalent to military ranks. Ranks above inspector in the RCMP receive the Queen's commission in the same manner as military officers.

Educational qualifications for recruitment into policing include high school graduation, but about a third of recruits have university degrees on entry and more acquire them during their careers. Many recruits have also completed police training at a community college before applying for entry into a police force. Other prerequisites will include good character, possession of a driving license, and perhaps proficiency in swimming, word processing, or other skills. The minimum age of entry is usually nineteen years, and there are physical fitness requirements related to job performance.

The duration of basic training is twenty to twenty-four weeks. The training consists of classes in law, police practice, human rights, cultural sensitivity, ethics, and practical training in many aspects of police work. Former emphasis on drill and discipline is being replaced with adult learning techniques that encourage recruits to think and problem-solve. While they learn how to shoot, use force, and protect themselves, the emphasis is on learning community policing techniques and how to manage situations without confrontation.

After recruit training, they enter the field where they serve a number of months under the supervision of a field training officer or a mentor. Later in their careers, more advanced and specialized training is provided at a provincial police academy or at the Canadian Police College, which is a center for police management and advanced and specialized investigative training.

Complaints and Discipline

Police accountability is ensured by a variety of mechanisms. Police statutes set up governing mechanisms and prescribe principles of conduct. Most municipal police are governed by police boards, at arm's length to municipal government, comprising appointed members of the public. Federal and provincial ministers responsible for policing must answer to elected representatives for the actions of the police. There are also independent agencies with powers to hold audits of police forces and to hear public complaints. The courts also limit abuse of police powers by dismissing cases where due process or the rights of an accused have been violated. Police officers are liable to reprimand, loss of pay, or loss of employment or other penalties for wrongful actions, and, if they commit a criminal act, are charged criminally. Keen news media interest in the police also serves as an oversight mechanism.

While sometimes controversial, police are protected from undue political influence by the doctrine that governments give policy direction, but the police are independent in the enforcement of the law. A governing body can therefore direct a police service to implement community policing as a strategy, or pay more attention to traffic violations, but it cannot direct a police service to halt an investigation or to investigate a particular person.

Policing is becoming a highly regarded, well-paid profession in Canada. A first-class constable, attainable after three years of service, is paid between $45,000 and $65,000 a year, depending on the size and location of the police service. Salaries can be augmented with generous overtime pay. Police executives of large police services earn more than $100,000 a year. There are also comprehensive benefits. Given that more than 80% of a police budget is spent on labor costs, Canadian policing is expensive. In 2003, Canadians paid C$8.3 billion for policing services or C$263 per person. The advantage is that police organizations can select good recruits. Together with good training, internal codes of discipline and ethics, external oversight, and high rates of public approval, this means that there is little corruption among Canadian police, and generally a high level of service to the public. In general, Canadian police tend to be public spirited. They support worthy causes and do much volunteer work, particularly with youth.

International Cooperation

Canada is a member of the United Nations, Interpol, and G7.

Police Education, Research, and Publications

The main police training institutions in Canada are listed below.

The Atlantic Police Academy provides pre-employment, basic, and some intermediate training.

The École Nationale de Police du Québec trains Quebec police recruits and provides some advanced training.

The Ontario Police College trains Ontario police recruits and provides some advanced training.

The Saskatchewan Police Training Academy provides some basic training.

The Police Academy at the British Columbia Justice Institute provides basic and advanced training.

The RCMP Academy at Depot Division in Regina provides basic training to RCMP recruits and basic training for some regulatory law enforcement officers.

The Canadian Police College provides advanced and specialized training in management and law enforcement related to organized and multijurisdictional crime.

A number of community colleges offer policing and security courses for students wishing to become police officers. A few universities offer degrees in police studies in addition to degrees up to the doctoral level in criminology. There are centers of criminology, with faculty specializing in policing research at the University of Moncton, University of Montreal, University of Ottawa, University of Toronto, University of Manitoba, and Simon Fraser University.

Research activity in policing fluctuates depending on the amount of public money available. The federal ministries of Public Safety and Emergency Preparedness and Justice, the Social Sciences and Humanities Research Council, the Law Commission of Canada, provincial governments, and, occasionally, other government institutions, make financial contributions to support research on policing. Some of the larger police services also have small staffs of researchers or contract academics to do applied research.

Compared to the United Kingdom, the United States, or Australia, there is little original, academic, policing research taking place in Canada. Some leading criminologists such as Clifford Shearing and Phillip Stenning, who have done seminal research on private security and the policing of private space, and Richard Ericson, known for his definitive research on police work, police as knowledge workers, and policing in a risk society, are working in other countries. The reason cited for the dearth of original policing research is weak government interest and funding.

Some criminologists continuing research activity in Canada include Jean-Paul Brodeur and André Normandeau of the University of Montreal, who bring European perspectives to Canadian police research; Margaret Beare, of York University, who researches organized crime, money laundering, and corruption; Christopher Murphy of Dalhousie University, who has various policing research interests; Curt Griffiths of Simon Fraser University; and

Anthony Doob of Toronto University. Among a younger generation of criminologists who have published on policing are Kevin Haggerty of the University of Alberta, Curtis Clark of Athabasca University, George Rigarkos of Carleton University, Willelm de Lint of the University of Windsor, and Benoit Dupont of the University of Montreal, who researches police governance.

Police research journals and police magazines include:

Canadian Review of Policing Research
Canadian Journal of Police and Security Services
Canadian Journal of Criminology and Criminal Justice
The Blue Line Magazine
The Canadian Police Chief, published by the Canadian Association of Chiefs of Police
The Express, published by the Canadian Police Association
The RCMP Gazette
The RCMP Quarterly

The Canadian Centre for Justice Statistics, a part of Statistics Canada, publishes statistical studies on policing and annual police administrative statistics. There are also numerous in-service newsletters published by individual police services.

There are many Canadian policing websites. Most police forces maintain their own sites. A few providing reliable, current information on policing, and links to other important sites follow:

www.cpc.gc.ca
www.ipperwashinquiry.ca
www.ararcommission.ca
www.yorku.ca/nathanson/
www.criminology.utoronto.ca
www.rcmp-grc.gc.ca
www.cacp.ca
www.cppa.acpp.ca
www.capb.ca
www.statcan.ca
www.psepc-sppcc.ca
www.gc.ca

TONITA MURRAY

Bibliography

Biro, F., P. Campbell, P. McKenna, and T. Murray. *Police Executives Under Pressure: A Study and Discussion of the Issues.* Police Futures Group Study Series No. 3. Ottawa: Canadian Association of Chiefs of Police, 2000.

Ceyssens, P. *Legal Aspects of Policing.* 2 vols. Salt Spring Island, Canada: Earlscourt Legal Press, 1994.

Ericson, R. V., and K. D. Haggerty. *Policing the Risk Society.* Toronto: University of Toronto Press, 1997.

First Nations Chiefs of Police Association, Canada. *A Human Resource Study of First Nations Policing in Canada.* 5 vols. Financially supported by Human Resources Development Canada, and with the consulting services of Perivale and Taylor Consulting, Vision Quest Consulting and Sixdion. Ottawa: First Nations Chiefs of Police Association, 1999–2001.

Goff, C. *Criminal Justice in Canada,* 3rd ed. Scarborough, Ontario: Nelson, 2004.

Goudreau, J.-P., and J.-A. Brzozowski. *A Statistical Profile of Persons Working in Justice-Related Professions in Canada, 1996.* Ottawa: Statistics Canada, 2002.

Griffiths, C. T., R. B. Parent, and B. Whitelaw. *Community policing in Canada.* Scarborough, Ontario: Nelson Thomson Learning, 2001.

LeBeuf, M.-E. *Policing and Use of Information Technology.* Ottawa: Canadian Police College, 2000.

Marquis, G. *Policing Canada's Century: A History of the Canadian Association of Chiefs of Police.* Toronto: Toronto University Press, 1993.

McKenna, P. F. *Police Powers.* Toronto: Prentice Hall, 2002.

Murphy, C. *The Rationalization of Canadian Public Policing: A Study of the Impact and Implications of Resource Limits and Market Strategies.* Police Futures Group Electronic Series No. 1. Ottawa: Canadian Association of Chiefs of Police. Available at: http://www.policefutures.org.

Murray, T., and S. Alvaro. *A Profile of the Canadian Police Executive Community.* Police Futures Group Study Series No. 2. Ottawa: Canadian Association of Chiefs of Police, 2001.

Nancoo, S. E. *Contemporary Issues in Canadian Policing.* Mississauga, Ontario: Canadian Educators' Press, 2004.

Pelango, P. *The Last Guardians: The Crisis in the RCMP ... and in Canada.* Toronto: McClelland and Stewart, 1998.

Richardson, J., ed. *Police and Private Security: What the Future Holds.* Police Futures Group Study Series No. 1. Ottawa: Canadian Association of Chiefs of Police, 2000.

Rigakos, G. "In Search of Security: The Roles of Public Police and Private Agencies." Discussion Paper. Ottawa: Canadian Law Commission, 2002.

Roberts, J. V., ed. *Criminal Justice in Canada.* Toronto: Harcourt Brace Canada, 2000.

Schachhuber, D. *Ethics Training in Canadian Police Organizations.* Antigonish, Nova Scotia: St. Francis Xavier University, 2001.

Spencer, R., R. Stansfield. *Community Policing.* Toronto: Emond Montgomery, 2003.

Steering Committee for the Human Resources Study of Public Policing in Canada, with PricewaterhouseCoopers (consultant). *Strategic Human Resources Analysis of Public Policing in Canada.* Ottawa: Canadian Association of Chiefs of Police and Canadian Police Association, 2000.

Stenning, P. C. *Policing the Cultural Kaleidoscope: Recent Canadian Experience.* Jerusalem: Israel National Police, Community and Civil Guard Department, 2001.

Stenning, P. C., J. E. Briggs, and M. Crouch. *Police Governance in First Nations in Ontario.* Toronto: Centre of Criminology, University of Toronto, 1996.

Stenning, P. C., ed. *Accountability for Criminal Justice: Selected Essays.* Toronto: University of Toronto Press, 1995.

CAPE VERDE

Background Material

An uninhabited archipelago of ten islands and five rocky islets, 620 kilometers off the western coast of Africa, Cape Verde was discovered in 1462 and then colonized by the Portuguese. The Republic of Cape Verde subsequently became a trading center for African slaves, and later an important coaling and resupply stop for whaling and trans-Atlantic shipping. In the early 1800's, the nation suffered drought and famine along with government corruption and poor administration. In 1951, the islands' status was changed from that of a Portuguese colony to an overseas province. Following independence in 1975, and a tentative interest in unification with Guinea-Bissau, a one-party system was established and maintained until multiparty elections were held in 1990. Cape Verde continues to exhibit one of Africa's most stable democratic governments. Repeated droughts during the second half of the twentieth century caused significant hardship and prompted heavy emigration. As a result, Cape Verde's expatriate population is greater than its domestic one. Most Cape Verdeans have both African and Portuguese ancestors.

With a rather young population—40% are under fifteen years old—Cape Verde has an unemployment rate of 21% (2000 estimate). About 30% (2000 estimate) of the population remains below the poverty line, for whom migration is a solution.

The island's economy suffers from a poor natural resource base, including serious water shortages exacerbated by cycles of long-term drought. The economy is service oriented, with commerce, transport, tourism, and public services accounting for 72% of GDP. Although nearly 70% of the population lives in rural areas, the share of agriculture in GDP in 2001 was only 11%, of which fishing accounted for 1.5%. About 82% of food must be imported. The fishing potential, mostly lobster and tuna, is not fully exploited. Cape Verde annually runs a high trade deficit, financed by foreign aid and remittances from emigrants; remittances supplement GDP by more than 20%. Economic reforms are aimed at developing the private sector and attracting foreign investment to diversify the economy. Prospects for coming years depend heavily on the maintenance of aid flows, tourism, remit-

tances, and the momentum of the government's development program.

Moreover, although Cape Verde remains a rather safe and peaceful country, its strategic location is attractive for transnational and organized crime structures. It is located along major north–south sea routes, and acts as an important communications station and an important sea and air refueling site.

The total area of the Cape Verde islands is 4,033 square kilometers. The population is 415,294 (July 2004 estimate), with a projected growth rate of 0.73% (2004 estimate). The ethnic composition of the population is Creole (mulatto), 71%; African, 28%; and European, 1%. Primary religions are Roman Catholic (infused with indigenous beliefs) and Protestant (mostly Church of the Nazarene). The population speaks Portuguese and Crioulo (a blend of Portuguese and West African words).

Cape Verde has a GDP per capita of US$1,400 (2002 estimate). Primary industries include fish processing, shoes and garments, salt mining, and ship repair.

The branches of the military are the Army, Air Force and Navy (includes Marines). The police are structured in four branches: Public Order, Judiciary, Treasury, and Maritime Police, comprised of a total of 1,310 officers (as of 2004).

Contextual Features

With independence, the type of government adopted by Cape Verde was the parliamentary republic, with a reasonable balance between the Prime Minister and the President of the Republic and a certain degree of decentralization at the level of the town councils.

In terms of administrative divisions, the country has seventeen municipalities (concelhos). As regards the executive branch, the chief of state is the President of the Republic, elected by popular vote for a five-year term. The government also includes the Prime Minister, who is nominated by the National Assembly and appointed by the President; and the Council of Ministers, appointed by the President on recommendation of the Prime Minister.

The legislative branch includes a unicameral National Assembly (Assembleia Nacional), which has seventy-two seats. Its members are elected by popular vote to serve five-year terms.

The judicial branch includes three levels of tribunals with general powers: the Supreme Tribunal of Justice, also acting as Constitutional Tribunal; and Regional and Subregional Tribunals. Moreover, there are the following categories of specialized tribunals: Tribunal of Public Accounts (Tribunal de Contas), Military Tribunals, Finance and Customs Tribunals, and Family and Labor Tribunals.

The legal system derived from, and is still deeply influenced by the legal system of Portugal, whose public and private law belong to the matrix of the European continental legal system.

The constitution of the newly independent country was enacted in 1980, and was further reviewed in 1981, 1988, and 1990. A new constitution came into force on 25 September 1992, providing the country with a legal system based on the rule of law. It underwent a major revision on 23 November 1995, substantially increasing the powers of the President. A further revision in 1999, created the position of the national Ombudsman (Provedor de Justiça).

The country has been reporting, in the last years, a general increase of criminality, according to statistics published by the Public Order Police (Polícia de Ordem Pública).

According to data made available by the Public Order Police, reported crime has been increasing over the last decade. The rate is forty-two reported crimes per 1,000 inhabitants. In 2003, crimes against persons were the most important category, representing 57% of the total, while property crimes represented 43%. Within the first category, assaults were the most important category, representing 44% of the total. As regards the second category, thefts and robberies were the most important crimes, representing together more than two-thirds of the total. Also in this category, 18 homicides and 145 rapes were reported in 2003.

The reported data show that offenses committed in the capital and São Vicente increased 70% and 50%, respectively, but other municipalities also reported increases over the last decade, namely Santa Catarina, Santa Cruz, and Sal.

According to an Afrobarometer survey, titled "Opinion of the Public on Democracy and Markets in Cape Verde," when asked about crime and insecurity in the country, compared with the period before 1991, 41% of Cape Verdeans answered that the situation is worse or much worse, against 35% who estimate that the situation is better or much better. For 15% of respondents, the situation remains stable, and 8% have no opinion. Forty percent of those living in rural areas estimate that the situation is better or much better, while only 32% of those living in urban areas estimate that the situation is better now.

Several crime factors have been addressed, such as the fragile social conditions, unemployment, extreme poverty of a significant part of the population, social exclusion, and drug trafficking.

Cape Verde has established three categories of judicial tribunals: the Supreme Tribunal of Justice, and regional and subregional tribunals. Thus, as regards the judicial organization, the country is divided into regions and subregions. The Supreme Tribunal of Justice is the highest judicial instance of the Republic. With between three to six magistrates, this tribunal has jurisdiction throughout the national territory. On a transitory basis, and since 1994, this tribunal has been carrying out the powers of the Constitutional Tribunal, which was established but not implemented in practice thus far. The Supreme Tribunal also has relevant powers in the field of contested electoral results.

Regarding the lower categories of tribunals, in every judicial district there is a regional tribunal, which decides the appeals from the subregional ones. The parties involved can appeal their decisions to the Supreme Tribunal. In every subregion, there is a subregional tribunal.

The Attorney General's structure controls compliance with the rule of law in the courts, represents the public interest, and carries out the criminal procedure, although said structure is subject to the government's generic guidance. Included here are the Attorney General's Office, and regional and subregional attorneys.

The Superior Council of Magistrates (Conselho Superior da Magistratura) is assigned by the constitution to manage and discipline the magistrates, as well as to guide and control the activity of all the tribunals, including the military one. It also coop-

Statistics on Reported Crime (1991–2000)

	1991	1992	1993	1994	1995	1996	1997	1998	1999	2000	2001	2002	2003
Number	8.344	9.985	8.756	9.293	11.363	11.542	12.749	14.525	13.135	14.119	14862	15.974	17.412
Variation		+19,67	-12,31	+6,13	+22,27	+1,58	+10,46	+13,93	-9,57	+7,49	+5,26	+7,48	+9,00

erates with the government in the implementation of justice policy. It can determine judicial inspections and assess the performance of the magistrates, through the Judicial Inspectorate, and carries out the disciplinary jurisdiction on the magistrates and servants of the justice system. However, that Inspectorate is foreseen by the law but, so far, has not been set up.

Regarding the status of the magistrates, the law states three basic principles of their activity: they are independent, irresponsible, and irremovable.

The Ombudsman (Provedor de Justiça), introduced by the constitutional revision of 1999, is defined by the constitution as one of the bodies assisting the political power. With an independent status, this official is elected by the National Assembly, and considered as a relevant tool for the protection of the fundamental rights and liberties of citizens, having the power to address recommendations to the administration aimed at preventing and repairing illegal or unfair actions.

The reform of the corrections system is one of the main political objectives of the government. Among other measures, the government has proposed the improvement of security conditions and renewal of certain prisons, as well as assessment of the necessity to build new prisons; particular attention focused on the issue of parole; and a new statute for prison guards.

In the survey carried out within the provisional report on the situation of the justice system in Cape Verde, the predominant negative aspects of the respondents were, by order of importance: poor conditions of the prisons, as well as the overcrowd of the main prisons, connected with the nonsegregation of the prisoners according to the nature of the crime committed and their dangerousness, and the duality preventive/sentenced prisoners; the lack of monitoring of the prisoners by technicians, namely social workers; the absence of programs for effective social reintegration; and, finally, disrespect of human rights.

The total number of prisoners, according to official statistics, remained rather stable between 1998 and 2001: 443 (1998) to 755 (1999), and 703 (2000) to 689 (2001). The ratio of prisoners to population is approximately 1:600.

Nevertheless, the proportion of convicted prisoners versus those waiting for trial in preventive detention is a matter of major concern. In fact, in 1998 these percentages were 61% and 39%, respectively. These proportions remained stable in the next year, but increased in 2000 when preventive prisoners accounted for 44.7% of the total, and decreased slightly in 2001 to 41.6%.

Police Profile

Background

The Public Order Police is the oldest police service in Cape Verde. It was established on 28 July 1870, when the Governor of the Province decided that a committee should present a regulation draft proposal for a Police Corps. Two years later, the Governor signed a decree implementing the first police body in the capital of the province, Praia.

After the Carnation Revolution in Portugal (25 April 1974), which determined the fall of the colonial and authoritarian regime that ruled Portugal for approximately five decades, a council of Cape Verdean police officials decided to remove the Portuguese police officers from its hierarchy and assumed direction of the new Public Order Police.

In that period, a police school was established. In the late 1970s and throughout the 1980s, police education and training remained a priority and, with that purpose, many trainees attended police schools in Cuba, the German Democratic Republic (East Germany), and Portugal.

In 1990, two special units were created within the Public Order Police: the Riot Police (Corpo de Intervenção) and VIPs' Personal Protection Unit (Protecção de Entidades).

The democratic constitution states that the police shall defend the democratic rule of law; prevent crime; and ensure internal security, peace in the streets, and the exercise of fundamental rights by the citizens.

In 1998, with a view to modernize and dignify the police, a set of twenty-one internal regulations were enacted, namely police statutes and organics, disciplinary regulations, and ethic and honor codes, as well as the regulation of police stations, among others.

In the 1990s, the Cape Verdean police system underwent important changes. The creation of a rule of law state, the implementation of strong local councils and mayors, establishment of the Judiciary Police, creation of the Riot Police (Corpo de Intervenção) within the Public Order Police, dismantlement of the National Security General Directorate (Direcção Geral da Segurança Nacional), and events that occurred in the early 1990s, urged the review and update of the Internal Security System.

There are four police services sharing responsibilities in the fight against crime: Judiciary Police (Polícia Judiciária), Public Order Police (Polícia de Ordem Pública), Treasury Police (Guarda Fiscal), and the Maritime Police (Polícia Marítima). In the near future, the Public Order Police might be replaced by a National Police Directorate, depending on the Minister of Justice and Internal Affairs and gathering the Treasury Police in its structure, with a view to simplify and rationalize the internal security model.

Demographics

The strength of the four police services (number of citizens versus number of police) is 1,310 officers for 415,000 citizens, which means that the ratio is one police officer per 317 citizens.

The Judiciary Police is one of the smallest police services, in terms of human resources, having a total of sixty-three officers.

The Public Order Police is the most important one, having a total of more than 1,000 officers, of which 930 are on duty. Of the total, 10% are female, 81 are commanders or supervisors, 165 are sergeants, and 684 are police constables. Specific training is required to be promoted to all the ranks of the hierarchy, which means that there is a correspondence between the education and training obtained and the rank.

The Police School "Daniel Monteiro" (Escola da Polícia) carries out the education and training of all levels of the hierarchy, within the Public Order Police, and cooperates with other schools and institutions in activities of specific training. It also provides specialized training to the Armed Forces.

The Treasury Guard has a total of 188 officers, of which 145 are constables. The average age is thirty-three. More than 80% of its strength is attending different training courses in the country.

The Maritime Police has a total of about sixty officers.

Organizational Description

Within the internal security system, the Prime Minister, as the head of the government, is responsible for the overall definition and implementation of the internal security policy.

According to the program of the government, the Minister of Justice and Internal Affairs (Ministro da Justiça e Administração Interna) proposes, coordinates, and carries out the policies in the fields of justice, internal security, and police. This Minister has political direction over the Public Order Police and the Judiciary Police.

Law-decree 54/98 enacted the organic law of the Public Order Police. It states that the force is headed by a General-Commander (Comandante-General), assisted by Deputy-General-Commanders, and the hierarchic organization includes the National Headquarters' Command, the Special Units Command, and the six Regional Commands. Next

in the hierarchy are police stations and, at the lowest level are small police offices and traffic stations when necessary.

Functions

The Judiciary Police was established in 1993 and started its activity in January 1995. This service is a national body for crime prevention and investigation, assisting in the administration of criminal justice, and depends, hierarchically and administratively, upon the Minister of Justice and Internal Affairs.

The Public Order Police is a uniformed public force, with very broad police powers. It is essentially an administrative police force, but it also carries out criminal investigation powers when the foreseen abstract sanction is up to three years of imprisonment. Its personnel have civilian status, but some military-type principles are applied, namely as regards hierarchy, discipline, and military honors and salutes.

This force includes the Immigration and Borders Directorate and two special units, which are its reserve services: the Riot Police (Corpo de Intervenção) and the VIPs' Personal Protection Unit (Protecção de Entidades).

The Treasury Guard is a civilian service of a special nature, armed and uniformed, notwithstanding that some military-type principles are applied, namely as regards hierarchy, discipline, and military honors and salutes. Its essential mission is to prevent and repress financial and customs offenses, ensuring a special surveillance and control of the customs territory, and cooperating with the treasury administration in the fight against fraud and tax evasion. In the field of national security, the Treasury Guard works jointly with other security services in the prevention and fight against criminality in general, and against drug and weapons and explosives trafficking in particular. There are offices of the Treasury Guard on every inhabited island of the archipelago, although the vast majority of its personnel (about 90%) are concentrated on the islands of Santiago, São Vicente, and Sal.

The Maritime Police is basically the armed force of the maritime authorities, the harbor captaincies. It depends on the Navy and Harbors General Directorate, and has the following missions: control the maritime, harbors, and ships activity; ensure compliance with all maritime laws and regulations; and promote sailing security, environment protection, and security and safety at work.

It is concentrated in the capital and in Mindelo, but lacks its own command. The territorial services of the Maritime Police are the captaincies of the harbors of windward and leeward, as well as their maritime delegations, subdelegations, and local representatives.

This service cooperates with the Treasury Guard in repressing customs offenses and with the Public Order Police, Judiciary Police, and Coast Guard in the prevention and repression of crime.

Training

The main requirements for enrolling in the basic second-class police officer's course, at the Public Order Police School are the following: Cape Verdeans citizenship; between twenty-one and twenty-seven years of age; height of at least 1.7 meters (men) or 1.6 meters (women); necessary physical strength to carry out police officer activities; clean criminal record; good moral and civil behavior; and completion of ten years of formal schooling or equivalent.

The academic requirement for joining the Portuguese Police Staff College is the possession of the grammar school certificate (secondary school).

Police Public Projects

Crime prevention and neighborhood policing are among the main priorities of the internal security police and the Public Order Police activity, with a view to reduce crime and victimization rates and increase the feeling of security of the population.

On several islands, such as Santo Antão, relevant neighborhood policing schemes have been implemented. These schemes are addressed to bring police officers closer to the most vulnerable groups of the population, such as the most hidden communities on the islands, or children at school.

In addition, and in order to facilitate contacts between victims and police, it is already possible to formalize a complaint directly through the police website.

Regarding traffic control, several prevention programs have been implemented with a view to reduce road accidents, such as the campaign against the use of mobile phones while driving.

Police Use of Firearms

The use of firearms by the police is covered in a specific regulation, which states the specific and restricted situations in which a police officer is able to use his gun: legitimate defense of himself or a third person, or the interception of a prisoner.

Every police officer has firearms training at the police school and throughout his or her career. Police staff are provided with a gun, and they are responsible for storage, use, and maintenance of their firearms. Police officers are subject to aggravated liability in case of excessive use of force involving firearms.

Complaints and Discipline

According to the law, every citizen has the right to register complaints against a police officer for criminal, civil, administrative, and disciplinary offenses. In general, a citizen can present a complaint before an Attorney General's office, a court, or a police station, or directly to the police national headquarters.

In the case of disciplinary liability, the police services have specific disciplinary regulations that provide commanders with disciplinary powers. Within the Public Order Police, a Discipline Consultative Council, depending directly on the General Commander, gives advice on disciplinary sanctions and rewards, and controls the disciplinary procedures within the force.

Both the Police School and the Portuguese Police Staff College provide officers with human rights training. As regards the training of police officers, the Portuguese five-year course includes, besides several law and police courses addressing this topic, a specific 120-hour course on human rights.

Terrorism

There are no terrorist organizations, whether domestic or with international connections. The police agencies charged with responding to terrorism are the Public Order Police for the tactical response to any terrorist incident that might occur, and the Judiciary Police for the criminal investigation.

International Cooperation

There are several bilateral agreements in the field of technical police cooperation, namely in the area of education and training, signed with Portugal, Angola, and Senegal, among others.

Police Education, Research, and Publications

The Public Order Police School (Escola da Polícia) carries out education and training of all levels, and ensures police research and publications, as well as bilateral cooperation with other police schools abroad.

The basic training courses allow police officers to follow several specialized branches, such as criminal investigation, traffic police, and immigration and border control.

Regarding bilateral cooperation with Portugal in the field of police education, most Cape Verdean senior police officers have attended a five-year course at the Portuguese Police Staff College since the early 1990s. The number of Cape Verdean police officers attending this course in Lisbon has been increasing year after year. The Police College in Lisbon also provides further training courses for the promotion to senior police officers, as well as specialized courses, since the late 1990's.

Cooperation with Angola includes training courses for officers from both countries, with theoretical and practical phases.

For further information, see the Polícia de Ordem Pública de Cabo Verde website at *www.pop.cv/*.

P. V. GOMES

Useful Websites

www.presidenciarepublica.cv/
www.parlamento.cv/
www.governo.cv
www.stj.cv/
www.pop.cv/
www.snpc.cv/
www.ine.cv/

Bibliography

Central Intelligence Agency. *The World Factbook, 2004.* Available at: www.cia.gov.org. Accessed 11 May 2004.

CENTRAL AFRICAN REPUBLIC

Background Material

Situated in the middle of the African continent, the Central African Republic (CAR) occupies close to 625,000 square kilometers. It is a landlocked country with Sudan at its northeast border; Democratic Republic of Congo (formerly known as Zaire) bordering the country to the south, and Cameroon and Chad bordering it to the west and northwest, respectively. The population numbers around 3,800,000 (2004 estimate). The official language is French, but Sangho, Arabic, Hunsa, and Swahili are also widely spoken. There are several ethnic groups in the country. The Baya make up 34% of the population; Banda, 27%, Mandjia, 21%; Sara, 10%, Mboum, 4%; and M'Baka, 4%. Nearly 7,000 Europeans (more than half of which are French nationals) reside in the CAR. Of the major religions observed in the country, 25% the population identify as Catholic (this would include most of the Europeans in the country); 25% as Protestant, and 25% identify as observing an indigenous religious system. There are roughly 15% who identify as Muslim, and another 10% who identify with some other belief system. The per capita annual income is estimated at US$250. The CAR's major trade partners are France, Cote d'Ivoire, and Cameroon; minor trade partners include Germany, Spain, Egypt, Japan, and China. The country exports diamonds, timber, cotton, coffee, and tobacco, and imports a variety of machinery, foodstuffs, consumer goods, textiles, and chemicals.

Contextual Features

The Central African Republic has a republic-style government with a legal system largely based on French law, its colonizing European power. CAR formerly became independent from France in August 1960. Its constitution passed by referendum in December 1994, and was adopted in January 1995. This constitution was suspended by decree in March 2003. A referendum on a new constitution scheduled for November 2004 took place December 2004, and passed by an overwhelming majority. The newly adopted constitution retained many features from the previously suspended 1995 version, including a five-year term for the head of state, which is renewable only once. The president retained the authority to appoint the prime minister and other members of the Council of Ministers in his or her administration. It also established February 2005 as the date for presidential and parliamentary elections.

There were twenty-eight ministries in the president's cabinet, but that was reduced by President Francois Bozize to twenty-two in 2003. Under the suspended constitution, the president presides over a strong executive branch, and has the power to appoint and dismiss ministers in his council, administrators in the country's sixteen administrative units (known as prefet), top military leaders, and other influential persons in administrative positions throughout the country. Among the ministries in the president's council are National Education, Youth, Sports, Arts, and Culture; Agriculture and Livestock; Foreign Affairs; Communications; Mines and Energy, and Foreign Affairs.

The country's judiciary system falls under the Ministry of Justice, Human Rights, and Good Governance. This part of the government contains the courts of various levels including the Constitutional Court, Court of Appeals, and Criminal Courts. Judges are appointed by the president, which has led to charges of executive control over the judiciary in CAR. As is the case in many African countries, there is a traditional court system that citizens have the option of using to resolve domestic matters, land and property disputes, and arbitration issues. There is also a separate military court system that assumes judicial control over military personnel of higher ranks (for instance, those involved in coup attempts or similar infractions). The Central African Republic has at least fifteen active political parties, and most were expected to put forward candidates in the February 2005 presidential election.

After seizing power in a March 2003 military coup, Francois Bozize (a former general and army chief of staff in the administration he ousted) took over the portfolio as defense minister as well as serving as head of state. There is a standing army numbering about 3,000 personnel, with the navy, air force, and national police force ranging between 1,200 and 1,500. There are other paramilitary organizations, such as the Presidential Guard (also known as the Presidential Security Unit); precise numbers of officers are not known. Since its negotiated independence from France in 1960, the Central African Republic has known relatively little political stability, and from that time to the present, it has experienced several military coup attempts that have contributed to instability of successive governments.

Police Profile

Background

As early as the mid-1940s, a small indigenous police force was established in the Central African Republic. Although there was a police presence made up of indigenous inhabitants, the movement to establish a national police force accelerated when the French Constitution was amended to grant the inhabitants of CAR French citizenship in 1946. Subsequently, General Charles de Gaulle made moves that would lead to formal independence of the territory, but the French presence (both militarily and economically) was very pronounced. After CAR became independent in 1960, the military assumed greater authority, with the police being limited to routine duties such as traffic patrol, investigating crimes such as property theft, and enforcing basic laws, among other standard duties.

The national police were politicized in the mid-1960s under the presidency of David Dacko. The Chief of Police (gendarmerie), Jean Izamo, enjoyed President Dacko's confidence far more than that of his cousin, Army Chief of Staff Jean Bedel Bokassa. Dacko's plan was to strengthen the power of the police and weaken that of the army. He also initiated a Presidential Guard for his personal security. Combined with the police force, the presidential guard numbered no more than 500, with the army numbering at least four times that number. Seizing an opportunity, Bokassa took control of the government in a coup d'etat at the end of December 1965. He imprisoned David Dacko (forcing him to resign from the presidency); assassinated Jean Izamo; and although there was some limited gunfire exchanged between the police and the army, without their leader, the police quickly capitulated. After Bokassa declared himself the head of state, he set aside the 1959 constitution, dissolved the governing legislative assembly, and assumed total legislative, judicial, and executive power by decree. In terms of influence, authority, and exercise of power, the national police force was minimized.

The thirteen-year reign of Jean Bedel Bokassa marked one of the cruelest and most repressive periods in the country's history. He oversaw massive human rights abuses, survived numerous assassination attempts and coup plots, put to death several military personnel for disloyalty (including several family members), and ultimately proclaimed himself emperor of the Central African Empire in 1977. To these ends, the police were used to spy on citizens and foreigners (known as *cooperant*), maintain secret surveillance on dissidents (whether actual or perceived), and engage in similar practices as directed by Bokassa's regime. The police were also used to suppress student gatherings, as well as infiltrate their organizations because they were seen as breeding grounds of agitation and sedition.

After several particularly brutal events, including the slaughter of many school-age children in 1979 (which was revealed to the world by the London-based Amnesty International), Bokassa was toppled in a coup d'etat by his predecessor David Dacko with the military backing of the French. Lasting only two years in power, Dacko was once again overthrown in another bloodless coup in 1981 by General Andre Kolingba. Kolingba initially led the country as a military leader, but moved Central African Republic back in the direction of civilian rule. He abandoned his military career, and won the presidency as a constitutionally elected president in 1986.

Again, the police seem to have returned to their former duties as peacekeepers and as the primary law enforcers. At some point in the 1980s, President Kolingba attempted to restore credibility to the national police by increasing their profile vis-à-vis the civilian public. He revamped police training and instituted civilian review panels to guard against certain abuses. Under the successive administration of Ange-Felix Patasse, the national police continued to rebuild some of its lost prestige by participating in joint Interpol exercises. In 1998, the organization joined the regional Conference of Central African Police Chiefs (CCAPC) as part of Interpol's worldwide strategy to combat international crimes such as car theft, smuggling of precious goods such as diamonds, and other transborder criminal activity.

Organizational Description

As part of his election to a second term in 1999, President Patasse embarked on a strategy of reorganizing the entire law enforcement branches in the Central African Republic, which included the army, navy, air force, Presidential Security Guard, and the national police. Under this restructuring plan, these forces would be overseen by a civilian Minister of Defense. In 2001, however, a failed coup attempt staged by former President Kolingba resulted in more than 1,000 members of the various armed branches (mostly within the army and national police who were loyal to Andre Kolingba) fleeing across the river into the Democratic Republic of Congo. The following year, the recently dismissed Army Chief of Staff, Francois Bozize, staged yet another coup attempt with the assistance of Chadian soldiers. This conflict, which lasted several months, resulted in the coup d'etat that removed President Ange-Felix Patasse from office in March 2003.

Since proclaiming the presidency in 2003, Francois Bozize has continued to rely on Chadian soldiers for military support. This situation led to tense standoffs between the Chadians and the na-

tional police on several occasions throughout 2003 and 2004.

Police Training

The major training center for police in the Central African Republic is the Gendarmerie Training School in Kolongo (an area near the capital Bangui). The training consists of basic weapon skills, crowd and traffic control, and basic conflict resolution. More recently, there have been requests for more stylized training in the area of refugee rights and obligations. This has been facilitated through the United Nations High Commission for Refugees (UNHCR). This specialized training has typically been offered in seminars.

In 1999, the national police force received training under the United Nations Mission in the Central African Republic, a civilian police component with the aim of instructing police on how to handle domestic disturbances with limited use of force. This effort was also designed to combat the complaints of professional truck drivers who frequently accuse the police at various checkpoints of extortion (mostly fuel and money) while transporting their goods to neighboring Cameroon. The current Minister for Public Security Paulin Bondeboli maintains that such training will enhance the delivery of police services to the public.

Even though the Central African Republic is approaching its forty-fifth year as an independent country, it has faced the troubled past and present of many of its surrounding neighbors (specifically Democratic Republic of Congo and Sudan). Most of these challenges have been of a political nature or human rights nature (that is, multiple military takeovers of several civilian-installed governments; the horrors of the Bokassa era; and continued practices such as harsh prison conditions, arbitrary tortures, and summary executions by its armed forces), but there have also been natural disasters that have contributed to country's impeded progress (like the continuing troubles brought on by regional drought and soil erosion). Because of consistent military involvement in the affairs of state (often with the aid and assistance of the French government), there is more information to be found about that organization than that of the comparatively smaller national and local police.

Laura Moriarty and Christopher Brooks

Bibliography

Decalo, S. *Psychoses of Power: African Personal Dictatorship*. Gainesville: Florida Academic Press, 1998.

Grinker, R. R. *Houses in the Rain Forest: Ethnicity and Inequality Among Farmers and Foragers in Central Africa.* Berkeley: University of California Press, 1994.

Kalck, P. *Historical Dictionary of Central African Republic.* Trans. T. O'Toole. Metuchen, NJ: Scarecrow Press, 1980.

Ramsay, F. J. *Global Studies: Africa*, 8th ed. Guilford, CT: Dushkin/McGraw-Hill, 1999.

Titley, B. *Dark Age: The Political Odyssey of Emperor Bokassa.* Montreal and Kingston: McGill-Queen's University Press, 1997.

CHAD

Background Material

Chad is located in Central Africa, and is bordered by Libya, Sudan, the Central African Republic, Niger, Cameroon, and Nigeria. The capital city is N'Djamena, with Abeche and Sarh being other major cities. It has a total population of 8,210,000 (2004 estimate), and occupies a land area of 1,284,000 square kilometers. There are four main languages: French, Arabic, Sara, and Sango. Three religious traditions coexist in Chad: traditional African religions, Islam, and Christianity.

Much about Chad's early beginnings is unknown. As most of the Saharan area is arid, early settlements found it difficult to sustain viable life. Scientific research on archaeological finds has indicated that human settlements date back to more than 1 million years ago. Seven thousand years ago, in the northern central basin, which now makes up most of the Saharan area, was filled with water, and Chad's early settlers lived and farmed around its shores.

From 1500 to 1900, Arab slave raids were commonplace. The French first occupied Chad in 1891, establishing their authority through military expeditions against the Muslim kingdoms. In 1905, administrative responsibility for Chad was placed under a governor general stationed at Brazzaville in what is now known as Congo. Although Chad joined the French colonies of Gabon, Oubangui-Charo, and Moyen Congo to form the Federation of French Equatorial Africa (AEF) in 1910, it did not have colonial status until 1920. In 1959, the territory of French Equatorial Africa was dissolved and along with three other states, Chad became independent under its first president, Francois Tombalbaye. A long civil war broke out in the country in the mid-1960s between the Muslim north and the southern-led government over tax rules. Even with the assistance of French combat forces, the insurgents were not quelled. Due to civil unrest with Tombalbaye's rule, in 1975 there was a national revolt leading to a military coup. In 1978, General Felix Malloum, a southerner, was installed as Head of State; however, his government was more inclusive than his predecessor, having a northerner Prime Minister, Hissein Habré. Internal dissent within the government led to the Prime Minister having to send his forces against the national army at N'Djamena in February 1979. This inevitably led to intense fighting among the eleven factions that emerged. Due to the fact that civil war was so widespread, regional governments decided that there was no effective central government and stepped in. A series of four international conferences held first under Nigerian and then Organisation of African Unity (OAU) sponsorship attempted to bring the Chadian factions together.

At the fourth conference held in Lagos, Nigeria in August 1979, the Lagos accord was signed. This accord established a transitional government pending national elections. In November 1979, the National Union Transition Government (GUNT) was created with a mandate to govern for eighteen months. Goukouni Oueddei, a northerner, was named President; Colonel Kamougue, a southerner, Vice President; and Habré, Minister of Defense. This coalition proved fragile; in March 1980, fighting broke out again between Goukouni's and Habré's forces. The war dragged on inconclusively until Goukouni sought and obtained Libyan intervention. More than 7,000 Libyan troops entered Chad. Although Goukouni requested complete withdrawal of external forces in October 1981, the Libyans pulled back only to the Aozou Strip in northern Chad. An OAU peacekeeping force of 3,500 troops replaced the Libyan forces in the rest of Chad. The force, consisting of troops from Nigeria, Senegal, and Zaire, received funding from the United States. A special summit of the OAU ad hoc committee on the Chad/Libya dispute in February 1982 called for reconciliation among all factions, particularly those led by Goukouni and Habré, who had resumed fighting in eastern Chad. Although Habré agreed to participate, Goukouni refused to negotiate with Habré on an equal basis. In the series of battles that followed, Habré's forces defeated the GUNT, and Habré occupied N'Djamena on June 7, 1982. The OAU force remained neutral during the conflict, and all of its elements were withdrawn from Chad at the end of June. In the summer of 1983, GUNT forces launched an offensive against government positions in northern and eastern Chad. Following a series of initial defeats, government forces succeeded in stopping the rebels.

At this point, Libyan forces directly intervened once again, bombing government forces at Faya Largeau. Ground attacks followed the bombings, forcing government troops to abandon N'Djamena and withdraw to the south. In response to Libya's direct intervention, French and Zairian forces were sent to Chad to assist in defending the government.

With the deployment of French troops, the military situation stabilized, leaving the Libyans and rebels in control of Chad north of the 16th parallel. In September 1984, the French and the Libyan governments announced an agreement for the mutual withdrawal of their forces from Chad. By the end of the year, all French and Zairian troops were withdrawn. Libya did not honor the withdrawal accord, however, and its forces continued to occupy the northern third of Chad.

President Habré's efforts to deal with his opposition were aided by a number of African leaders, especially Gabon President Omar Bongo. During accords held in Libreville, Gabon, in 1985, two of the chief exile opposition groups, the Chadian Democratic Front and the Coordinating Action Committee of the Democratic Revolutionary Council, made peace with the Habré government. By 1986, all of the rebel commando (CODO) groups in southern Chad came in from the forests, rallied to President Habré's side, and were reintegrated into the Forces Armees Nationales Chadiennes (FANT). In the fall of 1986, fighters loyal to Goukouni Oueddei, leader of the GUNT, began defecting to the FANT. Although Libyan forces were more heavily equipped than were the Chadians, Habré's FANT, with considerable assistance from ex-GUNT forces, began attacks against the Libyan occupiers in November 1986 and won victories in all the important cities. The Chadian offensive ended in August 1987, with the taking of Aozou Town, the principal village in the Aozou Strip. Chad government forces held the village for a month, but lost it to a heavy Libyan counterattack. The OAU ad hoc committee continued to seek a peaceful solution to the Chad–Libya conflict, holding meetings over the years with heads of state or ministerial-level officials. In October 1988, Chad resumed formal diplomatic relations with Libya, in accordance with recommendations made by the OAU. A month later, Habré's reconciliation efforts succeeded, and he took power in N'Djamena. In April 1989, Idriss Deby, one of Habré's leading generals, defected and fled to Darfur in Sudan, from which he mounted a series of attacks on the eastern region of Chad. In November 1990, he invaded; on December 2, 1990, his forces entered N'Djamena without a battle, President Habré and forces loyal to him having fled. After three months of provisional government, a national charter was approved by the Patriotic Salvation Movement (MPS) on February 28, 1991, with Deby as President.

Chad is a member of the Central African Economic and Monetary Union (CEMAC), a regional organization dedicated to economic integration. Common to most African countries, Chad's economy has historically been one of the poorest in the world; however, recent progress in the oil sector is likely to impact the local economy. The Chadian government has sought to avoid the mistakes of oil-rich countries where people still live in poverty despite large revenues from oil. Cotton and livestock are important export products, and in 2002, agriculture accounted for 35.8% of GDP. Industry and services made up 17.5% and 46.7% of GDP, respectively, and GDP totaled US$2 billion. Chad as a third-world country relies heavily on the contributions from international donors, who have attached conditions to aid; as a result, economic reforms have been implemented and transparency has improved. Chad attracted US$80 million worth of foreign direct investment in 2001, and there has been increased investment in the oil sector. Despite the resulting economic development, the pressures of inflation have served to negate much of the progress made.

Agriculture provides employment for almost 80% of the country's labor force with most farming taking place at subsistence level. The oil sector has the potential to change the future of Chad. The Doba Oil Basin is the center of oil-sector construction, and production estimates have been set at up to 250,000 barrels a day. This should result in annual government revenues of between $80 million and $100 million.

Contextual Features

Chad gained its independence from France in 1960, and following its independence experienced thirty years of tribal violence and instability. In 1990, Idriss Deby declared himself President; he enjoyed good relations with Libya and Sudan, gained power after a lengthy military offensive launched from bases in Chad and Sudan. President Deby began to implement multiparty democracy, a process that has been hampered by civil unrest and dissension among politicians. The process gained impetus in 1992 when opposition parties were legalized and was followed by the establishment of a transitional legislature in 1993. The year 1996 saw the holding of democratically contested elections in which 77% of the voting population cast their ballot. President Deby was reelected in 2001 for another nonrenewable five-year term. Isolated actions threaten political stability in the country. There are usually instances of soldiers expressing their satisfaction with the program of their integration into civilian society. Some analysts have stated that the government should speed up the disarmament process in order to guarantee a lasting peace. The government's track record has remained poor, with security forces engaged in extrajudicial killings, torture beatings, arbitrary arrests, and detention without trial. In January 2003, a peace agreement between the Chadian government and the National Resistance Army rebel group initiated the creation of a relatively stable state with little violence throughout 2004, and showed positive signs of brighter future for Chad. A fundamental aspect of the agreement is the recognition and respect for human rights, the right to life, protection from torture, and the establishment of fair public trials, which will act as the basis for constructing an open democratic society.

Chad's legal system was based on the French civil law system modified to a variety of traditional and Islamic interpretations. In the late 1980s, the civilian and military court systems overlapped at several levels, an effect of Chad's years of warfare. Civilian justice often deferred to the military system, and in some areas, military courts, many of which were established by rebel armies during the late 1970s, were the only operating courts. In the late 1980s, the government was working to reassert civilian jurisdiction over these areas. Chad's Supreme Court was abolished following the coup in 1975, and had not been reestablished by 1988. The highest court in the land was the Court of State Security, comprised of eight justices, including both civilian and military officers, all appointed by the President. In addition, a court of appeals in N'Djamena reviewed decisions of lower courts, and a special court of justice established in 1984 heard cases involving the misappropriation of public funds. Criminal courts convened in N'Djamena, Sarh, Moundou, and Abeche, and criminal judges traveled to other towns as necessary. In addition, each of the fourteen prefectures had a magistrate's court, in which civil cases and minor criminal cases were tried. In 1988, forty-three justices of the peace served as courts of first resort in some areas. Chad also had an unofficial but widely accepted system of Islamic sharia courts in the north and east, which had operated for a century or more. Most cases involved family obligations and religious teachings. In other areas, traditional custom required family elders to mediate disputes involving members of their descent group. In June 2002, President Deby signed a decree authorizing the creation of a five-judge Judicial Oversight Commission to conduct investigations of judicial decisions and correct infractions, highlighting the possibility that Chad is heading in the direction of becoming an open democratic republic.

Police Profile

Background

During more than twenty years of domestic conflict, the agencies of public order and the judiciary in Chad were severely disrupted. In areas of rebel activity in the south and in regions of the north under Libyan domination, the forces of civil protection and the system of criminal justice disintegrated. Where the national government was able to reimpose its authority, harsh and arbitrary martial law often resulted in mistreatment, torture, and extrajudicial detentions and executions. Chad has emerged as a centralized republic with a strong presidency.

Organizational Description and Functions

Police functions in Chad were the responsibility of the National Military Police (Police Militaire Nationale—[PMN]), the Territorial Military Police (Police Militaire Territoriale—[PMT]), and the National Security Police, known as the Sûreté. Certain internal security, intelligence, and antiterrorism operations were conducted by the Presidential Guard (Sécurité Presiclentielle—[SP]). The Bureau of Documentation and Security (Direction de la

Documentation et de la Sécurité—[DDS]) was a separate intelligence organization and political police force that sometimes engaged in covert operations against opponents of the government. The Special Rapid Intervention Brigade performed similar functions within the military, although it was controlled by the DDS, and was not formally part of FANT.

The Sûreté was originally part of a unified force that, until 1961, served all four countries of the former AEF. With about 800 agents, the Sûreté comprised the national civil police and the municipal police force of the major towns. Its duties included maintenance of law and order, crime prevention, maintenance of criminal records and identification files, investigations and arrests, and traffic control.

Until 1979, the National Gendarmerie, a paramilitary body created in 1960, had primary responsibility for maintaining order in the countryside. The force had remained under the command of a French officer until 1971. Later, in 1979, headed by Habré's political rival, Kamougué, and composed mainly of southerners, the National Gendarmerie had been involved in the fighting around N'Djamena. It remained active as part of the southern resistance to Habré after the overthrow of the Malloum regime. The National Gendarmerie's basic units were twenty-five–man mobile platoons, which had responsibility for internal security and crowd control, and "brigades" (squads) of four to eight gendarmes, who performed ordinary police work in small towns and rural areas. Another force, the paramilitary Chadian Security Companies (Compagnies Tchadiens de Sécurité—[CTS]), organized by Tombalbaye in 1967, performed mainly constabulary functions in eastern Chad against smugglers, cattle rustlers, and dissidents. The CTS resisted the 1975 coup that overthrew Tombalbaye, and it was subsequently disbanded.

To replace the National Gendarmerie, the 1979 GUNT coalition formed a police unit of soldiers drawn from FAN and FAP, with token contributions from the other military factions. Mixed military patrols attempted to maintain order in the capital among the contending factions. After the Habré government had been installed in 1982, most of the previous functions of the National Gendarmerie were entrusted to the newly created PMT. Many of the latter's personnel were southerners who had rallied to the government; it was often popularly referred to as the "gendarmerie."

In 1987, the PMT had an authorized strength of 1,600, but its personnel were poorly equipped, often armed with confiscated weapons. The PMT was nominally subject to the Ministry of Interior, and its field units were subject to the local prefect. In practice, the force came under military authority, and individual units were under jurisdiction of FANT military zone and subzone commanders.

The PMN, which in 1987 was under a military commander, Youssef Galmaye, was a branch of FANT; the force performed regular military police duties, assisted in control of prisoners of war, provided route and rear area security, and often took part in combat operations. Its authorized strength was 1,900, and the soldiers serving in it were better equipped than those of the PMT. Training was provided at a military police school organized by the French in 1986.

Police Education, Research, and Publications

Chad has begun the transitional period from its violent conflictual past into a fully democratic society with a government that is representative of all political views in Chad. With the peace agreement signed, and its apparent success with a continued reduction of violence, much development is now promising to bring the rebel factions into the political process. Little information is available on current police practices, research, and training techniques. The opportunity appears to be prevailing for the development of an accountable civilian police force and a move away from its current semimilitaristic-styled gendarme. The ensuing political settlement will undoubtedly begin a time in Chad for the development of human rights norms in policing practices.

NOEL MC GUIRK

Police-Related Websites
http://allafrica.com/chad/
www.sas.upenn.edu/African_Studies/Country_Specific/Chad.html
www.faqs.org/docs/factbook/geos/cd.html
www.ploughshares.ca/content/ACR/ACR00/ACR00-Chad.html
www.chadembassy.org/site/?CFID=226653&CFTOKEN=51563eb70dd466e7-D3B14A69-B346-6AE4-7CD6D033669F55B5

Bibliography

Azevedo, M. J. *Roots of Violence: A History of War in Chad.* New York: Taylor and Francis, 1998.

Mays, T. M. *Africa's First Peacekeeping Operation: The OAU in Chad, 1981–1982.* Westport, CT: Greenwood Press, 2002.

Thompson, V., and R. Adloff. *Conflict in Chad.* London: C. Hurst & Co., 1981.

CHILE

Background Material

The history of Chile as an independent republic begins with its declaration of independence from Spain in 1810. Although full independence did not come for another fifteen years, and both internal and external strife characterized political life during the rest of the century, Chile nevertheless succeeded in developing its administrative structures during this period, marking out an important position in the Southern Cone region.

By the dawn of the twentieth century, the country's economy was expanding and prosperity was on the rise, with heavy foreign investment fueling industrial development and mining activities, particularly in nitrate. However, falling nitrate prices and a global economic depression during the 1930s inspired political strife during the first half of the century. One result of the changes was the declaration of a new republic with the Constitution of 1925.

By mid-century, Chile enjoyed a well-developed educational system as well as a significant industrial sector for a country of its size. However, high rates of poverty continued with a tremendous gap between the incomes of rich and poor. This uneven distribution of wealth inspired social movements that gradually became both more powerful and radical, culminating in the presidency of the left-wing coalition candidate Salvador Allende in 1970. Allende's Popular Unity government began a program of deep social and economic reforms based on both communist and socialist principles. These reforms inspired further strife, eventually resulting in Allende's death during a bloody 1973 military coup that brought a conservative military junta, or governing council, to power.

The military junta held unrestricted power for the next seven years until a new constitution was approved in 1980, which made General Augusto Pinochet the official President of Chile. However, the new charter did little to change the undemocratic nature of the Chilean government's strict controls on the media and general restrictions on political dissent still in place. Pinochet remained in power until 1989 after he was defeated in a plebiscite held in 1988 to determine the future of the regime. Thus began the rule of a wide coalition of political parties that would gradually bring the democratic process back to Chile. President Ricardo Lagos, a socialist, was the third to hold office from this coalition; he remains in office until the elections in 2006.

The majority of Chile's 15.6 million inhabitants are of mixed Hispanic origins. Since the nineteenth century, Chile has also been home to an important immigrant population from countries as diverse as Germany, China, Korea, Italy, Yugoslavia, Cuba, and Peru. While indigenous communities still exist, their populations constitute only about 3% of the total, and are mostly confined to the southern regions of the country. These populations have long lived in relative peace, but incipient violent conflicts began to appear in the late 1990s as a result of poverty, discrimination, and the radicalization of groups often with the aid of political opportunists.

Spanish is the official language of Chile, but some native languages still remain in use. Quechua remains an important language in northern frontier regions formerly within the Inca Empire; Mapudungun is used in the south, as is Rapanui on Easter Island. Life expectancy for all Chileans is 75.8 years (up 0.5% from year 2000 figures). Adult literacy rates are nearly 96% for those 15 years of age and older.

Chile is a secular country, but religion nevertheless remains an important part of daily life. The majority Christian population is dominated by Roman Catholics who make up about 76% of all Christians, but a number of Protestant denominations exist, representing about 16% of the Christian total. Chile also has significant populations of Jews and Muslims.

Chile's average per capita income ranges between US$5,000 and $6,000, with a per capita GDP of US$9,190. Chile's major economic activities are mining, logging, farming, fishing, cellulose, and paper production. The country's service sector of banks, insurance, medicine, social services, and transport is extensive, and employs the majority of Chileans.

Contextual Features

Political Structure

The Chilean system of government features a democratically elected President who heads a strong executive branch. The President proposes major legislative initiatives, nominates officials for the most strategically important administration posts, and participates in the nomination of judges to the Supreme Court. The Parliament is comprised of the Senate and Chamber of Deputies. Each is comprised of members who, like the President, are directly elected, but in different years. In addition to these elected representatives, the Senate contains a number of members who are either nominated (so-called "Institutional Senators") or hold seats because they are former Presidents, who remain senators for life.

The judiciary consists of judges who have spent their entire careers in the service, from the lowest post all the way up to the Supreme Court. To earn a position on the Supreme Court, judges must not only have years of experience and sterling reputations, but also sufficient political support from both the executive branch and a majority of Senators who must approve the candidates nominated by the President.

Chilean jurisprudence is based on the continental Roman law tradition. There are three levels of tribunals—basic courts, courts of appeal, and Supreme Court. These tribunals vary from those that deal with a diversity of issues to those with responsibilities for specific matters such as revenues, customs, constitutional law, or elections.

In the field of criminal justice, the behavior of the courts is more circumscribed. Comprehensive reform of the courts has taken place since the late 1990s in order to modernize the exercise of justice. By 2002, the consequences of that reform were already significant. For instance, new institutions were created to lead investigations and provide professional defense for the accused, and trials are held in public where all allegations must be made orally. This new system, which has been designed to be more efficient, transparent, and respectful of human rights, was expected to be fully in place throughout the country by 2005.

Under the former system of criminal justice, a single judge was responsible for investigating all the facts and legal controversies of a given case. The new system brought in a prosecutor from the Public Ministry who is now in charge of carrying out an investigation of the facts, and ultimately providing the evidence that will be used against the defendant. The accused now benefits from the presence of a full-time professional lawyer almost immediately, and the judge's primary responsibility is to ensure the observance of civil rights during the investigation. The court is dedicated exclusively to the trial that would take place in case the investigation leads to a major crime, and the prosecutor is ready to open debate and pursue a sentence. This court is now integrated by three specialized judges, who hear the allegations from the prosecutor and the arguments of the defense and eventually private lawyers hired by particular individuals with specific interests, in the context of a continuous, open-to-the-public audience where the arguments are presented orally by each participant. At the end, the court determines a guilty or not guilty sentence at once, or a short time after the case, and the actions against it are reduced to a nullity action to be seen by the Supreme Court.

In 2002, a total of 294,529 accusations were registered, corresponding to a rate of 1,878.2 per 100,000 population. This is related to the 135,626 arrests made in the same period, corresponding to a rate of 862.9 for every 100,000 inhabitants. In general terms, this represents an increase of 176.2 cases per 100,000 inhabitants, an increase of 10.4%. Regarding arrests, the increase was 92.6 per 100,000 inhabitants, or 12.0%.

Chile's penitentiary system is run by an arm of the Ministry of Justice called the Gendarmería de Chile, which combines both military and civilian organizational structures. Military officials are responsible for guard and supervisory duties, and civilians are assigned to technical, administrative, and research activities. A presidential appointee runs the Gendarmería, and can thereby be removed from office at any moment with no need for consultation with any other government authorities.

Major Crime Statistics (1997–2002)

	1998–1997	1999–1998	2000–1999	2001–2000	2002–2001
Theft	37.6	30.4	25.6	31.7	12.2
Assault	−3.0	14.8	−1.8	13.0	12.5
Burglary	2.0	13.5	18.7	17.2	16.5
Injuries	3.1	0	20.8	26.1	1.2
Homicide	−5.9	−31.3	36.4	24.8	1.5
Rape	−3.3	7.9	4.2	22.9	−8.9

Source: División de Seguridad Ciudadana del Ministerio del Interior, Gobierno de Chile

All management and supervisory functions are carried out by the Gendarmería. However, reforms are planned that would turn some of these functions over to private firms contracted to construct the prisons, while the Gendarmería would retain only security and custody responsibilities.

Police Profile

Organizational Description and Functions

Two main bodies comprise Chile's police forces: the Carabineros and the Policía de Investigaciones. About 35,000 officers make up the former, which is a force designed on a military model and aimed principally at crime prevention. The latter is a civil force of about 6,000, charged primarily with investigative duties.

The official founding of the Carabineros de Chile dates to April 27, 1927, although the foundations for the force were really put in place two decades before. In 1902, during the presidency of Germán Riesco, a new integrated body of police was created when members of different squadrons like the cavalry's Dragones, the Lanceros, and the Guias y Cazadores were united into a single force. Later regiments from the so-called Gendarmes (who at the time were actually called the Carabineros) were added as were men from the Gendarmes de Colonias. The creation of a police academy for these forces—the Escuela de Carabineros—by President Pedro Montt in 1908 stands as truly the first step in creating the modern Carabinero force as it exists today. However, full integration is not considered to have happened until President Carlos Ibañez del Campo added several more forces to the unit in 1927. At that moment today's Carabineros were truly born.

The chief responsibilities of the Carabineros include maintaining public order, providing security to the community, investigating certain criminal cases as instructed by the courts, providing security for government officials and diplomats, and emergency aid and rescue.

The Carabineros are organized on a hierarchical military model. At the head, sits the General Director followed directly in rank by a Subdirector, a Directorate of Planning and Development, the General Director's Cabinet, and a General Inspector. In addition, there is a Justice Service that provides legal advice and defense for the force.

The next level down is the Directorate of Personnel, which is responsible for recruiting, selecting, training, distributing, and evaluating the active force. Also under the control of Personnel is the Directorate of Education, which directs activities at the various training schools and academies, and watches for the fulfillment of the institution's educational goals. Below personnel there is a Directorate of Order and Security that controls the force's operations and security functions at the community level. Its responsibilities are to prevent crime, maintain public order, and carry out investigative functions when requested to do so by the courts. To accomplish this function, the Directorate of Order and Security is directly responsible for the following public bodies:

- Directorate of Transit and Special Services, in charge of planning and directing road security and transportation through other specialized units such as the Transit Service, Frontiers, Air Police, VIP protection, and Police Operations.
- Directorate of Crime Investigation and Drugs.
- Directorate of Family Protection.
- Directorate of Police Intelligence.
- Directorate of Logistics, in charge of acquiring and maintaining the tools and materials used by the various forces in their work.
- Directorate of Finance does auditing and accounting work for the entire unit.

A number of special forces are also integrated into the Carabinero structure:

- CENCO (Central de Comunicaciones, Communication Center): the communications coordination unit
- Special Forces (Fuerzas Especiales, FF EE): crowd and riot control as well as disaster aid, and assistance and security for the Presidential Palace and important politicians and dignitaries
- GOPE (Grupo de Operaciones Policiales Especiales, Special Police Operations Group): high-risk operations such as bomb threats and rescue efforts
- SIAT (Sección de Investigación de Accidentes de Tránsito, Transit Accident Investigation Section): investigates traffic accidents
- SIP (Sección de Investigaciones Policiales, Police Investigations Section): responsible for investigating crimes at the request of the courts, Public Ministry, or independently
- SEBV (Sección de Búsqueda de Vehículos, Vehicle Search Section): a task force in charge of recovering stolen vehicles
- Air police prefecture: operations with airplanes and helicopters, for patrolling, rescue operations, and emergency transportation
- LABOCAR (Laboratorio de Carabineros, Carabineros Laboratory): forensic laboratory

- OS7, Crime and Drug investigation unit, for various aspects of drug-related crime prevention and investigation. In addition, OS7 offers seminars, talks, exhibitions, and conferences related to drug crimes

As in the case of the Gendarmería, the official founding date of the civil police (Policía de Investigaciones de Chile) came decades after the beginnings of the organization. In the nineteenth century, a plainclothes (thus the later designation of "civil") police had been organized on the model of the French Sureté. Even at that early date, this force was on the cutting edge, using the latest police technologies like photography and fingerprinting, and by 1896 added the first female officer to the ranks. However, it was not until the passage of a law in 1933 that the Civil Police is considered to have been officially born. The Civil Police are charged with a single task—the use of scientific techniques to investigate crimes. To this end, the force works throughout the country and employs a number of brigades specialized to investigate particular types of crime such as assault, sexual assault, financial crimes, and cybercrime.

The tradition of maintaining a state-of-the-art force continues to the present with a number of efforts to modernize techniques and improve capabilities. The announcement of a new law in 1979 began a process that was greatly accelerated with the return of democratic government in the 1990s. In 1999, a new police academy was inaugurated featuring a police studies curriculum officially recognized as a full-fledged academic discipline. And in response to judiciary reforms, an overall effort has been undertaken to educate and prepare officers to act within the new context, with new laboratories and specialized units also being added throughout the country.

Training

To become a Carabinero, each candidate must fulfill the following basic requirements:

1. Chilean citizenship, single marital status, no children, and maintain this status throughout the training period at the Academy. Candidates must be between seventeen and twenty-three years old, fulfill minimum height requirements, be in good health, and have completed high school or be on the verge of doing so, with military service requirements accomplished and an unexceptionable personal background.
2. Once accepted into the Police Academy, Escuela de Carabineros General Carlos Ibañez del Campo,

the officer candidate must complete a five-year program of courses including the following:

- Professional and institutional: institutional principles and essentials, police instruction, formal police procedure, law application of police procedure, methodology of investigation, applied police investigation, police practice, and police handling
- Law: introduction to law and principles of civil law, constitutional law and human conflicts, penal law, legal procedure, administrative law, and military justice

Throughout their studies, candidates must also pursue courses in English, communication techniques, and psychosociological fundamentals, as well as physical training and self-defense. The fourth year is spent in a full-time, one-year applications and research project that must eventually be presented and approved in order to gain the rank of lieutenant and the professional title of public security administrator.

Candidates may also pursue an alternative course of study emphasizing administrative rather than operational skills. This alternative track, which ultimately provides successful students with the title of institutional finance administrator, includes work in accounting, commercial law, taxes, labor regulations, economics, and math. Carabineros are offered a range of possibilities as career specializations, from criminal investigation, criminology, special operations, intelligence, and aviation, to traffic accident investigation and police instruction.

All candidates for the Policía de Investigaciones Academy must fulfill the following basic requirements:

1. Chilean citizenship, single marital status, twenty-seven years old or younger, have finished high school or must be on the verge of doing so, taken standardized university admissions tests, have completed their military service, and be in good health and physical condition.

2. Candidates must complete five years of coursework in the following fields:

- Required courses: introduction to law, institutional organization, research methodology, police procedure, social psychology, constitutional law, fingerprinting analysis, police and criminal psychology, penal law, international policing, human rights, forensic medicine, methodology of police investigation, ballistics, ethics, logic, legal penal procedure, criminology, practice of police proceedings, police investigation

- Additional elective courses: physical training, culture and sports, techniques of personal safety, gun handling and police shooting, English, institutional history, oral and written communication, computing, manners and human relations, scientific police laboratory, communication techniques, forensic oral expression

In the fourth year of study, students dedicate their activities fully to practice, and in the fifth, candidates choose a specialization. The specializations include homicide, narcotics, robbery or financial crime investigation, international policing, police intelligence, sexual crimes investigation, ballistics, fingerprinting analysis, organized crime, environmental crime, and internal affairs investigation.

Police Public Projects

Criminal Procedure Reform The new Criminal Procedure Reform has required significant adaptation by the police, particularly with respect to interactions among the various forces, and new training for the general teams, specialization for the technical forces, infrastructure, and resources dedicated to scientific projects. These new requirements are reflected in recent reforms carried out within the Carabineros and Policía de Investigaciones force.

Plan Cuadrante (Carabineros de Chile) Plan Cuadrante is a new system implemented by the Carabineros in 1998, and aimed at more efficiently fighting delinquency in metropolitan areas. The basis of the program is a greater efficiency in data evaluation (including the use of a regionally organized database) and the building of community support. In addition, the new program includes high standards for personnel evaluation based on performance in achieving crime prevention goals. This contrasts with the former system of evaluation that focused on maintaining military discipline within the force. Under the new plan, career promotions are based on crime prevention goal achievement rather than the maintenance of internal discipline.

Police Use of Firearms

Firearms possession is dictated by the Law of Control of Weapons and Explosives, which states: "The Ministry of National Defense through the General Directorate of National Mobilization will be in charge of the surveillance and control of weapons, explosive, artificial fire and pyrotechnic devices and other similar elements treated in this law.

The following bodies will be in charge of enforcing these regulations: The Commands of Garnish of the Armed Forces, the Authorities of the Carabineros de Chile, the Bank of Tests of Chile and the Specialized Services of the Armed forces." These same regulations dictate that private citizens desiring to own firearms must receive authorization from the Directorate of National Mobilization. Once authorized, firearms must be registered and only hunters, collectors, and merchants are permitted to own more than one gun.

Human Rights

In 1990, the Rettig Commission was created to investigate and inform the public on the human rights abuses of the former military regime, particularly cases of illegal detentions and disappearances. The Committee's confirmation of many of the worst fears of activists and average citizens alike helped make human rights a key issue in the democratic restoration efforts of subsequent years. The Reparation Commission has labored to restore a culture of respect for human rights in Chile, and this issue has been crucial within the dynamic of military–civilian relations. As part of the military environment, police have held an important place within this debate.

Despite significant police involvement in major abuses during the years of military rule, the Carabineros and Policía de Investigaciones have nevertheless been associated with efforts to improve and assume this new culture of human rights as part of its own doctrine and institutional values. This seemingly paradoxical association is not surprising, however, because despite past abuses the Carabineros have long been one of the most widely respected institutions in Chile, with a reputation for transparency, efficiency, and honesty that transcended even the events of the darkest years of the dictatorship.

Complaints and Discipline

During the late 1970s and the 1980s, the core of the conflict between police forces and civilians was alleged constant human rights violations: torture, illegal detentions, abductions, and forced disappearance of people. Even if hundreds of thousands of habeas corpus were presented at the courts, almost none were heard or resulted in any further investigation. Nevertheless, most of those judiciary activities were taken later as the base of longer trials that in some cases eventually found responsible parties and punished them. With the return of democracy, there have been several initiatives aimed at concentrating and accelerating those efforts, including the possibility of giving some compensation (sentence reduction or suspension, witness protection) to those who could give key information related to the cases. Later efforts have gone in the direction of establishing a group of judges fully dedicated to emblematic trials, so that they are run with complete competence to their respective ends. All these initiatives have been resisted by both sides: the military and former agents of intelligence agencies involved in human rights violation, who claim that Chile was under "civil war conditions," and by human rights violation victims and human rights organizations, who claim that special treatment ("compensation") to guilty parties leads ultimately to impunity.

Today, the allegations against police can be presented directly to the official superior in rank, for an internal administrative disciplinary procedure, or at the courts. This latter possibility presents the disadvantage of the Military Court excluding competence.

Terrorism

Chile's antiterrorist activities are concentrated on the protection of military and police outposts, the preservation of territorial integrity, national security, internal security, and public order. Each branch of the armed forces, the Carabineros, and the Policía de Investigaciones have intelligence units dedicated to foreseeing threats to security at both the national and international levels.

Efforts to combat the traffic in narcotics have also inspired a number of specialized organizations aimed at organized crime, money laundering, and financial and computer crimes. Oftentimes the work of these special units overlaps with those under the Attorney General that deal with official corruption. Civilian intelligence gathering is under the auspices of the Ministry of Interior through its Division of Citizen Security and Directorate of Public Security and Information.

International Cooperation

Both the Carabineros and the Policía de Investigaciones have long promoted educational and scientific exchanges with diverse institutions and international bodies, opening doors to personnel from other nations who want to enroll in Police Academy training courses. At the same time, the Chilean police have gone abroad to help train police forces from other Latin American nations and sent teams of advisory and support personnel to diverse destinations. The Carabineros have also participated in United Nations peacekeeping missions.

Police Education, Research, and Publications

Institutions

Academia Superior de Estudios Policiales
Academia de Ciencias Policiales

- Academia Nacional de Estudios Políticos y Estratégicos, ANEPE
- Centro de Estudios en Seguridad Ciudadana del Instituto de Asuntos Públicos de la Universidad de Chile, CESC
- Centro de Estudios de la Justicia de la Facultad de Derecho de la Universidad de Chile, CEJ
- Centro de Análisis de Políticas Públicas de la Universidad de Chile
- Centro de Estudios Jurídico Legislativos CEJIL, Escuela de Derecho, Universidad Diego Portales
- Centro de Estudios Públicos, CEP
- Centro de Estudios para el Desarrollo, CED
- Fundación Paz Ciudadana
- Corporación Ciudadanía y Justicia
- Corporación de Estudios Sociales y Educación, SUR
- Corporación de Promoción Universitaria, CPU
- Corporación FORJA
- Centro de Estudios de Justicia para las Américas, CEJA
- Fundación Ciudadanía y Justicia
- Corporación CHILE XXI
- Comité de Defensa de los Derechos del Pueblo, CODEPU
- Servicio Paz y Justicia, SERPAJ
- Fundación Asociación de Iglesias Cristianas, FASIC
- Comisión Económica para América Latina y el Caribe, CEPAL
- Programa de Naciones Unidas para el Desarrollo, PNUD

Leading Police Publications

Cuadernos de Criminología (Instituto de Criminología Policía de Investigaciones de Chile)
Cuadernos CED (Centro de Estudios para el Desarrollo, CED)
Temas Sociales (SUR, Corporación de Estudios Sociales y Educación)
Política y Estrategia (Academia Nacional de Estudios Políticos y Estratégicos, ANEPE)
Informes de Estadísticas Delitos de Mayor Connotación Social (Dirección de Seguridad Ciudadana Ministerio del Interior)

Anuario de Estadísticas Criminales (Fundación Paz Ciudadana)

Informe Desarrollo Humano (Programa Naciones Unidas para el Desarrollo, PNUD)

Other Publications

Programa Naciones Unidas para el Desarrollo. *Desarrollo humano en Chile 1998. Las paradojas de la modernización.* Santiago: PNUD, 1998.

Tudela, P. "Prevención del delito y seguridad ciudadana en democracia." *Cuadernos de Criminología*, no. 8 (1998) (Santiago: Policía de Investigaciones de Chile).

Oviedo, E., and A. Rodríguez. "Santiago, una ciudad con temor." *Temas Sociales*, no. 26 (1998) (Santiago: SUR).

Oviedo, E., and A. Rodríguez. "Santiago, una ciudad con temor. Inseguridad ciudadana y pérdida del espacio público." *Revista de la Organización Panamericana de la Salud* nos. 4–5 (1999).

Silva, I. *Costo económico de los delitos, niveles de vigilancia y políticas de seguridad ciudadana en las comunas del Gran Santiago.* Santiago: ILPES, 1999.

Arraigada, I., and L. Godoy. "Seguridad ciudadana y violencia en América Latina: diagnóstico y política en los años noventa." *Políticas sociales* no. 32 (1999).

Arraigada, I., and L. Godoy. "¿Prevención o represión? Falso dilema de la seguridad ciudadana." *Revista de la CEPAL*, April 2000.

Programa Naciones Unidas para el Desarrollo. *Desarrollo humano en Chile 2000. Más sociedad para gobernar el futuro.* Santiago: PNUD, 2000.

Acero, H., S. Bruneau, J. Burgos, S. Galilea, et al. *Conversaciones públicas para ciudades más seguras.* Santiago: Ediciones SUR, 2000.

Ramos, M. and J. Guzmán. *La guerra y la paz ciudadana.* Santiago: LOM, 2000.

Fruhling, H., and A. Candina, eds. *Policía, Sociedad y Estado: Modernización y Reforma Policial en América del Sur.* Santiago: CED, 2001.

Torres, E. and P. De la Puente. "Modelos internacionales y políticas públicas de seguridad ciudadana en Chile durante la última década." *Revista MAD* no. 4 (2001) (Santiago: Departamento de Antropología de la Universidad de Chile).

Tudela, P. *Seguridad y políticas públicas.* Política y Estrategia No. 83. Santiago: Academia Nacional de Estudios Políticos y Estratégicos, 2001.

Chalom, M., L. Léonard, F. Vanderschueren, and C. Vézina, eds. *Seguridad ciudadana, participación social y buen gobierno: el papel de la policía.* Santiago: Ediciones SUR, 2001.

Oviedo, E. "Policías de proximidad para las ciudades chilenas." *Temas Sociales* no. 35 (2001) (Santiago: SUR).

Burgos, J., and P. Tudela. *Políticas públicas y seguridad ciudadana.* Santiago: Corporación de Promoción Universitaria, 2001.

Burgos, J., and P. Tudela. "Seguridad ciudadana en Chile: Los desafíos de la participación y la modernización para una política pública." In *Seguridad ciudadana, ¿espejismo o realidad?* Quito: FLACSO Ecuador, OPS/OMS, 2002.

Barros, L. *Planificación de la actividad delictual en casos de robos con violencia o intimidación.* Santiago: CESC, Universidad de Chile, 2003.

FELIPE ABBOTT

Bibliography

See "Other Publications" above.

CHINA

Background Material

Despite holding a position for several centuries as an innovator in the arts and sciences and a leading civilization, in the nineteenth and early twentieth centuries China was undermined by famines, military defeats, and foreign occupation. After World War II, the communists under Mao Zedong established a strict, autocratic socialist administration that was responsible for the deaths of tens of millions of people. After 1978, Mao's successor, Deng Xiaoping, focused on market-oriented economic development. By 2000, economic output had quadrupled. Although living standards have risen and controls on personal choice have been relaxed, political controls remain tight.

China is located in Eastern Asia, bordering the East China Sea, Korea Bay, the Yellow Sea, and the South China Sea, between North Korea and Vietnam. It has a total area of 9,596,960 square kilometers and a population of 1,298,847,624 (2004 estimate). The ethnic composition of the population is Han Chinese 91.9%; with Zhuang, Uygur, Hui, Yi, Tibetan, Miao, Manchu, Mongol, Buyi, Korean, and other nationalities together accounting for 8.1%. The religious composition of the population is Daoist (Taoist), Buddhist, and Muslim, 1% to 2%, and Christian 3% to 4%. The nation is officially atheist. Languages spoken are Standard Chinese or Mandarin (Putonghua, based on the Beijing dialect); Yue (Cantonese); Wu (Shanghaiese); Minbei (Fuzhou); Minnan (Hokkien-Taiwanese); Xiang, Gan, and Hakka dialects; and minority languages.

With a purchasing power parity of US$5,000 (2003 estimate), China stood as the second-largest economy in the world after the United States, although in per capita terms the country is still poor.

Contextual Features

China is a communist state, with twenty-three provinces (*sheng*, singular and plural), five autonomous regions (*zizhiqu*, singular and plural), and four municipalities (*shi*, singular and plural). The legal system is a complex blend of customs and statutes. A basic civil code has been in effect since 1 January 1987. New legal codes have been in effect since 1 January 1980.

The president is the chief of state; he is assisted by a vice president. The premier is the head of the government. The cabinet, named the State Council, is composed of members appointed by the National People's Congress (NPC). The legislative branch of the government is represented by the unicameral National People's Congress (*Quanguo Renmin Daibiao Dahui*).

The judiciary is represented by the Supreme People's Courts; Local People's Courts, which are higher, intermediate, and local courts; and the Special People's Courts, which are primarily military, maritime, and railway transport courts.

The Criminal Law took effect on 1 January 1980. It took the power to mete out criminal punishment away from the discretion of officials, whose arbitrary decisions were based on party lines. The law listed eight categories of offenses.

The Statute on Punishment for Counterrevolutionary Activity approved under the Common Program in 1951 listed a wide range of counterrevolutionary offenses, punishable in most cases by the death penalty or life imprisonment. In subsequent years, especially during the Cultural Revolution, any activity that the party or government at any level considered a challenge to its authority could be termed counterrevolutionary. The 1980 law narrowed the scope of counterrevolutionary activity considerably, and defined it as "any act jeopardizing the People's Republic of China, aimed at overthrowing the political power of the dictatorship of the proletariat and the socialist state." Under this category it included such specific offenses as espionage, insurrection, conspiracy to overthrow the government, instigating a member of the armed forces to turn traitor, or carrying out sabotage directed against the government.

Other offenses, in the order listed in the 1980 law, were transgressions of public security, defined as any acts that endanger people or public property; illegal possession of arms and ammunition; offenses against the socialist economic order, including smuggling and speculation; offenses against both the personal rights and the democratic rights of citizens, which range from homicide, rape, and kidnapping to libel; and offenses of encroachment on property, including robbery, theft, embezzlement, and fraud. There were also offenses against the public order, including obstruction of official business; mob disturbances; manufacture, sale, or transport of illegal drugs or pornography; vandalizing or illegally exporting cultural relics; offenses against marriage and the family, which include interference with the freedom of marriage and abandoning or maltreating children or aged or infirm relatives; and malfeasance, which specifically relates to state functionaries and includes such offenses as accepting bribes, divulging state secrets, dereliction of duty, and maltreatment of persons under detention or surveillance.

China retained the death penalty in the 1980s for certain serious crimes. The overwhelming majority of prisoners were sentenced to hard labor.

In the early 1980s, the people's procuratorates supervised the prisons, ensuring compliance with the law. Prisoners were told that their sentences could be reduced if they showed signs of repentance and rendered meritorious service. Any number of reductions could be earned, totaling up to one-half the original sentence, but at least ten years of a life sentence had to be served. Probation or parole involved surveillance by the public security bureau or a grassroots organization to which the convict periodically reported.

Crime by youthful offenders has been a matter of grave concern to the post-Mao leadership. In common with most societies, nearly all those charged with violent crime have been under thirty-five years of age. Criminal law makes special provisions for juvenile offenders. Offenders between fourteen and sixteen years of age are to be held criminally liable only if they commit homicide, robbery, arson, or "other offenses which gravely jeopardize public order," and offenders between fourteen and eighteen years of age "shall be given a lighter or mitigated penalty." In most cases, juvenile offenders charged with minor infractions are dealt with by neighborhood committees or other administrative means. In serious cases juvenile offenders usually are sent to one of the numerous reformatories reopened in most cities under the Ministry of Education beginning in 1978.

In 1987, the crime rate remained low by international standards, and Chinese cities were among the safest in the world. The court system had been reestablished, and standard criminal, procedural, civil, and economic codes had been developed. Law schools, closed since the late 1950s, had been reopened, and new ones had been established to meet the growing need for lawyers and judges. Law enforcement organizations had been reorganized, civilianized, and made answerable to the courts and the procuratorates.

Opposition to the changes was pervasive at every level of the party and the government. Even its strongest supporters insisted that the legal system must be developed in accordance with the four cardinal principles—upholding socialism, the dictatorship of the proletariat, the leadership of the Chinese Communist Party, and Marxism-Leninism-Mao Zedong thought. Given these limitations, it was clear that although much progress had been made in replacing the Mao era's arbitrary rule with a solid legal system, much still remained to be done.

Police Profile

In the mid-1980s and early 1990s, China had an extensive public security system backed up by a wide variety of enforcement procedures. Along with the courts, the country's judicial and security agencies included the Ministry of Public Security and the Ministry of State Security.

The security and policing system of China has been influenced by communist ideology and practice. However, even more so, it remains rooted in the traditional Chinese concept of governmental control through imposed collective responsibility.

In 1932, Chiang Kai-shek's government reinstituted the traditional *bao jia* (tithing) system. Family households were organized into groups of ten, each unit being organized successively into a larger unit up to the county level of administration. Each family sent a representative to the monthly meeting of its unit, and each unit elected a leader to represent it at the next higher level.

When the communists came to power in 1949, they liberally borrowed from historical examples, adhering to traditions of mutual surveillance and responsibility. Communist control moved beyond the *bao jia* system. To achieve near-total control, a large number of administrative agencies and social organizations were established or adapted. Police forces resembling the Soviet police in organization, power, and activities were organized with the aid of Soviet advisers.

From 1949 to 1953, the newly established government of the People's Republic made use of the People's Liberation Army (PLA) to maintain order. The PLA was composed of militia units, and the members were demobilized soldiers and other civilians, the police, and loyal citizens.

The PLA under Mao continued to assume public security functions, establishing its own committees to replace the government bureaucracy, and to quell public resistance. By 1968, the Red Guards were in the process of being disbanded. Those who had taken part in riots were tried in and punished by mass trials.

PLA commanders came to assume leadership of nineteen of the country's twenty-nine provincial people's revolutionary committees. Thus, the military was effectively in charge of administration and security throughout the country. The PLA recruited both experienced police officers and inexperienced people to form auxiliary police units. These units were mass organizations with a variety of names reflecting their factional orientation.

The PLA began helping to remove millions of urbanites to rural areas, to alleviate urban overcrowding, in 1968. These forced moves were met with discontent. However, crime declined in the 1970s. In that decade, the PLA turned its attention to a perceived increased threat from the Soviet Union, given recent armed clashes on the shared border between the two nations in 1969. Thus, overall control of China reverted to civilian leadership.

During the PLA's time in power, one of its key units was the Beijing-based Central Security Regiment, also known as the 8341 Unit, which was responsible for the personal security of Mao Zedong and other party and state leaders. In addition to performing bodyguard duties, the Regiment also maintained a national intelligence network, focused on uncovering plots or threats against Mao.

In 1973 the Gang of Four, concerned over the transformation of the PLA into a more professional, less political, military force, took control of the urban militia from the PLA and placed it under local party committees loyal to them. For the next three years, the urban militia was used to enforce radical political and social policies. This urban militia dissolved demonstrations in Tiananmen Square honoring the memory of Zhou Enlai in April 1976.

From 1 January 1980, laws on police powers regarding arrests, investigations, and searches have been in effect. Any accused individual being held had to be questioned within twenty-four hours, and his or her family or work unit notified of his or her detention. Any premeditated arrest required a court or procuratorate warrant. The time that an accused could be held pending investigation was limited to three to seven days, and incarceration without due process was illegal. Two officials were needed to conduct a criminal investigation. They were required to show identification, and inform the accused of the crime regarding which he or she was being questioned. The suspect could refuse to answer questions irrelevant to the case. Torture was illegal. The 1980 laws also provided that, in conjunction with an arrest, the police could conduct an emergency search. In nonemergency cases, a warrant was required for search.

In July 1980, the government approved new regulations overseeing police use of weapons and force. Police could use their batons only in self-defense, or when necessary to subdue or prevent the escape of violent criminals or rioters. Lethal weapons, such as pistols, could be used if necessary to stop violent riots, to reduce overall loss of life, or to subdue resisting criminals.

In the mid-1980s, the Ministry of Public Security was the main police authority. The Ministry oversaw departments focused on areas such as intelligence; police operations; prisons; and political, economic, and communications security. The Ministry also oversaw province-level public security departments; public security bureaus and sub-bureaus at the county level; and public security stations at the township level. The security concerns of the Ministry were influential at all governmental levels, although the police seemed to be especially influential at the lower levels of government.

In the 1980s, the public security station was the police body most closely in direct contact with the civilian population. The public security station was maintained by the public security sub-bureau, the local government, and the procuratorates, the last of whom could assume direct responsibility for any case it chose. The public security stations, the security sub-bureaus, the procuratorates, and the courts coordinated closely, so that the outcome of a given trial was generally preestablished.

The public security station generally had broad areas of responsibility, involving itself in virtually every aspect of the civilians' lives. For example, the public security station controlled and oversaw any civilian change of residence. This was necessary as, otherwise, large numbers of rural residents would move to already overcrowded cities, seeking better work, education, and standards of living.

Secret police units employed agents, informers, and spies in the 1980s. Spies were posted at bus and railroad stations and other public places. Police informers assisted in surveillance of suspected political criminals.

After a trial period conducted in specific districts, the People's Armed Police Force (PAPF) was officially established at the national level in 1983. This unit was created as a response to a general new policy of reducing the size of the armed forces and security units, and transferring at least some of their powers to the civilian administrative units. The PAPF was formed by reassigning internal security units from the PLA, and customs, border defense, and firefighting units. In the mid-1980s, the PAPF was composed of approximately 600,000 volunteers and conscripts. The PAPF had a military organization, with a national general headquarters, subordinate provincial and specialized units, and detachments and brigades.

Those PAPF units assigned to internal security guarded party and state organizations, as well as foreign embassies and consulates. They were also charged with maintaining law and order and responding to emergency situations.

PAPF border units performed customs-related tasks, which included inspecting vehicles and ships leaving and entering China. These units also did surveillance to find and prevent smugglers and drug traffickers.

The PAPF also maintained firefighting units. All PAPF units at every level cooperated with the armed forces and other security organizations.

Bibliography

Library of Congress. "China." Library of Congress Country Studies. Available at: http://lcweb2.loc.gov/frd/cs/.

COLOMBIA

Background Material

In 1830, three countries were formed upon the dissolution of Gran Colombia: Ecuador, Venezuela, and Colombia. Over the course of the last forty years, insurgents led a campaign to overthrow the government, a campaign that grew more heated in the 1990s, thanks in part to monetary support from the drug trade. An opposing paramilitary army has grown in recent years, standing at several thousand strong. This army has clashed with the guerilla insurgents, fighting for control of both land and the drug trade. The administration in Bogotá is increasing efforts to regain government control of the country.

Colombia is located in northern South America, bordering the Caribbean Sea, between Panama and Venezuela, and bordering the North Pacific Ocean, between Ecuador and Panama. Its land area totals 1,138,910 square kilometers. The population of Colombia is 42,310,775 (July 2004 estimate). The ethnic compostion of the country is mestizo 58%, white 20%, mulatto 14%, black 4%, mixed black—Amerindian 3%, and Amerindian 1%. Ninety percent of the population identifies as Roman Catholic. The language is Spanish.

Colombia's economy suffers from weak demand, austere government budgets, and the armed conflict between the insurgents and the paramilitaries. Coffee, one of Colombia's primary exports, faces an uncertain future, as both harvests and prices are depressed. However, several international financial institutions have praised recent economic reforms, such as plans to reduce the public sector deficit. Government policies have created a growing confidence in the economy. As a result, in 2003, GDP growth was among the highest in Latin America. The GDP per capita stood at $6,300 that year.

Contextual Features

Colombia is a republic. The executive branch is the dominant one. The legal system is based on Spanish law. A new criminal code, modeled on U.S. legal standards and practices, was adopted in 1992–1993.

The president is the chief of state, as well as the head of the government. A bicameral Congress (Congreso) consists of the Senate (Senado) and the House of Representatives (Camara de Representantes).

There are four judicial bodies, approximately equal in stature. They are the Supreme Court of Justice, which is the highest court of criminal law; the Council of State, which is the highest court of administrative law; the Constitutional Court, which rules on the constitutionality of laws; and the Superior Judicial Council, which resolves jurisdictional conflicts arising between other courts.

The activities of Colombian narcotics traffickers have traditionally been a serious internal security problem. During the 1980s, government officials were murdered on numerous occasions for their efforts to combat the drug trade, including a former head of the Antinarcotics Police. In addition, scores of police personnel have been murdered by drug traffickers' hired assassins (sicarios). By the late 1980s, the narcotics traffickers had organized their own death squad, the Extraditables. They issued threats against or murdered persons seen as abetting the government's attempt to comply with outstanding U.S. extradition warrants.

Influential drug traffickers were able to obtain release from prison or escape conviction by paying off magistrates. The drug trade has created widespread corruption in the judicial system.

During the late 1950s and early 1960s, Colombia had the third highest rate of homicide in the world. In the 1980s, Colombia was still among the top countries in the world in terms of the ratio of murders to the total population. In 1985, murder was the fourth most common cause of death. In 1987, approximately 16,000 Colombians were murdered.

Throughout the late 1980s and early 1990s, the crime rate rose, reflecting spikes in both political violence as well as criminal violence. Data published by the Colombian government in 1987 estimated that nearly 80% of the crimes committed in the nation went unreported. In turn, of the 20% reported to the authorities, only 1% resulted in conviction and sentencing. In addition to the poor conviction rate, the administration of criminal justice was complicated by the mounting backlog of cases.

The Penal Code of 1938, as subsequently revised, regulated the country's penal system. Crimes were classifiable as either felonies or misdemeanors, and were divided into six categories: crimes against property, crimes against persons, crimes against individual liberties, sex-related crimes, crimes against public administration, and miscellaneous crimes.

In the early 1980s, the capacity of the country's prison system was only 12,000 prisoners, yet the size of the country's prison population was estimated at 30,000.

Police Profile

Background

The National Police is Colombia's principal law enforcement organization. Current reliable information on Colombian police forces is not readily available; however, data and information summarizing the force's status over the last fifty years are presented here.

During the 1950s, the government put the police force under the jurisdiction of the Ministry of National Defense. In 1962, the National Police assumed control of the separate police forces that had been maintained by each of the country's administrative divisions up until that time.

Demographics

In 1969, the National Police was estimated to include approximately 42,000 personnel. Recruitment plans were announced during the mid-1970s, and suggested a projected increase in the force to approximately 75,000 individuals by 1980. Although challenges to internal security rose, given the guerrilla warfare and the drug trade, the size of the force did not increase as planned, remaining constant at approximately 50,000 members between 1974 and 1984. In 1988, the size of the National Police was estimated at approximately 55,000, of whom approximately 10% were civilians.

Organizational Description

During the 1980s, the National Police remained directly subordinate to the Minister of National Defense. Officers holding military rank filled key posts within the National Police.

The force's organization mimicked that of the military. It was divided into separate departments, including personnel, intelligence, operations, and logistics. Force members not attached to one of these departments were stationed in each of the administrative departments of the country, where a commander served as the ranking police officer. In addition to his own staff, the departmental police commander supervised police personnel assigned to the various districts maintained throughout the department. Mayors and civil magistrates were also suspected of having influence in law enforcement matters, which, it has been suggested by observers, led to corruption within the National Police.

A number of special units functioned under the overall jurisdiction of the National Police headquarters as well, including the Radio Patrol Group, Antimugging Group, Private Surveillance Group, Highway Police, Tourist Police, Juvenile Police, Railroad Police, and Operational Group Against Extortion and Kidnappings.

The Antinarcotics police played a key role in the seizure of illegal narcotics, the arrest of drug traffickers, and destroying concealed air landing strips and processing laboratories used by traffickers. The Carabineros were a special rural police force of the National Police that carried out counterinsurgency missions, frequently in conjunction with army units. The National Police also oversaw and manned the fire departments.

During the 1980s, the National Police reportedly also assumed control of the Directorate of the Judicial Police and Investigation (Dirección de la Policía Judicial y Investigación [Dijin]), or, as it is more commonly referred to, the Judicial Police. This body was originally under the administration of the Ministry of Justice. The Judicial Police, along with the national Criminal Statistics Archives (Archivos de Estadística Criminal), is the principal repository of information required for the prosecution of criminal cases. The Criminal Statistics Archives also was transferred to the National Police.

The Judicial Police assumed a significant role in Colombia's National Antinarcotics Campaign in the 1980s. It carried out criminal investigations and assisted in the preparation of court cases against narcotics traffickers.

In addition to the National Police, the Administrative Security Department (Departamento Administrativo de Seguridad [DAS]) had important law enforcement responsibilities in the 1980s. The DAS was responsible for enforcement of laws relating to national security. The formal responsibilities of the DAS were investigating crimes against the internal security of the state, fraud against the state and its financial institutions, breaches of public faith, and crimes affecting individual liberty and human rights.

Functions

The National Police is charged with handling all duties relating to common crime. Its other main function included combating the drug trade, arresting narcotics traffickers, counterinsurgency tasks, and riot control. Other duties included traffic regulation enforcement, supervision of public recreation areas, mine security, and prison security.

Training

The National Police maintained its own professional education system, administered by the instructional division. The two principal professional schools for members of the National Police were the General Santander Police Cadet School and the Jiménez de Quesada Noncommissioned Officers School, both located in Bogotá. Completion of the cadet school's rigorous two-year program was required of all recruits who aspired to obtain a commission in the National Police. Completion of additional training was required for promotions. Noncommissioned officers were required to complete a five-month course for each advance-

ment in rank from corporal to sergeant major. The National Police also operated seven smaller police schools in various locations throughout the country. These schools offered a five-month basic training course for recruits as well as in-service training; coursework included subjects as diverse as Colombian history and riot control. Members of the Carabineros were required to undergo a special three-month training program at the National School of Carabineros, also located in the national capital.

Bibliography

Central Intelligence Agency. "Colombia." In *CIA World Factbook*. Available at: www.cia.gov/cia/publications/factbook/geos/co.html.

Library of Congress. "Colombia." Library of Congress Country Studies. Available at: http://lcweb2.loc.gov/frd/cs/.

COMOROS

Background Information

The Union of the Comoros is an independent republic located in the Mozambique Channel between northwestern Madagascar and southeast Africa. It consists of three semiautonomous islands: Grande Comore (Njazidja), Anjouan (Nzwani), and Moheli (Mwali). The Union claims a fourth, Mayotte, which is governed by France. The capital, Moroni, is located on Grande Comore. The nation covers an area of 2,170 square miles.

In 2004, the estimated population was 651,901. It is of African-Arab origins. The official languages are French, Arabic, and Shikomoro, a blend of Swahili and Arabic. Languages, dialects, ethnic distinctions, immigration patterns, and the relative isolation of island populations, have contributed significantly to the creation of strong island identities, which are becoming more nationalistic over time.

The official religion is Islam. Ninety-eight percent of the population is Sunni Muslim and 2% Christian. The government discourages religions other

than Islam, and there are reports of discrimination and police action against practicing Christians.

Comoros is a poor country. The economy is dominated by agriculture. French settlers, French-owned companies, and Arab merchants established a plantation-based economy that now uses about one-third of the land for export crops. France remains the major trading partner of Comoros. The main exports are vanilla, cloves, perfume oil, and copra; however, Comoros is not self-sufficient in food, and imports mainly rice. Its infrastructure cannot support economic development. It has only one deep water port, and many of its towns are not connected by roads. An estimated 60% live below the poverty line, and per capita income in 2004 was US$720. Life expectancy is 61.57 years, and the literacy rate is 57%.

France established colonial rule over the four islands in the mid-nineteenth century and placed the islands under the administration of the Governor General of Madagascar. After World War II, the islands became a French overseas territory, and were represented in the French National Assembly. In 1975, the islands declared independence from France and became the Federal Islamic Republic of the Comoros. Mayotte remained under French administration.

The postindependence government was a multiparty democracy, but it was overthrown in 1976. Coups and overthrow attempts have continued since then and number in excess of twenty. This pattern has impeded both economic and political development. Between 1990 and 2001, the islands were under military governments, during which time Anjouan seceded. It returned to the fold in 2001, and later in the same year a new constitution was approved. The incumbent President resigned from the army and ran as a civilian for election to the new presidency. He was elected in 2002, in what was considered a flawed but fair election.

Contextual Features

Under the constitution each of the islands has considerable autonomy, while the union government has authority over religion, nationality, money, external relations, exterior defense, and national symbols. In the case of shared responsibility, it also has the residual power in matters that cannot be settled by the islands. This power-sharing formula has been problematic and the constitution has not been completely adopted as a result. Contentious questions include revenue-sharing, particularly of customs duties, and the control of the police. Under the constitution, the Union controls the army and the islands have their own police, but the Gendarmerie is both a police force and a part of the army. An underlying problem is that Comoros is a poor country with a very small population, yet it has four governments.

There is a unicameral National Assembly of thirty-three seats, fifteen selected by the assemblies of the islands and eighteen elected by universal suffrage. The members serve for five years. The presidency rotates every four years among the elected presidents of the islands. There are two Union vice presidents from each of the two islands not supplying the president. The Union president is chief of government and the army. There is one woman in the Cabinet, another is the President of the Tribunal of First Instance, and another is legal counsel to the President.

The legal system incorporates both French and Shari'a (Islamic) law into a new consolidated code. The constitution provides for a judiciary independent of the executive and legislature; however, there have been reports of the executive and other elites exerting influence over court cases.

The constitution provides for a constitutional court to rule on jurisdictional matters between the Union and the islands, elections, and individual rights. There is a single Appeal Court situated in Moroni. The Supreme Court is charged with supervising elections and examining constitutional issues. It has seven members, two of which are chosen by the president, two by the Assembly, and one by each of the three island councils.

Courts are divided into criminal and civil. The criminal court is further divided into lower courts, which reflect a mixture of local customs and French law, and the upper and appeals courts, which reflect greater influences of the Napoleonic Code. Lower courts and jails are located on all islands. Higher courts are located in Moroni.

There are very few lawyers in the country, making it difficult to obtain legal representation. Government does not provide legal counsel to the accused. Disputes are often presented to village elders for possible resolution before being taken to court.

Prison conditions are poor. There is overcrowding, inadequate food and medical facilities, and a lack of proper sanitation. Female prisoners are held separately from males but pretrial detainees are not separated from convicted prisoners. Youths are not imprisoned, but are returned to the custody of their parents.

There is little crime in Comoros, particularly crimes of violence. Domestic violence occurs but is rare. Prostitution is illegal, but not considered a problem. Child abuse is rare, and child prostitution and pornography are illegal. Children under thirteen are protected, and there appears to be no trafficking in persons, although some families place their children in the homes of others, where they work long hours in exchange for food or shelter. Drug offenses carry heavy penalties.

Police Profile

Background and Organizational Description

Comoros has a small standing army and, under a 1996 agreement, a permanent French military contingent. Internal security is the responsibility of a defense force and the presidential guard, which are under the direct control of the civilian president. At times in the past, the presidential guard has functioned as a private army and has been controlled by mercenaries. It is now largely under the direction of the French. The defense force has approximately 500 members, including an armed and well-equipped sixty-member paramilitary mobile unit. The military provides support in quelling violence and disturbances, such as that encountered during the 2002 elections, and in restoring law and order.

There is a 500-member paramilitary police force, or gendarmerie, with its headquarters in Moroni. It is organized in detachments that are dispersed among the three islands. In addition to the gendarmerie, on Grande Comore there are local police forces under the jurisdiction of the island government, who are also responsible for immigration. The combination of French and Muslim law and military rule has created a national police force with significant power; however, international observers have not found any widespread, systemic violation of human rights by the police.

Functions

The policing function is divided into "administrative" or "preventive" policing, and "judicial" or "repressive" policing. The administrative police are responsible for maintaining order and applying the laws. In this role, they carry out such duties as patrol, criminal investigation, and intelligence operations. The national intelligence agency is called the Security and Information Bureau. Other regulatory functions such as immigration or customs are also considered to be administrative policing. In this role, the police come under the authority of the Minister of the Interior.

The judicial police come under the jurisdiction of the Minister of Justice and Islamic Affairs, and are responsible for identifying crimes, collecting evidence, and apprehending offenders. As soon as sufficient information is assembled, an "information" is "opened," and the judicial police then act under the authority of the court and directly for the examining magistrate, or *juge d'instruction*. They can also act as delegates of the examining magistrate and, in that role, exercise all the same powers as an examining magistrate. The judicial police therefore have considerable authority.

The status of judicial police is possessed by a wide range of public functionaries such as customs officers; forestry, environment, and fisheries officers; the joint antidrug brigade; court officials; and many members of the gendarmerie. This means that judicial police come under the jurisdiction of their functional ministries as well as of the Minister of Justice. In the case of the gendarmerie, this situation makes the judicial police of the gendarmerie virtually autonomous. Their administrative and judicial powers are not clearly distinguished and, with respect to discipline, promotion, training, and other matters, it is the regulations of the gendarmerie operating under the Minister of the Interior that prevail. Moreover, they often earn more than the magistrates who supervise them in their judicial role, thus creating an anomaly in the status of the two groups. In effect, despite the authority of the Minister of Justice for the control and direction of the judicial police, there is no means by which the authority can be enforced. It is generally recognized, however, that the gendarmerie is more effective than other judicial police, mainly because it is better equipped.

Training

All police training takes place at the National Armed Forces and Gendarmerie School. The training is military in philosophy as well as application. The presidential guard is the best-trained and equipped of the security services. Efforts to raise awareness of human rights among police officers are taking place.

Police Use of Firearms

The police are armed, and are assisted by the military to control riots and political dissidents. In 2001–2002, under a UN policy, the Organization of African Unity engaged in an initiative to combat the proliferation and trafficking of small arms. As a part of the program, the police of the Comoran island of Anjouan have collected, catalogued and, where necessary, stockpiled the weapons they discovered. At the time of the initiative there were a total of 415 weapons on the island, of which 346 were inspected and collected. The rest were retained by the gendarmerie and the defense force. Each official was allocated one weapon and a set amount of ammunition, and there were inspections of the four defense posts and the eleven gendarmerie detachments on the island to ensure that weapons were not being hoarded. The three armories on the island were checked, inventoried, and secured with a dual-key system.

International Cooperation

Comoros joined Interpol in 1998. In 2003–2004, Interpol launched plans to install the necessary electronic networks to bring West Africa and the East and South African regions into its I-24/7 Global Communication System. Comoros will be part of the network. Comoros is also a member of the United Nations.

RUTH MONTGOMERY

Bibliography

Agence Intergouvernementale de la Francophonie. Constitution de l'Union des Comores, 23-12-2001, Association des cours constitutionnelles ayant en partage l'usage du français, 2001. DFKMCO 1. Available at: http://droit.franco phonie.org/doc/html/km/con/fr/2001/2001dfkmco1.html. Accessed November 22, 2004.

Becker, H. K., and D. Lee. *Handbook of the World's Police.* Metuchen, N.J. and London: Scarecrow Press, 1986.

British Broadcast Corporation. "Country Profile: Comoros." BBC News (UK Edition). Available at: http://news.bbc.co/uk/l/hi/world/africa/country_profiles/1070727.stm. Accessed July 24, 2003.

Central Intelligence Agency. "Cormoros." In *CIA World Fackbook*, 2004. Available at: www.cia.gov.cia/publica tions/factbook/geos/cn.html. Accessed November 22, 2004.

Gale Group. *Countries of the World and Their Leaders Yearbook 2003*, Vol. 1. Detroit: Thomson Gale, 2003.

Institut International de Droit d'Expression et d'Inspiration Françaises. La direction de la police judiciare et son contrôle par les autorities judiciaires en République fédérale islamique des Comores, Juriscope, 1999. Available at: http://juriscope.org/publications/etudes/police.htm. Accessed November 11, 2004.

International Institute for Strategic Studies. *Military Balance 1997–98*. London: Oxford University Press, 1998.

Park, K. *World Almanac and Book of Facts, 2002*. New York: World Almanac Books, 2002.

Reeve, R. "Country Summary, Comoros." Jane's Terrorism Intelligence Centre, Jane's Information Group 2002, posted 6 September 2002. Available at: www4.janes.com. Accessed January 17, 2003.

United Nations Committee on the Rights of the Child. "Summary Record of Meeting" (CRC/C/SR.666), 25th session, 666th meeting held October 4, 2000, Geneva, Switzerland. CountryWatch.com, "Country Review: Comoros," 2001–2002. Available at: www.country watch.com. Accessed November 28, 2003.

United Nations Office for the Coordination of Humanitarian Affairs. "Comoros: AU Delegation—Recommendations but no Solution." IRINnews.org, posted 21 July 2003. Available at: www.irinnews.org. Accessed July 24, 2003.

U.S. Department of State. "Cormoros." In Country Reports on Human Rights Practices—. Bureau of Democracy, Human Rights and Labor, March 31, 2003. Available at: www.state.gov. Accessed July 24, 2003.

U.S. Department of State. "Background Note: Comoros." Bureau of African Affairs, November 2004. Available at: www.state.gov/r/pa/ei/bgn/5236.htm. Accessed November 22, 2004.

THE DEMOCRATIC REPUBLIC OF CONGO

Background Material

The Democratic Republic of the Congo (DRC), formerly known as Zaire, is located in central Africa, northeast of Angola. The nation achieved independence from Belgium on 30 June 1960. It has an area of 2,345,410 square kilometers, and a population of 58,317,930 (*The World Factbook* 2004). The capital is Kinshasa. Languages spoken include French (official), Lingala, Kingwana, Kikongo, and Tshiluba. Religions include Roman Catholicism (50%), Protestantism (20%), Kimbanguism (10%), Islam (10%), and other syncretic sects and indigenous beliefs (10%).

The government is a dictatorship, presumably undergoing a transition to representative government. The legislative branch, the Transitional Constituent Assembly, was established in 2000. The legal system is based on the Belgian civil law system, and tribal law. The DRC holds membership in the following international organizations: United Nations, African Union, World Health Organization, International Monetary Fund, Interpol, African Development Bank (ADB), and Economic Community of Central African States (ECOCAS). GDP purchasing power parity is US$35.62 billion (2003 estimate).

The shape of the DRC has been likened to that of a heart. Based on its appearance as represented on topical maps, it has been sometimes referred to as the heart of the African tropics. DRC's geographical setting makes it one of the strategic countries in Africa. Nine countries border it: Angola, Zambia, Tanzania, Burundi, Rwanda, Uganda, Sudan, the Central African Republic, and the Republic of the Congo. It has also been suggested by environmentalists that the DRC possesses some of the most significant tropical rainforests in the world. In addition, mountains, volcanoes, and rivers cover the country. It is rich with wildlife, including elephants, gorillas, and wildfowl, and various species of plant and animal life, many yet to be studied by scientists.

The early history of the country indicates that around 1000 BC, the ancestors of the Bantu speaking people from present-day Nigeria were the first to inhabit the area. In 1482, European interests in the area were invigorated, due, primarily, to the writings of early explorers, such as Henry Morton Stanley and the hard work of navigator Diego Cao. In 1885, the area was officially conquered by Belgium—under the leadership of King Leopold II, who was seeking business ventures and African possessions—as the Congo Free State. In 1907, the country's name was changed to Belgian Congo, and its administration was ceded to the Belgian government. Because of the uncontrollable political turmoil that faced the Belgian government, the country became independent in 1960 and conducted parliamentary elections, which elevated Patrice Lumumba, a sizzling orator, as its first Prime Minister. Subsequently, the country was renamed the Democratic Republic of the Congo. Lumumba died mysteriously in January 1961, and Col. Joseph Desire Mobutu (Mobutu Sese Seko) gained control over the administration, yielding power to President Joseph Kasavubu.

Political turbulence and revolts inundated the country until 1965, when Mobutu seized power again and declared himself president for five years. He also changed the country's name to Zaire, his own name to Mobutu Sese Seko, the capital's name from Leopoldville to Kinshasa, and forced Zairian citizens to assume African names. His reign in Africa lasted for thirty-two years. He was, undeniably, a dictator, a political tin god, and president-for-life. Mobutu continued his one-party rule until the late 1980s and early 1990s when his supremacy was weakened by opposition parties' demands, domestic protests, human rights violations, a tattered economy, and strong international condemnation of his arbitrary use of power.

In 1996, two significant events ensued. First, the Mobutu government expelled the Zairian Tutsis for fomenting trouble in Zaire. Additionally, Laurent Kabila, a rebel leader allied with the anti-Mobutu movement, joined with Rwandan troops for the purpose of ousting Mobutu from power. Supported by the Ugandan military, Mobutu was forced out of power in May 1997. Kabila declared himself president and assassinated several political opponents and supporters of Mobutu. However, Kabila's efforts to expel his own foreign cliques led to his assassination on January 16, 2001.

Following the death of Kabila, his son, Joseph Kabila, was asked to succeed him. On January 26, 2001, the younger Kabila was sworn in as head of state of the tumultuous DRC. He quickly dismantled various negative policies of his father, engaged in peace negotiations in both Addis Ababa and South Africa with many Inter-Congolese entities, improved external relations, and negotiated power sharing that led to the inclusion of four vice presidents in his government. These vice presidents took office on 17 July 2003. Additionally, the president appointed many ministers to their respective offices in the same year. Many have argued that President Kabila has made excellent use of his executive powers by calming political movements and commissioning progressive economic developments with the World Bank and the International Monetary Fund (IMF) that will improve the quality of life of the Congolese people.

Although the DRC is not densely populated, it maintains the status of the third-largest populated country in Sub-Saharan Africa and its second largest land area. It possesses enormous natural resources, such as copper, cobalt, diamonds, gold, and uranium. Agriculture accounted for about 56.3% of the Congolese GDP in 2002. The nation's primary export crops include coffee, tea, palm oil, and cotton, and it also produces food crops, such as cassava, groundnuts, maize, bananas, and rice. Sadly, because of many years of political instability, it is still one of the poorest countries in the world. It has been reported that corruption, negligence, and many years of war have created a dual economy controlled by the private sector and the government. According to published reports, in 2002, the government employed about 600,000 Congolese, and about 230,000 people worked for private enterprises.

In 2004, the Congolese population was estimated to be slightly over 58 million. The country is made up of people from about 250 different ethnic groups, who speak about 700 languages and dialects. French is the official language of the DRC. About two thirds of the population subscribes to the Christian faith, most with ties to the Catholic Church. The people are free to practice their respective religions in as much as it is not seditious and offensive to other citizens. However, in 1972, Mobutu's doctrine of "authenticity," discussed earlier, encouraged citizens to reject their Christian given names, and replace them with bona fide African names.

DRC's strategic location, population, size, and rich mineral deposits have made the country an important power in the region. It also received tremendous economic support during the Cold War period from the United States. However, due to the demise of the Cold War and reports about human right violations, Washington discontinued its aid to the country. Relations with surrounding African countries serve as a fundamental source of insecurity for the state. Domestic insurrections in countries like Rwanda, Uganda, the Central African Republic, Angola, and Burundi have initiated tensions in the region. The United States supports the current transitional government in the Congo as well as democratic initiatives and respect for human rights in the country. However, the United States does not provide significant economic aid to the DRC.

Contextual Features

Since the nation gained its independence in 1960, the Congo's electoral process has been elusive for the people of the DRC. Under current government arrangements, President Kabila is both the chief of state and head of government and is assisted by four Vice Presidents: Jean–Pierre Bemba, Arthur Z'ahidi Ngoma, Azarias Ruberwa, and Abdoulaye Yerodia Ndombasi. The transitional constitution that was adopted on April 4, 2003 gave the President broad powers over executive, legislative, and military matters. The republic has a highly centralized government structure. The cabinet is composed of thirty-five members, and the president possesses the power to appoint and fire them. Some of the significant ministerial presidential cabinets include Foreign Affairs, Defense, Interior, Justice, Finance, and Information and Press. The current administrative structure of the government has no provisions for a Prime Minister.

Currently, the DRC's legislative branch is made up of a 300-member Transitional Constituent Assembly that was established in August 2000. Based in Kinshasa, members of the legislative body were appointed by signatories to the December 17, 2002 all-inclusive agreement. As in other parliamentary bodies, the legislature has the power to debate and make laws, but it does not have the authority to alter the administration through a vote of no confidence. There is a Supreme Court (Cour Supreme); however, although the judiciary is independent, the President is vested with the power to dismiss and appoint judges without the checks and balances that characterize most of the democratic governments in the world. Generally, judges in the DRC have the discretion to reduce and increase criminal sanctions.

Indeed, prison conditions and penalties in the DRC are harsher than those in the United States. It has been reported that the situation in the former is deplorable and is characterized by overcrowding, inadequate financing, beatings, deaths from diseases, and poorly trained personnel. In addition, sometimes prisoners depend on their respective families for their daily meals, clothing, and medicine.

Since even after several amendments to the law, Congo continues to be defined by some of the harshest colonial codes, the roots of its criminal law and procedures can be traced to its Belgian origins. The Administration of Prisons is vested with the Ministry of Justice. Most penitentiaries are located in urban areas such as Kinshasa, but smaller prisons are also located in other large towns. There are separate detention centers for juveniles. There are also secret prisons that were developed under the leadership of Mobutu and reserved for the harshest treatment of political dissidents.

According to published reports, poor economic conditions that promote crime persist, especially in the regions near the country's capital, Kinshasa. Today, auto thefts, burglaries, and armed robberies are the most common predatory crimes in the country. The government does not tolerate trafficking and possession of illegal drugs, and violators of the criminal code face severe criminal sanctions. When apprehended by the police, offenders have the right to legal representation but will face jail sentences and fines if convicted.

Police Profile

Background

The DRC police institution has its root in the Belgian colonial administration. Under colonial rule, the Force Pulique was vested with both military and police functions. Created in 1885 by Leopold II to police the Congo Free State, the Force Pulique was charged with maintaining order and the enforcement of tax and labor laws in the territory. It regularly used punitive force against citizens, which led to international condemnation of Belgian imperialism. As a result, the force was dissolved after World War I and replaced with Garrison Troops and Territorial Service Troops (TST). The Garrison Troops were charged with military functions, while the TST was assigned the sole responsibility of performing police functions.

In 1959, the TST was renamed the Gendarmerie Nationale, a force of about 3,000 members. Immediately after Congolese independence was established, the force was integrated into the Armee

Nationale Congolaise (ANC). Following various mutinies, the force was later deserted by Belgian officers, leaving only African police officers in the force. In addition, both Chief's Police and Territorial Police existed under colonial management. They became part of the security apparatus of the postindependence Congolese administration. The Chief's Police were minipolice units located in the rural areas of the country. It consisted, primarily, of messengers, detention officers, and judicial officials who carried no weapons, received meager salaries, and were not supplied with law enforcement uniforms. They also were charged with maintaining order in rural communities.

In contrast, the Territorial Police was a professional and paramilitary police force, which at independence, included over 6,000 armed and uniformed officers. The force was charged with the maintenance of law and order, as well as additional duties, such as providing security for prison and public buildings. Whenever needed, members of the force also provided assistance to the Chief's Police. Each province administered its own Territorial Police station. For instance, the mineral-rich province of Katanga commanded its own Gendarmerie Katangaise. It was a well-trained paramilitary organization that kept law and order in the province prior to independence. Indeed, the Gendarmerie Katangaise consisted mainly of members of the Lunda ethnic group that supported the secession ambitions of Katanga people in 1961. In 1963, the Gendarmerie Katangaise was incorporated into the Congolese armed forces.

Due to the exodus of Belgian officers from the Territorial Police force, many of the indigenous police also left the force and joined various rebel groups. As a result, the police force crumbled, and was characterized by corruption and inadequate training in the execution of police duties. Obviously, the force needed to be reformed and injected with doses of police professionalism and principles of good policing. Nigeria was one of the countries that answered the call by sending professional members of its police force to provide training to the Congolese police. The United States provided financial assistance, new police arsenals, and equipment as part of its broad support program to the country. Additionally, the United Nations and Belgium participated in the retraining of the Congolese police.

Organizational Structure and Functions

The proliferation of provincial police forces in the 1960s created problems for the DRC government.

Provincial police stations lacked duly trained professionals to run and manage the police. In 1961, President Mobutu responded to this dilemma by passing a string of laws that consolidated the Congolese police into a single centralized police command, known as the Police Nationale, which was controlled by the Ministry of Interior. Numbering about 25,000, the Police Nationale had police authority over all municipal and local police forces in the nation. Like in other police organizations, such as the United States and Nigeria, the force was responsible for crime prevention, the apprehension of criminals, providing security for citizens, and the preservation of law and order.

President Mobutu's actions in 1961 included the enactment of laws that established police ranks akin to those of military personnel. For example, the rank of Inspector General of Police was comparable to that of a Brigadier General in the U.S. armed forces. Entrance into the Gendarmerie is voluntary. While women are generally admitted, they make up a minuscule portion of the police force.

On 1 August 1972, President Mobutu issued an executive order that abolished the Police Nationale, and reassigned its duties to the Gendarmerie Nationale. Additionally, the operation of the centralized police command was transferred from the Ministry of Interior to the Department of Defense. Local police authorities were further undermined from having any influence over police activities. In 1976, the Inspector General's rank was elevated to the equivalent of that of the Chiefs of Staffs of the army, navy, and the air force. The Inspector General reported only to the President, who also acted as the Defense Minister and the Armed Forces Chief of Staff. Mobutu's goal was to consolidate power over all branches of the armed forces, a dictatorial tendency that destabilized the police.

Local authorities, such as mayors, lost their powers to effectively act and enforce the law within their respective jurisdictions. The entire police was under funded and lacked the resources necessary for professional law enforcement operations. Peace and security were threatened in urban neighborhoods. In order to keep the peace, urban authorities sought help from a local youth brigade to take over police functions. President Mobutu also created a civilian police force in 1984, known as the Civil Guard. The president used the Guard to repress his political opponents. After Mobutu's demise in 1997, President Kabila disbanded the Civil Guard and tried to establish a new police force with the backing of the South African government. (Information about any new police formation was not available at the time of writing.)

However, it must be noted that under the regime of Mobutu, the government established and operated different intelligence agencies that complemented the functions of the police force. The principal national security service was the Service National d'Intelligence et de Protection (SNIP), which became the Agence Nationale de Renseignements (ANR) under Kabila. Military intelligence was furnished under the command of the Service d'Action et de Renseignements Militaire (SARM). Moreover, the police also maintained an obscure intelligence component known as "Les Hiboux" (The Owls), which was allegedly involved in kidnappings and terrorist acts against political detractors.

Complaints

Due to the current protracted armed struggles and conflicts in the Congo, parts of the country still face sporadic violence that has claimed millions of lives, mainly in the eastern region of the DRC. It has also been reported that serious human rights violations remain endemic in the country. Reportedly, the eastern region of the nation has witnessed cruelties in the form of mass unlawful killings of innocent civilians, rapes, and the use of children as soldiers. The police have also been accused of capricious use of torture, unlawful detention tactics, and arbitrary arrests of citizens with utter impunity.

Terrorism

Similar to the situations of many other African countries that are confronted with ongoing internal strife, there is no evidence that the DRC is involved in international terrorism that is capable of threatening the security of powerful core nations, such as the United States. Rather, erratic patterns of domestic forms of terrorism exist in the country. Allegedly, extremist rebel factions, such as the Liberation Army of Rwanda, have engaged in violent acts against U.S. citizens and interests. Reportedly, this faction was responsible for the March 1999 abduction and killing of Western tourists in Uganda. Also, it was reported that six workers of the International Committee of the Red Cross were murdered in the eastern province of Congo-Kinshasa in 2001. Additionally, it was alleged that the irregular Congolese Ma-Mai forces kidnapped twenty employees of a Thai logging company, located in North Kivu Province in May of 2001.

Under Mobutu's administration, an investigative branch, known as the Surete Nationale, was transformed into a secret police unit of his administration. Basically, this clandestine police unit performed "dirty" duties for the president. Renamed the Center Nationale de Documentation (CND), in 1969, CND was entrusted with the power to arrest individuals without regard to legal safeguards, and the authority to maintain its own independent communication systems. The CND protected the presidency and was credited with unmasking several coup efforts against Mobutu. It guaranteed that opponents of the government would not be allowed to assemble a political following in the country. Moreover, covert police factions also infiltrated anti-Mobutu resistance groups abroad.

Police Education, Research, and Publications

The DRC has experienced tremendous progress and improvement in its educational system since it regained independence from the Belgian administrators. Like other colonized African countries, education under colonial management was designed to serve the interests of the colonizers. Indeed, colonial powers placed emphasis on primary education, which only prepared Congolese citizens for clerical and secretarial duties. However, after independence, a pedagogical strategy was developed for primary and secondary levels and focused on training individuals to address the needs of the country. Today, there are educational institutions, such as the University of Lumumbashi and the University of Kisangani, founded in the 1960s to prepare Congolese people for professional careers in all areas of life, including police work. The DRC also has a police academy in Kisangani. Training centers were also created with Belgian and U.S. assistance in Kinshasa and Lubumbashi.

Historically, other countries have been involved in the training of the Congolese police. Nigeria, for example has played a pivotal role in the training of the Congolese police, sometimes with the financial and logistic support of the United States under the supervision of the United Nations. Beginning in the 1970s, Mobutu maintained excellent relations with the state of Israel, and the Israeli police helped train the Congolese armed forces. Israel also provided military assistance to Mobutu's government in the 1980s and the 1990s, and granted aid in the training of the Congolese security forces, with particular emphasis on Mobutu's personal guards. In 1990, Egypt signed a bilateral agreement with the Congolese government that enabled Egypt to train Zaire's Civil Guard. Egypt also provided Egyptian-built military equipment to the Congolese armed forces.

Recently, South Africa, Tanzania, and Uganda began providing new uniforms and training for Congo's civilian police force. The United Nations, through the MONUC office (its mission in the DRC), is also heavily involved in the training of the civilian police. Kofi Annan, the U.N. Secretary General, appointed Ambassador William Swing as a special representative to the United Nations to monitor and implement programs designed to train the Congolese National Police. Currently, MONUC has trained 1,200 police officers with assistance from the Congolese government. The U. N. relies on countries to aid in the training and integration of the national police. Meanwhile, Bangladesh, India, Uruguay, and Pakistan have all sent forces for the successful implementation of MONUC's mandates.

IHEKWOABA D. ONWUDIWE

Bibliography

Amnesty International. "Democratic Republic of Congo: Torture, A Weapon of War Against Unarmed Civilians," 2003. Available at: http://web.amnestyusa.org/stoptoture/document.do?id. Accessed September 9, 2004.

Banks, S. A., and Muller, T. C. *Political Handbook of the World: Governments and Intergovernmental Organizations*. New York: CSA Publications, 1998.

Bobb, F. S. *Historical Dictionary of Democratic Republic of the Congo (Zaire)*. Metuchen, N.J. and London: Scarecrow Press, 1999.

Central Intelligence Agency. "Democratic Republic of the Congo: Country Facts Sheet," in *The World Fact Book*, 2004. Available at: www.cia.gov/cia/publications/factbook/geos/cg.htm. Accessed September 9, 2004.

The Europa World Year Book. London: Europa Publications, 1999.

Ingleton, D. R. *Police of the World*. New York: Charles Scribner's Sons, 1979.

Kurian, G. T. *World Encyclopedia of Police Forces and Penal Systems*. New York: Facts on File, 1989.

Legun, C. *Africa: Contemporary Record*. New York and London: African Publishing Company, 1992–1994.

Mars-Proietti, L. *Nations of the World: A Political, Economic and Business Handbook*. Millerton, NY: Grey House Publishing, 2004.

Onwudiwe, I. D. *The Globalization of Terrorism*. Aldershot: Ashgate Publishers, 2001.

Ramsay, J. *Global Studies: Africa*, 5th ed. Guilford, CT: Dushkin Publishing Group, 1993.

U.S. Department of State. "Background Note: Democratic Republic of Congo," 2003. Available at: www.state.gov/r/pa/ei/bgn/2853.htm. Accessed September 9, 2004.

REPUBLIC OF THE CONGO

Background Material

Located in the heart of the African continent, the Republic of the Congo shares borders with Central Africa, Cameroon, Angola, The Democratic Republic of Congo, and Gabon. Its territory is about 342,000 square kilometers, with an ocean front 170 kilometers long. Brazzaville is its capital city, and "La Congolaise" its national anthem.

The territory of today's Republic of the Congo consisted of several kingdoms and chiefdoms. First reached by the Portuguese sailor Diego Cao in 1492, this territory would be placed under France's tutelage on October 3, 1880, with a treaty signed in MBé between Makoko, then King of the Anzico Kingdom, and Pierre Savorgnan de Brazza, a French explorer of Italian descent.

The colony of the Congo was officially created in 1881. It became autonomous in 1903, under the name of Moyen-Congo (Middle Congo) with Pointe-Noire for capital, a town founded by the Lieutenant Cordier in 1883. Moyen-Congo belonged to the Fédération de l'Afrique Equatoriale Francaise (French Equatorial Africa Federation [AEF]), along with Gabon, Oubangui-Chari (Central Africa), and Chad. Brazzaville has been the capital of the AEF since 1910. Following the German occupation of France in 1939 and the rallying of the AEF to General de Gaulle in 1940, Brazzaville became the capital of Free France.

Congo obtained its independence on August 15, 1960, two years after a referendum on self-rule organized by the French community on November 28, 1958.

The Republic of the Congo is a country of water and forests. It owes its name to the River Congo, the largest river in the world after the Amazon. Its 20 million hectares of forests make up 60% of the national territory, and about 10% of the dense forests of Africa. There are about 300 different species of forest wood. For a long time, the forests were the main source of revenue for the country.

The great biodiversity of the Congo Basin makes it, after the Amazon region, the greatest green lung of the planet. It is now the core of a collaborative project with the United States, South Africa, and the European Union. As for the climate, high temperatures and rain alternate with dry seasons with milder temperatures.

After years of strife and a civil war that erupted in 1997, the economy, which had suffered greatly, is now being rebuilt. Growth and development efforts rest on the economic policies' main supports and systems, reform of investments (judicially and institutionally), and investment opportunities in key areas.

Agriculture is characterized by rudimentary techniques and little mechanization, and only 3% out of the 8 million hectares of arable land is used. Coffee and cocoa exports have become almost nonexistent. This lack of commercialization has led to the abandonment of plantations covering thousands of hectares. Growing tobacco also has been abandoned, even though the country has the industrial means to transform the product. Likewise, animal husbandry is underdeveloped. Meat production reaches 5,000 tons compared to consumption of 25,000 tons; hence, the importance of meat imports.

Continental fishing is characterized by lack of storage structures and of means to rapidly move the production. Sea fishing has the potential to reach 80,000 tons per year, but production is only 20,000 tons.

The industrialization of forest products is still in a mechanical stage, and the transformation rate is 40% instead of the standard 60%.

There is, however, a great industrial potential due to the availability of arable land, water resources, forests, geographical location, and membership in the Economic Community of the Central African States (CEEAC) and the Economic and Monetary Community of the Central African States (CEMAC).

Industries can be created in the following areas: foodstuffs, wood products, building materials, metallurgy, engineering, electricity, electronics, chemicals, and petroleum-based products.

Oil fields are mostly situated along the shore and represent the bulk of the country's annual exports. Further, geological maps have indicated that there may be deposits of gold, diamond, potash, base metals, iron, sandstone, and other mineral substances of agricultural and industrial use.

In 2004, Congo counted 2,846,279 inhabitants across 342,000 square kilometers, that is, an average of 7.6 inhabitants per square kilometer. The rate of growth is around 3%, and life expectancy is 50 years. Congo is one of the most urbanized countries of Black Africa, with about 60% of its population living in cities.

The population of the Congo includes four groups who speak Bantu languages. The main one is the Bakongo, who live between Brazzaville and the coast. The Mboshi live in the north of the country. The Sanga live in the wooded zone in the north, between the Sangha and Ubangi Rivers, where the Baka pygmies also live. Nine ethnic groups can be found in Congo:

- Fang (Pahouin)
- Mekée (Djem, Kwélé, Bomouali, and Lino)
- Sanga (Pandé, Kaka, Bakoro, Ikenga, Bomassa, Kabonga, Pomo, Babolé, and Bonguli)
- Ubangian (NGbaka, Bandza, Moundjombo, Enyellé, Bandjombo, Bomitaba, and Bondjo)
- Kota (Bokiba, Kota, and Ongon)
- Mboshi (Mboko, Akoua; Bonga, NGaré, Koyo, Likouala, Bangala, Likouba, Mboshi, and Moye)
- Téké (MBamba, Mbeti, Tégué alima, NDzikou, NGangoulou, Koukouya, Mbon, Téké laalé, NDzabi, Tsnagui, Téké, Tsayi, Voumbou, Yaka, and Oumou)
- Kongo (Kougni, Bémbé, Kengué, Hangala, Kamba, Lari, Soundi, Kongo, Dondo, Yombé, and Vili)
- Eshira (Bouissi, Loumbou, and Punu)

French is the official language of Congo, and Lingala is the language most spoken. Of Bantu origins, Lingala is a common and vernacular language with dialectal variations.

Congo is a syncretistic country. Christianity is the main religion (Catholicism and Protestantism), but there are some sects, such as the Kimbanguist Church, as well as animism and other traditional religions. Islam is a minor presence in the country.

School is free and mandatory for children from six to sixteen. The Marien Ngouabi University, founded in 1961 and located in Brazzaville, is host to about 10,000 students.

The very rich tradition of Congolese art has been known since the early European trading posts. In the Kingdom of Loango, ivory was sculpted into ghosts, trunks, and statuettes. Congolese masks inspired the creators of modern art. Bakongo statues studded with nails or bearing a mirror to send back evil spells and Kwele dishes with polychrome abstract motifs could be found in painter's studios at the beginning of the twentieth century (Braque, Picasso).

Contextual Features

An electoral process sanctioned the new constitution (adopted by referendum on January 10, 2002) and the President of the Republic who was elected on March 10, 2002. The Republic of the Congo now operates under a presidential regime characterized by a balance of powers (executive, legislative, and judicial). As per the constitution, the executive branch is made up of the President of the Republic (Head of State, Head of Government, Supreme Army Chief), government, cabinet, and advisers.

The legislative branch consists of the Parliament (National Assembly and Senate). The judicial branch consists of the Supreme Court, the Constitutional Court, and the High Court of Justice (Mediator of the Republic, Economic and Social Council, High Council on Freedom of Communication, and National Human Rights Commission).

The Republic of Congo is administratively organized in ten prefectures (regions), six communes (smaller territorial divisions), and eighty-six subprefectures (districts and PCA) as per law 009/90 dated September 6, 1990, and amended by law 09/95 dated March 25, 1995.

Repressive Congolese justice is part of the judiciary system of Congo established by Article 1 of law 19-99 dated August 15, 1999, which modified and completed some provisions found in law 022-92 and dated August 20, 1992 that concerned the organization of the judicial system. Repressive justice must be carefully differentiated from the following courts.

The Supreme Court is the highest jurisdiction, with the power to control all other jurisdictions across the entire national territory. Its headquarters are in Brazzaville (Article 5).

The Audit Office is materially competent to examine the budgeting and accounting of public funds, local organizations, the state's economic endeavors, mixed economic endeavors, savings and social security agencies, subsidized agencies, and all agencies subjected to its jurisdiction or control by law. Its headquarters are in Brazzaville. It can

practice judicial attributions, budgetary discipline, and control of activity. By law, it serves the President of the Republic, President of National Assembly, President of Senate, Prime Minister, Minister of Finance, Minister of Justice, and ministers regarding matters related to civil servants and agents under their authority.

The competence of the Court of Appeals (Article 46f) is limited to the Region or the autonomous administrative community. (Since Congo is divided into nine administrative regions and the autonomous community of Brazzaville, nine Courts of Appeal should be created. Due to the scarcity of staff and logistic support, however, only four Courts of Appeals were created.) The Court of Appeals has second-instance jurisdiction, as it hears judgments rendered by lower courts.

In principle, County Courts (Article 61f) can be created in each county or arrondissement seat. Here again, insufficient staff and logistics have only allowed for a few to be created, with extended authority over one or more counties and arrondissements. County Courts rule over civil and penal matters.

Administrative Courts (Article 80f) with territorial authority that should extend over the territory of the county or the arrondissement, are yet to be created. They will rule over administrative disputes.

Commerce Courts (Article 91f) rule over the entire territory of the county or the arrondissement. By 2004, there were only a few, notably in Brazzaville, Pointe-Noire, and Dolisie, with extended authority over several counties or arrondissements. They are common law judges and hear disputes related to commerce.

The Magistrate's Courts (Article 119f) rule over the territory of the district or region, but as of 2004 only a few were in place. They hear civil cases in conciliation of all actions. They also hear all real estate disputes up to 1 million francs in capital and 300,000 francs in revenue, rents, or lease costs.

Labor Courts (Article 129f) have authority over the territory of the region, community, arrondissement, or county. Their creation is justified by the economic activity of the localities in question. In 2004, they only existed in areas with greater economic activity, such as Brazzaville, Pointe-Noire, and Dolisie. They are common law judges ruling individual or collective disputes stemming from work or apprenticeship contracts between worker and employer, and apprentice and master, as well as individual disputes relating to collective wage agreements, and disputes relating to social security matters.

Military Courts have authority over the territory of the military region or garrison. This authority can be extended to several regions or garrisons. By 2004, there were Military Courts in Brazzaville and Pointe-Noire, with extended authority over the territory, but they were not functional since the military code of justice had not yet been set.

The repressive justice system was inherited from French colonization in the second half of the nineteenth century. It was originally characterized by destruction based on race: on the one hand the French repressive justice dispensed to French nationals in Equatorial Africa, and, on the other, repressive justice dispensed to indigenous people across Moyen-Congo. These two forms of justice would be unified in 1947 and last until the independence in 1960. The penal proceedings code in use today was adopted by the Republic of Congo in January 1963.

The democratic period that began in May 1990, after a revolutionary period between 1960 and 1990, did not bring any significant changes. The penal code and the penal proceedings code remain in use. Consequently, the repressive judicial system in Congo remains antiquated and not adapted to modern times.

Recurring offenses are attacks against individuals, private property, public morals, and public property.

The repressive jurisdictions are part of the judicial system described above. They are organized and function according to the following general principles: legality of offenses and sanctions, equality of all citizens before the law, double degree of jurisdiction, collegiality of jurisdictional formations, contradictions, separation of the proceedings and judgment, and authority of the matter being judged.

The Magistrate's Court is structured as follows: a magistrate, who is also the president, is appointed by decree of the President of the Republic after recommendation by the Higher Council of the Magistrature. A Magistrate in the public prosecutor's department is appointed in the same manner, and serves as the substitute for the Public Prosecutor in the County Court. There is also a court clerk.

The Magistrate's Court rules over minor offenses and misdemeanors for which sanction would be imprisonment of one year or less.

The Court of Summary Jurisdiction is part of the County Court. It is presided over by the President. The public prosecution is done by the Public Prosecutor or one of his aides, and the clerk acts as court recorder. This court can hear misdemeanors and related minor offenses.

The County Court also includes:

- A Children's Court that has authority to judge offenses qualified as crimes or misdemeanors committed by minors under 18 years of age.
- One or more offices for judicial enquiries. It is a jurisdiction with a single judge, the examining judge, who is appointed by decree of the President of the Republic upon the recommendation of the Higher Council of Magistrature. He is assisted by a clerk. The examining judge carries out the information and the examination.

The Military Court is made up of magistrates appointed by decree of the President of the Republic upon the recommendation of the Higher Council of Magistrature and the advice of the Minister of Defense. It consists of a president who is a civil magistrate, two assessors who are military magistrates, a public prosecutor or substitutes who are all military magistrates, and a clerk.

The Military Court is composed of a Court of Summary Jurisdiction to learn about connected misdemeanors and minor offenses; a police office to rule on minor offenses; a Court of Summary Jurisdiction for minors to judge military schools students; and one or more investigation offices to process the information.

The Military Court can hear all offenses as defined in the code of military justice; offenses to the laws and customs of war; and offenses of common law committed by military personnel on duty or by anyone who has reached majority, by military or assimilated personnel within a military establishment. During wartime, they rule over all offenses.

The Court of Appeal has one or more Courts of Summary Jurisdiction. It includes a president, two councilors of the court, a public prosecutor, an assistant public prosecutor, and substitutes.

The Court of Summary Jurisdiction can hear appeals with regards to offenses from the Courts of Summary Jurisdictions, police, and military offices.

The Criminal Court is made up of a president, who is the president of the Court of Appeal, two assessors, and a body of jurors. It judges crimes committed by civilians or military personnel, within the realm of the Court of Appeal as well as related misdemeanors and offenses. It has full jurisdiction to judge defendants sent before it.

The Grand Jury is made up of a president and two councilors, the general prosecutor or his substitutes, and the clerk from the Court of Appeal. It is a second-instance jurisdiction of inquiry. Further, it rules on the activity of the officers of the criminal investigation department. The president of the grand jury has his own authority over the control of the offices of judicial enquiries, prison visits, and preventive custody.

The penal division of the Supreme Court hears in first and last resort crimes and common offenses by nonjusticiable magistrates from the High Court of Justice. It optionally exerts the right of evocation against Criminal Courts rulings. It has power of cassation against penal judgments made by the Court of Appeal.

The High Court of Justice is a jurisdiction of exemption. It consists of the president prosecutor of the Supreme Court; eight elected parliamentarians, eight elected deputies, six elected magistrates from the Supreme Court, and three elected deputies.

The High Court of Justice may judge government and parliament members; it can distrain upon acts qualified as crimes or offenses and committed while on duty as well as their accomplices in case of conspiracy against the state. It can also judge the President of the Republic in case of high treason.

Police Profile

Background

The history of Congolese police is that of the Congolese Police Force, which is bound to ancestral feuds. It has grown in synergy with societal evolution in Congo.

The following time line highlights key moments in the development and evolution of the Congolese Police force:

- During the time of the Kingdoms, Kings Anzico, Loango, and Kongo used their own armies to lead tribal wars and a police in charge of informing the Wise Men.
- Colonial era.
- 1960: National independence. The Congolese army is organized. Creation of the Congolese Army.
- 1966: Creation of the Armée Populaire Nationale (National Popular Army) (law 11/66, June 22, 1966). Single-party regime (Congolese Labor party).
- 1972: Dissolution and integration of the national police force into the National Popular Army. Single command. Members of the police had army training as well as technical and specialized training in various schools, including foreign schools in the case of executives. They also had political management.
- June 1990: Conférence Nationale Souveraine

(National Sovereign Conference). Creation of democracy, dissolution of the National Popular Army. The Force Publique Nationale (National Police Force) becomes apolitical and is made up of the Congolese Army, the Gendarmerie (State Police Force), and the Police Nationale (National Police), a civil force with paramilitary characteristics and the autonomy to manage its personnel.
- 1991: First States General of the Police.
- 1999: Reorganization of the Police Nationale (Ordinance 4-99, June 29, 1999).
- 2003: Publication of the texts about the structures under the authority of the Ministère de la Sécurité et de la Police (Ministry of Homeland Security and Police): agency, general inspection of the police force, administration of the Police Nationale, administration of homeland security, administration of public safety, and special units command.

Organizational Description

The Département de la Sécurité et de la Police (Department of Security and Police) is made up of one agency and six technical organizations.

The Inspection Générale des Services de Police (General Inspection of the Police Agencies) is a technical organ that helps the Minister assume his role with regards to the general control of the police personnel. This agency makes sure that deontological rules and statutes are respected. It leads inspections and controls to evaluate the functioning of operational, administrative, and technical services as well as that of any agency that answers to the ministry. It also leads administrative and disciplinary inquests on police agencies and personnel, conducts surveys on how to improve the functioning of the services, ensures that rules are respected with regards to police management and budget, and ensures the rational use of police personnel and their career management.

The Secrétariat Général des Services de Police (General Secretariat of the Police) is a technical organ that helps the Minister in charge of the police to manage human and financial resources as well as equipment. Its role is to follow up on the implementation of the police budget; centralize the needs of the police; organize and manage human resources; acquire and maintain heavy equipment; administer claims related to police personnel and estate; develop and maintain the police's real estate; manage police' administrative archives; manage schools; promote social, sanitary, cultural, and athletic action within the police services; and pre-process payroll operations and the liquidation of pension rights as well as the death capital on the account of police services.

The Direction Générale de la Police Nationale (General Management of the National Police) is the technical organ that assists the Minister with matters relating to police and safety. It participates in the safety of the institutions; maintains and restores public order; ensures the safety of people and goods; ensures peace and public health; prevents, researches, records, and checks fines, offenses, and crimes; ensures border safety; and leads any mission needed in a state of siege or war.

The Direction Générale de la Surveillance du Territoire (General Direction of the Surveillance of the Territory) is an intelligence agency whose role is to ensure the safety of the state. Its mission inside and outside the national territory is to safeguard and protect the vital interests of the state.

The Direction Générale de la Sécurité Civile (General Management of Public Safety) is the technical organ that assists the Minister in all matters of public safety. Its role is to develop and apply regulation with regards to preventing catastrophic events; study and plan the necessary conditions to prevent fires; ensure the safeguard and protection of the people, property, and the environment against accidents, fires, and disasters; lead civil defense missions in time of war; participate in disaster management; promote and popularize emergency relief plans; and develop programs and training of public safety personnel, businesses, and any establishment subject to the regulations.

The Commandement des Unités Spécialisées (Special Units Command) is the technical organ that helps the Minister with the management and control of the special units. It contributes to the safety of the institutions and ensures the impenetrability of the borders. It also takes part in the defense of the national territory; helps maintain and restore public order; leads all missions needed in states of emergency, siege, or war; contributes to the fight against national and international terrorism, and to the safety of high-ranking officials. It has at its disposal the following units:

- Criminal Investigation Units (Departmental Directions of the National Police)
- Fast Response Special Units (Special Units Commands)
- Intervention Units (Crime Fighting Brigades and Intervention Units)
- Logistic Support Units (General Secretariat of Police Services with all the administrative management, finance, and logistics of the technical services of the National Police)

Functions

Across the national territory, the Police Nationale:

- Contribute to protecting rights and defending the Republic's institutions, peacekeeping and maintaining public order, and protecting people and property.
- Fulfils its mission within the framework of the Declaration of Human Rights, the constitution, and international conventions and laws.
- Has a hierarchic structure. Subject to the rules set by the penal code with regard to judicial enquiries, the Police Nationale answers to the ministry in charge of the police.

To ensure the administration, coordination, orientation, and control of the Police Nationale, the ministry in charge of the police has at its disposal the Conseil de Commandement (Command Council) and the Conseil de Discipline (Disciplinary Council).

Training

Training of all police personnel is done through the École Nationale des Services de Police (National Police School), as well as police educational centers and some public establishments affiliated with Marien Ngouabi University (ENAM/Department of Judicial Careers), including the Military Academy Marien Ngouabi.

The curriculum is set by the Conseil de Commandement de la Police Nationale (National Police Command Council) after a proposal by the General Secretariat of the Police. There is a preliminary training for young recruits, which is basic training sanctioned by a diploma that leads to the rank of sergeant, and further education for officers and noncommissioned officers.

The latter consists of:

Qualification training to obtain the Certificat Interarmes (Interweapons Certificate) for those who have served as sergeants for at least two years, and which gives access to the rank of Sergent-Chef (staff sergeant).

Qualification training to obtain the Brevet Technique 1 (BT-1 Safety Technical Certificate), available only to staff sergeants who have served for two years as such, and who hold the CIA, to obtain the rank of Adjudant (Executive Officer) or Adjudant-Chef (Chief Executive Officer) after two years of service as Executive Officer.

Qualification training to obtain the Brevet Technique 2 (BT-2 Safety Technical Certificate), only for Executive and Chief Executive Officers who have served as such for at least two years and who hold the BT-1 Safety, to obtain the rank of Sous-Lieutenant (Second Lieutenant) for the two titulars, and the rank of Chief Executive Officer for the Executive Officer who does not pass the grade of Second Lieutenant.

Training to specialize in a specific police unit, available to any Officer and NCO wishing to improve his knowledge within his area of expertise.

Training to specialize in other areas useful to police work, with a qualification bonus, available to any Officer and NCO wishing to gain knowledge useful to the functioning of the police services.

Training to bring up to date NCOs who hold the BT-1 and BT-2 by recognizing the need to update training through the new acquisition of general police knowledge.

Training to bring up-to-date officers out of military school to update the training through the new acquisition of general police knowledge.

Retraining of any officer and NCO to renew and improve knowledge within the area of specialty or within general policing.

Refresher course for any superior officer to expand knowledge within a specific area of policing.

Information workshop for any officer and NCO selected by police command depending on the theme of the conference-debate, to acquire general knowledge needed for the development and modernization of the police, or within a specific area useful for improving police functions.

Conference-debate for any officer and NCO selected by police command, depending on the importance of the theme of the conference, to acquire general knowledge needed for the development and modernization of the police, or within a specific area useful for improving police functions.

Study and information trips for any officer selected by police command to acquire knowledge in an area useful to policing.

Basic training of police officers.

Police Public Projects

The main strategic interests found in the programming law of the Congolese police show its modernization through the adaptation of the judicial body of the police within a national and international context; implementation of recruiting and training policies; initiation of a coherent program of building and rehabilitating administrative structures and barracking; and purchase of equipment adapted to new technologies.

Police Use of Firearms

In the Republic of the Congo, the use of a weapon is a serious act that can only be justi-fied in extreme cases of self-defense or defense of another.

In accordance with the Penal Code and the decree of October 24, 1961 on maintaining public order, the use of weapons by the police can occur only under the following conditions:

1. In an isolated manner, the police officer can only make use of his weapon to respond to a serious attack on himself or on another person; his response must be proportional to the peril he is facing.
2. As part of an organized unit, the use of weapons when maintaining or restoring order is subject to the law and the command of the legitimate authority.

The ordinance 64/24 of October 16, 1962 ruled on the regime of war equipment, weapons, and munitions.

International Cooperation

The Republic of the Congo has signed and ratified the following texts and conventions:

Ratified

- Geneva Convention (1949)
- Convention on ban of biological weapons (1972)
- Additional protocols to the Geneva Convention (1977)
- Convention of the OUA for the elimination of mercenaries in Africa (1977)

Signed, but Not yet Ratified

- Convention against recruiting, using, financing, and training mercenaries (1989)
- Convention on the ban of chemical weapons (1993)
- Statute of Rome on the International Penal Court (1998)

Other Facts Relating to International Cooperation

- Zones of cooperation: no limit and no restriction
- Partner countries: Africa (Angola, Egypt, and Algeria); Europe (France); America (none);

Asia (China; see current cooperation project being drafted)

- Areas of intervention: Training and logistics support
- Information exchange: Interpol
- Current events research: IPES

Terrorism

On the national level, terrorist acts—including assassination, and destruction of works of art and of trains—are still being committed in certain areas of the Department of Pool, which still has pockets of insecurity. They are committed by the Reverend Pasteur Ntoumi and his followers.

The fight against terrorism in the Congo is led by the command of the Police's special units. On the international level, the Republic of the Congo is cooperating with the UN Security Council in the hunt for terrorists and terrorist organizations (see Act 1267, 1999).

Police Education, Research, and Publications

- Police Academy of Moukondo, "*Formation Initiale des Auxiliaires de Police* (Initial Training of Police Auxiliaries)," a document published with the assistance of the National Police of France from the French Embassy in Congo by Commandant Alain Donadieu and Colonel Marcel Ekouale, Director of the National Police Academy.
- University Marien Ngouabi Enam, "*Problèmes et perspectives de l'accroissement du phénomène d'immigration au Congo: cas de la ville de Brazzaville* (Problems and Perspectives on the Increase of Immigration in Congo: Case Study of Brazzaville), by Lieutenant Sosthène Bertrand Gobela. Newsletters, daily newspapers, and weekly papers: *Police Nouvelle* (New Police); *La Semaine Africaine* (The African Week); *Le Nouvel Observateur* (The New Observer); *Le Choc* (Impact).
- Selected publications: "*Mutations pour la police congolaise* (Changes for the Congolese Police)" by Colonel Albert Ngoto; and "*Crimes oubliés au Congo Brazzaville* (Forgotten Crimes in Congo Brazzaville)" by Colonel Alice Bienvenu Bayidikila.

JEAN-ETIENNE ELION

COSTA RICA

Background Material

Costa Rica is a Central American republic of 51,100 square kilometers located geographically between the countries of Panama to the south and Nicaragua on the north, and the Caribbean Sea and Pacific Ocean to the east and west. Colonized by the Spanish, it gained independence from Spain in 1821. While the period following independence was punctuated by episodes of authoritarianism, on the whole Costa Ricans did not experience the same type of repressive regimes as their Central American neighbors. Export-oriented economic policies relied on coffee and banana crops to spur growth, and this economic wealth was distributed more equitably than in other countries in the region. In the early 1900s, a strong labor movement and growing middle class began to pressure the government for reforms, which resulted in the implementation of policies that encouraged social welfare enhancement and stability. These policies addressed issues such as education, health care, labor rights, a minimum wage, and social insurance. In the 1940s tensions did arise, however, culminating in civil war in 1948. By 1949, Costa Rica had established a new constitution in which democratic rights and freedoms were firmly enshrined. The 1949 constitution guarantees all citizens equality before the law and protects fundamental civil liberties and political rights, such as freedom of speech, association, and the press. These constitutional rights have been upheld vigorously in Costa Rica. According to the Freedom House Organization, which has assessed nations' respect for civil liberties and political rights from 1972 to the present, Costa Rica has long protected

Costa Rica at a Glance

Population	3,811,000
Racial/ethnic composition	White (including mestizo) 94%, black 3%, Amerindian 1%, Chinese 1%, and other 1%
Urban population (percentage of total population)	52%
Language	Spanish (official)
Major religions	Roman Catholic 76%, Protestant 16%, other 5%, none 3%
Per capita income (GDP per capita, purchasing power parity)	US$8,650
Major economic activities	Employment in agriculture 20%, industry 23%, services 56%
Income distribution (income share of wealthiest 20% of population)	51%
Adult literacy rate (percentage of population aged 15 and older)	96%
Infant mortality (per 1,000 live births)	11
Life expectancy at birth	76 years

These data are based on the World Bank's World Development Indicators and the CIA World Factbook. Most data correspond to the year 2000, with the exceptions of income distribution (1997) and major economic activities (1999).

the fundamental rights of its citizens. Indeed, Costa Rica's freedom ranking has been on par with those of the United States and Western Europe from the time that Freedom House began rating countries.

Since 1953, Costa Rica has held fair and free democratic elections, followed by peaceful transitions of power. Costa Rica was one of the first countries in the region to establish a welfare state, and has been firmly committed to redistributive policies that promote economic equality. Costa Rica devotes a higher percentage of its resources to health care and education compared to other countries in the region, leading to levels of literacy and public health that are similar to those of high-income countries. The police have benefited from this political and social stability. While many Latin American police forces have been tainted by their associations with repressive governments and human rights abuses, in Costa Rica the police have escaped such infamy. The police of Costa Rica have a strong record of respecting human rights and earning citizens' trust.

Economically, Costa Rica has had bouts of instability. In particular, in the 1980s Costa Rica's economy was jolted by the economic crisis that plagued the entire Latin American region. Inflation and unemployment soared, and protests and strikes led to violence and social unrest. This economic and social instability was exacerbated by problems stemming from the political conflict between the Sandinistas and Contras in Nicaragua, its neighbor

to the north. By the late 1980s, however, tensions eased as the economy began to stabilize. A peace plan, brokered by Costa Rican President Oscar Arias, reduced political tensions in Nicaragua and the rest of Central America. The Costa Rican economy has maintained a healthy economic growth rate, averaging nearly 5% growth in gross domestic product (GDP) over the 1986 to 1996 period. While economic growth slowed somewhat in the late 1990s and averaged only 0.9% in 2001, organizations such as the World Bank are optimistic that its export-oriented economic policies will result in increased economic growth.

As the table indicates, Costa Rica is a relatively homogeneous nation. It has not been plagued by problems due to ethnic/racial tensions, and is classified as a middle-income country. Literacy and life expectancy rates are equivalent to those of wealthy countries; however, rates of infant mortality and income equality are higher and lower, respectively, than those of high-income nations. Still, Costa Rica does perform better on these indicators than the other Central American states.

Contextual Features

Costa Rica has a presidential system of democratic governance. It is divided into seven provinces, with San José as its capital. The 1949 constitution establishes three independent branches of government: executive, legislative, and judicial branches. The executive branch is comprised of the president (who is both chief of state and head of government), two vice presidents, and a cabinet appointed by the president. Both the president and vice presidents are elected by popular vote for four-year terms, and voting is mandatory for all adults over the age of eighteen. To be elected, a candidate must receive over 40% of the vote; otherwise a run-off election is held between the two leading candidates. As of 1969, an amendment prohibits the reelection of presidents, although presidents who served prior to 1969 may be elected for one more term.

The Costa Rican legislature is unicameral. Elections for the fifty-seven seats are held at the same time as presidential elections, and legislators, or *diputados*, are elected for four-year terms by proportional representation. Traditionally, the main two political parties have been the Social Christian Unity Party (PUSC) and the National Liberation Party (PLN). However, in the 2002 elections, the Citizen Action Party (PAC) captured a significant portion of the popular vote.

The judiciary has three divisions, or *ámbitos*: Jurisdictional, Justice Auxiliary, and Administrative. The Jurisdictional Division is entrusted with the actual administration of justice. The Justice Auxiliary consists of all individuals and organizations that assist with administering justice, such as the Organization of Judicial Investigations (OIJ), Public Ministry, and judicial schools. The Administrative Division consists of all departments that are indispensable for the practical functioning of the judiciary, such as personnel, accounting, and public relations. Since the role of the judiciary is intricately intertwined with that of the police, it is important to define each of its structures and roles clearly.

The Supreme Court sits at the top of the Jurisdictional Division. While there is no legal limit on the number of justices (or *magistrados*) that may preside on the Supreme Court, currently it is comprised of twenty-two members. These magistrados are elected by the Legislative Assembly for eight-year terms and can be reelected. The Supreme Court is divided into four chambers, or *salas*: Audit (Sala I), Administrative (Sala II), Judicial (Sala III), and Constitutional (Sala IV). Each chamber administers law in specific areas, and renders final rulings on the most important cases. Five magistrados sit on each of the first three salas, while the Constitutional Sala is comprised of seven justices.

The Audit Chamber hears financial cases related to property rights, houses, land, loans, and so on. The Administrative Chamber rules on civil cases, resolving labor disputes and family conflicts. The Judicial Chamber handles criminal law cases such as robbery, homicide, and assault, among others. Finally, the Constitutional Chamber exercises judicial review of legislative acts, which allows it to balance the power of the other two branches of government.

The Supreme Court magistrados are the highest members of the judicial branch. Magistrados must be Costa Rican by birth, or naturalized citizens with at least ten years of residency. They must be at least thirty-five years of age and be lawyers with at least ten years of experience practicing law, or at least five years of judicial practice. Magistrados may not be members of the other two branches of government, nor may they be religious authorities. These latter restrictions reinforce the independence of the judiciary from the executive and legislative branches of government, as well as the separation between church and state.

The lower tiers of the Jurisdictional Division mirror the Supreme Court's division of functions. In the judicial hierarchy, the magistrados are followed by the Superior Tribunals (*tribunales superiores*), lower courts (*juzgados*), and municipal courts (*alcaldías*), respectively. In criminal cases, Superior Tribunals typically hear cases for which the penalty is more than three years of incarceration. The lower courts try crimes whose penalties are less than three years, and municipal courts handle misdemeanors.

The Justice Auxiliary helps the Jurisdictional Division to administer justice effectively. It performs several functions vital to the operation of the criminal justice system. Three of its components are of particular importance: the OIJ, the Public Ministry, and Public Defenders. The OIJ plays a crucial role in the criminal justice system by assisting in the investigation of crimes. It has numerous departments to handle the many intricacies involved in criminal investigation, such as medical laboratories and forensic science facilities. While in countries like the United States police detectives would normally handle such investigations, in Costa Rica these tasks fall to the members of the OIJ. The OIJ works closely with the Public Ministry, which is the representative of the Costa Rican state in criminal trials. Finally, Public Defenders advise and defend individuals charged with crimes. This legal aid is provided free of charge by the Costa Rican government.

The Administrative Division carries out the practical functions of the judiciary a whole. It disseminates information, processes legal paperwork, and provides the administrative support structure.

Legal System

The Costa Rican legal system is based on the Spanish civil law system. The state serves as both the investigator of crimes as well as the arbiter. As Costa Rica has ratified the United Nations Convention on Children's Rights, it considers individuals over the age of eighteen to be legally accountable for their crimes. Offenders aged eighteen or less are tried and sentenced separately as juvenile offenders.

Crime falls into two main categories: felonies and misdemeanors. Felonies are crimes of a serious nature involving harm or threat, including homicide, sex offenses, human rights abuses, severe property damage or assault, and drug trafficking. While the penal code delineates the sentences that should correspond to crimes, judges can exercise some discretion in sentencing. Misdemeanors comprise less serious offenses, usually against property, and carry penalties of no more than one year in jail and/or fines (Giralt 1996).

According to government statistics, the number of reported crimes increased in the decade from 1990 to 2000. In 1990, there were 32,003 crimes reported in Costa Rica. This number peaked at 50,218 in 1995, and then declined slightly to 48,357 in 2000. While these statistics indicate that overall crime rates rose in the 1990s, unfortunately these numbers do not reflect the actual incidence of crime since many citizens do not report victimization. Indeed, according to the United Nations International Crime Victim Surveys conducted in Costa Rica in 1992 and 1996, 60% of Costa Rican crime victims did not report the crime to police. Thus, official crime statistics substantially underestimate the occurrence of crime.

Due to the problems of unreported crimes, public opinion surveys provide a more accurate means of measuring crimes and crime trends. Many citizens do not report crimes to police, but they do tend to report them to survey researchers. The United

Common Crimes and Trends, United Nations International Crime Victim Surveys

Crime	Percent Victimized, 1992	Percent Victimized, 1996
Car theft	1	1
Bike theft	5	4
Personal theft	7	10
Burglary	4	8
Attempted burglary	6	9
Robbery	1	9
Assault	3	5
Fraud	18	17
Corruption	Not available	10

Homicide Rates 1980–2000

Year	Number of Homicides	Percent Solved
1980	101	Not available
1981	103	Not available
1982	84	Not available
1983	95	Not available
1984	98	Not available
1985	109	Not available
1986	103	Not available
1987	114	Not available
1988	117	92.3
1989	116	92.2
1990	139	80.6
1991	132	86.4
1992	160	81.3
1993	160	88.1
1994	182	90.1
1995	184	87.5
1996	189	80.4
1997	210	80.0
1998	224	75.4
1999	245	78.0
2000	238	78.5

These data are based on statistics published by the Department of Planning, Division of Police Statistics (available at: *www. poderjudicial.go.cr/planificacion/estadistica/policiales/index. htm*).

Nations conducted two surveys of the San José area in Costa Rica in 1992 and 1996, and additional surveys are planned. In this survey, respondents were asked if they had been victimized in various types of crimes. The table (above) shows the results of the surveys in 1992 and 1996.

As the table (above) indicates, overall victimization rates remained steady from 1992 to 1996. The notable exception to this trend is robbery. In 1992, only 1% of survey respondents indicated that they had been victimized by robbery, yet in 1996 this number climbed substantially to 9%. In both years, fraud was the most common crime, followed by personal theft. By 1996, robbery, burglary, and attempted burglary were also more common.

While public opinion surveys avoid the pitfalls of unreported crimes, they obviously cannot account for the most violent of crimes: homicide. Official crime statistics frequently underestimate the occurrence of most crimes, but homicides are a notable exception and tend to be reported.

The table (left) reports homicide trends in Costa Rica from 1990 through 2000. In 2000, Costa Rica had 6.3 homicides per 100,000 inhabitants. This rate shows a modest increase through the previous decade, as Costa Rica averaged approximately 4.7 homicides per 100,000 inhabitants in the early

1990s. According to *The Illustrated Book of World Rankings*, in 1998 the Costa Rican homicide rate ranked sixty-seventh in the world, considerably lower than that of other Central American nations. While the number of homicides has increased, the rate of solving these crimes has deteriorated somewhat. In 1988, Costa Rica solved an impressive 92.3% of its homicides. By 2000, however, this success rate had steadily declined to 78.5%.

The correctional system is administered by the Department of Social Adaptation and the Ministry of Justice; however, there is a movement toward privatization of the prison system. Costa Rica has embarked on efforts to reform its correctional system, but it remained plagued by problems of overcrowding, budgetary constraints, and personnel shortages in the early twenty-first century. According to the Human Rights Watch report, as of 1998 Costa Rica confined 5,247 inmates, and an additional 523 individuals served sentences in semi-institutional facilities. Roughly 60% of these prisoners lived in precarious conditions. According to reports in the national newspaper *La Nación*, there was roughly one guard for every 120 prisoners, a ratio that falls far short of the desired mark. In addition, many of these guards lack adequate training. In light of these deficiencies, the government debated the feasibility of several ambitious initiatives to overhaul the prison system. Despite these problems, Costa Rican prisons do have one notable feature distinguishing them from the other Latin American nations: the vast majority of its prison population have been convicted and sentenced.

Police Profile

Background

Since Costa Rica abolished its military forces in 1949, the police are the sole protectors of the nation and of public order and security within. In 1949, the military forces were converted into the Civil Guard and were entrusted with police functions and maintenance of domestic order and security. To foster the professionalization of the police force, the National Academy of the Police was created in 1964. In the 1970s and 1980s, the police underwent a series of restructuring measures. During this time new police divisions were created, such as the Rural Guard (GAR), which served to enhance security in rural areas. To improve efficiency, the Ministries of Public Security and of the Interior and Police were merged into one entity, the Ministry of Interior, then later split apart, and finally rejoined again in 1995 under the current name of Ministry of Interior, Police, and Public Security. This ministry falls under the auspices of the executive branch, and encompasses all preventive police forces. As mentioned above, investigative duties are the domain of the specialized OIJ, not the police.

In 1994, the General Law of the Police dramatically restructured the police with the aim of transforming it into an accountable, transparent, and professional institution. The General Law of the Police described the position of police officer as a professional career, codifying the legal requirements for advancement and salaries. This reform also emphasized the need to provide the police with enhanced training and opportunities for specialization. In 2001, this law was reinforced by a second piece of legislation, the Law of the Civil Police. The most notable provision in this latter reform was the creation of the department of Police Legal Assistance, which supports the police in their duties by providing legal counsel. The goal of the 2001 reform was to endow the police with a more civilian character, as its previous modes of operation had been criticized as too militaristic.

In 1998, Costa Rica had one police officer for every 480 people. The police force is comprised primarily of male officers, but Costa Rica has embarked on initiatives to increase the number of women in its ranks. One program in 2002 invited 170 female police officers to a three-day conference to identify the problems confronting female officers and their potential solutions.

Organizational Description

Costa Rica has been criticized for its excessive number of police divisions, particularly since coordination among these bodies is frequently minimal and faulty. Similar to the organization of the judicial branch, the police are divided into several smaller forces, each assuming duties in a specialized sphere. To facilitate coordination among these diverse police bodies, the 1994 police reforms created the National Council of Public Security, led by the President. This council is comprised of the President, presidential appointees, and the Ministers of the Departments of Justice and of the Interior, Police, and Public Security. The National Council of Public Security aims to be a centralizing force for police divisions. To this end, it defines the political directions of each of the specialized police forces and coordinates their crime control efforts.

Under the auspices of the National Council of Public Security and the Ministry of Interior, Police and Public Security, ten specialized police forces plus Police Reserves currently operate. The names

Police Forces and Their Primary Functions

Police Force	Primary Functions
Public Force	Ensure that citizens are free to exercise their rights
	Protect the constitutional order and citizens' safety
	Maintain peace and public order
	Guard the security, integrity, and property of the people
	Prevent and repress legal infractions
State Security Directorate	Detect, analyze, investigate, and disseminate information pertaining to physical security of the nation
	Coordinate with international organizations on matters of external security
Special Intervention Unit	Protect government officials and foreign dignitaries
	Detect and deactivate explosives
	Conduct antiterrorism and antidrug activities
Civil Guard and Rural Guard	Ensure that citizens are free to exercise their constitutional rights
	Protect the constitutional order, citizens' safety, national sovereignty, and territorial integrity
	Maintain peace and public order
	Guard the security, integrity, and goods of the people
	Maintain respect for property
	Prevent and repress legal infractions
Border Police	Monitor and protect land, air, and sea borders
	Promote international respect for the constitution, treaties, and laws concerning national territory, territorial waters, and airspace
Antinarcotics Police	Investigate the usage and distribution of illegal drugs
	Disseminate information concerning illegal drug use
	Seize illicit drugs with the approval of judicial authorities
Fiscal Control Police	Guarantee the fulfillment of fiscal laws
	Assist relevant ministries in cases of tax evasion
	Inspect commercial establishments
	Promote international respect for the constitution, treaties, and respective laws and regulations
Immigration Police	Promote respect for the constitution, treaties, and immigration laws and regulations
	Execute judicial and administrative decisions concerning immigration
Prison Police	Guard and control the nation's penitentiary centers
Transit Police	Monitor and maintain order on public transit routes
Police Reserves	The president has the right to form a temporary police unit of reserve forces in times of emergency
	As of 2002, the president has not exercised this right

These functions are derived from the 1994 General Law of the Police (available at: *www.cicad.oas.org/Desarrollo_Juridico/esp/Armas/Leyesarmas/CostaRica/Ley%207410CR.doc*).

and functions of each division are shown in the table (above). In addition to these police units, local communities may also form committees to fight crime in their neighborhoods.

The Public Force, or Fuerza Pública, is the most recognizable of the Costa Rican police units, and is responsible for the maintenance of peace and order. To join the Public Force, applicants must be citizens and at least eighteen years of age, and must comply with their civic duties (namely voting). Members of the Public Force must pledge their loyalty to the constitution and its laws and may not have criminal records. They must be physically and morally fit for police service, pass a series of tests administered by the Ministry of Interior, Police and Public Safety, and have completed the third cycle of their general basic education. After acceptance into the Public Force, applicants must satisfactorily complete a six-month probation period before becoming full-fledged police officers.

The hierarchy of the Public Force recognizes three main divisions: senior officers, official executives, and basic officers. Within the category of senior officials, there are three ranks: (1) Commissioner (Comisario), (2) Commissioned (Comisionado), and (3) Commander (Comandante). The official executives also have three ranks: (1) Captain of Police, (2) Superintendent (Intendente), and (3) Assistant Superintendent (Subintendente). Finally, at the basic level the ranks are (1) Sergeant of Police, (2) Inspector of Police, (3) Police Officer. The 1994 police reforms established legal criteria for promotion among these ranks. To be promoted, individuals must meet educational requirements, have the appropriate amount of service, and obtain other merits that correspond to each of the ranks.

Salary increases are awarded annually to all individuals who receive qualifications of good, very good, or excellent in their annual reviews.

Training

The Public Force has acknowledged that their training programs need improvement. Recent initiatives have begun to address deficits and have aimed to improve police training. In particular, the Public Force has created training programs that instruct police on how to respond in specific areas such as domestic violence, bank robberies, and airport security. The length of these training programs varies according to the topic. For example, the domestic violence training course required participants to attend ninety-six hours of classroom training over several weeks. While these training programs provide police with much needed skills, independent Costa Rican human rights organizations argue that such measures are not enough. Such groups maintain that there has been a rise in the number of allegations of arbitrary arrest and brutality. Indeed, international organizations such as the Freedom House concur that some human rights abuses persist, although not nearly to the same extent as in other Central American nations. While the Public Force has attempted to stress the importance of respecting human rights, concrete advances in practical human rights training have not yet materialized.

Police Public Projects

The Public Force has become increasingly more active in public projects. In 2002, it collaborated with civil society groups to promote domestic violence awareness, reduce the consumption of illegal drugs, and protect the rights of minors. As part of its transparency initiatives, the Public Force has developed and maintained a user-friendly website, which lists department activities, police objectives, police phone numbers, and legal forms. In addition to promoting transparency, such efforts are meant to reach out to members of civil society and encourage community involvement in crime prevention programs.

Complaints and Discipline

Attempts have also been made to improve police discipline and transparency. The 1994 reforms delineate exact procedures to be followed in the event of police infractions. Police infractions are grouped into two categories: minor and serious. Serious infractions include offenses such as carrying a firearm that does not meet regulations, acceptance of bribes, lack of cooperation with other governmental agencies, use of illegal drugs, habitual inebriation, and use of excessive force. Minor offenses are sanctioned with oral or written reprimands, while serious infractions result in suspension without pay (ranging from one to thirty days) or dismissal. Infractions are handled through the Personnel Council, an agency comprised of various police officials that investigate and rule on police offenses. In its efforts to increase transparency, the Public Force has publicized police infractions and subsequent disciplinary measures. For example, in 2002 police were subject to tests for illegal drugs. The Public Force published the results of the drug testing, including the number of violators and their punishment, in its press releases.

International Cooperation

Costa Rica has cooperated extensively with international organizations as well as other countries. In the international arena, Costa Rica was one of the principal advocates of a United Nations prison monitoring system in 1998. Costa Rica argued that an international system of prison monitors was essential for addressing the serious human rights abuses many prisoners face, and as of 2002 it continued to work with international groups to create such an agency.

Costa Rica has also cooperated with Nicaraguan officials to tighten security at its northern border. Exchanges and information sharing programs with Nicaraguan police agencies has been an important feature in Costa Rica's efforts to reduce drug trafficking. While it has cooperated with Nicaragua to reduce the distribution of illegal narcotics, Costa Rica's most extensive cooperation remains with the United States. In 1999, Costa Rica signed a treaty with the United States to conduct joint patrols of its coast. Between 2000 and 2002, sixty-eight U.S. boats patrolled Costa Rican shores in efforts to confiscate illegal narcotics. Costa Rican officials estimate that in addition to the confiscation of 9.842 kilograms of cocaine, these patrols contributed $4.3 million to the local Costa Rican economy.

Police Education, Research, and Publications

To promote transparency, Costa Rica has created a series of internet sites that disseminate information on its criminal justice system, judicial and police structures, and statistics. Two sites are particularly helpful in gathering information on the police and criminal justice system: the homepages of the Ministry of Interior, Police, and Public Security (*www.msp.go.cr*) and of the Judicial Branch (*www.poder-judicial.go.cr*). In addition to these Costa Rican websites, there are also regional organizations that provide valuable information, such as the Institute of Investigation of Crime and Justice in Latin America (IIDEJUAL) (*http://iidejual.jus.gov.ar*), and the United Nations International Justice Network (*www.uncjin.org/country/country.html*). Academics have not rigorously examined the police system or police reforms of Costa Rica, but there has been some important research in this area conducted by Henry Giralt (University of Alaska), Mitchell Seligson (University of Pittsburgh), and Peter Kassebaum (College of Marin). The relevant research of each author is listed in the bibliography.

MARY FRAN T. MALONE

Bibliography

Aguirre, C., and R. Buffington, eds. *Reconstructing Criminality in Latin America*. Wilmington, DE: Scholarly Resources, 2000.

Call, C. "War Transitions and the New Civilian Security in Latin America." *Comparative Politics* 33, no. 1 (2002).

Central Intelligence Agency. "Costa Rica." In *The World Factbook*, 2002. Available at: www.odci.gov/cia/publications/factbook/.Accessed 20 December 2002.

Chacón, R. M. "Saturación asfixia a cárceles." *La Nación*, 1998. Available at: www.nacion.co.cr/ln_ee/1998/noviembre/30/pais1.html. Accessed 20 December 2002.

Costa Rica, Republic of. Ministerio de Gobernabilidad, Policía, y Seguridad Pública. Website, home page, 2002. Available at: www.msp.go.cr/. Accessed 20 December 2002.

Costa Rica, Republic of. Poder Judicial, Gobierno de Costa Rica. Website, home page, 2002. Available at: www.poder-judicial.go.cr/. Accessed 20 December 2002.

Freedom House Organization. Home page. Available at: www.freedomhouse.org. Accessed 20 December 2002.

Giralt, H. "Costa Rica." In *World Factbook of Criminal Justice Systems*, 1996. Available at: www.ojp.usdoj.gov/bjs/pub/ascii/wfbcjcos.txt. Accessed 20 December 2002.

Huggins, M. *Political Policing: The United States and Latin America*. Durham, NC: Duke University Press, 1998.

Human Rights Watch. *Ending the Abusive Treatment of Prisoners: World Report 2002*. Available at: www.hrw.org/prisons. Accessed 20 December 2002.

Inter-American Institute of Human Rights. *View Points Regarding the Administration of Justice and Indigenous Populations*. San José, Costa Rica: Inter-American Institute of Human Rights, 1999.

Interpol. *International Crime Statistics, 2002*. Available at: www.interpol.int/Public/Statistics/ICS/. Accessed 20 December 2002.

Kassebaum, P. "Role of the Police in Costa Rica." Paper presented at Western Society of Criminology meetings, Las Vegas, NV, February 1990.

Krauss, C. *Inside Central America: Its People, Politics, and History*. New York: Touchstone, Simon & Schuster, 1991.

Kurian, G., ed. *The Illustrated Book of World Rankings*, 5th ed. Armonk, NY: Sharpe Reference, 2001.

Latin American Crime and Research Institute. Website, home page, 2002. Available at: http://iidejual.jus.gov.ar/Ingles.htm. Accessed 20 December 2002.

Rico, J. M. *Citizen Security in Latin America: Situational Diagnoses*. San José, Costa Rica: Inter-American Institute of Human Rights, 2000.

Rico, J. M. *La Justicia Penal en Costa Rica*. San José, Costa Rica: Editorial Universitaria Centroamericana, 1988.

Seligson, M. "Trouble in Paradise? The Erosion of System Support in Costa Rica, 1978–1999." *Latin American Research Review* 37, no. 1 (2002): 160–185.

Serbin, A., L. Salomón, and C. Sojo. *Gobernabilidad Democrática y Seguridad Ciudadana en Centroamérica*. Managua, Nicaragua: Coordinadora Regional de Investigaciones Económicas y Sociales, 2001.

United Nations Crime and Justice Information Network. Website, home page, 2000. Available at: www.uncjin.org/country/country.html. Accessed 20 December 2002.

United Nations Inter-Regional Crime and Justice Research Institute. *International Crime Victim Survey, 2002*. Available at: http://ruljis.leidenuniv.nl/group/jfcr/www/icvs/Index.htm. Accessed December 20, 2002.

Wilke, J., ed. *Statistical Abstract of Latin America*. Vol. 36. Los Angeles, CA: UCLA Latin American Center Publications, 2000.

World Bank. *World Development Indicators*. CD-ROM. Washington, DC: World Bank, 2001.

CÔTE D'IVOIRE

Background Material

Observers and sociopolitical thinkers have often described Côte d'Ivoire as different from the rest of Africa. In their attempts to distinguish Côte d'Ivoire from other African nations, the country has been variously described as an oasis of political stability and economic prosperity. Until the death of the father of the nation and its first president, Felix Houphouet-Biogny, in 1993, the country remained the most peaceful and the only country in West Africa without a military coup.

Côte d'Ivoire (also known as the Ivory Coast in English-speaking countries) has an area of 322,463 square kilometers. It is, after Nigeria, the largest country in the forest zone of West Africa. According to Griffith (1994), one of the famous cities within the confines of the present Ivory Coast was founded by the Senoufo people in the eleventh century.

The French government's contacts in Côte d'Ivoire were in three phases. The first was from 1637 to 1704, when there were rare visits by ships of several companies and by missionaries to Assinie, a town near the Ghana boundary destroyed in 1942. The second contact was when forts were established at Assinie, Grand Bassam, Dabou, and Aboisso, major towns in Côte d'Ivoire. The last phase started with the proclamation of the colony in 1893, with its capital at Grand Bassam. Later the capital was moved to Bingerville (1900 to 1934) and from there to Abidjan.

Côte d'Ivoire has more than sixty ethnic groups usually classified into five principal divisions: Akan (East and Center, including Lagoon), peoples of the Southeast, Krou (Southwest), Southern Mande (West), Northern Mande (Northwest), Senoufo/Lobi (North Center and Northeast). Of all ethnic groups in this French-speaking West African country, the Baoules in the Akan division comprise the largest single subgroup with 15% to 20% of the population. They are based in the central region around Bouake and Yamoussoukro (which later became the official political capital city of the country). Other tribes include the Betes in the Krou division, Senoufos in the North, and Maliukes in the Northwest.

Côte d'Ivoire has a population of about 19,393,221 (including immigrants) (Free Encyclopeadia 2005). Of this population, 76% are Ivorians, and are the French-speaking majority. About 20% of the Côte d'Ivoire's population consists of workers and immigrants from neighboring Liberia, Burkina Faso, Guinea, and Nigeria. More than half of the population is largely Christian, primarily Roman Catholic, and animist, while the rest (mainly from the North) are Muslims. Four percent of the population is of non-African ancestry, including French and British nationals, and Lebanese, who are mainly in the commercial sector of the economy.

Griffiths (1994) asserts that Felix Houphouet-Boigny had a great influence on Côte d'Ivoire's economy through his liberal policies. He stresses further that he made the Ivory Coast a client state of France, that is, the nation's economy is tied to that of France. Most Ivorians are farmers planting cocoa, coffee, timber, rubber, banana, and other tropical products. In the Ivory Coast, average life expectancy is fifty-three years, with a $660 per capita income (Griffiths 1994).

Other than agricultural products, the country is also blessed with petroleum (offshore) discovered in 1977. Production of this in commercial quantities did not, however, begin until 1980. Similarly, the country has diamonds, which are produced in commercial quantities.

French is the official language, and is used throughout the country. There are other languages spoken by the people in Côte d'Ivoire. This linguistic diversity reflects the ethnographic mosaic nature of Ivorian nationals. For instance, Agni and Baoule (both Kwa languages) are the most widely spoken languages in the South. In the same vein, Mande and Senoufo are most widely spoken in the North but are also heard in virtually all Southern trading areas (most especially in Adjame, 220 Lodgements, Cocody, Abobo Gare, Agban, Bromakoute, Williams' Ville, Yopougon, and so on). Interestingly, most Ivorians speak two or more languages fluently, but no single African language is spoken by a majority of the population. The English language is taught in secondary schools and in the university.

Contextual Features

In Côte d'Ivoire, the country's judicial system is greatly influenced by the legacy of the French colonial masters. The judicial system bears the imprint of French legal and judicial traditions and, to a lesser extent, customary law. It consisted of two levels. The lower courts, all of which were created by presidential decree and exercised limited jurisdiction, included the courts of appeals (located in Abidjan and Bouake), the courts of first instance, the courts of assize, and the justice of the peace courts.

There are five courts of first instance, and they handle the bulk of trials (including misdemeanors and minor criminal cases). The maximum sentence that the courts can impose is three months or less. The courts consist of a president, one or more vice presidents, and one or more examining magistrates and trial judges, all of whom are appointed by the president of the republic. The courts are located in Abidjan, Bouake, Daloa, Korhogo, and

Man. At the lowest level are justice of the peace courts, presided over by justices of the peace who handle petty cases in civil, criminal, and customary law.

The superior courts are mandated by the constitution and have a nationwide jurisdiction. They include the Supreme Court, the High Court of Justice and the State Security Court. The Supreme Court is divided into four sections: constitutionality of laws, administrative appeal, criminal appeal, and financial control of government services. The court is headed by one president, assisted by three vice presidents (one for each section except the constitutional), nine associate justices, one secretary general, and four secretaries.

The Judicial section was the highest court of appeals in criminal cases. The court consisted of one vice president, four associate justices, and two secretaries. The two other superior courts include the High Court of Justice and the State Security Court.

The influence of Felix Houphouet-Boigny on the political landscape of Côte d'Ivoire cannot be overemphasized. Houphouet-Boigny was the son of a Baoule chief. He organized African cocoa farmers like himself to form a trade union. He later rose to prominence, and within a year he was elected to the French Parliament in Paris. Subsequently, he became the first African to become a minister in a European government.

The above greatly influenced the type of government established in Côte d'Ivoire, which gained independence on August 7, 1960. Côte d'Ivoire adopted a one-party democracy, where the government controls the press, limits civil liberties, and allows no institutionalized opposition to frame debate.

The Côte d'Ivoire constitution operates a presidential–parliamentary system where the president has executive power and he is the head of government. The other arm of government is the legislature, which is a unicameral national assembly comprised of 225 members. The Prime Minister is appointed by the President from the national assembly. At the lower level, there are local governments (known as the Marie in French) headed by chairmen.

Recently, there has been an upsurge in the crime rate in Côte d'Ivoire occasioned by sociopolitical and ethnic dominance problems. A rider to this is the influx of a large volume of refugees from the neighboring Liberia, which had been engulfed in civil war since 1987. These have led to increases in arson, banditry, armed robbery, murder, rape, and battering, among others. The police and gendarmes appear unable to cope with the crime wave due to the large quantities of arms and ammunition available throughout the country.

Police Profile

Background

The police are men and women organized by the state (government) as a paramilitary force with the sole purpose of defending the status quo, that is, to enforce the laws, values, and ideologies that justify, legitimize, and defend the prevailing distribution of power and wealth in society (Alemika 1993). This adequately portrays the philosophy of policing in Côte d'Ivoire, which until recently has been the most peaceful country in Africa.

Organizational Description and Functions

Côte d'Ivoire has adopted a three-ministry multi layered organization patterned on the French colonial system. The Ministry of Interior was responsible primarily for territorial and local administration, and this included the local police forces (which were adequately functioning in the precolonial period); the Ministry of Internal Security and national police functions; and the Ministry of Defense and Maritime Affairs (primarily through the National Gendarmerie) that provided paramilitary forces throughout the country in coordination with respective regional and local authorities.

The Ministry of Interior (which oversees the running of the local police) has broad regulatory functions. These include regulation of public associations, gun control, emigration and immigration, foreign propaganda, foreign visitors, and passport control. The ministry also directed the National Security Police and supervised traditional chieftaincies. The National Security Police was later transferred to the Ministry of Internal Security in 1976.

The Ministry of Internal Security was established as part of a governmental reorganization in March 1976 to consolidate the national police and state security functions that had formerly been assigned to the Ministry of Interior. In 1985, the ministry was reorganized into the following groups: the minister's cabinet; eight directorates (National Security Police, Regional Security, Inspector General of Police Services, Materials, Financial Affairs, Personnel, Police Economics and Finances, and Judicial Affairs); the National Police Academy; and an intelligence service.

In Côte d'Ivoire, the National Security Police is an investigative bureau and a national police force.

It has about 15,300 officers of various ranks (male and female). The National Security Police enforce law and order, and provide special police services such as:

- Protecting lives and properties
- Detecting and preventing crimes
- Apprehending and prosecuting offenders
- Preserving law and order
- Enforcing law and regulations
- Performing any other function assigned in the areas of peacekeeping both locally and internationally

The police in Côte d'Ivoire are grouped under the central commissariat, that is, the National Police Headquarters in Abidjan. In a similar vein, the National Security Police Public Security Directorate is also the umbrella of the uniformed national police. The Directorate has police otherwise referred to as prefects and those called Compagnies Republicaines de Securite (CRS) (Companies for the Security of the Republic). In emergencies, police prefects could call upon the Minister to use any CRS in his or her jurisdiction. The CRS are most frequently used to handle certain kinds of local emergencies and rescue operations.

The above situation has shown that the police force in Côte d'Ivoire is strongly dynamic. Although the police are formally under the control of the Generale Inspecteur de Police (Inspector General of Police), the control of the National Police Force is still a political matter. This is because the chief of police and his lieutenants are nominees of the President of the Republic. It is therefore, rare for any police officer to disobey the President or the designated minister. The consequence is outright dismissal from the force.

In the Ivorian police force, ranks that are distinguished by V's are those of noncommissioned officers; one V designates a corporal, two V's a sergeant, and three V's a staff sergeant.

Training

The National Police Academy was opened in 1967 at Youpougon by Houphouet-Boigny as a training school for all cadres of police in Côte d'Ivoire. By 1988, about 6,000 officers had been trained at the academy. In the 1980s, the academy also graduated about 450 officers, who were then assigned to the Police Forces of the Ministry of Internal Security. In recent years, the academy has graduated police officers of Ivorian nationality as well as of other countries (such as Burkina Faso, Ca-

meroon, Central African Republic, Chad, Congo, Niger, and Senegal).

The national academy's basic courses of study vary from six months to two years (depending on the student's rank). The academy's courses include forensic medicine, judicial procedure, criminal investigation, criminology and criminal psychology, police administration, computer technology, and communications.

Admission to the National Police Academy is by direct recruitment or competitive entrance examinations. Prospective police candidates (police cadets) for the rank of Commissioner of Police are required to have credits toward a law degree to gain entrance, and to complete their law degrees in order to graduate. Candidates who fail to obtain the law degree within two years of training are dismissed from the academy.

The national academy also trains police officers of commissioner rank who have fulfilled certain mandatory length-of-service requirements set by police regulations. In the same vein, the academy also gives further training for junior police officers who had earlier completed a two-year junior officer training course for a bachelor's degree program. Nationally, the police academy admits qualified Ivorian nationals who have completed primary school (ecole primaire).

Complaints and Discipline

Recent reports indicate that police are used to detain, torture, and harass members of the political opposition and innocent citizens (including foreign nationals). Ivorian police have also been accused of using extreme forms of brutality and torture, resulting in the deaths of several young men.

According to Human Rights Watch (2005), the Ivorian police have assaulted civilians (including several foreigners) in Abobo, Treichville, Blokosso, and Youpougon. The brutality adopted by the police was in form of sexual abuse and torture.

Police Education, Research, and Publications

In Côte d'Ivoire, the police and policing systems and culture have not been the focus of scholarship. Hence, there is a complete dearth of literature on the police in Côte d'Ivoire. Existing information derives from journalists (local and foreign), and centers mainly on the human rights record of the Ivorian police.

A. OYESOJI AREMU

Bibliography

Alemika, E. E. O. "Criminology, Criminal Justice and the Philosophy of Policing." In *Policing Nigeria*, edited by T. N. Tamuno, I. Bashir, E. E. O. Alemika, and A. O. Akano, 30–78. Ikeja: Malthouse Press Ltd., 1993.

Free Encyclopeadia. Ivory Coast: History, 2005. Available at: www.htm.freencyclopeadia. Accessed 21 January 2005.

Griffiths, I. *The Atlas of African Affairs*. London: Routledge, 1994.

Human Rights Watch. Ivory Coast: Internal Security Organisation and Forces, 2005. Available at: www.htm.livory %20coast. Accessed 21 January 2005.

CROATIA

Background Material

The Republic of Croatia is both a Central European and a Mediterranean country covering 56,538 square kilometers with a population of 4,381,352. Eighty percent of all Croatians identify themselves as ethnic Croats and 78% as Roman Catholics. The official language is Croatian.

Croats have lived in southeastern Europe for more than thirteen centuries, in both an independent Croatian Kingdom and in a union with Hungary and Austria. Following the collapse of the Austro-Hungarian monarchy in 1918 at the end of World War I, Croatia became part of the Kingdom of Serbs, Croats, and Slovenians (subsequently renamed the Kingdom of Yugoslavia). After World War II, Croatia became a socialist republic within the newly formed communist-dominated Yugoslav federation. In the midst of the war in Croatia after the breakup of the federation, the Republic of Croatia was recognized in 1992 as an independent and sovereign country.

Croatia is currently in transition toward a democratic society and market economy. It features a small open economy, that is, its economy is characterized by a small internal market, a high share of trade in gross domestic product, a limited share in world trade, and little influence on global prices.

Contextual Features

The Republic of Croatia is an indivisible and democratic state. Freedom, equal rights, ethnic and gender equality, love of peace, social justice, respect for human rights, inviolability of ownership, conservation of nature and the human environment, the rule of law, and a democratic multiparty system are the highest values of the constitutional order of the Republic of Croatia and form the basis for interpreting the constitution.

Government in the Republic of Croatia is organized on the principle of the separation of powers into legislative (Parliament), executive (the President and the Government), and judicial (constitutional and court system). The principle of the separation of powers includes levels of mutual cooperation and reciprocal control of the holder of power prescribed by the constitution and law.

Judicial power exercised by the courts is autonomous and independent. Courts administer justice on the basis of the Constitution and law. The Supreme Court of the Republic of Croatia, as the highest court, ensures the uniform application of laws and the equality of all citizens. The Constitutional Court decides on the conformity of laws and other regulations with the constitution and on constitutional applications against individual decisions of state, administration, and regional self-government bodies and other public authority bodies when these decisions interfere with human rights and basic freedom as well as the rights of local self-government and administration bodies guaranteed by the Constitution of the Republic of Croatia.

Three new criminal laws—the Criminal Code, Criminal Procedure Act, and Law on Juvenile Courts—were adopted in early autumn 1997. In addition to the known basic principles of the law on criminal procedure, such as the accusatory principle, the principle of mandatory criminal prosecution, the principles of the subsidiarity and legality of criminal law, the principle of guilt and proportionality, the principle of officially controlled fact finding, and the principle of free evaluation of evidence, the new criminal law contained two important features: a legal attempt at the definition of the principle *in dubio pro reo*, and a determination of the concept of illegally obtained evidence and the prohibition of its use in a criminal proceeding.

With regard to the new forms of criminal behavior such as economic and organized crime, Croatian criminal legislation has introduced several measures to expand the range of repressive actions, even though this behavior is not as daunting as in other transitional countries. Thus, Croatian legislation has shown balance and concern for the prevention and repression of crime.

In 2002, the Republic of Croatia recorded 58,776 criminal acts of the most common type, primarily property-related crime, which accounts for 78% of all crime. An essential characteristic of these criminal acts is that the majority were committed in the larger urban centers (61%). In 2002, the trend of increasing crime committed by children and minors was halted; the rate decreased 18% in comparison with 2001, as 5,154 criminal acts were recorded.

Police Profile

Background

The Croatian police is one of the youngest forces in Europe, established in the early 1990s, and is a national police of approximately 20,000 sworn officers. Through the 1990s and into the twenty-first century, the Ministry of Interior has been going through a process of significant change. Postwar police have been transforming into a new force that is suitable for a modern democratic world.

Organizational Description

Within the Ministry of Interior, the Police Directorate is structured as the administrative organization for carrying out police activities. The General Police Directorate consists of the following organizational units: Police Directorate, Criminal Police Directorate, Border Police Directorate, Security Bureau, Command of Special Police, Operational-Communication Center of the Police, and Criminal Forensics Center.

The organization of the police is centralized, which implies a pyramidal structure with the General Police Directorate at the top, followed by twenty police administrations that cover Croatian territory according to the organization of local gov-ernment units (divided into four categories according to the size of the area, the number of inhabitants, the crime rates, the characteristics of traffic and roads, and the geographical position). Below them are approximately 200 police stations at the bottom of the organizational chart.

To be admitted to the police force, the individual must have completed at least the secondary level of education, be under twenty-five years of age, possess special mental and physical abilities, have completed regular military service (applicable to men only), and be worthy of performing police tasks. Police officers shall be admitted to the service by means of competition. The government of the Republic of Croatia may—by passing a decree—determine the posts in the Ministry that are to be filled other than by competitive means.

An employee gains the status of a police officer by receiving a rank. An officer's rank depends on his or her level of education, years of service and position, passing the examination for receiving rank, and annual evaluations. The following ranks have been established for police officers: Officer, Senior Officer, Sergeant, Senior Sergeant, Inspector, Senior Inspector, Independent Inspector, Chief Inspector, Advisor, and Chief Advisor.

Functions

According to the Police Act, the Croatian police force is a public service of the Croatian Ministry of Interior, which performs following tasks:

- Protection of life, rights, safety, and inviolability of persons
- Protection of property
- Prevention and investigation of criminal acts, misdemeanors, and offenses
- Searching for perpetrators of criminal acts, misdemeanors, and offenses and taking them to the competent authorities
- Control and regulation of road traffic
- Tasks relative to the movement of aliens (immigration)
- Control and securing of national borders

The police powers prescribed by the Police Act follow:

- Verify and establish the identity of persons and objects
- Issue summonses
- Make arrests
- Search for persons and objects
- Temporarily restrict freedom of movement
- Give warnings and orders
- Temporarily dispossess persons of objects

- Perform polygraph testing
- Inspect premises, areas, buildings, and documentation
- Inspect persons, objects, and means of transportation
- Secure and inspect venues
- Register reports
- Publicly announce awards
- Record in public places
- Use coercion
- Protect victims of criminal acts and other persons
- Gather, process, and use personal data

While applying police powers, a police officer is obliged to behave in a humane way and respect the dignity, reputation, and honor as well as other fundamental human rights and freedoms of every person. In undertaking measures to ensure the safety of citizens and property, the police must cooperate with local and regional self-government units as well as with other authorities, organizations, communities, nongovernmental organizations, and associations of citizens. In 2002, the Croatian Police began implementing a community policing strategy.

Training

Police training in Croatia is carried out by the Police Academy and consists of two fundamental components: basic education and training (schooling and retraining of new police officers); and professional improvement, specialization, and vocational training as part of a system of continuing lifelong education of police officers, which begins on entering the police and ends with retirement. Human rights are included in all educational and training programs for police officers.

Police Use of Firearms

A police officer is obliged to carry weapons and ammunition, and may use firearms when there is no other way to:

- Protect his or her own life as well as the lives of other people
- Prevent the commission of a criminal act for which a prison sentence lasting five years or more can be given
- Prevent the escape of a person caught committing a criminal act for which a prison sentence of more than ten years can be given, or of a person for whom there is an announced search on the grounds of having committed such a criminal act

Complaints and Discipline

When a Croatian citizen or a legal resident files a report against a police officer or an organizational unit charging that the individual's rights have been violated by an unlawful or improper activity performed by a police officer, the submitter of the report shall be notified about the state of facts and the measures undertaken within thirty days of the receipt of the report. First-instance and second-instance disciplinary courts are established at the Headquarters of the Ministry both for police officers working at the Headquarters and for police officers working at Police Administrations.

Terrorism

In 2002, there were no incidents of activities by persons and groups connected to terrorist organizations. Representatives from the Criminal Police Directorate participate in the activities of the Inter-departmental Task Force for implementation of resolution 1373 of the UN Security Council, established by decision of the Croatian government at the Ministry of Foreign Affairs. Their role is to determine if there are any regulations of the Croatian legislature that obstruct the effective fight against international terrorism and, if so, to modify them. Representatives from the Criminal Police Directorate also actively participate in a number of regional initiatives dealing with the problem of terrorism, including the task force for suppression of terrorism under the title of "Fusion" established by the General Secretary of Interpol. The Ministry of Interior was also a co-organizer of the international symposium in September 2002 on "Terrorism and Security in the twenty–first century—South Eastern Europe and the World," attended by 175 participants, including 85 from Croatia.

International Cooperation

The Republic of Croatia is situated along the so-called "Balkan route," known for smuggling people, narcotics, vehicles, cultural heritage objects, works of art, and weapons and explosives. From the beginning of independence and sovereignty in 1990, this situation has directed Croatia toward bilateral contacts and various kinds of regional and multilateral cooperation. With the finalization of the agreement on stabilization and association, Croatia began seeking membership in the European Union.

The Ministry of Interior has appreciated the support and assistance of other states and has had a significant role in international contacts. This is demonstrated by the fact that bilateral agreements on police cooperation have been concluded with twenty-three countries and are being discussed with some twenty other countries. The Ministry of Interior maintains police cooperation with neighboring countries and the countries in the region, and is an active member of a number of international regional police organizations and initiatives such as the Stability Pact, South Eastern European Cooperation Initiative (SECI), Adriatic–Ionic Initiative, Regional Task Force, and Central European Initiative.

Police Education, Research, and Publications

Police reform in Croatia is not yet finished, and it is recognized that such reform must begin with changes in police education and training. This gives particular meaning to the discussion about reform at the Police Academy and Police College.

The Police College in Croatia has been in existence for thirty years. It is a public school that is almost the only one not exclusively controlled by the Higher Education Law applicable to all other educational institutes in the country. The Police College is both a part of the Ministry of Interior and associated with the Higher Education Law.

The Police College offers three graduate programs:

- Specialist graduate study of criminology over five semesters
- Specialist graduate study of criminology over eight semesters
- University study of criminology over eight semesters

The Police College also offers postgraduate studies of criminology in the field of violent crime. This curriculum was also licensed by the Ministry of Science and Technology in 1998.

The following are the leading Croatian researchers and authors in the field of policing (in alphabetical order):

- Ljubica Bakic Tomic, Ph.D., Police College
- Irena Cajner Mraovic, Ph.D., Police College
- Zvonimir Dujmovic, Ph.D., Police College
- Vladimir Faber, General Police Directorate
- Stjepan Gluscic, M.Sc., Police College
- Mirjana Grubisic Ilic, Ph.D., Police College
- Drazen Ivanusec, Ministry of Interior
- Tatjana Kolar Gregoric M.Sc., Police College
- Irma Kovco Vukadin, Ph.D., Police College

- Tajana Ljubin, Ph.D., Police College
- Dusko Modly, Ph.D.
- Marijan Superina, Ph.D., Police College
- Petar Veic, Ph.D., Police College
- Goran Volarevic, Ministry of Interior
- Josko Vukosav, M.Sc., Police College

The majority of police research is funded by the Croatian Ministry of Interior. Some funding is available within the Ministry of Science and Technology's National Research Program. The most important areas of Croatian research in the policing field include police protection of vulnerable groups (children, women, minorities); police use of force; police integrity; the code of silence and police corruption; interdependence of organization, education, and management, and the quality of police work; psychological and physiological correlates of stress; police powers in investigations of rape; criminal investigation of robbery; methods of processing fingerprints at the scene of the crime; development of information systems used in crime intelligence analysis; and media coverage of crime.

The leading Croatian periodical in the field of policing is *Police and Safety*, published by the Ministry of Interior (editor: Josip Tulezi, Police Academy, Avenia G. Suska 1, 10040 Zagreb, Croatia). The Croatian police website is *www.mup.hr*.

IRENA CAJNER MRAOVIC AND PETAR VEIC

Bibliography

Cajner Mraovic, I., V. Faber, and G. Volarevic. *Community Policing Strategy*. Zagreb, Croatia: Ministry of Interior, 2003.

Cehok, I., and P. Veic. *Police Professional Ethics*. Zagreb, Croatia: Ministry of Interior, 2000.

1997 Croatian Almanac, 1998. Available at: www.hina.hr/almanah97.

Croatia, Republic of, Ministry of Foreign Affairs. Republic of Croatia: Geographical Characteristics, Political Structure, Economy, 2003. Available at: www.mvp.hr.

Croatia, Republic of, Ministry of Interior. *Country Report 2002*. Zagreb, Croatia: Ministry of Interior, General Police Directorate, Criminal Police Directorate, 2003.

Dujmovic, Z. "Police Education in the Republic of Croatia." *The Croatian Journal* 3 (1998): 564–570.

Dujmovic, Z. "Thirty Years of The Police College in Zagreb." *Police and Security* 3–6, no. 9 (2002): 249–251.

Jurina, M. "Trends in the Police Colleges' Education Innovations—A Comparative Review. *Police and Security* 6, no. 3 (1994): 531–542.

Krapac, Davor. "The Physiognomy of the New Croatian Criminal Legislation." *Croatian Annual of Criminal Law and Practice* 6, no. 1 (1999): 3–21.

Veic, P. *Police Law*. Zagreb, Croatia: Ministry of Interior, 2001.

CUBA

Background Material

Smaller than the state of Pennsylvania, yet at one time the wealthiest island in the Caribbean, Cuba lies just ninety miles south of Key West, Florida. In 1868, after some 400 years under Spanish rule, the people of Cuba began the fight for independence, and in 1898 was declared independent and under U. S. protection when the United States entered into conflict with Spain. In 1902, the Cuban people began to rule themselves as a united nation under the control of various leaders until 1934 when the reins of power were taken by Fulgencio Batista y Zaldivar. Widespread opposition to the Batista government led to the Cuban Revolution; in 1959 the rebel army was led to victory by Fidel Castro Ruiz, who governs the country today.

In 1961, Castro formally embraced the marxist ideals of communism and allied the country with the Soviet Union. The Cuban government was, and is, based on socialist ideals, with centralized control given to the Partido Comunista Cubano (PCC). Through such an allegiance, Cuba's economy was able to thrive due in part to some US$4 billion to US$5 billion per year in Soviet subsidies. With the fall of the former Soviet Union, the loss of Soviet financial support coupled with trade embargos imposed by the United States, forced the Cuban government to enact widespread measures to combat the ensuing economic crisis. Despite the modest increase in trade with other nations and rising tourism, economic hardships continued to plague the Cuban people. These hardships were compounded in 1993 when the government legalized the U.S. dollar, leading to increased division among the people who have access to dollars and those who do not, and an increase in crimes such as prostitution, official corruption, and black market activities. Growing public outcry prompted the Cuban Foreign Ministry in 1994 to seek agreement with the U.S. State Department to allow a small number of Cuban citizens to emigrate to the United States each year. Although only 20,000 individuals are officially allowed to emigrate each year, both countries recognize swelling numbers of illegal migrants. In 2002 alone, some 4,000 Cubans attempted illegal entry to the United States by sea, land, and air.

Cuba's population of 11,308,764 consists of roughly 51% mulatto, 37% white, 11% Black, and 1% Chinese. Throughout Cuba's fourteen provinces, and one *município especia* (special municipality), the literacy rate of the population remains at nearly 97%, and alongside the major language—Spanish—English, Russian, French Patois, and even Creole English can be heard. Prior to the Castro regime, the Roman Catholic Church held sway over 85% of the population, and today's average Cuban citizen professes Christianity as their faith. Nearly 30% classify themselves as strictly marxist, without traditional religious faith. Besides Christianity, one will find Protestants, Jehovah's Witnesses, Jews, and Santería—a mixture of Catholicism and African religious beliefs.

With a labor force of some 4.3 million and an unemployment rate of over 4%, Cuba still struggles to raise its economic standing and standard of living. Although sugar and tobacco production had made it the wealthiest of all Caribbean islands in the past, today the Cuban economy remains depressed. Beginning with the loss of economic and trade-related aid from the former Soviet Union in the early 1990s, compounded by the severe damage caused by hurricanes Isidore and Lili, and the extreme decline in tourism following the World Trade Center attacks of September 11, 2001, today's average Cuban citizen holds a standard of living no higher than that of over twenty years ago. While the island exports nearly $2 billion of sugar, nickel, tobacco, (shell)fish, medical products, citrus, and coffee, close to $5 billion are spent importing petroleum, machinery and equipment, chemicals, and even food.

Contextual Features

The Cuban government is modeled on the marxist ideal whose head remains the *lider máximo* (highest leader) and *comandante en jefe* (commander-in-chief) in Fidel Castro Ruiz. The government is based on a single-party system, specifically the Cuban Communist Party (PCC). Within the PCC is the Central Committee, whose purpose is to collect information and weigh official PCC decisions against communist ideology and advise policymakers based on the "ideological purity" of those decisions. Similar in structure to the government of the United States, Cuba's is divided into three branches: executive, legislative, and judicial.

The executive branch includes the Council of State and the Council of Ministers, the president of whom holds the office of President of Cuba, who is chief of state and head of the government.

The legislative branch consists of the elected 601-member Asemblea Nacional del Poder Popular (People's Power National Assembly), which every four years elects the President of Cuba. The Assembly, created by the 1976 constitution to better involve citizen participation in government, is comprised of individuals elected at the municipal, provincial, and national levels to pass and administer laws.

The judicial branch includes the Tribunal Supremo Popular (Supreme Court), provincial courts, municipal courts, and military courts. The court system is overseen by both the Council of State and the Ministry of Justice, and the citizenry obtain legal counsel at the municipal and provincial levels from law collectives. The 1960s and 1970s saw the creation of the Tribunales de Base (People's Courts), courts of law staffed with trained, ordinary citizens acting as prosecution, defense, and even the role of the judge, known as lay judges. These laypersons would receive training but not at the level of law school graduates, and eventually made up 95% of presiding judges. Elected to the bench, lay judges are put into place for their ability to view each case and its mitigating circumstances that may be overlooked by traditionally educated lawyers and judges.

The major source of influence for Cuban law comes from its long history under Spanish rule. Cuban criminal law stems from the Spanish Penal Code, Ley de la Sierra. This Code was well used and became the main impetus for the 1936 Código de Defensa Social (Social Defense Code, or CDS), which included the death penalty, but instead of life imprisonment, relied on incarceration of up to thirty years. Four years later a constitution was adopted that limited the use of the death penalty. Marxist influence and communist ideals intermingled with such American ideals as habeas corpus, and have had great influence on Cuban law.

The current civil law of Cuba relies on the written laws of the state rather than on legal precedent in deciding the outcomes of civil matters. In 1973, the government created the Law of Judicial Organization that, among other things, formalized the courts system, abolished the private practice of law, and created the *bufetes colectivos* ("law collectives").

When it comes to private, civil matters, Cuba's legal system strongly limits the "use of formal legal mechanisms" to prevent the overuse and abuse of the system. Instead, informal "social courts" are used in conjunction with lay practitioners of law, and the law collectives that provide affordable legal advice and services, to resolve interpersonal conflicts. The newer Código Civil (Civil Code) of 1987 recognized the limits of individual financial abilities to render compensation for damages of exorbitant amounts, and placed limits on an individual's financial liability to be repaid over the course of years, with the rest being paid by national or local entities.

In Cuba, actions that are prohibited by law, or are *socialmente peligrosa* (socially harmful), are considered crimes, with the age of criminal accountability being sixteen. Actions that violate the written law, but do not constitute socially harmful actions are *contravenciones* or infractions that only rise to that of a citation. Felonies and misdemeanors fall under the socially harmful category of crimes. Felony offenses (murder, rape, assault, death or injury by vehicle, robbery, burglary, larceny, vehicle theft, arson, and drug manufacturing, selling, and trafficking) are those with sentences over one year imprisonment or a fine of more than 300 *cuotas* (a variable unit of measurement for fines), and are brought before provincial court. Misdemeanor offenses (lesser actions of the abovementioned except murder, rape, and robbery) are those with sentences of less than one year or 300 *cuotas*.

The early 1990s saw a sharp increase in crimes committed by average citizens seeking means of subsistence. This period also saw a dramatic increase in government response to drugs and drug trafficking that culminated in the President's announcement in 1999 that persons apprehended on Cuban soil and convicted of drug trafficking in Cuban courts would suffer the death penalty. Also in 1999, three new classifications of crimes were added to the Penal Code: money laundering (*lavado de dinero*), trafficking in humans (*tráfico de personas*), and the sale and trafficking of minors (*venta y tráfico de menores*).

Under the current Penal Code, those accused of felony offenses have the right to trial in provincial courts in front of a panel of three formally trained judges and two lay judges, while misdemeanor offenders have the right to trial in municipal court with a panel of one formally trained and two lay judges. While at court, each citizen is guaranteed the right to counsel provided by the law collectives, discussed earlier. Initially, police and prosecutors assemble their evidence and witnesses, and if the state wishes to proceed, the state issues the *conclu-*

sions provisionales or bill of indictment. If the offense meets the level of felony, the case will be prosecuted by the provincial office of the attorney general, and if not (that is, in the case of a misdemeanor offense) will be prosecuted by a police investigator. Because all criminal cases are required to be heard at trial, the plea bargain alternative is not recognized by the Penal Code. All sentences are determined by the presiding panel, and all criminal cases are required by law to be completed within six months of the indictment being issued. The Penal Code in 1988 listed the available sentences to panels hearing criminal cases: execution, incarceration, correctional labor with confinement to the work site, correctional labor without confinement, probation, fines, and *la amonestación*, or public chastisement. The method of execution in Cuba is by firing squad, and reserved for offenders convicted of certain types of murder cases (multiple, of a child, or associated with torture) or treason, excluding those under the age of twenty and/or pregnant when the offense was committed.

Cuban correctional facilities are overseen by the Penal Directorate of the Ministry of Justice and are of two levels of security: prisons (which are fenced and walled) and *granjas* (which are minimum-security facilities for those convicted of relatively minor offenses). While incarcerated, all offenders are required to complete their high school educational equivalency or learn a trade, and are paid for their work at the same rates as would be found outside the facility. Fully one-third of the inmates' income, however, is turned over to the state to pay for upkeep and maintenance of the correctional facility.

Police Profile

Background and Organizational Description

Established on January 5, 1959, the *Policía Nacional Revolucionaria* (PNR) or National Revolutionary Police is Cuba's primary uniformed law enforcement agency, and by the mid-1980s numbered over 10,000 strong. The PNR operates under the auspices of the Vice Ministry of Internal Order, Ministry of Interior. The Ministry of Interior consists of the three subdivisions of Security, Technical Operations, and Internal Order and Crime Prevention. The Internal Order and Crime Prevention subdivision is further divided into the areas of Corrections, Fire Protection, and Policing, which is where the PNR organizationally lies. The duties of the PNR include uniform patrol and policing, criminal investigations, crime prevention, juvenile delinquency, and traffic control. The policing of crimes against the state such as espionage falls under the responsibility of the Security division of the Ministry of Interior, and generally does not directly involve the PNR. The PNR supports the Committees for the Defense of the Revolution (CDRs), in that the CDRs work closely with the populace in preventive measures against crime, such as *la guardia*, or neighborhood watch, issues involving juvenile delinquency, and criminal victims' assistance.

Acting as an unofficial intelligence gathering organization, members of the CDRs (*cederistas*) act as the eyes and ears of the PNR and help by gathering information from the community regarding criminal or deviant behavior. The CDRs also act as localized neighborhood organizations not only for the prevention of crime, but as places where crime victims can obtain the support they need whether it be medical, social, or emotional, from one of their many "polyclinics."

Functions

The discretionary limits of the PNR in regards to suspects and criminal investigations are such that Cuban law does not as heavily restrict officers in the stopping and apprehending of suspects because the Penal Code assumes that once a *fase preparatoria* has been initiated, given the investigative measures taken to that point, the suspect is the probable offender. However, steps dictated by the Law of Penal Procedures to be followed once an arrest is made are quite stringent. A detainee's case must be turned over to criminal investigators no later than twenty-four hours after the arrest, formal charges must be filed against the suspect within ninety-six hours of the arrest, and the detainee must be provided legal counsel within seven days of the initial detainment.

The laws restricting the police power of search and seizure, however, follow along similar lines as the American system. The Cuban constitution dictates that search warrants must be specific in detailing what is being searched for, where the search will take place, and for what reason the search will take place—unless, that is, the search will take place at the scene of a crime, and then only to gather evidence supporting the investigation of that crime. When it comes to confessions, though, Cuban law dictates that a suspect cannot be convicted of a crime based solely on one's admission of guilt. Evidence supporting both the confession and the suspect's guilt must be presented in a court of law and be weighed accordingly.

Following a speech given by Castro in 1999, the government proceeded to bolster the fight on crime by adding new crime headings to the Penal Code, and to further improve the PNR with increased training for officers, increased manpower and patrols, and improvements in police communications. One outcome of the increased personnel initiative was the creation of the Brigada Especial, or Special Brigade, whose primary mission is to fulfill the proactive, preventive intelligence role. Working under the Sistema Unificado de Prevención y Vigilancia (SUPV), or Unified Prevention and Vigilance System, and in conjunction with the PNR, the Special Brigade coordinates numerous neighborhood-based anticrime groups to combat economic-related crime and to improve vigilance in relation to "antisocial" behavior. The community-based antidrug initiative that is spelled out in the Integrated Drug Prevention Plan also gains support from the PNR and works jointly with anticrime patrols made by civilian residents of urban areas who are supported by the police nationwide. The SUPV bolsters the existing Comisiones de Prevención y Atención Social, or Commissions for Social Attention and Prevention (CPAS), which were created in 1986 as groups of teachers, professors, lawyers, and other professionals who actively seek out municipal and provincial conflicts to intervene and assist communities, families, and individuals. While a great deal of literature exists in regards to Cuba's government and legal system, information detailing the Policía Nacional Revolucionaria was found to be over twenty years old and too general to aid in this analysis.

- Training: information unavailable
- Use of firearms: information unavailable
- Complaints and discipline: information unavailable

- Terrorism: information unavailable
- International cooperation: information unavailable

ERIC C. SCHULTZ

Bibliography

Azicri, M. "Crime, Penal Law, and the Cuban Revolutionary Process." *Crime and Social Justice Issues* 23 (1985): 51–79.

British Broadcasting Corporation. *Country Profile—Cuba.* BBC News (UK edition), 10 October 2003. Available at: http://news.bbc.co.uk/1/hi/world/americas/country_profiles/1203299.stm. Accessed May 7, 2004.

Central Intelligence Agency. *CIA World Factbook—Cuba.* 18 December 2003. Available at: www.cia.gov/cia/pub lications/factbook/geos/cu.html. Accessed May 7, 2004.

CubaPoliData. A Gateway to Cuba's Political and Military Data. Home page. Available at: www.cubapolidata.com/. Accessed May 7, 2004.

Cuba, Republic of. Official website of Cuban government. Home page. Available at: www.cubagov.cu/. Accessed May 7, 2004.

Michalowski, R. J. "Between Citizens and the Socialist State: The Negotiation of Legal Practice in Socialist Cuba." *Law and Society Review* 29, no. 1 (1995): 65–101.

Michalowski, R. J. "Cuba." In *World Factbook of Criminal Justice Systems.* U.S. Department of Justice, Office of Justice Programs, Bureau of Justice Statistics. Available at: www.ojp.usdoj.gov/bjs/abstract/wfcj.htm. Accessed May 7, 2004.

Treto, R. G. "Thirty Years of Cuban Revolutionary Penal Law." *Latin American Perspectives* 18, no. 69 (1991): 114–125.

U.S. Library of Congress. *Cuba: A Country Study.* Washington, DC: Federal Research Division, Library of Congress, 2002.

CYPRUS

Background Material

Cyprus, with its nine millennia of civilization, is an island of 9,250 square kilometers in the Mediterranean Sea, south of Turkey. It became an independent state in 1960 after eighty-two years of British rule, and an armed liberation struggle led by the Greek-Cypriot EOKA organization in the late 1950s. The apportionment of power by the 1960 constitution disproportionately favored the Turkish-Cypriot minority, and the constitution proved unworkable. Intercommunal fighting broke out in December 1963, and the Turkish-Cypriots withdrew from government, including the police, and fortified themselves in enclaves. In 2003, Cyprus remained a divided country, as it has been since

1974 when Turkey invaded the island and forcefully partitioned it into a Greek-Cypriot part (the Republic of Cyprus) in the south and a Turkish-Cypriot part in the north. The only internationally recognized government in Cyprus is the Republic of Cyprus, or the Republic. Unless otherwise stated, all references to police and policing do not include the northern part of the country occupied by Turkey, and Cyprus is used to refer to the territory policed by the Republic of Cyprus. Also, references to the population of Cyprus do not include 115,000 Turkish settlers illegally residing in the Turkish-occupied part of Cyprus.

In April 2003 the Republic of Cyprus signed an accession agreement with the European Union (EU), and in May 2004, Cyprus became a full member of the EU. Constitutionally, the official languages are Greek and Turkish, but the majority of the population speaks English. The major religions are Christian, primarily Greek Orthodox (78%); 18% of the population is Muslim, and the remaining 4% is Armenian Apostolic, Maronite (Christian Arabs), and Roman Catholic. The population in July 2002 was estimated at 758,363. Cyprus is a prosperous country enjoying a high standard of living. In 2002, life expectancy at birth was 76.1 years for males and 81 years for females; the number of licensed passenger cars per 1,000 population was 416. In the same year, the proportion of foreigners (including foreign workers) residing legally in Cyprus was 8.3% of the population.

As far as the economy is concerned, the largest source of revenue is tourism. The major economic activities in order of importance are trade, restaurants, and hotels; real estate, renting, and business activities; manufacturing; transport, storage, and communication; education; and agriculture and fisheries. In 2002, the real growth of the economy was contained at about 2.2%, the inflation rate was 2.8% (Accountancy Cyprus 2003), and unemployment was 3%. According to the Bank of Cyprus (2002), the gross domestic product (GDP) per capita in the free areas of the Republic was Cyprus pounds (CY£) 8,696 (approximately US$16,470). Government revenue was CY£2,076,500 (US$3,925,415), and expenditure, CY£2,240,700 (US$4,235, 819).

Contextual Features

As an ex-British colony, Cyprus's legal system is adversarial and largely modeled on the British common law system. Cyprus, however, does not have jury trials. The independence of the judiciary is established in Article 163 of the Constitution.

Compared with other countries, Cyprus enjoys relatively low crime rates. Using the latest available figures (1999), the number of serious offenses reported to the police per 100,000 population was Cyprus (16.9), Spain (23.4), Greece (68.2), France (162.7), and Israel (491.8). The numbers and types of serious offenses in 2002 were as follows: 14 homicides/attempted homicides (67% cleared); 106 cases of arson (26% cleared); 38 robberies/extortions (68% cleared); 436 narcotics cases (98% cleared); 23 cases of property damage with explosives (9% cleared); 1,228 burglaries (56% cleared); 948 thefts (65% cleared); and 1,987 other serious offenses (87% cleared).

The continuing long-term increase in crime rates is largely attributable to urbanization, tourism, and drugs, and the increasing involvement of non-Cypriots in serious offenses in the free areas of the Republic. For example, the number of such persons involved in cases of illicit narcotics in 1997 was 70, increasing to 203 in 2001.

The legal system is headed by the Supreme Court. Lower courts include district courts and assize courts. In the first instance, criminal offenses are tried by the pertinent District Court or Assize Court. Serious criminal offenses are heard by the Assize Court, which consists of President of a District Court, a Senior District judge, and a District Judge.

The Central Prison, administered by the Ministry of Justice and Public Order, is the only prison and correctional institution. It includes a maximum security block, a medium-security section, an "open" prison, and a halfway house for those on an outside employment program as part of their pre-release preparation. Prisoners are allowed frequent visits, and a system of both escorted and unescorted home visits are basic features of the prison regime. The administration and enforcement of such noncustodial sanctions as probation and supervision orders are the responsibility of the Welfare Department in the Ministry of Labor. The existing system of corrections is lacking any rehabilitation programs per se.

Police Profile

Background

Due to the fact that Cyprus was under British rule from 1878 to 1960, the police embody significant British influences in both structure and policing methods. Upon taking control of Cyprus, as part of the reform of the Ottoman system of criminal justice that had existed since 1571 when the Ottoman Turks occupied Cyprus, the British established the Cyprus Military Police, an organ of social control (Kapardis 2001). The colonial model of policing associated with the Royal Irish Constabulary—and not the London Metropolitan Police as established by Sir Robert Peel's Metropolitan (London) Police Act of 1829—was introduced (Jeffries 1952). Following an unsuccessful uprising by Greek-Cypriots in October 1931 and the burning of Government House, the name of the police was changed to the Cyprus Police Force in 1935.

Articles 130(1) and 130(2) of the 1960 Constitution of the Republic of Cyprus provided for the Cyprus Police Force and a gendarmerie (Chorofilaki). The latter had responsibility for law and order in rural areas. Both police forces consisted of 70% Greek-Cypriots and 30% Turkish-Cypriots, overrepresented since they made up 18% of the population. According to the Annual Police Report for 1960, selected police members were sent for specialist training overseas, mainly to England. In order to deal with the state of emergency in December 1963, the government merged the two police forces with law 21/1964 and quickly recruited 700 police officers to fill the vacuum created by the sudden desertion of its Turkish-Cypriot members and to deal with the continuing violent conflict.

Organizational Description

In 2002, the Cyprus police had 4,858 members, including 545 special constables and 22 civilian public servants. Of those who joined during the period 1995–2002, 4% held a university degree, 11% a college diploma, and 85% a high school certificate. In June 2003, the gender distribution was 85% males and 15% females. The absence of female officers is most noticeable among the high echelons of the police hierarchy (*Phileleftheros*, 26 May 2003, p. 4). Of the total number of serving personnel in 2002, 32.9% are involved in such nonpolice duties as guarding of foreign embassies and semigovernmental organizations, immigration, central information service, and overseas postings. According to the Koulentis and Zacharias (2003) report on the personnel needs of the Cyprus Police, the effective rate of police involved in strictly defined police duties is 380 per 100,000 of the population. The Chief of Police enjoys a great deal of autonomy, but the Minister of Justice and Public Order, who is responsible for the police, presents the budget of the service in parliament. The Chief of Police and the Deputy Chief of Police are appointed by the President of the Republic, nor-

mally after consulting with the Minister of Justice and Public Order.

There are ten ranks: constable, sergeant, inspector, chief inspector, assistant superintendent, superintendent, chief superintendent, assistant chief of police, deputy chief of police, and chief of police. The structure of the service consists of the Chief of Police, Deputy Chief of Police (research and development and computer departments), four Assistant Chiefs of Police responsible for the departments of education, administration and inspections, operations, and support. Administratively, the police serve in the following districts, each one headed by a District Police Officer: Nicosia, Limassol, Paphos, Larnaca, Famagusta, and Morphou. (The Kyrenia district has been occupied by the Turkish army.) There is also a separate category of special constable with no promotion prospects unless one applies and joins the force as a constable.

The requirements for selection as a constable include being no more than twenty-five years of age and at least a high school graduate or up to age thirty-five if a degree holder, successful performance in a written examination set by the Ministry of Education, an interview, a medical examination, and a physical fitness test. Promotion up to the rank of inspector is on the basis of a written examination, assessment of one's performance by one's superiors, and interview by the Police Board. Promotion to the rank of chief inspector and above rests with the Chief of Police. For all ranks, there is a minimum years of service requirement. Police officers have a right of appeal to the Supreme Court of the Republic against the promotion decisions of the Police Board and/or the Police Chief.

According to a Ministry of Justice and Public Order report, 688 more police are needed as a result of new departments and positions being created in the context of Cyprus's compliance with EU norms (*Phileleftheros*, 23 May 2003, p. 6). It is worth noting in this context that the *EU Progress Report for Cyprus Towards Accession* (1999:44) stated that "the Cyprus Police is a well established and stable institution. Officers are well trained and instances of corruption are rare...." The new era for the Cyprus Police has been under way for a few years, and there continue to be challenges (Christofides 2003:8).

Functions

The missions of the Cyprus Police are to

- Maintain law and order
- Preserve the peace

- Prevent and detect crime
- Arrest offenders

In the event of a declared state of emergency, their mission is to defend the Republic of Cyprus. Among other miscellaneous duties, the police provide a range of social services and humanitarian assistance to the public, deliver military orders to their recipients, and enforce court orders. The police enforce both the criminal law and local by-laws.

Training

The duration of formal training for probationary constables is three years (one at the Police Academy and two on placement in normal police duties). For sergeants and inspectors, the training is six weeks; and for more senior ranks, there are specialist training seminars and workshops. The curriculum for constables and sergeants includes English as a compulsory second language. In addition, the Police Academy regularly offers courses in Arabic, Turkish, French, Spanish, and Russian, as well as a broad range of specialist training courses.

Police Public Projects

In every police district, there is a Crime Prevention Squad. Local police regularly address students from the primary through university level, and national service recruits on crime prevention measures such as target hardening and minimizing the risk of traffic accidents. In addition, police liaise with local authorities and nongovernmental organizations (NGOs) in the context of community policing. Finally, police officers appear on regular public information programs on radio.

Police Use of Firearms

Active police officers are issued a service revolver, which they return upon retirement. The use of firearms is regulated by Article 7(3) of the Constitution and Police Regulation 5/26 (paragraph 15). In addition, criminal law provisions regarding self-defense also apply. In essence, police use of firearms is permitted only as a last resort in a few strictly defined cases. As far as it has been possible to ascertain, no statistics are available on police use of firearms, but suffice it to say that it is a rare event in Cyprus.

Complaints and Discipline

There is no independent authority to investigate complaints against the police. The Chief of Police is notified about any complaints against members of the police by a member of the public. Such complaints are normally the responsibility of the District Police Officer who appoints an "Investigative Officer" of a higher rank than the officer concerned to examine the complaint and submit a comprehensive report within thirty days. The officer is informed of the complaint and the investigation and has a right to make a statement. If a serious violation of the provisions of the Police Act (Law 53/89) and/or the Police Discipline Regulations (Police Discipline Offenses, Chapter 285), and Police Standing Orders 1/19 and/or the Police Code of Ethical Conduct (legislated in September 2003) is documented, the officer concerned is charged and a Disciplinary Committee appointed by the Chief of Police to hear the case and pass sentence. In such a case, the police officer under investigation has a right to legal counsel. If no serious disciplinary infraction is documented, the matter is referred back to the District Police Officer for action. The Minister of Justice and Public Order approves the three members of the Disciplinary Committee and its Chairman. The Committee has the power to subpoena witnesses and documents (paragraph 14 (1)a). A police officer can appeal against the decision of the Disciplinary Committee to the Appeals Board. If the investigation against an officer documents a serious criminal offense, the Chief of Police may order a criminal investigation while the officer is suspended from duty pending the investigation.

A member of the public can also complain about police behavior to the Attorney General who can appoint an "investigative officer." In addition, a police member can institute civil legal proceedings against a colleague in the courts. Complaints by a police officer against a colleague as well as claimed violations of the Police Discipline Regulations are dealt with following the same procedure used in complaints filed by the public. Legislation pending in Parliament in 2003 would provide for a new Department of Internal Affairs, which is meant to fight corruption within the police, and to provide more efficient and effective investigations and prosecutions in cases of police misconduct. The extent to which a police service thoroughly investigates complaints by and against its active members is an indication of the degree to which it embodies and safeguards human rights.

In compliance with the UNESCO decision in its 21st Congress in October 1980, the police code of ethics that is taught to new recruits includes training in human rights and includes the UN Universal Declaration of Human Rights, the European Convention on Human Rights (ratified via Law 39/

1962), and relevant articles of the Constitution of Cyprus. Nonpolice experts teach courses on human rights at the Police Academy. The Attorney General's Office, the Ombudsman, and the Commissioner for Human Rights investigate violations of human rights. Furthermore, allegations of human rights violations within the police and vis-à-vis the public are also investigated by the aforementioned agencies.

Terrorism

There are no terrorist organizations in Cyprus. Inside the police and in collaboration with the Attorney General's office, the agencies charged with responding to terrorism are the Central Information Service, the Office for Combating Terrorism, Crime Intelligence Bureau, Criminal Investigation Department, and the Financial Crime Unit. Outside the police, the responsible agencies are the Cyprus Financial Intelligence Unit and the Coordinating Committee Against Terrorism in the Attorney General's office, headed by the Deputy Attorney General.

International Cooperation

The Cyprus Police Force is a member of Europol, and part of the network of the EU police services and police cooperation. In addition, Cyprus has signed bilateral agreements for police cooperation with fourteen countries, namely the Czech Republic, Malta, Cuba, Lebanon, Romania, Israel, China, Egypt, Greece, Poland, Hungary, Italy, Russia, and Syria. International assistance in training has been received from the United Kingdom, United States, Greece, Russia, Germany, and France. No program for the exchange of officers with other countries has been established.

Police Education, Research, and Publications

Cyprus police personnel have attended higher education courses at the University of Cyprus, Staff College Bramshill (United Kingdom), University of Exeter (United Kingdom), FBI National Academy (United States), and the National Defense College of Greece.

Leading researchers include:

Chief Inspector M. Hadjidimitriou, PhD
    (Middlesex University)
Chief Inspector Z. Zacharia, BA (Psychology)
M. Iordanous, PhD, Director of Studies, Police
    Academy

The web address for the Police Academy is *www.police.gov.cy*.

Funding applications for police research can, in the main, be made to the Ministry of Justice and Public Order. In addition, the Research Advancement Foundation in Cyprus and various law enforcement research programs of the European Union advertize research grants on police-related topics.

Police publications include the periodical *Astynomika Chronika* (Police Chronicle), which is published regularly and contains a variety of articles on police-related topics by local and foreign authors. The two-volume work by the late P. Machlouzarides (1973) provides interesting material on policing and crime for the period up to 1960.

ANDREAS KAPARDIS

Bibliography

Accountancy Cyprus . "International and Cyprus economy." *Accountancy Cyprus, The Journal of the Institute of Certified Public Accountants of Cyprus* 71 (2003): 64–66.

Bank of Cyprus. *The Cyprus Economy in Figures 2002.* Bank of Cuprus. 2003. Available at: www.bankofcyprus.com.

Bogden, M. "The Emergence of Police—The Colonial Dimension." *British Journal of Criminology* 27, no. 1 (1987): 4–14.

Christofides, M. "Astinomia kai evropaiki enosi: prooptikes, efthines kai ipoxrewseis" (Police and the European Union: Scope, Responsibilities, and Obligations). Nicosia: European Union Office, Research and Development Department, Police Headquarters, 2003.

Cyprus, Republic of, Statistical Service. *Criminal Statistics.* Nicosia: Government Printing Office, 2000.

European Union. "EU Progress Report for Cyprus Towards Accession."

Hadjidimitriou, M. "Obtaining Money by Deception: An Overview of the Situation in Cyprus." In *Economika Egklimata stin Kipro: Mia Polithematiki Proseggisi* (Economic Crimes in Cyprus: A Multidisciplinary Approach), edited by M. Krambia-Kapardis, A. Kapardis, and N. Kourakis, 39–59). Athens: Sakkoulas Publishers, 2001.

Hadjidimitriou, M. "Askisi vias kata ton melon tis astinomias Kyprou, 1996–2000" (Violence Against Cyprus Police Personnel, 1996–2000). Nicosia: Police Headquarters, 2001.

Hill, G. Sir, ed. *A History of Cyprus.* Cambridge: Cambridge University Press, 1952.

Iordanous, M. "Isigitiki ekthesi gia themata ekpethefsis tis kipriakis astinomias" (Issues Pertaining to the Education of Cyprus Police Personnel: A Report). Nicosia: Police Headquarters, 2003.

Jeffries, S. C. *The Colonial Police.* London: Max Parish, 1952.

Kapardis, A. *Society, Crime and Criminal Justice in Cyprus, 1878–1900.* Athens: A.N. Sakkoulas, 2001.

Koulentis, C. and Zacharia, Z. "I anagkes tis astinomias se anthropino dinamiko" (The Personnel Needs of the Police). Nicosia: Research and Development Department, Police Headquarters, 2003.

Machlouzarides, P. *Criminality in Cyprus.* 2 vols. Nicosia: Police Headquarters, 1973.

THE CZECH REPUBLIC

Background Material

The Czech Republic was established as a modern state in 1918 (known then as the Czechoslovak Republic) when the Austrian-Hungarian Empire split. At that time, the country was largely formed from three historical territories—Bohemia, Moravia, and Slovakia. In the elections in 1948, the Communist Party won, and the Czechoslovak Socialistic Republic (the name was changed in 1960s) became part of the socialist bloc. In 1968, Czechoslovakia attempted to implement significant changes in the socialistic system, and to create "socialism with human a face." These attempts ended with the occupation of Czechoslovakia by armies of the Soviet Union and other socialist countries, on August 21, 1968. This occupation continued for the following twenty-three years. *Perestroika* in the Soviet Union in the 1980s gave Czechoslovakia the opportunity to attempt to implement the changes attempted in the late 1960s. In 1989, the political system was changed and the Czech and Slovak Federative Republic started building a market economy. An independent Czech Republic (consisting of Bohemia and Moravia) and an independent Slovak Republic were established on the January 1, 1993. The Czech Republic is a member-state of the United Nations, Organization for Security and Co-operation in Europe, NATO, Council of Europe, and European Union.

The Czech Republic is located in central Europe; it borders Germany on the west, Austria on the south, Poland on the north, and Slovakia on the east. It has a total area of 78,864 square kilometers, and a population of 10,246,178 (2004 estimate). The capital is Prague. The ethnic composition of the population is as follows: Czechs 94.2%; Slovaks 1.9%; Poles 0.5%; Germans 0.4%; Ukrainians 0.2%; and others 2.8%. Czech is the official language, but Slovak is also spoken. A majority (59%) of the population professes atheism, while 32% adheres to Christianity. The per capita GDP purchasing power parity is US $15,700 (2003 estimate).

Contextual Features

The head of state is the president. The legislative branch of the government is a bicameral parliament. The parliament consists of the Chamber of Deputies, which has 200 MPs and a proportional voting system, and a Senate, with 81 senators and a majority voting system.

The Czech Republic employs a continental system of law. The Ministry of Justice, the supreme judiciary body, oversees the Constitutional Court, the Supreme Court, the Supreme State Prosecutor Office, the Supreme Administrative Court, the High Court (Prague, Olomouc), the High State Prosecutor Office (Prague, Olomouc), Regional Courts (8), Regional State Prosecutor Offices (8), District Courts (86), and District State Prosecutor Offices (86).

The corrections system is part of the Ministry of Justice. The Prison Service is a special armed force designated for the administration of all prisons, transport of all prisoners, and protection of the courts. The service is responsible for pre-trial custody, custody during prosecution, and execution of sentences after trials. The Service is divided into the Prison Guard, Judicial Guard, and Administrative Service.

There are thirty-five prisons in the Czech Republic, divided into the following four categories:

- Prison with supervision
- Prison with surveillance
- Prison with security
- Prison with top security

Each prison is designated for various classes of prisoners, including men, women, underage, pre-trial custody, serious and dangerous criminals, and life sentences.

The total capacity of prisons in the Czech Republic is 15,400 inmates. At the end of 2003, the total number of persons held in prison was 17,270. Consequently, the prison system is overloaded by approximately 12%. As a result, a number of alternative forms of punishment are being introduced such as community service and fines.

Drugs are the largest growing area of illegal activity. By comparison with recent years, there is a significant difference. The Czech Republic used to be primarily a transit country for drugs streaming from the Middle East through the Balkan Peninsula to Middle Europe and heading to the West. Today, the Czech Republic has become a target country, and the street price for heroin and cocaine has decreased significantly in recent years. The inevitable effect has been an increase in the number of local addicts.

Relatively few organized crime activities appear to have originated from within the Czech Republic by Czech criminals. The few organized domestic crime activities include:

Organized prostitution of Czech girls
Production and distribution of Czech
    methamphetamine, known as a "pervitin"
Counterfeiting of Czech currency

More common is evidence of collaborative criminality between Czechs and foreigners, that have been either controlled from abroad, and the illegal goods or proceeds of crime have come from abroad or have been directed abroad. It is estimated that approximately 90% of all organized crime activities are international in character.

Foreigners in the Czech Republic operate mostly within groups from the former Soviet Union (generally called "Russian-speaking groups," including groups from White Russia, Ukraine, Georgia, Chechnya, and so on); and from Balkan (Kosovo Albanians) and from East Asia (Chinese and Vietnamese). They have connections to criminal organizations throughout Europe, the United States, Canada, China, Vietnam, and other countries of East Asia.

The activities of a number of these groups activities have merged with the activities of domestic Czech groups. Small groups or individual Czech citizens have been usually serving as "support services" in foreign structures. They provide legal services and counseling, and arrange and perform contacts with authorities and institutions. They cover purchases and the rental of facilities and properties, and they establish small limited or share companies to cover illegal business activities of criminal groups. (It is impossible for foreigners to establish a business company in the Czech Republic without somebody with Czech citizenship.)

The most significant problems in the Czech Republic in terms of serious economic crimes include:

- Privatization frauds (often connected with controlled bankruptcy of privatized enterprises, not paid loans)
- Loan frauds (valueless deposits, counterfeit deposits, multiple use of the same deposit for several loans in different banks)
- Frauds involving shares (artificial price increase, manufactured credibility of shareholders, illegal transfers of assets)
- Tax frauds (frauds involving value added tax, income tax evasion, failure by employer to pay social and health insurance contributions after they were paid by employees)
- Frauds involving donations, grants, and funds (abuse of funds, usage for other purposes, embezzlement)
- Corruption in political parties (illegal funding of parties, tax frauds with taxable donations, misuse of cash gifts, abuse of in kind support—cars, phones, copy machines)
- Corruption in state administration (fraud and illicit manipulation of state contracts; abuse of privileges by judges, state prosecutors, police officers, and other civil servants)
- Corruption in private sector (providing illegal advantages, damaging of employer)

The Czech mass media uses a special term for very large financial frauds—*tunneling*. The origin of the word is very simple. In the nineteenth century and earlier, when somebody wanted to rob a bank, he had to dig a tunnel to the safe and to steal the gold and money. Nowadays it is not necessary to dig tunnels; paper and a computer are the most powerful tools. But the result is the same—just empty a financial institution (or any other enterprise). To date the largest financial crimes in the Czech Republic have been committed mostly by Czech citizens, by individual perpetrators or small groups of associates.

What the real problem is and where the international factor lies in these cases is the fact that the proceeds of these crimes are usually transferred from the Czech Republic via offshore banks to tax havens. The perpetrators themselves escape from the Czech Republic at the moment when they feel danger of disclosure. They try to obtain new citizenship in other countries, mainly the countries that do not cooperate in legal matters and investigation, such as the Bahamas. Commonly, small companies are established with the assistance of Czech citizens or foreigners who obtained Czech citizenship (mostly limited companies, with a minimum deposit 200,000 CZK or approximately US$6,500). The owner of the company has the right to register other persons as "company associates" in the Czech Business Register. On the basis of official invitation by the company, new "associates" arrive into the country and ask for permission for long-term residency on the basis of establishing a business connection. After they establish new companies, they invite other "associates." Usually the companies have no audited profit, and very often there are no business activities; they serve only to cover other firms, bank accounts, and money transfers to cover criminal activities and money laundering.

Also increasingly popular is the use of fictitious marriages, where the wife of a person involved in activities of organized crime in a foreign country with a recent divorce certificate comes to the Czech Republic as a tourist. She meets a Czech man, very often also with a new/recent divorce certificate, and sometimes also just several weeks out of jail. They fall in love and in a week they arrange to be married. Before the marriage clerk, they have to use an official interpreter, because she does not speak Czech and he does not speak her language. After they are married, she does not live with her new husband. She starts business activities, and the former husband is invited to the Czech Republic as a business associate. After receiving Czech citizenship and another new divorce, she and her former husband are remarried.

Police Profile

Background

The police of the Czech Republic are an armed centralized security force, fulfilling the tasks in the matter of public order, security, and other tasks as determined by Czech law. In the performance of their tasks, the police function in accordance with national and international agreements as approved and ratified by the parliament.

Demographics

The total number of police officers stands at 7,000 (out of which approximately 30,000 are uniformed). There are 11,500 civilian employees affiliated with the police. Approximately 10% of police officers and 50% of civilian employees are females. Ethnic representation of the minorities is not monitored, as it does not have real significance in principle due to a very small percentage of minorities present.

Organizational Description

The police are subordinate to the Interior Ministry. The police are composed of the Police Presidium, central departments, and units with countrywide authority, and departments and units with territory-limited authority (Regional Headquarters, District Directorates). Police departments are constituted by the Minister of Interior after proposal by the Police President.

Generally, the police are divided into different services such as Public Order Police Service, Criminal Police and Investigation Service, Traffic Police Service, Administrative Matters Service, Protection Service, Alien and Border Police Service, Rapid Response Unit, Railway Police Service, and Aviation Service. Police activities are managed by the Police Presidium of the Czech Republic according to Police Act 283/1991.

The Police President is the most senior-ranking officer and is head of the Police Presidium. The Police President is appointed and may be removed by the Minister of Interior upon approval of the Czech Republic Government. He/she is responsible in police matters to the Minister of Interior.

Each Police Service or Unit has its own Director. These Directors are appointed by the Police President. One exception is the Director of the Protection Service of the Czech Republic. Its President is appointed and removed by the Minister of Interior upon assent of the Czech Republic President.

There are no regional or city police forces with similar tasks, only municipal police constabularies responsible for traffic and public order within the framework of the municipality. The municipal police have no right to arrest or to investigate crimes.

There is a small Military Police Force of approximately 250 officers who operate within the Czech Army. This force has limited rights to investigate crimes and accidents within the Army where the offense is believed to have been committed by army personnel. In the case of an emergency Army officers can be seconded to the Police mainly to reinforce fulfilling of protective tasks.

There are a number of specialist units that have roles in crime investigation. The Unit Combating Organized Crime consists of the Organizational Branch, Violent Crime Branch, Branch of Firearms, Explosives and Nuclear Materials, Branch of Trade with Human Beings and Smuggling of Refugees, Branch of Criminal Organizations, Branch of Counterfeiting, Branch of Terrorism and Branch of Investigation and Documentation. There are six regional units located in regional capitol towns outside of Middle Bohemia. The Unit has approximately 435 police officers and 35 civil servants.

The National Drug Central Unit is divided into specialized drug branches (heroin, cocaine, synthetic drugs, and so on). The Unit has approximately 160 police officers and 20 civil servants, including 6 regional units located in regional capital towns.

Both units are experiencing an increase in the number of reported incidents of drug trafficking; trade in human beings; smuggling of refugees and weapons; and counterfeiting of Czech currency.

The Unit Combating Corruption and Financial Crime is located in downtown Prague, close to other government and financial institutions. The directorate of the Unit comprises of the Organizational and Logistical Section, Internal Affairs Section, Special Projects and International Cooperation Section, and the Central Operational Branch. There are seven regional units controlled by the directorate, the largest in Prague (but at various locations), and the other six in regional capital towns of the Czech Republic. Some of these regional units have small satellite detachments. The Unit has approximately 285 police officers and employs 20 civil servants.

The Unit performs police tasks in the area of combating various forms of corruption and large financial crimes, such as privatization and financial frauds, where the state was damaged or where the damage within the private sector was greater than 50 million CZK (approximately US$1.5 million), and crimes within capital and financial markets.

The Unit Combating Illicit Proceeds and Tax Crime, also located in downtown Prague, investigates all cases of money laundering and various tax frauds. The Unit has approximately 280 police officers and 20 civil servants located in central and regional branches.

There is a direct connection between these units and the responsibilities of Czech National Bank as a regulatory body of the national banking system and the Ministry of Finance. They cooperate very closely with the General Directorate of Customs, the Finance Ministry's Financial Analytical Unit, and Commission for Securities and Bank Association. They collaborate with other ministries, government agencies, intelligence services, and the biggest financial institutions in the Czech Republic. Both units obtain information from their own operations and investigations as well as information provided by foreign police bodies. All information is checked, analyzed, and loaded into the analytical information system of the units.

The Czech Republic police force has the following ranks:

Noncommissioned officers (high school education required)

- Junior sergeant
- Sergeant
- Senior sergeant

- Junior warrant officer
- Warrant officer
- Chief warrant officer

Commissioned officers

- Junior lieutenant (associate degree level of education required)
- Lieutenant
- Senior lieutenant
- Captain
- Major (full university degree required)
- Lieutenant-colonel
- Colonel

Generals (full university degree required)

- Major-general (deputy police presidents, heads of special units, and so on)
- Lieutenant-general (police president)

Functions

According to Police Act # 283/1991, the police fulfill the following tasks:

Protect the security of people and property

Secure public order

Fight against terrorism

Detect criminal acts and locate offenders

Investigate criminal acts

Protect national borders in a limited framework

Protect constitutional principles of the Czech Republic and persons who are protected according to international agreements during their stay in the Czech Republic

Protect embassies, parliament buildings, the Constitutional Court, Ministry of Foreign Affairs, Ministry of Internal Affairs, other buildings of special interest for internal order and security, and buildings that are protected according to international agreements that the Czech Republic is obligated to fulfill

Supervise security and smoothness of the road traffic

Detect misdeeds and if determined by special law also solve them

Maintain registers and statistics necessary to fulfill police tasks

Announce nationwide search, including publication of data necessary to identify fugitives

Help the Prison Service in searches for escaped prisoners

Search for and arrest people who have been ordered into custodial care and escaped

Provide emergency protection of nuclear facilities and protection of nuclear material transports according to special law

Check policy certificates proving validity of liability insurance for damages caused by vehicle use

Training

According to Czech law, any applicant who fulfills the following criteria can join the Police:

- Minimum 18 years of age
- No criminal record
- Has obtained the degree required for the position of interest
- Has the ability to serve as a policeman according to his/her health, physical condition, and personality
- Has served in the military, if obliged to do so according to Czech law
- Has the competence to perform legal acts
- Is entitled to become acquainted with classified information according to Czech law, if this entitlement is required for the position that he/she is applying for
- Is not a member of any political party
- Is not an entrepreneur or involved in a similar gainful activity, nor member of a managerial board of any corporation

After joining the police, each recruit with a high school education has to pass a twelve-month basic police training program at one of the Interior Ministry's Secondary Police Schools. The Police Academy of the Czech Republic provides law and security education at both bachelor and master's levels.

Police Use of Firearms

A police officer has the right to use a firearm in the following situations:

Deflect an imminent or ongoing attack against him or an attack against the life or health of another person in the case of inevitable protection or during an assistance in inevitable protection

When a dangerous offender, against whom the officer intervenes, does not give up after the officer's summons or is reluctant to leave his hideaway

When there is no other way to break the resistance at preventing the police officer's duty to act

Prevent a dangerous offender from escaping, who cannot be captured any other way

Deflect a dangerous attack against a guarded or protected object, after would-be attacker has failed to heed summons to stand down

When there is no other way to stop a means of transport, when the driver seriously endangers the life or health of other people by reckless driving, and who does not stop on repeated summons or a sign given in accordance with special regulations

Force a means of transport to stop, when driver does not stop after repeated summons or warning sign given in accordance with special regulations, in the area close to national border

When a person against whom the coercive measure of threatened use of a firearm or the coercive measure of a warning shot was used does not obey instructions of a police officer whose aim is to ensure the security of his own person or that of another person

When needed to neutralize an animal endangering the life or health of people

In brief, a police officer can use a weapon only when it is obvious that any other coercive measures would not be effective.

The police of the Czech Republic are an armed security force. Therefore, all officers keep their own personal guns (since 2002, all police officers were issued the CZ 75 D Compact Model, 9mm-caliber Luger, developed according to Czech Police requirements). Special Services of the Czech Police have at their disposal other nonstandard models.

Before a police officer is issued a weapon, he/she is obligated to attend training, and pass tests containing a theoretical part focused on legal terms of use of the gun, secure operations with the gun including maintenance, and practical shooting.

According to internal rules, each policeman has to take all the abovementioned tests and practical shooting annually. Depending on their duties, policemen are divided into three groups: policemen enlisted in the first group are obliged to undertake shooting training every month, and policemen enlisted in the second and third group are obliged to undertake shooting training at least three times a year.

Complaints and Discipline

The Inspection unit of the Minister of Interior fulfills its tasks on the basis of the Code of Criminal Procedure and the Police Act 283/1991. The Police Act determines the Inspection unit's main task, which is detection of crimes perpetrated by policemen and its investigation. When involved in the penal proceeding against policemen, the Inspection unit fulfills the duties that are usually fulfilled according to the Code of Criminal Procedure by standard police units against other perpetrators.

The amendment of the Code of Criminal Procedure, which came into force on July 1, 2002, brought remarkable changes to the area of policing criminal investigations. A fundamental change was the transfer of responsibility for investigation from the police investigators to state prosecutors. This change is expected to improve the impartiality and proficiency of investigation.

The Control and Complaints Section of the Police Presidium is responsible for the supervision of police service activities, and dealing with citizen complaints. This section's principal responsibilities follow:

Analyze whether a crime has occurred, and whether the perpetrator is a police officer;

Analyze information in cases of missing police officers and suicides of police officers, and suicides and self-injury of citizens connected to policing;

Check work of police units to document the level of following the law and internal rules, and to propose solutions to correct any deficiencies;

Deal with complaints related to procedural incorrectness of police officers;

Analyze and interpret results of surveys

Cooperate with the Inspection unit of the Minister of Interior.

International Cooperation

All activities in the field of international police cooperation are provided by the Police Presidium's International Police Cooperation Division, which is divided into sections as described below.

Europol National Unit

On March 5, 2002, the Czech Republic and Europol signed a Cooperation Agreement, which came in force on August 16, 2002. This agreement provides guidelines for cooperation in the field of combating serious international organized crime, and sets conditions for strategic intelligence and personal data exchange.

The Europol National Unit has been built within the Police Presidium; operational readiness was expected to be reached at the time of the Czech Republic's accession to the Europol Convention, that is, September 1, 2004.

Interpol National Central Bureau

The main tasks of the National Central Bureau of Interpol follow:

1. Provision and improvement of cooperation of all law enforcement agencies in the limits of their national law and with respect to the General Declaration of Human Rights, that is, provision of the Czech Police's communication and cooperation with foreign organizations and security forces combating crime, with the exception of military- and religion-related, racial, and political crimes.

2. Support of institutions contributing to combating crime, especially in the areas of: obtaining and exchange of information related to criminal cases, searches of missing people and belongings, extradition of perpetrators to the Czech Republic, and handing over of perpetrators abroad.

One of the most important Interpol tasks is provision of operational cooperation and information exchange between the Czech Police and foreign partners. In this area, its position is essential and irreplaceable.

International Relations Branch

This branch is responsible for cooperation in international agreements and treaties (Council of Europe, bilateral and multilateral treaties), ensuring preparedness of the Czech Police to join the European security structures (Schengen cooperation), and organizing sending liaison officers (Slovakia, Russia, Ukraine, and Europol) and police officers posted abroad, especially within international security structures, and police and peacekeeping missions.

Police Education, Research, and Publications

Basic police training is provided by Secondary Police Schools of the Ministry of Interior of the Czech Republic.

The schools in Prague, Brno, and Holesov provide twelve months of basic police training for new recruits with a high school education.

The school in Prague-Ruzyne provides special surveillance training; the school in Jihlava, traffic police training; and the school in Pardubice, criminal investigation training. A university level of law and security education is provided by the Police Academy of the Czech Republic, both bachelor and master's degree. The Academy is also open for police officers and for civilian students. The Department of Education and Administration of Police Schools of the Ministry of Interior of the Czech Republic is responsible for the entire training system.

In addition to standard school training activities, special international courses, seminars, workshops, and conferences have also been organized, especially in the areas of combating organized crime, financial crime, money laundering, and the financing of terrorism. These events are organized in cooperation with experts from various U.S. law enforcement agencies (FBI, DEA, ATF, U.S. Marshals Service, Customs, Secret Service) and police of other countries (such as Royal Canadian Mounted Police, United Kingdom NCIS, Germany, Denmark, The Netherlands, and Norway).

Police Journals (Czech Language)

Kriminalistika, quarterly journal for criminology theory and practice. Available at: *www.mvcr. cz/casopisy/kriminal.htm*.

Policista, monthly journal for police officers. Available at: *www.mvcr.cz/casopisy/policista/ index.html*.

PAVEL CINCAR

D

DENMARK

Background Material

The kingdom of Denmark includes Denmark, the Faroe Islands, and Greenland. The area of Denmark covers 43,000 sq km, including the Jutland peninsula—bordering Germany—and 482 islands, of which one hundred are inhabited. Denmark has a population of 5.4 million, distributed over 2.9 million households. Copenhagen—the capital—is situated on the island of Zealand; 1.1 million people live in the metropolitan area of Copenhagen.

The great majority of the population of Denmark has a Danish background; 8.2% has a foreign background (6.3% immigrants and 1.9% second generation immigrants). The largest immigrant groups come from Turkey (54,000), Iraq (26,000), and Lebanon (22,000). Most immigrants from neighboring countries originate from Germany (25,000).

The language is Danish, which is part of the Nordic subdivision of the Germanic group. The national church is Christian (Lutheran). The great majority (84%) are members of the national church, but only a fraction professes their religion. Islam is the second largest religion in Denmark.

Denmark is a welfare state. Medical treatment and education are free. Those who are not able to generate an income (including unemployment, pen-sion) are financially supported by the state. The gross national product for 2003 was 1,182.7 billion DKK (159.6 billion Euro) or 258,000 DKK (34,800 Euro) per inhabitant. The average income per household—before tax—is 417,500 DKK (56,300 Euro).

Just over half of the population (54%) belongs to the labor force. Denmark is a typical service society. Only 4% of the labor force is employed in the agricultural sector, and 16% in manufacturing. The Danish economy is traditionally based on high quality agricultural products. However, industrial products make up the largest export category.

The Faroe Islands consist of 18 islands and a number of islets and skerries. The Faroe Islands cover an area of 1,400 sq km, and have a population of 44.000 people. The capital is Torshavn. The world's largest island, Greenland, covers 2,175,000 sq km, and has a population of 56,000 inhabitants. The capital of Greenland is Nuuk. Both the Faroe Islands and Greenland are self-governed and represented in the Danish Parliament.

Contextual Features

Denmark is a constitutional monarchy. The fundament of the Danish political system is the Consti-

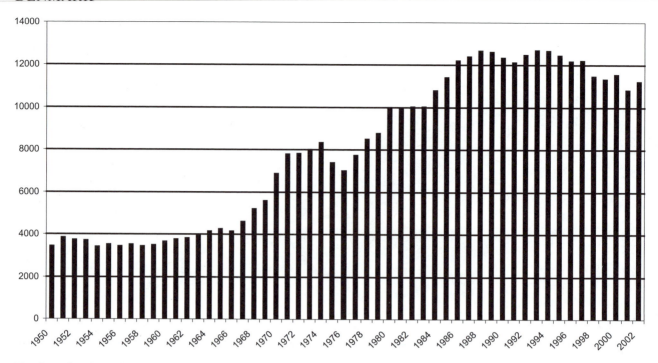

Number of registered penal law violations in Denmark pr. 100,000 inhabitants age 15 or older (1950–2002).
Source: Statistics Denmark, Criminality 2001, Table 1.1

tutional Act of 1849 (revised in 1953). According to the Constitution, the political system is separated in three powers: legislative, executive and judiciary. The Parliament consists of one chamber with 179 members (175 from Denmark, two from the Faroe Islands, and two from Greenland).

Denmark utilizes a civil law system. There is judicial review of legislative acts, and compulsory jurisdiction of the International Court of Justice is accepted with reservations. The Danish police register around half a million penal code violations per year. This number corresponds with around 11,000 registered crimes per hundred thousand inhabitants age 15 or older. Registered crime accelerated in the late 1960s up to the mid-1980s. In the 1990s, the number of registered penal law violations was rather constant and started to fall in the late 1990s.

The great majority of registered penal law violations are for property crimes. In the period 1950–2002, around 95 percent of all penal law crimes were classified as such. About 60 percent of the property crimes were thefts, while burglary stood for 20 percent of the registered property crimes.

A closer look at these crime trends shows that the number of registered violent crimes increased in the 1990s, while the number of property crimes fell. The table (above) indicates that registered crimes in the period 1996–2002 were distributed over the major categories of penal law violations. This table underscores the fact that the number of violent crimes has increased; partly due to an increased willingness to report these kind of offences.

When a defendant pleads guilty, cases are tried by a single professional judge in one of the 82 District

Registered penal law violations in Denmark (1996–2002)

	1996	1997	1998	1999	2000	2001	2002
Sexual crimes	2,536	2,706	2,688	2,981	2,800	2,738	2,919
Violent crimes	13,016	13,581	13,422	14,255	15,157	15,781	16,825
Property crimes	506,461	508,283	476,269	470,280	479,190	447,377	463,479
Other penal crimes	6,475	6,532	6,788	6,675	7,084	7,394	8,288
Total	528,488	531,102	499,167	494,191	504,231	473,290	491,511

Source: Statistics Denmark, Criminality 2001, Table 1.2

Courts. These 82 District Courts have a legal staff of 458 persons. Cases are also tried in the District Court when a defendant pleads not guilty. But in these cases, two lay assessors assist the professional judge. There are around 8,000 lay assessors in Denmark. In exceptional cases, the High Court is used as the court of first instance, for example, in homicide cases. There are two High Courts in Denmark (the Eastern and Western High Courts). In such cases, three professional judges and a jury of 12 citizens are present. The High Courts are also Courts of Appeal for cases started in a District Court. The High Courts have a legal staff of 143 persons. The Supreme Court is the Court of Appeal for cases started in a High Court. By exception, a case started in a District Court may be appealed to the Supreme Court. The Supreme Court has a legal staff of 29 persons.

In general, inmates are placed in so-called open prisons (no external ring wall). Denmark has eight open prisons. In cases where the inmate is considered dangerous, or a risk for escape, he is placed in one of Denmark's five closed prisons. In addition to prisons, there are 40 local jails and eight half-way houses. Total cell capacity was 3,774 in 2003, but only 3,641 cells were used on average.

Nineteen local offices of the Probation Service carry out supervision of persons subject to suspended sentences and inmates on parole. This work is based on four principles: (a) early assistance, (b) proximity to probation officer and family, (c) continuity in probation work, and (d) coordination between prison, probation and social welfare.

The Prison and Probation Service had 4,400 employees in 2003. About one third belongs to the civil staff, while two thirds work as uniformed officers.

Police Profile

Background

The first Danish law concerning the police is dated October 22, 1701. This law was aimed at Copenhagen and described superficially the structure and duties of the Copenhagen police. The duties of the police were primarily maintenance of public order. At that time, criminal investigation was left to citizens themselves.

The 1849 Constitutional Act provides a separation of power in the legislature (Parliament), the executive branch (government), and the judiciary (courts of justice). According to this model, the Parliament makes laws which determine the framework within which the police operate and the duties of the Minister of Justice, who is responsible for the Danish police.

Until 1911, municipalities employed police officers. The Chief of Police was Judge and Mayor as well. In 1919, the Chief of Police was no longer Judge anymore—as demanded by the Constitution, but first put into practice by the Administration Act of Justice. In the years 1911–1938, the Danish police was reformed to a national corps. The principles underlying the national corps are effectiveness, cooperation, and a single system for recruitment, education, and equipment.

Organizational Description and Demographics

Today the Danish police are a national corps under the authority of the Minister of Justice. The country is divided into 54 police districts. In 1973, the number of police districts was reduced from 72 to 54. The rationale for the reform was to provide every district with a 24-hour service. To compensate for the negative side effects of this centralization, "community police stations" were established in 1985 following a pilot program in nine police districts.

The Chief Constable is the autonomous head of a district. In addition, he or she is the public prosecutor in the District Court. The Chief Constable must have a university degree in law. Every police district is divided into four major sections: the Uniform Branch, Criminal Investigation Department (CID), Public Prosecution Section, and Administration.

The Uniform Branch is—depending of the size of the district—divided into several sections. Taking the Police District of Hillerød (in Northern Zealand) as an example, the Uniform Branch is split into the Patrol Services, Front Desk, Community Police, Crime Prevention, and Traffic Police. The Criminal Investigation Department is divided into three geographical sections and two specialists sections: Fraud and Narcotics. The CID also includes the Criminal Intelligence Section.

In general, police officers work for the Uniform Branch and detectives for the CID. Both the Uniform Branch and the CID utilize seven ranks. After completing the primary education at the Police College, a police officer will start as a Constable. The next rank, Sergeant, is achievable for everyone after some years of duty. The Uniform Branch is the starting position for every newly educated police officer. Eighty-four percent of the officers in the Uniform Branch hold one of these two ranks. With time, police officers may apply for a job at the CID, though their rank will remain the same. Seventy-seven percent of CID officers hold one of these two lowest ranks.

The next rank, Chief Inspector, generally pertains to a position in lower management. This position demands additional courses at the Police College. Ten percent of Uniform Branch officers

Personnel of the Danish Police (2002)

	National police	Copenhagen	Rest of Denmark	Faroe Islands and Greenland	Total
Legal Staff	60	62	329	10	461
Uniform Branch	1,748*	1,469	4,938	204	8,359
CID	520	390	1,142	-	2,052
Office Personnel	538	315	1,310	48	2,211
Total	2,866	2,236	7,719	262	13,083

* Including 909 aspiring police officers (Police College)
Source: National Police (www.politi.dk)

and 12 percent of CID officers hold the rank of Chief Inspector.

The remaining four ranks are reserved for middle and top management workers. Respectively, these ranks are Superintendent, Deputy Chief Superintendent, Chief Superintendent, and Commander. Four percent of Uniform Branch officers and 11 percent of CID officers hold one of these top ranks.

The number of executive police officers (Uniform Branch plus CID) increased from 6,575 officers in 1950 to 10,411 officers in 2002. Yet this increase is less dramatic when considered in relative terms. In 1950, there was one police officer per 650 Danish inhabitants while in 2001, there was one police officer per 525 inhabitants.

Seen in comparison to the increase in penal law violations, the number of police officers has increased very moderately during the period 1950–2002.

The head of the National Police is the National Commissioner. The National Commissioner's Office was established in 1938. The Chief Constables were concerned that the function of the National Commissioner would jeopardize their independence. Nonetheless, in the 1950s, a proposal of a working group under the authority of the Ministry of Finance to eliminate the function of the National Commissioner was not

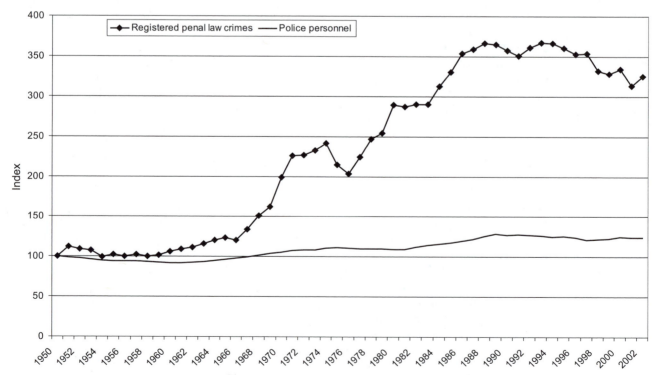

Changes in registered penal law crimes and police officers per 100,000 inhabitants (1950 = 100).
Source: Statistics Denmark and the National Police

put into effect. Instead of eliminating the function of the National Commissioner, more tasks of the Ministry of Justice were delegated to this function. Today the National Commissioner's Office consists of eight departments. The National Commissioner is not only responsible for these eight departments, but is also empowered to supervise and establish guidelines for the general organization, administration, and performance of duties. The National Commissioner may not direct or interfere with concrete law enforcement activities in the districts. In that sense, the Chief Constables remain independent.

Operational Support under Department A includes, for example, cases concerning homicide, organized crime (e.g., smuggling narcotics or human beings), and serious economic crimes like VAT-fraud. Formally, Operational Support functions under the authority of the local Chief Constable.

The National Security Intelligence Service may be compared, with limitations, to the American CIA, while Department A may be compared to the FBI. The National Security Intelligence Service is under the authority of the Minister of Justice and controlled by a special committee. This committee consists of five members. Each represents a political party in the Parliament. Everything discussed in this committee is considered confidential.

Functions

The 1919 Administration Act of Justice provides the fundamentals for the duties of the police. Section 108 states:

1) The duties of the police are to maintain security, peace, and order; to ensure that laws and regulations are complied with; to take the necessary steps to prevent crime; to investigate crimes and to prosecute offenders.
2) Other duties may be imposed on the police with the consent of the Minister of Justice.

The first part of Section 108 refers to the function of the Uniform Branch: to maintain security, peace, and order, and to ensure compliance of laws and regulations. A key strategy to fulfilling this task is patrol. This might be done by car, motorcycle, horse, bicycle, or on foot.

The police are also supposed to prevent crime. At the national level, the Crime Prevention Council was established in 1971. The General Assembly of the Council consists of 40 private and public organizations. The Secretariat of the Council employs 32 persons and is organizationally placed under the National Police. The Council is concerned with technical, tactical, and environmental crime prevention. Police Districts have incorporated crime prevention in the Uniform Branch.

By law, crimes reported to, or detected by, the police should be investigated. In reality, however, this is a question of priority. The CID has primary responsibility for criminal investigation. When a suspect is identified, the police may prosecute the case, yet not all cases are prosecuted. This largely reflects the principle of expediency in the Danish criminal law.

The second part of Section 108 refers to other duties that may be imposed on the police. The police have several administrative functions. The police conduct driving tests and issue driver's licenses and passports, administrate lost property, and take care of the registration of motor vehicles. The police are also responsible for cases concerning the custody of minors and matrimonial law, as well as for bringing debtors before the so-called "Bailiff's Courts," and serving summonses and court orders to offenders and witnesses. Finally, the police are part of Denmark's "total defense structure," which means performing duties in connection with early warnings and evacuation of civilians in case of major peace- or war-time emergencies.

Training

Requirements for joining the Danish police force are:

- Danish citizenship or right to citizenship

Departments of the National Commissioner's Office

Department A	International cooperation, operational support, and analysis of crime intelligence
Department B	Personnel and recruitment
Department C	Finances
Department D	Computerized data systems
Department E	Immigrants and refugees
Department F	Police College
Department G	National Security Service
Department H	Maintenance (buildings)

- Minimum age of 21 years
- Good health with normal hearing and no colorblindness
- Driver's license

Besides the above requirements, the following aspects are considered important:

- Under the age of 29 years
- Reasonably tall and physically suited to police work
- Sight no worse than 6/12–6/24
- Good school record
- Orderly personal and economic conditions
- No criminal record
- Some knowledge of foreign languages

About one out of ten applicants is selected for primary education at the police academy. Basic police training is provided in four stages: The first part consists of eight months' training at the Police College in Copenhagen. This is followed by twelve months of in-service training in a large police district. The third part consists of an additional eight months of training at the Police College, which is concluded with an examination. The last part of the basic training is practical service at a police station and service in the Tactical Support Unit of the Copenhagen Police. In total, basic police training takes four years.

Greenland has its own training requirements for police officers. The Faroe Islands recruit their own officers, but they are educated at the Police College in Copenhagen.

Police Public Projects

There are several police public projects in Denmark. Some projects are of an incidental nature, while others are of a more structural nature. A few examples of the latter are mentioned below. Many communities have neighborhood watch programs, in some cases supported by civil patrols during the evening and night.

A widely used preventive measure is the so-called SSP-Cooperation Program. This program is directed at young people and aims to promote cooperation between Social arrangements, Schools, and the Police. A recent offshoot is the SSP-Plus-Coordination Program, which is aimed at youth from 18 to 24 years old.

Victim support may also be considered as a police public project. In 1998, the National Commissioner initiated the establishment of the Victim Counselling Service on request of the Minister of Justice. This service works independently of the authorities, and all support personnel work on a voluntary basis receiving no remuneration. The police are responsible for informing victims as to the activities and location of victim counselling services.

Police Use of Firearms

Until 1965, the Danish Police generally patrolled unarmed. A shooting incident—whereby four police were killed—changed that situation. Today the standard equipment of a regular patrol officer consists of a 9 mm. Hecker & Koch, USP Compact firearm with Action-3 ammunition, a truncheon and handcuffs. Police officers' combat equipment includes a teargas gun, in addition to fireproof clothing, shield, and helmet.

Danish Police officers are entitled to use force with reference to §§ 13 and 14 of the Danish Penal Law. These paragraphs refer to the right to self-defence and to the right to prevent potential injury or material damage. Firearm use is, however, also guided by internal regulations. When a police officer uses a firearm, regardless of whether it is discharged, the incident must be reported to the National Commissioner. On average, 250 incidents of use are reported per year (see figure, next page). Between 1985 and 2002, the police killed 12 persons and injured an additional 78 persons with firearms—adding to an average of approximately one killing and four injuries per year.

Complaints and Discipline

Regional Public Prosecutors – six in total – deal with complaints regarding the conduct of police officers, investigate criminal cases involving police officers, and decide which charges, if any, should be brought. These Regional Public Prosecutors are supervised by the Police Complaints Board, which consists of one lawyer and two laymen.

As the table (next page) shows, the majority of complaints are dismissed as unfounded. In public debate, it is often suggested that the Regional Public Prosecutor is not the proper authority to deal with complaints concerning police conduct. In this view, the Regional Public Prosecutor is too closely related to the police to be reliable.

An example of the criticism of Regional Public Prosecutors in connection with the investigation of criminal cases involving police officers can be found in the 2003 annual report of Amnesty International. They refer to a police shooting in December, 2001 during which two men, suspected of robbery, were shot dead. The Regional Public Prosecutor decided not to prosecute either of the officers involved, despite the finding by the Police Complaints Board that charges should be brought against one of the officers.

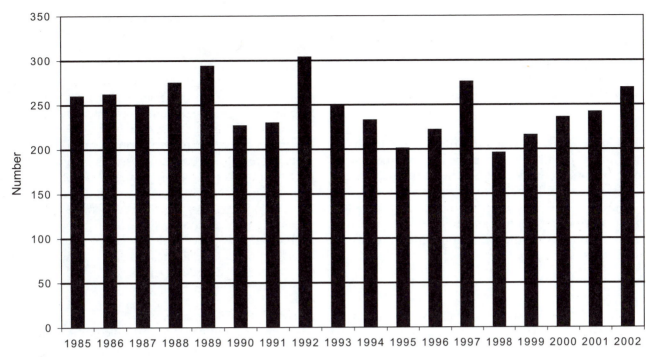

Police use of firearms (1985–2002).
Source: Holmberg, 2004, Table 1, p. 11

On average, 75 disciplinary cases are brought each year (see table, next page). Disciplinary cases may be raised whenever a police officer is suspected of abusing his or her authority or of committing a criminal offense—whether on or off duty. Disciplinary sanctions may vary from a warning to dismissal.

Denmark has ratified the European Convention on Human Rights and Fundamental Freedoms signed by members of the Council of Europe in 1950. Denmark has been frequently criticized by international organizations for its use of solitary confinement. In September 2002, the European Committee for the Prevention of Torture published a report concerning its visit to Denmark in early 2002. The Committee expressed concern about remand detainees being locked in their cells for up to 21 hours a day without access to purposeful activities, as well as the use of solitary confinement.

Safeguards have been introduced to limit the use of court-ordered solitary confinement during pretrial detention, although no limits on maximum duration are set. Similar safeguards are, however, completely unavailable for convicted prisoners who are also denied access to a judicial review of deci-

Conduct cases completed 1996-2001

	1996	1997	1998	1999	2000	2001
Settled in police district(Minor cases)	39	45	48	52	44	52
Complaint withdrawn	32	24	11	18	11	18
Complaint dismissed	12	4	5	7	12	9
Complaint dismissed as unfounded	145	206	162	255	197	241
No criticism but incident regretted	15	10	22	17	12	12
Criticism	4	6	11	12	16	9
Criticism of 'system errors'	1	0	0	0	1	1
Other	12	25	23	19	9	21
Total	260	320	282	380	302	363

Source: Director of Public Prosecutions (Rigsadvokaten), 2002, p. 181

Number of discipline cases

1997	1998	1999	2000	2001	2002	2003
66	58	86	79	83	85	79

Source: National Police (www.politi.dk)

sions made by the prison authorities to hold them indefinitely in solitary confinement. Detainees in court-ordered solitary confinement continue to be locked in their cells for up to 23 hours a day.

Another point of contention concerns the fact that torture is not defined as an offence in Danish law, as noticed by the UN Committee Against Torture in May 2002.

Terrorism

The National Security Intelligence Service is responsible for identifying, investigating, and preventing actions or plans that are or have the potential to develop into threats to the independence and security of Denmark and to the legal order of its society. Operational efforts in this connection are divided into three areas: counter-terrorism, counter-extremism, and counter-espionage.

Denmark cooperates with international approaches to combating terrorism, among other ways through UN Security Council Resolution 1373 and EU Framework Decision 2002/475/RIA. Within the framework of this cooperation, Denmark has an obligation to prevent the preparation of terrorist actions and to ensure that Denmark is not a so-called "safe haven," or place where terrorists have the possibility of setting up bases from which terrorist actions can be planned or implemented. Furthermore, Denmark is committed to ensuring the diligent prosecution of terrorists, as well as to assisting other countries in investigating criminal cases regarding terrorism. The Security Council Resolution and EU Framework Decision, together with the UN Convention on Terrorism Financing, among other things, constitute the basis of the "anti-terror package" passed by the Danish Parliament on May 31, 2002.

The National Security Intelligence Service has no authority to indict in criminal cases. Should an investigation initiate legal proceedings in a criminal case, the case would be passed on to the ordinary police or the prosecution service.

The staff—approximately 400 persons—consists of police officers, office staff, legal advisers, and other academic as well as communications staff, translators and technicians.

Today the major terrorist threat is from international terrorism, particularly due to the terrorist network Al-Qaeda. According to the National Security Intelligence Service, there are persons or circles in Denmark who sympathize with or have links to organizations involved in terrorist activities. It is the objective of the National Security Intelligence Service to monitor any such persons and circles to see whether they are breaking the law or seem likely to do so. The aim is to prevent terrorist activities from being planned and carried out in Denmark, and to prevent Denmark from being used as a base of support for the planning or implementation of terrorist activities in other parts of the world. A central element in counter-terrorism is the cooperation between the immigration authorities and the National Security Intelligence Service with the aim of ensuring that foreigners considered a threat to national security are not granted residence in Denmark.

International Cooperation

Denmark is not just a European country, but first and foremost a Scandinavian country. Police cooperation between Scandinavian countries is based on the Nordic Police Agreement (1968). Danish police officers and prosecutors are allowed to contact their colleagues in other Scandinavian countries without any formal barriers or procedures.

In the context of organized crime, the Police and Customs Cooperation (PCC) agreement is important to mention. In 1984, the PCC agreement was established consisting of two basic elements: (1) a corps of Scandinavian liaison officers with the competence to act on behalf of all Scandinavian countries in cases of drug crimes, and (2) training in the strategic analysis of drug crimes. In 1996, PCC cooperation was broadened to include all forms of international and cross-border crime.

Denmark also participates in coordinated police activities in the Baltic Sea Region. In 1996, the Task Force on Organized Crime in the Baltic Sea Region was founded and has resulted in information exchange centers and joint control activities in connection with smuggling.

As a member of the European Union, Denmark cooperates with the European police agency, Europol, established in 1998. Since 2001, Denmark has also cooperated with the Schengen Agreement.

Finally, Denmark's contribution to peacekeeping missions, generally on request of the United Nations, should be mentioned.

Police Education, Research, and Publications

In Denmark, police education is centralized at the Police College. The Police College provides primarily training for aspiring officers, as well as all sorts of specialty and management courses for functioning officers. Officers demonstrating high potential are sent to a so-called "leader course."

Lawyers constitute the top management of the police. They are educated at the university (faculty of law) and afterwards undergo a special training program at the Ministry of Justice. This training program is not limited to police lawyers; it also includes public prosecutors and lawyers trained to work in the prison and probation service.

Leading Researchers

- Prof. Dr. Flemming Bavig (University of Copenhagen)
- Dr. Lars Holmberg (University of Copenhagen)
- Dr. Britta Kyvsgaard (Ministry of Justice)

Research Funding

- Ministry of Justice, Research Department
- Danish Research Agency
- Scandinavian Research Council for Criminology

Police Journals

- *Dansk Politi.* Editor: Nicolai Scharling. Address: H.C. Andersens Boulevard 38, 1553 København V (blad@politiforbund.dk)
- *Nordisk Tidsskrift for Kriminalvidenskab.* Editor: Britta Kyvsgaard. Address: Justitsministeriet, Slotsholmsgade 10, DK-1216 København K.
- *Scandinavian Journal of Criminology and Crime Prevention.* Editor: Felipe Estrada. Address: Department of Criminology, Stockholm University, SE-10691 Stockholm.

Major Police Publications

- Balvig, Flemming and Lars Holmberg. *Politi og tryghed: Forsøg med nærpoliti i Danmark.* København: Jurist- og Økonomforbundets Forlag, 2004 (in Danish).
- Holmberg, Lars. *Policing Stereotypes: A qualitative study of police work in Denmark.* Berlin: Galda & Wilch Verlag, 2003.

- Kruize, Peter. *Beviskrav, ressourcer og opportunitet: En retssociologisk analyse af påtaleopgivelse og tiltalefrafald.* København: Jurist- og Økonomforbundets Forlag, 2004 (in Danish).
- Politikommissionen. *Betænkning om politiets struktur (betænkning 1409).* København: Statens Information, 2002 (in Danish).
- Politikommissionen. *Betænkning om politilovgivning (betænkning 1410).* København: Statens Information, 2002 (in Danish).

Police-related websites

www.politi.dk (Danish Police)
www.pet.dk (National Security Intelligence Service)
www.jm.dk (Ministry of Justice)
www.danskpoliti.dk (Police Magazine)
www.nsfk.org (Scandinavian Research Council of Criminology)
station2.tv2.dk (Television program about crime and policing)
www.crimprev.dk (Crime Preventive Council)

PETER KRUIZE

Bibliography

Abacci Atlas. www.abacci.com/atlas.
Amnesty International. *Report 2003.* http://web.amnesty.org/report2003/Dnk-summary-eng.
Danmarks Statistik. *Kriminalitet 2001.* København: Danmarks Statistiks trykkeri, 2003.
Danmarks Statistik. *Den lille årbog 2004.* København: Danmarks Statistiks trykkeri, 2004.
Henricson, Ib. *Politiret.* 2nd. udgave. København: Jurist- og Økonomforbundets Forlag, 1999.
Holmberg, Lars. *Politiets brug af skydevåben i Danmark 1985-2002.* Københavns Universitet, 2004.
Kruize, Peter. Denmark. In: Monica den Boer. *Organised Crime: A Catalyst in the Europeanisation of National Police and Prosecution Agencies?* Maastricht: EIPA, 2002, 159–178.
Langsted, Lars Bo, Peter Garde, and Vagn Greve. *Criminal Law in Denmark.* Copenhagen: DJØFPublishing, 1998.
National Commissioner. *The Police in Denmark in the Faroes and in Greenland.* Copenhagen, 1992/2001. www.politi.dk.
National Security Intelligence Service. www.pet.dk.
Rigsadvokaten. *Beretning 2001, Behandling af klager over politiet.* København, 2002.

DJIBOUTI

Background Material

The Republic of Djibouti is a small East African republic in the Horn of Africa bordering the Red Sea and the Gulf of Aden. Its neighbours are Somalia to the south, Eritrea to the north, and Ethiopia to the west. It was formerly part of French Somaliland and, for a while, was known as the French Territory of the Afars and Issas. Its land mass of 23,000 sq km consists of torrid coastal desert, subject to occasional devastating floods. Ten percent of the land is pasture; 1% is forested, and the rest is desert wasteland. Salt and a few other minerals are the extent of its natural resources.

Somalis, consisting of Issas, Issaks, and Gadaboursis, represent 60% of the population; Afars 35 percent; and Ethiopians, Arabs, French and Italians make up the remaining 5%. The official languages are Arabic and French, although Somali and Afar are widely used. Ninety-four percent of the population is Muslim, and Djibouti is an officially Muslim country.

The police organizations are the National Police and the National Gendarmerie. The ministries responsible for policing are the Ministry of the Interior (National Police), and the Ministry of Defense (National Gendarmerie). Djibouti is a member of Interpol and the United Nations.

The estimated population in 2004 was 466,900. Two thirds live in the capital, also called Djibouti, while most of the rest are nomads. At different times, incursions of refugees from Somalia and Ethiopia have swelled the population, put pressure on the economy, and threatened the stability of the country. The fertility rate is almost 5.5, and life expectancy slightly more than 43 years. Seventy-eight percent of men and 58.4% of women are literate.

The economy of the country depends mainly on its port, which lies on major shipping routes between the Mediterranean Sea and the Indian Ocean, and on its railway, which runs from the port to Addis Abba, the capital of landlocked Ethiopia. These make Djibouti integral to the transhipment of goods to the East African highlands. French and American military bases in Djibouti also contribute to the economy. Nevertheless, the economy has been declining, and the country has a substantial international debt. In 2002, 50% of the population was unemployed, and per capita income was $450 a year. Women represent 32.2% of the labour force, particularly in the informal and small enterprise sector.

While there are occasional turbulence and claims of government repression of free speech and the press, Djibouti is striving to become a well-governed democracy. It gained its independence in 1977 and adopted a new constitution in 1992. Between 1991 and 2001, there was a civil war between the dominant Issa and the Afars. This ended with an agreement between the government and the Front for the Restoration of Unity and Democracy (FRUD), which allowed for greater decentralization, more representative local bodies, and a more extensive multi-party system. There is universal suffrage for those over 18 years of age. Under the constitution, women must comprise at least 10% of the candidates of any political party, and, in 2004, they formed 11% of the National Assembly. Both the President of the Supreme Court, who also acts as Interim President of the Republic when the position is vacant, and the Minister of Women's Affairs are women.

Although government finances are overburdened and the pay of public employees is often delayed, there is free health care, and the government is trying to provide primary education to all. There is some discrimination against women in education, property inheritance, and mobility, and close to 98% of women have been subjected to female genital mutilation as young girls. Female genital mutilation is now illegal, and the government has launched an awareness campaign to eradicate it.

Contextual Features

The legal system of Djibouti is a combination of French civil, Islamic (Shari'a), and customary (Xeer) law, the latter of which incorporates nomadic traditions. The French civil law is used for urban crime and civil actions; the Shari'a law is applied in civil and family matters; while the Xeer is used for conflict resolution and victim compensation, such as blood price for murder or rape.

The 1992 constitution established a democratic republic with an executive headed by a president, a unicameral legislative branch, and an independent judiciary. Four existing political parties were given constitutional recognition. All persons were guaranteed equality before the law; freedom of expression, communication and association; presumption of innocence; the right to legal assistance; inviolability of the home; mobility; and freedom from torture or other inhumane treatment. There has been no death penalty since 1995.

In reality, there is some falling short of these high ideals. Various international observers report that traditional Djiboutian practices discriminate against women in inheritance, divorce, and mobility. Political protest is not always tolerated; the media are tightly controlled; security forces arrest dissidents without the required judicial decree, and reports suggest that the independence of the judiciary has been compromised by a 2000 law on judicial organization.

There are four levels of courts. The lower-level courts hear only civil cases. The Superior Appeals Court hears only criminal cases. There are courts with religious judges, or *qadis*, who hear cases governed by the Shari'a law, and the Supreme Court, which is the court of final resort.

There are no official statistics on the crime rate, but the lack of reports suggests that it is relatively low. There are accounts of domestic violence against women, sporadic attacks against the Djibouti-Ethiopian railway, rising petty crime and pick-pocketing in the capital of Djibouti, and prostitution practiced mainly by Ethiopian women which, it is feared, will affect the relatively low incidence of HIV/AIDS infection in Djibouti. While it is suspected there is some drug smuggling through the port, drug use does not seem to be a problem in Djibouti itself. *Khat*, a leaf with a mild stimulant effect imported from Ethiopia, is legal and widely used. Of more concern to Djiboutians is the instability at the borders and the potential for terrorist attacks, particularly from Somalia.

Prisons are overcrowded, and services such as medical care, rehabilitation or education are in short supply or non-existent. Women and men are separated, but juveniles and pre-trial detainees are not always separated from the general prison population. It is reported that inmates must pay for their own food and that prisoners may be beaten or tortured and female prisoners raped by prison guards. Because of overcrowding, on occasion the government has freed prisoners serving short sentences and shortened the prison sentences of others.

Police Profile

Background

The National Police of Djibouti is a hierarchically organized state police organization. It was formed in 1977 as the National Security Force and, later, as the National Police Force. It became the National Police in 2004 with the passage of the *National Police Law*. In 1979, the National Gendarmerie was established as a part of the Djiboutian military forces and reorganized in 1998. Both organizations are modelled on the French policing system.

Demographics

Recruitment into the National Police is open to both men and women and all ethnic groups. There are two levels of entry: the officer level and the subordinate agent level. Candidates are required to be citizens of Djibouti, between the ages of 18 and 25 years, able to read and write in French or Arabic, be at least five feet four inches tall for men or five feet two inches tall for women, be medically fit and of good character.

Both the National Police and the Gendarmerie are uniformed organizations. Only the head of the National Police, pregnant female police members, or those undertaking work incompatible to wearing uniforms are not uniformed.

Organizational Description

The strength of the National Police is roughly 8,000. With a population size of roughly 500,000 people, this means that the police to population ratio is about 1: 62.5 persons. This ratio, which does not include the Gendarmerie, is high compared to western countries.

The National Police come under the jurisdiction of the Minister of the Interior, and the Gendarmerie under the Minister of Defence. The most senior officer of the National Police is the Director General, who reports directly to the Minister of the Interior. The Director General has two deputies. At the lowest level are second and first class agents. Corporals and senior corporals are one step up. There are four ranks of non-commissioned officers: sergeants, staff sergeants, adjutants, and chief adjutants; three ranks of subaltern officers: sub-lieutenants, lieutenants, and captains; and three ranks of superior officer: commanders, lieutenant-colonels, and colonels.

Promotion is generally by seniority, a given number of years in a particular rank, and demonstrated knowledge and professionalism. Training is given and examinations taken for promotion to corporal, sergeant, and adjutant. Sub-lieutenants are direct entrants into the officer class, and promotion from thereon is by the number of years spent in a rank. Chief adjutants can be promoted to sub-lieutenants if they show aptitude for command and pass a professional examination. Two and a half percent of the National Police are officers;

7.5% are adjutants and chief adjutants; 17% sergeants and staff sergeants; 14% corporals and senior corporals; and 59% are agents and cadets.

Although the National Police is a civilian organization, it has many characteristics of a para-military organization. It is rigidly hierarchical, and has a strong code of conduct and discipline. It requires members to seek permission to marry but provides lodging, supplies, and medical services to members and their families.

Functions

The National Police has a general mandate for law and regulatory enforcement, maintenance of public order, the protection of people and property, the collection of intelligence, superintendence of penitentiaries, and investigation. Following French legal practice, investigations are carried out by "judicial police." These are members of the National Police designated and trained to do criminal investigations under the direction of the Attorney General and the examining magistrate or *juge d'instruction*. The National Gendarmerie has similar responsibilities but appears to function in a complementary way. In particular, the Gendarmerie has a special responsibility for presidential security.

The Intelligence Directorate of the National Police contains a unit which collects information on organized crime, economic and financial services, entertainment establishments, liquor outlets, and hotels. It also develops intelligence outlooks. Intelligence information is filed in a national card index. The Immigration Branch in the Intelligence Directorate is responsible for the land, rail, sea, and air borders, and it controls passports, visas, and other travel documents, and maintains an immigration card index.

Public security functions are divided into two sectors responsible respectively for the city and the interior. Apart from the judicial police, there is an urban police branch, which is responsible for peace in the capital, patrol, and traffic control, and accident investigation. There are a number of geographically located detachments which are responsible for neighbourhood policing, calls for service, accident investigation, traffic, investigation, and juvenile and social protection. In addition, there are detachments of static guards at vulnerable points, a detachment of static guards responsible for the National Assembly and the ministerial precinct, and a detachment responsible for guarding the penitentiaries and transferring prisoners. There are also special mobile intervention units for re-establishing order and for responding to attacks on vital points, hostage takings, and similar serious incidents.

Training

Candidates destined to become officers in the National Police are required to have a baccalaureate degree on entry. As recruits, they receive three years of police training. The entry requirements for those destined to become agents require no diploma. They receive one year of recruit training. There is workplace learning and continuous development throughout their careers.

Judicial police are selected by examination after a number of years of service and are given a further six months' training in the police school. Successful completion is dependent on passing two written and two oral examinations. The program includes training in general and special criminal law, criminal procedure, knowledge of crime and investigative techniques, and knowledge of the constitution, government, criminal justice system, human rights and police conduct.

Police Use of Firearms

Under the 2004 police law, the National Police holds a variety of armaments which are issued only when needed for special missions and interventions. In principle, every police officer or agent is issued an individual firearm. An arms inspection is held twice a year by the Assistant Director General of Administration, and periodic inspections are held by detachment commanders.

Complaints and Discipline

There is no mechanism for external oversight or public complaints against the police. However, the code of conduct in the 2004 police law requires police to comply with all laws; to serve the public equally irrespective of nationality, origin, social status or beliefs; to act in a dignified, respectful and courteous manner; to demonstrate exemplary conduct; to employ no more force than necessary; and not to consume *khat* or alcohol during duty hours. Demonstration of political affiliation is also forbidden. Penalties for violating the code of conduct range from warnings and reprimands to transfer, demotion, suspension, house arrest, confinement in a police lock-up (for drunkenness for example), preventive detention, and dismissal. As late as 2003, there were still reports of police violation of human rights, but they tended to be sporadic rather than systematic. A recurring concern is the misuse of force in police control of protests.

Terrorism

Djibouti is not a source of terrorism, but since September 11, 2001, it has become a centre for antiterrorist operations in East Africa and the Arabian Peninsula. Apart from 2,700 French troops, there are 1,800 American, 800 German, and 50 Spanish troops in the country, many of whom are involved in an anti-terrorist operation called "Enduring Freedom." In early 2004, the government of Djibouti became signatory to a number of international conventions and protocols for the suppression of terrorism.

International Cooperation

Djibouti has strong ties with France, which provide considerable financial and technical aid. The United States has also provided aid for the upgrade of infrastructure. Djibouti is also a member of the East African section of Interpol and a member of the United Nations.

Police Education, Research, and Publications

Djibouti has a police academy, but only a rudimentary post secondary educational system, so most post-secondary education takes place overseas, including legal education. Police officers are also permitted to take their training overseas after the first year of training at the police school in Djibouti. Given that policing in Djibouti is built on the French model, there is emphasis on formal training, and examinations to qualify for certain types of police work and to become eligible for promotion. There is only the nucleus of a university in Djibouti. This is Pôle University. There is a daily newspaper, *La Nation*, a rudimentary government website with links to the *Gazeteer*, which publishes the texts of government legislation, and to the Ministry of Women's Affairs, but there is no website or newsletter for the Minister of the Interior or the police. It also appears that no research on the Djiboutian police has been published.

TONITA MURRAY

Bibliography

Djibouti, Government of. Loi no. 46/AN/04/5éme L Portant Statut et Organisation de la Direction de la Police Nationale. *Journal officiel de la République de Djibouti.* March 2004.

Djibouti, Government of. Décret no. 98-0080/PR/DEF Portant Réorganisation de lagendarmerie nationale. *Journal officiel de la République de Djibouti*, 1998.

Djibouti, Government of. *Décret no. 95-0119/PR/MI Fixant les modalities de l'examen d'officier de Police judiciare de la FNP et la composition de la Commission d'examen, le*, November 7, 1995.

Djibouti, Government of. *Constitution de la République de Djibouti*. le 4 septembre 1992, http://droit.francophone. org/doc/html/dj/con/fr/1992/1992dfdjco1.html, November 20, 2004.

Freedom House. *Freedom in the World.* "Political Rights and Civil Liberties." www.freedomhouse.org/research/ freeworld/2002/countryratings/djibouti2.htm, November 20, 2004.

Politinfo. Country Profile: Djibouti, 2003.http://us.poli tinfo.com/information/country.profiles/country_profile_184.html, November 20, 2004.

Politinfo. Country Reports on Human Rights Practices – 2002, March 31, 2003, http://us.politinfo.com/informa tion/human_rights/country_report_2003_014.html, November 20, 2004.

United Nations Development Programme. "Djibouti : Judiciary." *Programme on Governance in the Arab Regions.* www.pogar.org/countries/djibouti/judiciary.html, November 20, 2004.

United Nations General Assembly. "Assistance for the reconstruction and developmentof Djibouti: Report of the Secretary General." Fifty-sixth session, Item 20 (b) of the provisional agenda, August 6, 2001.

United States, Central Intelligence Agency. *The World Factbook*, "Djibouti." www.cia.gov/cia/publications/fact book/ dj.html, 2004.

DOMINICA

Background Material

Dominica was the last of the Caribbean islands to be colonized by Europeans, due chiefly to the fierce resistance of the local Carib populace. France ceded possession to Great Britain in 1763, which made the island a colony in 1805. Dominica achieved independence in 1978.

Dominica is located in the Caribbean. It is an island between the Caribbean Sea and the North Atlantic Ocean, approximately half of the way from Puerto Rico to Trinidad and Tobago. It has a total area of 754 sq km, and a population of 69,278 (2004 est.). The population is composed of black, mixed black and European, European, Syrian, and Carib Amerindian ethnicities. The religious composition of the population is as follows: Roman Catholic 77%; Protestant 15% (Methodist 5%, Pentecostal 3%, Seventh-Day Adventist 3%, Baptist 2%, other 2%); none 2%; and other 6%.

English is the official language. French patois is commonly spoken. The Dominican economy depends on agriculture, primarily bananas, and remains highly vulnerable to climatic conditions and international economic developments. The GDP per capita is $5,400 (2002 est.).

Contextual Features

Dominica is a parliamentary democracy. It is a republic within the Commonwealth, divided administratively into ten parishes. The chief of state is the president, and the head of government is the prime minister. The members of the cabinet are appointed by the president on the advice of the prime minister.

The legistative branch of the government is represented by a unicameral House of Assembly. It has 30 seats, nine appointed senators, and 21 senators elected by popular vote.

Dominica is a member of the Eastern Caribbean Supreme Court, consisting of the Court of Appeal and the High Court. The Eastern Caribbean Supreme Court is located in Saint Lucia. One of the six judges must reside in Dominica and preside over the Court of Summary Jurisdiction.

The crime rate has steadily increased since the 1990s, with burglary being the most prevalent crime. Approximately 1200 burglaries are committed annually, which equals roughly one burglary per every 20 households in Dominica. Rates of robbery, forgery, and grievous bodily harm have also all significantly increased.

Firearms are increasingly used in robberies. The importation of illegal firearms is a growing problem.

Drug trafficking is another major concerns. Marijuana is grown on the island, and both marijuana and cocaine are trafficked.

Police Profile

Background

The Dominica Police Force was founded in 1840. In 1907, the Federal Police Act was passed, which created a single force in the Windward Islands. From 1960, Dominica's police force was managed locally by a British officer.

Demographics

The police force has 412 members, up from 282 in 1978. This is not significant progress, considering that the forces of other Caribbean forces generally number near 1,000.

Challenges

The Dominica Police Force faces a number of challenges. It lacks resources of transportation, storage, funding, equipment, technology, and office space.

Bibliography

"Dominica." *CIA World Factbook.* www.cia.gov/cia/publications/factbook.

"Dominica." *Consular Information Sheet.* US Department of State. http://travel.state.gov/travel/cis_pa_tw/cis/cis_1102.html.

Lestrade, Matthias. "Crime Management and Challenges in the 21st Century." National Symposium on Crime, Commonwealth of Dominica. Research and Development Sub-committee of the Dominica Academy of Arts and Sciences. www.da-academy.org/crimesympo_2.html.

DOMINICAN REPUBLIC

Background Material

The island of Hispaniola was first claimed by Christopher Columbus in 1492. In 1697, Spain recognized French dominion over the western third of the island, which in 1804 became Haiti. The remainder of the island, by then known as Santo Domingo, sought to gain its own independence in 1821, but was conquered and ruled by the Haitians for 22 years. It finally attained independence as the Dominican Republic in 1844.

In 1861, the Dominicans voluntarily returned to the Spanish Empire, but two years later they launched a war that restored independence in 1865.

A long period of unsettled, mostly non-representative, rule was brought to an end in 1966, when Joaquin Balague became president. He maintained a tight grip on power for most of the next 30 years when international reaction to flawed elections forced him to curtail his term in 1996. Since then, regular competitive elections have been held in which opposition candidates have won the presidency. The Dominican economy has had one of the fastest growth rates in the hemisphere over the past decade.

The Dominican Republic is located in the Caribbean. It is composed of the eastern two thirds of the island of Hispaniola, between the Caribbean Sea and the North Atlantic Ocean, east of Haiti. It has a total area of 48,730 sq km and a population of 8,833,634. (July 2004 est.). The population is 16% white, 11% black, and 73% mixed. Ninety-five percent of the population is Roman Catholic. The language of the Dominican Republic is Spanish. The capital is Santo Domingo.

Although the country has long been viewed primarily as an exporter of sugar, coffee, and tobacco, in recent years the service sector has overtaken agriculture as the economy's largest employer, due to growth in tourism and free trade zones. The GDP per capita is $6,000 (2003 est.).

Contextual Features

The Dominican Republic is a representative democracy. The legal system is based on French civil codes. The president is both chief of state and head of the government. There is also a vice-president. The members of the Cabinet are nominated by the president.

The bicameral National Congress or *Congreso Nacional* consists of the Senate or *Senado* and the Chamber of Deputies or *Camara de Diputados*. The Senate has 32 seats. Members are elected by popular vote to serve four-year terms. The Chamber of Deputies has 150 seats. Members are elected by popular vote to serve four-year terms.

There is a Supreme Court or *Corte Suprema*. The Supreme Court serves as the nation's ultimate court of appeal. It exercises original jurisdiction in cases involving the president, the vice president, members of the cabinet and Congress, and judges and prosecutors of the higher courts. The court consists of nine members, one of whom is designated president of the Supreme Court.

The 1966 Constitution guarantees several basic legal rights to all citizens. These include the rights to due process, to public trial, and to *habeas corpus* protection. An accused person is also guaranteed protection against double jeopardy and self-incrimination. A written order from a competent judicial authority is required, if any person is to be detained more than 48 hours or if an individual's home or property is to be searched.

The government does not publish statistics on the national incidence of crime, but the daily newspapers of Santo Domingo regularly report criminal acts. The crimes listed include murder, rape, robbery, fraud, counterfeiting, and extortion. According to the newspapers, rural crime accounts for only a small portion of the total. One manifestation of urban crime is criminal activity by juvenile street gangs.

According to the newspapers, rural crimes have accounted for only a small portion of the total. Crime in urban areas was believed to have risen during the 1980s as a result of growing unemployment, pervasive underemployment, and migration from rural to urban areas One manifestation of urban crime was criminal activity by juvenile street gangs. This problem was deemed sufficiently serious in 1988 to merit a campaign that targeted juvenile delinquents for detention.

Crimes associated with narcotics presented a growing problem in the 1980s, as drug traffickers attempted to use the Dominican Republic as a transshipment point between various Latin American countries and the United States. The police were on the front line of the war against drugs, but elements of the military took part as well. The navy, for instance, intercepted several boats carrying cocaine and marijuana during the late 1970s, and air force patrols were given the task of spotting seaborne drug traffickers. In 1988, the government created the National Economic Council for the Control of Drugs to coordinate domestic and international narcotics programs and to integrate the efforts of all police and military elements involved in antinarcotics activities.

Police Force

Background

The country's first police organization was a municipal force set up in 1844 in Santo Domingo. Beginning in 1847, other towns formed similar organizations. Eventually, there were independent police forces in every province. These forces were largely controlled by local *caudillos*, and the national executive branch had only nominal influence over them. These local forces were disbanded in 1916 during the United States occupation; the United States Marines, and later members of the Dominican Constabulary Guard, assumed police duties. The National Police was created in 1936. After that time, police activities in the nation were completely centralized, and no independent provincial or municipal forces existed.

In 1989, police personnel numbered some 10,000; the strength of the police had remained relatively constant since the 1950s. The director general of the National Police was a police major general, who was directly subordinate to the secretary of state of interior and police. The police maintained a close relationship with the armed forces, and until the 1980s, the chief of the National Police was quite often a senior officer from one of the armed services. The director general was assisted by a deputy director and two sections: internal affairs and planning, and special operations. Three sections, each headed by an assistant director general, carried out the administration and operation of the National Police. These were the Administration and Support Section, the Police Operations Section, and the Special Operations Section.

Organizational Description

The National Police, numbering more than 27,000, serve throughout the country; there are no separate municipal forces. The Ministry of the Interior and Police is responsible for making policy decisions affecting the police force. The military is also charged with providing internal security. The National Police, the National Department of Investigations (DNI), the National Drug Control Directorate (DNCD), the Airport Security Authority (CESA), Port Security Authority (CESEP), and the armed forces (army, air force, and navy) form the security forces. The National Police maintains internal security in conjunction with the military. The military's domestic responsibilities include maintaining public order and protecting persons and property. The police are under the Secretary of the Interior and Police; the military, CESA, and CESEP are under the Secretary of the Armed Forces; and the DNI and the DNCD, which have personnel both from the police and from the military, report directly to the President.

The Administration and Support Section supervised personnel, police education and training, and finances. It was responsible for the logistical system, communications, transportation, records, the police radio station, the police laboratory, and the data processing center. This section administered

the police academy at Hatillo in San Cristóbal Province. The Police Operations Section oversaw normal police operations. It was segmented into several functional departments, including robbery investigation, homicide investigation, felonies and misdemeanors against private property, highway patrol, and narcotics and dangerous drugs. Police patrolled on foot, on horseback, and by motorcycle and automobile. The customs and harbor police employed a small number of boats.

The deputy director of police functioned as the immediate superior of five regional directors. These officers, usually police brigadier generals, were responsible for five territorial zones: the Northeastern Zone (headquartered at San Francisco de Macorís), the Northern Zone (Santiago), the Southern Zone (Barahona), the Central Zone (San Cristóbal), and the Eastern Zone (San Pedro de Marcorís). The police regions each covered several provinces; forces within the regions were broken down into provincial, company, detachment, and local police post divisions.

The Special Operations Section was responsible for the administration of the secret service, which in 1989 was headed by a police brigadier general. The secret service performed undercover surveillance of domestic political groups and foreigners suspected of espionage or of inciting political or economic disorder. In this capacity, the secret service coordinated its efforts with the National Department of Investigations (Departamento Nacional de Investigaciones–DNI), which was under the direct control of the president. Created in 1962, the DNI was authorized to "investigate any act committed by persons, groups, or associations that conflict with the Constitution, laws, or state institutions, or that attempt to establish any totalitarian form of government." The DNI was an investigative body and, unlike the police, it did not generally have arrest authority. The functions of the DNI were closely coordinated with those of the armed forces' intelligence units, as well as with the functions of the police. In 1989, the DNI was commanded by a retired army general.

Approximately half of all police personnel were stationed in the capital area, both because Santo Domingo was by far the nation's largest city and because police headquarters, as well as several special police units, were located there. Among the special units garrisoned in the capital was a paramilitary special operations battalion with some 1,000 personnel. The unit was used for riot-control in Santo Domingo, although elements could also be deployed rapidly to any section of the country. Other specialized police units included a specialized bank guard corps and a sappers corps that performed firefighting and civil defense duties.

Like the armed forces, the police participated actively in civic-action projects. Police medical and dental teams provided services for poor residents throughout the country. The police also made donations to organizations set up to assist the poor.

The public image of the police had improved since the 1970s, but excesses on the part of police personnel, including beatings of suspects, continued to receive media publicity. Both government and police officials had announced their intent to monitor such activities and to take corrective measures, but complaints about such abuses continued to surface during the late 1980s. The role of the police in quelling disturbances and in supporting the government's political agenda also continued to spark controversy.

The Dominican police may be depicted as semi-democratic, engaging in violent measures that fail a full-democratic test, but which are not especially violent or repressive. The head of the police is a national cabinet officer, the Interior and Police Minister. The police perform routine repression of wildcat or general strikes, protests against austerity measures and the government generally by oppositions, and for police shootings. Frequently, protestors are killed, with claims and counter-claims of unprovoked violence from both sides rationalizing counter-violence, usually shooting. Often, the police arrest hundreds, and dozens are injured. They are known to enter houses, schools, and churches in search of opposition demonstrators.

As a then-candidate before his successful 2000 presidential election, Hipolito Mejía claimed that the secret police had eavesdropped on his telephone conversations. Mejía established a new Police Reform Commission made up of the Chief of Police, the Attorney General, the Secretary of the Armed Forces, the Legal adviser to the President, as well as representatives of human rights organizations and legislators. Under the new commission, which is designed to investigate any charges brought against security officials by the citizenry, extra-judicial killings fell from an estimated 20 per month in 1999 to around one a month in 2001.

In May 2001, the Dominican police arrested at least 16 leaders of FALPO, a leftist group, for their alleged involvement in the "armed uprising" against the northern regional government of Navarrete. Mejia's administration faced criticism from human rights organizations that Dominican police have summarily executed as many as 100 suspects. In January 2002, the president dismissed the national police chief after allegations of systematic police brutality. Pedro de Jesus Candelier was acting police chief for three years, and human rights activists blamed his 25,700-member force for the shooting deaths of 600 civilians while he was in charge. Candelier was replaced by 25-year veteran officer Jaime Martes Martinez, who headed the anti-riot police. In May and June of 2001, Candelier's National Police were accused of excessive force in quelling street protests that left at least 10 people dead.

Complaints and Discipline

The police are widely accused of torture and arbitrary arrests, as well as extrajudcial executions, particularly by security forces. The latter act through its military structure outside of civilian command and accountability. The mediaare discouraged from covering such problems, lest it harm the tourism industry. The police and, to a lesser degree, the military, have tortured, beaten, or otherwise abused suspects, detainees, and prisoners. Police arbitrarily arrested and detained suspects and suspects' relatives. Significant problems of this nature remained, in part, because of insufficient vetting of the backgrounds of police recruits. It was alleged that many persons with prior criminal records were incorporated into police ranks, either under false names or with identification or recommendations from other state institutions, such as the army. Many members of the police force lacked basic education, had received inadequate training, and showed weak discipline, all factors that directly contributed to unlawful or unwarranted killings and to cruel or inhuman treatment.

Police continued the practice of making frequent sweeps or roundups in low-income, high-crime communities, where they arrested and detained individuals arbitrarily, allegedly to fight delinquency. During these sweeps, police arrested large numbers of residents and seized property, including motorcycles, other vehicles, and weapons. Following the indiscriminate arrests, police regularly detained individuals for 20 days or more while they looked for a reason to charge them. Police stated that they relied upon unlawful detention without presentation to a court because some cases involved more complicated investigations. However, there was a clear pattern of police arrests of individuals before undertaking adequate investigation, and reliance on confessions obtained under questionable circumstances to make the cases. Prosecutors generally did not actively investigate cases; they often depended on police reports, many of which were based on forced confessions.

A related problem was the police practice of arresting and detaining individuals solely because of a familial or marital relationship to a suspect. A suspect's parents, siblings, or spouse was particularly vulnerable to this practice, the goal of which was to compel an at-large suspect to surrender, or to coerce a confession from one already arrested. The National Commission on Human Rights reported 100 such cases as of August; however, it reported no additional cases after the appointment of General Perez Sanchez as police chief.

By 2004, there were no politically motivated killings by the Government or its agents; however, security forces were involved in many killings that were unlawful, unwarranted, or involved excessive use of force. Security forces killed between 250 and 350 people during that year. In the majority of killings by police, the police stated that the deaths resulted from a gunfire exchange in the course of an arrest, which required officers to act in self-defense. A number of eyewitness accounts corroborated police reports; others did not. Many killings were related to aggressive tactics on the part of the police.

The National Commission on Human Rights reported approximately 300 killings by security forces, 20 of which occurred after a new National Police chief took control of the police department. A major newspaper reported 360 deaths in "exchanges of gunfire" with police during 2004, including 74 such deaths from August until the end of the year. The National Police reported 75 deaths at the hands of officers between August and the end of the year, compared with 167 such killings during the same time period in 2003. According to the National Police, three of the post-August killings were unlawful. Accounts of incidents varied, and some went unreported.

According to the National Police, authorities had referred 30 cases to civilian courts for accusations of unlawful killings as of October 2004. However, human rights organizations stated that the police employed unwarranted deadly force about as often against criminal suspects as in previous years, and uniformed vigilantism persisted on a less-than-deadly level. The lack of qualified investigators and the nontransparent conduct of investigations of killings in "exchanges of gunfire" resulted in impunity in a number of cases.

Detainees at police headquarters in Santo Domingo reported that they were held for 15 to 21 days. Juveniles held at the Department for Minors at the Villa Juana police station commonly were held well beyond the 12-hour limit for sending the case to the district attorney's Office. The law prohibits interrogation of juveniles by the police or in the presence of police.

Human rights groups report repeated instances of physical abuse of detainees, including various forms of torture, beatings, and sexual abuse. Certain police units, called "the surgeons," intentionally shot young men in the lower extremities during nighttime patrols as part of a strategy to deter crime, resulting in a number of serious injuries and amputations. According to human rights organizations, both the National Police and prison officials used forms of torture. The method most often used was beating. Other forms included asphyxiation with plastic bags to elicit confessions and a method called "roasting the chicken" in which the victim was placed over hot coals and turned.

In some instances, authorities interpreted the presence of prosecutors as meaning that detainees could be held more than 48 hours after being transferred from police custody to prosecutorial custody. However, with the implementation of the new Criminal Procedures Code in September 2004, detainees receive additional protections, and respect for detainee rights improved, including through increased enforcement of time limits for pretrial detention. Both the National Police and armed forces offered training courses for human rights.

Reform efforts have only had limited success. Local *ad hoc* justice is often seen as a more effective deterrent to crime than through police. By 1997, the Supreme Court of Justice was restructured to root out corruption and to reduce human rights abuses of the police. Supposedly toward that end, the number of judges was set at 16. In reality, the courts have not changed much, with limited judicial access for those without money or influence, to seek justice for police abuses. The Institute of Human Dignity, a branch of the National Police, monitors human rights abuses committed by members of the National Police. The Institute held more than 100 courses, seminars, and conferences, which were attended by more than 5,500 participants, including members of the National Police, armed forces, and civilians.

According to the National Commission on Human Rights, the military and police collaborated with their Haitian counterparts at the border to accept bribes from Haitians attempting to cross illegally. Local human rights observers reported roundups of Haitian and Dominican-Haitian construction workers. Officials allegedly took groups of darker-skinned or "Haitian-looking" individuals to empty buildings soon after they were paid, in order to extort money from them.

The Constitution provides for freedom of travel, and the Government generally respected these provisions in practice; however, there were some exceptions. For example, human rights groups alleged that many Haitians were not allowed to leave the sugarcane plantations where they worked. Local and international human rights groups cited discrimination against Haitian migrants, who were subject to arbitrary and unilateral action by the authorities.

HENRY F. CAREY

Bibliography

Atkins, G. Pope. *Arms and Politics in the Dominican Republic*. Westview Press: Boulder, 1980.

Bell, Ian. *The Dominican Republic*. Westview Press: Boulder, 1981.

Black, Jan Knippers. *The Dominican Republic: Politics and Development in an Unsovereign State*. Allen & Unwin: Boston, 1986.

Ferguson, James. *The Dominican Republic: Beyond the Lighthouse*. Monthly Review: New York, 1992.

Hartlyn, Jonathan, *The Struggle for Democratic Politics in the Dominican Republic*. University of North Carolina Press: Chapel Hill and London, 1998.

Pons, Frank Moya. *The Dominican Republic: A National History*. Hispaniola Book: New York, 1995.

Rodman, Seldon. Quisqueya. *A History of the Dominican Republic*. University of Washington Press: Seattle, 1964.

Tucker, Jack, and Ursula Eberhard. *Insiders' Guide to the Dominican Republic*. Hippocrene Books: New York, 1993.

Wiarda, Howard J., and Michael J. Kryzanek. *The Dominican Republic: A Caribbean Crucible*. Westview Press: Boulder, 1982.

E

ECUADOR

Background Material

The Republic of Ecuador is located on the northwest part of South America. It is bounded to the north by Colombia, to the east and south by Peru, and to the west by the Pacific Ocean. Ecuador owes his name to the imaginary line which crosses the country and divides the earth into two hemispheres. The Galápagos Islands, or Archipiélago de Colón, located in the Pacific Ocean approximately 1,050 kilometers off the coast, belong to Ecuador. Ecuador has a total area of 272,045 sq km, which includes the Galápagos Islands. The capital is Quito, one of the most ancient cities of South America.

Ecuador is divided into four geographic regions: the Costa, which has an extension equivalent to a little more than a fourth of the country's area; the Sierra, which consists of mountain chains between which lies a narrow uninhabited plateau known as Valle Interandino (Andean valley); the East or Amazonian region to the east of the Andes; and the Insular region, integrated by the Galápagos Islands, which consists of several volcanic islands.

The forests constitute the most important natural resource of the country, since they cover 38% of the territory. Other resources are: gold, petroleum, silver, copper, iron, lead, zinc, salt, and sulphur.

Ecuador's population is composed of 52% natives (mainly *quechuas*) and 40% *mestizos* (mix of Spanish colonizers and South American Indians); the remaining 8% are are mainly Spaniards and African descendants. Approximately 65% of the population lives in urban centers, and 35% in rural areas. Ecuador has 13,212,742 inhabitants (2004 est.); 47% of the population lives in the region of the Sierra, and 49% in the Costa; the rest of the population lives in the Amazonian region or the Galápagos Islands.

The official language of Ecuador is Spanish, although the indigenous populations speak other languages, mainly *quechua* or *quichua*, which is the language of the Incas. The indigenous population was converted to the Catholic religion after the Spanish conquest of Peru and Ecuador. At the end of the nineteenth century, the liberal revolution established the partial separation of Church and State, and in 1906 an anticlerical Constitution was promulgated, which caused clergy's properties to be confiscated and total freedom of creed to be promulgated. At present, more than 95% of the Ecuadorian population professes the Catholic Religion, and less than one percent practices Protestantism.

Ecuador is a country of highly contrasting cultural models, because it has an enormous ethnic diversity within its different regions. The natives of the Sierra, who are descendants of towns conquered by the Incas, still practice their musical traditions, which they interpret with native instruments, like the *siku, güiro, rondador,* and *quena.* On the east side live the Amazonian natives who have their own cultures and languages. In the region of the Costa, diverse degrees of mestization between descendants of Spaniards and African black slaves had been produced, which has given rise to a peculiar Afro-Ecuadorian culture.

Traditionally, the base of the Ecuadorian economy has been agriculture. Nevertheless, in 1965 a law on industrial development was passed to facilitate the establishment of factories of textiles, electrical and pharmaceutical articles, and other products. In 1970 Ecuador registered an important increase in the production and export of petroleum, which was enhanced by the construction of the pipe line "*transecuatoriano*" with the purpose of improving the supply from deposits located on the east side to Puerto the Esmeraldas. In 2000, the gross domestic product was $13,607 million. The entrance of Ecuador into the World Trade Organization (WTO) in 1995 was a great boost to its economy.

The arable land, covering less than 10 percent of the country's area (approximately 3,001,000 sq km), is exploited in a very tradition form in the regions of the Sierra and the Costa. Bananas are the main crop, followed by sugar cane, with a production of 5,962,310 t in 2001, rice (1,377,180 t), corn (642,444 t), potato (689,770 t), coffee (146, 457 t), cocoa (106,714 t) and citric fruits. The production of flowers, either tropical or of cold climate, has a great importance.

From 1884 to 2000, the monetary unit of Ecuador was the Sucre, which was divided into 100 cent units. The deepening of the economic crisis drove the dollarization of the Ecuadorian economy throughout 2000, which culminated on September 10 of that year with the substitution of the aforementioned national currency by the American dollar as store of value, unit of account, and medium of payment and exchange. This fact implied indeed a redefinition of the functions of the Ecuadorian Central Bank, which was created in 1927 and had been until then the banking organization responsible for currency printing. Also, numerous national and foreign private banks operate in Ecuador.

The value of Ecuador's exports generally outweighs the value of imports. In 2000, annual exports reached 4,846 million dollars, and imports reached 3,465 million. More than 60% of the income came from exports of crude petroleum, bananas, shrimp, cocoa, and coffee. Ecuador imports industrial raw materials, capital assets, transport equipment, and consumer goods. The United States is the main importer of Ecuadorian products, followed by Colombia, Chile, Italy, and Germany. Ecuador imports products from the United States, Japan, Colombia, Venezuela, Germany, Mexico, and Italy.

Contextual Features

Ecuador is divided in provinces (*provincias*), corners (*cantones*), and parishes (*parroquias*). Each province is administered by a governor appointed by the President of the Republic and a Provincial Council, which is headed by a prefect, who has only a deciding vote in case of ties in the Council; both are elected by universal vote. Each corner constitutes a municipality. The government and administration of the municipality are in charge of the Municipal Council. The councils of the province's capitals are formed by a Municipal Council and a mayor who presides over it, also elected by popular vote. The councils of the corners that are not capitals of provinces are governed by a president, except those corners that have more than 5,000 inhabitants. In each parish the governor of the province appoints a political lieutenant.

Ecuador is ruled by a Constitution promulgated in 1978 and reformed in 1984, 1992, and 1995, under which the country is a unitary and democratic republic.

The Ecuadorian Constitution confers the executive power upon the president, elected by direct universal suffrage to a four-year period. The president may run for re-election but not consecutively; he presides over the cabinet and appoints the provinces' governors. In addition to being the head of the State, he is supreme commander of the Armed Forces and has extraordinary powers in cases of national emergency.

The legislative branch is the National Congress, a unicameral legislative body formed by 125 members chosen to a five-year period. The legislators are elected under a system of proportional representation (105) and territorial representation (20). The deputies under the system of territorial representation are elected according to the percentage of votes cast in each province.

The Supreme Court of Justice is the most important body of the judicial branch. There are a total of 17 Superior Courts and numerous provincial courts. The criminal cases are studied by a "special jury" confirmed by a judge and three members of the court, after having received the instruction by a penal court. Capital punishment has been abolished.

The Ecuadorian legal system is the set of norms that constitute the effective legal order in Ecuador. It is based on the law as can be read in the first article of the Civil Code: "the Law is a declaration of the sovereign will that declared in the form prescribed by the Constitution, orders, prohibits or allows."

It is shown that customs do not constitute a right but in the cases in which the law refers to them. In the Ecuadorian Legislation, the Constitution prevails as the fundamental law of the State, over any other regulation. As for numerous countries, it can be noticed that jurisprudence does not reach the hierarchical rank of a source of right inasmuch as its mandatory force only concerns the litigation parts. Article 3, Clause 2 established it in the following way: "The judicial sentences do not have mandatory force but for the causes they will be pronounced for," but whenever there is uniformity of criteria and reiteration in time on the jurisprudential parameters to be followed as a possible source of Ecuadorian law.

Every legal norm is based on one of superior hierarchy. In the Ecuadorian Right, it is the Constitution, followed by ordinary laws, statutory laws, regulations, and other complementary rules.

Because of integration and development reasons, Ecuador has been immersed in the need of adapting new norms according to international treaties, especially those that refer to the Cartagena Agreement. It is in this way that diverse regulations have arisen, which have been gradually integrated to the internal legal order and have become part of the Ecuadorian Right and in some cases even with a superior hierarchy than the one of its respective ordinary laws.

The constitution in Ecuador was approved on January 15, 1978 and reformed to its present context on June 4, 1984. It is reflected in its Article 137, which states: "The Constitution is the supreme law of the country. The secondary norms and the others of smaller hierarchy must be in accordance with the constitutional rules. International laws, decrees, regulations, treaties or agreements that in any way should contradict the Constitution or should alter its prescriptions, do not have any legal value."

Like in most of the constitutions governing life in other countries, the Constitution of Ecuador specifies the functions of each one of the branches of the state in its Title I Section I. In Articles 56 and following it is stated that: "the legislative function is executed by the National Congress." In Title II, Section I, Articles 73 and follwing, it is stated that "the executive function is executed by the President of the Republic who represents the State."

Finally, Title III Section I in its Articles 92 to 108 explains the jurisdictional power, based on a basic principle stated in Article 93, by affirming that: "the procedural system is a means for administration of justice..."

Other Governmental Organisms are the Electoral Supreme Court, the Office of the Judge Advocate General, and the Court of Constitutional Guarantees. The Electoral Supreme Court has the duty of organizing, supervising, and guaranteeing the diverse electoral processes in the whole national territory.

The Office of the Judge Advocate General is in fact the Public Ministry. The main function of the Court of Constitutional Guarantees is to monitor compliance with the Constitution. This statement is clearly specified in Article 2 of the Constitution: " It is a fundamental function of the State to fortify the national unity, assure respect for the fundamental rights of individuals and promote the economic, social and cultural progress of its inhabitants."

According to the constitutional order, on July 13, 2001, the oral system for judgment of crimes typified in the Penal Code will be put into effect, establishing that the Public Ministry will conduct and promote the pre-trial and procedural penitentiary investigation, and the Judicial Police will be an auxiliary body of the Public Ministry, integrated by specialized personnel of the National Police, and its functions will be subject to the regulations stated in the Political Constitution of the Republic, in the Code of Penal Procedure, and in the Judicial Police Regulation created for this aim.

Police Profile

Background

The National Police can be considered within the context of different historical stages, starting from the Colonial Period (1534–1822). During this period, the 6th of December 1534, the National Police came into operation in the Spanish foundation of Quito and in later years in the remaining cities. The Colonial Period concluded in 1822 with the battle of Pichincha. Afterwards came the period "Gran Colombino" (1822–1830) during which, on October 2, 1827, the Colombian Congress issued the decree for the creation of police headquarters in the principal cities of the country, and the first Police Regulation was promulgated by the executive branch. These headquarters were established in Quito, Guayaquil, and Cuenca.

In the Republican Period (1830–1884), the 13th of May of 1830, when the Republic of Ecuador was already established, the police regulations were enacted; in 1831 for Quito and in 1833 for Guayaquil. These regulations established an institutional structure composed of a head, commissioners, and watchman, all of them controlled by the Municipal Council and with "cantonal" jurisdiction. Between 1835 and 1884, new regulations for Quito and Guayaquil, as well as for Cuenca, Loja, Latacunga, Otavalo, Ambato, Riobamba, and Azoguez were enacted, all of them proposed by the respective Municipal Councils and approved by the President of the Republic and the National Congress. On the 25th of November of 1865, the Police Headquarters were abolished, and in their place Police Intendances were created, which were composed of intendants, commissioners, watchman, and gendarmes.

On June 14, 1884, a key event in the history of the National Police of Ecuador took place: the Police of the Republic or Police of the State was created by order of President Jose Maria Placido Caamaño. This organization was officially named Police of Order and Security, and was divided into provincial bodies, each of which was commanded by a quartermaster general. In spite of its civil nature, on August 15, 1885 the Police of Order and Security was militarily organized, when their members decided to name themselves Police Soldiers. Soon afterwards, on August 3, 1892, the police was demilitarized by decree of president Luis Cordero Davila, and the service of Rural Police was created in the provinces of Guayas, Manabi, and Los Rios.

By enacting a new General Regulation for the Police Organization and Service by order of President Jose Luis Tamayo, the Police of Order and Security changed its name to National Police.

On January 4, 1938, General Alberto Enriquez Gallo, Supreme Head of the Republic, issued a new statutory law, which decreed a militarily organization in structure and hierarchies for the National Police and assigned a new name to it: the Police Forces. Furthermore, the first Law of Personnel, which considered only the existence of urban, rural, and transit services, being the latter integrated as a squad for urban service, was enacted under the title of Law of Military Condition and Promotions of the Police Forces.

March 2, 1938 brought the promulgation of the decree that established the creation of the Military School of Gendarmes for the officers training. Due to this decree, the professionalism of the National Police was a fact, which was reinforced by a new Statutory Law promulgated on July 8, 1938; the Policy Forces changed to Gendarmes Forces, keeping their military character; the General Investigative Police was abolished and replaced by the Commandant General Office. When Dr. Jose Maria Velasco Ibarra assumed control of the Republic, the Gendarmes Forces disappeared (June 6, 1944), and were transformed into a civil institution named National Civil Guard.

In 1951, the National Congress introduced diverse reforms, one of which substituted the name of Civil Guard by the new identity of National Police and also established the following officers' hierarchic ranks: Chief Prefect, Prefect, Under-Prefect, Inspector, First Under-Inspector, and Second Under-Inspector. On November 9, 1964, the name was changed from National Civil Police to National Police, whose structure was divided into urban, rural, transit, and investigation services.

On March 21, 1973, a new Statutory Law for the institution was issued by decree of General Guillermo Rodriguez Lara, Supreme Head of the Republic. The new law changed the name of National Police to National Civil Police and organized it into the following services: urban, rural, transit, criminal investigation, migration, public security and information, and narcotics and INTERPOL.

On February 28, 1975, a new Statutory Law was enacted by decree of General Guillermo Rodriguez Lara, which definitively restituted the name of NATIONAL POLICE. The new organization is structured to provide services within the following fields: urban, rural, transit, criminal investigation, migration, public security, narcotics and Interpol, Penitentiary and Prisons Police, and Judicial Police.

On February 28, 1975, the names of the hierarchical ranks of the organization's members changed to Police General, Police Colonel, Police Lieutenant Colonel, Police Major, Police Captain, Police Lieutenant, Police Second Lieutenant, Police Cadet, Police First Sub-Officer, Police Second Sub-Officer, Police First Sergeant, Police Second Sergeant, Police First Corporal, Police Second Corporal, and Policeman.

On July 28, 1994, the Anti-Kidnapping and Extortion Division was created; on December 3, 1997, the National Directorate of Police specializing in Children and Adolescents was created; on January 9, 1999, the Parks Police was formed; on January 21, 2000, the Environmental Protection Division was created.

Organizational Description

The National Police reports directly to the Ministry of Government and Police, and its organizational chart is represent in the following diagram:

The National Police is structured into the following divisions:

Antinarcotics;
Anti-Kidnapping and Extortion;
Judicial and Investigative Police;
Intelligence;
Migration;
Children and Teenagers;
Tourism;
Land Transport and Transit;
Intervention and Rescue;
Special Operations;
Air-Police Unit.

The organizational structure encompasses a Commanding General; an Inspector General; five General Directorates: Personnel, Intelligence, Operations, Logistics, and Civil and Community Matters; thirteen National Directions: Antinarcotics, Dinapen, Migration, Judicial and Investigation Police, Public Security, Land Transport and Transit, Urban and Rural Service, Health, Finance, Communications, Educations, Social Welfare, and Legal Advisory; five Special Divisions: Group of Intervention and Rescue (GIR), Group of Special Operations (GOE), Air-Police Service (SAP), Riding Division (UER), Anti-Kidnapping Division (UNASE), and the Institute of Social Security of the National Police (ISSPOL).

Functions

The National Police have the fundamental mission of guaranteeing internal order and individual and collective security. In the next five-year period (2005–2010), it will be an institution based on excellence and quality, with adequate and modern logistic resources, a leader in internal security and directed to

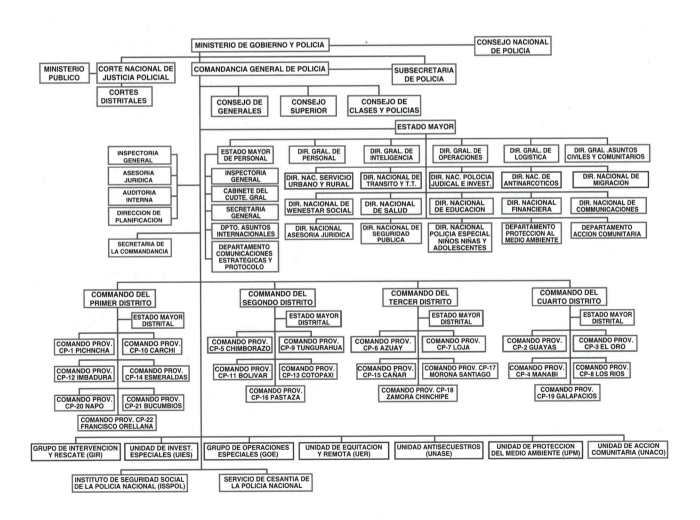

the community service; it will be professional, scientific, technical, and specialized, with women and men with integral training. To achieve these objectives, the higher ranks of the police have been carrying out diverse projects taking into account the institution's competence within its role in national context, always in compliance with the legal regulations in force and proclaiming human rights as the essential norm for the application of the law.

The general mission of the police is to achieve a scientific, technical, and specialized Police Organization, leader in internal security, with a modern legal and organizational framework, and with sufficient resources to guarantee peace and order in the country. Some of the strategic objectives to be pursued are described following:

I. To continue with the improvement of the National Police's Education System, in order to contribute to the effective and efficient fulfillment of the institutional mission.

II. To modernize the operational administration of all the police services by improving the necessary human, logistic, and economic resources.

III. To up-date, modernize, and reform the institutional legal framework.

IV. To modernize and decentralize the police administration and operation in order to attain greater efficiency in the community service.

V. To achieve the community active participation in the internal security and in environmental protection.

VI. To improve the life quality of the Police Institution's members and their families.

VII. To control, inspect, and penalize the corruption activities in all levels and forms that may be discovered.

VIII. To strengthen the institutional image through an ethic, moral, and professional behavior of all its members.

Training

Ecuador has two instructional facilities: the officer training school, which is the Superior Police School Alberto Enriquez Gallo; and the police training schools, which are distributed in every region of Ecuador. A four-year and one-year training program are required to graduate as Sub-lieutenant and Policeman, respectively.

Officers can also take specialization and improvement courses, which are compulsory for obtaining a promotion and finally, the course of the Major State for the level of Coronal Lieutenant, with training essentially in the administration field. In the last reforms, within the sections assigned to training and specialization matters, the need to include several courses as requirement for police promotion has been pointed out, based on the belief that attaining higher levels of professionalism is a symptom of effectiveness.

Ecuador also has the Technological Institute of the National Police, where the technicians specializing in police functions, especially in the criminology related fields, are graduated.

Terrorism

There is no evidence to suggest the existence of terrorist groups in Ecuador. The primary concern is the Revolutionary Armed Forces of Colombia (FARC), which uses parts of Ecuador as supply centers.

International Cooperation

The international organizations that support the police of Ecuador are many, especially concerning drug-trafficking, a crime that has been increasing in Ecuador. The United States, through the FBI; Spain, through the Internal Ministry; Great Britain, through its Customs Service; Colombia; France; Interpol; and Europol are among those providing assistance.

JAVIER GALARZA

Bibliography

Biblioteca de Consulta Encarta, 2004 Edition.
Código De Procedimiento Penal.
Código Penal Ecuatoriano.
Colección de Obras Policiales, Promociones XVIII, XIX, XX y XXI, de la Escuela de Estado Mayor, 1996 Edition.
Constitución Política del Estado.
Enciclopedia Lexus, 2000 Edition.
La Historia del Ecuador, Casa de la Cultura Ecuatoriana, 2003 Edition.
La Historia de la Policía Nacional, Capitán de Policía (S.P) Marío Villalobos, 1998 Edition.
National Institute of the National Police History.
Procedimientos de Comando Planas Mayores y Operaciones **Policiales, General Superior (S.P) Lenín Vinueza Mideros, 1999 Edition.**
Procedimientos Policiales y Derechos Humanos, Aldhu, 1999 Edition.
Recopilación de Leyes y Reglamentos, Escuela de Estado Mayor, 2000 Edition.
www.cibercentro.com.
www.ecuador.com.
www.monografias.com.
www.policíaecuador.gov.ec.
www.presidencia.gov.ec.

EGYPT

Background Material

Egypt is the largest populated nation in the Arab world, and the second most populous country in the continent of Africa. Egypt is a moderately unified society of Hamitic heritage. It is one of the world's greatest and earliest civilizations known for its historic pyramids and rich literature. Archeological evidence indicates that human beings resided along the Nile before the emergence of dynastic rule of the pharaohs. Known as the world's oldest incessant nation, which has existed for over six thousand years, its organized agriculture started around 6000 B.C. Indeed, the River Nile played a major role in human habitation by sustaining the people, their animals, and their crops. The Nile also was utilized for transportation of the people and their products from one corner of the country to another.

In 341 B.C., the Egyptian dynasty was conquered by the Persians. Subsequently, the Persians were replaced by the Greeks, Romans, and Byzantines. The Mamluks took control of Egypt in 1250, and helped Egypt evade defeat from the Mongol invasions that destroyed much of Central and Southwest Asia. These Mamluks, a neighboring military class, governed Egypt even after Egypt fell to the Ottoman Turks in 1517. In June 1798, Napoleon Bonaparte and his French army, scientists and scholars, conquered lower Egypt from the Mamluks and ruled it for a brief period. Mohammed Ali the Great, a protégé of the Ottoman Empire, governed Egypt until 1848, and in 1882, Britain seized control of Egypt's government for economic reasons and maintained allegiance to the Ottoman Empire until 1914. Because of growing Egyptian nationalism, Britain granted independence to Egypt in 1992.

Egypt served as a military base for Britain during World War II. In 1952, under the command of Lt. Col. Gamal Abdel Nasser and other disaffected soldiers, King Farouk's administration was deposed. King Farouk was held responsible for Egypt's inability to defeat Israel in the war of 1948. Nasser became a captivating head of state, briefly tried civilian rule, encouraged "Arab socialism," and advanced public-sector economy. Vice President Anwar el-Sadat was elected president after Nassers's death, and in 1971 and 1973, respectively, he signed a treaty of Friendship with the Soviet Union and ordered the October war with Israel. President Sadat later made peace with Israel and participated in the historic Camp David accords between Israel and Egypt in the United States, which led to his assassination on October 6, 1981. He was succeeded by Hosni Mubarak, who is the current president of Egypt.

President Mubarak subscribes to the Camp David agreements, and he endorses several economic reforms such as relaxing many price controls, decreasing financial assistance, and liberalization of trade and investments. His administration has also promoted private sector economy and privatization of some of the industries in the country. The Egyptian economy centers mainly on tourism, oil and gas, and profits generated from the Suez Canal. In addition to petroleum and natural gas, other natural resources include iron ore, phosphates, manganese, limestone, gypsum, talc, asbestos, lead, and zinc. About one third of the population relies on agriculture for their income by producing crops such as cotton, rice, wheat, corn, sugarcane, sugar beets, onions, and beans. The United States exports wheat, corn, and soybean products to Egypt. According to published reports, Egypt would be nothing but a "dessert wasteland" without the River Nile.

The Arab Republic of Egypt is located in Northern Africa, with a total area of area of 1,001,450 sq km. The population is 76,117,421 (July, 2004 estimate). The capital is Cairo. The ethnic composition of the population is Eastern Hamitic stock (Egyptians, Bedouins, and Berbers), 99%; Greek, Nubian, Armenian, and other Europeans (primarily Italian and French), one percent. The religious composition of the population is Muslim (mostly Sunni), 94%; Coptic Christian and other, 6%.

Contextual Features

Egypt has a powerful branch of an executive government. The Egyptian Constitution provides the president with the authority to appoint a cabinet, one or more vice presidents, and a prime minister. The People's Assembly nominates the president for a term of six years, which must be confirmed by a popular national referendum. Egypt's bicameral system consists of the People's Assembly or *Majlis al-Sha'b*. This legislative body has 454 members, of whom 444 are popularly elected, and 10 of whom are appointed by the president. They serve in office for a period of five years. Also, the Egyptian Constitution sets aside 50% of legislative seats for the wage earners and the poor. Additionally, there is a consultative council known as *Shura* with 264 members. The 1971 Constitution expanded the powers of the assembly to include originating and voting on legislations.

The judiciary mostly derives its criminal codes and legal methods from the British, Italian, and Napoleonic legal systems. Under the provisions of the Constitution, the executive president is prohibited from interfering in judicial proceedings. In order to insulate the judges from arbitrary and capricious influence, they are granted life tenures in office. Comparatively, this is true with the constitutional or Article 111 judges in the United States of America. According to public accounts, the Mubarak administration (unlike Nasser's regime that purged judges who defended citizens' rights from office in the late 1960s) respects judicial independence, and the doctrines of due process and judicial review. Egypt's *Sharia* or Islamic courts may have jurisdiction over family matters such as marriage, divorce, and inheritance, depending on the individuals involved. Prior to the 1952 Revolution, the *Sharia* courts had jurisdiction over Muslims while the Coptic community had its own communal courts.

The Egyptian courts also consist of district tribunals and single-judge courts. These lower courts have jurisdiction over civil and criminal matters. Egypt's criminal code has three primary types of crime, such as contraventions (insignificant crimes), misdemeanors, and felonies. Individuals involved in some serious felonies like murder, manslaughter, rape, arson, and treason may receive the death sentence. In 1987, six convicted murderers, and two rapists were executed by the Egyptian authorities. In addition to the lower courts, there are also courts of appeals, state security courts, and a three-level hierarchy of administrative courts under the leadership of the Council of State. The highest appellate court in Egypt is the Supreme Constitutional Court, which has a Chief Justice and nine associate justices. The Supreme Court is the final arbiter in important issues that require constitutional interpretations and protection of human rights.

Indeed, Egypt endeavors to play a pivotal role not only in the Arab World, but in the global society as a whole. The Arab League has its headquarters in Egypt, and Egypt is a formidable member of the African Union. Egypt is an important ally in the many challenges to find peace and harmony in the Middle East and in attempts to resolve the Israeli-Palestinian conflict. Egypt also organized and deployed (about 35,000) its troops in the war against Iraq to liberate Kuwait. Despite its domestic terrorism problems, the government of Egypt condemned the September 11, 2001 terrorist assault against the United States of America, and declared its strong support for America to defeat terrorist groups such as the al-Qaeda network. Based on much authoritative evidence, Egypt and the United States have outstanding and affable relations.

Police Profile

Background

Historically, Egypt has had an organized police regimen dating back close to 5,000 years; however, modern police formations emerged in the country after the demise of the monarchy in 1952. Under Nasser's regime, the police reigned to protect the interests of the wealthy caste, and the citizens' approach to the police was based on fear, disaffection, distrust, and violence. Nasser's administration was characterized by strict control of the population, leading to a police state. When Anwar Sadat took over power, he endeavored to relax some of the draconian measures instituted by his predecessor. Both leaders were, indeed, credited with reducing the prevalence of crimes because of their strategic policies that fortified police organization and security.

Demographics

Generally, like in most of the other African countries akin to Zambia, the Egyptian police personnel are underpaid, which creates an opportunity for the police to receive bribes while performing their functions. The abysmal low salary of the police led to a police mutiny on February 25, 1986. The rampage was quashed by the army on February 27. According to published accounts, the police force consisted primarily of uneducated youths from rural regions who were recruited for three-year terms and were paid only $4.00 a month. About 122,000 personnel, of whom

10,000 are sworn officers, make up the strength of the Egyptian police force, including additional 60,000 security officers and local village watchmen. There is also a paramilitary body estimated to reach 300,000, mostly conscripts, which supplement regular police in protecting buildings and controlling riots and disorder. Reportedly, disciplinary measures in the police regiment may be administrative or judicial. The legal aspect of it is based on the Military Justice Law of 1996, which superseded a code of military justice enacted by the British in 1893. The 1996 law mandated the death penalty for treason, murder, and the destruction or sabotage of weapons or property of the armed forces.

Organizational Description

Structurally, Egypt's police organization followed the pattern of both the French and Turkish police formations until the late nineteenth century, when the British adjustment of the police system occurred. In 1883, the national police force received instructions from the British officials, and the police personnel were selected by the British administrators. The British influence on the Egyptian police remained the philosophy of the police until 1990. Egypt's national police ranks resembled positions along military lines. Authority flowed from the Minister of Interior to the lower ranks of the police command.

Under Sadat's governance, a presidential decree in 1971 restructured police and security concerns under eight divisions of the Ministry of Interior. These departments include: State Security Investigations; Emigration and Nationality; Administrative Affairs; Criminal Investigation; Inspection; Transport and Communications; Personnel Affairs; Officers' Affairs; and Police Support. In August 1971, the Minister himself retained responsibility for State Security Investigations, Organization, and Public Relations. Responsibilities allocated to the deputy minister for public security included Port Security, Criminal Evidence Investigations, Emergency Police Rescue, Ministerial Guards, and Central Police Reserves. The deputy minister for special police was given responsibilities for Prison Administration, Civil Defense, the Central Security Forces, Police Transport, Communications, Traffic, and Tourism. Under the leadership of the deputy minister for personnel affairs and training were Police Training Institutions, Police Personnel, and the Policemen's Sports Association. The deputy minister for administrative and financial affairs had control over General Administration,

Budgets, Supplies, Accounting, Construction, and Legal Issues.

On February 22, 1972, Egypt's legislative body enacted the Police Authority Law, which established that the president would act as the chief of police and mandated that the Minister of Interior be known as the superior of police. The law also created the office of the Supreme Police Council and charged it with the responsibility of aiding the Minister to devise police rules and procedures. The law also established new police positions such as first undersecretary and undersecretary, which would be occupied by superior police generals. Furthermore, the new law of 1972 stipulated guidelines for police ranks; commissioned police ranks resembled grades in the military. The highest-ranking police officer begins with a major general and ranks descend to the first lieutenant. Below first lieutenant, is the grade of lieutenant chief warrant officer, followed by three descending ranks of warrant officers. The constables are assigned the grades of first or second assistant police officers. Enlisted police were allocated ranks of master sergeant, sergeant, corporal, and private. Police grade insignia were the same as those used by the military, and police uniforms were also identical. The basic police uniform consists of a khaki closed-neck tunic worn over matching trousers, with a khaki peaked cap. A Sam Browne belt completes the uniform. The police generally carry weapons such as hand guns in the performance of their duties.

The 1972 law also mandated that each police officer's personal history be kept on file, and every year additional information is added to the files. Annual reports of this kind are used to determine promotions to higher ranks in the force. To be promoted to the rank of brigadier general, seniority and vacancy are considered; promotion to the rank of major general is by selection. The retirement age for the members of the force is 60; however, an extension of three years could be given to the major generals. Police can receive 80% of their salary in pensions and 85% if they sustain injuries that lead to disability.

Operationally, the Egyptian national police force is deployed over police *mudiriyas* or provinces, which are situated in many governorates of the country. Each governorate has a director of police in charge of all police activities in the governorate. Both the governor (a presidential appointee) and the director of police implement the Ministry of Interior's policies within the jurisdiction of the governorate and are structured like the centralized police command. Both these officials are responsible to the minister of interior on all security matters of their various boundaries. The governor reports directly to the minister or a deputy, and the director reports to the ministry through standard official police guidelines. There are also police subdivisions located within the territorial boundaries of the governorates. Within these subdivisions, district police commandants have jurisdictional authority, and their duties are identical to those of the director of the governorate. Reportedly, the urban areas have modern police technology such as computers and communication equipment and modern facilities. On the other hand, police commands at the hinterlands lack modern facilities and police tools.

Functions

The Egyptian national police, a centralized police command, under the auspices of the Ministry of Interior, have various functions and responsibilities. The police are responsible for maintaining law and order, criminal investigation, preventing and detecting crime, and supporting the judicial system by serving to collect evidence of infractions. Additionally, the police have the duties to control traffic and provide emergency relief, process passports, prison administration, screening immigrants, and suppression of smuggling, defense intelligence, protecting celebrities, and participation in public security. Other broad functions include management of elections, combating narcotics operations, political sabotage, and providing assistance during the *haj* or pilgrimage to the holy land of Mecca.

Police Education, Research, and Publications

The Police Training College is located in Al Abbasiyay, near Cairo, the capital city of Egypt. Police officers receive their instructions at the college and must be graduates of the institution with a few exceptions. All recruits joining the police force are expected to finish a three-month course administered by the college. While some notable officers are sent abroad annually for additional police training, the Cairo training institute emphasizes modern procedures, practice, and contemporary methods of policing. The police training college is equipped with a laboratory and other facilities for police dogs and horses.

Officer candidates of the college, who must be citizens of Egypt, are required to complete 55% of secondary education, except for the descendants of those who died while serving in the armed forces and offspring of police and military personnel. The broad curriculum of the college includes divergent courses such as security administration, French and English languages, army drill, public security, fire fighting, criminal investigation, forensic science, sociology, radio communication, first aid, anatomy, and cryptology. Other courses include public relations and political science, infantry and cavalry exercise, marksmanship, group management, and internship. After completing a two-year curriculum, graduates are awarded a bachelor of police studies and are promoted to police lieutenants. It is estimated that at least 700 new officers a year are produced by the college. Another arm of the training institution is the Advanced Police Studies, which is responsible for advanced candidate training. Successful graduates of this superior institute qualify for ranks beyond the grade of lieutenant colonel. Enlisted police officers receive a vital three-month instruction at the Police College on military environment, police activities, and methods. After finishing their training, the students are deployed to their respective police posts, where they receive practical experience.

Most importantly, a doctoral program in criminology was added to the institute in 1975. Some prominent individuals with prior degrees in medicine, law, and engineering may also take advantage of a two-year program that will guarantee them the ranks of first lieutenants in the force. Candidates of the police force may also receive training in other police institutes that are established at various other centers in the country. Particularly, the criminal evidence investigation institute and police communications institute offer police education to potential students. Generally, newly commissioned officers receive police assignments with their local directorates after receiving required instructions from the college institutions. However, the urban police divisions receive priority of police assignments and receive more officers than the rural police stations.

IHEKWOABA D. ONWUDIWE

Bibliography

Arthur, Goldschmidt. *Historical Dictionary of Egypt*. The Scarecrow Press, Inc.: London, 1994.

Banks, S. Arthur, and thomas C. Muller. *Political Handbook of the World: Governments and Intergovernmental Organizations*. CSA Publications: New York, 1998.

Becker, Susan. 1990. "Library of Congress Country Studies: Cairo Street Scene with Traffic Police Officer." http://1cweb2.1oc.gov/cgi-bin/quey/r?frd/cstdy:@field (DOCID+eg0173).

Ingleton, D. Roy. *Police of the World*. Charles Scribner's Sons: New York, 1979.

Kurian, George Thomas. *World Encyclopedia of Police Forces and Penal Systems*. Facts on File: New York, 1989.

Legun, Colin. *Africa: Contemporary Record*. African Publishing Company: New York and London, 1992–1994.

Mars-Proietti, Laura. *Nations of the World: A Political, Economic and Business Handbook*. Grey House Publishing: Millerton, New York, 2004.

Onwudiwe, Ihekwoaba D. *The Globalization of Terrorism*. Ashgate Publishers: Aldershot, 2001.

Ramsay, Jeffress. 1993. Global Studies: Africa. An Annual edition's Publications. Connecticut: The Dushkin Publishing Group: Connecticut.

The Europa World Year Book. Europa Publications Limited: London, 1999.

The World Fact Book. "Egypt: Country Facts Sheet." 2004. www.cia.gov/cia/publications/factbook/geos/eg.html, Accessed January 23, 2005.

U.S. Department of State. "Background Note: Egypt." 2004. www.state.gov/r/pa/ei/bgn/5309.htm (23 January, 2005).

EL SALVADOR

Background Material

The Republic of El Salvador is geographically the smallest country Central America (21,040 sg km), and yet it has the largest population of any country in the region (6,353,681 as of July of 2002). Its territorial boundaries are formed to the west with the Republic of Guatemala; to the north and east with the Republic of Honduras; to the east with the Republic of Honduras and Nicaragua at the Gulf of Fonseca; and to the south with the Pacific Ocean.

The official language of El Salvador is Spanish, and the predominant religion is Catholicism.

The Gross Domestic Product per capita is US$4,497. The GDP per sector breaks down approximately as agriculture 10%, industry 30%, and services 60%.

The inhabitants of the Salvadoran territory before the arrival of the Spaniards to the New World in 1492 were of Mayan origin. El Salvador achieved its independence from Spain in 1821. Since then, its history has been marked by extensive social conflict.

Contextual Features

El Salvador is a unified state that is administratively divided in 14 departments. The Government's system is presidential, republican, democratic, and representative. The political system is pluralistic, with representation expressed through the political parties. The government's main bodies are legislative, executive, and judicial.

The juridical system has its basis in civil law, with the Constitution of the Republic as the supreme law of the land.

The Salvadoran criminal justice system is accusatory. The General Prosecutor's Office of the Republic, with support of the Police, is in charge of the functional management of the investigation; and the role of the penal judges is limited to the control of the activity of the state prosecutors and the mounting of the defense. In this structure, the functions of the judges are divided: there are judges who control the investigative phase exclusively (Judges of Peace and Instruction) and judges who pronounce the definitive sentence (Sentencing Judges).

The Judicial System is vertically structured and is composed of the Supreme Court of Justice, the Appellate Courts of Second Instance, the Tribunals of First Instance, and the Tribunals of Peace. The jurisdiction of the Tribunals of Peace is varied; and includes criminal, civil, family matter, traffic, and other jurisdictions. The Tribunals of First Instance are specialized in specific jurisdictions, and in criminal cases they have jurisdiction over the investigation and sentence phase. The Appellate Courts of Second Instance have jurisdiction over interlocutory appeals and appeals of definitive sentences that were imposed by the Tribunals of First Instance. In criminal cases, cassation is provided as an action for the definitive sentence.

The resource of cassation in civil, family, and labor matters is in the jurisdiction of the Civil Body of the Supreme Court of Justice, and in criminal cases, the Penal Body of the same institution has jurisdiction. Two bodies that form part of the Supreme Court of Justice are: the Administrative Contentious Court, which has jurisdiction over trials against the public administrators; and the Constitutional Court, which has jurisdiction mainly over the constitutional pro-

Five most common crimes in the period 1999–2001

N°	Crime	Protected Good or Right	Description
1	Theft	Property	Removal of personal property without violence
2	Robbery	Property, Personal Integrity	Removal of personal property with violence toward the person
3	Threats or Intimidation	Personal Autonomy	To threaten a person that he or his family will be harmed
4	Assault	Personal Integrity	Cause a physical damage to another
5	Homicide	Life	Deprive intentionally the life of another

Source: Unit of Operations and Statistics of the PNC.

cesses, such as the writ of *Hábeas Corpus* and questions of the unconstitutionality of laws.

The corrections system is divided in separate systems for adults and minors.

Some common aspects of both systems include the following: Their ultimate goal is the reeducation and the reinsertion into society of persons prosecuted for criminal offenses. Additionally, both systems depend upon the Executive Body. The adult system falls under the responsibility of the Ministry of Government, specifically under the General Administration of Penal Centers; and the system for minors falls under the direction of the National Department of the Family, and is assigned specifically to the Salvadorzan Institute of Protection of Minors (ISPM).

The tasks of the General Administration of Penal Centers and of the ISPM can be summarized as: the execution of policies for the treatment of prisoners, design and application of programs directed to the prisoner's reeducation and reinsertion, and the supervision of the guarantees of the rights of the prisoners.

The Judicial Body has special tribunals that supervise the guarantee of the rights of the prisoners during the trial phase and the punishment phase. These tribunals are: Penitentiary Observation and Execution of the Punishment, for adults; and Tribunals of Execution of Measures, for Minors.

Police Profile

Background

Between 1990 and 1992, peace agreements were signed between the Government and the insurgent group called *Farabundo Martí* for the National Liberation (FMLN), ending 12 years of civil war (1980–1992). The end of the civil war signified the transformation of the militaristic Public Security regime that had reigned until that time.

The system of Public Security before the Peace Agreements was composed of three security bodies of the Armed Forces: The Police of Treasury (PH), the National Guard (GN), and the National Police (PN).

The peace agreement of 1992, signed in Chapultepec, Mexico, opened the way to constitutional reform in the same year, which redefined the idea of National Defense and Public Security. The first reform was attributed to the Ministry of the National Defense, and was responsible for changing the mission of the Armed Forces to the defense of the sovereignty of the State and of the integrity of the territory. The second reform focused on Public Security, creating the National Civil Police (PNC) within the Ministry of Government. The main purpose of this reform was to subject the military and Public Security authority to civil authority.

According to Article 159 of the Constitution of the Republic, the National Civil Police is a professional body, independent of the Armed Forces and free from partisan influences. The PNC is also responsible for urban and rural police functions and works to guarantee order, security, and public peace. The PNC also collaborates in the procedure of criminal investigations. The PNC is responsible for performing these duties with due respect for the law and a strict respect for human rights.

The constitutional regulation of the PNC was developed for the first time, by the Legislative Ordinance #269 of June 25, 1992, published in the Official Diary number 144, volume 316 of August 10, 1992, containing the Organic Law of the Civil National Police that was effective until December 28, 2001, when a new Organic Law of the PNC entered in force. Both laws have been developed by a regulation and other dispersed laws. From the first Law, the PNC was created as a corporation of public law.

Organizational Description

The organizational description of the PNC can be seen from two perspectives: institutional, which is concerned with the hierarchical structuring of each one of the branch offices of the Corporation;

Administrative and operative personnel of the PNC and their gender

Administrative personnel	4,424	Total
		20,257
Operative personnel	15,833	
Female	2,188	
Male	18,069	

Source: Memory of works PNC June 2000–May 2001.

and professional, which is concerned with the hierarchy of their members, according to the level of the police career.

The structure and organization is of hierarchical nature, under the leadership of the President of the Republic through the Secretary of Government. In reality, the ordinary control of the police corporation is exercised by the General Director, who acts as the maximum administrative authority and legal representative.

The General Management is divided in different branches. These are:

General sub-bureau: This unit supports the General Management in the supervision and coordination of activities and in the transmission of orders to the sub-bureaus;

Sub-bureaus: specialized units of police service.

General Inspection: This unit supervises and controls the operative services of the institution in general, and also manages questions concerning the respect of human rights. It directs the control and disciplinary investigation units. It also prepares and presents cases at the disciplinary tribunals.

Technical Council: This unit develops a process of institutional strengthening through strategic planning, organizational development, consulting, and legal, technical and administrative matters. This unit determines the necessities of the police and their professional formation as well as of the institutional relationships with the community.

Center of Intelligence: This unit generates intelligence analysis through the collection, analysis, control, and diffusion of the information concerning the decision-making process of all the control levels.

Unit of Internal Audit: This unit makes audits of the operations, activities and programs of the police entity and it dependences.

Tribunals: This unit has jurisdiction over disciplinary matters, appeals, revenues, promotions, and scholarships.

In 1996, the police training began to be regulated through a special law: the Law of the Police Career of July 18, 1996 (LCP). This legislation contains the hierarchy of the PNC which includes three levels:

1) Basic level: Agent, Corporal, and Sergeant. In general their activities entail the execution of the police operative activities.
2) Executive level: Subinspector, Inspector, and Inspector in Chief. Their activities entail the direct and immediate supervision in the execution of the services and management functions.
3) Superior level: Subcomissioner, Commissioner, and General Commissioner. Their activities entail the managing, planning, coordination, and supervision of the divisions, units and police services.

With respect to promotions, the LCP and the "Regulation of Promotions of the PNC" of March 19, 1999, regulate the basic requirements. These are:

The applicant is in active service.

There is a vacancy for the position desired.

Applicant has served a minimum of established time in the category or level immediately below that which is desired.

Possession of the academic requirements for the level that is desired.

A lack of serious disciplinary sanctions or less serious sanctions that have not been canceled.

The promotion procedure consists of three phases:

1) Contest: In this phase, the Tribunal of Entrance and Promotions selects those who meet the requirements established in the law and the Regulation.
2) Theoretical and practical exams: It includes two eliminatory exercises: the first one, a personal interview to determine the applicant's aptitude for the category that he or she seeks; the second, practical theoretical exams on professional knowledge in the judicial, operative, and administration environments and police management.
3) To pass the course of Promotion of the National Academy of Public Security (ANSP): After passing the previous phases, the applicants with more qualifications undergo a course dictated by the ANSP whose content will be determined by the applicants' level and respective category. While the course is carried out, the applicant can't perform police services, unless exceptional circumstances exist.

In the case of the promotion to General Commissioner, in addition to the three phases, the presentation, defense, and approval of a masterful, unpublished thesis in Public Security, that will be exposed and defended openly in front of a tribunal composed of the Secretary of Government or his representative, the General Director of the PNC, the General Director of the ANSP, the President of the Penal Court of the Supreme Court of Justice and the General District Attorney of the Republic is required.

Functions

The most important functions are guaranteeing the general execution of laws, protecting and guaranteeing the free exercise of the rights of all the people in the whole national territory; maintaining the internal peace, tranquility, order and public security; preventing and combatting all kinds of crimes with strict respect of the law; collaborating in the procedure of investigation of crimes; and performing duties related to auxiliary to the citizenship in cases of public calamity; and other duties (Article 4, Organic Law PNC).

Starting from this enumeration, the functions can be classified by their nature in two classes:

a) Administrative: activities directed toward the management of the PNC;
b) Operative: These functions involve the execution of activities proper of the police regime. They can be summarized as: the surveillance of the execution of the laws in general, in the administrative field (breaches) as in the judicial field (support to the General Office of the Republic in the investigation of crimes); the other types of operative functions that do not have to do with the execution of the laws are the support tasks to the community in difficult situations such as earthquakes or floods.

For the execution of their different functions, the Corporation Police work with specific sub-bureaus for each of the tasks that the law mandates that it complete. The sub-bureaus and their attributions are:

Sub-bureau of Public Security: coordinates and evaluates the execution of strategies and police plans for prevention of the crime.
Sub-bureau of Investigations: coordinates and evaluates the process of investigation of crime, including organized crime, under the functional direction of the General Office of the Republic.

Sub-bureau of Specialized Operative Areas: coordinates and evaluates the execution of the operative activities of support for the maintenance public order and public security.
Sub-bureau of Ground Traffic: coordinates the police actions at national level in order to supervise ground traffic for the purpose of guaranteeing the road security, in addition to the supports that are necessary for the public security.
Sub-bureau of Administration and Finances: supports the operative function of the institution through the implementation and maintenance of administrative, logistical, and technical systems.

Training

The admission to the police training process can only be made at the Basic Levels, in Agent and Executive category, to the category of Subinspector.

The requirements for entrance are of two types:

1. General: They describe the conditions that all the applicants should complete, without attention at the chosen level. These are:

   a. Institutional:
   Approval of a course taught by the ANSP
   Approval by the Tribunal of Entrance and Promotions of the PNC.

   b. Personal:
   The individual who applies for this type of entrance must display a capacity for human relationships and emotional maturity, as well as the physical, moral and intellectual conditions needed to act as a police agent. The individual must also:

   Be Salvadoran from birth and in the full possession of citizen's rights;
   Have no criminal record;
   Fulfill the academic requirements for each level.

2. Specific: They describe the conditions peculiar of the entrance in the chosen level. For the basic level, the applicant must be older than 18 and younger than 28 at the time of the application, and have a high school diploma. For the executive level, the applicant must be younger than 30 years old when presenting the application, and have a university degree.

There are two institutions in charge of the police personnel's internal training. These are the Unit of Professional Formation (clerk of the General Secretary of the PNC) and the National Academy of Public Security (entity with own juridical personality, separate from the PNC).

As part of the instruction that the ANSP offers to police's applicants, there is included a course on human rights whose duration is of 40 hours for the basic level and of 80 hours for the executive level. Also in the courses of promotions human rights information is taught. The duration of this instruction depends on the level.

People who teach these courses are qualified in turn by other institutions. In 1997, the High Commissioner of the United Nations for the Human Rights taught several training days in human rights for the educational of the ANSP.

In January of 2000, the international organization *Rädda Barnen* of Sweden (Save the Children Sweden) subscribed to a cooperation agreement for the invigoration of the ANSP and the PNC regarding promotion, training, and protection of human rights.

In 2001, special courses on human rights were carried out, including the Graduate Program in Human Rights coordinated by the Institute of Human Rights of the Central American University José Simeón Cañas, UCA (IDHUCA). Thirty-six police agents of the basic level have graduated from this program. In the same year the international organization Save the Children Sweden supported the organization of several courses, including: Course of Youth, Violence and Delinquency, Course of Domestic Violence in judicial and administrative headquarters, Problems of the Childhood, and other courses.

The institutions that supervise the respect of human rights in the police activity are the General Inspection of the PNC (IGPNC), and the Attorney's Office for the Defense of the Human Rights PDDH (Ombudsman). Both institutions receive complaints of violations to human rights made by the police.

From January to December of 2001, the IGPNC received a total of 1,089 complaints for supposed violations to human rights on the part of police agents. The PDDH received in the same period a total of 1,142 accusations.

Police Public Projects

The Police have developed different projects in several areas:

Police effectiveness: Implemented in 1999, the project consists in the holding of periodic meetings to analyze the criminal behavior in certain territorial areas.

Deployment of Patrol cars for Community Intervention: This project seeks to offer an approach to the community and at the same time promote crime prevention measures.

Support to Areas of Disasters: This project offers help to areas that have suffered damages due to floods or earthquakes.

Safe vacations: This project seeks to ensure the security of people during the periods of national vacations.

DARE program (Drug Abuse Resistance Education): This program is directed to schoolchildren in order to discourage them from consuming drugs.

PEPAD program (Educational Program against the Abuse of Drugs): This program seeks to inform families, parents, and students about the damage caused by the consumption of drugs.

Ground traffic: Alcohol Detection, Firefly (Night Control of Vehicular Lights), and Highway Security: This project seeks to diminish the number of traffic accidents through vehicular control.

Police Uses of Firearms

The regulation of the use and possession of firearms is contained in the Law of Control and Regulation of Firearms, Ammunition, Explosive, and Similar Articles (LCRAF), of July 1, 1999. According to the LCRAF, persons older than 21 years of age, who are citizens or foreigners who reside permanently in the country, can obtain a license for the use or a registration for possession and carrying of the weapons. Even members of the PNC should have a license or registration for firearm possession outside of the hours of police service.

The Criminal Code establishes a sanction of three to five years of prison for individuals who possess, carry or control weapons of war. According to the LCRAF, the main characteristics of a war weapon are: that it possesses a fire selector for the shot in blast or those classified for light or heavy support, mines, and grenades. The Armed forces, certain units of the PNC, and the ANSP in the training of special units of the PNC are excluded from this prohibition.

The Police share jointly with the Ministry of National Defense the responsibility of verifying the execution of the LCRAF, for that which has a Division of Weapons and Explosive (DAE).

The Organic Law of the PNC and the Criminal Code establish certain norms for the use of weapons:

1. Preliminary exhaustion of all other means prior to the use of the weapons, and only

when other means that guarantee the foreseen result do not exist.

2. Use in self-defense or for the defense of others when a danger that can cause severe damages exists.
3. Proportionality of the use to the danger, attempt to cause the smallest damage.
4. Obligation of giving notice to superiors when the firearms were used
5. Not to use the force to dissolve meetings or peaceful gatherings.
6. It is forbidden to invoke political uncertainty as justification for not applying the present rules of use of weapons.

Complaints and Discipline

The personal responsibility of Police agents can be divided in the following areas:

Common responsibility:

Criminal: If they are accused of a crime, police agents are judged by the common tribunals, but their punishment is completely separated from that of the common convicted persons.

Civil: Civil responsibility for criminal or civil offenses is determined by the common tribunals.

Administrative: The responsibility for failure to fulfill a duty or infraction of administrative laws is determined by the authorities that the respective law imposes.

Special responsibility:

Disciplinary: Infractions of laws, regulations, norms in general and the inherent orders to the police duty.

The regulation of the disciplinary responsibility—type and classification of the infractions, procedure, competent authorities and sanction—is contained in the Disciplinary Regulation of the PNC of August 15, 2000.
The infractions and their sanction are:

a) Simple nonfeasance whose sanction can be oral or written warning, arrest for five days or suspension of the position without salary for not longer than fifteen days.
b) Serious nonfeasance, whose sanction can be suspension of the position without salary for up to one hundred eighty days, or demotion.

An important aspect that should stand out is that the Legislative Assembly can recommend to the President of the Republic the demotion of the Director of the Police Corporation. When the demotion is due to violations of human rights, this is obligatory.

Terrorism

The Criminal Code defines as criminal "Acts of terrorism," including a group of activities, among others, such as acts against the life, personal integrity, or freedom of the President of the Republic; destruction of public property; production of weapons to commit acts of terrorism. Although terrorist organizations do not exist currently within Salvadoran territory, there are cases in which people have been accused of carrying out acts of terrorism.

The PNC does not have a specific unit to combat terrorism, although it has a Group of Police Reaction (GRP) that offers support to the different police dependences in critic situations. The Armed forces has a special unit to combat terrorism.

International Cooperation

Among the countries that give support to the PNC are: Spain, France, Japan, the United States, the European Union, Colombia, and Chile. Besides these countries, other types of reciprocal cooperation exist, specifically with countries of the Central American Region and the Caribbean.

Some areas of international cooperation during the 2001 were:

Criminal investigation: Events were developed to combat kidnapping. The Organized Crime unit provided to the police controls and agents, effective techniques for the eradication of this crime. This area oversees Forensic ballistics, Basic Anti-drug operations, Investigation of Computer Crimes, Economic Crimes, and others. The developments were advised by the United States, France, and the European Union.

Administration, Management and Police Proceeding: Courses of Administration and Supervision were developed, directed to the Executive and Superior Level of the police force. This work was developed by the ICITAP (International Criminal Investigation and Training Program of the U.S. Government). In this same area, the European Community carried out a series of courses about Police Administration, directed to the Executive and Superior level of the police force, concerned with the handling of personnel. Other similar courses were carried out by the European Union through the National Police Body of Spain.

Specialized units: The Unit of Maintenance of the Order (UMO) was the beneficiary of cooperation with the Republican Company of Security of France that conducted the "3rd Central American Course for the Maintenance of the Order," carried out in El Salvador.

Other areas that have benefited from international cooperation are:

Patrol cars of Community Intervention (PIP-COM) that received donations from the governments of the United States, Japan, and Spain. The donations of the first patrols consisted in bicycles for patrolling; the third donation consisted in computer equipment to expedite the processing of information and the upgrade of detention orders.

Part of the cooperation and international assistance is the exchange of police personnel. Chile and Colombia have offered police courses. Also, there are frequent trips to share experiences with other police forces in the Central American Region and the Caribbean. Most of these activities are directed toward the Executive and Superior levels, although some exchanges are also given in the Basic Level.

Police Education, Research, and Publications

Institutions

National Academy of Public Security (ANSP). This institution was created in 1992 as an autonomous institution of public law with its own juridical personality, in charge of the permanent formation of the members of the PNC. It elaborates the plans for applicant selection and the promotion of agents of the PNC. It also is in charge of investigating, studying and disclosing significant matters to the PNC and the Public Security.

Central American Institute of Superior Studies of Police (ICESPO). This institution was created in 1996 by an international agreement as part of the plan of Central American integration, among the governments of the Republic of Costa Rica, El Salvador, Guatemala, Honduras, Nicaragua and Panama. Its headquarters is in San Salvador, El Salvador.

Some of their objectives include contributing to the analysis of the national judicial ordinances governing Police Forces, cooperating for the respect of human rights as the base of police performance, and strengthening the civil and apolitical character of the police institutions and others.

Leading Researchers

Jeannette Aguilar Villamariona, independent consultant

Edgardo Amaya Cóbar, Center of Penal Studies of El Salvador, CEPES/FESPAD.

Jaime Martínez Ventura, Center of Penal Studies of El Salvador, CEPES/FESPAD.

Salvador Samayoa, National Council of Public Security

Miguel Cruz, Institute of Human rights of the Central American University José Simeón Canes, IDHUCA.

Sandra Rivera Flores, Commission of the European Communities.

Gino Costa, Consultant, Peru

William Stanley, Hemisphere Initiatives, USA.

Charles Call, Brown University, USA.

The Police Corporation does not have a unit specially dedicated to investigation. Instead, this task is carried out by its various units and concentrated on the Unit of Institutional Planning, a dependence of the General Secretary of the PNC. (The Unit of Police Statistic [UEP], clerk of the Center of Police Intelligence, is one of the entities that generates information with the purpose of monitoring criminal activity.)

Other institutions that carry out investigations are the National Academy of Public Security and the National Council of Public Security, which are concerned with Public Security, the prevention of crime, police procedure, and other issues; the Foundation of Studies of Applied Law; FESPAD, a non-government organization that carries out studies as concerning Public Security and police reform, under the auspice of the Kingdom of the Low Countries and the Washington Office for Latin American, WOLA.

Also the Program of Strengthening of the Police Institutions of El Salvador, supported by the European Union, carries out investigations on the subject.

NELSON ARMANDO VAQUERANO

Bibliography

Police. El Salvador.

Editor: National Civil Police of El Salvador.

Address: Central barracks, 6th Street, between 8th and 10th Avenue South, number 42, Neighborhood Vega, San Salvador, El Salvador.

National Civil Police. Memory of Works. Second phase, June 2000–May 2001.

Description: The memory of works is presented every year as a report of the activities carried out by the PNC (publication in Spanish).

National Civil Police. Division of Juvenile Services and Family. *Statistical Report of Nonfeasance and Domestic Crimes. First and second trimester of 2001.*

Description: Analysis of statistical figures with the purpose of monitoring delinquent activity. This is one of the several reports that are prepared by the Units of the PNC (publication in Spanish).

National Academy of Public Security and Civil National Police. *Module for civil protection.* San Salvador, 2001.

Description: This publication seeks to improve police performance in several areas through manuals of criminal investigation, procedures customs officers, etc. This specific document refers to the legal procedures, treatments, and intervention in cases of emergencies, natural disasters and prevention (publication in Spanish).

Ministry of Public Security. General Inspection of the PNC. *Annual evaluation on the grade of knowledge that the members of the PNC have on human rights. 1999 Final report.* March 2000.

Description: This publication evaluates the knowledge in human rights of the members of the PNC in different areas such as criminal investigation, detentions, etc (publication in Spanish).

Police website:
www.pncelsalvador.gob.sv

EQUATORIAL GUINEA

Background Material

Equatorial Guinea has been an independent country since 1968, after 190 years of Spanish rule. President Obiang Nguem Mbasogo has ruled the country for over two decades, after seizing power from his uncle, then President Macias, in a 1979 coup. Although the country has been a nominal constitutional democracy since 1991, the country's presidential elections in 1996 and 2002 were considered internationally to be widely flawed. The president handles opposition parties through the judicious use of patronage. The country has undergone an economic windfall in recent years, due to oil production. While this has resulted in a massive increase in government revenue, there have been few improvements in living standards for the country's inhabitants. Equatorial Guinea has received international attention recently after Mark Thatcher, the son of Britain's former Prime Minister Margaret Thatcher, pleaded guilty in a South African court to helping finance a failed coup plot.

Equatorial Guinea is a tiny country, composed of a mainland and five inhabited islands. It is located in Western Africa, bordering the Bight of Biafra. The country of Cameroon borders Equatorial Guinea to the north, and Gabon borders the country to the south and east. The total area of Equatorial Guinea is 28,051 sq km, with a population of 523,051 (2004 est.). The capital is Malabo on the island of Bioko. The country is comprised of two ethnic groups: Bioko (primarily Bubi, some Fernandinos), and Rio Muni (primarily Fang). There are also fewer than 1000 European inhabitants, most of whom are Spanish. Religious affiliation in the country is nominally Christian and predominantly Roman Catholic, along with pagan practices as well. The official languages are Spanish and French; however, pidgin English, Fang, Bubi, and Ibo are also spoken.

The GDP per capita is $2,700 (2002 est.). The discovery and exploitation of large oil reserves have led to dramatic economic growth in recent years. Forestry, farming, and fishing are also major components of GDP. Before gaining independence, Equatorial Guinea was dependent on cocoa production for hard currency earnings. However, neglect of the rural economy under successive regimes has diminished the potential for agricultural growth (though the government has stated its intention to reinvest some oil revenue into agriculture). A number of aid programs sponsored by the World Bank and the IMF have been cut off since 1993, because of corruption and mismanagement. The government is no longer eligible for concessional financing because of the country's large oil revenues. The government has been unsuccessfully trying to agree on a "shadow" fiscal management program with the World Bank and IMF. Businesses, for the most part, are owned by government officials and their family members. Undeveloped natural resources include titanium, iron ore, manganese, uranium, and alluvial gold. It is predicted that economic growth in the country will remain strong, because of oil export.

Contextual Features

Equatorial Guinea has a legal system that is partly based on Spanish civil law and tribal custom. The executive branch is led by the President and Prime Minister, First Deputy Prime Minister, and Deputy Prime Minister. A Council of Ministers is appointed by the president. The President is elected by popular vote for a seven-year term. The Prime Minister and Deputy Prime Ministers are also appointed by the President.

The legislative branch is the unicameral House of People's Representatives, or *Camara de Representantes del Pueblo*. The House of People's Representatives holds 80 seats, and the members are elected directly by popular vote to serve five-year terms. The Parliament has little power, since the constitution vests all executive authority in the President. Power of the judiciary branch is placed in the Supreme Tribunal.

Police Profile

Reliable and easily accessible information on the police in Equatorial Guinea is not readily available. The number of police has been estimated as consisting of 400 paramilitary men.

Bibliography

"Equatorial Guinea." *CIA World Fact Book* www.cia.gov/cia/publications/factbook/geos/ek.html.

"Mark Thatcher Admits Equatorial Guinea Coup Plans." *Afrol News*, January 13, 2005. www.afrol.com/articles/15309.

"Military of Equatorial Guinea." *Answers.com* www.answers.com/topic/military-of-equatorial-guinea.

ERITREA

Background Material

Ethiopia's annexation of Eritrea as a province in 1962 led to a 30-year war that ended in 1991, with Eritrean rebels defeating governmental forces. Independence for Eritrea was approved in a 1993 referendum. A two-and-a-half-year border war with Ethiopia that began in 1998 ended on December 12, 2000.

Eritrea currently hosts a UN peacekeeping operation that is monitoring a 25 km-wide Temporary Security Zone on the border with Ethiopia. An international commission, organized to resolve the border dispute, posted its findings in 2002, but final demarcation is on hold due to Ethiopian objections.

Eritrea is located in eastern Africa, bordering the Red Sea, between Djibouti and Sudan. It covers a total area of 121,320 sq km, and has a population of 4,447,307 (July 2004 est.). The population is composed of the following ethnic groups, by percentage of the total population: Tigrinya, 50%; Tigre and Kunama, 40%; Afar, 4%; Saho (Red Sea coast dwellers), 3%; and other, 3%. Muslims, Coptic Christians, Roman Catholics, and Protestants are all present in the population. Afar, Arabic, Tigre, Kunama, Tigrinya, and other Cushitic languages are spoken.

The GDP per capita is $700 (2002 est.).

Contextual Features

Eritrea has a transitional government. After the referendum on independence passed, a National Assembly, composed entirely of members of the People's Front for Democracy and Justice (PFDJ), was established as a transitional legislature. A Constitutional Commission was also established to draft a constitution. The constitution was ratified in May 1997, but it did not take effect, pending parliamentary and presidential elections. Parliamentary elections had been scheduled for December, 2001, but they were postponed indefinitely. Currently, the only legally recognized political party is the PFDJ.

The legal system is mainly based in the Ethiopian legal code of 1957. Civil, commercial, and penal codes have not yet been promulgated.

The president is both the chief of state and the head of government. The president is head of the State

Council and the National Assembly. The State Council is composed of members appointed by the president.

The unicameral National Assembly has 150 seats. Term limits have not yet been established. In 1997, members of the PFDJ Central Committee, the Constituent Assembly (which had been established to ratify the constitution), and representatives of Eritreans living abroad formed a Transitional National Assembly, intended to serve as the nationallegislative body until elections for the National Assembly were held. National Assembly elections scheduled for December 2001 were postponed indefinitely.

The High Court is the supreme branch of the judiciary. Eritrea also has regional, subregional, village, military, and special courts.

Police Profile

Information on the police in Eritrea is difficult to access. Given that most governmental and administrative bodies in Eritrea are in transition or in development, it seems unlikely that the police force is an effective nationalized and organized body.

In early 2004, the International Committee of the Red Cross (ICRC) conducted a workshop with the Eritrean police. The workshop focused on issues of international humanitarian law and human rights law. It also focused on topics of law enforcement, ethical conduct, prevention and detection of crime, arrest and detention, asylum, refugees, and use of firearms. Twenty-one senior police officers took part, including several full-time training professionals at the Eritrean Police Training Centre in Asmara.

Bibliography

"Eritrea." *CIA World Fact Book*. www.cia.gov/cia/publica tions/factbook/geos/er.html.

"Eritrea: First workshop with Eritrean police force." *ICRC News* 01/13 www.icrc.org/Web/Eng/siteeng0.nsf/htmlall/ 57JQXH.

ESTONIA

Background Material

After centuries of Danish, Swedish, German, and Russian rule, Estonia attained independence in 1918. Estonian territory was taken over by Russia for the first time in 1721, when Russia defeated Sweden in the Great Northern War, and the second time by the then-Soviet Union in 1939 in World War II. The occupation by the Soviet Union (USSR) lasted more than a half century. Estonia restored its independence on August 20, 1991, with the collapse of the Soviet Union. Since the last Russian troops left in 1994, the Republic of Estonia has been free to promote economic and political ties with Western Europe. Russia continues to reject signing and ratifying the joint December, 1996 technical border agreement with Estonia. Estonia has been a member of NATO and the European Union (EU) since 2004.

The population of Estonia is 1,356,045 (2003 est.). The ethnic composition of the population is 65.3% Estonians, 28.1% Russians, 2.5% Ukrainians, 1.5% Byelorussians, one percent Finns, and 1.6% others (1998). The official language is Estonian, but 108 other languages are spoken in Estonia as mother tongues. The most commonly spoken are Russian, Ukrainian, Byelorussian, Finnish, Latvian, and Lithuanian (2000).

Religions represented include Evangelical Lutheran, Russian Orthodox, Estonian Orthodox, Baptist, Methodist, Seventh-Day Adventist, Roman Catholic, Pentecostal, Word of Life, and Jewish.

The Per capita income (purchasing power parity) is US$12,300 (2004 est.). Major economic activities are engineering, electronics, wood and wood products, textile, and information technology and telecommunications. Services, particularly financial, transit, and tourism, have grown in importance compared to the historically more prominent light industry and food production.

Contextual Features

Under the Constitution adopted on June 28, 1992, Estonia has a parliamentary system of government, with a Prime Minister as chief executive. The executive power of the state—the Government—is responsible to the *Riigikogu* (Parliament). The *Riigikogu* elects a President, whose duties are largely ceremonial.

The Estonian judicial system is based primarily on the German model, especially within the field of civil law with which it has direct historical links. Estonian law and order are subject to international law, whose general principles are incorporated into Estonian law. According to its Constitution, Estonia is an independent sovereign state whose international agreements take precedence over national law.

In 1992, the Criminal Code and the Code of Criminal Procedure of the Estonian Republic were adopted, and they considerably modified criminal law and criminal procedure law. Capital punishment was abolished in 1998 and replaced by life imprisonment. The Penal Code, which took effect in 2002, reforms the whole penal policy. The unified penal law combines the earlier criminal law and administrative offence law, which has resulted in the elimination of earlier distinctions between criminal and administrative offences. The new law stipulates the responsibility not only for criminal offences but also for wrongdoings.

The number of crimes recorded has almost doubled in Estonia since regaining independence in 1991. Alongside of the quantitative changes that took place, there have been relevant changes in the incidences of crime. Crimes against property comprise the majority of all registered crimes. Concealed thefts form the biggest part of crimes against property. Fraud is presently the fastest growing type of property crime. However, the number and percentages of crimes against the person have noticeably dropped. Increasing drug-related crime and drug use are prompting concern in Estonia, as these types of crime have skyrocketed during the past years. The crime problems associated with drug trafficking are growing steadily. The number of economic crimes has grown more than four times since the beginning of 1990s.

In the first decade of the 2000s, the total number of crimes recorded by the police was 53,595 (3,952 crimes per capita). The number of homicides recorded by the police was 147, which made up 10.8 homicides per capita and constituted 0.3% of all recorded crimes.

The court system is divided into three levels: (a) county, city, and administrative courts, (b) circuit courts of appeal, and (c) the Supreme Court, which also functions as the constitutional court. County and city courts are the courts of first instance and hear all civil, criminal, and misdemeanour matters. There are three city and 15 county courts in Estonia. Four administrative courts as courts of first instance hear administrative matters. Three circuit courts are the courts of second instance and review judgments of county, city, and administrative courts on the basis of appeals against judgments and rulings. Appeals against judgments of circuit courts may be submitted to the Supreme Court. The Supreme Court decides on granting leave to appeal in the determination of at least three justices. The Supreme Court is composed of the Civil Chamber, Criminal Chamber, Administrative Law Chamber, and the Constitutional Review Chamber. Appeals may also be heard by Special (*ad hoc*) Panels or by the Supreme Court *en banc*. The Supreme Court *en banc*, composed of all justices of the Supreme Court, is the highest body of the Court.

The Department of Prisons of the Ministry of Justice manages and supervises prison administration and operations of the institutions involved. The main task of the Department of Prisons is to organise the work of prisons, places of preliminary detention, and of extradition camps; and the supervision and execution of pre-trial investigation of prison crimes and surveillance work. There are nine prison institutions in Estonia: four of the prisons are closed; three semi-closed; and two institutions are for young offenders. According to 2003 data, the prison population in Estonia is 4,636 (342 per capita). Some 3% of all prisoners are women. The Imprisonment Act provided two types of prisons in the Estonian prison system—closed and open ones.

Police Profile

Background

The Estonian Police was founded on November 12, 1918, and it existed until the summer of 1940. The Estonian Police was re-established within the jurisdiction of the Ministry of the Interior in March 1, 1991 by the Police Act. In 1993, the Security Police Board gained the status of an independent institution within the jurisdiction of the Ministry of the Interior.

The Police Act, which regulates police activity, was passed in 1990, during the crumbling phase of the Soviet regime. The Act set out the transition period during which the dissolution of the Soviet Militia and the formation of the Estonian Police had to be completed. This law remained in effect until 1998, when a new Police Service Act was passed. The passage of this Act was a very important step in the development of the Estonian Police, since it laid the basis for stabilizing the personnel of the police force. Also, the Police Service Act Amendment Act, which provides for the pension of policemen, was adopted in 2000.

Demographics

The number of personnel in the Estonian Police is 4,802 (2004 data). The number of police officers employed by the Estonian Police is 3,529 (206 per capita). Female police officers constitute 30.1 percent of the sworn police personnel. Non-sworn staff (civilian and contracted employees) constitutes 26.5% of the Estonian Police personnel, out of whom women make up 56.7%.

Before police reform in 1991, ethnic Russians constituted approximately two-thirds of the police forces. Currently, the proportionate representation has substantially declined in favour of ethnic Estonians.

An equal opportunities policy exists in the Estonian Police. No minimum or maximum quotas have been set for the number of both sexes in the police. There are neither any sections within the police that both sexes cannot join nor any shifts that are not open for both sexes. To get promoted, officers have to have served a certain number of years in the police service, and they have to meet evaluated requirements for police officers.

Organizational Description

A police officer is a person employed in the police service. The basic categories of police officers are: (1) higher police officers; (2) senior police officers; and (3) junior police officers. Higher police officers are: national police commissioner and national security police commissioner; deputy national police commissioner and deputy national security police commissioner; police chief and police prefect; deputy police chief, deputy police prefect and police counselor; chief superintendent; and superintendent. Senior police officers are: leading police inspector, and leading constable; senior police inspector, and senior constable; and police inspector, and constable. Junior police officers are junior police inspector and junior constable. The titles of assistants are only applicable in the Security Police Board.

Police officers are selected according to the evaluation requirements of the Police Service Act, and civilian employees are selected according to the requirements of the Public Service Act.

The Security Police Board is subordinate to the Interior Minister but also reports to the Prime Min-

ister. The main tasks of the Security Police are supporting independent statehood; the prevention, obstruction, and detection of certain crimes; and the pre-trial proceeding of criminal cases having initiated on such basis. The structure and operations of the Security Police are classified.

The central and supervisory authority of the Estonian Police is the Police Board, which manages, directs, and co-ordinates the activities of all police agencies under its administration. The Estonian Police has four territorial police units called Police Prefectures, each serving several counties and towns. A Police Prefecture maintains public order and ensures internal security in its area; it prevents, combats and detects criminal acts and wrongdoings; and it conducts preliminary investigations of criminal matters and processes misdemeanors. There are four national units: the Central Criminal Police, the Central Law Enforcement Police, the Forensic Service Centre, and the Police College.

The Central Criminal Police co-ordinates the activities of the criminal police in the whole state and the international co-operation of the criminal police. It investigates: crimes committed by criminal organisations; drug crimes, economic crimes and IT crimes exceeding the service areas of Police Prefectures; crimes related to money laundering; and crimes requiring extensive international co-operation or central proceeding because of their danger to society. The main tasks of the Forensic Service Center are to conduct forensic examinations (18 main areas), participate in gathering evidence as an impartial specialist, keep relevant databases and data collections, conduct professional training, and equip police agencies with forensic equipment. The main tasks of the Central Law Enforcement Police are to analyse and co-ordinate the activities of the police in the area of law enforcement (e.g., crime prevention; to participate in ensuring public order and performing traffic supervision together with Police Prefectures; to follow up on misdemeanours; to protect the President, the Chairman of the *Riigikogu*, the Prime Minister, and the official guests of the state; to guard the objects assigned by the Government; and to train police dogs).

The main task of the SWAT Team ("K-komando"), subordinated to the Central Criminal Police, is to conduct police operations for apprehending criminals who are believed, based on prior information, to be armed and who may resist arrest. The Central Criminal Police tend to employ the SWAT Team for their police operations more often than other units of the police, but the Criminal Police Departments of the Police Prefectures and Security Police Board utilize them as well, although not so commonly.

The Crowd Control Unit ("*Märulipolitsei*") of the Law Enforcement Department is subordinated to the Central Law Enforcement Police. This special unit consists of police officers from different departments of the Estonian Police, who have joined the unit on voluntary basis, and who are specially trained, equipped, and utilized for maintenance of order at public events and meetings, and crowd control at mass disturbances and riots.

Functions

According to the Police Act para.2, the police can be considered an institution. On the other hand, police functions are assignments in which the law entitles the executors the special rights to carry out these assignments. Thus, in order to fulfil assignments that don't need special police rights, un-sworn staff can be used in Estonian Police. The police functions are fulfilled by sworn police officers. Although around 27 percent of the police personnel are non-sworn, the new trend of involving more civilian or contracted employees has been developing during recent years.

The main task of the Estonian Police is to maintain public order and ensure security; prevent, detect and investigate crimes and wrongdoings; conduct pre-trial investigations into criminal matters; and process misdemeanours. While doing so, the Police are in close cooperation with inhabitants and communities of different regions.

There are nine core jobs within the police organization:

1) Patrol officer: patrolling in the assigned area, responding to emergency calls, protecting crime scenes, and detecting and clearing wrongdoings;
2) Constable: community policing, clearing citizens' applications, settling disputes and re solving various issues, conducting prelimina ry criminal investigation procedures, and detecting and clearing wrongdoings;
3) Detention house and convoying officer: securing the arresting regimes of police cells and court, convoying detainees;
4) Duty officer: receiving, registering, and reacting to 110 calls (this is the national police number as Estonia has a separate emergency number for rescue service, both similar to 911 in the United States); receiving, registering and forwarding information; guarding police agencies' premises

and the property, and delivering the arms and equipment of the police;
5) Juvenile police officer: conducting preliminary criminal investigation procedures involving juveniles and detecting and clearing juveniles' wrongdoings, clearing citizens' applications concerning juveniles, community policing;
6) Investigator: pre-trial investigation of criminal cases;
7) Surveillance officer (criminal intelligence): conducting surveillance procedures using undercover techniques and methods, conducting preliminary criminal investigation procedures;
8) Forensic expert: making use of expert knowledge and equipment in preliminary investigation procedures;
9) Personal protection officer: guarding persons and objects as determined by the government of Estonia.

Training

The Estonian Police accepts citizens of the Republic of Estonia, who are at least 19 years old, have at least secondary education, and have not been punished for intentional criminal action. The candidates should be able to fulfil the obligations of police in all aspects—their personal and moral capacities, level of education, physical fitness, and condition of health. A police officer candidate has to be fluent in the national language and while on duty must be able to communicate in the most common language of the respective area, which can be Russian or English. Candidates for the entrance tests to the Police College have to submit their applications with relevant documentation to the staff department of their local police institution.

While the Police School of the Police College prepares junior and senior police officials, the graduates of the Police College are enabled to work at the position of a senior police officer.

Police Public Projects

For enhancing public security crime prevention at national, local, and population levels, the police organize public events (presentations, courses, joint activities, etc.), motivating activities (contests and competitions dealing with prevention), and develop cooperation with population and local authorities.

Police Use of Firearms

The police in Estonia are routinely armed. The SWAT team members receive special, intensive training; they have distinctive weaponry and clothing.

Complaints and Discipline

Police personnel commit random acts of human rights abuses. The most common complaints concern the police use of excessive force and verbal abuse during the arrest and questioning of suspects, and mistreatment of prisoners and detainees.

Estonia is a member of the Council of Europe and has signed and ratified the European Convention for the Protection of Human Rights and Fundamental Freedoms. Estonian Institute for Human Rights (EIHR) was founded in 1992. One of the purposes of EIHR is monitoring the situation in the field of individual and collective human rights. The Legal Chancellor has the power to ensure legislative compliance with the Constitution by the State; in addition, she/he also acts as Ombudsman to deal with specific complaints by citizens regarding the work of the State or State officials (e.g., police officers). There is a Police Control Unit of the Personnel Department subordinated to the Police Board, which is responsible for carrying out investigations of abuses committed by the police.

In 1998, a new subject, Police and Human Rights, was introduced in all specialties taught at the Public Service Academy, and all the graduates from 1998 and 1999 received corresponding training. Since 2000, the new syllabus of the Academy no longer includes the subject and the related training courses.

Terrorism

In Estonia, the Security Police is in charge of fighting terrorism. There have not been any terrorist aimed bomb explosions on the territory of the Republic of Estonia, brought about by political or religious views and ideologies.

International Cooperation

Estonia is a member of Interpol and Europol. The Estonian Police has posted its liaison officers in Finland, Russia, and in The Hague at Europol. A United States Federal Bureau of Investigation (FBI) representation operates in Tallinn. Other foreign liaison officers posted in Estonia are the attaché in judicial matters from Finnish Ministry of Justice and Nordic police liaison officer in the Swedish Embassy to Estonia. Since 2002, the Police College of the Public Service Academy has been a member of the Association of European Police Colleges. An international law enforcement training centre for the International Police Academy has been set up at the Public Service Academy.

There has been a range of foreign assistance in relation to the Police School: Sweden has provided an exchange program; Strathclyde police from Scotland, United Kingdom, has provided assistance in teaching methods; and Germany has provided individual programs for teachers. Foreign specialists have come to teach in Estonia, for example from Denmark, Holland, Sweden, Germany, Finland, and Ireland. There have also been links with the Nordic Baltic Police Academy.

Many police officers at any level study in foreign countries; seminars, lectures and training trips are organised; experts are invited to Estonia, etc. European police academies, colleges, schools or training centres are involved in this process.

In order to improve the structure of the police training system and the quality of the education, support was requested from the EU. The Phare project "Police training and educational system," assisted by the twinning-partners from Swedish and the Netherlands police, was approved and started at the end of 2001. The final report of the project was published in December 2002. As a result of the project, a new competencies-based police education was formulated.

Police Education, Research, and Publications

The Police College organizes courses at the Police School and the Public Service Academy. The provision of basic training is concentrated at the Police School at Paikuse in Pärnu County, and it provides vocational secondary education. Successful graduates can continue their studies at the Police College of the Public Service Academy in Tallinn.

The Public Service Academy is an institution of applied higher education subordinated to the Ministry of the Interior, which prepares officials for the state, and local self-governments, giving them applied higher education on the bachelor level. Since it is also the Estonian civil service training and development centre, the Academy carries out continuous education and applied research work. The fields of activities of the Academy are: (1) public safety (police, border guard, rescue service); (2) legal administration (corrections, court officers); (3) tax administration (customs, taxation); and (4) public administration.

A master's degree in public administration can be acquired after two years of extramural studies. Graduate courses were started at the Academy in the year 2001 and were organized in cooperation with the Tallinn Technical University. The purpose of these studies is preparation and development of leaders for Estonian public service institutions (e.g., police).

Many police officers are enrolled at the Faculty of Law and the Institute of Law at the University of Tartu, or have graduated from these institutions.

Leading Police Researchers

A. Ahven, Adviser, Internal Security Analysis Department, Ministry of the Interior.

I. Aimre, Professor, Department Chair, Department of Criminology and Sociology, Public Service Academy.

J. Ginter, Assistant Dean, Faculty of Law, University of Tartu.

A. Markina, Lecturer, Institute of Law, University of Tartu.

A. Resetnikova, Researcher, Institute of Law, University of Tartu.

J. Saar, Docent, Institute of Law, University of Tartu.

J. Sootak, Professor, Department of Criminal Law, Faulty of Law, University of Tartu.

J. Strömpl, Docent, Department of Sociology, University of Tartu.

U. Traat, Lecturer, Faculty of Criminology and Sociology, Public Service Academy.

Leading Journals, Periodicals, and Magazines

Politseileht (Police Journal). M. Rüga (Ed.), Pagari 1, 15060 Tallinn, Estonia. (Estonian)

Juridica. K. Prükk (Ed.), Näituse 20, 50409 Tartu, Estonia. (Estonian)

Juridica International. K. Prükk (Ed.), Näituse 20, 50409 Tartu, Estonia. (English)

Süüdistaja (Prosecutor). S. Pärmann (Ed.), Wismari 7, 15188 Tallinn, Estonia. (Estonian)

Verbis Aut Re. K. Tääker & E. Jalakas (Eds.), Kase 61, 12012 Tallinn, Estonia. (Estonian) Publications

Saar, J., Markina, A., Ahven, A., Annist, A. & Ginter, J. (2003). Kuritegevus Eestis 1991-2001: *Crime in Estonia 1991-2001*. Tallinn, Estonia: Juura, Õigusteabe AS. (Estonian, summary in English)

Saar, J., Markina, A., Resetnikova, A., Ginter, J., Sootak, J. & Parmas, A. (2003). *Eesti õiguskaitseasutuste koostöö Euroopa Liidu liikmesriikidega piiriülese kuritegevuse tõkestamisel (olukord enne ja pärast liitumist Euroopa Liiduga) (Cooperation of Estonian legal protection agencies with European Union Member States in combating cross-border crime* (Situation before and after accession to the European Union)) (110 p.). Report conducted within the framework of public contract 03-175 in the Institute of International and Social Studies of the Tallinn Pedagogical University and the Faculty of Law of the University of Tartu. (Estonian)

Police-Related Websites:

Estonian Police: *www.pol.ee/*
Security Police Board: *www.kapo.ee/*
Ministry of the Interior: *www.sisemin.gov.ee/*
Ministry of Justice: *www.just.ee/*
Public Service Academy: *www.sisekaitse.ee/*

AIGI RESETNIKOVA

Bibliography

Hebenton, B., and J. Spencer. (2001). *Assessing international assistance in law enforcement: Themes, findings, and recommendations from case-study of the Republic of Estonia* Tampere, Finland: Tammer-Paino Oy. www.heuni.fi/uploads/ai1xeg7glsj9.pdf (01/15/2005).

Kangaspunta, K., M. Joutsen, N. Ollus, and S. Nevala, (Eds.). (1999). *Profiles of criminal justice systems in Europe and North America 1990-1994*. HEUNI Publication Series, 33.

Resetnikova, A. (June, 2003). *Emerging issues in the transition from a militia to a national police service: The case of Estonia*. Unpublished theses presented in partial fulfillment of the requirements for the degree of Master of Arts in criminal justice, John Jay College of the City University of New York. www.enut.ee/enut.php?keel=ENG&id=24&uid=60 (01/15/2005).

Saar, J. (1999). *Criminal justice system and process of democratization in Estonia* NATO Democratic Institutions Research Fellowship Final Report. www.nato.int/acad/fellow/97-99/saar.pdf (01/15/2005).

Saar, J., A. Markina, A. Ahven, A. Annist, and J. Ginter, J. (2003). *Kuritegevus Eestis 1991-2001: Crime in Estonia 1991-2001*. Tallinn, Estonia: Juura, Õigusteabe AS.

Saar, J. (2004). "Crime, control and criminology in post-communist Estonia." *European Journal of Criminology*, 1, pp. 505-531.

Sepp, M. (2002). *"New public management" elements: Case study of human resources allocation to achieve the goals in the Estonian Police* Tallinn, Estonia: Faculty of Social Sciences of the Tallinn Pedagogical University. http://www.unpan1.un.org/intradoc/groups/public/documents/nispacee/unpan007843.pdf (01/15/2005).

ETHIOPIA

Background Material

Ethiopia is unique among African countries, with an ancient monarchy that maintained freedom from colonial rule. The sole exception to Ethiopia's presiding monarchy occurred during the Italian occupation of 1936–1941. In 1974, a military *junta*, the Derg, deposed Emperor Haile Selassie (who had ruled since 1930) and established a socialist state. Torn by bloody coups, uprisings, wide-scale drought, and massive refugee problems, the regime was finally toppled by a coalition of rebel forces, the Ethiopian People's Revolutionary Democratic Front (EPRDF), in 1991. A constitution was adopted in 1994, and Ethiopia's first multiparty elections were held in 1995. A two and a half year border war with Eritrea concluded with a peace treaty on December 12, 2000. The final demarcation of the boundary is currently on hold, due to Ethiopian objections to an international commission's requirement to surrender sensitive territory.

Ethiopia is located in Eastern Africa, bordering Djibouti, Eritrea, Kenya, Somalia, and Sudan. It comprises a total area of 1,127,127 sq km, and has a population of 67,851,281 (2004 est.). The population is composed of the following ethnic groups, by percentage of the total population: Oromo (40%); Amhara and Tigre (32%); Sidamo (9%); Somali (6%); Afar (4%); Gurage (2%); and other (1%). Muslims, Ethiopian Orthodox, and animist comprise the predominant religions. Languages spoken include Amharic, Tigrinya, Oromigna, Guaragigna, Somali, Arabic, and other local languages (English and major foreign languages are taught in schools).

The GDP per capita is $700 (2003 est.). Ethiopia's poverty-stricken economy is dependant on agriculture, which accounts for half of the GDP, 60% of exports, and 80% of total employment. Farming in the country suffers from frequent drought and poor cultivation. Coffee is critical to the Ethiopian economy with estimated exports of $156 million in 2002. In November 2001, Ethiopia qualified for debt relief from the Highly Indebted Poor Countries (HIPC) initiative. The government estimates that an annual growth of 7% is necessary in order to reduce poverty.

Contextual Features

Ethiopia is the oldest independent country in Africa and one of the oldest in the world (at least 2000 years). The country's legal system is currently made up of a transitional mix of national and regional counts. The Executive Branch is headed by the President (chief of state), and the Prime Minister (head of government). The President is elected by the House of People's Representatives for a six-year term; the Prime Minister is designated by the party in power following legislative elections. The Council of Ministers, as outlined in the December 1994 constitution, are selected by the Prime Minister and approved by the House of People's Representatives.

The bicameral Parliament consists of the House of Federation or upper chamber, which holds 108 seats. Members of the upper chamber are chosen by state assemblies to serve five-year terms. The House of People's Representatives, or lower chamber, holds 548 seats, and members are directly elected by popular vote from single-member districts to serve five-year terms. In the past, irregularities and violence at some polling stations have necessitated the rescheduling of voting in certain constituencies.

Ethiopia's judicial system is composed of the Federal Supreme Court. The President and Vice President of the Federal Supreme Court are recommended by the Prime Minister and appointed by the House of People's Representatives. For other federal judges, the Prime Minister submits candidates to the House of People's Representatives for appointment, and they are selected by the Federal Judicial Administrative Council.

Police Profile

Background

In traditional Ethiopian society, conflicts were resolved by customary law, and families usually avenged wrongs against their members. In 1935, the emperor authorized the establishment of formal, British-trained police forces in Addis Ababa and four other cities. In 1946, the authorities opened the Ethiopian Police College in Sendafa, near Addis Ababa.

Demographics

The number of national police, including the paramilitary Mobile Emergency Police Force, was estimated at 9,000 in 1991.

Organizational Description

Initially administered as a department of the Ministry of Interior, by the early 1970s the national police had evolved into an independent agency. The national police were commanded by a police commissioner, who answered to the emperor. Thus local control over police was minimal. The Federal Republic of Germany (West Germany) supplied the paramilitary police with weapons and vehicles and installed a nationwide teleprinter system, and Israeli counterinsurgency experts trained commandos and frontier guards.

After the 1974 overthrow of Haile Selassie, the new Marxist government severely altered the authority of the national police, which were identified by the old regime. In 1977, the Mengistu regime reorganized the national police and placed a politically stable commissioner in command. The army was given a larger role in investigation and maintaining public order, and as a result the number of national police declined.

The government began a policy of recruiting police at an early age and training in their native regions. Training standards were not uniform among regions, and training was less exacting in rural areas. A high percentage of rural police could neither read nor write, and therefore they did not keep records of their activities. The Addis Ababa police, by contrast, were organized into uniformed, detective, and traffic units, and also housed a police laboratory. A small number of women served in police units in larger cities, usually in administrative positions or as guards for female prisoners.

Police Use of Firearms

As a rule, police were armed only with batons, though small arms were kept in designated armories. Paramilitary units, however, used heavy machine guns, mortars, grenades, and tear gas. In many rural areas, horses and mules were often the sole means of police transportation.

Training

Officers usually were commissioned after completion of a cadet course at the Ethiopian Police College at Sendafa. Initially staffed by Swedish instructors, since 1960 the faculty has consisted entirely of Ethiopians who are police college graduates. Candidates for the two-year course have to have a secondary school education or its equivalent. Instruction at the college includes general courses in police science, criminal law, tactics, traffic control, sociology, criminology, physical education, and first aid, as well as political indoctrination. Practical training is offered midway in the program, which sometimes entails field service in troubled areas. The few cadets who pass their final examinations with distinction are selected for further specialized training. By the end of 1990, the police college had graduated a total of 3,951 officer cadets in the years since its establishment in 1946.

Bibliography

"A Country Study: Ethiopia." *Library of Congress Country Studies.* http://lcweb2.loc.gov/frd/cs/ettoc.html.

"Ethiopia." *CIA World Fact Book.* www.cia.gov/cia/publications/factbook/geos/et.html.

EUROPEAN UNION

Background Material

At the end of 2004, the European Union consisted of 25 member states with approximately 450 million inhabitants.

European integration started after World War II in an attempt to prevent further wars by linking the basic industries and economies of the former enemies. Belgium, Germany, France, Italy, Luxembourg, and The Netherlands thus created the European Coal and Steel Community in 1951 and the European Economic Community in 1957. In 1992, the integration process was extended to further political fields, including those of justice and home affairs. Today, there are fifteen Member States (Denmark, Ireland, United Kingdom since 1973, Greece since 1981, Spain and Portugal since 1986, Austria, Finland and Sweden since 1995). In 2004, Cyprus, the Czech Republic, Estonia, Hungary, Latvia, Lithuania, Malta, Poland, Slovakia, and Slovenia joined the Union.

Within the European Union (EU), there are currently 21 official working languages, including English, French and German, in which the legislative acts of the Union are published. The majority of the EU's population belongs to Christian religions, but there are numerous other religions present, with in particular important Islamic minorities in some countries. For details, please refer to the reports on individual EU countries. The average per capita income in the EU is approximately US$25,000 (2002).

Contextual Features

The political structure of the EU in 2003 is situated somewhere between that of an international organization and a federal state. Mainly in the economic field, member states have conferred considerable legislative responsibility to the EU. This represents an evolving process with a gradually increasing number of areas falling under the EU domain, including internal and external security.

According to the Amsterdam Treaty, in force since May 1, 1999, a priority objective of the EU is "to provide citizens with a high level of security within an area of freedom, security and justice," in particular through the development of police and judicial cooperation in criminal matters.

The recent enlargement to 25 members requires new instruments for decision making, division of institutional powers, etc. In this context, it is expected that a forthcoming new Treaty (Constitution) for the EU will further strengthen the legislative powers in the internal security field.

The EU is founded on the rule of law, democracy, and separation of powers. Legislative power is mainly exercised by the EU Council, composed of representatives of national governments, with a growing role being played by the directly elected European Parliament. The European Commission exercises the executive functions of a government, with its directorates-general playing the role of ministries at national level; it holds the right of legislative initiative. Jurisdiction lies with the European Court of Justice.

European Union law in criminal justice consists of a set of rules mainly on the inter-operability of law systems of the Member States or setting minimum criteria for national criminal legislation, including for penalties and sanctions. Furthermore, it serves to strengthen law enforcement cooperation between the police forces of the Member States.

So far, there are no formal EU crime statistics, although it is planned to develop statistics in certain fields (e.g., money-laundering, counterfeiting, drug trafficking, fraud, vehicle theft, and sexual exploitation). Meanwhile, the annual report on organized crime by Europol provides an overall picture of the crime situation in the European Union.

The European Court of Justice has so far no authority in penal matters. Penal jurisdiction lies with the courts of the Member States. However, the Union facilitates Europe-wide cooperation on criminal justice cases by means of Eurojust, a body established in 2002 to help authorities within Member States when they are dealing with the investigation and prosecution of serious cross-border crime, particularly when it is organized. Eurojust is seated in The Hague and is composed of 25 national members, mainly experienced judges or prosecutors. Work under way on procedural safeguards for suspects and defendants in criminal proceedings will further promote the implementation of the principle of mutual recognition of judicial decisions in criminal matters.

Police Profile

Background

The role of the EU in police matters lies in the promotion and facilitation of cooperation between the Member States police forces. The EU has no police force of its own but operates a number of services with important support and policy development functions to policing. Europol is the most important, but services within the Commission (i.e., Directorate-General Justice and Home Affairs and the anti fraud office OLAF) should be mentioned. Furthermore, the Council's Secretariat General plays a significant support role in the legislative and police development process.

Organizational Description

Discussions on legislative initiatives and policy development take place within the working groups of the EU Council; that is, primarily the following:

- Police Co-operation Working Party (PCWG),
- Multidisciplinary Working Party on Organized Crime (MDG)

- Horizontal Narcotics Group (HNG).

At the political level, legislative projects and other high-level initiatives are examined by

- Article 36 Committee
- Committee of Permanent Representatives (COREPER)
- Council of Ministers of the Interior and Justice, in charge of adopting legislation.

Outside the Council framework, a Task Force of Member States Police Chiefs (EU PCTF) has been set up. Since April 2000, it meets on a regular basis. The objective is to bring together the police chiefs in an informal way in order to promote police cooperation.

Training

In December, 2000, the European Police College (CEPOL) was set up by a Council decision. CEPOL focuses training on cooperation between national law enforcement services In 2004, the council was evaluating the achievements of CEPOL, with a view to establish it as a permanent organization with headquarters in one Member State.

Police Public Projects

The Union also plays an important role in funding police projects under various justice and home affairs programs, both within the EU and in relation to countries and regions outside the EU. The EU financially supports many projects and activities in connection to police and policing. This includes *inter alia* awareness campaigns on trafficking in human beings.

Terrorism and International Cooperation

EU police cooperation began in the mid-1970s as a reaction to a series of terrorist attacks by leftist groups in various Member States (TREVI cooperation). It was formally introduced into the Union framework through the Maastricht Treaty of 1992 in response to the risk of serious cross border criminality after the abolition of internal borders, as part of the intergovernmental "Third Pillar" (so-called compensatory measures). Further upgrades occurred through the Amsterdam Treaty of 1997, stipulating in Article 29 that "the Union's objective shall be to provide citizens with a high level of safety within an area of freedom, security and justice by developing common action in the fields of police and judicial co-operation in criminal matter," and the European Council of Tampere in October 1999, introducing new features of cooperation such as the European Police College and the scoreboard mechanism to measure progress.

A cornerstone of European police cooperation lies in the Schengen mechanism, formally part of the Union framework since May, 1999 and developed to cope with the security risks of free movement within the common territory.

The main EU contribution to policing lies in the field of the legal and logistic infrastructure provided to cooperation between national services. In particular, the 2000 *Convention on Mutual Legal Assistance* (building upon a Convention of the Council of Europe of 1959), allows *inter alia* police authorities the following:

- direct operational contacts between services;
- hearing of suspects and witnesses by videoconference or telephone;
- interception of telecommunications;
- exchange of bank information;
- Joint Investigative Teams for criminal investigations in several Member States;
- Controlled deliveries.

Partly as a response to terrorist threats after September 11, 2001, the *European Arrest Warrant* was introduced in December 2001. It simplifies cumbersome extradition procedures by requiring the surrender of suspects or convicted persons within not more than 90 days. The warrant applies to a list of 32 serious offences, other offences with a lowest penalty of three years imprisonment, and to persons convicted for more than four months imprisonment.

Closer security cooperation started in the 1980s as the so-called Schengen mechanism, named after the town in Luxembourg where the first agreement was signed. By 2001, all Member States (except UK and Ireland) plus the non-EU members Norway and Iceland joined this operation, based on the acceptance of one common external border and the abolition of all internal border checks. Similar to the situation in the United States, once a traveler who has completed immigration formalities in one of the Schengen countries, he/she can freely move around to other Schengen countries.

In order to compensate for possible security risks arising from this principle of single entry and visa formality, police services established a sophisticated cooperation mechanism along the following lines:

- Common rules for crossing of external borders, including at air and sea ports;
- Coordination of the rules regarding conditions of entry and visas for short stays;

- Coordination on surveillance of borders (liaison officers, harmonisation of instructions and staff training);
- Rights granted to police services to conduct surveillance and hot pursuit operations across the internal borders;
- The creation of the Schengen Information System (SIS), a combined database and communication system allowing police and border services as well as consular authorities to access data on specific individuals, or vehicles and objects which are lost or stolen.

The EU also maintains a mechanism for mutual evaluation of police systems, providing for peer reviews by evaluation teams which visit the various Member States. So far, two rounds of evaluation have been completed, including mutual legal assistance and the role of law enforcement in combating drugs. The third round will mainly address exchange of information between Member States and Europol.

Various individual issues of efficient police cooperation have been addressed at Union level. This includes *inter alia* the following:

- Exchange of information and best practice concerning violence and hooliganism in connection with football (soccer) matches within the EU;
- Exchange of information on DNA analysis;
- Registration of colour codes on car paint;
- Standardized routines for registration in the field of missing or unidentified persons;
- Guidelines on closer cooperation with Russia on stolen vehicles;
- Protection of public persons;
- System for common use of liaison officers;
- Fight against drugs on the Internet;
- System for forensic profile analysis of synthetic drugs;
- Transportation of samples between law enforcement authorities;
- Tracing of chemical precursors used for drug production.

Since 1996, several police and justice-related funding programs have supported development in the area. In June, 2002, the programs were replaced by a broad framework program for police and judicial cooperation in criminal matters, the AGIS-program, with an annual amount of 11 million available. The Commission was given the role as manager of the programme.

Police cooperation in the EU was originally born under the effect of terrorism in the 1970s (TREVI). It has always remained on the agenda, but obtained special attention again after the events in New York on September 11, 2001.

To implement Security Council Resolution 1373 at EU level, the Justice and Home Affairs Council adopted a road map already on September 21, 2001, and several concrete measures such as the European Arrest Warrant and a Framework Decision on the approximation of criminal law in the field of terrorism as early as December 2001.

The death of 200 innocent people in Madrid on March 11, 2004, strengthened further the commitment among EU leaders to address terrorism. Several measures were envisaged in the conclusions of the summit held in Brussels on March 25–26, 2004, among them improving the exchange of information as a key issue for law enforcement cooperation.

Protection of fundamental rights and non-discrimination are key objectives for the EU, which seeks to guide the creation of an area of freedom, security, and justice. All Member States agree to high standards on human rights, and EU leaders proclaimed in December 2000, the European Union Charter on Fundamental Rights. The charter builds on Treaties, European Court of Justice case law, the Member States constitutional traditions, and the Council of Europe Convention on Human Rights.

Human rights can form part of a training project under the AGIS Program and other programs in countries outside the Union.

Democratic control of law enforcement cooperation is a matter for the EU. The protection of personal data is a crucial issue for law enforcement cooperation and is permanently monitored by the Council structures, the European Parliament, national law enforcement services and within the Europol and Schengen contexts.

Besides the obvious priority given to enlargement, the EU is very active in its relations with non Member States. Several programs such as TACIS for Russia and the Newly Independent States and CARDS for the Balkans have been set up.

Justice and Home Affairs form part of the strategic priorities and aims for instance at capacity building, not least including police services, and the promotion of the rule of law. Cooperation agreements with many countries also include sections on law enforcement cooperation, for instance with countries in the Mediterranean region. The EU has also developed action plans on organized crime with Russia and the Ukraine, and as a player at the international level, the Union addresses law enforcement issues with many countries such as the United States and Canada, and in international fora such as the UN, OSCE and G8.

In recent years, the EU has also stepped up its activities and involvement in civil crisis management. The EU continues to develop its ability to participate in future missions in the field of civil crisis management. Within the European Security and Defense Policy, a capacity of deploying up to 5,000 police officers has been established. Out of the 5,000 officers, 1,400 are organized in police units capable to take up executive tasks within 30 days. Currently, the EU has police missions in Macedonia (Proxima) and in Bosnia (EUPM).

Police Education, Research, and Publications

Police education at the EU level is provided in particular by CEPOL, Europol and through the funding programme AGIS. Research can be funded through various programs (AGIS, Sixth framework program on research).

ANDREW JACKSON AND HENRIK SJÖLINDER

Police-Related Websites

Description of EU police cooperation: *http://europa.eu.int/comm/justice_home/fsj/police/fsj_police_intro_en.htm.*
Commission DG JAI: *http://europa.eu.int/comm/dgs/justice_home/organigramme_en.pdf.*
Europol: *www.europol.eu.int.*
Eurojust: *www.eurojust.eu.int.*

Legislation: *www.europa.eu.int/comm/justice_home/doc_centre/police/acquis/doc_police_acquis_en.htm.*

Project funding AGIS: *http://europa.eu.int/comm/justice_home/funding/agis/funding_agis_en.htm*
Research program: *www.europa.eu.int/comm/research/fp6/index_en.html.*

Bibliography

Apap, Joanna, ed. *Justice and Home Affairs in the EU — Liberty and Security Issues after Enlargement.* Brussels: CEPS, 2004.
Jean, Carlo. *An Integrated Civil Police Force for the European Union.* Brussels: CEPS, 2002.

F

FIJI

Background Material

On October 10, 1874, a convention of chiefs ceded Fiji unconditionally to the United Kingdom. The country remained a British colony until October 1970 when it became a fully sovereign and independent nation. Democratic rule existed for the next 17 years, but came to an end in May 1987 when Lt. Col. Sitiveni Rambuka staged a military coup to restore the balance of political power to Melanesian Fijians. It had been lost through a democratic election process in which Indian Fijians had become the preeminent power in government. A period of confusion followed the coup, but appeared to be resolved when the Governor-General and the two main political groups agreed to form a government of national unity. Rambuka opposed the decision and was angered by the military's exclusion from the negotiation process. He staged another coup in September 1987 and the newly formed military government declared Fiji a republic. In December 1987, Rambuka voluntarily ceded government to civilian control, but military officers, including Rambuka, held four cabinet posts in the new civilian government.

The civilian government's first term expired in September 1990 and a smaller government, which excluded active-duty military personnel, was formed. A new constitution that favoured Melanesian Fijians was introduced 1990. In 1997, the constitution was amended to make it more equitable. In 1999, a democratic election process resulted in an Indo–Fijian-led government.

An attempted coup in May 2000 by a group of armed ethnic Fijians led by a civilian businessman, George Speight, heralded a period of civil and political turmoil. Indo-Fijian Prime Minister Chaudry and his government were held hostage for fifty-six days. In August 2001, a democratic parliamentary election resulted in the election of the Qarase government (*www.odci. gov/cia/publications/factbook.geos/fj.html*).

With two military coups and one attempted coup since 1987, political stability and ethnic tensions remain a constant threat to the peace and economic prosperity of Fiji. The political and civil turmoil that accompanied the coups and attempted coups have created opportunities for organised crime and terrorist organizations. International organised crime gangs have begun using Pacific Island countries including Fiji for criminal activities such as drug trafficking, people smuggling and credit card fraud.

As of July 2002, the population was estimated to be 844,330, with 51% Melanesian Fijians and 44%

Indo-Fijian. The remainder of the population consists of people with European, Chinese, or other Pacific Island origins.

The official language is English, with Fijian and Hindustani also being spoken.

Fifty two percent of the population are Christians, 38% are Hindus, and 8% are Muslims. Other religions form the remaining 2%. Ethnic Melanesian Fijians are mainly Christians, and Indo-Fijians are predominantly Hindus.

In 1999, the GDP per capita was estimated at US$7,300.

Fiji has substantial forestry, mineral, and fishing resources. The sugar and tourism industries are also important sources of foreign exchange. However, political instability has had a negative impact on tourism and investor confidence.

Contextual Features

The legal system is based on the British common law system. Broadly speaking, the basic law of Fiji is derived from the 1997 constitution (as amended in 1998), which the Fijian High Court found to be in force, despite attempts by the military government to abrogate it. Supplementing the constitution is a body of legislation, presidential decrees, military decrees, emergency proclamations, and acts and ordinances inherited from colonial times. There is also a body of subsidiary legislation. Customary law is part of the law of Fiji except where it is constitutionally incompatible or in breach of human rights.

Between 1997 and 2001 assault occasioning actual bodily harm was the most recorded offence. In 2002, the most common crimes were serious assaults (3766), theft (3259), breaking and entering (3016), and aggravated theft (1478). A zero-tolerance policy has been recently introduced in relation to domestic crimes.

The Supreme Court is the final appellate court in civil and criminal matters. It has exclusive jurisdiction to hear and determine appeals from all final judgments of the Court of Appeal. The President, on the advice of the Cabinet, can refer constitutional questions to the Supreme Court for an opinion.

The Court of Appeal has jurisdiction to hear and determine appeal judgments of the High Court.

A person convicted on trial before the High Court may appeal to the Court of Appeal against their conviction on any ground involving questions of law; with leave of the Court of Appeal; and with leave of the Court of Appeal against a sentence unless it is one that is fixed by law.

Any party who wants to "further appeal" from a criminal appeal to the High Court can only do so if the High Court did not affirm a verdict of acquittal by a Magistrates' court. The grounds for appeal can only be in relation to a question of law not severity of sentence.

The High Court has unlimited jurisdiction to hear and determine civil proceedings. It has an appellate jurisdiction in relation to decisions of the Magistrates' courts. Criminal appeals can be made in relation to matters of fact and law. Magistrates can refer any question of law to the High Court.

Magistrates' courts are divided into three classes: resident magistrate, second-class magistrate, and third-class magistrate. The division of Magistrates' courts is limited to the division in which they are situated. Magistrates have civil jurisdiction to hear certain minor claims in contract or tort, proceedings between landlords and tenants, all cases involving trespass or recovery of land with the exception of landlord and tenant disputes, habeas corpus applications, and applications for the appointment of guardians or custody. Magistrates have a criminal jurisdiction as defined in Sections 4 to 9 of the Criminal Procedure Code and in the First Schedule of the Code. Criminal sentences are also imposed by magistrates according to their class. A resident magistrate has jurisdiction to hear appeals from the decisions of second- and third-class magistrates.

In mid-2001, the Fijian prison system housed some 1,102 prisoners in 13 institutions.

Police Profile

The police force in Fiji is known as the Royal Fiji Police Force.

Background

The Fiji Police Force has it origins in the Armed Native Constabulary which was created by the colonial administration in 1874. By 1884, it consisted of 45 police including a superintendent, sub-inspector, 5 Europeans, 34 Fijians, and 4 Indian officers. In 1906, a new force known as the Fiji Constabulary was established, which was headed by an inspector-general. At the time of independence in 1970, the name was changed to the Royal Fiji Police. The first local commissioner, P. U. Raman, was appointed in 1981.

Demographics

In 2001, the Fiji Police Force consisted of 1,863 police officers, including 1,685 men and

178 women. The overwhelming majority were Fijians (1,155), with the remainder comprised of 670 Indians and 38 others. Following an agreement between the Australian and Fijian governments in 2001, the Australian Federal Police (AFP) have had two AFP officers stationed in Suva.

Organisational Description

In October 2001, the ratio of police to population was 1:436. The ranks of the Royal Fijian Police Force are categorised as gazetted officers, inspectorate officers, and subordinator officers. There is provision in the Police Act for special constables to be appointed when necessary and they are vested with the same powers and privileges as police officers.

Gazetted officers, the most senior, are comprised of the following ranks:

- Commissioner of Police
- Deputy Commissioner of Police
- Senior Superintendent
- Superintendent
- Deputy Superintendent
- Assistant Superintendent

Inspectorate officers form a narrow middle band. They hold the ranks of:

- Senior Inspector
- Inspector

Subordinate officers hold the ranks of:

- Sergeant Major
- Sergeant
- Corporal
- Constable

The commissioner is vested with the general control and operation of the force, including control over promotions and demotions of nongazetted members. The commissioner may promote all police officers other than gazetted officers as he/she sees fit.

Functions

The Fijian Police Act (Cap. 85 in the 1978 Revised Laws of Fiji) states that the functions of the Royal Fijian Police Force are:

- Maintenance of law and order
- Preservation of the peace
- Protection of life and property
- The prevention and detection of crime
- The enforcement of all laws and regulations with which it is directly charged
- The regulation and control of traffic

- In times of war or other emergencies, to act in the defence of Fiji

Training

Police training takes place at the Police Academy. Training is also conducted by the Australian Federal Police, Victoria Police (Australia), and the Federal Bureau of Investigation (United States).

Police Academy training extends beyond recruits. Officers wishing to be detectives have to successfully complete a detectives' course at the Academy.

Australian and New Zealand police departments are also engaged in basic and advanced training programs including crime scene investigation, community policing, and fraud. A training project for Fiji Police funded by AusAID and a $4 million project that ran from 1996 to 1999, which focused on strengthening the Fiji Police Force, included a restructure of the Police Academy, the establishment of a training development section, and the creation of a better career structure for police members. Three full-time and eight short-term officers from the Victorian Police Force were involved in staffing the project.

In the lead-up to the annual Pacific Island Forum in Auckland in August 2003, Australian's Prime Minister John Howard announced that Australia would be contributing $15 million toward establishing a Pacific police training college in Fiji. This commitment is designed to help counter a breakdown in law and order across the Pacific region.

Police Public Projects

The Neighbourhood Watch Scheme is part of the community crime prevention program. There are also civil instructions in schools designed to enhance the public's support for community policing initiatives. Police also help to regulate and control traffic and to divert traffic when it is in the public interest to do so.

Police Use of Firearms

Police are authorised by the Police Act to carry firearms.

Complaints and Discipline

In 2001, as a result of complaints, 68 police (37 regular and 31 special constables) were dismissed from the force. All complaints against police officers are investigated immediately. If there is corroborating evidence, the complaint is found and the officer is suspended awaiting trial. If found guilty, the officer's employment with the Royal Fiji Police Force is terminated.

The Police Act contains numerous provisions relating to discipline. Mutiny, sedition, desertion, violent insubordination, and allowing riot are all serious offences rendering the offending police officer(s) liable to imprisonment. Police officers are able to arrest officers of lower rank for disciplinary offences.

As outlined in the Police Act, the Commissioner of Police may impose any of the following penalties: admonishment, reprimand, severe reprimand, confinement to quarters (for subordinate officers only), a fine of up to seven days' pay, demotion, dismissal. However, dismissal requires the consent of the Police Services Commission.

The commissioner can review the decision of any discretionary tribunal other than those presided over by him or herself. He or she may confirm, quash, alter the findings, or remit them to another tribunal for rehearing. The commissioner can also find the offending police officer guilty of another offence, and has the power to punish.

Fiji's Human Rights Commission is drafting a Human Rights Handbook specifically for disciplined forces, including the police.

Terrorism

The most recent coup (2000) was initiated by George Speight, a Fijian businessman. Speight was sentenced to death for his role in the coup, but in February 2002 this was commuted to life imprisonment. No other incident that could be defined as terrorism has taken place as of this writing, but recent reports suggest that the Police Force is concerned that terrorists might use Fiji as a place to prepare terrorist strikes. They are asking for amendments to the immigration law to help counter any weaknesses in this area. Fiji has also expressed its willingness to cooperate in international policing efforts to counter terrorism.

Fiji has supported the UN Security Council Resolution 1373 in the fight against terrorism and implemented internationally agreed antiterrorism policies. The 2002 Nasinoni Declaration recommitted Pacific nations to the fight against terrorism, money laundering, drug trafficking, and people smuggling and trafficking.

Fiji is a founding member of the annual South Pacific Chiefs of Police Conference, which has resolved to focus on the prevention of terrorism and to introduce legislative changes relating to terrorism, transnational crime, and drug laws. Members have also resolved to commit to the development of standardised legislation within South Pacific jurisdictions.

International Cooperation

The Honiara Declaration is the basis for law enforcement cooperation in the Pacific. The Royal Fiji Police Force is a member of Interpol, the global police organization established to facilitate cooperation among police forces at an international level. Fiji is also a member of the South Pacific Island Criminal Intelligence Network. It acts as a clearinghouse for information to assist in the detection and combating of drug trafficking, white-collar crime, organised crime, money laundering, and terrorism. It is also a member of the Pacific Island Forum, a founding member of the South Pacific Chiefs of Police, and member of the Pacific Islands Forum's Regional Law Enforcement Capacity Development and Cooperation Program. These forums exist, in part, to develop a number of cooperative antiterrorist initiatives among Pacific Island Police Forces. In 2003, delegates to the annual South Pacific Chiefs of Police conference finalised a four-year strategic plan that establishes key law enforcement priorities for the region.

The Royal Fiji Police Force has been involved in peacekeeping missions in Bougainville (PNG), the Solomon Islands, Namibia, Iraq, Cambodia, Lebanon, and Sinai.

Police Education, Research, and Publication

Institutions

University of the South Pacific, *www.usp.ac.fj* (Institute of Justice and Applied Legal Studies (IJALS), Laucala Campus, Fiji)

Researchers

Yunus, Rashid, "Crime and punishment," *Pacific Islands Monthly* 65, no. 3 (March 1995): 16–19. Fiji's growing crime rate, comments by Police Commissioner Isikia Savua; increase in crime related to youth unemployment, and a lack of equipment and resources for police.

Newton, T. *An Introduction to Policing in the South Pacific Region.* University of the South Pacific School of Law, 1998.

Leading Journals

Journal of South Pacific Law, *http://easol.vanuatu.usp.ac.fj/ jspl/current.*

Major Police Publications

Brown, S. *History of the Fiji Police*. Suva: Fiji Police Force, 1998.

Police-Related Websites

Fiji Law Reform Commission: *www.lawreform.gov.fj/*
Fiji Ombudsman: *www.fiji.gov.fj/publish/pm_office.shtml*
Fiji Police Training Project: Overseas Projects Corporation of Victoria, *www.opc.vic.gov.au/psja/Content/fiji.html*
Fiji Women's Crisis Centre: *www.fijiwomen.com/*

COLLEEN LEWIS AND DAVID BAKER

Bibliography

Brown, S. B. *From Fiji to the Balkans: History of the Fiji Police*. Suva: Fiji Police Force, 1998.
Public Service Commission. Ministry of Finance and National Planning. 2001. Available at: *www.fijichris.gov/fj/Home.htm*.
Senate Committee on Foreign Affairs, Defence and Trade. A Pacific Engaged: Australia's Relations with Papua New Guinea and the Island States of the South-West Pacific, Commonwealth Parliament of Australia, Sub. 29, 12 August 2003.

FINLAND

Background Material

Finland is a Scandinavian country, sharing borders with Denmark, Iceland, Norway, and Sweden. Up until 1809, Finland was a part of the Swedish kingdom; from then until 1917, it remained annexed to imperial Russia as a Grand Duchy, or an autonomous area. In 1906, Finland became a parliamentary democracy, and parliaments of 200 members were elected every four years. Shortly after the Bolshevik revolution in Russia, Finland declared its independence on December 6, 1917. In 1919, Finland became a republic, headed by a president elected every six years. Finland joined the European Union (EU) in 1995.

The total area of Finland is 338,145 square kilometers. The population of the country is just over 5 million. Administratively, the country was divided into five provinces (originally twelve) in 1996. In addition, an autonomous Province of Åland (the Åland Islands) is part of Finland. The majority of the inhabitants are nominal members of the Lutheran Church, which is an official state church, the other being the Orthodox Church.

Finland is a bilingual country. The official languages are Finnish and Swedish, but the Swedish-speaking people constitute only 6% of the whole population. Two other traditional ethnic groups are the gypsies (Roma) and the Lapps. These latter groups, however, account for only a few thousand people. Particularly during the 1990s, some tens of thousands of refugees have come into the country, mainly from Africa and the former Soviet Union.

The GNP per capita at market prices was 26,210 euros in 2001. The value of the gross national product is distributed in the following way: services 28%; industry 27.7%; trade, hotels, and restaurants 11.1%; transport, storage, and communications 10.7%; operation and rental of dwellings 9.3%; and all other fields 13.2%. Major industrial activities include electrical and electronics manufacturing, representing 24% of all industrial output in 2000, followed by the pulp and paper industry (16.6%), machinery and equipment production (9.7%), and chemicals and chemical products (9.4%). The lumber industry has traditionally been a pillar of Finnish production, but its share is now only 4% of industrial output. Finland is a high-tech country that requires a high level of education, which is a challenge for the country. Another major challenge is the relatively high number of unemployed people. The unemployment rate was 9% in 2002.

Contextual Features

In 2002, the number of political parties in Finland was twenty-one. However, in Parliament only seven parties have representatives. The leading political parties in governments between the end of World War II in 1945 and 1968 were the Center Party (Agrarians) and the Social Democratic Party. Since 1966, the People's Democrats (with a core formed from the Communist Party) or their successor party, the Left Alliance, have sometimes participated in coalition governments. From 1995 to 2003 there were coalition governments of Social Democrats and Conservatives, the Left Alliance, the Swedish People's Party, and the Greens. After the 2003 elections, the government parties were the Center Party, Social Democrats, and the Swedish People's Party.

The Finnish legal system is based on the German-Roman system, which is common in most European countries. According to the Finnish Constitution, legislative power is vested in Parliament, in conjunction with the President of the Republic. Draft bills emanate from the ministry with responsibility for the matter in question. Projects of wider general significance are prepared in committees with representatives from the various organs of government, political parties and other interest groups. The bills drafted in the Ministries are scrutinized by the Council of State in general session prior to their submission to Parliament by the President. The most important duty of Parliament is to pass legislation. A new act is adopted or an old one amended on the basis of a governmental bill or of a motion submitted by a representative, which must be reviewed and considered by a select committee and presented to the Parliament for adoption or rejection. The President of the Republic, the government, and the ministries may also issue decrees pursuant to an act adopted by Parliament.

As of this writing, a special procedure is in place to enable Parliament to participate in the preparation of EU legislation in time to affect the outcome. Parliament is in the drafting phase, having been notified of new EU proposals and the pertinent positions taken by the Finnish government. This preliminary decision making is delegated to Parliament's Grand Committee.

Recorded crime in general increased during the 1960s and the 1970s due to rapid urbanization and the large postwar age cohorts reaching a crime-intensive age. During the 1980s, there were new increases in some categories of recorded crime. However, with the economic recession in the early 1990s, many major crime categories including theft began to decrease. As the economy has recovered, there are new increases in some crime categories (Rikollisuustlanne 2001). Major crimes reported to the police in 2001 are listed in the table (above). Note that almost 50% of all crimes are traffic offenses, and most of the rest are property crimes.

The Finnish Constitution guarantees to everyone the right to have a case heard appropriately and without undue delay by a court or other public authority. Everyone also has the right to have a

Types and numbers of crimes reported to police in 2001

Type of crime	Count
Property crimes	286,953
Crimes against life and health	29,974
Sex crimes	1,224
Narcotics offenses	12,970
Drunkenness in traffic	25,423
Other traffic offenses	341,490
Other crimes	49,470
Total	747,774

decision affecting rights and duties reviewed by a court or other judicial organ. The independence of the judiciary is constitutionally guaranteed. Judges are appointed by the President of the Republic.

The age of criminal responsibility in Finland is fifteen years. A younger person cannot be sentenced for a crime, but other measures such as the Child Welfare Act and/or the Law on Compensation for Damage can be used. The court system is diagrammed in the figure on the next page.

The highest prosecuting authority in Finland is the Prosecutor General who is appointed by the President. The State Prosecutors appraise the evidence and decide on prosecution in cases with wider national significance. There are also District Prosecutors. Administratively, prosecutors are part of the Ministry of Justice. The police come under the control of the Ministry of the Interior.

Most crimes are handled in the District Courts. In addition to judges, the District Courts have lay members who take part in hearing criminal cases and certain disputes under family law. In a District Court a civil case is divided into a preliminary preparation and a main hearing. The preliminary preparation commences with the written submissions of the parties. If the case cannot be resolved at this point, a separate main hearing is scheduled. In a main hearing, the composition of the District Court is three judges, except for family law cases, where the Court is composed of a panel of one judge and three lay members. In a criminal case, the composition of the District Court varies in accordance with the offense in question; cases of petty infractions are heard by one judge and those of more serious offenses by a panel of one judge and three lay members. Criminal procedure follows the same principles as in civil cases. All evidence is presented in the main hearing. If the Court does not reach a consensus on the judgment, a vote is taken. Each member of the panel has an individual vote.

The Criminal Sanctions Agency is a new central administrative board that started its work on August 1, 2001. It is responsible for directing and

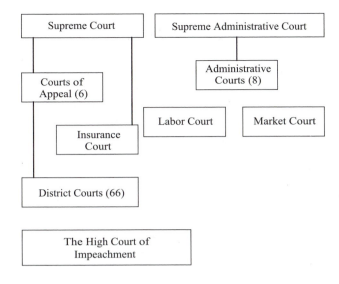

developing the enforcement of community sanctions and prison sentences (the Enforcement of Sentences Administration Act 135/2001).

The Criminal Sanctions Agency consists of four units that are responsible for:

- Directing the work of the Probation Service
- Directing the work of the Prison Service
- Enforcement of prison sentences and community sanctions
- Joint administration of the Probation Service and the Prison Service

The Criminal Policy Department of the Ministry of Justice is in charge of the strategic direction in this field of administration. The Prison Court is a special court belonging to the central administration of the administrative sector of the Ministry of Justice. It decides on whether to incarcerate dangerous recidivists and on whether young offenders are to serve their sentence in a juvenile prison.

Closed prisons accommodate inmates sentenced to prison and persons serving imprisonment for nonpayment of fines. Open institutions accommodate persons working or taking part in some other activity and who are considered suitable for the freer conditions in open institutions compared to closed institutions. The Mental Hospital for Prisoners is a nationwide institution intended for prisoners in need of psychiatric treatment. It also carries out mental examinations of persons accused of offenses. The Prison Staff Training Centre is responsible for basic and advanced training leading to an examination in correctional treatment. At year-end 2002, there were 3,433 confirmed prison beds in the penal institutions (an average daily number); 74 of these were assigned to people with life imprisonment sentences, including six female inmates. The total number of female inmates was 204, about 6% of the total.

Police Profile

Background

After Finland became part of the Russian Empire in 1809, the Governor-General made a proclamation on sheriffs' duties in 1814, which remained in effect until 1898 when the rural police were given their own statutes and regulations (Sinisalo 1971). With independence in 1917, the police became civil servants under the jurisdiction of the Ministry of the Interior. The town and rural police were brought under the same set of regulations by the Police Act of 1925. In 1926, a Crime Research Centre was set up, which was also entrusted with the local Interpol responsibilities. Criminal investigation facilities improved in 1927, following the creation of additional positions for detectives in the provinces. These positions were transferred to provincial criminal investigation police units started in 1938. In 1955, the Central Criminal Investigation Department was formed. Until the end of World War II, a police unit called the State Police existed in Finland. Their main task was to deal with activities against the state.

Finland was at war with the Soviet Union from 1939 to 1940, and from 1941 to 1944. After the armistice with the Soviet Union in 1944, the State Police unit was led by communists or leftist officials until 1949. During this postwar period, the main duty of this branch of the police forces was the investigation of activities against the Soviet Union. The branch was abolished in 1949. A unit of the Security Police without an overt political agenda was established in its place.

The first comprehensive police law, the Police Act (No. 84/1966), came into effect in 1967. In 1973, the Act was amended and provisions were made for advisory boards in units. This allowed members of the public to cooperate with the police (Jousimaa 1986). In 1973, the Police Department of the Ministry of the Interior became the Supreme Command of the Police in Finland, while police bureaus were given command of the police in the provinces. A new Police Law enacted in 1995 changed the organization and structure of the police, and took into account certain demands of international human rights organizations. Although these rights were previously observed in Finland, they were not officially covered in the laws governing the police. The new law brought agreement between police legislation and international requirements.

Organizational Description

The Finnish police are subordinate to the Ministry of the Interior. The police organization is at three levels. It is supervised and coordinated by the Police Department of the Ministry of the Interior, acting as the Supreme Police Command. The Supreme Police Command develops and supervises police work throughout Finland. The Supreme Police Command develops the legislation, administration, training, and research for the police sector.

At the regional level, there are provincial administration units of the police in five Provincial State Offices and the ninety Local Police Departments. The police district of the Åland Islands is an autonomous unit.

The following National Police units that are directly subordinate to the Ministry of the Interior: the National Bureau of Investigation, Security Police, Mobile Police, Police School, Police College of Finland and Police Technical Center. The Police Department of the Helsinki Local District is also operationally subordinate to the Ministry of the Interior, and is responsible for some special national duties.

1. National Bureau of Investigation: combats international, organized, professional, economic, and other serious crime; carries out investigations; develops crime prevention and investigation methods and police information systems.
2. Security Police: works to prevent schemes and crimes that may endanger the established social order or the internal or external security of the state and carries out the investigation of such crime.
3. Mobile Police: maintains public order and security; controls traffic; works to promote traffic safety.
4. Police Technical Center: supports police work by acquiring, maintaining, and developing the equipment and material needed in police work.

Police training institutions are described in more detail below under the heading "Police Education, Research, and Publications."

The Civilian Police are not part of the regular Finnish police forces. Finland has participated in international civilian police operations since 1994, and all civilian police officers sent from Finland have completed civilian police training that conforms with the United Nations training standards.

In 2001, the police force employed some 10,800 personnel, most of whom (7,685) were officers, senior officers, commanding officers, and police chiefs in local police units. Women represented about 24% of total police personnel, and 8% of police officers. Students studying to become police officers accounted for 502 of all police personnel. The number of police officers per capita in Finland is low by international standards.

Functions

The main duties of the Finnish police are to maintain public order and security, to prevent and solve crimes, and to forward investigated cases for prosecution (Police Act 493/1995). They also carry out other duties assigned to the police by law, such as providing license services for driving licenses and weapon permits. Police work is guided by legislation, agreements on human rights, international police ethical norms, research data on people's expectations, and established police practice. The police work in close cooperation with various authorities and sectors such as the rescue services, frontier guards, customs, social services and health authorities, schools, and traffic organizations.

Police Use of Firearms

The police administration issues instructions or guidelines about police use of firearms. The first official *Instruction for the Use of Firearms of the Police* was given by the Ministry of the Interior, and the most recent and revised instructions were given in 2000. The use of firearms is only allowed if a police officer is in a dangerous situation and can assume that the threat of violence is probable. A police officer may stop the activities of a person who is threatening someone's life or health. The new regulations do not define exactly when the use of firearms *is allowed*, but it gives a detailed list of the situations when their use *is prohibited* (Kolehmainen 2001:42–49). On a more general level, the use of force by the police has been regulated in the Police Law. The above-described instructions are, of course, in accordance with that law.

Complaints and Discipline

Every Finnish citizen or person who lives in the country has a right to make a verbal or written complaint about police actions. It is possible to lodge a complaint first at the national level, second at the provincial level, and third at the local level. Complaints may also be lodged either with the Parliamentary Ombudsman or the Chancellor of

Justice. From 1999 to 2002, the annual number of police complaints to the Parliamentary Ombudsman was a bit more than 300, that is, 11% to 12% of all complaints. The number of complaints to the Chancellor of Justice was lower.

The most common reason for the complaints has been preliminary investigations made by the police. The second most common reason has been the use of coercion. The misbehavior of a policeman or inadequate service (human rights violation and racist attitudes) make up only 0% to 3% of complaints. The Parliamentary Ombudsman has several possible responses to complaints: no measures, serving a notice of the issue involved, reprimand, and a claim for legal proceedings. The most common reaction has been "no measures," given in approximately 85% of cases. The second most common reaction has been a reprimand. The responses of the Chancellor of Justice to complaints against the police have been similar to those of the Parliamentary Ombudsman.

The police see their behavior as nonracist and in accordance with human rights standards. However, human rights organizations (the Finnish League of Human Rights and Amnesty International) have pointed out that the most important human rights problems for the police are linked to foreign immigrants and refugees. At the end of 2000, some 90,074 foreign citizens were living in Finland, that is, 1.8% of the Finnish population. The role of the police is important for refugees and immigrants because the police represent the first authority that they meet. The problems pointed out by human rights organizations primarily concern immigrants who are African and Islamic. The two main issues are, first, the attitudes of the police, or how foreigners perceive these attitudes, and, second, the short time for dealing with cases of immigrants or refugees. The latter, however, is a greater problem for other authorities (Jasinskaja-Lahti et al. 2002).

Generally, immigrants feel that making a criminal report on racial crimes may not produce results. The threshold for making a criminal report is high when the suspect is a police officer. Some immigrants also are afraid of going to the police, and therefore the majority of cases go unreported. According to various polls, approximately 75% to 80% of Finland's citizens trust the police. In comparison to other state authorities such as courts, Parliament, church, and so on, the police are at the top of the list (Lappi-Seppälä 2000:36).

There are two orders concerning the police and racism: The decision in principle of the Council of the State on administrative measures for the increase in tolerance and prevention of racism (6.2; 1997) and the instructions of the Ministry of the Interior on Increase in tolerance and prevention of racism in the police force (30.6.1997, 15/011/97). The last-mentioned instructions were being updated as of year-end 2002. These two orders give a strong message to administration, including the police, to abstain from racist behavior and human rights violations. The follow-up and control of these decisions is a matter for each ministry, which is the Ministry of Interior in the case of the police.

Terrorism

Terrorism does not exist in Finland, although the Finnish Government has prepared for terrorist incidents. On September 1, 2002, the Ministry of Foreign Affairs published an updated report entitled *Terrorism and Finland*. Based on a decision made by the EU, the government of Finland prepared a proposal for a Law on Terrorist Crimes that was passed by Parliament on January 24, 2003 (Amendment to the Criminal Law 17/2003) and came into force on February 1, 2003. According to the amendment, specifically defined crimes that are included in the law are terrorist acts if "the intention of the crime is terrorism, that is, to cause serious fear among people, to compel illegally the government or administration of some country, or an international organization to do something, or illegally revoke the constitution or legal system of some country, or to cause very extensive damage to a country or an international organization." Terrorist crimes include menace, aggravated damage to property, sabotage, health endangerment, ignoring the prohibition on using chemical or biological weapons, aggravated impairment of the environment, aggravated assault, hostage taking, hijacking, homicide, and murder. Attempting these crimes is also punishable.

Planning a terrorist crime is also punishable. Before the law, the preparation of a crime was punishable in a few cases, such as genocide and high treason. Since passage of the law, the police have the right to use coercive measures in investigating the preparation of a terrorist crime.

Finland has also cooperated on terrorism with the North Atlantic Treaty Organization (NATO), the Council of Europe, and the Organization of Economic Cooperation and Development (OECD).

International Cooperation

The Supreme Police Command draws up guidelines for international police cooperation and prepares matters involving police cooperation between the EU member-states at the national level. Police cooperation among the Nordic countries has a long tradition. In addition, the national police commissioners of Finland and the Baltic countries and the highest law enforcement authorities of Finland and Russia cooperate on a regular basis. As mentioned before, Finland has been involved in international civilian police operations since 1994. Membership in the European Union has also affected Finnish police activities. In 1998, Finland joined EUROPOL, the common European police (established 1996), and this has imposed more duties on the Finnish police. EUROPOL started its activities on 1 July 1999. In 2000, Europol's mandate was extended to money laundering. Even before this, the fight against international drug crimes, organized crime, control of smuggling, and other corresponding issues have been key duties for EUROPOL (EYVL Nr. C 316, 27. 11.1995). In 2000, the ministers of the interior and justice agreed to establish a European Police Chiefs Operational Task Force and a "Eurojust" unit to aid in the prosecution and investigation of crime.

Toward promoting free movement in Europe, five European countries signed the so-called Schengen Agreement in 1990. This meant, for example, more open national borders. In 1995 five more European countries joined the agreement. Finland, Sweden, and Denmark signed the agreement in 1996. The agreement came into full force five years later. Finland joined the Schengen area on March 25, 2001. Great Britain and Ireland are the only European Union countries that are outside the Schengen agreement.

Finland began applying the Schengen Information System (SIS) regulations on January 1, 2001. The SIS, common to all Schengen countries, is one of the key tools in the cooperation between authorities. All alerts in the SIS are delivered through SIRENE (Supplementary Information Request at the National Entries) bureaus. Finland's twenty-four-hour SIRENE bureau is part of the National Bureau of Investigation's Criminal Intelligence Division's Communications Centre. Most of the work involved in establishing Finland's SIRENE bureau took place in 2000.

Within the framework of the Council of Europe, the Supreme Police Command takes part in the work of the Committee on Prevention of Torture, Group of States Established Against Corruption, Human Rights Steering Committee, and the Committee on Spectator Violence. (This section is based on information provided by the Ministry of the Interior and Police Department; website *www.intermin.fi*).

Police Education, Research, and Publications

The Police School in Tampere and the Police College of Finland in Espoo provide vocational training. A special division of the Police School, the police dog-training center, trains police dogs and their instructors. The Police School provides basic police training and training for non-commissioned officers, as well as specialized professional training related to its field of activities. During recent years, the annual number of police graduates from the Police School has been about 320.

The Police College provides studies at the polytechnic level. It also provides specialized professional studies in policing, and is responsible for commanding officers' training and other command-level training. The Police College is also responsible for research and development related to police work. Only those who have completed the basic training can apply to the Police College. In the College, the teaching and degree requirements for a commanding officer's degree resemble those of an undergraduate university degree. Students who graduate from the Police College have a chance to take a higher degree in a university cooperating with the Police College and to continue their studies up to the level of the doctorate. An educational cooperation agreement has been made with the Universities of Turku (criminology and sociology of law) and Tampere (security administration).

The leading police researchers are in the Research Unit of the Police College of Finland, University of Tampere, and University of Turku.

Finland has adhered to all international human rights agreements, and these resolutions have been taken seriously in police training as well. The Finnish police adopted an Ethical Oath of the Police at the beginning of 2001, which the new graduating police officers from the Police School have to take. Furthermore, there are courses and a textbook on police ethics (Ellonen et al. 2000).

Publications

Timo Korander and Seppo Soine-Rajanummi, eds. "Koskarille—samantien sakot." Research Communications No. 13, Police College of Finland, 2002. Evaluates the zero tolerance experiment and other crime prevention operations in the city of Tampere during 1999 and 2000.

Anne Jokinen, Janne Häyrynen, and Anne Alvesalo. "Yritykset talousrikollisuuden uhreina." Research Communications No. 19, Police College of Finland, 2002. This study is about major economic crime, the victims of which are enterprises, not natural persons.

Risto Honkonen. "Komisarioksi oppiminen. Koulutuksen vaikuttavuus ja työssä oppiminen." Research No. 13, Police College of Finland, 2001. Makes comparisons between learning of the police by training and learning by working.

Ahti Laitinen. "Police and Democracy in Finland." In *Policing, Security and Democracy: Theory and Practice*, edited by Menachem Amir and Stanley Einstein, 157–186. Huntsville, TX: Office of International Criminal Justice (OICJ), 2001. The study is concerned with police work, police duties, and organizations in Finland. It also evaluates complaints against the police.

Markku Ranta-aho. "Juppi, bulvaani, talonpoika, huijari." Turku: Department of Criminal Law and Legal Procedure, University of Turku, 2000. This study deals with fraud and other illegalities against the financial interests of the European Union. The role of various police operations is discussed as well as working through legislative means. The focal point is the prevention of crimes and other irregularities.

Leading Journals, Periodicals, and Magazines

Poliisi ja oikeus (The Police and Justice, in Finnish). Chief editor Seppo Yrjönen. Asemamiehenkatu 2, 00520 Helsinki, Finland. Publisher: The Union of Finland's Police Organizations.

Suomen poliisilehti (Finland's Police Magazine, in Finnish). Chief editor Jaakko Kares, Raision kihlakunnan poliisilaitos, PL 15, 21201 Raisio, Finland. Publisher: The Union of Police Officers.

Rikosuhri (The Victim of Crime, in Finnish). Chief editor Petra Kjällman, PL 168, 00141 Helsinki, Finland. Publisher: Service for the Victims of Crime.

Poliisi-info (Info of the Police, in Finnish). Chief editor Jukka Hämäläinen, Kirkkokatu 12, 00023 Valtioneuvosto, Finland. Publisher: Ministry of the Interior, Police Department. Content: information about new laws linked to the police activities, information about amendments of legislation, crime prevention, information about new publications, and so on.

Internet Resources

www.ihmisoikeusliitto.fi/php/varjoraportit/cerd_2002.doc
Ministry of the Interior: www.intermin.fi/
Ministry of Justice: www.om.fi/
www.poliisi.fi/
www.stat.fi

AHTI LAITINEN

Bibliography

Ellonen, Erkki, et al. *Etiikka ja poliisin työ* (Ethics and Police Work). Textbook No. 6. Helsinki: The Police College of Finland, 2000.

Helminen, Klaus, Kuusimäki, Matti, and Salminen, Markku. *Poliisioikeus* (Law for the Police). Helsinki: Kauppakaari Oyj, 2000.

Jasinskaja-Lahti, Inga, Liebkind, Karmela, and Vesala, Tiina. *Rasismi ja syrjintä Suomessa* (Racism and Discrimination in Finland: The Experiences of Immigrants). Helsinki: Gaudeamus, 2002.

Jousimaa, Kyösti. *The History of the Finnish Police*. Helsinki: The Police of Finland, 1986.

Kolehmainen, Seppo. "Tunnelman kohottamisesta hallittuun aseenkäyttöön. Seenkäyttömääräysten eräitä vakutuksia poliisitoimintaan" (From the Presentation of Arms towards a Controlled Use of Arms: Some Effects of the Orders for Using Arms in Police Activities). Master's thesis, University of Turku, 2001.

Lappi-Seppälä, Tapio. "Luottamus tuomioistuimiin" (Trust in the Courts). In *Legal Circumstances 2000*, edited by Litmala, Marjukka. Publication 173. Helsinki: National Research Institute of Legal Policy, 2000.

National Research Institute of Legal Policy. *Rikollisuustilanne 2001* (The Crime Situation 2001). Publication No. 190/2002. Helsinki: National Research Institute of Legal Policy, 2002. Parts of the section Police Profile concerning contemporary legislation on the police and police organization were derived from this source, as well as the websites of the Ministry of the Interior and the Ministry of Justice.

Sinisalo, Kari. "Poliisin toimivallan määräytyminen" (Defining of the Powers of the Police). 1971.

FRANCE

Background Material

France is one of the oldest European nations. Initially called the "Gaule," its state structures developed soon after the Middle Ages under the rule of the monarchy and centered around Paris.

The monarchy was abolished during the French Revolution of 1789 when the country became a republic. Until the twentieth century, France was one of the most powerful and influential countries in the world with many colonies in Africa and Asia. Traditionally, agriculture has been very important, but fundamental changes have occurred since the end of World War II. France is now a country with strong industries and international trade, and tourism is a significant business.

France is a founding member of the European Union (EU). Its territory is approximately 551,500 square kilometers. "Overseas" or non-European France consists of four departments (Guadeloupe, Martinique, Guyane, and Reunion Island) and various territories including New Caledonia and Polynesia. Metropolitan and Overseas France constitute territories under French sovereignty. The political and administrative capital is Paris.

The population of France is approximately 60 million, and the official language is French. The majority of inhabitants are Roman Catholic, but there are also many Protestants and about 5 million Muslims. France's Muslim population is made up of three distinct ethnic groups, North Africans, black Africans, and Turks, who arrived in three waves of immigration, the first of which began in the 1950s. North Africans (Algerians, Moroccans, and Tunisians) are the largest group, and Algerians are dominant within it.

Per capita GNP in 2002 was US$22,690. France is among the most industrialized countries in the world. It is a member of the European Union and the so-called Group of Seven (G7) industrialized nations. The official currency is the euro. France is part of the European Union (EU) and Schengen Agreement area in which all internal border controls have been abolished.

Contextual Features

France is a constitutional parliamentary republic, functioning on the basis of the separation of powers. Legislative power is exercised by Parliament with its two chambers (Senate and National Assembly). The 321 Senators are elected by indirect vote, and the 577 Deputies in the National Assembly are elected by direct vote. France also has deputies in the European Parliament. The executive power is exercised by the President of the French Republic who is the head of state and the Prime Minister who is the head of government.

The independence of the judiciary is guaranteed by the constitution. France has the statutory legal system of continental European tradition.

In 2002, 60.94% of the crimes reported to the police and gendarmerie were thefts; 8.64% were economic and financial crimes; 7.38% were crimes against persons (assault, etc.); and 23.04% were other crimes including drug trafficking.

In France, criminal courts of the first instance handle violations of the law listed in the Penal Code, and they are divided into three categories: "contraventions" (minor offenses), "délits" (misdemeanors), and "crimes" (capital offenses or felonies).

"Contraventions" are handled by Tribunaux de Police (Police Courts), which sit with a single judge. "Délits," which comprise most offenses, are handled by Tribunaux Correctionnels (Criminal Courts), which usually sit with three judges unless the law specifically provides for a single one. Crimes, described as serious offenses such as murder, are tried by the Cours d'Assises (Assizes Court), composed of three judges and a jury of nine citizens drawn by lot from a list of names. The judges and jury together decide on innocence or guilt and on the sentence to be passed. However, for certain particularly "sensitive" cases, such as those concerning terrorist crimes, there are special Cours d'Assises composed of seven judges sitting without a jury.

Appeals are handled by the Cour d'Appel (Court of Appeal) initially and ultimately in the Cour de Cassation, or supreme court for the judiciary.

The judicial investigation of crimes and of some délits is controlled by the juge d'instruction, or examining magistrate. When the prosecutor turns over a case to an examining magistrate, the latter will delegate some of his powers of investigation and coercion, within strict limits and under his direct supervision, to police or gendarmerie officers.

The task of the prosecutors (officials of the French Parquet, or ministère public) is to defend society by acting as its advocate and to ask the judges to apply the criminal law. They decide on the advisability of instituting criminal proceedings and initiate them by transferring cases to an examining magistrate. However, they supervise and control all police investigations before such transfers.

The penitentiary administration is a part of the Ministry of Justice. There are 185 prisons of different types:

- Maisons d'arrêt, 117 : Prisons for short penalties and pre-trial detention
- Centres de detention, 23: Prisons for middle-term penalties
- Maisons centrals, 6: Prisons for the most lengthy penalties
- Centres penitentiaries, 26: Mixed, including a section for short-term prisoners and a department for long sentences

- Centres de semi-liberté, 13: Centers for prisoners allowed to work outside during the day (half-liberty)

On June 1, 2003, there were 60,513 persons in prison in France, of which 38,072 persons were convicted and 22,441 were awaiting trial.

The death penalty was abolished in France in 1981. Penal sanctions are mainly imprisonment (six months for minor offenses to thirty years for particularly serious crimes, and life sentences are possible for the most serious crimes) and fines. Other sanctions such as confiscation of assets or property are possible in certain cases.

Police Profile

Background

Since the Middle Ages, policing in France was handled by the Guêt (watchmen), a body of civilian foot-patrol agents in the cities that later became municipal police forces, and by the Gens d'Armes (men at arms), military police who patrolled the rural areas on horseback. The two entities remained, although developing and changing with the times and related changes in government. At the end of a long evolution, France chose a legal status that makes these two police forces directly subordinate to the state.

Organizational Description and Functions

Today internal security is the responsibility of two major forces: national police, governed by a civil statute and under the supervision of the Ministry of Interior; and national gendarmerie with a military statute under the Ministry of Defense.

Other government institutions are responsible for law enforcement in their particular sectors. Two main examples are the Customs Directorate General (Direction générale des Douanes et Droits indirects) and the Directorate General of Competition, Consumption and Repression of Fraud (Direction générale de la Concurrence, de la Consommation et de la Repression des Fraudes), both of which are departments of the Ministry of Finance.

Police personnel number 264,000, resulting in about one officer for every 229 inhabitants. The types and staffing of various police forces follow:

- National police: 145,000 in large towns (including about 15,000 security adjuncts and 13,000 administrative staff) under the Ministry of the Interior.
- National gendarmerie: 101,000 (including about 15,000 gendarmerie adjuncts and about 1,900 civilian staff) under the Ministry of Defense. Municipal police forces and rural police: 18,000 in some municipalities. Customs: 20,000, nder the Ministry of Finance.
- Other: National penitentiary administration (18,000 under the Ministry of Justice); gendarmerie reserves (11,000); two railway special police forces (2,250)

The National Police constitute one of the three Directorates General at the Ministry of the Interior. Its staff is divided into two categories, police officers and administrative employees, and comprises eleven Directorates and Central Departments. Nine of them are "active," and therefore engaged in operational police tasks. The most important operational Directorates are the Central Directorate of Judicial Police and the Central Directorate of Public Security, which, under the law are responsible for assisting the judiciary in investigating crimes under the supervision and control of the relevant judicial authorities.

The task of the Central Directorate of Judicial Police is to investigate crimes. It plays an essential role in the effort to combat crime thanks to its centralized organization with, in particular, the various Central Offices. These centralized institutions operate at national level with interministerial responsibilities to combat certain types of organized crime with the assistance of the Regional Services of Judicial Police (Services régionaux de Police judiciaire) located in various locations throughout France.

Furthermore, since the Central Director of the Judicial Police is also the Head of France's Interpol National Central Bureau, the Central Directorate of Judicial Police plays an important role in combating international organized crime.

The Companies for Republican Security (CRS) are mobile units that form the general reserve of the national police. The main mission of the CRS is to maintain public order and road security, and to contribute to the protection of people and buildings. CRS employs about 14,000 people.

The Central Directorate of General Intelligence (Direction centrale des Renseignements généraux, DCRG) is responsible for research and centralization of information for the government. It employs about 3,850 people.

The National Gendarmerie is an integral part of the armed forces. It comes under the responsibility of the Ministry of Defense for administrative and organizational purposes. It is divided into two major subdivisions with different tasks. Its total manpower (commissioned and noncommissioned officers and gendarmes) is nearly 101,000.

The Mobile Gendarmerie, with a force of about 20,000, is essentially responsible for maintaining public order during peacetime. The Territorial Gendarmerie conducts crime investigations under the same laws and regulations as the National Police. Its staff is distributed throughout the territory of France and concentrated mainly in rural areas. Its members also perform certain military tasks.

The Directorate General of Customs and Indirect Taxation under the Ministry of Finance has specific control and enforcement duties in connection with customs and tax matters. In addition, it cooperates with the National Police and the Gendarmerie on crime investigation operations, especially in cases of traffic in drugs and arms, so that information is shared. Officers from the Judicial Police and National Police are, in fact, seconded to the Customs Administration.

Pretrial police and judicial powers when an offender is caught in a criminal act (flagrante delicto) are listed in the table below. Police powers under a rogatory commission are listed in the table to the right.

Training

Recruitment for police and gendarmerie service is open to both male and female candidates. There are several levels of recruitment in the Police Nationale. The applicants must be French and pass a selection exam. There are schools for different levels:

- 14 Police Schools (Ecoles de police, ENP)
- 12 Police Training Centers (Centres de formation de police, CFP)
- 1 Higher National Police Officer School (Ecole Nationale supérieure des officiers de police, ENSOP)

Pre-trial police and judicial powers

Police	Police	Prosecutor
Identity check	X	X
Arrest	X	X
Questioning	X	X
Detention by police	2 × 24 hours*	X**
Custody (on judicial order)	–	X
Search of person	X	–
Search of premises	X	X
Confiscation of property	X	X

* For twenty-four hours initially and for a further twenty-four hours with the agreement of the Public Prosecutor.
** May be extended to four days in drug and terrorism cases.

Power of police services under a Rogatory Commission

Police	Magistrate	Judge
Identity check	X	X
Arrest	X	X
Questioning	X	X
Detention by police	2 × 24 hours*	
Custody (on judicial order)	–	X
Search of person	X	–
Search of premises	X	X
Confiscation of property	X	X

* For 24 hours initially and a further 24 hours with the agreement of the Examining Magistrate.

- For the highest ranks, the Higher National Police School (Ecole Nationale supérieure de police, ENSP), located in Saint-Cyr au Mont d'Or, near Lyon (Address: 9, rue Carnot 69450 Saint-Cyr au Mont D'Or, France)

The Ecole nationale supérieure de la police (ENSP) is under the authority of the Minister of Interior. This school is for the commissaires de police. There are two options for the recruitment of commissaires de police: The first competitive exam for students under age thirty who are university graduates (60%). The second competitive exam is open to National Police personnel. The basic training in ENSP is two years: one year in the school and a one-year practicuum in the police.

Various levels of recruitment exist also in the schools of the Gendarmerie Nationale. Under the authority of a general, there is a school headquarters in Charenton, near Paris, and the Training Centers of Auxiliary Gendarmes (Centres d'instruction des gendarmes auxiliaries, CIGA).

Police Use of Firearms

All police officers and gendarmes are equipped with individual handguns. Other kinds of firearms may also be used for particularly dangerous operations. The law stipulates conditions for the legal use of firearms. A police officer may carry his gun at any time, but may make use of it only in case of legitimate self-defense or defense. A police officer firing under any other circumstances is subject to disciplinary and penal sanctions.

Complaints and Discipline

The state requires a strong service commitment from the members of the Police Nationale and the

Gendarmerie Nationale. This commitment includes responsibility, obedience, a professional and dignified demeanor (including in private life), professional confidentiality, and the obligation of exclusive public service. There is a code of ethics for all officers of the National Police, and there are sanctions for violations of duties.

The activities of police officers and gendarmes are subject to several types of control, including hierarchical control; internal control by the Inspection Générale de la Police Nationale, the Inspection Générale de la Prefecture de Police de Paris, and the Inspection Générale de la Gendarmerie Nationale; and control by the Judiciary.

France is a party to the international human rights treaty (International Covenant on Civil and Political Rights and its protocols) and the Convention for the Protection of Human Rights and Fundamental Freedoms (treaty open for signature by the member-states of the Council of Europe). France respects the rights contained there and has ratified most of the thirteen protocols of this Convention. The death penalty was abolished in France in 1981 for all crimes, and France has ratified the Treaty on the International Criminal Court.

Terrorism

France has had to deal with two kinds of terrorism. In the past, there was a period of Marxist-Leninist terrorism, but the country has struggled more recently with separatist terrorism. Action Directe (AD) was the most important extreme leftist terrorist organization founded in the 1970s. AD was responsible for the murder of Georges Barse, the president of the Renault Company. During the 1990s, one source of terrorism in France was Algeria where the military canceled elections in 1991, fearing victory by the fundamentalist organization FIS. The first attempt to export terrorism into France took place at Christmas 1994. Four mujahedin from the GIA (Armed Islamic Group) hijacked an Air France plane at the airport in Algiers. French antiterrorist police stormed the plane during the Marseille stopover and killed the hijackers . The next wave of terrorism to hit France was in the summer of 1995, and the actors were French. Eight bomb attacks left seven dead and over 130 injured. These attacks were carried out by alienated North African youths with a history of petty crime.

Separatist terrorism is mainly active in Corsica, where the Corsica FLNC Organization is claiming independence, but groups with a terrorist potential exist in other parts of France (Revolutionary Army of Bretons, Separatist Basque Organization, Revolutionist Alliance of the Caribbean).

France has a comprehensive and coherent body of anti-terrorist legislation. Terrorism is legally defined, and terrorist offenses within the meaning of the definition are subject to special procedures. Terrorist offenses are defined in Articles 421-1 to 421-2-2 of the Penal Code, which distinguish among four types of offenses:

- Terrorism resulting from infringements of ordinary law (Article 421-1 of the Penal Code) committed in a particular context; it is the context that makes them terrorist offenses (deliberate assault on the life or integrity of a person, kidnapping, hijacking of aircraft or any other means of transport, manufacture and use of biological and chemical weapons, and so on).
- Environmental terrorism
- Conspiracy to commit terrorist acts
- Financing terrorism

Terrorism is, in principle, subject to the ordinary rules of procedure, but there are exceptions that apply to terrorist offenses listed in Articles 706-16 to 706-25 of the Code of Criminal Procedure. They include the centralization of proceedings in Paris and some special features during investigations.

For example, Article 706-23 states that the total length of time spent in police custody may be increased to four days when terrorism is involved, whereas the usual maximum is forty-eight hours. The additional forty-eight hours may be authorized only by the judge of liberties and detention or the examining magistrate; it may occur during a preliminary investigation, an expedited police investigation, or a written order from an examining judge.

Special rules also apply during the trial. There is a special assize court consisting exclusively of judges (a president and six assessors). Terrorist criminals are not tried by jury. In the court, decisions against the accused, such as the pronouncement of a maximum sentence (Articles 698-6-3 and 362) are taken by a simple majority.

Under Article 706-17-1, in exceptional circumstances and for reasons of security, hearings may take place in any location other than those where they are usually held within the venue of the Paris Appeal Court.

Time limits and statutes of limitations for prosecution and enforcement of sentence have been extended for terrorist offenses. Article 706-25-1 sets a thirty-year limit for felonies involving terrorist acts. The limit for membership in a terrorist organization is twenty years. For other terrorist offenses, the time limits for prosecution and enforcement of sentence are those of ordinary law, namely, three years for prosecution (Article 8 of the Code of Criminal Procedure) and five years for enforcement of sentence (Article 133-3 of the Penal Code).

International Cooperation

France is a member of the European Union and participates in the organization of police and justice structures in Europe through the following entities:

- Europol is a European police coordination center for the collection, analysis, and dissemination of information. It was established to help law enforcement agencies (mainly police and customs) when they have to carry investigations in two or more EU countries.
- Eurojust is a European institution for the judiciary composed of legal and judicial experts. Their mission is to help coordinate the investigation and prosecution of serious cross-border crime within the EU.
- The Office européen de Lutte Anti-Fraude (OLAF, European Anti-Fraud Office) is an agency of the European Commission in charge of administrative investigations on fraud against the interests of the European Community and certain forms of corruption.

France is also a part of the Schengen area. The first convention among the five original group members (France, Germany, Belgium, The Netherlands, and Luxembourg) was signed on June 14, 1985. A further convention was drafted and signed on January 19, 1990. When it came into effect in 1995, it abolished the internal borders of the signatory states, plus Spain and Portugal, and it created a single external border where immigration checks for the Schengen area are carried out in accordance with a joint set of rules. Common rules regarding visas, asylum rights, and checks at external borders were adopted to allow the free movement of persons within the signatory states without disturbing law and order. Accordingly, in order to reconcile freedom and security, this freedom of movement was accompanied by so-called "compensatory" measures. This involved improving coordination between the police, customs, and the judiciary and taking necessary measures to combat terrorism and organized crime. In order to make this possible, a complex information system known as the Schengen Information System (SIS) was set up to exchange data on people's identities as well as descriptions of objects which were either stolen or lost. The Schengen area was gradually extended to Austria and Italy (1998), Greece (2000), and Denmark, Finland, and Sweden, together with the non-EU members Norway and Iceland (2001).

On January 1, 2004, the European arrest warrant replaced the traditional extradition system within the EU. This greatly simplified the procedure by substituting the entire political and administrative phase with a judicial mechanism. A European arrest warrant is considered to be any judicial decision issued by a member-state with a view to the arrest or surrender by another member-states of a requested person for the purposes of:

- Conducting a criminal prosecution;
- Executing a custodial sentence;
- Executing a detention order.

The warrant applies in the following cases:

- Where a final sentence of imprisonment or a detention order has been imposed for a period of at least four months;
- For offenses punishable by imprisonment or a detention order for a maximum period of at least one year.

If they are punishable in the issuing member-state by a custodial sentence of at least three years, the following offenses, among others, may give rise to surrender without verification of the double criminality of the act: terrorism, trafficking in human beings, corruption, participation in a criminal organization, counterfeiting currency, murder, racism and xenophobia, rape, trafficking in stolen vehicles, and fraud, including that affecting the financial interests of the Communities.

For criminal acts other than those mentioned above, surrender may be subject to the condition that the act for which surrender is requested constitutes an offense under the law of the executing member-state (double criminality rule).

As a general rule, the issuing authority transmits the European arrest warrant directly to the executing judicial authority.

Further international cooperation is governed by the constitutional principle that treaties prevail over domestic law on condition of reciprocity (Article 55 of the French Constitution). Pursuant to Article 55, duly ratified international conventions or agreements are incorporated directly into the domestic legal system. Certain provisions, however, may need to be "transposed" into domestic law in order to define legal and/or practical arrangements or to incorporate or extend the requested assistance.

Bilateral police cooperation agreements exist with many countries, in particular Hungary (1996), Switzerland (1998), Italy (1997), Germany (1997), Belgium (2001), and Spain (1998).

French liaison officers are posted, in particular, in Belgium, Colombia, Cyprus, Germany, Italy, Lebanon, Morocco, The Netherlands, Pakistan, Romania, Spain, Thailand, Turkey, United Kingdom, United States, and Venezuela. In turn, foreign liaison officers are posted in France from Belgium, Canada, South Korea, Germany, Israel, Italy, The Netherlands, Spain, Tunisia, United Kingdom, and United States.

The International Technical Cooperation Service of the French police (SCTIP) operates almost sixty delegations abroad.

Most exchanges relating to mutual legal assistance in criminal matters take place on the basis of either the European Convention of April 20, 1959, the Convention implementing the Schengen Agreement, or bilateral conventions. The majority of extraditions are carried out on the basis of the European Convention of December 13, 1957, or bilateral conventions.

Within the European Union, a convention on mutual assistance in criminal matters was adopted in 2000, but was not yet in force as of this writing.

If no convention or EU rule applies, requests for legal assistance and extradition are governed by the Act of March 10, 1927, pursuant to the French Code of Criminal Procedure, but with a view to meeting the legal requirements of the foreign country.

Dual Criminality Rule In mutual legal assistance matters, dual criminality is not generally required. However, such a requirement may arise from the relevant convention or from the Act passed to implement the convention in French law.

As far as extradition is concerned, the Act of March 10, 1927 requires dual criminality, and France issued a reservation along these lines when filing its instrument ratifying the 1957 European Convention. France does not therefore grant extradition for offenses that are not criminal offenses in France. However, it is not necessary for the definition of the offense in the law of the requesting State to be exactly the same as the definition in French law. It should be noted that the trend in recent EU conventions is toward reducing the scope of the dual criminality rule.

Mutual Legal Assistance, Extradition, and Public Policy Regarding mutual legal assistance, the general rule is that requests from foreign authorities are treated in the same way as identical measures from domestic authorities. However, it is possible to refuse to execute the request under the terms of Article 2 of the 1959 European Convention, in particular on the grounds of the country's essential interests or of a similar provision in another convention.

Likewise, France may refuse to extradite a person from its territory on public order grounds (declaration made by France when depositing its instrument ratifying the 1957 European Convention).

It is deemed to be contrary to French public order, and extradition is not granted, if the person sought would be tried in the requesting state by a court that does not ensure fundamental procedural guarantees and the protection of the rights of defense or by a court created for that person's particular case, or if extradition is requested for the enforcement of a sentence or detention order imposed by such a tribunal.

Extradition of Nationals France currently avails itself of the option to refuse extradition of its nationals offered by Article 6.1 of the European Convention on Extradition. The principle of the nonextradition of nationals is also set out in the Act of March 10, 1927. In accordance with the declaration made when depositing the instrument ratifying the above Convention, the nationality of the person sought is determined at the date of the offense in respect of which extradition is requested.

Political Offenses If the person claimed has obtained political refugee status from the relevant authorities in France with regard to the requesting state, extradition is systematically refused as being contrary to the general rules of law relating to refugees. However, refugee status is no obstacle to extradition to a third country.

Regarding political offenses, France applies Article 3 of the European Convention on Extradition pertaining to the signatory states. Accordingly, extradition is therefore not granted if the offense for which it is requested is regarded as a political offense by the requested State.

In French law, extradition can be refused when the person claimed is sought for a political offense or an offense of a political character. Nevertheless, the notion of political offense, which has no legal definition, is strictly interpreted by case law.

It is an established practice that French courts insist on the seriousness of the crime committed, by the person claimed, and for political or ideological reasons or motivations in order to give their consent on extradition.

While appreciating the political character of the offense for which extradition is sought, French courts also take into consideration whether the offense has been committed in a state respecting human rights.

Minimum Penalties for Extradition   Within the Schengen framework, the penalty incurred must be at least one year's deprivation of liberty under the law of the requesting state, and two years under French law (Article 61 of the 1990 Schengen Convention).

Under the European Convention on Extradition, the offenses must be punishable under the law of the requesting state, and under French law by deprivation of liberty for at least two years (reservation expressed with regard to Article 2 of the above Convention).

For other states, France applies the minimum penalties set forth in the relevant multilateral or bilateral convention.

With regard to offenses for which the sentence was imposed, France applies the four-month deprivation of liberty threshold stipulated at Article 2.1 of the European Convention on Extradition.

Extradition and the Death Penalty   France is a party to the Protocol 6 of April 28, 1983, to the European Convention for the Protection of Human Rights and Fundamental Freedoms, which states that the death penalty has been abolished and that no one may be condemned to such penalty or executed.

On this basis, pursuant to Article 11 of the above European Convention on Extradition, France does not grant extradition for offenses punishable by death under the laws of the requesting state unless the state concerned gives sufficient assurances that a death sentence will not be imposed or, if it is imposed, will not be carried out. The French government will take such assurances into consideration only if they are binding on both the government and the criminal courts of the requesting state.

Extradition and Infringements of Human Rights
France is party to the European Convention for the Protection of Human Rights and Fundamental Freedoms of November 4, 1950, and ensures that the rights of individuals derived from the convention are guaranteed during extradition procedures. In addition, under the *ne bis in idem* principle, pursuant to Article 9 of the European Convention on Extradition, France does not grant extradition if its courts have passed final judgment on the person claimed in respect to the offense or offenses for which extradition is requested.

Requests for Mutual Assistance   With regard to mutual legal assistance in criminal matters, French domestic law makes no provision for divulging the content of a request for assistance from another country without prejudice to the rights of the defense and entailing access to the file when an investigation is instituted (Article 116 of the Code of Criminal Procedure).

With regard to extradition, Article 13 of the Act of March 10, 1927, provides that the warrant pursuant to which the person is arrested is served on him by the principal public prosecutor. Then, and before the case is heard by the examining court competent to issue an opinion on all extradition requests, the entire file is made available to the claimed person's attorney. This requirement must be complied with, otherwise the procedure is void.

France does not require requests for legal assistance or extradition to be made in French or to be accompanied with a translation. In practice, however, it is in the foreign authority's interest to attach a translation to its request so that it can be processed more quickly.

Police Education, Research, and Publications

For research in police matters and security, the most competent state institution is the Institut des hautes études de sécurité intérieure (IHESI, Institute for Studies on Internal Security). It is located at 19, rue Peclet 75015 Paris, France.

The following are the major centers for documents and research:

- National Police: Centre de documentation de la Police Nationale, Ministère de l'Intérieur, de la sécurité intérieure et des libertés locales, Direction de la formation de la Police Nationale, 73 rue Paul Diomède, BP 144, 63020 Clermond-Ferrand cedex, France (Tél 00 33 1 49 27 49 27)
- Police of Paris: Archives de la Préfecture de police, 1 bis rue des Carmes 75195 Paris RP, France
- National Gendarmerie: Service historique de la Gendarmerie Nationale, Fort de Charenton 94706 Maisons-Alfort cedex, France (Tél: 00 33 1 41 79 25 33)
- Customs: Centre de documentation historique des douanes, 1 quai de la douane BP 60 33024, Bordeaux cedex, France

Police-related periodicals:

- *Civic*, edited by the Ministry of Interior, 1bis place des Saussaies 75008 Paris, France
- *Tribune du Commissaire de police*, Syndicat des commissaires et hauts fonctionnaires, 3 boulevard de l'Hôpital 73013 Paris, France
- *La revue de la Gendarmerie*, edited by the National Gendarmerie, 35 rue Saint-Didier, Paris cedex 16, France
- *L'essor de la Gendarmerie Nationale*, 132 rue du Faubourg Saint-Denis Paris cedex 10, France

DANIEL FONTANAUD

Websites

Ministère de l'Intérieur: *www.interieur.gouv.fr*
IHESI: *www.ihesi.interieur.gouv.fr.html*
Prefecture de police de Paris: *www.prefecture-police-paris. interieur.gouv.fr*
Gendarmerie Nationale: *www.defense.gouv.fr/gendarmerie/*
Ministère de la Justice: *www.justice.gouv.fr*
Direction Générale des douanes et droits indirects: *www. finances.gouv.fr/douanes/*
www.police.online.fr
www.globalsecurity.org/intell/world/france

Bibliography

Alary, E. *Histoire de la Gendarmerie*. Paris: Calmann Levy, 2000.

Aspects de la criminalité et de la délinquance constatées en France en 2002 par les services de police et les unités de gendarmerie en 2003. Paris: La Documentation française, 2003.

Belorgey, J. M. *La police au rapport*. Nancy: Presses Universitaires de Nancy, 1991.

Buitrong, L. *La Police dans la société française*. Paris: Presses Universitaires de France, 2003.

Carnot, G. *Histoire de la police française: des origines à nos jours*. Tallandier/Approches, 1992.

De Hert, P. *La Police française en l'an 2000*. Politeia n° 4–95, 1995.

De Bousquet, and Alary, E. *La Gendarmerie Nationale*. Paris: Le Cherche Midi Editeurs, 2001.

European Union. Council Framework Decision 2002/584/JHA of 13 June 2002 on the European Arrest Warrant, *Official Journal L* 190, 18 July 2002.

Pichon, R., and Haenel, H. *La Gendarmerie*. Paris: Presses Universitaires de France, 1999.

"Police nationale et polices municipales." *Cahiers de la Fonction publique et de l'Administration* no. 166 (1998): 4–16.

Queant, A. *Le Commissaire de police dans la société française*. Economica, collection "mieux connaître," Paris: 1998.

G

GABON

Background Material

It is estimated that between 3000 and 1000 BC, the Bantu arrived in the current territory of Gabon from the West African savannas. When the Portuguese commander Lopo Gonçalvès arrived in 1742 at the Estuary level, three Bantu groups lived on the coasts, the Mpongwe in the Estuary, the Orungu in the Port Gentil region (Cap Lopez), and the Nkomi further to the south; all three spoke Myene (and were consequently called the Myene ethnic group). For three and a half centuries, the Dutch, English, French, and then the Americans engaged in trade with the Myene ethnic group—mostly slave trade—with the slaves originating from inland territories. The ethnic distribution in Ga-bon was significantly altered by the arrival of the Fang ethnic group hailing from the north at the beginning of the nineteenth century. The Fangs were part of the Pahouin group, and settled predominantly in Gabon.

The Gabonese Republic is located in western Africa, bordering the Atlantic Ocean at the Equator, between Republic of the Congo and Equatorial Guinea. It has a population of 1,355,246 (2004 estimate) and a total area of 267,667 square kilometers.

The population is Bantu, comprised of four major tribal groupings (Fang, Bapounou, Nzebi, Obamba). There are minority populations of other Africans and Europeans, primarily French.

Christianity is practiced by 55% to 75% of the population. The rest of the population adheres to traditional animist beliefs. Less than 1% of the population identifies as Muslim.

French is the official language, although Fang, Myene, Nzebi, Bapounou/Eschira, and Bandjabi are also spoken.

The capital is Libreville.

GDP per capita (purchasing power parity) is US$5,500 (2003 estimate).

Contextual Features

Only two autocratic presidents have ruled Gabon since independence from France in 1960. Gabon's current president, El Hadj Omar Bongo—one of the longest-serving heads of state in the world—has dominated Gabon's political scene for almost four decades. President Bongo introduced a nominal multiparty system and a new constitution in the early 1990s. However, the low turnout and allegations of electoral fraud during the most recent local elections in 2002–2003 have exposed the weaknesses of formal political structures in Gabon. In addition, recent strikes have underscored popular disenchantment with the political system. As of this writing, presidential elections scheduled for 2005 were considered unlikely to bring change since the opposition remains weak, divided, and financially dependent on the current regime. Despite political conditions, a small population, abundant natural resources, and considerable foreign support have helped make Gabon one of the more prosperous and stable African countries.

Gabon is a republic with a multiparty presidential regime. Opposition parties were legalized in 1990. Gabon is administratively organized into nine provinces: Estuaire, Haut-Ogooue, Moyen-Ogooue, Ngounie, Nyanga, Ogooue-Ivindo, Ogooue-Lolo, Ogooue-Maritime, and Woleu-Ntem.

Gabon has a legal system based on French civil law system and customary law; judicial review of legislative acts occurs in the Constitutional Chamber of the Supreme Court.

The bicameral legislature consists of the Senate (ninety-one seats; members elected by members of municipal councils and departmental assemblies) and the National Assembly or Assemblee Nationale (120 seats; members are elected by direct, popular vote to serve five-year terms).

The president is the chief of state, while the prime minister acts as the head of the government. The prime minister appoints a Council of Ministers in consultation with the president. The Supreme Court consists of the judicial, administrative, and accounts branches. The judiciary system also has a Constitutional Court, courts of appeal, the Court of State Security, and county courts.

COLONEL JEAN-ETIENNE ELION

THE GAMBIA

Background Material

The Republic of The Gambia is located in Western Africa, bordering the North Atlantic Ocean and Senegal, and covering an area of 11,300 square kilometers. The population numbers 1,546,848 (July 2004 estimate), and the capital is Banjul. Languages spoken include English (official), Mandinka, Wolof, Fula, and other indigenous vernaculars.

The Gambia's GDP per capita (purchasing power parity) is US$1,700 (2003 estimate). The Gambia participates in the following international organizations: United Nations, Economic Community of West African States, African Union, World Health Organization, International Monetary Fund, and Interpol.

Gambia, a small multiparty democratic republic, is located in western Africa and is bordered by Senegal. It was originally part of the Empire of Ghana, the Kingdom of the Songhais, and the Kingdom of Mali. The Arab traders documented the first known record of the country in the ninth and tenth centuries. Without regard for Gambia's ethnic lines of demarcation, French and British colonizers drew the boundaries for Gambia in 1889. A failure on the part of the colonizers to adhere to those boundaries has resulted in the people of Gambia being restricted to a small serpentine state, a mere ten kilometers from either side of the Gambia River.

During the latter part of the seventeenth century and the entire eighteenth century, England and France engaged in geopolitical and geoeconomic mêlées in Senegal and the area around the Gambia River. It has been reported that about 3 million Africans may have been removed from the region during the trans-Atlantic slave trade. Initially, Africans were uprooted from their homeland and taken to Europe where they worked as servants. Later, in the eighteenth century, Africans were taken to the West Indies and North America to perform physical and commercial labor. After two centuries of British domination, Gambia became an independent nation on February 18, 1965. Later, in April 1970, it became a republic. Between 1982 and 1989, Gambia formed a confederation with Senegal, and in 1991, both countries signed a friendship and cooperation treaty.

Sir Dawda Jawara, leader of the Protectorates People's Party (PPP), ruled the country from its independence until 1994, when the military, led by Lt. Yahya Jammeh, overthrew the president and banned all political activities. In 1996, a Gambian constitution was developed and presidential elections were conducted. The nation held parliamentary elections in 1997, which completed a titular return to civilian rule. In 2001 and early 2002, the country conducted another round of presidential and parliamentary elections that returned Yahya Jammeh to the executive office of the presidency.

The Gambia is composed of various ethnic groups, including the Mandinka, Fula, Wolof, and Serahuli. Unlike many other African nations with troubled ethnic relations, Gambians engage in few intertribal hostilities; rather, the people generally respect the nation's divergent languages, religions, and traditions. The Gambia has a population of 1,546,848 people, of which only about 2,500 are non-Africans, including Europeans and Lebanese. More than 92% of the nation's citizens are Muslim, while people of various Christian faiths constitute the remainder of the population. Officially, the government celebrates both Muslim and Christian holidays and is tolerant of various religions. Although young people are increasingly migrating to the cities in pursuit of education and employment opportunities, most Gambians still dwell in the rural areas of the country. Indeed, without disregarding Western lifestyles and ideals, Gambians subscribe to the extended family principles common to other West African countries.

Economically, unlike many other African countries, Gambia lacks important mineral or other natural resources. While agriculture accounts for 23% of the nation's gross domestic product (GDP), and employs about 75% of the workforce, Gambia has a limited farming foundation. According to published documents, the population relies on peanut production, livestock, fish, forestry, and hides for its sources of revenue. Manufacturing, which is primarily agriculturally based, and services account for 6% and 19%, respectively, of the GDP.

It has been reported that tourism, which constitutes a significant portion of the economic activity of the country, has been declining since 2000, resulting in widespread unemployment. Yet, despite these serious economic conditions, some optimism can be expressed regarding Gambia's economic future. The United Kingdom and other European Union member-states, Asia, the United States, and other African countries constitute The Gambia's economic export trading partners. While the International Monetary Fund (IMF) provides technical help and advice for the improvement of the nation's economy, economic development in The Gambia still relies heavily on sound economic policies of the government. With foreign aid from various donor countries, along with disciplined economic management, such as a revitalization of the tourist industry, Gambia's economy will expand.

Since civilian rule was restored between 2001 and 2002, U.S. policy toward The Gambia has improved significantly. Based on past relations, mutual respect, democratic rule, devotion to counter terrorism collaboration, and other pressing international affairs, the United States has sought to enhance its strong relationship with The Gambia. To that end, U.S. assistance to The Gambia supports democratic and civil society operations, efforts to control and eradicate the HIV and AIDS epidemic in the country, and equality in education for females. In 2003, The Gambia was selected by U.S. authorities to receive economic preference under the African Growth and Opportunity ACT (AGOA).

It should be noted that, historically, The Gambia has played pivotal roles in peacekeeping operations in Africa and other regions of the world. Therefore, Gambia also maintains cordial relations with many other African, Asian, and European countries. For instance, it is a member of the African Union and the Economic Community of West African States (ECOWAS), and it played a significant role by contributing troops in 1990 and 2003 to help squash the conflict in the Liberian Civil War. The Gambian army also participated in peacekeeping operations in Bosnia, Kosovo, the Democratic Republic of the Congo (DROC), Sierra Leone, Eritrea, and East Timor.

Contextual Features

Before the July 1994 military coup in Gambia that revoked the 1970 constitution, the nation was one of the oldest and most respected multidemocracies on the African continent, having a reputation throughout Africa for maintaining and sustaining the fundamental principles of democratic government. On August 8, 1996, the Constitution of the Second Republic of the Gambia was approved in a national referendum. It was implemented on January 16, 1997. The constitution provides for a strong presidential government, a unicameral legislature, an independent judiciary, and the protection of human rights.

Under the provisions, the head of state serves as the executive president of the Republic and is elected by universal adult suffrage for a five-year term. The president is vested with the authority to appoint a vice president and other cabinet ministers from the ranks of the members of the House of Representatives. The unicameral National Assembly is vested with legislative power. The constitution limits membership of the National Assembly to fifty-three, from which forty-eight members are directly elected by the people and five appointed by the president. Representatives of the legislature serve for a period of five years.

Despite a few amendments made by the present administration to the constitution, the provisions of the Gambia judiciary remain intact. Moreover, the judiciary resembles the structure and administration of other countries with common law principles. In the Gambia, there is only one hierarchical system that is composed of lower and upper courts. The lower level courts include Khadis (Muslim) courts, District tribunals, and Magistrate courts. Together they have jurisdictions over criminal and civil litigations. At the apex of the judiciary are the Supreme Court and the Gambia Court of Appeal. These courts have appellate jurisdictions over judicial matters. The Gambia has an independent judicial system that maintains a high degree of respect for and protection of human rights.

While Gambia is not known for egregious violations of human rights, an Amnesty International Report (2003) alleges that the government has deliberately breached some human rights principles in violation of the mandates of the constitution. It claims that Gambia's new constitution threatens human rights, grants total immunity from prosecution to the country's authorities, denies Gambian citizens their constitutional right to address wrongs, and allows for both the retention of capital punishment and the detention of citizens incommunicado. In addition, it states that freedom of expression is under repeated attack in the Gambia, that female genital mutilation is still widespread, and that the ill treatment of citizens by the security forces remains unchecked.

Generally, The Gambia is a peaceful country, having the lowest crime rates in sub-Saharan Africa. Murder is a rarity in the nation, primarily because of the introduction of the death penalty. Stealing, burglary, and sexual offenses are the most commonly committed crimes in Gambia. It has been reported that between ten and fifteen sexual assaults (rape) occur annually, an offense that is punishable by life imprisonment.

There are three main prisons in Gambia: State Central Prison (Mile 2), Jeshwang Prison, and Janjangbureh Prison (formerly Georgetown). All three facilities fall under the auspices of the Ministry of Interior. Thematically, State Central Prison, which has a capacity of 500 inmates, serves as headquarters for the Gambian prison system. It houses both male and female offenders and employs 130 correctional officers. It is reported that the Jeshwang Prison has a capacity of 200 inmates. It warehouses only male inmates with relatively short prison sentences. It is a hygienic facility that resembles a minimum-security prison in the United States. The Janjanbureh prison is situated about 300 kilometers from Banjul, the capital of the Gambia. It is a rural prison and is operated under the Central River Division (CRD). It has a capacity of 80 and does not accept political or death penalty offenders. Primarily, it functions as a camp for prisoners who are later transferred to Banjul.

Inmates in Gambia's prisons are given complete access to medical treatment, receive three meals a day, and rarely experience cruel and unusual punishment, such as living in overcrowded conditions. Except at Mile 2, which has held as many as six female inmates at once, women are separated from male prisoners. Detention of suspects before trial generally does not exceed seventy-two hours. Prison guards receive adequate training. Gambia's identifiable major problems are a lack of adequate transportation needed to carry prisoners to court, an appropriate process for the rehabilitation of offenders, and more buildings to hold juvenile offenders, who enter the criminal justice system by way of contact with the police.

Police Profile

Background

Like many other former colonized African countries, Gambia first fell under British rule in 1783 before becoming a colony in 1843. Consequently, the nation's initial police regiment was a product of its colonial past. Police authority in the country was established in 1855, primarily to foil the smuggling that was occurring around the River Gambia, to enforce the taxation of the Gambia citizenry, and to contain dissident insurgency in the territory. Scholars generally regard the River Police force as Gambia's first professional law enforcement agency. It consisted of an armed militia, imperial troops, and ten male river police officers. In 1866, Britain added forty armed constabulary men to the existing force. Subsequently, in 1870, the constabulary force was enhanced to a level of 100 men, and Britain removed all the imperial troops from The Gambia. The River Police were essentially responsible for the maintenance of public order in the region.

Although it has grown dramatically, in 1901 the Gambian police force consisted of only two officers and eighty other ranks. In 1909, badge messengers were created by a protectorate ordinance of Britain that authorized chiefs and local leaders to appoint men for the preservation of peace in their jurisdictions. They possessed the rights, obligations, and tasks of normal police who functioned in a particular district of the protectorate. Prior to Gambia's gaining its independence, badge messengers performed duties such as the enforcement of the Native Authorities Decrees.

On the eve of Gambia's independence, police manpower was increased to 284 officers, which resulted in a markedly more efficient force. In 1958, the Gambia Regiment was deactivated, leading to the creation of the Field Force, generally referred to as the Gambia Police Force. Subsequently, the Gambia Police Force, under the guidance of an Inspector General, took over the defense responsibilities of the country.

Organizational Description

In contemporary Gambia, a police force with many stations and cells maintains law and order. Responsibilities for internal security and law enforcement fall within the jurisdiction of the Gambian police. Organizationally, the police force is divided into nine operational divisions. The Kanify Division is the divisional police headquarters and serves as the Kariba police station. One division of the police covers the capital city of Banjul. Other police stations are located in Mansankonko, Janjanbureh, Bundung, Kotu, Brikama, Serekunda, Yundum, and Bakau.

Other functional police divisions include a Criminal Investigation Department (CID), which is responsible for investigating crimes, a licensing and traffic division, an immigration and criminal records office, and a special branch office. The police also command the various fire brigades, such as the Banjul Fire Station, the Yundun Airport Fire, and the Bakau Fire Station. In addition, the Inspector General of Police is responsible for the Military Field Force that is charged with maintaining internal security and supervision over ceremonial duties. The military field force is also available to aid the police in controlling rebellions.

The police uniform consists of khaki drill, short-sleeved, open-necked tunics, in combination with matching or black trousers and a gray bush shirt. During "graveyard" shifts (night duties), officers wear black, closed-neck tunics with matching trousers. The uniforms of night officers also include black pointed hats and black leather belts.

Police Public Projects

As noted earlier, The Gambia is a relatively peaceful society with a constitution that respects the duties and rights of individuals. In order to protect its tourist industry and attract foreign investment, the country has introduced a Sea Police unit to help maintain an atmosphere of tranquility on its beaches and streets, and to assist its citizens and visitors. Recently, community policing, with an emphasis on citizen involvement, was introduced in Gambia. Its objective is to prevent and detect crime in a proactive manner. Furthermore, in order to restore public trust in the police, the government has introduced bicycle patrols as part of its strategy to regain the public's confidence. It is hoped that this strategy of "pedal power" in the Banjul area will help to reduce crime and bring the police closer to the citizens. It is also intended to alleviate some of the occupational hazards associated with police foot patrols (such as exposure to extreme heat in The Gambia's hot, sunny climate).

Police Use of Firearms

The police are not normally armed. However, the Field Force is equipped with small police arsenals, such as rifles and automatic guns. As in other nations, police ranks follow a hierarchical structure as follows:

Inspector General
Deputy Inspector-General
Commander
Deputy Commander
Assistant Commander
Chief Inspector
Inspector
Subinspector
Sergeant
Corporal
First Class Constables

Terrorism

Regarding terrorism, Gambia supports U.S. efforts to eradicate the terrorist havens around the globe that threaten peace and stability. In short, the government of Gambia is committed to the global struggle against such problems as international terrorism. Like its other African counterparts (Niger, Togo, and so on), Gambia's foreign policy goal is dedicated to national development interests and the promotion of international peace and security. It is widely believed that internal economic problems preclude most African countries from engaging in terrorism against core nations of the world. However, Gambia is not immune from internal tribulations, which could lead to political instability and internal struggles in the country. Therefore, the military wing of the police provides needed assistance that dictates and combats terrorism with support, training, and aid from developed nations.

Police Education, Research, and Publications

During the colonial era, Britain developed a Garrison School dedicated to the education and training of African soldiers positioned in Gambia. A second school, situated at Bathurst, was particularly significant in producing a small number of trained, noncommissioned African officers. These competent elites served the interest of the metropolis. Generally, the Gambia National Police Force, augmented by the Gambia College, provided police training in the nation.

Recently, the Canadian International Development Agency (CIDA) provided a grant of $1 million to Mount Saint Vincent University (MS VU) to train Gambian police. The grant emphasizes the introduction of community policing and adherence to restorative justice in Gambia. The program is headed by Stephen Perrott and is designed to strengthen good governance and democratic institutions in Gambia. The Halifax Regional Police Service is a major partner of the project and will provide both technical training and education on the principles of good policing to the Gambian Police Force. Other partners of the project include Gambia College, the Gambia Police Force, the African Center for Democracy, the Nova Scotia Department of Justice, and the Nova Scotia Gambia Association, Human Rights Studies, and the Dalhousie Law School.

IHEKWOABA D. ONWUDIWE
AND THOMAS S. MOSLEY

Internet Resources

Amnesty International. 2003. "Gambia." Available at: *http:// web.amnesty.org/web/web.nsf/print/2004-gmb-summary-eng.* Accessed September 13, 2004.

Central Intelligence Agency. "Gambia." In *The World Factbook.* 2004. Available at: *www.cia.gov/cia/pub lications/ factbook/geos/ga.htm.* Accessed August 31, 2004.

Gambia Information Site. "Gambian Government." 2004. Available at: *http://gambianinformation.tripod.com/gam bia-government.html.* Accessed August 31, 2004.

The Nova Scotia-Gambia Association. "Canadian and Gambians Working Together on Programs for Youth." 2004. Available at: *www.novascotiagambia.ca/communi ty_Based_Policing.htm.* Accessed September 31, 2004.

U.S. Department of State. "Background Note: The Gambia." 2003. Available at: *www.state.gov/r/pa/ei/bgn/5459. htm.* Accessed August 31, 2004.

Bibliography

Banks, S. Arthur, and Muller, Thomas C. *Political Handbook of the World*: Governments and Intergovernmental Organizations. New York: CSA Publications, 1998.

Dankwa, E. V. O. *Prisons in The Gambia: Report of the Special Rapporteur on Prisons and Conditions of Detention in Africa.* Series 1V. Banjul: African Commission on Human and Peoples' Rights, 2000.

The Europa World Year Book. London: Europa Publications Limited, 1999.

Gailey, A. Harry. *Historical Dictionary of The Gambia.* Metuchen, NJ: Scarecrow Press, 1987.

Ingleton, D. Roy. *Police of the World.* New York: Charles Scribner's Sons, 1979.

Kurian, George Thomas. *World Encyclopedia of Police Forces and Penal Systems.* New York: Facts on File, 1989.

Legun, Colin. *Africa: Contemporary Record.* New York: African Publishing Company, 1992–1994.

Mars-Proietti, Laura. *Nations of the World: A Political, Economic and Business Handbook.* New York: Grey House Publishing, 2004.

Onwudiwe, Ihekwoaba D. *The Globalization of Terrorism.* Aldershot: Ashgate Publishers, 2001.

GEORGIA

Background Material

Georgia is located in the South Caucasus; it covers an area of 69,700 square kilometers, and has a population of 4.4 million. The capital is Tbilisi, and the principal towns are Kutaisi (population 241,100), Rustavi (158,000), Batumi (137,100), Zugdidi (105,000), Chiatura (70,000), Gori (70,000), and Poti (50,900). The country is divided into nine districts, sixty-five regions, and five towns of Republic Dependence (without Abkhazia and Tskhinvali).

The national currency is the Georgian lari (US $1=1.8 lari). GDP per capita is US$995 (1998). Georgia's official language is Georgian, and in the territory of Abkhazia, both Georgian and Abkhazian. The main religion is Greek Orthodoxy. Other religious groups represented include Shiite and Sunni Muslims, Armenian Gregorians, Catholics, Baptists, and Jews.

Contextual Features

Georgia is a republic with a constitution that provides for a strong executive branch that reports to the president. The president appoints ministers with the consent of Parliament. Eduard Shevardnadze was reelected to a second term as president in a 2000 election with serious irregularities that was criticized by international observers. Parliamentary elections held on November 2 were also marred by serious irregularities. Two major opposition parties organized peaceful street protests, and on November 23, 2003, President Shevardnadze resigned and opposition leader Michael Saakashvili became president in January 4, 2004.

The Ministry of Internal Affairs (MIA) and the Prosecutor General's Office have primary responsibility for law enforcement, and the Ministry of State Security plays a significant role in internal security. In times of internal disorder, the government may call on the MIA or the military. While civilian authorities generally maintained effective control of the security forces, there were some instances in which elements of the security forces acted independently of government authority. Some members of the security forces committed a number of serious human rights abuses.

Constitutional courts were established according the Law on the Constitutional Court of Georgia of 31 January 1996.

The Constitutional Court of Georgia (herein after the Constitutional Court) is the body of constitutional supervision, which guarantees the supremacy of the Constitution of Georgia, constitutional justice, and the protection of the constitutional rights and freedoms of individuals.

The organization of the Constitutional Court, its jurisdiction, and procedure are determined by the constitution and the present law. Other procedures of organization and the administration of

constitutional justice of the Constitutional Court are determined by law and the regulations of the Constitutional Court.

The Constitutional Court consists of nine judges—members of the Constitutional Court, who shall elect among themselves the president of the Constitutional Court, two vice presidents, and the secretary. Three members of the Court are appointed by the president, three members are elected by the Parliament of Georgia by not less than three-fifths of the total number of deputies, and three members are appointed by the Supreme Court.

The structure and competence of the Supreme Court are set forth in the Organic Law of Georgia on the Supreme Court of Georgia, adopted on 12 May 1999. The Supreme Court is comprised of the Plenum, Grand Chamber, Chambers, Collegium, and Board. Thirty judges perform the judicial activities of the Supreme Court. Judges are elected to the Collegium and Chambers by resolution of the Supreme Court Plenum. The Plenum of the Supreme Court of Georgia consists of the chairman, the first deputy chairman, two other deputy chairmen, the chairmen of the highest courts of the Ajara and Abkhazia Autonomous Republics, and the chairmen of the Tbilisi and Kutaisi District Courts. The Prosecutor-General of Georgia and the Minister of Justice of Georgia may be invited to attend the sessions of the Plenum and to exercise consultative votes. The members of the Consultative Board of the Supreme Court and appropriate experts can be invited to sessions of the Plenum.

The penitentiary system of Georgia includes eighteen prisons. As of February 2004, 2,620 people were imprisoned, and 3,761 were awaiting judicial process.

Police Profile

Background

The Republic of Georgia was a part of the Soviet Union until 1990. The basic law enforcement bodies were the Ministry of Internal Affairs, the State Office of the Public Prosecutor, and Committee of State Security. All of these ministries were subordinated to ministries in Moscow.

After independence in 1990, all law enforcement bodies in Georgia became independent. In 2004, the new authority, headed by President M. Saakashvili, initiated radical reforms. Reforms have changed the structure of the Ministry of Internal Affairs (MIA), such as.

- Division of police and civilian functions of the Ministry of Internal Affairs

Crime data, 2003

Type of Crime	Registered Crime	Detected Crime
Murder	302	222
Attempt of murder	197	151
Body injury	253	188
Robbery	1013	494
Theft of motor vehicle	190	157

- Decentralization and demilitarization of the Ministry of Internal Affairs
- Establishment of a municipal police on the basis of regional and patrol police units of the Ministry of Internal Affairs
- Merging of inquiry and preliminary investigation services after implementing appropriate amendments to legislation
- Harmonizing the number of personnel of the Ministry of Internal Affairs with European standards (one police officer per 240 to 400 citizens in developed countries)

Demographics

Before the reorganization, Ministry personnel totaled 53,691. Given the population of 4,771,535, the ratio was one police officer per eighty-nine citizens. Currently Ministry personnel totals 22,229, and the ratio is 1:214.

Functions

At present, protection of the public order is provided by appropriate regional units and the Patrol Police of the Ministry of Internal Affairs. Inquiry and preliminary investigation of crimes in vehicles or other means of transport is implemented by the regional units of the Ministry of Internal Affairs. Protection of travelers and cargo is transferred to a Legal Entity of the Ministry of Internal Affairs of the Protection Police Department. Combating environmental crimes is implemented by regional and Patrol Police units.

The recently formed National Gendarmerie has 4,000 personnel, including conscripts. Tasks of the National Gendarmerie will be protection of public order and assistance to the police. A number of units have merged with the main administrative board of the criminal police, as outlined below. For instance, regarding the Service for Combating Corruption:

- Combating economic crimes was transferred to the Financial Police of the Ministry of Finance on 15 April 2004
- As a result of reorganization the Main Administrative Board of Combating Economic Crimes and Corruption was transformed into the Service for Combating Corruption
- Personnel declined by 180
- The Service for Combating Corruption is included into the Main Administrative Board of Criminal Police

Service for Combating Drug Addiction and Narcobusiness:

- As a result of reorganization, the National Bureau for Combating Drug Addiction and Narcobusiness was transformed into the Service for Combating Drug Addiction and Narcobusiness
- Personnel decreased by 170

State Border Protection Department:

- Became a structural unit of the Ministry of Internal Affairs in February 2004
- Decreased personnel by 2,000
- Additional reduction by 1,500 persons is planned
- Department will be reorganized from a military into a police unit
- As a result, the Ministry of Internal Affairs will be completely demilitarized

Department of State Reserves:

- Became Legal Entity of the Ministry of Internal Affairs in February 2004
- Elimination is planned

Highway Patrol Police:

- Established on 15 August 2004
- Number of personnel is 2,467
- For the Patrol Police units, the following equipment was purchased (US$4,700,000):
  - 140 patrol cars (130 Volkswagen-Passat, 10 Niva)
  - New uniforms

Training

In accordance with Decree No. 1039 of 1 October 1994 issued by President Eduard Shevardnadze with the purpose of strengthening the financial standing and technical basis of the educational institutions under the Ministry of Internal Affairs of Georgia, and in regard with Article 15 and Article 24 in the Georgian Law on Education, the Academy of the Ministry of Internal Affairs of Georgia was founded as a juridical person subject to public law.

The Academy of the Ministry of Internal Affairs of Georgia has a long history and old traditions. Its founding was preceded by a long period of development of educational institutions within the system of law enforcement agencies of the country.

In 1925, by the initiative of the Administrative Board of the People's Commissariat of the Internal Affairs of the Georgian SSR, a militia school was founded in Tbilisi. The school provided training of qualified leading personnel of militia corps for the Soviet Socialist Republic of Georgia within the USSR.

In 1932, by the decision of the Transcaucasus Regional Committee of the Communist Party, the militia schools in Tbilisi, Baku, and Yerevan were merged. The educational institution provided training of the-top level personnel for the internal affairs agencies of the Caucasus Federation. Students represented citizens of all three republics.

In 1937, the united militia school was disbanded, resulting in independent militia schools in Baku and Yerevan. It should be noted that apart from Georgian citizens, representatives of the North Caucasian republics, territories, and regions were also allowed to study at the Tbilisi school. The structure of the militia school underwent some changes, and one-year refreshment courses were started for training of leading personnel.

In 1940, the above-mentioned educational institution was transferred under the subordination of the Commissariat of Internal Affairs of the USSR, and was named Tbilisi Militia School under the Commissariat of the Internal Affairs of the USSR.

In 1949, as a result of transferring militia organs to the authority of the Ministry of State Security of the USSR, the school was transferred to the above-mentioned Ministry and was renamed the Tbilisi Militia School with a total of 100 employees.

From 1963 to 1968, the school was renamed the Tbilisi Specialized High School of the Ministry of Public Order of the Georgian SSR, and from 1968 to 1979, it was renamed the Tbilisi Specialized High School of the Ministry of Internal Affairs of the USSR.

In 1979, in accordance with the order of the Ministry of Internal Affairs of the USSR, the Tbilisi Department of Moscow Higher Militia School of the Ministry of Internal Affairs of the USSR was opened in Tbilisi on the basis of Tbilisi Specialized Militia High School. The language of instruction was Russian.

In 1990, according to Resolution No. 572 of 23 October 1990, of the Council of Ministers of the Georgian SSR, the Tbilisi Department of Moscow Higher Militia School was transformed into the Higher Militia School of the Georgian Ministry of Internal Affairs. During 1991 through 1993 throughout the ethnic conflicts in Abkhazia and the war for territorial unity of Georgia), two officers and twenty students of the Higher School of the Ministry of Internal Affairs were killed.

From 1991 to 1993, the Higher School closed, due to a number of factors, including the permanent involvement of officers and students in international disputes or in operations necessary to maintain public order; change in language of instruction from Russian to Georgian; lack of instructional and methodological literature or technical equipment; and insufficient funding.

Since 1 October 1994, the Higher School has been called the Academy of the Ministry of Internal Affairs of Georgia. At present, employees number 323, including 156 officers, 47 privates, and 120 civilians. The annual enrollment of students in the academy is 220, including 110 students enrolled in the extramural program of the Department of Law and the Technical Department.

The Academy provides training of specialists for the Internal Affairs Agencies of Georgia in the following fields: lawyer/jurisprudence, lawyer/traffic safety, and engineer/fire protection. At the same time, the Academy is actively involved in the activities of making improvements in the country and maintaining public order.

Since 1999, a postgraduate training program has been functioning at the Academy, in which fifteen police officers were enrolled. Numerous events, conferences, and seminars were held at the Academy in recent years, with the participation of prominent Georgian scholars and practitioners, as well as foreign specialists.

The Academy maintains contacts with a number of foreign educational centers at law enforcement agencies. The principal foreign partners of the Academy are higher educational institutions in Commonwealth of Independent States (former USSR) countries and in Turkey, located in Mos-

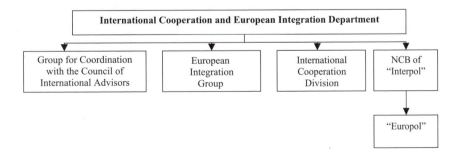

cow, Kiev, Minsk, and Ankara, where Georgian students undergo training courses.

International Cooperation

For the purpose of cooperation with the Council of International Advisors, coordination of the reform process, and integration into the European structures, a European Integration Department will be established. The following diagram summarizes international cooperation.

In early 2005, the Georgian government decided to merge the MIA and Ministry of State Security. This is a strategy intended to subsequently reduce the number of law enforcement personnel.

GEORGI GLONTI

GERMANY

Background Material

The Federal Republic of Germany is located in the heart of Europe, linking the west with the east, and the north with the south. The most densely populated country in Europe, Germany has been flanked by nine neighboring states since the unification of the two German states in 1990. An integral part of the European Union and NATO, Germany is a partner to the central and eastern European states that are en route to becoming part of a united Europe.

The Federal Republic of Germany covers an area of 357,022 square kilometers. The longest distance from north to south as the crow files is 876 kilometers, and from west to east, 640 kilometers. There are some 82.6 million people living in Germany. Germany has become a home for more than 8 million aliens, migrants, and asylum-seeking persons. Germany has four national minorities: Sorben (60,000), Danes (50,000) and the German Sinti and Roma (70,000). The official language is German, but there are numerous dialects spoken in the sixteen federal states and the regions of the country.

Germany is one of the most important industrial and economic states in the world economy, and has achieved international renown in information systems and biotechnology, as well as in energy and environmental technologies.

Contextual Features

Germany is a democratic and socially responsible federal country. The nationwide constitutional order of the basic law is expressed in the country's constitutional bodies, in the country's federalism, and in its legal order and electoral system. These determine not only everyday political routines, but also the lives of the people in Germany.

German law applies to virtually all aspects of life; as a result, legislation today consists of adjustments and amendments to existing laws to take social developments into account and to cope with social problems. Germany's legal system has been shaped by constitutional law but is also influenced by the law of the European Union and by international law. The body of federal laws now encompasses approximately 1,900 acts and 3,000 statutory instruments. Laws are passed by the Bundestag, and decrees on the basis of laws are enacted by the federal government. State law is mainly concerned with such matters as schools and universities, the press, radio, and television, as well as the police and local government.

Historically speaking, German law in part goes back to Roman law and in part dates back to numerous other legal sources in the German regions. A uniform system of private law was created for the entire German Reich for the first time in the nineteenth century. To this day, the Civil Code and the Commercial Code have preserved the liberal spirit of those times. Their underlying principle is the freedom of contract.

As its name suggests, the Federal Republic of Germany is a federation consisting of several individual states (the Laender). The federal nature of the system of government in the Republic is reflected in the fact that these sixteen Laender are not mere provinces but states endowed with their own powers. They have their own state constitutions, which must be consistent with the principles of a republican, democratic, and socially constitutional state as laid out in the Basic Law so that all Germans may enjoy uniform rights and duties and the same living conditions. Within this framework, the Laender largely have a free hand as to what they particularly wish to stress or specify in their individual constitutions.

This form of federalism is one of the sacrosanct principles of the German institution. But this does not mean that the boundaries of the constituent states may not be changed, as long as the citizens affected by any such changes or amalgamations are in agreement. Provisions have been made in the Basic Law for boundary adjustments within the Federal Republic.

Direct federal administration is basically limited to the Foreign Service, the labor offices, customs, the Federal Border Guard, and the Federal Armed Forces. Most administrative tasks are dealt with by the states independently. The federal government's scope is basically limited to the federal Constitutional Court and the supreme courts. These courts ensure uniform interpretation of the law. All other courts come under the jurisdiction of the individual states.

The individual states are responsible for those areas of legislation not covered by the federal government or which the Basic Law does not place within the ambit of the federal government. Thus, they enact legislation on education and cultural policy almost in its entirety, as a manifestation of their "cultural sovereignty." They are also in charge of local authority government and police law.

The real strength of the states lies in their administrative functions and participation in the legislative process at federal level through the Bundesrat. The states are responsible for all internal administration, and their bureaucracy actually implements most federal laws and regulations. State administration performs a threefold task: (1) it handles matters that fall exclusively within its jurisdiction (such as schools, police, and regional planning); (2) it implements federal law in its own right and on its own responsibility (for example, laws on planning building projects, trade and industry and environmental protection); and (3) it implements federal law on behalf of the federal government (for instance, construction of national highways, promotion of youth training). Thus, in constitutional practice, in the course of its development the Federal Republic has become a state where most legislation is enacted centrally, whereas the bulk of administration is conducted at the state level.

In the case of federal legislation, this principle is stated in Article 70 of the constitution. Accordingly, the states have the right to enact legislation as long as the Basic Law itself does not empower central government to do so.

Consequently, in principle, federal legislation is in the hands of the individual states—unless it is expressly stated that responsibility at the federal government level appears more appropriate. For this reason, responsibility for legislation is divided into three categories at the federal level—exclusive, concurrent, and framework. Areas of legislation that fall exclusively within the purview of the federal government, for example, are foreign affairs, defense, monetary matters, aviation, and some areas of taxation.

In the case of concurrent legislation, the states have the right to pass their own laws on matters not governed by federal law. Simultaneously, in such cases, the federal government may only legislate here if this is in the common interest in order to ensure equal living conditions for all or to maintain a uniform legal or economic situation. Areas that fall into the category of concurrent legislation include, among others, civil and criminal law, commercial law and nuclear energy, and labor and land law, as well as the laws concerning aliens, housing, shipping, road transport, refuse disposal, air pollution, and noise abatement. Since, in practice, the constitution has shown that uniform laws are necessary for these matters, the states have practically ceased to have any jurisdiction in these areas.

Organized crime has become a challenge to the government and society in Germany. Because of its legal system, economy, currency, infrastructure, and geographical position, the FRG faces special danger from organized crime. This type of crime is concentrated in certain spheres guaranteeing high profits where, at the same time, the risk of detection is reduced because there are either no immediate victims or victims are not willing to press charges and make statements to the prosecuting authorities.

In the first place, the development of organized crime in the past was marked by an alarming increase in drug trafficking. Internationally organized drug syndicates brought drugs into the FRG by means of couriers, built marketing organizations, and took steps to launder the money earned from drug trafficking.

Money earned from illegal drug trafficking was quite often transferred to other lines of criminal activity yielding particularly high profits, such as in the field of money and check forgery, or "red-light" crime, which is largely impermeable (pimp rings, operation of illegal gambling casinos).

Also, in other spheres of crime we can see the development of a substantive qualitative change: the increasingly organized mode of commission. To a growing extent, criminal organizations are coming to the fore in special spheres of crime such as counterfeiting money, gang theft and theft by burgling, with handling rings waiting in the background, and particularly as regards removal of high-grade assets to foreign countries, illegal arms trafficking, "red-light" crime connected with prostitution and "night business," and extorting protection money. As far as possible, the activities of such organizations are arranged so that the main figures are not conspicuous. It is usually only the crimes of peripheral figures that can be identified via traditional means of investigation, and these persons typically lack knowledge of the structure and composition of the organization as a whole. These peripheral offenders are interchangeable and replaceable at will, with the result that their arrest does not really disturb the criminal activities of the organization. Persons who inevitably know of the crimes committed are restrained from making statements by hush money, by orders not to talk, and by threats and intimidation. When a lone offender is caught, the organization quite often renders material support to members of that person's family and ensures responsibility for defense costs so as to obtain compliance and to prevent disclosure of information concerning the organization. Altogether, the crimes committed show that criminal offenders—who are usually interconnected on the international level—exploit personal and business connections with enormous energy and financial strength in order to make large illegal profits. Conspiratorial preparation and execution of criminal offenses make the fight against crime more difficult. Its success depends on the extent to which the people acting behind the scenes and the organizers concerned are convicted of committing criminal offenses and are deprived of the financial resources to commit further crimes.

In 2001, a total of 6,363,865 cases were recorded in the FRG. Compared to the previous year, this represents an increase of 99,142 cases or 1.6%. Although the number of theft cases has decreased continuously in recent years, theft still dominates overall crime statistics with a share of about 47%. On average, about half of all crimes are solved, but the solve rate varies substantially by type of crime. The solve rate for breaking in and stealing from cars is about 10%, compared to 95% for murder and manslaughter.

Police Profile

Demographics

The BGS has a good 40,000 employees, including about 30,000 male and female police officers. Of these officers, about 21,000 are employed at border-crossing points, about 6,000 serve in units as standby police, and 3,000 officers work in the special units Aviation Service, GSG 9, Central Office for Information and Communication, and other organizations. The police officers are supported by about 2,400 salaried employees mainly in border police matters and flight passenger checks. About 6,800 civil servants are available for administration and service matters.

Organizational Description and Functions

Maintaining public security and order is one of the most important tasks of government. In Germany, this task is shared by the states and federal government. For the most part, the police come under the jurisdiction of the states, but in certain areas, the Basic Law assigns responsibility to the federal government.

The jurisdiction of the states for the police encompasses all organizational and personnel matters pertaining to their state police forces. The branches of the police forces include the general police forces, criminal police, alert forces, and waterway police.

The general police forces are essentially responsible for ensuring public safety and order. Their duties range from warding off dangers to prosecuting crime.

The criminal police have special police units—in some cases jointly with the general forces—to combat terrorism and hostage-taking as well as for protective measures at special events and for observation and searches.

The alert forces of the states, which are deployed as whole units, were instituted pursuant to administrative agreements between the federation and the states in order to be available in case of internal emergencies, natural disasters, and major accidents, in a state of tension or in a state of defense. In some states, the alert forces are responsible for the training of new police recruits. They also provide support for individual police forces during demonstrations, sporting events, and other major events, traffic surveillance, police raids, and large-scale search operations, and can be deployed to combat organized crime.

The president of the German Bundestag is the "police president" of the House Inspection. He has the so-called "home-right" and the police power for his inspection (Basic Law of the

FRG, Article 40 section 2) about the houses of the German Federal Parliament in Berlin. He guarantees with this police force the public order and security in this area. No other police force can work without his permission in the houses of the German Bundestag. If he is unable to solve a problem with his own police officers, he can order the police force of the land Berlin or another one or another federal police force for help and assistance. When there are sessions outside the rooms of the houses of the German Federal Parliament, he is always the chief for the guarantee of public and inner security and order for the politicians. Moreover, he is responsible for the whole region in property of the federal government around the German Bundestag.

The Bundesgrenzschutz (BGS) is a federal police force. It carries out special police duties in the security system of the FRG, and is subordinate to the federal Ministry of the Interior.

It is the duty of the police forces of the individual federal Laender, together with other authorities, to maintain public safety and order. They must protect individual citizens and the general public and law and order in general, and remove any disturbances. The focal points of their duties set down by law are the protection of the liberal-democratic basis of order of the government, and ensuring the basic rights guaranteed under constitutional law.

Constitutional and federal law charge the federal government with police duties in important areas of public security and order. These duties are carried out by the BGS and the federal Office of Criminal Investigation (Bundeskriminalamt, BKA). In addition, there are authorities within the sphere of other federal ministries that have police duties, such as Customs at the federal Ministry of Finance, and the Water and Shipping Directorates at the federal Ministry of Transport.

Due to its special duties, particularly at external borders, the BGS today already has manifold experience in international collaboration that gains greater significance through time for the internal security in Europe.

The extensive duties of the BGS are regulated above all in the law on the Bundesgrenzschutz (Bundesgrenzschutz Act, BGSG) of 19 October 1994 (Federal Gazette I, p. 2978), supplemented by amendment laws of 25 August 1998 (Federal Gazette I, p. 2486), and of 22 December 1999 (Federal Gazette I, p. 2534), as well as in numerous other legal regulations, such as the Alien Act, the Asylum Procedure Act, and the Air Traffic Law.

Under this law, the Bundesgrenzschutz has the following duties:

- Border police protection of federal territory
- Railway police duties
- Air traffic security
- Protection of constitutional institutions of the federal government and ministries
- Duties on North Sea and Baltic Sea
- Police duties in states of emergency and in case of defense
- Involvement in police duties abroad under responsibility of United Nations, European or West European Union, or any other international organizations
- Support of police service in house inspection of the German Parliament
- Support of Ministry of Foreign Affairs in protecting German diplomatic and consular missions abroad
- Support of federal Office of Criminal Investigation in protection and escort services (protection of persons)
- Support of federal Office for the Protection of the Constitution in the field of radio communication
- Support of police forces for federal Laender, particularly in large-scale operations
- Assistance in cases of catastrophes or particular accidents including airborne rescue services

The BGS is a federal police force of high operational value that is available nationwide, and which makes an important contribution to maintaining domestic security in the Federal Republic of Germany and Europe.

The federal Border Police, being a national police force, is subordinate to the federal Ministry of the Interior. It is headed by its own Bundesgrenzschutz Section within the Ministry. The following are directly subordinate to the federal Ministry of the Interior.

As regionally competent federal intermediate authorities the following five Grenzschutzpraesidien (regional offices)

- Grenzschutzpraesidium North, having its seat in Bad Bramstedt
- Grenzschutzpraesidium East having its seat in Berlin
- Grenzschutzpraesidium Middle having its seat in Fuldatal
- Grenzschutzpraesidium South having its seat in Munich
- Grenzschutzpraesidium West having its seat in Sankt Augustin

As authorities with central duties:

- Border Police Directorate having its seat in Koblenz
- Border Police College having its seat in Luebeck

Moreover, under the direction of the Grenzschutzpraesidien as federal subauthorities, a total of nineteen Bundesgrenzschutzaemter (district offices) are set up all over the country, including the Bundesgrenzschutzamt Sea, the maritime component of the Bundesgrenzschutz at the Grenzschutzpraesidium North (northern regional office).

The regional offices, with eighteen integrated criminality combatting companies and 99 subordinate regional companies, five protection duty companies, and three maritime companies carry out their duties integratively according to the Bundesgrenzschutz Act (particularly the border police, railway police, and aviation security duties) in the framework of their local competence. Along with these offices that are organized as units, the BGS has eleven operational sections in the whole of the Republic that are subordinate to the Grenzschutzpraesidien. These are police groups that can be called on when the need arises to reinforce the Bundesgrenzschutzaemter in all spheres of border police duties, and also to support the police forces of the federal Laender. These operational sections make up the police standby component of the BGS. They are divided into a central headquarters, three operational squadrons, and one support unit for central duties. Moreover, depending on the task, an operational unit with light or heavy technical apparatus is allocated to each section, and, per Grenzschutzpraesidium, instead of a third operational squadron, there is one unit that is responsible for securing evidence and for arrests at one of the sections. The squadrons are divided into squads, which in turn are divided into groups and troops as the smallest organizational unit.

The duties and organization of the Grenzschutzpraesidien and the authorities and offices that are subordinate to them are essentially of the same structure. Each Grenzschutzpraesidium thus has at its disposal an instruction and further training center for all decentralized education and a border police aviation squadron for carrying out police duties.

There are exceptions to this where special duties are carried out: The Grenzschutzpraesidien North, East, and South each have a musical corps for public relations work. The Grenzschutzpraesidium North is responsible for the Bundesgrenzschutzamt Sea, the Grenzschutzpraesidium South for the Border Police College of Physical Education Bad Endorf. The Grenzschutzpraesidium West in the greater Bonn area is responsible for the Border police aviation group, Border police group 9 (GSG 9), and Central Office for Information and Communication.

In its capacity as railway police, the Bundesgrenzschutz is responsible for averting danger in the region of the facilities of the federal railways. This preventive police task serves to protect public order and safety against danger that might threaten the users, facilities, or running of the railway or danger that emanates from the railway facilities. It concludes prosecution measures and dealing with certain circumstantial facts of offenses. This results in the following operational focal points:

- Prevention and prosecution tasks at railway stations and railway facilities, such as against vandalism, offenses against property and crimes of violence (such as graffiti, theft, and bodily harm) and dangerous interference in railway traffic
- Patrol in trains of the German Railway Company, particularly in trans-border traffic and in connection with journeys on the occasion of demonstrations
- Targeted patrols and search measures in trains that are vulnerable to crime, particularly in short-distant passenger traffic but also in goods traffic
- Protective measures at railway stations in trains of the German Railway Company in connection with passenger transport to big events (such as escort of football fans)

Moreover, the BGS has duties in the field of aviation security. Aviation security tasks include all measures that are necessary according to the Aviation Traffic Law to protect civil aviation against attacks. In particular, hijacking and acts of sabotage must be prevented. The Bundesgrenzschutz fulfills this duty mainly through

- Checking flight passengers and their hand luggage and checked-in luggage using qualified trained staff and sophisticated aviation security technology
- Measures when objects are identified that could cause danger, such as by seizing forbidden objects such as weapons and ammunition or by deactivating unconventional explosives or incendiary devices
- Surveillance of entire airport grounds
- Carrying out protective measures for particularly vulnerable flights and airlines (high-risk clearance). The BGS carries out aviation se-

curity duties at the following fifteen German airports (as of March 1, 2001): Berlin-Schoenefeld, Berlin-Tegel, Bremen, Cologne/Bonn, Dresden, Duesseldorf, Erfurt, Frankfurt am Main, Hamburg, Hannover, Kassel-Calden, Leipzig/Halle, Saarbruecken, Stuttgart, and Munich (without flight passenger and luggage checks). At the twenty-one smaller airports, the Laender carry out aviation security duties on behalf of the federal government.

The Bundesgrenzschutzamt Sea—part of the German Coast Guard—with its seat in Neustadt/Holstein is subordinate to the Grenzschutzpraesidium North, and is responsible for border police protection of German territory in coastal areas. With its three Bundesgrenzschutzinspektionen in Cuxhaven, Neustadt/Holstein, and Warnemuende, the Bundesgrenzschutzamt Sea has the task of preventing illegal entry and combating human trafficking and facilitating crime at sea. It is entrusted with water police duties and protection of the environment, and also carries out fishery surveillance and surveillance of research activities at sea. Rescue and assistance measures at sea will be executed always in case of imminent danger. Outside German coastal areas, the Bundesgrenzschutzamt Sea is the police force responsible for general police duties, and can take measures which the Federal Republic of Germany is authorized to do according to international law.

Since 1994, this maritime component of the Bundesgrenzschutz has been a part of the federal Coast Guard, a coordinated network of federal maritime judicial staff, to which the Customs, Water and Shipping Administration, and Fishery Protection also belong. The Bundesgrenzamt Sea collaborates closely with the coastal Laender, that are represented by their own command offices at the Coast Guard centers North Sea (Cuxhaven) and the Baltic Sea (Neustadt/Holstein).

For carrying out duties at sea, at present nine water vessels are at the disposal of the Bundesgrenzschutzamt Sea. Additionally, for surveillance purposes, special helicopters of the Bundesgrenzschutz Aviation squad North are suitable for flight operations at sea under their command and in service. The sea borders, which are also Schengen external borders, have a total length of about 700 kilometers.

As a central office of the BGS, the Border Police Directorate with its seat in Koblenz is responsible in the entire federal territory for supraregional specialized duties and coordination. These include inter alia the collection and evaluation of intelligence, documents, and information; the development of concepts for fulfillment of the duties of the federal Border Police in the field of the border police, railway police, and aviation security; the coordination and steering of police duties in the field of prosecution; and if there is no legal regulation providing otherwise, the official communication with foreign and intergovernmental offices.

In the fields of prevention of illegal entry, combat of facilitating crime, combat of document abuse, return of aliens including the procurement of emergency travel documents and the prevention of illegal carriage, the Border Police Directorate carries out central missions and collaborates therefore closely with authorities in the Federal Republic of Germany as well with foreign border authorities and police authorities.

It is also a centre for the handling of questions with regard to equipping the federal Border Police and the standby police of the federal Laender with technical command and operational resources, particularly vehicles, weapons, apparatus for the control of aviation security, border surveillance equipment and technical services. Moreover, the Border Police Directorate plans and coordinates the development, adoption, use and maintenance of modern information and communication systems for the entire federal Border Police.

On the basis of international and bilateral agreements, the Border Police Directorate cooperates with at present more than thirty foreign governments and intergovernmental organizations, supervises the border police liaison officers of the BGS in Germany and abroad, coordinates the deployment of document advisers, and also offers international training measures in the recognition of falsified and counterfeit documents in the framework of combating border-related document crime.

There are special federal police agencies like the Bundesgrenzschutz that were responsible for the protection of the borders when Germany had no army. It was for the protection of the eastern border. Now, what the border police of the former time perform as their main duty is to protect the federal dignitaries, embassies in foreign countries, function as a special task force against terrorism, and provide security to the airport. They also give help to the states (Laender) in times of emergencies.

The tasks and powers of the federal Criminal Bureau (Bundeskriminalamt) are governed by the Law on the Bundeskriminalamt of 7 July 1997. The following tasks are assigned to the BKA:

- Central agency for police information and communications
- International cooperation

- Prosecution of criminal offences in certain cases
- Protection of members of the constitutional bodies at federal level
- Witness protection in certain cases

The BKA is Germany's central police agency. In a federal system where the federation and the states bear equal responsibility for combating crime, the BKA works side by side with other police forces at federation and state levels. As a federal police agency, it is the task of the BKA to ensure cooperation in crime prevention at the national and international levels. The BKA provides support to police forces at the state and federal levels for the purpose of preventing and prosecuting offenses that cross state or national borders or are of considerable significance. This support is provided by making central facilities and services available in the following areas:

- Collection, analysis, and dissemination of information
- Electronic data communications network
- Identification services
- Forensic science
- Crime-fighting strategy
- Technology
- Basic and advanced police training

In addition, the BKA also provides training for civil servants at the state and federal levels to qualify them as experts in the fields of forensic science and fingerprinting. Special courses of training, advanced training in scientific and technical fields, foreign language courses, and task-oriented training for police operations complete the BKA educational program. The BKA also provides basic and advanced training for police officers from other countries.

The BKA carries out significant tasks in the field of criminal prosecution. However, these tasks are clearly defined, and their number is limited. In addition to crimes directed against the life or freedom of certain members of the constitutional organs at the federal level, such tasks include law enforcement work that targets internationally organized terrorist associations. The Bundeskriminalamt has original jurisdiction in other areas as well, above all with regard to suppression of internationally organized trafficking in weapons, ammunition, explosives, and drugs, as well as internationally organized production of counterfeit currency and its distribution. However, the BKA is only responsible for pursuing such offenses if clarification of the respective matter is necessary in other countries.

In addition, the BKA can take action for the purpose of criminal prosecution

- At the request of competent state authorities
- If ordered by the Minister of the Interior for significant reasons
- If requested or ordered to do so by the federal Prosecutor General

Within the scope of its original jurisdiction in the field of internationally organized terrorism and of its secondary jurisdiction, the BKA is involved in prevention of leftwing and rightwing extremism and terrorism, in prevention of politically motivated crime committed by foreigners, and in police work aimed at prevention of espionage. The main targets of investigations in the field of organized crime are prevention of narcotics-related crime, money laundering, and economic/financial crime.

Training

Since World War II, emphasis has been placed on training that teaches how democracy works, the separation of powers, and so on. Police reform after World War II has attempted to include demilitarization, communalization, democratization, and improved community relations and public accountability (Fairschild 1988). The latest reforms involve having a community-oriented strategy, communication, conflict resolution, and modern management skills and techniques (Feltes 2002). In police training, students learn a great deal of police law, which cannot be learned at university because courses for law degrees contain more information and knowledge of general laws. The police laws also tend to be taught with a greater focus on the importance of the principle that the state must be built on the rule of law (Rechtsstaat) and that the democracy (Demokratischer Staat) must coexist with it. Law is the primary focus in all forms of training, especially in the training of lower ranks, with less emphasis on social sciences. Senior superintendents had criminal sections. There used to be a strong emphasis on militaristic discipline. Now, particularly with wo-men coming in, there is more stress on practical police training, and less on militarism. There are even a lot of programs geared toward training police officers as social workers (Steinhilper 1986).

Basic police training is imparted at the Police Technical College (Polizeifachhochschule). There exist some models of police training. One model is the former common police school, more of a theoretical school. Another model is the training provided by the Emergency Police, as it is done in the Laender where the academy part is separate from the operational police. But the trainees see the work of the operational part. Another model is that people go to the police station, take leave from police work, and then come to the police school training. This model is very much practice oriented.

The Police Technical College (Fachhochschule) is for regular training. There they do training for three years. If officers do not have university entrance qualifications, they must have a certificate from the Police Technical College. They have to study in the Technical College for four years (because one year is taken up by studies to get the certificate from the Technical Police College). After finishing the Technical Police College, students must go to work with the Emergency Police. However, they are sent to the police stations to work when there is no emergency. They also may be sent to other states. According to the German constitution, one state is required to help another. They are also deployed for special projects like drug operations and to control demonstrations.

In Germany, the training of higher police officials is for one year at Police Technical School of the land and another year at the Police Command School (Polizeifuehrungsakademie) in Muenster. Candidates with the professional background and examinations can enter the school this way until they are thirty-nine years of age. Other personnel possess university entrance qualifications and have passed the government civil service examination. They are in the school for thirty-six months; they must pass the test next year if they cannot do so the first time. The best among them can go to Police Command School. They stay at school during the training.

The Probationary Advisors (Rat) Training or Command Level Training (Ratsanwaerterlehrgang oder Ausbildung zum Hoeheren Dienst) at the Police Command School is a two-year course: one year, as prescribed by the school, in the states, and another year in theoretical training in the Police Command School.

At the Police Command School in Muenster, most of the training is in law, sports, computers, and techniques in traffic and investigation. Recent changes in training have led to increased attention on psychology to minimize conflicts between the police and the public. There are also antistress, communication, and action training for managers. They are given education for six months in various training centers. They offer training on attitudes, anxiety, motivation, relaxation, and stress management.

At the Police Command School there are thirty-three police officers and civilian officers as teachers in the PFA (Polizeifuehrungsakademie); they are on loan from state governments. They are given the rank of directors, which attracts people to the PFA. Seventy percent of regular training is conducted by their own staff (30% by outsiders). External personnel teach 80% of refresher courses. They come from universities, industries, and governments. Out of these 80%, half come from the police outside the PFA's own staff. In Germany, the police themselves largely engage in police training.

The federal Criminal Bureau brings police officers from Africa, South America, and Asia to provide training in prevention of specific crimes (economic crime, for example).

The BKA trains its own officers (in addition to providing for federal Border Guard officers). The Border Police College in Luebeck is the central instruction and further education institution of the Bundesgrenzschutz. Its duties include particularly the specialized general instruction of management staff in the higher and senior police services in the BGS and the specialized further training in the field of the border police, the railway police and aviation security, further training in technical police matters, police sports, medical care and foreign languages. Demand-driven seminars on topical police-related, political, sociological, and ethnic subjects for various addressees of the government, the federal Laender and foreign countries complete the extensive training offer of the Border Police College.

The central selection service of the Border Police College is responsible for preparing and carrying out selection procedures for applicants for careers in the higher and senior service, and also for specific duties and functions of all careers.

Moreover, the Border Police College supports the five instruction and continuing education training centers of the Grenzschutzpraesidien for the decentralized instruction and further training for example by analysis of police action, by developing operational and training. Officer candidates receive their training during a three-year course of study at the federal College of Public Administration as preparation for police service. The three-year course is divided into a theoretical phase and a practical phase, each of which lasts eighteen months. Officer candidates receive hands-on training at police agencies in the federal states and in specialized departments of the Bundeskriminalamt.

In addition, the BKA also provides training for civil servants at the state and federal levels to qualify them as experts in the fields of forensic science and fingerprinting. Special courses of training, advanced training in scientific and technical fields, foreign language courses, and task-oriented training for police operations complete the BKA educational program. The BKA also provides basic and advanced training for police officers from other countries.

The Border Police College in Luebeck is the central instruction and continuing education institution of the Bundesgrenzschutz. Its duties include particularly the specialized general instruction of management staff in the higher and senior police services in the BGS and the specialized further training in the field of the border police, the railway police and aviation security, further training in technical police matters, police sports, medical care, and foreign languages. Demand-driven seminars on topical police-related, political, sociological, and ethnic subjects for various addressees of the government, the federal Laender and foreign countries complete the extensive training offer of the Border Police College.

The central selection service of the Border Police College is responsible for preparing and carrying out selection procedures for applicants for careers in the higher and senior service, and also for specific duties and functions of all careers.

Terrorism

The events of September 11, 2001, have changed the world. Since then, a new division was set up in New York and Washington, the SIZ (Sicherheitszentrum or Security Center). Its task is observing all trends and developments of crime nationwide and internationally, especially terrorism, organized crime, drug trafficking, and so on. These crime networks are analyzed with the specific aim of providing police with data on near and far future trends. Police and intelligence services staffs now work together to exchange information and experiences.

International Cooperation

For the purpose of intensifying international cooperation, the BKA currently has 58 liaison officers in 43 countries at 46 locations, who contribute to establishing an international communication network for crime prevention. In addition to the work of liaison officers, efforts aimed at controlling organized crime, in particular drug trafficking in countries of production and transit, make it necessary in many cases to assist local police agencies by providing training and equipment assistance, which is also handled by the BKA.

The wanted persons database, part of the electronic information system at the BKA (known as INPOL), currently contains about 892,000 arrest requests, including 667,000 expulsion orders/deportations of foreigners, as well as 187,000 circulars issued for the purpose of locating persons. The INPOL property database includes approximately 8.7 million items that are the subject of searches because of possible links to crime. This number includes, among others, the following items:

> 249,000 passenger cars
> 39,000 lorries, including trailers
> 113,000 mopeds, motorized bicycles, and
>   motorcycles
> 884,000 bicycles
> 3,935,000 identity documents, driving licenses,
>   and so on
> 184,000 firearms

An additional computer-assisted information system designed to store and retrieve data on persons and property is the Schengen Information System (SIS), which can be used for searches in countries that are parties to the Convention Applying the Schengen Agreement (CAS). Establishment of the SIS is a significant compensatory measure following elimination of border controls at the internal borders of the CAS countries. SIRENE (Supplementary Information Request at the National Entry) at the BKA is the national central office for information exchange relating to SIS searches. Within seconds, the search data can be accessed from more than 30,000 terminals located throughout the Schengen area.

At the present time, Germany, France, Belgium, the Netherlands, Luxembourg, Spain, Portugal, Italy, Austria, and Greece participate in the SIS. Since January 1, 2001, Sweden, Finland, Denmark, and associated countries of Norway and Iceland have also joined the SIS.

In early 2002, more than 10,541,000 wanted notices were included in the SIS. Of these, approximately 9,307,000 involved property searches and 1,234,000 involved searches for persons. About one-third of all wanted notices are submitted by Germany.

Since the 1950s, German police forces of the Laender and the federal government have engaged in contacts with police forces across the world. And after the big success of the GSG 9 in Mogadishu (Somalia) in 1977, this special police unit had many requests for training. The exchange of experiences and knowledge in fighting terrorism and organized crime are current topics of information exchange. German police forces are in the former Yugoslavia, Kosovo, Afghanistan, Kuwait, and elsewhere.

Police Education, Research, and Publications

Police Periodicals

Kriminalistik
Die Polizei
PolizeiInfoForum
Der Kriminalist
Die Bundespolizei
Die Polizeifuehrungsakademie
Das Polizeiblatt
Deutsche Polizei
Polizeispiegel
Die Kriminalpolizei
Polizeinachrichten
Die Bayerische Polizei
Hessische Polizeirundschau
Die Streife
Die Neue Polizei
Magazin für die Polizei
Die Kriminalpraevention
Bereitschaftspolizei-heute

Police-Related Websites

www.polizei.de
www.bka.de
www.bundesgrenzschutz.de
www.bundesinnenministerium.de
www.im.nrw.de
www.polizei.nrw.de
www.polizei.bayern.de
www.polizeifuehrungsakademie.de
www.europol.eu.int
www.eugefis.de

ROBERT F.J. HARNISCHMACHER

Bibliography

Bundeskriminalamt. *The Bundeskriminalamt*. Wiesbaden: Bundeskriminalamt, 1991.

Bundeskriminalamt. *Profile, Mandate, Facts and Figures*. Wiesbaden: Bundeskriminalamt, 2002.

Das, Dilip, and Pino, Nathan W. "A Comparative Account of Police Training in Five Countries." *EuroCriminology* 17 (2003): 47–74.

Europol. *Annual Report 2003*. The Hague: Europol, 2004.

Grenzschutzdirektion, Bundesgrenzschutz, Aufgaben und Organisation (Federal Border Police—Duties and Organization), 2nd ed. Koblenz, 2001.

Harnischmacher, Robert. "The Federal Border Guard—Group 9—Special: The German Response to Terrorism." *Royal Canadian Mounted Police Gazette* 49, no. 2 (1977): 1–5.

Harnischmacher, Robert. "Die Polizei in der DDR" (The Police in the GDR). Special Documentation for the German Federal Border Guard/Bundesgrenzschutz of the FRG. Luebeck: School of the Federal Border Guard, Luebeck, 1985.

Harnischmacher, Robert. "Insight into the GSG 9." *Garda Review* 15, no. 18 (1987): 18–24.

Harnischmacher, Robert. "The Police Security System in the German Democratic Republic." *International Journal of Comparative and Applied Criminal Justice* 18, no. 2 (1994): 277–299.

Harnischmacher, Robert. *Organized Crime in Germany* (in Japanese). Tokyo: Verlag Seibundoh, 2002.

Harnischmacher, Robert. *Deutsches Polizeijahrbuch 2003*. Luebeck: Verlag fuer Polizeipublikationen, 2003.

Harnischmacher, Robert. *Deutsches Polizeijahrbuch 2004*. Luebeck: Verlag fuer Polizeipublikationen, 2004.

Harnischmacher, Robert, and Heumann, Rolf. *Die Staatsschutzdelikte in der Bundesrepublik Deutschland*. Stuttgart: Verlag W. Kohlhammer, 1985.

Harnischmacher, Robert, and Semerak, Arved. *Deutsche Polizeigeschichte* (History of German Police). Stuttgart: Verlag W. Kohlhammer, 1986.

Hilger, Johan Peter Wilhelm. *Measures of Investigation in Cases of Organized Crime in the Criminal Process of Germany*.

Knieling, Volker. Germany. In Proceedings of 11th Annual Meeting of IPES, Criminal Exploitation of Women and Children, Vancouver, Canada, May 16–20, 2004, pp. 36–37.

Ministry of the Interior, North-Rhine Westphalia. *Polizei in Nordrhein-Westfalen* (Police in North-Rhine Westphalia).

GHANA

Background Material

When Ghana achieved independence from the British in 1957, it changed its name to Ghana from the colonial inscription "Gold Coast." It is also believed that the Gold Coast was renamed Ghana upon independence because of indications that the present-day inhabitants descended from migrants who moved south from the ancient kingdom of Ghana. The first contact with the colonial people was in 1470 when a group of Portuguese explorers landed in Gold Coast for trading with the natives. Around 1553, the first recorded English trading voyage to the coast was made, and during the next three centuries, the English, Danes, Dutch, Germans, and Portuguese controlled various parts of the coastal areas. Beginning the 1820s, the British government took control of the major trading activities on the Gold Coast. In the early 1900s, the British succeeded in establishing firm control over Ghana, and ruled until 1957 when they gained independence. The Portuguese were the first Europeans to arrive in Ghana, but the British were the last to leave.

Ghana is located in western Africa, bordering the Gulf of Guinea in the south, Burkina Faso at the north, Cote d'Ivoire to the west, and Togo in the east. The capital of Ghana is Accra. Ghana's first postindependence population census was in 1960, which estimated about 6.7 million people. By 2004, the country's population was estimated at 20,757,032. Ghana's population was estimated to have increased to about 15 million in 1990 and to an estimated 17.2 million in mid-1994. With an annual growth rate of 2.2% for the period between 1965 and 1980, a 3.4% growth rate for 1981 through 1989 and a 1992 growth rate of 3.2%, the country's population is projected to surpass 35 million by 2025 (LaVerle 1995). The life expectancy for the total population is 56.27 years (2004 estimate); with 55.36 years for men, and 57.22 years for women.

During the early part of the 1960s, Ghana had roughly 100 linguistic and cultural groups. The major ethnic groups are black African, 98.5% (major tribes: Akan 44%, Moshi-Dagomba 16%, Ewe 13%, Ga 8%, Gurma 3%, and Yoruba 1%); and European and others 1.5% (CIA 2004). The subdivisions of each group share a common cultural heritage, history, language, and origin. English is the official language, as it facilitates communication among the diverse ethnic groups.

Ghanaian languages could be categorized into two major linguistic subfamilies of the Niger–Congo language family, one of the large language groups in Africa. These are the Kwa (found to the south of the Volta River) and Gur (found to the north of the Volta River) groups. The Kwa group comprised about 75% of the country's population, which includes the Akan, Ga-Adangbe, Ada, and Krobo or Kloli. Ewe is not left out in this language stratification. In spite of the fact that Ewe constitutes a single linguistic group, it is divided into Nkonya, Tafi, Logba, Son-trokofi, Lolobi, and Likpe. On the northern part of the Volta River are the three subdivisions of the Gur-speaking people: Gurma, Grusi, and Mole-Dagbane. Like the Kwa subfamilies, further divisions exist within the principal Gur groups. It is important to mention that no part of Ghana is ethnically homogeneous. In the rural areas, the population tends to reflect more traditional group settings, while urban areas are ethnically mixed because of migration from rural to urban areas in search of employment.

The major religions in Ghana are indigenous beliefs, Muslim, Christian, and other. The religious composition in the first postindependence population census of 1960 was 41% Christian, 38% indigenous beliefs, 12% Muslim, and 9% no religious affiliation. Contemporary Ghana has indicated Christian 63%, Muslim 16%, and indigenous beliefs 21%. Religious tolerance is very high.

Ghana is rich with natural resources. When Ghana became independent in 1957, the economy was stable and prosperous. It was the world's leading producer of cocoa, which boasted a well-developed infrastructure to support trade and a relatively advanced education system. By the mid-1960s through the early 1990s, Ghana experienced economic turbulence, and recovery has been slow and steady. In the early 1990s, Ghana's economic recovery still appeared uneven, and was geared primarily toward export rather than the domestic market.

The economy of the country is more stable compared to other poorer countries in West Africa. Even so, Ghana remains heavily dependent on international financial and technical assistance. The major sources of foreign exchange are gold, timber, and cocoa. The domestic economy continues to revolve around subsistence agriculture, which accounts for 35% of the GDP and employs 60% of the workforce. Economic policy priorities include tighter monetary and fiscal policies, accelerated privatization, and improved social services. According to a 2003 estimate, the gross domestic product (GDP) of Ghana was $44.49 billon, and real growth was 4.8%. Population below poverty line was 31.4%, and the inflation rate was 26.4%. Overall, Ghana's economy is on the recovery path, and the potential for sustained long-term growth is the commitment of the present government.

The Republic of Ghana operates as a constitutional democracy. For administrative purposes, the country is divided into ten regions: Ashanti, Brong-Ahafo, Central, Eastern, Greater Accra, Northern, Upper East, Upper West, Volta, and Western. These regions are further subdivided into 110 district assemblies to ensure adequate representation of the people in government. The Constitution of Ghana protects each Ghanaian's right to be represented by legitimately elected public officials by providing for partisan national elections and nonpartisan district elections. It also guarantees the freedom and independence of the media and makes any form of censorship unconstitutional. Every citizen of Ghana eighteen years of age or above has the right to vote. The right to form political parties is guaranteed. Political parties must have a national character, and membership is not to be based on ethnic, religious, regional, or other sectional divisions.

The 1992 Constitution of Ghana, which went into effect on January 7, 1993, declares the country to be a unitary republic with sovereignty residing in the Ghanaian people. The constitution is regarded as the supreme law of the land, provides for sharing of powers among a president, parliament, cabinet, council of state, and independent judiciary. The 1992 constitution ensures that executive authority is shared by the president, the twenty-five-member council of state, and numerous advisory bodies, including the National Security Council. The president is the head of state, head of government, and commander-in-chief of the armed forces of Ghana. The National Parliament, which consists of a unicameral 200-member body plus the president, is vested with legislative functions. For legislation to become law, it must have the assent of the president, who could sign or veto all bills except those to which a veto of urgency is attached. Members of parliament are elected for terms of four years, except in wartime, when terms may be extended for not more than twelve months at a time beyond the four years.

The judiciary is the last arm of the government. According to the constitution, the judiciary is independent of the two other branches of government. The Supreme Court has broad powers of judicial review. The Supreme Court has the constitutional mandate to rule on the constitutionality of any legislative or executive action at the request of an aggrieved citizen. The Ghana court system is reflective of British juridical forms with some modification. Accordingly, the hierarchy called the Superior Court of Judicature is composed of the Supreme Court of Ghana, the Court of Appeal, the High Court of Justice, regional tribunals, and lower courts as Parliament may establish. The courts have jurisdiction over civil as well as criminal cases.

Contextual Features

The legal system of Ghana is based on the constitution, common law (Ghanaian), statutory enactments of parliament, and assimilated rules of customary (traditional) law. The criminal justice system in Ghana is centralized, thereby giving the government the exclusive power to control the police, courts, and prisons. The Chief Justice of the Supreme Court, the Inspector General of Police, and the Director of Prisons are all appointed by the president to serve the entire country. The adjudicatory process is adversarial, where the accused is presumed innocent until proven guilty. In the rural areas and villages, the informal criminal justice system is observed. Primarily, this is where the traditional chiefs and elders administer justice based on Ghanaian customary law.

Crimes are classified according to the seriousness of the act. Serious acts are classified as felonies, and the less serious as misdemeanors. The most serious crimes (felonies) are murder, armed robbery, abortion, rape, stealing (grand larceny), unlawful entry (burglary), possession of dangerous drugs, possession of cocaine, possession of marijuana (Indian hemp), abduction, extortion, forgery, smuggling contraband, and counterfeiting. The less serious crimes (misdemeanors) include tax evasion or violation of ordinances that can be disposed of by fines instead of imprisonment.

Crime statistics are provided by the Ghana Police Crime Data Services Bureau. The available crime data on murder, rape, theft, and drug offenses date back to 1991. There were a total of 282 murder cases and 408 cases of rape recorded by the Ghana Police in 1991. There were a total of 40,254 cases of theft and approximately 770 drug offenses recorded by the police. Crime incidents are concentrated more in the urban areas with high population density and commercial activities.

The structure and jurisdiction of the courts were defined by the Courts Act of 1971, which established the Supreme Court of Ghana, the Court of Appeal, and the High Court. There are two divisions of the Court of Appeal (ordinary bench and full bench), and the High Court possess both appellate and original jurisdiction. The court Act also established inferior and traditional courts, which, along with the above courts, constituted the judiciary of Ghana according to 1960, 1979, and 1992 constitutions. The superior courts handle English laws, as well as statutory law, common law, ordinances, and other laws that have been promulgated by Ghana postindependence legislatures. The inferior courts decide less serious felonies, misdemeanors, and cases involving customary law violations.

There are three levels of superior courts: Supreme Court, Court of Appeal, and High Court. The inferior courts in descending order are circuit courts, district courts (magistrate courts) grades I and II, and juvenile courts, existing mostly in cities and large urban areas. In mid-1993, the Ghanaian parliament created a new system of lower courts, consisting of circuit tribunals and community tribunals in place of the former circuit courts and district (magistrate) courts. Furthermore, the traditional courts are the National House of Chiefs, the regional houses of chiefs, and traditional councils. The traditional courts are constituted by the judicial committees of the various houses and councils. All courts, both superior and inferior, with the exception of the traditional courts, are vested with jurisdiction in civil and criminal matters. Judicial appointments are made by the chief justice on the recommendation of the independent Judicial Council of Ghana. The appointments must be approved by the government.

The prison system as a punishment technique was introduced by the British in the mid-nineteenth century. By the early 1900s, British colonial officials administered the country's prisons, and employed Europeans exclusively to work as guards in the prisons. By mid-1960s, prison administration was overtaken by Ghanaians who staffed all positions in the prison system. The constitution of 1969 established a prison service, the director of which is appointed by the chief executive (president) and is responsible to the minister of interior. The Prisons Service Board is responsible for formulating policy and administering the country's prisons. To ensure the welfare of prisoners, the constitution requires the Prisons Service Board to review at intervals of not less than two years the country's prison conditions.

According to available data in 1993, Ghana has approximately thirty-three correctional facilities. Most of these facilities are used for short-term incarceration. Furthermore, open prisons are used for less dangerous offenders, while medium prisons are used for people serving a one- to two-year prison sentence (Anson 1990). There are juvenile facilities in the country for young offenders who have committed less serious crimes. These facilities in addition to other rehabilitative services provide vocational and educational programs.

Police Profile

Background

The origin of Ghana's police can be traced to the efforts of the British council of merchants to protect trade routes and depots. These early pseudo-officers were hired as guards and escorts to protect British merchants. Around 1843, the British established the 120-member Gold Coast Militia and

Police (GCMP), which was replaced in 1860 by a 90-member corps called the Queen's Messengers. The Queen's Messengers joined the Hausa Constabulary (imported from Nigeria) during the Ashante wars to form the Gold Coast Armed Police Force. In 1876, this unit was reorganized by the British into the Gold Coast Constabulary, which was divided into two forces in 1901, with the paramilitary mission assigned to the Gold Coast Regiment and the police functions given to the Gold Coast Police. The Northern Territories Constabulary, which was created in 1907, joined the Gold Coast police force shortly after World War I. This amalgamation created a single police force, a situation that prevailed until the country's independence.

During the 1950s, the Gold Coast Police force experienced major changes in an effort to modernize, enlarge, and better equip the police. Up to this time, all senior positions in the Gold Coast Police force were dominated by the British. A major change instituted by the British was to Africanize the police. In 1951, sixty-four of eighty senior police officers were British, and by 1958, only eleven of 128 senior officers were British. After independence, the Africanization of Ghana Police continued especially under the new the President Kwame Nkrumah. As part of the developmental process, in 1952 a specialized squad composed of twelve was created. Their functions were to deal specifically with cases of juvenile delinquency and offenses committed by women. In 1998, the position of women in law enforcement was further buttressed when the police administration established "the Women and Juvenile Unit (WAJU)." This unit deals with domestic offenses, that is, cases pertaining to women and children. It seeks to promote domestic harmony and unity in Ghana.

After independence in 1957, President Nkrumah, under his Africanization policy, promoted Ghanaians to fill the positions previously held by Europeans and the first Ghanaian promoted to head the police force in 1958. In 1959, a new era was added to the development of law enforcement in Ghana. It was the year that an Armored Car Squadron unit was established to deal with instances of security threats to the state, and the establishment of a Police College to undertake the training of officers. Another milestone in the development of policing in Ghana was in 1965 when the Police Service Act (Act 284) was promulgated. This act provided for the organization of the police service, and the appointment, promotion, and retirement of police officers. It also spelled out conditions of service, disciplinary proceedings, and other pertinent administrative issues relating to the police service. In 1969, the new government in power passed Police Service Act (Act 350) in 1970, which went into effect in 1971. It incorporated all previous acts relating to the police service. This act clearly explains the functions of the force and duties of the Police Council. The duty of the police service was to prevent and detect crime, apprehend offenders, and maintain public order and safety of persons and property. The Police Council functioned as an advisory body on appointments, welfare, and discipline, selection and training, police public relations, and the adjudication of disciplinary appeals from officers.

Organizational Description

Contemporary policing in Ghana is called Ghana Police Service (GPS). It is a centralized police system with a unitary command structure. The president is authorized by the constitution (1960) to appoint the Inspector General of Police (that is, the chief executive of the Ghana Police Services). In the hierarchy of authority, the following ranks are under the leadership of the inspector general: deputy inspector general of police, commissioner of police, deputy commissioner of police, chief superintend, deputy superintend, assistant superintend, inspector, sub-inspector, sergeant, corporal, lance corporal, constable (private) and recruit. Accordingly, senior officers include positions from the inspector general to assistant superintend, while the ranks of inspectors to sub-inspector are regarded as junior officers. All the ranks below subinspector constitute the category of nonmcommissioned officers. The Ghana Police Service is under the authority of the Ministry of the Interior.

For administrative purposes, the Ghana Police Services are divided into ten regions including the Police Force Headquarters in Accra. The national headquarters of the police force is in Accra under the command of an inspector general. An eight-member Police Council established in 1969 advises the inspector general of police on all personnel and policy matters. The inspector general supervises ten police regions, and each region is commanded by an assistant commissioner of police. For efficient administration, the police regions are divided into districts, stations, and posts. The police service is composed of General Administration, Criminal Investigations Department, Special Branch, Police Hospital, and National Ambulance Service.

Functions

The functions of the Ghanaian Police Services are enumerated as follows: detection of crime, arresting offenders, law and order maintenance, protection of lives and property, automobile licensing and driver licensing, firearms licensing (hunting guns), inspection of vehicles for road worthiness, escort and bodyguard services for ministers and senior government officials, prosecution of offenders, riot control, collection of certain rates and taxes for the government, traffic control, and escort of convicted offenders to prisons.

Training

Recruitment into the police is conducted at the rank-and-file and commissioned officer levels. All recruits must be between eighteen and thirty-four years of age, must pass a medical examination, and must have no criminal record. Prospective escort officers must speak fluent English, and general police applicants must have completed middle school or junior secondary school, and officer corps applicants must be university graduates. Since 1975, the training requirement has been that new recruits must attend a nine-month course of instruction in physical training and drill, firearms use, unarmed combat, and first aid. Escort police are given general education and instruction in patrol and escort duties. General police are trained in criminal law and procedures, methods of investigation, current affairs, and social sciences.

Senior police officers are trained at the Police College in Accra. The Accra Police College, established in 1959, offers a nine-month officer cadet course, and two- to six-week refresher courses in general and technical subjects. Courses are taught by guest lecturers, government officials, university professors, and senior police officers. The courses taught include criminal law and procedures, laws of evidence, police administration, finance, social sciences, practical police work, and physical fitness. Upon graduation, cadets are sworn in and promoted to assistant superintendent of police.

Police Public Projects

The police personnel in Ghana are well trained to perform specific tasks as needed by the country. In addition to what has been identified under the functions of Ghanaian Police Service, specific units are created to ensure crime prevention, traffic control, and youth programs. The recent initiative to enhance crime prevention is the introduction of community policing. Community policing as a crime prevention initiative seeks to bridge the communication and interactive gaps between police institutions and the communities they serve. This method of policing facilitates conditions where the police can work in partnership with the local people in identifying potential crime problems and take proactive measures to avert crime.

In recent years, HIV/AIDS has become a major health menace in Africa. With the cooperation of the police, Ghana has taking strong measures to deal with the disease. The Ghana Police Service HIV/AIDS program enlisted more than 17,000 police personnel across the country through some 400 peer educators to combat the problems of HIV/AIDS. The program recently launched a voluntary counseling and testing facility at the police hospital, and has developed innovative behavior change materials including a "condom wallet" that is worn on the belt and is now a standard component of the Ghana police uniform. The program is also being expanded to reach the remaining police units across the country and to provide leadership for the introduction of a broader program aimed at all Ghana's uniformed services.

Police Use of Firearms

In 1964, an unsuccessful assassination attempt was made on President Kwame Nkrumah by a police constable. In reaction to this attempt on his life, he disarmed the police, discharged nine senior officers, detained eight others, and removed the Border Guards unit from the police and placed it under military control. Due to his distrust of the police, he reduced the size of the force from 13,247 in 1964 to 10,709 in 1965. After his administration, the size of the police force increased from 17,692 in 1966 to 19,895 in 1968. The Guards unit was restored to police control, and in 1972, it became autonomous. Contemporary policing in Ghana includes a special paramilitary unit called the mobile police. This special division is well armed with automatic rifles for controlling syndicated criminals, highway robbers, and land-based, armed international smugglers. The general duty police officers do not carry firearms, except in assignments where there is likelihood the police will encounter deadly force. The Ghana police use deadly force only when an offender resists arrest or is armed and refuses to surrender. In addition, police are equipped with patrol vehicles, radio communication devices, computer recording devices, and riot control devices.

Ghana has participated in International Criminal Investigative Training Program (ICITAP)

aimed at professionalizing law enforcement. It was a program sponsored by the U.S. government to provide institutional law enforcement developmental assistance to the Ghana Police Service (GPS), focusing on human dignity and civil disorder management training. This program enhanced police capability to deal effectively with civil disorder. This program also provided training in basic criminal investigations, sex crimes investigations, and media relations. The advantage of this training is sensitizing police personnel to respecting human rights.

The government of Ghana generally respects human rights of its citizens; however, there were serious problems in some areas. Police use of excessive force resulted in some unlawful killings and injuries. There were cases of police shooting and killing of armed robbers while trying to apprehend them. Police corruption, arbitrary arrest, and detention of citizens were serious problems with the Ghana Police Service. ICITAP's project was initiated to address these law enforcement issues, thereby enhancing a more civil society in Ghana.

Terrorism

Ghana has no history of terrorism, and for that reason has no specialized police unit to deal with the problem. Although Ghana remains generally trouble free, periodic internal conflicts do occur. There are occasionally localized outbreaks of interethnic violence around the country. In October 2001, Ghana established a Counter-Terrorism Intelligence Center in response to the terrorist attacks against the United States. The center is designed to ensure cooperation among all units of the National Security Council and reports to the National Security Coordinator. The goal is to facilitate the exchange of intelligence bordering on terrorism, narcotics trafficking, and money laundering. It is important to acknowledge that Ghana is committed to the global war against terrorism. Ghana is also a party to several international instruments on international terrorism and well committed to African efforts in combating terrorism. The government has made several sweeping changes in fighting terrorism such as (1) the denial of safe heaven for those who finance, plan, support, or commit terrorist acts; (2) improvement of border controls to prevent terrorism movement; and (3) installation of methods to freeze funds or other assets of persons who commit or attempt to commit terrorist acts or facilitate the commission of terrorist acts.

International Cooperation

Since the early 1990s, an increasing number of police officers have been deployed overseas to support Ghana's commitment to international peace-keeping operations. This peace mission has been in Africa as well as abroad. For example, in 1992–1993, a police contingent served with the United Nations Transitional Authority in Cambodia. In addition to supervising local police and maintaining law and order, this contingent worked to prevent gross violations of human rights and fundamental freedoms.

Police Education, Research, and Publications

As mentioned earlier (under police training), required education for enlistment into the force ranges from middle school or secondary school to university degree. The educational programs were aimed at producing general officers, escort officers, and cadet officers. It is difficult to find journals, magazines, or newsletters exclusively meant for policing in Ghana. Searches did not come up with credible sources worth mentioning.

JONATHAN C. ODO

Bibliography

Anson, C. A. "Responses to 1990 Survey." Accra: Ghana Ministry of Justice, Attorney General's Department, 1990.

Central Intelligence Agency. *The CIA World Factbook.* Washington, DC: CIA, 2004.

Ebbe, Obi N.I. "World Factbook of Criminal Justice Systems—Ghana." U.S. Department of Justice, Bureau of Justice Statistics. Available at: www.ojp.usdoj.gov/bjs/pub/ascii/wfbcgha.txt.

GoldSchmidt, Jenny E. *National and Indigenous Constitutional Law in Ghana.* Accra: Ghana Publishing Corporation, 1981.

Kaplan, Irving, J. L. McLaughlin, B. J. Marvin, P. W. Moeller, H. D. Nelson, and D. P. Whiteker, eds. *Area Handbook for Ghana.* Washington, DC: Government Printing Office, 1971.

LaVerle, Berry. *Ghana, A Country Study.* Washington, DC: Federal Research Division, Library of Congress, 1995.

GREECE (HELLENIC REPUBLIC)

Background Material

The Mediterranean nation of Greece has an area of 131,957 square kilometers. According to a 2004 estimate, the population is 10,964,020. The capital is Athens, and the nation enjoys a republic form of government. The official language is Greek. In terms of religion, the population breaks down as Eastern Orthodox 92%, Muslim 1%, and others 7%. GDP purchasing power parity is $189.7 billion. GDP per capita is $17,900. Greece is a member of the United Nations (UN), the North Atlantic Treaty Organization (NATO), and the European Union (EU).

Following the War of Independence (1821–1827) against the Ottomans, Greece declared its independence as the Kingdom of Greece in 1830. With an area of 47,515 square kilometers, approximately one-third of its present size, and a population of 753,000 people, Greece drafted its first constitution in 1844 and a second one in 1864, while in 1875 the parliamentary regime was established. Acquiring new land in 1864, 1881, 1913, and 1918, Greece finalized its borders in 1946.

Greece participated in the Balkan Wars, and entered World War I on the side of the Allies in 1917. The defeat of the Greeks by the Turkish Army in Asia Minor (1922), and forced expulsions in 1923 drove approximately 1.5 million Greeks living in the area to seek refuge in Greece. Rapid population increases particularly in urban areas intensified existing problems of poverty, poor living conditions, and social unrest.

Precipitated by the Italian invasion on 28 October 1940, Greece's participation in World War II was followed by a civil war that ended in 1949 leaving 100,000 dead, 700,000 displaced people, and a deep political division between the left and the right.

Political instability and infringements on democracy led to a military junta on 21 April 1967. In the summer of 1974, the Turkish invasion of Cyprus brought Greece and Turkey close to war, and accelerated the fall of the junta and the restoration of democracy. A referendum abolishing the monarchy, and national elections (1974) led to the country's constitution (amended in 1986 and 20 01) and the election of the first president under democracy (1975).

In 1980, Greece joined the EU, and in 1981 the first socialist government of Andreas Papandreou was elected. Political stability and democratic rule of law of the last twenty years have contributed to increasing rates of social and economic development. Since 2001, Greece has belonged to the Euro-zone.

Currently, the country is facing the challenges of maintaining economic stability, and improving growth rates and infrastructure, as well as modernizing, debureaucratizating, and decentralizing public administration. Declining fertility rates and aging of population pose another set of challenges while an unemployment rate of 10% has remained stable for at least five years. Legal and illegal migration during the 1990s contributed to increased social heterogeneity, while isolated instances of racism and prejudice elevated the issue of immigrants' socioeconomic and political integration to top priority. Rates of conventional crime and criminality continue to remain relatively low, albeit there are reports of increasing fear of victimization. All types of illegal activity related to narcotics, trafficking of people, and organized crime in general, present core challenges to the sense of public safety and security. National security continues to present a challenge for the country although significant efforts have been made toward national defense and international relations.

Contextual Features

The country's type of government is a presidential democracy headed by the president. Elected by the Parliament for a period of five years, the president represents the country; assembles and dissolves the Parliament; appoints the prime minister, and upon the prime minister's recommendation the members of the cabinet; signs treaties and agreements; and approves, signs, and publishes in the *Government Gazette* Parliamentary laws and governmental administrative and executive acts.

The head of the government is the prime minister, (usually) the head of the majority party. The cabinet is comprised of nineteen ministers, and one assistant and twenty-eight deputy ministers. Cabinet members tend to be elected members of the Hellenic Parliament. The Hellenic Parliament, *Vouli ton Ellinon*, is a unicameral body of 300 seats. Members are elected by direct popular vote to serve four-year terms.

Greek law is based on codified Roman law. The judiciary is divided into penal, civil, and administrative parts. There is no differentiation of duties for judges serving in civil or penal courts. Depending on the case introduced, higher courts may function either as first-instance or as appeals courts. The Areios Paghos (Supreme Court) decides civil and penal cases. A Special Court comprised by Supreme Court justices and other high-ranking judges, may try ministers and/or members of the government (currently serving or having concluded their service) for criminal acts committed during the course of their duties.

Penal courts try violations of the Penal Code (PC) and a number and other Special Penal Laws (that is, the codes of market regulations, traffic regulations, customs, and military) and laws of narcotics, environmental protection, certain labor regulations, and tax evasion.

Originally enacted in 1950, the PC (after several minor amendments) recognizes three types of penal offenses based on the prescribed penalties: petty offenses (fines to ten days imprisonment), misdemeanors (ten days to five years imprisonment), and felonies (five to ten years imprisonment). The capital penalty was abolished in 1993, although no death penalties were executed since 1972.

Penal courts are comprised by one or three members (including the presiding judge), the public prosecutor, and the secretary of the court. Penal Courts comprised of three judges and four jurors try serious felonies as well as felony appeals.

Based on official police data (arrests and offenses known to the police), crime in Greece is increasing. Between 1985 and 1999, the average rate of total offenses per 100,000 people was 2,237 with an average increase of 22.2%, while the rate of felonies was 51 per 100,000, and the rate of misdemeanors 2,256 per 100,000. Violent crime (homicide, robbery, arson and rape combined) accounts, on average, for less than 4% of all known offenses.

Approximately 66% of all crimes reported to the police occur in urban areas, and 85% of these are committed by men. The age distribution of arrestees shows that, on average 23.11% of all known offenders are aged thirty-five to forty-four, while 19.51% are aged thirty to thirty-four.

Notable is the increase of non-Greeks among known offenders (in 1999, almost 9% of known offenders were non-Greek). Conclusive evidence, however, does not exist as to whether these increases are due to non-Greeks' (primarily economic immigrants) actual increasing rates of criminal behavior, or to police and public responses to actual and/or perceived sociocriminal behavior of non-Greeks. Violations of immigration laws are included in the total number of arrests.

The following categories of correctional facilities exist in the country: three semi-open correctional facilities (rural prisons); three correctional institutions for minors; six closed-type correctional institutions (one for women); two hospitals (one general, one psychiatric) and one rehabilitation center for drug addicts; and thirteen detention facilities (for people awaiting trial and inmates serving short sentences).

Police Profile

Background

The need for public order and security was recognized as a priority in the country's first constitution (1822), which provided for the establishment of a Ministry of Police. Formation of the first police bodies began with a Royal Decree of 1833 which, following the French model, established a dual policing system of municipal police bodies and Chorofylake (Gendarmerie), a national police body.

Two subsequent Royal Decrees of 1834 and 1836 defined that municipal police bodies were to be headed by the mayor, be funded by the local community, and exercise administrative (law enforcement and crime prevention) and judicial (crime investigation, collection of evidence, and referrals of suspects to criminal justice authorities) duties. Lower-ranking personnel (*erenofylakes*, guardians of the peace and/or *agrofylakes*, rural guards) were hired by the mayor, while one or two police officers (*astynomos*) were appointed by the government at the mayor's suggestion. The size of these bodies depended on the population and the policing needs of the community; there was no training for police personnel.

The Chorofylake, established by the Royal Decree of 1833 as "complementary to the Army," had as duties establishment of public order and security, crime prevention and investigation, application of the rule of law, and guarding of the borders. With an authorized force of 1,054 gendarmes, and an actual force of 800, Chorofylake was given authority over the whole country and had as its first chief the Frenchman Francois Grailland.

In 1849, the Administrative Police of Athens and Piraeus was formed for policing the rapidly growing areas of Athens and Piraeus. It was governed by the same laws as municipal bodies but its personnel were appointed by the government.

In 1893, all municipal police bodies, accused of lack of professionalism and efficiency in establishing public order and security (although historical evidence exists to the contrary) were abolished, and all police powers were transferred to the Military Police. Under the order of the Army, the officers of the Administrative Police formed the Astyfylake (Urban Police). Chorofylake remained responsible for policing the whole country except Athens and Piraeus.

In 1906, Chorofylake became the country's sole police body, and until 1920 played a significant, albeit controversial, role in the political and military history of the county. Allied to conservative and right-wing governments and political powers, Chorofylake was instrumental in overthrowing democratically elected governments and suppressing civil liberties. Alongside the military, Chorofylake took part in various military operations such as the Balkan Wars (1912–1913), World War I, the Greek Campaign of Asia Minor, World War II, and the Civil War.

The losses of Chorofylake during military operations, the increase of population due to acquisition of new territories, and the increase of urban population due to internal migration and the influx of Asia Minor refugees, minimized Chorofylake's ability to police the interior of the country. In 1920, Astynomia Poleon (City Police), the first nonmilitary police body of the country was established (Law 2461/1920), and the country returned to a dual policing system.

Modeled after the London Metropolitan Police, Astynomia Poleon, responsible for policing Athens, Piraeus, Thessaloniki, Patras (large cities, industrial-commercial centers), and Corfu (preferred tourist destination of the time), hired personnel through specific selection processes, established its own training facilities and curricula, and was expected to exercise policing "scientifically and methodically." Chorofylake and Astynomia Poleon differed in wages, training, professionalism, and jurisdiction, and clashes emerged between their personnel over prestige, power, and authority.

The police's active involvement in military and state infringements on democracy and suppression of civil liberties of individuals and groups broadly defined as left-wing generated strong negative feelings among civilians. The paramount importance of restructuring, democratizing, and legitimizing policing became particularly evident after the fall of the military junta and the restoration of democracy.

To this end, and after a decade of political, civil, and police officials' efforts, Chorofylake and Astynomia Poleon were amalgamated into the Hellenic Police (HP) founded by Law 1481/1984 (minor amendments in 1999 and 2000) as a "special armed body following rules and regulations pertaining to its function ... organized in a military way ... [with] ... military hierarchy and discipline."

In order to fight a victorious "continuous war against crime" and guarantee public order and security, HP came under the authority of the then newly established Ministry of Public Order, and set as its immediate priorities the development of training and professionalism.

Demographics

HP's personnel is made up of police and civil personnel, Border Guards, and Special Guards. Police personnel are divided into general duties personnel (assigned to all police services), special duties personnel (primarily scientists of various specializations), and civilian (either permanent or contractual personnel) staff administrative positions. Border Guards dealing mainly with prevention of illegal migration and Special Guards assigned to duties of surveillance and guarding of sensitive targets constitute special categories of police personnel. There are no special provisions for ethnic or other representations.

Organizational Description

The current authorized strength of the HP is approximately 45,000 police personnel (425 police per 100,000 people in the population). Including Border and Special Guards, the actual strength of HP is approximately 52,000 (489 police per 100,000 people). Approximately 3,400 (3,900 including Border Guards) women occupy positions up to the rank of police major general, but tend to concentrate in the lower ranks. Of these, 56.62% perform various public order duties (police stations, Immediate Response Units, and so on), 14.25% are assigned to Public Security Units, while 9.07% serve in the Traffic Police.

For analytical purposes, the HP's organization can be addressed in two ways: geographically and operationally. Geographically, the HP is organized in fourteen General Police Directorates broadly corresponding to the country's administrative peripheries.

General police directorates are divided into fifty-four police directorates corresponding to the country's fifty-two prefectures (in Athens and Thessaloniki operate two police directorates). Finally, police directorates are divided into numerous police stations whose strength and location depend on the population and crime and surveillance needs of each area.

The HP's operatonal organization is the following:

- Chief of Police: Stategic Planning and Crisis Management Council, Press Bureau, and Directorates of Internal Affairs, Special Violent Crimes, Olympic Games Security
- Deputy Chief of Police
- General Inspector: Security Divisions of President of Democracy, Parliament, Prime Minister, Criminal Investigation Directorate, Aerial Transportation Division
- General Directorates: Fifty-four General Directorates throughout the country
- Chief of Staff: Public Order and Security and Order Division (Directorates of) General Policing, Traffic, Public Security, State Security, Immigration, International Police Cooperation
- Administrative Division: (Directorates of) Personnel, Education, Legal Provisions Management, Public Relations
- Economic, Technical and Information Division: (Directorates of) Finance, Technical Support, Informatics, Economic Inspections, Economic Management, Police Academy
- Health Directorate
- Directorate of Expenditures Control

The following ranks and hierarchy exist in HP: lieutenant general, major general, brigadier, colonel, lieutenant colonel, major, captain, first lieutenant, second lieutenant, warrant officer, sergeant, and constable.

Promotions, in general, are based either or seniority or merit. The chief of police is appointed by the government upon selection and recommendation by the autonomous body of Governmental Council of Foreign Policy and National Defense. The Council selects the chief of police from among officers holding the rank of police major general and police lieutenant general. Upon decision, if necessary, the chief of police is promoted to police lieutenant general and all officers preceding him in rank and seniority are discharged. The same holds true for other top ranks as well.

For all other promotions, the law requires that officers serve a specific number of years in each rank. Promotions are decided by police councils whose composition varies depending upon the ranks of officers to be evaluated. Assessment for each officer is based on commanding officers' annual evaluation for the evaluated officer's professional performance and attitude. Officers receiving negative evaluations can be dismissed.

For promotion to the rank of police sergeant, police constables need to have completed at least three years of service, be under thirty-five years of age, be positively evaluated by their commanding officers, and perform well in written examinations.

A number of specialized police functions are carried out under general directorates:

- HP's Directorate of Criminal Investigations is the country's National Service of Forensics. A member of the Network of Forensics Institutions (ENFSI) assists all crime fighting services in the country alongside the Subdirectorate of Northern Greece (located in Thessaloniki) and numerous local bureaus.
- The Directorate of Internal Affairs and the SubDirectorate of Northern Greece were founded in 1999 to combat instances of corruption within HP. Under the direct authority of the chief of police and the investigative supervision of the Public Prosecutor of Appeals Courts, the directorate's jurisdiction was expanded in 2003 to cases of bribery and extortion involving public servants in general.
- Under the Chief of Police, the Directorate of Olympic Games Security's goal is the organization, coordination, and execution of strategic safety plans for 2004 Olympic Games.
- Established in Athens in 1959, the Immediate Response Unit became publicly and widely recognizable by its telephone number "100." Synonymous almost to the word "police," 100 expanded to the entire county responding to emergencies. After 1984, the Attica unit was ungraded to directorate.
- Special Guards constitute a special category of police personnel (Law 1724/1999), and their duties include guarding of potential/sensitive targets, and patrolling and supporting police personnel in specific operations of search and seizure. Hiring procedures differ from those for regular police personnel. Candidates must be Greek citizens, high school graduates, and under twenty-eight years of age. Male candidates have to have served as reserve army officers or in any of the army's Special Forces.
- Border Guards constitute also a special category of police personnel (Law 2622/98), and their goal is to prevent and combat illegal migration and transnational crime. They operate in twenty-five prefectures either at the border or/and receiving large numbers of illegal immigrants. Hiring procedures differ from those for regular police personnel. Candidates must be Greek citizens, under the age of thirty-two (men) or the age of twenty-six (women), have a high school diploma, and good command of foreign languages. Men have to have served as reserve army officers or in any of the army's Special Forces. Residents of Border Guard operations areas are preferred.
- The Explosives Disposal Squad is staffed by specially trained volunteers, and equipped with robots, remote-control-operated vehicles, bullet-proof uniforms, and the like. A number of such units operate in Athens, Thessaloniki, and other large cities.
- The K-9 Unit's mission is to search, retrieve, and guard people and objects, narcotics, and explosives assisted by specially trained dogs.
- Since 1995, HP has acquired five helicopters for police operations and aerial support.

Functions

In addition to their criminal justice duties, police personnel have duties such as serving of summons, transferring of prisoners, guarding prisons, and issuing identification cards and passports as well as issuing weapon and hunting permits.

Training

Prior to 1994, recruitment, selection, and admission to the police served as a means of political control over the functions and operations of police. Police recruits, although participating in police-administered examinations, were in effect, selected by government and other public officials on the basis of political affiliations and for the promotion of personal and party politics, thereby negatively affecting relations between police and the public. Since 1994, admission to Police Academy follows the rules, regulations, and procedures of admission to universities and technical institutions of higher education, namely, per-formance in the University Entrance National Examinations.

In addition, candidates (Greek citizens, aged eighteen to twenty-six years) have to meet specific body structure requirements and perform satisfactorily in health, personality, and athletics tests as specified each year by the Ministry of Public Order. In year 2003, body structure and athletic requirements previously different for men and women were unified, and the relevant gender quota was annulled. Depending on performance in written and other tests, candidates enter one of Police Academy's training institutions.

Police Public Projects

In order to develop and strengthen police–public relations, the Ministry of Public Order has initiated various projects such as the following:

- *Safe cities:* Initiated in 1999, this project upgraded the functions and operations of foot patrols in several cities of the country aimed at enhancing the sense of security among citizens through increased police visibility.
- *Neighborhood Police Officer:* Initiated in March 2003, this project establishes direct lines of communication among residents, relevant police stations, and responsible police officers, and aims at petty criminality prevention, dispute resolution, coping with emergencies, and small-scale social and neighborhood problems. Staffed with specially trained police officers, this pilot project is implemented in 354 neighborhoods in Athens, Pireaus, and Thessaloniki.
- *Local Crime Prevention Councils:* Initiated in 1999, this project aims at contextualizing, designing, and implementing crime prevention programs at the local level. Designed as consultation bodies, these Councils can be established in municipalities with over 3,000 residents, are headed by the mayor, while their members (five to eleven permanent residents of the municipality) are to have expertise on issues of crime, social work, public safety, and public health, and closely collaborate with the police.
- *On the Road:* This joint project of five ministries, universities, and local authorities aims at strategic planning for traffic accident reduction, a significant social problem in the country (leading cause of death for men eighteen to twenty-five years of age) through infrastructure interventions, continuing education of drivers, effective policing, and responding to accidents. Already exhibiting positive results, the project aims at 20% reduction of traffic accident–related deaths for the years 2001 to 2005 and 40% (compared to 2000) by the end of 2015.
- *School Traffic Regulator:* Particularly popular among police and the public, and effective in changing pedestrians' and drivers' attitudes toward safety, this project engages civilians (parents or other interested individuals) in the control of traffic around school areas during arrival and departure of students. Training is provided by traffic police officers.

Police Use of Firearms

Law 3169/2000 provides the framework of police use of firearms. According to the law, the police can legally discharge a firearm only when faced with imminent and unavoidable threat of death or severe bodily harm and only against armed persons. Prior to discharging a firearm, police are required to identity themselves and announce their intention to fire, give ample time for response, exhaust all nonviolent means of apprehension, and apply the rules of necessity and analogy. A weapon cannot be fired (1) when uninvolved third parties may be injured; (2) when firing against armed crowds may injure unarmed persons within or outside the crowds; (3) against minors under the age of eighteen (unless necessary for preventing imminent danger of death); (4) and against persons fleeing only to avoid routine police controls.

Police cadets' failure in training in the use of firearms constitutes reason for dismissal. A special committee will, at regular intervals, evaluate all personnel charged with firearms as to their technical and psychological ability to carry firearms and weapons. Penalties are provided for improper use and guarding of professional and personal firearms while until 2008 all currently serving police officers will undergo evaluation as to their ability to carry and use firearms.

Complaints and Discipline

According to Police Disciplinary Law and depending on the degree of punishable behavior the following penalties may by administered to police officers:

- Reprimand
- Fine up to the amount of three monthly salaries
- Temporary suspension (fifteen days to four months)
- Suspension (two to six months)
- Dismissal

As a general rule, police accountability lasts for the duration of service except for certain violations and/or illegal acts for which prosecution after discharge is possible. Penalties may be assigned either by superior officers or by disciplinary boards. Charges against police officers can be filed by superior officers or other officers as well as civilians.

Violations of human rights (particularly the rights of illegal immigrants) in the form of use of excessive force have attracted public attention and are documented by Amnesty International. Charges against police officers have been dealt with by the police as well as the courts, while the independent body Citizens' Advocate has noted relative unwillingness on the part of the police to administer strict penalties to violating officers despite the fact that torture and use of excessive physical force and/or psychological abuse constitute reasons for dismissal.

Terrorism

Terrorism in Greece is characterized by the actions of two terrorist organizations for which no international connections have been established: Ellinikos Laikos Agonas-ELA (Revolutionary People's Struggle) and 17 November.

ELA initiated action in 1974, and after a 1994 bombing that killed one and injured five police officers waiting at a bus stop, publicly announced (through a letter to a newspaper) that they were ceasing their operations. During summer 2002, three members of ELA were arrested and are awaiting trial.

17 November started action in 1975, and remained active until the summer of 2000. The organization is considered responsible for twenty-four deaths and numerous bombings of public and police buildings, vehicles, and so on. In summer 2002, several members of 17 November were arrested and are presently on trial pending court decisions.

To combat terrorism and terrorist attacks, HP has established the Special Violent Crimes Directorate, which deals primarily with acts of terrorism and other special violent crimes, receives orders directly from the Chief of Police and operates throughout the country. Additionally, the Terrorist Acts Response Unit considered among the elites of HP, deals with emergencies and dangerous situations such as terrorist acts, highjackings, kidnappings, and so on, as well as performs rescue operations during natural disasters and/or other extreme conditions. Staffed by volunteers who meet strict criteria and undergo specific training, the Unit's operation is authorized by the Chief of Police.

International Cooperation

The Directorate of International Police Cooperation is responsible for establishing and maintaining cooperation with international organizations such as the Council of Europe, United Nations, OECD, EDU/Europol, Interpol, Teldrug, HE, SECI, FBI, and DEA. It further implements all treaties signed between Greece and other countries on issues of organized crime, illegal migration, and police functions and cooperation.

On a regular basis, one or two police officers are trained each year in the FBI Academy/Quantico, Virginia, United States, and in Europol/The Hague/The Netherlands. Occasionally, officers are trained in Police Staff College, Bramshill, United Kingdom, and various police academies in the United States. Greece provides training assistance to Balkan countries.

Police Education, Research, and Publications

Police Education

The following schools and institutions within Police Academy provide police education in Greece:

School of Police Lieutenants: Located in Athens, admits approximately 100 cadets annually. During their studies, men fulfill their mandatory military obligation. All cadets receive salaries and have full medical insurance. After completing eight semesters of studies, they graduate at the rank of police second lieutenant.

Schools of Police Constables: Approximately 1,100 recruits are admitted annually to any of the nine schools. During their studies, male recruits serve their mandatory military service. All cadets receive salaries and have full medical insurance. After five semesters of studies, they graduate at the rank of police constable.

School of National Security: Established in 1997, provides prostgraduate studies to high-ranking police, military, coast guard and fire-fighting officers and personnel in matters of strategy and politics of national security. Studies last six months.

School of Postgraduate Studies and Continuing Education: Depending on the subject, hundreds of police personnel each year receive training (from one to six months) on matters of police and general interest.

Researchers and Affiliations

Dimopoulos, Charalambos. Assistant Professor. Department of Law. Dimokritio University.

Zarafonitou, Christina. Assistant Professor. Department of Sociology. Panteion University.

Kampanakis, Joseph. Police Major. Analyst/ Trainer Europol. Analysis Unit of Serious Crime Department.

Lambropoulou, Effie. Assistant Professor. Department of Sociology. Panteion University.

Panousis, Yannis. Professor. Department of Communication and Mass Media. National and Kapodistrian University.

Papakonstandis, Georgios. Police Lieutenant Colonel. Director of School of Constables in Rethymno.

Stergioulis, Evagelos. Police Major. Head of Public Relations Office. Europol.

Vidali, Sofia. Lecturer. Department of Social Administration, Dimokritio University.

Funding and Research

There are no regular sources of funding for police research in the country. The Ministry of Public Order has at times allocated research monies to selected research projects, such as the following:

Farsedakis, I., Kalogeropoulos, D., Lampropoulou, Effie, and Papagiannopoulou, M. 2002. *Restructuring of Services of Hellenic Police*. Funded by the Panellenic Association of Police Officers, this project studied the existing organizational structure and functions of the HP, and made suggestions for reorganization of certain services.

Zopounidis, Konstantinos, Nikolarakis, Mixail, Petoussi, Vassiliki, Doumbos, Mixail, and Tzekis, Konstantinos. 2002. *Causes of Traffic Accidents in Greece*. Employing official police data and interview data, this project addresses the causes of traffic accidents in Greece approaching issues such as infrastructure, emergency

response units, law application, and their interdependencies.

Police Journals, Magazines

Police Review. Bimonthly magazine of Hellenic Police Headquarters. 23 Kifisias Ave, Marousi, GR 151 23. astepi@otenet.gr

Criminal Justice. Nomiki Vivliothiki, Mavromihali 51, 106 80 Athens, Greece. legalinn@otenet.gr

IPA News. On-line magazine of IPA. *www.ipa. gr/greek/magazine.html*

New Police. Journal of the Panellenic Association of Police Officers. *www.poasy.gr*

Police Publications

Dimopoulos, Charalambos. *Police and the Policeman*. Athens-Komotini Ant. N. Sakkoulas Publishers, 2000 (in Greek).

Kampanakis, Joseph. "Organizational, Managerial, and Human Resource Aspects of Policing in the 21st Century." *Police Review* 18, (July–August 2001): 420–426 (in Greek).

Papaioannou, Zoi. *The Principle of Analogy during Exercise of Police Authority*. Athens: Sakkoulas, 2003 (in Greek).

Papakonstandis, Georgios. *Hellenic Police: Organization, Politics and Ideology*. Athens: Ant. N. Sakkoulas Publishers, 2003 (in Greek).

Petoussi, Vassiliki. "Views on the Relations Between Youth and the Police." In *Social Developments in Contemporary Greece: Work, Education, Family, Deviance*, edited by Sokratis Koniordos, Laoura Maratou-Alimpranti, and Roi Panagiotopoulou. Athens: National Center of Social Research, 2003 (in Greek).

Stergioulis, Evangelos. *The Greek Police in the Post-Junta Period 1975–1995*. Athens: Nomiki Vivliothiki, 2001 (in Greek).

Rigakos, George S., and Georgios Papanicolaou. "The Political Economy of Greek Policing: Between Neo-Liberalism and the Sovereign State." *Policing and Society* 13, no. 3 (2003): 271–304.

Police-Related Websites

www.ydt.gr or *www.astynomia.gr*, Department of Public Order (Greek)

www.policenet.gr, (Greek, English)

www.adh.gr, Police Directorate of Iraklio, Crete (Greek)

www.ipa.gr, International Police Association Greek Division (Greek, English)

www.p.en.a.a.tripod.com, Panellenic Union of Police Officers (Greek)

www.upoc.gr, Police Officers' Association of Crete (Greek)

www.poasy.gr, Union of Police Personnel (Greek)

www.sefaa.gr, Special Guards (Greek, English)

VASSILIKI PETOUSSI

Websites

Michigan State University. "Greece." Available at: *www.globaledge.msu.edu/ibrd/*. Accessed May 6, 2003.

Ministry of Foreign Affairs. "Greece Today, Politics." Available at: *www.mfa.gr/english/greece/today/politics/, www.mfa.gr/english/greece/today/politics/parlia ment.html*.

Ministry of Public Order. Available at: *www.ydt.gr*.

United Nations Convention to Combat Desertification. "Greece: Economic Outlook." Available at: *www.gm-unccd.org/FIELD/Countries/Greece/ST_outlook.htm*. Accessed May 6, 2003.

Unicef. "Greece." Unicef Statistics. Available at: *www.unicef.org/statis/Country_1Page69.html*. Accessed May 6, 2003.

Bibliography

Daskalakis, A. B. *History of the Greek Gendarmerie, 1936–1950*. Athens: Chrorofylake Headquarters, 1973 (in Greek).

Dimopoulos Kampanakis, Joseph. "Interactive Multimedia in Police Training: A Study in the Area of Crime Witness Interviewing." In *Policing in Central and Eastern Europe: Organizational, Managerial, and Human Resource Aspects*, edited by Pagon Milan, 131–144. Ljubljana: College of Police and Security Studies, 2000.

———. "Police Organizational Culture and Policemen's Integrity." In *Policing in Central and Eastern Europe: Organizational, Managerial, and Human Resource Aspects*, edited by Pagon Milan, 131–144. Ljubljana: College of Police and Security Studies, 2000.

Lambropoulou, Effi. "The 'End' of Correctional Policy and the Management of the Correctional 'Problem' in Greece." *European Journal of Crime, Criminal Law and Criminal Justice* 9, no. 1 (2001): 33–55.

———. "Greece." In *Organised Crime: A Catalyst in the Europeanisation of National Police and Prosecution Agencies?* Edited by Monica den Boer, 261–307. Maastricht: European Institute of Public Administration, 2002.

Panousis, Yannis, and Vasilis Karydis. "Fear of Victimization, Insecurity and Police Efficiency." In *Public Opinion in Greece: 1999–2000*, edited by VProject Research Consulting. Athens: Nea Synora-A. A. Livani, 1999 (in Greek).

Papakonstandis, Georgios. *Hellenic Police: Organization, Politics and Ideology*. Athens: Ant. N. Sakkoulas Publishers, 2003 (in Greek).

Papatheothorou, Theodoros P. *Public Safety and Crime Prevention Politics: Comparative Approach*. Athens: Nomiki Vivliothiki, 2002 (in Greek).

Petoussi, Vassiliki, and Georgios Papakonstandis. "Officially Recorded Violent Crime in Greece." Paper presented at the II European Society of Criminology Conference, Madrid, September 2002.

———. "Police Organization in Greece: Current State and Future Potential." Paper presented at the II European Society of Criminology Conference, Madrid, September 2002.

Petoussi, Vassiliki, and Georgios Papakonstandis and Kalliopi Stavrou. "The Juvenile Justice System in Greece." In *International Handbook of Juvenile Justice System*, edited by Donald J. Shoemaker, 146–159. Westport, CT: Greenwood Publishing Group, 1996.

Rigakos, George S., and Georgios Papanicolaou. "The Political Economy of Greek Policing: Between Neo-Liberalism and the Sovereign State." *Policing and Society* 13, no. 3 (2003): 271–304.

Spinellis, Dionysios, and Calliope D. Spinellis. "Greece." In *Criminal Justice Systems in Europe and North America*. Helsinki, Finland: HEUNI, 1999. Available at: www.heuni.fi/uploads/7gb012.pdf. Accessed 29 October 2003.

Spinellis, Calliope D. *Crime in Greece in Perspective*. Athens-Komotini: Ant. N. Sakkoulas Publishers, 1997.

Stamatis, Ch. Th. *History of the Astynomia Poleon, 1921–1971*. Athens: M. Frangoulis Publications, 1971 (in Greek).

Vidali, Sofia. "Greek Police of the 21st Century: A Mediterranean Model of Crime Prevention Policy." In *Texts of Police and Policing*, edited by Yannis Panousis and Sofia Vidali. Athens-Komotini: Ant. N. Sakkoulas Publishers, 2001 (in Greek).

Zarafonitou, Christina. "'New' Tendencies in Prevention Policy in Greece: Local Crime Prevention Councils and the Partnership Model." Paper presented at the II European Society of Criminology Conference, Madrid, September 2002.

———. *Fear of Crime: A Criminological Approach and Inquiry Based on an Empirical Study of the Phenomenon within the City of Athens*. Athens: Ant. N. Sakkoulas Publishers, 2002 (in Greek and English).

Zianikas, Ch. *The Police Today*. Athens. Estia Booksellers, 1990 (in Greek).

GRENADA

Background Material

On his third voyage to America, Columbus landed on Grenada in 1498. Grenada was colonized more than 100 years later. Early English attempts at discovery were unsuccessful. In 1650, a French company purchased the island from the English. The island remained under French control until 1762 when it was captured by the English, during the Seven Years War. Except for a short period, 1779 to 1783, the English controlled Grenada until it became an independent country.

During the eighteenth century, nutmeg and cocoa were introduced into the economy which led to the development of small holdings. In 1834, slavery was outlawed. Grenada was governed under several different forms of administration until independence in 1974.

Upon obtaining independence, Grenada became a member of the British Commonwealth. Grenada adopted a parliamentary form of government with a governor-general appointed by and represented by the British monarch and a prime minister. In 1979, a Marxist-Leninist government came into power and established close ties with Cuba, the Soviet Union, and other communist bloc countries. This government was removed from power in 1983. The governor-general administered the country until elections could be held in 1984. The country has been operating as a democracy since 1984.

The population of Grenada in the first part of the twenty-first century is approximately 90,000 people. About 35.5% of the population is under fifteen, 62% range from 15 to 64 and approximately 3.5% are over 64.

The official language is English with French patois as a secondary language. Fifty-three percent of the people are Catholic, almost 14% are Anglican, and the rest are other Protestant denominations. The per capita income is $5,000, with the major industry being agriculture and services.

Contextual Features

Grenada is a constitutional monarchy with Queen Elizabeth as the chief of state represented by a governor-general. The head of government is represented by the prime minister. The governor-general appoints the cabinet on the advice of the prime minister. A parliament with two houses is elected. The leader of the majority party or the leader of the majority coalition is usually appointed prime minister by the governor general.

The basis of Grenada law is English common law. The judicial basis is the West Indies Associate States Supreme Court resides in Grenada. The primary concerns of crime trends in Grenada are:

- The increasing tendency toward violence among young people, believed to be a significant factor in the public's fear of crime in Grenada
- The bad influence that deported criminals from first-world countries have upon the local criminal element
- Corruption at all levels and the need to enact legislation enabling the country to effectively deal with perpetrators
- Financial crimes and money laundering, and the need to continue enforcing legislation for compulsory reporting and against secrecy
- The ongoing threat of terrorist activity and the devastating effects that an incident could have
- The increase in domestic violence and sex crimes, including incest, rape, child molestation, and harassment, and the need to highlight these issues in crime prevention strategies, training, and data collection. In addition, the reluctance to report these crimes, possibly due to the lack of capabilities and/or coordination of agencies involved in service delivery for victims, is also a major concern
- The trafficking of illegal drugs through Grenada, and the country's need for increased international cooperation of air and maritime patrol capabilities to intercept those using Grenada as a transhipment point
- The increase of kidnapping and other crimes in larger, trend-setting countries such as Guyana, Trinidad, and Jamaica
- The scarcity of resources to combat crime and finance capital improvements, intelligence capabilities, and training

The criminal procedural system of Grenada is based on common law, and is oral and adversarial.

All minor offenses are heard by a magistrate court. Criminal procedures in these cases have a pretrial hearing and if the offender pleads guilty, the judge issues a sentence with the case not going to trial. Crimes of a serious nature have a preliminary investigation, a hearing before the magistrates court, and a trial held in the High Court with a jury of twelve.

Current crime statistics were first done by the Canadian International Development Agency. A study consisted of criminal, civil and family cases heard by the Magistrate Courts and published in 2002. The study collected and analyzed 4,159 cases in Grenada. The crime statistics follow:

- Fourteen percent were crimes against property, 17% traffic disputes, 9% drug offenses, and 7% use of firearms against persons.
- Sixty-one percent of cases were resolved in a pretrial hearing, 26% were overturned, 10% were dismissed for lack of merit, and in 3% of cases charges were withdrawn.
- Of the 2,566 cases resolved by pretrial hearing, 51% of the defendants pleaded guilty; in 34% defendants were found guilty; 6% of the hearings were still in press when the study was ended; and 2.3% were sent to trial.
- Arrest warrants were issued for defendants in 671 cases. Upon completion of the study, 78% of the arrests warrants had been executed and 22% were pending.
- In Grenada, 92% of case records did not provide information regarding whether or not the accused had legal counsel. The scant information provided showed that 7% of these defendants had a defense attorney and 1.14% had no legal counsel.
- An analysis of Grenada's criminal cases indicates that 33% received sentences or convictions that combined fines and incarceration.

Police Profile

Policing in Grenada can be traced back to 1853 when policing was a part-time occupation, and town magistrates were given charge of the police in their district. The modern Grenada police force began to take shape in 1705 when they were given firearms and given authority to administer their own affairs. There are 755 sworn police officers and 130 rural constables.

The chief executive is known as the commissioner and is appointed by the governor general on the advice of the Public Service Commission in consultation with the prime minister. The commissioner is responsible for the general administration and policy direction of the police and reports to the Minister of National Security. The deputy commissioner has responsibility for the day-to-day operations of the police force. This office is responsible for discipline, community relations, and complaints against the police.

An executive committee assists the commissioner in managing the organization. The committee has nineteen members including the commissioner, deputy commissioner, two assistant commissioners, four divisional commanders, and twelve department commanders/managers. The Royal Grenada Police force organizationally has four divisions and twelve departments, and is administered from the Office of the Commissioner at Fort George St. George Police Headquarters.

MICHAEL PALMIOTTO
AND PAUL IBBETSON

Bibliography

Central Intelligence Agency. "Grenada." In *The World Factbook*. Available at: www.odci.gov/cia/publications/factbook/geos/gi.html. Accessed January 18, 2005.

Consulate General of Grenada. "Crime Reduction Strategy for Grenada." October 2003. Available at: www.grenadaconsulate.org/grenada%20government/Constitution%20Review/constitutionreview.htm.

Geography IQ, *World Atlas*. Available at: w.geoghyiq.com/counties/gi/Grenada_history_summary-htm. Accessed January 18, 2005.

Justice Studies Center of the Americas. *Report to the Nation*, 5th ed. Available at: www.cejamaericas.org/reporte/muestra_pais.php?idioma=ingl. Accessed March 1, 2005.

Royal Grenada Police Force. Available at: www.spicisle.com/rgpf/historical_background.

GUATEMALA

Background Material

The Republic of Guatemala is situated in Central America, bordering the Caribbean Sea, between Honduras and Belize and bordering the North Pacific Ocean, between El Salvador and Mexico. The country's borders total 1,687 kilometers, and the border countries are Belize 266 kilometers, El Salvador 203 kilometers, Honduras 256 kilometers, and Mexico 962 kilometers. The country's total area is 108,890 square kilometers.

Spanish is the official language, although twenty-three indigenous idioms are also spoken. The primary religions are Catholicism, Protestantism, and Mayan traditional religions.

Guatemala's government is a constitutional democratic republic. The nation has 22 departments and 330 municipalities. Guatemala has a civil law system, with judicial review of legislative acts.

Guatemala was freed from Spanish colonial rule in 1821. During the second half of the twentieth century, it experienced a variety of military and civilian governments, as well as a thirty-six-year guerrilla war. In 1996, the government signed a peace agreement formally ending the conflict, which had led to the death of more than 100,000 people, and created some 1 million refugees.

The population of Guatemala is 13,314,079 (July 2002 estimate).

Contextual Features

The government of Guatemala is formed by three powers: the executive (president, vice president, and cabinet of ministers); the legislative (Chamber of Representatives) and the judicial (Supreme Court of Justice). The first two are constituted by popular election, and the judicial by designation of the Congress.

The executive branch consists of the president (chief of state and head of government); vice president; and cabinet, the Council of Ministers, which is appointed by the president. The president is elected by popular vote for a four-year term.

The legislative branch is comprised of the unicameral Congress (113 seats). Members are elected to serve four-year terms.

The judiciary is headed by the Supreme Court of Justice and Constitutional Court. The Supreme Court of Justice is composed of thirteen members who serve concurrent five-year terms and elect a president each year among their members; the president of the Supreme Court of Justice also supervises trial judges around the country, who are named for five-year terms. For the Constitutional Court, five judges are elected for concurrent five-year terms by the Congress, each serving one year as president of the Constitutional Court.

Justice in Guatemala is applied through the judicial branch, which is independent from the rest of the powers of state. Its structure is formed by the Courts of Peace, at a local level, in which misdemeanors are solved, and where they determine when an offense constitutes a crime. In the same way, they dictate and execute cases concerning the civil area of the law. In its order and according to the seriousness of the misdemeanor (if this is criminal), cases are transferred to the Courts of First Instance. If the Attorney General presents enough elements of proof to create a doubt about the innocence of the accused, the process is transferred to a Court of Sentence, where trials can be public and the decision is taken by a jury. If the case is not transferred to the Court of Sentence, the Judge of First Instance decides. As a further recourse, there is an Appeal Court Room and the Supreme Court of Justice. There is the Institute of Public Defense, a mechanism to guarantee an attorney for every person.

In regard to the correctional subsystem, there is only a penitentiary system. It is still not regulated by law. It is headed by the General Office of the Penitentiary System, dependent on the Interior Ministry.

The basic principle of the procedural penal system valid in Guatemala states that in order to carry out the opening for an oral trial, an accusation is needed. That requires that the commission of the crime is investigated to gather the evidence and elements of proof. That allows requesting the legal prosecution (accusation). The preparatory procedure (instruction) corresponds to the Attorney General, while the police have to help in carrying out the investigative tasks within the criminal process.

The following table summarizes crime in Guatemala.

Statistical Report of Criminal Acts Registered in Guatemala 1996–2002

Criminal Acts	1995	1996	1997	1998	1999	2000	2001	2002	Total
Homicides By									
Firearms	2,295	2,436	2,806	2,392	1,839	2,109	2,404	2,171	18,452
Bladed weapons	726	833	833	646	605	555	545	447	5,190
Crushing weapons	203	265	241	158	123	165	171	175	1,501
Explosives	0	0	0	19	15	6	10	1	51
Strangulation	36	60	72	67	42	38	59	64	438
Lynch	0	25	36	28	31	32	21	19	173
Total	3,260	3,619	3,988	3,310	2,655	2,905	3,210	2,877	25,824
Injured By									
Firearms	2,831	3,228	3,592	2,616	2,456	3,056	3,211	3,143	24,133
Bladed weapons	1,531	1,829	1,795	1,736	1,816	1,809	1,866	1,551	13,933
Crushing weapons	16	204	98	284	358	466	661	540	2,627
Explosives	0	0	0	45	45	39	32	18	179
Lynching	0	19	76	47	29	31	28	15	245
Total	4,378	5,280	5,561	4,728	4,704	5,401	5,798	5,267	41,117
Kidnappings and Rape									
Kidnapping	5	233	148	61	37	28	32	35	579
Rape	44	110	167	220	323	366	416	303	1,949
Crimes Against Property									
Residences	1,059	1,234	1,225	1,448	2,055	2,193	1,720	1,233	12,167
Businesses	1,326	1,366	1,746	1,682	1,868	2,033	1,557	1,365	12,943
Vehicles	6,426	5,411	5,529	5,894	6,262	7,072	7,784	7,132	51,510
Motorcycles	953	916	1,191	1,369	1,241	1,409	1,287	1,143	9,509
Firearms	744	1,003	1,177	1,338	1,555	1,528	1,357	1,037	9,739
Tourists	31	31	65	65	40	185	147	145	709
Pedestrians	727	1,039	926	1171	1,421	3,856	3,372	2,714	15,226
Buses	84	65	136	119	108	95	171	154	932
Banks	0	7	35	21	33	25	21	10	152
Armored vehicles	0	0	0	0	14	10	10	1	35
Churches	0	0	0	0	31	199	127	12	369
Total	11,350	11,072	12,030	13,107	14,628	18,605	17,553	15,072	113,417
General Total	19,037	20,314	21,894	21,426	22,347	27,305	27,009	23,554	182,886

Police Profile

Background

The National Civil Police (NCP) is the result of several historical stages, during which it changed from being a corps at the service of landowners, until it became the mechanism of control of citizens and state security defense. Although, institutionally, the police depend on the Ministry of Government, during the internal thirty-six-year armed conflict, the police corps was used by the army for the control of the population and for repression in urban areas. At that time, the police totally lost its natural function of defense of citizens to become an arm of terror of the state, within the prevailing doctrine of national security.

During that period three police corps were created: the Treasury Guard (Guardia de Hacienda), in charge of everything related to borders and customs; Mobile Military Police (Policía Militar Ambulante), in charge of roadway security; and the National Police (Policía Nacional), in charge of the citizen security.

The current National Civil Police is a product of the Peace Agreements signed on December 29, 1996, by the government and the guerrillas unified under the National Guatemalan Revolutionary Unit (Unidad Revolucionaria Nacional Guatemalteca). The National Civil Police was created on February 4, 1997, through congressional Decree 11-97. This law considers the organization and functioning of a single police force and recognizes the existence of several ethnicities and cultures, which will have to be represented in the new police corps, in the fulfillment of its mission. It is important to point out that in the new concept of internal security; the *police are in charge of internal security, leaving to the army the function of external defense.*

Organizational Description

The organization of the NCP Office is clearly stipulated by law, which establishes a General Administrative Office, in charge of the Office of Social and Informative Relations, Juridical Advisory, the Section of Petition Rights and Recourses, and the Secretary of Dispatch.

Additionally, there is a General Attached Office, which represents the second hierarchical step within the institution, with a range of General Subadministrative Office, in charge of the following:

- The General Operations Administrative Office, under the command of the General Commissioner, who is in charge of the Technical Department, Operations Service, Service of Antinarcotics Analysis and Information, Service of Information, Service of Criminal Investigation, Customs and Borders Service, Special Police Forces, and Service of Traffic and the Units of Specialists
- The General Personnel Administrative Office, which has a Technical Department, and which directs the Teaching Headquarters, Personnel Section, Disciplinary Regime, Section of Assistance to Personnel, Service of Publications and Central Archive
- The General Administrative Office of Support, whose structure is composed of the Secretary, Legislative Studies and Professional Doctrine Area, Selection and Training Area, Training for Promotions Area, Specialization Area, and Physical Education and Sports Area

The Attached General Director is in charge of the General Technical Department, Professional Responsibility Office, Office for Private Security Entities, and Department of Traffic.

In the organizational regulation of the NCP, there is a title related to the Peripheral Organization of the National Civil Police, which refers to the organization of the District Headquarters, stations, and substations.

The NCP has twenty-seven police stations; six are in the city of Guatemala, and one per department (province) account for the rest. In other words, the NCP has complete geographical coverage at the level of department capitals, but not in all municipalities.

The Intelligence Corps consist of the Service of Police Information (SPI); the Service of Antinarcotic Analysis and Investigation (SAIA); and as an investigatory department, the Service of Criminal Investigation (SCI).

The SAIA centers all its efforts in the antinarcotics operations and works in close cooperation with the U.S. Drug Enforcement Agency. The Service of Criminal Investigation has as its main mission to "gather the elements of investigation useful to be the base of the accusation in a criminal process." Its specific mission is (a) to gather the objects, instruments and proofs of the crime, handing them to the corresponding authority to serve as a base for the criminal prosecution; and (b) to investigate the crime, discover and capture the criminal, by its own initiative or by the request of the Attorney General or of the judicial authority and to comply with the requests of both authorities. For the fulfillment of its missions, the SCI is under the command of the general commissioner, and depends hierarchically on the General Operations Administrative Office. The organization is formed by a general headquarters and twenty sections located in the capital city, from which nine are supportive and eleven are operative.

The Cabinet of Identification is the organ in charge of preparing evidence reports, those obtained by their agents of visual inspections, as well as those sent by the Public Attorney, and which are the bases for clarification of criminal acts. The Service of Police Information is the least developed of all; in some cases, the SCI and SAIA fulfill its tasks of information gathering.

Functions

The Peace Agreements define the functions and main characteristics of the NCP as follows:

> The National Civil Police is a professional and hierarchical institution. It is the only armed police corps with national competence, whose function is to protect and guarantee the exercise of the rights and freedoms of people, to prevent, investigate and attack crime and set the public order and the internal security. It leads its actions with strict observance of the respect of the human rights and under the direction of civil authorities...

The Police Law also mentions the following principal functions, among others: investigation by their own initiative or behind the Public Attorney prosecution; help and protect the persons and their possessions; maintain public order; prevent crime; apprehend persons by judicial order; recollect and analyze information for the elaboration of preventive techniques; civil protection in case of disasters; participate in international relationships with other police forces; oversee the private security corps; transit; personal identification service;

and the promotion of civil society participation in security plans.

Training

After the Peace Agreements, the new police force was integrated in training new personnel and reeducating part of the members of the National Police and the Treasury Guard. Political formation was assumed by the European Union and developed by the "Program of Support to the National Politics of Security" through the Spanish Civil Guard (SCG) in 1998, which had a major influence in organizing the academic curriculum of the basic education and continuing education courses, as well as the promotion and specialty courses. Regarding criminal investigation, the Academy received since the beginning the support of ICITAP (International Criminal Investigative Training Assistance Program), which organized the Criminal Investigation School. Training and education in human rights, elaboration of databases of personnel and the evaluating board, and organization of the computer area and library, were undertaken in the program of strengthening the NCP.

The Academy is in charge of teaching all career and basic courses, as well as the specialization courses. The basic education of agents lasts six months. By 2001, the Academy had trained 8,568 new police agents (which represents 45% of the total), and 10,463 old police agents (55%). In the same way, six promotion courses had been granted, and seventy specialization courses for fourteen disciplines. The programs for the majority of the courses were developed by the European Union, which elaborated a total of forty-seven handbooks to support the teaching activity in the various courses and subjects. ICITAP was responsible for the criminal investigation curriculum, and the U.N. Verification Mission in Guatemala (MINUGUA), for human rights materials.

Basic police training consists of police training, judical training, humanistic training, administrative police, physical education and practices, and complementary subjects.

There is no organ within the NCP or the Ministry of Government in charge of carrying out the holding of examinations. This situation affects the number of applicants that guarantees an adequate candidate selection. Regarding the selection of personnel to enter the Academy, this is developed by the Evaluation Board, under the command of the General Commissioner of the NCP. The tests pertain to medical evaluation, physical exam, psychotechnical, and general culture areas.

Police Public Projects

Among the main programs under development by NCP are community policing and the Victim Attention Unit. The first project is being developed in coordination with the Guatemala City Municipality and the Local Boards of Security, formed by residents who volunteer to work with police to end the delinquency in their neighborhoods. The second project is related to restructuring police methodology to provide better responses to crime victims, and particularly women and children. This effort includes training personnel to specialize in psychological support techniques, as well as support for adding women to this unit.

Police Use of Firearms

The control of weapons and ammunition is overseen by the Guatemalan Army. According to the Peace Agreements, this control should be transferred to the Ministry of Government, for which the Law of Weapons and Ammunitions must be reformed. In Guatemala, the possession and bearing of weapons is a constitutional right, although it should be regulated.

The NCP has substantially improved its weaponry. Every police officer has his or her own weapon, although problems remain in terms of effective distribution by weapon type by territorial unit and maintenance.

A related issue is the number of private security companies whose agents triple the total number of national police agents. Legislation for oversight of such agents is inadequate; a reform project is underway to grant the NCP the possibility of better supervision and control of weapons. At present, the private security companies use offensive weaponry, while the NCP uses defensive weapons.

Complaints and Discipline

Guatemala has a long history as a violator of human rights and fundamental freedoms. Before the signature of the Peace Agreements, on several occasions the UN Human Rights Commission reported on the practice of serious and systematic abuses and violations to these rights. For many years, and particularly during military dictatorships, Guatemala had a UN Special Rapporteur assigned to investigate the human rights situation. Military and police agents who acted with impunity were responsible for systematic abuses against citizens.

The constitution of 1985 created important institutions to guarantee the respect and validity of human rights. At this time, the Human Rights Office was created, which along with the Constitutional Court and the Supreme Electoral Court, comprise the main pillars of the rule of law.

After the signing of the Peace Agreements, with the support of new institutions and legal reforms, substantial improvements in the respect and validity of the human rights were expected, as well as the eradication of impunity. However, even with a clear legal framework and with the commitment of the government derived from the regional and international organizations to which it belongs, observance of human rights remains problematic.

The NCP has been singled out for its responsibility in the execution of serious human rights violations. With regard to this matter, in recent years the MINUGUA has verified the following:

- Responsibility of members of the NCP in extralegal executions and execution attempts, as well as in attempts against personal integrity
- Excessive use of force or illegal use of weapons against prisoners or people who died in custody
- Detentions without judicial order
- Application of torture, cruel, inhuman or degrading treatment, and mistreatment during interrogation
- Failure to investigate attempts or threats against members of the political opposition and human rights advocates
- Evidence and report tampering to protect criminals
- Failure to investigate the possible participation of soldiers in cases of extrajudicial executions

As a demonstration of concerns regarding human rights, the NCP has created the Office for the Prevention of Crime, formed by the Human Rights Office, Gender Equality Office, and Community Policing Office. In this context, the Human Rights Office is in charge of introducing and updating the training in this matter at the Police Academy, as well as special courses for officers of various police stations and services.

The Agreement for the Strengthening of Civil Power establishes the police profession, which according to Article 27 should be guided by the following criteria:

> Establish that all the members of the new police structure should be trained in the Police Academy, where they will receive a highly professional preparation, a

culture of peace and respect of human rights and democracy and obedient of the law.

The International Red Cross provides training courses on the proportional use of force, and several organizations of the civil society in coordination with the Human Rights Officer accompany the training of instructors in subjects related to human rights, gender equity, children's rights, community policing, and democratic security.

The law pertaining to the congressional Human Rights Commission and the Human Rights Office establishes that the Human Rights Attorney has a duty to protect individual social, civil, and political rights, along with the life, freedom, justice, peace, dignity, and equality of the human person, as well as rights defined in international treaties or conventions accepted and signed by Guatemala.

Among the functions assigned to the Ombudsman, the following stand out: to investigate and report administrative behavior harmful to the interests of the people; investigate all types of reports presented by any person about violations to human rights; make private or public recommendations to public officials so that they modify reported incorrect behavior; publicly censor acts or behaviors against institutional rights; and promote actions or judicial or administrative recourse in cases that they are required.

The organ in charge of controlling the fulfillment of the mission and functions of the army and the NCP and of all the entities and public services is the Congress, while the political constitution assigns to it the function of controlling the actions of the executive branch and its dependencies. To achieve this task, the Congress has the faculty to call on respective ministers to interrogate them about their jobs.

The NCP has two disciplinary instances: the Professional Responsibility Office (PRO), which investigates the behavior contrary to professional ethics, and the Disciplinary Regime Section, whose job is to apply disciplinary procedures for serious and minor infractions.

Terrorism

Under the constitution, the Guatemalan Army is responsible of guaranteeing the internal and external security of the country. With the signature of the Peace Agreements, the separation of the functions of the Police and the Army was established. Because of the events of September 11, 2001, in the United States, in Guatemala the

Commissioner against Terrorism post was created, and a retired military man was named for it. Terrorism is not considered a major threat against the stability of the country, although it is well known that Guatemala due to its geographical situation is a channel to the United States, so controls at the country's borders and in immigration offices have been increased; the NCP and the Migration Office of the Government Ministry are responsible for such controls.

International Cooperation

The NCP's international cooperation is summarized in the following table.

Police Education, Research, and Publications

There are no institutions for professional police training, other than the Police Academy.

Activity or Working Area	Donor(s)
Support to NCP	European Commission
Support to NCP (Academy), training in problem solving	Sweden, Norway
Support to the NCP, multicultural	Norway
Support and equipment for the Academy and other dependencies, such as the language laboratory, computer equipment, and so on	Japan
Support to NCP specialized units	Norway
Support for investigative function	United States
Support to SAIA	United States (DEA, ICITAP); Chilean Carabineers
Transition toward NCP of programs executed by MINUGUA	UN Development Programme, Norway
Training seminars directed to the national police corps of the status of Central America	France
Training NCP Academy instructors under the Coordinadora de Apoyo a la Academia de la Policía, based on various nongovernmental and governmental organizations	Information provided by NGOs and Attorney for Human Rights

Source: Elaborated with information from MINUGUA/UN Development Programme

Research

Research focused on the police in Guatemala is rare. Investigators have centered on the task of supervising and monitoring police reforms and on defining public policies that support police actions. For this reason, it is more appropriate to talk about entities devoted to citizen security and the police task.

Regarding the historical view of security, Facultad Latinoamericana de Ciencias Sociales (FLACSO) was the first institution to focus on that issue. The Institute for Teaching Sustainable Development (IEPADES), under the guidance of Carmen Rosa de León-Escribano, has developed research and publications on police intelligence and police–community relations, and handbooks on human rights and communitarian police for the Academy, and has carried out the diagnosis on gender equity for the NCP, as well as contributed to systematization of information in ballistics and the Cabinet of Identification. At present, it is developing investigations centered on weapons and ammunitions.

The Guatemalan Institute of Comparative Studies in Criminal Sciences has developed studies mainly about prisons, and Worried Mothers (Madres Angustiadas) and Families and Friends Against Disappearances and Kidnappings (Familiares y Amigos Contra la Desaparición y el Secuestro), have centered their efforts on influencing police reforms. The Washington Office for Latin America (WOLA) has developed, under the guidance of Rachel Nield, comparative studies about police reform in Latin America and the Caribbean.

Sources of Funding for Police Research and Areas of Research

The financial resources for research are practically nonexistent. However, the abovementioned organizations are seeking financial as-sistance from their donors to develop research projects. Donors include the SOROS Foundation, Canada, UN Development Programme, Norway, Sweden, Holland, Finland, Switzerland, International Action Network on Small Arms, OXFAM, U.S. Agency for International Development, Inter-American Development Bank, and WOLA itself.

The main areas of investigation are weapons and munitions, police intelligence, police–community relations, preventive security, police and human rights, prison system, and police reform.

There are no periodicals specialized in police topics.

CARMEN ROSA DE LEÓN-ESCRIBANO

GUINEA

Background Material

The Republic of Guinea lies on the Atlantic Ocean, in West Africa. It is bordered to the north and northwest by Guinea-Bissau, Senegal, and Mali; to the east and southeast by Ivory Coast; and to the southwest by Liberia and Sierra Leone. It covers an area of 245,900 square kilometers, or 94,000 square miles, and its landscape ranges from coastal plain to a hilly to mountainous interior. The climate is hot and humid, with wet and dry seasons. The capital city, Conakry, is located on the coast.

In 2004, the estimated population was variously reported at 8.6 to 9.2 million. Population growth is over 2% a year, and those in the zero to fourteen-year age group constitute 42.8% of the population. The median age is 17.7 years. The fertility rate is 5.87 children per woman, and life expectancy is 49.7 years.

There are three major ethnic groups in Guinea: the Puhlar, also called Peuhl or Fulani, which represents 40% of the population; the Malinke, which represents 30%; and Soussou, 20%. A number of smaller ethnic groups constitute the remaining 10%. French is the official language, but the various ethnic groups have their own. The male literacy rate is close to 50%, while that of women is less than 22%. Eighty-five percent of Guineans are Muslim, 8% Christian, and 7% have indigenous beliefs.

Guinea has been populated by various peoples over the millennia. The Soussou and Malinke moved into the area in the tenth century. From then until the end of the eleventh century, Guinea was part of the Ghana Empire, and then part of the Mali Empire until the end of the fourteenth century, and of the Songhai Empire until the nineteenth century. The Fulani moved into Guinea in the eleventh century, bringing Islam with them and pushing the Soussou to the coastal plain. French rule began in the nineteenth century.

In 1958, Guinea declared unilateral independence from France and embraced the Soviet Union. Its dictatorial president pursued a revolutionary social program, crushing political opposition. Tens of thousands of people were tortured, executed, or disappeared during his regime. He survived many assassination attempts and died in 1984, whereupon the present president seized power in a bloodless coup. Despite instituting civilian government, he has kept a tight hold on the reins of power and, in 2001, engineered an amendment to the 1990 constitution that allows him to run for an unlimited number of terms of seven years each. These actions created considerable tension and distrust. In protest, all but one opposition party boycotted the legislative elections which followed, so that his party also dominates the National Assembly.

Guinea has rich natural resources and a large extractive industry. It produces gold, diamonds, and 25% of the world's bauxite, and engages in alumina refining, light manufacturing, and agricultural processing. The country also has great hydroelectric potential. Primary sector products include rice, coffee, pineapples, palm kernels, cassava, bananas, sweet potatoes, cattle, sheep, goats, and timber. Women are the major agricultural producers, and account for 80% of food production. While economic performance has been slowly improving, Guinea is nevertheless the recipient of foreign aid, has a large foreign debt, and its social indicators compare poorly with those of its neighbors in Sub-Saharan Africa. Forty percent of the population lives below the poverty line. Some of the factors contributing to this situation are low literacy rates, political instability, and government mismanagement. The government provides six years of free compulsory education, but enrollment rates are low because of school fees and lax enforcement of school attendance laws.

In the late 1990s and early twenty-first century, the borders with Sierra Leone, Liberia, and Ivory Coast were destabilized at different times as refugees fled into Guinea from the turmoil in their own countries. While Guinea has been welcoming in some instances, it has also repelled refugees, and there are many reports of Guinean security forces and police abusing, raping, and killing refugees.

Contextual Features

Under the Fundamental Law, or constitution, Guinea is a unitary democratic republic assuring universal suffrage, equality under the law for both men and women, and the right to protest, form associations, and to circulate freely. Citizens also have religious, health, education, and employment rights, and children are protected from exploitation. In reality, the freedom of the press is limited, and there is considerable abuse of human rights.

The president has executive power. He appoints the prime minister, who is the head of government, and the council of ministers. Government decisions are subject to approval by the People's National Assembly, but opposition can be overruled by decree. The unicameral National Assembly has 114 seats. Members are elected for a term of five years. There are nineteen female deputies in the Assembly, and three women hold seats in the twenty-six-member council of ministers.

Guinea's legal system is based on French civil law, but incorporates aspects of customary law and can be modified by decree. The judiciary is independent under the Fundamental Law, but in reality is dominated by the president. Judicial officials routinely defer to the executive in political cases. There is a shortage of qualified lawyers and magistrates, the penal code is outdated and restrictive, and there are many reports that the judiciary is riddled with corruption and nepotism. Capital punishment is still in effect. Distrust of the formal legal system encourages people to use the customary law practiced in villages and neighborhoods by local leaders. Some victims impatient of justice have resorted to vigilantism and dealt out their own retribution to offenders.

There are reports of street crime and breaking and entering in urban neighborhoods, but no firm figures to indicate the seriousness of the problem. There is diamond smuggling through Guinea from Sierra Leone, despite the introduction of an international diamond identification system to deter the illicit trade. Smuggling profits are used to buy arms for the various warring factions in the region that, in turn, contribute to human rights abuses. According to the United Nations, there are over 7 million military-style small arms and light weapons in West Africa that have facilitated civil strife and rebellions, and the abduction and exploitation of over 25,000 children as soldiers. The turmoil has claimed over 2 million lives in ten years in the region.

Crimes against the person in Guinea appear common. Assaults, sexual assaults, and murders, particularly in the border regions, are frequently reported. There is trafficking in women and children for labor and sexual exploitation, both within Guinea and across its borders. Domestic violence against women is prevalent, and female genital mutilation is practiced by "wise" women. While government campaigns to persuade the women to "lay down their knives" have had some success, progress is slow because the practice is lucrative.

There is also widespread corruption in the public life of Guinea. The judiciary, ports, customs, and police are all reported to engage in corrupt practices. Officials responsible for weapons stockpiles are known to "rent" out firearms and police routinely extort bribes at the many roadblocks throughout the country.

The Supreme Court has the highest level of jurisdiction and the highest court of appeal. It also decides constitutional and election matters. It has three chambers: administrative and constitutional; civil, criminal, commercial, and social matters; and accounts.

There are two courts of appeal: courts of the first instance and justices of the peace. There is also a military tribunal for military personnel, to whom the penal code does not apply. In addition, there is a State Security Court composed of magistrates appointed by the president, which tries cases involving the security of the state.

There are thirty-three official detention centers in the country with a population of 3,070 in 2002. Prison conditions are reported to be inhumane and life-threatening. While men and women are housed separately, juveniles are housed with adults and pretrial detainees are not separated from convicted prisoners. The prison system is not always able to track pretrial detainees and some have remained in prison for up to two years without trial. Overcrowding is common, and some prisoners have reported having to sleep on their knees because their cells were so small. Sanitation and diet are so poor that prisoners have died from disease and malnutrition. Beatings, threats, torture, and rape of female prisoners by guards have been reported. Homosexual activity is also prevalent. To help reduce the spread of HIV/AIDS, condoms are sold in prison hospitals. The International Committee of the Red Cross has prison access and is able to provide some basic sanitary supplies and food.

Police Profile

Background and Organizational Description

Policing in Guinea is based on the French model. There is a National Gendarmerie, which is part of the army and falls under the responsibility of the Defense Minister. The National Police comes within the jurisdiction of the Minister of Security. There is also a Presidential Guard that answers directly to the President. The role of both the Gendarmerie and the National Police is order maintenance and administrative control. In general, the Gendarmerie operates in rural areas and the National Police in urban areas; however, the distinction is not always clear. For example, a member of officer rank in the National Gendarmerie may be an officer in the National Police, although not the other way around. They also mount joint operations and share training.

Certain members of the Gendarmerie and the National Police are nominated to act as judicial police. In this role, they come under the authority and direction of the Attorney General and the Public Prosecutor. They identify infractions against the law, collect evidence, and seek out offenders on behalf of an examining magistrate.

Women seem to have formed part of the police for at least forty years, dating back to the period of affiliation with the Soviet Union. There is a report of a Guinean jazz band called the Amazons, well known in the 1960s and 1970s, which was comprised of women from the Guinean Gendarmerie. In November 2004, sixty-two war-seasoned police officers and police managers of both sexes were selected by examinations supervised by the United Nations for civilian police missions in Haiti, Burundi, and the Democratic Republic of Congo.

Training

The National Police and the National Gendarmerie have similar training programs offered at two separate academies in the capital. Training can last from eighteen months to two years. The International Committee of the Red Cross (ICRC) has provided financial and technical support as well as training in the academies and in the field on humanitarian principles and international human rights law. In 2003, a total of 750 new police officers were trained by the ICRC. During the same year, in cooperation with the UN High Commission for Refugees (UNHCR), the Royal Canadian Mounted Police provided training to a mixed brigade of Gendarmerie and National Police on maintaining security in refugee camps on the borders of Guinea.

Police Use of Firearms

Members of both the National Police and the Gendarmerie are issued with firearms for the duration of their careers. They can be required to undergo periodic requalification. As a member of the Economic Community of West African States

(ECOWAS), Guinea has engaged with other member-states and the United Nations in strengthening control of illicit small-arms trafficking at border posts and in building the capacities of military, police, customs, and others in controlling small arms. This includes controlling arms used by security officials and ensuring that security forces returning from missions abroad return their weapons to the state armories. Police have also been provided with training in arms control.

Complaints and Discipline

Police effectiveness is uneven. In the capital city, police service is adequate during the day, and a police emergency service introduced in 2004 functions well. The same cannot be said for the night hours or outside the capital. Moreover, there are reports that police have beaten, tortured, and raped civilians with impunity, although they have been punished or paid compensation on occasion. There are also reports of their having fired on peaceful demonstrations and killed unarmed students and others. The police have also made arrests without warrants and held people for long periods in detention in contravention of the Penal Code. Amnesty International accuses the Guinean security forces of having contravened international standards and the UN Basic Principles on the Use of Force and Firearms by Law Enforcement Officials.

International Cooperation

Some international aid has been provided to the police. In 2001, for example, Guinea received 210,000 euros as part of a multiyear program for equipping the Gendarmerie and, in 2002, a total of 920,000 euros for military information technology, transmission infrastructure, and support of the Gendarmerie. Up until the end of April 2004, Guinea also received aid totaling US$1.4 billion from the World Bank, some of which was being spent on law, justice, and administrative programs.

Guinea is a member of the United Nations, the Economic Community of West African States (ECOWAS), and Interpol.

ERICA MCKIM

Bibliography

"Africa—West Africa." *Jane's Intelligence Review*. Available at: www.janes.com/search97. www. Accessed October 18, 2002.

African Development Bank. "Basic Indicators of African Countries: Comparison." Available at: www.afdb.org/african_countries/information_comparison.htm. Accessed December 1, 2004.

Amnesty International. "Guinea: Maintaining Order with Contempt for the Right to Life." Amnesty International Publications, 2002, AI Index 29/001/2002. Available at: http://web.amesty.org/library/print/ENGAFR 290012002. Accessed November 28, 2004.

Amnesty International. "Report 2000 (Guinea)," January to December 2001. AI Index: POL10/001/2002. New York: Amnesty International, 2002.

Bureau of Democracy, Human Rights and Labor. "Guinea." Country Reports on Human Rights Practices—2002. Available at: www.nationbynation.com/Guinea/Human.html. Accessed November 29, 2004.

Canada, Department of Foreign Affairs and International Trade. "Sub-Saharan Africa: Country Profile Guinea." Available at: www.dfait-maeci.gc.ca/africa/guinea_ background-en.asp. Accessed December 1, 2004.

Canadian International Development Agency. "Guinea: Facts at a Glance." Available at: www.acdi-cida.gc.ca/CIDAWEB/webcountry.nsf. Accessed December 1, 2004.

Central Intelligence Agency. "Guinea." In *The World Factbook 2004*. Available at: www.cia.gov/cia/publications/factbook/geos/gv.html. Accessed November 28, 2004.

Diallo, Mamadou. "A Time Bomb Ready to Explode, A Looming Rwanda-Type Genocide." West Africa—Republic of Guinea. Available at: www.guinea-forum.org/analyses/index.asp?Lang = en.htm. Accessed December 1, 2004.

Droit Francophone. "Guinée: Description du droit national." Encyclopédie universelle des droits de l'Homme (E.U.D.H.), Agence intergouvernementale de la francophonie, September 14, 2001. Available at: http://portail.droit.francophonie.org/doc/html/gn/dtn/fr/2001/2001dfgndn1.html. Accessed November 29, 2004.

Guinea, Government of. "Loi fondamentale du République de Guinée, le 3 avril 1984." Droit francophone, Agence intergouvernementale de la francophonie. Available at: http://portail.droit.francophonie.org/doc/html/gn/. Accessed November 29, 2004.

Guinea, Government of. Les Institutions Républicaines. Available at: www.guinee.gov.gn/7_institutions/instituti.htm. Accessed November 28, 2004.

Human Rights Watch. "Trapped Between Two Wars: Violence Against Civilians in Western Côte d'Ivoire, Chapter XI. The Regional and International Response." Human Rights Watch, 2003. Available at: www.hrw.org/reports/2003/coted. Accessed November 28, 2004.

International Centre for Prison Studies, Africa. "Prison Brief for Republic of Guinea." World Prison Brief of International Centre for Prison Studies, Africa. Available at: www.kcl.ac.uk/depsta/rel/icps/worldbrief/africa_records.php?code = 23. Accessed December 1, 2004.

Seck, Cheikh Yérim. "Conakry sans Lansana Conté." *J.A./L'Intelligent*, no. 2192, January 12–18, 2003.

United Nations Integrated Regional Information Networks. "Guinea: NRC Update on Displaced Guineans." AllAfrica Global Media. Available at: http://allafrica.com/stories/printable/200301170773.html. Accessed January 17, 2003.

U.S. Committee for Refugees. "Sierra Leone and Liberia Violence Spills into Guinea." AllAfrica Global Media. Available at: http://allafrica.com/stories/20009140046.html. Accessed September 14, 2000.

World Bank. "Guinea—Country Brief." Updated September 2004. Available at: http://web.worldbank.org/wbsite/external/countries/africaext/guinea. Accessed November 29, 2004.

GUINEA-BISSAU

Background Material

Beginning in September 2000, the Revolutionary United Front (RUF) rebel army, backed by Liberian President Charles Taylor, commenced large-scale attacks into Guinea from Sierra Leone and Liberia. The RUF, known for their brutal tactics in the near decade-long civil war in Sierra Leone, operated with financial and material support from the Liberian government and its allies. These attacks destroyed the town of Gueckedou as well as a number of villages, causing large-scale damage and the displacement of tens of thousands of Guineans from their homes. The attacks also forced the UN High Commissioner for Refugees (UNHCR) to relocate many of the 200,000 Sierra Leonean and Liberian refugees residing in Guinea. As a result of the attacks, legislative elections scheduled for 2000 were postponed.

After the initial attacks in September 2000, President Conté, in a radio address, accused Liberian and Sierra Leonean refugees living in the country of fomenting war against the government. Soldiers, police, and civilian militia groups rounded up thousands of refugees, some of whom they beat and raped. Approximately 3,000 refugees were detained, although most were released by the end of 2000.

In November 2001, a nationwide referendum, which some observers believe was flawed, amended the constitution to permit the president to run for an unlimited number of terms, and to extend the presidential term from five to seven years. The country's second legislative election, originally scheduled for 2000, was held in June 2002. President Conté's Party of Unity and Progress (PUP) and associated parties won 91 of the 114 seats. Most major opposition parties boycotted the legislative elections, objecting to inequities in the existing electoral system.

Guinea has four main ethnic groups:

- Peuhl (Foula or Foulani), who inhabit the mountainous Fouta Djallon
- Malinke (or Mandingo), in the savannah and forest regions
- Soussous in the coastal areas
- Several small groups (Gerzé, Toma, and so on) in the forest region

West Africans make up the largest non-Guinean population. Non-Africans total about 10,000 (mostly Lebanese, French, and other Europeans). Seven national languages are used extensively; major written languages are French, Peuhl, and Arabic.

Guinea-Bissau is one of the world's poorest nations. Farming is by far the leading occupation; rice, corn, beans, cassava, and cotton are the main crops grown for domestic use. The population of 1.2 million relies largely on subsistence agriculture and the export of cashew nuts. Both activities were affected negatively by the fighting. Annual per capita gross domestic product (GDP) prior to 1998 has been estimated at $840. Due to the conflict, GDP declined by 28% in 1998, but was expected to reach 80% of pre-1998 levels by the end of the year. Exports of cashew nuts returned to 70% of pre-conflict levels. Commercial banks and other monetary institutions, which had ceased operations with the outbreak of hostilities in June 1998, reopened in July. The country remains burdened by heavy external debt and massive underemployment.

Much of the land is state owned. Bauxite is mined, and there are unexploited petroleum deposits. Industrial activity is mostly limited to the processing of agricultural products. Guinea-Bissau is a member of the Franc Zone.

Contextual Features

Guinea-Bissau has a republican government with a multiparty system currently in a transitional period. According to Guinea-Bissau's constitution, last modified in 1993, and the Pact of Transition, the newly selected prime minister serves as the head of government. Tasks facing the new government include determining whether to modify the April 2001 constitution before the president promulgates it.

The Constitution provides for an independent judiciary; however, it is subject to political influence and corruption. The judiciary, which ceased to function at the onset of fighting in June 1998, resumed minimal responsibilities with the inauguration of a government of national unity in February. Judges are trained and paid poorly, and sometimes are subject to political pressure and corruption. The Supreme Court is especially vulnerable to political pressure, as its members are appointed by the president and serve at his pleasure. The judiciary is reluctant to decide cases of a political nature. Cases against several former and current members of the government were delayed. The Supreme Court failed to deal impartially with highly charged political cases. In 1997, the Court took up the issue of the constitutionality of the manner in which the president named his new government. The decision ultimately rendered was in favor of allowing the government to remain in office, but was issued only after the president brought significant pressure to bear on the Court.

Trials involving state security are conducted by civilian courts. Under the Code of Military Justice, military courts try only crimes committed by armed forces personnel. The Supreme Court is the final court of appeal for both military and civilian cases. The president has the authority to grant pardons and reduce sentences.

Citizens who cannot afford an attorney have the right to a court-appointed lawyer. Traditional law still prevails in most rural areas, and urban dwellers often bring judicial disputes to traditional counselors to avoid the costs and bureaucratic impediments of the official system. The police often resolve disputes.

The law provides for procedural rights, such as the right to counsel, the right to release if no timely indictment is brought, and the right to a speedy trial. In practice, the judicial system generally failed to provide these rights. The constitution provides for the inviolability of domicile, person, and correspondence; however, the government does not always respect these rights.

Prison conditions are poor, but generally not life-threatening. Beatings and deprivation have been used as a means of coercion. The June 1998 rebellion effectively stopped a program aimed at halting such methods. Prison authorities had very little control over inmates, many of whom simply left during the day. Following a request in 1998 by the Ministry of the Interior for international donor assistance to rehabilitate the prisons, the European Union renovated two of them. However, many prisons were damaged during the fighting, and the inmates escaped and have not been recaptured. Human rights monitors reported several incidents in which police accused of rape or the mistreatment of prisoners were not prosecuted.

Police Profile

The police, under the direction of the Ministry of the Interior, have primary responsibility for the nation's internal security. However, following the June 1998 revolt, the police became ineffective, as the military junta, Economic Community of West African States Military Observer Group (ECO-MOG) peacekeeping forces, and troops defending President Vieira were better equipped and openly carried arms on highly visible patrols and checkpoints. Following Vieira's ouster in May, the withdrawal of all foreign troops, and efforts of the interim government to reinstate the rule of law, the police resumed many of their responsibilities; however, lack of resources and training continue to hamper their effectiveness. The armed forces are responsible for external security and may be called upon to assist the police in internal emergencies.

A clear majority of soldiers joined the rebellion against President Vieira. Those who remained loyal, numbering no more than 300, generally took a secondary role to Senegalese and Guinean troops who entered the conflict at Vieira's request.

ECOMOG peacekeeping forces were introduced, and all Senegalese and Guinean troops were withdrawn by the end of March as agreed in the Abuja accords. ECOMOG forces were withdrawn in June following the defeat of loyalist forces and Vieira's departure to exile.

The police, the military (both loyal and rebel), the Senegalese, and the Guineans were responsible for serious human rights abuses.

The constitution prohibits cruel and inhuman punishment, and evidence obtained through torture or coercion is invalid; however, prior to the May coup, the government often ignored these provisions, and security forces beat, mistreated, and otherwise abused persons. Security and police authorities historically have employed abusive interrogation methods, usually in the form of severe beatings or deprivation. The government rarely enforced provisions for punishment of abuses committed by security forces.

The police do not always use judicial warrants and have forced entry into some private homes. Police also detained suspects without judicial authority or warrants, occasionally through the device of house arrest. Prior to the May coup, the government held detainees without charges or trial for extended periods of time, sometimes incommunicado. The authorities did not routinely observe bail procedures.

MINTIE DAS

Bibliography

Central Intelligence Agency. "Country Report." 2005. Available at: www.cia.gov/cia/publications/factbook.
U.S. Department of Justice. "Background Note." 2005. Available at: www.travel.state.gove/travel.

GUYANA

Background Material

Guyana comprises an area of 216,000 square kilometres (83,000 square miles) and is situated on the northern coast of South America. Following the so-called voyages of "discovery" by Christopher Columbus in 1492, competition between Holland, Britain and France for the plunder and control of the area ended when the country was formally ceded to the British by the Treaty of Paris in 1814 (Shahabuddeen 1978). The colonial period finally came to an end when Guyana became a sovereign, democratic state by virtue of the Guyana Independence Act, 1966. In 1970, Guyana became a Co-operative Republic.

The most recent Statistical Bulletin (2001) for the country reports a huge increase in the country's public debt, steadily increasing inflation rates, and a significant decline in public sector employment over the period 1998–2001. Controlling the spread of AIDS is also a serious problem facing Guyana. AIDS and AIDS-related complex have consistently ranked among the top three leading causes of death in Guyana during the most recent years for which official statistics are available (1997–1999). On the subject of the environment, there is grave concern at the increased incidence of flooding due to global warming and higher precipitation intensity, as well as accelerated deforestation and the drainage of existing wetlands.

The total estimated population for Guyana was 777,200 at mid-year 2000 (Guyana Bureau of Statistics 2001: 92). Based on the results of the 1990/1991 population census, ethnic composition of the total population of 718,406 follows: black, 234,765; Amerindian, 45,379; East Indian, 347,110; Chinese, 1,338; Portuguese, 1,964; Syrian/Lebanese, 19; White, 318; Mixed, 87,402; Other, 90; Not stated, 21 (Caricom Secretary-General 1992: 3).

The language spoken is English. Major religions are Anglican, Baptist (Spiritual), Church of God, Jehovah Witness, Methodist, Pentecostal, Roman Catholic, Adventist, Hindu, and Muslim. The per capita income for the year 2000 was US$850.

Contextual Features

The legal system is based on the English common law and is adversarial in nature.

A review of the crime statistics for each year during the period 1974–2000 reveals that burglary and house breaking and larceny occur with much greater frequency than all other crimes combined (Guyana Police Force 1974–2000).

Between 1999 and 2000, there were also significant increases in the amount of illegal drugs seized by police. Current media reports and press releases by the police and the Guyana Human Rights Association indicate that this trend is continuing, accompanied by a dramatic increase in violent crime, the possession and use of illegal firearms, the slaying of police officers, and extrajudicial killings by police. On June 5, 2003, the Kidnapping Bill (No. 15 of 2002) was passed in Parliament to deal with the emerging problem of kidnappings for ransom.

The judicial system of Guyana consists of a hierarchy of courts: the Magistrate's Court, the High/Supreme Court, the Full Court of the Supreme Court and the Court of Appeal, which is the Court of last resort. There are a total of thirty-seven Courts consisting of twenty-three Magistrate's Courts, thirteen High Courts, and one Court of Appeal. Courts perform the adjudication function in the justice system using an adversarial system that is executed in both a written and oral manner.

The legal tradition upon which the criminal law is based consists of the English common law and a series of indictable and summary offences created by statute. Summary offences are all conducted in the Magistrate's Court. Indictable matters, after a preliminary inquiry takes place in the Magistrate's Court, are heard in the High/Supreme Court. Appeals go to the Full Court of the Supreme Court and finally to the Court of Appeal.

Civil practice and procedure is based on the English common law as well as statutory law (High Court/Court of Appeal Rules). The majority of civil litigation takes place in the High/Supreme Court.

The correctional system consists of the Guyana Prison Service and the Parole Board, both of which are under the jurisdiction of the Ministry of Home Affairs. The Guyana Prison Service was established under the Prison Act, No. 26 of 1975 of the Laws of Guyana (as amended). Responsibility for the administration of all prisons, lockups, and detention centres in Guyana rests with a Director of Prisons and Deputy Director of Prisons. Rehabilitation initiatives include educational programmes for literacy development and technical training, as well as treatment for drug and sex offenders.

The Parole Board was constituted under the provisions of the Parole Act, No. 24 of 1991. Its mission is to promote the rehabilitation of prisoners by affording early release on specified conditions, and parole supervision/aftercare. In addition to receiving and processing parole applications and preparing quarterly reports, Parole Board members are expected to carry out the following functions: liaise with the probation service for home study, liaise with the police to obtain records on the prospective parolees, visit prisons, meet with legal personnel, assist in facilities for rehabilitation in and out of prison, engage in discussions with prisoners about parole, and sensitize the public about parole (Ministry of Home Affairs 1995:27–28).

Police Profile

Background

The Guyana Police Force was established by British colonial authorities in 1839 under the advice of the commissioners of the London Metropolitan Police. Frequent incidences of social unrest resulted in the gradual transformation of the Force from a civilian into a semimilitary operation. The model adopted was that of the Royal Irish Constabulary, and the militarization process was completed in 1891 when British troops withdrew from the colony (Mars 2002). Throughout the colonial period, semimilitary policing continued in Guyana with emphasis on coercion and crowd control rather than protection of and service to citizens.

In August 1957, the Police Act (No. 39) was passed "to amend and consolidate the law relating to the Guyana Police Force." The objectives of the Force are outlined in Section 3(2) of the Act, and include crime prevention and detection, peacekeeping, law enforcement, repression of internal disturbances, and performance of military duties when required to do so by the Minister of Home Affairs. This Act, as amended, is currently in force.

Demographics

In the absence of specific data on gender and ethnic representation, it appears that women are fairly well represented in the Force, but no steps have yet been taken to correct the acute ethnic imbalance due to the severe underrepresentation of East Indians at all levels of the Force (International Commission of Jurists 1965). The educational attainment of commissioned and non-commissioned ranks in the Force ranges from primary school graduation to four-year college degrees.

Organizational Description

In 2000 (the most recent year for which statistics are currently available), the establishment of the regular Police Force was 3,570 members and the strength was 3,146 members, an increase of 135 over the previous year (Guyana Police Force 2000: 7). A total of 157 were enlisted into the Special Constabulary. Eighteen persons were performing full time duties in the Rural Constabulary, and 425 were enlisted in the Supernumerary Constabulary. Civilian personnel consisted of 45 barrack labourers who were employed by the Guyana Police Force. In 2000, the police/population ratio was one policeman to every 319 people.

The Force is commanded by the commissioner of police who by virtue of the Police Act, 1957 (as amended), is directly responsible to the Minister of Home Affairs. In discharging his responsibilities, the commissioner is assisted by a headquarters staff, comprising a deputy commissioner operations, deputy commissioner law enforcement, assistant commissioner finance and stores, staff officer administration I, staff officer administration II, and divisional and branch commanders. For the purpose of police administration, the country is divided into seven geographical police divisions, code lettered A to G.

Members of the Force are recruited and trained at the Felix Austin Police College in Georgetown, Berbice, and Essequibo. After training, the ranks are deployed to work either at the Force Headquarters or in a Division. Ranks with the relevant academic qualifications, CXC (Caribbean Examinations Certificate) or GCE (General Certificate of Education), and other requisite requirements may be appointed cadet officers.

The commissioner of police is responsible for the promotion and control of members of the Force below the rank of inspector. The Police Service Commission, which is established under the constitution, is responsible for the promotion of police officers from the rank of inspector to deputy commissioner. Under the constitution, the president appoints the commissioner of police and every deputy commissioner of police, after consultation with the Police Service Commission.

The Criminal Investigation Department includes the Anti-Crime Task Force Unit, Quick Reaction Group, Homicide Squad, Fraud Squad, Narcotics Branch, Juvenile Branch, Criminal Records Office, Fingerprint Branch, Scenes of Crime Unit, and a forensic laboratory. It is also assisted by Impact Bases in A, B, C, D, and E Divisions, and 403 functional Community Policing Groups.

The Anti-crime Task Force Unit and the Quick Reaction Group are specially designed to manage the crime situation and keep the crime rate down. The Anti-crime Task Force Unit operates on a twenty-four-hour basis and utilizes vehicular patrols as well as foot and cycle patrols. Ranks can conduct field interrogations, searches, and seizures. The Quick Reaction Group is a special response unit, and maintains foot and mobile patrols in the capital city of Georgetown and its environs. Support services in crime fighting include tactical, impact, and plainclothes patrols in all divisions, coastal patrols, cordon and search operations, and roadblock exercises.

Functions

The Guyana Police Force provides service and protection by preventing and detecting crime, maintaining law and order, controlling traffic, and preserving the public peace. The police may also perform military duties when called upon to do so.

The police also serve in areas not directly related to core functions in policing, including the following: postal agents, Guyana Airways

Corporation agents, customs officers, licensing and certifying officers, road marking and painting of traffic signs, building construction and repairs, sentries at vulnerable points and key points, lands and mines officers, manufacturing shotgun cartridges, escorts of senior government officials and head of states, and prison wardens for juveniles and female prisoners at locations in the interior of Guyana.

Training

The entrance requirement for the Police Force is primary school graduation. There is also a written entrance examination. The Assistant Commissioner "Administration" is responsible for training members of the Guyana Police Force. The training policy of the Force is implemented by a Board of Training, which deals with both internal and overseas training for members of the Force.

Police Public Projects

Police public projects include the Children's Outreach Programme, Traffic Education Programme, and School Safety Patrols.

Police Use of Firearms

Police Special Order, No. 7 of 1963 provides that the police may use "offensive weapons" when, in "the honest opinion of the police present ... less extreme measures will not suffice" (Section (a)(i)). The Force does not release data relating to the frequency of the use of firearms. The current policy on firearm ownership requires that applications for firearms licenses be made to the Commissioner of Police. Applications are then sent to the relevant divisional commanders for processing. After an investigation is carried out, a report is prepared and sent to Force Headquarters, and the Commissioner of Police makes the ultimate decision whether to grant or refuse the application. Information relating to the number and types of firearms licensed yearly is provided in the Guyana Police Force Annual Report.

Complaints and Discipline

The Commissioner of Police is responsible for the discipline of members of the Force below the rank of inspector. The Police Service Commission is charged with the responsibility for the discipline of police officers from the rank of inspector to deputy commissioner.

By virtue of the Police Complaints Authority Act, No. 9 of 1989, an independent Authority was established to receive and inquire into allegations of misconduct by members of the Police Force. The Authority may direct the police to record and investigate such complaints in accordance with the Police Discipline Act, but can only provide "comments" on the decisions taken under police internal disciplinary procedures as set out in the Police Discipline Act.

The Guyana Human Rights Association provides training to the police on human rights. A team of human rights educators provides the training free of charge to the police at least once a year on average, and upon special request. Human rights documents and instructional materials are also provided free of charge to participants. Members of the Force also attend international human rights training seminars.

The Guyana Police Force has repeatedly been criticized for human rights violations. The U.S. Department of State disseminates information on human rights violations by police in its annual report on Guyana. At the local level, the Guyana Human Rights Association and Amnesty International (Guyana Section) monitor human rights violations in Guyana, and intercede on behalf of persons whose rights have allegedly been violated by police. Victims of human rights abuses also have recourse to the courts where such abuses also amount to violations of the laws or the Constitution of the Cooperative Republic of Guyana.

Terrorism

There are no known terrorist organizations in Guyana. There are no specific police agencies charged solely with responding to terrorism.

International Cooperation

The Guyana Police Force participates in the exchange of information and cooperation with reference to the apprehension and prosecution of crime suspects, with police forces throughout the world through the International Police Organization (INTERPOL). Several police organizations provide technical assistance and training such as the Royal Canadian Mounted Police; Scotland Yard; and the U.S. Federal Bureau of Investigation and Drug Enforcement Administration. In addition, officers regularly attend seminars and training programmes in several Latin American and Caribbean countries such as Argentina, Bolivia, Brazil, Barbados, Jamaica, Martinique, Trinidad and Tobago, Grenada, and St. Lucia.

Police Education, Research, and Publications

Institutions for Higher Education for Police

Apart from the Felix Austin Police College, there are several institutions for higher education in Guyana that are also attended by members of the Police Force. These include the Government Technical Institute, the Critchlow Labour College, the Institute of Adult and Distance Education, Business College, Computer World, Global Technology, and the University of Guyana.

Leading Police Journals/Magazines/Newsletters

The Copper (Magazine/Newsletter)—Guyana Police Force, Force Headquarters, Eve Leary, Georgetown, Guyana.

JOAN R. MARS

Bibliography

Campbell, John. *History of Policing in Guyana*. Georgetown, Guyana: Guyana Police Force, 1987.

Caricom Secretary-General. *1990/91 Population and Housing Census of the Commonwealth Caribbean—National Census Report: Guyana*. Trinidad and Tobago: Central Statistical Office Printing Unit, 1992.

Danns, George K. *Domination and Power in Guyana: A Study of the Police in a Third World Context*. New Brunswick, NJ: Transaction, 1982.

Guyana Bureau of Statistics. *Statistical Bulletin*. Trinidad and Tobago: Central Statistical Office Printing Unit, 2001.

Guyana Police Force. *Guyana Police Force Annual Report*. Georgetown, Guyana: Guyana Police Force, 1974–2000.

Harris, Adam, ed. *Kaieteur News*. Georgetown, Guyana: National Media and Publishing Co. Ltd., 2003.

Jeffries, Sir Charles. *The Colonial Police*. London: Max Parrish & Co., 1952.

Khan, Sharief, ed. *Guyana Chronicle*. Georgetown, Guyana: Guyana National Newspapers Ltd., 2003.

Mars, Joan. *Deadly Force, Colonialism and the Rule of Law: Police Violence in Guyana*. Westport, CT: Greenwood Press, 2002.

Ministry of Home Affairs. *Ministry of Home Affairs Annual Report 1995*. Co-operative Republic of Guyana: Ministry of Home Affairs, 1995.

Orrett, W.A. *The History of the British Guiana Police*. Georgetown, Guyana: Daily Chronicle Ltd., Printers and Publishers, 1951.

Persaud, Anand, ed. *Stabroek News*. Georgetown, Guyana: Guyana Publications Inc., 2003.

Shahabuddeen, Mohammed. *Constitutional Development in Guyana: 1621–1978*. Georgetown, Guyana: Guyana Printers Ltd., 1978.

HAITI

Background Material

Haiti is the poorest country in the Western Hemisphere. More than half the population earns less than $100 per year as either marginalized peasants or underemployed urban migrants. The entire population speaks Kreyol and most practice a combination of the Catholicism and Voudon religions. A rich elite also speaks French as a first language, and increasing numbers of the middle class and rich speak English as a second language. About 95% of the population is of pure African origin, their ancestors having been slaves on sugar plantations. The remainder are mulattos and combinations of Syrian, Lebanese, Polish, German, and other non-African ethnicity. The elite consists primarily of this non-African segment, although there is a black middle class, as well as remnants of the black aristocracy in the north dating to the country's 1804 revolution.

In the late eighteenth century, the then-sugar producing, French colony was the wealthiest in the world. The world's first and only successful slave uprising led to independence in 1804. Civil war in the early nineteenth century was followed by regime instability. Following the nineteen-year U.S. occupation from 1915 to 1934, Haiti has varied between periods of rapid instability and long periods of autocratic rule, including under Paul Magloire (1950–1956), and François and Jean Claude Duvalier (1957–1986).

Under pressure from the United States, domestic protests, and an army coup, Jean Claude Duvalier left Haiti on February 7, 1986. The United States recognized a civilian-military transitional junta, which held elections in November 1987; the elections were marked by violence, leaving the country without legitimate authority. In elections sponsored by the United Nations, the Organization of American States (OAS), and the United States in December 1990 and January 1991, Jean-Bertrand Aristide, a former Roman Catholic priest and popular anti-Duvalier activist, became president. It was the first democratic transfer of power in Haitian history. However, only seven months after his inauguration, the army deposed Aristide, which left an inchoate, but autocratic authoritarian regime in power. About three years later, Aristide returned to power, following a U.S. invasion sanctioned by United Nations Security Council Resolution 940.

President Aristide served the remaining fifteen months of his term in office until the 1995 elections. Aristide's protégé, René Préval, won the presidency in the name of the Lavalas party. Haiti has been without a legitimate government since 1997 when controversial legislative elections led to the resignation of the prime minister. Préval's subsequent nominees for prime minister were rejected by Parliament, which was in turn disbanded by Préval in January 1999. New elections were initially announced for December of that year, but in the end did not take place until May 2000. They were mired in controversy, the opposition correctly claiming that at least seven senate seats had been accorded to Lavalas members when they should have faced a run-off election. The elections were described by the United States, European Union, and OAS as deeply flawed, and up to US$500 million in foreign loans assistance has been frozen since (as of August 2003), pending a political resolution and holding of credible elections.

Contextual Features

Haiti has a civil law system with inquisitorial trials, based on models derived from French colonialism. The system has been somewhat modified since the 1994–2000 U.S./UN intervention. Its 1987 Gaullist constitution is based on the French Fifth Republic, based on a semipresidential system, with power shared between a directly elected president and an prime minister indirectly elected and theoretically accountable to Parliament. Its criminal justice system has been modernized by the establishment of a new National Police force established in the mid-1990s by the UN peace mission. However, the courts and prison system are comparatively antiquated, with large backlogs of cases and prisoners held after the new police force made numerous arrests.

François Duvalier created a notorious paramilitary force, the Volunteers for National Security (VSN), colloquially known as the Tonton Macoutes, which counterbalanced the power of the army that had been created by the United States during its first occupation. The Macoutes, along with an army purged of all anti-Duvalier elements, repressed all opposition. Duvalier maintained a mesmerizing power over the people of Haiti through a combination of VSN paramilitary terror, conventional police-state repression, and appeals to voodoo. After the 1986 end to the Duvalier dictatorship, the VSN was disbanded, although informal elements of repression have persisted since.

Since 1987, the police had been a 1,000-man force in Port-au-Prince, without formal separation from the army and reporting to the Justice Minister. In the rest of the country, rural sheriffs reporting to one of the nine Army departments reigned via havoc or terror, while expropriating economic output. UN interim police monitor, Raymond Kelly,

soon after arriving commented in his diary on October 5, 1994: "The Haitian police know they are not much of a police force. Few are trained. Few have sidearms, fewer have radios, and there are no vehicles to speak of. What we do find are machine guns, grenade launchers, and other weapons of war. The Haitian police have been an army occupying their own country."

The attempt to establish a new justice system following the 1994 arrival of U.S. troops was focused primarily on separating the police from the army. With Aristide returned to the presidency on October 15, 1994, the old military was initially allowed to remain in power. However, when Aristide announced layoffs in December and there was resistance, he immediately announced the army's dissolution, against the wishes of the United States. The subsequent UN (MINUHA) mission initially led by an American, Daniel Schroeder, was ordered by President Aristide to demobilize the Haitian officer corps. The decision came after rioting at military headquarters by soldiers demanding their paychecks led to four deaths. Aristide considered the situation tantamount to mutiny, and simply considered the army insubordinate or inept. The National Haitian Police will be more difficult to develop, since training a recruit in a new force in a few months and a justice system in a year seems unrealistic. An interim police force, composed of former army officers, which had also included the police, was used until a new national police force was trained and replaced it, beginning in 1995. Haiti's demilitarization plan has succeeded in the best way imaginable, by eliminating a hierarchical army that had been rich in generals, intrigue, corruption, and insubordination. The United States withdrew in late March 1995, and the UN was present until 2000, eventually focusing on infrastructure and rule of law programs.

Police Profile

Background

The new National Civil Police (PNC) formally came into existence in 1996 with 6,000 members envisioned, although the number was about 4,000 by 2003. It was not simply the retraining of the same corrupt military established by the United States in 1915–1934, which had replaced the army established by Touissant L'Ouverture during the Revolution. The PNC was chosen to a significant extent on the basis of loyalty to Aristide alone, rather than merit. Among Aristide, initial appointments included known criminals or army personnel, such as Lt. Col. Pierre Neptune, twice Aristide's Port-au-Prince Police Chief; Lt. Col. Pierre Cherubin, once Aristide's national security adviser; and Captain Richard Solomon, once Aristide's Director of the "Anti-Gang Investigations" unit. At the same time, 90% of criminals from the 1991–1994 coup regime and before, who are not rich enough to have escaped Haiti, were never arrested.

By any objective measure, U.S.-sponsored police reform did well in Panama and El Salvador, less well elsewhere, and least well in Haiti. Most commentators have concluded that this project has failed to move beyond establishing a force that is both effective in crime control and accountable for human rights protection. The consensus is that the force is corrupt and politicized, while foreign assistance was uncoordinated internally with the judiciary and penal agencies and externally with disparate foreign agencies. The long-term project had a short-term focus because of the lack of political consensus in Haiti, resulting from the lack of any government enjoying a consensus since 1997. After the initial introduction of an interim police force from 1994–1995, the new permanent force was established in 1996–1997 at a time when there was no functioning majority in parliament able to enact reforms, beyond the initial police law, which had been decreed several years before.

The impetus for such an ambitious project in Haiti came from the successful multilateral training for the national police force in El Salvador several years before the Haitian peace mission was established with Aristide's return to power on October 15, 1994. By comparison, the missing conditions in Haiti become apparent. El Salvador had a peace treaty, consensus, and the political will to establish an apolitical, professional police force over the long term. By merging a force with some experienced police officers from the previous agency with demobilized combatants from the FMLN guerrillas, the new Salvadoran police force included some experienced officers, as well as internal checks against abuse by dint of divided political allegiances. In Haiti, almost none of the new recruits came from the demobilized armed forces or the interim police force. While this reduced problems of legitimacy, it suffered from incompetence and leadership gaps. Haitian officers were promoted on the basis of initial performance and political loyalty, not a long-term track record.

Complaints and Discipline

In a country with few functional institutions, it has been difficult to make the police more effective and accountable than other institutions in the country, even if the police are well paid. The various countries involved in training the PNH made it more difficult to establish coherence in policing and with other criminal justice agencies because of their differing priorities and philosophies. The United States has been primarily interested in controlling drugs and capturing Haitian boat people, which the United States considers to be migrants, not refugees. Obtaining cooperation on these two scores initially, the United States was happy to cede political control to President Aristide in 1995–1996, even though that has led to promotions and assignments on the basis of political loyalty, not competence. Thus, the first head of the PNC was one of Aristide's bodyguards. While the French preached a centralized form of control, U.S. trainers endorsed decentralization of management with community policing emphasized. Meanwhile, it was difficult for Haitian officials to feel ownership of the PNC when foreign governments, along with the UN Mission in Haiti, were giving their own preferred version of the type of policing believed necessary.

The appointment of Calixte Delatour in October 2002 as Justice Minister, a man with a notorious Duvalierist past with paramilitary Macoute connections, has strained credulity of the Aristide presidency's commitment to equal justice. Instead of a reformer of the police and judicial processes, which might attract domestic and international support, the signal has been one of little interest in changing policing and other criminal justice activities along professional apolitical lines. This makes problematic the prospect of building police, judiciary, and penal institutions on the basis of long-term continuity with sufficient resources and support from the two constituencies that Haiti needs most: a loyal opposition and the international community.

In retrospect, it takes longer than five years (1995–2000) to establish an effective, new police force, such as was created in El Salvador. Nine small Haitian National Police forces effectively were created in the country's nine departments. The police command structure reflects orders from the president or his loyalists, as much as by professional officers. The lack of economic development has increased the temptation for police corruption. The lack of accounting controls and transparency has rendered the police force into just another instrument of political power and personal fiefdoms for private gain. The similarities between the former army and current police with organized crime are more remarkable in their similarities, even if the current methods are less autocratic and less threatening to the civilian government's survival. More alarming, the trend has been declining effectiveness. While some of the multilateral training and monitoring of police was well structured and implemented, the failure to prevent its politicization may be the consequence of the justified claim that the police is an instrument of national sovereignty and ought to be judged by the populace in holding the president and the government that he appoints accountable. Because the United States has been so divided over Aristide, it has never been willing to give him full authority over the police, and never gave him cause to believe that elements of the United States, in collaboration with paramilitary elements, are not plotting to undermine or remove him.

Another problem is the lack of judicial or penal institutions to manage the larger number of criminals apprehended by the new police force. Multilateral assistance to new police forces, such as in Bosnia and Haiti, have not used the "full triangle," as Jacques Paul Klein, the former UN administrator for its police mission in Bosnia, puts it. Haiti's prisons are stuffed with illegally detained prisoners, for whom human rights nongovernmental organizations could easily ask under habeas corpus why they have been charged. Adding to their numbers of criminals, who take advantage of the opening society under democratization, are many individuals linked to the opposition, whom the Aristide presidency has sought to intimidate with trumped-up charges.

Bernard Miyet, UN Undersecretary-General for Peacekeeping Operations, called the police not just an appendix to peacekeeping operations, but rather an increasingly crucial tool for peace building and institution building. Yet, in Haiti like Bosnia, East Timor, Kosovo, and other peace-building missions, "the absence of a functioning judicial system has severely hindered the ability of the Haitian Police to carry out its tasks." Most of the assistance for the judiciary was provided by U.S. Agency for International Development, and was far less extensive than what the United States financed and the UN and OAS provided to the new National Police. The freeze on aid funding has limited the ability to assist the police in developing its professional competence and autonomy, as well as of monitoring human rights and helping justices of the peace to improve the capabilities of the Haitian judiciary. This resulted from the selfishness of Haitian political society, both Aristide's Fanmi Lavalas party and Gerard Pierre Charles's Democratic Convergence, to put their own interests aside for the sake of the country. The failure to use Haitian NGOs in the planning process of the UN and OAS missions has also inhibited the country's ability to sustain the changes sought throughout both police and judicial institutions.

The establishment of a corrupt and partisan police force has resulted in massive increases in drug trafficking and repression of opposition demonstrations with impunity. Inadequate police presence in rural areas has contributed to the formation of local vigilante groups and poorly trained private security agencies who operate with impunity. Former members of the armed forces, disbanded in 1995, also began to become more active in their opposition to Aristide in 2001, raising fears of a coup attempt. The PNC has been unwilling and unable to stop the development of new paramilitary forces. While there were secret arrests of two police superintendents who were involved in drug trafficking in late 2002, the vast majority of corrupt police officers have operated with impunity. While some opposition protests occur, the Aristide government has been implicated in violent disruptions with police collaboration. While there is much more freedom than under the long periods of dictatorial rule, the opposition does not trust the police to contain violence.

For example, in 2002, Amnesty International criticized the police and judiciary for failing to guarantee security and justice. After armed men attacked police targets in an apparent coup attempt in July 2001, forty-one people were arrested and then released without being charged. Amnesty International admits that the situation is not as bad as it was in the years immediately following the ousting of Aristide in the 1991 coup, but there is a serious danger that all the progress made since his return in 1994 may quickly be undone.

Human rights activists are also concerned about "zero tolerance" policing encouraged by Aristide in a speech in 2001. Aristide encouraged police officers to bypass the courts in pursuing justice for petty offenders, and police claim that street crime has dropped 60%. However, there is also evidence that the new policy has sparked a wave of at least twenty-seven vigilante killings and given free reign to a police force already accused of killing more than 150 without cause. The murder of radio journalist Brignol Lindor in December 2001 was alleged to have resulted from this "zero tolerance" policy, as he and others were named on the radio as potential targets. In the same month, a radio director was stoned and hacked to death by government supporters in the town of Petit-Goave after he broadcast an interview with local opposition leaders. Although authorities identified the alleged assassins, police refused to execute arrest warrants.

An apparent coup attempt on December 17, 2001 left ten people dead after gunmen attacked the national palace. Police retook control and violent reprisals were launched on opposition targets. Human rights groups protested the barbaric suppression of the revolt, which many suspect was an excuse to kill or intimidate opposition leaders as well as those with knowledge of the April 2001 murder of independent journalist Jean Dominique. Following international criticism, the government attempted to crack down on the leaders of the December violence, notably Amiot Métayer. Métayer, who claims that his gangs were armed by the government, was arrested in September 2002, sparking riots that culminated with him being broken out of jail in Gonnaives, along with 158 other prisoners, following a bulldozer attack. In response, the government stepped up its intimidation. Radio Kiskeya, an independent radio station based in Haiti's capital, stopped broadcasting following threats, and riot police halted a concert by musicians who played a song viewed as critical of President Aristide.

In a final example, in July 2003, Jean-Robert Faveur, Haiti's third national chief of police in as many months, walked into the Dominican Republic and boarded a plane to south Florida, after only two weeks into the job. International observers had hoped that the career officer would reform Haiti's struggling police force. Faveur presented pages of letters and evidence detailing how President Jean-Bertrand Aristide and aides allegedly tried to run the police from the National Palace. They usurped so many of his functions, Faveur charged, that he hardly had more authority than a patrol officer. Faveur said that he was ordered by a Haitian congressman to hire eighteen armed men as officers, even though they lacked police academy training.

Various proposals to end Haiti's ongoing political crisis since 1987 have been based on proposals that have always included protocols on civil disarmament and professionalization of the police, as well as establishing a professional electoral commission. Until the Haitian government fields a professional police force of its own that is not corrupt at its core, Haiti will continue to fail at building democratic institutions and economic development. The establishment of a national police force after Aristide effectively ended the army has had some positive consequences, but the costs seemed to have outweighed their benefits—a relationship that is intolerable in a country where incomes have been declining for over a decade and where the relatively large amounts of foreign aid have made few positive differences. The effect has been humane, but has also propped up an electoral authoritarian regime. The elimination of the army and the establishment of a civilian police force have reduced the chances of another coup and reduced political repression, but the police are corrupt and politicized. There is no comparable investment in the more difficult task of developing a criminal justice system for prosecution and punishment.

HENRY F. CAREY

Bibliography

Kelly, Raymond "Learning When to Wear Gloves," *New York Times*, April 2, 1995, p. 1.

Stromsem, Janice M., and Joseph Trinccellito, "Peacebuilding in Haiti: Lessons Learned in Building the Haitian National Police." Paper presented at seminar, International Peace Academy, New York, January 23–24, 2002.

UN Development Programme. "Lessons Learned: Exercise Undertaken by the Emergency Response Division." 2001. Available at: www.undp.org.

Ziegler, Melissa, and Rachel Nield. *From Peace to Governance: Police Reform and the International Community*. Washington, DC: Washington Office on Latin America, 2002.

HONDURAS

Background Material

Honduras is located in Central America, with Guatemala to the west, El Salvador to the south, and Nicaragua to the east. It has a long northern coastline on the Caribbean Sea, and a short southern coastline on the Pacific Ocean. It has an area of 112,100 square kilometers (43,270 square miles), about the size of the U.S. state of Louisiana.

The current population is 6.7 million, and the growth rate is 2.39%. About 90% of the people are mestizo, a mix of indigenous and Europeans, and about 7% are indigenous, mainly from the Mosquita group, living primarily in the north. The Afro-Honduran community, called the Garifuna, makes up about 2% of the population and also lives primarily in the north. The remainder of the population is of Arab and European descent. The majority religion is Roman Catholic, although there is a growing Protestant minority. Six years of education are compulsory, with 88% overall attendance, but just 31% at the junior high level. The literacy rate is 81%. The infant mortality rate is 34 per 1,000, and life expectancy is 71.8 years.

The capital and largest city is Tegucigalpa, with 1,150,000 residents. The second biggest city is San Pedro Sula, with a population between 800,000 and 900,000, and the third biggest city is La Cebia on the Caribbean Coast, with approximately 90,000 people. Most of the country is mountainous, and the southern and northern coastal areas are tropical.

Honduras is one of the poorest countries in Latin America, with a 2003 GDP of US$6.9 billion and per capita GPP of just US$958. The economy, whose growth rate is 3.2%, is based primarily on agriculture, minerals, and other raw materials. Agricultural exports, comprising 11% of GDP, include coffee, bananas, shrimp, lobster, sugar, fruits, grains, and livestock. Principal manufacturing exports, which contribute 18% of GDP, are textiles, apparel, cement, wood products, cigars, and foodstuffs. Of the 2.3 million-strong labor force, 42.2% work in services, particularly in factories of multinational companies, 35.9% in natural resources and agriculture, 16.3% in manufacturing, and 5.6% in construction and housing. Unemployment in 2003 was 27.5%, and well over 55% of the population is below the poverty line. Inequality is also high: the poorest 10% of households consume only 0.6% of income and the highest 10% consume nearly 43%.

Contextual Features

The Honduran legal system is based on civil law, with many common law features being introduced. Civil procedures, which continue to be based on written documents, are comprised of summary, ordinary, and executive proceedings, along with injunctions and prejudicial actions. Criminal law has undergone more changes in the modern era than have civil or commercial law, but remains centered on civil law procedures. The investigative police (DGIC: Dirección Nacional de Investigación) detain and investigate criminal suspects for twenty-four hours, but can ask the judge in charge of the case (the *juzgado*) to extend the period of investigation for up to six days. In areas of the country without DGIC detention facilities, the National Preventive Police (PNP: Policía Nacional Preventiva, or simply Policía Nacional) may hold defendants instead. If the defendant cannot afford a lawyer, the *juzgado* can assign a court-appointed attorney (*abogado de oficio*). Only in some minor cases can the *juzgado* grant bail, and there is no kind of "plea bargaining." When the DGIC completes an investigation, the juzgado determines whether there is sufficient evidence for a trial. The remainder of the case is divided into the "discovery" phase and the trial. The discovery phase follows the investigation and is comprised of further investigation by the DGIC, the *juzgado*, the defendant's attorney, the prosecutor (*fiscal*), and the accuser's attorney. Although the discovery period is legally limited to thirty days, it usually takes much longer, often because judges, lawyers and police deviate from established procedures. The trial begins when the discovery period concludes. Although the courts are now adopting a more efficient system of oral arguments, they still rely on a series of written submissions to the *juzgado* based on information obtained during the discovery. Although there are time limits on trials, the constant backlog of cases and lack of judicial personnel causes them to last months and often years. The *juzgado*'s sentence of "guilty" or "not guilty" is sent to the Court of Appeals (Corte de Apelaciones) for ratification. The prosecutor can appeal a "not guilty" ruling, and the defendant can appeal a "guilty" verdict at the Appeal Court. With no time deadlines for these steps, delays are frequent.

This system has been overhauled by a new penal process code that came into effect in March 2002. The new code created oral trails, enhanced the powers of the prosecutor, alternative resolution mechanisms like mediation, and established new courts at the investigation and sentencing stages, such as the Juez de Ejecución to oversee pretrial procedures. This new code has already sped up the criminal justice process. But many officials assert that the new code is being adopted without adequate training, causing a continuation of practices such as mass raids and extended preventive detention. Under the new code, judges must have scientific evidence to move forward, but since such evidence is often lacking, many detainees are released. This has antagonized the government and the police, who often respond with mistreatment and forced confessions. The Human Rights Commission estimates that over 80% of detainees are beaten.

Honduras has one of Latin America's highest crime rates, and Tegucigalpa is one of the region's most crime-ridden cities. For every 100,000 habitants, according to the most reliable statistics, per year there are 154.2 homicides, 44.10 assaults, 5.12 robberies and violent thefts, and 1.17 rapes (Interpol 1998). The main morgues in Tegucigalpa and San Pedro Sula reported that 2,205 persons were killed in those two cities in 2002, a number universally regarded as a major underestimate. In the first six months of 2003, there were 1,305 killings in San Pedro Sula, but only 3% of cases reached the courts (*La Prensa*, San Pedro Sula, July 21, 2003). The police estimate that about a third of violent crimes are committed by the country's youth gangs, which together have between 60,000 and 70,000 members, collaborators, and sympathizers—about 12% of whom are criminally violent. The few state institutions for rehabilitation serve only about 100 gang members (*La Prensa*, San Pedro Sula, July 17, 2003).

Structure and Role of Courts

The judiciary is headed by the Supreme Court of Justice (Corte Suprema de Justicia), whose thirteen judges are elected for seven-year terms and handle both civil and criminal cases. Below the Supreme Courts are the Courts of Appeal, courts of first instance at the level of each of the country's eighteen regional departments, and justices of the peace at municipal level. The judicial council selects and appoints most judges and judicial personnel. There are also a range of specialized courts in the following legal areas: penal, family, children and adolescence, housing and rent, administration, and labor. In 2002, Honduras had 550 judges (8.2 per 100,000 inhabitants), 435 courts, 209 public defenders (3.1 per 100,000 inhabitants) and 364 public prosecutors (5.4 per 100,000 inhabitants). That year, the judiciary received 7.16% of the annual fiscal budget, equivalent to 1.97% of GDP.

Correction System Structure and Role

The penal system is made up of twenty-four prisons, holding nearly 13,000 prisoners—twice the system's intended capacity and well over double the 1992 prison population of 5,717. Because of delays in the courts, well over 90% of these prisoners wait nearly two years for trial. Health and food are inadequate, with just 46 cents allocated per prisoner for both (author interview, Mauricio Guardado, Administrative Director of the Centro Penal of San Pedro Sula, March 1, 2004). Basic rules—such as the new penal code's provision that prisoners must be separated by crime and be sentenced within 4.5 years—are largely unenforced. The few months of training given to prison personnel have left them unprepared for the violence and killings that have swept through most facilities. In April 2002, for example, sixty-eight inmates were killed in a fire at the El Porvenir agricultural penal colony on the Caribbean coast, a 300-inmate-capacity facility that held 500 prisoners. It appears that officials shot at prisoners fleeing the fire, only days after the sudden transfer to the prison of members from one gang without notification of the small twenty-person staff—even though members of the rival gang were being held there. The government also operates three juvenile detention centers, which, like the prisons, are characterized by poor conditions and inadequate services.

Police Profile

Background

The National Police of Honduras was founded in 15 January 1882. Beginning in the early 1960s, it was directed along with the military by the National Defense Secretary. With the onset of democratization in the 1990s, though, the force began to be civilianized and reformed. In 1996, a constitutional reform officially transferred public security authority from the armed forces to a newly created civilian police force, with standards and structures similar to those that peace accords introduced to neighboring countries. The following year, a new Police Law and Organic Police Law were enacted, which included a new internal affairs unit to increase accountability.

Demographic

As of 2002, there were 6,663 police officers, which corresponds to a ratio of 92.7 per 100,000 inhabitants. The police had an additional 567 administrative, technical, and service personnel, bringing the total to 7,230 (Rivera 2002: 6). But just 397 of all police officers, under 6% of the total, were women, and only 15 of those women were officers.

Organizational Description

The police are all directed by the national Security Secretariat, which was established in 1997. The secretariat is divided into the Subsecretariat of Prevention and the Subsecretariat of Investigation. Under the Prevention Subsecretariat is the, the Police Education Unit (DGEP, *Dirección General de Educación Policial*), and the Office of Special Preventative Services (DGSEP), and the National Preventive Police (PNP, *Policía Nacional Preventiva*). The PNP is the largest police body. Headed by the Comisionado General, the Preventive Police has four major ranks. The top rank is the Executive, followed by the ranks of Investigation, Basic, Cadets, and Auxiliary. The Investigative Subsecretariat is divided into the Investigative Police, the DGIC, and the General Office of Special Investigative Services. The annual police budget is approximately $35 million, the majority of which goes to the PNP. There is also a Transit Police unit and a special women's unit, the Feminine Auxiliary Police (Policía Auxiliar Femenina), which was formed in 1977. The military has also become increasingly involved in policing, mainly with sweeps of gang-controlled areas and repression of prison riots, as well as with combined military-police units to fight international crimes like drug trafficking.

There are also several police oversight and accountability agencies. The principal ones are the National Council of Interior Security (CONASIN, Consejo Nacional de Seguridad Interior) and the Internal Affairs Unit (UAI, Unidad de Asuntos Internos). In 1996, the Public Ministry (Ministerio Público), the country's prosecutorial office, created the office of Human Rights Inspector within the DGIC to monitor the behavior of its agents, reporting to the Attorney General, who directs the Ministry, as well as to the agency's human rights section. The Security Secretariat's Office of Professional Responsibility (OPR) investigates allegations of torture and abuse, and can recommend sanctions against police agents found guilty of such abuses, but only the accused officer's immediate superior can actually punish them. The OPR, accused by the Public Ministry and human rights groups for not pushing for more objective investigations of police wrongdoing, was supposed to be eliminated under the new police law, but still continues to exist. The UAI, meanwhile, has been debilitated by a weak structure, deficient resources, and unclear regulations. But these agencies have been restricted after the Security Secretariat was formed and took control over nearly all police agencies. There has been a sharp drop in internal investigations of wrongdoing in the DGIC after Congress moved it from the Public Ministry to the new Secretariat, for example, and little follow-up on accusations brought by CONASIN. According to one analyst, the creation of the Security Secretariat began a "process of counter-reform and deterioration of the police ... characterized by halting the process of purging of corrupt officers

and those involved in right violations and in death squads." In addition, the Security Minister "strengthened the Preventive Police and weakened the Investigation Police, which also halted the purge" (*El Heraldo*, October 8, 2002).

Functions

The police are involved in nearly every aspect of public order and the criminal justice process, including crime prevention, support for the judiciary, prison security and transport, and social services such as aid for children and youth. The PNP patrols the streets and carries out arrests. The DGIC, which has about 570 officials, conducts criminal investigations.

Investigation is generally poor, however, since the DGIC lacks sufficient resources and reliable statistics, with no centralized information or network of information. The DGIC is also encumbered by rivalry with an ineffective PNP. Many PNP officers intimidate witnesses, inadequately protect crime scenes, and conduct their own parallel investigations, even though they have practically no investigative background. As a result of these deficiencies, officials estimate, about 90% of all serious crimes are not investigated.

With nearly 2,000 new officers joining the police since 2002, in some areas the number of police officers has risen by up to 80%. But the police presence varies widely within the country. The DGIC has no presence in many areas, and the PNP does not function in over 50 of the country's 299 municipalities. There is a chronic lack of personnel, as a result, such as in the high-crime San Pedro Sula neighborhood of Choloma, which has just ten officers and one permanent vehicle for 70,000 people. Most small municipalities also lack an adequate number of prosecutors, public defenders, and judges, human rights commission officials, and nongovernmental organization (NGO) representatives. Rural Yoro state, for example, had just three prosecutors to handle forty-seven killings in 2003. Many police functions are also being shared with local security committees, which mayors may create and fund themselves. Nearly 600 committees have been formed throughout the country, but still lack a clear and uniform national legal status. Police officers lack professional security or decent wages. The average salary of US$225 per month is inadequate for a middle-class lifestyle, and many officers live up to eight hours of travel time from their station, often in shifts from 7:00 a.m. to 12:00 midnight with only every other weekend free.

Despite major reforms, police abuse continues to be a major problem. Members of the security forces are suspected of direct involvement in many of the estimated 1,600 extrajudicial and summary killings of youth and children from 1998 to 2003 (Amnesty International 2003). According to press reports and the NGO Casa Alianza, 549 people aged twenty-three and younger were killed in 2002, and 557 in 2003, often with AK-47 machine guns. Of these killings, 61% have not been adequately investigated, and 39% of cases had evidence of police responsibility (*La Prensa*, Tegucigalpa, July 17, 2003). In 2002, no perpetrator was identified in 60% to 70% of the killings, and gangs were suspected in 15% to 20% of them. Youth living on the street uniformly complain of continual attacks (author interviews, Tegucigalpa street youth, July 16, 2003), and residents of most poor neighborhoods report unmarked grey vans roaming basketball courts and other areas where youth congregate.

As the principal police accountable, the UAI took the initiative in investigating these deaths. UAI director María Luisa Borjas documented and compiled a list of apparent victims of police killings (author interview, María Luisa Borjas, July 18, 2003), and in September 2002 denounced the participation of members of the Security Ministry and National Police in at least twenty extrajudicial executions of children and youth. Soon afterward, her staff was reduced, and, two months later, she was suspended, allegedly for having failed to present proof of her claims, and legal claims were filed against her. But continuing outside attention on youth killings led the government to create the Commission on Summary Executions, while the Security Ministry set up a Special Investigative Unit to investigate killings of youth and children. Prosecutors also investigate police wrongdoing, but since they generally lack institutional, political, and legal power, there has been little or no progress in bringing charges in most of the youth killings. The Human Rights Prosecutor complains that any investigation into the police faces constant delay and obstruction (author interview, Aída Estella Romero, July 22, 2003), while the prosecutor for youth issues (Fiscal de la Niñez) asserts that "there are neither human nor logistical resources" to handle "the enormous quantity   of cases" (author interview, Eduardo Villanueva, July 15, 2003).

Training

The Organic Police Law gave the DGEP the authority to define the objectives, strategies, and professional development policies of the police at each level. There are two main training academies. The highest-level officers train at the National Police Academy (ANAPO, Academía Nacional de Policía), formed in 1976, where they receive forensic and other investigation training for a period of three years. ANAPO has inadequate resources, however, with only a barely functioning forensics laboratory. Most lower-ranking street officers attend the Center for Police Instruction (CIP, Centro de Instrucción Policial), which was formed in 1982. CIP cadets receive training in transit accidents, criminal investigation, special police operations, prison control, and tourism. But the six months of training lack adequate legal or sociological education, and many police remain functionally illiterate even after being admitted to the PNP. The other training academies are the Training School of Police Officials (ECOP, *Escuela de Capacitación de Oficiales de Policía*), founded in 1984, and the Superior Institute of Police Studies (ISEP, *Instituto Superior de Estudios Policial*), created in 1996, from which police obtain advanced degrees in areas such as police strategy, police operations, and criminal investigation.

Police Public Projects

Honduras is in the process of introducing manynew crime prevention programs, most of which follow two different and often contradictory approaches. On the one hand, many new laws empower citizens to fight crime and participate in crime-fighting policy. The most ambitious of these is the 2002 Safer Communities (Comunidad Más Segura) community policing program, based on preventive strategies such as installing street lights, having regular community meetings, and stopping domestic violence. It operates in thirty of the country's most crime-ridden areas, with marked reductions in homicides, robberies, and domestic violence. In the San Pedro Sula barrio of Choloma, for example, well-attended community policing committees meet every fifteen days. Choloma had nine murders in January 2002, but in the first four months of 2003, and only four per month and seventeen robberies in January 2002, but none at all in the first four months of 2003 ("Presidente Maduro inaugura programa 'Comunidad Segura' en Choloma, Cortés," May 3, 2003, *www.casapresidencial.hn/seguridad*). There has been resistance by other police toward the program (author interview, Carlos Chincilla, July 22, 2003), but more serious is abuse by participating citizens, including vigilante killings of suspected criminals. Prosecutors and human rights commissioners, in fact, estimate that there have been tens of thousands of unreported vigilante attacks since 2002 (author interviews: Prosecutor Eduardo Villanueva, July 15, 2003; Prosecutor Walter Menjivar Mendoza, February 26, 2004; northern regional human rights commissioner Victor Parelló, February 20, 2004). In the poor neighborhood of Confite, the main testing ground in the La Ceiba region of community policing, the head of the local group says that it is sometimes used as a front to attack local delinquents (author interview, Céleo Santo Sosa, February 25, 2004).

In part to support community policing, local commissioners are being given more leeway to adopt policing to their areas, such as declaring curfews. In neighborhoods plagued by powerful narco traffickers, for example, officers now alternate shift schedules and visit every single house to avoid having anyone targeted as cooperating with the police. Another innovative program is to provide street lighting for the many urban neighborhoods darkened by neglect, vandalism, and robbery of lights, particularly in the areas with heavy gang membership. These efforts have been funded and organized by Congress, the National Company of Electric Energy (ENEE, Empresa Nacional de Energía Eléctrica), and the Central America Bank of Economic Integration, with many residents providing metal cages for protection of individual lights. In San Pedro Sula, it has led to the repair of nearly 30,000 of the city's 57,000 street lights (*La Prensa*, San Pedro Sula, July 22, 2003).

On the other hand, the National Party government of President Ricardo Maduro is enacting tough "iron fist" policies to clamp down on crime. The focus of his policy is youth gangs (*maras*), who even police acknowledge commit less than a third of all crimes, but are blamed for almost all of them. New "social control" laws are being introduced to increase police power on the street. The 2002 Law of Police and Social Coexistence (Ley de Convivencia Social), for instance, allows the police to "control" the people in any given area in order to fight crime and to detain "vagabonds," that is, people who lack an honest means of living or are suspected of having illicit purposes in the neighborhood in which they are found. More drastic and constitutionally questionable is the Law of Illicit Association, an August 2003 amendment to the penal code that punishes mere membership in a gang with a nine- to twelve-year prison term. In two of the country's main prisons, about 40% of gang members are now incarcerated under 322 (author interviews: warden,

officials, and prisoners in the Centro Penal de La Ceiba, February 24, 2004, and of the Centro Penal of San Pedro Sula, March 1, 2004). Many gang members now shun the trademarks of gang membership – particularly tattoos and particular clothing styles, which, in more and more cases, is leading prosecutors and judges to declare a lack of the higher level of proof required for conviction under the penal code. Such conflicts between new laws and legal guarantees has led government officials, including Security Minister Óscar Álvarez (author interview, July 18, 2003), to criticize the new penal process code as being ineffective against violent crime in Honduras.

Police Use of Firearms

Regulations on the use of force are determined by four sources: the Penal Process Code, the Organic Police Law, the Law of Peace and Citizen Existence, and United Nations norms. These laws state that the police may use firearms when nonviolent means have failed, they follow a judge's orders, to prevent imminent or actual commission of crimes, to ensure the capture of a suspect, to overcome resistance of someone resisting legitimate police order, to avoid worse public dangers, to defend others from physical or psychological harm, and to maintain or restore public order.

Terrorism and International Cooperation

Although there are no known terrorist groups operating in or moving through Honduras, the U.S. government has stepped up funding to bolster the government's ability to fight terrorism, such as through the State Department's International Military Education and Training (IMET). Such funding is based on long-standing suspicion that Honduras may become a refuge or recruitment ground for international terrorists. In August 2003, in fact, Honduras tightened security at foreign embassies and declared a national terrorism alert after receiving information that Al Qaeda was trying to recruit Hondurans to attack embassies of the United States, Britain, Spain, and El Salvador. Some Hondurans reportedly were offered money to carry out attacks, while others were approached on ideological grounds. The Security Ministry said a Saudi-born terrorism suspect sought by the United States was spotted in July 2004 at a Tegucigalpa Internet cafe.

The primary international threat in Honduras, though, derives from a high level of penetration of its territory and institutions by international drug traffickers. Cartels based in Colombia have use Honduran territory, particularly the sparsely populated northeast coastal areas, as a transit route to North America. As a result, most of Honduran international cooperation on policing is centered on U.S. funds, which have risen from approximately $1.17 million in 2001 to an estimated $3.62 million in 2004, for police and military antinarcotics operations. In 2003, Honduras received $170,000 in foreign military financing, and $620,000 from Section 1004 Counterdrug (counternarcotics program of the Defense Department), and received part of the $2.75 million earmarked for Central America for international narcotics control. Between fiscal years 2000 and 2003, Honduras also received $1.93 million from the U.S. International Criminal Investigative Training Assistance Program. Since the mid-1990s, Honduran military and police personnel have also received training from the School of the Americas, the U.S. Army training school for Latin American military officers; the Navy Small Craft and Technical Training School, the U.S. Navy's training school for Latin American militaries; the Inter-American Air Forces Academy; and the Center for Hemispheric Defense Studies, a Defense Department initiative to improve civilian defense planning and management (Center for International Policy).

Honduras also receives aid from European and Asian countries, but primarily in development assistance. Germany has provided about EUR 300 million in bilateral financial and technical cooperation, while Japan, Sweden, and Spain also provide funds. Some specific programs are also funded by other countries; for instance, the Republic of China (Taiwan) has bought many of the Honduran police force's cars.

Finally, the Inter-American Development Bank approved a loan agreement in November 2002 to support Honduras's new penal process code by helping train personnel in the Public Ministry, the public defender's office (Defensoría Pública), and the Court Inspector's office (Inspectoría de Tribunales), and by reducing the backlog of cases through defining administrative and organizational methodologies for court offices and advancing automation of all court offices, police investigations offices and prosecutor and public defender offices, leading to an operating system that allows judicial operators to process case files via e-mail. The World Bank, the U.S. Agency for International Development, and the Japan International Cooperation Agency also have supported judicial reform.

Police Education, Research, and Publications

Leading Researchers, Authors, Reports, and Columnists

Honduran police specialists work in both governmental and nongovernmental organizations. Casa Alianza, the NGO that works with youth, publishes regular reports on police activity, and the director of its Legal Aid program, José Gustavo Zelaya, writes frequently on policing. The other NGO that works extensively with youth is a San Pedro Sula organization called Honduras Youth Forward—Together We Advance (JHA–JA, Jóvenes Hondureños Adelante—Juntos Avancemos). Its director, Ernesto Bardales, writes extensively on youth and policing. The Center for the Prevention, Treatment and Rehabilitation of Torture Victims and their Families (CPTRT, Centro de Prevención, Tratamiento y Rehabilitación de las Víctimas de la Tortura y sus Familiares) is a well-established NGO with regular reports on police abuse. Its executive director, Juan Almendarez, is a respected rights activist. Another organization working on policing is the Committee for the Defense of Human Rights of Honduras (CODEH, Comité para la Defensa de los Derechos Humanos de Honduras), and its president, Andrés Pavón, is active in the monitoring of police activity.

Academic sources on policing in Honduras include the Autonomous National University and Documentation Center of Honduras (CEDOH, Centro de Documentación de Honduras). Leticia Salomón, a leading Honduran expert on the country's police, is affiliated with CEDOH. The National Library of Honduras and the Biblioteca Nacional de Honduras also have written collections on police history, policy, and operations.

Within the government, one of the major sources of publications on criminal justice is the Supreme Court's Electronic Center of Documentation and Judicial Information. It writes annual and other regular reports on the functioning of the criminal justice system. The Security Commission of Congress also publishes reports. The Inter-Institutional Commission of Penal Justice also publishes work on policing, such as in its *Information Bulletin*. But the biggest source of policing publications comes from Ramón Custodio López, head of the National Commission of Human Rights Protection.

Funding for Police Research

The extent and sources of funding for research on police come from international NGOs. The

Washington Office on Latin America has supported research on policing in Honduras, such as the project Citizen Security and Civil Society in Central America, which provided funds to Honduran NGOs to carry out research. European governments have also supported Honduran NGOs working on police reform. The Danish International Development Agency (DANIDA), for example, has funded several of the CPTRT's studies on policing.

Leading police journals, magazines, and newsletters include *Justicia Penal*, published by the Technical Penal Reform Unit (UTR, Unidad Técnica de Reforma Penal) of the Supreme Court. Major police publications include many pamphlets on citizen security, such as "Vigilancia de Vencinadrio" (Neighborhood Security), which informs residents about measures that they can take to protect their own areas.

Police-related websites include a section of the Presidential Palace website, *www.casapresidencial. hn/seguridad/index.php*, which has crime news and updates on security policies. The Secretariat of Government and Justice (Gobernación y Justicia), which functions as the country's Interior Ministry, also has information on security issues. Its website is *www.gobernacion.gob.hn*. The Human Rights Commission (Comisionado Nacional de los Derechos Humanos), at *www.conadeh.hn*, also reports on security developments, as well as criticisms of police activity. The National Institute of Statistics (INE, Instituto Nacional de Estadística) has information on social conditions and state services. Finally, Congress has legal updates and legislative analysis. Many of its documents are placed on the congressional website, *www.congreso.gob.hn/principal3.asp*.

MARK UNGAR

Further Reading

Amnesty International. *Honduras: Zero Tolerance ... For Impunity: Extrajudicial Executions of Children and Youths since 1998*. New York: Amnesty International, 2003.

Castellanos, Julieta. "El Tortuoso Camino de la Reforma Policial." *El Heraldo*, October 8, 2002.

Center for International Policy, et al. *Just the Facts: A Civilian's Guide to U.S. Defense and Security Assistance to Latin America and the Caribbean.*. Available at: www. ciponline.org/facts/ho.htm.

Interpol. International Crime Statistics. Report on Justice Center of the Americas. Available at: www.cejamericas. org.

Inestroza M., Jesús Evelio. *Historia de la Policía Nacional de Honduras*. Tegucigalpa: Ediciones Nai, 2002.

La Prensa, February 26, 2004, p. 14, "Álvarez molesto con fiscalía de Derechos Humanos."

La Prensa, July 17, 2003, p. 18, "'Reformas contra maras es cacería de brujas'."

La Prensa, July 17, 2003, p. 10, "Garzón: 'Espeluznante situación de derechos humanos en Honduras."

La Prensa, July 21, 2003, p. 70, "No hay investigación policial."

La Prensa, July 22, 2003, p. 41, "Luz contra la inseguridad."

Meza, Víctor, et al. *Corrupción y Transparencia en Honduras*. Tegucigalpa: Centro de Documentación de Honduras, 2002.

Neild, Rachel. "Sustaining Reform: Democratic Policing in Central America." In *Citizen Security Monitor*. Washington, DC: Washington Office on Latin America, October 2002.

Rivera, Morelia. "Incorporación del Enfoque de Género en la Modernización de la Policía Preventiva de Honduras." Paper presented at Centroamericana: Reducción de Pobreza, Gobernabilidad Democrática y Equidad de Género Conference, Managua, Nicaragua, August 2002.

Romero, Ramón, and Leticia Salomón. *La Reforma Judicial*. Tegucigalpa: Centro de Documentación de Honduras, 2000.

Washington Office on Latin America (WOLA). *Demilitarizing Public Order: The International Community, Police Reform and Human Rights in Central America and Haiti*. Washington, DC: WOLA, 1995.

HUNGARY

Background Material

Hungarian history is summed up in one word: invasion. Even the Hungarians invaded Hungary, after the Romans and Huns, and before the Turks, Austrians, Germans, and Soviets. The Hungarians remained, while other cultures came and went from all points of the compass. So, Hungarian history is easily divided into different periods.

A devastating but short-lived Mongol invasion in 1241—the invaders went home on the news of the death of the Great Khan a year later—left much of Hungary in need of drastic reconstruction. Furthermore, the Arpad Dynasty ended in 1301, and allowed for a period of foreign rulers. Charles Robert of Anjou, Louis the Great, Sigismund of Luxemburg, and the Turks were a raising threat to Europe for several centuries until they were defeated by a powerful Hungarian lord, Janos Hunyadi, at Belgrade in 1456. The Turks were gradually forced out of Hungary by the turn of the eighteenth century.

The eighteenth century is marked by the Germanization of Hungary. The Austro-Hungarian Empire allied itself with the Germans during World War I. With the defeat of Germany in the west, and the end of the monarchies in Austria and Russia, Hungary was in tatters. It declared itself a republic in November 1918.

Huge domestic problems after the war led to the brief tenure of a Republic of Councils, which was forced to stand down a year later due to foreign pressure. Romanian troops occupied Budapest. The rightwing Admiral Miklos Horthy formed a counterrevolutionary army, which instigated a reign of terror against communist sympathizers. For all its twenty-five-year rule, the Horthy administration is best remembered for the signing of the Treaty of Trianon in 1920. Hungary ceded a third of its people and more than two-thirds of its territory to neighbouring countries. The presence of large Hungarian minorities in Slovakia, Serbia, and Romania is still a concern. The regaining of the lost territories took preference over more pressing domestic affairs.

As World War II approached, Hungary regained some of its lost territory through its pro-Nazi policy. Terrible Hungarian losses at Stalingrad and forced labour at home caused Horthy to try and declare neutrality. The Germans invaded Hungary in March 1944. When Horthy tried to pull out again, and with Soviet troops crossing the border, Germany set up the fascist Arrow Cross party.

With the fall of the Horthy regime, an even greater reign of terror ensued against Jews and Gypsies. The Red Army blockaded Budapest and drove the Nazis out after a long and bloody siege. A provisional government was formed under Soviet auspices. Separate elections took place in November 1945, but the Soviet did not recognize the winning Smallholders' Party. The communists and Social Democrats joined to form the Workers' Party, which seized power in 1948.

Hungary suffered the misfortunes of a one-party system along Stalinist lines: five-year plans, terror tactics from a secret police, and the cult of personality. With Stalin's death in 1953, a more relaxed leadership took over under Imre Nagy. Nagy's return and a mass student demonstration led to the two-week uprising of 1956, when Soviet tanks put down the rebellion.

In 1989, Hungary had begun to dismantle the barbed wire around its border, allowing thousands of East Germans to seek refuge in the West. Protest at the resealing of the border led to mass demonstrations and the fall of the Berlin Wall. This was proclaimed live on national television on the thirty-third anniversary of the 1956 Uprising. An election was scheduled for the following spring.

All has not been rosy since the fall of communism, however. Certain elements remain from the old system, including an intimidating bureaucracy. In addition, the currency has yet to be fully convertible. In the 1990 elections, the conservative nationalist MDF beat the liberal SZDSZ. The government became increasingly unpopular as inflation reached 35% in 1992. The 1994 elections duly returned the MSZP to power. In the next election in 1998, the Hungarian bourgeois parties came to power. In 2002, again the MSZP and SZDSZ coalition won the election.

Since 1989, Hungary has made significant progress both in economic and political democratisation. Hungary joined NATO in 1999 and the European Union in 2004.

Hungary has a population of 10,374,822. The following race/ethnic groups reside in Hungary: Armenians, Bulgarians, Croatians, Greeks, Gypsies, Hungarians, Polish, Romanians, Russians, Serbians, Slovakians, Slovenians, and Ukrainians. Almost all Hungarians speak Hungarian; approximately 2% speak the Gypsy language. In terms of religion, the population breaks down as follows: Roman Catholic 67.5%, Calvinist 20%, Lutheran 5%, atheist and other 7.5% (Greek Catholic, Jewish, and Orthodox). The per capita income is US $5,280 (2003 estimate).

Contextual Features

The Parliament is the supreme body of state power and popular representation in the Republic of Hungary. Hungary's head of state is the president of the republic. The president of the republic is the commander-in-chief of the armed forces. Hungary also has a prime minister. The system of law is modern continental.

The number of crimes committed showed a steady increase after 1995, until in 1998 it exceeded all previous numbers, reaching 600,000. In the years following regime change, the number of reported and concluded crimes oscillated around 400,000. The last three years, the number of reported crimes has gone back down between

400,000 and 500,000 a year; in 2004, the total was 420,782.

The abovementioned changes required the transformation of the police as well. From an organization alienated from the citizens and standing above them and distanced from them, the police turned into a service working for the taxpayers.

Police Profile

Background

In general, the relevant literature dates the first appearance of an organization and persons carrying out independent policing activity to the 1848 war of independence. Up to World War I, different types of law enforcement organizations existed simultaneously: pluralistic law enforcement system, state and municipal police, centralized and decentralized forms, and organizations based on civilian and military principles. Before World War II, the dualistic model (police and gendarmerie) and centralized structures were preferred. From 1945 until 1989, based on the monistic model, a single state police force with a centralized militaristic structure was in place, acting under the direction of the Hungarian Socialist Labour Party.

Since 1989 a single, centralized police force has been in place, based on the monistic model.

Demographics

Authorized strength of the police force totals 38,500, compared to current strength (as of January 8, 2004) of 29,446. The force includes 4,708 women. There are no records available regarding ethnic representation.

A total of 17,780 are uniformed, 11,660 plainclothes, and 8,870 civilian. There is a single centralized state police force. Basic training consists of two years. Officer training is a three-year course, unless the candidate is a university or college graduate, in which case the training is one year.

Organizational Description

The Ministry of the Interior supervises the Hungarian National Police, National Border Guards Service, Counter Disaster Service, Counter Organized Crime Coordination Centre, and the Police College.

The Criminal Investigation Division maintains national supervision and professional control of regional CID units, and is responsible for detection and investigation of certain serious major crimes, or of crimes arousing great public interest, and for detection and arrest of perpetrators. It contributes to the development and execution of local crime-prevention programs, coordination of the search for missing children, DADA program, Telephone Witness Program.

The National Investigation Bureau oversees actions against drug-related crime, money laundering, vehicle crime, arms smuggling, and trafficking in human beings. It investigates certain white-collar crimes (bankruptcy fraud, violation of the rules of accounting, tax and social security fraud, related forgery of documents, and so on).

The International Law Enforcement Cooperation Centre coordinates cooperation with international law enforcement organizations, and the exchange of information.

The Republican Guard Regiment (RGR) is a special response unit. The tasks of RGR are enhanced protection of the President of the Republic and of the Prime Minister, guarding the Holy Crown and the Coronation Jewels, protection of cabinet members and other senior officials of the state, protection of diplomats, cooperation with foreign counterpart agencies, and during the reception of foreign delegations, physical security of designated facilities.

The Criminal Logistics Directorate focuses on logistic support of criminal investigations, special tasks related to covert intelligence gathering, and the Witness Protection Program. The Criminal Analysis, Evaluation, and Coordination Directorate is responsible for strategic and operational crime analysis, profiling, and analysis of telephone call lists.

Functions

The primary functions of the Hungarian police force are investigation, criminal intelligence, crime prevention, and traffic control. Police powers pertaining to the conduct of each function are arrest and detention. The Hungarian National Police has an administrative function, and handles criminal law as well.

Police Public Projects

Areas of police crime prevention include crime prevention counselling and development of recommendations for various target groups of the community and institutions that propagate the program Neighbours for One Another (aimed at increasing security of local communities), child and youth protection, DADA program, victim protection, property protection, and the Telephone Witness Program.

Areas of traffic enforcement are assistance for road traffic, air traffic enforcement, waterway traffic enforcement, and accident prevention.

Police Use of Firearms

Police use of firearms is regulated by the following laws and regulations:

- Act XX of 1949 on the Constitution of the Republic of Hungary
- Act XXXIV of 1994 on the Police
- Ministry of Interior Decree No. 3 of 1995 on the Service Regulation of the Police
- Act XLIII of 1996 on the Service Relations of Members of the Career Active Duty Personnel of Armed Organizations

Complaints and Discipline

Each Chief of Police once a year has to report in front of the Local Government Law Enforcement Committee. There is a Main Complaint Office at the National Police Headquarters, and Ombudsman available for citizens. The police are trained in internationally recognized human rights, at the Basic Police Schools in a six-hour course, and at the Police College in a thirty-two-hour curriculum.

The police sometimes come under criticism for human rights violations against the Gypsy populations.

Programs that exist to control and investigate human rights violations include the Parliamentary Ombudsman for Civil Rights, and the Parliamentary Ombudsman for the Rights of National and Ethnic Minorities.

The Parliamentary Ombudsman for Civil Rights is responsible for investigating or initiating the investigation of cases involving the infringement of constitutional rights that come to his attention and initiating general or specific measures for their remedy. The Parliamentary Ombudsman for the Rights of National and Ethnic Minorities is responsible for investigating or initiating the investigation of cases involving the infringement of the rights of national or ethnic minorities that come to his attention and initiating general or specific measures for their remedy.

The police conduct internal investigations to ensure a climate of respect for human rights inside its organizations.

Terrorism

There are no known terrorist organizations in Hungary. The police agencies charged with responding to terrorism are the National Investigation Bureau and the Law Enforcement Security Service, Counter-terrorist Unit.

International Cooperation

International assistance received in training is provided by: International Law Enforcement Academy (Budapest, Hungary), Middle-European Police Academy (Vienna-Budapest), European Police Academy (Bramshill, England), Federal Bureau of Investigation National Academy (Quantico, United States), French Police College, and German Police Academy (Munster).

There are exchanges of officers among the following countries:

- German-speaking officers exchange program between Hungary and Germany
- Police peacekeeping trainers and observers exchange programs with Austria and Sweden

Police Education, Research, and Publications

Institutions for higher education of the police (local and frequently used foreign institutions) follow:

Hungarian Defence University (HDU)
Hungarian Police College (HPC)
International Training Centre (Ministry of Interior, Hungary)
FBI National Academy (FBI NA)
International Law Enforcement Academy (ILEA)
Middle-European Police Academy (MEPA)
European Police College (CEPOL)

Leading researchers/authors/reporters/columnists include:

Andras Szabo, member of Hungarian Academy of Sciences
Laszlo Korinek, chief editor of *Hungarian Internal Bulletin*
Geza Katona, doctor of forensic sciences
Istvan Szikinger, expert in constitutional and law enforcement sciences
Geza Finszter, head of department, Hungarian Criminology Institution
Ferenc Irk, director, Hungarian Criminology Institution
Imre Kertesz, doctor of criminal law
Gabor Szakacs, director, Ministry of Interior, Directorate of Education
Janos Sallai, head of Research Department, Police College
Bela Blasko, director, Police College

Jozsef Paradi, president, SZB Hungarian
Law Enforcement Historical Scientific
Association

Regarding recent research, a textbook on police
sciences, which covered the definition of police
sciences, notion and structure of police sciences,
police management, modernization, and the constitutional framework of law enforcement, was
published in 2004.

Leading police journals follow:

Police Magazine
Internal Bulletin
Law Enforcement Bulletin
Prison Bulletin
Prison Journal

Major recent publications (all in Hungarian) are
listed below:

Ernyes, Mihaly. *The History of the Hungarian
National Police*, 2002.
Finszter, Geza. *The Theory of Law
Enforcement*, 2003.

Kaiser, Ferenc. *The History of the Royal
Hungarian Gendarmes between the Two World
Wars*, 2002.
Korinek, Laszlo. *Directions in the Development
of Criminology Theory*, 2003.
Katona, Geza. *The Police and the Criminal
Sciences in the Third Millennium*, 2004.
Katona, Geza. *The Forensic and Crime Sciences*,
2002.
Paradi, Jozsef. *Law Enforcement at Borders in
the XIX–XX Centuries.*, 2003.
Sallai, Janos. *Internal and Justice Affairs Co-
operation*, 2004.

Police-related websites:

www.police.hu/
www.worldwide-tax.com/hungary/hungov.asp
www.adminet.com/world/hu/
*www.vam.hu/data/vpop_altalanos/
vpop_tortenet_e.html*
www.borderpol.com/page4.htm

JÓZSEF BODA

I

ICELAND

Background Material

An independent island nation in the north Atlantic, Iceland was first settled by Celtic (Irish and Scottish) immigrants in the late ninth century. After centuries of independence, in 1262 it entered into a union with Norway, and in the late fourteenth century passed to Denmark when Norway and Denmark were united under Danish rule. Granted limited home rule in 1874, Iceland remained part of Denmark until 1944, when it became fully independent. Iceland became a charter member of NATO in 1949, and is the only member with no standing military. Since 1951, Iceland's defense is provided by the United States-manned Icelandic Defense Force (IDF) headquartered at Keflavik.

Iceland's capital is Reykjavik. The country is a constitutional republic. It has an area of 103,000 sq km and a population of 290,570 (December 2003). Iceland has a homogeneous population of descendents of Norwegians and Celts. The population's religious preferences are: Evangelical Lutheran (87.1%), other Protestant (4.1%), Roman Catholic (1.7%), and other (7.1%). Major industries include fishing, (75% of exports employing 12% of workforce), manufacturing, software production, biotechnology, ecotourism, and whalewatching.

Contextual Features

Iceland is a constitutional republic with a written constitution and a parliamentary form of government, with the Prime Minister as head of governme0nt. Both the President (a largely ceremonial position) and the 63 members of the *Althingi* (parliament) are elected by direct popular vote every four years, and there are no term limits for president. Established in 930, the *Althingi* is the oldest functioning parliament in the world. With the exception of the President and judges of the Supreme Court, any citizen 18 years of age or older can run for the *Althingi*. Until 1991, the *Althingi* was divided between an upper and lower house, but this was changed to a unicameral system. The legal system in Iceland is a civil law system, inquisitorial in nature, based on Danish law. Iceland does not accept compulsory International Court of Justice Jurisdiction.

Crime rates are relatively low in Iceland, but indications are that drug offenses and residential burglaries are on the rise. The most common crime is theft; the least common (besides homicide) are robbery, embezzlement and rape.

Few illegal drugs are produced in Iceland, and the harsh climate and lack of arable land makes

373

outdoor cultivation of cannabis impossible. The majority of illegal drugs originate from Denmark, Germany, and The Netherlands. There are, however, indications that while alcohol abuse dropped sharply during the 1990s, illegal drug use has increased dramatically. To deal with the problem, the National Police Commission divided the country into five operational areas and assigned a specially trained narcotics officer to each. Since 1997, 18 new drug officer positions have been established.

Judicial power in Iceland lies with the Supreme Court and the district courts, and the judiciary is independent. There are eight district courts and approximately five to ten percent of cases originating here are appealed to the Supreme Court. One of the more interesting aspects of the Icelandic system is that when a defendant is convicted of more than one offense, the judge will impose one sentence, rather than a separate sentence for each offense; usually reflecting the most serious crime, which carries the heaviest penalty.

The Director of Public Prosecutions has primary responsibility for criminal investigations and prosecutions. Fully independent and appointed for life, his decisions are generally not subject to review. His chief duties are to supervise the Commissioners of Police in their prosecutions and to supervise police investigations. The Director of Public Prosecutions deals directly with the more serious offenses, including corruption and offenses committed by public officials, and prosecutes all cases heard by the Supreme Court.

There are five prisons in Iceland: two in the Reykjavik area, two on the southwest coast, and one in the north, housing some 138 inmates. The largest can hold up to 87 inmates. None of these is classified as maximum security. The unit at Kopavogur is a separate minimum-security facility for female inmates, but because so few women are incarcerated in Iceland, some non-violent men are held there as well. There is no separate facility for juvenile inmates, but few are sentenced to prison terms; instead, they are given probation, suspended sentences, or are sentenced to treatment programs. In the few instances where juveniles are sentenced to prison, they are held with adults. By law, pretrial detainees may be held with the general prison population.

Police Profile

Background

Although it is uncertain when organized policing began in Iceland, in 1778 two night watchmen/patrolmen were issued letters of appointment by the *Innrettingar*, a private company in charge of a large social improvement project in Reykjavik. In addition to patrolling the properties of the *Innrettingar* and raising the alarm in cases of fire, they were also expected to be on the lookout for criminal activities. They carried a long club with a spiked head called the "morning star" for protection.

Modern policing dates to the late eithgteenth century, when a constable was appointed for night patrol in Reykjavik. Other constables followed, and policing throughout Iceland remained a municipal responsibility until 1972. With the passage of Police Act 56/1972, the police throughout Iceland were reorganized as a state service.

Organizational Description and Functions

The Minister of Justice is the supreme commander of the police in Iceland, while the National Commissioner directly oversees the police under the authority of the Minister. The Office of the National Commissioner was established by Police Act 90/1997 on July 1, 1997, and he is directly appointed by the Minister of Justice. To hold this position, as well as that of Deputy Commissioner, a university law degree is required. This Act replaced earlier police legislation and also abolished the State Criminal Investigation Police, whose functions were transferred to the local police commissioners. The primary functions of the National Commissioner are:

- To relay the decisions of the government that deal with the police to the police commissioners and to ensure that these decisions are put into effect.
- To provide the Minister of Justice with information on police matters.
- To supervise the systematic collection of crime data for use in criminological studies and law enforcement.
- To handle international liaison on law enforcement.
- To attend to matters which by their nature call for nationwide coordination or collaboration with police officials in another country.
- To assist special police departments concerned with the investigation of tax and economic crimes, forensic studies, and treason and activities against the national government.

For police purposes, Iceland is divided into 26 police districts that correspond to the administrative districts of the executive branch, each supervised by a regional commissioner. There are 35 separate stations within the districts. The Keflavik

Airport Police are under the direction of the Minister of Foreign Affairs. In the 26 districts, there are approximately 800 sworn officers, of whom 15 percent are part-time, and less than 10 percent are women. Members of the police force must be at least 20 years of age and must retire when they reach the age of 65.

The rank structure of the Icelandic Police is similar to that of the police in Great Britain. Subordinate to the National Commissioner and Deputy, are Police Commissioner, Deputy Commissioner, Chief Superintendent, Superintendent, Chief Inspector, Inspector, Sergeaant, Policeman (Constable), and Trainee (and reservist). There are detective ranks as well within the Superintendent and Inspector levels.

The number of police in each administrative district is determined by the Minister of Justice, in consultation with the National Commissioner, based on recommendations from each local commissioner. The Icelandic police forces is organized under five divisions, each headed by a Chief Superintendent, except Division 1, which is overseen by the Deputy National Commissioner.

Division 1 houses the Administrative and Financial Section, the International Section (INTERPOL, Sirene, PTN, and Baltcom), Police Control on Foreigners Border Control Section, and the Legal Section.

Division 2 contains the State Security Section, which is responsible for security of the parliament, state officials and embassies, the Police Tactical Team (counter terrorist unit), International Police Participation (PTF) Section, Traffic Section, Police Equipment Section and Vehicle Center, Police Communication Center including the Search and Rescue Section, and the Civil Protection Section.

Division 3 houses the Personnel Section, Organization of Police Forces in the Districts, Computer Section, Driving License Registry, and License Control for Alcohol and Firearms.

Division 4 contains the Technical Section, Intelligence Unit including Drug Intelligence, Units devoted to crime prevention and police education, Statistical Section (Police Manuals and Annual Reports Statistics), and Internal Affairs.

Division 5 houses the Unit for investigation and prosecution of economic and environmental crime, the Unit for processing of information on money laundering, financial and economic crimes, the Investigative Unit, and a section devoted to assistance to the districts.

Police Act 90/1997 specifies the following duties of the Icelandic Police Officer:

- Preventing crime and the maintenance of public safety;
- Investigating crime and the arrest of criminal suspects;
- Safeguarding human rights, private ownership and private interest;
- Assisting the public when appropriate especially when they are in danger;
- Cooperating with other authorities and assisting them according to the law or other traditions;
- Upholding the Constitution and laws of Iceland.

Although police officers in Iceland are permitted to register and own firearms, and are trained in their use, most carry only batons and pepper mace. In emergencies, members of the Viking Squad, a special armed response team, are called. Icelandic citizens are not authorized to own firearms, except under special circumstances.

Training

The National Police College, an independent institution under the Minister of Justice, is responsible for basic police education and training in Iceland. The organizational structure and administration is outlined in Chapter VIII of the Police Act (30/1997).

To qualify for admission to the College and be a member of the Icelandic police forces, applicants must be Icelandic citizens between the ages of 20 and 35, in good physical and mental health, have successfully completed two years of post-compulsory education (or the equivalent), have good language and swimming skills, and possess a valid driving license. A clean criminal record is necessary. The entrance examination emphasizes the Icelandic language and general physical stamina. In July, 1997, height restrictions were abolished. A selection committee consisting of five members is in charge of choosing students for admission. The number of trainees selected ranges between 40 and 50 each year.

Trainees receive a comprehensive introduction to police work in the General Department of the College, structured in three terms of study. The first course of study at the National Police College consists of an initial 14-week term, during which the recruits do not receive wages, but do qualify for grants from the Icelandic Student Loan Fund. Eight to twelve months of practical training in the field follow. After completing the field training, all recruits return to the College for an additional eighteen weeks, during which time the students are paid. In the third term, trainees may be used to reinforce the regular police as necessary. The following curriculum is standard:

- The Constitution
- Criminal Law and Criminal Procedure
- Police Theory
- Criminal Investigation
- Crime Scene Investigation
- Report Writing
- Traffic law enforcement
- Icelandic
- Typewriting
- English
- Psychology
- Police Tactics
- Physical Training
- First Aid
- Firearms Training

After completing the course of study, short courses are available in the Further Studies Department with specializations in various areas. Unlike the United States and other European systems, there are no mandatory in-service courses for police officers to maintain their police certification. The National Police College is also a source for scholarly studies of policing and related areas. In this regard, it acts in an advisory capacity to the government on matters concerning the police as needed.

As mandated in the Police Act and subsequent regulations, the day-to-day operations of the College are under the control of a director with the assistance of two chief superintendents.

Complaints and Discipline

Police corruption does not seem to be a problem in Iceland, nor does it widely exist within the government as a whole. On a 2002 Transparency International Corruption Perceptions Index, Iceland ranked fourth (behind Finland, Denmark, and New Zealand) on the Index, scoring 9.4 out of a possible ten, positioning it among the least corrupt nations in the world. In June, 2003, a new Police Code of Ethics was adopted, which addressed the many responsibilities of police officials and officers, other police personnel, and prosecutors in the offices of Chiefs of Police.

Iceland generally has an exceptional human rights record, and there are very few complaints of ill treatment or brutality by citizens. Article 68 of Iceland's Constitution specifically states: "No person may be subjected to torture or other inhuman or degrading treatment or punishment." Most of the complaints (usually less than 20 per year) against the police are the in

areas of illegal seizure of evidence and illegal searches of premises.

The Constitution also prohibits arbitrary arrest and detention, and the police generally adhere to these restrictions. An exception occurred in June, 2002, during a visit of Chinese President Jiang Zemin, when about 100 members of the Falun Gong religious movement (illegal in China) were detained for several hours and prevented from entering the country for a short time. This provoked much criticism within the country from the public, media, and several political figures.

International Cooperation

On March 25, 2001, Iceland joined 14 other European states in Schengen, whereby identification checks at the common borders were abolished. In an attempt to combat international crime, border controls were tightened on perimeter non-Schengen states. Iceland has also been a signatory to the United Nations Convention against Transnational Organized Crime, the Protocol to Prevent, Suppress and Punish Trafficking in Persons, and the Protocol against the smuggling of Migrants.

In the early 1980s, Iceland joined the other Nordic countries in establishing a formal system of police and customs cooperation (PTN). The PTN systematically gathers, processes, and shares data on drug trafficking, and in July 2001, Iceland assumed the chairmanship of the PTN for the first time. In September 2000, Iceland joined the Council of Europe's Pompidou Group, bringing together 33 other European countries to monitor trends in the use and trafficking of drugs, and to develop common strategies to combat it. Iceland also participates in the European Union's *Mercure* project, which focuses specifically on dealing with the production and trafficking of ecstasy in Europe.

Beginning in 1950, when two United Nations-trained Icelandic policemen were dispatched to Palestine to serve in "no man's land" between the Arab and Jewish populations, Iceland has been involved in numerous international police and peacekeeping activities. More recently, police from Iceland have participated in United Nations peacekeeping activities in Bosnia/Herzegovina and Kosovo. Their duties in Bosnia/Herzegovina consisted primarily of monitoring the local authorities, teaching, training, and investigative work. They were unarmed and not authorized to use force. In Kosovo, they were armed and had full police powers. In the National Commissioner's office, there is an International Department which acts as liaison with other national police authorities.

CHUCK FIELDS

Bibliography

Baumer, Eric P., Richard Wright, Kristrún Kristinsdóttir, and Helgi Gunnlaugsson (2002) "Crime, Shame and Recidivism: The Case of Iceland." *British Journal of Criminology* 41: 40–59.

Gunnlaugsson, Helgi (2000) "Crime and Criminal Policy in Iceland" *Norrkisk tidsskrift forkriminalvidenskab* 87 (1) (In Danish).

Gunnlaugsson, Helgi (2000) *Icelanders and Crime: A Collection of Essays on Criminology*. Reykjavík: Háskólaútgáfan (In Icelandic).

Gunnlaugsson, Helgi, and John F. Galliher (2000) *Wayward Icelanders: Punishment, Boundary Maintenance, and the Creation of Crime*. Madison, WI: University of Wisconsin Press. www.logreglan.is (website of the National Commissioner of the Icelandic Police—English and Icelandic).

National Commissioner of Police (2004) *The Icelandic Police: A Historical Sketch*. Reykjavik: Office of the National Commissioner of the Icelandic Police.

Police Act No. 90 (13 June, 1996) Reykjavik: Ministry of Justice and Ecclesiastical Affairs (English and Icelandic).

Police Code of Ethics (26 June, 2003) Reykjavik: Office of the National Commissioner of the Icelandic Police (English and Icelandic).

Sigurdsson, Jon Fridrik (1998) *The Icelandic Criminal Justice System*. Unpublished Paper. U.S. Department of State (25 February, 2004) *Iceland: Country Reports on Human Rights Practices–2003*.

INDIA

Background Material

India, a Republic in South Asia, is the seventh largest and second most populous country in the world. It covers an area of 1,261,810 sq mi (3,268,090 sq km) with a land frontier of 9245 miles and coastline of 3535 miles. It is marked off from the rest of Asia by mountains and seas, which give the country a distinct geographical entity. Countries having a common border with India are Afghanistan and Pakistan to the northwest; China, Nepal, and Bhutan to the north; Bangladesh and Myanmar to the east; and Sri Lanka to the south. India's population on March 1, 2001 stood at 1027 million, (531.3 million males and 495.7 million females). Thus India, which accounts for 2.4% of surface area of the world, supports and sustains little more than 16% of the world's population. The birth bulge constitutes one of the most serious problems of the country.

India is the cradle of an ancient civilization and birthplace of four major religions. People of all major religions with their diverse sects and subsects reside in India. There are more than a dozen of major, and hundreds of minor linguistic groups in India. However, in the midst of bewildering diversities there is a thread of unity, which binds the people of the subcontinent together.

India is a sovereign democratic republic. It consists of 28 states and 7 union territories. The constitution of India, which came into force on January 26, 1950, is the lengthiest written constitution in the world. It envisions a Parliamentary form of government, which is federal in structure but unitary in features. The constitution distributes legislative power between parliament and state legislatures, and provides for vesting residual powers in the parliament.

The census of 2001 reveals that there has been an increase in literacy in the country. The literacy rate in the country is 65.38% (75.85% for males and 54.16% for females). There is, thus, a steady improvement in the literacy rate. The literacy rate in the country was 18.33% immediately after independence in 1947.

Contextual Features

In India, the criminal law consists of the substantive law contained in the Indian Penal Code (IPC) of 1860, as well as the special and local laws enacted by the Central and State Legislatures from time to time. A variety of criminal offences are registered under these laws. The Indian Penal Code deals with all types of criminal offences. It identifies acts of omission and commission that constitute the offences and make them punishable under the Code. Over the years, the scope of the Code has been enlarged by few amendments and insertions of specific provisions. The code of Criminal Procedure (1973) lays down the procedures to be adopted by the courts for dispensation of justice. The Indian Evidence Act (1872) lays down the quality and quantum of evidence required for proving or disproving facts constituting the ingredients of an offence. Indian criminal law makes a distinction between two categories of offences: cognizable and non-cognizable. In respect to cognizable offences, the police have the responsibility to undertake investigation and the power to arrest a person without a warrant. In respect to non-cognizable offences, the police can undertake the investigation only after receiving the direction of the court.

As many as 5,344,538 cognizable crimes were reported in the country during 2001. These consist of 1,769,308 cases under the Indian Penal Code (IPC) and 3,575,230 cases under the special and local laws, known as SLL crimes. Cognizable crimes registered during the period 1996–2001 are indicated in the table given below along with other details (Crime in India 2001).

There were 6.2 million cases pending in the courts for trial. This indicates mounting dependency in the trial of criminal cases in the various courts of the country, affecting seriously the justice delivery system. The conviction rate (i.e., the ratio of cases convicted to the total cases tried in courts) in 2001 was 40.8%, which was marginally lower as compared to 41.8% in 2000. The conviction rate was highest (67%) in cases relating to sexual harassment.

To accelerate disposal of cases, Fast Track Courts (FTCs) have been set up. FTCs will take up cases pending for two years or more and the cases of undertrials in jails. At present, there are about two *lakh* undertrials in jails on whose maintenance, the state governments are spending about Rs.400 *crores* per annum. As of August 2003, 1366 fast courts have been established, of which 1139 are functional. The courts have disposed of 203221 numbers of cases out of 378071 cases transferred to them.

There are 41.9 policemen per 100 sq km, and the police public ratio is 1,360 policemen per million population.

Police Profile

Background

Although not much is known about police system in ancient India, on the basis of ancient Hindu religious texts and Kautilya's *Arthashastra* (310 BC), it can be said that the Hindus had developed a very elaborate system of law enforcement and dispensation of justice. In *Arthashastra* (Manual of Statecraft) written by Kautilaya, who was the minister of Indian emperor Chandragupta Maurya, there is detailed description of various functionaries of law enforcement and the nature of jobs performed by them. *Arthashastra* is a monumental work yielding systematic information about "investigation patterns," "punishment agencies," and "vice control devices" (Singh 17). But India is always a country of villages, and the basic unit of the traditional police system has been the village. Responsibility for village security, for prevention and detection of crime, was in the hands of the village headman. The autonomy of the village headman depended upon the structure of land-holding.

During the Muslim period from the twelfth century onwards, policing of the vast rural areas was left to be done by the village headman with the help of local *chowkidars*. But the cities and the towns had a more elaborate law enforcement system because they were the centres of trade and communications, and were tied more closely with the imperial administrative structure. The head of the town police was *Kotwal* "who was to raise and maintain the police force, arrange surveillance over the strangers and visitors, arrest criminals, control prostitution and consumption of alcoholic beverages" (Jadunath).

During the British rule in India from the eighteenth century onwards, police were organized on the model of the Royal Irish Constabulary (RIC). It was the model for the colonial police set up by the British rulers in their different colonies.

Demographics

Women now form part of the police forces of all states and Union Territories. Some states have also set up police stations run exclusively by women police personnel. There are 166 women police stations in the country. Women police are utilized not

Cognizable Crimes Registered During 1996–2001

| Year | Number of Offences | | | Ratio (IPC:SLL) | Rate Per 1,00,000 Inhabitants |
	IPC	SLL (Special Local Laws)	Total		
1996	17,09,576	45,86,986	62,96,562	1:2.68	675.6
1997	17,19,820	46,91,439	64,11,259	1:2.73	671.2
1998	17,78,815	44,03,288	61,82,103	1:2.47	636.7
1999	17,64,629	31,47,101	49,11,730	1:1.78	497.8
2000	17,71,084	33,96,666	51,67,750	1:1.92	515.7
2001	17,69,308	35,75,230	53,44,538	1:2.02	520.4

only for dealing with situations where women and children are involved, but also for mainstream duties like investigation of cases, detection of offenders, and other law enforcement duties. On 1/1/2001 the total strength of the women police in the states was 26,018, and they constituted only 1.78% of the total police strength of the country.

Organizational Description

The Police Act of 1861, which even now governs the structure of Indian policing, established the following principles of police organization:

(a) Military police were to be eliminated, and policing was to be entrusted to a civil authority.
(b) Civil police were to have their own separate administrative establishment headed by an Inspector General in each province.
(c) The Inspector General of Police was to be responsible to the provincial government.
(d) The Superintendent of the Police was to supervise policing in the district.

Section 3 of the Police Act of 1861 vested the superintendence of the police in the state government. A system of dual control at district level was introduced by section 4 of the Act. It placed the police forces under the District Superintendent of Police subject to the "general control and direction of the District Magistrate" and the court. But for the presidency towns of Calcutta, Bombay, and Madras, the colonial rulers developed a police organization centering around the Police Commissioner. Here the British administrators were influenced by the example of London Metropolitan Police. They realized that the system of dual control at the district level would not work efficiently in the Metropolitan areas, where problems were different and prompt interventions necessary, and therefore the Commissioner of Police was given magisterial powers. During the British rule in India, the Commissioner of Police existed in three cities. In post-independence India, it has been extended to many other cities all over the country.

Under the Indian Constitution, the police force is a state subject. Article 246 of the constitution distributes legislative powers between the Parliament and State Legislative Assemblies. It mentions the three lists of subjects given in the Seventh Schedule of the constitution:

(a) List 1—Union List—it includes subjects in respect of which the Parliament has the sole power to make laws.
(b) List 2—State List—it includes subjects in respect of which state legislatures have powers to make laws.
(c) List 3—is the concurrent list. It consists of subjects of which both Parliament and State Legislatures enjoy concurrent powers to make laws.

Article 246 of the Constitution of India places police, public order, prisons, and other allied institutions in the state list.

As the police force is a state subject, its organization and functioning are governed by rules and regulations framed by the state governments. These rules and regulations are normally embodied in the Police Manuals of different states. In the police forces all over India, despite diversities arising out of different local conditions and situations, there are certain notable common features. These are:

(a) The structure and working of the police forces are governed by the Police Act of 1861 or by State Police Acts modeled on 1861 legislation.
(b) Major criminal laws, viz., Indian Penal Code, the Code of Criminal Procedure, Indian Evidence Act etc. are uniformly applicable to all parts of India.
(c) Indian Police Service, an all-India police service, recruited trained and managed by the central government, provides senior officers occupying leadership positions in the state police forces.
(d) Provisions of Indian constitution allow an important coordinating and counseling role for the Central government in police matters and authorize it to set up certain central police organizations.

Thus, it may be seen that in Indian police, diversities in operational control are combined with remarkable organizational similarity. "India has managed to avoid both the fragmentation of police under a system of local control such as in the United States, with its 40,000 separate forces, and the rigidity of a national police directed by a central government" (Bayley 35).

There has been a rapid growth in police manpower since independence. In 1947, the total strength of the police force in different states and union territories was 381,000. By 2001, the strength had increased to 1,449,000. The strength of the police varies from state to state. The table below shows the strength of the police forces in the state and union territories as on 2001.

Under the Police Act of 1861, superintendence over the Police in the state is exercised by the state government. The head of the police force is now called Director General of Police, who is entrusted with the overall responsibility of administration of the police force. The senior administrative Police set up in the state consists of Director General, Inspector General, Deputy Inspector General, Superintendent, Assistant Superintendent, and Deputy Superintendent of Police, and they are assigned to different departments of the Police organization on the basis of the work load. The structure of the organization is hierarchical, with the Director General at the top of the pyramid and Constable at the bottom.

The number of policemen available per 100,000 of population on an average has remained almost static around 130 during the decade (1991–2001).

States are divided into administrative units called districts. An officer of the rank of Superintendent Police heads the district Police force. In each district, there are a number of police stations, which constitute the basic units of police administration. The police station is the reporting center for all crimes occurring in its jurisdiction. Under the criminal procedure code, all crimes are to be recorded in the police stations in whose jurisdiction they have occurred. The officer in charge of the police station, who is known as the station officer, is either of the rank of the sub-inspector

Sanctioned strength of the police forces in states/union territories (as on 1.1.2001)

Sl.	State / UTs	Civil Police	Armed Police	Total Strength	Police per 10,000 Population	Police per 100 Sq Kms
1	Andhra Pradesh	68,889	13,483	82,372	10.88	29.95
2	Arunachal Pradesh	2,985	2,383	5,368	49.20	6.41
3	Assam	18,533	35,838	54,371	20.41	69.31
4	Bihar	68,937	15,499	84,436	10.19	89.67
5	Chhatisgarh	15,296	9,698	24,994	12.02	18.49
6	Goa	3,306	723	4,029	29.98	108.83
7	Gujarat	51,056	12,419	63,475	12.55	32.38
8	Haryana	37,949	4,707	42,656	20.23	96.48
9	Himachal Pradesh	8,822	5,238	14,060	23.14	25.25
10	Jammu & Kashmir	40,278	18,759	59,037	58.63	58.23
11	Jharkhand	26,917	6,202	33,119	12.31	41.55
12	Karnataka	55,597	9,509	65,106	12.35	33.95
13	Kerala	44,468	8,248	52,716	16.56	135.65
14	Madhya Pradesh	51,280	19,494	70,774	11.72	22.96
15	Maharashtra	144,581	15,307	159,888	16.53	51.96
16	Manipur	5,425	8,209	13,634	57.07	61.07
17	Meghalaya	9,367	2,995	12,362	53.61	55.12
18	Mizoram	3,266	4,745	8,011	89.91	38.00
19	Nagaland	7,544	8,462	16,006	80.47	96.54
20	Orissa	28,973	8,245	37,218	10.14	23.90
21	Punjab	52,322	17,972	70,294	28.94	139.58
22	Rajasthan	44,899	25,442	70,341	12.46	20.55
23	Sikkim	2,040	1,439	3,479	64.43	49.03
24	Tamil Nadu	80,110	11,669	91,779	14.78	70.57
25	Tripura	8,666	8,810	17,476	54.77	166.66
26	Uttar Pradesh	89,297	65,577	154,874	9.33	64.28
27	Uttaranchal	9,485	3,182	12,667	14.94	23.68
28	West Bengal	41,776	15,633	57,409	7.16	64.67
29	A & N Islands	2,155	527	2,682	75.34	32.51
30	Chandigarh	4,190	419	4,609	51.15	4042.98
31	D & N Haveli	118	95	213	9.68	43.38
32	Daman & Diu	264	-	264	16.71	235.71
33	Delhi	46,383	10,622	57,005	41.36	3843.90
34	Lakshadweep	351	-	351	57.54	1096.88
35	Pondicherry	1,890	796	2,686	27.58	559.58
	TOTAL	1,077,415	372,346	1,449,761	14.12	45.79

Data on Police Organization in India. Published by the Bureau of Police Research & Development, 2001 or Inspector of police. Besides prevention and detection of crimes, other important police functions include patrolling, surveillance over criminals, execution of warrants, service of processes, collection of intelligence, etc.

State police has two main components: Civil police and armed police. The primary function of the civil police is to control crime, while the armed police mainly deal with law and order situations The civil police staff police stations and departments of criminal investigation agencies. They are uniformed but unarmed, though sometimes they carry a short baton or a bamboo stick called "*lathi.*" The armed police organized in the form of battalions are used as striking reserves to deal with sudden law and order situations. Armed police battalions, which are called by different names in different states, are established under the Acts passed by the State Governments. Their organization, broadly speaking, is on the lines of armed infantry battalions, though their armaments are more limited. The district police forces also have armed units, mainly used to meet the requirements of armed guards and escorts. They are also deployed to meet emergency law and order situations.

On January 1, 2001, the strength of the armed police was 372,346, and there were as many as 307 armed police battalions all over the country. Each battalion is commanded by a Commandant of the rank of Superintendent of Police, and each battalion has between four to six companies; the strength of each company varies between 100 to 120 men.

Functions

Important duties of police officers are laid down by the Police Act of 1861. Following are some of the important duties to be discharged by police officers:

1. Obey and execute all warrants and orders lawfully issued by a competent authority;
2. Prevention and detection of crime and bringing offenders to justice;
3. Collect and communicate intelligence affecting public peace;
4. Apprehend all persons whom an officer is legally authorized to apprehend and for whose apprehension sufficient ground exists.

Training

Recruitment to the state police is generally done at the levels of constable, Sub-inspector, and Deputy Superintendent of Police. Some proportions of vacancies at these levels are left open to be filled up by promotion. In addition, there is recruitment to the Indian Police Service at the level of Assistant Superintendent of Police.

For recruitment to the rank of constable, most states have prescribed high-school certificate as the minimum educational qualification. The Committee on Police Training (1973), which is also known as Gore Committee (after the name of its chairman MS Gore, a distinguished sociologist) strongly recommended this. But its recommendations regarding minimum qualification have not been implemented by some of the states. The minimum qualification for recruitment of the sub-inspectors and the Superintendent of Police is a Bachelor's degree (graduation) in most of the states.

The minimum age limit for recruitment in police is 18 years in almost all the states, while upper age limit varies from 24 to 35 years. There is age relaxation for candidates belonging to Scheduled Castes and Scheduled Tribes. Recruitment of the constables in districts or armed police battalions is done by a Board, presided over by the Superintendent of Police or the Commandant of the Battalion. In some states, the selection board is headed by an officer in the rank of Deputy Inspector General of Police. The selection process consists of physical measurements, efficiency tests, written and oral interview, and medical examination. Sub-inspectors usually in most of the states are recruited by State Public Service Commissions. Recruitment to the post of Deputy Superintendent of Police similarly is also done by the State Public Service Commission. There is always keen competition for recruitment in the rank of sub-inspectors and constables, and there is no dearth of applicants for these posts.

At the time of independence, India inherited from the British government two all-India services: Indian Civil Service (ICS) and Indian Police (IP). After independence, they were renamed as Indian Administrative Services (IAS) and Indian Police Service (IPS). These two services were constituted under Article 312 of the Indian Constitution, and legislation was framed to govern them. Recruitment in the IPS is done by the Union Government on the basis of an All India Examination, conducted annually by the Union Public Service Commission. After selection, the officers receive their training at the National Police Academy, Hydrabad (NPA). After completion of training, they are allotted to different states to hold senior leadership positions. Though posting, promotion, and transfer of IPS officers are controlled by the Governments of the states where they are posted, an IPS officer can be removed or dismissed from service only by the Central Government. Because the rules and conditions of service are laid down by the central government, IPS officers, although they act under the state governments, are to a large extent immune from the threats and pressures of the state authorities. The minimum academic qualification of an IPS officer is graduation, but most of the officers of the service have much higher academic accomplishments. Most of them hold first-class university degrees, and some are engineers and doctors or have management degrees from prestigious Management Institutes. The total sanctioned cadre strength of IPS on January 4, 2000 was 3,516.

Most of the states have their own Police Training Colleges or Academies to impart training to Sub-Inspectors and Deputy Superintendents of Police. For the training of the Constables, there are training schools in all the states.

Most of the Central Police Organizations also have their training institutions, which organize basic training for their officers and men, and also specialized courses and in-service training programs for them. In summary, four types of training courses are organized by police training institutions. They include:

1. Basic induction course for the fresh recruits;
2. Specialized courses;
3. In-service courses;
4. Refresher courses.

The Committee on Police Training set up by Government of India in 1973 reviewed the existing facilities in different training institutions and made some concrete well-thought-out recommendations for improving the training syllabi, organization of training, and instructional methods. Some of these recommendations have been implemented. However, police training institutions in many of the states are not in good shape and suffer from many constraints, including shortage of capable trainers, and they have become dumping grounds for officers who are not required elsewhere. The state governments on their part have not been able to spare adequate resources for bringing about desired improvements for police training. The percentage of expenditure incurred on police training to total expenditure reads between 1.09 to 1.41 during the last decade.

The Committee on Police Training (1973) rightly shifted the focus of the training from drill and regimentation to the development of proper attitudes through study of social and behavioral sciences, and modern management norms and techniques. In the opinion of the Committee, police training is very often patterned on the model of training given in the military training establishments. The military model was accepted by the training institutes due to historical reasons. The Committee, however, felt that police training should make adequate provisions for sensitizing police personnel to the changing social situation in the country and its implications for the role of the police.

The Central government has also set up a number of Central Police Organizations (CPOs), which function under the control of the Ministry of Home Affairs, Government of India. The CPOs can be broadly divided into two groups: one consists of the armed police organizations known as Para Military Forces, such as Border Security Force, Central Reserve Police Force, Assam Rifles, etc.; and the other group includes organizations like the Bureau of Police Research and Development, Central Bureau of Investigation, Intelligence Bureau, National Police Academy, etc.

The Ministry of Home Affairs extends financial support to the state governments for modernization of police forces. The Home Ministry also annually convenes a conference of the Directors General of Police of different states. This body provides a forum for discussions of important issues pertaining to police forces all over the country.

Complaints and Discipline

Police accountability in the country has three spheres. The police are:

1. accountable to the people;
2. accountable to the laws of the land;
3. accountable to the organization.

The ultimate accountability of the police is to the people. The police have proximate accountability to the law of the land, which is the expression of popular will. For violation of laws of the land, the police are answerable to the courts of law. In India, there is constant judicial supervision over the functioning of the police. The Criminal Procedure Code (1973) provides for magisterial enquiries into all cases of death in police custody.

In India, the National and State Human Rights Commissions were set up under the Protection of Human Rights Act 1993 to look into complaints of human rights violation by the police and to enforce police accountability. The police on their part, to quote the words of National Police Commission, (8th Report of the National Police Commission, May 1981) must realize that "their ultimate responsibility to the people and to the people alone, Their accountability to law and organization are only complementary in this ultimate objective of accountability to the people." For ensuring accountability of the police, the National Human Rights Commission has suggested formation of District Complaints Authorities to examine complaints of police excesses by the public, and the institutions of lay visitors for visiting jails and police lockups.

Unfortunately, in India there is considerable extraneous interference in the discharge of duties by the police. For improving the functioning of the police there is need for both autonomy and accountability. They are the two sides of the same coin. For ensuring accountability people also should be aware of their rights, and they should be willing to exercise them in a responsible manner. Public awareness should further include realization of the constraints and difficulties under which the police function.

There is a direct and critical relationship and interdependence between policing and human rights. Effective law enforcement and order maintenance by the police enable the people to enjoy their rights, while thoughtless and unlawful policing can cause suppression of these rights. Thus, though human rights are protected by law, in practice they are often imperilled by the enforcers of law. Many serious claims of violations of human rights by the police are being reported from different parts of the country, and these include false arrest, non-registration of cases, various forms of torture, and custodial violence, etc. During the year 2001, 183 cases of human rights violations by the police were reported throughout the country. For these violations, 135 policemen were charge-sheeted, and two of them were convicted. However, National and State Human Rights Commissions receive many more complaints of human rights violations by the police.

The National Human Rights Commission, since its inception in 1993, has viewed torture in police custody as one of the most outrageous violations of human rights and taken a number of measures to curb it. Further, the Supreme Court in its landmark judgement *viz.* DK Basu *vs.* State of West Bengal*- has issued detailed guidelines to be followed by the police in case of arrest and detention. The guidelines lay down the following:

1. Police personnel carrying out an arrest and handling interrogation of an arrestee must wear clear, visible, identifiable nametags giving their designation;
2. The arrestee should be medically examined at the time of arrest;
3. The arrestee should be permitted to meet his lawyer during interrogation;

4. The arrested person should undergo a medical examination by a trained doctor every 48 hours of his detention in custody;
5. The person arrested or detained shall be entitled to have a friend or relative or another person known to him informed of his arrest as soon as practical.

The Supreme Court imparted a new dimension to the enforceability of these provisions by attaching the sanction of contempt for breach of violations of these requirements. The Supreme Court has also made the immunity against torture and inhuman treatment as a fundamental right by an expansive interpretation of Article 21 of the Constitution. Article 7 of the International Covenant on Civil and Political Rights is thus woven into the constitutional jurisprudence of the country.

Terrorism

The spectre of terrorism has haunted India for last three decades. No foolproof remedies against this persistent and difficult feature of international violence are yet visible. Terrorist groups are active in Jammu and Kashmir, Northeastern India, and in other parts of the country, such as Andhra Pradesh, Bihar, Madhya Pradesh, etc. Terrorists operating in Jammu and Kashmir belong to international terrorist group like *Jaish-i-Muhammad, Laskar-e-Toiba* etc., who receive training, arms and financial resources from Pakistan. Pakistan has encouraged and abetted the terrorists by presenting them as freedom fighters working for liberation of Kashmir from Indian domination. Induction of *Fidayeen* (suicide squads) has introduced a new dimension in Kashmir militancy. The Central and State governments have taken a series of measures to contain terrorism. A stiff anti terrorist law—Prevention of Terrorism Act (POTA)—has been passed to contain terrorism. The United Nations has mandated that all states must adopt necessary legal instruments to prevent terrorism and strengthen international cooperation in combating terrorism. For combating terrorism, the security forces have to be equipped with stringent, anti-terrorist laws, but it has to be endeavored at the same time that they act within the four corners of law and do not misuse the authority. For this constant monitoring by the courts, review authorities and civil oversight agencies are called for.

However, there are criticisms against the police and security forces for violation of human rights while carrying out counter terrorist operations. Police have been advised by the Courts and National Human Rights Commission to guard against this form of abuse. Police response must be well defined and controlled. Any repressive over-reaction serves the interests of the terrorists, who seek to alienate the police from the community.

Indian Police, despite many constraints and occasional aberrations, have played an important role in maintaining the country's unity and integrity, and in keeping at bay the forces of disruption and disintegration. Showing exemplary dedication to duty and discipline of a high order, many policemen have made supreme sacrifices for the cause of the country. During the year 2001, 828 policemen were killed, and 3936 sustained injuries in line of duty. Many of them were victims of terrorist attacks.

Police Education, Research, and Publications

For study and research of police problems in a changing society, the Bureau of Police Research and Development (BPR&D) was established by the Ministry of Home Affairs, Government of India. Later, on the basis of recommendations of the Committee on Police Training (1973), a Directorate of Training in BPR&D to aid and advise the states on the training of the police officers was set up. The research and publications division of BPRD carries on research on subjects of importance and concern for the police forces of the country. It also undertakes various studies of practical utility on problems pertaining to police organization and administration, crime and delinquency, enforcement of laws, and security, etc. It publishes a quarterly journal titled *Indian Police Journal*, which disseminates information and ideas about latest police problems and developments. It also brings out a *Documenta-tion Bulletin* relating to police science, forensic science, and criminology for the use of police institutions and forces of the country. It further organizes each year the Police Science Congress, which provides an important forum for discussing issues concerning policing and forensic science.

The National Institute of Criminology, New Delhi, was set up in 1972, to undertake teaching, training and research in criminology and forensic science. It conducts integrated in-service training programs for the functionaries of the criminal justice system. During the year 2002–2003, 68 courses were conducted by the Institute in which 1812 officers participated.

SANKAR SEN

Bibliography

Bayle, David. *The Police and Political Development in India.* Princeton University Press, 1969.

Crime in India 2001. National Crime Record Bureau, The Ministry of Home Affairs. MP Singh. Police Problems and Dilemmas in India. Mittal Publications, New Delhi.

Data on Police Organisation in India. Published by the Bureau of Police Research & Development, 2001.

Dhillon, K.S. *Defenders of Establishment – Ruler-Supported Police Force in South Asia.* Indian Institute of Advance Studies, 1998.

India a Reference Manual, Publication Division Ministry of Broadcasting, Government of India. India 2004—A Reference Annual, Publication Division, Ministry of Information & Broadcasting, Government of India.

Police Organisation in India—Some Basic Information. Commonwealth Human Rights Initiatives, New Delhi, 2002.

Report of the Committee on Police Training, Ministry of Home Affairs, Government of India. 1973.

Sarkar Jadunath, Mughal Administration. *Orient Longmans.* New Delhi, 1972.

INDONESIA

Background Material

Indonesia is located at the crossroads between two continents, Asia and Australia, and two oceans, the Indian and the Pacific. The Republic of Indonesia is the largest archipelago-nation in the world, consisting of 17,508 islands stretching along 5,120 km from east to west, and 1,760 km from north to south. The islands scatter over more than one tenth of the equator between Southeast Asia and Australia, covering a land area of around two million sq km and territorial waters nearly four times that size.

As a whole, the territory covered by Indonesia contains more water than land. The land area of 1,766,163 sq km consists of approximately 17,508 large and small islands scattered across the archipelago as chains or isolated islands. Only 956 islands are inhabited. The main islands are Java, Bali Sumatera, Kalimantan, Sulawesi, and Papua. There are two groupings of smaller islands: Maluku and Nusa Tenggara.

The population of Indonesia is 238,452,952 (July 2004 est.), consisting of 250 ethnic groups with 250 local dialects. Indonesia has one national language, Bahasa Indonesia. The religions officially recognized are Islam (majority), Christian (Catholic and Protestant), Hinduism, and Buddhism.

The major economic activity is agriculture. The GDP is $654 billion, and per capita income is $3,000 (2001).

Indonesia is divided into several administrative regions consisting of 30 provinces with 357 districts. Jakarta, the capital of Indonesia, is located on the northwest coast of Java, and acts as the administrative and economic center of Indonesia.

Contextual Features

The Republic of Indonesia was founded on August 17, 1945, when its independence was proclaimed just days after the Japanese surrender to the allied forces, at the end of World War II. On August 18, 1945, the constitution was adopted as the basic law of the country.

Following the provisions of the constitution, the president is the chief executive who heads the country. The president is assisted by the vice president and a cabinet of ministers. The sovereignty of the people rests with the people's consultative assembly (MPR). Hence, the president is accountable to the MPR. The legislative power is vested in the House of Representatives (DPR). Other institutions of the state are the Supreme Court, the supreme advisory council, and the supreme audit board.

Under the 1945 constitution, the form of government is a republic, and the people's power is represented by the People's Consultative Assembly (MPR). The President of the Republic of Indonesia is elected by MPR every five years, and he is given mandate to run the government for a five-year term.

The Indonesian judicial system is independent from the executive and legislative arms of the government. The system is composed of five types of lower courts, and a Supreme Court. The lower courts include: General Courts, Military Courts, Administrative Courts, and Religious Courts, all of which are all two-tiered systems featuring High Courts, which preside over the lower court of the same type, as well as the Commercial Court, which specializes in hearing insolvency cases with the possibility of appeal to a special bankruptcy tribunal of the Supreme Court.

The Supreme Court is the highest judicial tribunal and the final court of appeal in Indonesia. Existing beside the legislative and the executive branches, the Supreme Court enjoys an independent status in the socio-political fabric. It was not until 1968 that the restructuring of the Supreme Court was completed to meet the conditions set out in the 1945 Constitution, (i.e., to be free from government intervention in the exercise of justification).

The system of law is based on Roman-Dutch law, substantially modified by indigenous concepts and by a new criminal procedures code and the other specialized criminal law.

Police Profile

Background

On August 21, 1945 in Surabaya, police troops firmly proclaimed themselves as the Indonesian National Police Troop under the leadership of first lieutenant Mochammad Jassin. The troop's initial step was to disarm the Japanese soldiers who remained and to boost the moral and patriotic spirit of the nation, including other armed troops who were suffering from desperation and war fatigue.

The Indonesian National Police were born simultaneously with Indonesian independence. The committee on the preparation of Indonesian Independence (PPKI) in their meeting on August 18, 1945, clearly stated that in addition to forming the 1945 Constitution, they have also created the State Police. The appointment of General R.S. Soekanto Tjokrodiatmodjo as Chief of Police on September 29, 1945, was simply a confirmation that the Indonesian National Police cannot be divorced from the history of Indonesia's independence.

Therefore, determining July 1, 1946 as Police Day has raised some questions, as many people think July 1, 1946 was the birth of the Indonesian National Police. In fact, this is Bhayangkara Day (Police Day). Although historically the Indonesian National Police were formed on August 18, 1945, administratively they were not yet fully completed. On July 1, 1946 it was decreed that the institution called the Indonesian National Police were equal to a Department within the Government, and the Chief of Police was the counterpart of a minister. In the development, the institution of the police has been changed, but in 2001 the Indonesian National Police were equal to a Department. The Police should be directly under the President on the same level as other law-enforcement bodies, The Indonesian Office of Attorney General and Ministry of Justice.

Demographics

In 1998, the Indonesian National Police personnel had a total of 194,904 persons, consisting of 89 General Officers, 3,973 Medium Officers, 14,878 First Line Officers, 142,433 Sergeants, and 33,525 Enlisted Men. There were 6,551 Police Women: two General Officers, 274 Medium Officers, 1,508 First Line Officers, and 4,765 Sergeants.

Deployed throughout police regions, the increased role of police women in policing cannot be denied. Few Indonesian police women have reached the rank of one star general, while some young police women have been given the trust of holding a post to become heads of Police Station in Greater Jakarta and other big cities in Indonesia.

Today, the role of the Indonesian police women has developed to almost the same level as that enjoyed by men. They are assigned at all fields of job areas without any discrimination.

Organizational Description

The Indonesian National Police have four dominant functions, categorized as prominent, organic, techniques, and special functions. Prominent functions include law enforcement, the establishment of police, and maintaining security. Organic functions relate to two things: organic function of establishment and organic function of police operation. The latter, whether it is regular or special, involves the operation of society security and order, or even technical and tactical administration assistance. Organic functions in establishment matters cover research and development, planning, and organism to the control level. Techniques functions basically cover the element of police operational action, which consists of intelligence and security, investigation, police patrol (samapta), traffic police, and communication relations. Moreover, techniques functions include education and logistic; and techniques functions include history, psychology, medical, and Interpol. Police special functions cover finance, establishment of information, communication, and electronic systems, public relations, information, law, and mental establishments, and SAR (search and rescue) (see INP structure).

The hierarchy of rank in the Indonesian National Police is as follows:

Officers:
Police General

Police Inspector General
Police Commissioner General
Police Brigadier General
Komisaris Besar Polisi (Police Colonel)
Ajun Komisaris Besar Polisi (Police Lieutenant Colonel)
Komisaris Polisi (Police Major)
Ajun Komisaris Polisi (Police Captain)
Inspektur Satu Polisi (Police First Lieutenant)
Inspektur Dua Polisi (Police Second Lieutenant)
Non-Commissioned Officers:
Assistant First Lieutenant (AIPTU)
Assistant Second Lieutenant (AIPDA)
Sergeant Major
Chief Sergeant (Brigadier *polisi kepala*)
First Sergeant (Brigadier *Polisi satu*)
Second Sergeant (Brigadier *polisi dua*)
Enlisted men:
Chief Corporal
First Corporal
Second CorporalFirst Soldier (*Bharatu*)
Second Soldier (*Bharada*)

Functions

The Criminal Investigation Corps (CIC) is the Indonesian National Police Core Business, so the implementation of tasks is very complex. In the organization CIC is separated into several directorates:

- Directorate of Criminal Corruption, which has the task of building and organizing the function of criminal corruption for CIC that is centralized to support the police operational in the region.
- Directorate of Criminal Drugs, which has the task of building and executing the function of criminal drugs and national/centralize to support the police operational in the region unit.
- Directorate of Criminal Public, which has the task of building and executing the function of criminal public that is national/centralized to support the police operational in the region level.
- Directorate of Specific Criminals, which has the task of investigating criminal acts/violations of specific law/ordinance beside that criminal act which is regulated criminal code, the law of drugs and psychotropic, and the law of corruption.
- Directorate Identification, which has the task of operational assistance, which proves the identity of a victim or crime perpetrator by means of police identification methods. This ranges from the most simple methods of identification, such as fingerprinting, signal methods, police photography, and odontology, to

current modern identification methods such as genetic (DNA) investigation.

Police intelligence is an integral part of the Indonesian National police organic function, including early detection and early warning, as well as identifying sources of social threats and unrest or disruptions, especially those of criminal nature.

Police security is an important element of police intelligence function to maintain security within the INP itself. This includes security of personnel, material, and information; threats from inside and outside of the INP force; and also security of the military and the INP secret code.

Traffic Police are responsible for the maintenance of law and order on the road, minimizing traffic accidents, and helping to create safer and smoother flow of traffic in the street.

These functions are broken down into four main tasks, namely:

- Traffic law enforcement
- Traffic education
- Traffic engineering
- Registration and identification of drivers and vehicles.

Traffic policemen are also called the front line of the Police, so they must appear in their best performance.

In order to implement public security and order, the Indonesian National Police hold the security of developing the members of the public as protectors of security and order, and to enhance, to serve, and to instruct the public. Hence, the Indonesian National Police not only implements law enforcement in a narrow sense, which includes law enforcement by taking measures against every kind of violation, but must also execute their function so as to guide and protect the public from existing or potential harm.

In general, pre-emptive efforts are aimed at enhancing public resistance against every from of public security and order activities enhancement.

A concrete implementation of the Police Community Relation function includes self-initiative of security measures among communities, public order, youth-child-student and juvenile, and technical development of specific police equipment.

Within an ever developing human civilization, Police Community Relation members are required to be able to improve themselves as the implementers of the Indonesian National Police's main function to prevent crime.

This activity determines the attitude of the public in facing public security and order threats. According to the Broad Outlines of the Nation's Direction, creating a system of public security and order which is aimed at

self-initiative is a main duty of the Community Relation Unit (General Assembly Decree No.11/1998).

The success of this function will create three effects in a society which supports public security and order. These areas shall form a society that automatically possesses an instinctive antipathy against violation, all forms of disobedience, social defense, and crime.

SABHARA stands for *Samapta Bhayangkara*, which means an every day police force. They perform in uniform and mainly cover preventive duties such as guarding, patrolling, and escorting. They also come to crime scenes prior to the primary polic force to preserve the scenes, executing first degree repressive measures, and performing other emergency actions.

The dominant task of Police Patrol is patrolling. Proper patrolling not only prevents the criminal or would-be criminal from committing crimes, but also attracts the sympathy of the people who, in turn, will show their best participation.

The Mobile Brigade of the Indonesian Police (BRIMOB) is a technical function of a tactical operational back-up within the Police operation as well as the combat element within the defense and security operations.

The Mobile Brigade is present at almost every critical event of high intensity, mass disruptions, and major incidents that require rapid and emergency actions with high degree of accessibility.

The Mobile Brigade is manned with specially trained policemen to cope with any law violation of high caliber and intensity.

They are trained to exercise S.A.R., riot control, and anti-terror. Those who are highly specialized in this field are organized in a special unit called GEGANA.

If the Marine Police are not as widely known, this does not necessarily mean that their existence is unimportant. This is just a matter of popularity in relation to the frequency of their public appearance. In reality, the Marine Police are not new within the Indonesian Police; being established on December 1, 1950, they are almost the same age as the Republic.

The Marine Police are an operational technical function of the police that uphold the law on the Indonesian waters to ensure security and order, and to prevent and act against criminality or threats to disrupt order and security within the community.

The Marine Police therefore have conducted various efforts, such as implementing security and developing island communities. Apart from that, they also act as guards, conduct escorts, patrol, chase, arrest, and investigate all activities which violate marine laws.

At present, Marine Police possess 15 type A 500 and four type 900 German made patrol ships. There are also nine B 600 Type patrol ships made by PT PAL Surabaya, two Australian made ships, and 198 smaller patrol ships.

The Marine Police were founded on the order of the State Police Chief to prevent smuggling. The State Police Chief, on the basis of Order No.48 dated November 1, 1950, Commissioner RP Soedarsono became the commander, while Commissioner Van Gulpen was in charge of training. At that time, the Marine Police was part of the State Police, with maintenance duty of ships to patrol the waters and execute all other duties related to contraband trade and smuggling.

The Air Police, abbreviated as *Pol Udara*, are an operational technical air back-up to all other operational technical functions of the Police forces. Their duty is to provide tactical air back-up to all other operational technical functions, such as the Marine Police, Traffic Police, Detective Unit, etc.

To provide tactical operational assistance, the Air Police are involved in various kinds of activities, such as air patrol, air escort, and assisting in traffic regulations by air. They also assist the Police Detective Unit in chasing and arresting criminals (i.e., bandits, car thieves, and smugglers), preventing illegal fishing at sea, assisting S.A.R. on land as well as sea, and logistically backing up air transport.

The Air Police currently possess 17 helicopters (913 NBD 105, a product of IPTN Bandung) and one Bell 206 B (made in the USA) and five fixed wing aircrafts (including five piston engines and one turbine engine of Piper Cheyenne type made in the USA).

Utilizing the natural instinct of certain animals such as dogs and horses, the Police have developed the Police Animal Squad. This squad provides operational assistance to other police operational functions, mainly to CID in searching for evidence and criminals, and to Police Patrol in riot control operations.

Dogs are very effective in searching for drugs and narcotics, since they have a sense of smell which is 300 times sharper than human, and this enables them to be aware of every molecular change around them. Moreover, they cannot be influenced by any gratuities.

Modern policing is characterized by modern techniques, especially in the field of criminal investigation. The utilization of science and technology is essential in order to reach a high degree of accuracy and expedient process of investigation.

The Forensic Laboratory plays a very important role in scientific crime investigation, where physical evidence is examined by experts in a sophisticated laboratory with a high degree of accuracy. In this way, testimony made by forensic experts can be part of evidence which substantiates or disproves a criminal case in any court proceeding.

Identification is a technical function of police operational assistance that proves the identity of a victim or crime-doer by means of police identification method.

These methods continue to progress rapidly in line with developments in technology. This ranges from the most simple methods of identification, such as fingerprinting, signal methods, police photography, and odontology, to current modern identification methods such as genetic (DNA) investigation. The police try to find other scientific evidence at the scene of crime. The role of police identification becomes more prominent in a modern society. Not only has crime become more sophisticated, but as the ever-increasing global culture of the world results in increased civil cases, it will be increasingly vital to the efforts of giving evidence in any crime related matters.

Training

The department of human resources oversees the promotion process, by a section of the office called Personnel Control. The function of personnel control is implemented by directorate personnel control; they formulate the policy and organize the function of selection, education, development of the police and technical development.

Supplying the human resources is the preliminary task of subdirector of human resources. The tasks of the subdirector are:

a. Selection for society of being police member
   Requirements:

   - graduated from junior high school for enlisted man
   - graduated from senior high school and police academy for non-commissioned officer
   - graduated from three-year university and academy degree for officer

Requirements for the each grade are different, but still have the same requirement such as; healthy, anatomy, academic ability and condition.

b. Posting for the first graduate
c. Proceeding the police member who cannot do their tasks caused by the sickness, those who are in sentence or desertion.

The tasks of sub director of career controller are:

a. Proceeding mission (job transfer)

b. Proceeding the rising rank

c. Proceeding the mission of staff both in the country and overseas

The tasks of subdirector of educational selection are to select the qualified personnel based on the job and rank to improve the ability and skill for the implementation of work and have a chance to be promoted to higher rank.

The levels of education are as follows:

b. General development education:

1. High rank officer college
2. Staff and command college
3. College of Police science
4. Advance officer college
5. Diploma 3 year for Police Woman

c. Establishment of education:

1. Regular school establishment
2. Special school establishment

d. Specialization for educational development/ science and technology in Indonesia and overseas. A sample:

1. Master and doctoral program in police science at University of Indonesia
2. Course for position chief of police resort
3. Traffic education and investigation
4. FBI course
5. Master degree Central police university

Educational institution within the Indonesian National Police is symbolized as *Kawah Condrodimuko* (the Condrodimuko Crater is a symbol of burning crater in which police leaders are developed to be mature leaders). The quality of graduates will very much depend upon the success the students experience through their learning process in three following stages:

- Forming
- Developing
- Scientific & Technology

Forming is a stage whereby the substance of the training is geared to changing the student's status from civilian to that of police. In this way, a police "officer" possesses the ability, physical endurance and qualification according to the existing hierarchical rank in the wide force. This rank commences from Seta (school for enlisted man), Seba (school for non-commissioned officers), and Secapa (school for candidate officers).

Developing is the next stage of the training, which is geared to develop the abilities, physical endurance, and qualification of Police officers in the level appropriate for "officer" rank in the force. This stage of training or education is more directed at specific issues to meet the ever-developing challenges of holding a post. This includes:

1. Specialized education aimed at broadening one's knowledge of specialized job areas through operational or practical approaches.
2. Positional education aimed at certain prepared positions held by the student in his/her career in the police.
3. Expert education aimed at broadening a certain expertise to enhance competence at a certain position (maintenance approach).

Included in this category are Police College (PTIK), officers continuing education (Selapa) of the Indonesian National Police, staff and Command College of the Indonesian National Police (Sespimpol), and (Seskogab) Integrated Command School of the Indonesian Armed Forces.

Scientific and technological education is more focused on increasing expertise in science and technology development, especially police technology development and state security.

International Cooperation

On October 5, 1954, the Government appointed the Indonesian National Police as NCB/Interpol Indonesia, and the Chief of the Indonesian National Police was appointed as the Chief of the NCB/Interpol Indonesia. Hence, the Indonesian National Police, as NCB/ Interpol, acts on behalf of the Government of Indonesia in relation to ICPO-Interpol (International Criminal Police Organization). To implement NCB/ Interpol Indonesia functions, an NCB/Interpol Secretariat was established and abbreviated as NCB Interpol Indonesia.

In accordance with the resolution of the ICPO-Interpol General Assembly at Rio de Janeiro in 1964, it has been determined that the main objective of NCB is to assist in fighting crime against the existing law at the international level by exchanging information and opening international investigations.

NCB duties may also be implemented on request of an Indonesian law enforcer or other related institutions that submit an investigation request for the purpose of supervision or arrest for extradition and deportation to NCB of other countries.

NCB duties also include submitting requests to the NCB of other countries or to receive requests of the NCB of other countries to identify a person or prisoner and to check out a person's criminal record.

In various international activities, NCB plays a role in preparing Indonesian NCB participation in

INDONESIA

various conferences, seminars, symposiums, and so on, set in the calendar without prior notice. NCB also prepares materials for ICPO Interpol assembly results at Asian Regional Conferences. NCB also monitors the implementation of ICPO-Interpol General Assembly Resolutions, and resolution of Regional Asian conferences as well as regular meeting of *Aseanapol*.

Within an increasingly modern and global police force, the latest development shows that the Indonesian National Police not only maintain internal order and security, but have commenced involvement in regional as well as international issues of order and security. This is in agreement with UN policy, which has requested police forces, including those from Indonesia, to participate in various police peace-keeping operations, such as those in Namibia, Somalia (Africa), Bosnia, Slovenia (Europe), and Kampuchea (Asia).

For facing future challenges, the global and regional strategic environment needs accurate attention. This is important because it impacts national situations in politics, economics, and social culture. The impacts on law matters are security interference and democracy issues, human rights, and environment.

International democracy issues drew the attention of some societal groups, resulting in social political power demanding some change in the political policy of the government, which is not appropriate

with or ignorant of the demand of society. Law developing and constitution especially in politics matter; freedom of unity or speech had increased the political awareness of society. Demonstrations and human rights demands are a part of society. To anticipate that matter, INP upgraded the ability, system, and method in order to facilitate the right of democracy to society and still pay attention to law supremacy, ethics, and police techniques.

The INP has anticipated several international crimes; for example, money laundering, drugs and trafficking, smuggler, hijack, patent, money counterfeit, and terrorist activities are expected. The INP has established several investigation units in criminal investigation corps to solve these problems. Recently, INP has anti-terrorist and bomb units: their task is early detection, prevention, and investigation of terrorist acts.

ENDANG USMAN

Bibliography

Indonesian National Police Profile, published by Public Relation & information unit INP, 1998.
Indonesian National Police Profile, published by Public Relation & information unit INP, October 2001.
www.polri.go.id/; Indonesian National Police website.
www.indonesia.go.id/, Indonesia Government website.

IRAN

Background Material

The Islamic Republic of Iran is a Middle Eastern country whose written history covers 25 centuries of continuous existence, with periods of war and foreign invasion as well as periods of social and economic progress and cultural efflorescence. Iran is located between the Caspian Sea on the north, and the Persian Gulf and the Sea of Oman on the south. Turkey and Iraq are Iran's two neighbors on the west; the former Soviet Republics of Azerbaijan and Armenia are Iran's new neighbors on the northwest; and other former Soviet Republic of Turkmenistan is on the northeast. Afghanistan and Pakistan are Iran's two other neighbors on the east and southeast, respectively. With a total

land mass of 1,648,000 sq km, Iran is the world's sixteenth largest country in terms of the area it covers. As of July 2004, Iran's population was estimated at 69,018,924. The birth rate is estimated at 34.85 births/1,000 population, and the death rate is estimated at 6.85 deaths/1,000 population. From an ethnic perspective, Iran is a multiethnic country composed of the following groups: Persians (51%); Aaerbaijanis (24%); Gilakis and Mazandaranis (8%); Kurds and Arabs (3%): Lurs (2%); Baluchis (2%); and Turkmens (2%). Administratively, Iran is divided into 28 provinces, each headed by a Provincial Governor appointed by the Office of Jurist Council, the highest executive authority in the Islamic Republic of Iran, formed after the 1979 revolution.

Iran's climate is of a varied nature, with considerable regional differences in vegetation and rain fall. This feature of the country's climate has affected population density as well as settlement patterns in Iran's long history. The northern and western parts of Iran, covered with arable lands, lush vegetation and forests and large rivers, have been more amenable to large settlements. Eastern, southern, and southeastern regions of Iran have been more arid and less arable, thus less populated. There are two central deserts which are extremely arid with salt basins which are extremely hostile to agriculture and sustainable settlement, except in their peripheral oases. However, the Iranian Plateau is endowed with rich mineral resources such as oil, natural gas, coal, and different ores scattered in different regions of the country. Oil was discovered in 1906 in southwestern Iran, and ever since it has played a central role in Iran's economy as well as political developments, making Iran one of the most important regional powers in the Middle East.

Until 1979, Iran was a constitutional monarchy. With the success of what is customarily been identified as an Islamic Revolution under the auspices of the Ayatollah Khomeini (d. 1989), the country has been transformed into an Islamic Republic with a cadre of Iranian clerics at the helm of the state and economy. Iran adheres to Shii Islam, which is a minority branch as opposed to Sunni Islam, which is practiced by the majority of Muslims in the world. Scholars have analyzed the impacts of different factors that led to the 1979 uprising in Iran in order to provide comprehensive explanations for the overthrow of the relatively modern, secular, and yet oppressive Pahlavi monarchy, and for its replacement with an Islamic form of governance. One view is that the uprising was due to oppressive policies that the two Pahlavi monarchs (r. 1925–1971) pursued as they tried to initiated a number of modernization and development programs in Iran to uplift the country's social and economic conditions. For example, Reza Shah (r. 1925–1941) is generally credited as the one who built Iran's modern education, health, army, aviation, and communication networks during his reign (1925–1941). However, he ruled with iron fist and did not tolerate any dissention to his rule.

During Wold War II, Iran was invaded by the Allied Forces in 1941, and subsequently Reza Shah was forced to abdicate his thrown in favor of his eldest son, Muhamamd Reza Pahlavi. He was proclaimed the shah. Later, the young shah initiated an ambitious modernization and development program titled The White Revolution of the Shah and the People, which commenced in 1963 and contin-ued until his overthrow in 1979. This program, implemented through stages, dramatically changed Iranian society and economy and was financed by Iran's crude oil and natural gas exports to the West. The revenues reached around US$20 billion in the 1970s. However, Muhammad Reza Shah gradually turned into another tyrant with no tolerance for dissent or for the primacy of the rule of law. These aspects of his rule gradually led to much public resentment against the state and the persona of the monarch. Starting from the mid 1960s, Iranian dissident groups started waging city-guerrilla warfare against the monarchy to topple it and to replace it with a democratic and pluralistic regime, at least in theory. These groups were ruthlessly pursued and eliminated by Iran's police, gendarmerie, or the dreaded secret police, the SAVAK. The state, however, could not touch Iran's powerful Shii establishment or its dissidents clerics, like the Ayatullah Khumaini, who in exile in Iraq called for an Islamic form of government to replace the monarchy. The 1979 uprising is seen by many as a final culmination of these factors leading putatively to the overthrow of the monarchy in Iran and its replacement by an Islamic form of governance.

The Constitution of the Islamic Republic has replaced Iran's modern Constitution of 1906. The new constitution is composed of 175 articles and a Preamble. It gives primacy to an Islamic theocratic form of governance based on (1) belief in God; (2) belief in heavenly revelations; (3) belief in life after death; (4) belief in justice; (5) belief in perpetual religious leadership; and (6) belief in freedom, human responsibility toward God made possible through perpetual leadership of religious jurors of highest competency based on the Koran, and the Tradition of the Prophet Muhammad and Shii Imams. Other articles of the Constitution implore the use of modern technology, how to improve social conditions, how to achieve national unity through, how to establish equity, justice among the general populace so as to garner social, political, and economic independence. Much stress is placed on moral virtues based on Islam and how such a virtuous state of affairs is to be established by the Islamic government that the Ayatollah Khomeini called it the Government of God. The highest authority in the Islamic Republic is the Office of the Jurist Council which, based on the Constitution's Article (110), must be filled with a religious figure of the highest credentials authorized to give *Fatwa* (religious edicts). The Jurist Council also assumes the mantle of the Leader of the Islamic Revolution, whose range of powers includes appointments and dismissals of both elected and non-elected officials at the highest levels of the government. The Jurist Council, as the Commander in Chief of Iran's Armed Forces, is also authorized to declare war and peace, call for general mobilization, or commute capital punishments. Next is the Council of Guardians, which is composed of a number of high ranking Shi'ite clerics, who help the Jurist Council in carrying out his immense powers. In addition, the Guardian Council is legally and religiously duty-bound to ensure that all civil, criminal, financial, economic, administrative, cultural, military, and political laws and regulations of the country are based on purely Islamic criteria. Thus, the main responsibility of the Council is vetting the legislative bills that are presented to the parliament so that they do not contravene Islam's Sacred Law in both letter and spirit. There is the Islamic Consultive Assembly, which acts in the capacity of an Islamic parliament. The bills do not become law unless they are ratified by the Council of Guardians and are subsequently approved by the Jurist Council.

The second part of the Constitution specifies Iran's official language, script, calendar, and national flag. The third part of the Constitution provides for the nation's rights, despite the fact that the thrust of the Constitution is to transform the Iranian nation into a religious entity, the Islamic Community of Believers. The nation's rights are enunciated in 24 articles (Articles 19 through 42). These pertain to the rights of nationalities (Article 19), gender-related rights (Article 20), women's rights (Article 21), individual rights (Article 22), freedom of expression and belief (Article 23), freedom of print (Article 24), inviolability of communication rights through post, telephone and telegraph services (Article 25), freedom of assembly and formation of political parties, gathering and demonstrations (Articles 26 and 27), freedom of choice in career (Article 28), and the right to social security, retirement and unemployment benefits (Article 29). The exercise of some of these articles (e.g., 20, 21, 24, 26, 27 and 28) is contingent upon a vague and unspecified premise, the non-violation of Islamic criteria.

Articles 32, 34, 35, 36, 37, 38, and 39 pertain to the operational dynamics of the Islamic criminal justice system which cover the criteria for arrest, arraignment, appearance before the judge, right to counsel, right to cross-examination of the witness, and right to appeal. Ironically, though, none of these later articles is contingent upon any Islamic criterion.

Through Articles 156–174, the Islamic Constitution provides for an Islamic system of judiciary. Article 156 provides for an independent judiciary in disseminating justice and safeguarding individual and social rights and freedoms. The judiciary has been entrusted with five main responsibilities: (1) presiding over grievances; (2) dissemination of justice; (3) detection of crimes and criminals based on the due process of law; (4) providing a suitable medium for crime prevention and rehabilitation of criminals; and (5) observance of the Islamic criteria in these efforts.

The Criminal Justice System

In August, 1982, the Supreme Judicial Council abolished Iran's secular civil and criminal codes as the basis of both civil and criminal prosecutions that had been institutionalized under the two Pahlavi monarchs' regimes. The Council believed that the codes did not conform to Islam's notion of law, crime, justice, or penology. In October of the same year, the modern civil and criminal courts were abolished. Also, in June 1987, a tribunal named the Special Court of the Clergy was established with the sole duty of presiding over cases that involve offences of the Shii clergy. This special court, of course, contravenes the Constitution in both its letter and spirit because it treats the clergy as a privileged group whose offenses are treated differently from those of other citizens. Next to theses courts, the Islamic revolutionary tribunals are scattered all over the country under the direct jurisdiction of the Supreme Judicial Council. Initially formed on an *ad hoc* basis to safeguard the Revolution and to combat the remnants of the *ancien regime*, these tribunals became a political arm of the state, neutralizing social and political dissent. In May 1983, the Law on Jurisdiction of Islamic Revolution Courts and Prosecutor's Office was passed by the clergy-dominated parliament in order to give some shape to these primitive and unruly tribunals, which had been responsible for tens of thousands of illegal arrests, misappropriation of funds, confiscation of lands and houses, and outright illegal and criminal executions. The Law puts these tribunals under the supervision of the Supreme Judicial Council. However, to date, these primitive tribunals continue to operate in the most arbitrary style. The jurisdiction of these tribunals covers three types of offense: drug pushing and smuggling, political and anti-state activities, and economic offences (hoarding, black-marketing, price fixing, etc.).

Contextual Features

Historians have divided Iran's long history into two macro periods, with Islam as the cutting point between the two. During the pre-Islamic period (708 BC–642 AD), five major dynasties reigned in Iran. These were: the Medes (r. 708–550 BC), the Achaemenids (r.550–330 BC), the Seleucids (r. 312–247 BC), the Parthians, (r. 247 BC–224 AD), and the Sasanids (AD 224–642). During the post-Islamic era (650–present), around 40 dynasties ruled Iran, the last one being the Pahlavi dynasty discussed above. Thus, Iran's written history covers 25 centuries of social and historical evolution. There are those historians who have argued that the history of Iranian police and law enforcement runs parallel to this long social and historical development of the country; thus, the two are inseparable from one another.

The pre-Islamic era came to its end in mid-seventh-century AD, when Iran was invaded by MuSlim Arabs, who brought the religion of Islam to Iran and created a vast Islamic empire during the reign of the Umayyad (r. 661–749) and Abbasid (750–1258) caliphs. From mid-ninth-century AD, semi-autonomous kingdoms, headed by local elites of Iranian origin, emerged in different localities of the vast Islamic empire, whose frontiers now had reached Morocco in the west and India in South East Asia. This was a world of high civilization and cultural efflorescence under a relatively tolerant Islam, with a penchant for knowledge that allowed Muslim literati and scientists to study the so-called Ancient Sciences (Chines, Indian, Persian, Greek and Byzantine) that included alchemy, medicine, astronomy, public administration, surgery, navigation, and militarism into a new brand of Islamic sciences. Of importance for our discussion here is a vast number of law enforcement apparatuses and philosophies that Muslim administrators discovered as they studied the Ancient Sciences to subsequently apply to impose order and security in large urban areas of the Islamic empire, including in Iran (to be analyzed below).

Police Profile

First, starting from the time of the Medes, and especially during the Achaemenids, the Persian emperors and local kings employed various "means of legitimate coercion," to borrow the term from German sociologist Max Weber, to impose order in the realm. These legitimate means of coercion and order-imposing ranged from professional standing armies to local military garrisons or militias groups who performed these duties throughout the realm. More specifically, a number of quasi-military and quasi-administrativeunits, to be explained below, performed policing duties in cities, or highways that linked the four

corners of the Persian empire that at times covered several millions of square miles stretching from the Indus River on the Indian sub-continent to the Aegean See shores of Asia Minor. These included the following:

Arkpat. This was the commander of military garrison, whose main duty was to police cities and highways. Being different than regular military commander, the *Arkpat* had the authority to imprison thieves and highway robbers before their case were hared by trial judges, known as *Dat*. Capital cases were brought before the local kings (shah) or the emperor himself.

The Ears and Eyes of the Monarch. These were surveillance officials appointed by the Persian emperors whose main responsibility was to travel throughout the empire, to conduct surveillance on local authorities, and to report to the emperor of the manner in which the *Arkpats* performed their policing duties. The actual identity of the "Ears" and "Eyes" were kept secret, only known by few individuals very close to the emperor.

Polis. This was adapted from the Greek system of local administration after the Achaemenid empire was conquered by Alexander, the Great in 330 B.C. The Office of the Polis oversaw the management of the city, including policing and other security-related matters. An official named *Epistat*, appointed by the monarch, oversaw the manner in which the *Polis* performed its duties.

Shahrik and Dayhik. The *Shahrik* and the *Dayhik* were two administrative and governing bodies whose development goes to the time of the Sasanid empire. The *Shahrik* was responsible for law enforcement and security matters pertaining to cities, whereas the *Dayhik* performed these duties in villages. It is logical to assume that these order-imposing institutions borrowed legal and administrative concepts and technical know-how form their predecessors, for instance from the Hellenistic notion of *Polis* mentioned above. It is an established fact that the efficacy of these institutions rested on the strength and efficacy of the central government, the economic prosperity of the realm, and a general notion of justice that linked the average free taxpaying citizens with the local and imperial governing structures in pre-Islamic Iran.

In the post-Islamic period, a commixture of Islamic and Sasanid-Byzantine notions of law, justice, crime, and punishment, including various structures for law-enforcement, were adapted and developed by the Muslim Caliphs after the Prophet Muhammad died in 632 AD. The most prominent among these were the following that developed in Iran's long post-Islamic history:

- *Shorteh*: Local police;
- *Shabgard*: Night watches and vigils;
- *Saahib al-Barid*: Postal authority who also conducted surveillance;
- *Gazmeh*: A Turk-Mongol institution of mobile quasi-legal vigilantes at the service of local authorities;
- *Saaheb-e Diwaan*: A Turk-Mongol invention that oversaw financial as well as legal security of the realm;
- *Yarghu*: A Turk-Mongol invention created to hear allegations of wrong doings of those in the position of authority;
- *Diwaan Beygi*: Acted as the order-imposing council of the chieftains responsible for hearing public grievances; and
- *Darugheh*: A Turkish invention that represents the main law enforcement authority in the capital city.

Again, the efficacy of these law enforcement institutions largely depended on factors such as the strength of the central government as well as the personal character of the monarch on the throne in conjunction with the security of the frontiers. In addition, Iranian culture has historically been of a humanist nature at the same time that it has been geared towards respect for authority, aversion to law-infracting behavior, and concern for the honor of the family, making imposing order on both individual and society a relatively easy task for power holders, including the police. It also should be emphasized that Islam's view of crime and punishment helped these agencies in their order-imposing process. For example, the Islamic notion of propriety in punishment based on the Koran, is a regime that is swift, certain, and of an egalitarian basis so as to garner general aversion to crime and deviance; thus, the policing philosophy has theoretically been one of harmony between efficacy in enforcement so as to achieve efficacy in punishment. Thus, whereas during the tenure of strong-willed, effective Persian kings the cause of justice was effectively served through law and order imposing institutions mentioned above, the same became quite oppressive, and criminogenic during the reign of ineffective rulers.

Modern Police

Iran's modern police was created in the 1930s during the reign of Reza Shah. However, of significance was also the role of the Qajar monarch, Nasser al-Din Shah (r.1848–1895), who inaugurated a kind of cyclical periods of reforms and modernization in Iran impacting Iran's traditional policing and order-im-

posing organs of the state. The Qajar monarch appointed a number of able Prime Ministers, like Mirza Taqhi Khan Amir Kabir (1848–1851), Moshir ad-Dowlah (1871), who were cognizant of the European supremacy and advancements in many fields, including in the field of modern policing. During the tenure of Moshir ad-Dowlah, the old police system known as the *Nazmiyeh* (literally, an order-imposing organ) went through a number of reforms first modeled after a the Austrian system of policing. The first head of the newly established *Nazmiyeh* police was Count de Mount Fur, an Italian officer then serving the Austrian police. The Count accepted an official invitation and offer to relocate to Iran to organize the first modern *Nazmiyeh* police in the capital city, Tehran. Upon arrival, he studied the structure and the lay out of the city, gave a report to the shah in which he proposed how to impose order in the city with about 400 foot patrol, and 60 mounted, officers. He also wrote a Police Charter (*Nezaam-Naameh*) that was signed by the shah and put into commission.

The reformed *Nazmiyeh* police was put under the authority of the Governor of Tehran, rather than under the Minister of War, as it was customary with the police of the past decades. The Police Charter had a preamble and 58 items detailing the responsibilities of the police. Each administration units of the *Nazmiyeh*, modeled after the Vienna police, were composed of several bureaus such as:

- Bureau of Public Adjudication and Claims (*Daayereh-e Mohakemat wa Daavi*),
- Bureau of Stolen Goods (*Daftar-e Tabt-e Esm wa Masruqaat*),
- Courier of Imperial Edicts to the Police (*Mamur-e eblaagh-e Ahkaam-e Homaaynu beh Nazmiyeh*),
- City Manager (*Rais-e Gardesh-e Shahr wa Nazm wa Tartib*),
- The Bureau of Investigation and Interrogation (*Raise Majles-e Tahqiq wa Estentaaq*) etc.

The Count also uniformed the police. However, from the beginning of his tenure, the Count's reforms of the police were met with much suspicion and outright hostility of two groups of people in Iran: (1) the Qajar bureaucratic elite, (2) the Shii clergy. Both had a very anarchic view of law enforcement. Both resented any tightening of their arbitrary power base by the new police, whose aforementioned Charter gave a new and disciplined view to the notion of policing, one that was in stark contrast to the vigilante style of law and order of the pre-reform period. The clergy was also resentful of the notion that the authority to enforce law in a Muslim society had been delegated to a non-Muslim (i.e., a Christian). The resentment was also due to the Count's law enforcement strategy, which was strict and of an anti-vice in nature. After 14 years of trial and error, he was forced to resign.

With the departure of the Count, the reformed *Naz-miyeh* police reverted back to some of its old malaise under 13 Director Generals, who followed each other's short and ineffective tenures until the beginning of Iran's Constitutional Revolution, during 1906–1911. This was a tumultuous period in Iran's long history, and an epoch-making event in Iran's more than a century of trial and error to modernize her economic, social, and legal relations as well as police structure and philosophy. To explain this, a synopsis of Iran's system of conflict resolution is provided.

Iran's modern police, as part of Iran's secular criminal justice system, was formed under the two Pahlavi monarchs as previously mentioned. A modern police as a fully integrated part of a secular criminal justice system posed a direct challenge to Iran's traditional law enforcement structure and philosophy that, as noted above, were nothing more than instruments of power at the service of the governing class. The police administrators never gave much attention to due process as it was understood in Anglo-American policing. The traditional style of imposing order was not open to the strategic call of policing in modern democracies as one whose motto is to protect and to serve the public. The modern police force is not just modern in its investigative tools, or in its scientific approach to patrol and investigate crime; the modern police force is also modern in its perception of what constitutes service, clientele, the police and community relationship, the place of police in social and legal relations. Modern police are subjected to the following:

- code of honor and professionalism;
- constitutional checks and balances;
- code of dedication to cause of justice;
- code of public protection and service to community;
- code of equity, social justice and impartiality in law enforcement.

Modern secular law, as the base of these codes, is operative in modern policing in most democratic societies; it conceives of persons as citizens who have real and legal status equal in the proverbial eye of law, regardless of sex, creed, and religious affiliations. Monarchs, presidents, and state functionaries are subjected to constitutional limitations in the same manner that average citizens are. Most scholars agree that it was Sir Robert Peel who first proposed the code of honor and professionalism for police as he organized the London Metropolitan Police in 1829. Peel introduced 11 points as to how

make policing an honorable profession. Iran was, of course, a late comer to the general arena of social, economic, and legal modernization. Those who promoted these ideas in the late nineteenth-century Iran (to whom references has been made above) gradually realized their irreconcilable differences with the traditionalist forces. This situation led to Iran's first modern revolution, the Constitutional Revolution that occurred between 1905–1911. Although many factors were responsible for this event, one factor of primary significance was the general perception that the Qajar shahs, and their functionaries, regularly and egregiously abused the power of the state for their own benefit, an abuse that by the time of the Constitutional Revolution had already affected, quite negatively, the efficacy of Iran's traditional system of conflict resolution.

Iran's first modern constitution was drafted in 1906. Consisting of 51 articles, the Constitution of 1906 established a Parliament (*Majlis*), and a Senate defining the state organs' duties and responsibilities. A Supplementary Law was enacted in 1907 to clarify the rights of the people, the members of the Parliament, the powers of the Shah, the ministers, the judiciary, and the army. Under the "Power of the Courts," there were 19 Articles (Articles 71 through 89) and five Clauses in the Constitution of 1906 that defined the power, nature, and operational dynamics of the judiciary and courts. These articles, once implemented, changed Iranian judiciary, court structure, and procedure describing how judges were to be employed, assigned to districts with jurisdiction. In short, the 1906 Constitution created a temporal and secular judiciary. In addition, modern concepts and categories of offense and punishment were adapted from different European penal codes. These offenses were hierarchical as:

- Offenses against the state, the person of the sovereign, the constitution, and the government.
- Offenses against public order and security.
- Offenses against public property and/or state officials.
- Offenses against a person's physical well being, followed by those committed against a person's freedom.
- Offenses against children and deceased.
- Offenses against family and public norms of morality.
- Offenses that injure the public's sense of fiduciary trust and responsibility, such as lies, perjury.
- Offenses against private goods, or the individual rights of private ownership.

- Alcohol and drug related offenses.
- Rural offenses.

Next to a modern criminal code, Iran's secular criminal justice system followed a modern view of conflict resolution in the context of duly appointed courts of law. Criminal cases were referred to ordinary and/or special courts, depending on the nature of the case under consideration.

The ordinary courts were composed of the following:

- The Police Courts
- The Houses of Equity
- The Arbitration Councils
- The Criminal Courts
- The Assize Courts

The special courts were composed of the following:

- The Military Tribunals
- The Juvenile Courts
- The Criminal Court of Governmental Officials
- Financial Court

Iran, under the two Pahlavi monarchs, was among "nations not obsessed with crime" to use Freda Adler's famous title of a comparative study, in which she has discussed the issue of crime in third world and Islamic, as well as ex-Iron Curtain, societies. Although Iran was not included in that study, Adler's rationale applies to Iran under the Pahlavi monarchs.

Police Mandate and Philosophy 1925–1979

The Iranian modern police force was charged with urban policing, named as the National Police head quartered in the capital city, Tehran, and was put directly under the Ministry of Interior. Officially, its main function was to serve and protect the citizens against crime, to regulate traffic, to investigate crime scenes, and to enforce laws in the urban areas. In the rural areas, it was the National Gendarmerie created in mid 1940s that was charged with law enforcement functions and responsibilities. In case of large operations against drug smugglers, the National Police and Gendarmerie would collaborate with the army unites.

Despite its modern mandate (to serve and to protect), the police force was a very important instrument of Reza Shah's dictatorial power base. Under the Directorate General Mukhtari in the 1930s, the police gained a notorious reputation for outright illegal internal intelligence gathering against average Iranian citizens and especially for manhandling the political dissidents. Under the Muhammad Reza Shah, the police were also responsible for internal security throughout the country, which the police carried out in collaboration with local and foreign intelligence-gathering organizations, such as the Federal Bureau of Investigation and American military advisers stationed in Iran. The most prominent among the local ones were the Army Intelligence Unit, and the National Information and Security Organization, the SAVAK. Created in 1957 and approved by an act of Iranian Parliament, the SAVAK had a wide range of powers in relation to intelligence gathering, arrest, and investigation. To enhance the power of its Directorate, it was given the administrative rank of the Assistant to the Prime Minister to be appointed directly by a decree of the Shah. By the passage of the time, the SAVAK became a notorious organization involved in the illegal arrest, imprisonment, and torture and execution of hundreds of Iranian political dissidents and a main impetus to popular hate of the shah and Muhammad Reza's dictatorial reign. With the rise of the Islamic Republic, the Iranian police force has changed in structure but has remained as an oppressive instrument of power in the hands of the new power holders.

HAMID R. KUSHA

IRAQ

Background Material

Formerly part of the Ottoman Empire, Iraq was occupied by Britain during the course of World War I. In 1920, it was declared in a League of Nations mandate to be under UK administration. In stages over the next dozen years, Iraq attained its independence as a kingdom. A "republic" was proclaimed in 1958, but dictatorial regimes prevailed, most recently with Saddam Hussein at the helm. Territorial disputes with Iran led to an inconclusive and expensive war (1980–1988), and in August 1990, Iraq seized Kuwait, generating the First Gulf War of January–February 1991.

Following Kuwait's liberation, the UN Security Council (UNSC) required Iraq to destroy all weapons of mass destruction and to allow UN inspections. Continued Iraqi noncompliance with UNSC resolutions resulted in the US-led invasion of Iraq in March 2003.

Iraq, since 2003, is an occupied country, tasked with supplementing the efforts of Coalition Forces after the demise of Saddam Hussein and the fall of the Ba'athist regime. To date, Coalition forces remain in Iraq, helping to restore a viable police force and facilitating the establishment of a freely elected government. The Coalition Provisional Authority transferred sovereignty to the Interim Government on June 28, 2004.

Police Profile

The new Iraqi police force was created based on the mandate of the Coalition Provisional Authority in order to assist in the restoration of conditions of security and stability. The newly formed organization, like many others around the world, falls under the authority of the Ministry of Interior. It faces enormous challenges and is essentially a municipal force which, under normal circumstances, would provide basic police services. The interim government, led since summer 2004 by Prime Minister Ayad Alawi, has authorized the police force to assist coalition forces on raids against the rising level of insurgency throughout the country. It is not technically assigned the functions of terrorist pursuit, authority over alleged military crimes, or any investigative function whatsoever. The current government has announced that it will staff the force with about 75,000 officers and supporting staff which evidenced an increase of about 10,000 members between November 2003 and February 2004. By their own admission, the Iraqis' ability to fight crime, not to mention corruption, in their own ranks is in its infancy.

The five critical Iraqi forces supplementing US forces are: the Iraqi police, the Facilities Protection Service, the Border and Customs police, the new Iraqi Army, and the Iraqi Civil Defense Corps. The actual police force is divided into two parts: the Iraqi Police Service (IPS) and the Facility Protection Service (FPS). The IPS will eventually include a highway patrol and more traditional policing types of units. Initial recruits received training in January 2004 when 466 of 35,000 new officers

underwent tailored instruction and graduated from a multinational-taught program. The FPS is a holdover from the Hussein regime. It is actually a conglomerate of security guard operations, each of which is technically controlled by a different government ministry. The largest is claimed by the oil Ministry, which is tasked with guarding thousands of miles of pipeline. Additionally, 250 women have signed up to train with the Facilities Protection Services. So far, 100 female trainees have graduated, but getting them out on the job in male-dominated Iraqi society has been a struggle. To date, only around 20 women are working. The Border and Customs force is brand new and has started to protect a few key crossing points along the 2,000-mile border.

Specifically, in a press statement from the US government, it was announced that on January 29, 2004, the first class of 466 Iraqi police recruits graduated from an intensive eight-week training program conducted in Jordan, and they have returned home to begin policing duties in the new Iraq. Under an agreement with the former Coalition Provisional Authority, Jordan is providing facilities and other support to enable the training. (US Government Press Release, January 30, 2004) The Iraqi Police (IP) were a cornerstone of the Graner Office of Reconstruction and Humanitarian Assistance (ORHA) process and seen as a critical requirement very early on. Jay Garner, a retired lieutenant general, headed the first occupation authority. As the ORHA transitioned to the CPA, the transition process centered around building a government, and the IP were placed below the New Iraqi Army, and Iraqi Civil Defense Corp as priorities. The former police commissioner of New York, Bernard B. Kerik, was leading the effort to rebuild Iraq's police force. However, Major General Paul Eaton, who initially had the responsibility for training the Iraqi Army, was later given the responsibility for training the Iraq police force. In October, he was quoted in the *New York Times* as indicating he had inherited a "disjointed fiasco."

The training focuses on modern, democratically based policing methods, and it includes subjects such as human rights, community policing, domestic violence, search and seizure, and firearms training. Additionally, Germany originally agreed to train Iraqis in the forensic sciences to enhance capability in crime scene investigation. The Coalition also had started to develop some special training capabilities, including counterterrorism protocols and criminal investigation. The endeavor has proved to be less than successful. Unfortunately, in testimony before the Senate Foreign Relations

Committee, on September 14, 2004, Joseph Bowab, Deputy Assistant Secretary of State for Foreign Assistance Programs and Budget, acknowledged that none of the Iraqi Officers put in place since the occupation have completed a full training program. A second class of approximately 500 recruits followed the first, and another 1,000 recruits arrived February 8, 2004. When the facility reaches full capacity, as many as 3,000 recruits are to be in training concomitantly. Once graduated, the police are supposed to work side by side with American military forces and to gradually asume total responsibility for maintaining law and order.

The United States named a veteran Iraqi cop as interim police chief. In a surprise move, they later fired him. The former interior minister responsible for rebuilding Iraq's shattered police force said on June 4, 2004 that the police are crippled by poor training, haphazard recruitment, corruption, and paralyzing delays in procuring essential equipment that have driven police to buy weapons on the black market. Without major reforms, Samir Shakir Sumaiday warned, the police force is bound to turn in a dismal performance and undermine the new interim government's chance of winning credibility. Before his dismissal, he said, he had been planning to purge at least 10,000 police from the nation's 70,000-strong force. Nevertheless, Major General Tariq, the deputy in charge of the special crimes units at the Interior Ministry, has high hopes. "We want to make this department like the FBI or Scotland Yard," he declared. In August 2004, Ahmed Ibrahim was appointed Iraq's deputy minister of the interior. During the 1980's he was a member of the Iraqi police but was later imprisoned and tortured.

The broader nationwide effort to rebuild the Iraqi police and justice system has just begun. The US Justice Department sent a 26-member assessment team, including judges, prosecutors, police, and corrections officials, into Iraq to help the US State Department figure out how much of the Iraqi police and justice system needed to be rebuilt. In reality, it all does, and interim efforts are failing. The United States is hampered by its lack of any fulltime peacekeeping forces. Unlike almost every other nation in the world, the United States does not have a national police force, nor does the US military have any large-scale units that specialize solely in domestic day to day police functions. Instead, the US has turned to a private company, in this case, Dyncorp International to fill the gaps. The State Department has awarded a $50 million contract to Dyncorp to hire about 1,000 US civilians who will work as advisers in setting up the Iraqi police, courts, and correctional system. By whom and how they will be equipped, as well as financing to rebuild the Iraqi resources, will be expensive. The logistics problems remain unsolved, and it appears that the US will bear most of the burden of the costs of rebuilding the force.

Iraqi exile groups have estimated that the country has some 500 judicially qualified judges. The same groups estimate that significant numbers will need to be replaced because of former ties to the previous regime, according to Bathsheba Crocker, a fellow with the Center for Strategic and International Services in Washington. Iraq already has a modern legal code and a constitution, but it was often ignored by Saddam, who overruled it by decree. Additionally, while most prison buildings were not physically destroyed, many of the corrections officials participated in torturing prisoners. "It may be that you have to get rid of all of the prison officials," said Crocker. Experts agree that all of Saddam's various national security services must be disbanded, and few if any of their officers will be eligible for other police work. But many of the lower ranks of the former 20,000-strong border patrol and the 50,000 members of the national police force have sought reemployment.

The relationship between US military forces and the Iraqi police force has been strained during the transition. Building a reputable, efficient, and professional force in Iraq presents enormous challenges. However, the success of a credible domestic police force is critical in the establishment of a potentially democratic Iraq. The nascent Iraqi security forces must appear to be willing to bring the raging insurgency under control, permitting the withdrawal of US forces. The former Iraqi police force under Saddam Hussein could be characterized as an enforcing component of a brutal regime. They were paid a very small salary and expected to subsidize that income by stealing from those they were supposed to protect. This mindset, of corruption and laziness, will have to be overcome, both by the police themselves and the citizens they are sworn to serve. Another problem bedeviling Iraq's police is the history of corruption tied to nepotism. Before leaving, the top US administrator, L. Paul Bremer III, appointed an inspector general to the Interior Ministry, an official with a five-year term and subpoena power charged with eliminating corruption. In central Iraq alone, Inspector General Hassan al-Saray had opened 500 corruption investigations against police officers.

Current officers are paid about $120 to $140 per month, but some SWAT teams receive about $200 a month. In Western terms, this monthly income seems very small, but within the Iraqi economy the paychecks are significantly higher than income available as a street vendor or other part-time employment. Getting hired, however, is problematic, and nepotism is rampant. The necessity to feed a family is more the reason for high numbers of applicants than dedication to a policeman's life and duties. Iraqi police officials are confronting some intimidating agenda items, including the vetting of 70,000 existing officers, most of them untrained, and many suspected as criminals by their own supervisors. The ministry has barely begun to examine the records of the 70,000 police officers recruited during the occupation, tens of thousands of whom have been deemed unreliable in times of crisis.

Members generally can be identified by their chocolate brown flak vests, but underneath they wear a hodge-podge of different uniforms or civilian attire. Modern police equipment, standard among Western police units, is scarce, even though some equipment has been delivered. Camaraderie is weak, except among family members, and the risks are high. But the breakdown in authority and police loyalty exceeded even the fears of some of the force's fiercest critics. In Shi'ite strongholds in Baghdad, most notably Sadr City and Shula, uniformed police officers openly joined ranks with the Mahdi, taping posters of Sadr to their vehicles and taking orders from clerics at their offices.

At the same time, many officers refused to help when police stations in Sunni areas came under attack by insurgents. In Aadhamiya, for example, a Baghdad neighborhood with a history of anti-American resistance, more than 100 heavily-armed men attacked the police station several nights running at the beginning of April. More recently, the first election returns from the Sunni majority heartland north of Baghdad showed that a low Sunni turnout in Saddam Hussein's home province has given a lead in the voting there to a Shiite political alliance. The Sunni rejection of the political process was underscored recently by two suicide bombings on Iraqi police targets in Sunni insurgent strongholds that killed at least 27 people.

So far, they have also been disinclined to engage members of Muqtada al-Sadr's well-trained Shiite forces or former regime loyalists. The motives of those willing to take Iraq's most dangerous jobs reflect not only a desire to feed their families, but hopefully in the future a deep commitment to create a self-sufficient nation that does not rely on American troops for its security.

A cursory look at the security environment in Iraq in the fall of 2004 reveals that a traffic cop in the street does not necessarily cooperate with vehicular patrol police, who do not often communicate with the other division of IP. There is clearly a lack of lateral communications, direction, and authority. On top of that, their authority can be challenged by the neighborhood Mullahs as well as Mayors, and Ba'athist had begun to creep back into the IP the previous April. Efforts to partially ferret out former Hussein regime members that support IP tasks from sunrise to sunset indicate that at dusk, they are just as likely to trade their uniforms for masks.

Over 700 police officers have perished since the invasion. Alarmed at the deteriorating security environment and in a major push to improve the situation, the United States announced it would shift $1.8 billion from reconstruction programs to add more security forces. Some Iraqi scholars have argued that the US committed a huge mistake by completely dissolving the former Iraqi military and police force, thereby necessitating building the force from scratch. (Riyadh Aziz Hadi, Dean of the College of Political Sciences at Baghdad University.) Dr. Hadi has said, Iraqis want their own security forces, "so that the Americans can leave. No one can accept to see his own country occupied."

Consequently, in September 2004, the Bush administration announced plans to divert $3.5 billion of $18 billion in reconstruction funds from infrastructure projects. Specifically, about $1.8 billion of the money would go to create 80,000 new posts in local security forces: 45,000 new police, 20,000 additional national guardsmen, and 16,000 additional border police. Unfortunately, attacks have proliferated, regardless of US efforts to get the situation under control. On October 16, 2004, two car bomb attacks killed at least 17 Iraqi security officers in what has become known as the Sunni Triangle. Recently, six Americans were wounded in a separate attack on a military convoy shortly after dawn in Baghdad on the same day.

The Bush Administration decided to initiate the establishment of a secret police force. The Administration will fund the agency in its latest bid to root out the Ba'athist loyalists behind the insurgency in parts of Iraq. The force will cost up to US$3 billion over the next three years. Its ranks are composed of members of Iraqi exile groups, Kurdish and Shiite forces, and former intelligence agents who are now working for the Americans. It has been suggested that CIA officers in Baghdad will play a leading role in directing their operations. The United States hopes to organize the various groups into one force with the local knowledge, motivation, and authority to hunt down resistance fighters. According to Washington, the new agency could number 10,000. The force is intended to have a crucial role in post-Saddam Iraq, but the violence appears to be increasing instead of diminishing.

Progress has been slow, and efforts have been made to publicly show the Iraqi people that the police force is indeed assuming routine domestic police functions. For instance, in a test of their professionalism, Saddam Hussein was formally, if not operationally, turned over to Iraqi control in July 2004, as publicized by Iraq's national security adviser, Muwaffaq al Rubaie in a televised interview on *CBS Evening News*. He was quoted as saying, "We wanted to show our people that this miserable soul is in the hands of Iraqis now." Rubaie went on to say that when the time came, two American soldiers would take a handcuffed Saddam from his cell and turn him over to four Iraqi policemen. Saddam was indeed taken before a judge and formally charged with crimes against humanity, highlighting the initiation of an Iraqi criminal justice system. The official transfer of power from the United States to the interim government took place on June 30, and the Iraqis accepted jurisdiction over Saddam Hussein in early July.

However, it became evident that the Iraqi police force needs to be increased in order to maintain the peace or risk losing control to Kurdish and Shi'ite militia and gangs controlled by hard-core Saddam Hussein loyalists. Additionally, more than criminal gangs are threatening public security in Iraq. In cities such as Kirkuk and Mosul in northern Iraq, where the United States still has little military presence, some 300,000 Kurds who were evicted from their homes by Saddam a decade ago are beginning to return and try to reclaim their old property from the Arab families who now live there, raising the specter of revenge killings. The two major Kurdish groups in northern Iraq each have a militia, while several of the Shiite clerics vying for power in southern Iraq are also arming their followers.

KATHLEEN SWEET

Bibliography

Congressional Research Service Reports

23 April 2003 (Update) *Iraq: Regime Change Efforts and Post-War Governance*. Congressional Research Service Report. http://fpc.state.gov/documents/organization/19708.pdf (PDF).

12 June 2003 *Beyond Iraq: Repercussions of Iraq Stabilization and Reconstruction Policies*. Hearing before the U.S. Senate Committee on Foreign Relations Senate Hearing, 108-167. http://purl.access.gpo.gov/GPO/LPS41159 (Text) http://purl.access.gpo.gov/GPO/LPS41160 (PDF).

2003 "Iraq." *CIA World Factbook* 2003. www.cia.gov/cia/publications/factbook/index.html.

Iraqi Army & Police

30 January 2004 *Nearly 500 New Police Officers join ranks of Iraqis Protecting Iraq*. Volition Provisional Authority Press Release. http://cpa.gov/pressreleases/20040130_new_cops.html.

31 July 2003 *Coalition Provisional Authority Update Briefing, Law Enforcement Issues in Iraq*. U.S. Army V Corps. www.vcorps.army.mil/www/CJTF7/Transcripts/cjtf7_trans_030805a.htm.

18 July 2003 *First Baghdad Police Graduate Civil Retraining*.

September 2004 "Iraqi Police Service" John Pike http://www.globalsecurity.org/intell/world/iraq/ips.htm. U.S. Army Public Affairs. www.4army.mil/ocpa/read.php?story_id_key=5061.

9 January 2004 *Decisions on Trial of Saddam Hussein Up to Iraqis, Powell Says*. Text of CBS Radio Interview with U.S. Secretary of State Colin Powell, U.S. Department of State, http://usinfo.state.gov/dhr/Archive/2004/Jan/12-12208.html.

30 December 2003 "The U.S. Defense Department December 30 named retired generals and current and retired attorneys general to fill positions in its new Office of Military Commissions. The office will oversee the legal proceedings involving detainees taken into custody during military operations in Afghanistan and Iraq and held in U.S. military custody at Guantanamo Bay, Cuba, and elsewhere." U.S. Department of State. http://usinfo.state.gov/dhr/Archive/2003/Dec/31-861825.html.

10 December 2003 *The Statute of the Iraqi Special Tribunal*. Coalition Provisional Authority. http://cpa.gov/audio/20031210_Dec10_Special_Tribunal.htm.

27 November 2003 "Justice in Iraq." *Voice of America* Editorial. www.voanews.com/Editorials/article.cfm?ObjectID=85712D0007D3-47F5-A28E60FC9AF95E02.

20 November 2003 "Iraq's New Constitution." *Voice of America* Editorial http://www.voanews.com/Editorials/article.cfm?ObjectID=F5883D7F-8AE5-47FC-8077ABB9759012FE.

16 November 2003 *Agreement announced between the Coalition Provisional Authority and the Iraqi Governing Council re the process of restoring Iraq's sovereignty and the adoption of a permanent constitution*. U.S. Department of Defense. www.defendamerica.mil/iraq/nov2003/tni-ig111803.html.

13 October 2003 *Iraq's Central Criminal Court convicts two Oil Smugglers*. Press Release - Coalition Provisional Authority. http://cpa.gov/pressreleases/20031014_OCT14-Conviction.htm (English) http://cpa.gov/pressreleases/20031014_Oct-13Conviction-arabic.htm (Arabic).

4 October 2003 *Council of Judges begins work again in Iraq*. Press Release - Coalition Provisional Authority. http://cpa.gov/pressreleases/20031007_Oct-04-CouncilofJudges.html.

11 August 2003 *Reappointment of Eight Iraqi Justices Shows Commitment to Independent Judiciary*. News Release - Iraqi Ministry of Justice.Coalition Provisional Authority. http://cpa.gov/pressreleases/11Aug03PRjustices.pdf (PDF).

23 May 2003 *Iraqi Jurists Propose Plan for Transitional Justice, Rule of Law in Iraq*. Washington File Report - U.S. Department of State. http://usinfo.state.gov/regional/nea/iraq/text2003/0522jur.htm.

1 April 2003 (Update) *Iraq*. (Legal resources about Iraq) Law Library of Congress. www.loc.gov/law/guide/iraq.html.

March 2003 *Transitional Justice In Post-Saddam Iraq : The Road to Re-establishing Rule of Law and Restoring Civil Society : A Blueprint* Working Group on Transitional

Justice in Iraq and Iraqi Jurists' Association. The Judge Advocate General's Corps, U.S. Army. http://purl.access.gpo.gov/GPO/LPS36686 (PDF).

Undated, but 1996 or after *Legal System/History of the Republic of Iraq.* Draft Article as part of the Islamic Family Law Resource. Emory University School of Law www.law.emory.edu/IFL/legal/iraq.htm.

Michael R. Gordon, *New York Times*, "For Training Iraq's Police, the Main Problem was Time," 21 October 2004, pg. A 13.

Amy Waldman, *New York Times*, "US Struggles to Transform a Tainted Iraq Police Force," 30 June 2004, pg. A1.

KurdSat TV, Al-Sulaymaniyah, in Sorani Kurdish. 9 Oct 04.

IRELAND

Background Material

Irish society was, for much of the twentieth century, characterized by stasis and homogeneity. Since the 1990s in particular, however, Ireland has undergone significant changes in terms of demography, economy, and culture. In 2002, the population of the Republic of Ireland was estimated to be 3,917,000 people, the highest figure recorded since 1871. While the population has been steadily increasing since the 1960s, this followed a century-long decline in population from the 1840s until the 1950s that arose from a devastating potato famine and ensuing emigration. This rise in population is particularly concentrated in the Dublin region.

Although Irish ("*gaeilge*") is the first official language, its usage is generally restricted to a number of western regions formally designated as an Irish-speaking area or "*gaeltacht*" (with a total population of over 60,000) and to ceremonial occasions. English remains the everyday language of Ireland.

In terms of religious affiliation, Roman Catholics are by far the largest religious group, consisting of 3,462,000 persons, over 88 percent of the population. The next most populous religions in Ireland are Church of Ireland (116,000), unspecified Christians (21,000), Presbyterians (21,000), and Muslims (19,000). Initially, the Irish constitution "recognised" the "special position" of the Catholic Church in Irish society, effectively privileging its status. That clause was deleted through a constitutional amendment in 1973.

During the 1990s, the Irish economy expanded dramatically, achieving growth rates of 10 percent in successive years and leading to the designation of Ireland as the "Celtic Tiger." Much of this growth was based on establishing Ireland as a low-tax corporate base, and an international hub for the information technology industry, particularly in terms of being a gateway for US business to the EU. This resulted in Ireland being rated in a 2002 survey as one of the most globalized countries in the world.

The population is strikingly homogenous in terms of race and ethnicity. No Irish census to date has gathered information on race/ethnicity, and traditionally—and in spite of longstanding, if small, ethnic minority communities—Irishness has been synonymous with whiteness. Irish Travellers, an indigenous minority group of approximately 25,000 people, are characterized by a nomadic lifestyle and a culture distinct from that of the settled population. Travellers consistently rank far worse than the settled population in terms of child mortality, life expectancy, illiteracy, and other measures of health and welfare. Since the early 1990s, there has been a rapid expansion in the numbers of ethnic minorities in Ireland. The number of asylum applications made in Ireland increased from 39 in 1992, to 1,179 in 1996 and to 10,325 in 2001, with Nigerians and Romanians constituting the largest of the "new" ethnic groups. As a consequence of these changes, Ireland has, within a relatively short period of time, shifted from being a society of net emigration to one of net immigration, from an almost exclusively white society to one with a sizeable ethnic minority population, and from a relatively poor country to a relatively wealthy one.

Contextual Features

The criminal law is based on an adversarial system, and the Office of the Director of Public Prosecutions has responsibility for prosecuting those against whom criminal charges have been made. The Irish legal system derives from a combination of sources that includes common law, parliamentary legislation, the Irish constitution, and the European Union. Common law is based on legal precedent and longstanding tradition. The government of the day enacts legislation in the Irish legislature—the *Oireachtas*—which consists of *Dáil Eireann* (the Irish parliament), and *Seanad Eireann* (the Irish Senate, whose role is largely advisory). The President is the formal head of state, but this is a largely symbolic position and carries no executive powers. The Irish Constitution was enacted in 1937 and can only be amended by referendum. Upon accession to the European Economic Community in 1973, the European Court of Justice took precedence over Irish domestic law. In 2003, the government announced that it was actively considering ways to establish a penal code, given the disparate sources of criminal law in existence.

In 2000, the police classification of crimes was amended from "indictable" and "summary" (or "non-indictable") to the roughly corresponding categories of "headline" and "non-headline" offenses. Headline offenses are grouped under ten headings: homicide, assault, sexual offences, arson, drugs, larcenies, burglaries, robberies, frauds, and remaining offences listed as "other." Other changes in the recording of crime accompanied this, based on the introduction of an integrated police computer system called PULSE (Police Using Leading Systems Effectively). While this makes long-term historical analysis problematic, some clear patterns are nonetheless evident. For much of the twentieth century, Ireland's levels of recorded crime were negligible compared with other countries. Although a number of victimisation studies from the 1980s onwards suggested that Ireland's crime levels may be closer to international norms than was hitherto thought to be the case, by most indices Ireland remains very much a "low-crime" society. From the mid-1960s onwards, however, the crime level increased sharply, rising from 16,203 indictable offenses in 1963 to 102,387 in 1983. Thereafter, the crime level dropped until the late 1980s, at which point it rose again until a new all-time high of 102,484 offenses was reached in 1995. Since then, recorded crime levels have fallen somewhat—to 73,276 headline offenses in 2000, but then up to 86,693 offenses in 2001—although this decline masks a number of important trends, most notably an increase in the proportion of violent crimes.

The increase in crime levels from the mid-1960s onwards was likely due to a number of factors, including the expansion of the Irish economy, a reduction in emigration, higher mobility within Ireland, an increasing secularisation of Irish society, and the emergence of a serious heroin problem in Dublin in the early 1980s. Additionally, the impact of the Northern Ireland conflict was significant, not least through the attention and resources it absorbed. While the increase in overall crime levels that can reasonably be attributed to the conflict is probably quite modest, its impact on the levels of specific high-profile crimes such as armed robberies was much more marked (Mulcahy 2002).

As the table (below) shows, the vast majority of recorded crime in Ireland is property related. Analyses of historical trends demonstrate that this is a longstanding feature of crime in Ireland. Between 1976 and 1995, violent crime (officially described as "offenses against the person") accounted for an average of 2.5 percent of recorded crime, and the highest level it reached during this period was 3.7 percent of crimes in 1978 (Brewer, Lockhart and Rodgers, 1997). In recent years, levels of violent crime have increased as a proportion of overall crime (it amounts to 6.7% of violent crime in the 2001 figures), although the vast majority of crimes continue to be property-related and non-violent (see table, below).

The court system is based on the historical distinction between "indictable" and "summary" (or "non-indictable") offenses. Summary offenses are relatively minor in nature and can be heard before a judge sitting alone in the lower level District Courts. The maximum penalty for conviction of a summary offence is imprisonment for one year. Indictable (now referred to as "headline") offenses

Recorded Headline Offences in Ireland for 2001

Group	Number of Offences	Percentage of Total	Number Detected	Percentage Detected
1. Homicide	74	0.1	64	86
2. Assault	3,802	4.4	2,861	75
3. Sexual Offences	1,939	2.2	1,386	71
4. Arson	1,407	1.6	320	23
5. Drugs	2,380	2.7	2,372	100
6. Larcenies	45,652	52.7	17,630	39
7. Burglaries	24,015	27.7	6,691	28
8. Robberies	2,880	3.3	1,139	40
9. Frauds	3,492	4.0	2,770	79
10. Other	992	1.1	678	68
TOTAL	86,633	99.8*	35,911	41

Source: Garda Síochána Annual Report for 2001.

* Does not add up to 100% because of rounding.

are more serious in nature and, although these are first brought before a District Court, they must then be brought before the Circuit Criminal Court. The more serious indictable offenses are heard before the Central Criminal Court. Serious offenses involving threats to national security or, more recently, organized crime are heard before the Special Criminal Court.

Appeals from the Circuit Criminal Court, the Central Criminal Court, and the Special Criminal Court may be heard before the Court of Criminal Appeal. The court of final appeal domestically is the Supreme Court, and it is here that the constitutionality of legislative powers may be determined.

There are 18 prisons and detention centres in Ireland, and in April, 2003 these held a total prison population of 3,200 individuals (with a further 287 on temporary release). The prison population has been growing steadily since the 1970s, and severe overcrowding is a persistent feature of several prisons. By 1980, the prison system held approximately 1,200 inmates, rising to approximately 2,200 inmates by the early 1990s. Since 1995, the prison population has increased by approximately 50%. Much of this increase is due to the Irish Government's "zero tolerance" crime control policies from the mid-1990s (O'Donnell and O'Sullivan 2001 2003).

The first report of the newly established Independent Inspector of Prisons and Places of Detention was published in 2003, and it recommended that Mountjoy and Portlaoise prisons be closed because of their generally poor condition. Mountjoy prison, for instance, dates back to 1850, and although the installation of televisions in each cell commenced in 2003, there are no toilets or running water in the prison cells. There are a number of reintegration programs for prisoners who are about to be released, but the welfare component of the prison system remains underdeveloped.

Police Profile

Background

An *Garda Síochána* (known colloquially as "the guards") emerged in the aftermath of the partition of Ireland in 1922 into two states—the Irish Free State (becoming the Republic of Ireland in 1949) and Northern Ireland. The Irish Free State government established "the Civic Guard" as the national police force, renaming it "*An Garda Síochána*" (Irish for "Guardians of the Peace") in 1923. In 1925, the Dublin Metropolitan Police Force (which had existed as a separate police force for the capital since its establishment by legislation in 1786) was amalgamated into the *Garda Síochána*.

The Free State government sought to ensure that the state's institutions would reflect its new-found independence. This involved distinguishing the *Garda Síochána* from its predecessor, the Royal Irish Constabulary, and establishing it as an indigenous police force responsive and responsible to the local population rather than to a colonial administration. The first *Garda* Commissioner, Michael Staines, outlined the ethos he sought to permeate the force, stating that: "The *Garda Síochána* will succeed, not by force of arms or numbers, but by their moral authority as servants of the people." In line with this, although the force borrowed heavily from the RIC's organizational structure, important symbolic changes were introduced to emphasize the *Garda Síochána's* role as a civic (rather than paramilitary) police force. For example, officers were to be unarmed, and numerous cultural initiatives were undertaken to establish the force as an expression of national identity—by providing training through the Irish language for a period, maintaining close links with the Catholic church, and promoting widespread involvement in gaelic sports (a feature of policing in Ireland to the present day).

From the 1970s onwards, as crime levels increased and political violence in Northern Ireland escalated, the *Garda Síochána* came under greater scrutiny. Other factors also increased the public and political salience of policing, including a number of inquiries into allegations of police misconduct, a decline in levels of quiescence towards authority structures generally, and a growing governmental interest in cost-effectiveness in and modernisation of the public sector (especially through the Strategic Management Initiative from the mid-1990s onwards).

Demographics

The size of the force in June, 2003 was 11,749 officers, with a further 1,747 civilian staff. The table (previous page) provides a breakdown of these figures by rank. During the 1950s and 1960s, the force was frequently allowed to fall below its establishment size, as low levels of recorded crime, the general absence of social upheaval, and a poor state of pubic finances gave little urgency to calls for increasing policing levels. During the 1970s in particular, the pressures of crime and political violence led to a sustained increase in the force's size. Since the mid-1990s, the coalition government of the

Strength of An Garda Síochána in June 2003

Rank/Status	No. of Personnel
Commissioner	1
Deputy Commissioner	2
Assistant Commissioner	9
Chief Superintendent	49
Superintendent	168
Inspector	292
Sergeant	1,965
Garda	9,263
TOTAL POLICE	11,749
Civilian Staff*	1,747
TOTAL PERSONNEL	13,361

Source: Garda website (*www.garda.ie*), November 2003.
*Approximately one third of whom work part-time.

Fianna Fáil and Progressive Democrat political parties has committed itself to increasing the size of the force to an all-time high of 12,000 officers (see table, above).

Women were first admitted to the force in 1959 with the title of *Bangharda* (meaning "female police"), a term which was discontinued in 1991. In June 2003, there were 1,713 female *garda* officers, comprising 15% of the force. In September 2003, a female officer was promoted to the rank of Assistant Commissioner, the highest rank held to date by a woman.

In terms of ethnicity, the *Garda Síochána* is almost exclusively white. There is estimated to be only a single Irish traveller within the force, and Walsh (2000) noted that only two *garda* officers were "visible" ethnic minorities.

Organizational Description

The organizational structure of *An Garda Síochána* is largely inherited from its predecessor, the RIC. *Garda* headquarters is situated in a former RIC barracks in Dublin's Phoenix Park. With its centralized command structure and its status as a unitary, national police force, it appears increasingly anachronistic in terms of the proliferation of policing agencies in Europe and the West generally. This situation, however, is likely to change in the near future as the diversification of policing agencies in Ireland gathers pace (Vaughan 2004). In 2002, a scheme of community wardens was established on a pilot basis in a number of local authority areas, and under legislation published in 2003, a *Garda* Reserve—consisting of a part-time police force—will soon be established also.

The force is divided into six separate regions, each headed by an Assistant Commissioner, and each region is turn is divided into a number of divisions (headed by a Chief Superintendent), which in turn are divided into a number of districts (headed by a Superintendent). In all, there are approximately 700 *garda* stations throughout Ireland, although most of the specialist units are based in Dublin.

Although the *Garda* Commissioner is in formal charge of the force and has operational responsibility for its actions, the relationship between the force and the Minister for Justice is problematic. The Commissioner reports to, and is answerable to *Dáil Éireann* (the Irish parliament), through the Minister for Justice. However, pursuing matters of concern about policing through parliamentary debates or parliamentary questions is difficult because of the lack of clarity in distinguishing an operational policing matter from force policy.

During the 1990s, the force was increasingly subjected to a new regime of audit, especially through the Government's Strategic Management Initiative, which sought to modernise and increase the effectiveness of the public sector. As a result, mission statements and strategy documents have become increasingly prominent features of the organization's culture and practice.

Several specialized units have recently been established to reflect the changing social and legal environment of policing in Ireland. These include the Criminal Assets Bureau, which is primarily used to target the assets of those involved in serious or organised crime, and other initiatives, such as the Human Rights Office and the *Garda* Racial and Intercultural Office.

Functions

An Garda Síochána performs the familiar police functions of crime prevention and detection. Because of its undifferentiated character as the national police force, its responsibilities include state security as well as ordinary crime. The increased number of support service posts held by civilians, and imminent creation of a *Garda* Reserve Force (provided for in the 2003 legislation) may mean that *garda* officers will increasingly be expected to focus on crime-related issues rather than service provision more generally.

Training

Historically, training for *Garda* recruits was characterised by militaristic levels of discipline and rote learning of relevant legislation. In the late 1980s, the training regime was significantly revamped to ensure that recruits were better prepared for the realities of police work. Training is now provided at the *Garda* College in Templemore in County Tipperary. The development of a campus-style policing training college mirrored the changes to the training curriculum. Currently, *garda* training is a two-year program based around five separate phases. These cover: (1) a twenty-week training program based in Templemore; (2) a twenty-two week period in a *garda* station as a student *garda* under the instruction of a tutor *garda*; (3) a sixteen-week training program in Templemore; (4) a thirty-eight week period working as a regular guard in a *garda* station; and (5) a final four-week program in Templemore. Upon completion of this two year training program, successful graduates are awarded a National Diploma in Police Studies.

The training modules generally emphasize contemporary issues relating to the role of the police in modern society, including such topics as community policing, political conflict, prejudice and discrimination, and aspects of modern Irish society. The training curriculum also "emphasises such issues as human rights" (Dunn, Murray and Walsh 2003), but in a general sense rather than through any dedicated modules on this topic. The incorporation of the EU Convention on Human Rights into Irish domestic law has provided an impetus for a greater focus on human rights in *garda* training, and a working group is currently investigating ways of achieving this.

Police Public Projects

Surveys of public attitudes towards the police have consistently reported high levels of satisfaction. A recent large-scale postal survey conducted by the *Garda* Research Unit found that 87 percent of respondents reported being satisfied with the *Garda Síochána*. This is largely consistent with previous studies and suggests that *An Garda Síochána* appears to enjoy levels of public support and satisfaction higher than that found in Britain and many other European countries.

Since 1963, the force has operated a system of youth diversion, largely operating through programs established by juvenile liaison officers. One of the most prominent features of this is a cautioning scheme for juveniles who admit their involvement and for whom the incident in question is a first offense. Recently, the force has established a system of restorative justice conferences under the provisions of the *Children's Act 2001*. These conferences are held in circumstances where the victim and offender both agree to participate, and these meetings are chaired by a trained mediator. The *garda* juvenile liaison officer usually is involved in ensuring that the program of action which is agreed on is duly implemented. The *Garda Síochána* also has operated a scheme of "Special Projects" which function as crime-prevention measures in what typically are socially-deprived communities (Bowden and Higgins 2000).

There is no tradition of structured police-public consultation in Ireland, although some consultation has operated—albeit on a very limited basis—through a pilot Community Policing Forum established in Dublin in 2001. This involves regular meetings between local police officers/commanders and a variety of local representatives, community leaders, etc., at which issues relating to crime, safety and quality of life are discussed. This scheme is likely to be extended to other areas in the future. Under the draft provisions of the *Garda Síochána Bill 2003*, the force will have a statutory requirement to obtain the views of the public. This will, for the first time, provide a legislative footing for police-public consultation in Ireland.

Police Use of Firearms

An Garda Síochána is, in routine terms, an unarmed police force. *Gardaí* are issued with wooden batons as their only day-to-day weapon. Detectives, who comprise about 15% of the force, are issued with firearms (usually revolvers), and also have access to more powerful weaponry. Specialist units such as the Emergency Response Unit are heavily armed, and are deployed in circumstances such as hostage situations.

Complaints and Discipline

Up until 1987, complaints against *garda* conduct were dealt with internally. Following a number of prominent incidents in the late 1970s and 1980s that featured allegations of police malpractice, the *Garda Síochána* Complaints Board (GCSB) was established under the provisions of the *Garda Síochána (Complaints) Act 1986*. Although the GSCB emerged from a period of heated debate about policing, the responsibilities of the Board were largely limited to supervising investigations that continued to be carried out by *garda* officers. Moreover, the GCSB's remit was firmly directed towards complaints made against individual officers rather than against general force policy. Additionally, although it was established independently of the police, the GCSB's annual reports persistently criticized government for failing to provide it with the organisational resources or legal powers necessary to enable it to function effectively as a police oversight body.

A number of issues and scandals in recent years have placed the force under unprecedented levels of scrutiny. In May 2002, *garda* officers engaged in what video footage clearly showed was excessive force when confronting individuals participating in a "traffic-free" protest in Dublin city centre. Other prominent inquiries include the Barr Tribunal into the fatal police shooting of a mentally unstable man in the town of Abbeylara in 2000, and the Morris Tribunal into allegations of police misconduct in County Donegal (including allegations that officers sought to secure promotion by manufacturing explosives, and later "finding" them).

In legislation put before the Irish parliament in 2003, the Minister for Justice outlined proposals for the establishment of a *Garda* Inspectorate, which will be modelled in many respects on the structure and functions of the Office of the Police Ombudsman in Northern Ireland. The Inspectorate's powers will extend beyond those of the GCSB in significant ways, most notably by being able to conduct the investigations itself rather than reviewing investigations carried out by *Gardaí*. Moreover, the Inspectorate will have the discretion to initiate investigations even when no complaint has been made. Although much public concern around policing may centre on general force policy rather than from the misconduct of a specific officer, the draft legislation did not specify any means by which the Inspectorate could address policy issues.

The Northern Ireland conflict (often referred to as "the troubles") emerged in the late 1960s from widespread disturbances surrounding the civil rights movement. Although the vast majority of troubles-related incidents have occurred in Northern Ireland, the conflict has nevertheless had a considerable impact on policing in Ireland. Since 1970, 12 of the 14 *Gardaí* killed in Ireland have died in circumstances directly related to the conflict. Republican paramilitaries have posed the most serious threat to the Irish police. Loyalist paramilitaries have, with the exception of a number of incidents such as the 1974 Dublin and Monaghan bombings in which a total of 33 people were killed, largely confined their activities to Northern Ireland.

In addition to the dangers associated with the conflict, its impact has also been evident in relation to the huge amount of resources absorbed by policing the conflict, and a number of specializations that have developed in response to the paramilitary activity (aspects of criminal investigations involving forensic science, improvised weaponry, etc.).

The conflict has also implicated the force in various scandals, particularly in relation to alleged abuses of police powers. This was particularly so in the 1970s, when persistent allegations of police brutality led to an Amnesty International mission in 1977 and a subsequent official inquiry. Additionally, as part of the Northern Ireland peace process, an investigation is underway into allegations that *garda* officers assisted republican paramilitaries by providing them with intelligence subsequently used in a number of fatal republican operations.

International Cooperation

The most immediate dimension of international cooperation relates to cross-border police cooperation between the Northern Ireland and the Irish Republic. The development of links between the *Garda Síochána* and the Royal Ulster Constabulary was minimal up until the 1980s. The 1985 Anglo-Irish Agreement provided for formalized arrangements for cooperation, and these were supplemented by informal relationships formed between officers on either side of the border. The levels of cooperation this yielded, however, remained basic, a point noted in the 1999 Patten Report on policing in Northern Ireland, which provided enormous impetus for the development of closer links between the two forces (Dunn, Murray, and Walsh 2002).

For several decades, *garda* officers have been involved in numerous policing operations as part of various United Nations peacekeeping missions. This has included service in Cyprus, Croatia and Bosnia/Herzegovina, East Timor, and other locations.

Police Education, Research, and Publications

The *Garda* College at Templemore in County Tipperary is the main centre for police training in Ireland. While some police training courses are provided in Dublin and elsewhere, all recruit training is based in Templemore, which is recognized as a third level educational institution. Degrees in Police Management are offered through the college.

In Ireland, specialized training in criminology remains sparse. In 2003, University College Cork offered a masters degree in Criminal Justice, the first and only dedicated postgraduate criminology course in the country to date. The Institute of

Public Administration in Dublin offered its first Masters in Public Administration (Criminal Justice) in 2002. In 1999, University College Dublin established Ireland's first Institute of Criminology, and there are also criminology research programs in the Dublin Institute of Technology and at the University of Limerick.

In addition to in-house training, *garda* officers attend a range of courses provided at John Jay College of Criminal Justice in New York. A number of senior officers have also attended advanced courses provided at the FBI academy in the US. In addition, a small number of officers have attended courses at the National Police Training College at Bramshill in England, as well as a range of courses in other EU states.

The number of researchers in Ireland actively working on policing—as with criminology generally—remains quite small, although it is increasing. The Irish policing literature includes several important works in social and political history (Allen 1999; Brady 2000; Breathnach 1974; McNiffe 1997), and this has been complemented by a number of analyses of contemporary policing arrangements.

Dermot Walsh (1998) has written the most comprehensive discussion on police powers and accountability structures of *An Garda Síochána*. He and his colleagues have also written on cross-border and international issues generally (Dunn, Murray, and Walsh 2002). Connolly has written trenchant analyses of the development of policing in Ireland and on local accountability (2002). O'Donnell and O'Sullivan (2001, 2003) have examined recent policing policies of "zero tolerance." Vaughan (2004) has explored the changing framework of policing, and the present author is doing research exploring the relationship between policing, social marginalisation and social change in Ireland.

After decades of neglect, the funding situation for social science research, and particularly criminological research, has greatly improved since the late 1990s. The Department of Justice, Equality and Law Reform (*www.justice.ie*) and the National Crime Council (*www.crimecouncil.ie*) provide funding for crime-related research. More generic funding opportunities are provided by the Royal Irish Academy (*www.ria.ie*), the Combat Poverty Agency (*www.cpa.ie*), and especially the Irish Research Council for the Humanities and Social Sciences (*www.irchss.ie*). The level of funding available, however, varies considerably from year to year.

Information on crime levels and organizational developments is provided in the *Garda* Commissioner's *Annual Report of An Garda Síochána*. An *Garda Síochána* also publishes *Communique: The Garda Management Journal*, first appearing in 2001 and now established as a quarterly periodical. *Garda Review* is published by the *Garda* Representative Association (the representative body for rank-and-file *garda* officers) on a monthly basis. A number of Irish-based academic periodicals, including the *Irish Criminal Law Journal*, the *Jurist*, and the *Irish Journal of Sociology*, regularly publish material on crime/policing matters. *Magill*, a monthly current affairs magazine, had a long tradition of investigative reporting on policing issues, but it ceased publication in 2003 due to financial difficulties.

The following websites provide useful material on policing and related matters.

garda.www.garda.ie – *An Garda Síochána*.
www.justice.ie – Department of Justice, Equality and Law Reform
www.iccl.ie – Irish Council for Civil Liberties
www.esatclear.ie/~garda/histsoc.html – *Garda Síochána* Historical Society
www.agsi.ie – Association of *Garda* Sergeants and Inspectors
www.gra.cc – *Garda* Representative Association
www.amnesty.ie – Amnesty International (Irish Section)
www.gov.ie/crimecouncil/ – National Crime Council
www.ireland.com – *Irish Times* newspaper

AOGÁN MULCAHY

Bibliography

Allen, Gregory. *The Garda Síochána: Policing Independent Ireland 1922–82*. Dublin: Gill and Macmillan, 1999.

Bowden, Matt, and Louise Higgins. *The Impact and Effectiveness of the Garda Special Projects*. Dublin: Stationary Office, 2000.

Brady, Conor. *Guardians of the Peace*. London: Prendeville, 2000. [Originally published in Dublin in 1974 by Gill and Macmillan.]

Breathnach, Seamus. *The Irish Police: From Earliest Times to the Present Day*. Dublin: Anvil, 1974.

Brewer, John, Bill Lockhart, and Paula Rodgers. *Crime in Ireland 1945–95*. Oxford: Clarendon, 1997.

Connolly, Johnny. "Policing Ireland: Past, Present and Future." *Criminal Justice in Ireland*, edited by Paul O'Mahony, 483–519. Dublin: Institute of Public Administration, 2002.

Dunn, Seamus, Dominic Murray, and Dermot Walsh. *Cross Border Police Co-operation in Ireland*. Limerick: University of Limerick/University of Ulster, 2002.

Institute of Criminology. *Crime in Ireland: Issues and Trends, 1950–1998*. Dublin: Stationary Office, 2001.

McNiffe, Liam. *A History of the Garda Síochána*. Dublin: Wolfhound, 1997.

Mulcahy, Aogán. "The Impact of the Northern 'Troubles' on Criminal Justice in the Irish Republic." *Criminal Justice in Ireland*, edited by Paul O'Mahony, 275–296. Dublin: Institute of Public Administration, 2002.

National Crime Council. *A Crime Prevention Strategy for Ireland: Tackling the Concerns of Local Communities.* Dublin: Stationary Office, 2003.

O'Donnell, Ian, and Eoin O'Sullivan. "The Politics of Intolerance—Irish Style." *British Journal of Criminology* 43, no.1 (2003): 41–62.

———. *Crime Control in Ireland: The Politics of Intolerance.* Cork: Cork University Press, 2001.

O'Mahony, Paul, ed. *Criminal Justice in Ireland.* Dublin: Institute of Public Administration, 2002.

Vaughan, Barry. "Accounting for the Diversity of Policing in Ireland." *Irish Journal of Sociology* (2004): In Press.

Walsh, David. "Policing Pluralism." *Cultivating Pluralism*, edited by Malcolm MacLachlan and Michael O'Connell, 152–174. Dublin: Oak Tree Press, 2000.

Walsh, Dermot. *The Irish Police: A Legal and Constitutional Perspective.* Dublin: Round Hall/Sweet and Maxwell, 1998.

ISRAEL

Background Material

Israel received its independence in 1948. Its total area measures some 28,000 sq km, and its population is about seven million. About 80% of the population are Jews; 20% are Arabs. Over half of Israeli Jews are native-born, while the rest hail from over 80 countries around the world. Some 90% of Israel's inhabitants live in over 100 urban centers, including the country's four major cities: Jerusalem—the capital city—Tel Aviv, Haifa, and Beer-Sheba. The language of the country is Hebrew, and Arabic is the second official tongue.

The GDP of Israel in 2001 was 105,425 million dollars. The per capita GDP was 16,364 million dollars. Seventeen percent of the GDP is from industry; more than half of the high-tech product is exported. Forty-three percent of the GDP comes from imports, while 34% comes from exports. Israel's diamond industry produces about 80% of the world output of small polished stones. The average inflation has decreased to 3% to 4% in recent years.

The major challenge for Israel is to arrive at a peace settlement with the Palestinians and with other neighboring Arab States (Syria and Lebanon). The insecurity which exists in the country and the constant state of war and terror cause discontent within the population, and also a decrease in investments from abroad, a complete standstill in the tourism industry, and generally, a decrease in economic growth.

Israel is a democratic republic with a parliamentary multiparty system of government. The principle of separation of powers is maintained, with three branches of government: the legislature (the *Knesset* is a 120-member, single chamber legislature whose members are elected every four years); the executive (the Government of Israel, in which the Prime Minister leads a coalition government); and the judiciary (Israeli courts). The *Knesset* elects the President (elected for a seven-year term, not renewable), who is the Head of State and exercises mainly ceremonial functions.

Israel does not have a formal written constitution, although the Declaration of Independence and a body of legislation provide for a gradual build up for a future planned Constitution. Israel's Supreme Court—acting as a High Court of Justice—can suggest the desirability of legislative changes and can rule on constitutional and administrative matters.

Contextual Features

The Israeli criminal justice system is adversarial in nature, and the judicial proceedings are in the hands of professional judges, elected by a public committee. Like in many other western systems, the criminal process in Israel is composed of two stages: the trial and the sentencing process. The judge decides if the accused is found guilty or innocent, based on the indictment and the material evidence. During the sentencing process, the judge is allowed to sentence the accused to any length of imprisonment below the maximum limit or to apply more lenient alternatives to imprisonment. Death penalty as criminal punishment for murder, was in existence until 1954, when it was abolished and replaced by a mandatory life sentence.

In criminal hearings, district attorneys represent the State, and the Attorney General heads the Prosecutorial Branch. During the entire prosecutorial process, the prosecutor invokes the process of indictment and has the right to offer a plea bargain to the suspect or his/her attorneys. In magistrate courts, police prosecutors usually prosecute misdemeanors.

Children between the ages of 14 to 18 can be prosecuted, but are tried in special juvenile courts.

Every criminal suspect or accused has the right to choose an attorney who will represent him/her. The court has the right to appoint an attorney, free of charge, if the defendant cannot afford one. In 1996, the Office of Public Defender was established, and it employs both in-house and private attorneys.

The court system is three-tiered: 1. Magistrates' (or Peace) Courts, which exercise criminal jurisdiction on crimes punishable by no more than seven years of imprisonment or by a fine. Most of the proceedings in these courts are conducted before a single judge; 2. District Courts, which deal with all criminal cases beyond the jurisdiction of the Magistrates' Courts, and also serve as appellate courts for the District Courts' verdicts and other decision. A three-judge panel is appointed in serious cases; 3. The Supreme Court exercises jurisdiction over the District Courts' decisions. In addition, this court serves as the state's Supreme Court, sitting as a High Court of Justice. In this case, it functions as an administrative law court to provide judicial review of official administrative actions.

There is only one national prison system in Israel, which includes maximum, medium, and minimum security prisons, which serve general or particular populations (e.g., women and youth). Its principal role is the safe incarceration of the inmates and prevention of the inmates from causing harm to the society. This system also claims to have a role in the rehabilitation of the incarcerated population (The Prison Ordinance 1971). The system is headed by the Prisons Commissioner, who is appointed by the Minister of Public Security.

The Ministry of Labour and Social Affairs is responsible for correctional services and for the probation systems—both juvenile and adult (Hasin and Horovitz 1998). The Ministry also deals with correctional and treatment services for youths at-risk and at-risk families (including the institutions, hostels and half-way houses used for these populations) and adolescents who have been placed outside their home environment by a juvenile court order, and who were designated as "minors in need of protection" because of serious physical, social or emotional neglect (Sebba et al. 2003).

The Anti-Drug Authority (ADA) coordinates all anti-drug strategy throughout the country, including enforcement activity with the police, education and publicity campaigns, legislation, treatment, and community prevention activity (www.antidrug.org.il; Sebba and Horovitz 2000).

Crimes in Israel are classified into three categories: crimes/felonies, misdemeanors, and administrative violations. The police compile the daily number of complaints reported by victims or offenses detected by the police, and record and transfer the data to the Central Bureau of Statistics (CBS), which publishes them monthly.

After a relatively steady climb in crime rates for 15 years (until 1997) (Rahav 1998)—especially in property crime, which constitutes, on average, about 60% of the total recorded crime—there was some decline in recorded crime (in absolute numbers) as well as in the crime rate (files recorded per capita) from 1998 to 2002. However, in 2003 there was again an increase in reported overall crime (up 4.2% from the previous year) (see table, below).

Property crime (including all thefts and break-ins) increased during the early 1990s and reached a peak in 1997–1998. Car theft, for instance, rose due to the relative ease in moving the stolen cars and dismantling or changing their identities within the Palestinian Territories, where the Israeli police had difficulty entering. In an endeavor to decrease this problem, a law has been passed which allows the legal selling of car parts only by authorized dealers who trade in parts that have been marked and registered. Anyone selling un-marked parts will be prosecuted for selling stolen parts. House and business burglary and thefts of all kinds constitute a serious problem, both in terms of the economic impact on society and the traumatic effect these have on the victims, throughout the years. During periods in which there is increased terrorist activity—as in the present "Intifada" (Palestinian uprising)—(since the fall of 2000)—various anti-terrorist techniques are put into place, such as the closure of the West Bank and Gaza Strip to Palestinian workers, who would otherwise come to work in Israel. There seems to be a correlation between the decrease in crime rates and these periods of "closure"—probably because of the increase in police patrolling presence, increased police and army personnel surveillance at check-points, and the decrease in the number of Israeli offenders, who, prior to the Intifada, committed crimes together with Palestinian offenders, freely entering and exiting the Palestinian territories (Herzog 2003).

Violent crime has also been on the rise in the last few years—especially perpetrated by youth and orga-

Reported crime and crime rates in Israel: 1994–2003

Year	Total Reported Files*	% Change in Reported Crime from Previous Year	Average Population**	Crime Rate (per 1,000 population)
1994	386,066		5,471,500	70.5
1995	411,531	6.60	5,612,300	73.3
1996	438,063	6.45	5,685,100	77.0
1997	498,550	13.81	5,826,900	85.5
1998	516,435	3.59	5,970,700	85.5
1999	484,950	-6.10	6,125,300	79.2
2000	466,038	-3.90	6,289,200	74.1
2001	469,073	0.65	6,439,000	72.8
2002	464,854	-0.90	6,570,000	70.7
2003	484,688	4.27	6,750,000	71.8

Sources: *http://www.police.gov.il/english/Crime/Trend_Analysis/xx_trends.asp; **http://147.237.248.51/shnaton54/st02_01.pdf

nized gangs—perhaps also due to increased use of alcohol and drugs and culture-conflict of new immigrants. There was a steady rise in domestic violence in the mid 1990s—which may be due to an increased reporting rate because of increased public awareness to the problem of domestic and spouse abuse. However, in the last few years there has been a decrease in such cases, perhaps due to increased enforcement policy of the police and immediate arrest of abusing men.

Other major changes that have occurred in the last five years include the strengthening and infiltration of organized groups of criminals (many from abroad), who use Israel as a base for money laundering and for setting up gambling, prostitution, and drug-trafficking rings (Amir 1998; Landau 1998). Furthermore, there is an increase in fraud and so-called "white collar crimes"—especially within financial institutions. In recent years, there is an increase in the number of illegal foreign workers living and working in Israel. Their status precipitates other illegal activity—such as forgery of documents and fraud, trafficking in women for prostitution, property crime, and violent offences. In 2002, a special unit in the Police was established to deal expressly with enforcement issues regarding illegal workers.

Drug trafficking and drug abuse have also been on the rise, although in the last few years there has been a slight decrease in drug abuse by youth. However, there has also been a decrease in the age in which drug abuse begins (Anti-Drug Authority Annual Reports: www.antidrugs.org.il).

Traffic accidents pose a continuous problem, causing about 500 fatalities a year and between thirty to forty thousand injured. Since 2000, there has been a slight but steady decline in the number of fatal and other accidents around the country each year (www.police.gov.il).

There have been four victim surveys made by the Ministry of Public Security since 1979 and until 2001. During the last survey (2001) (Central Bureau of Statistics 2002), it was found that the victimization rate against persons is 10.2 and 7.3 pertaining to property crime, while only 37.5% reported crimes against the person and 45% reported property crime to the police.

Police Profile

Background

After the foundation of the state in 1948, a Ministry of Police was founded, to supervise both the Israel Police (henceforth, IP) and the Israel Prison Service; a single Commissioner for both the Israel Police and the Israel Prison Service reported directly to the Israeli Cabinet. From 1952, however, these functions were split.

In 1953, the Border Guard was set up within the IP to combat the problem of terrorist infiltrators and to patrol the State's frontiers. In the mid 1950s, the police force was organized geographically into districts. In 1958, the growing demand for police services forced the police to separate national staff work from field units. Its manpower and equipment establishment was codified; its investigations department went over to a proactive crime prevention strategy; beat policemen and juvenile crime units made their first appearance, and policewomen were given operational duties. In the 1950s and 1960s, the Forensic Laboratory was upgraded, and a mobile scene-of-crime laboratory introduced. In the early 1970s, candidates with a university education and ex-army officers were recruited directly to officer-rank positions. Technological and scientific advances were absorbed more and more into police work. Due to numerous Palestinian terrorist attacks, the government, in April 1974, decided to hand over responsibility for internal security within Israel to the IP, and this in turn compelled the IP to make wide-ranging organizational changes to accommodate its new responsibilities. The Civil Guard was set up to mobilize, train, and equip tens of thousands of volunteers for patrolling neighborhood streets. The Special Anti-Terrorist Unit and the Bomb Disposal Division were set up. The IP created its Operations Division in 1975 to coordinate and streamline the work of all operational branches. In the early 1980s the Community Relations Unit was set up. By the mid 1990s, police officers' working conditions and welfare improved. Applications for recruitment had risen, and the service set out to reevaluate its recruitment, placement, and training system, placing the emphasis on efficient and reliable service to the public, and encouraging ordinary citizens to extend their confidence in, and cooperation with, the police. IP intelligence services were overhauled, putting emphasis on drug-trafficking detection and enforcement. Special units were deployed on the borders and ports of the country. Early in 1995, the Community Policing Unit was created, whose function was to make policing more responsive to the needs of the ordinary citizen and to integrate the resources and goals of the police with those of Local Government Authorities and community agencies and services. 1995 saw also the creation of the Traffic Administration to coordinate the handling of urban and inter-city road traffic. In 1997, the IP's new Code of Ethics was officially introduced. Since 2000 to date, many police officers have been killed in the line of duty by terrorists, and a majority of the patrolling police are occupied with security matters. However, other problems plague the country: increased youth violence, computer and internet crime, white-collar crime, trafficking in drugs and drug-abuse, and trafficking in women and arms—some by organized crime rings. These have made it necessary for the police to set up special intelligence and operative units along the borders of the country, to upgrade international cooperation, to upgrade the computerized data bases of the IP, and to set-up computer crime units to deal more efficiently with a variety of new types of crimes.

Organizational Description

The force is commanded and directed, operationally and organizationally, by its Commissioner (known as "Inspector-General"), who is appointed by the Government on the recommendation of the Minister of Public Security. The Commissioner has no political affiliations and is usually a veteran police officer. Units attached to the national headquarters and directly responsible to the Commissioner are: the Office of the Legal Counsel, the Office of the Spokesperson, Accounting, the Office of the Internal Auditor and Ombudsperson, the Disciplinary Court, and Disciplinary Appeals Court, the Operational Safety Unit the Quality Service Unit, and the Illegal Immigrant Unit.

Eight Departments constitute the IP's national headquarters, which is situated in Jerusalem, the capital of Israel: Investigations and Crime Fighting, Patrol and Security, Intelligence, Traffic, Logistics, Personnel, Planning, and the Community and Civil Guard.

The functions of the IP's national HQ Departments—each in its field of expertise—include professional guidance and training to the units in the field, policy and decision making, gathering and analyzing data, research and development, logistic support, resource allocation, review of operations and procedures, and coordination with other departments and with external agencies.

The main computer systems are at HQ—containing the criminal files, ten-print fingerprint and palm print files of all convicted offenders, stolen vehicle files, and many other data bases, received from other Ministries—such as names, addresses and identification numbers of all adults in Israel, registration of all weapons and their ownership, vehicle registration, and driving licenses.

There are nationally based units, which are under the direct supervision of the Patrol and Operations Department: The Helicopter Unit, the National Vehicle Theft Prevention Unit, and a National Negotiation Team—used when hostage situations arise.

There are two national investigation units: one for serious and international crimes, (such as the operation of car theft rings, and drug-trafficking) and the second for dealing with white-collar crime, fraud and computer crime.

Divided into geographic areas, the IP is organized into District Commands (in 2004—there were seven Districts; however, the number has changed over the years—sometimes through integration and sometimes through separation). The District Commanders are directly responsible to the Police Commissioner. The District Commanders and the Department Heads at HQ all hold the rank of Major General and comprise the Senior Command Staff of the Commissioner.

These Districts are divided again into Sub-Districts, each of which is under the direction of a Police Commander. These are, in turn, divided into large Regional Police Stations or smaller Police Stations and Police Sub-Stations. To date (2004), there are ten large Regional Stations (mostly in the metropolitan centers), 53 stations, about 100 sub-stations, about 360 community policing centers (usually, one-man police centers in neighborhoods or rural villages, but sometimes a mobile or temporary centers set up in a specific area to deal with specific problems), and about 400 neighborhood Civil Guard Bases. The commanding officers of the police units are all selected by national and regional headquarters: town mayors or other heads of locally elected councils have no say in these appointments.

Each of the Districts and Sub-Districts is managed by an administrative and operational headquarters that parallels the organization of the central IP Headquarters in Jerusalem (i.e. Police functions such as investigations, patrol and security, traffic, personnel management, community and [volunteer] Civil Guard affairs, are all carried out at national, district, sub-district and station levels). There has been an attempt to flatten out the organizational structure and do away with the middle management (Sub-District) levels. This is a slow process that has yet to be completed. Furthermore, a strategic plan, set up by the Community and Civil Guard Dept., will decrease the number of Civil Guard Bases by joining them up with the existing and planned Community Policing Centers.

The budget of the IP is provided by the National Budget, and none is provided by municipal or other taxes. However, there are some services, provided by the police, that are paid for by the bodies or agencies receiving these services. These funds are channeled through the Ministry of Finance, to the IP.

In the last ten years the budget distribution has been as follows: over 75% for salaries; 22% for procurement; about 3% for R & D.

Demographics and Training

As of 2004, the Israel Police employs some 25,700 policemen and women, including soldiers doing their compulsory military service in the IP; 20% of this total are women. Virtually all staff is enlisted to the Police. Only since 1999 has the organization begun to civilianize some of the jobs—especially secretarial and logistical support jobs. This trend increases each year.

On an average (since 1995 to 2000), more than 1,000 men and women are recruited to the IP each year, the majority for the core duties of patrol work, investigations, intelligence, traffic control, bomb disposal, and the Community and Civil Guard. There are some 8,000 Border Guard police officers, 12% of whom are police officers from the ethnic minorities in Israel (Bedouin, Circassian, Christians, Druze and Moslems). Some of the police officers are recruited to the Border Guard as part of their compulsory military training (three years

for males, and two years for females), after completing their high-school studies at 18. Some of these continue on to a police career as regular police officers. In 1995, an amendment to the Security Service Act came into effect, enabling young men and women to do their compulsory military service in other branches of the police. Since then, hundreds each year have made this choice.

The Organizational Behavior Division at HQ is responsible for the selection process of all recruits - covering psychological and physical health, security clearance, schooling, and intelligence testing of candidates, who are examined for general suitability and for suitability to a particular area of activity of the IP. All candidates are obligated to have completed High School (12 years) and taken their matriculation exams. Police officers are assessed for placement and for promotion using testing, interviews, simulations—individually and in groups— and by the use of "assessment centers." An officer leaves the Service by personal request, retirement, or dismissal. The age for compulsory retirement is 55, but many retire at the age of 50 as well—receiving pension payments according to the years which they served (2% of their present salary, for each year of service).

On the whole, the working salary and the working conditions of the police officers are above the average in the Israeli public sector workforce. The Commissioned Officers' salary is "linked" to that of army personnel.

A new police officer, once recruited, participates in a basic 25-week training course, which consists of four weeks of physical training, seven weeks of general police training, and 14 weeks of specific police training. An officer must work for at least three years on the job before possible promotion to the next rank. A proficiency test in his area of work must be passed. After another year on the job, the officer can be recommended by his/her commanders to go to the "Advanced Police-Officers' Course"—a four to six weeks' specialized training course. During the fifth year in the service, the officer is also eligible to go to the "Senior Police-Officers' Course" for those police officers who are slated to become commanders of units. This five-to-ten-week course concentrates on material pertaining to the particular field of specialty of the police officer. Only after this second training course can a police officer be recommended for promotion to Commissioned Officer (CO) status and take part in the CO Course, which takes 30 weeks. During this training course, the officers also take part in academic studies for one semester at the Haifa University (for those who do not have academic degrees). For those who are slated to become Commanders of bureaus in police stations, a further six weeks' training in their particular area of work is necessary. For Police Station Commanders, a 13-week command and leadership course is given. For those appointed to be Sub-Division or a Regional Station Commander, there is a further six-week Senior Management Course.

Promotion from rank to rank is achieved by seniority, completion of training courses, and individual evaluation—both by commanders and peers. There are seven non-commissioned officer ranks and nine CO ranks.

Police officers having academic degrees are also recruited to the lowest rank, but can advance to Commissioned Officer, if they pass the assessment center and complete the Commissioned-Officer's Course, after about one year of service.

A new National Police Training Academy is being built and will include specially designed training areas for different police activities. There is a separate Senior Officer's Training Academy, which provides the training in management and planning, and The Operational Fitness Academy, which trains the police officers for self-defense, crowd dispersal, use of firearms and non-lethal weapons, moving around an urban environment, and subduing a suspect.

Functions

The Israel Police, from its inception in 1948, has been a national, highly centralized force. Under the Israel National Police Ordinance (Revised Version), 1971, which defines functions and powers of the IP, the Police force is responsible for the maintenance of law and order, for crime prevention, for traffic control, for the apprehension and remanding of criminals and suspected criminals, for securing public order, for safeguarding life and property; and for providing a secure environment for detainees (IP internet web site: *www.police.gov.il*, 2003).

In 1974, an additional responsibility was given to the IP—maintaining internal security and providing anti-terrorist activity within the borders of the country.

There are approximately 2,500 investigators (2003) and prosecutors. Police prosecutors present criminal cases to the Magistrate Courts, when dealing with all misdemeanors and some felonies. When a complaint has been reported to the police, and when there is reasonable belief that a crime has been committed, the police open a file and start an investigation. If the suspected offense is a misdemeanour or contravention, a police Commissioned Officer, with the rank of Captain (Chief Inspector) or higher, has the authority to decide that an inquiry falls within the jurisdiction of another agency having investigative and enforcement powers. In certain cases, there may be grounds for deciding not to investigate further or not to indict the suspect. In this case, the person who reported the offense receives a letter from the police stating the reasons for the decision.

After gathering the evidence, the police file is forwarded to the District Attorney's office or to the police prosecution unit or to other legal administrative units responsible for the prosecution of the crime. The responsible agency must then review the evidence and decide whether to request further clarification or investigation by the police, and whether there is a strong enough case to go to trial.

The investigative work is backed up by forensic science and criminal identification units at subdistrict and most police levels, and by various specialist units. The Investigation Department is also responsible for dealing with juveniles—both as suspects and as victims—from ages 12 (the age of criminal responsibility) until the age of 18. Youth police investigators, at the various levels, are specially trained, and in addition to their investigative work, they also work on preventive activity in the schools and exercise oversight on places of entertainment that are considered of high-risk to youth. They coordinate their activity with youth and community social services at the city and neighborhood levels. There are also specially trained "domestic violence investigators" to deal with this offense.

A Victim Support Unit provides the professional input on all policy and its implementation regarding the support given to victims of crime—especially regarding special groups, such as those of domestic abuse, sexual abuse, "helpless" victims (such as the mentally retarded) or the aged.

The Division of Identification and Forensic Sciences analyzes evidence using a range of tests (DNA, fingerprints, drugs, explosives and flammable materials, ballistics, etc.) in its specialized laboratories at HQ. Each regional subdivision has forensic technicians who are sent to gather evidence from crime scenes. The evidence is sent to the IP's central laboratories for further examination and for presentation by forensic experts as evidence in court. In addition, testing and evidence-gathering kits have been developed in-house and with collaboration with academic institutions. There is an Automatic Fingerprint Identification System (AFIS) at HQ, which helps compare latent fingerprints, found at the scenes of crime, with the fingerprints in the central data bank of known criminals and to authenticate the identification of suspects with the help of their fingerprints.

Intelligence efforts are concentrated on serious "target criminals" in accordance with an evaluation that is made at the various strata of the police hierarchy. All intelligence data are centrally computerized. The intelligence units are responsible for all drug-related enforcement work, as well as for international cooperation with foreign police forces. Since 1949, Israel has been a member of INTERPOL, and extensive operational cooperation takes place on a regular basis. Several police representatives are stationed abroad, in order to facilitate international investigations.

At the district level, there are centralized intelligence units, whose task is to gather evidence and do undercover work. Detectives work out of the stations at the local level, doing surveillance work, undercover operations, and gathering and analyzing intelligence.

Police officers can detain, question, arrest, and search a suspect, without a warrant, if they have reasonable suspicion that an offense has been committed, and if not arrested or detained, the suspect may cause harm to a person, to the public or to the security of the country. Furthermore, a police officer may arrest a suspect without a warrant if he believes that the suspect may disrupt an investigation or tamper with evidence or try to influence witnesses.

Upon the suspect's arrest, the police officer must identify himself, notify the suspect that he/she is under arrest, explain to him/her the reason for the arrest, and provide the arrestee with a copy of the warrant, if such exists. According to the new Criminal Procedure Law (Law Enforcement Powers and Arrest) 1996, the police have to bring the detained suspect before a judge, in order to extend remand in detention, no later than 24 hours after the initial arrest if the suspect is an adult, and no later than 12 hours, if the suspect is a minor under 14 years of age. The court may extend the period of detention for up to a maximum of 15 days. Usually, however, the court extends the period for five days at a time (Haberfeld and Herzog 2000; Sebba et al. 2003).

The IP has 10 detention centers (cells for holding suspects while they are under investigation and before prosecution or trial) at its disposal throughout the country. Most police stations also have some detention cells. Youths, adult men, and adult women are each confined separately, as required by law.

The patrol and operations unit's chief responsibility is to respond to public calls for assistance, usually telephoned into the Emergency Calls Center by dialing 100. They are the first line of response to any emergency, whether road accident, natural disaster, or terrorist attack.

At major events and large gatherings, the patrol units take charge of maintaining public order. If necessary, they are reinforced by officers drawn from other units. In certain events that are run by a profit-making body, the services of police officers can be hired for an hourly fee, in order to upgrade the standard police presence.

The Special Patrol Units were established to give the IP a rapid response capacity to incidents of particular severity or danger. Together with the Border Guard's Special Units, they are the first to respond to any life-endangering security incident or mass-casualty disaster. They are routinely deployed against particularly dangerous criminal targets or where there are geographical concentrations of criminal activity. Any arm of the IP can call on them for immediate reinforcement.

The patrol function uses cars, jeeps, motorcycles, scooters, dune-buggies, boats, and helicopters as well as horse patrol.

To help prevent terrorist and criminal activity in residential areas, the Civil Guard maintains a network of neighborhood Civil Guard Bases, run by a police officer, whose task is to recruit and operate armed mobile and foot patrols of volunteer citizens, run training programs, and organize rapid response teams for emergency duty.

Civil Guard volunteers, aged 17 to 90, number annually approximately 70,000. While on duty, the volunteers have police authority, and they are usually armed with police rifles and portable radio transmitters and identification vests given them only while on duty. Regular volunteers must volunteer for at least four hours per month, and they must undergo regular target practice and other police training courses. The Civil Guard also includes "special units" that provide volunteer aid to regular police units in traffic control and enforcement, patrol functions, emergency rescue units, and agricultural theft prevention. These uniformed volunteer units undergo specialized training and volunteer between four to six hours per week.

In 1994, the IP began to implement the Community Policing strategy. The essence of this approach is that the police should work in partnership with local authorities and community agencies, all pooling their resources to prevent or minimize crime, social problems that lead to crime, and incivilities that decrease the quality of life. Community Police Officers were deployed to Community Policing Centers in the rural areas and in the neighborhoods of large cities. Multiagency models for tackling different types of crimes are being implemented. (Geva 1995; 1998; 2003; Geva and Shem-Tov 2002).

In 1999, based on the COMPSTAT method used by the NYPD, computerization of all policing activities was implemented, linking the stations to the central computer at HQ. This allows the local police commanders, as well as the management staff, to keep track of changing crime and traffic accident patterns, and helps them plan preventive and enforcement strategies.

The traffic units enforce road traffic laws, investigate road accidents, and educate and inform the public in road discipline.

In the Traffic Department, specialists instruct other staff in traffic law enforcement, handle prosecutions, and investigate accidents; a strategic arm looks for ways to upgrade staff skills and develop new detection and enforcement technologies; an operational arm, the National Traffic Police, is responsible for enforcement and traffic flow on inter-urban roads and, together with local city traffic units, for enforcement campaigns inside towns. Specialized traffic units at all levels from station to district are assisted by thousands of Civil Guard volunteers.

The "2000 Traffic Command Center" updates the public on traffic conditions, by use of a system of CCTVs on major intersections and roadways. Other technological advances, such as an automated traffic-light camera ticket-issuing system, attempt to deal with the high rate of traffic accidents in the country.

The Planning Department manages all IP resources, its budget, its staff, and its data-banks. It coordinates all short- and long-range staff work and planning, and also designs systems and tools for planning, and for the collection and analysis of statistics. It also draws up and disseminates Police Orders and NHQ Directives.

The Technological Administration is responsible for developing and maintaining computer systems, building databanks, and supplying data processing services as well as communications systems to all police units. The IP is presently working to computerize all patrol vehicles, all border crossing checks by persons and vehicles, all police station work, the Investigations and Intelligence Departments, and other units.

The Logistical Support Department is charged with the management and care of the IP's material supplies, building projects, vehicle and other equipment procurement and maintenance, and the provision of logistical support to all IP operations and staff.

Dogs are used mainly for drug and explosive detection, search and rescue operations. Horses are used for patrol and crowd control.

Complaints and Discipline

At each District level, there is a Public Complaints Officer, who can receive complaints from the public and investigate them. The public can also send a complaint to the Police HQ Ombudsperson or to the Ministry of Public Security Ombudsperson. The Discipline Division draws up indictments for the IP's Disciplinary Court, where hearings are heard before the Police Judge, two additional Officers (who act as judges), and a "public representative" (a lawyer from another agency). There is also an Appeals Court.

Complaints which deal with suspected criminal matters or the un-lawful use of force are dealt with by the external "Department for the Investigation of Complaints Against Police Officers," under the supervision of the Ministry of Justice. It was set up in 1992 following public pressure and a gradual change in the attitudes regarding the issue of police accountability. Earlier, all complaints against police officers were handled internally by the IP. Less serious cases continue to be dealt with by the Internal Investigations Unit within the IP. If the complaint is sustained, then a Disciplinary Board hears the case and provides judgment. All verdicts are subject to appeal and are then passed onto the Disciplinary Appeals Board for further decision.

Training in police ethics is a part of all police training courses, at all stages of the police career (Geva 1995; Herzog 2000a; 2000b).

Terrorism

The IP is directly responsible for anti-terrorist activity and for security of the population within the country's borders. Thus, in 1995 responsibility for school perimeter security and, in 1997, for public transport security was also added. For this assignment, the IP has allocated a fleet of vehicle patrol units, briefed to patrol the perimeter and vicinity of schools and other educational institutions; and of bus, train, and taxi stations, to detect and prevent terrorist or criminal activity.

The Patrol and Operations Department is also responsible for providing input regarding the security standards needed to enable the licensing (by the local authority) of business premises, considered to be of "high-risk." At the local level, "business licensing officers" make visits to business premises to check the attainment of such standards, both before and upon renewal of licenses.

The IP's Anti-Terrorist Special Combat Unit, which organizationally belongs to the Border Guard, deals with terrorist activities within the borders of the country, operates in hostage-taking situations (both terrorist and criminal in nature), and sometimes assists in the handling of serious public disturbances.

The Border Guard Police is the para-military "gendarmerie" force within the IP, working under the supervision of the District Commanders. Its tasks are to deal with security and anti-terrorist duties, to guard and patrol the Israel-Palestinian Autonomous Area border, to deal with public order disruptions, and to prevent agricultural theft.

Established in 1975, the Bomb Disposal Division operates in the realm of both criminal and terrorist sabotage activities. The bomb disposal technicians, at the local level, handle about 100,000 calls per year to check suspicious objects, parcels, cars, and, lately, suspected persons carrying bombs on their person. On average, less than one percent of these calls involve actual incendiary or explosive devices. An important aspect of their work is the prevention program, which includes surveillance of crowded public areas and facilities, and educational programs in the schools.

The HQ Division has its own R&D Unit, to develop specialized equipment and techniques as well as a separate laboratory to provide analysis of explosive devices and *modus operandi*. The Israel Bomb Disposal Information Center gathers, analyzes, and disseminates information to police sappers and to other security organizations in the country and worldwide.

International Cooperation

Since the early 1970s, there has been much international cooperation between the IP and counterparts around the world in the area of forensic science, in which there is on-going collaboration, and also in research and development, with many major laboratories around the world. Joint projects have brought about development of new methods in the area of fingerprint identification, explosive analysis, etc.

Another major area of international cooperation—and especially since the early 1990s—is in bomb disposal and anti-terrorist tactics, equipment, and technologies. Numerous international Memoranda of Understandings have been signed with European and Asian countries in this respect, and these have brought about exchanges of police officers to study methods and techniques in the relevant countries (Geva 1995).

Since the late 1990s, Community Policing, especially the mobilization of police volunteers, has been another major field of cooperation with other countries (e.g., an exchange program with the State of Georgia).

Police Research and Publications

No formal police research institute exists in Israel at present. However, the Office of the Chief Scientist at the Ministry of Public Security is responsible for the planning, coordination, and analysis of police-related research. Each year, the Chief Scientist solicits Requests for Proposals (RFPs) from the IP and then chooses research groups (public or private) or agencies, through a tender process, to undergo the research which was decided upon for that year. This research varies from technological and forensic R & D to the social sciences and management areas. Within the police, various police departments have Research Sections, which undertake small-scale research projects in their field of activity. These include: forensic sciences, traffic enforcement, and technological and computer development projects, as well as in the management areas, and community policing.

The Community and Civil Guard Department at IP HQ publishes:

Marot Hamishtara (Police Sights): a bi-monthly journal, disseminated to all IP staff and IP pensioners as well as to journalists, judges, Members of Knesset, and libraries. No subscription. In Hebrew.

Mishtara Ve'Hevra (Police and Society): A reviewed academic annual publication, including articles and research reports. No Subscription. In Hebrew with English abstracts. Since its inception in 1997, it has produced eight issues. Since 2000, it is published in cooperation with the Senior Command School of the Israel Defense Forces (IDF). Distributed to libraries, academic institutions, and the Senior Command of the IP and the IDF.

The Ministry of Public Security-Information Services Division publishes a yearly journal in English called: *Innovation Exchange*. This publication publishes articles on the latest innovations in crime prevention, law enforcement, corrections, and incarceration. A major chapter in this journal contains articles on innovations and implementations in the IP. Since its inception in 1990 to date (2004), it has put out 11 issues.

The following are notable websites devoted to Israeli policing:

American Israel Public Affairs Committee (AIPAC): *www.us-israel.org*
Central Bureau of Statistics: *www.cbs.gov.il*
Israel Police: *www.police.gov.il*

Israel Prison Service: *http://ips.gov.il*
Israel Anti Drug Authority: *www.antidrugs.org.il*
Ministry of Foreign Affairs: *www.mfa.gov.il*

RUTH GEVA AND SERGIO HERZOG

Bibliography

Amir, Menahem. "Organized Crime in Israel." *Crime and Criminal Justice in Israel: Assessing the Knowledge Base Toward the Twenty-First Century*. Edited by Robert R. Friedmann. State University of New York Press, Albany, USA, SUNY Series in Israeli Studies, 1998. 121–138.

Bein, D. "Criminal Law." *The Law of Israel: General Survey*. Edited by Israel Zamir and S. Colombo, Haifa: University of Haifa, Israel, 1995.

Bensinger, Gad. *Justice in Israel: A Survey of Criminal Justice*. Chicago: University of Illinois, Office of International Criminal Justice, 1989.

———. "Crime and Criminal Justice." *Crime and Criminal Justice in Israel: Assessing the Knowledge Base Toward the Twenty-First Century*. Edited by Robert R. Friedmann. State University of New York Press, Albany, USA, SUNY Series in Israeli Studies, 1998. 43–61.

Central Bureau of Statistics. *Victimization Survey 2001*. October, Jerusalem, Israel, 2002 (Hebrew).

Friedmann, Robert R. (ed.). *Crime and Criminal Justice in Israel: Assessing the Knowledge Base Toward the Twenty-First Century*. State University of New York Press, Albany, USA, SUNY Series in Israeli Studies, 1998.

———. *An Annotated Bibliography of English Language Publications, 1948–1993*. Westport, CT: Greenwood Press, 1995.

Geva, R. "Innovative Methods for Crime Prevention in Israel and International Cooperation as the Means for Furthering These Methods." *The Prevention of Crime and the Treatment of Offenders in Israel – A Report*. Prepared for the Eighth UN Congress on the Prevention of Crime and the Treatment of Offenders, Cuba, August, 1990, 48–55. 1990.

———. "The Founding and Recent Activities of the National Crime Reduction Council in Israel." *The Prevention of Crime and the Treatment of Offenders in Israel – A Report*. Prepared for the Eighth UN Congress on the Prevention of Crime and the Treatment of Offenders, Cuba, 1990. 56–64. 1990.

———. "Feelings of Insecurity and Fear and Cooperation with the Police: The Israeli Experience." *International Faces of Victimology*. Edited by Sarah Ben David, and G.F. Kirchoff. WSV Publishing, Monchengladbach, 1992. 281–291.

———. "Crime Prevention Strategies: Twenty-Year Summary." *Innovation Exchange*, Issue 7 Jerusalem: Ministry of Public Security, Israel (1998), 28–37.

Geva, R. "The Principles of Professional Ethics in Law Enforcement in Israel as Pertaining to the Use of Force." *The Prevention of Crime and the Treatment of Offenders in Israel – A Report*. Prepared for the Eighth UN Congress on the Prevention of Crime and the Treatment of Offenders, Cuba, Aug. 1990, 80–86. Jerusalem: Ministry of Police, 1990.

———. "Effective national and international action against terrorism: the Israeli experience." *The Prevention of Crime and the Treatment of Offenders in Israel*. Edited by Ruth Geva. Prepared for the Eighth UN Congress on the Prevention of Crime and the Treatment of Offenders, Cairo, Egypt, August, 1995, 71–84, 1995.

———. (1995). "The Ministry of Police and the Israel National Police." *Police and Government Security Technology*. (1995):98–101.

———. "Community Policing in Israel." *The Police Chief* vol. LXV, no. 12 (1998): 77–82.

———. "Crime Prevention: The Community Policing Approach in Israel." *International Perspective on Community Policing and Crime Prevention*. Edited by Stanley Lab and Dilip Das, Prentice Hall, 2002.

Haberfeld, Maki, and Sergio Herzog. (2000). "The Criminal Justice System in Israel." *Comparative and International Criminal Justice Systems: Policing, Judiciary and Corrections*. Edited by Ebbe Obi, 55–78, New York: Butterworth / Heinemman, 2000.

Hasin, Yael, and Menaham Horovitz. "Juvenile and Adult Probation in Israel." *Crime and Criminal Justice in Israel*. Edited by Robert R. Friedmann. State University of New York Press, Albany, USA, SUNY Series in Israeli Studies, 1998. 315–336.

Herzog, Sergio. (2000a). "The Treatment of Illegal-Use-of-Force Complaints Against Police Officers in Israel: The Beleaguered Path to Civilian Involvement." *Police Quarterly*, vol. 2, no.4 (2000a): 477–501.

———. "Evaluating the New Civilian Police Complaints Board in Israel." *Civilian Oversight of Complaints Against Police: Governance, Democracy and Human Rights*. Edited by Andrew Goldsmith and Colleen Lewis. Oxford: Hart Publishing Co., 2000b. 125–146.

———. "Border Closures as a Reliable Method for the Measurement of Palestinian Involvement in Crime in Israel: A Quasi-Experimental Analysis." *International Journal of Comparative Criminology*, vol. 3, no.1 (2003): 18–41.

Horovitz, Menaham. "Juvenile Justice in Israel." *The Prevention of Crime and the Treatment of Offenders in Israel–A Report*. Prepared for the Eighth UN Congress on the Prevention of Crime and the Treatment of Offenders, Cuba, August, 1990. 105–114. 1990.

Israel Police, *Annual Reports*.

Israel Prison Service, *Annual Reports*.

Kremnitzer, Mordechai, "Criminal Law in Israel." *Crime and Criminal Justice in Israel: Assessing the Knowledge Base Toward the Twenty-First Century*. Edited by Robert R. Friedmann. State University of New York Press, Albany, USA, SUNY Series in Israeli Studies, 1998. 185–205.

Landau, Simcha. F. "Crimes of Violence In Israel: Theoretical and Empirical Perspectives." *Crime and Criminal Justice in Israel: Assessing the Knowledge Base Toward the Twenty-First Century*. Edited by Robert R. Friedmann. State University of New York Press, 1998. 97–120.

Ohana, D. "Sentencing Reform in Israel: The Goldberg Committee Report." *Israel Law Review*, vol. 32, (1998): 591–643.

Rahav, Giora. "Criminal Statistics." *Crime and Criminal Justice in Israel: Assessing the Knowledge Base Toward* the *Twenty-First Century*. Edited by Robert R. Fried-mann. State University of New York Press, Albany, USA, SUNY Series in Israeli Studies, 1998. 65–78.

Sebba, Leslie. "[Prison Labour in] Israel." *Prison Labour: Salvation or Slavery? International Perspectives*. Edited by F Dunkel and D. VanZyl Smit. Darmouth, Aldershot, 1999. 115–144.

Sebba, Leslie., Menahem Horovitz, and Ruth Geva. *Israel, Criminal Justice Systems in Europe and North America*, HEUNI, Finland, 2003.

Sebba, Leslie. "Sanctioning Policy in Israel – an Historical Overview." *Israel Law Review*, vol. 30, (1996): 234-275.

———. "Victims' Rights and Legal Strategies: Israel as a Case Study." *Criminal Law Forum*, vol. 11, (2000): 47–100.

Shadmi, Erella. "Police and Police Reform in Israel: The Formative Role of the State." *Crime and Criminal Justice in Israel: Assessing the Knowledge Base Toward the*

Twenty-First Century. Edited by Robert R. Friedmann. State University of New York Press, 1998. 217–241.

Shavitt, Gabriel. "The Israeli Prison System." *Crime and Criminal Justice in Israel*. Edited by Robert R. Friedmann. State University of New York Press, Albany, USA, SUNY Series in Israeli Studies, 1998. 275–313.

Weiss, Shoshana. *The National Anti-Drug Authority*. www.antidrugs.org.il, 2002.

Weisburd, David., Orit Shalev, and Menahem Amir. *Community Policing in Israel: A National Evaluation* Bureau of the Chief Scientist, Jerusalem: Ministry of Public Security, Israel, 2001. (English summary).

Wozner, Yochanan. "Rehabilitation Efforts in the Israel Prison Service." *Crime and Criminal Justice in Israel: Assessing the Knowledge Base Toward the Twenty-First Century*. Edited by Robert R. Friedmann. State University of New York Press, Albany, USA, SUNY Series in Israeli Studies, 1998. 337–355.

ITALY

Background Material

The Italian nation dates back to 1861. In the early nineteenth century, a nationalist movement developed and led to the reunification of Italy (excluding Rome) in the 1860s. In 1861, Victor Emmanuel II of the House of Savoy was proclaimed King of Italy. Rome was annexed in 1870. Between 1870 and 1922, Italy was a constitutional monarchy with a parliament elected under limited suffrage. In 1922, Benito Mussolini came to power and, over the next few years, eliminated political parties, curtailed personal liberties, and installed a fascist dictatorship termed the Corporate State. The king, with little or no effective power, remained titular head of state. Italy allied with Germany and declared war on the United Kingdom and France in 1940. In 1943, when the defeat in the war and the failure of the dictatorship project seemed highly probable, the King dismissed Mussolini and appointed Marshal Pietro Badoglio as prime minister. The Badoglio government declared war on Germany, which quickly occupied most of the country and freed Mussolini. For two years, until April 1945, when German forces were driven out, Italy was the site of a civil war. After the end of World War II, in 1946, a plebiscite ended the monarchy, and a constituent assembly was elected to draw up plans for the republic.

Italy is a founding member of the European Union. Its territory measures approximately 301,200 sq km, with a population of currently 57 million. The presence of settled immigrants is increasing. The citizens of other countries with regular residence permits numbered approximately 1.3 million, somewhat more than 2% of the resident population. Compared to previous records, the foreign population increased by about 5%. The most numerous communities are, in decreasing order, Moroccan, Albanian, Philippine, Yugoslavian, Tunisian, and Chinese. The language mainly taught and spoken is High Italian (although in Alto Adige and Valle d'Aosta, also German, Ladino and French are spoken). The citizens are obliged to attend school until ninth grade. The majority of inhabitants are Catholic, but there is a small Muslim community (1.2%). The average per capita income is 24,019, on an annual basis. Italy is among the most industrialized countries in the world. It is a member of the European Union and G8, and part of the European Union-Schengen area, in which all internal border controls have been abolished. The official currency is the Euro.

Contextual Features

Italy is a constitutional parliamentary republic functioning on the basis of the separation of powers. Legislative power is exercised by a Parliament formed by two chambers ("*Senato*" and "*Camera dei deputati*"). Both the Chambers (composed of 315 "*Senatori*" and 630 "*Deputati*") are elected by a majority system, with the exception of 25 percent of the *Deputati* who are elected through a proportional system. Italy has also deputies in the European Parliament. The executive power is exercised by the "*Governo della Repubblica*" (Government of the Republic), composed by the "*Presidente del Consiglio*" (President of the Council) and by the "*Ministri*" (Ministers). The President and the Ministers constitute, together, the Council of Ministers. The President of the Council is nominated by the "*Presidente della Repubblica*" (President of the Republic); the Ministers are also nominated by the President of the Republic, on the recommendation of the President of the Council. Usually, the nomination of the President of the Council by the President of the Republic is determined by the result of the elections; the political leader of the winning coalition is nominated as President of the Council. After the nomination of the President and the Ministers, and their oath in the hands of the President of the Republic, the Government must receive the "*fiducia*" (a vote of confidence) by each Chamber of the Parliament. If one of the Chambers—or both—denies the confidence, the Government is obliged to resign. In the Italian System, the President of the Republic lacks of executive powers and operates as an impartial entity, with the duty to watch over the constitutional guarantees and rights. The President of the Republic is elected by the Parliament, in "*seduta comune*" (plenary session, in which the Chambers vote together), is the Head of the Italian State, and represents the National unity.

The independence of the judiciary is guaranteed by the Constitution.

Italy has the statutory legal system of continental European tradition. From a statistical point of view, in the last 30 years crimes against persons have generally not increased. An exception is represented by murders and most serious crimes, whose number has grown since 1978. In recent years, almost 75% of the crimes reported to the police were thefts. Only 6.7% were crimes against persons. A large part of the crimes related to drug trafficking. About eight percent of the offenses were economic and financial violations, often connected to the powers and functions of public administration.

Criminal courts of first instance handle violations of the law listed in the Penal Code or in other sources of law (the so called "special legislation"); they are divided into two categories: "*contravven-zioni*" (minor offences) and "*delitti*" (misdemeanors and felonies).

Less serious offenses, including both *contravvenzioni* and *delitti*, are handled either by the "*Giudice di Pace*" ("Justice of Peace") or by a "*Tribunale in composizione monocratica*" ("Court in monocratic composition"), which both sit as a single judge. The Justice of the Peace, created in 2001, has an *ad hoc* jurisdiction. In other words, his/her jurisdiction is delimited *per nomina delicti*, because there are specific crimes—both "*contravvenzioni*" and "*delitti*"—expressly assigned to this judge. All other minor offenses, punished with the imprisonment up to 10 years, fall within the jurisdiction of the "*Tribunale in composizione monocratica.*" The crimes punished with imprisonment for more than 10 years in the maximum are assigned to the "*Tribunale in composizione collegiale*" ("Court in collegial composition"), which sits with three judges. For the most serious crimes (major offenses like murder), the jurisdiction lies with the "*Corte d'Assise*" (Assizes Court), composed of two professional judges and six lay judges, citizens drawn by lot from a list. The professional and lay judges decide jointly whether the accused is innocent or guilty and which sentence is to be passed. Instances of appeal are the "*Corte d'Appello*" (Court of appeal), and the "*Corte d'Assise d'Appello*" (Assizes Court of Appeal), which is responsible for the crimes assigned in first instance to the *Corte d'Assise*. The minor offenses and the misdemeanors under the jurisdiction of the Justice of Peace are in second instance examined by the Tribunal in single composition. The supreme instance is the "*Corte di Cassazione*" (Supreme court for the judiciary). Under Art. 111 of the Constitution, it is possible to file appeal to the *Corte di Cassazione* against all judgments and decisions in the field of personal freedom. The role of the *Corte di Cassazione* is to control the correct application and interpretation of the law by the other courts and judges; the *Corte di Cassazione* has no power to review the facts of a case, but only the exact application of the legal rules.

Notwithstanding its inquisitorial traditions, Italy, since 1989, has had a new Code of Criminal Procedure, modeled on the adversarial system typical of common law. As a consequence of this political choice, a general distinction between the investigation phase and the trial is provided for, and, in general, all the information collected in the first phase of the proceeding—the investigations—is not admitted at the Trial as evidence. This principle stems from the need to ensure the right to confrontation and cross-examination of the defendant in the criminal process, which could be frustrated by the admission of untested statements collected by the police, unilaterally, in the course of the investigations. For the same reason, a particular rule against hearsay in relation of the police testimony at Trial is provided for, according to which the police cannot be examined on the statements collected or on the declarations received during the first phase of the proceedings by persons informed on the facts investigated.

Since the adoption of the Constitution in 1948, the prosecutors belong to the Judiciary and are independent of any other power. They are entitled to the same guarantees of independence and irremovability as the judges. Both prosecutors and judges are classified as "*magistrati*" (judicial officials). They are selected through the same competitive examinations and follow the same career, and once appointed they may move from one function to the other, of course only at their own request. To fully guarantee the independence of the prosecutor, the Constitution provides that the police, during the investigations of a criminal case, act under the control of the prosecutor, even though every police institution belongs to the executive branch, from an administrative point of view. In other words, the prosecutor's orders are binding for the police forces in criminal proceedings and investigations, notwithstanding their belonging to the executive branch.

The administration of prisons is part of the Ministry of Justice. Article 59 of Law No 354 of 26 July 1975 establishes four types of prisons:

1. *Istituti di custodia cautelare* (Preventive Detention Institutes) are intended for the detention of persons indicted in criminal cases, pending the investigations or the Trial.
2. *Istituti per l'esecuzione delle pene* (Penitentiary Institutes) serve to the execution of the sentence after the end of the criminal process.
3. *Istituti per l'esecuzione delle misure di sicurezza* (Institutes for Preventive Measures) serve to the execution of measures applied by the judge, at the end of the criminal cases, to dangerous persons either convicted or acquitted for mental insanity.
4. *Centri di Osservazione* (Observation Centers) are intended for the observation of the personality of detained persons. They can also be used for the purposes of medical reports or psychiatric examination during the criminal process.

In Italy, there are 256 prisons of different types. Currently, approx. 56,000 persons are detained in Italian jails, five percent of whom are women.

The death penalty was abolished in 1948, after the ratification of the Constitution, which, in Article 27, paragraph 4, excludes the death penalty from the field of penal sanctions. This provision prohibits the death penalty only in period of peace. One might object that this sanction would not be illegal in terms of the Italian Constitution if applied during a war period. However, in 1994, the Legislator abolished the death penalty even in the penal military code. The penal sanctions are mainly imprisonment (one day, for minor offenses, to 30 years for particularly serious crimes; a life sentence is possible for the most serious crimes) and fines. Other sanctions, such as confiscation of assets or property, are possible in certain cases.

Police Profile

Background, Organizational Description, and Functions

Since the reunification of the Italian state, there have been three policing bodies: the *Carabinieri*, the *Polizia di Stato*, and the *Guardia di Finanza*.

The *Arma dei Carabinieri* (*Carabinieri* force) was created in 1814, after the Vienna Congress, by the King of Sardinia. From the very beginning, the duty and the power to protect the state and to enforce domestic law in the field of criminal and public law (internal security) were attributed to this police institution. The dual character of this military body, with duties and powers in state defense and internal security, was confirmed through the years, from the reunification of Italy (in 1861) to the Constitution (1948) and up to now. The *Carabinieri* force is the most widespread enforcement body in the Italian territory, given that their offices are located in every municipal district. Just as all the other police bodies mentioned above, the *Carabinieri* force belongs to the executive branch. As a special feature, the *Carabinieri* are placed under the control of the Ministry of the Defense (whereas State Police belong to the Ministry of Home Affairs and the *Guardia di Finanza* to the Finance Ministry).

The founding of the *Polizia di Stato* (State Police) dates back to 1848, by a decision of the King of Sardinia, who gave to this body a structure not too different from the present organization. The task of the State Police is to act as a National Security Authority. It is responsible for public order and security maintenance.

In the carrying out of his/her function of high direction and co-ordination of the police forces' tasks and activities, the Minister of Home Affairs, under which the *Polizia* are put, is supported by the Public Order and Security Committee, an advisory body consisting of an Undersecretary of the Interior—(as its deputy chairman), of the Chief of

Police—(Director General of Public Security), and of the heads of the other Police Forces.

The function of Public Security Administration is exercised, at the central level, by the Public Security Department and, at the local level, by provincial and local authorities, public security officials, and local officers. The public security provincial authorities are the following: the Prefect, in charge of the Territorial Government Office, having the general responsibility of public order and security; and the "*Questore*," the senior official of the State Police, responsible for the direction and technical and operational coordination of public order and security services, and of police force employment.

Local public security authorities are State Police officials in charge of detached *Commissariati di pubblica sicurezza* (police stations). Where the latter are not present, the functions of local public security authorities are exercised by the mayor in his/her role of government official. The State Police staff carrying out police functions amounts to 109,144 officials belonging to the ranks of managers, executives, inspectors, sergeants (*sovrintendenti*), assistants (*assistenti*), and agents. The technical-scientific activity or technical activity is performed by further 5,720 officers.

The *Guardia di Finanza* (Financial Police) act under the control of the Minister of Finance. They are organized as a military body. The tasks of the *Guardia di Finanza* include prevention, investigation, and law enforcement in the field of the financial infringements, and, in general terms, enforcement of all the laws and rules of economical or financial interest. Its fundamental duties are the investigation and the reporting of cases of tax evasion and financial violations. Moreover, this body has powers regarding public security (in the field of money laundering, smuggling, trade of stolen works of art, drug trafficking) and regarding the political-military defense field. In recent years, the protection of financial interests was extended to the protection, in Italian territory, of those of the European Union. The *Guardia di Finanza* can thus initiate investigation, under criminal and administrative law, in view of the protection and enforcement of the European law, as far as it may be infringed on Italian soil.

As an EU member, Italy participates in the police and justice structures at the European level. The European police coordination center, Europol, is in charge of the collection, analysis, and dissemination of law enforcement information. It has been set up to help law enforcement agencies (mainly police and customs) when carrying out investigations in two or more EU countries.

Eurojust, as the European agency responsible for improving cooperation between the EU member states' judiciary, is composed of legal and judicial experts. Their mission is to help coordinate the investigation and prosecution of serious cross-border crimes within the EU.

OLAF, the Anti-Fraud Office, as a special agency of the European Commission, is in charge of administrative investigations of infringements against financial and other interests of the European Community, including certain forms of corruption.

Italy is also a party to the Schengen conventions. These conventions, while abolishing passport controls at the internal borders of the signatory states, created a single external border at which immigration checks for the Schengen area are carried out in accordance with a common set of rules. All European citizens have the right of moving freely in the entire EU territory. This freedom of movement is accompanied by so-called "compensatory" measures, involving the efforts to improve the coordination between the police, customs, and the judiciary and to take the necessary measures to combat terrorism and organized crime. In order to make this possible, a complex information system known as the Schengen Information System (SIS) was set up to exchange data on the identities of persons and descriptions of objects stolen or lost.

In the criminal process, the police operate under the control and guidance (or supervision, in practice) of the prosecutor. The police stations acting under the prosecutorial control are called juridical police stations. There are thus *carabinieri* army juridical stations, police juridical stations, and financial police juridical stations. In the first stages of investigation, the police are partially independent of the prosecutor. In fact, when researching the *notitia criminis* (information of the existence of a crime) and conducting on-site investigations, the police can act without the control of the prosecutor. Once the commission of an offense is discovered, the police must report it to the prosecutor without delay. Under the supervision of the prosecutor, the police may carry out specific acts of investigation, such as summoning and questioning suspects, witnesses, and victims. Only in cases provided for by the law may the police search persons and premises. When a person is found in the act of committing a serious crime, or where there is the risk that the suspect may escape, the police have the power to arrest him provisionally ("*arresto in flagranza*"), but, within 24 hours, they must communicate the arrest to the prosecutor (who, within the following 24 hours, must request that a judge validate the arrest).

Once the investigation is concluded, the prosecutor may either file an indictment or request permission to dismiss the case from to the "*Giudice per le indagini preliminari*" (Preliminary Judge) The judge has the power to oblige the prosecutor to perform further investigations, or he can order to the prosecutor to take action against the suspect. According to the Constitution, the prosecutor is obliged to take action in criminal cases; the principle of legality strictly rules. No discretion is allowed to the prosecutor by the law, no matter how slight the offense is. The prosecutor has no choice on whether to prosecute or not, nor can he suspend or withdraw the action, which must always end in a judicial decision. Nevertheless, as a matter of fact enough room is left for prosecutorial discretion. Whereas the obligation to bring a proceeding has no stated exceptions, the law does not settle any priority to the prosecutor when dealing with pending cases; consequently, he may choose the investigations to be put forward, as well as the resources to be employed in every single case. The judicial control concerns only the decision not to prosecute, and not the time or the manner in which the prosecution takes place.

Within 48 hours from the arrest, the police must place the person arrested at the disposal of the president of the court of appeal of the district in which the person was arrested. The president of the court of appeal must validate the arrest within 96 hours from the very beginning of the measures adopted by the police. When 96 hours from the arrest have passed without any judicial confirmation, the person has to be released.

Training

Recruitment for the *carabinieri, polizia di stato* and *guardia di finanza* service is open to both male and female candidates.

There are several levels of recruitment. The applicants must be Italian and pass a selection exam. There are schools for different levels.

For the *polizia di stato*, the *Direzione Centrale per gli istituti di istruzione* (Central Directorate for School Institutes) is in charge of the management and coordination of all police schools. There are several police schools throughout the territory, including on the islands.

Regarding the *carabinieri*, the necessary training is provided by facilities for individual and collective preparation, ranging from basic military training to more specialized career training. The Training School is required to prepare participants to carry out their military and public order duties to the best of their ability, thereby maintaining the high standards of the Institution. Furthermore, there is the *Carabinieri* Officers' College with headquarters in Rome; the Warrant Officer and Brigadier Training School, based in Florence with detachments at Velletri (Rome) and Vicenza for the training of Warrant Officers and Brigadiers of the *Carabinieri* Force; and finally, *Carabinieri* Cadet Training Schools provide basic military, technical-professional training for young people who join the Force. There is an 11-month course for permanent *Carabinieri*, a five-month course for auxiliaries who are enlisted for a four-year period of service, and a three-month course for those enlisted for one year.

The *guardia di finanza* has two main educational institutions. The most important is the "*Accademia*" (academy), with headquarters in Bergamo and Roma, in charge of the organization of all basic training activities for the officials of the corps and for the apprentices. The second one is the "*Scuola di Polizia Tributaria*" (Police Tax School), located in Roma, for all the training activities connected with fiscal law.

Throughout their careers, all police officers have to periodically attend training events.

Police Use of Firearms

All police officers are equipped with handguns. There may also be other kinds of firearms for particularly dangerous operations. The law establishes the conditions for the legal use of firearms. A police officer may carry his gun at any time but may use it only in case of self-defense (article 52 of the Penal Code). Moreover, a special case of justification is provided article 53 of the Penal Code) for the police officer who uses a firearm with the purpose of performing a duty imposed by the law. In this case, however, the officer, in order to be excused, has to demonstrate that he/she was obliged to use the firearm by the strict necessity to respond to violence and in general to prevent the commission of a crime. A police officer firing in any other circumstances is subject to disciplinary and penal sanctions.

Complaints and Discipline

The state requires a strong service commitment from all police corps members. The commitment includes non-stop duty, obligation of obedience, obligation of dignity (even in private life), duty of reserve, professional secrecy, and the obligation of exclusive public service. There is a code of deontology of the National Police for police officers. There are sanctions in case of the violation of duties.

The activities of police officers are subject to several types of control (hierarchical control, internal control, and judicial control).

It is important to mention that the prosecutor has some limited powers with regard to the organization of police, particularly in disciplinary matters. The approval of the Prosecutor of the Republic and of General Prosecutor to the Court of Appeals is necessary in order to remove chief constables of the police and for their promotions. The prosecutor lacks hierarchical powers to sanction the misconduct of the police, but the General Prosecutor to the Court of Appeals has the power to initiate disciplinary proceedings. When such action is taken, a Commission composed of two judicial officers and one police officer decides whether there has been misconduct and which sanctions must be applied.

Italy is a party to the international human rights treaties (International Covenant on Civil and political Rights and its protocols) and to the European Convention of Human Rights and Fundamental Freedoms (treaty open for signature by the member States of the Council of Europe). Italy respects, through its Constitution and its laws, the rights therein contained.

As said above, the death penalty was abolished in Italy in 1948, after the entry in force of the Constitution. Italy has ratified the Treaty on the International Criminal Court in 1999.

Terrorism

In the past, Italy has experienced the threat of terrorism, although terrorist organizations have become, in the last 30 years, progressively weaker and more isolated. There was a period of Marxist-Leninist terrorism in the 1970s, with the "Red Brigades" (*Brigate Rosse*) being the most important extreme leftist terrorist organization. The most relevant action of the BR was the murder of Aldo Moro, former President of the Council of Ministers and, at the time of the murder, Secretary General of the "*Democrazia Cristiana*," the most important Italian political party. But it would be incorrect to mention the murder of President Moro only, because, during the 1970s and the first half of the 1980s, there were many murders and assaults of other politicians, judges, policemen, and citizens with important roles in the democratic society. In the recent past, there were two murders attributed to the BR terrorists: the targets were two scholars (Prof. Marco Biagi, on March 10, 2003, and Prof. Massimo D'Antona, on May 20, 1999), experts in the field of the labor law, who were cooperating

with the government to draft reforms in the field of the labor market and social security.

Italy has a comprehensive and coherent body of anti-terrorist legislation. Terrorism is legally defined, and terrorist offenses within the meaning of the definition are subject to special procedures. Terrorist offenses are defined in Articles 270 *bis* (conspiracy for the purpose of committing acts of terrorism or subversion of the democratic order; and also for the purpose of committing acts of international terrorism, introduced in 2001, after the September 11 attack), 270 *ter* (aid to terrorist conspirators, introduced in 2001), 280 (terrorist attack) of the Penal Code.

Terrorism is partially subject to the ordinary rules of procedure, except when otherwise provided. These exceptions are applied to the terrorist offenses as well as to the organized crime. Among many provisions, it is important to remember the rules about the duration of the investigations, which can last up to 24 months (usually the maximum period of investigation is 18 months). Another important divergence from the ordinary procedure is the use of hearsay evidence at trial. Usually, in the Italian system, the investigation file is not admitted as evidence at trial, and all the witnesses have to testify orally before the judge, and be cross-examined. In terrorism cases, the law allows the admission as evidence of police reports and investigation acts (Article 190 *bis* of the Italian Code of Criminal Procedure). Finally, the use of wiretapping is easier, in the investigation of such crimes. In ordinary investigations, wiretapping is admitted, with the consent of the judge, only when it is "absolutely necessary" for moving on with the investigations, and if there are "serious reasons to believe that a crime has been committed"; instead, in terrorism and organized crime investigations, wiretapping is allowed when it is simply "necessary" to carry on the investigation, and if there are "sufficient reasons to believe that a crime has been committed." Other particular provisions were approved, after September 11, 2001, for undercover investigations by police, with the purpose to improve the element of evidence gathered by investigators and enforcement agencies.

International Cooperation

With regard to cooperation within the European Union, Italy fully participates in the police cooperation developed in that framework, in particular the Schengen agreements.

In general, at the European level, the Italian system of police and judicial cooperation is very similar to those provided for in other European Countries, like France and Germany. Particularly, Italy has signed, and, at present, has almost implemented, the European Arrest Warrant, an instrument of judicial cooperation greatly simplifying the procedure by replacing the whole political and administrative phase of extradition within a simple judicial mechanism. If the facts for which the European Arrest warrant is issued are punishable in the issuing Member State by a custodial sentence of at least three years, the following offenses, among others, may give rise to surrender without verification of the double criminality of the act: terrorism, trafficking in human beings, corruption, participation in a criminal organization, counterfeiting currency, murder, racism and xenophobia, rape, trafficking in stolen vehicles, and fraud, including that affecting the financial interests of the Communities. For criminal acts other than those mentioned above, surrender may be subject to the condition that the act for which surrender is requested constitutes an offense under the law of executing Member State (double criminality rule).

As a general rule, the issuing authority transmits the European arrest warrant directly to the executing judicial authority.

Further international cooperation is governed by the constitutional principle that treaties prevail over domestic law on condition of reciprocity. Most exchanges relating to mutual legal assistance in criminal matters take place on the basis of either the European Convention of April 20, 1959, the convention implementing the Schengen agreement, or bilateral conventions. The majority of extraditions are carried out on the basis of the European convention of 13 December 1957 or bilateral conventions.

If no convention or European Union rule applies, requests for legal assistance and extradition are governed by Italian Code of Criminal Procedure (articles from 697 to 713). It is important to observe that, where it is requested that the dual criminality rule, it is not necessary for the definition of the offense in the law of the requesting State to be exactly the same as the definition in Italian law.

Police Education, Research, and Publications

For research in police matters and security, the most relevant state institutions are as follows.

For police, the *Direzione Generale per gli Istituti di Istruzione* (General Directorate for Training Institutes), with the Central Library located in Viminale Palace (Ministry of Home Affairs), Piazzale del Viminale, 1-00184 Roma (RM).

For the *carabinieri*, the *Centro Alti Studi per la Difesa* (CASD—High Studies Center for the Defence) is the highest institution for the education and training in the field of the State Defense and State security. The Center is located in Roma, Piazza Della Rovere, 83-00165 Roma (RM).

For the *Guardia di Finanza*, the *Accademia della Guardia di Finanza* (Guardia di Finanza Academy), located in Bergamo, Via Statuto 21, 24100 Bergamo.

Police-related periodicals :

Rassegna dell'Arma dei Carabinieri (Carabinieri Force Review), Scuola Ufficiali Carabinieri ed., Via Aurelia n.511-00165 Roma;
Polizia moderna (*Modern Police*), official review of the State Police, piazza del Viminale, 7 00184 Roma;
Rivista giuridica di polizia (*Police Law Review*), Maggioli ed., Rimini;
Rivista della Guardia di Finanza (*Finance Police Review*), Viale XXI aprile, 51–00162, Roma

Websites:

Carabinieri: *www.carabinieri.it*
State Police (*Polizia di Stato*): *www. poliziadistato.it*
Guardia di Finanza (Guardia di Finanza): *www. gdf.it*
Penitentiary Police (*Polizia penitenziaria*): *www. polizia-penitenziaria.it*

MICHELE CAIANIELLO

Bibliography

Cantagalli, Raffaello, and Tindari Baglione. *Manuale pratico della polizia giudiziaria* (Practical Judicial Police Handbook). Roma: Laurus Robuffo, 2000.

Carofiglio, Giovanni. *La testimonianza dell'ufficiale e dell'agente di polizia giudiziaria* (Judicial Police Officers Testimony in Criminal Process). Milano: Giuffrè, 1998.

Ceresa-Gastaldo, Massimo. *Le dichiarazioni spontanee dell'indagato alla polizia giudiziaria* (Spontaneous Statements by the Suspect to Judicial Police During Criminal Investigations). Torino: Giappichelli, 2002.

Conso, Giovanni, and Vittorio Grevi, (Eds.). *Compendio di procedura penale* (Criminal Procedure Digest). Padova: Cedam, 2003.

Cordero, Franco. *Procedura penale* (Criminal Procedure). Milano: Giuffrè, 2003.

D'ambrosio, Loris. *Diritto penale per l'attività di polizia giudiziaria* (Criminal Law and Juridical Police Activity). Padova: Cedam, 1999.

Gaggiotti Antonella, and Maurizio Marinelli. *Gli atti della polizia giudiziaria* (Judicial Police Deeds). Rimini: Maggioli, 1999.

Ingletti, Vito. *Diritto di polizia giudiziaria : diritto penale, procedura penale, diritto di polizia*, Laurus Robuffo,

(Judicial Police Law: Criminal Law, Criminal Process, Police Law). Roma: Laurus Robuffo, 2004.

Morgigni, Aldo. *L'attività della polizia giudiziaria* (The Activity of the Judicial Police). Milano: Giuffrè, 2002.

Rinella, Leonardo, and Enrico Sgambati. *Manuale di polizia giudiziaria : guida-prontuario agli atti di polizia giudi-ziaria* (Judicial Police Handbook: a Practical Guide to the Judicial Police Deeds). Rimini: Maggioli, 1994.

Scaglione, Antonio. *L' attività ad iniziativa della polizia giudiziaria* (The Activity of the Judicial Police in the Criminal Proceeding). Torino: Giappichelli, 2001.

J

JAMAICA

Background Material

The written history of Jamaica usually begins with the "discovery" of the island by Christopher Columbus in 1492. The Spanish were not disinterested explorers. On his arrival in the Caribbean, Columbus noted in his journal, "I was attentive and took trouble to ascertain if there was gold" (Williams 1983:23). But Jamaica was not rich in precious metals, and was conquered and settled primarily for agricultural exploitation. Sugarcane production was organized on the system of plantation slavery. This system and fatalities from exposure to new diseases brought from Europe, led to Spanish extermination of the indigenous population and their replacement by slaves imported from Africa. Like the other Caribbean Islands, Jamaica emerged as a society based on transplanted populations drawn initially from Europe and Africa and later from India and China (as indentured labourers after the end of slavery).

When the British captured Jamaica in 1655, plantation slavery was already established (although there were less than 2,000 African slaves on the island at the time). Jamaica remained a fairly lucrative slave society built on the misery of the majority of the population and its wealth extracted and sent to England. In the mid- to late eighteenth century, the wealth of the average white Jamaican was ten times greater than the wealth of the average free person in the southern plantation colonies of America (Coclanis 1990, cited in Burnard 2002:76). Indeed, Kingston, the present capital of Jamaica, was still one of the richest cities in the New World— richer than Philadelphia, then the richest city in British North America. Jews and nonwhites, including elements of the coloured population did acquire considerable wealth, but the economy and political institutions were dominated by whites. Universal adult suffrage did not occur until 1944, and prior to this the political administration was completely dominated by whites (although after 1891, as a proportion of the population, their number did not exceed 2.3%).

Given the harsh social realities and the demographic make-up of the society, force was always a visible and fairly overt organizing principle of the state. Like the population, the laws, system of policing, entire criminal justice system, and institutions of state were transplanted from Britain and served the colonial administration as tools for dominating the subject populations.

Resistance in various forms was sustained over a long duration—from the maroon wars of the seventeenth and eighteenth centuries, which began against the Spanish and resumed under the British. Slave uprisings of the eighteenth and nineteenth century, and national strikes and labour riots of the 1930s and similar resistance in other parts of the Empire, including the other Caribbean islands, led to the abolition of slavery in 1838, internal self-government in 1944, and eventually to the end of British colonial rule and independence in 1962.

Periodic public opinion surveys indicate that Jamaicans regard unemployment and violent crime as the major challenges facing the country. Over the last two decades the Jamaican (formal) economy has stagnated. The number of new jobs created each year has tended to be fewer than the number of persons joining the labour force. Unemployment has thus remained at or higher than 16% for the last two decades. Youth unemployment is particularly high. The crime problem is discussed below.

Jamaica's population for the year 2000 was estimated at 2,597,600. According to the 1991 census, racial/ethnic composition is as follows: blacks 90%, East Indians 1.2%, Chinese 0.2%, whites 0.2%, and mixed 7.7% and "Other."

Languages spoken are English and Jamaican Creole or "patois" (local dialect).

In terms of number of converts, the major religions are Christianity in its various denominations and Rastafari. There are also a number of folk religions such as Pukkumina that are a part of the people's African cultural heritage. The main Christian groupings are Pentecostal, Anglican, Baptist, Church of God, and Roman Catholic.

Per capita income is US$2,750 (2001). Major economic activities are tourism, mining (mainly bauxite and alumina production for export), manufacturing and processing (includes food processing, alcoholic beverages, and chemicals), and agriculture (export crops such as sugarcane, coffee, and bananas as well as domestic crops and livestock).

Contextual Features

The legal system is based on the English common law and is adversarial in nature.

Jamaica's aggregate crime rate is relatively low by Caribbean and hemispheric standards. In 2002, its crime rate was 1,118 incidents per 100,000 citizens. Its rate of violent crime is, however, the highest in the Caribbean, and its homicide rate among the highest in the world. In 2002, Jamaica's homicide rate was 40 incidents per 100,000 citizens, up from 9.6 per 100,000 in 1974. Other frequently occurring crimes are shootings, rape, robberies, and possession of illegal drugs. Most violent crimes are committed with the aid of a firearm. For example, in 2002, 69% of all homicides were committed with a firearm. Given the high rate of violent crime, especially gun violence, as would be expected, significant sections of the population are gripped by fear of violent victimization. The incidence of violent crimes is highly concentrated in the major urban centres and particularly in the capital city of Kingston. Some 60% to 70% of all violent crimes are committed in the Kingston metropolitan area where only 26% of the population resides. Despite the high level of violent crime against the local urban population, crimes against tourists tend to be rare. In 2000, only 0.05% of the 2.23 million tourists who visited Jamaica were criminally victimized, violently or otherwise.

Policing is conducted within the context of a stable yet competitive democratic system. Since the end of British colonial rule in the early 1960s, the Commonwealth Caribbean has been distinguished as a region by the democratic character of most of its governments. Jamaica has had a competitive two-party system since universal adult suffrage in 1944. The Jamaican system of government is modelled on the British system. There is an elected Lower House and nominated Upper House or Senate. Government is highly centralized but there is an accompanying system of local government. The constitution guarantees the basic rights of all citizens, but contains a "grandfather clause" that subjects these rights to previous colonial laws when the two are in conflict.

The judicial system consists of a hierarchy of courts. At the lowest level is the Resident Magistrate's Court and next is the Supreme Court. Appeals against the judgments of the Supreme Court are heard by the Court of Appeal. Although Jamaica is an independent country, as is the case with a number of Commonwealth countries, the final court of appeal is the Judicial Committee of the Privy Council in the United Kingdom. There are special Magistrates Courts such as the Family Court and the Drug Court. With the exception of the Drug Court, the system is adversarial.

The correctional system consists of the prisons, probation services, and approved schools. In 1975, all three elements were consolidated as the Department of Correctional Services and were accountable to the Ministry of National Security and Justice. The primary concern of the system is social defence. There are, however, programmes that are designed to assist in the rehabilitation of persons serving custodial and noncustodial sentences. A number of nongovernmental organisations (NGOs) are actively involved in prisoner rehabilitation programmes. Rehabilitation "strategies" include weekend, day release, and work release programmes; skills training; and a variety of work programmes that are designed to foster work discipline. In addition, there is an "aftercare programme" that includes the disbursement of small rehabilitation grants to assist selected ex-convicts in establishing microenterprises.

There are six male and one female adult prisons and four correctional institutions for juveniles. In 2000, there were 3,397 prisoners in the adult correctional centres and 398 in the juvenile centres. In 2000, the prisoner-to-population ratio was approximately 1:684. Some 94% of all adult prisoners are males—mainly young, poorly educated, unskilled, and unemployed or underemployed.

Due to overcrowding and new thinking within the criminal justice system, there has been increasing resort to "community treatment as an alternative to incarceration." In December 2002, there were 4,533 community service cases. In recent years, the number of community services orders has been increasing while the prison population has been declining.

Police Profile

Background

Jamaica is policed by three state security forces: the Jamaica Constabulary Force (JCF); the Island Special Constabulary Force, which is an auxiliary of the JCF; and the Jamaica Defence Force (JDF), which includes the regular army, its reserves, and the coast guard that polices the territorial waters of the country. The JDF does not enjoy police powers, and polices only in joint operations with the JCF. The primary responsibility for policing rests with the JCF.

The Jamaica Constabulary Force (JCF) was established by the British colonial authorities in 1866, and has its legal authority in the JCF Act of that year. Its formation as an act of colonial state building was precipitated by the Morant Bay Rebellion of 1865, which was the first major violent resistance to the colonial regime after the end of slavery in 1838. From the British point of view, the performance of the previous police force was poor. It had been a disaster in terms of its failure to detect the organization of the rebellion and to forewarn the authorities, its competence was doubtful, and loyalty to the regime was considered suspect.

Unlike the earlier police, the JCF was more centralized and tightly controlled by the administration, and was modelled on the RUC. It developed primarily as an instrument of colonial domination, and was primarily concerned with public order, the suppression of riots and various forms of resistance to the colonial regime. Consistent with its political functions, the JCF was, for most of the colonial period, subjectively controlled by the British; that is, its officers and even NCOs were largely white and British. Despite the fact that the vast majority of the population (90%) was of African descent, it was not until after internal self-government in 1944 when Jamaica entered an independence preparation period that the first black Jamaican constable was admitted to the rank of officer. It was not until after independence, and almost 100 years after the formation of the JCF that the first black Jamaican commissioner of police was appointed. The colonial legacy with respect to policing was thus one of a politicized, subjectively controlled, order maintenance instrument that was fixed on regime protection rather than law enforcement and service to and protection of the rights of the population. In short, it was an authoritarian rather than a democratic tradition of policing.

The challenge of independence was to truly democratize the police, but colonial traditions have persisted. Police forces are all profoundly political institutions. They, however, do not all operate on the political model of policing, that is, being overtly involved in competitive party politics and regime maintenance security policing, and thus engaged not just in the control of deviants, but of whole populations or sectors of those populations. On this model of policing, as noted above, control of the police force is achieved via subjective modes. And while under the colonial power, this involved appointments based on race/ethnic solidarity and nationality. After independence, this method of control was now based on the principle of party affiliation, and involved the determination of appointments (particularly to sensitive posts such as the leadership of the Intelligence and Special Operations Units) largely on the basis of political affiliation.

This mode of control allows the political directorate to determine detailed operational matters. This includes, in addition to personnel selection and deployment, the type of operations appropriate in various situations and their timing and targets, and to determine rewards and punishment within the force. In the Jamaican expression of the model, no sphere of police activity is beyond the reach of the minister in charge.

Efforts at seriously reforming the JPF have come very late—some four decades after Independence. With the radical changes in the local and international environment (the end of the Cold War and new patterns of crime), public concerns with crime control have now superseded concerns about political subversion. But the role of the police and its strategies and structures have not been substantially changed, resulting in the JCF being largely unfit for the crime-preventive, problem-solving, accountable, and democratically oriented policing that is being demanded of it. But there have been efforts in this direction and the mission statement of the JCF has been recently revised to indicate a more service-oriented intent.

Demographics

In 2002, the establishment of the JCF was 8,500 and its actual strength was 6,937, the latter representing a police density of one per 376 citizens. Some 31% of the members of the Force are females. They are represented in all ranks, including the senior managerial ranks, albeit not sufficiently. Consistent with the racial/ethnic composition of the population, which is 90% black, the Force is almost entirely composed of blacks.

The educational requirements for entry to the JCF are fairly basic. Preference is given to recruits who have been able to secure passes at the CXC O level, but the JCF sets its own test, comprised of basic mathematics and the English language. An initial screening of applicants is done at four centres across the country. About 15% of all candidates are recruited. For most of the 1990s, recruitment was almost perfectly balanced with the attrition rate. Recently, however, there has been an increase in the size of the Force.

Organizational Description

The JCF is highly centralized and consists of a hierarchy of eleven ranks. A distinction is made between officers and other ranks. The highest rank in the officer class is that of commissioner of police. He is assisted by four deputy commissioners, who usually have specific responsibilities for crime, operations, intelligence, and administration. There are approximately eight assistant commissioners, which completes the top tier of the command structure. Below them are three ranks of superintendents. The supervisory ranks are composed of inspectors, sergeants, and corporals. The JCF therefore has a multitiered decision-making system that makes the organization somewhat ineffective and unresponsive to local demands. Consis-

tent with its centralizing dynamic, resources are largely concentrated at Police Headquarters, and not the geographic divisions or key points of service delivery.

According to official policy, promotions are based on a system of examinations and on the job performance. Performance assessments are routinely done. The commissioner of police (CP) is responsible for all promotions up to and including the rank of sergeant. At the level of the senior supervisors (inspectors) and managers or officers (deputy superintendent to commissioner), the CP recommends, but the Police Services Commission, which is appointed by the governor-general on the recommendation of the prime minister (after consultation with the leader of the opposition), must approve all such promotions. The Commission appoints the commissioner.

The Criminal Investigation Bureau (CIB) is responsible for all major criminal investigations. It was formed in 1936 and consists of various units of specialist investigators based on crime type. There is a Homicide Unit, a Fraud Squad, a unit responsible for the investigation of motor vehicle theft, and an Organized Crime Unit. The CIB also had a Criminal Intelligence Unit, but this has now become part of the Consolidated Intelligence Department based on a merger of Criminal Intelligence and the Special Branch. Investigators from the CIB are also assigned to the various geographic commands of the Force. The CIB accounts for approximately 5% of the Force. They tend to have a high case load. In 2002, the "cleared-up" or arrest rates for serious violent crimes varied from 54% in the case of murder to a low of 41% in the case of robbery. The arrest rates for property crimes ranged from a high of 75% for larceny of motor cars to a low of 39% for house breaking.

Recently, there has been considerable effort to improve the work of this section of the Force via more specialized training, especially in the use of more advanced criminalistics with the aim of reducing dependence on witnesses (who are vulnerable to pressures from powerful criminal networks) and increasing the use of physical evidence in developing cases. This is likely to give greater impetus to professionalization and efforts to improve the educational level of investigators.

There are a number of special operations units within the Force. These include the Mobile Reserve, which has primary responsibility for riot control and the control of civil disorders more generally. It may also be called on in particularly dangerous situations where there is open armed conflict with criminal groups. It is organized in a paramilitary mode, trained in military type tactics, and domiciled in barracks. It is thus easily mobilized.

The JCF also employs special anticrime units, the most recent of which is the Crime Management Unit. This unit operates nationally, and is able to pull officers from other units of the Force depending on its operational needs. The responsibilities of the CMU include recovery of illegal firearms and neutralization of gangs and organized crime networks. These units usually attract the attention of the public, the press, and human rights groups, as they tend to be repeatedly involved in the controversial use of violence directed at alleged criminals.

Functions

The aims of the JCF are expressed in its mission statement. The mission statement manifests the aim to serve and protect the people of Jamaica. It also reassures them that this would be done through the delivery of impartial and professional services aimed at maintaining law and order, protecting life and property, and preventing and detecting crime and preserving peace. Historically, the police was primarily concerned with public order and the protection of the state, but there are efforts to make the Force service oriented.

Training

The JCF operates an Academy and Staff College. The Academy is responsible for the training of recruits, and also provides specialized courses for investigators and other specialists. All training officers are members of the JCF. Recruit training is residential, and is of approximately twenty-six weeks duration. It consists of an introduction to the laws of Jamaica, basic psychology, drill and physical training, firearm use, and a module in "human dignity."

The Staff College provides education and training for senior supervisors and managers. It offers high-quality junior command, command, and senior command/strategic management courses. These are typically intensive full-time courses, and therefore the participants are relieved of their normal duties. At the junior command level, the contents of the courses include problem-solving exercises based on the current problems of policing in the region, application of information technology to policing, and drug interdiction. The strategic management course focuses on policymaking and planning processes, project implementation, and leadership issues.

Unlike the Academy, this facility serves all regional police forces, and the courses offer opportunities for senior officers from the various Caribbean territories to share their experiences and expertise with their Caribbean colleagues.

Police Public Projects

The most noteworthy police projects are a new community policing project and traffic control. Community policing is seen as a way of operationalising the shift from being purely reactive to being proactive and more engaged in crime prevention and problem solving. Since 1998, this has been highlighted as a major initiative. There has been much training, but thus far the attempts at implementing this style of policing have been exploratory. In the mid 1990s, there was some early success with a pilot project in community policing, measured in terms of reducing some types of crime, increasing the relationship between police and citizens and their active cooperation in crime control. This was of great interest as it took place in a typical Kingston inner-city community that was regarded as too violent for this style of policing. But this project was never properly evaluated and the appropriate lessons drawn so that the effort could have been replicated in other communities. At the time of writing, a new initiative is being planned.

During the last decade there was a significant increase in the number of motor vehicles in the country. Against this background, the incidence of traffic accidents has increased. In 2000, there were 11,145 traffic accidents resulting in 334 fatalities. The JCF maintains a Division that is completely dedicated to traffic control. In addition, there are traffic units within the geographic divisions. Consistent with the general style of policing, in this area the method of work is largely reactive. While some effort is made to analyse the data on motor vehicle accidents and to determine "black spots," not enough effort is made to reduce the accident rate by preventive measures based on these analyses.

Police Use of Firearms

The following standing orders of the JCF endorse the principle of minimum force. First, members of the Force, in carrying out their duty, shall make every effort to apply alternative measures before resorting to the use of force or firearms. Second, in those circumstances where the lawful use of force or firearms is justifiable, members shall use such force or firearms with restraint and in proportion to the legitimate objective to be achieved" (FO #2248). In situations of violent confrontation, members of the JCF are instructed to "meet force with no more force than is necessary in protecting the lives of the members and of others." This suggests that the use of lethal violence to protecting property is inappropriate and should be discouraged.

Despite these standing orders, the level of police violence, especially lethal violence, is extraordinarily high. In 2000, Jamaican police officers killed 140 persons, that is, a killing rate of 5.4 persons per 100,000 citizens. This represents some 16% of all homicides in that year. These figures, as alarming as they may seem, reflect an improvement in the situation. Police killings were lower in the decade of the 1990s than they were in the 1980s. The highest level of police killings was in 1984 when 355 persons were killed, representing a rate of 15.6 persons per 100,000 citizens, and accounting for 42% of all homicides in that year.

In Jamaica (and the Commonwealth Caribbean), police violence is primarily directed at criminals and criminal suspects. It is not politically repressive violence, although occasionally the opposition may treat community invasions as the political targeting of such communities.

Complaints and Discipline

The high rate of police killings of criminal suspects has led to repeated criticisms by human rights activists and concerned citizens (see, for example, the reports by Amnesty International). The JCF has responded to this by instituting new training programmes in human rights, humanitarian law, and human dignity (discussed above). These courses are conducted at both the level of new recruits and managers and supervisors; the first is done at the Academy and involves thirty hours of contact time, and the second, at the Staff College and involves eight hours of contact time. The trainers include local human rights activists. Since 1998, the International Committee of the Red Cross has also been involved in the training of JCF trainers.

In order to ensure a climate of greater respect for human rights, in addition to the new training courses, the JCF has instituted the following:

- Closer on-the-job guidance and counselling of police personnel.
- Briefing and debriefing of personnel before and after duties.
- Members who are involved in questionable incidents are removed from "frontline" duties until the investigation of these incidents are completed.
- Team leaders are generally held responsible for the conduct of personnel under their command.

Terrorism

As in the case of drug trafficking, an important area for international cooperation is antiterrorism. However, there are no terrorist organizations in Jamaica; neither did any terrorist organizations emerge during the long anticolonial struggle or at any time after independence. There have been episodes of political violence, but no terrorist groups.

International Cooperation

Jamaica has become an important transhipment point for hard drugs that are produced in Latin America and marketed in the United States and Europe. Jamaican traffickers therefore tend to have strong international ties, and some crime networks have gained notoriety as "yardies" in England and "posses" in America. These networks also engage in arms trafficking from the producer countries of the north to Jamaica. International police cooperation is thus of great importance for public safety in Jamaica.

The JCF is a member of the Association of Commissioners of Police (ACCP), which promotes active cooperation among the police forces of the region. Members of the JCF have served as advisors and trainers, along with other police forces in the region. They have, for example, assisted with the reorganization of the Grenada Police Force after 1979. On the international level, the JCF has participated in peacekeeping and policing in Namibia in the period immediately after its independence. The JCF also participates in the work of Interpol. At the bilateral level, it has had a long and mutually beneficial relationship with English police services, and long-standing relations with Canadian and U.S. law enforcement. The governments of Jamaica and Colombia recently signed an important agreement on cooperation in the field of law enforcement, which was preceded by active cooperation by the law enforcement agencies of both countries.

Police Education, Research, and Publications

There is a "graduate entry programme" which facilitates the direct entry into the officer ranks of recruits with a first degree. This is done on an *ad hoc* basis depending on the need for specialized skills. From time to time, there is debate about recruiting all officers in this way, but thus far it has been settled in favour of promotion from the lower ranks.

Unfortunately the literature on the JCF does not do justice to its long history and importance in the political and social life of Jamaica and indeed the Caribbean. A number of biographies have been written by officers who served in the Force during the colonial period, spanning from the immediate post–World War I period to the immediate pre-independence period in the 1950s. These include *The Story of a West Indian Policeman or 47 Years in the JCF*, written by H. Thomas, and *Reckoning with the Force—Stories of the Jamaica Constabulary Force in the 1950s* by David Godfrey. More recent literature is limited to a single book, *Police and Crime Control in Jamaica: Problems of Reforming Ex-Colonial Constabularies* by Anthony Harriot, which examines post-independence attempts at reforming the Force; and one monograph, *Patriarchy in the JCF: Its Impact on Gender Equality*, by Gladys Brown-Campbell, who currently serves as a sergeant in the Force. In addition, there are a number of doctoral and master's theses that are held at the Main Library of the University of the West Indies, Mona Campus, and articles on various aspects of policing in Jamaica that have been published in Caribbean and international criminology journals.

The website of the Jamaica Constabulary Force may be found at *www.jamaicapolice.org.jm*.

ANTHONY HARRIOT

Bibliography

Brown-Campbell, G. *Patriarchy in the JCF: Its Impact on Gender Equality*. Kingston: Canoe Press, 1998.

Burnard, T. "Not a Place for Whites? Demographic Failure and Settlement, 1655–1780." In *Jamaica in Slavery and Freedom—History, Heritage and Culture*, edited by K. Monteith and G. Richards. Kingston: University of the West Indies Press, 2002a.

Burnard, T. "The Grand Mart of the Island: The Economic Function of Kingston, Jamaica in the Mid-Eighteenth Century." In *Jamaica in Slavery and Freedom—History, Heritage and Culture*, edited by K. Monteith and G. Richards. Kingston: University of the West Indies Press, 2002b.

Coclanis, P. "The Wealth of British America on the Eve of Revolution." *Journal of Interdisciplinary History* 21 (1990): 259.

Godfrey, G. *Reckoning with the Force—Stories of the Jamaica Constabulary Force in the 1950s*. Kingston: The Mill Press, 1996.

Harriott, A. *Police and Crime Control: Problems of Reforming Ex-Colonial Constabularies*. Kingston: University of the West Indies Press, 2000.

Harriott, A. "Police and Society in the Caribbean: The Application of United Nations Standards for Law Enforcement." Paper presented at Conference on the Application of UN Standards and Norms in Crime Prevention and Criminal Justice. Peace Center, Castle Schlaining, Stadtschaining, Austria, 10–13 February 2003.

Thomas, H. *The Story of a West Indian Policeman or 47 Years in the JCF*. Kingston: The Gleaner Co., 1927.

Williams, E. *From Columbus to Castro: The History of the Caribbean, 1492–1969*. New York: Vintage Books, 1984.

JAPAN

Background Material

As of 2004, the total population of Japan was 127,333,002. The only official language in the nation is Japanese. Students in junior and senior high schools study English as the "first foreign language." The two major religions are Buddhism and Shinto (Japanese original polytheism).

In 2002, the per capita income was US$33,550. The gross domestic product totaled 513 trillion yen, of which manufacturing accounted for 21.8%, followed by service industries (20.2%), and wholesale and retail businesses (13.6%).

Contextual Features

The system of criminal law in Japan is classified as civil and adversarial. At every criminal procedure stage, innocence is presumed until the determination of guilt applies. The prosecutor bears the burden of proving facts relating to all elements of the crime, and in case of doubt, the presumption is always in favor of the defendant.

Article 76 of the Japanese Constitution vests all judicial authority in the Supreme Court and inferior courts, and Article 81 empowers the Supreme Court, as the court of last resort, to determine the constitutionality of any law, order, regulation or official affairs.

All courts are incorporated into a unitary national judicial system, in which any criminal case is, without exception, heard and determined. There are five types of courts: Supreme Court, High Courts, District Courts, Family Courts, and Summary Courts.

The Supreme Court, the highest court in Japan, is located in Tokyo, and deals with final appeals from High Courts. The High Courts are located in eight major cities, and have jurisdiction over intermediate appeals filed against judgments made by lower courts. There are fifty District Courts whose territorial jurisdiction is mostly identical to each of the forty-seven prefectures. They are generally in charge of all cases in the first instance with few exceptions. Family Courts are located in the same places as the District Courts, and handle family disputes and juvenile delinquency cases. There are 438 Summary courts in cities and towns, dealing with minor civil and criminal cases.

The Ministry of Justice administers both prisons and juvenile training schools according to the Prison Law and the Juvenile Training School Law. Prisons have the rehabilitative function of resocializing offenders, based on the progressive treatment program and classification system. Prisoners are also provided with various vocational training and educational programs. The average daily population of convicted prisoners is 55,132 in 2002, while that used to be 40,977 in 1997. The average occupancy rate accounts for 116.5% of the capacity and most prisons suffer from overcrowding.

Juvenile training schools are classified as primary, secondary, special and medical, based on the conditions of juveniles, and offer rehabilitative services until they become twenty years of age. Guidance programs, such as group activities, counseling, lectures and psychotherapy sessions, are provided in order to let them achieve more socialized way of thinking and behavior. The schools daily accommodate 4,794 juvenile delinquents on average in 2002, while that used to be 3,358 in 1997.

The number of Penal Code offenses has been increasing since 1995. In 2003, there were about 2,790,136 reported Penal Code offenses, excluding death or injury cases from traffic accidents. This is the largest number since World War II. The police cleared 592,359 cases (up 9.3%), and arrested 347,558 persons (up 6.8%).

Among the Penal Code offenses, larceny is by far the most common and accounts for 83.3% of the reported offenses. The number of felonious offenses, such as homicide, robbery, arson, and rape, is relatively small and accounts for 0.4%. For example, there were 1,396 homicide cases reported in 2002.

The most widely abused drug in Japan is stimulants, primarily methamphetamine, which accounts for about 90% of the drug-related offenses. The number of persons arrested for stimulant cases was 16,771 (down 6.4%) in 2002. Most of stimulants are smuggled from foreign countries, such as China and North Korea, by transnational crime organizations.

The number of seized MDMA and other synthetic drugs is over 170,000 tablets (up 55.1%), an all-time record and there is much concern about its extending abuse. They are mostly shipped from the Netherlands and Belgium.

In Japan, the possession of firearms is strictly controlled by the Firearms and Swords Control Law. To possess hunting rifles or shotguns, one must obtain a license, which is not granted to those suffering from mental disorder, organized crime group members, and so on. As of 2002, approximately 400,000 hunting rifles, shotguns, or air rifles are owned by licensees. Regulations for handguns are the most restrictive and only police officers and other public officials such as Self-Defense Forces personnel on duty can carry handguns.

Due to the strict regulations, there were only 375 crimes involving firearms in 2002, resulting in twenty-four deaths and thirty-four injuries. The police seized 747 handguns, of which U.S.-made handguns account for the largest share of 28.3%, followed by Japanese (12.0%), Chinese (6.2%), and Russian (5.3%).

By the end of 2001, automobile ownership in Japan had risen to about 90 million, with a ratio of one car for every 1.4 persons. There were about 7.8 million violations of the Road Traffic Law in 2002. Speeding accounts for 2.6 million cases, followed by illegal parking of 1.7 million cases. There were about 937,000 traffic accidents, resulting in 1,168,000 injuries and 8,326 fatalities.

Boryokudan, commonly referred as Yakuza, are anti-social groups indigenous to Japan. As of the end of 2002, Boryokudan membership was about 85,300, with 43,600 full members and 41,700 associates. The three major Boryokudan groups are Yamaguchi-gumi, Inagawa-kai, and Sumiyoshi-kai. These three groups have about 31,200 full members representing more than 70% of the national membership.

In 2002, the police arrested 30,824 Boryokudan members in 49,217 cases. Bodily injury, theft, extortion, and stimulant drug-related cases account for approximately 60% of them. For example, 40.2% of the stimulant drug offenders are Boryokudan members. In addition to traditional fund-raising activities, they are intervening in civil affairs. Especially in Japan's prolonged economic recession, Boryokudan have been active in interfering with financial institutions holding the bulk of bad loans.

In 2002, the police cleared 34,746 offenses (up 25.2% from the previous year) by visiting foreigners, and arrested 16,212 people (up 10.6%). The number of the cleared cases is 1.8 times as many as that in 1993. A total of 51.9% of the arrested foreigners had illegally remained in Japan. They are more likely to commit thefts and robberies as a group, and pose a serious threat to public security. Chinese account for 40.0% of the arrested, followed by Koreans (10.7%), Brazilians (7.3%), and Filipinos (6.6%).

Juvenile delinquency has become serious in Japan. In 2002, there were about 142,000 juveniles committing Penal Code offenses, representing 40.8% of all offenders. Among them, senior high school students account for 43.0%, followed by junior high school students (26.8%). A total of 58.8% committed larceny offenses, such as shoplifting, and motorcycle and bicycle thefts. About 70% of the street crimes such as purse snatching and street robbery were committed by juveniles.

Police Profile

Background

In Japan, the Interior Ministry of the central government used to have total control over the nationwide police. After World War II, there was significant reform of the police structure, and each town and city came to have its own municipal police. However, that resulted in the police split into too many small organizations working independently, which proved to be a serious obstacle to solving cases. Therefore, there was another reform to launch the current police structure in 1954. The police system is now centered on local police forces established in each prefecture. There are forty-seven prefecture police forces to carry out entire aspects of police duties including those of a national nature.

The former Code of Criminal Procedure stipulated that criminal investigation was the duty of prosecutors attached to the courts, and police officers used to be involved in criminal investigation only under prosecutors' supervision. However, after World War II, the Code of Criminal Procedure was extensively revised, and prosecutors were separated from the courts and placed under the Ministry of Justice.

Now the police and other investigative organizations have their own investigative authority, and prosecutors no longer preside over criminal investigation. Prosecutors can also conduct investigations for themselves, if necessary, but the number of those cases is quite small. The typical cases that prosecutors investigate directly are tax evasion, corporate crime, and bribery. Only 446 suspects were arrested by the prosecutorial authorities in 2001.

Most investigative powers (that is, arrest, search and seizure, inspection of evidence, and telecommunications interception) are given to the police as well as prosecutors, but only prosecutors are authorized to request the court for detention of a suspect. In addition, prosecutors have the exclusive power to decide whether to prosecute, and close communication between the police and prosecutors is indispensable.

Maritime safety officials, narcotics agents, and postal inspectors also have the authority to conduct criminal investigation. In contrast to the general investigative authority of the police, the jurisdiction of these special investigative organizations is restricted in terms of areas or types of crimes. Even where special investigative organizations exist, the police legally maintain their own investigative authority. On the other hand, the police are not involved in cases under the purview of specific organizations (such as the Fair Trade Commission and the National Tax Administration Agency).

The Maritime Safety Agency, the largest investigative organization other than the police, is a national organization in the Ministry of Land, Infrastructure and Transport, and is concerned with maintaining public security on the ocean. It employs about 12,000 staff altogether, of which around 3,000 are involved in security duties. The Maritime Safety Agency dealt with about 7,000 maritime crimes during 2001.

The Japanese Self-Defense Forces do not normally conduct any police activities. But when the general police forces are unable to keep public order in emergency situations, the prime minister is authorized to use them. Prefecture governors can also request the prime minister to use military forces.

Demographics

As of 2003, the prescribed strength of the Japanese police totaled 278,307, in which there were 243,276 police officers protecting the population of 127,291,000, for a ratio of one police officer per 523 people. The forty-seven prefecture police forces differ considerably in scale. In terms of the number of police officers, the Metropolitan Police

Department in charge of Tokyo is the largest with about 41,700 personnel, while the Tottori prefecture police force is the smallest with 1,100.

Detailed demographics for the National Police Agency of 7,498 personnel follow: police officers, 1,544; Imperial guards, 928; and clerical and technical officials, 5,036. Prefecture police personnel total 270,077, of which police officers account for 241,732, and clerical and technical officials, 29,077.

The number of female police officers is about 10,200 nationwide. The ratio of female recruits is 10.2% in 2002, and their number has been steadily increasing. More than 70% of the newly recruited officers are university graduates, and the others are high school graduates.

Organizational Description

One of the major characteristics of the Japanese police is that public safety commissions have administrative supervision over the police. The public safety commission system was established during the postwar police reform in order to maintain political impartiality and keep police from being self-centered by letting citizens' representatives control the police.

At the national level, the National Public Safety Commission exercises administrative supervision over the National Police Agency. The Commission formulates basic policies and regulations, coordinates police management on matters of national concern, and authorizes general standards for training, communication, criminal identification, criminal statistics, and equipment. While the Commission is under the jurisdiction of the prime minister, its independence and political neutrality are legally guaranteed.

Prefecture Public Safety Commissions exercise administrative supervision over prefecture police forces by formulating basic policies and regulations for police operations. While the commissions are under the jurisdiction of elected prefecture governors, neither the commissions nor governors are authorized to supervise individual cases or enforcement activities of the prefecture police.

The National Police Agency, the police organization of the national government, is subordinate to the National Public Safety Commission, and headed by the Commissioner General. It does not carry out enforcement activities, except for the operations of the Imperial Guard, but plans the policing system, provides the bases of police activities, such as police communications, police training, police equipment, and criminal identification, and supervises and coordinates

prefecture police forces for national or transprefecture concerns.

One of the major duties of the National Police Agency is to provide a nationwide police communications system comprised of multiplex radio circuits, dedicated lines rented from private carriers, and a satellite network for prefecture police forces. All circuits from the National Police Agency to local police stations are digitized and double-tracked to be effective even in emergencies.

Three organizations are attached to the National Police Agency: the National Police Academy, the National Research Institute of Police Science, and the Imperial Guard Headquarters.

The National Police Academy provides various training programs to senior officers from prefecture police and conducts academic researches on police issues. The Academy has six institutes: the Police Policy Research Center, the Highest Training Institute for Investigation Leaders, the International Research and Training Institute for Criminal Investigation, the Police Communications Research Center, the Police Info-Communications Academy, and the Research and Training Center for Financial Crime Investigation.

The National Research Institute of Police Science conducts research in forensic science, prevention of juvenile crimes, and traffic accidents. The Imperial Guard Headquarters provides escorts for the Emperor and other Imperial family members, and is also responsible for the security of the Imperial Palace and other imperial facilities.

Regional Police Bureaus are subordinate to the National Police Agency. There are seven Bureaus nationwide, each of which is located in a major city of the region. All Bureaus have a Regional Police School that provides training programs for newly promoted police sergeants and assistant police inspectors from the prefecture police forces in its region.

According to the Police Law, each of forty-seven prefecture governments has its own police organization. The prefecture police of Tokyo are called the Metropolitan Police Department, while all other prefectures have Prefecture Police Headquarters. The Metropolitan Police Department and Prefecture Police Headquarters have identical functions and authority with respect to their jurisdictions.

Although each prefecture police force works independently, it is stipulated that they have to cooperate mutually. In the event of a disaster or when a large number of police officers are required for an important international conference or other reasons, the assistance of other prefecture police forces can be requested. Whenever the dispatch of support staff or the close cooperation among prefecture police forces is necessary, the National Police Agency acts as the coordinator.

Police stations are placed under the command of prefecture headquarters. There are about 1,270 police stations nationwide. In Japan, both investigators and uniformed officers are working in the same police station. Police stations handle everyday police affairs in their district, but the investigation of important cases or cases requiring specialist knowledge are directly carried out by the headquarters.

Police officers are classified into the following nine ranks in Japan:

Superintendent general (Keishi-sokan)
Superintendent supervisor (Keishi-kan)
Chief superintendent (Keishi-cho)
Senior superintendent (Keishi-sei)
Superintendent (Keishi)
Police inspector (Keibu)
Assistant police inspector (Keibu-ho)
Police sergeant (Junsa-bucho)
Police officer (Junsa)

The Commissioner General of the National Police Agency holds the highest position of the Japanese police, but his title is not a police rank. The Superintendent General represents not only the highest police rank, but also the head of the Metropolitan Police Department.

Superintendent supervisor is equivalent to chief of a larger prefecture police force or director general in the National Police Agency. Chief superintendent is equivalent to chief of a prefecture police force or director in the National Police Agency. Senior superintendent is equivalent to director of a department in a prefecture police headquarters or chief of a larger police station.

Superintendent is equivalent to director of a division in a prefecture police headquarters or chief of a police station, and they make up 3% of police personnel. Police inspectors account for about 7% of all officers and are field supervisors, such as chief of a section in a police station. Ranks of assistant police inspector and below account for about 30% each.

Police officers in prefecture police forces are employed by each prefecture as local public servants, and most work for the same prefecture police force until retirement. They start their career as the rank of police officer, and are generally promoted to higher ranks after passing promotion tests. Their performance and seniority are also considered in the promotion process, and those with good performance for years have a better chance of promotion.

Those who successively pass promotion tests can be promoted to police inspector in their early thirties. Then they can be promoted to superintendent and senior superintendent after screening of years of performance. Officers recruited by prefecture police forces are hardly ever promoted to chief superintendent or higher. The officers who are supposed to be leading members of the prefecture police are dispatched to the National Police Agency for two or three years.

The National Police Agency annually employs about twenty recruits among those who have passed the National Public Service Category Examination; those who pass this exam are also employed as officers of mid-level rank. Another exam conducted by the National Personnel Authority selects prospective executives in government organs; police candidates who pass this test will have executive positions in prefecture police forces several times in their career.

The national police budget covers costs to run the National Police Agency, expenses for prefecture police activities of national concern, and subsidies to supplement prefecture budgets. In fiscal year 2002, the national budget totaled about 268 billion yen, and the total sum of forty-seven prefecture police force budgets is 3,430 billion yen, of which more than 80% is for personnel expenses.

There are about 35,000 police vehicles and 200 police boats ranging from five to twenty-three meters in length. As a mobile force in the air, the police operate about eighty small and medium-sized helicopters.

Functions

The responsibilities of the Japanese police described in the Police Law are protecting life and property, preventing and investigating crimes, traffic enforcement, and maintaining public safety and order.

The community safety branch deals with crime prevention, prevention of juvenile delinquency (including activities to provide juvenile delinquents with guidance), control of firearms and drugs, and investigating special law offenses. It also has a wide variety of administrative authorities like licensing and supervising specific businesses and actions related to public order (that is, amusement, private security, pawnbroker businesses, and so on).

The community police branch is involved in all aspects of police matters. There are some 84,000 uniformed officers carrying out patrols and responding to emergency calls (#110), as well as maintaining the safety and peace of community life and dealing with various requests of the general public.

The criminal investigation branch is in charge of investigating Penal Code offenses and implementing countermeasures against organized crime groups. The traffic branch deals with investigations of Road Traffic Law offenses, including traffic accident fatalities and injuries and traffic management (that is, traffic regulations and drivers' licenses).

The security branch covers crime investigation related to terrorists, extreme leftists and ultranationalists (rightists), escort of VIPs, counterespionage, investigation of Foreign Resident Control Law offenses, prevention of mob lawbreaking, and disaster relief operations. To deal with these issues, well-trained riot police units are organized.

The allocation of police officers as of April 2002 is as follows: 7% community safety branch, 36% community police branch, 15% criminal investigation branch, 15% traffic branch, 11% security branch, and 16% others.

Training

Newly recruited prefecture police officers undergo a twenty-one-month (fifteen months for university graduates) initial training program. First they attend ten (six) months of a pre-service training course at their prefecture police school so that they can acquire basic knowledge and disciplined behavior. Then they are assigned to a police station for eight (seven) months of an on-the-job training course to practice community policing under the guidance of a senior officer. Finally, they return to the police school for three (two) months of a comprehensive training course to further develop their professional knowledge and skills.

Police Public Projects

The Japanese police have a unique community police system, the Koban, comprised of around 6,600 police "boxes," or one-room stations (Koban) and 7,900 residential police "boxes" (Chuzaisho) nationwide, each of which has its own beat, and plays a role as the base for community police activities. Koban are mostly deployed in urban areas, and Chuzaisho are located in rural towns and villages.

The Koban system has made a substantial contribution to securing safe and peaceful communities. Police officers watch and patrol their beats, responding to cases and accidents, and arresting suspects. In 2002, around 270,000 suspects that account for 77.5% of the offenders of the Penal Code are arrested by community police officers.

Koban police prevent crimes, control traffic, offer juvenile guidance, protect lost children, and provide various counseling services to troubled citizens. The Koban system ensures a high level of officer visibility, imparting peace of mind to community residents. In order to build a good relationship with citizens and secure their cooperation with the police, community police officers make routine visits to homes and offices in their precinct. During these visits, they listen to residents' requests and give advice on crime prevention.

The following are the most representative public projects of the Japanese police.

Assistance for Crime Victims   In Japan, the Crime Victims Benefit Payment Law took effect in 1981, and the police have been playing a substantial role in assistance for crime victims. According to the law, victims who have been severely injured or become disabled, as well as bereaved family members of victims, can apply to a Prefecture Public Safety Commission for benefits of the national government. The police are expected to deal with victims without causing "secondary victimization," while also taking the following measures of victim relief:

1. Assigning specially trained crisis intervention officers and counselors to help victims of felony crimes
2. Providing special support for possible cases of repeated victimization
3. Assigning a victim liaison to ensure timely dissemination of important information
4. Establishing a section in charge of planning, research, and coordination of victim support measures at each prefecture police headquarters
5. Developing networks with other administrative authorities, medical institutions, and victim support organizations
6. Assisting the establishment of private victim support organizations

Juvenile Delinquency   The Japanese police detect juvenile delinquents and provide guidance in a timely manner through on-the-spot activities with volunteers and school authorities. Each prefecture police headquarters has a Juvenile Support Center staffed with specialized juvenile guidance officials to offer systematic and expert support to juvenile delinquents and their families.

Harmful social environments have proved to be a major factor for juvenile delinquency, and the police, in cooperation with the community and other public authorities, are taking measures to control the flow of information on sex-related issues. The police have also managed the Young Telephone Corner, which provides counseling services for troubled youths, and there were about 88,000 consultation cases in 2002.

Anti-Boryokudan Campaign The Japanese police actively support local communities and private enterprises in their anti-Boryokudan movements. They also conduct door-to-door visits to businesses and construction companies susceptible to extortion, and encourage them to reject unreasonable demands of Boryokudan members. According to the Anti-Boryokudan Law enacted in 1991, each prefecture has a Prefecture Center to Promote Movements for Elimination of Violence, which holds anti-Boryokudan seminars and gives support to people in trouble with Boryokudan in cooperation with the police and other administrative agencies.

Universal Traffic Management System The National Police Agency promotes the Universal Traffic Management Systems (UTMS) that are designed to create a safe, comfortable, and environment-friendly motorized society. The UTMS provide traffic information to drivers in real time, and control traffic flows through two-way communication with each vehicle via infrared beacons. The UTMS encompass the Integrated Traffic Control Systems (ITCS), the operational core, and the following subsystems:

1. Advanced Mobile Information Systems (AMIS)
2. Public Transportation Priority Systems (PTPS)
3. Mobile Operation Control Systems (MOCS)
4. Help System for Emergency Life Saving and Public Safety (HELP)
5. Environment Protection Management Systems (EPMS)
6. Driving Safety Support Systems (DSSS)
7. Pedestrian Information and Communication Systems (PICS)
8. Fast Emergency Vehicle Preemption Systems (FAST)

Police Use of Firearms

In Japan, the Police Duties Execution Law provides the necessary measures for police officers to perform their authorities and duties. Article 7 grants a police officer use of his weapon including a firearm in case there are reasonable grounds to deem it necessary for the apprehension of a criminal or the prevention of his escape, self-protection or protection of others, or suppression of resistance to the execution of his official duty. At the same time, use of weapons must be done within the limits judged reasonably necessary according to the situation.

There were fifty-four incidents of firearm use by police in 2002, comprised as follows:

Actual shot incidents: 10
Warning shot incidents: 20
Holding at the ready (no firing) incidents: 24

Among the ten actual shooting incidents, there were two fatalities. The most typical case of firearm use is shooting a suspect who recklessly drives his car at police officers. The number of firearm use cases is relatively small, but twice as many as that in the previous year, mostly due to the increase of incidents involving assault of police officers.

Complaints and Discipline

There were 433 officers reprimanded in 2003, of whom thirty-six were dismissed. Responding to the increase in misconduct by police officers, in 2000 the police established a program handling complaints against police officers' inappropriate actions in order to make police administration open to the public and restore good discipline. The police are also putting much emphasis on disciplinary training, and newly recruited police officers have to undergo 134 hours of disciplinary courses in the initial training program.

Terrorism

Since Aum Shinrikyo carried out the sarin attack in 1995, the police have arrested more than 500 followers, including its leader Chizuo Matsumoto, and its membership has declined to about 1,650 in 2002. However, the cult still clings to antisocial teachings established by Matsumoto. In January 2003, the Public Security Examination Commission reconfirmed the fact that the cult retains dangerous elements who are capable of conducting indiscriminate mass murders, and decided to impose another three-year-term of supervisory measures.

After its leader Fusako Shigenobu was arrested in November 2000, the Japanese Red Army has sought to maintain and rebuild its organization in spite of its statement of disbandment in May 2001. The Yodo-go Group, which hijacked a Japan Airlines flight and defected to North Korea in 1970, has often traveled abroad with forged or illegally obtained passports to carry out clandestine operations under the protection or support of North Korea officials.

Violent ultraleftist groups have sought to achieve a communist or socialist revolution by violence. Members are estimated at about 22,000 people in several factions, such as Chukaku-ha, Kakurokyo, and Kakumaru-ha. Attacks have been in the form of planting time bombs, setting fires with inflammable devices connected to timers, and shooting metal shells toward governmental facilities. Additionally, they have committed illegal intelligence activities such as wiretapping.

International Cooperation

The National Police Agency hosts international seminars to provide technical assistance, independently or in cooperation with the Japan International Cooperation Agency. Around 200 law enforcement officials from fifty countries are invited to the seminars each year. The Japanese police also dispatch identification experts and others to developing countries as instructors.

Police Education, Research, and Publications

Institute for Higher Education of the Police

Newly promoted police sergeants and assistant police inspectors attend six- and eight-week training courses, respectively, at a Regional Police School, which is attached to each Regional Police Bureau of the National Police Agency.

Those promoted to police inspector enter the National Police Academy attached to the National Police Agency for a three- or six-month training course to master management skills. The National Police Academy also provides a supervisory training program for superintendents newly designated as either chief of a police station or director of Prefecture Police Headquarters.

The National Police Academy includes the Highest Training Institute for Investigation Leaders and the International Research and Training Institute for Criminal Investigation. The former trains police inspectors and higher ranks in criminal investigation, and the latter provides both foreign language training for Japanese police officers and seminars to officers from other countries.

Leading Researchers

- Toyo Atsumi (Chuo University)
- Masahide Maeda (Toritsu University)
- Koichi Miyazawa (Keio University)
- Masahiro Tamura (Cabinet counselor)

Leading Police Journals

Keisatsugaku-Ronshu (Journal of Police Science), monthly journal; Editor: The National Police Academy; Publisher: Tachibana-shobo; 3-28-2 Kandaogawa-cho, Chiyoda-ku, Tokyo 101-0052, Japan; *http://tachibanashobo.co.jp*

Keisatsu-Koron, monthly journal; Editor: Seiichi Shiraishi; Publisher: Tachibana-shobo

Keisatsu-Jiho, monthly journal; Editor: Tetsuya Arai; Publisher: Keisatsujihosha; 1-22-3 Ehara-cho, Nakano-ku; Tokyo 165-0023, Japan

Sosa-Kenkyu, monthly journal; Publisher: Tokyohorei-shuppan; 5-17-3 Koishikawa, Bunkyo-ku; Tokyo 112-0002, Japan

Major Police Publications

Keisatsu-Hakusho (The White Paper on Police), published annually by National Police Academy [NPA])

Police of Japan (published annually by NPA)

Police Policy Research (published annually by the Police Policy Research Center)

Police Communications Technical Review (published annually by the Police Info-Communications Research Center)

Reports of the National Research Institute of Police Science on Prevention of Crime and Delinquency (published twice a year by National Research Institute of Police Science [NRIPS])

Reports of the NRIPS on Forensic Science (published twice a year by NRIPS)

Reports of the NRIPS on Traffic Safety and Regulation (published twice a year by NRIPS)

Keisatsukaikaku-no-Michisuji (The Way to Police Reform), Hiroto Yoshimura (published by Tachibana-shobo in 2002)

Keisatsugyosei-no-Aratanarutenkai (The New Development of Police Administration) (published by Tokyohorei-shuppan in 2001)

Police-Related Websites

National Public Safety Commission *www.npsc.go.jp*

National Police Agency *www.npa.go.jp*

National Police Academy *www.npa.go.jp/keidai/keidai.html*

National Research Institute of Police Science *www.nrips.go.jp*

Courts *www.courts.go.jp*

Public Prosecutors Offices *www.kensatsu.go.jp*

The addresses of Prefectural Public Safety Commissions and Prefectural Police Headquarters can be found at the website of the National Police Agency.

HARUHIKO HIGUCHI

Bibliography

Asia and Far East Institute for the Prevention of Crime and the Treatment of Offenders (UNAFEI). *Criminal Justice in Japan.* UNAFEI.

Hidemine, Takahashi. "It Started in Japan: Koban." Available at: http://web-japan.org/nipponia/nipponia11/start.html.

Ministry of Internal Affairs and Communications, Japan. *Japan in Figures 2005*. Statistics Bureau. Available at: www.stat.go.jp/english/data/figures/#w.

Ministry of Justice, Japan. *Hanzai-Hakusho* (The White Paper on Crime). Ministry of Justice, 2003.

National Police Agency, Japan. *Police of Japan 2003*. Tokyo: National Police Agency, 2003.

National Police Agency, Japan. *Keisatsu-Hakusho* (The White Paper on Police). Tokyo: National Police Agency, 2003.

JORDAN

Background Material

From 1953 to 1999, King Hussein ruled Jordan, surviving several challenges to his rule, drawing on the loyalty of his military, and eventually serving as a symbol of unity and stability for both the East Bank and Palestinian communities in Jordan. Significant events during his reign include the signing of the peace agreement between Jordan and Israel in 1994, which ended the official state of war between the two nations. In 1989 and 1993, free and fair parliamentary elections were held. King Hussein ended martial law in 1991, and legalized political parties in 1992. However, the government became less tolerant of dissent as the country's economy continued to decline. Laws restricting the freedom of press were instituted in 1997. Islamic parties boycotted the legislative elections, claiming that they were unfair that same year. Following his death in February 1999, King Abdullah II succeeded his father Hussein.

Various political parties emerged due to Jordan's continuing economic difficulties, open political environment, and burgeoning population. Jordan's Parliament investigated corruption charges against several regime figures, and had become a leading forum for the expression of diverse political views. The king dissolved Parliament in June 2001 only to reinstate parliamentary elections in June 2003. In October 2003, the king dissolved the government, appointing a new prime minister and appointed three women as ministers (unprecedented) along with several young technocrats. A year later, the cabinet was reshuffled.

The population of Jordan is 5,611,202 (2004 estimate). Except for a few small communities of Circassians, Armenians, and Kurds who have adapted to Arab culture, Jordanians are Arabs. Arabic is the official language, but English is widely spoken in government and commerce. Over 95% of the 5.48 million people living in Jordan are Sunni Muslims, and 5% are Christians, most of whom are Greek Orthodox. Approximately 70% of the population is urban.

The World Bank classifies Jordan as a "lower middle–income country." In 2003, per capita GDP was approximately $1,817, and 14.5% of the population was unemployed. Education, literacy rates, and measures of social welfare are relatively high compared to other countries with similar incomes.

Contextual Features

Jordan is a constitutional monarchy, based on the 1952 constitution. The king is granted both executive and legislative powers. The bicameral legislature, called the National Assembly, consists of the Senate, members of which are appointed by the king, and the popularly elected House of Representatives.

There are three categories of courts: civil, religious, and special. Within the realm of criminal jurisprudence, Jordan retains a nominal application of Islamic law (Sharia). Although codified laws are based on Islamic principles and prescribe penalties for acts such as adultery and libel, they have been modified to reflect French codes in an effort to adapt to the requirements of a changing economy and culture. A specially provided High Tribunal reviews legislative acts. There is no jury system. Judges decide matters of fact and law.

In traditional French form, the criminal code adopted in 1955 divides criminal offenses into felonies, misdemeanors, and minor violations. Felonies are punishable by death from hanging to imprisonment for periods ranging from three years to life.

The penal system is a responsibility of the Ministry of Interior, and administered by the Prisons

Department of the Public Security Directorate. The system is composed of approximately twenty-five jails and prisons. All of these institutions, except for the largest, Amman Central Prison, is under the management of police chiefs. They are sometimes referred to as police jails. Smaller jails are located at or near regional police stations.

The Prison Law of 1953 provides for the decent treatment of prisoners and comprehensive regulations governing facilities and administration of the prison system. Jordan was one of the first Arab countries to take a rehabilitative approach as the basis for punishment of lawbreakers. The concept that crime is caused by human weakness resulting from poor social conditions rather than immorality is emphasized. This approach stands in direct contradiction to the traditional Muslim custom of personal revenge by the family of the victim. However, in practice, the lack of facilities and professionally trained staff make it difficult to take a rehabilitative approach in Jordan's penal system.

According to Jordanian submissions to Interpol, national criminal statistics recorded 16,215 offenses for 1984. Ordinary theft (3,850 cases reported), aggravated theft (1,208 cases), and breaking and entering (1,164 cases) were the most common crimes.

According to the annual human rights reports of the U.S. Department of State, prison conditions are harsh but not intentionally degrading. A 1985 royal amnesty that resulted in the release of more than 1,000 inmates helped to relieve crowded prisons. A 1988 Amnesty International report cited several prisoner abuse cases, notably at Al Mahatta and Az Zarqa military prison. The Jordanian government notes that the education and training in human rights is a main priority for the Public Security Force.

Police Profile

Background

During his reign, Hussein stressed that the concept of public order founded by the supremacy of law is a prerequisite to internal stability and the achievement of national development goals. In accordance with the constitution, comprehensive codes of law enforced by a professional police force have helped to maintain public order. The police and General Intelligence Department (GID), a civilian agency, have been given a broad range of powers in monitoring Jordanians.

The Public Security Force was created by law in July 1956 as an outgrowth of the Arab legion when it was separated into distinct police and army units. From April 1957 to November 1958, the police were again subordinated to army control during the twenty months of martial law instituted by Hussein. In July 1958, as domestic and internal threats to Hashimite rule were brought under control, a new law permanently established the separation of the two security forces.

Organizational Description

Routine maintenance of law and order is exercised by the Public Security Force, the national police establishment. Centralized under the Public Security Directorate of the Ministry of Interior, the police are commanded by an officer with the title of director general of public security. The director general is traditionally selected by the king on the basis of their military record, leadership qualifications, and loyalty to the crown.

The police are classified according to areas of geographic responsibility. The three major divisions are metropolitan (Amman), rural, and desert contingents. Amman houses central police headquarters where administrative control and technical functions are carried out in order to support the countrywide system. The three-tiered structure consists of a Public Security Directorate above ten regional directorates. The ten regions are subdivided into fifty-nine security centers and serve approximately 50,000 people.

Jordan was the first country to admit women into its police establishment. A women's police academy was opened in Amman in 1972. Primarily, women serve in the police laboratory, accounting, public relations, and prison operations, with relatively smaller numbers serving in street patrols and traffic control as well as border security.

Functions

The basic functions of the Public Security Force are to maintain public order, protect life and property, investigate criminal activity, and apprehend suspected offenders. In additions to these tasks, special services are performed such as operating the country's penal institutions, assisting customs and immigration officials, traffic control, licensing of vehicles and businesses, enforcing trade prohibition and zoning ordinances, locating missing persons, and guarding shrines and other public places. In 1987, following a reorganization of the police, a more active social role and community policing initiatives were adopted.

Police responsibilities are carried out according to administrative, judicial, and support operations. Prevention of crime and maintenance of public order are assigned to the administrative police. Judicial police handle criminal offenses, conducting criminal investigations, apprehending suspects and assisting the public prosecutor. Support police perform logistic functions, training, public affairs, accounting and planning. Regional police activities also follow this division of responsibility.

The police force operates on the same capacity as European law enforcement agencies in that they are fully motorized and technologically modernized. Rural areas are customarily less modern, with the traditional system of camel-mounted desert patrol supplemented by improved communications gear and fully equipped four-wheel-drive vehicles.

Training

Police personnel are recruited through voluntary enlistment. The National Service Law of 1976 requires new police recruits to have prior military training. The Royal Police Academy in Amman provides training for both officers and enlisted ranks. There is also separate police training in Az Zarqa, which welcomes large numbers of police trainees from friendly Arab countries. Cadets study the country's legal system, general and administrative work, undergo physical training, and are instructed on the use of firearms and other police equipment. Courses on court operations, criminal code and investigation procedures are also required. In 1987, the government mandated that Public Security Force officers must have a university degree.

Although job titles differ, rank and insignia of the Public Security Force are identical to those of the army. Like the Royal Jordanian Air Force, police uniforms in the Amman metropolitan area are light tan in summer and dark blue in winter. The Desert Police Force wear traditional Arab garb. Police pay scales are similar to those in the army, but the authorization of special allowances differs. Attracting and retaining personnel is not a problem due to the favorable conditions of service.

Police Use of Firearms

The police are armed with pistols, rifles, light automatic weapons, and nightsticks, depending on their location. Special riot control equipment is available in Amman and larger towns.

Terrorism

Countering terrorism is the function of the Special Police Force, which is a division within the Public Security Directorate. In 1988, as part of its antiterrorism program, a multimillion-dollar project to improve police communications was announced.

MINTIE DAS

Bibliography

Central Intelligence Agency. *World Factbook*. 2005. Available at: www.cia.gov/cia/publications/factbook.

Library of Congress. "Country Reports." 1989. Available at: www.lcweb2.loc.gov/rfd/cs.

U.S. Department of Justice. 2005. "Background Note." www.travel.gov/travel.

K

KAZAKHSTAN

Background Material

The Republic of Kazakhstan is located in the middle of the Eurasia landmass. Extending over a territory of 2,725,000 square kilometers, it is the second largest republic of the former Soviet Union, and the ninth largest country in the world. The republic borders Russia to the north and northeast, China to the southeast, and Turkmenistan, Uzbekistan, and Kyrgyzstan to the south.

The population is 15,143,704 (July 2004 estimate), 56% of whom live in urban areas. The Kazakhs comprise the majority ethnic group (53.4%), although Russians account for a significant minority (30%). The former capital, Almaty, remains a financial, cultural, and business centre. Astanam became the new capital in 1998, and the city is growing rapidly. Kazakh is the official language, but is used co-extensively with Russian.

Contextual Features

In Kazakhstan there are fourteen *oblast* (regions), two cities with special status (Almaty and Astana); eighty-four cities, thirty-nine of which are subordinate to national and oblast jurisdictions; 160 *raion* (districts); ten city districts; 200 towns; and 2,150 rural counties.

Kazakhstan is divided into the following tiers of local government:

Third (*oblast*) tier, which includes the local state administrations, that is, the executive and representative bodies in fourteen oblasts and the cities of Almaty and Astana

Second (*raion*) tier, which includes the local state administration, that is, the executive and representative bodies in 160 raion and seventy-nine cities of *raion* status

First (rural) tier, which includes to the local administrations, that is, executive bodies in towns, villages (*auls*), and rural counties.

The Ministry of Internal Affairs (MIA) is the central agency of Kazakhstan, which oversees the management system for law enforcement bodies. The MIA, as stipulated by legislation, performs interbranch coordination of protection of public order and maintenance of public safety, participating in development and realizing a state policy of law enforcement.

According to the 1995 constitution, Kazakhstan is a democratic, secular, legal, and social state that values the life and liberty of the individual.

The legal system borrows from the Roman, German, and Russian systems. Like other formerly Soviet republics, Kazakhstan has experienced radical transformation since the early 1990s (having independence in 1991). The nation has expressed a commitment to ideological and political pluralism, a socially focused market economy, and an expansion of human rights and personal freedom.

Kazakhstan has passed numerous legal reforms, and has one of the best rates of such reform among former Soviet republics. It has established a record of rapid legal reform among post-Soviet republics.

The judicial system is composed of the Supreme Court and the local courts. The establishment of specialized or any other courts is barred by current law, although the constitution dictates when exceptions can be made, and military, economic, administrative and juvenile courts can be created. Judges have the power to administer justice as established by law and the constitution.

The local courts include the regional courts, city court of capital, courts of cities, specialized military court of armed forces, district courts, specialized military court of the garrison, specialized interdistrict economic court, and administrative court.

The criminal-executive system of Kazakhstan is a component of the Ministry of Justice, and represents establishments and the bodies providing execution of criminal punishments. There are seventy-nine establishments function in structure of criminal-executive system now: fifty corrective colonies of the general, strict, and special modes; twenty-four colonies-settlements; four educational colonies for minors; and one prison.

Prompt and practical development of capitalist, pro-market attitudes adopted in the transition to independence has not been supported by adequate legislative maintenance, and overall dissatisfaction and unrest has led to a sharp growth in crime. More than half of all crime (in 2003) fell into crimes against property (robbery, theft, burglary, extortion, fraud).

Unemployment is higher among people convicted of crimes; in 1998, the unemployed accounted for

two-thirds of crimes, and in 2003, 87.5%. The general crime rate increased 20% between 1990 and 1995. In 1998, the rate was 9.1 per 100,000 persons, and in 2001, 10.3 per 100,000. From 2003 to 2004, the crime rate increased 18.6%.

Police Profile

Organizational Description

Law enforcement bodies include the Ministry of Internal Affairs, and Internal Affairs departments. The minister of internal affairs is chairman of the board of the Ministry of Internal Affairs, and also the commander of the army. The chiefs of the departments of Internal Affairs are the senior operative chiefs, overseeing commanders of divisions and parts of internal armies.

The Kuzet is one of the structural divisions of the Ministry of Internal Affairs. The Kuzet carries out functions related to the protection of the government, property, and public order to maintain public safety and keep the crime rate down. According to existing law, the Kuzet is the specialized security division of law enforcement bodies, carrying out security activity in Kazakhstan. The Kuzet also offers protection services to both individuals and valuable cargo. The Kuzet also carries out duties relating to the installation, adjustment, service, and repair of protection systems and signal systems.

Functions

Law enforcement bodies cooperate with other law enforcement bodies, including with the special state bodies, as well as the general population and the mass media to maintain and enhance public order and safety.

The state bodies and their officials are obliged to assist law enforcement bodies in protecting the rights and freedom of the person and citizen, protection of public order, and maintenance of public safety, in the prevention, revealing, suppression, disclosing, and investigation of crimes and other offences.

Training

In higher education institutions of the Ministry of Internal Affairs, citizens are accepted when they have average general, initial professional, average professional, or professional higher education, meet requirements of employees of the law enforcement bodies, and have a suitable state of health for military service and study. The acceptance of citizens into higher education institutions of the Ministry of Internal Affairs of Republic Kazakh-

Type of Crime	Percent Convicted
Larceny	33.6
Murder	12.2
Robbery	9.1
Looting	8.6
Assault	6.5
Violation	4.3
Hooliganism	2.4
Extortion	1.5
Fraud	1.2
Other crimes	20.6

Source: Republic of Kazakhstan Agency of Statistics

stan under the authorized plan of reception is carried out in three stages:

At the first stage, selection committees form an entrants contingent, carrying out selections based on medical, physical, and psychophysical characteristics

At the second stage, the education institutions carry out selection based on results of uniform national testing or the complex testing related to technologies, the national center of state standards of formation, and testing by the Ministry of Education and Science

At the third stage, credentials committees of the education institutions determine student numbers

Police Use of Firearms

In accordance with Kazakhstan legislation, the following groups hold the right to bear firearms: armed forces, other troops and military units, security services; state public authorities and officials who have a right to keep and bear firearms; legal entities with specific duties that require use of firearms by charter; legal entities and individuals who collect of display arms; legal entities that produce or trade arms; organizations that work in the hunting business; sport organizations; educational organizations; citizens of Republic of Kazakhstan; and foreigners.

Terrorism

According to N. Dutbaev, chairman of the Committee of National Safety, Kazakhstan is the site of cells of some international terrorist organizations. Recently, a cell of the Islamic East Turkistan group was discovered, headed by citizens of Kazakhstan. The organization was found to have explosive materials, weapons, and ammunition. Contact and communications between the Kazakhstan cell of East Turkistan and Afghanistan, Iran, Kyrgyzstan, and Uzbekistan cells have been confirmed.

International Cooperation

The Ministry of Internal Affairs is a member of the following international organizations:

- Commonwealth of Independent States
- Central Asian Cooperation Organization
- Collective Safety Treaty Organization
- Shanghai Organization of Co-operation
- Interpol
- European Union
- Organization on Safety and Cooperation in Europe

Bases of interaction of government participants in the struggle against crime are incorporated in the international contracts that are made at various levels (interstate, intergovernmental, and interdepartmental), and cover practically all aspects of law enforcement operations.

Kazakhstan, Kyrgyzstan, Uzbekistan, Turkmenistan, and the Russian Federation have created mobile joint groups to control railway junctions and train stations, highways, airports, and shared borders.

The Central Asian Cooperation Organization is regulated by an agreement among the governments of Kazakhstan, Kyrgyzstan, and Uzbekistan, binding them in a cooperative struggle against the illegal drug trade. A contract has also been agreed to between Kazakhstan, Kyrgyzstan, Tajikistan, and Uzbekistan, which outlines joint actions against terrorism, political and religious extremism, transnational organized crime, and other threats to national stability.

Police Education, Research, and Publications

Institutions of Higher Education

Semipalatinsk Law College
Kustanay Law Institute
Shimkent Law College, Ministry of Internal Affairs, named after B. Momishuli
Kazakh Humanitarian Law University
High Police School of Almaty
Law faculty, Kazakh National University, named after Al-Farabi
Academy of the Committee of National Security (KNB)
The KNB Military Institute

Police Websites

- *www.mvd.kz* (official site of Ministry of Internal Affairs)
- *www.police.kz* (official site of Almaty *oblast* police)
- *www.uvdvko.kz* (official site of East Kazakhstan *oblast* police)
- *www.guvd.kustanai.info* (official site of Kustanay *oblast* police)
- *www.krg-guvd.kz* (official site of Karaganda *oblast* police)
- *www.zakon.kz* (Kazakhstan law site)
- *www.government.kz* (official site of Republic of Kazakhstan government)

MERUERT MAKHMUTOVA

Bibliography

Makhmutova, M. "Local Government in Kazakhstan: Developing New Rules in the Old Environment." In *Local Government in Eastern Europe, the Caucasus and Central Asia*, vol. 3, edited by I. Munteanu and V. Popa, 407–408. Budapest, Hungary: Open Society Institute, 2001.

KENYA

Background Material

The Republic of Kenya, sometimes referred to as the "cradle of mankind," is situated along the Indian Ocean and the East African littoral, and is bordered by Sudan and Ethiopia. It has an extensive and complex history that dates backs many centuries. The nation's strategic location has attracted numerous foreigners, including people from the United States, England, China, Germany, Portugal, and Arab nations. Like most of its fellow African nations, Kenya has had an abundance of social, political, and economic problems. Many of them were a result of English colonization from July 1, 1895 to December 12, 1963.

Called the East Africa Protectorate until July 1, 1920, Kenya became the nation's official name when its status was changed from protectorate to colony. Led by founding president and liberation fighter Jomo Kenyatta, Kenya gained its independence on December 12, 1963, and became a republic exactly one year later on December 12, 1964. Following Kenyatta's death in 1978, Daniel Toroitich arap Moi assumed the presidency.

After Kenya had existed as a de facto one-party state from 1969 until 1982, the Kenya Africa National Union (KANU) imposed itself as the country's exclusive legal political party. Opposition factions failed to dislodge KANU in 1992 and 1997 elections that were characterized by fraud and violence. Among the catastrophes that have plagued Kenya in recent years were terrorist bombings in 1998 and 2002, and the devastating drought of 1999 and 2000 that severely affected the nation's agricultural production while creating a necessity to ration water and energy.

As East Africa's regional hub for finance and trade, Kenya has long been troubled by judicial corruption as well as by its dependence on several primary commodities whose prices on the world market have been in long-term decline. International Monetary Fund loans were requested in 2000 to aid Kenya with its drought problems, but were discontinued in 2001 as a sanction against the nation for failing to institute anticorruption measures. Strong rains in 2001 did little to offset the impact of weak commodity prices, infectious corruption, and low investment, all of which served to restrict economic growth in Kenya. And with the irregular rain patterns, political infighting, and other critical problems that ensued in Kenya in 2002, economic growth was further retarded. Campaigning as an anticorruption candidate, Mwai Kibaki was elected as Kenya's president in 2002. Although signs of progress—increased donor support and stepped-up anticorruption campaigns—were detected in 2003, creating a slight growth in economic activity, Kenya remains a quagmire of social, political, and economic turmoil.

The population of Kenya is 32,021,856 (July 2004 estimate). It has an area of 582,650 square kilometers (land 569,250, and water 13,400). The capital is Nairobi. Kenya has the following ethnic composition: Kikuyu 22%, Luhya 14%, Luo 13%, Kalenjin 12%, Kamba 11%, Kisii 6%, Meru 6%, other Africans 15%, non-African (Asian, European, and Arab) 1%. Languages spoken include English (official), Kiswahili (official), and numerous indigenous languages. The religions practiced include Protestantism (45%), Roman Catholicism (33%), indigenous beliefs (10%), Islam (10%), and other 2%.

Gross domestic purchasing power parity in 2003 was estimated at $33.03 billion. Per capita income totaled US$271. Major economic activities include agriculture, industry, mining, and tourism.

Contextual Features

The Republic of Kenya is a republic consisting of executive, legislative, and judicial branches of government. The nation's president serves as both the chief of state and head of government. The president is elected by popular vote and serves a five-year term. However, a run-off election is held if no candidate receives at least 25% of the popular vote in each of at least five of Kenya's seven provinces and one area. The president appoints the vice president and a presidential cabinet. A unicameral National Assembly (or Bunge) comprises Kenya's legislative branch of government. It is a 224-seat body, of which 210 members are elected by popular vote. Another twelve members are appointed by the president, and selected by the parties in proportion to their parliamentary vote totals. These members carry the title (or label) of "nominated" members. Ex-officio members occupy the remaining two seats of parliament.

Kenya's court system is comprised of the Court of Appeal, High Court, and Magistrate Courts that serve at two levels. The majority of Kenya's civil and criminal court cases are initiated in the Magistrate Courts. In Kenyan courts, judges determine the fate of convicted defendants in criminal cases. However, in the more serious murder and treason cases, up to three assessors can be designated by the High Court's deputy registrar to sit with the judge.

The Kenyan president holds executive power over some of the nation's most prominent and powerful appointees, including the Chief Justice, the Attorney General, and the judges of the High Court. The Chief Justice is a member of both the Court of Appeals and the High Court. Courts martial are employed to try individuals in the Kenyan military, who may appeal their verdicts by way of military court networks. Traditional and customary courts are not a part of the Kenyan court system; however, Kenyans who enter into matrimony may choose either customary or national law, and in the event of disputes, the type of law that is applied is determined by the courts. The impoverished nature of Kenyan society negates access to legal counsel for most Kenyan citizens, and only in capital cases do defendants gain access to government legal representation.

Crime is a major concern in virtually every Kenyan city. It is particularly high in Nairobi, Kisumu, and Mombasa, as well as along coastal beach resorts. Depending on the offense, criminal offenses in Kenya are classified as either felonies or misdemeanors. Sanctions for youth seven to twelve years of age are significantly more lenient than those designated for older individuals, and no one under the age of seven is criminally liable for his or her actions. The maximum and minimum penalties for felonies in Kenya are death and three years imprisonment, respectively.

Among the most common crimes in Kenya are incidents—many of them involving tourists—that include pick-pocketing, muggings, carjackings, burglarizing hotel rooms, thievery from automobiles, residential burglaries, con artistry, and highway banditry. According to several sources, including a study conducted by the United Nations Human Settlements Programme (UN-HABITAT) and the Technology Development Corporation, which works in underprivileged areas to expand their access to technologies, the majority of crimes reported by the police take place in Nairobi, the capital of Kenya. In addition, *Crime in Nairobi*, a 2002 study, revealed that among 10,500 individuals interviewed, nearly four in ten people had been robbed, and nearly two in ten people had been victims of physical assault.

The corrections system in Kenya is overseen by several different organizations, including the Kenya Prisons Service, the Children's Department, and the Probation Department of the Ministry of Home Affairs. Corrections staff are employed by the civil service system and are paid on a level comparable to that of Kenya's police. The Prisons Training School, located in Nairobi, is the institution where corrections personnel are trained. In Kenya there are both general and special-purpose prisons, approved schools and re-mand houses for youth offenders, and detention camps (temporary barracks or tent compounds, work camps, prison farms, and so on). Overcrowding in all correctional facilities has long been one of the most salient problems characterizing Kenya's corrections system, in part because the majority of Kenya's prisoners fall uner the category of "for safe custody" and includes vagrants, debtors, and individuals held in pretrial or preventive detention.

Compared to other developing nations, Kenya's corrections system is more humane and has embraced rehabilitation as a penal policy. Inmates are encouraged to learn trades such as tailoring, metalwork, carpentry, and shoemaking. There are also literacy trai-ning and education courses available to prisoners. Except for inmates sentenced to life in prison or those under preventive detention, sentences may be reduced by a third for good behavior. Periodically, there is a review of the records of all prisoners serving sentences of seven or more years. Reduced sentences are sometimes recommended to the president by a review board, and inmates serving long sentences may have their sentences reduced by three months for good behavior.

After being released from prison in Kenya, individuals may turn to the probation service program to aid them in their transition back into general society. There are also halfway houses in both Nairobi and Mombasa, and the Prisoners' Aid Society, which operates in conjunction with probation and parole officials, to help former inmates. The Society, which was established in the 1950s, aids ex-prisoners with small loans, helps them to buy materials for work, and assists their families until they can resume their roles as heads of household.

Police Profile

Background

The contemporary Kenyan police system was created and has evolved, largely, as a result of a variety of influences that England had on the whole of East Africa. It was transformed during the colonial period as the nation's social conditions and problems matured. To protect their interests along the caravan route from Mombasa to Uganda, the British Imperial East Africa Company employed a defense operation in 1887 called Askaris, composed of armed guards, and developed, ultimately, to become Kenya's first organized security force.

By 1896, Kenya had put in place a police force with headquarters in Mombasa, and by 1901 it included a variety of resources and specialized personnel, including a European superintendent, several European, Indian, and Somali inspectors, and 150 lower-ranked individuals. Smaller police stations were positioned in Vanga, Rabai, Malindi, Lamu, and Kismayu. In 1897, the Uganda Railway Police, another independent law enforcement unit, was established to protect workers who were constructing railroad lines.

Police forces in Nairobi and Kisumu were also among the early systems. All of these affiliations were merged in 1902 by European colonizers to form the British East Africa Police, headed by Inspector General C.G.D. Farquhar. In 1920, the organization's name was changed officially to the Kenya Police. The next half-decade witnessed the establishment of no less than eighty-eight police stations and outposts scattered throughout the country. During the era of the Mau Mau uprising, the Kenyan police force doubled its size to 13,000 officers, while maintaining a reserve force of about 9,000 police.

Authority over the police force was ceded to the Kenyan government after the nation became an independent state. By the mid-1980s, Kenya's police force had grown to 19,000 and included female officers. In addition, the force included administrative and reserve personnel. General duty officers, a General Services Unit (GSU), and the Railways and Harbours Police were included among the organizational structure of Kenya's police operations. There were also specialized units that included the Criminal Investigative Directorate (CID), the Intelligence Directorate, the Police Air Wing, and stock theft and dog units.

There has not been any significant change in the British-influenced police grade structures since Kenya's pre-independence period. Cadet assistant superintendents to commissioners constitute the range of appointed officers, cadet assistant inspectors to chiefs encompass inspectorate officers, and constable to sergeant comprises subordinate officers. The rank and pay scale of the Administrative Police are subordinate to those of the regular Kenya Police. For example, the ranks of the former include only those of constables and noncommissioned officers. Because they are part of the civil service system, Kenya's police are not permitted to join trade unions. That has not resulted in many serious problems, however, because police salaries are considered fair when compared to local standards.

The Kenyan Police wear military-style tropical uniforms—blue-gray short-sleeved shirts worn with either long or short pants and garrison hats (plastic helmets for the lower-ranked personnel). GSU officers wear green camouflaged jackets and deep red berets. Like the British, uniformed police in Kenya's urban areas carry batons only, but are issued firearms in emergency situations. Plainclothes officers are issued pistols, while officers in the outlying rural areas are equipped with rifles.

Demographics

Kenya's police force, including administrative and reserve staff, consists of both male and female officers. The majority of the force—about 76%—is made up of rank and file officers, with senior rank officials and inspectors constituting about 8% and noncommissioned officers representing about 16%, respectively, of the organization. Those respective proportions have remained relatively constant since Kenya's independence. Relative to other developing nations, the Kenyan police technical staff is large. About one in three individuals employed by the Kenyan Police are assigned to technical and support jobs.

Organizational Description and Functions

The paramilitary GSU, a domestic mobile security operation, created and specially trained in 1953 to deal with the opposition Mau Mau faction, remains a heavily armed force with Bren guns, rifles, and light mortars. Its various units are strategically situated throughout Kenya to deal with civil disturbances. With units in Nairobi, Nakuru, and Kisumu, GSU forces are self-contained and operate in the field, and are provided with their personal equipment, transportation vehicles, and communication systems.

Known throughout Kenya as the "formation," and with units in Mombasa, Lake Victoria, and Kisumu, the Railways and Harbors Police are responsible for dealing with violations associated with land or transportation lines or installations. Headed by an assistant commissioner, this special force is divided into three divisions and consists of about 1,000 constables, and 300 officers and non-commissioned officers, including an independent criminal investigation division known as the "formation crime branch."

All tasks associated with the investigation of crimes and maintenance of criminal files falls to the CID, a force of plainclothes detectives. It operates throughout Kenya's various police headquarters, and its chain of command extends to the national headquarters. The Intelligence Di-rectorate is charged with gathering intelligence related to domestic issues and subversive criminal activities.

The Police Air Wing provides communications, supply, and evacuation services and performs reconnaissance operations. Developed in 1959 and first utilized in the mid-1960s during the *shifta* insurgency, the Air Wing unit is comprised of several aircraft. Among its most highly regarded capabilities is its ability to operate under harsh conditions from very underdeveloped airstrips.

Originally known as the Tribal Police, the Administrative Police was organized to supplement Kenya's regular police force. The Administrative Police operates in rural Kenya where regular forces and police stations and posts are absent. Recruits are generally enlisted from the same areas where they serve. Centrally involved in both the arrests of criminal suspects and the maintenance of public order, indigenous chiefs and subchiefs assume daily operational authority over Administrative Police officers. However, administrative control over the force remains the domain of the district commissioner, and the provincial commissioner provides general directions for the officers. Because murders and other serious crimes are considered beyond the capability of the Administrative Police, Kenya's regular police are usually called on to handle such incidents.

An all-volunteer unit created in 1948, the Reserve Police also serves as a support force to the regular police in emergency situations. Members serve minimum terms of 2 years and must be at least 18 years of age. Unlike the standing Administrative Police force, the reserve officers constitute an ad hoc force of sorts that is only operational when needed. The power of the Reserve Police as a law enforcing entity reached its height during the insurgency of the Mau Mau when its ranks totaled around 9,000. It is now a mere fraction of that number.

The police headquarters in Nairobi serves as the core of Kenya's police communications operations, which is considered to be among the most technologically advanced systems on the African continent. Well equipped to sustain armed attacks, the headquarters is a self-contained bunker installation that serves as an emergency national communications and operations center. In 1975, a VHF communications network was established, allowing patrol cars traveling major thoroughfares throughout Kenya to connect with central control in the police headquarters. There is also a regional Interpol police communications system that opened in Nairobi in 1973.

Complaints and Discipline

International and domestic accusations of immorality, corruption, and human rights violations against the Kenyan police were rampant by the early 1990s. Those complaints have ensued into present-day Kenya. In one incident, the police killing of three college students over a 2-day period in late 1996 prompted President Daniel arap Moi to appoint Duncan Wachira as police commissioner. Wachira's primary task was to refine the image and competency of the Kenyan police. However, minimal progress has been made, and many Kenyans citizens still list the police among their greatest fears.

Police Education, Research, and Publications

Recruiting teams enlist police recruits on a national voluntary basis. Although Kenya's national policy calls for an ethnically diverse police force, it is widely believed that the Kikuyu dominate Kenya's police force in the same manner as they do in other public service jobs. There has been a steady rise in the overall educational level of police recruits, including an increase in the number of high school and college graduates who apply for police jobs in Kenya. Generally, the social status of the country's law enforcement personnel is good, but their overall status has suffered some as a result of their tax collection practices.

Established in Kiganjo, near Nyeri, in 1948, the Kenya Police College serves as the primary institution for the training of police recruits and officers as well as for teaching courses for reservists. In addition, there are several other institutions—both inside and outside the police establishment—that provide specialized instruction in policing. Police personnel from the CID enroll in courses in Nairobi at the Criminal Investigation Directorate Training

School. Police communications personnel study and train at the Kenya Polytechnic Institute, and there are provincial training centers where refresher and other kinds of training are conducted, including instruction in literacy and continuing education courses for field personnel. The Administrative Police enroll in six-week courses at the Armed Forces Training College at Lanet, near Nakuru, in the Rift Valley. Their studies include basic refresher training and weapon familiarization.

Although some Railways and Harbours Police officers are sent away to the Railways Training College for specialized training, the majority of officers take refresher and technical courses at their own training centers. The Kenya Institute of Administration is the site where senior police personnel receive management and supervisory training.

THOMAS S. MOSELEY AND
IHEKWOABA D. ONWUDIWE

Bibliography

Abreo, Rosendo P. *Historical Review of the Kenya Prisons Service (From 1911–1970)*. Nairobi: Kenya Prisons Service, 1972.

Banks, S. Arthur, and Muller, Thomas C. "Governments and Intergovernmental Organizations." In *Political Handbook of the World*. New York: CSA Publications, 1998.

Bienen, H. *Kenya: The Politics of Participation and Control*. Princeton, NJ: Princeton University Press, 1974.

BBC News. "Mob Justice Acceptable." October 13, 2000. Available at: http://newsvote.bbc.co.uk/hi/english/talking_point/debates/african/newsid_965000/965299.stm. Accessed May 18, 2002.

Central Intelligence Agency. *The World Factbook*. Available at: www.cia.gov/cia/publications/factbook/geos/ke.html. Accessed March 22, 2002, and October 5, 2004.

"CJ Pledges Change in Judiciary." *Daily Nation*, March 26, 2002. Available at: www.nationaudio.com/News/DailyNation/Today/News/News46.html. Accessed March 26, 2002.

Dilley, M.R. *British Policy in Kenya Colony*, 2d ed. London: Frank Cass, 1966.

Ebbe, Obi N.I. *Crime in Nigeria*. Ann Arbor, MI: University Microfilms International, 1982.

Ebbe, Obi N.I. "Crime and Delinquency in Metropolitan Lagos: A Study of Crime and Delinquency Area Theory," *Social Forces* 67, no. 3 (1989): 751–765.

Gertzel, C.J., GoldSchmidt, M., and Rothchild, D., eds. *Government and Politics in Kenya*. Nairobi: East African Publishing House, 1969.

Ghai, Y.P., and McAuslin, J.P.W.B. *Public Law and Political Change in Kenya*. Nairobi: Oxford University Press, 1970.

Ingleton, D. Roy. *Police of the World*. New York: Charles Scribner's Sons, 1979.

Kamoche, J.G. *Imperial Trusteeship and Political Evolution in Kenya, 1923–1963*. Washington, DC: University Press of America, 1981.

"Kenya: A Case for Reform." Available at: http://law.cua.edu/classes/comparative_law/johnson/. Accessed March 19, 2002.

Kercher, Leonard C. *The Kenya Penal System: Past, Present, and Prospect*. Washington, DC: University Press of America, 1981.

Kinuthia, Waithera. Interview by author. Rochester Institute of Technology, Rochester, NY, 1993.

Kurian, George Thomas. *World Encyclopedia of Police Forces and Penal Systems*. New York: Facts on File, 1989.

Legun, Colin. *Africa: Contemporary Record*. New York and London: African Publishing Company, 1992–1994.

Leys, Norman. *Kenya*, 8th ed. London: Frank Cass, 1973.

Mars-Proietti, Laura. *Nations of the World: A Political, Economic and Business Handbook*. Millerton, NY: Grey House Publishing, 2004.

Mungeam, G.H. *British Rule in Kenya 1895–1912*. Oxford: Clarendon Press, 1966.

Nelson, H.D., ed. *Kenya: A Country Study*, 4th ed. Washington, DC: Government Printing Office, 1984.

Nyachae, Samuel. Interview by author. State University of New York, Brockport, NY, 1993.

Transparency International Kenya. Frequently Asked Questions. Available at: www.tikenya.org/faqs.asp. Accessed March 26, 2002.

KIRIBATI

Background Material

The Republic of Kiribati is a small (by population) island state of the Micronesian group in the South Pacific. Its important defining characteristic is the large ocean area included within its geographical boundaries. The population is mostly of Micronesian descent. Contact with Western Europe and consequent changes marked the development of this island state. The chief languages spoken are Kiribati and English. The main industries of the islands are fishing and mining. Kiribati people remain very religious with most denominations represented among the population. Catholics dominate with Congregational Protestants forming the second largest grouping. Next are Bahai', Adventists, and Latter-Day Saints, among others.

The population totals 85,000, according to the last census (2000). Kiribati has a land area of 811 square kilometers.

Contextual Features

The supreme law of the land is the constitution. The laws that applied before independence (from British colonial rule, 12 July 1979) are retained. Thus, the law of the land comprises the doctrines of English common law and equity, the statutes of general application in force in England as of January 1, 1961, except insofar as they are inconsistent with the circumstances of Kiribati, and the laws of Kiribati, such as the ordinances, orders and subsidiary legislation having effect immediately before independence and the acts made thereafter. Local custom may also apply in the manner provided by statute (Constitution of Kiribati 1979).

Kiribati's crime rate is low, and there are no general crime trends.

Crime statistics are only available for 1999 (personal communication, Crime Unit, 1999). These statistics reported age and gender rates of convicted cases, as well as those discharged and pending prosecution, but do not show a single common crime in Kiribati. However, according to police sources, there is suspicion that violence against parents by their own children is increasing.

There are twenty Magistrates' Court corresponding with the number of islands scattered throughout the Republic, and including urban centers such as Betio and South Tarawa. There is also the Magistrates Court (Land), located throughout the Gilbert Group. There is no such Court for the Line Islands. The Magistrates' Court consist of a bench of three lay magistrates, appointed and subject to the approval by the President, acting on the advice of the Chief Justice who selects nominees from village representatives. The Magistrates are normally respected *unimwane* (elders). The jurisdiction of the Magistrates Court includes criminal matters where the maximum penalty does not exceed five years imprisonment or a fine not exceeding $500. The Magistrates Court also presides over civil matters where there may be a claim of less than $3,000. In addition, the Court is empowered to order and enforce payment and maintenance, and can hear petitions for divorce between I-Kiribati under the Native Divorce Ordinance (Kiribati Government 1977).

The Magistrates' Courts (Land) consist of a bench of at least five magistrates who are appointed from a panel of magistrates, in the same manner as members of the Magistrates Courts. However, in making recommendation for appointment the Chief Justice is required to consult with the Chief Lands Officer. Land Magistrates have no legal qualifications. They are required, however, to have extensive knowledge of local land tenure. The Magistrates Courts (Land) has jurisdiction over the application of the Lands Code or local customary law residing over all cases concerning: land boundaries, transfers of registered Native Land, and disputes concerning the possession and utilization of land; application of customary law to all cases arising from the administration and partition of estates of I-Kiribati and related conveyances; paternity orders and care of children and single women; and, the adjudication of cases involving customary fishing rights. A court clerk employed by the Judiciary Department and responsible to the Chief Registrar, serves both the Magistrate Court and the Magistrates Court (Land).

A Court higher than the two Magistrates Court is the Single Magistrate Court, which is empowered to hear cases as the Chief Justice may direct. The Single Magistrate Court is used regularly to hear serious criminal cases including sex crimes, fraud, or cases of some complexity.

Appeals from the Magistrates Court and Single Magistrate go to the High Court. The High Court comprises the Chief Justice or a Single High Court Judge. There is limited right of appeal to the Kiribati Court of Appeal, which was established by the Court of Appeal Act 1980. Judges of the Court of Appeal are appointed by the Beretitenti, acting on the advice of the Chief Justice and the Public Service Commission. The Chief Justice is ex officio president of the Court of Appeal. The constitution provides for a Chief Justice and for a High Court judge. The Beretitenti appoints them on the advice of the Chief Justice and the Public Service Commission (Kiribati Government 1979).

With regard to the Magistrates Court (Land), appeal goes to the High Court judge, consisting of the Chief Justice or a High Court judge sitting with at least two Lands Magistrates. There is no further appeal from the High Court in land matters. The High Court sits either in Betio or South Tarawa when hearing land appeals or periodically tours the outer islands. Commissioners of the High Court may also be appointed and have such powers of a High court as the Chief Justice may confer.

The Prison Ordinance regulates the administration of the prisons in Kiribati. The Superintendent of Prisons who reports to the Commissioner of Police heads the Prison service. There are four main prisons in the country. The largest prison is located in Betio, the main commercial center of the country, and houses male inmates. Another larger prison is situated in Bairiki, the seat of central government, and houses female inmates. The remaining two prisons are located on Tabiteuea North and Kiritimati. One of these houses prisoners of North and South Tabiteuea, including adjacent islands in the Southern Gilbert. The other is used for Line Islands inmates.

Prison officers number less than thirty, and with the Superintendent of Prisons, are responsible for the day-to-day operation of the Prison.

Police Profile

Background

Before becoming a British protectorate in 1892, the indigenous population of Kiribati lived in clan structures governed by rules created by clan elders. In the absence of formal rules binding the people at both the local and macro levels, wars were often fought in order to gain more land or to create chieftains. During this period there was widespread turbulence, regularly culminating in sporadic reigns of terror throughout the islands.

The colonial period brought significant developments in terms of "law and order."

From headquarters on Butaritari Island, colonial officers visited numerous islands, introducing simple laws and punishing deviants. This marked the beginning of policing. Early policing initiatives encouraged different clans to cohabit in villages, deliberately breaking down the clan structures that had been a source of social conflict.

From the early days of colonialism until the establishment of the Armed Constabulary Ordinance in 1916, the type of policing was carried out by village wardens who were appointed specifically to individuals or villages. The wardens were later renamed village constables. The modern police, the Kiribati Police Force, originated in the constabulary, although it became a formal police force at independence in 1979. Entry requirements for the police force are completion of high school or its equivalent.

Demographics

The national police force consists of 293 officers, less than twenty of whom are female. About 95% of officers are uniformed; the rest, particularly members of the crime branch, are not uniformed. There is no designation of police according to federal; regional/state, or local municipal status.

Organizational Description

The organizational hierarchy of the police force consists of one police commissioner, two assistant police commissioners, three police superintendents, five assistant superintendents, nineteen police inspectors, twenty sergeants, thirty-six corporals, and 207 constables. The commissioner of police has overall command of the police, while the assistant commissioner of police is in charge of operations.

Police are distributed as follows: Makin island (population less than 2000) 2 constables; Butaritari (population over 2000) 3 constables; Marakei island (population over two 2000) 2; Abaiang (population over 2000) 3 constables; Abemama (population over 2000) 3; Maiana island (population less than 2000) 2 constables; Aranuka island (population less than 2000) 1; Kuria (population less than 2000) 1; Nonouti island (population over 2000) 3; Tabiteuea North island (population over 2000) 4; Tabiteuea South island (population less than 2000) 2 constables; Onotoa island (population over 2000) 2 constables; Beru island (population over 2000) 2 constables; Nikunau island (population over 2000) 2 constables; Tamana island (population less than 2000) 1 constable; Arorae (population less than 2000) 1 constable; Banaba island (population less than 1000) 1 constable; Betio (population over 10,000) constables 20; South Tarawa (population over 20,000) 40 constables; Kanton island (population less than 1000), in the Phoenix Group, 1; Orona island (population less than 1000), in the Phoenix group, 1 constable; Tabuaeran island (population less than 2000), in the Line Group, 2 constables; Teraina (population less than 2000) in the Line Group, 2 constables; and Kiritimati island (population over than 2000) in the Line Group 14 constables.

Fire service is also provided by the police, which is additional to the main functions that are provided under the police law.

Functions

The preservation of public order is the primary responsibility of the police (police ordinance Chapter 73, Section 21 (1) (a)), which includes prevention of obstruction of roads. Recently, the same responsibility included policing of Kiribati Exclusive Economic Zone (EEZ) with only one patrol boat. Australia and New Zealand police have occasionally provided coastal surveillance assistance.

Police Public Projects

There are currently no police/public initiatives. However, the Kiribati Police Force is considering the development of a crime prevention project, which would involve community participation, as well as technical and financial assistance from aid donors. Among other things, the project would focus on violence against women and parents/the elderly, and drug abuse, the incidence of which are considered by local authorities to be rapidly increasing, particularly in the urban growth centers.

Police Use of Firearms

Kiribati police have no access to firearms.

Complaints and Discipline

The General Orders (Sommerville 1989) allow for complaints against police by members of the public. The commissioner, based of the substance of reported complaints, takes any necessary action. If necessary, criminal charges can be laid against an officer, following investigations. To date, there have been no human rights complaints made against police officers.

Terrorism

The police are not currently engaged in any anti-terrorist activities.

International Cooperation

Institutions providing for the training and education of the police include the following local and frequently used foreign institutions: Kiribati Technical Institute; Kiribati Centre of the University of the South Pacific, particularly with regard to basic skills in English, management and other leadership programs; and training institutions in Australia and New Zealand for specialized police training such as patrol boat operations and police middle-management-level courses.

Police Education, Research, and Publications

To date, there has no funding for research on police and policing. Hence, substantive publications on policing in Kiribati do not exist.

NII-K PLANGE AND NGUTU AWIRA

Bibliography

Kiribati, Government of. *Constitution of Kiribati*. Tarawa: Kiribati, 1979.
Sommerville, P. *Police Standing Orders and Instructions*. 1989.
United Nations Development Programme. *Pacific Human Development Report*. Suva, Fiji: UNDP, 1999.

NORTH KOREA

Background Information

Following World War II, Korea was divided, with the northern half coming under communist domination and the southern portion under Western influence. North Korea has remained a communist republic since 1948. In the conflict with South Korea from 1950 to 1953, a ceasefire was negotiated and a demilitarized zone of 1,262 square kilometers was established between the two Koreas. Kim Jong Il has ruled North Korea since his father and the country's founder, president Kim Il Sung, died in 1994. After decades of mismanagement, the North relies heavily on international food aid to feed its population, while continuing to expend resources to maintain an army of approximately 1 million. North Korea's long-range missile development and research into nuclear, chemical, and biological weapons, and massive conventional armed forces are of major concern to the international community.

The Democratic People's Republic of Korea (or North Korea) occupies a total area of 120,540 square kilometers (water 130 square kilometers, and land 120,410 square kilometers). It is located in eastern Asia, in the northern half of the Korean Peninsula, bordering the Korea Bay and the Sea of Japan, between China and South Korea. It has a population of 22,224,195 (July 2002 estimate). The population is racially homogeneous; there is a small Chinese community and a few ethnic Japanese. The capital is Pyongyang, and Korean is the primary language spoken. All religion has been effectively prohibited since the 1950s. Traditionally, the nation was Buddhist and Confucianist, with some Christian and syncretic Chondogyo (Religion of the Heavenly Way). Note that autonomous religious activities are now almost nonexistent; government-sponsored religious groups exist to provide the illusion of religious freedom.

The government is a communist "dynasty," or one-man dictatorship. The chairman of the National Defense Commission (highest post held by a living person) is Kim Jong Il, while the eternal president is Kim Il Sung.

North Korea's GDP is US$22 billion, and GDP per capita in purchasing power parity is $1,000 (2002 estimates). Major industries are military products, machinery, electric power, chemicals, mining, metallurgy, textiles, and food processing. Major trading partners are China, Japan, South Korea, Germany, Hong Kong, and Russia. North Korea is involved in an international dispute with China regarding a thirty-three-kilometer section of the boundary in the Paektu-san (mountain) area. The demarcation line with South Korea is also contested. The military branches are the Korean People's Army (includes army, navy, air force), and the Civil Security Forces.

Contextual Features

North Korea, one of the world's most centrally planned and isolated economies, faces desperate economic conditions. Industrial capital stock is nearly beyond repair as a result of years of underinvestment and spare parts shortages. Industrial and power output has declined in parallel. Despite a good harvest in 2001, the nation faced its ninth year of food shortages because of a lack of arable land, collective farming policies, weather-related problems including major drought in 2000, and chronic shortages of fertilizer and fuel. Massive international food aid deliveries have allowed the regime to escape mass starvation since 1995–1996, but the population remains vulnerable to prolonged malnutrition and deteriorating living conditions. Large-scale military spending eats up resources needed for investment and civilian consumption. In the late 1990s, the regime placed an emphasis on earning hard currency, developing information technology, addressing power shortages, and attracting foreign aid, but in no way was this at the expense of relinquishing central control over key national assets or undergoing widespread market-oriented reforms. In 2002, heightened political tensions with key donor countries and general donor fatigue held down the flow of desperately needed food aid and threatened fuel aid as well (*www.cia. gov/cia/publications/factbook/geos/kn.html*).

The chief of state of North Korea since July 1994 is Kim Jong Il; in September 1998 he was reelected chairman of the National Defense Commission, a position accorded the nation's "highest administrative authority." Kim Yong-nam was named president of the Supreme People's Assembly Presidium and given the responsibility of representing the state and receiving diplomatic credentials. The premier, elected by the Supreme People's Assembly in September 1998, is Hong Song-nam. Cabinet members, except for the minister of the People's Army, are appointed by the Supreme People's Assembly (*www. cia.gov/cia/publications/factbook/geos/kn.html*).

Administratively, the 1972 constitution provides a two-tier system in which nine provinces and three province-level special cities are under direct central control. Seventeen ordinary cities are under provincial control (*http://memory.loc.gov/cgi-bin/query/r? frd/cstdy:@field(DOCID + kp0009)*).

The legislative branch of government is a unicameral Supreme People's Assembly of 687 seats. Members are elected by popular vote to serve five-year terms. The last election was held in 2003. In general, the election results reflect a system in which the Korean Workers' Party (KWP) approves a single list of candidates who are elected without opposition. Minority parties hold a few seats (*www.cia. gov/cia/publications/factbook/geos/kn.html*).

In the North Korean judicial process, both adjudicative and prosecuting bodies function as powerful weapons for the proletarian dictatorship. The constitution states that justice is administered by a three-tiered court system of a Central Court, Provincial Courts (or Court of the Province), and People's Courts at the county level.

The Central Court, the highest court of appeal, stands at the apex of the court system. As of July 1992, it had two associate chief judges, or vice presidents, Choe Yong-song and Hyon Hongsam. Pang Hak Se, who died in July 1992, had been chief judge or president, since 1972. In the case of special cities directly under central authority, provincial or municipal courts serve as the courts of first instance for civil and criminal cases at the intermediate level. At the lowest level are the people's courts, established in ordinary cities, counties, and urban districts. Special courts exist for the armed forces and for railroad workers. The military courts have jurisdiction over all crimes committed by members of the armed forces or security organs of the Ministry of Public Security. The railroad courts have jurisdiction over criminal cases involving rail and water transport workers. In addition, the Korean Maritime Arbitration Committee adjudicates maritime legal affairs.

Judges and people's assessors, or lay judges, are elected by the organs of state power at their corresponding levels, those of the Central Court by the Supreme People's Assembly (SPA) Standing Committee and those of the lower courts by the province-level and county-level people's assemblies. Neither legal education nor practical legal experience is required for judgeship. In addition to administering justice based on criminal and civil codes, the courts are in charge of political indoctrination through "reeducation." The issue of punishment is not expressly stated in the constitution or the criminal code.

The appeal process is based on the principle of a single appeal to the next highest court. The Central Court is the final court of appeal for criminal and civil cases, and it has initial jurisdiction for grievous crimes against the state. According to the 1992 constitution, the Supreme People's Assembly has the power to elect and recall the president of the Central Court and to appoint or remove the president of the Central Procurator's Office (Article 91, items 12–13). The Standing Committee of the Supreme People's Assembly interprets the laws and ordinances in force and elects and recalls judges and people's assessors of the Central Court (Article 101, items 3, 9). The Central Court supervises all lower courts and the training of judges. It does not exercise the power of judicial review over the constitutionality of executive or legislative actions, nor does it have an activist role in protecting the constitutionally guaranteed rights of individuals against state actions.

Below the Central Court are the courts of the provinces and cities under central authority—courts that serve as the courts of first and only appeal for decisions made by the People's Courts. They are staffed in the same manner as the Central Court. Like the Central Court, provincial courts have initial jurisdiction for certain serious crimes. In addition, provincial courts supervise the People's Courts.

The People's Courts are at the lowest level of the judicial system. They are organized at the county level, even though they may have jurisdiction over more than one county or smaller city. They have initial jurisdiction for most criminal and civil cases. Unlike the high courts, they are staffed with a single judge, who is assisted by two "people's assessors," laypeople who are temporarily selected for the judiciary. An initial trial typically is presided over by one judge and two people's assessors. If the case is appealed, three judges preside, and a decision is made by consultation.

Socialist law guidance committees were established in 1977 in the Central People's Committee, and in the people's committees at the provincial, city, and county levels. These ad hoc committees meet once a month, and are chaired by the president of the people's committee. The committees are a control measure for ensuring respect for public authority and conformity to the dictates of socialist society. The committees are empowered to implement state power, monitor the observance of law by state and economic institutions, and prevent the abuse of power by the leading cadre of these institutions. To this end, they have oversight of state inspection agencies, the procurator, and the police; they also have supervision and control of all organizations, workplaces, social groups, and citizens in their jurisdiction. The committees can apply strict legal sanctions to all violations short of crimes.

The 1992 constitution guarantees judicial independence and requires that court proceedings be carried out in accordance with laws containing elaborate procedural guarantees. Article 157 of the constitution states that "cases are heard in public, and the accused is guaranteed the right to a defense; hearings may be closed to the public as stipulated by law. However practice is another matter, according to the U.S. Department of State's report on human rights practices for 1990, and a 1988 report by Asia Watch and the Minnesota Lawyers International Human Rights Committee. Additionally, according to the Criminal Code, defense attorneys are not proxies for the defendant but are charged with ensuring that the accused take full responsibility for their actions.

The Penal Code adopted in 1987 simplifies the 1974 code without making substantial changes in the definitions of crimes or penalties. The entire section, entitled "Military Crimes," in Part 5 of the previous code, was deleted. It is likely that military crimes still are treated as a criminal category, and are covered by another separate code. In general, the 1987 code covers fewer types of crimes. Crimes eliminated from the general heading of treason include armed incursions, hostile crimes against the socialist state, and antirevolutionary sabotage. Penalties have also been relaxed. The number of crimes for which the death penalty can be applied has been reduced from twenty civil crimes to five offenses in addition to those offenses covered under the military crimes section. Retained as capital offenses are plots against national sovereignty (Article 44), terrorism (Article 45), treason against the motherland by citizens (Article 47), treason against the people (Article 52), and murder (Article 141). The death penalty no longer applies to propaganda and sedition against the government; espionage; armed intervention and instigating the severance of foreign relations; antirevolutionary disturbances; theft of government or public property; violation of railway, water, or air transportation regulations; mob violence; unauthorized disclosure of or loss of official secrets; rape; and robbery of personal property. The maximum sentence has been reduced from twenty to fifteen years.

The definition of the most serious political crimes—reforms notwithstanding—is ambiguous and includes both counterrevolutionary crimes and more general political offenses. Punishment for counterrevolutionary crimes is severe, and includes capital punishment, loss of property, and even summary execution for almost any dissident activity. Furthermore, these cases are often decided without recourse to the appropriate legal procedures. Most political offenses do not go through the criminal justice system but are handled by the State Security Department. Trials are closed, and there is no provision for appeal. Punishment is often broadened to include the offender's immediate and extended family (*http://memory.loc.gov/cgi-bin/query/r?frd/cstdy:@field(DOCID+kp0162)*).

Punishment for criminal behavior is determined by both the type of crime—political or nonpolitical—and the status of the individual. The underlying philosophy of punishment reflects both Marxist influences and Confucian moral precepts. According to the 1950 Penal Code, the purpose of punishment is explicitly Marxist, that is, to suppress class enemies, educate the population in the spirit of "socialist patriotism," and re-educate and punish individuals for crimes stemming from "capitalist" thinking. However, the code's ambiguity, the clear official preference for rehabilitating individuals through a combination of punishment and reeducation, and additional severity for crimes against the state or family, reflect the lack of distinction among politics, morality, and law in neo-Confucian thought.

Penalties for various types of crimes range from imprisonment, forced labor, banishment to remote areas, forfeiture of property, fines, loss of privileges or work status, and reeducation, to death. With the exception of political criminals, the objective is to return a reformed individual to an active societal role.

There are indications that criminal law is applied differentially. An accused person's class and category can have a substantial effect on the treatment meted out by the justice system. The severity of punishment for common crimes such as rape, robbery, and homicide apparently is influenced by such considerations. There also is considerable leeway in the classification of crime; a robbery can be classified as either a common crime with minor punishment or a political-economic crime with far harsher punishment. The classification of crimes also is open to political considerations.

There apparently are several types of detention camps for convicted prisoners. Political criminals are sent to separate concentration camps managed by the State Security Department. Twelve such camps, holding between 100,000 and 150,000 prisoners, and covering some 1,200 square kilometers, were reported to exist in 1991. They are located in remote, isolated areas at Tongsin and Hich'n in Chagang Province; Onsng, Hoeryng, and Kyngsng in North Hamgyng Province; Tksng, Chongpyng, and Yodk in South Hamgyng Province; Yngbyn and Yongch'n in North P'yngan Province; and Kaech'n and Pukch'ang in South P'yngan Province. Convicted prisoners and their families are sent to these camps, where they are prohibited from marrying, required to grow their own food, and cut off from external communication (which was apparently once allowed). Detainees are classified as antiparty factionalists, antirevolutionary elements, or those opposed to Kim Jong Il's succession. There is conflicting information as to whether individuals sent to these camps ever reenter society.

A second set of prisons, or camps, is concerned with more traditional punishment and rehabilitation. Prisoners sent to these camps can reenter society after serving their sentences. Among these facilities are prisons, prison labor centers, travel violation centers, and sanatoriums. The basic prison is located at the city or province level; some seventeen of these prisons were identified in 1991. They are managed by the Ministry of Public Security for the incarceration of "normal" criminals.

Labor prisons are found at the city or province level. Adult and youth centers house those convicted of common crimes. There apparently are separate facilities for the incarceration of those who have attempted to violate travel restrictions or leave the country illegally. It is unclear, however, if these are in fact separate centers, or if those convicted of travel violations are placed in normal prisons. Lastly, minor political or ideological offenders or persons with religious convictions may be sent to sanatoriums where the offenses are treated as symptoms of mental illness. North Korean officials deny the existence of these camps, although they do admit to the existence of "education centers" for people who "commit crimes by mistake" (*http://memory.loc.gov/cgi-bin/query/r?frd/cstdy:@field(DOCID+kp0163)*).

The North Korean government does not re-lease statistics on crime, but street crime appears to be uncommon. Petty thefts, however, have been reported, especially at the airport in Pyongyang. Lost or stolen passports should be re-ported to the local police and to the Swedish Embassy (*http://travel.state.gov/nkorea.html*).

Police Profile

Background

The Democratic People's Republic of Korea is a unique system of totalitarian control, even when compared to the communist systems in the former Soviet Union and Eastern Europe. The population of North Korea is rigidly controlled. Individual rights are subordinate to the rights of the state and party. The government uses education, mass mobilization, persuasion, and coercion to guarantee political and social conformity. Massive propaganda and political indoctrination are reinforced by extensive police and public security forces.

Government control mechanisms are quite extensive. Security ratings are established for individuals and influence access to employment, schools, medical facilities, stores, admission to the KWP, and so on. The system in its most elaborate form consists of three general groupings and fifty-one subcategories. Over time, however, the use of subcategories has diminished.

The population is divided into a core class, the basic masses, and the "impure class." The core class, which includes those with revolutionary lineage, makes up approximately 20% to 25% of the population. The basic masses—primarily workers and peasants—account for around 50%. The impure class consists of descendants of pro-Japanese collaborators, landowners, or those with relatives who have defected. In the past, restraints on the impure class were strict, but they have been relaxed as time has passed, although the core class continues to receive preferential treatment. Nonetheless, by the 1980s even a member of the impure class could become a party member.

Since the late 1950s, all households have been organized into people's neighborhood units. The units, originally called the five-family system, consist of about 100 individuals living in close proximity. The ward people's committee selects the people's neighborhood unit chief, generally from pensioners in the unit. Meetings are held once a month or as necessary. The primary function of the ward people's committee is social control. There are five categories of social control: residence, travel, employment, clothing and food, and family life. Change of residence is possible only with party approval. Those who move without a permit are not eligible for food rations or housing allotments and are subject to criminal prosecution. Travel is controlled by the Ministry of Public Security, and a travel pass is necessary. Travel on other than official business is limited strictly to attending family functions, and obtaining approval normally is a long and complicated process. The ration system does not recognize individuals while they are traveling, which further curtails movement. Employment is governed by the party, with assignments made on the basis of political reliability and family background. A change in employment is made at the party's convenience

(*http://memory.loc.gov/cgi-bin/query/r?frd/cstdy:@field (DOCID+kp0159)*).

Organizational Description and Functions

The Ministry of Public Security and the State Security Department are responsible for internal security. Although both are government organs, they are tightly controlled by the party apparatus through the Justice and Security Commission and the penetration of their structures by the party apparatus at all levels. The formal public security structure is augmented by a pervasive system of informers throughout the society. Surveillance of citizens, both physical and electronic, also is routine.

The Ministry of Public Security, responsible for internal security, social control, and basic police functions, is one of the most powerful organizations in North Korea, and operates with an estimated 144,000 public security personnel. It maintains law and order; investigates common criminal cases; manages the prison system and traffic control; monitors citizens' political attitudes; conducts background investigations, census, and civil registrations; controls individual travel; manages the government's classified documents; protects government and party officials; and patrols government buildings and some government and party construction activities. In general, the North Korea police system is similar to that of China, with a strong Soviet influence (*http://memory.loc.gov/ cgi-bin/query/r?frd/cstdy:@field(DOCID+kp0160)*).

The Ministry of Public Security has vice ministers for personnel, political affairs, legal counseling, security, surveillance, internal affairs, and engineering. There are approximately twenty-seven bureaus, but the functional responsibilities of only some of the bureaus are known. The Security Bureau is responsible for ordinary law enforcement and most police functions. The Investigation Bureau handles investigations of criminal and economic crimes. The Protection Bureau is responsible for fire protection, traffic control, public health, and customs. The Registration Bureau issues citizen identification cards and maintains public records on births, deaths, marriages, residence registration, and passports.

Below the ministry level, there are public security bureaus for each province and directly administered city. These bureaus are headed by either a senior colonel or a lieutenant colonel of police, depending on the size of the population. Public security departments at each city or county and smaller substations throughout the country are staffed by about 100 personnel. They are organized roughly parallel to the ministry itself, and have several divisions responsible for carrying out various functions.

In 1973, political security responsibilities were transferred from the Ministry of Public Security to the State Security Department, an autonomous agency reporting directly to Kim Il Sung. The State Security Department carries out a wide range of counterintelligence and internal security functions normally associated with so-called secret police. It is charged with searching out anti-state criminals—a general category that includes those accused of antigovernment and dissident activities, economic crimes, and slander of the political leadership. Camps for political prisoners are under its jurisdiction. It has counterintelligence responsibilities at home and abroad, and runs overseas intelligence collection operations. It monitors political attitudes and maintains surveillance of returnees. The ministry guards national borders and monitors international entry points. Ministry personnel also escort high-ranking officials.

The Border Guards are the paramilitary force of the Ministry of Public Security. They are primarily concerned with monitoring the border and with internal security. The latter activities include physical protection of government buildings and facilities. During a conflict, they would probably be used in border and rear area security missions (*http://memory.loc.gov/cgi-bin/query/r?frd/cstdy:@field(DOCID+kp0160)*).

Lessons learned from the Korean War still shaped military planning in mid-1993. Because Pyongyang determined that inadequate reserve forces were a critical deficiency, Kim Il Sung decided to arm the entire population. The Four Military Guidelines formulated in 1962 created a nonactive duty force of between 5 million and 6 million persons.

All soldiers serve in the reserves; there were an estimated 1.2 million reservists in mid-1993. The primary reserve forces pool consists of persons who either have finished their active military service or are exempted and are attached to the reserve forces until age forty (age thirty for single women). Reserve training consists of approximately 500 hours annually. Afterward, reservists along with unmarried women join the paramilitary Worker-Peasant Red Guards and receive approximately 160 hours of training annually until age sixty.

There are four general categories of reserve forces: reserve military training units, Red Guard Youth, College Training Units, and Worker-Peasant Red Guards. Unit organizations essentially parallel active-duty forces. Some military training units are organized around factories or administrative organizations.

In 1990, the reserve military training units had approximately 720,000 men and women, and included as many as 48,000 active-duty troops assigned to between 22 and 26 divisions, at least 18 independent brigades, and many smaller units. All maneuver units are believed to have individual weapons for all troops. Transportation assets probably are much lower.

Approximately 480,000 college students have been organized into College Training Units. These units have individual weapons. Training is geared toward individual replacement, and soldiers called to active duty are parceled out as needed as a manpower pool rather than as organized forces.

Red Guard Youth units are composed of some 850,000 students between the ages of fourteen and seventeen at the senior middle-school level. Emphasis is on pre-induction military familiarization.

The Worker-Peasant Red Guard is composed of some 3.89 million persons between the ages of forty and sixty. They receive 160 hours of military training annually. Unit structure is small and decentralized, and focuses on homeland defense. Units are equipped with individual small arms, and have a limited number of antiaircraft guns.

The overall quality of the North Korean reserve structure is difficult to evaluate. Through strong societal controls, Pyongyang is able to regulate forces and maintain unit cohesion to a greater degree than is possible in more open societies. Reserve military training units probably are good-quality forces with the ability to take on limited regular force responsibilities during wartime.

The reserve force structure apparently was fleshed out in the 1980s when many older weapons were phased out of the regular forces and passed on to the reserves. Weapons refitting led to restructuring and development of the Military District Command system. Turning over the homeland defense mission to the command system has allowed North Korean force planners the freedom to forward deploy a greater proportion of the regular forces toward the Demarcation Line with South Korea (*http://memory.loc.gov/cgi-bin/query/r?frd/cstdy:@field(DOCID+kp0142)*).

Police Education, Research, and Publications

Information on police education, research, and publications in North Korea is not available.

MARK MING-CHWANG CHEN

Websites

Lonely Planet. Available at: www.lonelyplanet.com/destinations/north_east_asia/north_korea/.

U.S. Library of Congress. "Country Reports." Available at: http://memory.loc.gov/frd/cs/kptoc.html#kp0009.

Central Intelligence Agency. *World Factbook*. Available at: www.cia.gov/cia/publications/factbook/geos/kn.html.

U.S. State Department. Travel Advisories, North Korea. Available at: http://travel.state.gov/nkorea.html.

Bibliography

Andrade, John. *World Police & Paramilitary Forces.* New York: Stockton Press, 1985.

Kurian, George Thomas. *World Encyclopedia of Police Forces and Penal Systems.* New York: Facts on File, 1988.

SOUTH KOREA

Background Materials

Korea's history goes back more than 4,000 years. According to myth, in 2,333 B.C.E., Tangun established the first Korean kingdom. Korean history separates into the following periods: primitive society, Three Kingdoms (Paikche, Silla, and Koguryo), Late Silla, Koryo Dynasty, Yi Dynasty, and modern Korea.

Korea's central geographical position has served as a bridge over which in early times higher civilization passed from China to Japan. Japan's history and culture are heavily indebted to Korea. Two new metal cultures were transmitted to Korea in the fourth century B.C.E. from China. The two cultures intermingled in Manchuria and spread into Korea. Moreover, these cultural waves went on to cross the sea and penetrate into Japan. Economic and cultural interchange also took place with Japan; Paikche in particular, because of its confrontation with Silla, communicated frequently with Japan. Shilla, moreover, even had contacts with Arab merchants and their culture.

Throughout history, Korea has been a meeting place of influences, not only from China and Japan but also from the northern areas. The clash of the cultural, political, and military forces from these larger areas have made Korea a strategic zone of contact in East Asian history. Thus, Korea was invaded many times by the abovementioned countries. About 400 years ago in Japan, Toyotomi Hideyosi brought an end to internal disorders. He had been ambitious to invade the Ming Empire through Korea. The Japanese army landed at Korea in 1592. Japan benefited from the kidnapping of skilled Korean potters who then became the instruments of great advances in ceramics. The numerous books and scholars seized by the Japanese in Korea also contributed to the development of learning in Japan, especially the study of neo-Confucianism.

The population of Korea is 48,598,175 (July 2004 estimate). Korean is the official language. Just less than half the population is Christian and almost the same number is Buddhist. GDP per capita is $17,800 (2004 estimate).

Contextual Features

On August 15, 1948, the government of the First Republic was born. It was created through the first ever peaceful transfer of power between the ruling and opposition parties in the fifty years of modern Korean political history since its liberation from Japan on August 15, 1945. The country is divided administratively into the following: capital city, six metropolitan cities, and nine provinces (*do*), with seventy-two cities (*shi*), and ninety-one counties (*gun*).

Korea is a democratic republic with a strong presidential system. Regional autonomy was established in 1995.

Standing at the apex of the executive branch of government, the president not only functions as the head of state in domestic affairs, but also represents the state in foreign relations. He has the constitutional duty to safeguard the nation's independence and work for the peaceful reunification of the country. He is chairman of the state council (cabinet), and has the power to appoint and dismiss the prime minister and cabinet ministers, as well as other senior officials, including heads of government agencies and offices, and ambassadors. He serves as the commander-in-chief of the armed forces, and is empowered to grant amnesty, commutation, and restoration of civil rights as prescribed by law. The president is elected through direct popular vote to serve a five-year term. He cannot be re-elected.

The president performs his executive functions through the state council, which is made up of fifteen to thirty members presided over by the president, who is responsible for deciding all important government policies. The present state council consists of the president (chair), prime minister (vice chair), and seventeen heads of executive ministries. The prime minister is appointed by the president with the approval of the National Assembly. The prime minister supervises the executive ministers as the principal executive assistant to the president under the direction of the president.

There are three administrative tiers in Korea. The highest tier includes seven metropolitan cities and nine provinces (*do*). Metropolitan cities refer to urban areas with a population of over 1 million. Seoul, the capital of Korea, is the largest urban center, having over 10 million residents. Pusan is the second largest city, with a population of over 4 million. Taegu, Inchon, Kwangju, Taejon, and Ulsan are each home of over 1 million people. At the second administrative tier, provinces are subdivided into small cities (*shi*) and counties (*gun*). Although they are administrative units, provinces also play an important role in the regional identification of the people, and many Koreans often identify themselves by the province in which they were born and raised. The last administrative tier consists of subdivisions of *shi* which are called dong. In rural areas, however, counties (*gun*) are subdivided into towns (*up*) and townships (*myon*). A town (*up*) has a population of 20,000 people or less.

The highest tribunal in the country, the Supreme Court examines and issues final decisions on appeals of the decisions of appellate courts in civil and criminal cases. Its decisions are final and indisputable, forming judicial precedents. The chief justice is appointed by the president to a single six-year term with the consent of the National Assembly, and the justices of the Supreme Court are appointed by the president on the recommendation of the chief justice. Judges at all lower courts are appointed by the chief justice with the consent of the Conference of Supreme Court Justices.

There are five appellate courts that hear appeals of verdicts by district courts in civil and criminal cases. They hold their own trials and pass decisions for or against lower court verdicts. They may also pass decisions on administrative litigation filed by individuals or organizations against government decisions, orders, or actions. District courts are established in major cities and exercise jurisdiction over all civil and criminal cases filed in the first instance. The Family Court hears matrimonial problems and cases involving juveniles. Its sessions are closed to the public in order to protect the privacy of individuals.

The traditional legal system has existed throughout the history of Korea, stretching back some 5,000 years. However, when Korea began to adopt the Western legal system in the late nineteenth century, judicial functions become separate from administrative power. Later, in 1948, the Ministry of Justice and the Supreme Court were established separately.

In Korea, constitutional power is divided into three branches—administration, legislature, and judiciary. The Ministry of Justice belongs to the administration, and is thus separate from the judiciary.

The judiciary is composed of the Supreme Court, High Courts, District Courts, Family Court, and Branch Courts. The courts are empowered to adjudicate civil, criminal, and administrative cases as well as election suits and other judicial cases as stipulated by law.

Prosecutors have the authority to investigate criminal cases, and take final responsibility for pertinent investigations.

The judicial police conduct investigation under the supervision of prosecutors. The judicial police consist of general judicial police, dealing with criminal cases in general and special judicial police in charge of cases specifically related to railway facilities, forest, fire fighting, marine, and labor.

When a crime occurs, the judicial police usually initiate the investigation. The cases are then transferred to the Prosecutors' Office where prosecutors continue with the investigation by questioning the suspect, examining the documents and evidence, and conducting additional investigation as necessary. Upon completion of the investigative procedure, they make a decision on whether to file for prosecution.

A suspect can be arrested only with a warrant issued by the court, except in cases in which the suspect is caught at the scene of crime, and in other cases of emergency. If a suspect has been arrested without a warrant, a detention warrant should be filed within forty-eight hours; if the warrant is not filed, the suspect should be released immediately.

The prosecutor can submit the request for issuance of a warrant to the court. The judicial police officer, however, submits the request for issuance of a detention warrant to the prosecutor, not directly to the judge. In cases involving the issuance of a detention warrant, the judge can schedule a preliminary hearing in which the accused must participate.

At the conclusion of the investigation, the prosecutor decides whether the suspect should be prosecuted. When the prosecutor believes that the alleged facts do not constitute a crime or that there is no sufficient evidence to prove the commission of crime, she or he can exercise discretionary power not to bring the case to the court. The prosecutor is also authorized to suspend prosecution in consideration of the suspect's age, character, or motive, or because of other circumstances, even if incriminating evidence against the suspect sufficient for prosecution.

Cases involving possible capital punishment, life imprisonment, or sentences in excess of one-year imprisonment, are tried by a three-judge court. A single-judge court tries other cases. After a case is referred to the court, the prosecutor, as the representative of the state, questions the defendant, examines witnesses, introduces evidence to the court, and performs other duties in an effort to uncover the truth.

In order to fully guarantee the right of defendant to have the assistance of legal counsel, the defendant should be assisted by defense counsel appointed by the court, when the defendant is a minor, seventy years of age or older or suspected of mental illness, or when the defendant cannot afford to hire a counsel for other reasons such as poverty.

In the closing statement, the prosecutor suggests a suitable form and amount of punishment. The judge finally determines whether the defendant is guilty and, on finding the defendant guilty, decides the penalty.

A prosecutor or a defendant who is dissatisfied with the judgment rendered by the trial court has the right to appeal to a higher court. The High Court tries the appeals, which are raised against the judgment, rendered by a three-judge court, whereas the appellate division of a District Court tries the appeals against the judgments of a single-judge court. A prosecutor and/or a defendant have the right to re-appeal to the Supreme Court when dissatisfied with the judgment for the appeal. When a sentence becomes final, the prosecutor directs and supervises its execution.

The prosecutor may bring a case before a court by a summary indictment when the offense is punishable by a fine. In such a case, the judge may either give summary judgment without holding any hearing, or transfer the case to the normal procedure of trial. In addition, the dissatisfied defendant can request a formal trial within seven days from the date of receiving the summary judgment.

A speedy trial procedure is available in certain cases for the brevity and expeditiousness of proceedings without formal investigation and trial. The procedure is applicable to minor offenses such as the violation of administrative regulations. Such cases are referred to the court by the chief of police station without the engagement of the prosecutor. A speedy trial is presided over by a judge, and open to the public at a court other than the police station. The judge, when deciding that such proceedings are not applicable to the case referred, dismisses the application, whereby the chief of the police station immediately transfers the case to the prosecutor for formal criminal proceedings. Any defendant dissatisfied with the outcome of the speedy trial can request a formal trial within seven days from the receipt of the judgment. With the sentence of speedy trial confirmed, it is executed by the chief of police and then reported to the prosecutor.

The greater part of a prosecutor's job is the prosecutorial function in criminal proceedings. In view of the importance of a prosecutor's role in criminal proceedings, the Public Prosecutors' Office Act states that the minister of justice, as the chief supervisor on prosecution functions, generally directs and supervises prosecutors, but, for specific cases, he can only direct and supervise the prosecutor general in order to secure the prosecutor's quasijudicial status.

The president has the authority to appoint and assign prosecutors upon the recommendation of the minister of justice. Qualifications for a prosecutor are identical to those of a judge: passing the judicial examination and completion of a two-year training course at the Judicial Research and Training Institute. In addition to this requirement, some professional experience is needed to be appointed as a high-ranking prosecutor.

There are three ranks of prosecutor: prosecutor general, senior chief prosecutor, and prosecutor. The status of a prosecutor, like that of a judge, is guaranteed by law. Prosecutors may not be dismissed; suspended from the exercise of their powers; or subjected to a reduction in salary other than through impeachment, conviction of crimes punishable by imprisonment or more severe penalties, or disciplinary actions.

Police Profile

Background

After an abortive attempt to employ the existing Japanese colonial police in Korea to maintain public order after World War II, the U.S. occupation authorities established in October 1945 a new force under a Police Affairs Division within the military government. This force was placed under the Ministry of Home Affairs upon the establishment of the First Republic on August 15, 1984. This force was a paramilitary constabulary in which police and military functions were combined. Even after the formal establishment of a discrete military service by the Armed Forces Organization Act of November 1984, differentiation between the police and the military in the maintenance of domestic order remained unclear. During the Korean War, the police forces were employed in military operations.

The new force was plagued from the beginning by a low degree of professionalism, the retention of Japanese-trained cadets in the higher ranks, endemic corruption, and flagrant use of police power for partisan political activity. Major reforms did not take place until the revolutionary military junta seized power in 1961. The new regime reorganized the structure of the force, placing it on a sound institutional basis; instituted recruitment by examination and merit promotion; and introduced modern concepts of management, administration, and training.

Organizational Description

The Police Agency is divided into six departments, five offices, one consultant office, nine direct offices, twenty-four sections, and the regional police agency is seven departments, two direct offices, sections sections in the Seoul Metropolitan Regional Police Agency, three direct offices, nine sections in Pusan Metropolitan Regional Police Agency, three divisions two direct offices, nine sections in Kyunggi Province Regional Police Agency, and other regional police agencies are organized by three direct offices and sections sections. Police stations are divided from one- to three-level stations, consisting of four to nine sections.

The National Scientific Investigation Institute and three regional centers, although under the name of the Ministry of Government Administration and Home Affairs, are operated under the conducted supervision of the chief of the Police Agency, and perform the core role of scientific police investigation. In addition, the Police Commission installed under the Ministry of Government Administration and Home Affairs, which is the highest order consultation/legislative organ of the police administration, is responsible for securing the political neutrality and the democracy of the police. The police organization is structured in ways similar to regional governments, but because security conditions differ by region, they are not exactly the same across regional governments, and as security demand increases, additional police stations and police stands are being installed.

Terrorism

Terrorism has not been reported in Korea, but its potential is very high due to the country's unique geological formations. Thus, the government is developing comprehensive antiterrorism efforts that include both police and military forces.

The SWAT (Special Weapon and Tactics) Team, established in 1983, is subordinate to the Seoul Metropolitan Regional Police Agency. SWAT is becoming the vanguard of the police forces in terms of responding swiftly to the war on terrorism with advanced knowledge and apparatus.

Complaints and Discipline, and International Cooperation

In a landmark step toward safeguarding the human rights of Korean citizens, the National Assembly passed (April 30, 2001) a new law establishing a National Human Rights Commission. The commission will provide Koreans with an additional recourse to protect and promote their human rights as guaranteed under the nation's constitution and laws. The eleven-member commission began work in November 2001 to protect the rights of citizens, and is empowered to investigate human rights violations and provide compensation to victims whose rights have been violated. The new panel will conduct investigations into all types of discrimination, including sex, race/ethnic, and religious, as well as discrimination against the mentally or physically handicapped. The bill also includes provisions to prevent the abuse of human rights in cases of unlawful arrest, torture, intimidation, punishment, and detention of citizens by public service personnel, including employees of psychiatric hospitals.

After receiving a complaint, the commission will initiate an investigation to decide whether to recommend relief, file for prosecution, or recommend changes in law or policy. False testimony or refusal to cooperate with the commission's investigation will be punishable by a fine of up to 10 million won (US$8,000).

Due to the fact that citizens can now submit petitions directly and confidentially to the commission instead of going through the more cumbersome litigation process, it is hoped that cases of wrongful application of criminal code provisions and excessively broad interpretation of the laws will be sharply reduced.

Korea is a signatory of the International Bill of Human Rights, which includes the Universal Declaration of Human Rights, International Covenant on Civil and Political Rights, and International Covenant on Economic, Social and Cultural Rights. Korea has also filed annual human rights reports with the UN Commission on Human Rights. (North Korea, in contrast, failed to file the report for sixteen years between 1985 and 1999.)

The government has created the human rights commission to provide citizens with an additional means to guarantee their fundamental human rights and to simplify the filing of complaints. The opening of the new human rights protection agency is expected to promote the quality of life and respect for human dignity in Korea.

The police exercise extreme care with respect to individual privacy and confidential communications. Wiretapping for investigative purposes has been kept to a minimum, in accordance with the law. A recent crackdown on illegal wiretapping by private individuals resulted in the arrest of 401

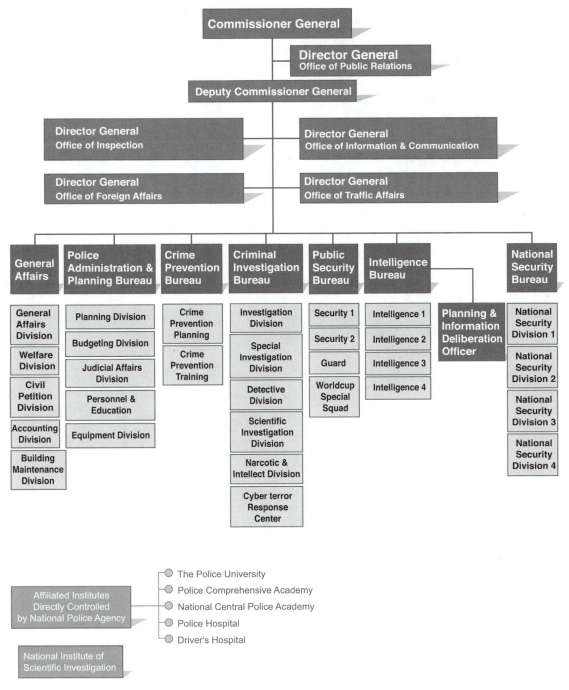

National Structures

persons in 277 cases in 1999 and in 223 persons in 131 cases in 2000.

To provide more humane treatment of inmates, shackles are no longer used. Less intrusive physical examinations are now given to nonviolent suspects before they are imprisoned.

To protect the human rights of suspects, the right to defense counsel is now guaranteed from the outset of an investigation. Also, to eliminate illegal investigations, an internal affairs system is now in operation, and to discourage unfair investigations, an outside investigation appeals system has been introduced.

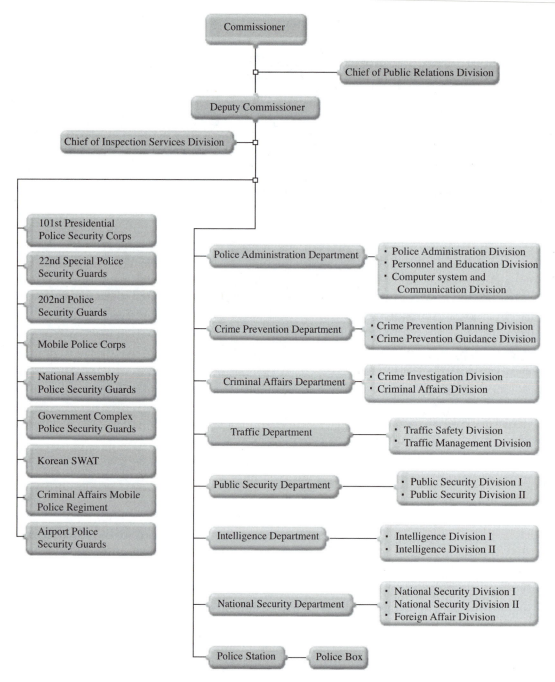

Regional Structures

Police Education, Research, and Publications

Police Academy

Purposes: Continuous recruitment and education

Courses: Recruits for the entering grade of constable must have completed high school and military service. All newly recruited police cadets participate in six months of training programs in the Academy, comprised of three weeks of close-order drill, seventeen weeks of preliminary education including continuous physical training, four weeks of actual on-the-job training, and other extra curriculums provided for an entire six months.

Police University

Purposes: Training police officers through university courses

Frequency and arrests of five common crimes.

Types		1997	1998	1999	2000	2001
Total	Frequency	294,569	330,304	383,976	520,763	532,243
	Arrests	244,007	290,160	349,653	385,087	396,885
Murder	Frequency	784	963	976	941	1,051
	Arrests	770	975	993	955	1,076
Robbery	Frequency	4,420	5,516	4,972	5,461	5,692
	Arrests	4,027	5,316	4,885	4,524	4,670
Rape	Frequency	5,627	5,978	6,359	6,855	6,751
	Arrests	5,327	5,745	6,164	6,139	6,021
Theft	Frequency	83,063	91,438	89,395	173,876	180,704
	Arrests	41,427	57,393	60,315	68,564	78,777
Violence	Frequency	200,675	226,409	282,274	333,630	338,045
	Arrests	192,456	220,731	277,296	304,905	306,341

Courses: The regular course grants a bachelor in law and in public administration. Graduates fulfill their military service as commanders of the combatant police unit and mobile police forces, and then they are placed in the police offices all over the country.

YONGSANG KIM

Bibliography

Andrade, John. *World Police & Paramilitary Forces*. New York: Stockton Press, 1985.

Kurian, George Thomas. *World Encyclopedia of Police Forces and Penal Systems* New York: Facts on File, 1988.

National Police College. "National Police College." Seoul: National Police College, 1990.

National Police Headquarters. "Korean National Police." Seoul: National Police Headquarters, 1990.

Websites

Korean Police Agency: *www.police.ac.kr*
Korea Infogate: *www.koreainfogate.com*
www.sie.edu/offices
Ministry of Justice: *www.moj.go.kr*
KOREA.net: *www.kois.go.kr*
National Police Academy: *www.npa.go.kr*
Internet crime archives: *www.mayhem.net*

KUWAIT

Background Material

In 1989, then-Iraqi President Saddam Hussein accused Kuwait of flooding the international oil market, and consequently forcing oil prices down. Iraq invaded Kuwait on August 2, 1990, and Hussein declared Kuwait annexed. Many native Kuwaitis, including the royal family, fled. Western and Arab coalition forces, the largest part of which were American, drove Iraqi forces from Kuwait in the Persian Gulf War. Thousands of foreign workers who were based in Kuwait fled to Iran, Turkey, and Jordan, or were housed in temporary refugee camps throughout the Middle East. Iraqi forces devastated the country, setting fire to Kuwaiti oil wells before retreating. Over 80% of all wells were destroyed or damaged, causing phenomenal environmental hazards. The sheikh returned to Kuwait from Saudi Arabia in March 1991. The Palestinians remaining in Kuwait after the war were expelled because of the Palestine Liberation Organization's support of Iraq.

In the war's wake, Kuwait concentrated on restoring its oil industry and rebuilding the country. Parliamentary elections in 1992 resulted in the victory of a majority of opposition candidates, but despite promises of democratic reform, the al Sabah family continued to dominate the government. In October 1994, Iraq massed elite troops along the border with

Kuwait, but they were removed when Kuwait and the United States moved forces into the area. Parliament was dissolved by the sheikh in May 1999; new elections held in July gave Islamist and liberal candidates the most seats. Also in 1999, the sheikh issued an edict giving Kuwaiti women the right to vote and run for office, but parliament failed to ratify it. In the July 2003 parliamentary elections, Islamists won 42% of the seats, while liberals retained only a handful. Government supporters won 28% of the seats.

Over 90% of the population lives within a 500-square kilometer area surrounding Kuwait City and its harbor. Although the majority of people residing in Kuwait are of Arab origin, less than half are originally from the Arabian Peninsula. The discovery of oil in 1938 drew many Arabs from nearby states. Following the liberation of Kuwait from Iraqi occupation in 1991, the Kuwaiti government undertook a serious effort to reduce the expatriate population by specifically limiting the entry of workers from nations whose leaders had supported Iraq during the Gulf War. Kuwait later abandoned this policy, and it currently has a sizable foreign labor force (over 60% of the total population).

The national census does not distinguish between Sunni and Shi'a adherents, but an estimated 1.6 million residents, including the ruling family and 600,000 Kuwaiti nationals, belong to the Sunni branch of Islam. An estimated 400,000 Muslims are Shi'a, including about 300,000 Kuwaitis. Estimates of the Christian population range from 250,000 to 500,000 residents, including about 200 citizens. There are also communities of Hindus (estimated at 100,000) and Sikhs (estimated at 10,000).

Kuwait's 83% literacy rate, one of the Arab world's highest, is the result of extensive government support for the education system. Native Kuwaitis have an extremely high per capita income, pay no taxes, and enjoy numerous social services. Arabic is the official language, but English is widely spoken.

Kuwait has about 96.5 billion barrels of recoverable oil; only Saudi Arabia and Iraq have larger proven reserves. Following Operation Iraqi Freedom, Kuwait enjoyed a limited economic boom. The banking and construction sector, in particular, have grown. Sustained high oil prices have also provided the Kuwaiti government with a substantial windfall in 2003 and 2004.

Contextual Features

The country is a monarchy governed under a constitution promulgated in 1963. The sheikh, the hereditary monarch of the Mubarak line of the ruling al Sabah family, serves as head of state. A prime minister is appointed by the sheikh to head the government; until 2003 the prime minister traditionally was the crown prince. The unicameral national assembly has fifty members who are elected by popular vote. There are no official political parties, although several political groups act as de facto parties. Administratively, the country is divided into five governorates.

The general election held in July 2003 was considered free and fair, although there were some credible reports of vote buying by the government and the opposition. The government bans formal political parties, but de facto political blocs exist and are typically organized along ideological lines. Although the Amir maintains the final word on most government policies, the National Assembly plays a real role in decision making, with powers to initiate legislation, question cabinet ministers, and express lack of confidence in individual ministers. For example, in May 1999, the Amir issued several landmark decrees dealing with women's suffrage, economic liberalization, and nationality. The National Assembly later rejected all of these decrees as a matter of principle, and then reintroduced most of them as parliamentary legislation.

The Kuwaiti judicial system generally provides fair public trials and an adequate appeals mechanism. Under Kuwaiti law, no detainee can be held for more than four days without being charged; after being charged by a prosecutor, detention for up to an additional twenty-one days is possible. Persons held under the State Security Law can be detained. Bail is commonly set in all cases. The lowest level courts, aside from traffic courts, are the misdemeanor courts that judge offenses subject to imprisonment not exceeding three years. Courts of first instance hear felony cases in which the punishment can exceed three years. All defendants in felony cases are required to be represented by attorneys, appointed by the court if necessary. Legal counsel is optional in misdemeanor cases, and the court is not obliged to provide an attorney.

Two separate State Security Court panels, each composed of three justices, hear crimes against state security or other cases referred to it by the Council of Ministers. Trials in the State Security Court initially are held in closed session but subsequently are opened to the press and others. They do not, in the judgment of the Department of State, meet international standards for fair trials. Military courts, which ordinarily have jurisdiction only over members of the armed services or security forces, can try offenses charged against civilians under conditions of martial law. Martial law was imposed for the first time after the liberation of the country from Iraqi occupation. About 300 persons suspected of collaboration with Iraq were tried by military courts in May and June 1991, and 115 were convicted. Twenty-nine received death sentences that were later commuted to life imprisonment after international criticism of the trials. Human rights groups drew attention to the failure to provide adequate legal safeguards to defendants and an unwillingness to accept the defense that collaboration with Iraqi forces had been coerced. Many of the accused alleged that their confessions had been extracted under torture.

Prison conditions, including conditions for those held for security offenses, meet minimum international standards in terms of food, access to basic health care, scheduled family visits, cleanliness, and opportunities for work and exercise. Continuing problems include overcrowding and the lack of available specialized medical care. Approximately 1,300 persons are serving sentences or awaiting trial in the central prison. An estimated additional 250 prisoners are being held at the state security facility in Shuwaikh, which also operates as a deportation center.

Following charges of corruption at the central prison in 1998, prison officials were punished and the senior prison official lost his position. The Ministry of Interior maintained oversight of central prison officials during the year, but there were no new charges of corruption.

The government reopened Talha prison in 1998, and it is now being used as a prison for persons convicted of civil crimes and those awaiting trial, some of whom subsequently are processed for administrative deportations. Since its reopening, Talha has not been criticized by human rights groups for prisoner mistreatment. The government also began construction of a new maximum security facility. The National Assembly's Human Rights Committee closely monitored prison conditions throughout the year, and the

government allowed the International Committee of the Red Cross access to all detention facilities.

Police Profile

Organizational Description and Functions

The Ministry of Interior has overall responsibility for public security and law and order. Under the ministry, the Criminal Investigation Department (CID) and Kuwait State Security (KSS) investigate internal security–related offenses, in addition to the regular police. The national police have primary responsibility for maintaining public order and preventing and investigating crimes. The National Guard a semiautonomous body has guard duties on the border and at oil fields, utilities, and other strategic locations. The Guard acts as a reserve for the regular forces and reinforces the metropolitan police as needed.

The principal police divisions are criminal investigation, traffic, emergency police, nationality and passports, immigration, prisons, civil defense, and trials and courtsmartial. The criminal investigation division is responsible for ordinary criminal cases; Kuwait State Security investigates security-related offenses. Both are involved in investigations of terrorism and those suspected of collaboration with Iraq.

Training

Police selected for officer rank attend a three-year program at the Police Academy. National Guard officer candidates attend the Kuwaiti Military College, after which they receive specialized guard

Felonies and misdemeanors by governorates, 2002–1998

	Percentage					Years				
	2002	2001	2000	1999	1998	2002	2001	2000	1999	1998
Capital	27.2	28.4	28.2	19.9	21.3	2,843	2,969	3,586	1,865	2,931
Hawally	26.5	24.9	19.4	29.2	30.2	2,766	2,601	2,465	2,745	4,164
A-Ahmadi	9.8	10.0	8.5	12.1	12.2	1,029	1,050	1,084	1,139	1,683
Al-Jahra	11.9	11.3	7.7	9.3	9.7	1,247	1,186	975	872	1,332
Farwaniya	19.3	19.7	16.3	20.7	20.3	2,018	2,059	2,074	1,945	2,799
Mubarak Al-Kabeer*	5.4	0.0	0.0	0.0	0.0	566	590	612	0	0
Total	100.0	100.0	100.0	100.0	100.0	10,469	10,455	12,724	9,388	13,776
Capital	19.7	17.2	17.4	27.9	19.5	1,752	1,582	1,605	2,774	2,666
Hawally	21.2	24.6	24.7	37.4	26.6	1,884	2,263	2,272	3,720	3,631
A-Ahmadi	12.6	11.7	13.5	17.1	14.7	1,114	1,083	1,245	1,703	2,013
Al-Jahra	16.1	15.7	17.4	22.0	16.0	1,426	1,443	1,605	2,190	2,185
Farwaniya	24.1	23.6	26.2	32.5	22.1	2,141	2,177	2,409	3,232	3,019
Mubarak Al-Kabeer*	6.3	7.2	0.0	0.0	0.0	564	663	772	0	0
Total	100.0	100.0	100.0	100.0	100.0	8,881	9,211	9,954	13,651	13,549

*Including Mubarak Al-Kabeer governate for 2000.

training. Women work in certain police departments, such as criminal investigation, inquiries, and airport security.

Complaints and Discipline

The constitution prohibits torture; however, there continue to be credible reports that some police and members of the security forces abuse detainees during interrogation. Reported abuses include blindfolding, verbal threats, stepping on toes, and slaps and blows. Police and security forces were more likely to inflict such abuse on noncitizens, particularly citizens of other non-Gulf Arab nations and Asians, than on citizens.

The government states that it investigates all allegations of abuse, and that it has punished at least some of the offenders. However, the government does not make public either the findings of its investigations or what, if any, punishments are imposed. This omission creates a climate of impunity, which diminishes deterrence against abuse.

Defendants have the right to present evidence in court that they have been mistreated during interrogation. However, the courts frequently dismiss abuse complaints because defendants are unable to substantiate their complaints with physical evidence. Members of the security forces routinely decline to reveal their identity during interrogation, a practice that further complicates confirmation of abuse.

The constitution provides for freedom from arbitrary arrest and detention; however, the government occasionally arbitrarily arrests and detains persons. There also were incidents of prolonged detention.

Police officers must obtain an arrest warrant from state prosecutors before making an arrest, although in misdemeanor cases the arresting officer may issue them. Security forces occasionally detain persons at checkpoints in Kuwait City.

Under the Penal Code, a suspect may not be held for more than four days without charge. Security officers sometimes prevent families from visiting detainees during this confinement. After four days, prosecutors must either release the suspect or file charges. If charges are filed, prosecutors may remand a suspect to detention for an additional twenty-one days. Prosecutors also may obtain court orders for further detention pending trial.

The constitution provides for individual privacy and sanctity of the home; however, the government infringes on these rights in some areas. The police must obtain a warrant to search both public and private property unless they are in hot pursuit of a suspect fleeing the scene of a crime, or if alcohol or illegal narcotics are suspected on the premises. The warrant may be obtained from the state prosecutor or, in the case of private property, from a judge. In May 2004 an Amiri decree was issued that gives the police under warrant the right to conduct searches for illegal firearms by neighborhood. The National Assembly rejected the decree during its fall session; no similar legislation was introduced to take its place. The security forces occasionally monitor the activities of individuals and their communications.

MINTIE DAS

Bibliography

Central Intelligence Agency. *The World Factbook*. 2005. Available at: www.cia.gov/cia/publications/factbook.

Library of Congress. "Country Reports." 1993. Available at: www.lcweb2.loc.gov/rfd/cs.

Ministry of Interior, Kuwait. "Felonies and Misdemeanors." Kuwait Ministry of Interior, 2003.

U.S. Department of State. "Background Note." 2005. Available at: www.travel.state.gov/travel.

KYRGYZSTAN

Background Material

The modern Kyrgyz Republic (Kyrgyz Respublikasy) became independent on August 31, 1991, when it declared its separation from the Soviet Union. It is a landlocked country, bordering China on the East, Kazakhstan on the North, Uzbekistan on the West, and Tajikistan on the South. Its territory covers 198,500 square kilometers, of which 7,100 are water. Its capital city is Bishkek. The other major cities are Jalalabad, Kara-Balta, Karakol, Osh, and Tokmok.

In 2004, Kyrgyzstan's population was estimated at 5,081,429, with a 1.25% annual growth rate. The population is concentrated in small areas in the north and southwest, with about two-thirds in the Chu, Fergana, and Talas Valleys. About 60% of the population lives in rural areas. In 2004, about 32% of the population was 14 years of age or younger, and 6% was 65 years of age or older. Life expectancy was 67.8 years (72.1 years for females and 63.8 years for males) and the fertility rate was 2.7 births per woman. Kyrgyzstan's population is based on a mixture of Central Asian nomadic tribes. According to 2003 estimates of ethnicity, 67% of the people are Kyrgyz, 14% Uzbek, 11% Russian, 1% Dungan (Chinese Muslim), 1% Tatar, and 1% Uyghur.

Since Kyrgyzstan's economy was highly dependent on the Soviet Union prior to 1991, the loss of key Soviet inputs caused severe economic decline, and has required substantial restructuring. Emigration of Russians and other minorities with technical expertise has also hurt the economy. Agriculture and services are the most important sectors, as industry remains concentrated in specific regions and outputs. The government launched two major programs to privatize state enterprises, which by 2003 had shifted about 7,000 enterprises to the private sector.

Contextual Features

Kyrgyzstan is a unitary presidential republic that began the post-Soviet era as the least authoritarian of the five Central Asian states. The constitution, which calls for three separate branches of government, has been amended several times to change the structure of the legislative branch.

The executive branch is comprised of the president, the prime minister, and a cabinet of twelve ministers, and the heads of nineteen national agencies, commissions, and committees. The prime minister is appointed by the president, subject to parliamentary approval. The president also appoints cabinet members.

The second constitutional branch is the legislative branch. Members of both houses of the bicameral Supreme Council (Zhogorku Kenesh) are directly elected to five-year terms. The Supreme Council consists of a seventy-seat lower house, the People's Assembly, which meets twice a year to consider regional issues, and a thirty-five-seat upper house, the Legislative Assembly, which is in permanent session.

The Supreme Court is the highest appeals court for civil and criminal cases. The Constitutional Court rules on constitutional interpretations and on the validity of presidential elections. The members of those courts are elected to ten-year terms by the Supreme Council, after being nominated by the president. The president appoints judges to seven-year terms at the subnational level.

Kyrgyzstan is divided into seven provinces and the municipality of Bishkek, the capital. Each province is headed by a governor (akim), appointed by the president. The provinces are divided into districts whose administrators are appointed by the central government. Rural communities, comprising up to 20 small settlements, are governed by directly elected mayors and councils.

Kyrgyzstan's crime problem is generally regarded as serious to the point of being out of control. In particular, police corruption and incompetence are blamed for high crime rates in urban areas. Kyrgyzstan's location between Tajikistan and Russia has also made the western part of Kyrgyzstan (particularly Osh) a major transit region for trafficking in narcotics and people. Since the early 2000s, domestic narcotics production and abuse have grown sharply. In the Fergana Valley, in addition, tension continues between Kyrgyz and Uzbek citizens over land and housing rights. According to Seventh United Nations Survey of Crime Trends and Operations of Criminal Justice Systems, reported crimes between 1998 and 2000 broke down as follows:

- Adults prosecuted: 21,373, 4.36 per 1,000 people
- Females prosecuted: 2,396, 0.48 per 1,000 people
- Assault: 208, 0.04 per 1,000 people
- Car theft: 163, 0.03 per 1,000 people
- Embezzlement: 1189, 0.24 per 1,000 people
- Fraud: 1156, 0.23 per 1,000 people
- Murder: 413, 0.08 per 1,000 people
- Rape: 321, 0.06 per 1,000 people
- Robberies: 1497, 0.30 per 1,000 people
- Total crimes: 38,620, 7.89 per 1,000 people

In addition, four people were executed by the state in this period.

Police Profile

Demographics

The main law enforcement agencies are the Ministry of Internal Affairs (for general crime), the National Security Service (for state-level crime), and the National Prosecutor's Office, which handles all types of crime. About 25,000 police officers were active in 2004.

Organizational Description

The Ministry of Internal Affairs is responsible for tasks assigned to the ministry, the law enforcement bodies subordinate to the ministry, and to internal armies. He is appointed and dismissed by the president after consultation with the Prime Minister. Deputy ministers are appointed and dismissed by the prime minister on recommendation of the minister.

The minister of internal affairs is supported by the Board of the Ministry, which he chairs. Other members are deputy ministers, representatives of the staff of the prime minister of Kyrgyz Republic, supervising employees, and soldiers of the Ministry's system, among others; the total number of board members has been established by the government of the Kyrgyz Republic. The board considers the most important issues of activities related to law enforcement bodies and internal armies. Decisions are made by a majority of votes of its members, are registered by minutes, and brought into practice by orders of the minister. In case of disagreement between the minister and the board, the minister brings into practice his decision and reports on disagreements to the president and the government of the Kyrgyz Republic. Members of the board have the right to submit their opinion in written form to the government.

The Ministry in Bishkek contains thirty-four functional departments, each headed by a chief and a deputy. The eight provincial headquarters, which support operational militia stations, comprise around twenty-five functional departments. In one particular province, there are 100 personnel at the headquarters. These territorial militia units follow:

- Bishkek Directorate with four district stations and 26 city precincts
- Chui Provincial Directorate with eight district stations
- Issyk-Kul Provincial Directorate with two city departments and four district stations
- Talas Provincial Directorate with one city department and four district stations
- Naryn Provincial Directorate with four district stations
- Osh Provincial Directorate with one city department and seven district stations
- Jalal-Abad Provincial Directorate with one city department and eleven district stations
- Batken Provincial Directorate with two city departments and three district stations

There are four district stations in Bishkek: Leninsky, Octiabrsky, Pervomayksy, and Sverdlovsky. An example of a station's administrative structure is that of Pervomayksy, which serves approximately 200,000 people. The Pervomayksy police station's structure is depicted in the following figure.

The structure of the militia remains entrenched in ex-Soviet military forms. Duties of the militia are defined in current laws on policing, but except for the regulation on ethics, there is no statement of purpose or values that provides guidance on how policing should be conducted. Control is from the center, the Ministry of Internal Affairs that, by virtue of the 2002 "Regulations about the Ministry," is responsible for all matters of any importance. Even senior officers, heads of departmental and operational units, are given little discretion, and are not always consulted on policy and personnel.

Functions

The nature and function of the Kyrgyz militia is spelled out in the Regulation about the Ministry of Internal Affairs of the Kyrgyz Republic. Clause 1, "Law-enforcement bodies of the Kyrgyz Republic," spells out the police structure. The unified system of the law-enforcement bodies of the Kyrgyz Republic consists of the Ministry of Internal Affairs; district and Bishkek city departments of internal affairs (part of the Ministry); subdivisions on transport, city, provinces, provinces in cities, village subdivisions of law enforcement bodies; and special and operating facilities, educational institutions, establishments, and organizations. The structure of law enforcement bodies is determined by the Minister of Internal Affairs and approved by the government. Supervision of the police is carried out by the minister of internal affairs, who is appointed by the president in coordination with the prime minister. The minister of internal affairs is responsible to the president and government.

Clause 2 states that the primary goals of law enforcement bodies are maintenance of public order, safety of the individual and society, crime fighting, execution of criminal punishments and official penalties within the limits of competence; controlling and licensing activities in traffic safety; and registration and examination. This clause also forbids law enforcement bodies to be involved in tasks that have not been assigned to it by legislation. No one, except for bodies and officials authorized by the law, has a right to interfere in law enforcement activities.

Clause 3, "Activities of law enforcement bodies and rights of citizens," states that law enforcement bodies in their activities proceed out of respect for the rights of citizens and are the guarantor of protection of each person irrespective of his/her citizenship; social, property, and other position; racial and national identity; gender; age; education; language; religion; political and other beliefs; and field and character of occupation. It also states that any restriction of citizen rights is allowed only on the basis of law, and that citizens have the right to receive an explanation concerning restriction of their rights and freedom from police officials. Any person who believes that actions of a law enforcement officer

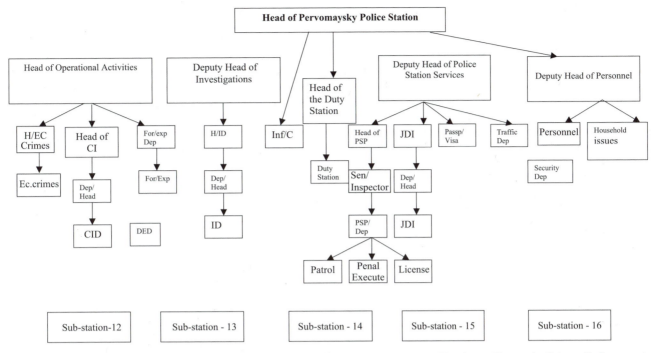

Explanatory notes: H/Ec.crimes, Head of Economic Crimes Enforcement Department; Ec.crimes, Economic Crimes Enforcement Department; CI, Criminal Investigation; Dep/Head, Deputy Head; CID, Criminal Investigation Department; For/Exp, Forensic Expert Department; H/ID, Head of Investigation Department; ID, Investigations Department; Inf/C, Information Center; Head of PSP, Head of Public Security Provision Department; Sen/Inspector, Senior Inspector; Patroll, Patrolling and Point Duty Service (security provision at buildings and organizations); Penal Execut, Penal Executive; License, Licensing Service (giving permission or license for carrying/storing/collecting weapons); JDI, Juvenile Delinquency Inspection; Passp/Visa, Passport and Visa Department; Traffic Dep, Traffic Police Department; Securit.Dep, Security Department; Personn, Personnnel/Staff selection department; Household, Householding issues within police station (procurement officer); DED, Drug Enforcement Department.

have infringed on his/her rights, freedoms, or legitimate interests, has the right to appeal against these actions to a higher body, the law enforcement body, the public prosecutor, or a court. All police bodies must allow arrested, imprisoned, and convicted persons to fulfill the right for legal protection, inform relatives, and the place of the person's work or study. When necessary, law enforcement bodies must provide medical and other forms of assistance.

The 2004 budget was 384.67 million soms (around US$8.82 million), falling far short of the 1.7 billion soms requested by the Ministry. The Police Academy, which trains officer ranks, has its own budget.

Training

Officer ranks occupy management or specialist posts while sergeant ranks or noncommissioned officers are engaged as traffic police, guards, or patrol officers in street-level work. There is a direct-entry system for officers who enter their posts directly from the Police Academy or from some other academic institutions without serving at the street level. There is a system for calculating forthcoming vacancies in order to assess

recruiting needs. Official selection criteria take into account academic achievement, fitness, previous character, and family history. Ranks are military based, and awarded according to education and years of service. Promotion through officer ranks is almost always automatic after specified periods of service. However, the rank an officer holds does not necessarily reflect his/her position in the management hierarchy. An officer of a higher rank often becomes subordinate to an officer of lower rank as she moves around the organization. Transfers are relatively regular, affecting the continuity of service to a community.

Separate training exists for officers and junior ranks. The Police Academy has higher academic institution status, conferred by the Minister of Education, and students graduate with a law degree. Men and women can enter the militia officer ranks direct with diverse degrees from higher educational establishments without undergoing this course. Officer recruits are then required only to undertake this shortened course. Sergeant ranks are recruited by and trained at the Centers for Induction Training in the ordinary police schools of Bishkek and Osh.

Police Public Projects

Kyrgyzstan has a very strong centralized government, and so the structure of the police is also centralized. However, a pilot decentralization project has begun in Issyk-Kul Province to give more autonomy to the state chief of administration. Although the Department of Internal Affairs is not included in this project, there have been efforts to alter police structure in recent years. These efforts were initiated when the president set up the State Commission on Police Reform to engineer change in the militia. Progress has been slow—the chairman is no longer in that post and it has not met in a long time. But the Ministry has played its part by drafting a "concept" document entitled "Reform in the System of Ministry of the Internal Affairs in the Kyrgyz Republic for the Period to 2010." There is much room for improvement in many areas, yet there is resistance to change. Rules and regulations are so high on the agenda that few are willing to risk challenging the process or taking the bold steps needed to bring about durable change.

Complaints and Discipline

An inescapable feature of the Kyrgyz Ministry is corruption, the extent of which is difficult to estimate. There is little doubt that it is widespread. The wide range of corrupt activities by the police—manipulation of crime and detection figures, offer or receipt of bribes, extortion, involvement in crime—are regarded by honest police officers, politicians, nongovernmental organizations (NGOs), and other public bodies as the major hurdle in the path of reform. Since corruption also exists in other areas of public life, it is the view of some officers, lawyers, and at least one public prosecutor that police reform needs, as a prerequisite, the reform of the prosecutor's office.

The use of police to disrupt political demonstrations is also a problem. Violent demonstrations in 2002, when demonstrators were shot by officers facing a difficult public order situation, led to a police reform program to improve public perceptions of a force known for taking bribes, criminal ties, and violence, and plagued by low pay.

Not all officers, of course, are corrupt. Many are committed to serving the public, want their professionalism to be recognized, and are anxious to experience change. They continue to serve, working twelve to fourteen hours a day, every day, without basic support services, and often using their own resources in order to complete their tasks. Recent researches have suggested that even many of those lower ranks who do participate in supplementary income schemes would prefer not to do so, given the opportunity to earn an honest living wage.

According to a 2004 Organization for Security and Cooperation in Europe (OSCE) report, relationships between the militia and the public are described as having never been worse, and the mistreatment of offenders is seen as one of the most important human rights issues. NGOs warn of impending revolt, particularly if there are more violent clashes with demonstrators, such as in 2002. However, some senior officers at least, view that incident as shameful for the militia and hope that lessons have been learned. Nevertheless, NGOs warn of the possibility for unrest, particularly during the impending presidential elections in 2005 if policing policies deny the right to peacefully demonstrate.

Terrorism

In the late 1990s and early 2000s, Kyrgyzstan suffered incursions by terrorist groups from hotbeds of insurgent activity in nearby Tajikistan and the Fergana Valley. In 1999, terrorists took a group of Japanese and Kyrgyz hostages in Kyrgyzstan, and insurgent activities continued in Batken and Osh in 2000. In 2003, a series of minor incidents in Osh were attributed to terrorists. Those events showed that Kyrgyzstan did not have sufficient security forces to prevent major terrorist incursions. Domestic forces were upgraded somewhat in the early 2000s, but Kyrgyzstan likely would need assistance from Russia or Uzbekistan to counter a serious insurgency. The OSCE has held seminars in Kyrgyzstan on money laundering and terrorism.

International Cooperation

In the post-Soviet era, Kyrgyzstan has joined several regional organizations in an effort to improve its security and economic conditions. In addition to the OSCE, which has set up office in Bishkek, are the Shanghai Cooperation Organization and the Collective Security Treaty Organization of the Commonwealth of Independent States. Because of these institutions' limited impact, Kyrgyzstan's more substantive foreign relations have largely been bilateral. Relations with Russia have remained a primary concern because Kyrgyzstan had been unusually dependent on Soviet structures in security and economic matters. Relations with China have improved steadily since 1991, as trade has flourished and border issues have been settled. Kyrgyzstan's large population of Uyghur emigrants concerns China, however, because of separatism in adjoining Xingjiang Province, from which they migrated.

SAMIH TEYMUR, ISMAIL DINCER GUNES, AND RECEP GULTEKIN

Bibliography

Brown, Raymond. *Kyrgyzstan Militia: A Question of Reform.* Organization for Security and Cooperation in Europe, 2004.

Central Intelligence Agency. *The World Factbook.* Available at: www.cia.gov/cia/publications/factbook/geos/kg.html. Accessed.

Library of Congress, Federal Research Division. "Country Profile: Kyrgyzstan." Washington, DC: Library of Congress, September 2004.

Sonmez, M. Murat. *Traffic Policing in Kyrgyzstan.* Organization for Security and Cooperation in Europe, 2004.

United Nations. *Seventh United Nations Survey of Crime Trends and Operations of Criminal Justice Systems (Covering the Period 1998–2000).* United Nations Office on Drugs and Crime, Centre for International Crime Prevention, 2000.

INDEX

D

F

H

N